International Encyclopedia of the SOCIAL SCIENCES

International Encyclopedia of the SOCIAL SCIENCES

DAVID L. SILLS EDITOR

VOLUME 4

The Macmillan Company & The Free Press

International Encyclopedia of the SOCIAL SCIENCES

[CONTINUED]

CUMULATIVE DISTRIBUTION FUNCTION
See PROBABILITY.

CUNNINGHAM, WILLIAM

William Cunningham (1849–1919), British economic historian, was born in Edinburgh, Scotland, the third son of James Cunningham, a prominent Edinburgh solicitor. After attending Edinburgh Academy, Cunningham became a student at Edinburgh University and studied for a short time in Tübingen. In 1869 he entered Caius College of Cambridge University to read moral science, and upon his graduation in 1872 he was bracketed top with F. W. Maitland, an honor that earned Cunningham a scholarship to Trinity College. He was a man of "overflowing vitality" (Scott 1920); this trait enabled him, after his ordination in 1873, to combine, with outstanding success, clerical and academic work. Between 1874 and 1878 he served in the industrial cities of Yorkshire and Lancashire as one of the first lecturers in the Cambridge University extension scheme. Before this time his academic training and interests had been mainly philosophical, but he now turned increasingly toward economics and history.

He returned to Cambridge in 1878. The following year he was appointed an examiner in the Cambridge history tripos and found that the examination included a paper on political economy and economic history, although the latter subject was not being taught. Cunningham decided to teach economic history, and the first edition of *The Growth of English Industry and Commerce* (1882)

was prepared as a textbook for his courses. From 1884 to 1888 he was a university lecturer in history and from 1888 to 1891 a lecturer at Trinity College. His appointment as Tooke professor of economics at King's College, London, from 1891 to 1897, was a tribute to a rapidly established reputation. He would have resided in London had he not been elected in 1891 to a fellowship of Trinity College. An honorary fellowship of Caius College followed in 1895. In 1899 he was lecturer in economic history at Harvard; he returned to Harvard as Lowell lecturer in 1914. He was active in the economic section of the British Association (president in 1891 and 1905) and was a foundation member of the British Academy, president of the Royal Historical Society from 1910 to 1913, and proctor for the clergy in convocation (helping to write, in 1906, an important report on clerical poverty).

It was at Cambridge that Cunningham's great and enduring work in economic history was done. He was, more than anyone else, responsible for the recognition and establishment of economic history as an independent discipline in the universities of Britain, where it is the only branch of history with, usually, its own department and, often, its own degree. Cunningham's achievements were, first, to demonstrate the importance of economic history for both history and economics and, second, to stimulate research and teaching in economic history by a stream of publications of high quality. Cunningham gave economic history in Britain both status and content: before him, only J. Thorold Rogers could claim to have been an economic historian in the professional sense; after him, economic history attracted some of the most talented of historians and inspired some of the best historical writing.

Cunningham, with his contemporary W. J. Ashley, outlined the subject matter of economic history, established its methods of inquiry, and defined its problems for at least the next half century. Cunningham's *Growth* was the first major historical work to sketch systematically the periods and features of English economic history. Cunningham was responsible for many revisions of accepted historical opinion, the most enduring being his favorable revaluation of mercantilism. His economic history suffered, however, from being too simply conceived as the story of national development within a framework largely established by the political historians. Economic legislation, and the policy behind it, played the major role in Cunningham's economic history. This led him into bias; for example, he believed mistakenly that Edward III had pursued a consistent economic policy and, for a later period, he exaggerated the extent of the transition in England from state control to laissez-faire.

All of Cunningham's views were carefully established and strongly held, and he was constantly involved in controversy about history, economics, theology, and academic and clerical administration. Two controversies, one academic and one political, were particularly important. The academic controversy concerned method. Cunningham believed that history was essential to economics in order to prevent economics from becoming an abstract branch of social philosophy, and his advocacy of the historical method precipitated a minor *Methodenstreit* in England. He argued that economists were unable to give guidance on contemporary affairs because of their ignorance of facts and of "the empirical study of the phenomena of the past." He believed in "the relativity of economic doctrine" and that economic history was "the best propaedeutic to political economy." In a famous article Cunningham attacked the economists for what he called "the perversion of economic history" by the neglect of "the serious study of facts" (1892); this provoked a pained reply from Alfred Marshall and caused him to revise the economic history in Book I of his *Principles of Economics*. It also established more firmly the claims of economic history to a place in the training of economists.

The second controversy concerned protection. Cunningham was an early critic of laissez-faire and had much sympathy for the *Sozialpolitik* of the German nationalist economists. He was, indeed, a patriot, with a strong sense of Britain's greatness and imperial responsibilities. This greatness, he believed, was based mainly on industrial strength, which in the long run could only be preserved by trade protection within an imperialist framework. He was thus for many years one of the few academics who vigorously supported the protectionist movement. He did not live long enough, however, to see either the resurgence of empirical economics or the end of free trade.

R. M. Hartwell

[*Directly related is the entry* History, *article on* economic history.]

WORKS BY CUNNINGHAM

(1882) 1910–1912 *The Growth of English Industry and Commerce.* 3 vols., 5th ed. Cambridge Univ. Press.

1892 The Perversion of Economic History. *Economic Journal* 2:491–506.

(1895) 1904 Cunningham, William; and McArthur, Ellen A. *Outlines of English Industrial History.* Cambridge Historical Series. New York and London: Macmillan.

1896 *Modern Civilization in Some of Its Economic Aspects.* London: Methuen.

1897 *Alien Immigrants to England.* London: Sonnenschein; New York: Macmillan.

1902 Economic Change. Volume 1, pages 493–531 in *Cambridge Modern History.* New York and London: Macmillan.

(1904) 1905 *The Rise and Decline of the Free Trade Movement.* 2d ed. London: Clay.

1911 *The Case Against Free Trade.* Preface by Joseph Chamberlain. London: Murray.

(1916) 1925 *The Progress of Capitalism in England.* New York and London: Macmillan.

WORKS ABOUT CUNNINGHAM

Cunningham, Audrey 1950 *William Cunningham: Teacher and Priest.* Preface by F. R. Salter. London: Society for Promoting Christian Knowledge.

Foxwell, Herbert S. 1919 Archdeacon Cunningham (obituary). *Economic Journal* 29:382–390.

Knowles, Lilian 1919 Archdeacon Cunningham (obituary). *Economic Journal* 29:390–393.

Scott, William R. 1920 William Cunningham, 1849–1919. British Academy, *Proceedings* 9:465–474.

William Cunningham [obituary]. 1919 *The Times* (London) June 11, p. 16, col. 3.

CURIOSITY
See Stimulation drives.

CURRENCY
See Money.

CURVE FITTING
See Goodness of fit; Linear hypotheses, *article on* regression.

CUSTODY
See Internment and custody; Penology; Slavery.

CUSTOM

See CULTURE; NORMS.

CUSTOMS

See INTERNATIONAL INTEGRATION, *article on* ECONOMIC UNIONS; INTERNATIONAL TRADE CONTROLS.

CUVILLIER, ARMAND

Armand Joseph Cuvillier was born in Paris in 1887. He entered the École Normale Supérieure in 1908 and became *agrégé de philosophie* in 1919. After holding positions at *collèges* in Montluçon, Bourges, Strasbourg, Laon, and Paris, he taught sociology at the Sorbonne from 1945 to 1953.

Cuvillier is primarily a historian of ideas. His interest in French socialism at the time of the revolution of 1848 goes back to 1919, when he published his thesis on *L'Atelier*, a workers' periodical edited between 1840 and 1850 by followers of Philippe Buchez. In 1937 he wrote an essay on the differences between Proudhon and Marx (1937*a*), and in his article "Les antagonismes de classes dans la littérature sociale française de Saint-Simon à 1848" (1956*b*) he showed to what extent the notion that class antagonism is inherent in industrial society had developed prior to the earliest Marxist writings.

Another major concern of Cuvillier's has been to introduce the work of Durkheim and his followers to a larger public. Anxious as he has been to preserve Durkheim's heritage, Cuvillier has found it necessary to separate the properly scientific part of Durkheim's work from what he has called his "sociologism": thus, he has denounced Durkheim's attempt to arrive at moral conclusions on the basis of the study of social facts, and he has accused Durkheim of transforming society itself into the fundamental value. In spite of such criticism, Cuvillier has defended Durkheim repeatedly against more extreme critics. In an article, "Durkheim et Marx" (1948*a*), he concluded that Durkheimism and Marxism cannot be simply opposed as conservative and revolutionary sociology, respectively, or as idealist and materialist conceptions: they have common elements, and both are forerunners of the sociology of knowledge.

Cuvillier has done useful work both as an editor and as a writer of teaching documents. He has edited the works of Proudhon, Spinoza, Roustan, Condillac, Malebranche, and Durkheim; particularly valuable is his reconstruction of Durkheim's course on pragmatism and sociology from the notes of two students. His textbook, *Introduction à la sociologie*, was first published in 1936 and has since been revised six times and translated into several languages. A handbook of sociology in two volumes, *Manuel de sociologie* (1950), has become a useful tool for sociologists because of its great wealth of references.

In 1953 Cuvillier warned that the traditional French conception of sociology as an objective science based on empirical investigation was in danger (*Où va la sociologie française?...*). Asserting the importance of the formula attributed to François Simiand, "no facts without ideas, no ideas without facts," he focused his attack on the work of Georges Gurvitch, whom he berated for having created an arbitrary, formalistic sociological typology, divorced from facts. Simultaneously, he deplored a tendency in French sociology to conduct empirical research without theoretical foundations.

JOSEF GUGLER

[*For the historical context of Cuvillier's work, see* MARXIST SOCIOLOGY; *and the biographies of* DURKHEIM; MARX; PROUDHON; SIMIAND.]

WORKS BY CUVILLIER

(1919) 1954 *Un journal d'ouvriers: L'Atelier (1840–1850)*. Paris: Éditions Ouvrières.
(1936) 1960 *Introduction à la sociologie*. 6th ed., rev. Paris: Colin.
(1937*a*) 1956 Marx et Proudhon. Pages 145–226 in Armand Cuvillier, *Hommes et idéologies de 1840*. Paris: Rivière.
1937*b* *Proudhon*. Paris: Éditions Sociales Internationales.
1948*a* Durkheim et Marx. *Cahiers internationaux de sociologie* 4:75–97.
1948*b* *P. J. B. Buchez et les origines du socialisme chrétien*. Paris: Presses Universitaires de France.
(1950) 1962–1963 *Manuel de sociologie: Avec notices bibliographiques*. 2 vols. Paris: Presses Universitaires de France.
1953 *Où va la sociologie française? Avec une étude d'Émile Durkheim sur la sociologie formaliste*. Paris: Rivière.
1956*a* *Partis pris sur l'art, la philosophie, l'histoire*. Paris: Colin.
(1956*b*) 1961 Sociologie et histoire sociale: Les antagonismes de classes dans la littérature sociale française de Saint-Simon à 1848. Pages 108–156 in Armand Cuvillier, *Sociologie et problèmes actuels*. 2d ed., enl. Paris: Vrin.
1958 Trends Abroad: France. Pages 716–736 in Joseph S. Rouček (editor), *Contemporary Sociology*. New York: Philosophical Library.

CYBERNETICS

The term "cybernetics," designating a distinct field of activity, appeared on the scientific scene at the close of World War II, with the publication of Norbert Wiener's book *Cybernetics: Or Control and Communication in the Animal and the Machine*. Wiener defined the term "cybernetics" as "the entire field of control and communication theory, whether in the machine or the animal" (Wiener 1948, p. 19); he was unaware that the term had been used, in a more limited sense, a century earlier by André Ampère (1834).

Since 1948, research and publications related to cybernetics have proliferated, unfolding the content of cybernetic concepts and their impact on fields ranging from psychology and neurophysiology to sociology and philosophy of science. This continuing clarification of the meaning and implications of cybernetics has influenced attitudes toward and usage of the term, as well as our understanding of it, thereby blurring Wiener's initial definition. A brief look at some of the forces that shaped its development will help in understanding what "cybernetics" means today.

In his personal review of the subject, Wiener recounts that while working on the theory of an automatic system for aiming antiaircraft guns he and his colleagues were impressed with the critical role of feedback in the proper functioning of a control system. This led them to conjecture that in order for a person to perform motor activities, his cerebellum must embody types of feedback and associated information processes comparable to those used in an artificial control system. If this were so, then the brain could be viewed as a complex communication, computer, and control system; and the concepts of feedback and control theory could account for internal homeostatic control (for temperature, blood-sugar concentration, heart action, etc.), as well as for control of those motor actions required for purposeful manipulation of external objects. Implicit in these notions was the further thesis that those cognitive activities involved in higher-level problem-solving behavior also could be interpreted mechanistically in terms of the flow and processing of information.

The concepts of cybernetics, emphasizing an information-processing analysis of the mechanisms that generate purposeful behavior, excited the interest of some psychologists, physiologists, and even psychiatrists. Psychologists saw a way of relating behavior to the underlying information processes that control behavior. Neurophysiologists found that the brain and nervous system could be analyzed as a special-purpose computing machine "designed" to generate adaptive, intelligent behavior. And for psychiatrists, Wiener argued that functional mental disorders in the human are primarily diseases of memory caused by errors introduced in the processing of information and are not necessarily indicative of a physiological or anatomical breakdown of the brain mechanism. Thus, Wiener's writings suggested that problems in the psychology of behavior, the physiology of the nervous system, and the psychopathology of mental disorders could all be described in the neutral language of information processing and control.

Because of the central importance of the concept of information, a second major force behind the development of cybernetics was the publication in 1948 of Shannon's paper "The Mathematical Theory of Communication." Here was a theory that explicated quantitatively one measure for the amount of information conveyed by messages. The theory showed how to determine the capacity of a communication channel. One could now compute how much more information one channel could transmit than another. Shannon's theory clarified the important concept of a code and showed how to determine the efficiency of a given coding system. The theory also demonstrated how to combat the destructive effects of noise by introducing redundancy into coding schemes. Shannon's mathematical theory of communication not only explicated all of these key concepts but also proved some surprising mathematical relationships between noise, redundancy, channel capacity, and error-free transmission of messages [see INFORMATION THEORY].

Clearly, the digital computer was a third force pushing and molding the development of cybernetics. The first electronic digital computer was completed in 1946, and the following years brought swift advances in computer theory, technology, and applications. Switching speeds and memory capacities increased by several orders of magnitude. Input–output devices and information conversion equipment of great diversity were developed. Theoretical foundations emerged in the form of a theory of automata and information machines. More reliable equipment, more flexible programming languages, and a steady decline in costs all contributed to the ever widening use of computers. The application of computing machines spread from scientific calculations to automatic control and business-data processing—in fact, into almost every facet of government, industrial, and military information processing. One of the most interesting applications is simulation, where the computer is used as a general-purpose research vehicle to generate the logical consequences of arbitrary assumptions about a complex process. Thus, one can get new insights about a complex process by having a computer simulate its behavior, whether the model be for some aspects of the economy or for some neurophysiological structure. In this way psychologists searching for theories of problem-solving behavior (for example, the cognitive behavior associated with proving theorems of logic) have attempted to simulate aspects of such behavior by using a computer. Similarly, neurophysiologists seeking an understanding of the neural organizational principles that give rise to pattern recognition, learning, and similar processes have simulated with computers the behavior of networks of idealized neurons [*see* COMPUTATION; SIMULATION].

Wiener's notions about the brain and the computer, Shannon's theory of information, and the new computing technology created optimism about new ways to attack the formidable problems of thinking and knowing. This atmosphere of excitement and ferment, accentuated by hopes of interdisciplinary unification, generated much competent work. Unfortunately, it also produced serious intellectual and semantic misunderstandings about computers, brains, and people; and confusions between information and meaning, between amount of information and entropy. These difficulties caused some nonsensical claims to be offered under the banner of cybernetics. The more responsible workers criticized this pseudoscientific fringe, thereby contributing to a reversal in attitudes. The new tendency was to regard cybernetics with suspicion and disdain.

Thus, there developed—and still exist—conflicting attitudes toward cybernetics and what its subject matter really is. Vagueness about the meaning of "cybernetics" has been compounded by the fact that since around 1955 the subject of cybernetics has enjoyed a wide acceptance and publicity in the Soviet Union, where it is now interpreted most broadly and used to describe all studies and techniques that relate even in the most remote way to computers, information processing, communications, or control systems.

Today, almost two decades after Wiener's book, "cybernetics" still means different things to different people. For some, cybernetics is not a "new science" but merely a collection of techniques, studies, and devices clustering around information processing. For those who accept this interpretation, "cybernetics" is but a fancy name for the application of certain techniques to related fields—for example, the application of information theory to analysis of coding and redundancy in the visual sensory system.

Others equate cybernetics with automation and its accelerating thrust into all facets of human activity. They recognize that cybernetics not only changes favorably the face of our society but also initiates sociological problems of great magnitude —such as technological unemployment and social conflict resulting from the increasing replacement of men by machines.

Finally, many interpret cybernetics as a new, all-inclusive, and powerful way of analyzing complex systems, from machines to society itself, in terms of the flow and processing of information. Some of these see a deeper significance to the underlying logical structure of cybernetics. The concepts of cybernetics do, in fact, offer hope for a new unity in our understanding of those processes that underlie the activities of knowing.

For some, the real intellectual wealth of cybernetics lies not in its analogies between the computer and the brain—though these analogies are fruitful—but rather in the realization that both systems, natural and artificial, can be analyzed in terms of the same cybernetic language, the language of information and control (see MacKay 1957 for a more detailed discussion). The concepts of this language are potentially rewarding because they span the traditional gap between the psychology of behavior and the physiology of those mechanisms that generate behavior, including cognitive behavior. Thus, cybernetics offers an effective new language for analyzing those information mechanisms and processes associated with behavioral aspects of thinking and knowing. The language of cybernetics may prove rich and versatile enough to permit a theory of knowing—a science of knowledge—to be expressed in terms of cybernetic concepts.

Those concepts suggest even more than how to grasp and formulate the relationship between the information-flow organization of the brain and intelligent behavior. There is no reason to believe that the human brain and nervous system is optimally organized. One might find principles, framed in cybernetic language, that show how to design an artifact able to learn more quickly, remember and associate better, act faster and more reliably, or solve problems more ingeniously than humans. One might find design principles radically different from those embodied in the human, and build (or grow) highly intelligent artifacts. All of this presupposes, of course, a theory of thinking and knowing (as exists for engineering communications) that can be used to judge which cognitive system is optimal relative to some aspect of information processing. Be clear about what this means. Cybernetics today offers no laws describing what kinds of information-flow structures are necessary to produce various dimensions of intelligent (mindlike) behavior.

There exist only the faintest outlines of such organizational principles. Nothing, however, contradicts the thesis that such design principles exist, can be described, and can be implemented. Cybernetics offers both a language and a set of concepts to use in molding these principles into a theory relating information processing to the activities of learning, thinking, knowing, and understanding (see Maron 1965).

M. E. MARON

[*Directly related is the biography of* WIENER. *Other relevant material may be found in* COMPUTATION; INFORMATION THEORY; SIMULATION.]

BIBLIOGRAPHY

AMPÈRE, ANDRÉ MARIE (1834) 1856 *Essai sur la philosophie des sciences: Ou exposition analytique d'une classification naturelle de toutes les connaissances humaines.* 2d ed. Paris: Mallet-Bachelier.

ASHBY, WILLIAM R. (1956) 1961 *An Introduction to Cybernetics.* London: Chapman.

GEORGE, FRANK H. 1961 *The Brain as a Computer.* New York: Pergamon.

Kybernetik. → Published since 1960, mostly in German; the emphasis is on bio-cybernetics.

MACKAY, D. M. (1957) 1964 Information Theory in the Study of Man. Pages 214–235 in John Cohen (editor), *Readings in Psychology.* London: Allen & Unwin.

MARON, M. E. 1965 On Cybernetics, Information Processing, and Thinking. Pages 118–138 in Norbert Wiener and J. P. Schadé (editors), *Cybernetics of the Nervous System.* Progress in Brain Research, Vol. 17. Amsterdam: Elsevier.

SHANNON, CLAUDE E. 1948 The Mathematical Theory of Communication. *Bell System Technical Journal* 27: 379–423, 623–656.

SHANNON, CLAUDE E.; and WEAVER, WARREN (1949) 1959 *Mathematical Theory of Communication.* Urbana: Univ. of Illinois.

WIENER, NORBERT (1948) 1962 *Cybernetics: Or Control and Communication in the Animal and the Machine.* 2d ed. Cambridge, Mass.: M.I.T. Press.

WIENER, NORBERT (1950) 1954 *The Human Use of Human Beings: Cybernetics and Society.* 2d ed. Boston: Houghton Mifflin.

CYCLES

See BUSINESS CYCLES; PERIODIZATION; TIME SERIES.

D

DARWIN, CHARLES

Charles Robert Darwin was born in 1809 at Shrewsbury and died in 1882 in Down House in Kent. He was the next to youngest child in a family of four sisters and an older brother. His father, Robert Darwin, was a physician of imposing presence and severe character. His paternal grandfather, Erasmus, had also been a doctor by profession. By avocation, however, Erasmus Darwin was a naturalist, whose *Zoönomia*, a disquisition in verse on the course of nature, has usually been considered, quite incorrectly, to have been an anticipation of Charles Darwin's theory of evolution. Darwin's maternal grandfather was Josiah Wedgwood, founder of the pottery firm and friend of Erasmus Darwin in the Birmingham scientific circle known as the Lunar Society. Darwin belonged, in short, to a provincial family of means and intelligence which associated itself with the professions, intellectual pursuits, and commerce. Although his father expected him to choose a profession, he never needed to earn a living. In 1839 Darwin, too, married a Wedgwood, his cousin Emma. The seven (of ten) children who survived infancy and their descendants have sustained the notable literary and scientific tradition which distinguishes the family.

Originally intended for medicine in his turn, Darwin detested the study of it at the University of Edinburgh. His father allowed him to move to Cambridge, with a view to his becoming a clergyman. At both universities the hobby of natural history absorbed him. He read; he collected beetles and prepared specimens; he went on geological and entomological forays. He might have become a clerical naturalist like Gilbert White, whose *Natural History and Antiquities of Selborne* had charmed him in boyhood. Instead, a decisive opportunity intervened. In 1831 he was offered the (unpaid) post of naturalist aboard H. M. S. *Beagle*, then outfitting for a voyage to collect geographical information. This was to be no mere trip around the world. The expedition lasted five years. It was the making of Darwin as a scientist, and it cost him his health. Sir Gavin de Beer's biography has established the strong probability that the chronic physical prostration which debilitated Darwin throughout the rest of his life was the manifestation of Chagas' disease, a malady identified only in 1909, which involves infestation of the heart muscle and intestines by *Trypanosoma cruzi*. These bacteria are carried by the great black bug of the pampas, *benchuca* (*Triatoma infestans*), and while in Peru Darwin recorded having watched with careful interest one of these insects biting his finger and engorging itself on his blood.

Darwin returned to England in 1836. *On the Origin of Species* appeared in 1859. In the interval of over twenty years Darwin published descriptive accounts of the zoological and geological findings of the voyage. His *Journal of Researches* in 1839 was followed by a series of geological treatises: one on coral reefs in 1842, a second on volcanic islands in 1844, and a third on South America in 1846. These writings won him the reputation of an accurate, thorough, and reliable naturalist. In the early 1850s he published in four volumes a complete study of fossil and living barnacles. Here his work was that of a descriptive biologist of great finesse, capable also in experimental inquiry. Meanwhile, he was quietly maturing his views on evolution, these too deriving from observations and reflections started on the voyage of the *Beagle*.

Theory in biology. The theoretical originality of Darwin's central work is more difficult to appreciate than its content is difficult to understand. *On the Origin of Species* does not on the face of it read like a book animated by theory, either abstruse or abstract. Paragraphs follow one out of another setting forth evidence for the mutability of animals. That notion was not in itself a new one. Intimations and even evidence of the transformation of species had often before been adduced—by Lamarck, by Darwin's grandfather, and by many others. Certainly Darwin marshaled his materials with a fidelity to fact and a range of relevance that proved telling. Nevertheless, what was original was not the assertion but the explanation of evolution in the theory of natural selection. For that theory constituted a new notion of biological order. Although Darwin's mundane style tended to obscure its novelty, the *Origin* is in fact a work of theory; it changed the way of seeing the phenomena of life.

Prior to the assimilation of Darwin's work, no consensus existed about the mode of biological explanation. Only in the early nineteenth century did biology as a professional discipline emerge from the combination of the tradition of natural history with that of the medical or mechanistic study of anatomy and physiology. In Darwin's youth two distinct traditions governed the modeling of theory —the one organismic and the other teleological. The former arose in eighteenth-century romantic feeling about nature and harked back to ancient Stoicism. According to that philosophy, nature is the source of vitality, morality, and destiny. Goethe's vision of universal metamorphosis exemplified this cast of mind, and its foremost scientific exponent was Lamarck. In post-Darwinian polemics Lamarck has often been represented by those hostile to the theory of natural selection as the predecessor who had formulated whatever was original and valid in the doctrine of evolution. That argument is untrue to the facts and unfair to the thought of both Lamarck and Darwin. In Lamarck's view, cyclic equilibrium obtains in the world between the continuously constitutive forms of activity (electricity, fire, life itself) and the perpetually disintegrating tendency of the physical environment. The innate self-perfecting drive of living beings never altogether prevails over the dead hand of inorganic matter, and the tableau of animals each in its kind represents the highest point to which every species has attained in the continuous process of becoming. Assertions of the inheritance of acquired characters and the law of use and disuse (these are later terms) may, indeed, be found in Lamarck's writings, although only as incidental to his view of flux and process in the progression of life, not as explaining actual evidence of variations.

Over against this conception of life as plastic power, novel in emphasis and appeal if not in principle, persisted the strong tradition of teleology. Engrained since Aristotle, that habit of mind had survived the scientific revolution of the seventeenth century with its scope reduced to the degree that it had become the mode of explanation appropriate to the description of organisms. Within this restricted domain teleology had if anything been fortified by the popularity in eighteenth-century natural theology of the argument from design, which held that the existence of God is demonstrable in the ease and skill with which He had specially created each species to fit its own environment and manner of life. In scientific practice, moreover, teleology answered in detail to the problems of functional analysis of anatomical structure, exhibiting how in plants and animals the part serves in exact respects the purposes of the whole. Such was Cuvier's method in comparative anatomy.

Background of "Origin of Species." The problem of adaptation, in short, was the crux of biological explanation. Aboard the *Beagle* Darwin already saw it to be so. Leaving home a believer in the fixity of species, like Cuvier or Paley, he had the facts of geographical variation of species continuously borne in upon him throughout the extensive experience of the voyage. He told in his *Autobiography* what lines of evidence led him first to doubt and then to change his mind:

. . . I had been deeply impressed by discovering in the Pampean formation great fossil animals covered with armour like that on the existing armadillos; secondly, by the manner in which closely allied animals replace one another in proceeding southwards over the [South American] Continent; and thirdly, by the South American character of most of the productions of the Galapagos archipelago, and more especially by the manner in which they differ slightly on each island of the group. ([1876*a*] 1958, p. 118)

Upon these manifold indications of variation of species in geographical space the new science of geology superimposed evidence of their modification in time. Stratigraphy had become a definitive science in the decades between 1810 and 1830. The first truly historical science, stratigraphy systematically ordered the geological succession according to the fossil population characteristic of the several formations and systems of the rocks. While an undergraduate, Darwin had worked one summer as assistant to one of the founders of stratigraphy, the

Reverend Adam Sedgwick, a professor at Cambridge. Sedgwick, like many among the early geologists, held that the evidence for geological revolutions confirmed Biblical accounts of the Creation and the Flood. That view proved venial scientifically, however, for their intensive study of the fossil record made clear the progression of forms of life in the course of the ages.

Catastrophists of Sedgwick's persuasion took those ages to be brief and punctuated by cataclysms. Increasingly, however, skeptical critics came to think of the span of the past as very long—long enough for all changes to come about gradually. Indeed, the mentor to whom Darwin professed the deepest of his scientific obligations was not a biologist at all. He was Sir Charles Lyell, whose *Principles of Geology*, published in three volumes between 1830 and 1833, was the earliest fully comprehensive work in that science. It combated the doctrine of geological catastrophes in the name of the uniformity and virtual eternity of nature and taught Darwin to think of the cumulative efficacy of minute changes operating progressively across vast reaches of time.

Further insights came to Darwin as he puzzled over the problem of species in the months following his return to England in the autumn of 1836. Soon thereafter he started a notebook on the subject, the first in what was to become a voluminous series. He worked the while, so he later said, on Baconian principles, collecting facts wholesale. One of his concerns was inheritable modifications. Such modifications are not to be confused with characteristics acquired, in the Neo-Lamarckian sense, as a consequence of a creature's individual necessities —the biceps in a blacksmith's arm, for example. Any theory of evolution must, of course, suppose that the variations which are its subject matter are cumulative over generations. From the outset Darwin had the wit to see that if a theory of evolution were not to beg the question, variations must be supposed random in origin, cumulative in effect, and indefinite in extent. In thinking about how they may be accumulated, Darwin meditated often upon the way in which kennel owners, cattle farmers, stablemen, nurserymen, and pigeon fanciers select stock for breeding—how, operating upon successive generations of domesticated animals and plants, the breeder picks for reproduction those individuals that exhibit the characters desired and thus appears to mold the species.

As early as 1837, then, Darwin had all this: geographical evidence of variation; geological proof of succession; a uniformitarian sense of the history of nature; and the notion of random, heritable, and cumulative modifications in form, modifications produced by a process of selection, albeit an artificial one. Even so, he saw no prospect of oversetting by means of such indirect evidence the well-nigh universal conviction that species are fixed in nature itself, based as that belief was on the universal observation that within the experience of everyone like reproduces like, as well as on the plausible supposition that the adaptation of species to all sorts of specialized lives argues the creation of each to lead just that life we see it living.

Darwin disposed of a set of facts and ideas, in other words, and needed a theory; indeed, he was constantly looking for one. It came in one of those flashes of insight which is better called catalytic than coincidental or subconscious. In October 1838 he chanced to read for distraction Malthus' essay on population. The argument persuaded him at once [*see* POPULATION, *article on* POPULATION THEORIES; *and the biography of* MALTHUS]. It must, indeed, have been familiar, for it was one of the commonplaces of contemporary political economy, requiring only to be brought together with Darwin's problem for its relevance to flash into his mind:

. . . being well prepared to appreciate the struggle for existence which everywhere goes on from long-continued observation of the habits of animals and plants, it at once struck me that under these circumstances favourable variations would tend to be preserved, and unfavourable ones to be destroyed. The result of this would be the formation of new species. Here, then, I had at last got a theory by which to work.   ([1876a] 1958, p. 120)

He worked for twenty years before publishing, although he did write out a draft in 1844 for circulation among friends and colleagues, notably Lyell and J. D. Hooker, the botanist. In May 1856 he at last began writing on an exhaustive scale and completed some ten or eleven chapters in the next year and a half. He thought to call the work "Natural Selection." Then on June 18, 1858, Darwin had the shock of receiving from Alfred Russel Wallace, a young naturalist who had been investigating the flora and fauna of the Malayan jungle, the manuscript of an evolutionary theory identical with his own although based on much less extensive material, together with a request to send it along to Lyell if it should seem worthy. This coincidence precipitated Darwin's decision to come before the public. On the advice of Lyell and Hooker he prepared a brief summary of his views to be published jointly with Wallace's paper. Thereupon he settled down to compose an account that should be full enough to do justice to his materials although reduced in scale from what he had initially intended.

It took eight months to write the *Origin of Species*, which appeared in November 1859.

The circumstances of the publication of the *Origin* belong, of course, to Darwin's personal history, not to an account of his science. Suffice it to say that his behavior throughout was entirely honorable. It offers no grounds for the imputation repeated by detractors that he slighted Wallace. (For a general discussion of multiple discoveries in science, see Merton 1961.)

"Origin of Species." The full title summarizes the argument: *On the Origin of Species by Means of Natural Selection, or the Preservation of Favoured Races in the Struggle for Life.* Addressing himself to the general public, Darwin began with the most familiar matter, the great variations evident among domesticated animals. He thereby called attention to the variability which exists within what are commonly taken to be fixed species and observed that in the breeder's hands they are malleable: "The key is man's power of accumulative selection: nature gives successive variations; man adds them up in certain directions useful to him" ([1859] 1964, p. 105). The second chapter extends consideration of the ambiguity of species into nature, and the third attributes the function of selection to the struggle for existence. "Owing to this struggle, variations, however slight, and from whatever cause proceeding, if they be in any degree profitable to the individuals of a species, in their infinitely complex relations to other organic beings and to their physical conditions of life, will tend to the preservation of such individuals, and will generally be inherited by the offspring" (p. 145). Within the species the proportion of favored individuals will increase in successive generations, since by definition these individuals have characteristics with survival value that enable their possessors, merely by living longer than less favored competitors, to produce more descendants similarly equipped. Thus will species alter as time goes on.

The middle chapters of the *Origin* discuss the laws of variation. Darwin's masterful control over detail is particularly evident here. There are acute observations on the effects of use and disuse of organs, on the influence of climate, and on the greater variability of species than of genera, the last offering a consideration peculiarly difficult to comprehend on any basis other than his. Darwin expressly excluded the problem of cause. Given the evidence that variations have in fact occurred and are heritable, the theory of natural selection explains the course of variation or change. Indeed, the success of the theory turned on dropping the question of cause, not as uninteresting, but as cur-

rently unanswerable, although not necessarily forever so.

In the later chapters Darwin anticipated difficulties and objections. He dealt with instinct, which hardly seems a bodily matter. He acknowledged the problem of extreme specialization and discussed the spectacular beauty of the male in certain species of birds as an extravagance that seems to surpass the humdrum effects of selection. He ascribed the absence of transitional forms to the imperfection of the geological record. He treated sexual preferences and choices as a special case of natural selection rather than as an auxiliary or extraneous factor. In summary let it be said that contemporary evolutionists bear him out on all essential matters. The degree of confirmation of his reasoning and its fidelity to vast reaches of fact is extraordinary when it is also considered that he was necessarily unaware of the twentieth-century discoveries about the fine structure and workings of heredity.

Publication of the *Origin* was the great event, indeed the *raison d'être*, of Darwin's career. His single-mindedness invested the book with a kind of power—a power deriving from the scope as well as from the depth of his thought. Iconoclastic critics have sometimes described the book as dull. Nor does it invite stylistic appreciation. It will repay structural analysis, however, and this is the way to understand Darwin's merit as a theorist. For this is a work of theory, even though any given sentence expresses only fact or deduction. The art lies in the deployment, not in the expression, and it creates its effect in the way a mosaic does rather than a painting. Each element is a mere bit of stone, every sentence a mere statement; yet a design governs the arrangement and the disposition. There are not many books in just this genre. Burckhardt's *Civilization of the Renaissance in Italy*, for example, and perhaps Marx's *Capital* (setting aside the disgust which often overlays statements in Marx) are also works in the mid-nineteenth-century mode of factual argumentation which, in the literature of science, Darwin represents at its most powerful.

Darwin did not abandon further science in order to defend his views in the discussion that followed the publication of the *Origin*, although the pattern of the remaining half of his career was inevitably determined by the response to his book. He followed criticism closely and modified later editions of the *Origin* in numerous respects which either met or accepted objections without abandoning the position. Not all the revisions proved fortunate. Least felicitous was one he introduced into the subtitle as well as into the text. At Wallace's urging he substituted Herbert Spencer's formula, "survival of the fittest," for his own phrase, "preservation of favoured races" to describe what transpires in the struggle for life in consequence of natural selection. Both the tautology—i.e., survival in a struggle for life—and the ambiguity of the superlative "fittest" confused his proper meaning and obscured the point he had originally emphasized: that the essential feature in the operation of natural selection is not mere survival for its own sake. It is the differential reproductivity of individuals favored adaptively by chance variation, which effect entails an increasing proportion of similarly constituted offspring in a population.

Darwin's later work.   Thenceforth, Darwin was more effective in his other writings, both in substantiation of the theory of natural selection and in affirmation of his remarkable virtuosity in research. He chose problems which combined an appeal to his taste with relevance to evolution. Three major books develop central evolutionary themes more fully than does the *Origin*. *The Variation of Plants and Animals Under Domestication* (1868) tells in full zoological and archeological detail how man has bent to his uses very variable breeds—dog and horse, for example, sheep and goat, peacock and guinea fowl—and attributes the contrasting stability of the goose to its never having been taken in as a pet or servant and of the donkey to its having served only the classes of society whose members cannot afford experiments [*see* DOMESTICATION, *article on* ANIMAL DOMESTICATION]. By way of excursion, at the end of his book Darwin advanced the hypothesis of pangenesis to account for the phenomena of heredity. Here he addressed himself to the complaint that he had not explained how variations are transmitted. The speculation with which he met the criticism has only increased his vulnerability before later critics, for in imagining that the basis of heredity might be generalized throughout the organism ("gemmules" in each structure and organ governing the formation of its counterpart in the offspring), Darwin appeared to have conceded inheritance of acquired characters taken in a Lamarckian sense. It is to be appreciated, however, that Darwin suggested this speculation as a parenthetical aside.

In *The Descent of Man* (1871) Darwin directed his theory explicitly to the single species *Homo sapiens*. Much of the book is devoted to developing the evolutionary significance of sexual selection—i.e., the preferential choice of reproductive partner. Apart from that, the argument follows two main lines. The first is physical. The immediate evolutionary forebears of mankind are unknown. Darwin never represented man as deriving from apes. He did establish that man must in all probability be descended from species that are classified among primates, and further, that man and the higher apes resemble each other anatomically more closely than the latter resemble the lower primates.

The second line of argument is behavioristic. Intellectual and social faculties are themselves adaptive and in their variations make for the greater or lesser survival of the creatures that possess them. Other species besides man subsist with the aid of rudimentary or developed forms of social organization and communication, and Darwin could see only differences of degree between these and the characteristics of human community and moral awareness.

The last of Darwin's expressly evolutionary treatises carries behavioristic comparisons even further. Probably *The Expression of the Emotions in Man and Animals* (1872) is the most dated of Darwin's writings. Nevertheless, in comparing phenomena like the physical manifestation of hostility in dog and master—the similarity of the snarling jaw to the drawn lip—and many other states of temper, Darwin did carry biology into treatment of faculties traditionally reserved for moral studies. Reciprocally, he introduced the study of animal behavior into psychology [*see* SOCIAL BEHAVIOR, ANIMAL].

In the last decade of his life Darwin put in hand a train of experimental researches mainly botanical in character and published a final series of monographs exhibiting a great variety of novel observations and phenomena. He had already brought out a study of fertilization in orchids—in 1862; in 1877 he issued a second edition, much enlarged in detail. In the same year he published a very acute work on hermaphroditic reproduction in trees and plants. Two years previously, in 1875, he had issued two quite new studies, one on climbing plants (first published in journal form in 1865) and one on insectivorous plants. In 1880 he generalized the former in a book about the power of movement in plants as it resides in root, leaf, stem, and flower. In 1881 he concluded his lifework with an account of the process by which earthworms contribute to the formation of humus: the originality of the subject is characteristic of his acumen, while its choice reflects the modesty of his temperament.

To appreciate the full range of Darwin's accomplishment as a scientist one must read in these experimental writings as well as in the *Origin*. The comparison to Newton is often adduced. It is justified. Notable scientists normally excel either in theoretical insight or in experimental virtuosity.

Newton and Darwin were capable as very few have ever been, and perhaps none in equal measure, of combining those veins and thereby achieving the foremost stature in all aspects that distinguish science. It is true that, given the state of the science, comprehensiveness had to do the work in theory for Darwin that mathematical power did for Newton, which is only to say that the one was suited by his abilities to accomplish for biology what the other had done for physics, and that both of them made the most of those abilities.

Professional response to the "Origin." The theory of natural selection polarized opinion among biologists more radically than is the common effect of scientific theories. Those who adopted it tended to do so straightaway in something like a conversion. "How extremely stupid not to have thought of that," was T. H. Huxley's often quoted reaction as the pieces suddenly fell into place on reading Darwin. Yet even the professional response was influenced by philosophical taste and cultural tradition. Then, as now, the English-speaking scientific world was empirically minded after the manner of Bacon, Locke, and Mill. In Darwin's own milieu, what immediately persuaded was his resolution of the question of biological adaptation. Not that he solved the problem. He did better. He dispelled it, by turning adaptation from final cause into present effect. Instead of a wonder so intricate as to bespeak Providence or purpose, adaptation became merely the outcome of the whole life history of the species in its relation to circumstance and environment, a phenomenon or set of phenomena to be analyzed and explained in evolutionary terms. In Huxley's hands, therefore, Darwin became the protagonist of the drama of scientific fact undoing theological prejudice.

In Germany, where Darwin's work enjoyed a success if anything more influential than in England and the United States, what appealed was less its empiricism than its historicism. The sense of history as indwelling process, whether in the successive versions of Herder, Hegel, or Marx, had in the course of the romantic movement of thought become deeply engrained in the German sense of the world. Philosophically speaking, such historiography treats the past in a mode exactly counter to Darwin's, the one being a realist and the other a nominalist approach to nature. Oblivious to these distinctions, German historicists misread Darwin and took him for their own. It is well known that Marx spoke of dedicating the second book of *Capital* to Darwin, an intention which makes a curious contrast to the Lamarckian position of some subsequent Marxists. The professional champion and self-appointed spokesman, however, was Ernst Haeckel, who tried to make over all biology into the study of evolution. He governed his embryology, for example, by the doctrine that the development of every individual in the womb recapitulates the evolution of the species. Not only does evolution govern all biology, but all truth too: Haeckel's *Riddle of the Universe* is the cardinal document of the movement to make something like a religion out of evolutionary thought itself.

Only in France was Darwin's work initially greeted by indifference (except among anthropologists who did take it up with very great benefit to their science). Not so the biologists. Among them the writ of Cuvier still ran. There was also a problem of language. In French, the word *évolution* refers to the development of an individual; *transformisme* connotes the doctrine as affecting species in general, and at that time involved visionary connotations. A self-defeating semantic objection also supervened—to explain the origin of species in a book which questioned their reality seemed an inadmissible mode of discourse. The greatest of physiologists, Claude Bernard, never even seized the differences between the Darwinian theory and its speculative predecessors. "We must doubtless admire," he wrote disdainfully, "those great horizons dimly seen by the genius of a Goethe, an Oken, a Carus, a Geoffroy Saint-Hilaire, a Darwin, in which a general conception shows us all living beings as the expression of types ceaselessly transformed in the evolution of organisms and species, —types in which every living being individually disappears like a reflection of the whole to which it belongs" ([1865] 1957, pp. 91–92). In general, Darwin expressed himself pragmatically in a manner characteristically English and characteristically unconvincing, not to say irritating, to the French.

The nonprofessional response. Darwin himself took no part in the social Darwinist movement of ideas and gave it no countenance [*see* SOCIAL DARWINISM]. Something must here be said, nevertheless, about the pattern of nonprofessional response, insofar as it has been hostile, for these attitudes greatly amplified for a time certain scientific difficulties left unresolved by Darwin, and they have also contributed to persistent misunderstandings of the status of the theory in science—misunderstandings arising from repugnance toward its political and social derivations.

The pattern has two distinct aspects, theological and moralistic, which turn on different implications of the theory of evolution. The former, the theological issue between the Biblical story of the Creation and the Darwinian account of the origin of species, is the more famous. It is also the more literal and has proved the more ephemeral, concerned as it is with the wide historical fact of evolution rather than with the theory of natural selection, by which Darwin explained and thereby established the fact. The science of geology had, indeed, already faced theology with the necessity of regarding the scriptural account of earth history in an allegorical fashion, and the confrontation between Darwinists and religious believers settled rather than initiated that matter among informed persons. The *Origin of Species* did cause additional shock and distress, of course, chiefly in regard to the question of whether the reality of a spiritual component of human existence requires that man be biologically unique and specially created. This is a dilemma which may be resolved in one of two ways: either by considering the whole universe as contingent and composed of physical and spiritual aspects; or, in a more restricted way, by appreciating that the theory of evolution treats man as an evolved animal, but it does not and in principle cannot assert that he is nothing but an animal. At all events, within a relatively short space of time theologians learned to contemplate evolution without dismay, as clearly a matter of fact; significant religious minds have not felt impelled to gird against the facts, although fundamentalist rejection of them persists in diminishing backwaters.

What has persisted in recurrent and often serious manifestations is a second aspect of resistance to Darwin's work. This kind of resistance is serious because it obtains among educated persons and reveals the occasional inability of highly intelligent people to respect the force and limitations of scientific demonstration. In this tradition the tenor has been to accept and even celebrate the phenomenon of evolution while denigrating the theory of natural selection. Sometimes this denigration has taken the form of an attack on Darwin's character and probity, as in the instances of Barzun (1941) and Himmelfarb (1959). Sometimes it has taken the form of a revival, more or less garbled, of the views of Lamarck, as in the writings of Samuel Butler and George Bernard Shaw. Sometimes it has taken the form of proposing an alternative formula, metaphorical in character, for the purpose of replenishing evolution with intelligence, will, or choice. Such were the notions of "creative evolution," the *élan vital* of Bergson, or entelechy of Driesch. Sometimes it has taken on ideological and political dress, as in the refusal of Lysenko's adherents to admit the irrelevance to heredity of manipulation of the physical and social environment. As, indeed, in any complex of opinions, some proportion of

these several elements, some mixture of these motivations, may be discerned in all types of educated refusal to be persuaded by the theory of natural selection.

What unifies these hostile views into a tradition of romantic resistance is the common complaint that the theory of natural selection deprives the history of nature of any sanctions for man as a social or moral being. These critics hold a different conception of the function of a scientific explanation. They want more out of nature than Darwin, or science generally, has found there. They want reasons, and Darwin gave them circumstance. They want causes, and he gave them accidental variation. They want purpose and direction, and he gave them an indefinite sequence of indifferent results. They want a science which seizes on unity and deep process, and he fragmented nature into a congeries of discrete events connected only by proximity and happenstance. What has proved profound, therefore, is not the incompatibility between evolutionary science and theology, considered intellectually at least. Much deeper and more persistent, partly because of common commitment to the natural with different understandings of what it signifies, has been the incompatibility between the Darwinian theory and any form of naturalistic social or moral philosophy. For the moralist knows what sort of nature he requires of science. And the theory of natural selection has succeeded precisely in consequence of limiting its purview to the indifferent event. While the present state of scientific understanding is not the touchstone by which to judge theories of the past, it is important to emphasize, nevertheless, that the theory of natural selection is part of working evolutionary thought. To refuse to admit its force is not only to question the actual state of scientific knowledge, but it is also to impugn the current mode of scientific explanation.

CHARLES C. GILLISPIE

[*Directly related are the entries* EVOLUTION; GENETICS; RACE. *Other relevant material may be found in the biographies of* COOLEY; GALTON; GIDDINGS; LUBBOCK; MORGAN, LEWIS HENRY; SPENCER; TYLOR.]

WORKS BY DARWIN

(1839) 1952 *Journal of Researches Into the Geology and Natural History of the Various Countries Visited by H.M.S. Beagle.* New York: Hafner. → A facsimile reprint of the first edition. A second edition was published in 1845.

(1842) 1962 *The Structure and Distribution of Coral Reefs.* Berkeley: Univ. of California Press. → A second edition was published in 1874.

(1842–1858) 1958 DARWIN, CHARLES R.; and WALLACE, ALFRED R. *Evolution by Natural Selection.* With a foreword by Gavin de Beer. Cambridge Univ. Press. → The Darwin and Wallace papers of 1858, together with Darwin's other early drafts.

(1844–1846) 1900 *Geological Observations on the Volcanic Islands and Parts of South America Visited During the Voyage of H.M.S. "Beagle."* 3d ed. New York: Appleton. → First published as *Geological Observations on the Volcanic Islands, Visited During the Voyage of H.M.S. Beagle* (1844) and *Geological Observations of South America* (1846).

1851 *A Monograph on the Fossil Lepadidae: Or, Pedunculated Cirripedes of Great Britain.* London: Palaeontological Society.

1851–1854 *A Monograph on the Sub-class Cirripedia, With Figures of All the Species.* 2 vols. London: Ray Society. → Volume 1: *The Lepadidae: or, Pedunculated Cirripedes.* Volume 2: *The Balanidae (or Sessile Cirripedes), the Verrucidae,* etc.

1854 *A Monograph on the Fossil Balanidae and Verrucidae of Great Britain.* London: Palaeontological Society.

(1859) 1964 *On the Origin of Species.* Cambridge, Mass.: Harvard Univ. Press. → A facsimile of the first edition. Numerous editions have been published, including a reprint of the sixth edition in 1927 by Macmillan, and a variorum text edited by Morse Peckham, published by the Univ. of Pennsylvania Press in 1959.

(1862) 1903 *The Various Contrivances by Which Orchids Are Fertilized by Insects.* 2d ed., rev. New York: Appleton. → First published as *On the Various Contrivances by Which British and Foreign Orchids Are Fertilised by Insects.*

(1865) 1893 *The Movements and Habits of Climbing Plants.* 2d ed., rev. New York: Appleton. → First published in Volume 9 of the *Journal of the Linnean Society.*

(1868) 1900 *The Variation of Animals and Plants Under Domestication.* New York: Appleton.

(1871) 1930 *The Descent of Man and Selection in Relation to Sex.* 2d ed., rev. enl. New York: Appleton.

(1872) 1965 *The Expression of the Emotions in Man and Animals.* Edited by Francis Darwin. Univ. of Chicago Press.

(1875) 1900 *Insectivorous Plants.* 2d ed., rev. Edited by Francis Darwin. New York: Appleton.

(1876a) 1958 *Autobiography of Charles Darwin, 1809–1882.* Edited by his granddaughter Nora Barlow. London: Collins. → Written in 1876; first published posthumously in 1887.

(1876b) 1902 *The Effects of Cross and Self Fertilisation in the Vegetable Kingdom.* New York: Appleton.

(1877) 1896 *The Different Forms of Flowers on Plants of the Same Species.* New York: Appleton.

1880 *The Power of Movement in Plants.* London: Murray.

(1881) 1892 *The Formation of Vegetable Mould Through the Action of Worms, With Observations on Their Habits.* New York: Appleton.

(1887) 1959 *The Life and Letters of Charles Darwin.* 2 vols. New York: Basic Books. → Includes an autobiographical chapter, edited by Francis Darwin.

SUPPLEMENTARY BIBLIOGRAPHY

BARZUN, JACQUES (1941) 1958 *Darwin, Marx, and Wagner: Critique of a Heritage.* 2d ed. Garden City, N.Y.: Doubleday.

BERNARD, CLAUDE (1865) 1957 *An Introduction to the Study of Experimental Medicine.* New York: Dover. → First published in French.

DE BEER, GAVIN R. 1964 *Charles Darwin: Evolution by Natural Selection.* New York: Doubleday. → The most authoritative biography.

EISELEY, LOREN 1959 *Darwin's Century: Evolution and the Men Who Discovered It.* Garden City, N.Y.: Doubleday.

GILLISPIE, CHARLES C. 1951 *Genesis and Geology: A Study in the Relations of Scientific Thought, Natural Theology, and Social Opinion in Great Britain, 1790–1850.* Harvard Historical Studies, Vol. 58. Cambridge, Mass.: Harvard Univ. Press. → A paperback edition was published in 1959 by Harper.

GLASS, BENTLEY (editor) 1959 *Forerunners of Darwin: 1745–1859.* Baltimore: Johns Hopkins Press.

HIMMELFARB, GERTRUDE 1959 *Darwin and the Darwinian Revolution.* Garden City, N.Y.: Doubleday.

MERTON, ROBERT K. 1961 Singletons and Multiples in Scientific Discovery: A Chapter in the Sociology of Science. American Philosophical Society, *Proceedings* 105:470–486.

DATA BANKS

See INFORMATION STORAGE AND RETRIEVAL, *article on* INFORMATION SERVICES.

DATING

See ARCHEOLOGY; HISTORIOGRAPHY; PERIODIZATION; TIME.

DAVENANT, CHARLES

Charles Davenant (1656–1714) was one of the leading economic and political pamphleteers in the England of William III and Queen Anne. His writings have a literary distinction far above that of the average pamphlet of the time, and they show considerable skill in the use of the new techniques of "political arithmetic." These qualities, combined with the air of judicious detachment that the author often succeeded in imparting, have misled many commentators into considering Davenant an independent and objective thinker. His pamphlets, however, are essentially occasional pieces, concerned with advancing a particular partisan cause and indeed frequently concerned with advancing the author's own personal interests. Nevertheless, they are interesting examples of early economic analysis and were influential in promoting the increased use of quantitative argument on political and economic questions.

From 1678 to 1689 Davenant served as a commissioner of excise, but when a new commission was named after the accession of William III, he was omitted. This must have been a serious financial blow to him, and for the next five years he applied, without success, for reinstatement in the revenue service. His early writings represent a new approach to the same end. His first pamphlet, published in 1695, *An Essay Upon Ways and Means of Supplying the War* (1771, vol. 1, pp. 1–81), a number of unpublished "memorials" of that and the following year, and his *Discourses on the Public Revenues, and on the Trade of England, Part I* of 1698 (1771, vol. 1, pp. 125–302) can be regarded as an attempt to bring about an alteration in policy likely to redound to his own benefit. These works express disapproval of the financial measures of the Whig ministry and in particular of its use of long-term loans, which Davenant argued would prove detrimental to the economy. His counterproposal was an increase in excise taxation —the branch in which he had had experience.

But he had also a political objection to the loans, for they brought profits to the moneyed men, whom Davenant identified with the Whigs, and the greatest burden of taxation fell on the landed gentry, who were mainly Tories and whose interests Davenant came to espouse. This political side became more prominent, and at the end of *An Essay Upon the Probable Methods of Making a People Gainers in the Balance of Trade* (1771, vol. 2, pp. 163–382), published in 1699, Davenant gave up proposing changes in policy and launched an out-and-out attack on the ministry and all its works. He was presumably convinced that his chances of advancement were better with the Tory opposition, and he went on to write several purely political pamphlets, the most celebrated being *The True Picture of a Modern Whig* (1771, vol. 4, pp. 125–180), published in 1701. These established him as the leading Tory pamphleteer. He was also identified with the extreme Tories in Parliament, where he sat from 1698 to 1701.

When his friends came to power on the accession of Anne in 1702, he was rewarded with the customs post of inspector-general of exports and imports, which he held until his death in 1714. This was not, however, enough to keep him out of financial difficulties, and he lived his last years largely on the charity of friends. His next work, in 1704, *Essays Upon Peace at Home and War Abroad* (1771, vol. 4, pp. 267–439; vol. 5, pp. 1–69), supported the new ministerial policy of "moderation" and infuriated his former extremist associates. When they returned to power in 1710, Davenant had to conciliate them with two partisan dialogues in his old style and with two *Reports to the . . . Commissioners for . . . Public Accounts* (1771, vol. 5, pp. 345–463) on the trade with France and Holland, which, although in the guise of impartial statistical studies, constituted in fact an economic argument in justification of the minis-

terial policy of deserting the Dutch and other allies and making a separate peace with France.

Davenant's earlier writings on foreign trade are less political, but they reveal the same fears of the threat of Dutch rivalry to England's trade. In *An Essay on the East India Trade* (1771, vol. 1, pp. 83–123) published in 1696, he argued that English textiles need not be protected against Indian goods. Some passages in this work have given rise to the myth that Davenant was an early free trader. His whole argument, however, is conceived in terms of the balance of trade, and he takes the line, as did earlier writers, such as Thomas Mun, that even if the "particular" balance with India is adverse, this is more than compensated for through the interdependence of different branches of international trade and that it is the country's "general" balance of trade alone that matters. Two years later, in 1698, he elaborated this argument and applied it also to the "losing" trade with France in *Discourses on the Public Revenues, and on the Trade of England, Part II* (1771, vol. 1, pp. 343–459; vol. 2, pp. 1–162). He obtained some reward for these services from the East India Company and may also have been remunerated for his strong advocacy of the case of the Royal African Company in *Reflections Upon the Constitution and Management of the Trade to Africa* (1771, vol. 5, pp. 71–343), published in 1709.

Although Davenant's personal career was not very successful, although he was on the losing side in almost every controversy he joined, and although his enemies had some grounds for regarding him as a self-seeking, mercenary timeserver, his writings have a place in the history of economic thought and analysis; they set out tenable points of view held by significant bodies of minority opinion and often suggest a very genuine concern for the welfare of his country.

D. A. G. WADDELL

WORKS BY DAVENANT

For a complete list of works, see Waddell 1956. *With the exception of* Davenant 1710, *all of Davenant's important published works, including all titles mentioned in the text, are collected in* Davenant 1771.

(1695–1696) 1942   *Two Manuscripts by Charles Davenant.* Edited by A. P. Usher. Baltimore: Johns Hopkins Press. → Contains *A Memorial Concerning the Coyn of England,* 1695, and *A Memorial Concerning Creditt,* 1696.

1710   *Sir Thomas Double at Court, and in High Preferments.* Volume 2: New Dialogues Upon the Present Posture of Affairs. London: Morphew.

1771   *The Political and Commercial Works of That Celebrated Writer Charles D'Avenant.* Edited by Charles Whitworth. 5 vols. London: Horsfield.

WORKS ABOUT DAVENANT

Biographical information is summarized in Waddell 1958. No satisfactory critical work has been published. Casper 1930 is an attempt to analyze Davenant's economic ideas, and Ballière 1913 is a bald summary of his economic writings.

BALLIÈRE, YVON 1913 *L'oeuvre économique de Charles Davenant.* Paris: Rivière.

CASPER, WILLY 1930 *Charles Davenant: Ein Beitrag zur Kenntnis des englischen Merkantilismus.* Beiträge zur Geschichte der Nationalökonomie, No. 7. Jena (Germany): Fischer.

WADDELL, D. A. G. 1956 The Writings of Charles Davenant. *Library: A Quarterly Review of Bibliography* 5th Series 11:206–212.

WADDELL, D. A. G. 1958 Charles Davenant (1656–1714) —A Biographical Sketch. *Economic History Review* 2d Series 11:279–288.

DAVENPORT, HERBERT J.

Herbert Joseph Davenport, American economist, was born in Wilmington, Vermont, in 1861 and died in New York City in 1931. His father, a leading lawyer, had been a Democrat in Republican Vermont, and the father and son shared a good measure of rugged individualism. Davenport's forebears on both sides were members of old New England families that included the founders of New Haven, Connecticut, and Salem, Massachusetts.

While in his twenties Davenport went to South Dakota, invested his parental legacy in real estate, and made and lost a fortune. He studied successively at the University of South Dakota, Harvard Law School, the University of Leipzig, the École des Sciences Politiques at Paris, and eventually at the University of Chicago, where he obtained his doctorate in economics in 1898. After serving as a high school principal in the Midwest, he taught at the University of Chicago from 1902 to 1908, then at the University of Missouri, where he was head of the department of economics and from 1914 to 1916 dean of the School of Commerce, and finally, from 1916 to 1929, at Cornell University.

Davenport was a man of strong personal loyalties that correspond to the complex nature of his position in American economic thought. When he published *Value and Distribution* in 1908, he dedicated it to J. Laurence Laughlin, soundest of economists, who had served as the first chairman of the department of economics at the newly founded University of Chicago. When, a dozen or so years later, Davenport was under consideration for the presidency of the American Economic Association, his loyalty to Laughlin was strong enough to cause him misgivings about accepting the post, because

Laughlin had never held this high office. No less durable was the attachment that connected Davenport with the unorthodox and scintillating Thorstein Veblen, who was first his teacher and later his colleague at Chicago. Veblen considered Davenport one of his outstanding pupils, second only to Wesley Clair Mitchell. Davenport, in turn, stood by Veblen on many occasions when Veblen was in difficulties, securing employment for him at the University of Missouri in 1910, taking him into his home, and in later years more than once trying to find a place for him at Cornell.

Davenport claimed, half in jest, that he was drawn to the study of economics because he was sure that something was wrong with socialism and he wanted to find out what it was. As a young man at Chicago, he had sought out Veblen after class, eager to hear his frank opinion on this subject, but the great skeptic never gave him a direct answer. Again, in 1920, in his presidential address (1921), Davenport touched on the subject of socialism, saying that he was not a socialist because he was unable to predict what the socialist ideal would concretely turn out to be. He did not doubt, however, that political democracy was as readily possible in a collective as in a competitive economic order.

In his own way Davenport was as bitter a critic of business civilization as his master Veblen. He was convinced of the relative character of most economic doctrines, but his bent was not an institutional one. Rather than tracing changes in institutions, he set out to develop a theory that was to shed light on the economic environment in which he found himself. This theory was to be purged of the moralizing and psychologizing tendencies characteristic of the thought of Alfred Marshall and of the Austrians. It was to have no place for such concepts as utility, real costs, and the "social organism." Instead, it was to be, more narrowly, "the science which treats phenomena from the standpoint of price" (1913, p. 25). On this basis, Davenport developed his economic theory in a "sound," although not entirely conventional, manner, with such occasional shockers as the inclusion of abortionists and prostitutes among the ranks of producers and of burglars' jimmies among wealth. At the end of this work, he stated the need for a new economics that is not "a system of apologetics, the creed of the reactionary, a defense of privilege, a social soothing sirup, a smug pronouncement of the righteousness of whatever is" (1913, p. 528). Economists, he claimed, have wrongly identified private gain with social welfare. There are echoes of John A. Hobson here as well as of Thorstein Veblen. It was no wonder that

Davenport advised his students to take Veblen's course, to which he considered his own work a prelude. Although Davenport's views did not prevent his election as president of the American Economic Association in 1920, they scandalized not a few of his colleagues.

Davenport is remembered best as an early exponent of the concept of opportunity cost, which defines cost in terms of opportunities foregone. Underlying his system is the notion of a general interdependence of all prices, but this idea was not connected with the general-equilibrium approach of the mathematical school of Lausanne. Davenport's critical view of utility, which, of course, he shared with others, prepared the ground for the acceptance of the indifference-curve approach, a theory developed by mathematical economists. In still other ways he was ahead of his time—for example, when he considered the problem of unemployment as "the most important practically and perhaps the most difficult theoretically" (1896, p. 355), when he developed what was then one of the best explanations of the multiple expansion of credit through the banking system (1913, chapter 17, pp. 260–266), or when he related the interest rate to the operations of the commercial banks rather than to psychological factors (1913, chapter 8, pp. 349 ff.).

HENRY W. SPIEGEL

[*For the historical context of Davenport's work, see the biographies of* HOBSON *and* VEBLEN.]

WORKS BY DAVENPORT

For a list of Davenport's contributions to economic periodicals, see American Economic Association 1961.

1896   *Outlines of Economic Theory.* New York: Macmillan.
1908   *Value and Distribution.* Univ. of Chicago Press.
(1913) 1943   *The Economics of Enterprise.* New York: Macmillan.
1921   The Post-war Outlook. *American Economic Review* 11:1–15.
1935   *The Economics of Alfred Marshall.* Ithaca, N.Y.: Cornell Univ. Press; Oxford Univ. Press.

SUPPLEMENTARY BIBLIOGRAPHY

AMERICAN ECONOMIC ASSOCIATION   1961   Herbert Joseph Davenport. Volume 1, page 185, and Volume 2, page 302 in *Index of Economic Journals.* Homewood, Ill.: Irwin. → Volume 1 contains 30 items by Davenport published from 1894 to 1921. Volume 2 contains 3 items published from 1925 to 1930.
COPELAND, MORRIS A.   1931   Herbert Joseph Davenport (obituary). *Economic Journal* 41:496–500.
DORFMAN, JOSEPH   (1934) 1961   *Thorstein Veblen and His America.* New York: Viking; Kelley Reprints.
DORFMAN, JOSEPH   1949   Herbert Joseph Davenport: Conflict of Loyalties. Volume 3, pages 375–390 in Joseph Dorfman, *The Economic Mind in American Civilization.* New York: Viking.
HOMAN, PAUL T.   1931   Herbert Joseph Davenport 1861–1931 (obituary). *American Economic Review* 21:696–700.
HUTCHISON, TERENCE W.   (1953) 1962   *A Review of Economic Doctrines, 1870–1929.* 2d ed. Oxford: Clarendon.
KENDRICK, M. SLADE   1944   Herbert Joseph Davenport. Volume 21, page 224 in *Dictionary of American Biography.* New York: Scribner.
KNIGHT, FRANK H.   1931   Herbert Joseph Davenport. Volume 5, pages 8–9 in *Encyclopaedia of the Social Sciences.* New York: Macmillan.

DAVIDSON, DAVID

The Swedish economist David Davidson (1854–1942) established his reputation with the publication of his dissertation, *Bidrag till läran om de ekonomiska lagarna för kapitalbildningen* ("Contributions to the Doctrine of the Laws of Capital Formation" 1878). Written at the completion of his law studies at the University of Uppsala (1871–1877), the book made him, with Gustav Cassel and Knut Wicksell, one of the founders of neoclassical economics in Sweden.

Although the main part of the book is devoted to an analysis of the concept of capital along classical lines, the second part is an attempt to base an economic theory upon the structure of wants. Thus the main part of the book continues the tradition of Turgot, Adam Smith, F. B. W. Hermann, and others, whereas the second part shows the strong influence of Carl Menger. Davidson accepted Menger's theory of subjective value, a doctrine implying that wants are measurable, that the wants of individual consumers are comparable, and that economic activity represents a striving to maximize utility ("the value of things"). There is also a trace of marginalistic reasoning in the book.

Davidson's discussion of capital formation emphasizes the factors that determine saving, whereas investment is given little attention. Among the factors that influence saving, he mentioned provision for one's family, provision for old age, the size of one's income, and the efficiency of credit institutions. He did not treat the rate of interest. His views on capital have certain similarities with those of Eugen von Böhm-Bawerk, who was also a student of Menger's.

Davidson's next book, *Bidrag till jordränteteoriens historia* ("Contributions to the Theory of Rent" 1880), attempts to show, among other things, that the classical form of the doctrine of rent was developed before Ricardo (for example, by West). This book was responsible for stimulating Davidson's strong interest in Ricardo, and his theoretical work after this point was, to a large extent, involved with analyses of Ricardo. Davidson also published works on monetary and fiscal theory (1886; 1889).

In 1899 he made his major contribution to the development of economics with the founding of the *Ekonomisk tidskrift*, Sweden's first scientific economic journal. He served as editor of the journal until 1939, and from 1900 on published almost all his own writings in it. Davidson was often involved in controversies with Cassel and Wicksell; Wicksell acknowledged the extent to which his own ideas were developed as a result of sharpening his wits against Davidson's.

Davidson's writing was characterized by its analytical rigor. An example of the kind of analytical work identified with him is his concept of "stable money value." He saw stable money as something that could be achieved by decreasing the price level during times of increasing productivity. Later, he also developed the idea of an "absolute money value," but this does not seem to have been a fruitful one.

Davidson was appointed professor of economics and public finance at the University of Uppsala in 1890. One of his students was Per Jacobsson, later president of the International Monetary Fund.

KARL GUSTAV LANDGREN

[*For the historical context of Davidson's work, see the biographies of* CASSEL; MENGER; RICARDO; SMITH, ADAM; TURGOT; WEST; WICKSELL.]

WORKS BY DAVIDSON

1878 Bidrag till läran om de ekonomiska lagarna för kapitalbildningen. Ph.D. dissertation, Uppsala (Sweden) Univ.
1880 *Bidrag till jordränteteoriens historia.* Uppsala Universitets Årsskrift. Rätts-och statsvetenskaper, No. 2. Uppsala (Sweden) Univ.
1886 *Europas centralbanker.* Uppsala (Sweden): Almqvist.
1889 *Om beskattningsnormen vid inkomstskatten.* Uppsala (Sweden): Lundequist.

SUPPLEMENTARY BIBLIOGRAPHY

BRINLEY, THOMAS 1935 The Monetary Doctrines of Professor Davidson. *Economic Journal* 45:36–50.
HECKSCHER, ELI F. (1951) 1952 David Davidson. *International Economic Papers* 2:111–135. → In English; first published in Swedish.
JACOBSSON, PER 1939 David Davidson. *Economisk tidskrift* 41:1–10. → In Swedish.

DAVY, GEORGES

Georges Ambroise Davy, French sociologist, was born in Bernay (Eure) in 1883. He entered the École Normale Supérieure in 1905 and became *agrégé de philosophie* in 1908 and *docteur ès lettres* in 1922. After teaching at *collèges* in Nice and Lyons, Davy joined the University of Dijon in a teaching capacity in 1919 and in 1931 entered university administration as rector of the university division of Rennes. In 1938 he became general inspector of public instruction in France. He returned to teaching in 1944, occupying the chair of sociology at the Sorbonne until 1955.

Davy may be considered a member of the Durkheim school. His early book reviews in *L'année sociologique* (from 1910 on), particularly the reviews of books in the fields of the sociology of morals and of law, discussed the judicial theories of the time in the light of Durkheim's ideas. In 1922 he published *Le droit, l'idéalisme et l'expérience* (1922*a*), a collection of essays on Raymond Saleilles, Maurice Hauriou, Léon Duguit, François Gény, and Emmanuel Lévy, asserting that the postulate of the reality of a collective mind permits the sociological explanation of the idea-content of the law.

In the debate between sociologists and psychologists that took place in France after Durkheim's death, Davy's position was a dogmatically "sociological" one: His article "La sociologie" (1924) presented Durkheim's approach without even the occasional restrictions imposed by Durkheim himself. Yet Davy later modified his position. In an inaugural address at the First World Congress of the International Sociological Association, he stressed that psychology must also play a part in the explanation of social facts, and he asserted that the way the conscious individual determines his behavior must be related to the way social conditions determine his behavior (1950).

Davy's most significant work, *La foi jurée* (1922*b*), was an attempt to reconstruct the formation of contractual law. Davy argued that there is a continual change from statute to contract and that even before a contractual relationship comes into existence, its function is performed by the adaptation of relationships established by statute. Specifically contractual relationships appear only when certain social transformations have taken place: a transformation of totemism that turns names and blazons into objects of exchange introduces a contractual element into social status; a change in descent patterns conduces to male heredity and supremacy and the emergence of a kind of male individualism characteristic of feudalism. Davy's analysis, based largely on the accounts of the potlatch that became known in France through the work of Marcel Mauss, interprets Kwakiutl society as being in a state of transition and revealing the transformations requisite to the development of contractual law.

JOSEF GUGLER

[Other relevant material may be found in the biographies of DURKHEIM; MAINE; MAUSS.*]*

WORKS BY DAVY

1919–1920   Émile Durkheim *Revue de métaphysique et de morale* 26:181–198; 27:71–112.
1922a   *Le droit, l'idéalisme et l'expérience.* Paris: Alcan.
1922b   *La foi jurée: Étude sociologique du problème du contrat, la formation du lien contractuel.* Paris: Alcan.
(1923) 1926   MORET, ALEXANDRE; and DAVY, GEORGES *From Tribe to Empire: Social Organization Among Primitives and in the Ancient East.* London: Routledge; New York: Knopf. → First published in French.
1924   *La sociologie.* Volume 2, pages 765–810 in Georges Dumas (editor), *Traité de psychologie.* Paris: Alcan.
(1931) 1950   *Sociologues d'hier et d'aujourd'hui.* 2d ed. Paris: Presses Universitaires de France. → A collection of essays on Espinas, Durkheim, McDougall, and Lucien Lévy-Bruhl, with an introduction on French sociology from 1918 to 1925.
1939   *Les sentiments sociaux et les sentiments moraux.* Volume 6, pages 153–240 in Georges Dumas (editor), *Nouveau traité de psychologie.* Paris: Alcan.
1950   *La recherche sociologique et les relations internationales. Cahiers internationaux de sociologie* 9:3–16.
1952   *Le social et l'humain dans la sociologie durkheimienne. Revue philosophique* 142:321–350.
1956   *Droit et changement social.* Volume 1, pages 33–46 in World Congress of Sociology, Third, Amsterdam, 1956, *Transactions.* London: International Sociological Association.

DE GOBINEAU, JOSEPH ARTHUR
See GOBINEAU, JOSEPH ARTHUR DE.

DE MAN, HENDRIK
See MAN, HENDRIK (HENRI) DE.

DE MOIVRE, ABRAHAM
See MOIVRE, ABRAHAM DE.

DE SAUSSURE, FERDINAND
See SAUSSURE, FERDINAND DE.

DE TOCQUEVILLE, ALEXIS
See TOCQUEVILLE, ALEXIS DE.

DE TOURVILLE, HENRI
See TOURVILLE, HENRI DE.

DE VITI DE MARCO, ANTONIO
See VITI DE MARCO, ANTONIO DE.

DEAFNESS
See HEARING.

DEATH

I. DEATH AND BEREAVEMENT   *John W. Riley, Jr.*
II. THE SOCIAL ORGANIZATION
    OF DEATH   *Robert W. Habenstein*

I
DEATH AND BEREAVEMENT

Death is a personal event that man cannot describe for himself. As far back as we can tell, man has been both intrigued by death and fearful of it; he has been motivated to seek answers to the mystery and to seek solutions to his anxiety. Every known culture has provided some answer to the meaning of death; for death, like birth or marriage, is universally regarded as a socially significant event, set off by ritual and supported by institutions. It is the final *rite de passage.*

The social and psychological aspects of death have been studied by anthropologists, sociologists, psychologists, and psychiatrists; and the main outlines of their understandings can be summarized on three levels—cultural, social, and individual. The meanings which have been attached to death in most cultures include beliefs in some kind of existence after death; most peoples—save the nonliterate—have entertained theories of personal salvation; and religion, philosophy, and political ideology have provided some answers to man's quest for the meaning of death. The relationship between death and the social structure has received little systematic attention from social scientists, although there is much research on the social prescriptions for bereavement, especially as these relate to ritualistic mourning and individual grief. Scattered empirical studies suggest that, for the individual in the contemporary Western world, matters of death are less salient than those of living, although there are clear traces of a latent and underlying ambivalence.

Although between fifty and sixty million people die each year, growing proportions of people in the world live into the later years. Thus, many people have the opportunity to contemplate their death, and unknown but even greater numbers of persons are affected by bereavement. For a phenomenon of such wide and pervasive significance, it is curious that the most recent systematic bibliography on the subject of Western social science literature on death and bereavement (Kalish 1965) does not exceed four hundred entries—many of them recent. In our time death has been largely a taboo topic (e.g., see Feifel 1959; Fulton 1965). But attention is now being directed to various social problems involving man's relationship to death: the problem of death and bereavement for the aged, dilemmas faced by the practitioners who deal with death, risk taking by both nations and individuals, and the social and moral implications of scientific advance in the control of death.

Death and culture

Death raises two kinds of problems that require cultural definitions and norms: those pertaining to one's own death, and those pertaining to the obligations imposed upon others by the fact of a death. In no known culture is the individual left to face death completely uninitiated. He is provided with beliefs about "the dead" and about his own probable fate after death. Similarly, all these cultures include norms governing the imperatives imposed by death: a corpse must be looked after; the deceased must be placed in a new status; his vacated roles must be filled and his property disposed of; the solidarity of his group must be reaffirmed; and his bereaved must be re-established and comforted (Blauner 1966).

Death in nonliterate society. Systematic analysis of the records on nonliterate peoples shows various recurrent components in their belief systems (Simmons 1945). Belief in a spirit world inhabited by the dead is practically universal among them. There is no clear theory of "natural" death; they believe that death results from the intervention of an outside agent. The culture typically includes a conception, implicit or explicit, of a relationship between the living and the dead. Death is viewed as a crisis through which the deceased enters upon a new status. Symbols of power, either malevolent or benevolent, are attached to the dead. Among the Navajo, for example, actions of the spirits of the dead are generally perceived as being hostile toward the living; while among the Tikopia, where cohesion and continuity between the two worlds is a central theme, the relationship between quick and dead is believed to be benign. Belief in personal salvation appears rare; and, in contrast to the pervasive concerns of civilized man, primitive man seems to have developed no eschatology of rewards and punishments in the worlds populated by the dead (Bellah 1964).

In respect to bereavement practices, anthropologists report great diversity. The actual bereavement period may extend, as it does for the Cocopa, over a period of years; or, as among the Pueblo, it may be but brief and perfunctory. In some cultures, bereavement begins with illness (which may be tantamount to death); in others, it begins only after the disposal of the corpse. In some cultures, the bereaved are required to idolize and placate the deceased, who is certain "to return"; in others, the deceased is held in such great fear that elaborate rituals are required to prevent his taking up his former role in the community (Krupp & Kligfeld 1962). There is, however, no satisfactory general theory to account for these cultural variations.

Historical perspectives. Within recorded history, answers to problems raised by death are found in religion, philosophy, and, to some extent, in political ideology. The major world religions include varying beliefs in a relationship between man's life on earth and his ultimate fate after death. Rabbinic Judaism developed a detailed theory of a day of judgment. According to the teachings of Zoroaster, the soul is directed at death to balance its good and evil deeds. In the Islamic scheme, Allah is ready to prepare a happy place for the true believer. Buddhism postulates that *nirvana* (a final beatitude, oblivion) is attainable through a long succession of reincarnations, each mystically related to the *karma* (deeds) of preceding lives. Similarly, Hinduism rests upon a complex and philosophical relationship between *dharma* (civic and religious piety) and *moksa* (the attainment of salvation). The teachings of both Confucius and Lao-tzu carry an implication of salvation in that man must adapt both to the expectations of his ancestors and to cosmic moral law. The religions of East and West differ fundamentally with regard to death and life after death on only two main points. First, for the East, the route to salvation tends to be either contemplative or mystical; for the West, it tends to be ascetic and active. Second, the East views the ultimate outcome as an undifferentiated and impersonal "oneness" with the universe, while the West sees it as the continuation of the integrity of the personal self.

In the history of Western religion, the emergent Christian conception of salvation gave emphasis to an afterlife in which the individual's identity continues essentially intact. The Roman Catholic church institutionalized the problem of salvation in the relationship of the individual to the priest; anxiety about death is reduced as the individual experiences sin, repentance, atonement, and release. In contrast, the Calvinist concept of predestination intensified anxiety about death and the afterlife, since it regarded man as powerless to control his fate. Thus new forms of conduct and social organization evolved, as Max Weber (1904–1905, pp. 99–128, 155–183 in 1958 edition) points out, to help the early Protestant deal with this increased anxiety; and, to ensure his salvation, the individual turned to a life that emphasized methodical, rational conduct in work and a disciplined family life. In present-day religious thinking, however, the clear connection between death and salvation has become blurred. Schneider and Dornbusch's (1958) study of popular religion in America (an analysis of the inspirational writings by Norman Vincent Peale, Joshua Loth Liebman, and others) shows a predominant stress on salvation in this life rather than in the next and small preoccupation—since man is assumed to be essentially good—with spiritual preparation for death.

The most active periods of philosophical concern with death tend to coincide with periods of relative inactivity in formal religious institutions (Choron 1963). In Greece during the fifth and fourth centuries B.C., for example, death was a central theme of philosophical speculation. Plato developed his theories of the interlocking relationship of knowledge and the immortality of the soul—a juxtaposition of ideas destined to play a dramatic role in the history of Christendom. During the second and first centuries B.C. in Rome, the problem of death again became a major focus for philosophy; to the Stoics, for example, preparation for death was considered the only proper end of philosophy.

Although the history of Christian belief in eternal life seems to have largely inhibited widespread philosophical treatments of the problem of death in the West, a notable development took shape toward the end of the nineteenth century in the form of existentialism. Contemporary existentialist theories, often obscure and contradictory, are of special interest because of their emphasis upon death. Jean-Paul Sartre, in one view, echoes several earlier philosophical traditions in his argument that the self is finite, that nonbeing follows death, and that the immortality of the soul is a fiction. Sartre thus ignores and despises "the stranger," which is death. Martin Heidegger, in another view, wants to "disarm" death by taking it into the consciousness. Hence, the individual's search for the meaning of existence (*Dasein*) points to death as the ultimate phenomenon of life (Choron 1963). In still another existentialist view, the question posed by death has been reinterpreted to ask: Can the individual cope with the threat of nothingness by replacing his belief in personal immortality with a belief in social immortality?

Various ideologies throughout history have involved such higher principles as patriotism or work in seeking answers to the meaning of death. The Homeric singers extolled death for warriors, promising that they would not be forgotten. The ideology of the Greek *polis* offered the individual a kind of immortality if his life was sacrificed for the common good—an element in political ideology that has changed little over the centuries. Man has always been willing to die for the state; in the extreme case, even by his own hand (for example, Durkheim's conception of altruistic suicide). The stress on death for the state typically gains currency during wartime. War consecrates the meaning of death (Warner 1959), and the similarity between the soldier and the man who perishes "in his calling" foreshadows an important element in the ideology of the monolithic state. According to communist doctrine, the individual can reduce his anxiety about death through work and identification with the party. Thus the Russians, like the Puritans, have incorporated work into their ideology as one answer to the threat of death.

Death and society

Death and the changing patterns of mortality are reflected in the structure of society. With the exception of a number of highly significant and institutionalized practices—war, infanticide, cannibalism, ceremonial human sacrifice, capital punishment—social institutions have evolved to facilitate life and to prevent death. The demographic history of man bears out the generalization that he has been more interested in death control than in birth control. Thus, mortality rates have tended to fall faster than fertility rates. Yet, despite an impressive literature on the means for controlling demographic changes, relatively little attention has been paid to the larger problems inherent in the relationship between death and social structure. Two examples will illustrate the range of developing theoretical concern with such problems, although no general theory is yet at hand.

First, the recent work of Blauner (1966) points to the fact that mortality operates on society as a variable, not as a constant. According to this theory, the higher the mortality, the greater the threat to the social system, a threat which is reflected both in ritualistic mourning practices and in the social prescriptions that are activated when deaths occur. In high mortality societies, social relationships tend to be diffuse and widely dispersed throughout the group (everyone knows everyone else), and, when someone dies, the entire community mourns along with the next of kin and close associates. Similarly, in such societies there tend to be prescriptions that "solve" the social problems created by individual deaths. Thus, elaborate kinship rules provide new families for orphaned children, just as such customs as the levirate and sororate provide new spouses for widows and widowers.

In societies with low mortality rates, however, death poses a greater threat to the personality system. In the West today, for example, the small family tends to socialize its members for interpersonal competence, giving bereavement an especially personal significance. Furthermore, since a person's significant others are concentrated among his close relatives and friends, bereavement reactions tend to be highly varied and individually therapeutic. The most striking exceptions to this tendency are the highly ritualistic occasions produced by the deaths of heads of state and other prominent figures, such as the funeral of President Kennedy.

Findings of recent studies in the United States and Great Britain support such an individualistic emphasis in bereavement practices. In the United States, the appropriate expressions of grief and the length of the bereavement period, rather than following a widely accepted pattern, are found to vary greatly with the circumstances of the death, the status of the deceased, the status of the bereaved, the nature of their former relationship, and the age and sex of both the bereaved and the deceased (although women are permitted a greater display of sorrow than men, the general prescription is "to be brave"). Bereavement, with few social limitations, is susceptible to individual definition to fit individual needs (Bowman 1959). Similarly, a study of bereavement in Britain concludes that "the majority of the population lack common patterns or ritual to deal with bereavement" (Gorer 1965).

A second theoretical approach, developed by Parsons (1963), calls attention to the changing context of death in American society; it notes that increasing proportions of any birth cohort live to the approximate completion of the life cycle and that death has been largely separated from its long and complex relationship to suffering. Thus, the twin threats of suffering and prematurity have been greatly reduced by medical advances. Death is now more often inevitable than adventitious; as early as the beginning of the twentieth century, Sir William Osler was able to report that few of his dying patients died in agony. Within this context, Parsons argues, new orientations toward death are developing that are less influenced by these traditional anxieties.

Parsons classifies the developing orientations into two types: a "normal" or active orientation (consistent with the high evaluation placed by contemporary society on science and activity) that stresses the moral significance of death as the termination of a completed life cycle of effort and achievement; and a deviant orientation that is essentially regressive and fatalistic. To the extent that this "normal" orientation prevails in American society, the individual is expected to "face up" to death in realistic terms, and his bereaved are expected to do their "grief work" quickly and privately—within the intimate circle of family and close associates. At the same time, the deviant orientation to death is also clearly in evidence, and to this Parsons relegates the denial of the reality of death, which some scholars have regarded as the modal American view (as indicated by such phenomena as the impermeability of caskets, the practice of cosmetic embalming, and the lifelike presentation of the corpse). How widespread each type of orientation actually is becomes an empirical question to which studies have only recently begun to be directed.

Apart from such special theories, the over-all relationships between human death and human society have recently been probed by a few writers (for example, Choron 1963; Hoffman 1964; Sulzberger 1961; Brown 1959) but have not yet received systematic theoretical attention from social scientists. Yet the fact of death raises problems on several levels of social structure (Blauner 1966). Mortality challenges social continuity—and societies are universally characterized by institutions for transmitting the heritage from one generation to the next. Mortality threatens the orderly functioning of society—and social structures are universally characterized by mechanisms for replacing deceased performers of social roles. Mortality weakens the group—and groups have traditionally established means, in the face of death, for reassembly and restoration.

Mannheim (1923–1929) pursues one theoretical approach that begins to deal with such broader issues by asking the disarmingly hypothetical question of what society would be like if there were no death. He points to connections between death and other basic processes: as participants in society die, there are roles to be filled by new participants; moreover, since the accumulated heritage can be only imperfectly transmitted, there is a continual process of transition from generation to generation. Consequently, as new participants are able to take a fresh look at society, social change is facilitated. New approaches and solutions are constantly being developed, and old solutions are discarded and forgotten when they are no longer necessary or effective.

While Mannheim's provocative essay probes a wide range of social phenomena, a more complete theoretical formulation of the adaptive and selective mechanisms implicit in the relationship of death to society might well be possible. Such widely used social science concepts as those pertaining to political succession, property inheritance, kinship structure, socialization—to list but a few—might be transferable to a more general sociological theory of death.

Death and the individual

The historical shift in bereavement practices from a social to an individual emphasis holds important implications for the individual, who must face not only his own death but also the possible loss of close relatives and associates. Despite the importance of the topic, empirical studies of the individual's relationship to death have been comparatively few and recent. Great obstacles to research are posed by people's reluctance to discuss so private a matter, as well as by their underlying ambivalence toward death itself. Nevertheless, attempts are now being made to examine different aspects of the individual's feelings and attitudes, using a variety of research techniques, from projective tests and physiological response measures to interviews of cross-section samples. Reactions have been obtained from several special segments of the population—children, the aged, the dying, the mentally and the physically ill. Certain characteristics of the individual (sex, age, religiosity, education, health, etc.) have been studied as possible factors affecting attitudes toward death. And, although some of the first findings appear inconclusive or confusing, efforts are underway to explain individual attitudes through their interrelationships with the norms of the culture (Volkart & Michael 1957) and to design new research within a broader conceptual framework.

The image of death. While the empirical studies cannot yet support any over-all formulation of individual attitudes toward death, a few examples will illustrate the many clues and suggestive findings now beginning to emerge. One set of studies focuses on children, indicating, for example, that the child's conception of death develops in stages. Thus, among very young children, prior to the development of the sense of causality, death is seen as reversible, not final (Nagy 1948). Emotional involvement with death tends to vary with stages in the development of the ego structure and with changing cultural pressures and expectations, so that involvement is greater during early childhood and adolescence than during the preadolescent period (Alexander & Adlerstein 1958). Fear of death in children (as well as in adults) has been related in various studies to such disparate phenomena as separation anxiety, sex guilt, physical restraint, fear of the dark, sibling rivalry, and the castration complex.

Another set of studies emphasizes the impor-

tance, for the dying individual, of a secure environment and a return to primordial kinship ties. Most subjects who know they are to die say they prefer to die at home and to be surrounded by families and friends (Fulton 1965; Feifel 1959). Elderly subjects are less apprehensive about death if they live in familiar surroundings and with relatives (or even in homes for the aged) rather than alone. Such indications point to a need for social support that may be out of keeping with present tendencies toward hospitalizing and isolating the dying individual (Glaser & Strauss 1965). And the increasing majority of people do, in fact, die in hospitals (Fulton 1965).

A series of small studies attempting to connect a person's religion with his attitudes toward death has thus far produced inconclusive findings—in part because of conceptual differences in the attitudes studied and the specialized populations examined. Thus, fear of death is variously reported to increase with religious orientation, or to decline with religious activity. Some studies report that more thought is given to death by the religiously inclined. Other studies show no association whatsoever between religious conviction and attitudes toward death. While there are no satisfactory empirical data at hand to link these apparently conflicting findings, greater consistency will undoubtedly be found as research takes into account the differing definitions of death emphasized by the several religions and the differing needs met by religion in the various sectors of society.

Two other types of research offer preliminary support for Parsons' argument regarding the development of an active orientation toward death as contrasted with the denial of its reality. In one strand, a few small but cogent studies suggest that many persons fear their own death largely because death eliminates the opportunity to achieve goals important to self-esteem and that death may appear appropriate to the dying under conditions of dignity and personal fulfillment (e.g., Diggory & Rothman 1961). The second type of research deals with people's concerns with death in comparison with their concerns about the problems of life and studies the modes of their adaptation to death. A cross-section study of the adult population of the United States by Rosalie Goldwater and John W. Riley, Jr. (the results of this study were being analyzed in 1966, but had not yet been published) shows that large majorities report frequent concern with such problems as health (76 per cent) and money matters (74 per cent), in contrast to a minority who say they think often about the uncertainty of their own lives or about the possible death of someone else (32 per cent). That this lack of concern does not reflect a general "denial" of death is indicated by the finding that 85 per cent, in response to a question concerning different ways of adjusting to the uncertainty of life, concur that people should "try to make some plans about death." Although relatively few adult Americans have executed wills (24 per cent) or made funeral or cemetery arrangements (28 per cent), eight out of ten have purchased life insurance, and half have made a point of talking about death with those closest to them (for a preliminary account of some of these findings, see Riley 1964).

Further analysis shows connections in this study between these views of death and the respondents' educational attainment and age (analyzed jointly). The higher the education, the less negative the respondent's image of death, the less his expressed anxiety about death, and the more active his adaptation to death. This suggests that, as the general level of education in the Western world rises, a new orientation toward death may be in the making, however many defense mechanisms may be operative. Furthermore, older people are more likely than their younger counterparts (at any given educational level) to reveal an active orientation to death and to disavow the idea that one should ignore death or avoid making plans. Similarly, other studies note that, among the aged, approaching death seems to provoke less anxiety (Cumming & Henry 1961); whereas among the young (adolescents), there is little structuring of the future and low tolerance for the idea of death (Kastenbaum 1964). Thus, an active adaptation to death seems to become greater as individuals come nearer to completing the life cycle.

Bereavement. Death means to the individual not only his own demise but also the loss of other people who are significant to him. From a psychological standpoint, bereavement—generally held to signify the emotional state and behavior of the survivor following the death of a person who fulfilled dependency needs—is a temporary condition from which the individual is expected to recover. Studies of grief reactions to death have identified such syndromes of associated psychological and physiological symptoms as somatic distress, preoccupation with the image of the deceased, guilt, hostile reactions, and loss of established patterns of conduct (Lindemann 1944). Freud (1915), whose classic work has afforded the theoretical foundation for the psychiatric literature on melancholia, paranoid reactions, and other emotional concomitants of bereavement, argued that recov-

ery from the grief syndrome requires a process of reality testing to demonstrate that the loved object no longer exists; only when this process is complete is the ego free again. Mourning, then, is a psychological task to be performed (Krupp & Kligfeld 1962).

From a sociological standpoint, the bereaved individual may be aided through rituals and the support of family and friends to resume his usual social obligations after the mourning period (Eliot 1932). In this perspective, the task is to re-establish the systems of relationships interrupted by death or to develop new ones. Durkheim originally specified the function of ritual in enabling bereaved persons to cope with death (1912, pp. 445, 448 in 1961 edition): "When someone dies, the family group to which he belongs feels itself lessened and, to react against this loss, it assembles. . . . The group feels its strength gradually returning to it; it begins to hope and to live again." Various studies suggest, however, that such social supports often work imperfectly. A large-scale British survey, for example, shows that the help afforded by family gatherings and religious ceremonies is limited to the period of initial shock; for the subsequent period of intense mourning and physiological stress, the bereaved is typically left alone, bereft of attention or affect from the external world (Gorer 1965). Thus societal supports may be ill designed to meet the needs of those who must live through bereavement and come to terms with grief.

The psychological response of the survivor and his need for social support depend upon many factors, and especially upon *who* has been lost—a child, a parent, a distant friend; in particular, many studies have focused upon the loss of a spouse. The majority of the widowed are older people, for whom the death of a spouse can leave a void that may never be filled, and research has called attention to the associated problems of financial support, changes in housing and daily routine, and social isolation. To be sure, the most extreme sense of desolation occurs with recency of bereavement and tends to decrease over the subsequent years (Kutner et al. 1956). Yet, numerous studies comparing widowed with married persons have consistently shown that the widowed have reduced contacts with their children, intensified feelings of loneliness, higher suicide rates, and higher death rates.

Some current issues

Two specific problems related to the meaning of death are engaging the research efforts of social scientists: the problems of an aging population, who are approaching death, and the role conflicts experienced by those who must deal with death (doctors, nurses, ministers, life insurance agents, undertakers). There is increasing concern with the morale and living conditions of the aged. For instance, with death imminent, is disengagement from social relations to be preferred over continued activity (Cumming & Henry 1961)? Should age-homogeneous retirement facilities for the elderly be gradually developed? What are the relative responsibilities of public and private pension plans? Of the family? The solutions to such problems (of which there are many) are being sought by a wide variety of social science researchers.

Role conflicts among those who deal professionally with death are also being increasingly identified and studied. The clergy ponder the distinction between faith and therapy; doctors debate the Hippocratic mandate that life must be preserved at all costs; and nurses are caught between the demands of recuperating and dying patients. Life insurance agents attempt both euphemistic and realistic approaches in their efforts to bring into salience the uncertainty of life; while undertakers, constant reminders of the certainty of death, are berated as "grief therapists" and commercializers of ritual (Mitford 1963; Fulton 1965).

The ambiguity of death is also to be seen in various other fields of scientific advance. Although the law generally holds that death occurs when auscultation can no longer detect a heartbeat, such a definition is frequently made obsolete in routine medical practice. Distinctions are drawn between clinical death (of the organism) and biological death (of the organs), so that the time of death is increasingly a matter for decision, and moral questions arise as to the individual's "right to die with dignity." An important issue in the ethics of birth control is also involved—does the intrauterine device cause an abortion and hence a death? Furthermore, while science can neither prove nor disprove the hypothesis of some form of communication between living and dead, recent research in the field of parapsychology, reactivating an old tradition of psychic research (Myers 1903), is demanding attention from reputable scientists. To be sure, the "findings" of such research have not yet earned a place in the framework of modern science, but such efforts cannot be completely ignored. Finally, with the discovery that cells can be kept alive (apparently indefinitely) in a nutrient medium and that such cells can perhaps be reconstituted through the process of genetic transformation, biological immortality itself can no longer be entirely ruled out. Thus science in various ways challenges the social definition of death.

JOHN W. RILEY, JR.

[*Directly related is the entry* AGING. *Other relevant material may be found in* KINSHIP, *article on* DESCENT GROUPS; LIFE CYCLE; LIFE TABLES; MORTALITY; RITUAL.]

BIBLIOGRAPHY

ALEXANDER, IRVING E.; and ADLERSTEIN, ARTHUR M. 1958 Affective Responses to the Concept of Death in a Population of Children and Early Adolescents. *Journal of Genetic Psychology* 93:167–177.

BELLAH, ROBERT N. 1964 Religious Evolution. *American Sociological Review* 29:358–374.

BLAUNER, ROBERT 1966 Death and Social Structure. *Psychiatry* 29:378–394.

BOWMAN, LEROY 1959 *The American Funeral: A Study in Guilt, Extravagance, and Sublimity.* Washington: Public Affairs Press.

BROWN, NORMAN O. 1959 *Life Against Death: The Psychoanalytic Meaning of History.* Middletown, Conn.: Wesleyan Univ. Press.

CHORON, JACQUES 1963 *Death and Western Thought.* New York: Collier.

CHORON, JACQUES 1964 *Modern Man and Mortality.* New York: Macmillan.

CUMMING, ELAINE; and HENRY, WILLIAM E. 1961 *Growing Old: The Process of Disengagement.* New York: Basic Books.

DIGGORY, JAMES C.; and ROTHMAN, DOREEN Z. 1961 Values Destroyed by Death. *Journal of Abnormal and Social Psychology* 63:205–210.

DURKHEIM, ÉMILE (1912) 1954 *The Elementary Forms of the Religious Life.* London: Allen & Unwin; New York: Macmillan. → First published as *Les formes élémentaires de la vie religieuse, le système totémique en Australie.* A paperback edition was published in 1961 by Collier.

ELIOT, THOMAS D. 1932 The Bereaved Family. American Academy of Political and Social Science, *Annals* 160:184–190.

FEIFEL, HERMAN (editor) 1959 *The Meaning of Death.* New York: McGraw-Hill.

FREUD, SIGMUND (1915) 1959 Thoughts for the Times on War and Death. Volume 4, pages 288–317 in Sigmund Freud, *Collected Papers.* International Psychoanalytic Library, No. 10. New York: Basic Books; London: Hogarth. → First published as "Zeitgemässes über Krieg und Tod."

FULTON, ROBERT L. (editor) 1965 *Death and Identity.* New York: Wiley.

GLASER, BARNEY; and STRAUSS, ANSELM 1965 *Awareness of Dying: A Study of Social Interaction.* Chicago: Aldine.

GOODY, J. R. 1962 *Death, Property and the Ancestors: A Study of the Mortuary Customs of the Lodagaa of West Africa.* Stanford Univ. Press.

GORER, GEOFFREY 1965 *Death, Grief, and Mourning.* New York: Doubleday.

HERTZ, ROBERT (1907–1909) 1960 *Death and The Right Hand.* Glencoe, Ill.: Free Press. → First published as "La représentation collective de la mort" in Volume 10 of *L'année sociologique* and as "La prééminence de la main droite" in Volume 34 of *Revue philosophique*.

HOCKING, WILLIAM E. 1957 *The Meaning of Immortality in Human Experience*. New York: Harper.

HOFFMAN, FREDERICK J. 1964 *The Mortal No: Death and the Modern Imagination*. Princeton Univ. Press.

KALISH, RICHARD A. 1965 Death and Bereavement: A Bibliography. *Journal of Human Relations* 13:118–141.

KASTENBAUM, ROBERT (editor) 1964 *New Thoughts on Old Age*. New York: Springer.

KRUPP, GEORGE R.; and KLIGFELD, BERNARD 1962 The Bereavement Reaction: A Cross-cultural Evaluation. *Journal of Religion and Health* 1:222–246.

KUTNER, BERNARD et al. 1956 *Five Hundred Over Sixty: A Community Survey on Aging*. New York: Russell Sage Foundation.

LINDEMANN, ERICH 1944 Symptomatology and Management of Acute Grief. *American Journal of Psychiatry* 101:141–148.

MANNHEIM, KARL (1923–1929) 1952 *Essays on the Sociology of Knowledge*. Edited by Paul Kecskemeti. New York: Oxford Univ. Press.

MITFORD, JESSICA 1963 *The American Way of Death*. New York: Simon & Schuster.

MYERS, FREDERICK W. H. (1903) 1954 *Human Personality and Its Survival of Bodily Death*. 2 vols. New York: Longmans.

NAGY, MARIA 1948 The Child's Theories Concerning Death. *Journal of Genetic Psychology* 73:3–27.

PARSONS, TALCOTT 1963 Death in American Society: A Brief Working Paper. *American Behavioral Scientist* 6:61–65.

RILEY, JOHN W. JR. 1964 Contemporary Society and the Institution of Life Insurance. *Journal of the American Society of Chartered Life Underwriters* 18, no. 2:93–103.

SCHNEIDER, LOUIS; and DORNBUSCH, SANFORD M. 1958 *Popular Religion: Inspirational Books in America*. Univ. of Chicago Press.

SIMMONS, LEO W. 1945 *The Role of the Aged in Primitive Society*. New Haven: Yale Univ. Press.

SULZBERGER, CYRUS 1961 *My Brother Death*. New York: Harper.

VOLKART, EDMUND H.; and MICHAEL, STANLEY T. 1957 Bereavement and Mental Health. Pages 281–304 in Alexander H. Leighton et al. (editors), *Explorations in Social Psychiatry*. New York: Basic Books.

WARNER, W. LLOYD 1959 *The Living and the Dead: A Study of the Symbolic Life of Americans*. New Haven: Yale Univ. Press.

WEBER, MAX (1904–1905) 1930 *The Protestant Ethic and the Spirit of Capitalism*. Translated by Talcott Parsons, with a foreword by R. H. Tawney. London: Allen & Unwin; New York: Scribner. → First published in German. The 1930 edition has been reprinted frequently.

II

THE SOCIAL ORGANIZATION OF DEATH

The physical extinction of its members, not all at the same time but all eventually, is a contingency that every human group must face. Each death initiates significant responses from those survivors who in some way have personally or vicariously related to the deceased. Inevitably, the collectivities in which the dead person held membership also react. Despite the social (symbolic) ambiguity presented by the dead body, the survivors continue to relate to it for some time with predeath imagery. At the same time, they must attempt to cope with emotions no longer secured within the pre-existing balance of interpersonal relations.

The reciprocal problem for the social group or collectivity remains the reassigning and reassembling of social roles and statuses, optimally in such fashion that not only is the social order in some measure re-established but the survivors affected by the death are re-equipped with images and symbols appropriate for building and sustaining an altered yet viable self-conception. This group problem forms the basis for the treatment of mortuary behavior that follows. No categorical separation is attempted between the personal and organizational dimensions of the subject. The emphasis remains, however, on the latter.

Death as passage. No social group socializes and controls members with a cosmology that categorically holds out death as nothing more than the total eclipse of the person. To the primitive and preliterate, the opposite orientation is more likely. The belief that life is not the end underlies some of the ritual behavior of all peoples. It is perhaps a necessary premise to the development of human culture.

A corollary premise suggests that the death of a society is inconceivable by its members, inasmuch as their belief and symbol systems link man and society reciprocally. Total obliteration of the person would so challenge the grounds for society's existence that the very idea constitutes, in effect, a sacrilege.

Possibly the most elementary and universal response is found in the conception of death as a transition or journey, as a series of happenings rather than an event complete in itself. The notion of transition implies qualitative changes in time and place. Consequent to death, secular time and location are replaced by sacred time and existence in another world, in which the spirit is either absorbed or exists with some measure of individuality. Recognition cannot help but be given to physical dissolution of the dead body, but the force or entity that gave the body life is held to be only transformed but never extinguished. All great religious systems seemingly build on this principle; its universality directs attention, then, to death as a passage or as stages in the career of some life force that for a time inhabits the body but neither begins nor ends with it.

Channeling of death responses. For the survivors the death of an intimate has its most immediate consequence in vaguely or distinctly felt ambiguity and confusion. The intensity of the individual response will be roughly proportionate to the intensity of the interpersonal interaction, vicarious as well as face-to-face, that the survivor enjoyed with the deceased. For these individuals, as well as for the group, the response will in great measure vary with the difficulty of replacing the departed member in an ongoing system of role and status relationships.

The channeling of basic human sentiments is never an automatic process, nor is it possible to guarantee that the collectivity suffering such rupture in its affairs will not react so violently as to threaten all operating institutions. Whatever the rationale or general belief about the nature of death, elaboration into a set of operative prescriptions for behavior proceeds expeditiously in the context of symbolically ritualized ceremonials. The social prescriptions surrounding death do not unequivocally control the responses of individuals and groups to the phenomenon of death. Personal reactions where these prescriptions are embracing, as in preliterate, tribal societies, may seem reflexive. But it would be incorrect to assume that the emotional responses of the survivors must and do coincide exactly with the demands of a socially prescribed mortuary etiquette. Death of an intimate always results in some loss of the bereaved ego—an impoverishment of self—and when the association has been close, whether characterized by positive or negative sentiments, the loss will trigger off emotional responses that can overflow the channels for appropriate mortuary behavior provided by the culture.

The effectiveness of death rituals stems from the fact that, through the medium of a sacred-symbol system, they assist man in defining his relations to himself, his fellow man, and the cosmos. Rites are for the most part performed or engaged in collectively; the representations thus evoked and expressed in ritual carry the authority and sanction of society itself. Mortuary rites characteristically operate to give meaning and sanction to the separation of the dead person from the living, to help effect the transition of the spirit, soul, or life force into an otherworldly realm, and to assist in the incorporation of the spirit of the dead into its new existence.

Ritualization and the drama of funerals. Ritualization of mortuary behavior evokes new or changed self-conceptions, insofar as it serves to move people from moments of personal confusion and ego impoverishment toward a restructuring of identity. Through such ritualization the "work of

grief," as postulated in dynamic psychology, is expedited by the meaningful social interaction of the bereaved survivors. Since this interaction involves role playing, such rearrangement as occurs through the emergence of new or different roles resolves the anomaly of the incumbentless role created by death.

The actual disposal of the dead body is generally handled in a number of ritual-bearing scenes or episodes. Once properly prepared for the funeral, the corpse will receive some form of attention from the survivors. Family and close kin, friends and neighbors, usually have the greatest emotional involvement, although where kin, sib, and clan bonds are strong, more extensive prescriptions for mortuary behavior channel and sanction the emotional and physical behavior of the most closely, as well as the most distantly, related.

Funerals for the dead are matters of dramatic and sacred moment. The manner of disposal of the body, the role of the corpse in the ritual, and the utilitarian care of the dead is highly variable from group to group. Despite preliminary magico-religious prophylactic and propitiatory acts of the survivors, bodies may still be considered so representative of virulence and danger that, as in the case of the Kaingang in South America, they may be abandoned in terror. In like manner, the Navajo and other Indian tribes in the southwestern United States quickly bury the body along with many, if not all, of its earthly effects; the deceased's dwelling, if he died there, is abandoned and never reused. At another extreme, common among the Malayo-Polynesians, the corpse may for a long period of time be kept on display close at hand, seemingly benign or positive in its influence, or be temporarily sequestered until the remaining burial rites are performed.

Disposal of the dead emphasizes the separation of the physical dead from the society of the living. The role of the specialist, such as the priest, medicine man, shaman, or spiritual intercessor, is crucial at this juncture, since it is through ritualized actions, organized into episodes or scenes, that both the dead and the living are moved on to new points of orientation and to new status positions. The point to be emphasized is that mortuary ceremonials affect the individual's sense of identity, or self, and provide entry into and departure from the system of roles and status relationships in the society. It is for this reason that funerals have the basic potential for the highest order of social significance. Within the framework of mortuary ceremonies, society-specific patterns of belief and action centering on death and burial arise to express or achieve other purposes, among which are the descent of property, authority, and sexual privilege and the enhancement of a popular aesthetic of beauty in death; or the projection of cults of personality, rationality, or pragmatism. Dramatization of all such purposes—even that of expressing indifference—may achieve a measure of functional autonomy.

ROBERT W. HABENSTEIN

BIBLIOGRAPHY

FEIFEL, HERMAN (editor) 1959 *The Meaning of Death.* New York: McGraw-Hill.

FREUD, SIGMUND (1917) 1959 Mourning and Melancholia. Volume 4, pages 152–170 in Sigmund Freud, *Collected Papers.* International Psycho-analytic Library, No. 10. New York: Basic Books; London: Hogarth.

FULTON, ROBERT L. (editor) 1965 *Death and Identity.* New York: Wiley.

GENNEP, ARNOLD VAN (1908) 1960 *The Rites of Passage.* London: Routledge; Univ. of Chicago Press. → First published in French. A classic anthropological essay on birth, puberty, marriage, childbirth, and death.

GLUCKMAN, MAX (editor) 1962 *Essays on the Ritual of Social Relations.* Manchester (England) Univ. Press.

GOODY, J. R. 1962 *Death, Property and the Ancestors: A Study of the Mortuary Customs of the Lodagaa of West Africa.* Stanford (Calif.) Univ. Press.

GORER, GEOFFREY 1965 *Death, Grief, and Mourning.* New York: Doubleday.

HABENSTEIN, ROBERT W. 1954 The American Funeral Director: A Study in the Sociology of Work. Ph.D. dissertation, Univ. of Chicago.

HABENSTEIN, ROBERT W.; and LAMERS, WILLIAM M. 1961 *Funeral Customs the World Over.* Milwaukee, Wis.: Bulfin.

HENRY, JULES 1964 *Jungle People: A Kaingang Tribe of the Highlands of Brazil.* New York: Random House.

HERTZ, ROBERT (1907–1909) 1960 *Death* and *The Right Hand.* Glencoe, Ill.: Free Press. → First published as "La représentation collective de la mort" in Volume 10 of *L'année sociologique,* and "La prééminence de la main droite" in Volume 34 of *Revue philosophique.*

KEPHART, WILLIAM M. 1950 Status After Death. *American Sociological Review* 15:635–643.

LINDEMANN, ERICH 1944 Symptomatology and Management of Acute Grief. *American Journal of Psychiatry* 101:141–148.

MALINOWSKI, BRONISLAW (1916–1941) 1948 *Magic, Science and Religion, and Other Essays.* Glencoe, Ill.: Free Press. → A paperback edition was published in 1954 by Doubleday.

RADCLIFFE-BROWN, A. R. (1922) 1948 *The Andaman Islanders.* Glencoe, Ill.: Free Press.

SIMMONS, LEO W. 1945 *The Role of the Aged in Primitive Society.* New Haven: Yale Univ. Press.

VOLKART, EDMUND H.; and MICHAEL, STANLEY T. 1957 Bereavement and Mental Health. Pages 281–304 in Alexander H. Leighton et al. (editors), *Explorations in Social Psychiatry.* New York: Basic Books.

WARNER, W. LLOYD 1959 *The Living and the Dead: A Study of the Symbolic Life of Americans.* New Haven: Yale Univ. Press.

DEATH RATES

See LIFE TABLES; MORTALITY; *and the biographies of* KŐRÖSY *and* WILLCOX.

DEATH TAXES

See under TAXATION.

DEATH WISH

See PSYCHOANALYSIS.

DEBT, PUBLIC

Public debt is an obligation on the part of a governmental unit to pay specific monetary sums to holders of legally designated claims at particular points in time. The sums owed to creditors may be defined in standard monetary units of the debtor government or in units of an external currency. The United States national debt represents, predominantly, an obligation of the federal government to pay specific sums of United States dollars to creditors. On the other hand, national debts may, and local debts must, be defined in units of external currency. The monetary obligation may be that of paying either interest or a return of principal, or both. Specific issues of debt may or may not be characterized by definite maturity schedules. Consols, which represent obligations to pay interest in perpetuity, involve no obligation for a return of principal.

Public debt must be distinguished from currency outstanding. The obligation on the part of a money-issuing governmental authority to the holder of currency is not public debt, since the claim can also be met in currency units.

Public debt is created by the act of public borrowing, or, in other words, the act of floating public loans, the act of selling government securities. This is a process through which governmental units, in exchange for money (currency or demand deposits) give promises to pay, this exchange being normally voluntary on the part of the lender. For governments the purpose of the exchange is that of securing current purchasing power with which they may purchase resource services, or final products. The issue of public debt is one means of financing government expenditures, alternative to taxation and to direct currency creation.

Public debt is amortized, or retired, by a reverse transfer in which government gives up money for debt instruments, either through purchase on the open market or through scheduled maturity payments.

Measurement. Public debt is normally measured in nominal maturity values. This does not represent the "size" of the public debt in such a manner as to make comparisons over time and among separate governmental units fully accurate. Varying composition of debt can affect its degree of liquidity for holders, as well as other characteristics. To the extent that debt instruments are valued for these nondebt features, the effective size of public debt, as such, is reduced. A more accurate measure of debt is produced by capitalizing the annual interest charges at some appropriate rate of discount, normally that rate which approximates the return on risk-free investment in the economy. An example will clarify this point. In terms of nominal maturity value, national debt may be of equal size, say $300,000 million, at two points in time. In the one case, however, if the debt is composed primarily of short-term issues possessing a high degree of "moneyness," the annual interest charges may amount to, say, only $6,000 million. In the other case, if the debt is largely funded, the interest charges may be as high as, say, $12,000 million. Clearly, the "size" of the public debt is not identical in the two cases; other dimensions than nominal maturity values must be included in any appropriate measure. For purposes of making intertemporal and international comparisons, the most appropriate measure is perhaps the ratio of annual interest charges to gross national or gross domestic product.

Table 1 — National debt in selected countries, 1960

	NATIONAL DEBT, 1960[a] (In millions of dollars)	RATIO OF DEBT TO GNP[b] (Per cent)
Brazil	4,911	19
Canada	17,679	49
France	24,925	40
Germany	611	1
India	13,159	35
Japan	2,551	7
Norway	1,293	29
United Kingdom	77,652	124
United States	286,471	57

a. Includes intragovernmental debt. Converted to U.S. dollars at official rates.
b. Rounded to nearest percentage point.

Source: International Financial Statistics.

Public debt may characterize both national and local fiscal systems. Data are much more readily available for national debts, and that of some selected countries may be introduced for illustrative purposes. Table 1 shows the national debts of several selected countries in 1960, defined in nominal maturity values, local currency units being con-

verted into United States dollar equivalents at official exchange rates. The right-hand column of Table 1 indicates the ratio of national debt to gross national product of the issuing country.

The most significant fact that emerges from any comparative survey of national debts in the various countries, and one that is indicated from the data summarized in Table 1, is that no single country was, in 1960, dangerously "overburdened" with national debt. Among the major countries of the world, only for the United Kingdom was the size of the national debt larger than GNP. And for relatively few countries, developed or underdeveloped, is the ratio of national debt to GNP more than 50 per cent. There are several reasons for these results, some of which make their significance less than it might initially seem to be.

Countries that are characterized by large national debts, measured proportionately to GNP, tend to be those that have enjoyed reasonably stable government, that have been victorious in wars, and that have experienced reasonable monetary stability over a relatively long period. Great Britain and the United States, both victorious in two world wars and both characterized by political stability and relatively moderate inflation, carry relatively heavier national debts than most other countries. Causality seems to work in only one direction here, however. Political and monetary stability do not result from large national debts; instead, large national debts emerge only in conditions of reasonable political and monetary stability. In the absence of these conditions, public borrowing will rarely be important as a means of financing public spending, and, even when it is successfully carried out, the creditors of the state may be subject to confiscation through inflation or through default.

Historically, the large increases in national debts have been associated with the financing of war emergencies. This is illustrated by the growth of the United States national debt, shown for selected years in Table 2.

Table 2 — Growth of United States national debt, selected years

YEAR	NOMINAL MATURITY VALUE (In millions of dollars)
1917	1,023
1919	26,349
1930	15,774
1940	42,376
1946	277,912
1949	249,509
1960	286,471
1965	317,270

Source: U.S. Treasury Department data.

Composition.   Public debt assumes many forms, ranging from consols at the one extreme to treasury bills of very short maturity at the other, with other characteristics not relating to maturity schedules. The form in which debt is marketed affects the interest rate that must be paid, since various features, desired in themselves, may be offered complementary to what may be called "pure debt." Consols, which have no maturity and which obligate the issuing government only to pay a specific interest charge periodically and in perpetuity, provide a useful bench mark for comparative purposes. These come close to representing "pure debt," and as other features are added the cost of carrying debt tends to decrease. The fixing of a definite maturity, which obligates the government to return the principal to the holder of claims, increases the liquidity of the claim, especially as maturity is approached. Hence, as maturities are shortened, liquidity is increased to the point at which short-term treasury bills take on a high degree of "moneyness." For this reason bills can normally be sold at considerably lower rates of interest than long-term bonds.

Certain countries have been successful in floating issues of debt that obligate the government to return monetary sums of fixed purchasing power to holders of claims. These constant-value bonds, which provide holders with apparent protection against inflationary erosion in value, have been marketed at very low rates of interest. Great Britain, in the years since World War II, has successfully introduced "premium bonds," which incorporate certain features of a lottery.

The terms "funded debt" and "floating debt" have been used, historically, to refer to long-term and to short-term debt, respectively. Any definitions are, to an extent, arbitrary, but all issues of more than five-years maturity are generally called "long-term," and all issues with shorter maturities are called "short-term." The rubric "floating debt" is most explicitly used with reference to issues of less than one year maturity.

The names given to specific debt instruments reflect the maturity category. Bonds are securities issued for long term. Notes and certificates are intermediate-term, and treasury bills are short-term. The term "government securities" is used to refer to the whole range of public debt instruments.

Ownership.   The pattern of ownership of public debt is an important factor in determining its impact on the national economy. In almost all countries national debt is held in significant amounts by various governmental or quasi-governmental agencies. For some purposes it is desirable to include only debt held outside the governmental sector in measuring total debt. For other purposes intragovernmental debt should be included. Insofar as the agencies holding debt are, in fact, treated as being independently accountable units, both in their investing and in their paying functions, the public debt that these agencies hold is not different in effect from that held by the nongovernmental public. However, insofar as these agencies holding debt are not independent of direct treasury control, their holding does not constitute debt at all and could as well have been canceled at the outset. For the most part, intragovernmental debt represents some combination of these two institutional situations.

It is also important to distinguish between the debt held by the nonbanking public and that held by the banking system and by certain categories within the banking system. To the extent that government securities are held by the central banks, they provide reserves for the commercial banking system, and changes in central bank holdings are indicative of important monetary movements in the economy. To the extent that commercial banks hold securities, potential reserves are available to them.

Traditionally, debt held internally and debt held externally have been sharply distinguished. In a national accounting sense, the servicing of internally held debt does not require the transfer of income resources out of the national economy, whereas, of course, such a transfer is required for the servicing of an externally held debt. This point is relevant, even though it must be kept in mind that, other things being equal, the income base from which the transfers are to be made must be larger in the case of externally held debt, precisely by the amount of the necessary interest transfer.

Management.   Public debt management may be defined as that set of operations required to maintain an existing nominal debt. Again, consols provide a useful reference point; if all public debt should consist of consols, management reduces to the payment of interest charges. Significant problems of management arise because issues must be refinanced, must be "rolled over," at periodic intervals. These problems become more difficult as the proportion of floating debt in the total becomes larger and also as economic conditions over time become less stable.

Recognition of management difficulties explains the traditional policy objective of funding the national debt to the maximum extent that is possible. This objective may conflict with other objectives that have been introduced into public policy. As national debts grow in importance, the annual interest payments assume relatively large shares of the governmental expenditure budget. This fact prompts recognition of the minimization of interest cost as an objective of debt management, one that is sharply in conflict with funding. Modern developments in the theory of macroeconomic policy have also forced the recognition that debt management exerts significant over-all effects on the economy. This produces a third possible management objective, that of supplementing macroeconomic policy in promoting stabilization–growth aims.

In a period of threatened inflation both the funding and the macroeconomic objectives would dictate a shift out of short-term into long-term issues, but this would increase interest costs. By contrast, during a period of recession both the interest-cost and the macroeconomic objectives dictate a shift into short-term issues from long-term, but this runs afoul of traditional notions about funding. The experience of the United States since World War II suggests that the best explanatory hypothesis is that management has been directed toward maintaining substantially the same maturity structure over time.

Monetization. Interest costs on national debt could, of course, be reduced to zero through direct monetization of public debt. This is a process through which interest-bearing issues are refinanced through the issue of money, currency, or bank deposits. Because of the interest saving alone, monetization is always to be recommended insofar as it can be accomplished without inflation. Only the threat of inflation provides a barrier to monetization.

As the national economy grows, an increasing stock of money is required in order to maintain a constant level of product and service prices. One means of injecting increments to the money stock into the system is through debt monetization. Given the improbability that modern governments will retire public debts through the deliberate creation of budgetary surpluses, monetization provides the primary means through which national debts will be reduced. Monetization of debt is possible only for governmental units that possess independent money-creating powers.

National debt and fiscal policy. There is no simple connection between fiscal policy and the issue or retirement of national debt. Budgetary deficits need not be financed by the issue of debt, defined in a meaningful way. And, if such deficits are generated purposefully for the supplementing of aggregate demand, national debt should not be used as the means of financing. Instead, money should be directly created, which is always an alternative means of financing. In such a setting, the issue of debt exerts a deflationary, and undesirable, impact on total demand.

The elementary confusion about all this arises because, institutionally, national governments tend to disguise money creation through so-called "borrowing" from the central banks, and "public debt" is, nominally, created in this money-creating process. It is essential, however, that these two methods of financing deficits, which are conceptually quite different, be distinguished in the analysis.

The same analysis applies, in reverse, when budgetary surpluses are created. If the purpose of generating the surplus is that of reducing total demand, debt held outside the central banks should not be retired. Instead, the surplus should be disposed of by drawing down treasury balances or retiring debt held by central banks, which is the institutional equivalent of destroying money.

Principles of public debt. The preceding sections of this article summarize the institutional elements of "public debt," on which there exists broad agreement among professional experts. It is the "theory," or "principles," of public debt that has traditionally generated controversy, and the debate shows little sign of being resolved, although essentially the same arguments have been advanced for two centuries. For those who remain skeptical about the progress of economic science, the debt-theory controversy provides ample corroboration.

Nominally, the central question has been: *Who* bears the burden of public debt, and *when*? Analysis is clarified if this question is more carefully stated as follows: Who bears the real cost, or burden, of the public-expenditure projects that are financed by the issue of public loans, and when is this real cost incurred? What is sought is the incidence of debt, and the problem is comparable to that of locating the incidence of taxation, should this alternative financing device be employed.

This question is important because only if it is answered properly can a rational choice be made between debt issue and alternative financing devices. When should government borrow? This ultimate policy question cannot be answered until and unless the consequences of public borrowing can be predicted. Public spending may be financed in any of three ways: (1) taxation, (2) public borrowing, and (3) money creation. The appropriate situations for the use of the second alternative cannot be identified until the differences between this and the remaining alternatives are analyzed.

For whom is the central question relevant? Failure to clarify this point has also led to ambiguity.

In any broadly democratic political structure, "government" is the institutional process through which people make "public" decisions. Therefore, "When should government borrow?" becomes merely a shorthand manner of asking, "When should individual citizens, as participants in the governmental decision process, as prospective taxpayers, borrowers, or beneficiaries, borrow?" The question of the appropriateness of public debt issue becomes analogous to the question concerning private debt issue for the individual in his private capacity.

The answer to the central question posed above seems obvious. Public borrowing should take place when it is desirable to put off or to postpone the incurring of real cost until some later period, in return for which, as in any act of borrowing, an interest charge must normally be paid. The desire to postpone the incurring of real cost or incidence of the public expenditure project may or may not be related to the characteristics of the project itself. Public or collective consumption may, in some cases, be legitimately financed from public loans, just as private consumption may be legitimately financed from private loans. A more normal or standard reason for public borrowing is found, however, in the temporal pattern of benefits that are expected to be produced by the public spending project. If the project involves a large and concentrated outlay that is anticipated to yield benefits over a whole sequence of time periods in the future, considerations of both efficiency and equity suggest resort to public loans, provided only that direct money creation is predicted to cause inflation. Traditionally, public debt has been discussed with reference to the financing of extraordinary expenditure needs, and specifically with reference to public capital formation. Historically, national debts have been created largely during periods of war emergency, when spending needs have indeed been extraordinary, even if the result has not been public capital formation of the orthodox variety.

The controversy.   Little more would need to be said with respect to the "principles" of public debt were it not for the fact that the straightforward analysis has been recurrently challenged, and by economists of great eminence. Ricardo's logic led him to enunciate the proposition that the public loan and an extraordinary tax of equivalent amount exert identical effects on the rational individual. Under conditions of perfect certainty, perfect capital markets, and under the assumption that individuals act "as if" they will live forever, the future tax liabilities that are inherent in a public debt obligation will be fully capitalized at the time of debt issue, and the effects on individual behavior

patterns will be identical to those that would be produced by a tax of the same capital sum (Ricardo 1817). Within his own restricted model Ricardo's basic proposition cannot be challenged, but its validity does not contradict the elementary notions on public debt outlined above. The individual, as prospective taxpayer–borrower–beneficiary, confronts two financing alternatives—current taxation and public debt issue. And to the extent that he interprets these two alternatives correctly, he knows that each of the two will impose upon him a real cost, a burden that in a present-value sense is substantially the same. This Ricardian equivalence does not suggest, however, that the objective pattern of cost payments remains the same over the two alternatives. Taxation and debt issue remain different, not similar, financing institutions, between which the individual may choose, for the simple reason that taxes require a transfer of resource services from the individual to the fisc during the initial period, whereas debt issue postpones such transfer until later periods. Whether or not the individual, under debt financing, correctly or incorrectly anticipates or "capitalizes" future tax liabilities as he "should" in the normative Ricardian model, is not relevant to the determination of the objective pattern of real cost payments over time.

A common fallacy.   The most pervasive and recurring fallacy in the discussion of public debt has been that which summarizes the theory of internally held debt by the statement "We owe it to ourselves." The fallacy here is not a new one; it was widely held by both scholars and publicists in the eighteenth century. It almost faded out of the literature during the nineteenth and early twentieth centuries, only to reappear and to gain predominance after the so-called Keynesian revolution of the 1930s. In the immediate post-Keynesian decades the fallacy came to be almost universally accepted by economists. Therefore, if for no other reason, the importance that this fallacy has held in the literature warrants some consideration of it here. For purposes of discussion it may be labeled the "national accounting fallacy."

If the government borrows funds internally, so the theory goes, the public expenditure project is financed from internal resources. These cannot be brought from future time periods into the present; hence, the opportunity costs of the public project, regardless of the method of finance, must be borne during the period in which the resources are actually used. Public debt involves no postponement of cost or burden in time, and the view that it does so is based on a crudely drawn analogy with private debt. In periods after public debt issue, the required interest payments represent nothing more than transfers from taxpayers to bondholders, and, so long as both groups are members of the community, no real cost is incurred. External public debt, by contrast, because of the necessity to transfer interest payments to outsiders, is seen as wholly different from internal debt and analogous to private debt.

This conception of national debt contains a fundamental flaw in its failure to translate opportunity cost or burden from aggregative components into something that is meaningful to individual members of the community. What is the behavioral relevance of the fact that the resources actually used up in the public project are taken from current consumption or investment within the community until and unless those members of the community who must undergo the sacrifice of alternatives can be identified? Once this question is raised, however, and such identification is attempted, the fallacy is clearly revealed.

The members of the group who actually surrender purchasing power, command over current resource services, which is used by the government to carry out the public purpose, are those who purchase the public debt instruments, the government securities. No other members of the group sacrifice or "give up" anything directly during the initial period. But do the bond purchasers bear the real costs or burden of the project? That they do not becomes clear when it is recognized that their surrender of current funds is a wholly voluntary and private transaction in which they exchange current purchasing power for promises, on the part of the fisc, of income in future periods. These bond purchasers, or persons acting in this capacity, do not in any way consider themselves to be exchanging purchasing power for the benefits of the public spending, which would be the case if they should be really bearing the real cost. If, however, it is acknowledged that bond purchasers do not bear the real cost of the public spending, and if no other members of the group bear such cost during the initial period, who does pay for the project that is debt-financed? If, as the national accounting fallacy suggests, none of this cost is shifted to future periods, public debt might seem to provide for "fiscal perpetual motion," since a means would have been located for financing beneficial public projects without cost.

The core of the fallacy lies in the equating of the community as a unit, in some aggregated national accounting sense, with the individuals-in-the-community, in some political sense as participants, direct or indirect, in collective decision making. In their capacities as prospective taxpayers–borrowers–beneficiaries, individual members of a political community can postpone the objective real costs of public spending through resort to debt finance, even though they may sell the debt instruments, bonds, to "themselves," acting in a wholly different capacity as bond purchasers. There are two exchanges, not one, involved, and it is the neglect of this basic duality that has clouded much of the discussion and analysis. Individuals, as taxpayers–borrowers–beneficiaries, through the political decision process, "exchange" the future tax liabilities that debt issue embodies for the promise of expected benefits of the public spending, current or in future. They are enabled to do this because individuals, in their capacities as prospective bond purchasers, are willing to exchange current purchasing power for the promise of future payments. The second group makes an intertemporal exchange that is the opposite of that made by the first group. And it is grossly misleading to think of these two exchanges as canceling in effect merely because the two groups may be partially coincident in membership.

The alleged differences between internal and external debt disappear in a model that corrects for this national accounting fallacy. In either situation individuals in their roles as participants in collective fiscal choice secure command over resource services initially without the necessity of giving up purchasing power. Whether other parties to the exchange be foreigners or some subset of individuals acting in their private capacity as bond purchasers makes no essential difference, secondary transfer considerations aside.

For individuals as they participate in fiscal choice, public debt is the institutional analogue to private debt as these same individuals act privately. Basically, the same principles apply in each case, despite all the disclaimers made by economists. This is not, of course, to equate public finance with private finance in all respects. The important difference lies, however, not in the effects of borrowing but in the fact that national governments possess powers of money creation whereas private persons, and local governments, do not. The power to create money allows national governments to generate budgetary deficits without at the same time issuing debt. The principles of public borrowing, which are at base simple, have been obscured by the failure of economists to make this elemental point clear. In part, as suggested before, this has been the result of institutional complexities present in modern fiscal–financial structures. Modern governments create money through issuing what they commonly call "public debt"; they do so by "borrowing" from central banks. This disguised money creation does not, of course, have the same effects as genuine debt issue.

The analysis of public debt which was dominant in the 1940s and 1950s, as a result of the Keynesian and post-Keynesian emphasis on deficit financing combined with the confusion between debt issue and money creation, was subjected to critical attack in the late 1950s and early 1960s. Predictions as to the development of analysis or the acceptance of ideas are risky at best, but it seems reasonable to suggest that the principles of public debt are on the verge of synthesis. Undue optimism is, however, surely to be avoided, especially if the history of debt theory is to be used as a guide.

JAMES M. BUCHANAN

[*See also* FISCAL POLICY; *and the biography of* RICARDO.]

BIBLIOGRAPHY

ADAMS, HENRY C. 1887 *Public Debts: An Essay in the Science of Finance.* New York: Appleton.

BASTABLE, CHARLES F. (1892) 1895 *Public Finance.* 2d ed. London and New York: Macmillan.

BUCHANAN, JAMES M. 1958 *Public Principles of Public Debt: A Defense and Restatement.* Homewood, Ill.: Irwin.

FERGUSON, JAMES M. (editor) 1964 *Public Debt and Future Generations.* Chapel Hill: Univ. of North Carolina Press.

GREAT BRITAIN, COMMITTEE ON NATIONAL DEBT AND TAXATION 1927 *Report.* London: H.M. Stationery Office. → Known as the Colwyn Committee Report.

HARRIS, SEYMOUR E. 1947 *The National Debt and the New Economics.* New York: McGraw-Hill.

International Financial Statistics. → Published monthly since January 1948 by the International Monetary Fund.

LERNER, ABBA P. 1948 The Burden of the National Debt. Pages 255–275 in *Income, Employment and Public Policy: Essays in Honor of Alvin H. Hansen.* New York: Norton.

LEROY-BEAULIEU, PAUL (1877) 1912 *Traité de la science des finances.* Volume 2: Le budget et le crédit public. 8th ed. Paris: Alcan. → Volume 1 is entitled *Des revenus publics.*

MAFFEZZONI, FEDERICO (1950) 1962 The Comparative Fiscal Burden of Public Debt and Taxation. *International Economic Papers* 11:75–101. → First published as "Ancora della diversa pressione tributaria del prestito e dell'imposta" in Volume 9 of the *Rivista di diritto finanziario e scienza delle finanze.*

RICARDO, DAVID (1817) 1951 *Works and Correspondence.* Volume 1: On the Principles of Political Economy and Taxation. Cambridge: Royal Economic Society.

VITI DE MARCO, ANTONIO DE (1934) 1950 *First Principles of Public Finance.* London: Cape. → First published in Italian.

DECENTRALIZATION

See CENTRALIZATION AND DECENTRALIZATION.

DECISION MAKING

I. PSYCHOLOGICAL ASPECTS   *Ward Edwards*
II. ECONOMIC ASPECTS   *Jacob Marschak*
III. POLITICAL ASPECTS   *James A. Robinson*

I
PSYCHOLOGICAL ASPECTS

Men must choose what to do. Often, choices must be made in the absence of certain knowledge of their consequences. However, an abundance of fallible, peripheral, and perhaps irrelevant information is usually available at the time of an important choice; the effectiveness with which this information is processed may control the appropriateness of the resulting decision. This article is concerned with laboratory studies of human choices and of certain kinds of human information processing leading up to these choices. It is organized around two concepts and two principles. The two concepts are utility, or the subjective value of an outcome, and probability, or how likely it seems to the decision maker that a particular outcome will occur if he makes a particular decision. Both of the principles are normative or prescriptive; they specify what an ideal decision maker would do and thus invite comparison between performances of ideal and of real decision makers. One, the principle of maximizing expected utility, in essence asserts that you should choose the action that on the average will leave you best off. The other, a principle of probability theory called Bayes' theorem, is a formally optimal rule for transforming opinions in the light of new information, and so specifies how you should process information. The basic conclusions reached as a result of comparison of actual human performance with these two principles is that men do remarkably well at conforming intuitively to ideal rules, except for a consistent inefficiency in information processing.

Utility

Utility measurement and expected utility. The concepts of utility and probability have been with us since at least the eighteenth century. But serious psychological interest in any version of them did not begin until the 1930s, when Kurt Lewin wrote about valence (utility) and several probability-like concepts. Lewin had apparently been influenced by some lectures on decision theory that the mathematician John von Neumann had given in Berlin in 1928. But the Lewinian formulations were not very quantitative, and the resulting research did not lead to explicit psychological concern with decision processes. However, in 1944 von Neumann and Morgenstern published their epochal book *Theory of Games and Economic Behavior*. The theory of games as such has been remarkably unfruitful in psychological research, mostly because of its dependence on the absurdly conservative minimax principle that in effect instructs you to deal with your opponent as though he were going to play optimally, no matter how inept you may know him to be. But von Neumann and Morgenstern rather incidentally proposed an idea that made utility measurable; that proposal is the historical origin of most psychological research on decision processes since then. Their proposal amounts to assuming that men are rational, in a rather specific sense, and to designing a set of procedures exploiting that assumption to measure the basic subjective quantities that enter into a decision.

Since the origin of probability theory, the idea has been obvious that bets (and risky acts more generally) can be compared in attractiveness. Formally, every bet has an expectation, or expected value (EV), which is simply the average gain or loss or money per bet that you might expect to accrue if you played the bet many times. To calculate the EV, you multiply each possible dollar outcome of the bet by the probability of that outcome, and sum the products. In symbols, the EV of the *i*th bet is calculated as follows, where V_{ij} is the payoff for the *j*th outcome of the *i*th bet and p_j is the probability of obtaining that payoff:

$$(1) \qquad EV_i = \sum_j p_j V_{ij}.$$

Bets can be ordered in terms of their EV, and it seems plausible to suppose that men should prefer a bet with a higher EV to a bet with a lower one. But a little thought shows that men buy insurance in spite of the fact that the insurance companies pay their employees and build buildings, and thus must take in more money in premiums than they pay out in benefits. Thus insurance companies are in the business of selling bets that are favorable to themselves and unfavorable to their customers. Nevertheless, it is doubtful that anyone would call buying insurance irrational. This and other considerations led to a reformulation of the notion that men should order bets in terms of EV. The seventeenth-century British utilitarian philosophers had distinguished between objective value, or price, and subjective value, or utility. If the utility of some object to you is different from its price, then surely your behavior should attempt to maximize not expected value in dollars but expected utility. That is, you should substitute $u(V_{ij})$, the *utility* of

the payoff, for the *j*th outcome of bet *i*, for the payoff itself, V_{ij} in equation (1). Since it is utility, not payoff, that you attempt to maximize in this model, it is called the expected utility maximization model, or *EU* model. In symbols,

$$(2) \qquad EU_i = \sum_j p_j u(V_{ij}).$$

Von Neumann and Morgenstern proposed simply that one should use equation (2) to measure utility, by assuming that men make choices rationally. Several specific implementations of this idea will be examined below.

Freud and psychiatry have taught us, perhaps too stridently, to look for irrational motivations behind human acts, and introspection confirms this lesson of thousands of years of human folly. Why bother, then, with measurement based on the assumption that men are rational? Three kinds of answers seem clear. First, rationality, as decision theorists think of it, has nothing to do with what you want, but only with how you go about implementing your wants. If you would rather commit rape than get married and rather get drunk than commit rape, the decision theorist tells you only that, to be rational, you should get drunk rather than get married. The compatibility of your tastes with your, or society's, survival or welfare is not his concern. So it is easy to be irrational in Freud's sense, and yet rational from a standpoint of decision theory. Second, men often want to implement their tastes in a consistent (which means rational) way, and when large issues are at stake, they often manage to do so. In fact, knowledge of the rules of rational behavior can help one make rational decisions, that is, knowledge of the theory helps make the theory true. Third, the most important practical justification of these or any other scientific procedures is that they work. Methods based on von Neumann and Morgenstern's ideas do produce measurements, and those measurements provide predictors of behavior. The following review of experiments supports this statement.

The Mosteller and Nogee experiment. The von Neumann–Morgenstern proposal was elaborated by Friedman and Savage (1948), a mathematical economist and a statistician writing for economists, and then was implemented experimentally by Mosteller and Nogee (1951), a statistician and a graduate student in social psychology. (No discipline within the social or mathematical sciences has failed to contribute to, or use, decision theory.) Mosteller and Nogee asked subjects to accept or reject bets of the form "If you beat the following poker-dice hand, you will win $X; otherwise, you will lose $0.05." A value of *X* was found such that the subject was indifferent between accepting and rejecting the bet. Arbitrary assignment of 0 utiles (the name for the unit of utility, as gram is the name for a unit of weight) to no transaction (rejection of the bet) and of −1 utile to losing a nickel fixed the origin and unit of measurement of the utility scale, and the calculated probability *p* of beating the poker-dice hand was substituted into the following equation:

$$p\,u(\$X) + (1-p)\,u(-\$0.05) = u(\$0).$$

Since $u(\$X)$, the utility of $X, is the only unknown in this equation, it is directly solvable. Mosteller and Nogee used two groups of subjects in this experiment: Harvard undergraduates and National Guardsmen. For the Harvard undergraduates, they found the expected decreasing marginal utility; that is, the utility function rose less and less rapidly as the amount of money increased. For the National Guardsmen, they found the opposite; the larger the amount of money, the steeper the slope of the utility function.

Perhaps the most important of the many criticisms of the Mosteller–Nogee experiment is about the role that probabilities display in it. The probability of beating the specified poker-dice hand is not at all easy to calculate; still, it is substituted into equation (2), which is supposed to represent the decision-making processes of the subject. Actually, Mosteller and Nogee did display these probabilities as numbers to their subjects. But they also displayed as numbers the values of the amounts of money for which the subjects were gambling. Why should we assume that the subjects make some subjective transformation that changes those numbers called dollars into subjective quantities called utilities, while the numbers called probabilities remain unchanged? Mosteller and Nogee made the point themselves, and reanalyzed their data using equation (2), but treating *p* rather than $u(\$X)$ as the unknown quantity. But this is no more satisfactory. The fundamental fact is that equation (2) has at least two unknowns, *p* and $u(\$X)$. This fact has been recognized by renaming the *EU* model; it is now called the *SEU* (subjectively expected utility) model. The addition of the S means only that the probabilities which enter into equation (2) must be inferred from behavior of the person making the decision, rather than calculated from some formal mathematical model. Of course, the person making the decision may not have had a very orderly set of probabilities. In particular, his probabilities for an exhaustive set of

mutually exclusive events may not add up to 1. Thus there are really two different *SEU* models, depending on whether or not the probabilities are assumed to add up to 1. (In the latter case, the utilities must be measured on a ratio, not an interval, scale.) This article will examine the topic of subjective probabilities at length later.

In the *SEU* model every equation like equation (2) has at least two unknowns. A single equation with two unknowns is ordinarily insoluble. All subsequent work on utility and probability measurement has been addressed in one way or another to solution of this problem of too many unknowns. Edwards (1953; 1954*a*; 1954*b*) gave impetus to further analysis of the problem by exhibiting sets of preferences among bets that could not be easily accounted for by any plausible utility function for money but that seemed to require instead the notion that subjects simply prefer to gamble at some probabilities rather than others, and indeed will accept less favorable bets embodying preferred probabilities over more favorable bets embodying less preferred probabilities.

The Davidson, Suppes, and Siegel experiment. The next major experiment in the utility measurement literature was performed by Davidson, Suppes, and Siegel (see Davidson & Suppes 1957), two philosophers and a graduate student in psychology. The key idea in their experiment—the pair of subjectively equally likely events—was taken from a neglected paper by the philosopher Ramsey (1926). Suppose that you find yourself committed to a bet in which you stand to win some large sum if event *A* occurs and to lose some other large sum if it does not occur. Now suppose it is found that by paying you a penny I could induce you to substitute for the original bet another one exactly like it except that now you are betting on *A* not occurring. Now, after the substitution, suppose that I could induce you to switch back to the original bet by offering you yet another penny. Clearly, for you, the probability that *A* will occur is equal to the probability that it will not, that is, the two events are subjectively equally likely.

If we assume that either *A* or not-*A* must happen, and if we assume that for you (as for any probability theorist) the probabilities of any set of events no more than one of which can happen and some one of which must happen—that is, an exhaustive set of mutually exclusive events—add up to 1, then the sum of the probabilities of *A* and not-*A* must be 1. Now, if those two numbers are equal, then each must be 0.5.

Davidson, Suppes, and Siegel hunted for subjectively equally likely events, and finally used a die with one nonsense syllable (e.g., *ZEJ*) on three of its faces and another (*ZOJ*) on the other three. (They were very lucky that the same event turned out equally likely for all subjects.) They fixed two amounts of money, −4 cents and 6 cents. They found an amount of money, X cents, such that the subject was indifferent to receiving 6 cents if, say, *ZOJ* occurred and X cents if *ZEJ* occurred, and receiving −4 cents for sure. It follows from the *SEU* model that

$$p(ZOJ)u(6\text{¢}) + p(ZEJ)u(X\text{¢}) = u(-4\text{¢}).$$

A little algebra shows that

$$u(6\text{¢}) - u(-4\text{¢}) = u(-4\text{¢}) - u(X\text{¢}).$$

That is, the distance on the utility-of-money scale from 6 cents to −4 cents is equal to the distance from −4 cents to X cents (of course X cents is a larger loss than −4 cents). Once two equal intervals on the utility scale have been determined, it is no longer necessary to use a sure thing as one of the options. If A, B, C, and D are decreasing amounts of money, if the distance from B to C is equal to the distance from C to D, and if the subject is indifferent between a subjectively equally likely bet in which he wins A for *ZOJ* and D otherwise, and another in which he wins B for *ZOJ* and C otherwise, then the distance from A to B is equal to the other two distances. Davidson, Suppes, and Siegel used this procedure to construct a set of equally spaced points on their subjects' utility-for-money functions. Thereafter, they used the resulting utility functions as a basis for measuring the probability that one face of a symmetrical four-faced die would come up. (If the four faces were considered equally likely and if their probabilities added to 1, then that probability would be 0.25.)

The most important finding of the Davidson, Suppes, and Siegel experiment was that a good many internal consistency checks on their utility functions worked out well. Once a number of equal intervals on the utility function have been determined, many predictions can be made about preferences among new bets; some of these were tested, and in general they were successful. The utility functions were typically more complicated than those of the Mosteller–Nogee experiment and differed from subject to subject; they were seldom linearly related to money. The subjective probability of the face of the four-faced die was typically found to be in the region of 0.20.

The Davidson–Suppes–Siegel procedure remains intellectually valid, though criticisms of details are easy to make. However, it is unlikely that future utility measurement experiments will use it. The prior determination of the subjectively equally likely event is less attractive than procedures now available for determination of both utilities and probabilities from the same set of choices.

Among a substantial set of utility-measurement experiments, only two others are reviewed here. They both embody sophisticated ideas taken from recent developments in measurement theory, and they both use what amounts to a simultaneous-equations approach to the solution of a system of equations like equation (2) for utilities and probabilities, treating both as unknowns.

The Lindman experiment. Harold Lindman (1965) began by giving a subject a two-outcome bet of the form that if a spinner stopped in a specified region, the subject would win $X, while if it did not, he would win $Y. Then he invited the subject to state the minimum price for which he would sell the bet back to the experimenter. After the subject had stated that amount, $Z, Lindman operated a random device that specified an experimenter's price. If the experimenter's price was at least as favorable to the subject as the subject's price, then the sale took place, the experimenter paid his price to the subject, and the bet was not played. Otherwise, the sale did not take place, and the subject played the bet. Since the sale, if it took place, always took place at the experimenter's price, it was to the subject's advantage to name the actual minimum amount of money that he considered just as valuable as the bet. Thus Lindman could write

$$pu(\$X) + (1 - p)u(\$Y) = u(\$Z).$$

This equation has at least four unknowns, three utilities and a probability. If we question whether subjects unsophisticated about probability theory make their probabilities add up to 1, it may have five unknowns, since then both the probability of the event and the probability of its complement can be treated as unknowns. Thus, in a system of such equations there will always be many more unknowns than equations, even though the same probabilities and amounts of money are used in many different bets. However, the system can be rendered soluble, and even overdetermined, by taking advantage of the fact that if $Z is between $X and $Y (as it will be in the example), then u($Z) will be between u($X) and u($Y). In more formal language, the relation between u($X) and $X is monotonic. Lindman exploited this fact by fitting a series of line segments to his utility functions;

by controlling the number of line segments, he controlled both the number of unknowns and the amount of curvilinearity (more precisely, changes in slope) he could introduce into the utility function.

Lindman's results are complex, orderly, and pretty. He obtained a variety of shapes of utility functions for money from his different subjects. When he analyzed the data without assuming additivity of probabilities, he found that the actual sums were very close to 1; the data strongly support the idea that his subjects do in fact make probability judgments that add to 1. The probability and utility functions that were found predicted choices among bets very well indeed. There were some interactions between probabilities and utilities of a kind not appropriate to the *EU* model, but they were not major ones.

The Tversky experiment. Deviating from the nearly universal use of college student subjects, Amos Tversky used prisoners at Jackson Prison, the largest state prison in Michigan, as subjects (1964). He used cigarettes, candy bars, and money, rather than money alone, as the valuable objects whose utilities were to be measured. Tversky's research was based on an application of simultaneous conjoint measurement, a new approach to fundamental measurement which emphasizes the idea of additive structures. Consider a bet in which with probability p you win X and with probability $1 - p$ no money changes hands. Suppose such a bet is worth just Z to you. A matrix with different values of p on one axis and different values of X on the other defines a family of such bets. If the utility of no money changing hands is taken to be 0, then the *EU* model can be written for any such bet in logarithmic form as follows:

$$\log p_j + \log u(\$X_{ij}) = \log u(\$Z_{ij}).$$

That is, in logarithmic form this is an additive model. If all the values of Z_{ij} for such a matrix of bets are known, then the rules for additive representations of two-dimensional matrices permit solution (by complex computer methods) of a system of inequalities that give close values of p_j and $u(\$X_{ij})$. Tversky did just this, both for gambles and for commodity bundles consisting of so many packs of cigarettes and so many candy bars.

The main finding of Tversky's study was a consistent discrepancy between behavior under risky and riskless conditions. If probabilities are not forced to add to 1 in the data analysis, then the form that this discrepancy takes is that the probabilities of winning are consistently overestimated relative to the probabilities of losing. If probabilities are forced to add to 1, then the utilities measured under risky conditions are consistently higher than those measured under riskless conditions. The latter finding would normally be interpreted as reflecting the attractiveness or utility of gambling as an activity, independently of the attractiveness of the stakes and prizes. The discrepancy between Tversky's finding and Lindman's remains unexplained.

Summary. In all of these studies, the choices among bets made under well-defined experimental conditions turn out to be linked via some form or other of the *SEU* model to choices among other bets made by the same subjects under more or less the same conditions. That is, the *SEU* model permits observation of coherence among aspects of subjects' gambling behavior. Of course it would be attractive to find that such coherence would hold over a larger range of risk-taking activity. A substantial disappointment of these studies is that the individual utility and probability functions vary so much from one person to another. It would be scientifically convenient if different people had the same tastes—but experience offers no reason for hoping that they will, and the data clearly say that they do not.

At any rate, these studies offer no support for those who reject a priori the idea that men make "rational" decisions. An a priori model of such decision making turns out to predict very well the behavior of a variety of subjects in a variety of experiments. Nor is this finding surprising. A very general and intuitively appealing model of almost any kind of human behavior is contained in the following dialogue:

> Question: What is he doing?
> Answer: He's doing the best he can.

Probability

Identification rules for probability. The previous discussion has probably been somewhat confusing to many readers not familiar with what is now going on in statistical theory. It has consistently treated probability as a quantity to be inferred from the behavior of subjects, rather than calculated from such observations as the ratio of heads to total flips of a coin. It is intuitively reasonable to think that men make probability judgments just as they make value judgments and that these judgments can be discovered from men's behavior. But how might such subjective probabilities relate to the more familiar quantities that we estimate by means of relative frequencies?

This question is a controversial one in contemporary statistics. Considered as a mathematical quantity, a probability is a value that obeys three quite simple rules: it remains between 0 and 1; 0 means impossibility and 1 means certainty; and the probability of an event's taking place plus the probability of its not taking place add up to 1. These three properties are basic to all of the elaborate formal structure of probability theory considered as a topic in mathematics. Nor are they, or their consequences, at all controversial. What are controversial are the identification rules linking these abstract numbers with observations made or makable in the real world. The usual relative-frequency rules suffer from a number of intellectual difficulties. They require an act of faith that a sequence of relative frequencies will in fact approach a limit as the number of observations increases without limit. They are very vague and subjective while pretending to be otherwise; this fact is most conspicuous in the specification that relative frequencies are supposed to be observed under "substantially similar conditions," which means that the conditions should be similar enough but not too similar. (A coin always tossed in *exactly* the same way would presumably fall with the same face up every time.) Perhaps most important, the frequentistic set of rules is just not applicable to many, perhaps most, of the questions about which men might be uncertain. What is the probability that your son will be a straight-A student in his senior year in high school? While an estimate might be made by counting the fraction of senior boys in the high school he is likely to attend who have straight-A records, a much better estimate would be based primarily on his own personal characteristics, past grade record, family background, and the like.

The Bayesian approach.   Dissatisfaction with the frequentistic set of identification rules, for these and other more technical reasons, has caused a set of statisticians, probability theorists, and philosophers led by Leonard J. Savage, author of *The Foundations of Statistics* (1954), to adopt a different, personalistic, set of such rules. According to the personalistic set of identification rules, a probability is an opinion about how likely an event is. If it is an opinion, it must be someone's opinion; I will remind you of this from time to time by reference to your probability for something, and by calling such probabilities personal. Not any old opinion can be a probability; probabilities are orderly, which mostly means that they add up to 1. This requirement of orderliness is extremely constraining, so much so that no real man is likely to be able to conform to it in his spontaneous opinions. Thus the "you" whose opinions I shall refer to is a slightly idealized you, the person you would presumably like to be rather than the person you are.

Those who use the personalistic identification rules for probabilities are usually called Bayesians, for the rather unsatisfactory reason that they make heavier use of a mathematical triviality named Bayes' theorem than do nonpersonalists. Bayes' theorem, an elementary consequence of the fact that probabilities add up to 1, is important to Bayesians because it is a formally optimal rule for revising opinions on the basis of evidence. Consider some hypothesis H. Your opinion that it is true at some given time is expressed by a number $p(H)$, called the prior probability of H. Now you observe some datum D, with unconditional probability $p(D)$ and with conditional probability $p(D|H)$ of occurring if H is true. After that, your former opinion about H, $p(H)$, is revised into a new opinion about H, $p(H|D)$, called the posterior probability of H on the basis of D. Bayes' theorem says these quantities are related by the equation

$$(3) \qquad p(H|D) = \frac{p(D|H)\,p(H)}{p(D)}.$$

An especially useful form of Bayes' theorem is obtained by writing it for two different hypotheses, H_A and H_B, on the basis of the same datum D, and then dividing one equation by the other:

$$p(H_A|D) = \frac{p(D|H_A)}{p(D)} p(H_A),$$

$$p(H_B|D) = \frac{p(D|H_B)}{p(D)} p(H_B),$$

$$\frac{p(H_A|D)}{p(H_B|D)} = \frac{p(D|H_A)}{p(D|H_B)} \frac{p(H_A)}{p(H_B)},$$

or, in simpler notation,

$$(4) \qquad \Omega_1 = L\Omega_0.$$

In equation (4), Ω_0, the ratio of $p(H_A)$ to $p(H_B)$, is called the prior odds, Ω_1 is called the posterior odds, and L is the likelihood ratio. Equation (4) is perhaps the most widely useful form of Bayes' theorem.

Conservatism in information processing.   Bayes' theorem is of importance to psychologists as well as to statisticians. Psychologists are very much interested in the revision of opinion in the light of information. If equation (3) or equation (4) is an optimal rule for how such revisions should be made, it is appropriate to compare its prescriptions with actual human behavior.

Consider a very simple experiment by Phillips and Edwards (1966). Subjects were presented with a bookbag full of poker chips. They were told that it had been chosen at random, with 0.5 probability, from two bookbags, one containing 700 red and 300 blue chips, while the other contained 700 blue and 300 red. The question of interest is which bag this one is. Subjects were to answer the question by estimating the probability that this was the predominantly red bookbag. On the basis of the information so far available, that probability is 0.5, as all subjects agreed.

Now, the experimenter samples randomly with replacement from the bookbag. At this point let me invite you to be a subject in this experiment. Suppose that in 12 samples, with replacement, the experimenter gets red, red, red, blue, red, blue, red, blue, red, red, blue, red—that is, 8 reds and 4 blues. Now, on the basis of all the evidence you have, what is the probability that this is the predominantly red bookbag? Write down an intuitive guess before starting to read the next paragraph.

Let us apply equation (4) to the problem. The prior odds are 1:1, so all we need is the likelihood ratio. To derive that is straightforward; for the general binomial case of r reds in n samples, where H_A says that the probability of a red is p_A (and of a blue is q_A) and H_B says the probability of a red is p_B (and of a blue is q_B),

$$L = \frac{p_A^r q_A^{n-r}}{p_B^r q_B^{n-r}}.$$

In this particular case, made much simpler by the fact that $p_A = q_B$ and vice versa, it is simply

$$L = \left(\frac{p_A}{q_A}\right)^{2r-n}.$$

Of course $2r - n = r - (n - r)$ and is the difference between the number of reds and the number of blues in the sample—in this case, 4. So the likelihood ratio is $(7/3)^4 = 29.64$. Since the prior odds are 1:1, the posterior odds are then 29.64:1. And so the posterior probability that this is the predominantly red bookbag is 0.97.

If you are like Phillips and Edwards' subjects, the number you wrote down wasn't nearly so high as 0.97. It was probably about 0.70 or 0.80. Phillips and Edwards' subjects, and indeed all subjects who have been studied in experiments of this general variety, are conservative information processors, unable to extract from data anything like as much certainty as the data justify. A variety of experiments has been devoted to this conservatism phenomenon. It is a function of response mode; Phil-

lips and Edwards have shown that people are a bit less conservative when estimating odds than when estimating probability. It is a function of the diagnosticity of the information; Peterson, Schneider, and Miller (1965) have shown that the larger the number of poker chips presented at one time, the greater is the conservatism, and a number of studies by various investigators have shown that the more diagnostic each individual poker chip, the greater the conservatism.

Conservatism could be attributed to either or both of two possible failures in the course of human information processing. First, the subjects might be unable to perceive the data-generating process accurately; they might attribute to data less diagnostic value than the data in fact have. Or the subjects might be unable to combine information properly, as Bayes' theorem prescribes, even though they may perceive the diagnostic value of any individual datum correctly. Data collected by Beach (1966) favor the former hypothesis; data collected by Edwards (1966) and by Phillips (1965) favor the latter. It seems clear by now that this formulation of the possible causes of conservatism is too simple to account for the known facts, but no one has yet proposed a better one.

Probabilistic information processing. If men are conservative information processors, then it seems reasonable to expect that this fact has practical consequences. One practical consequence is familiar to anyone who has ever grumbled over a hospital bill: human conservatism in processing available diagnostic information may lead to collection of too much information, where the collection process is costly. An even more serious consequence may arise in situations in which speed of a response is crucial: a conservative information processor may wait too long to respond because he is too uncertain what response is appropriate. This consequence of conservatism is especially important in the design of large military information-processing systems. In the North American Air Defense System, for example, the speed with which the system declares we are under attack, if we are, may make a difference of millions of lives.

Edwards (1962; 1965b) has proposed a design for diagnostic systems that overcomes the deficiency of human conservatism. A probabilistic information processing system (PIP) is designed in terms of Bayes' theorem. For vague, verbal data and vague, verbal hypotheses, experts must estimate $p(D|H)$ or L as appropriate (usually L rather than $p(D|H)$ will be appropriate). They make these estimates separately for each datum and each hypothesis or pair of hypotheses of interest to the system. Then a computer uses equation (3) or equation (4) to synthesize these separate judgments into a posterior distribution that reflects how all the hypotheses stand in the light of all the data. This distribution is of course revised each time a new datum becomes available.

A number of studies of PIP have been performed (see, e.g., Schum, Goldstein, & Southard 1966; Kaplan & Newman 1966; Edwards 1966). The studies have generally found it more efficient than competitive systems faced with the same information. In a large unpublished simulation study, Edwards and his associates found that data that would lead PIP to give 99:1 odds in favor of some hypothesis would lead its next-best competitor to give less than 5:1 odds in favor of that hypothesis. Even larger discrepancies in favor of PIP appear in Phillips' study. Thus a combination of human judgment and Bayes' theorem seems to be capable of doing a better job of information processing than either alone.

Are men rational?

All in all, the evidence favors rationality. Men seem to be able to maximize expected utility rather well, in a too-restricted range of laboratory tasks. There are, of course, a number of well-known counterexamples to the idea that men consistently do what is best for them. More detailed analysis of such experiments (e.g., probability learning experiments) indicates that substantial deviations from rationality seldom occur unless they cost little; when a lot is at stake and the task isn't too complex for comprehension, men behave in such a way as to maximize expected utility.

The comparison of men with Bayes' theorem is less favorable to men. The conservatism phenomenon is a large, consistent deviation from optimal information-processing performance. Nevertheless, it is surprising to those newly looking at this area that men can do as well as they do at probability or odds estimation.

The topic of the articulation between diagnosis and action selection will receive much more study in the next few years than it has so far. What little evidence is available suggests that men do remarkably well at doing what they should, given the information on hand. But the surface of this topic has scarcely been scratched.

Total rejection of the notion that men behave rationally is as inappropriate as total acceptance would be. On the whole, men do well; exactly how well they do, depends in detail on the situation they are in, what's at stake, how much information they have, and so on. The main thrust of psychological theory in this area is likely to be a detailed spelling out of just how nearly rational men can be expected to be under given circumstances.

WARD EDWARDS

[*Directly related are the entries* DECISION THEORY; PROBLEM SOLVING; REASONING AND LOGIC. *Other relevant material may be found in* BAYESIAN INFERENCE; GAMBLING; GAME THEORY; INFORMATION THEORY; MODELS, MATHEMATICAL; PROBABILITY; UTILITARIANISM; UTILITY; *and in the biographies of* BAYES; BENTHAM; VON NEUMANN.]

BIBLIOGRAPHY

Edwards 1954c; 1961 *provide two reviews of decision theory from a psychological point of view; these constitute a good starting point for more intensive study. For those who find these papers too difficult,* Edwards, Lindman, & Phillips 1965 *is an easier and more up-to-date but less thorough introduction to the topic.* Luce & Raiffa 1957, *though somewhat out-of-date, remains unique for its clear and coherent exposition of the mathematical content of decision theory.* Luce & Suppes 1965 *performs a similar job at chapter rather than book length and much more recently; its emphasis is on the probabilistic models of choice and decision. The easiest introduction to Bayesian statistics is* Edwards, Lindman, & Savage 1963 *or* Schlaifer 1961. *By far the most authoritative treatment of the topic is* Raiffa & Schlaifer 1961, *but* Lindley 1965 *and* Good 1965 *are also important. No review of the more recent psychological work on subjective probability structured around the Bayesian ideas exists yet, though one is in preparation.* Beach 1966; Kaplan & Newman 1966; Phillips, Hays, & Edwards 1966; Schum, Goldstein, & Southard 1966; Slovic 1966; Peterson & Phillips 1966 *provide a good sample of that work, comparing men with Bayes' theorem as information processors.* Wasserman & Silander 1958 *is an annotated bibliography that emphasizes the sorts of interpersonal topics and social applications here ignored; it is a good guide to older parts of that literature. There is a much more up-to-date supplement, but it is not widely available.* Rapoport & Orwant 1962 *reviews the literature on experimental games.* Kogan & Wallach 1964 *is on personality variables in decision making.*

BEACH, LEE ROY 1966 Accuracy and Consistency in the Revision of Subjective Probabilities. *IEEE Transactions on Human Factors in Electronics* HFE-7:29–37.

BRIGGS, GEORGE E.; and SCHUM, DAVID A. 1965 Automated Bayesian Hypothesis-selection in a Simulated Threat-diagnosis System. Pages 169–176 in Congress on the Information System Sciences, Second, *Proceedings.* Washington: Spartan.

DAVIDSON, DONALD; and SUPPES, PATRICK 1957 *Decision Making: An Experimental Approach.* In collaboration with Sidney Siegel. Stanford Univ. Press.

EDWARDS, WARD 1953 Probability-preferences in Gambling. *American Journal of Psychology* 66:349–364.

EDWARDS, WARD 1954a Probability-preferences Among Bets With Differing Expected Values. *American Journal of Psychology* 67:56–67.

EDWARDS, WARD 1954b The Reliability of Probability-preferences. *American Journal of Psychology* 67:68–95.

EDWARDS, WARD 1954c The Theory of Decision Making. *Psychological Bulletin* 51:380–417.

EDWARDS, WARD 1961 Behavioral Decision Theory. *Annual Review of Psychology* 12:473–498.

EDWARDS, WARD 1962 Dynamic Decision Theory and Probabilistic Information Processing. *Human Factors* 4:59–73.

EDWARDS, WARD 1965a Optimal Strategies for Seeking Information: Models for Statistics, Choice Reaction Times, and Human Information Processing. *Journal of Mathematical Psychology* 2:312–329.

EDWARDS, WARD 1965b Probabilistic Information Processing Systems for Diagnosis and Action Selection. Pages 141–155 in Congress on the Information System Sciences, Second, *Proceedings*. Washington: Spartan.

EDWARDS, WARD 1966 Non-conservative Probabilistic Information Processing Systems Final Report. ESD Final Report No. 05893-22-F. Unpublished manuscript.

EDWARDS, WARD; LINDMAN, HAROLD; and PHILLIPS, LAWRENCE D. 1965 Emerging Technologies for Making Decisions. Pages 261–325 in *New Directions in Psychology*, II. New York: Holt.

EDWARDS, WARD; LINDMAN, HAROLD; and SAVAGE, LEONARD Y. 1963 Bayesian Statistical Inference for Psychological Research. *Psychological Review* 70:193–242.

EDWARDS, WARD; and PHILLIPS, LAWRENCE D. 1964 Man as Transducer for Probabilities in Bayesian Command and Control Systems. Pages 360–401 in Maynard W. Shelly and Glenn L. Bryan (editors), *Human Judgments and Optimality*. New York: Wiley.

FRIEDMAN, MILTON; and SAVAGE, L. J. 1948 The Utility Analysis of Choices Involving Risk. *Journal of Political Economy* 56:279–304.

GOOD, I. J. 1965 *The Estimation of Probabilities: An Essay on Modern Bayesian Methods*. Cambridge, Mass.: M.I.T. Press.

KAPLAN, R. J.; and NEWMAN, J. R. 1966 Studies in Probabilistic Information Processing. *IEEE Transactions on Human Factors in Electronics* HFE-7:49–63.

KOGAN, NATHAN; and WALLACH, MICHAEL A. 1964 *Risk Taking: A Study in Cognition and Personality*. New York: Holt.

LINDLEY, DENNIS V. 1965 *Introduction to Probability and Statistics From a Bayesian Viewpoint*. 2 vols. Cambridge Univ. Press.

LINDMAN, HAROLD R. 1965 The Simultaneous Measurement of Utilities and Subjective Probabilities. Ph.D. dissertation, Univ. of Michigan.

LUCE, R. DUNCAN; and RAIFFA, HOWARD 1957 *Games and Decisions: Introduction and Critical Survey*. A study of the Behavioral Models Project, Bureau of Applied Social Research, Columbia University. New York: Wiley.

LUCE, R. DUNCAN; and SUPPES, PATRICK 1965 Preference, Utility, and Subjective Probability. Volume 3, pages 249–410 in R. Duncan Luce, Robert R. Bush, and Eugene Galanter (editors), *Handbook of Mathematical Psychology*. New York: Wiley.

MOSTELLER, FREDERICK; and NOGEE, PHILIP 1951 An Experimental Measurement of Utility. *Journal of Political Economy* 59:371–404.

PETERSON, CAMERON R.; and MILLER, ALAN J. 1965 Sensitivity of Subjective Probability Revision. *Journal of Experimental Psychology* 70:117–121.

PETERSON, CAMERON R.; and PHILLIPS, LAWRENCE D. 1966 Revision of Continuous Subjective Probability Distributions. *IEEE Transactions on Human Factors in Electronics* HFE-7:19–22.

PETERSON, CAMERON R.; SCHNEIDER, ROBERT J.; and MILLER, ALAN J. 1965 Sample Size and the Revision of Subjective Probabilities. *Journal of Experimental Psychology* 69:522–527.

PETERSON, CAMERON R. et al. 1965 Internal Consistency of Subjective Probabilities. *Journal of Experimental Psychology* 70:526–533.

PHILLIPS, LAWRENCE D. 1965 Some Components of Probabilistic Inference. Ph.D. dissertation, Univ. of Michigan.

PHILLIPS, LAWRENCE D.; and EDWARDS, WARD 1966 Conservatism in a Simple Probability Inference Task. Unpublished manuscript, Univ. of Michigan, Institute of Science and Technology.

PHILLIPS, LAWRENCE D.; HAYS, WILLIAM L.; and EDWARDS, WARD 1966 Conservatism in Complex Probabilistic Inference. *IEEE Transactions on Human Factors in Electronics* HFE-7:7–18.

RAIFFA, HOWARD; and SCHLAIFER, ROBERT 1961 *Applied Statistical Decision Theory*. Graduate School of Business Administration, Studies in Managerial Economics. Boston: Harvard Univ., Division of Research.

RAMSEY, FRANK P. (1926) 1964 Truth and Probability. Pages 61–92 in Henry E. Kyburg, Jr. and Howard E. Smokler (editors), *Studies in Subjective Probabilities*. New York: Wiley.

RAPOPORT, ANATOL; and ORWANT, CAROL 1962 Experimental Games: A Review. *Behavioral Science* 7:1–37.

SAVAGE, LEONARD J. 1954 *The Foundations of Statistics*. New York: Wiley.

SCHLAIFER, ROBERT 1961 *Introduction to Statistics for Business Decisions*. New York: McGraw-Hill.

SCHUM, D. A.; GOLDSTEIN, I. L.; and SOUTHARD, J. T. 1966 Research on a Simulated Bayesian Information-processing System. *IEEE Transactions on Human Factors in Electronics* HFE-7:37–48.

SLOVIC, PAUL 1966 Value as a Determiner of Subjective Probability. *IEEE Transactions on Human Factors in Electronics* HFE-7:22–28.

TVERSKY, AMOS 1964 Additive Choice Structures. Ph.D. dissertation, Univ. of Michigan.

VON NEUMANN, JOHN; and MORGENSTERN, OSKAR (1944) 1964 *Theory of Games and Economic Behavior*. 3d ed. New York: Wiley.

WASSERMAN, PAUL S.; and SILANDER, FRED S. 1958 *Decision Making: An Annotated Bibliography*. Ithaca, N.Y.: Cornell Univ., Graduate School of Business and Public Administration.

II
ECONOMIC ASPECTS

The distinction between prescriptive and descriptive theories of decision is similar to that between logic—a system of formally consistent rules of thought—and the psychology of thinking. A logical rule prescribes, for example, that if you believe all X to be Y, you should also believe that all non-Y are non-X, but not that all Y are X; and if you believe, in addition, that all Y are Z, you should believe all X to be Z (a logical rule known as transitivity of inclusion). Here, X, Y, and Z are objects or propositions. Such prescriptive rules do not state that all people of a given culture, social position, age, and so forth, always comply with them. If, for example, the links in a chain of reasoning are numerous, the rule of transitivity will probably be broken, at least by children or by unschooled or impatient people.

Descriptions, and consequently predictions, of "illogical" behavior, as indeed of all human behavior, are presumably a task for psychologists or anthropologists. Such predictions are obviously important to practicing lawyers, politicians, salesmen, organizers, teachers, and others who work with people, just as predictions of the behavior of metals and animals are important to engineers and dairy farmers. These practitioners are well advised to know the frequencies of the various types of illogical behavior of their clients, adversaries, or students. But they are also well advised to avoid logical errors in their own behavior, as when they apply their knowledge of men (and of all nature, for that matter) to win lawsuits or elections or to be successful in organizing or teaching. For example, their propositions X, Y, and Z may be about another's madness, yet should obey the rule of transitivity of inclusion. Moreover, if you want to train future lawyers, statesmen, or businessmen, you are well advised to learn, from your own or other people's experiences, the techniques needed to make your pupil not only knowledgeable about other men's logical frailties but also strong in his own thinking and able to solve the brain twisters his future will offer. These pedagogical techniques are, of course, objects of descriptive study.

To illustrate the prescriptive–descriptive distinction in the domain of decisions, let us consider one of the rules proposed by prescriptive decision theory. We choose the rule called transitivity of preferences (other proposed rules will be discussed below) because of its special similarity with transitivity of inclusion. If you prefer a to b and b to c, you should prefer a to c. Here, a, b, and c are, in general, your actions with uncertain outcomes, although in the special case of "sure actions," the outcome, e.g., gaining or losing an object, is unique, in which case preferring action a is, in effect, the same as preferring the outcome of action a. If an individual disobeys the transitivity rule and prefers a to b, b to c, and c to a, we would say that he does not know what he wants. Surely we would advise or train a practitioner to develop the ability for concentrated deliberation, weighing advantages and disadvantages in some appropriate way. This should result in a consistent ranking, from the most to the least preferable, with ties (i.e., indifference between some alternatives) not excluded, of alternative actions from which the decision maker may be forced to choose.

The statement that "given a set of feasible alternatives, the 'reasonable' (rational) man should choose the best" and the parallel statement that "an actual man does choose the best (and if the best is not feasible, the second best, etc.)" are both empty if the ranking order is not supposed to be stable over a period long enough to make the statements of practical relevance. If the ranking order is stable, economics as the study of the best allocation of available resources becomes possible.

The boundary between descriptive and prescriptive economics did not worry early writers. Gresham's law, Ricardo's explanations of rent and of the high postwar price of bullion, and Böhm-Bawerk's theory of interest are deductions from the assumption of consistent ranking of alternatives by reasonable men. But those authors also practiced induction and looked for historical facts that confirmed their deductions. The two approaches are not inconsistent if one assumes that in the cultures considered, housewives and adult, gainfully occupied men have by and large been "reasonable," at least when deciding not on wars and divorces but on matters of major interest to the economists of the time—for example, quantities such as prices, demands, and outputs, as well as less quantifiable choices such as location and internal organization (division of labor) of a plant. These matters were studied under the assumption of a tolerably well-known future.

The descriptive and prescriptive approaches became more clearly distinguished as more attention was directed to economic decisions under uncertainty (Fisher 1906; Hicks 1939; Hart 1940) and, stimulated by the *Theory of Games and Economic Behavior* (von Neumann & Morgenstern 1944), to nonquantifiable decisions traditionally assigned to political and military science or to sociology. In search of tools for their descriptive work, economists were also influenced by modern statistical decision theory. [*See* DECISION THEORY.] It then appeared that the reasonable man was not sufficiently approached even by the *ideal type* of an industrial entrepreneur, who evidently must be aided by a sophisticated hypothesis tester, a statistician, or, more recently and generally, an expert in operations research. [*See* OPERATIONS RESEARCH.] As such experts, armed with computers, do indeed progressively penetrate the economic world, predictive and descriptive economics (e.g., the prediction of aggregate inventories) may again become closer to what can be deductively derived from rational decision rules.

To return to the analogy between theories of thinking and of decision, prescriptive theories of thinking and decision are concerned with formal consistency between sentences or decisions, not with their content. If one believes that Los Angeles is on the Moon and that the Moon is in Africa, it is logical for him to believe that Los Angeles is in Africa, although none of the three statements is true. Similarly, if a man prefers killing to stealing and stealing to drinking strong liquor, he should prefer killing to drinking, although none of these actions is laudable or hygienic. Hicks (1939) used Milton's "reason is also choice" as a motto to the theory of consumption. Ramsey (1923–1928) called his theory of decision an extension of logic, an attitude adopted more recently by other logicians, for example, Carnap (1962), von Wright (1963), and Jeffrey (1965). The mutual penetration of logic and decision theory will appear even more founded and urgent when we come to discuss the cost of thinking and deciding (section 8).

In sections 1, 3, 4, and 5 we shall discuss some prescriptive decision rules and outline some simple experiments whose outcomes determine whether the subject did or did not comply with these rules. Whenever such experiments or similar ones have actually been performed, we shall refer to available descriptive evidence, namely, the frequency of subjects' obeying these rules or obeying some other stated behavior patterns, such as the probabilistic decision models of section 2. In section 6 the expected utility theorem implied by the prescriptive rules is discussed. Sections 7 and 8 point to unsolved problems on the frontier of decision theory.

1. Complete ordering of actions

Before we consider the notion of a complete ordering of alternative actions or decisions (we need not distinguish between the two here), it is convenient to restate the *transitivity* of preferences by defining the relation "not preferred to" or "not better than," written symbolically as $\leqslant$. If $a \leqslant b$ and $b \leqslant c$, then $a \leqslant c$. It is a *reflexive* relation, i.e., $a \leqslant a$. A relation that is transitive and reflexive is called an *ordering* relation. When $a \leqslant b$ and $b \leqslant a$, we write $a \sim b$ and say that the decision maker is indifferent between a and b, even though a and b are not identical. For example, an investor may be indifferent between two different portfolios of securities. Thus "$\leqslant$" (unlike the relation "not larger than" applied to numbers) is a *weak ordering* relation. Further, when $a \leqslant b$ and not $b \leqslant a$, we write $a < b$ and say that b is preferred to, or is better than, a.

Shall we say that a reasonable man always either prefers b to a or a to b or is indifferent? Or can he, in addition, refuse to compare them? If

he can, the ordering of the actions by the relation "not better than" is only a *partial* one. This position has been taken, for example, by Aumann (1962), Chipman (in Interdisciplinary Research Conference 1960), and Wolfowitz (1962). But can one escape choosing? As in Pascal's (1670) famous immortality bet, "Il faut parier!" The avoiding of choice itself is a decision. Like other decisions, it is made more or less desirable by the prizes and penalties it entails. If this is granted, the transitive relation "$\leqslant$" is also *connective* and induces a *complete ordering*. Then any subset of actions can be arranged according to their desirabilities (with ties not excluded). Rank numbers, also called *ordinal utilities* (priorities), can then be assigned to the alternative actions provided that certain weak conditions are satisfied (Debreu 1959, section 4, note 2, and section 4.6).

Tests of transitivity of preferences. As a matter of descriptive theory we ask whether people (of a given culture, etc.) do act as if there exist complete orderings of their actions by preferences. In actual experiments the penalty for refusing to choose was assumed to be strong enough to force subjects to make genuine choices in the form of verbal statements of preferences or, in some cases, actually to stake money on one wager rather than another. With connectivity of the preference relation thus assured and its reflexivity assumed by definition, the transitivity of the relation remained to be tested. The alternative actions were represented by multidimensional objects—a bundle of tickets to various shows (Papandreou 1957), marriage partners classified by three three-valued characteristics (May 1954; Davis 1958), a monetary wager (Edwards 1953; Davidson & Marschak 1959), a price policy affecting both the firm's rate of return and its share of the market, an air trip varying in both cost and duration (MacCrimmon 1965), and so forth. The subject responded by a triad of binary choices—a or b? b or c? c or a?—but in most experiments these choices were separated in time by choices from other triads, that is, "a or b?" was followed by "a' or b'?" rather than by "b or c?" Moreover, neither of the two actions "dominated" the other (see section 3), and no subject could use paper and pencil.

In all experiments, the transitivity rule was violated with varying frequencies. The proportion of the number of violations by all subjects to the maximum theoretical number of intransitive triads that were possible in the given experimental designs ranged from .04 in MacCrimmon's tests of business executives to .27 in May's tests of students. Since the experiments record actual choices and not preferences, intransitivity might be exhibited by a person who, although consistent, is strictly indifferent among three alternatives. (To approach, more generally, the case of "near indifference," the hypothesis tested must be rephrased in probabilistic terms. This will be discussed in section 2.) Thus the outcome of an experiment depends on the nature of the alternatives offered, making the experiments mentioned not quite comparable.

It would also be of great interest to study the effects of the passage of time and the effects of learning, especially if different methods of training are applied, such as "post-mortem" discussion (a domain opened by MacCrimmon), sequential modifications of the list of choices, etc. In fact, what would be the effect of supplying the subjects with paper and pencil and training them to use these prerequisites of our culture to tabulate the decision problem in an "outcome matrix" as in Table 1 below?

It has been suggested (Quandt 1956; Simon 1957) that intransitivities of decisions occur when the subject is unable to pay simultaneous attention to the several dimensions of each object of choice. This is somewhat analogous to the psychophysical finding that discrimination is greater between sounds differing in pitch but of equal loudness than between sounds differing in both (Pollack 1955). This suggests that the probabilistic approach common in psychophysics might be tried in a description of decision behavior. As to prescriptive theory, one may recall Benjamin Franklin's suggestion to score the pros and cons of each decision or the practice of adding scores when grading students or judging young ladies in beauty contests. Again, these or any other ways of overcoming the multidimensionality of decisions through deliberate and simultaneous marshaling of all the dimensions will in general require paper and pencil.

2. Probabilistic ordering of actions

Since the prescriptive rule of transitivity is often violated, it is necessary to recast descriptive decision theory in different terms. The hypothesis that transitivity of decisions may be achieved by learning or training has already been mentioned. It is also traditional in experimental psychology, especially since Fechner's (1860) studies of perception, to describe behavior by probability distributions. Economists, by contrast, have succeeded in the past in making useful predictions of the aggregate behavior of large numbers of individuals based on the assumption that individuals are, by and large, "reasonable." The probabilistic approach is rather new in economics, perhaps as young as

the econometricians' attempts to test aggregate economic models statistically and to relate these models to observable behavior of sampled individual households and firms.

Luce and Suppes (1965) have comprehensively surveyed the literature and the experimental evidence relevant to probabilistic orderings. One model that implies all the others suggested so far is that presented by Luce (1959). Fixed positive numbers $v_a, v_b, v_c, \cdots$, called *strict utilities*, are attached to the alternative actions $a, b, c, \cdots$. The set of actions includes all alternatives that may ever be offered to a given subject. The strict utilities are assumed to have the following property: if the subject must choose from a particular subset of alternatives, he will choose each with a probability proportional to its strict utility. For example, suppose $v_a:v_b:v_c:v_d = 1:2:3:4$. Then, if asked to choose from the subset (a, b, c), the subject will choose a, b, or c with respective probabilities $\frac{1}{6}$, $\frac{2}{6}$, $\frac{3}{6}$; if he must choose from the pair (a, b), he will choose a or b with respective probabilities $\frac{1}{3}$, $\frac{2}{3}$. The hypothesis can be tested at least "in principle" (i.e., assuming that representative samples from the universe of all choice situations can be obtained). One would observe the relative frequencies of choices from various subsets and infer, for example, that the ratio of the probability of choosing a to the probability of choosing b from the pair (a, b) does or does not change if a third alternative is also offered.

In another model, constants $u_a, u_b, u_c, \cdots$, called *strong utilities*, are associated with the alternatives $a, b, c, \cdots$. The strong utilities are assumed to have the following property: in the binary choice between a and b, the probability $p(a, b)$ of choosing a is an increasing function of the difference $u_a - u_b$ (except when $p(a, b)$ is equal to 1 or 0).

It follows that $p(a, b) \underset{<}{\overset{>}{=}} \frac{1}{2}$ according as $u_a \underset{<}{\overset{>}{=}} u_b$.

Note that the case $p(a, b) = \frac{1}{2}$ provides an operational definition of "indifference" based on actual choices rather than on the verbal statement "I am indifferent." This model was used, in effect, in Thurstone's discussion of public opinion and of soldiers' food preferences (1927–1955). It is analogous to Fechner's perception model, which associates a physical stimulus a with a subjective "sensation" u_a; the subject perceives a to be heavier (or louder or brighter) than b with a probability $p(a, b)$ that increases with the difference $u_a - u_b$ (provided $p(a, b)$ is neither 0 nor 1).

It can be shown that if strict utilities exist, then strong utilities also exist (putting $u_a = \log v_a$, etc.), but not the converse. The strong utility model implies, in turn, the still less restrictive *weak utility* model, which assigns the ordinal numbers w_a, w_b, w_c, $\cdots$ to the alternatives $a, b, c, \cdots$, such that $p(a, b) \gtreqless \frac{1}{2}$ according as $w_a \gtreqless w_b$. Clearly, if the strong utilities exist, so do the weak utilities (putting $w_a = u_a$, etc.), but not the converse since differences between ordinal numbers are undefined. Both the weak utility model and the strong utility model can be tested in principle for possible rejection, for they have implications that involve choice probabilities only, avoiding the intervening utility concept. In particular, the models imply, respectively, the *weak stochastic transitivity*,

if $p(a, b) \geqslant \frac{1}{2}$ and $p(b, c) \geqslant \frac{1}{2}$,
then $p(a, c) \geqslant \frac{1}{2}$,

and the *strong stochastic transitivity*,

if $p(a, b) \geqslant \frac{1}{2}$ and $p(b, c) \geqslant \frac{1}{2}$,
then $p(a, c) \geqslant \max [p(a, b), p(b, c)]$.

Of these two forms of stochastic transitivity, the strong implies the weak one; it is, in turn, implied by the exact transitivity rule treated in section 1 if the choice probabilities are assumed to take on only three values: 0, $\frac{1}{2}$, and 1, corresponding to the preference relations $a < b$, $a \sim b$, and $b < a$.

Another probabilistic model also implied by, and less restrictive than, Luce's strict utility model is the *random utility* model. It does not imply, nor is it implied by, the strong or the weak utility model. It asserts, for a given subject, the existence of a fixed probability distribution on the set of all preference orderings of all alternatives, so that for a set of N alternatives, a probability is attached to each of their $N!$ permutations. In the nonprobabilistic economics of consumer's choice the (ordinal) utility function that attaches a constant rank to each commodity bundle is a fixed one. In the random utility model this function is, instead, visualized as drawn at random from a set of such functions, according to a probability distribution that is fixed for the given subject. Thus the word "utility" designates here a random number, not a constant as in the other probabilistic models described.

What relevance do these (and related) models have for a prescriptive theory of decision? Just as not all men are always consistent, not all men are always in good health. Doctors and nurses are busy measuring the temperatures and blood pressures of the sick ones. The probability distributions supposed to characterize a "stochastic decision maker" may vary in the degree of their closeness to the ideal limit—consistency. For example, consistency

is approached in the strong utility model as the values of $p(a, b)$ concentrate near 1 or 0 or $\frac{1}{2}$. We can thus trace the path of progress of learning or training for consistency.

3. Inadmissibility of dominated actions

An action's result (outcome) depends, in general, not only on the action but also on the "state of the world (nature or environment)," which is not in the decision maker's control. For our purposes an action (called an act by Savage [1954]) can be defined by the results it yields at various states of the world. Thus an action is a function from the set of states to the set of results. (This function has constant value if the action is a "sure action.") In a decision situation, only some such functions are available; their "feasible set" (the "offered set of alternatives" of section 2) depends, for example, on the decision maker's resources, technology, and market as he views them.

An *event* is a subset of the states of nature. In particular, the subset consisting of all states that, for any given feasible action, result in the same outcome is called an *outcome-relevant event*. In a decision situation the set of states is partitioned into such events, with all irrelevant details omitted.

Even if the well-disciplined decision maker can consistently rank multidimensional results according to his preferences, action under uncertainty remains multidimensional because of the multiplicity of events. Actions are bets, or wagers. Yet it seems reasonable to prescribe (as in section 1) that bets be ordered; indeed, some authors prescribe that bets be completely ordered (Ramsey 1923–1928; Savage 1954; de Finetti 1937). It will be shown in section 6 that a complete ordering corresponds to that of numerical "expected utilities" of actions *provided* that the decision maker is consistent in the sense of obeying both the traditional rules of logic and certain postulates that are plausible enough to qualify as extensions of logic. These postulates will be discussed in this and subsequent sections, essentially following Savage.

Action a is said to dominate action b if the results of a are sometimes (i.e., when some events take place) better than the results of b and are never worse. Is it not reasonable that you should prefer

Table 1 — *An outcome matrix (in dollars)*

Action	Event	
	Z_1	Z_2
a	1,000	1,500
a'	999	1,500
b	1,000	1,000

the dominating action? Any action that is dominated by some feasible action is thus inadmissible. Consider, for example, the actions listed in Table 1. If action a is taken and the state of the world is Z_1, a gain of \$1,000 will be realized; if action a is taken and the state of the world is Z_2, a gain of \$1,500 will be realized; and so on. Such a table is called an *outcome matrix*.

The inadmissibility postulate would order these actions as follows: $a' < a, b < a$. It does not, by itself, induce complete ordering of the actions. Thus, it is silent about the preference relation between actions a' and b in Table 1. The "expected utility" rule of section 6 will determine this relation roughly in the following manner: depending on the "probabilities" of events and on the "utilities" of results, the \$500 advantage of a' over b if Z_2 happens may or may not outweigh its \$1 disadvantage if Z_1 happens. This appeals to common sense but remains vague until, with help of other postulates, we define the concepts of "probability" and "utility."

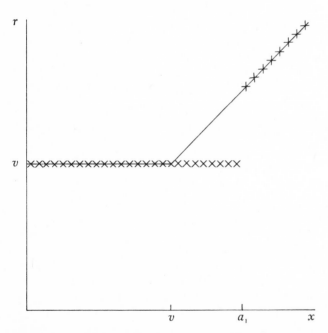

Figure 1 — *Result r as a function of bid x when the asking price is equal to v (solid line) and to $a_1 > v$ (crosses)*

Does the inadmissibility rule describe people's actual behavior? It is difficult to make an individual violate the rule when the decision situation is presented with clarity, for example, by an outcome matrix whose entries have an obvious ordering (sums of money, as in Table 1, or good health, light illness, and death). But consider the following experiment. A subject is given an envelope containing v dollars; he is permitted to convince himself that the envelope does contain v dollars. He writes, but does not tell the experimenter, his asking price, a, for the envelope and its contents. He will then receive a bid of x dollars. If x exceeds a, he will receive x dollars; otherwise, he will keep the v dollars. There will be no further negotiations. Subjects often ask more than the true value, setting $a = a_1 > v$. In Figure 1, the stipulated result r of such action is plotted against possible levels of the bid x (state of nature). Comparison with the corresponding plot for the "honest" asking price, $a = a_0 = v$, shows that a_1 is dominated by a_0. In fact, an asking price $a_2 < v$ (not shown in Figure 1) is also dominated by a_0. Hence the honest asking price is the only admissible one. It seems that some subjects expect further negotiations despite the explicit warning. We surmise that they would waive uncalled-for associations and habits if trained to plot or tabulate payoffs.

4. Irrelevance of nonaffected outcomes

Table 2 presents a matrix of outcomes measured in per cent of return on a firm's investment. We may interpret a, b, a', and b' as the firm's investing in the development of alternative products. The outcomes of these actions depend on the mutually exclusive events (say, business conditions) Z_1, Z_2, and Z_3. Suppose the firm prefers a to b. This preference cannot be due to any difference in the outcomes if the event Z_1 happens, for these outcomes are identically 5. Therefore, the firm's preference of a to b must be due to its preferring the wager "−200 if Z_2, 100 if Z_3" to the return of 5 with certainty. But then the firm should also prefer a' to b', for, again, if Z_1 happens, the outcome (−200) is not affected by the firm's choice. Its preference as between a' and b' must depend on its preference as between the wager "−200 if Z_2, 100 if Z_3" and the certainty of 5, just as in the previous case. By the same reasoning, if the firm is indifferent between a and b, it should be indifferent between a' and b'. The rule enunciated here can be regarded as a generalization of the admissibility rule of the previous section, with wagers admitted as a form of outcomes so that, for example, action a is described

Table 2 — *Outcome matrix for the return on a firm's investment (per cent)*

Event Action	Z_1	Z_2	Z_3
a	5	−200	100
b	5	5	5
a'	−200	−200	100
b'	−200	5	5

as follows: if Z_1 happens, you get 5; otherwise you get a lottery ticket, losing 200 if Z_2 happens and gaining 100 if Z_3 happens.

Tests of the irrelevance rule. Most business executives violated the irrelevance rule when Mac-Crimmon (1965) *verbally* gave them the choices in Table 2—first *a* versus *b*, then *a'* versus *b'*. However, a large majority of my students, who also never heard of the irrelevance principle but knew how to draw up a matrix of outcomes, complied with the rule. Allais (1953) performed a similar experiment, but instead of describing the three events as alternative business conditions, he gave them numerical probabilities (an extraneous notion in the present context), the probability of one of the events being only .01. Most of his respondents, including some decision theorists, violated the principle (but see Savage's pungent introspective discussion of his own second thought [1954, sec. 5.6g]).

The following type of experiment has been discussed widely. Funnel 1 contains an equal number of red and black balls, and the subject is invited to convince himself of this; but he is not permitted to look into funnel 2, which he only knows to contain one or more balls whose colors are either black or red. When a handle is pulled, each funnel will release only the bottom ball. In the following bets, he will win either $100 or nothing:

> Bet 1R: bottom ball in funnel 1 is red.
> Bet 1B: bottom ball in funnel 1 is black.
> Bet 2R: bottom ball in funnel 2 is red.
> Bet 2B: bottom ball in funnel 2 is black.

The outcomes are as indicated in Table 3, where, for example, event *RB* is "bottom ball in funnel 1 is red, bottom ball in funnel 2 is black." Suppose the subject always prefers to use funnel 1 rather than funnel 2, that is, he prefers bet 1R to 2R and also bet 1B to 2B. He will thus treat the results unaffected by his choice—namely, those earned when events *RR* and *BB* occur—as *relevant* to his choice! Yet similar experiments performed by Chipman (see Interdisciplinary Research Conference 1960) and Ellsberg (1961) suggest that many people do indeed prefer funnel 1 to funnel 2. Some of my

student subjects who did so motivated their choice by stating the sharp distinction between "risk" (funnel 1) and "uncertainty" (funnel 2), a distinction taught to economists since Knight (1921). Others stated that they could base their bets on more information when using funnel 1 than when using funnel 2. But information, although never harmful, can be useless. In experiments of Raiffa (1961) and Fellner (1965), subjects were, in effect, willing to pay for such useless information.

5. Definitions of probabilities

Having defined events $Z_1, Z_2, Z_3, \cdots$ as subsets of the set X of all states of nature, it is consistent with current mathematical language and current English to require that any numbers, $P(Z_1), P(Z_2), P(Z_3), \cdots$, claimed to be the probabilities of these events, satisfy the following conditions: (1) they should be nonnegative; (2) for any two mutually exclusive events, say Z_1 and Z_2, the number assigned to the event "Z_1 or Z_2" (meaning the occurrence of either Z_1 or Z_2) should equal the sum of $P(Z_1)$ and $P(Z_2)$; (3) $P(X)$, i.e., $P(Z_1$ or Z_2 or Z_3 or $\cdots$), should be equal to one.

Personal probabilities. The numbers $P(Z_1), P(Z_2), P(Z_3), \cdots$ are an individual's personal probabilities of these events if, in addition to having the mathematical properties just stated, they describe his behavior in the following sense: whenever $P(Z_1) > P(Z_2)$, for example, he will prefer betting on Z_1 to betting on Z_2, assuming he wants to win the bet. This, too, is consistent with ordinary English—he will prefer betting on the victory of the Democrats in the next election to betting on the truth of the proposition that California is longer than Norway if and only if he considers winning the former bet "more probable" than winning the latter one. Here, "betting on Z_1" means taking an action that yields a result s (for success) if Z_1 occurs, a result that is more desirable than the result f (for failure) if Z_1 does not occur. The probabilities of events must depend on the events only, i.e., the individual's preferences between bets must be the same for all pairs of results s, f ($100, $0; *status quo*, loss of prestige; etc.) provided only that s is better than f. This postulate of *independence of beliefs on rewards* must be added to those of sections 1, 3, and 4. Will the subject reverse his judgment about the comparative chances of any two events—as revealed by his choices between two bets—if the prizes are changed? If not, he satisfies the postulate. It seems to be satisfied by practically all subjects asked to rank several bets according to their preferences, the rewards being first a pair s, f, then a different pair s', f'.

Table 3 — Outcome matrix for the funnel experiment (in dollars)

Event Bet	RB	BR	RR	BB
1R	100	0	100	0
2R	0	100	100	0
2B	100	0	0	100
1B	0	100	0	100

Suppose a subject is indifferent to bets on any of the eight horses running a race. His preferences would thus imply that $P(Z_1) = P(Z_2) = \cdots = P(Z_s)$, where Z_i is the event that the ith horse wins (ties are excluded for simplicity). The nonnegativity property is satisfied if we put $P(Z_i) = \frac{1}{8}$ for all i. What about the other two mathematical properties required? Suppose the subject considers double bets with the same prizes s, f as for single bets. He will prefer every double bet, e.g., the bet on the event "Z_1 or Z_2," to any single bet (here he has, in effect, applied the inadmissibility postulate), and he will be indifferent between any two double bets (here the postulates of irrelevance and of intransitivity apply). Similarly, he will prefer triple bets to double bets and will be indifferent between any two triple bets, and so on. Consistent with these preferences, we can put

$$P(Z_i \text{ or } Z_j) = \frac{2}{8} = P(Z_i) + P(Z_j)$$

for any two horses i and j,

$$P(Z_i \text{ or } Z_j \text{ or } Z_k) = \frac{3}{8} = P(Z_i \text{ or } Z_j) + P(Z_k)$$

for any three horses i, j, and k, and so on. In general, we can assign probability $P(Z) = m/8$ to the event Z that one of the m specified horses will win (where $1 \leqslant m \leqslant 8$). Then the numbers $P(Z)$ are the subject's personal probabilities, for they agree with his preferences between bets and also satisfy the three mathematical requirements stated at the beginning of this section.

Instead of a horse race, a subject is asked to imagine a dial divided into n equal sectors. Suppose the hand of the dial is spun and comes to rest in the ith sector. We define this occurrence as event Z_i. If the subject is convinced that the dial's mechanism is "fair," i.e., that the events $Z_1, Z_2, \cdots, Z_n$ are symmetrical (exchangeable), he will be indifferent among bets on any one of these n events. [See PROBABILITY, *article on* INTERPRETATIONS.] Following Borel (1939, chapter 5), he can then assess his personal probability of any event T, say "rain tomorrow," by finding a number m ($1 \leqslant m \leqslant n$) such that betting on T is not more desirable than betting on "Z_1 or Z_2 or $\cdots$ or Z_m" and is not less desirable than betting on "Z_1 or Z_2 or $\cdots$ or Z_{m-1}." Then his personal probability of T, $P(T)$, satisfies the inequality

$$\frac{m-1}{n} \leqslant P(T) \leqslant \frac{m}{n}.$$

By making n arbitrarily large, one can assess $P(T)$ arbitrarily closely, and by using dial arcs which represent any fraction, rational or irrational, of the dial's circumference, one can define personal prob-

abilities ranging continuously from 0 to 1. Note that such assessments of personal probabilities, when determined in an experiment, are based not on the subject's verbal statement of numbers he calls probabilities but on his actual choices. They may therefore be useful in predicting actions provided that the subject is consistent. If he is not consistent, his violations may or may not be similar in principle to those incurred in any instrument readings—a theme of probabilistic psychology touched upon in section 2.

Objective probabilities. As a special case, personal probabilities of some real-world events may be "objective," i.e., the same for different people. This is particularly the case when there is agreement that the events come sufficiently close, for all practical purposes of those involved, to fulfilling certain symmetry requirements. Approximate symmetry is assumed for the positions of a roulette dial like Borel's and for the occurrences of death among many similar males of age 20. Such requirements are strictly satisfied only by idealized, mathematically defined events—events that are never observed empirically. A "fair" coin, a "fair" roulette dial, a "homogeneous" population of males aged 20 (or a "random" sample from such a population) are all mathematical constructs. The mathematical theory of probability applies rules of logic to situations in which strict symmetry and the three properties stated at the beginning of this section hold (refining property 2 in order to accommodate the case of an infinite X). If decision makers agree that certain events are approximately symmetric, and if they apply logical rules, then their choices between betting on (predicting) any two events will agree; their personal (in this case also objective) probabilities will coincide with those given by mathematical theory. Clarity requires us, however, to distinguish between mathematical probabilities and objective probabilities assigned by decision makers to empirical events, just as we distinguish between a geometric rectangle and the shape of an actual sheet of paper.

6. Expected utility

The four postulates discussed thus far—complete ordering of actions, inadmissibility of dominated actions, irrelevance of nonaffected outcomes, and independence of beliefs on rewards—appear about as convincing as the rules of logic (and about as subject to transgression by people not trained in untwisting brain twisters). Together with a "continuity" postulate (to be introduced presently), they imply the following rule, which is more complicated and less immediately convincing: The consistent man behaves as if he (1) assigned personal probabilities $P(Z)$ to events Z, (2) assigned numerical utilities $u(r)$ to the results r of his actions, and (3) chose the action with the highest "expected utility." The expected utility $\omega(a)$ of action a is the weighted average

$$\omega(a) = \sum_r u(r) \cdot P(Z_{ra}),$$

where the event Z_{ra} is the set of all states for which action a yields result r.

The rule is trivially true when the choice is among sure actions; if action a always yields result r, then $P(Z_{ra}) = 1$, so that $\omega(a) = u(r)$.

Consider now actions with two possible results —success s and failure f. This is the case, for example, when actions are two-prize bets (as in section 5) or when the decision maker is a "satisficer" (Simon 1957) for whom all outcomes below his "aspiration level" are equally bad and all others equally good. In section 5 we saw that of two two-prize bets, a consistent decision maker prefers the bet that has the higher probability of success. Since s is better than f, we can assign numerical utilities

$$u(s) = 1 > 0 = u(f),$$

and we see that the expected utility $\omega(b)$ of a two-prize bet b coincides with its probability of success $P(Z_{sb})$, since

$$\omega(b) = 1 \cdot P(Z_{sb}) + 0 \cdot P(Z_{fb}) = P(Z_{sb}).$$

Thus the satisficer maximizes the probability of reaching his aspiration level.

As the next step, we compute the probability of success and hence the expected utility $\omega(c)$ of a bet c compounded of n simple two-prize bets or lottery tickets $b_1, \cdots, b_n$ on n different (but not necessarily mutually exclusive) events $T_1, \cdots, T_n$. Lottery ticket b_i is a bet on the event T_i, and the subject will receive ticket b_i if Z_i happens. The events $Z_1, \cdots, Z_n$ are mutually exclusive events one of which must happen, and the events "Z_i and T_i" (the occurrence of Z_i and T_i) are pairwise independent in the sense that

$$P(Z_i \text{ and } T_i) = P(Z_i) \cdot P(T_i).$$

We can thus regard ticket b_i as the result yielded by action c when Z_i happens. Hence $P(Z_i) = P(Z_{b_ic})$ in the present notation. Moreover, we have just shown that the expected utility of a simple two-prize bet can be measured by its probability of success, so that $P(T_i) = \omega(b_i)$. Clearly, the probability of success of the compound bet c is the probability of the event "(Z_1 and T_1) or (Z_2 and T_2) or $\cdots$ or (Z_n and

T_n)"; by mathematical property 2 of probabilities (section 5), this is equal to $\sum_i P(T_i) \cdot P(Z_i)$. Hence,

$$\omega(c) = \sum_i \omega(b_i) \cdot P(Z_{b_ic}),$$

i.e., the expected utility rule is valid for the special case where each result of an action is a two-prize bet.

To extend this in a final step to the general case, let s be the best and f the worst of all results of an action. In the preference notation of section 1, $f \leqslant r \leqslant s$ for any result r. Consider the continuous range of all bets b whose two prizes are s and f and whose success probabilities take all the values between (and including) 1 and 0. Then, for any b, $f \leqslant b \leqslant s$, and for a given r, $r \leqslant b$ or $b \leqslant r$ depending on the bet's success probability. A plausible *continuity postulate* asserts, for each r, the existence of a bet, say b_r, such that $r \sim b_r$. We can therefore assign to r a utility $u(r) = \omega(b_r)$. A decision maker should then be indifferent between an action a that yields various results r with respective probabilities $P(Z_{ra})$ and a bet c compounded of the corresponding two-prize bets b_r just described entering with the same probabilities $P(Z_{ra})$. That is to say, $P(Z_{b_rc}) = P(Z_{ra})$. The expected utility rule follows, since

$$\omega(a) = \omega(c) = \sum_r \omega(b_r) \cdot P(Z_{b_rc})$$
$$= \sum_r u(r) \cdot P(Z_{ra}).$$

Some insight into this derivation of the expected utility rule is provided to the trainee in decision making by letting him rank his preferences among the tickets to four lotteries. Each ticket is described by prizes contingent on two alternative events, one of which must occur. An example of such a decision problem is presented in Table 4, where p is written for $P(Z)$ for brevity. If the event Z is "a coin is tossed and comes up heads" (we refer below to this event simply as "heads") and the subject regards the coin as "fair," then $p = \frac{1}{2}$. But Z may also

Table 4 — Decision problem involving lottery tickets

Lottery ticket	Prize if event Z happens	Prize if event Z does not happen	Probability of gaining $100
a	$100	$0	p
b	Lottery ticket a	$100	$p^2 + 1 - p > p$
c	Lottery ticket a	$0	$p^2 < p$
d	Lottery ticket b	Lottery ticket c	$p(p^2 + 1 - p) + (1 - p)p^2 = p$

be, for example, "the next sentence spoken in this room will contain the pronoun 'I.'" In any case, when the inadmissibility postulate is applied, it is evident from the last column of Table 4 that ticket *a* is better than *c* and worse than *b*. Furthermore, the decision maker should be indifferent between tickets *a* and *d*.

Cash equivalents and numerical utilities. Let us define the *cash equivalent* of ticket *a*, denoted $k(a)$, as the highest price the decision maker would offer for ticket *a*; $k(b)$, $k(c)$, and $k(d)$ are defined similarly. If asked to name his cash equivalent for each lottery ticket in Table 4, the decision maker should name amounts such that $k(b) > k(a) = k(d) > k(c)$. If he fails to do this, he is inconsistent, and no scale of numerical utilities can describe his behavior. If he is consistent, and if the event Z is "heads," the following utilities for some money gains can be ascribed to him:

$$\omega(\$100) = 1;$$
$$\omega[k(b)] = \tfrac{3}{4};$$
$$\omega[k(a)] = \omega[k(d)] = \tfrac{1}{2};$$
$$\omega[k(c)] = \tfrac{1}{4};$$
$$\omega(\$0) = 0.$$

Some but not all subjects conform with the required ranking of the lottery tickets. Therefore, in any empirical estimation of a subject's utilities and personal probabilities, one must check whether the subject is consistent, at least in some approximate sense. As pointed out in the simpler context of section 2, probabilistic models of decision and of learning to decide are needed for any descriptive theory, and they too may fail.

Behavior toward risk. Again suppose that the event Z in Table 4 is "heads." If the subject has named cash equivalents $k(a) = k(d) = \$50$, $k(c) = \$25$, and $k(b) = \$75$ (and similarly for further, easily conceived compound lotteries with utilities $\tfrac{1}{8}, \tfrac{3}{8}, \cdots, \tfrac{1}{16}, \cdots$), we would infer that over the observed range he is indifferent between a "fair bet" and the certainty of getting its expected gain. We would say that he is "indifferent to risk." His utility function of money gain is a straight line. On the other hand, if he has named cash equivalents $k(a) = k(d) < \$50$, $k(c) < \tfrac{1}{2}k(a)$, and $k(b) < \tfrac{1}{2}[100 + k(a)]$, his utility function of money gain will be a concave curve (any of its chords will lie below the corresponding arc), and we would say that he is "averse to risk." If the inequality signs in the preceding sentence are reversed, the utility function is convex (chords are above arcs), and we would say that over the observed range the subject "loves risk." When the utility function is either concave or convex, the decision maker maximizes the expected value, not of money gain, but of some nonlinear function of money gain.

Daniel Bernoulli (1738) pointed out that the utility function is concave in the case of the "Petersburg paradox." Marshall (1890) also assumed risk aversion as an economic fact (or perhaps as a prescription from Victorian morals) equivalent to that of "decreasing marginal utility of money." Some economic implications of risk aversion were given by Pratt (1964) and Arrow (1965). It should be noted that this assumption is inconsistent with the behavior of a satisficer for whom utility is a step-function of money gain and the behavior of a merchant for whom the disutility of bankruptcy is the same regardless of the amount owed.

The maxmin rule. In competition with the expected utility rule (and the postulates underlying it) is the "conservative" or "maxmin" rule, which states that the decision maker should maximize the minimum payoff; that is to say, the maxmin rule proposes that preferences among actions be based on each action's worst result only. Thus in the case of Table 1 the maxmin rule would prescribe that $a' < b$ even if Z_1 has the probability of, say, an earthquake, and presumably $b \sim a$, contradicting the inadmissibility postulate. However, because of the strong appeal of the inadmissibility postulate, it is usually proposed that the maxmin rule be applied only when domination is absent; this leads to the ordering $a' < b < a$ rather than $a' < b \sim a$. This proposal is not too satisfactory since it violates a plausible continuity principle (Milnor 1954). A small modification in outcomes —by \$1 in Table 1, or by 1 cent for that matter— can make or break domination and thus reverse the preference ordering. Indeed, should we advise people not to live in San Francisco or Tokyo because of possible but not very probable earthquakes? Should we advise pedestrians never to cross streets because of the possibility of being struck by an auto? Such considerations compel us to balance the advantages against the disadvantages of competing decisions, weighing them by appropriately defined probabilities—the expected utility principle.

A historical note. Early theories prescribing maximization of expected utility were confined to special cases. Two types of restrictions were imposed. First, the decision maker was advised to maximize the expected value of his money wealth or gain, i.e., utility was in effect identified with a money amount or some linear function of a money amount. Some other quantifiable good, such as the number of prisoners taken or the number of patients cured, might play the same role as money, but nonquantifiable rewards and penalties of actions were unnecessarily excluded from the set of results. Second, probabilities were restricted to objective ones—a special case of personal probabilities.

It is difficult to imagine that an experienced Bronze Age player who used dice that had "tooled edges and threw absolutely true" (David 1962) would bet much more than 1:5 on the coming of the ace. Cardano's efforts in computing the gambler's odds (Ore 1953) suggest at any rate that by the sixteenth century the rule of maximizing average money gains computed on the basis of objective probabilities was taken for granted.

We have already cited Bernoulli and Marshall as having proclaimed utility a nonlinear function of money, thus lifting the first of the above restrictions. Marshall also applied the utility concept to commodity bundles. Von Neumann and Morgenstern (1944) extended it further to all possible results of actions and derived the expected utility rule from simple consistency postulates. This was simplified by others, especially Herstein and Milnor (1953). All these writers dealt only with objective probabilities, leaving out the important cases in which symmetries between relevant events are not agreed upon.

Bayes (1764) can be credited with the idea of personal probabilities. He thought of them as being revealed by an individual's choices among wagers—not just on cards and coins, but on horses and fighting cocks as well! Thus Bayes removed the second restriction, but he retained the first in assuming that utility was in effect identified with money gains, so that betting 9 guineas against 1 implies a corresponding ratio of probabilities. In 1937, de Finetti provided mathematical rigor for this approach.

In 1926, Ramsey (1923–1928) stated, perhaps for the first time, simple consistency postulates that imply the existence of both personal probabilities (of any events, regardless of symmetries) and utilities (of any results of actions, quantifiable or not). Savage (1954) restated the consistency postulates and, partly following de Finetti and von Neumann and Morgenstern, proved that they imply the expected utility rule. For an original exposition, see Pratt, Raiffa, and Schlaifer (1964).

Reviews of the works of other contemporary authors are found in Arrow (1951), Luce and Suppes (1965), Ożga (1965), and Fishburn (1964). [See also ECONOMIC EXPECTATIONS.] Surveys and bibliographies as well as much original material by 21 leading authors on both the prescrip-tive and descriptive aspects of decision theory are found in Shelly and Bryan (1964).

7. Strategies

The existence of numerical utilities describing a decision maker's "tastes" and of probabilities describing his "beliefs" has been shown to follow from rules of consistency. To formulate and solve the problem of choosing a good decision, both tastes and beliefs must be assumed fixed over some given period of time (but see Koopmans [1964] on "flexibility"). In general, the probabilities the decision maker assigns at any time to the various states of nature and thus to the results of his actions depend on his information at that time. New information may also uncover new feasible actions. We shall generalize the decision concept accordingly in several steps.

A *strategy* (also called a decision function or response rule) is the assignment, in advance of information, of specific actions to respond to the different messages that the decision maker may receive from an information source. If, more generally, messages, actions, and results form time sequences (the case of "earning while learning"), we have a *sequential strategy* (also called an extensive or dynamic strategy). To each possible sequence of future messages, a sequential strategy assigns a sequence of actions (see, for example, Theil 1964). An optimal sequential strategy maximizes the weighted average of utilities assigned to all possible sequences of results, possibly taking into account "impatience" by means of a discount rate (Fisher 1930; Koopmans 1960). The weights are personal *joint* probabilities of sequences of events *and* messages. This amounts to the same thing as saying that the probabilities of events are revised each time a message is received.

It is still more general to redefine action in order to include in it the choice of information sources to be used and thus of "questions to be asked" at a given time. The resulting problem of finding an optimal *informational strategy* is a task of economic theories of information and organization and also of statistical decision theory (e.g., Raiffa & Schlaifer 1961) where events and information sources correspond to hypotheses and experiments, respectively.

Finally, if we allow the decision maker to receive messages about the feasibility and outcomes of actions he has not formerly considered, we obtain the still more general concept of *exploratory strategy*. True, it has been almost proverbially tenuous to assign probabilities to the results of industrial or scientific research; yet these undertakings are not different in principle from many other ventures and bets, such as those discussed in section 5.

The complex strategies noted here are hardly maximized by the actual entrepreneur, although the penetration of industry by professionals may again bring descriptive and prescriptive economics to their pristine closeness. Today many descriptive hypotheses in this field use the concept of aspiration level—the boundary between success and failure. The actual decision maker is said to revise his aspiration level upward or downward depending on whether he has or has not reached it by previous action; exploration for actions not previously considered is triggered by failure (Simon 1957). The sequence of actions generated by the dynamic aspiration-level model will, in general, differ from that prescribed by dynamic programming. [*See* PROGRAMMING.] Yet, with utilities assigned to results of actions in a particular way, it is possible that the aspiration-level mechanism is indeed optimal. It has been inspired, in fact, by adaptive feedbacks observed in live organisms; such feedbacks presumably have maximized the probability of the survival of species.

8. Cost of decision making

One action or strategy may appear better than another as long as we disregard the toil and trouble of decision making itself, i.e., the efforts of gathering information and of processing it into an optimal decision. The ranking of actions may be reversed when we take these efforts into account and deal, in this sense, with "net" rather than "gross" expected utilities of actions. A small increase in expected profit may not be worth a good night's sleep. In statistics, we stop sequential sampling earlier the higher the cost is of obtaining each observation. As an approximation to some logically required, but very complicated, decision rule, we may use a linear decision rule (e.g., prescribe inventories to be proportional to turnover) in order to lessen computational costs. The "incrementalism" observed and recommended by Lindblom (1965) in the field of political decisions corresponds to the common mathematical practice of searching for a global optimum in the neighborhood of a local optimum or possibly in the neighborhood of the *status quo*. How many local search steps one should undertake and how often he should jump (hopefully) toward a global optimum will presumably depend on the costs of searching (see, for example, Gel'fand & Tsetlin 1962). Indeed, some strategies may be too complex to be computable in a finite amount of time, even though they respond to each message by a feasible action.

There is, after all, a limit on the capacity of computers and on the brain capacity of decision makers. Hence, some strategies may have infinite costs.

The net utility of an action is often represented as the difference betwen "gross utility" and "decision cost." A prescriptive theory would presumably require that personal probabilities be assigned not only to the outcomes of the actions but also to the efforts of estimating the outcomes and of searching for the action with the highest expected utility.

On a more general level, it is not strictly permissible to represent net utility as a difference between gross utility and decision cost. Even if the two were measurable in dollars, say, utility may be a nonlinear function of money gains. Yet the assumption that net utility is separable into these components simplifies the theory—it reduces the cost of thinking! Almost all prescriptive theory to date deals with gross utility only. Little attention has been given to decision costs that might be subtractable and thus definable in arriving at a net utility concept. Still less attention has been given to a net utility concept that cannot be decomposed into gross-utility and decision-cost components.

The elements for a theory of the expected cost of using inanimate computers, given the (statistical) population of future problems, are probably available. However, the current classification of computation problems as "scientific" and "business" (differing in their comparative needs for speed and memory) is certainly much too rough. A theory of mechanical computation costs would resemble the theory of the cost of manufacturing with complex equipment and known technology when capacities and operations are scheduled optimally. On the other hand, so little is known about the "technology" of human brains! If economists would join forces with students of the psychology of problem solving, insights would undoubtedly be gained into both the descriptive and prescriptive aspects of decision making.

JACOB MARSCHAK

[*Directly related are the entries* DECISION THEORY; GAME THEORY, *article on* THEORETICAL ASPECTS; UTILITY.]

BIBLIOGRAPHY

ALLAIS, M. 1953 Le comportement de l'homme rationnel devant le risque: Critique des postulats et axiomes de l'école américaine. *Econometrica* 21:503–546.

ARROW, KENNETH J. 1951 Alternative Approaches to the Theory of Choice in Risk-taking Situations. *Econometrica* 19:404–437.

ARROW, KENNETH J. 1958 Utilities, Attitudes, Choices: A Review Note. *Econometrica* 26:1–23.

ARROW, KENNETH J. 1963 Utility and Expectation in Economic Behavior. Pages 724–752 in Sigmund Koch (editor), *Psychology: A Study of a Science*. Volume 6: Investigations of Man as Socius: Their Place in Psychology and the Social Sciences. New York: Mc-Graw-Hill.

ARROW, KENNETH J. 1965 *Aspects of the Theory of Risk-bearing*. Helsinki: Academic Bookstore.

AUMANN, ROBERT J. 1962 Utility Theory Without the Completeness Axiom. *Econometrica* 30:445–462. → Corrections in Volume 32 of *Econometrica*.

BAYES, THOMAS (1764) 1958 An Essay Towards Solving a Problem in the Doctrine of Chances. *Biometrika* 45:296–315.

BERNOULLI, DANIEL (1738) 1954 Exposition of a New Theory on the Measurement of Risk. *Econometrica* 22:23–36. → First published as "Specimen theoriae novae de mensura sortis."

BOREL, ÉMILE 1939 *Valeur pratique et philosophie des probabilités*. Paris: Gauthier-Villars.

CARNAP, R. 1962 The Aim of Inductive Logic. Pages 303–318 in International Congress for Logic, Methodology, and Philosophy of Science, Stanford, California, 1960, *Logic, Methodology, and Philosophy of Science: Proceedings*. Edited by Ernest Nagel, Patrick Suppes, and Alfred Tarski. Stanford Univ. Press.

CHERNOFF, HERMAN; and MOSES, LINCOLN E. 1959 *Elementary Decision Theory*. New York: Wiley.

DAVID, FLORENCE N. 1962 *Games, Gods and Gambling: The Origins and History of Probability and Statistical Ideas From the Earliest Times to the Newtonian Era*. New York: Hafner.

DAVIDSON, DONALD; and MARSCHAK, JACOB 1959 Experimental Tests of a Stochastic Decision Theory. Pages 233–269 in Charles W. Churchman and Philburn Ratoosh (editors), *Measurement: Definitions and Theories*. New York: Wiley.

DAVIS, JOHN M. 1958 The Transitivity of Preferences. *Behavioral Science* 3:26–33.

DEBREU, GERARD 1959 *Theory of Value*. New York: Wiley.

DE FINETTI, BRUNO (1937) 1964 Foresight: Its Logical Laws, Its Subjective Sources. Pages 93–158 in Henry E. Kyburg and Howard E. Smokler (editors), *Studies in Subjective Probabilities*. New York: Wiley. → First published in French.

EDWARDS, WARD 1953 Probability-preferences in Gambling. *American Journal of Psychology* 66:349–364.

ELLSBERG, DANIEL 1961 Risk, Ambiguity, and the Savage Axioms. *Quarterly Journal of Economics* 75:643–669.

FECHNER, GUSTAV T. (1860) 1907 *Elemente der Psychophysik*. 2 vols. 3d ed. Leipzig: Breitkopf & Härtel. → An English translation of Volume 1 was published by Holt in 1966.

FELLNER, WILLIAM 1965 *Probability and Profit*. Homewood, Ill.: Irwin.

FISHBURN, PETER C. 1964 *Decision and Value Theory*. New York: Wiley.

FISHER, IRVING 1906 The Risk Element. Pages 265–300 in Irving Fisher, *The Nature of Capital and Income*. New York: Macmillan.

FISHER, IRVING (1930) 1961 *The Theory of Interest*. New York: Kelley. → Revision of the author's *The Rate of Interest* (1907).

FRANKLIN, BENJAMIN (1772) 1945 How to Make a Decision. Page 786 in *A Benjamin Franklin Reader*. Edited by Nathan G. Goodman. New York: Crowell. → A letter to J. Priestly.

GEL'FAND, I. M.; and TSETLIN, M. L. 1962 Some Methods of Control for Complex Systems. *Russian Mathematical Surveys* 17, no. 1:95–117.

HART, ALBERT G. (1940) 1951 *Anticipations, Uncertainty and Dynamic Planning*. New York: Kelley.

HERSTEIN, I. N.; and MILNOR, JOHN 1953 An Axiomatic Approach to Measurable Utility. *Econometrica* 21:291–297.

HICKS, JOHN R. (1939) 1946 *Value and Capital: An Inquiry Into Some Fundamental Principles of Economic Theory*. 2d ed. Oxford: Clarendon.

INTERDISCIPLINARY RESEARCH CONFERENCE, UNIVERSITY OF NEW MEXICO 1960 *Decisions, Values and Groups: Proceedings*. Edited by D. Willner. New York: Pergamon. → See especially the article by J. S. Chipman, "Stochastic Choice and Subjective Probability."

JEFFREY, RICHARD C. 1965 *The Logic of Decision*. New York: McGraw-Hill.

KNIGHT, FRANK H. (1921) 1933 *Risk, Uncertainty and Profit*. London School of Economics and Political Science Series of Reprints of Scarce Tracts in Economic and Political Science, No. 16. London School of Economics.

KOOPMANS, TJALLING 1960 Stationary Ordinal Utility and Impatience. *Econometrica* 28:287–309.

KOOPMANS, TJALLING 1964 On Flexibility of Future Preference. Pages 243–254 in Maynard W. Shelly and Glenn L. Bryan (editors), *Human Judgments and Optimality*. New York: Wiley.

LINDBLOM, CHARLES E. 1965 *The Intelligence of Democracy: Decision Making Through Mutual Adjustment*. New York: Free Press.

LUCE, R. DUNCAN 1959 *Individual Choice Behavior: A Theoretical Analysis*. New York: Wiley.

LUCE, R. DUNCAN; and RAIFFA, HOWARD 1957 *Games and Decisions: Introduction and Critical Survey*. A study of the Behavioral Models Project, Bureau of Applied Social Research, Columbia University. New York: Wiley. → First issued in 1954 as *A Survey of the Theory of Games*, Columbia University, Bureau of Applied Social Research, Technical Report No. 5.

LUCE, R. DUNCAN; and SUPPES, PATRICK 1965 Preference, Utility, and Subjective Probability. Volume 3, pages 249–410 in R. Duncan Luce, Robert R. Bush, and Eugene Galanter (editors), *Handbook of Mathematical Psychology*. New York: Wiley.

MACCRIMMON, K. R. 1965 An Experimental Study of the Decision-making Behavior of Business Executives. Ph.D. dissertation, Univ. of California at Los Angeles.

MARSCHAK, JACOB 1950 Rational Behavior, Uncertain Prospects, and Measurable Utility. *Econometrica* 18:111–141.

MARSCHAK, JACOB (1954) 1964 Scaling of Utility and Probability. Pages 95–109 in Martin Shubik (editor), *Game Theory and Related Approaches to Social Behavior: Selections*. New York: Wiley.

MARSHALL, ALFRED (1890) 1961 *Principles of Economics*. 9th ed. New York: Macmillan. → See especially the Mathematical Appendix, note 9.

MAY, KENNETH O. 1954 Intransitivity, Utility and the Aggregation of Preference Patterns. *Econometrica* 22:1–13.

MILNOR, JOHN 1954 Games Against Nature. Pages 49–60 in Robert M. Thrall, C. H. Combs, and R. L. Davis (editor), *Decision Processes*. New York: Wiley.

NEYMAN, JERZY 1950 *First Course in Probability and Statistics*. New York: Holt.

ORE, OYSTEIN 1953 *Cardano, the Gambling Scholar*. Princeton Univ. Press; Oxford Univ. Press. → Includes a translation by Sidney Henry Gould from the Latin of Cardano's *Book on Games of Chance*.

OŻGA, S. ANDREW 1965 *Expectations in Economic Theory*. London: Weidenfeld & Nicolson.

PAPANDREOU, ANDREAS G. 1957 *A Test of a Stochastic Theory of Choice*. University of California Publications in Economics, Vol. 16, No. 1. Univ. of California Press. → In collaboration with O. H. Sauerlender, O. H. Brownlee, L. Hurwicz, and W. Franklin.

PASCAL, BLAISE (1670) 1961 *Pensées: Notes on Religion and Other Subjects*. New York: Doubleday. → See especially Section 3: De la nécessité du pari.

POLLACK, IRWIN 1955 Sound Level Discrimination and Variation of Reference Testing Conditions. *Journal of the Acoustical Society of America* 27:474–480.

PRATT, JOHN W. 1964 Risk Aversion in the Small and in the Large. *Econometrica* 32:122–136.

PRATT, JOHN W.; RAIFFA, HOWARD; and SCHLAIFER, ROBERT 1964 The Foundations of Decision Under Uncertainty: An Elementary Exposition. *Journal of the American Statistical Association* 59:353–375.

QUANDT, RICHARD 1956 A Probabilistic Theory of Consumer Behavior. *Quarterly Journal of Economics* 70:507–536.

RAIFFA, HOWARD 1961 Risk, Ambiguity, and the Savage Axioms: Comment. *Quarterly Journal of Economics* 75:690–694.

RAIFFA, HOWARD; and SCHLAIFER, ROBERT 1961 *Applied Statistical Decision Theory*. Graduate School of Business Administration, Studies in Managerial Economics. Boston: Harvard Univ., Division of Research.

RAMSEY, FRANK P. (1923–1928) 1950 *The Foundations of Mathematics and Other Logical Essays*. New York: Humanities. → See especially Chapter 7, "Truth and Probabilities," and Chapter 8, "Further Considerations."

SAVAGE, LEONARD J. 1954 *The Foundations of Statistics*. New York: Wiley.

SHACKLE, L. S. (1949) 1952 *Expectation in Economics*. 2d ed. Cambridge Univ. Press.

SHACKLE, L. S. 1955 *Uncertainty in Economics and Other Reflections*. Cambridge Univ. Press.

SHACKLE, L. S. 1961 *Decision, Order and Time in Human Affairs*. Cambridge Univ. Press.

SHELLY, MAYNARD W.; and BRYAN, GLENN L. (editors) 1964 *Human Judgments and Optimality*. New York: Wiley.

SIMON, HERBERT A. 1957 A Behavioral Model of Rational Choice. Pages 241–260 in Herbert A. Simon, *Models of Man*. New York: Wiley.

SIMON, HERBERT A. 1959 Theories of Decision-making in Economics and Behavioral Science. *American Economic Review* 49:253–283.

THEIL, HENRI 1964 *Optimal Decision Rules for Government and Industry*. Amsterdam: North Holland Publishing; Chicago: Rand McNally.

THURSTONE, LOUIS L. (1927–1955) 1959 *The Measurement of Values*. Univ. of Chicago Press. → Selections from previously published papers.

VON NEUMANN, JOHN; and MORGENSTERN, OSKAR (1944) 1964 *Theory of Games and Economic Behavior*. 3d ed. New York: Wiley.

WALD, ABRAHAM (1950) 1964 *Statistical Decision Functions*. New York: Wiley.

WOLFOWITZ, J. 1962 Bayesian Inference and Axioms of Consistent Decision. *Econometrica* 3:471–480.

WRIGHT, GEORGE H. VON 1963 *The Logic of Preference*. Edinburgh Univ. Press.

III
POLITICAL ASPECTS

Decision making is a social process that selects a problem for decision (i.e., choice) and produces a limited number of alternatives, from among which a particular alternative is selected for implementation and execution (Snyder et al. 1962, p. 90). Some writers use the term synonymously with *policy making*, although others distinguish the two, reserving decision making for choices that involve conscious action and are subject to sanctions and policy making for a collectivity of intersecting decisions that has no choice-making unit in a position to decide for all parties involved (Braybrooke & Lindblom 1963, p. 249). For example, one may refer to decision making by the presidency or by Congress, but together these institutions constitute part of the total policy-making process of the United States. Decision making is also distinguished from *problem solving*, which may refer either (1) to tasks in which both the problem for solution and the alternative solutions are given (Kelley & Thibaut 1954) or (2) to more abstract higher mental processes of thinking and information processing (Newell et al. 1958). Political decision making, however, is conceived of as involving the search for both problems and alternatives. Voting, however, is an exception, because electors have little, if any, power over the timing of elections and for all practical purposes only indirect, if any, participation in the selection of alternatives (candidates).

History. The intellectual origins of decision-making analysis are twofold. One line of its development, mathematical economics, has its beginnings in the eighteenth-century work of Bernoulli (1738) and in the modern formulations of theories of games by von Neumann and Morgenstern (1944). An important political successor was Downs' formulation of governmental decision making in terms of economic theories (1957). The origins of mathematical, economic, and game-theoretic decision making have been codified by Luce and Raiffa (1957) and give promise of including many further hypotheses for empirical investigation, as is illustrated by Riker's work on coalitions and coalition formation (1962). This root branched off into experimental studies, reviewed in two papers by Edwards (1954; 1961), to test hypotheses deduced from the mathematical models [*see* GAME THEORY].

The other historical root of decision-making analysis is in public administration, which so far has been the more influential strain in political decision making. Alexander Hamilton in America and Charles-Jean Bonnin in France identified the field at the turn of the nineteenth century (White [1926] 1955, pp. xiii, 10), and within a hundred years Woodrow Wilson in the United States and Max Weber in Germany had inaugurated academic studies of organizational decision making. The next major original works on organizations were those of Chester I. Barnard (1938) and Herbert A. Simon (1947), who were pioneers in calling for and introducing social scientific techniques to the study of the subject and also in indicating the relevance of psychological and sociological knowledge to the understanding of organizations and administration. Richard C. Snyder and his colleagues (1954; 1962) followed with a conceptual scheme that was designed for the study of foreign-policy making organizations but is applicable to organizational decision making in general [*see* PUBLIC ADMINISTRATION].

In political science, decision making—or, more broadly, policy making—has been studied in electoral voting, legislative roll calls, judicial opinions, public opinion, and virtually every other kind of political situation or setting.

Approaches

Among the most influential modern work on decision making is that of Simon. Beginning with his logical critique of "proverbs of administration," Simon challenged eighteenth-century assumptions about decision behavior. Classical economic theory assumed that decision makers know all alternatives, that they know the utilities (values) of all alternatives, and that they have an ordered preference among all alternatives. For such a demand for "rationality" Simon proposed to substitute the concept of "bounded rationality," which would more nearly comport with what is known about the psychological and physiological limits of decision makers. For the model of *optimizing* decisions, he substituted *satisficing*, that is, the adoption of a decision when an alternative seems to meet minimal standards or is good enough and is not dependent on the availability of all alternatives from which the best is chosen. These concepts and propositions have been researched primarily in industrial rather than in governmental organizations (see the systematic codification of theory in March & Simon

1958), although there is no theoretical reason to expect them to be any less applicable in the latter. [*See* ADMINISTRATION, *article on* ADMINISTRATIVE BEHAVIOR.]

Another important stimulus to studies of political decision making is the work of Snyder et al. (1954; 1962). The first presentation of Snyder's conceptual scheme was an outline of categories on which data for studying foreign policy decisions should be gathered. Although distributed initially only in a privately published paperback format, Snyder's study was soon cited in publications ranging from work on disturbed communication to studies in judicial behavior. Before Snyder's work was published in book form eight years after its first appearance, excerpts of it had been widely reprinted. Much of its impact, quite apart from its attention to decision-making analysis, undoubtedly stemmed from its explicit concern with a number of issues in methodology and the philosophy of science that were current in American political science during the 1950s.

Because Snyder's approach consisted largely of a conceptual scheme that identified clusters of variables for study without containing theory about their interrelations, propositions for empirical study could not logically be derived from the formulation as they had from more formal models, such as those of von Neumann and Morgenstern. However, Snyder and his associates formulated a number of hypotheses for empirical work based on the conceptual scheme that were capable of being studied in a number of contexts by different researchers (Snyder & Paige 1958; Snyder & Robinson 1961).

One of the great merits of the conceptual scheme originated by Snyder et al. was that it joined psychological and sociological levels of explanation; that is, it proposed to combine data and theory about both individual decision makers and the group or organizational context in which they operate. It offered a means of explaining group behavior in terms other than those strictly of personality. The aim was to combine the social and the psychological levels of analysis in order to increase the ability to predict variance. However, some critics felt that neither the state of psychology nor that of sociology permitted such hypothetical combinations. This point undoubtedly had merit, owing to the fact that few political scientists pursued Lasswell's initiatives in studying political personality (1930; 1935; 1948) and to the continuing separation of experimental social psychologists from field-oriented political scientists. One may expect that among the most active lines of future research on decision making will be studies of the interrelation of individual and organizational factors in producing decision outcomes.

A more descriptive and intellectualized model of the decision process is that of Lasswell (1956), who has identified seven stages or functions in the making of any decision. The first function is that of *intelligence*, which brings to the attention of the decisional unit problems for decision and information about these problems. There follow the *recommendation* function, in which alternatives are proposed; the *prescription* stage, in which one alternative is authoritatively selected; the *invocation* of the prescribed alternative; its *application* in particular cases by administrative or enforcement officers; the *appraisal* of its efficacy; and, finally, the *termination* of the original decision. This conception of decision making was designed on the basis of numerous investigations of judicial processes and has since been employed in a variety of legal contexts, including sanctioning systems in civil and criminal law, law of outer space, law of the seas, and public order [see POLICY SCIENCES]. Its usefulness has been demonstrated also in studies of legislative and foreign policy decisions. Like Snyder's conceptual scheme, Lasswell's descriptive model does not immediately generate hypotheses for empirical investigation. Many such hypotheses have been formulated and researched, however, among them propositions relating power advantages to decision makers who dominate the intelligence and recommendation functions.

Voting studies have only recently been cast in the language of decision making. Downs considered electoral decisions in terms of the postulates of economic behavior and deduced 25 propositions about party and governmental decision making (1957, pp. 296–300). For many of these data were independently available to confirm or disconfirm the predictions by their consistency or inconsistency with his model. In contrast to such quasi-mathematical models, the more typical voting study has emphasized the social-psychological variables acting to produce the voter's (and voters') decisions. An inventory of voting surveys (exclusive of ecological and gross data analyses) found 209 hypotheses on which some empirical evidence was available in one or more studies (Berelson et al. 1954). Contemporary voting theory considers the decision to vote and the direction of the vote to be products of party affiliation, orientation toward candidates, and orientation toward issues. Party affiliation is a stable factor, usually inherited from one's family, and generally subject to change only by dramatic social events (e.g., an economic depression). In the absence of unusual salience of either candidates or issues, party affiliation will determine the individual and aggregate vote. [*See* VOTING.]

Generic characteristics of decision making

Whether these different uses of decision terminology have anything in common remains to be seen. The answer depends on two kinds of effort. One is to search for congruence among specific, narrow-gauged propositions from contrasting kinds of decisions. For example, if organizations have relatively little information and have a deadline for decision, their decision makers tend to rely more heavily than otherwise on fundamental value orientations (Snyder & Paige 1958). Similarly, if voters have relatively little information about issues and candidates, they tend to rely more heavily on rather enduring and stable party affiliations (Michigan . . . 1960). These separate hypotheses suggest a transcendent one; that if information is low, evaluative criteria are likely to be more important than empirical or factual criteria. Another example of possible complementarity is the similarity between the dimensionality of attitudes in legislative voting and leadership and power in legislative bodies and the dimensionality of attitudes and roles among community decision makers. Legislative attitudes, at least among U.S. congressmen, seem to "scale" around several dimensions rather than along a single liberal–conservative continuum (MacRae 1958; Miller & Stokes 1963); that is, if an observer knows a legislator's vote on one bill, he can predict his vote on other bills in the scale, e.g., social welfare, but not on bills outside the scale, e.g., foreign affairs. Similarly, leadership on decisions is typically multidimensional; one set of leaders prevails on issue A, e.g., civil rights, and another set dominates issue B, e.g., education (Matthews 1960; Robinson 1962b). This finding is supported in studies of influence and decision making in communities of various size (Katz & Lazarsfeld 1955; Dahl 1961). [*See* LEGISLATION, *article on* LEGISLATIVE BEHAVIOR.] Still another apparently transcendent proposition is one that incorporates the "cross-pressures hypothesis" in voting and the frequent characterization of committee decisions. Voters receiving conflicting appeals from family, church, work group, and other sources tend to compromise by not voting or by split-ticket voting (Michigan . . . 1960). Committee or group decisions are similarly said to be compromised and ambiguous versions of originally clear and consistent alternatives

(Kelley & Thibaut 1954). Whether such apparently similar propositions have anything more than superficial commonality and whether many such congruities exist are questions for research that would help determine whether decision studies of various units and levels have much in common. [*See* CROSS PRESSURE.]

The second kind of effort that would clarify the generality of decision phenomena would be the construction of models of decision that would *both* generate new hypotheses for empirical investigation *and* accommodate existing, more or less confirmed propositions. Such attempts are apparent, for example, in the recent books by Downs, Riker, and Campbell et al. Downs, as already noted, has parsimoniously derived from his model a large number of propositions that had previously been investigated as parts of less general theories. Riker, too, has found that electoral and legislative decision studies fit his theory of coalition formation. And Campbell et al. have incorporated previous ecological and sociological voting hypotheses into their model of the American voter. However persuasive postdictive studies may be, that is, however consistent *ad hoc* propositions about historical events may be with the *post hoc* models, the stronger and more compelling evidence comes from predictive models from which derived hypotheses may be researched and verified. Decision models of this kind are less apparent in political science than in economics and psychology (Edwards 1954; 1961; Simon 1959).

The concept of occasion for decision. A conception of decision making that includes the identification of a problem or situation and is not confined to choice making treats the occasion for decision as a variable and not as a constant. Different kinds of decision situations involve participants and activate organizational structure in different ways. A number of dimensions of occasion for decision have been identified: uncertainty, risk, routine, unprogrammed (Snyder et al. 1962, p. 81; Simon 1960). Among typologies of decision situations is a three-dimensional one that identifies a range of situations varying between "crisis" and noncrisis. Crisis is a situation that (1) is regarded by decision makers as threatening to their organizational goals, (2) requires a relatively short response time, and (3) is unanticipated (Robinson 1962a; C. F. Hermann 1963, pp. 63–65). This conceptualization resembles social-psychological concepts of stress and threat but is more particular to the domain of decision making. It also is a more narrow definition than usually appears in historical and political science literature, which often defines a crisis as only

an important event. Further empirical work will be required to validate a workable concept; more than logic or a priori definitions are required [*see* CRISIS].

Personality and decision making

The relation between "personality" and decision making, historically of interest to political analysts but long confined to anecdotes and speculation, still awaits sustained systematic study. Lasswell's advocacy of the application of psychoanalytic and psychological concepts in the study of politicians in the 1930s remains to be heeded, except by a few political scientists. Research falls into two categories: (1) that dealing with political socialization and recruitment into decision-making roles, and (2) that relating personal characteristics of decision makers to the content of their decisions.

Political socialization studies are founded on Lasswell's dictum that everyone is born a politician, but some outgrow it. Three psychologically oriented biographies relate adolescent and preadolescent events to the eventual political careers of President Woodrow Wilson (George & George 1956), Mayor Anton Cermak of Chicago (Gottfried 1962), and James Forrestal, the first U.S. secretary of defense (Rogow 1963). Wilson illustrates the hypothesis that childhood deprivations of affection lead to low self-esteem, for which in adolescence and adulthood one compensates by seeking and exercising power over others. Wilson's compensation came first as speaker of college debating societies and later as chief executive of Princeton University, the state of New Jersey, and the United States. Efforts to find psychological characteristics to distinguish political types from apolitical types have been small in number and discouraging in results. For example, McConaughy's study of South Carolina legislators (1950), Hennessy's survey of Arizona party activities and nonactivists (1959), and Browning and Jacob's tests of politicians' motivations (1964) confirmed few of a number of hypotheses that psychological instruments would distinguish politicians from nonpoliticians. However, acknowledged methodological shortcomings in some of these studies make their results indecisive and inconclusive. Wahlke et al. (1962), in a comparison of four state legislatures, found that political interests of the elites they studied were activated at almost any stage of the life cycle, but that the most frequently crucial phase of political socialization occurs at a relatively early age—for many, as early as childhood. Similar conclusions are documented in Hyman (1959), Greenstein (1960), and Easton and Hess (1961; 1962). [*See* SOCIALIZATION.]

The other line of research on personality and decision making relates personal characteristics to decision content. One class of such studies searches for correlations between social backgrounds and prior experiences on the one hand and decisions or policies on the other. Matthews (1960) found that legislators who adhere more closely to the internal norms or folkways of the Senate are most successful in getting their bills adopted. And, in turn, senators who adhere most closely to the folkways tend to come from noncompetitive, homogeneous states. Nagel (1962) investigated the relations of more than fifteen variables, such as party affiliation, education, occupation, ethnicity, and group affiliations of judges, to a large number of different kinds of judicial decisions, including those involving administrative regulation, civil liberties, taxation, family relations, business, personal injury, and criminal cases. Statistically significant results of correlations of varying sizes have been obtained for many variables.

Another class of such studies relates unconscious motivations of decision makers to the outcomes of their decision process. A. George and J. George's biography of Wilson (1956) is a case in point, for the president's ambitions for power obscured his perception of the actual power situations and led him into self-defeating strategies. Almond and Lasswell (1948) reported that the interaction between the dominance or submissiveness of clients and welfare administrators was predictive of the decisions of the administrators; dominant clients were more likely to obtain favorable decisions from submissive agents than vice versa, and submissive clients were more likely to receive favorable decisions from dominant agents than vice versa. Margaret Hermann (1963) revived content analysis of public speeches as an indirect measure of legislators' motivations toward power, personal security, other people, tolerance of ambiguity, and ethnocentrism, and from knowledge of some of these unconscious motivations of twenty legislators, she successfully predicted their votes on a scale of foreign policy issues around the dimensions of nationalism–internationalism. Milbrath found that highly sociable citizens tended to make more contributions to political campaigns than nonsociable citizens, but he found that sociability was not associated with the behavior of Washington lobbyists (1963).

However elemental these personality studies are, they are more advanced than efforts to relate personal attitudes and values to political decisions. This line of research is only beginning to be opened up in American studies. However, the cross-cultural work of McClelland (1961) suggests strongly that motivations toward and values of achievement are related to a society's economic development; this finding is supported by an investigation of more than forty societies that is based on content analysis of educational materials and projective tests.

However discouraging the outcomes, to date, of research on personality and decision making may be, the disappointment owes more to the neglect of extensive effort than to any evidence that the task is fruitless or unpromising. The long-standing academic separation of political science from psychology and the diverse kinds of training given to political scientists have hindered the research. Recently completed and published studies once again reveal evidence that the interaction of personality and political decision is a fruitful subject of study. [See PERSONALITY, POLITICAL.]

Organizational context of decision making

With the possible exception of voting, all political decision making occurs in an organizational context. Organization is not easily defined [see ORGANIZATIONS], but it embraces a number of agreed-upon characteristics, including relatively formal rules of procedure, certain impersonal norms, indirect and mediated communication, relatively stable role expectations, and durability beyond the life of its members. Decision makers in organizations act under some influence from the rules, norms, and expectations of the large group to which they belong and in which they participate. Thus, organizational decision making is not merely individual or small-group decision making writ large.

The distinguishing characteristics of organization constitute dimensions that may vary from one organization to another. That is, rules of procedure in some organizations are different from those in others (for example, compare the voting procedures in Congress with decision rules in more hierarchically arranged organizations), and these procedures contribute to variations in the substantive content of policy or decision outcomes (e.g., Shuman 1957; Riker 1958). Communication patterns also vary from organization to organization. Mulder ([1958] 1963, pp. 65–110) has shown experimentally how centralized and decentralized groups differ in their approach to problem solving. Robinson (1962b, pp. 168–190) has related variations of frequency, source, mode, and kind of communication, together with satisfaction with communication processes, to the policy attitudes and votes of legislators.

Political scientists (and also industrial management analysts) have emphasized extent of centralization (and decentralization) as an important dimension of organizations. Some element of hierarchy accompanies all organizations (Simon 1962, pp. 468–469), although there may be variations in the organizational levels at which hierarchy is concentrated and these may be variations in the accuracy, frequency, and receptivity of upper echelons to feedback from lower ranks and vice versa.

Centralization is but one specific characteristic or dimension of organization. Others, such as division of labor and the criteria of recruitment, are increasingly being made operational and are researched in governmental organizations (Hall 1963). Former efforts to construct a priori gross typologies of organizations are yielding to empirical search for individual dimensions, which may or may not correlate highly enough to be thought of as constituting distinguishable types of organizations.

Political scientists studying decision making are concerned with whether differences in organization make any differences for decision outcomes. Probably the most studied problem of this type is the comparison of bureaucratic (i.e., executive or administrative) decision making with legislative decision making. Bureaucracies tend to be more impersonal and to have more "programmed" decision rules and more complex and hierarchical structures than legislatures. In general, executive agencies tend to be more innovative than legislatures, to be more capable of obtaining and processing larger amounts of technical information relevant to the problem for decision, and to exercise greater influence over policy (Robinson 1962*b*; Banks & Textor 1963, especially characteristics 174 and 179).

Methodology

In political science, most decisional studies have been *cases* of particular decisions or individual decision makers. Bailey (1950) inaugurated legislative case studies with the detailed history of the passage of a single bill in Congress. The Interuniversity Case Program pioneered in developing more than fifty cases of administrative, legislative, election, and party decisions. However, most case studies have been atheoretical and have not been directed at building a body of confirmed propositions across cases. Indeed, the possibilities of the case method usually have been regarded as limited to illustrating known principles or generating new ones, but as of little or no value for testing hypotheses. Efforts to use cases for testing hypotheses by generalizing across instances have been begun by Munger (1961) and Robinson (1962*b*, pp. 23–69).

Case studies of individual decision makers

through standard biographical techniques continue, but only a few have followed Lasswell's early examples of psychological inquiry.

Many national and some international political bodies produce large numbers of decisions and record many of them in a form readily susceptible to quantitative analysis. *Roll-call* data are especially useful for identifying voting blocs among members of these bodies and for identifying patterns of voting for individual members, whether persons or nations. In decision making analysis, such roll-call data may be regarded as dependent variables or as outcomes of decision-making processes. Hypotheses can readily be formulated that link these dependent variables to such independent variables as personality, social backgrounds, economic characteristics, and organizational variables. However, because legislatures, courts, and international organizations are essentially noncrisis organizations (as the term is used to designate one kind of decision occasion), these data are relevant only to a limited number of decision situations. Specific techniques used in organizing and interpreting roll-call data include cluster bloc, Guttman scaling, index of cohesion, factor analysis, party unity scores, and similar techniques familiar throughout the social sciences.

Survey techniques (i.e., a sampling of a population of respondents with whom personal interviews are conducted) have been used largely to study nonelite decision making (e.g., voting). The most ambitious of these studies include "panels" of respondents who are reinterviewed periodically during and/or after an election, and perhaps throughout a series of several elections. Although surveys have been confined mostly to nonelite studies, they are also applicable to investigations of elite decision making by interviews with samples of decision makers on one or more aspects of their processes Robinson 1962*b*, pp. 168–190, 220–234). [*See* SURVEY ANALYSIS.]

Simulation of political decision making has included both man-simulation (e.g., Guetzkow et al. 1963) and computer-simulation (e.g., Pool & Abelson 1961). Both forms constitute operating models of large-scale social processes. The functions of simulation are both heuristic and hypothesis-testing. To formalize models of decision processes requires logical and rigorous statements of the relationships among relevant variables and also of the relationships among propositions containing the variables. And, like any laboratory technique, simulation makes it possible to test hypotheses by controlling some factors while varying others. The use of simulation to study decisions developed later in political science than in the other social sciences, but it promises to be one of the increasingly used methods of the future. [See SIMULATION.]

Mathematics as a method in political science and decision-making analysis is also likely to increase in use, although, to date, its applications to this field have been less numerous than those in other parts of social science. The next generation of political scientists will have more opportunities to obtain training in mathematical analysis, and their training will include new developments in mathematics which make the tools of that subject more helpful for the social sciences. The functions of mathematics for studying political decision making are the same as its functions for studying other aspects of social or political phenomena. First, mathematics constitutes a formal language for making explicit statements of the relationships between variables and hypotheses. Second, it provides for the logical deduction of hypotheses from the rigorous statements that may be empirically researched by other methods, either experimental or field-observational. In short, mathematics serves both to integrate theory and to generate new hypotheses. After the deduction of new hypotheses, however, other techniques must be employed for conducting empirical tests of the hypotheses.

JAMES A. ROBINSON

[See also ADMINISTRATION; POLITICAL BEHAVIOR; POLITICAL PROCESS.]

BIBLIOGRAPHY

ALMOND, GABRIEL A.; and LASSWELL, HAROLD D. 1948 The Participant–Observer: A Study of Administrative Rules in Action. Pages 261–278 in Harold Lasswell (editor), *The Analysis of Political Behavior: An Empirical Approach.* New York: Oxford Univ. Press.

BAILEY, STEPHEN K. 1950 *Congress Makes a Law: The Story Behind the Employment Act of 1946.* New York: Columbia Univ. Press.

BANKS, ARTHUR S.; and TEXTOR, ROBERT B. 1963 *A Cross-polity Survey.* Cambridge, Mass.: M.I.T. Press.

BARNARD, CHESTER I. 1938 *The Functions of the Executive.* Cambridge, Mass.: Harvard Univ. Press.

BERELSON, BERNARD; LAZARSFELD, PAUL F.; and MCPHEE, WILLIAM N. 1954 *Voting: A Study of Opinion Formation in a Presidential Campaign.* Univ. of Chicago Press.

BERNOULLI, DANIEL (1738) 1954 Exposition of a New Theory on the Measurement of Risk. *Econometrica* 22:23–36. → First published in Latin.

BRAYBROOKE, DAVID; and LINDBLOM, CHARLES E. 1963 *A Strategy of Decision: Policy Evaluation as a Social Process.* New York: Free Press.

BROWNING, RUFUS P.; and JACOB, HERBERT 1964 Power Motivation and the Political Personality. *Public Opinion Quarterly* 28:75–90.

DAHL, ROBERT A. (1961) 1963 *Who Governs? Democracy and Power in an American City.* New Haven: Yale Univ. Press.

DOWNS, ANTHONY 1957 *An Economic Theory of Democracy.* New York: Harper.

EASTON, DAVID; and HESS, ROBERT D. 1961 Youth and the Political System. Pages 226–251 in Seymour M. Lipset and Leo Lowenthal (editors), *Culture and Social Character: The Work of David Riesman Reviewed.* New York: Free Press.

EASTON, DAVID; and HESS, ROBERT D. 1962 The Child's Political World. *Midwest Journal of Political Science* 6:229–246.

EDWARDS, WARD 1954 The Theory of Decision Making. *Psychological Bulletin* 51:380–417.

EDWARDS, WARD 1961 Behavioral Decision Theory. *Annual Review of Psychology* 12:473–498.

GEORGE, ALEXANDER L.; and GEORGE, JULIETTE L. 1956 *Woodrow Wilson and Colonel House.* New York: Day.

GOTTFRIED, ALEX 1962 *Boss Cermak of Chicago: A Study of Political Leadership.* Seattle: Univ. of Washington Press.

GREENSTEIN, F. I. 1960 The Benevolent Leader: Children's Images of Political Authority. *American Political Science Review* 54:934–943.

GUETZKOW, HAROLD et al. 1963 *Simulation in International Relations: Developments for Research and Teaching.* Englewood Cliffs, N.J.: Prentice-Hall.

HALL, RICHARD H. 1963 The Concept of Bureaucracy: An Empirical Assessment. *American Journal of Sociology* 69:32–40.

HENNESSY, BERNARD 1959 Politicals and Apoliticals: Some Measurements of Personality Traits. *Midwest Journal of Political Science* 3:336–355.

HERMANN, CHARLES F. 1963 Some Consequences of Crisis Which Limit the Viability of Organizations. *Administrative Science Quarterly* 8:61–82.

HERMANN, MARGARET G. 1963 Some Personal Characteristics Related to Foreign Aid Voting of Congressmen. M.A. thesis, Northwestern Univ.

HYMAN, HERBERT H. 1959 *Political Socialization: A Study in the Psychology of Political Behavior.* Glencoe, Ill.: Free Press.

KATZ, ELIHU; and LAZARSFELD, PAUL F. 1955 *Personal Influence: The Part Played by People in the Flow of Mass Communications.* Glencoe, Ill.: Free Press. → A paperback edition was published in 1964.

KELLEY, HAROLD H.; and THIBAUT, JOHN W. 1954 Experimental Studies of Group Problem Solving and Process. Volume 2, pages 735–785 in Gardner Lindzey (editor), *Handbook of Social Psychology.* Cambridge, Mass.: Addison-Wesley.

LASSWELL, HAROLD D. (1930) 1960 *Psychopathology and Politics.* New ed., with afterthoughts by the author. New York: Viking.

LASSWELL, HAROLD D. 1935 *World Politics and Personal Insecurity.* New York and London: McGraw-Hill.

LASSWELL, HAROLD D. 1948 *Power and Personality.* New York: Norton.

LASSWELL, HAROLD D. 1956 *The Decision Process: Seven Categories of Functional Analysis.* Bureau of Governmental Research, Studies in Government. College Park: Univ. of Maryland.

LUCE, R. DUNCAN; and RAIFFA, HOWARD 1957 *Games and Decisions: Introduction and Critical Survey.* New York: Wiley.

MCCLELLAND, DAVID C. 1961 *The Achieving Society.* Princeton, N.J.: Van Nostrand.

MCCONAUGHY, JOHN B. 1950 Certain Personality Factors of State Legislators in South Carolina. *American Political Science Review* 44:897–903.

MacRae, Duncan 1958 *Dimensions of Congressional Voting: A Statistical Study of the House of Representatives in the Eighty-first Congress.* University of California Publications in Sociology and Social Institutions, Vol. 1, No. 3. Berkeley: Univ. of California Press.

March, James G.; and Simon, Herbert A. 1958 *Organizations.* New York: Wiley. → Contains an extensive bibliography.

Matthews, Donald R. 1960 *U.S. Senators and Their World.* Chapel Hill: Univ. of North Carolina Press.

Michigan, University of, Survey Research Center 1960 *The American Voter,* by Angus Campbell et al. New York: Wiley.

Milbrath, Lester W. 1963 *The Washington Lobbyists.* Chicago: Rand McNally.

Miller, Warren E.; and Stokes, Donald E. 1963 · Constituency Influence in Congress. *American Political Science Review* 57:45–56.

Mulder, Mauk (1958) 1963 *Group Structure, Motivation and Group Performance.* Rev. ed. The Hague and Paris: Mouton. → First published in Dutch.

Munger, Frank J. 1961 Community Power and Metropolitan Decision-making. Pages 305–334 in Roscoe C. Martin et al. (editors), *Decisions in Syracuse.* Bloomington: Indiana Univ. Press.

Nagel, Stuart S. 1962 Judicial Backgrounds and Criminal Cases. *Journal of Criminal Law, Criminology, and Police Science* 53:333–339.

Newell, Allen; Shaw, J. C.; and Simon, Herbert A. 1958 Elements of a Theory of Human Problem Solving. *Psychological Review* 65:151–166.

Pool, Ithiel de Sola; and Abelson, Robert 1961 The Simulmatics Project. *Public Opinion Quarterly* 25:167–183.

Riker, William H. 1958 The Paradox of Voting and Congressional Rules for Voting on Amendments. *American Political Science Review* 52:349–366.

Riker, William H. 1962 *The Theory of Political Coalitions.* New Haven: Yale Univ. Press.

Robinson, James A. 1962a *The Concept of Crisis in Decision-making.* National Institute of Social and Behavioral Science, Symposia Studies Series, No. 11. Washington: The Institute.

Robinson, James A. 1962b *Congress and Foreign Policy-making: A Study in Legislative Influence and Initiative.* Homewood, Ill.: Dorsey.

Rogow, Arnold A. 1963 *James Forrestal: A Study of Personality, Politics, and Power.* New York: Macmillan.

Shuman, Howard E. 1957 Senate Rules and the Civil Rights Bill: A Case Study. *American Political Science Review* 51:955–975.

Simon, Herbert A. (1947) 1961 *Administrative Behavior.* 2d ed., with new introduction. New York: Macmillan.

Simon, Herbert A. 1959 Theories of Decision-making in Economics and Behavioral Science. *American Economic Review* 49:253–283.

Simon, Herbert A. 1960 *The New Science of Management Decision.* New York: Harper.

Simon, Herbert A. 1962 The Architecture of Complexity. American Philosophical Society, *Proceedings* 106:467–482.

Snyder, Richard C.; Bruck, H. W.; and Sapin, Burton 1954 *Decision-making as an Approach to the Study of International Politics.* Foreign Policy Analysis Series, No. 3. Princeton Univ. Organizational Behavior Section.

Snyder, Richard C. et al. (editors) 1962 *Foreign Policy Decision-making: An Approach to the Study of International Politics.* New York: Free Press.

Snyder, Richard C.; and Paige, Glenn D. 1958 The United States Decision to Resist Aggression in Korea: The Application of an Analytical Scheme. *Administrative Science Quarterly* 3:341–378.

Snyder, Richard C.; and Robinson, James A. 1961 *National and International Decision-making: Toward a General Research Strategy Related to the Problem of War and Peace.* New York: Institute for International Order.

von Neumann, John; and Morgenstern, Oskar (1944) 1964 *Theory of Games and Economic Behavior.* 3d ed. New York: Wiley.

Wahlke, John et al. 1962 *The Legislative System: Explorations in Legislative Behavior.* New York: Wiley.

White, Leonard D. (1926) 1955 *Introduction to the Study of Public Administration.* 4th ed. New York: Macmillan.

DECISION THEORY

Statistical decision theory was introduced by Abraham Wald (1939) as a generalization of the classic statistical theories of hypothesis testing and estimation. Ostensibly designed to put these theories in a common mathematical framework, it accomplished much more. It eliminated fundamental gaps in the previous theories and widened the scope of statistics to embrace the science of decision making under uncertainty. Although statistical decision theory represented a novel synthesis, many of its individual elements of novelty had been anticipated in spirit by Gauss and by the Neyman–Pearson theory of testing hypotheses. Furthermore, in formal structure it has much in common with game theory [see Game theory].

In a decision problem the statistician must select one action from a set of available actions. A strategy (also called a decision function) is a plan that tells how to use the data to select an action and is evaluated by reference to the cost of its expected consequences. The difficulty in selecting the best strategy derives from the fact that the consequences of an action depend on the unknown state of nature.

The proper role of decision theory is the subject of considerable controversy. Because it makes essential use of costs, many statisticians feel that decision theory may be suitable for problems of the marketplace but not those of pure science. Another issue is the difficulty in assigning costs or values to the consequences.

Crosscutting this controversy is another, which

concerns criteria for selecting a strategy; such criteria may be regarded as principles of statistical inference.

An example.   To illustrate the decision-theory formulation, consider a simplified and artificial example. An archeologist has recently uncovered a skull that may belong to one of two populations, A or B. A skull positively identified as A would set off an extensive and costly research effort; a skull positively identified as B would not justify any research effort. The archeologist proposes to take one of three actions, the extensive research effort (action a_1), a lesser research effort (action a_2), or dropping the inquiry (action a_3). The possibilities that the skull belongs to either population A or to population B are called states of nature and labeled θ_1 and θ_2 respectively. Assume that after considerable introspection the archeologist has attached values to the consequences. By tradition, statisticians think in terms of losses, so the best situation (action a_1 and state θ_1) will be treated as having zero loss. The losses are represented in Table 1.

Table 1 — Losses

		ACTION		
		a_1	a_2	a_3
STATE OF	θ_1	0	2	5
NATURE	θ_2	4	3	2

One may ask why the loss corresponding to θ_2 and a_3 is not zero since a_3 is the best action under state θ_2. If the situation (θ_2, a_3) is compared with the conceivable alternative (θ_1, a_1), the latter seems preferable and it is reasonable to assign a positive loss to (θ_2, a_3). To compare (θ_2, a_3) with the alternatives under θ_2, one uses *regret*. The regret for (θ_2, a_3) would be zero, while the regrets for (θ_2, a_1) and (θ_2, a_2) are 2 and 1 respectively.

Thus far three of the basic elements of decision theory have been presented: the available actions, the possible states of nature, and the consequences, or loss table. Because the state of nature is not known, the selection of a best action is not trivial. Ordinarily a scientist will perform some experiment to diminish the costly effect of ignorance.

Suppose that the archeologist decides to measure the cranial capacity of the skull and classify it as either large (z_1), medium (z_2), or small (z_3).

There would be no difficulty in using the data if all members of population A had large skulls and all members of population B had small ones. Unfortunately the experiment is not so informative: while skulls from A tend to be large and skulls from B tend to be small, there is appreciable overlap. Table 2 gives the fraction of skulls of population A and of population B that are large, medium, and small; this information, supposedly based on the results of extensive prior work, is not always readily available.

Table 2 — Probability of observing z given θ

	z_1	z_2	z_3
θ_1	.6	.3	.1
θ_2	.2	.3	.5

There are many ways in which the data can be used. Any rule that prescribes an action for each possible result of the experiment is called a strategy; Table 3 lists the 27 such rules for this problem. A discussion of the concept of strategy is given by Girshick (1954).

A typical reasonable strategy is s_6, which may be abbreviated (a_1, a_2, a_3). This strategy calls for action a_1 if z_1 is observed, a_2 if z_2 is observed, and a_3 if z_3 is observed. The strategies s_1, s_{14}, and s_{27} ignore the data; s_{22} seems to be unreasonable.

To determine how good a strategy is, it must be evaluated. How to evaluate the expected costs of $s_6 = (a_1, a_2, a_3)$ will be illustrated. If θ_1 is the true state of nature, z_1 is observed and a_1 taken with loss 0 and probability .6, z_2 is observed and a_2 taken with loss 2 and probability .3, and z_3 is observed and a_3 taken with loss 5 and probability .1. The expected loss is

$$(.6)0 + (.3)2 + (.1)5 = 1.1.$$

Similarly, if θ_2 is the true state, the expected loss is

$$(.2)4 + (.3)3 + (.5)2 = 2.7.$$

The expected losses for the 27 strategies are given in Table 4. Justification for the relevance of

Table 3 — Actions for the 27 strategies

		STRATEGIES																									
		s_1	s_2	s_3	s_4	s_5	s_6	s_7	s_8	s_9	s_{10}	s_{11}	s_{12}	s_{13}	s_{14}	s_{15}	s_{16}	s_{17}	s_{18}	s_{19}	s_{20}	s_{21}	s_{22}	s_{23}	s_{24}	s_{25}	s_{26}	s_{27}
	z_1	a_1	a_1	a_1	a_1	a_1	a_1	a_1	a_1	a_1	a_2	a_2	a_2	a_2	a_2	a_2	a_2	a_2	a_2	a_3	a_3	a_3	a_3	a_3	a_3	a_3	a_3	a_3
DATA	z_2	a_1	a_1	a_1	a_2	a_2	a_2	a_3	a_3	a_3	a_1	a_1	a_1	a_2	a_2	a_2	a_3	a_3	a_3	a_1	a_1	a_1	a_2	a_2	a_2	a_3	a_3	a_3
	z_3	a_1	a_2	a_3	a_1	a_2	a_3	a_1	a_2	a_3	a_1	a_2	a_3	a_1	a_2	a_3	a_1	a_2	a_3	a_1	a_2	a_3	a_1	a_2	a_3	a_1	a_2	a_3

Table 4 — Expected losses

STRATEGIES

		s_1	s_2	s_3	s_4	s_5	s_6	s_7	s_8	s_9	s_{10}	s_{11}	s_{12}	s_{13}	s_{14}	s_{15}	s_{16}	s_{17}	s_{18}	s_{19}	s_{20}	s_{21}	s_{22}	s_{23}	s_{24}	s_{25}	s_{26}	s_{27}
STATE OF NATURE	θ_1	0.0	0.2	0.5	0.6	0.8	1.1	1.5	1.7	2.0	1.2	1.4	1.7	1.8	2.0	2.3	2.7	2.9	3.2	3.0	3.2	3.5	3.6	3.8	4.1	4.5	4.7	5.0
	θ_2	4.0	3.5	3.0	3.7	3.2	2.7	3.4	2.9	2.4	3.8	3.3	2.8	3.5	3.0	2.5	3.2	2.7	2.2	3.6	3.1	2.6	3.3	2.8	2.3	3.0	2.5	2.0

expected loss derives from the theory of utility (Chernoff & Moses 1959, chapter 4; Luce & Raiffa 1957, chapter 2). [*See* UTILITY.]

Table 4 may be regarded as an extension of Table 1 with s_1, s_{14}, and s_{27} corresponding to a_1, a_2, and a_3. The increased size gives the appearance of greater complexity but implies that the archeologist has greater choice after performing the experiment than before. Since s_6 is obviously an improvement on s_{14}, having smaller expected losses under both θ_1 and θ_2, the experiment may be regarded as having succeeded in reducing the costly effects of ignorance.

The strategies and their expected losses are represented in Figure 1. Here each strategy is identified by a point whose coordinates are the expected losses under θ_1 and θ_2 respectively.

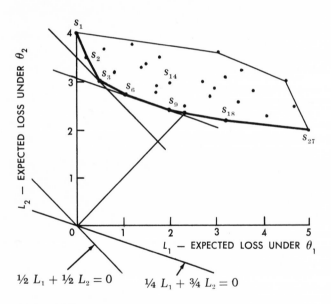

$$\tfrac{1}{2}\,L_1 + \tfrac{1}{2}\,L_2 = 0 \qquad \tfrac{1}{4}\,L_1 + \tfrac{3}{4}\,L_2 = 0$$

Figure 1 — Strategies and expected losses

The archeologist is not restricted to the 27 strategies mentioned above. He may decide to toss a fair coin and select s_1 if it falls heads and s_3 if it falls tails. Such a strategy is called a *randomized*, or *mixed*, strategy in contrast to the original *nonrandomized*, or *pure*, strategies. For the above mixed strategy the expected loss under θ_1 is 0 with probability $\tfrac{1}{2}$ and .5 with probability $\tfrac{1}{2}$ or .25, which is halfway between 0 and .5. In like manner, the expected loss under θ_2 is $\tfrac{1}{2}(4.0) + \tfrac{1}{2}(3.0) = 3.5$,

which is halfway between 4.0 and 3.0. It follows that the point representing this randomized strategy is halfway between the points representing s_1 and s_3 in Figure 1. By replacing the coin with a more general randomizing device, it is possible to find a strategy corresponding to any point on the line segment connecting any two strategies. Thus the set of available strategies (randomized and nonrandomized) has the property that every point of the line segment connecting two points of the set is in the set. Such a set is called *convex*. The fact that the set of strategies is the smallest convex set containing the nonrandomized strategies plays a fundamental role in the mathematics of decision theory.

To minimize loss, the statistician seeks a strategy whose representative point in Figure 1 is as low and as far to the left as possible. A strategy is said to dominate another strategy when the first is never more costly than the second and sometimes less costly. In Figure 1, s dominates s^* if s is below and to the left of s^*, directly below s^*, or directly to the left of s^*. A strategy that is not dominated is called admissible. The admissible strategies lie on the heavy line $s_1 s_2 s_3 s_6 s_9 s_{18} s_{27}$. The intuitively unreasonable strategy s_{22} is dominated by s_6; the strategy s_{14}, which ignores the result of the experiment, is also dominated by s_6.

Choice of good strategy. Clearly, the statistician can profitably confine his attention to the relatively few admissible strategies. How one should select from among these strategies is the subject of considerable controversy (Luce & Raiffa 1957, pp. 278–306). One criterion tentatively suggested by Wald was the *minimax criterion*, which may be described as follows: If nature is malevolent and the statistician picks s, nature will select the state θ that gives the greatest loss for s. Thus each strategy is evaluated by its maximum loss, and the statistician selects that strategy s for which the maximum loss is as small as possible. For the example, the minimax is found as the intersection of the line $L_1 = L_2$ with the segment $s_9 s_{18}$, and consists in selecting s_9 with probability $\tfrac{5}{7}$ and s_{18} with probability $\tfrac{2}{7}$, yielding expected losses 2.34 under both θ_1 and θ_2. For illustration of minimax strategies that do not lie on the line $L_1 = L_2$, see Luce and Raiffa (1957, p. 404).

The minimax criterion is generally regarded as too pessimistic. In the theory of two-person, zero-sum games, where a player has a malevolent opponent who is anxious to ruin him, minimax has justification; it seems unreasonable, however, to regard nature as a malevolent opponent.

An alternative view is that if the archeologist is in complete ignorance he ought to act as though each state of nature were equally likely and select the strategy that minimizes the average of the two losses (Luce & Raiffa 1957, p. 284). This strategy is s_3 and may be derived graphically by moving the line $\frac{1}{2}L_1 + \frac{1}{2}L_2 = 0$ parallel to itself until it touches the convex set of strategies. This objective approach has been criticized on the grounds that rarely, if ever, does a scientist approach a problem in complete ignorance.

A third approach (Savage 1954) consists in proving, under relatively weak assumptions describing restrictions of consistent and rational behavior, that such behavior leads one to act as though he had certain prior subjective or psychological probabilities for the states of nature. Thus if the archeologist had prior probabilities $\frac{1}{4}$ and $\frac{3}{4}$ for θ_1 and θ_2, he would minimize $\frac{1}{4}L_1 + \frac{3}{4}L_2$. Graphically, this may be achieved by moving the line $\frac{1}{4}L_1 + \frac{3}{4}L_2 = 0$ parallel to itself until it touches the set of strategies. In fact this line first touches the set of strategies along the line segment connecting s_6 and s_9, which means that s_6, s_9, and all their mixtures are equally good for the archeologist.

Other statisticians refuse to be bound by such restrictions in matters as sensitive and complex as inductive inference.

The decision-theory controversy.   The main objection to decision theory involves the losses. Some feel that in scientific problems where the only object is the satisfaction of scientific curiosity, it makes no sense to attach values or costs to the actions. Others, who are willing to accept a pragmatic approach, are overwhelmed at the difficulty in finding precise numbers to insert in the loss table. Still others feel that a statistician should not consider losses or actions but should confine himself to analyzing the inferential content of the data.

I feel that some conception of the value of consequences, be it based on personal gratification or on selfless consideration of the welfare of humanity, is necessary when faced with the problem of designing efficient experiments or when considering what data to gather and when to stop accumulating data. Since small deviations in the loss table have little effect on the relative merit of strategies when there is a substantial amount of data, precise values of losses are not vital; on the other hand, some rough conception of costs is required to understand the problem. By closing the gaps of previous formulations, decision theory has the advantage of focusing attention on all the major issues of a problem.

Another objection to decision theory is based on the requirement of a detailed model representing the preconception of the totality of possible states of nature. Common sense is necessary to avoid foolish results in the face of data indicating that the preconception was wrong. This issue is not peculiar to decision theory and lies at the heart of some of the current controversies over the comparative method in the social sciences.

Decision theory and classical statistics.   Testing hypotheses, estimation, and confidence intervals are the three main classical theories of statistical inference. A hypothesis-testing problem corresponds to a two-action problem. The possible actions are to accept a hypothesis or to reject it. The considerable difficulty that troubled novices over the choice between one-tailed and two-tailed tests was largely resolved by Neyman–Pearson theory. Decision theory added clarification by indicating that some problems traditionally formulated as testing problems really involve three actions.

In estimation problems one attaches a loss to estimating θ by t. A popular special case is the loss $(t - \theta)^2$. Then a good procedure tends to minimize the mean squared error, $E(t - \theta)^2$, which is the traditional measure of the goodness of an estimate. (See Chernoff & Moses 1959, pp. 207–233.)

The theory of confidence intervals is mathematically elegant, appealing, and popular but does not fit naturally into the decision-theory framework. The introduction of costs in a reasonable fashion would undoubtedly lead to substantial modification of the theory of confidence intervals.

Decision theory is wider than these classical theories. For example, in the archeological example, decision theory permits the consideration of the compromise action a_2, which is not optimal for any state of nature. This possibility does not exist in hypothesis testing. Decision theory also accommodates formulations involving sequential design of experiments.

Complete classes and Bayes solutions.   A complete class of strategies is one in which every strategy not in the class is dominated by some strategy in the class. A Bayes solution for certain prior probabilities is a strategy that minimizes the weighted average of the expected losses, with those prior probabilities as weights. In Figure 1, changing the prior probabilities changes the slope of the line that produces the Bayes solution; and by changing this slope, all admissible strategies are obtained. Thus, in the example, the class of all Bayes solutions is complete.

In many decision problems, in particular in all decision problems with a finite number of states of nature and a finite number of actions, the class of all Bayes solutions is complete. A consequence of this result is that one may restrict oneself to Bayes solutions whether one believes in psychological prior probabilities or not. The importance of this result is related to the fact that Bayes solutions are easily characterized using Bayes' theorem for posterior probabilities. If this theorem is used, the tedious task of listing all possible strategies before observations are obtained is no longer required to compute Bayes solutions [see PROBABILITY].

Compound decision problems. The Robbins theory of compound decision problems (Robbins 1951) can be partly illustrated by the following example: A subject is given a true–false question on an examination. An investigator wishes to classify the student as knowing the answer or not knowing it. The cost of misclassifying the subject is 1. It is assumed that a subject who knows the answer will answer correctly and that one who does not know the answer will guess at random. The traditional strategy of treating the subject as knowing the answer if he answers correctly seems reasonable.

Suppose now that several hundred students take the examination and about 50 per cent answer the question correctly. If a substantial proportion of the group knew the answer, one would expect considerably more than 50 per cent correct answers. Thus one may conclude that almost everyone should be treated as not knowing it.

This exotic approach illustrates that it is possible to use the data from many unrelated problems of the same type to improve over the results attained by analyzing each problem separately.

A variation of this approach yields Robbins' theory of empirical Bayes procedures (Robbins 1956), where past data on different examples of a problem are used to estimate empirical prior probabilities.

Further problems. Three other branches of decision theory in which interesting work has been done are comparison of experiments (Blackwell & Girshick 1954, chapter 12); invariance (Blackwell & Girshick 1954, pp. 223–236); the study of monotone procedures (Blackwell & Girshick 1954, pp. 179–195) and the extension of monotone procedures to problems involving Pólya type distributions (Karlin 1957–1958).

HERMAN CHERNOFF

[*Directly related are the entries* ESTIMATION; HYPOTHESIS TESTING; *and the biography of* WALD.]

BIBLIOGRAPHY

BLACKWELL, DAVID; and GIRSHICK, M. A. 1954 *Theory of Games and Statistical Decisions.* New York: Wiley.

BROSS, IRWIN D. J. 1953 *Design for Decision.* New York: Macmillan. → A paperback edition was published in 1965 by Free Press.

CHERNOFF, HERMAN; and MOSES, L. E. 1959 *Elementary Decision Theory.* New York: Wiley.

GIRSHICK, M. A. 1954 An Elementary Survey of Statistical Decision Theory. *Review of Educational Research* 24:448–466.

KARLIN, S. 1957–1958 Pólya Type Distributions. Parts 2–4. *Annals of Mathematical Statistics* 28:281–308, 839–860; 29:1–21.

LUCE, R. DUNCAN; and RAIFFA, HOWARD 1957 *Games and Decisions: Introduction and Critical Survey.* New York: Wiley.

ROBBINS, HERBERT E. 1951 Asymptotically Subminimax Solutions of Compound Statistical Decision Problems. Pages 131–148 in Berkeley Symposium on Mathematical Statistics and Probability, Second, University of California, 1950, *Proceedings.* Berkeley and Los Angeles: Univ. of California Press.

ROBBINS, HERBERT E. 1956 An Empirical Bayes Approach to Statistics. Volume 1, pages 157–163 in Berkeley Symposium on Mathematical Statistics and Probability, Third, University of California, 1954–1955, *Proceedings.* Berkeley and Los Angeles: Univ. of California Press.

SAVAGE, LEONARD J. 1954 *The Foundations of Statistics.* New York: Wiley.

VON NEUMANN, JOHN; and MORGENSTERN, OSKAR (1944) 1964 *Theory of Games and Economic Behavior.* 3d ed. New York: Wiley.

WALD, ABRAHAM 1939 Contributions to the Theory of Statistical Estimation and Testing Hypotheses. *Annals of Mathematical Statistics* 10:299–326.

WALD, ABRAHAM 1950 *Statistical Decision Functions.* New York: Wiley. → Reprinted in 1964.

DEFENSE MECHANISMS

The concept of defense mechanisms was originally proposed by Freud to explain the origins of socially handicapping symptoms, such as unreasonable fears or unjustified anger. Freud pictured symptoms as "derivatives," or indirect expressions, of impulses that cannot be expressed directly because they are incompatible either with other impulses or with one's moral standards. The blocking of expression elicits the unpleasant experience of anxiety, which varies with the strength of the impulses and tends to increase progressively until the conflict is resolved. Defenses represent predilections for particular distortions of unacceptable impulses. Torn between his impulse to hurt his father and his guilt, a son may *project* his anger to someone else. The boy is consequently relieved of both guilt and anxiety. If he *displaces* his anger to a safer target, he develops irrational angers at the scapegoat and is again saved from the discomfort of guilt and anxiety. If he *represses* the anger, he forgets about it; if he *isolates* it, he is aware of the idea that he wants to hurt someone but does not experience the feeling. He can also cancel the results of previous aggression by employing defenses like *undoing, reparation,* and *reversal,* the meanings of which are conveyed by the terms themselves.

What was first a clinical construct proved to be so fruitful in clarifying a large variety of social phenomena, both normal and abnormal, that it can be regarded as one of the most revolutionary influences on twentieth-century thought. Freud himself employed the construct in discussing such different topics as the content of art, the meaning of dreams, slips of the tongue, sources of prejudice, psychotherapists' errors, universal myths, the appeal of humor, religious ritual, and the child's view of his world. His papers on such topics have provided the foundations for numerous professional specialties in the arts and humanities as well as in medicine and the social sciences. It is difficult to picture what the novel, the play, or the painting of the twentieth century would be like if creative artists had not been exposed to the concepts of conflict, unconscious motives, and defensive distortions.

The ubiquitous interest in defenses is a tribute to their usefulness in explaining otherwise incomprehensible behavior in terms of the resolution of conflict, particularly internal conflict from which the person cannot escape. The clinician typically observes patients torn between moral standards and either sexual or aggressive impulses. The antagonistic forces are intense and have approximately the same strength. The conflict often develops a stable equilibrium characterized by protracted indecision and mounting anxiety. The inclination to forego either impulse tends to strengthen that impulse, by emphasizing the impending frustration, and to weaken the antagonist, which seems less important once it can be gratified. Anxiety may become so great that it interferes with the objective appraisal of events. At such times one can resort to the defenses, which permit resolutions without awareness of the nature of the choice or even of the conflict.

Definition and identification

In the more than half a century since the concept of defense was proposed, it has been subjected to considerable scrutiny both by partisan clinician and rigorous experimenter. People who study defenses empirically are immediately faced with a paradox. To conduct research on a mechanism, they have to be clear about ways of identifying it.

The attempt to attain clarity often makes the average investigator skeptical about the widespread enthusiasm for the concept, an enthusiasm buttressed more by faith in clinical observation than by a substantial body of experimental data or even by a theoretical system. What is available is a group of loosely defined descriptive labels. There is little agreement either about the definition of the mechanism or about the ways in which it affects perception. The label has been applied to such different phenomena as scotoma to visual details, the inability to report material whose recall is manifested indirectly, and the reinterpretation of events.

Critics often object to the "explaining" of forgetting by the invoking of the mechanism of repression, a practice they correctly label as a reification of the term. Postman (1953) makes another cogent criticism when he objects to the presumed assumption of a "Judas eye, scanning incoming concepts in order to decide what shall be permitted in consciousness" and apparently acting as a trigger that releases mechanisms employed to distort the unacceptable concepts. [*See* PERCEPTION, *article on* UNCONSCIOUS PERCEPTION.]

In the face of such phenomena as multiple personality, "forgotten" material that can be recovered under special conditions like hypnosis, and motivated errors in judgment, most skeptics concede that Freud was asking legitimate questions and that the perceptual system must often be split into subsystems, some of which are not accessible to awareness. But there is considerable disagreement about ways of describing such phenomena, and sympathetic critics often plead for hypotheses that are phrased in the language of the social scientist.

The vagueness of the concept of defense is suggested by Freud's definition: ". . . all the techniques of which the ego makes use in the conflicts which potentially lead to neurosis" ([1926] 1936, p. 144). This definition provides little help in discriminating between defense and other reactions that occur during conflict and ignores much of what Freud himself observed about the connections between defenses and normal phenomena, such as creativity, thinking, and humor.

Enumeration and criteria. The mechanisms labeled by Freud include repression, regression, reaction formation, reversal, isolation, undoing, introjection, identification, sublimation, denial, projection, and turning against the self. Many other psychoanalysts have proposed lists of defenses, few of which agree with Freud's in either content or length. The lack of consensus reflects some basic theoretical disagreements. Melanie Klein (1959), who founded her own psychoanalytic group, was very concerned with splitting and reparation, which are ignored by members of other groups. A more common reason for the lack of consensus is a casualness about definition of which Freud himself was often guilty. Later writers have been even less sensitive to the necessity of clear definition, extending the meaning of defense from a disposition to remotely related phenomena, such as neurotic symptoms; to stylistic trends, like resistance to change; and even to cultural products, like myths, which are neither defenses nor derivatives of impulses.

Anna Freud (1936) provided some useful criteria for definition when she noted that the "ego's defensive operations" are unconscious and that they repudiate "the claims of instinct" by keeping "ideational representatives of repressed instincts" from becoming conscious and by "creating a transformation" in the associated emotions. She suggested the additional functions of regulating needs by appropriate substitutions, altering the inappropriate strengths of needs, and preventing the recognition of painful events over which there is no control.

Miller and Swanson (1960) propose a group of specific criteria for recognizing defenses. They think that the observer must first identify an event, usually an impulse, that the person in conflict cannot acknowledge because the awareness of it would create objective difficulties or anxiety. The observer identifies the event on the basis of such indirect evidence as the content of dreams, subliminal perception, and unpleasant emotional states, such as excessive anxiety or guilt. Second, he must locate the substitute for the original impulse. The type of defense is inferred from the substitute, particularly the nature of the discrepancy between wish and act. If a son is constantly aggressive and his father responds by being very helpful, he is viewed as reversing his aggressive impulses if he has dreams that symbolize a murder of the son. If the father replaces aggression by fears that the son will be killed in an accident, these are interpreted as projections of the father's hostile wishes to auto drivers.

The nature of defense mechanisms

Of course the definition of terms is only a prelude to the raising of questions about the nature of defense mechanisms. How do the different defenses operate? Specifically, how does one project? Are there different kinds of projection? How does one repress? Do certain defenses have common characteristics? To what extent are different defenses learned? The literature on defense contains few deliberate attempts to answer such questions but many suggestive contributions.

Attempts at classification. Freud suggested a possible system of classification when he postulated that defenses are specific to particular pathologies: projection to paranoia, repression to conversion hysteria, turning against the self to depression. Such associations occur frequently but they are still not very strong. The same defense may be found in different pathologies; projection contributes to the irrational fear of the phobic, the obsessive's overconcern with his potential condemnation by others, and the depressive's feelings that he has lost all status in the eyes of others.

Another basis of classification was proposed by Anna Freud, who classified defenses with reference to eliciting conditions, such as anxiety, impulse, actual danger, forbidden emotion, and the pressure of conscience. Even though a single condition may sometimes elicit a large number of different defenses, there is some validity to the presumed association between the two. Turning against the self seems most appropriate to the distortion of aggressive impulses. Reversal, undoing, and reparation also seem appropriate to conflicts about aggression. Turning against the self seems inapplicable to anxiety, external threat, and sex. It seems more appropriate to think of denying anxiety and external threat or of repressing sexual impulses.

Employing a variety of criteria, Miller and Swanson (1960) propose two families of defense, differentiating them on the bases of complexity, distortion in derivatives, specificity to particular problems, and social effectiveness. The use of defenses in the first family, which is presumed to have developed early, leads to considerable distortion in the interpretation of events; they tend to be applicable to most problems; they are often socially handicapping; they are simple in that they require little previous learning. A defense like denial, for example, only requires that the person close his eyes and conjure up a wishful picture in his imagination. Common to such mechanisms is an obliteration of awareness and many kinds of information associated with it.

The use of defenses in the second family creates only minor distortions in the interpretation of events; they tend to be suited to particular problems; they are conducive to socially acceptable, even rewarded, behavior; they are relatively complex. A defense like projection requires that the person be able to recognize his impulses, that he have an awareness of self, and that he be able to apply a code of values.

Defenses in the second family have in common a displacement or shift on one or more dimensions of the forbidden impulse, such as the objects, affects, actions, agents, and goal states. When a boy who is angry at his father displaces his aggression to another object, he chooses something similar in certain respects to the original object. Sometimes the choice may be very remote as in the classical case of Freud's little Hans, who shifted his problem from his father to white horses, both being large, light-skinned, and strong and having dark structures around the eyes (glasses and blinders) and a dark area around the mouth (beard and snout).

Projection—an example

Research on the defense mechanisms has proliferated to such an extent as to require that a survey of the literature be restricted to one mechanism. Projection has been chosen because it has been the subject of the most fruitful investigations.

One problem that has plagued investigators is the variety of phenomena that have been labeled as projection. Freud recognized that, in addition to the unconscious attribution of traits, there is also a more "normal" kind of projection in which we "refer the cause of certain sensations to the external world instead of looking for them inside ourselves. . ." (1912–1913). As a result of his observations of psychotics, Federn (1953) identified still another type in which confusion about the body image leads a person to be uncertain about the location of either acceptable or unacceptable impulses, which might be attributed to self, another person, or some object in the intervening space. The literature contains references to still other phenomena that were called projection. [See BODY IMAGE.]

In designing research, most investigators begin with a conception of ways in which the mechanism affects perception. The commonest conceptions attribute projection to the breakdown in discrimination caused by the loss of ego boundaries, to displacement of unacceptable impulses from self to outside world, to a combination of increased sensitivity to the forbidden impulses in self and other and a denial of the impulses in self, to a diminution of the seriousness of one's problems by exaggerating them in others, and to displacements on dimensions of the agent of action. Some of these conceptions are compatible with one another; others are not. The version that attributes projection to poor discrimination is consistent with the version that explains it as a displacement of the experienced event from inside to outside the self. But one cannot postulate both an intact body image and a breakdown in its boundaries or explain the distortion as pathological and basic to all cognition.

Depending on their assumptions about the nature of projection, various investigators have become concerned with different problems. Assuming that the mechanism is learned during the child's struggles with toilet training, a number of investigators have devoted their efforts to studying the associations between anality, projection, and aggression. Others have studied the social implications of the defense by observing its use in different societies. Among the Dobuans (Fortune 1932), whose members are very competitive, poisoning, witchcraft, and other types of treachery are frequent enough, even in relations between close kin, to elicit universal suspicion of one's fellow man, and the person who does not project his aggression may not survive very long. Projection is also helpful to the Hopi (Goldfrank 1945), who have a highly organized cooperative economic system which could not function even in the presence of mild aggression. They project their anger to evil spirits. Although citizens of both communities favor the same defense, the difference in targets results in one group being homicidal and the other being exceptionally peaceful.

A concern with the social consequences of projection in American society has led a number of social scientists to study the vicious cycle that reinforces the paranoid's projection of aggression. He initially has little evidence to justify his suspicions, but if his fear leads him to withdraw or to be hostile, others soon begin to shy away. On the second encounter they are more wary, which confirms his suspicions of their intentions and enhances his fear and hostility. Each encounter reinforces the elements in the cycle, which consists of increased alarm and self-protective hostility on his part followed by puzzled retreat and, finally, anger on the part of others.

Epidemiological research on the incidence of different psychoses provides indirect evidence about the learning of defenses. Paranoid psychoses occur more often in the poorer than in the more affluent areas of large cities (Faris & Dunham 1939). Some investigators reason that the hardships faced by the poor reinforce the tendency to project; others that people with paranoid tendencies are economically handicapped and their downward mobility finally forces them to live in poorer sections. The disagreement has not yet been resolved, but evidence that psychotics in poor areas have not generally drifted there from other sections casts doubt on the latter hypothesis. [See PARANOID REACTIONS.]

A relatively new field of investigation, which represents a merging of Freudian theory, the sociology of communication, and certain epistemological principles, starts with the assumption that projection is an inherent part of all perception. On observing an object, a man organizes his visual sensations into meaningful categories and adds additional meanings and values in terms of the implications of the incident for his condition and his goals. The more concerned he is with what an object is like or how it ought to be, the greater is the likelihood that he will view it within a particular rubric of meanings and that he will impose qualities on it that others may not see.

Projection has a prominent role in many studies of the development of moral standards. It is assumed that the child first resists parental demands, such as those prohibiting attacks on his siblings. He then conforms because of fear. But then, each time he is tempted to misbehave he anticipates how the mother will judge him by projecting to her the feeling he would have if he were in her place. He then identifies with the disapproving mother and gradually comes to inhibit his impulses or to punish himself just as she might have done.

Underlying this type of speculation is the premise that we can never know what is in another person's mind on the basis of direct experience. We must project what we would feel if we were in his place in order to guess what he is experiencing. After we project, we usually test our resultant impression by comparing it with subsequent events. If these show the impression is wrong, we modify it and test the new one in turn. It is assumed that the paranoid projects no more than anyone else; he differs from other men in the inefficiency with which he tests the veridicality of his projections.

Experimental research on projection has helped to develop the outlines of a potential theory. Studies reveal, for example, that the incorrect attribution to others of unpleasant traits is a function of the situation as much as the predilections of the person. Bramel (1962) threatened his subjects by indicating that their homosexual tendencies were more marked than they had reported in their self-ratings. On obtaining his reports the subjects increased their ratings of the homosexual tendencies of people with whom they had been paired but whom they did not know very well. The more favorable were the original estimates, the greater was the tendency to see others more unfavorably. Posner (1940) asked a group of children to rate the attractiveness of pairs of toys, to give one of the pair to a friend, and then to guess which of the toys the friend would have given the subjects. They usually chose the preferred toy for themselves and projected the selfish choice to the friend. This pro-

jection was much less evident in a control group whose members did not have to give away one of the toys before estimating the friends' choices.

In a study of the contents and targets of projection Zimmer (1955), like a number of investigators, found that subjects project their acceptable personality traits to liked people and unacceptable traits to disliked people. Moreover, the degree of projection is related to conflict about the trait. According to Harvey (1958), people feel positively about raters who agree with their self-rating but deprecate the raters when they disagree. The subjects also show poor recall of the ratings, the distortions increasing with the discrepancies from self-rating up to a critical point.

The results of some studies help to explain the conditions under which people project similar and complementary traits to others. At a party arranged by Murray (1933) preadolescent girls rated a group of pictures before and after a frightening game called "murder." The maliciousness attributed to the people in the pictures increased markedly following the game. Similar rather than complementary projection was elicited by Bramel, whose study has been described above. A comparison of the two investigations suggests that subjects project complementary traits when they find their own qualities acceptable and similar traits when they dislike their qualities and need to de-emphasize them.

The projection of complementary attributes seems to require a particular cognitive style. Leventhal (1957) divided his subjects into two groups, depending on the number of different concepts they used in describing their friends. The complex perceivers used many concepts and typically reacted to others in terms of differences between them; simple perceivers used few concepts and were more prone to assume likenesses in others.

Still another determinant of the contents of projection is its appropriateness to the target. Menzies (1960) reports that nurses project irresponsible impulses to juniors and severe disciplinary attitudes to seniors. The resultant impressions tend to be accurate because they are consistent with the nurses' roles. The "social defense system" of the nursing service enables the women to "project and reify" relevant elements of their psychic defense systems. Some features of the social system that help to defend nurses against their many anxieties include the splitting of tasks in a manner that prevents intensive contact with any one patient, the denial of the patients' individuality by such practices as referring to them by number or by diagnostic category rather than by name, the encouragement of ritualistic performance of tasks, and the discouragement of discretion and initiative. Unless a new nurse can restructure her defenses in ways that are congruent with this social defense system, she has considerable difficulties in her professional relationships.

A number of recent papers have been devoted to the hypothesis that people with incompatible defenses have more difficulty getting work done than do people with less incompatible combinations. Cohen (1956) asked his subjects to work together on a task and to judge each other's interpersonal ability. As anticipated, people inclined to favor projection were more negative and hostile in interacting with one another than when paired with other subjects.

Recent research on the defenses has been dominated by the assumption that the mechanisms represent predilections for particular styles of interpreting one's environment. This cognitive viewpoint has led investigators to think of defenses as components of a general style of solving emotional problems. It has also concentrated people's interest on the self as a focus for the kinds of problems that elicit various defenses. Finally, it has prompted investigators to think of the possibility that all defenses, and possibly much of the process of thinking, can be analyzed into certain basic components. Some of these that are common to the defenses listed in the psychoanalytic literature include the tendency to do or think something that is opposite in meaning to the unacceptable event, to obliterate one's total awareness of a problem, and to displace awareness from one location on a dimension to another. Displacements from inside to outside the body may represent a special instance of oppositeness, other examples of which are reversal and denial of beliefs and undoing and reparation of action. It seems probable that within the next decade, research on defense mechanisms will permit close integration of the concept with theories of cognition and motivation.

DANIEL R. MILLER

[*For further general discussion of defense mechanisms, see* ANXIETY; PREJUDICE; PSYCHOANALYSIS; *and the biographies of* FREUD *and* KLEIN. *More specific treatment may be found in* AESTHETICS; DREAMS; FANTASY; HUMOR; LITERATURE, *article on* THE PSYCHOLOGY OF LITERATURE; MYTH AND SYMBOL; RELIGION.]

BIBLIOGRAPHY

BRAMEL, DANA 1962 A Dissonance Theory Approach to Defensive Projection. *Journal of Abnormal and Social Psychology* 64:121–129.

COHEN, ARTHUR R. 1956 Experimental Effects of Ego Defense Preference on Interpersonal Relations. *Journal of Abnormal and Social Psychology* 52:19–27.

FARIS, ROBERT E. L.; and DUNHAM, H. W. (1939) 1960 *Mental Disorders in Urban Areas: An Ecological Study of Schizophrenia and Other Psychoses.* New York: Hafner.

FEDERN, PAUL 1953 *Ego Psychology and the Psychoses.* New York: Basic Books.

FORTUNE, REO F. (1932) 1963 *Sorcerers of Dobu: The Social Anthropology of the Dobu Islanders of the Western Pacific.* Rev. ed. London: Routledge.

FREUD, ANNA (1936) 1957 *The Ego and the Mechanisms of Defense.* New York: International Universities Press. → First published as *Das Ich und die Abwehrmechanismen.*

FREUD, SIGMUND (1888–1938) 1959 *Collected Papers.* 5 vols. Authorized translation under the supervision of Joan Riviere. Vol. 5 edited by James Strachey. International Psycho-analytic Library, Nos. 7–10, 34. New York: Basic Books; London: Hogarth. → Translation of *Sammlung kleiner Schriften zur Neurosenlehre* and additional papers. A ten-volume paperback edition was published in 1963 by Collier Books.

FREUD, SIGMUND (1912–1913) 1938 *Totem and Taboo.* London and New York: Penguin.

FREUD, SIGMUND (1926) 1936 *The Problem of Anxiety.* New York: Norton. → First published as *Hemmung, Symptom und Angst.* A British edition was also published in 1936 by Hogarth as *Inhibitions, Symptoms and Anxiety.* Pages cited in text refer to the American edition.

GOLDFRANK, ESTHER S. 1945 Socialization, Personality, and the Structure of Pueblo Society. *American Anthropologist* New Series 47:516–539.

HARVEY, O. J. 1958 *Reactions to Negative Information About the Self . . .* Group Psychology Branch, Office of Naval Research, Technical Report No. 8. Washington: The Office.

KLEIN, MELANIE 1948 *Contributions to Psycho-analysis: 1921–1945.* International Psycho-analytic Library, No. 34. London: Hogarth.

KLEIN, MELANIE 1959 Our Adult World and Its Roots in Infancy. *Human Relations* 12:291–303.

LEVENTHAL, HOWARD 1957 Cognitive Processes and Interpersonal Predictions. *Journal of Abnormal and Social Psychology* 55:176–180.

MENZIES, ISABEL E. P. 1960 A Case-study in the Functioning of Social Systems as a Defense Against Anxiety. *Human Relations* 13:95–121.

MILLER, DANIEL R.; and SWANSON, GUY E. 1960 *Inner Conflict and Defense.* New York: Holt.

MURRAY, HENRY A. 1933 The Effect of Fear Upon Estimates of Maliciousness of Other Personalities. *Journal of Social Psychology* 4:310–329.

POSNER, B. A. 1940 Selfishness, Guilt Feelings and Social Distance. M.A. thesis, Univ. of Iowa.

POSTMAN, LEO 1953 On the Problem of Perceptual Defense. *Psychological Review* 60:298–306.

ZIMMER, HERBERT 1955 The Roles of Conflict and Internalized Demand in Projection. *Journal of Abnormal and Social Psychology* 50:188–192.

DEFLATION
See INFLATION AND DEFLATION.

DEGREES OF FREEDOM
See COUNTED DATA *and* LINEAR HYPOTHESES.

DELEGATION OF POWERS

Delegation of powers is the act whereby a political authority invested with certain powers turns over the exercise of those powers, in full or in part, to another authority. Accordingly, the powers of the delegate are precisely those that belonged to the delegant, and the actions performed in virtue of the delegation have the same juridical nature as if they had been performed by the delegant himself. Delegation should not, therefore, be regarded as permission or authorization; rather, it is a transfer of power. The fundamental problem then is to find out whether, and to what extent, that transfer is legitimate in the realm of public law.

When delegation is legally provided for there is no difficulty. This is often the case on the administrative level; the organizational regulations of a bureau authorize its head to turn the exercise of his powers over to another official. It should be noted, however, that even when delegation is authorized by existing law, it is subject to very precise conditions. In the first place, the right to exercise delegation cannot be presumed. Furthermore, those actions for which the right of delegation is granted must be clearly indicated. Finally, delegation must necessarily be limited in time.

In constitutional matters, the problem is more delicate. Since it arises in relations between legislative and executive branches of government, it has political implications that can lead to deviations from the strict application of legal principles. In practice the question is whether, in the absence of constitutional provisions authorizing the legislature (parliament or congress) to strip itself of its competence, it can entrust the executive with the right to take regulatory measures that will have the force of law. In cases where a constitution reserves certain areas to the competence of a legislative body, delegation would have the effect of bringing about *a transfer of functions* from the legislative branch to the executive; and in every case, delegation would achieve *a transfer of powers.*

Critique. Theoretically it is impossible to delegate the legislative power (or any other prerogative) given by a constitution to a legislature. This position is based both on a legal argument and on a consideration of common sense. Legally, one can only delegate a power that one possesses. But the power to legislate is not a right of the legislative houses; it is a function entrusted to them by a constitution, to exercise and not to dispose of at will. Common sense reinforces the legal principle. Locke was the first to show that when the people, by means of a constitution, grant the power of making laws to a given agency, it is because they have confidence in that agency. They feel that the way the agency is constituted and the procedures it has to follow will guarantee that the rules made will merit obedience. "The people," Locke wrote, "can[not] be bound by any Laws but such as are Enacted by those, whom they have Chosen, and Authorised to make Laws for them" (*Two Treatises of Government* [1690] 1960, II, sec. 141).

In opposition to delegation, one could also invoke the principle of the separation of powers, saying that it would be violated if, under cover of an invitation by parliament, the executive could adopt measures that, by their nature and object, were veritable laws. Finally, for those who, especially in France, identified democracy with the omnipotence of the houses of the legislature, delegation would endanger the very idea of democracy, since on the one hand it appeared to be a means of imposing obligations on individuals that their representatives would not have consented to; and on the other hand, by reinforcing the scope of the government's actions, it could justly be suspected of favoring the views approved of by the government.

Historical development. The theoretical force of these arguments opposing the concept of the delegation of power could not prevail against the actual necessities that have compelled governments to resort to it in almost every country. These necessities arose in two areas, war and economic catastrophe, and in two successive waves, World War I and the depression. The war of 1914–1918, when the bitterness of the struggle entailed mobilization of all the forces of the nation, made it necessary to concentrate all powers in the hands of an agency able to use them promptly. Since this agency could only be the executive, the latter was granted power by the parliaments to regulate affairs that in normal times would have called for a legislative vote. In France, the first laws extending the regulatory powers of the government were adopted on August 3 and 5, 1914; they regarded only matters of limited scope. Subsequently, although special laws had enlarged the government's power to act, it promulgated, on its own accord, measures called *décrets-lois*, which properly belonged exclusively within the competence of the parliament.

In England it has always been held that, in the absence of a written constitution, Parliament is sovereign and can therefore delegate to an agency of its choice any or all of its legislative competence. Nevertheless, although such instances of delegation were known for a long time (for example, by the Mutiny Act of 1717, Parliament transferred to the crown all regulation of discipline in the army), they remained exceptional and, furthermore, did not entirely divest Parliament of those powers. In point of fact, the historical practice of *delegated legislation* that had become fairly widespread during the nineteenth century came down to this: Parliament itself established the broad principles of regulation; the subordinate authority was empowered to adapt them to actual situations. In 1914 there was a clear-cut change; the Defence of the Realm (Consolidation) Act gives the government the broadest powers and introduces *crisis legislation* into the framework of delegated legislation. This category of delegation goes much farther since it does not in any way limit the liberty of the executive.

In the United States, the principle that Congress cannot delegate its legislative powers can be modified by a broad interpretation of the function of the president. It is admitted that in a period of crisis or war, the president can do anything that is needed to preserve the Union. Applying this idea, originally held by Lincoln and Theodore Roosevelt, President Wilson, during World War I, took steps that normally would come under the competence of Congress. Even among the neutrals, the international crisis led to a transfer of legislative powers from the legislative branch to the executive branch. Thus, in Switzerland, on August 3, 1914, the federal assembly granted full powers to the federal council.

Since the motive for the extensive delegation of power was war necessity, it might have been thought that the delegation would end when the war ended. Nothing of the sort happened. After the conflict, a new wave of delegation appeared, this time provoked by economic difficulties. In France, financial emergencies led successive governments to ask parliament for the power to legislate by decrees; in England, delegated legislation became a normal governmental procedure; in Switzerland, the economic crisis of 1930 led to a new extension of the powers of the federal council. In the United States, President Roosevelt had recourse to his statutory powers, i.e., those that a president has under an express delegation from Congress, to regulate by executive order matters that are normally reserved to formal law. The international tension from 1948 on has led American presidents to take similar actions.

Since that time it has become impossible to regard delegation of the legislative power as a mere expedient, legitimate only to meet a crisis situation. The volume of legislative measures taken by the executive in many states often exceeds the number of laws adopted by their legislatures. Experience has shown that even under normal conditions the legislative bodies can no longer claim a monopoly of legislation. In the ideal liberal state, the right to make laws is reserved solely to the national representatives because laws are few in number and very general in their content, being only a last resort intended to help overcome the inadequacies of the social order. But the modern conception of democracy calls more and more frequently for intervention by the state. The number of regulations required and their technical nature make legislatures increasingly incapable of issuing them. Furthermore, the executive, being obliged to act and to act quickly, can no longer wait for the legislative branch to decide whether to grant the government the laws it needs for its policies. Governments need to have the power to work out general policy and to issue freely the regulations necessary for its implementation.

These facts were recognized in England in 1932 by the Committee on Ministers' Powers (Donoughmore Committee), which was charged with studying the legality of delegated legislation. In the United States, these facts were recognized in 1949 by the Commission on Organization of the Executive Branch of the Government (Hoover Commission). In both countries, it was held that legislation by the executive was not unconstitutional so long as it left room for control a posteriori, either by parliament (in England) or by the courts (in the United States). This control can indeed be effective, as was shown in 1952 by the Supreme Court decision declaring unconstitutional President Truman's seizure of the steel mills. In Europe, some constitutions drafted between the two wars granted the executive the right to legislate by decree under exceptional circumstances (Polish constitution of April 23, 1935, articles 55 and 57; Austrian constitution of December 7, 1929, article 18; Spanish constitution of December 9, 1931, article 80; etc.). After World War II, the possibility of the delegation of the legislative power was expressly recognized by the Italian constitution (article 77) and the fundamental law of the German Federal Republic (article 80). In France, on the other hand, the obloquy that the use of decrees had cast on parliament, which was accused of evading its responsibilities, led the authors of the 1946 constitution to insert, in article 13, the rule that parliament alone makes law. In fact, however, from 1948 on, by more or less disguised procedures, all the governments of the Fourth Republic asked parliament for the power to legislate, and obtained it. The 1958 constitution, taking cognizance of what has become an unavoidable necessity in a modern state plainly incorporated legislation by the executive branch. Not only can the executive, by virtue of article 37, legislate by decree on any matters not reserved to parliament by article 34, but article 38 gives it the power of asking the houses of parliament for a delegation of power to legislate even on those matters that are reserved to parliament.

G. BURDEAU

[*See also* CONSTITUTIONAL LAW; CRISIS GOVERNMENT; LEGISLATION.]

BIBLIOGRAPHY

ALLEN, CARLETON K. (1945) 1956 *Law and Orders: An Inquiry Into the Nature and Scope of Delegated Legislation and Executive Powers in English Law.* 2d ed. London: Stevens.

BATELLI, MAURICE 1950 Chronique constitutionnelle étrangère: Suisse. *Revue du droit public et de la science politique en France et à l'étranger* 66:124–146.

BINKLEY, WILFRED E. (1937) 1947 *President and Congress.* 2d ed. New York: Knopf. → A third revised edition, in paperback, was published in 1962 by Vintage Books.

BURDEAU, GEORGES 1949–1957 *Traité de science politique.* 7 vols. Paris: Librairie Général de Droit et de Jurisprudence.

CARR, CECIL T. 1921 *Delegated Legislation.* Cambridge Univ. Press.

CORWIN, EDWARD S. (1940) 1957 *The President: Office and Powers.* 4th rev. ed. New York Univ. Press.

GÓMEZ-ACEBO, RICARDO 1951 El ejercicio de la función legislativa por el gobierno: Leyes delegadas y decretos-leyes. *Revista de estudios políticos* 40, no. 60:67–97.

LAFFERRIÈRE, J. 1956 La législation déléguée en Angleterre et le contrôle de son exercice par le Parlement. Pages 331–357 in *L'évolution du droit public: Études offertes à Achille Mestre.* Paris: Sirey.

LOCKE, JOHN (1690) 1960 *Two Treatises of Government.* Cambridge Univ. Press.

LOGAN, D. W. 1944 Post-war Machinery of Government. *Political Quarterly* 15:185–195.

MANUEL, ANDRÉ 1953 *Les pleins pouvoirs en droit public fédéral Suisse.* Lausanne (Switzerland): Jaunin.

NEUSTADT, RICHARD E. 1955 Presidency and Legislation: Planning the President's Program. *American Political Science Review* 49:980–1021.

ROCHE, JOHN P. 1952 Executive Power and Domestic Emergency: The Quest for Prerogative. *Western Political Quarterly* 5:592–618.

SOUBEYROL, JACQUES 1955 *Les décrets-lois sous la Quatrième République.* Bordeaux (France): Samie.

TINGSTEN, HERBERT 1934 *Les pleins pouvoirs: L'expansion des pouvoirs gouvernementaux pendant et après la grande guerre.* Publication du Fonds Descartes. Paris: Srock, Delamain & Boutelleau.

TUNC, ANDRÉ 1952 Les pouvoirs du président des États-Unis et l'arrêt de la Cour Suprême relatif à la saisie des aciéries. *Revue internationale de droit comparé* 4:735–751.

VISSCHER, PAUL DE 1947 *Les nouvelles tendances de la démocratie anglaise: L'expérience des pouvoirs spéciaux et de pleins pouvoirs.* Paris: Casterman.

WEYR, FRANÇOIS 1926 La question de la délégation de la puissance législative. *Revue internationale de la théorie du droit* 1:72–88.

DELINQUENCY

I.   THE STUDY OF DELINQUENCY   *James F. Short, Jr.*
II. SOCIOLOGICAL ASPECTS   *Stanton Wheeler*
III. PSYCHOLOGICAL ASPECTS   *William McCord*
IV. DELINQUENT GANGS   *Jackson Toby*

I
THE STUDY OF DELINQUENCY

Juvenile delinquency is that behavior on the part of children which may, under the law, subject those children to the juvenile court. As such, it is a relatively new and legal term for a very old phenomenon.

The term has both precise and diffuse referents. When a child is designated a juvenile delinquent by the court, this is a precise definition of his legal status. He is, by this act, a ward of the court, subject to its discretion. By contrast, except in a strictly legal sense, the term refers only vaguely to actual behavior, since what is delinquent varies greatly over time and from one part of the world to another.

Delinquency as legal status. Concern with misbehavior by children is at least as old as recorded history. The earliest known code of laws (the Code of Hammurabi) took specific note of the duties of children to parents and prescribed punishments for violations. As legal systems were elaborated, the age of offenders continued to be important in defining responsibility for criminal behavior. Ancient Roman law and English common law, for example, held that children under the age of seven were incapable of criminal intent and, therefore, of responsibility for crime; between age seven and the time of puberty (approximately), criminal responsibility was a matter for determination by the courts. When responsibility was assumed or "proven," however, children of any age were subject to the same laws and the same courts as were adults. It was this fact, and the related concern for the welfare of children rather than for specific types of behavior engaged in by errant youngsters, that motivated the early reformers to urge the passage of juvenile court legislation.

The establishment of the first juvenile court in Cook County, Illinois, in 1899 climaxed many years of legal and humanitarian concerns for the welfare of children held to be in violation of the law and concerns with the criteria by which they might be so adjudged (Van Waters 1932). This legislation created a new kind of machinery, outside the criminal law, for handling juvenile offenders. Every state in the United States and virtually all "modern," or "developed," societies have since established special legal procedures for handling juvenile offenders. Juvenile delinquency has emerged as a social problem only recently in some areas of the world, but there is evidence even in "new nations" and "underdeveloped countries" of increased concern with problems of youth under the law.

The defining features of the juvenile court are its informality, as compared to the rigorously formal procedures of the criminal court with its rules of evidence and adversary system, and its primary concern with the welfare of the child rather than with guilt or innocence. Under the law, and following the ancient doctrine of *parens patriae*, the court, as the agent of the state, has the right and the responsibility to intervene in cases of child need, including those where violation of the law is involved or likely to be involved. However, there is no unanimity over the world concerning the precise conditions under which courts may intervene. United Nations reports suggest that there is a tendency in many countries to broaden the jurisdiction of the courts to include children who for various reasons are considered to be potentially delinquent, as well as those directly in violation of the law. This tendency, and the lack of rigorously defined rules of "due process" by which a juvenile may be deprived of his liberty or a family of its children, has led to great and widespread concern with the rights of children and their parents.

The flexibility urged as essential to the proper functioning of the court confers great power on juvenile court judges. Concern with the rights of children and parents arises in countries with strong democratic political philosophies, not because miscarriage of justice is probable but rather because it is possible. Hence, a dilemma is built into the structure of juvenile courts: how to provide the discretion and flexibility necessary to the prevention of delinquency and the rehabilitation of delinquents while at the same time preserving due process under the law [see PENOLOGY].

Patterns of delinquency. The *legal status* of "juvenile delinquent" is important in defining, but does not fully encompass, the *social role* of "juvenile delinquent." That is, a youngster who has been taken into custody by the police, or committed to an institution, or otherwise disposed of by the court is likely to be defined as a delinquent by many people—his parents, friends, neighbors, teachers, or employers. The legal process, whether or not it officially defines a youngster as delinquent, may be important in establishing and reinforcing both the community's and the individual's definition of himself as a delinquent (Tannenbaum 1938). These, in turn, may be important factors in deter-

mining the nature of his subsequent experience, and hence the likelihood that he will engage in behavior that is considered delinquent.

Many youngsters take part in activities defined by the statutes as delinquent but are not detected or, if detected, are not brought to the attention of legal authorities. And some of these youngsters, who have not been legally designated as delinquent, are defined as delinquent by others significant to the community and to themselves. The behavioral sciences are concerned with the nature of delinquent behavior, whether or not that behavior has resulted in legal action. For purposes of scientific inquiry *delinquency* may be defined as behavior that is specified by law as grounds for an adjudication of delinquency, and *delinquents* as those young people who engage in such behavior.

The very broad specifications of behavior defined by the statutes as delinquent (some do not define delinquency in behavioral terms at all) give rise to the question: Who is *not* delinquent? The question is important, however, only if we assume that there are only two classes of children—"delinquent" and "nondelinquent"—that need to be described and understood. In reality, children vary in a great many ways in the types of delinquent behavior in which they engage and in the relative frequency, regularity, and versatility of such behavior. In other words, there are different patterns of delinquent behavior and different degrees of involvement in them. Social scientists are interested both in processes accounting for the development of the behavior of youngsters and in the manner in which behavior comes to be defined as delinquent.

The data of delinquency. Official counts of delinquents, or "offenses known," are limited in the extent to which they can contribute to knowledge concerning the extent and nature of delinquency or of the processes involved in becoming delinquent. They represent the actions of officials rather than of young people, and legal rather than scientific concepts of behavior. They provide little information about the characteristics of offenders or their behavior. The very flexibility of legal processes concerned with juveniles calls into question the comparability of official data from one jurisdiction to another. Despite these limitations, for some purposes official data are useful, and they are in any case the only data available for describing certain characteristics of the phenomena. They are particularly useful as reflections of official concern with juvenile delinquency over time, within and between societies. Sellin and Wolfgang (1964) have demonstrated that among broad groups of individuals (police, judges, and college students) there is widespread agreement concerning the perceived seriousness of many crimes; they propose that the seriousness of delinquency problems in different communities and over time be measured from police descriptions of delinquency events that are most likely to be officially recorded. Certainly, variations in official handling of offenders, by age, sex, and other theoretically meaningful categories, reflect varying degrees of social concern with the behavior of young people. In addition, they may provide crude indexes of the behavior of children, which are reliable perhaps only with respect to the most serious types of behavior, for these will most consistently be officially recorded.

Because of the limited usefulness of official data for treatment and etiological purposes, agencies and projects devoted to these ends also generate large bodies of data concerning delinquents. These take three principal forms: clinical reports, usually in the form of intensive case studies, which result from detailed interviews in a clinical setting, with treatment as the primary object of data collection (Hewitt & Jenkins 1947); self-reported behavior, obtained by completion of questionnaires by individuals or by interviewers, with research the primary object of inquiry (Short & Nye 1957–1958; Reiss & Rhodes 1961); and reports of participant and field observation made both by persons interested in treatment or prevention and by those committed primarily to scientific inquiry (Whyte 1943; Miller 1958).

The methodology of delinquency studies has been subject to extensive criticism (Hirschi & Selvin 1962). While it is true that most studies in any substantive field exhibit methodological weaknesses, the field of juvenile delinquency has perhaps been especially vulnerable in this respect. The more fundamental problem has not been methodological, however. Rather, delinquency studies have tended to lack both methodological and theoretical rigor because they have not been associated with the mainstream of behavioral science developments. This was not so much the case in the 1920s and early 1930s, when delinquency studies were an important part of the "Chicago school" of developing urban sociology. Following this period of intensive activity, the empirical study of delinquency dropped off sharply and was largely uninformed by the main body of sociological thought. Clinical studies also lacked the discipline of systematic inquiry, and their impact on sociological interpretations was minimal and marginal. Sociological theory concerning delinquency was greatly stimulated by the publication of Albert Cohen's *Delinquent Boys* in 1955. Still, empirical

inquiry lagged until grants from private and federal agencies made possible investigations of sufficient scope to contribute markedly to the development of knowledge in this field. Passage of the Juvenile Delinquency and Youth Offenses Control Act by the Congress of the United States in 1961 focused unprecedented public attention on juvenile delinquency and provided additional impetus for large-scale social action and research programs directed at the acquisition of new knowledge concerning juvenile delinquency and its control.

Age and sex differences. Throughout the world juvenile court cases tend to be in the older age categories specified by law. Official cases of delinquency thus tend to be a phenomenon of adolescence and young adulthood rather than of childhood. In countries that have experienced increases in delinquency, however, the average age of court appearance has tended to decrease. As services to delinquents and "potential" delinquents become more elaborate, younger children are brought before the court in the interest of delinquency prevention as well as rehabilitation.

In most countries young people are involved in a high proportion of property offenses. In the United States, offenses for which persons under the age of 18 contribute more than one-half of the arrests annually are typically auto theft, burglary, and larceny. Concern is great in some countries over the involvement of juveniles in crimes of violence, in the general disregard for social order, as in cases of property destruction and mass rioting, and in the use of alcohol and narcotics.

Boys and girls are not equally involved in delinquency, and sex ratios are not the same for all types of delinquency. The ratio of boys to girls appearing before juvenile courts is very much related to the over-all social structure of a society, as well as to variations within it. As the social status of women approaches that of men and women gain greater freedom to participate in the affairs of the larger society, socialization patterns in the family and other institutions change and more girls come to the attention of the courts. Present ratios in the United States, for example, are about five boys to each girl; this is a considerable decrease since the early 1900s, when ratios of 50 or 60 to 1 were common. Sex ratios tend to be lower among groups, and in areas, with high delinquency rates. Since World War II increasing proportions of female offenders have been noted especially in Japan and Turkey, where the emancipation of women has proceeded with considerable rapidity.

Boys tend to be arrested for offenses involving stealing and mischief of one sort or another. And while studies indicate that more boys than girls engage in illicit sex behavior, far higher proportions of girls are arrested and brought to court for sex offenses and for other offenses, such as running away, incorrigibility, and delinquent tendencies, which very often involve problems of sex behavior.

Ecological variations. There appears to be a direct relationship between urbanization and juvenile delinquency. Although it is not always true that urban areas with the largest populations and highest densities have the highest delinquency rates, urban areas tend to have higher rates than do "semiurban" areas, and these areas, in turn, have higher rates than do rural areas. Exceptions within the general pattern, at least in the United States, modify but confirm it. Thus, rural areas and smaller communities that are near urban centers have been shown to have higher delinquency rates than do those that are further removed from such centers. Similarly, delinquency rates in relatively less populated areas have been found to be directly related to the size of their nearest urban center. Other studies have found higher proportions of preadolescent and female offenders in more urbanized areas.

Within cities, juvenile delinquency tends to be concentrated in areas characterized by extreme physical deterioration, poverty, and social disorganization. These areas have been called "delinquency areas" because they have been found to be characterized by high delinquency rates and high rates of recidivism over time; they are usually areas in which major shifts have taken place in racial and ethnic residential composition (Shaw & McKay 1942). In high-rate as compared with low-rate areas, age at first delinquency of youngsters appears to be lower, and proportions of female offenders are higher. Organized vice and political corruption flourish in high-rate areas, but there are important variations in these respects between delinquency areas (Kobrin 1951).

Delinquency and race. Racial and ethnic groups have been shown by many studies to have widely varying delinquency rates. Numerous studies have found greater variation within than between these groups, however, depending especially on the type of community areas in which they are located. Newly arrived ethnic groups characteristically locate in high delinquency areas, and their delinquency rates reflect this fact. When these ethnic groups move to areas with lower delinquency rates, their rates become lower. Variations in this pattern serve only to confirm the hypothesis that the amount of delinquency in a racial group is a function of its basic socioeconomic position. Negroes

in the United States, despite some improvements in socioeconomic position (which are reflected in variations in delinquency rates within the Negro population), for many years have had high delinquency rates. These rates are closely associated today, as they have been historically, with high rates of unemployment and economic uncertainty and with family disorganization. By contrast, the Chinese in the United States have had very low delinquency rates. These have been associated with strong family and community organization and with the relative isolation of Chinese Americans from the mainstream of life in the United States.

The association of poverty with high delinquency areas and studies of the socioeconomic background of offenders have led to much speculation concerning the influence of social stratification patterns on young people. Studies suggest that both delinquency rates and the type of delinquency vary in different ecological areas. Delinquency rates even of middle-class and upper-class persons are higher in high-rate areas than in low-rate areas.

International trends. No source of data is adequate for the determination of how much delinquency there is in any country, much less for comparison of the volume of delinquency today with that of the past, or from one country to another. It is evident that public concern with the problem has increased in most countries, especially since World War II. Such published reports as are available from countries involved in both world wars indicate that delinquency rates increased *during* the conflicts (Middendorff 1960; U.S. Children's Bureau 1962; U.S. Federal Bureau of Investigation 1966).

Although a few countries reported stabilized or slightly decreasing delinquency rates during the late 1950s, these reports carried the caution of uncertainty. By contrast, most European countries, Japan, and the United States reported startling increases during this period, and reports filtering out of Russia, China, and various underdeveloped but rapidly changing countries, such as Ghana and Kenya, indicated a high level of public concern and probably actual increases in the incidence of juvenile delinquency. The United Nations has attempted to promote better standards of data gathering and reporting and to arrive at some international consensus as to the volume and nature of delinquency throughout the world.

Delinquency rates in the more technologically and economically advanced countries appear to be the highest in the world. Studies of the relation between delinquency rates and cycles of economic depression and prosperity have yielded inconsistent results (Bogen 1944; Fleisher 1963; Glaser & Rice 1959; Gibbs 1966). In large cities of these same countries high delinquency rates are associated with poverty, as reflected in ecological distributions and rates for persons in different social classes, but in smaller communities delinquency appears to be more evenly distributed throughout the class structure. There is growing interest, but little evidence, concerning increases in delinquent behavior on the part of "middle-class" youngsters in prosperous and technologically advanced countries.

Delinquent subcultures

Just as age, sex, ethnic, and social class distributions of those who come to the attention of authorities for delinquent behavior vary by ecological setting, so also the forms that delinquency takes have characteristic ecological distributions. Far more than delinquency that occurs in the midst of mass rioting, for example, gang delinquency tends to be concentrated in high delinquency areas.

Variations in gang organization and behavior are well documented (Thrasher 1927). There has been much speculation and some research on the existence of regularities amidst such variability. The concept of "delinquent subcultures" has been introduced, in part to describe and in part to account for the forms taken by gang delinquency. Here we are concerned with classifications of delinquency as descriptive categories and with what is known about them.

The term "delinquent subcultures" refers to delinquent behavior, with supporting norms, values, and structures, which is traditional among members of a group or several groups of young people (Cohen 1955). Although Cloward and Ohlin (1960) and others have suggested the following classification of delinquent subcultures, the extent to which concrete subcultures can be clearly differentiated in these terms is still uncertain. *Conflict* subcultures are described as consisting of networks of gangs engaged in periodic disputes over local territory (as within a particular neighborhood), real or imagined insults, proprietary interests in girls, etc. *Criminal* subcultures are oriented toward economic advantage by illegitimate means, through planning and organization, which often involve marketing arrangements and protection from police interference. The gang and these arrangements with adults are characteristic organizational features of criminal subcultures, in contrast with the networks of gangs making up conflict subcultures. *Retreatist* subcultures seek esoteric experience, or "kicks," as in the use of drugs, or participation in "deviant" sexual behavior; here gang organization is sub-ordinated to subcultural forms of experience, regardless of group identity. These three types of subcultures are described as involving chiefly lower-class males, although females are acknowledged to participate in each to some extent (Rice 1963; Short & Strodtbeck 1965).

Middle-class delinquency of a subcultural nature has also been hypothesized; it is said to involve deliberate courting of danger and excessive consumption of alcohol, but with less violence than is found in lower-class subcultures. There are also collective forms of delinquency that are neither gang oriented nor supported by a subcultural system. Of particular note are the mass riots of adolescents that have accompanied public concerts or motion pictures of teen-age "idols" in various Western countries [Middendorff 1960; *see also* DELINQUENCY, *article on* DELINQUENT GANGS]. While these are not common, when they have occurred their "epidemic" character, within countries and from one country to another, suggests the actions of "expressive crowds" which at times have been transformed into "acting crowds" bent on destruction [*see* COLLECTIVE BEHAVIOR]. Higher proportions of leaders than of followers in these crowds have been found to have previous records of delinquency. Participation has ranged broadly across the social class spectrum, however, and involves many youngsters without previous or subsequent participation in delinquency.

A second type of elementary collective behavior involving occasional delinquency has accompanied the spring holidays of students in various countries. Here property destruction and the defiance of adult authority and conventional morality also occur with a considerable element of spontaneity and collective excitement. Delinquency is not the object of those who participate, but it is a frequent result.

There is little research documenting the existence or the nature of delinquent subcultures or other collective forms of delinquency. On the basis of reports from several Western countries, the following conclusions seem warranted concerning subcultures and gangs:

(1) Delinquent gangs exist in many cities and are responsible for much theft, property damage, and violence against persons (themselves and others).

(2) Most but not all countries report that such gangs are especially common among youngsters in the most depressed socioeconomic areas of larger cities and in low-rent housing projects, which in many countries have been built to alleviate housing conditions for lower-class families.

(3) More boys than girls are members of gangs,

and boys are the acknowledged leaders, but girls frequently participate and, when they do, often "instigate" delinquent episodes. Sex relations within the gang most commonly occur between boys and girls who are "going steady," although shifts often occur in such alliances. Marriages, both common-law and legally formalized, frequently occur between gang boys and girls, but the courtship system is not exclusive for either, and many prefer mates who have not participated in any gang, or at least not in their own.

(4) It is evident that youngsters who participate in gangs gain status within the gang as a result of their participation, and in many cases they enjoy the notoriety of gang exploits that results from mass media coverage of delinquent episodes. The mass media thus help to perpetuate, and perhaps to create, both gangs and delinquent subcultures, for it is partially through their coverage of delinquent episodes that delinquents come to know of one another, and gang reputation as a status criterion is enhanced.

(5) Delinquent behavior by gangs is episodic in nature, and, except in rare instances, not all gang members participate in any given episode. Observation suggests that those youngsters who are core members of gangs, particularly those who occupy positions of leadership or are striving to do so, are most likely to be involved in a given episode.

(6) Gang size and structure vary greatly, but gangs with more than fifty members are relatively rare; structure tends to be weak and fluid; and the cohesion of gangs is weak except in times of crisis.

(7) The elaboration of gang "nations" through rough age-grading (senior, junior, midget, peewee branches of a larger gang) or across neighborhood or community lines (East Side and West Side branches, etc.), according to published reports, has occurred only in a few large cities of the United States (New York and Chicago, in particular).

(8) Similarly, hypothesized delinquent subcultures (conflict, criminal, retreatist) appear to exist in relatively pure form only in these large U.S. cities. European studies do not report them. From the United States, fragmentary evidence suggests that in rural areas and in small towns, and in larger cities without the huge concentrations of disadvantaged ethnic populations together with abject poverty such as exist in New York and Chicago, group delinquency does *not* assume the specialized forms described as delinquent subcultures.

This is not to say that delinquency in other areas may not be subcultural in nature. It seems likely, both theoretically and empirically, that in many instances it is. Youngsters who "get into trouble"

in any local institutional context tend to know one another and, through such processes as exclusion from circles of nontroublemakers, the search for solutions to common problems, and mutual attraction, they tend to be thrown into interaction with one another (Empey & Rabow 1961). Legal definitions seem crucial, for they provide a common identity of those processed, for themselves and for others.

In summary, the concept of delinquent subcultures requires greater theoretical and empirical specification. Whether it will prove to be a viable concept will depend upon demonstration of utility not otherwise provided by such concepts as personality, group and community process, collective behavior, and concepts of social class subcultures.

Class, personality, and group process

Discussions of collective patterns of delinquency are couched largely in terms of the position of lower-class adolescents in the social structure. Community and group-process variables, which are more immediate in the experience of individuals and groups, provide a possible linkage between theories couched in terms of social structural variables and those based on personality considerations.

Thus, Miller (1958) describes gang delinquency as a manifestation of various lower-class "focal concerns," such as *trouble, toughness, smartness, excitement, fate,* and *autonomy.* Similarly, Cloward and Ohlin (1960) describe relations between adolescents and adults at the community level as crucial in determining the nature of collective delinquent behavior on the part of juveniles. But in neither case are personality variables integrated either theoretically or empirically with social and cultural concepts.

The group has been described as the context of much delinquency, and Cohen (1955), especially, has stressed its catalytic nature by virtue of which more extreme behavior occurs than otherwise would be likely on the part of participating individuals. More recently, in experimentally manipulated groups in treatment cottages and in gangs in their natural community settings, such group processes as role playing and status striving have been found to be involved in the precipitation of delinquency episodes (Short & Strodtbeck 1965). Recruitment to particular group roles may prove, in part, to be a function of individual personality characteristics.

Role performance is likely also to be linked in important ways to personality. The observation that gang leaders often react to status threats by leading or attempting to lead the group in delinquency episodes is a case in point. It seems likely that what is considered threatening will in important ways be determined by the experience and the personality configuration of the individual leader. It can hardly be doubted that personality considerations, in addition to role and situational elements, are involved in a broader spectrum of delinquent behavior.

Psychological types of delinquents. Several psychological types of delinquents have been proposed. The classification with perhaps the greatest amount of theoretical and research specification is that which describes three major types and discusses their social correlates (Reiss 1952; cf. Hewitt & Jenkins 1947). *The relatively integrated delinquent*, characterized by adequate personal controls, accounts for nearly two-thirds of the boys classified. This offender often is a member of an organized group and characteristically resides in a high delinquency area; his family socialization is conventional and reasonably adequate. In contrast, *the relatively weak ego delinquent* is described as an insecure, internally conflicted, and anxious person. His offense pattern characteristically includes property destruction and other aggressive acts, but not gang membership. *The defective superego delinquent* has failed to internalize conventional standards of conduct and is, instead, oriented toward deviant groups. His offense pattern, like that of the integrated delinquent, typically involves property offenses and aggressive behavior in a gang context. He is described as having been socialized in a broken home characterized by much conflict and nonconventional behavior.

Repeated attempts to demonstrate that there is a "delinquent" personality type have failed. The few studies that have employed control groups have compared "delinquents" with "nondelinquents," without regard for more subtle differences in delinquency involvement. On the basis of such studies, it appears that delinquents are characterized by greater aggressive tendencies and less neuroticism than are nondelinquents (Glueck & Glueck 1950).

The relation between various personality characteristics and processes, on the one hand, and patterns of delinquency involvement, on the other hand, is unclear, theoretically and empirically. Viewed as a special case of collective adaptations by young people generally, this relation is one of the most significant unknowns in the behavioral sciences.

JAMES F. SHORT, JR.

[See also CRIME, *article on* CAUSES OF CRIME; DEVIANT BEHAVIOR.]

BIBLIOGRAPHY

BOGEN, DAVID 1944 Juvenile Delinquency and Economic Trend. *American Sociological Review* 9:178–184.

CLOWARD, RICHARD A.; and OHLIN, LLOYD E. 1960 *Delinquency and Opportunity: A Theory of Delinquent Gangs.* Glencoe, Ill.: Free Press.

COHEN, ALBERT K. (1955) 1963 *Delinquent Boys: The Culture of the Gang.* New York: Free Press.

EMPEY, LAMAR T.; and RABOW, JEROME 1961 The Provo Experiment in Delinquency Rehabilitation. *American Sociological Review* 26:679–695. → A discussion by E. P. Schwartz appears on pages 695–696.

FLEISHER, BELTON M. 1963 The Effect of Unemployment on Juvenile Delinquency. *Journal of Political Economy* 71:543–555.

GIBBS, JACK P. 1966 Crime, Unemployment and Status Integration. *British Journal of Criminology* 6:49–58.

GLASER, DANIEL; and RICE, KENT 1959 Crime, Age, and Employment. *American Sociological Review* 24:679–686.

GLUECK, SHELDON; and GLUECK, ELEANOR 1950 *Unraveling Juvenile Delinquency.* New York: Commonwealth Fund.

HEWITT, LESTER E.; and JENKINS, RICHARD L. 1947 *Fundamental Patterns of Maladjustment: The Dynamics of Their Origin.* Springfield, Ill.: Thomas.

HIRSCHI, TRAVIS; and SELVIN, HANAN C. 1962 The Methodological Adequacy of Delinquency Research. Unpublished manuscript, Univ. of California, Survey Research Center.

KOBRIN, SOLOMON 1951 The Conflict of Values in Delinquency Areas. *American Sociological Review* 16:653–661.

MIDDENDORFF, WOLF 1960 *New Forms of Juvenile Delinquency: Their Origin, Prevention and Treatment.* New York: United Nations, Department of Economic and Social Affairs.

MILLER, WALTER B. 1958 Lower Class Culture as a Generating Milieu of Gang Delinquency. *Journal of Social Issues* 14, no. 3:5–19.

REISS, ALBERT J. JR. 1952 Social Correlates of Psychological Types of Delinquency. *American Sociological Review* 17:710–718.

REISS, ALBERT J. JR.; and RHODES, ALBERT LEWIS 1961 Delinquency and Social Class Structure. *American Sociological Review* 26:720–732.

RICE, ROBERT 1963 The Persian Queens. *New Yorker* October 19:153–187.

SELLIN, THORSTEN; and WOLFGANG, MARVIN 1964 *The Measurement of Delinquency.* New York: Wiley.

SHAW, CLIFFORD R.; and McKAY, HENRY D. 1942 *Juvenile Delinquency and Urban Areas: A Study of Rates of Delinquents in Relation to Differential Characteristics of Local Communities in American Cities.* Univ. of Chicago Press.

SHORT, JAMES F. JR.; and NYE, F. IVAN 1957–1958 Reported Behavior as a Criterion of Deviant Behavior. *Social Problems* 5:207–213.

SHORT, JAMES F. JR.; and STRODTBECK, FRED L. 1965 *Group Process and Gang Delinquency.* Univ. of Chicago Press.

TANNENBAUM, FRANK (1938) 1963 *Crime and the Community.* New York: Columbia Univ. Press.

THRASHER, FREDERIC M. (1927) 1963 *The Gang: A Study of 1,313 Gangs in Chicago.* Abridged and with an introduction by James F. Short, Jr. Univ. of Chicago Press. → A revised edition of Thrasher's classic work, with a new introduction which appraises recent developments in theory and research on delinquent gangs.

U.S. CHILDREN'S BUREAU 1962 *Juvenile Court Statistics: 1961.* Washington: Government Printing Office.

U.S. FEDERAL BUREAU OF INVESTIGATION 1966 *Uniform Crime Reports for the United States and Its Possessions: 1965.* Washington: Government Printing Office.

VAN WATERS, MIRIAM 1932 Juvenile Delinquency and Juvenile Courts. Volume 8, pages 528–533 in *Encyclopaedia of the Social Sciences.* New York: Macmillan.

WHYTE, WILLIAM F. (1943) 1961 *Street Corner Society: The Social Structure of an Italian Slum.* 2d ed., enl. Univ. of Chicago Press. → Contains an extensive methodological statement.

II
SOCIOLOGICAL ASPECTS

Theories of delinquency causation can best be understood as a part of the social context in which they are developed. Two features of that social context seem crucial to an understanding of current theories. First, most of the systematic explanatory efforts have come from the United States, where a pragmatically oriented social science developed early in the twentieth century and has continued to flourish. Thus, despite the historically important theoretical works (Lombroso 1899; Bonger 1905) and systematic treatises on criminology (Hurwitz 1947) contributed by European scholars, as well as the growing number of careful empirical studies from Scandinavia (Christie 1960), England (Morris 1958), and other European countries, most of the systematic theories continue to reflect the dominant trends in American social science. Second, within American social science the subject matter of delinquency has been a primary concern of sociologists, who have done most of the research and written most of the texts, and a secondary but still important concern of psychologists; it has received less attention from the other social science disciplines.

Theories of delinquency causation

The following review of five theoretical emphases will illustrate the range of current efforts to understand the causation of delinquency. It will omit work done primarily from within a biological or physiological perspective, as well as that done within a psychoanalytic framework.

Psychogenic theories. Since shortly after the turn of the century a number of essays and studies have located the causal processes of delinquency within the individual delinquent. Many of these contributions have come from clinical experience with delinquent youths. The central argument is that delinquency is a "solution" to psychological problems stemming primarily from faulty or pathological family interaction patterns.

The research and theoretical interpretations of Healy and Bronner (1936) provide an excellent example of this approach. These investigators systematically compared delinquent youths with their nondelinquent siblings. The most important difference between them was that over 90 per cent of the delinquents, as compared to 13 per cent of their nondelinquent siblings, had unhappy home lives and felt discontented with their life circumstances. The nature of the unhappiness differed: some felt rejected by parents; others felt inadequate or inferior; others were jealous of siblings; still others were affected by a more deep-seated mental conflict. But whatever the nature of the unhappiness, delinquency was seen as a solution. It brought attention to those who suffered from parental neglect, provided support from peers for those who felt inadequate, and brought on punishment for those who sought to reduce guilt feelings. This study, though published in 1936, is still the prototype of studies following what may be called a psychogenic model, that is, studies that search for the causes of delinquency in the psychological make-up of the delinquent, which typically stems from specific styles of family interaction.

Later studies in this tradition have more clearly identified detailed aspects of family relations that seem important, but they have not altered the fundamental point of view. McCord, McCord, and Zola (1959) found that among youths from areas of low socioeconomic status, delinquents differed from nondelinquents in the extent of parental rejection and in the inconsistency of punishment and discipline. Bandura and Walters (1959) gathered detailed interview data from adolescents with records of highly aggressive actions and compared them with a control sample of nondelinquents. Their investigation suggested that the delinquent youths differed from the nondelinquent controls relatively little in their relationship with their mothers but that they had much less identification with their fathers. In addition, discipline was meted out in a harsher manner within the families of the delinquents. Also, the more aggressive, delinquent boys had poor relations with their peers, while the boys with more healthy family relations had stronger peer relations as well.

In the interpretations of these studies, the psychogenic model is clearly in operation: unfortunate, unhappy family circumstances lead to personal psychological problems of adjustment for the youth, which in turn are in some way solved by the commission of delinquent acts. Attention focuses on the boy, his family, and their problems. Delinquency is assumed to be a form of reaction to the problems.

Sociogenic theories.   At about the time that Healy and Bronner and others were studying the psychogenic sources of delinquency, social scientists at the University of Chicago were impressed by the force of culture and social disorganization in a rapidly expanding city filled with immigrants and other minorities. In a series of investigations of crime rates in the urban area, it was found that rates of delinquency were stable from one period to another, that the largest percentage of youths committed their delinquencies in companionship with others, and that a series of sociocultural characteristics were typically associated with the areas where high rates were found. These characteristics included rapid turnover of population; a sizable portion of the land used for industrial buildings; high rates of minority-group membership; and high rates of social disruption as reflected in broken homes, suicide, alcoholism, and related problems. The studies of Thrasher (1927), Shaw and McKay (1942), and Shaw and Moore (1931) report both evidence and argument in line with this tradition.

In the face of these characteristics, it was natural for students of delinquency to see important causes residing not in the youth's family alone but in the cultural context of his home and neighborhood. In such areas a boy's "natural history" was to participate in delinquent careers (Shaw 1929). No specific psychological block seemed necessary; patterns of delinquent and criminal action were all around. Joining in those patterns would be natural for all except those restrained by close family life or by strong ties to conventional community institutions such as the school.

In this research tradition the key concept for understanding why youths became delinquent was association with other youths already delinquent. This was later put most clearly by Sutherland, who developed the theory of *differential association* (Sutherland & Cressey 1960). This theory asserts that youths become delinquent to the extent that they participate in settings where delinquent ideas or techniques are viewed favorably: the earlier, the more frequently, the more intensely, and the longer the duration of the youths' association in such settings, the greater the probability of their becoming delinquent. Unlike the psychogenic theories this set of ideas focuses on *what is learned* and who it is learned from rather than on the problems that might produce a *motivation* to commit delinquencies. Support for this theory has been found both in studies using the method of self-reported delinquent behavior (Clark & Wenninger 1962; Akers 1964) and in those using official crime data (Reiss & Rhodes 1964).

Theories of delinquent subcultures.   At least until the early 1950s the two perspectives reviewed above were the dominant forms of theories attempting to link individuals with delinquency. In the decade of the 1950s, however, attention was drawn to organized-gang activities more insistently than in the past. Partly this was because of an apparent increase in the amount of violence and crime engaged in by such groups, and partly because it seemed to reflect the nearly universal importance of the gang in industrialized countries. In any event, there were enough differences between the formally organized gangs studied and reported on during the 1950s and the somewhat looser aggregates usually referred to in the earlier studies to generate a new series of theoretical efforts focused on the organized street gang.

The central concept that emerged to encompass the phenomenon of the gangs was that of the *delinquent subculture.* The concept "culture" refers to the set of values and norms that guide the behavior of group members; the prefix "sub" indicates that these cultures often emerge in the midst of a more inclusive system. Delinquent subculture refers, then, to a system of values and beliefs encouraging the commission of delinquencies, awarding status on the basis of such acts, and specifying typical relationships to persons who fall outside the delinquents' social world.

Several variations of the theory of subcultures have been formulated, each of which provides a distinctive way of locating the nature of the delinquent patterns, the sources that give rise to the patterns, and the functions the patterns serve for the groups where they are found. Leading statements of this theory include those of Cohen (1955), Cloward and Ohlin (1960), and Miller (1958). Variations or modifications have been suggested by Yablonsky (1962), Bordua (1961), and Spergel (1964). Detailed review of the various ideas cannot be provided here, but it is important to note the central line of argument, for it has something in common with both of its predecessors. Like the more general sociogenic theories, the sources of the problem are found in the nature of the social structure and the particular patterns of neighborhood and community life where delinquent gangs abound: high population density, low socioeconomic status, high rates of family disorganization. No matter how the particular argument is framed, there is agreement on the *general* source of delinquent subcultures within the broader context of urban slum life.

Unlike those involved in earlier sociogenic work, most subculture theorists have been unwilling to rest with the concept of differential association and the explanatory power it provides. Like the psychogenic theorists, they have seen the formation of delinquent gangs and subcultures as a *reaction* to the problems caused by low social status in a world where high status is valued and yet where access to the means to high status is relatively unavailable to them. In this feature, the explanatory model derives from the more general theory of deviant behavior and anomie (Merton 1938).

The situational delinquent. The theories outlined above have one quality in common. In all of them delinquency is viewed as having deep roots. In the psychogenic tradition these roots lie primarily within the individual, while in the sociogenic tradition they lie in the structure of the society, with emphasis either on the ecological areas where delinquency prevails or on the systematic way in which the social structure places some individuals in a poor position to compete for success. But no matter where the emphasis is laid, it is clear that in these theories delinquency is a serious business, requiring for its prevention or correction a fundamental reorganization of the psyche, the social structure, or the culture.

The conception of the situational delinquent provides a different perspective. Here, the assumption is that delinquency is not deeply rooted, that the motives for delinquency are often relatively simple. And if they are not so deep, then perhaps their causes do not lie in the deeper recesses of the psyche and the social order but are closer to the immediate contingencies of action in the everyday world. Such a conception of the nature of delinquent motives forces a closer examination of the immediate social context of delinquency and of the problems of adolescent youth rather than of the more distant problems of achieving middle-class status from lower-class origins.

This conception is receiving increased attention from students of delinquency. It is partially reflected in the provocative treatment by Matza (1964*a*; 1964*b*), who restores the concept of "will" to the study of delinquency and argues persuasively that potential and actual delinquents assess risks and engage in rationalizations in much the manner suggested by the traditional criminal law. He notes, for example, that when delinquents offer excuses for their acts, the excuses bear a close resemblance to those provided within the traditional law of crimes. And he emphasizes the shifting, transitory character of delinquent acts and actors.

Other students reflect a similar perspective in varying degrees. In one of the principal empirical studies of gang delinquency, sociologists James Short and Fred Strodtbeck (1965) began with the orientations suggested by the conception of a delinquent subculture but became increasingly persuaded of the necessity to study immediate group process and interaction. Briar and Piliavin (1965) provide further argument in favor of a situational approach.

Delinquency and secondary deviation. Tannenbaum (1938) suggested years ago that the formation of delinquent careers owed much to the stigma and labeling associated with the processing of delinquents by the police, courts, and other agencies. Since almost all adolescents engage in some form of delinquency, the interesting explanatory problem may be why some *continue* and others do not. Lemert (1964) speaks of *secondary deviation* to refer to the deviant acts that appear to have as their cause the limitations placed on normal functioning by the *prior* definition of the person as a deviant. The strong suggestion is that the development of a disciplined delinquent career is a response to the labeling and stigma that result from official treatment as a deviant. Whatever the source of the initial delinquent act, the labeling and stigma that result from the official processing provide important new stimulus toward delinquency, for the actor is invited, implicitly, to assume a delinquent *role*.

This emphasis directs attention to an underdeveloped area in the general theory of deviant behavior, the analysis of the deviant's response to the organized system of social control (Cohen 1965). In the case of delinquency there are still no definitive studies that clearly trace the consequences of official sanctions *per se* on the later conduct of the delinquent. The theoretical emphasis on secondary deviance points strongly to the need for such studies.

Social definitions of delinquency. In all of the theoretical schemes traced thus far, the emphasis remains on the delinquent and the forces that move him toward or away from delinquency. Yet one of the most interesting features of delinquency is the way it is socially defined by conventional people. Unlike some of the more traditional areas of criminal law, the concept of delinquency is only vaguely spelled out in legislation. The result is that much room is open for discretion in the designation of conduct patterns as "delinquent." This discretion is in the hands of police and judicial officials, with the result that delinquency is in a very real sense a product of the *interaction* between adolescents and officials and cannot easily be understood by focusing on only one side of the interaction (Wheeler 1965).

Thus, theories of delinquency are beginning to be concerned with the conduct of officials, since that conduct is an integral part of the official labeling of persons as delinquent. Political scientist James Q. Wilson has found, in comparative studies of police administration carried out in the mid-1960s, that variations in the juvenile arrest rate in two different cities may be largely a function of differences in the nature and type of police organization in the cities. These differences are not merely a function of differing degrees of police efficiency; rather, they reflect differences in what is conceived to be delinquent conduct. This view requires a radical reconstruction of theories of delinquency, one that focuses jointly on the behavior, background, and social setting of the delinquent *and* on the behavior, background, and social setting of those who are officially charged with responding to delinquency. This perspective, of course, is not limited to delinquency. It is equally applicable to a broad range of deviant behavior patterns (Becker 1963; Cicourel & Kitsuse 1963).

Limitations of current theories. Among the many problems and issues facing all those who would develop systematic theories of delinquency causation, the following seem most important.

Adequacy of data. The theories reviewed above all suffer heavily from a lack of adequate supportive data. Most of the theories require for their test the gathering of information about adolescents that is of a type not routinely collected by the official agencies that deal with youth. This is perhaps most true of the theories that emphasize collective enterprise among delinquents, as well as situational elements and structures. Record-keeping systems are designed to report individual acts of delinquency and typically provide very little information about the surrounding social context. It is an especially demanding and exacting enterprise to gather systematic data of a type that bears closely on the truth value of the various theories.

Reconciling divergent perspectives. The several perspectives described above may each be valid, but for differing sectors of the adolescent population. Delinquency is a blanket concept that of course conceals a variety of different types of delinquent acts. One way of harmonizing the various perspectives is to note their applicability to different types of delinquents. Hewitt and Jenkins (1947) have provided one such typology, Reiss (1952) has provided another, and Gibbons (1965) has reviewed a variety of such efforts for both delinquents and adult offenders.

Still another way of reconciling the divergent perspectives is to assume that they interact under appropriate conditions to produce delinquency. While most students would agree with Cohen's critique (1955) of multiple-causation theories as inadequate, most would also agree that the several processes described above may interact to produce effects that no one of them would produce operating alone. One or two empirical studies, for example, show the joint effects of socioeconomic status and family pathology on delinquency (Stanfield 1966). Yet this area of research is still grossly underdeveloped.

Practical implications. A seemingly important practical consequence of a theory of delinquency causation is that it might suggest action strategies for the prevention or control of delinquent conduct. Although the action implications of some of the above theories have never been spelled out clearly, there are at least a few instances in which preventive programs have developed (Powers & Witmer 1951; Miller 1962; Mobilization for Youth, Inc. 1961). Although it is too early to draw firm conclusions, most investigators would agree that the programs to date have not proved effective. A chief problem remains to spell out clearly the practical implications of the theories, to design preventive or corrective programs that embody those ideas, and to provide careful empirical tests of the results when the theories are applied.

Cross-national studies. The theories treated here find the causes of delinquency within the family, the neighborhood, the community, or in one's location in the social order. They do not relate delinquency directly to the forces of mass society itself. Yet it is the burden of argument of much serious social criticism and broader social theory that the problems ought to be couched at the level of mass society itself. The modern bureaucratized world, it is argued, produces a broad malaise, a sense of alienation from work and community, a loss of identity, and a decline in meaningful experience. The resulting anomie leads to many deviant reactions, among them delinquency.

These ideas are too broad and general to constitute a theory of delinquency that is subject to careful empirical test, but it is fitting to close this article by noting that problems of delinquency are indeed common to most of the industrialized world. A grave limitation of current theories lies in the absence of a genuine cross-national focus upon delinquency. Despite the technical problems that arise in cross-national research, it seems an essential ingredient if our theories are not to be highly limited in their scope and explanatory capacity.

Stanton Wheeler

[*Directly related are the entries* Crime, *article on* causes of crime; Criminology; Deviant behavior. *Other relevant material may be found in* ADOLESCENCE; *and in the biography of* SUTHER-LAND.]

BIBLIOGRAPHY

AKERS, RONALD L. 1964 Socio-economic Status and Delinquent Behavior: A Retest. *Journal of Research in Crime and Delinquency* 1:38–46.

BANDURA, ALBERT; and WALTERS, RICHARD H. 1959 *Adolescent Aggression: A Study of the Influence of Child-training Practices and Family Interrelationships.* New York: Ronald Press.

BECKER, HOWARD S. 1963 *Outsiders: Studies in the Sociology of Deviance.* New York and London: Free Press.

BONGER, WILLIAM A. (1905) 1916 *Criminality and Economic Conditions.* Boston: Little. → First published as *Criminalité et conditions économiques.*

BORDUA, DAVID J. 1961 Delinquent Subcultures: Sociological Interpretations of Gang Delinquency. American Academy of Political and Social Science, *Annals* 338:119–136.

BRIAR, SCOTT; and PILIAVIN, IRVING 1965 Delinquency, Situational Inducements, and Commitment to Conformity. *Social Problems* 13:35–45.

CHRISTIE, NELS 1960 *Unge Norske lovovertredere.* Universitetet ï Oslo, Institutt for Kriminologi og Strafferet, Skrifter, No. 4. Oslo and Bergen: Universitetsforlaget.

CICOUREL, AARON V.; and KITSUSE, JOHN I. 1963 A Note on the Uses of Official Statistics. *Social Problems* 11:131–139.

CLARK, JOHN P.; and WENNINGER, EUGENE P. 1962 Socio-economic Class and Area as Correlates of Illegal Behavior Among Juveniles. *American Sociological Review* 27:826–834.

CLOWARD, RICHARD A.; and OHLIN, LLOYD E. 1960 *Delinquency and Opportunity: A Theory of Delinquent Gangs.* Glencoe, Ill.: Free Press.

COHEN, ALBERT K. (1955) 1963 *Delinquent Boys: The Culture of the Gang.* New York: Free Press.

COHEN, ALBERT K. 1965 The Sociology of the Deviant Act: Anomie Theory and Beyond. *American Sociological Review* 30:5–14.

GIBBONS, DON C. 1965 *Changing the Lawbreaker: The Treatment of Delinquents and Criminals.* Englewood Cliffs, N.J.: Prentice-Hall.

HEALY, WILLIAM; and BRONNER, AUGUSTA F. 1936 *New Light on Delinquency and Its Treatment.* New Haven: Yale Univ. Press.

HEWITT, LESTER E.; and JENKINS, RICHARD L. 1947 *Fundamental Patterns of Maladjustment: The Dynamics of Their Origin.* Springfield, Ill.: Thomas.

HURWITZ, STEPHAN (1947) 1952 *Criminology.* London: Allen & Unwin. → First published in Danish.

LEMERT, EDWIN M. 1964 Social Structure, Social Control and Deviation. Pages 57–97 in Marshall B. Clinard (editor), *Anomie and Deviant Behavior: A Discussion and Critique.* New York: Free Press.

LOMBROSO, CESARE (1899) 1911 *Crime: Its Causes and Remedies.* Boston: Little. → First published in French.

McCORD, WILLIAM; McCORD, JOAN; and ZOLA, IRVING K. 1959 *Origins of Crime: A New Evaluation of the Cambridge–Somerville Youth Study.* New York: Columbia Univ. Press.

MATZA, DAVID 1964a *Delinquency and Drift.* New York: Wiley.

MATZA, DAVID 1964b Position and Behavior Patterns of Youth. Pages 191–216 in Robert E. L. Faris (editor), *Handbook of Modern Sociology.* Chicago: Rand McNally.

MERTON, ROBERT K. 1938 Social Structure and Anomie. *American Sociological Review* 3:672–682.

MILLER, WALTER B. 1958 Lower Class Culture as a Generating Milieu of Gang Delinquency. *Journal of Social Issues* 14, no. 3:5–19.

MILLER, WALTER B. 1962 The Impact of a "Total-community" Delinquency Control Project. *Social Problems* 10:168–191.

MOBILIZATION FOR YOUTH, INC. 1961 *A Proposal for the Prevention and Control of Delinquency by Expanding Opportunities.* New York: Mobilization for Youth, Training Department.

MORRIS, TERENCE 1958 *The Criminal Area: A Study in Social Ecology.* London: Routledge; New York: Humanities.

POWERS, EDWIN; and WITMER, HELEN 1951 *An Experiment in the Prevention of Delinquency: The Cambridge–Somerville Youth Study.* New York: Columbia Univ. Press; Oxford Univ. Press.

REISS, ALBERT J. JR. 1952 Social Correlates of Psychological Types of Delinquency. *American Sociological Review.* 17:717–718.

REISS, ALBERT J. JR.; and RHODES, A. LEWIS 1964 An Empirical Test of Differential Association Theory. *Journal of Research in Crime and Delinquency* 1:5–18.

SHAW, CLIFFORD R. 1929 *Delinquency Areas: A Study of the Geographic Distribution of School Truants, Juvenile Delinquents, and Adult Offenders in Chicago.* Univ. of Chicago Press.

SHAW, CLIFFORD R.; and McKAY, HENRY D. 1942 *Juvenile Delinquency and Urban Areas: A Study of Rates of Delinquents in Relation to Differential Characteristics of Local Communities in American Cities.* Univ. of Chicago Press.

SHAW, CLIFFORD R.; and MOORE, M. E. 1931 *Natural History of a Delinquent Career.* Univ. of Chicago Press.

SHORT, JAMES F. JR.; and STRODTBECK, FRED L. 1965 *Group Process and Gang Delinquency.* Univ. of Chicago Press.

SPERGEL, IRVING A. 1964 *Racketville, Slumtown, Haulburg: An Exploratory Study of Delinquent Subcultures.* Univ. of Chicago Press.

STANFIELD, ROBERT E. 1966 The Interaction of Family Variables and Gang Variables in the Aetiology of Delinquency. *Social Problems* 13:411–417.

SUTHERLAND, EDWIN H.; and CRESSEY, DONALD R. 1960 *Principles of Criminology.* 6th ed. New York: Lippincott. → First published in 1924 as a textbook, *Criminology,* under the sole authorship of Edwin H. Sutherland.

TANNENBAUM, FRANK (1938) 1963 *Crime and the Community.* New York: Columbia Univ. Press.

THRASHER, FREDERIC (1927) 1960 *The Gang: A Study of 1,313 Gangs in Chicago.* 2d ed., rev. Univ. of Chicago Press. → An abridged edition was published in 1963.

WHEELER, STANTON 1965 Criminal Statistics: A Reformulation of the Problem. American Statistical Association, Social Statistics Section, *Proceedings* [1965]: 29–35.

YABLONSKY, LEWIS 1962 *The Violent Gang.* New York: Macmillan.

III
PSYCHOLOGICAL ASPECTS

Ironically, as nations grow richer and the opportunities for youth multiply, juvenile delinquency seems to increase steadily. In almost every society, of course, adults have complained about the presumed immorality of children. Even Socrates in the fifth century B.C. sounded an alarm about the "delinquents" of his time. Editorialists today echo Socrates' opinion, but in our era, laments about the condition of young people may have more to sustain them.

Incidence of delinquency. While every statistic in the measurement of crime remains open to doubt, there seems little reason to deny that delinquency grows as a society becomes industrialized and urbanized (Bloch & Geis 1962). In England, for example, the best studies indicate that burglaries committed by delinquents climbed almost 200 per cent between 1938 and 1961; sex offenses, by about 300 per cent; and violent crimes by an astounding 2,200 per cent (Mays 1963). The United States, that classical arena for crime, exhibits a similar trend: juvenile crimes have gone up since 1940 by about 93 per cent (Bloch & Geis 1962, p. 186). These statistics refer only to officially recognized crimes. Many juvenile offenses remain undetected or, if recorded, go unpunished. Indeed, as John Mays's studies have shown, virtually every child in certain urban areas has participated in a wide range of delinquent activities even though only 10 per cent or 15 per cent of the youthful population are recognized by the courts as delinquents (Mays 1963).

Using official definitions of delinquency, it appears that as a society progresses materially, crime increasingly becomes the prerogative of youth. Thus, in the United States during the 1950s, crimes committed by boys under eighteen increased six times as rapidly as crimes committed by adults. By 1961, American children accounted for 8 per cent of the arrests for murders, 20 per cent of rapes, 51 per cent of burglaries, and 62 per cent of auto thefts. As many as one-fifth of American boys between the ages of ten and seventeen have appeared before courts or have been arrested by police (Bloch & Geis 1962).

Every affluent nation faces a similar problem. Juvenile crime has grown immoderately during the last fifty years and has outdistanced the rate of many types of adult crime. To understand this phenomenon requires some comprehension of the relation of culture, social structure, and early environmental experiences as they combine to produce psychological types prone to delinquency. The first step toward such knowledge is to review briefly the great fund of knowledge concerning the characteristics of delinquents.

General characteristics

Psychological studies of delinquents have traditionally been concerned with how delinquents differ from nondelinquents in intellectual structure, physiological constitution, and personality characteristics.

Intellectual structure of delinquents. In 1912, Henry H. Goddard initiated research on the intelligence of delinquents (Goddard 1921), and his original endeavors stimulated hundreds of similar studies. Goddard administered a crude test of intelligence to incarcerated delinquents and found that 50 per cent were "feeble-minded." Later research appeared to confirm this result. Edwin H. Sutherland, for example, surveyed 340 studies of delinquents conducted up to 1928 (Sutherland 1931). He reported that these studies found that from 50 per cent to 20 per cent of delinquents were feeble-minded.

More recent research utilizing more sophisticated tests has, however, tended not to support the earlier studies. L. A. Siebert, for example, tested 8,003 court cases. The average IQ of these delinquents was 91.4, slightly below the national average (Siebert 1962). Caplan, who has reviewed contemporary evidence, concludes that delinquents differ from nondelinquents only by approximately eight points on standard intelligence tests (Caplan 1965). This inconsequential difference can be explained in a number of ways: more intelligent delinquents may escape detection by the police, or perhaps the fact that the tests are normally administered in a stressful situation (such as a juvenile reformatory) may affect the performance of delinquents.

While the general intelligence of delinquents does not differ significantly from that of nondelinquents, there may be specific cognitive functions where differences exist. Wechsler has found that delinquents usually score higher on "performance" tasks than on those which require verbal skill (Wechsler 1939). This characteristic seems, however, to be a reflection of the lower socioeconomic status of delinquents, rather than specifically of their criminal activities (Caplan 1965). Baker and Sarbin have found that delinquents utilize a relatively limited number of cognitive categories in viewing the outside world (Baker & Sarbin 1956). In consequence, they are less able to tolerate ambiguities, less able to predict the behavior of others, and tend to deal with other human beings as if they were simply "mirror images" of the delinquents themselves. [See INTELLIGENCE AND INTELLIGENCE TESTING.]

Physique and physiology of delinquents. A number of investigators have long been concerned with examining the constitution of delinquents, on the assumption that certain physical traits might determine the character and actions of the delinquent. Lombroso may be considered the founder of this school of thought. He believed that delinquents were "moral idiots" who differed from normal men in basic and inborn physical characteristics (Lombroso 1899). Goring and others have subsequently disproved Lombroso's specific claims (Goring 1913), but more sophisticated researchers have found evidence to support the belief that the physique of delinquents differs from that of nondelinquents. These investigators have compared the total body structure of delinquents and nondelinquents and have found, generally, that delinquents tend more often to be "mesomorphs" (relatively muscular, tightly knit people). Work by Sheldon (Sheldon 1949) and by the Gluecks (Glueck & Glueck 1950) supports this view. The Gluecks, for example, found that 60 per cent of their sample of delinquents could be typed as mesomorphs. Although the matter remains in great dispute, there seems, on the whole, to be sufficient evidence to conclude that delinquents are more often mesomorphic. Such a finding may, of course, be interpreted in a number of different ways. Some scholars contend that mesomorphy may be considered as a reflection rather than a cause of delinquency, since obviously most delinquent acts require a fairly muscular physique. Other scholars would attribute greater significance to the research findings and would contend that the bodily constitution is a basic causal factor (e.g., mesomorphs, at birth, are presumably more aggressive; as they grow up, this higher level of aggression may push them toward delinquency). [See PSYCHOLOGY, *article on* CONSTITUTIONAL PSYCHOLOGY.]

Other investigators have been concerned with various specific neurological and physiological functions of delinquents. Lindner, for example, has noted that a high proportion of delinquents underreact to painful stimuli (Lindner 1942/1943). Stafford-Clark has found that delinquents exhibit more signs of physical immaturities or "developmental anomalies" than do nondelinquents (Stafford-Clark et al. 1951). The Ostrows, as well as other investigators, have reported that delinquents have more indications of neurological disorders than does a normal population (Ostrow & Ostrow 1946). These various results can again be interpreted in several ways. It could be that the higher rate of physical disorders is simply a result of environmental deprivation, or it may be that, in some cases, a physiological malfunction plays a causal role in producing delinquency.

Personality characteristics of delinquents. Many psychologists have been concerned with defining the particular personality traits which lead people to become delinquents. Siegman in Israel found, for example, that delinquents are highly "present-oriented" and do not plan for the future (Siegman 1961). In a series of studies Hathaway and Monachesi have utilized the Minnesota Multiphasic Personality Inventory to delineate various personality patterns of delinquents (Hathaway & Monachesi 1953). They have shown that many delinquents are emotionally disturbed, but equally important, that certain types of emotional disorder are negatively correlated with delinquency.

Dinitz and his colleagues have longitudinally studied a group of boys who had been exposed to social influences which, under usual circumstances, produce delinquency (Dinitz et al. 1958). The delinquents in this group were less "socialized," less responsible, and more often perceived themselves as likely "to get into trouble."

While these studies are highly provocative, the evidence suggests that there is no single personality pattern which characterizes all delinquents, or even a majority of delinquents. In 1950, Schuessler and Cressey reviewed 113 investigations and concluded that delinquency and specific personality traits were not related (Schuessler & Cressey 1950). More recently, Quay has examined the literature and decided that there are particular *types* of delinquents who differ from each other and have distinctive personality characteristics (Quay 1965). To understand fully the psychological aspects of delinquency, then, it is necessary to examine each of these various types.

Types of delinquency

With some precision and a degree of practical utility, juvenile delinquents can be categorized into three general classes: the socialized delinquent, the neurotic delinquent, and the psychopathic delinquent. Each of these types exhibits certain traits that distinguish it from the other types and from nondelinquents. Since the background and treatment of each variety of delinquent differs, an understanding of youthful crime should commence with an examination of these differences.

Socialized delinquency. The *socialized delinquent* has been analyzed by such researchers as Albert J. Reiss, R. L. Jenkins, and Lester Hewitt

(Reiss 1952; Hewitt & Jenkins 1947). Indeed, most research on delinquency has concentrated on this type—and rightfully so, since socialized delinquents account for the great majority of crimes. The socialized delinquent does not suffer from any particular psychological disorders, other than those which characterize the typical adolescent. His crimes are not motivated by deep-seated anxieties or unresolved conflicts, but rather by a simple desire to conform to the norms of his gang. Typically, such a boy comes from a transitional urban area where a gang subculture has become entrenched. In his immediate social environment, delinquency has evolved into an accepted, even honored, pattern of life, a legitimate way of achieving prestige in the juvenile community. Often, in early childhood the socialized delinquent joins a gang and imbibes the values and habits of a delinquent subculture. Put most simply, in the fashion of Edwin Sutherland, the child learns to become criminal through "differential association" with delinquents (Sutherland & Cressey 1924).

One should not conceptualize the process of becoming a socialized delinquent, however, as just a matter of chance learning. Only certain children seem to be drawn toward a gang culture. Specifically, as many pieces of research have demonstrated, the socialized delinquent seems to be produced by a frustrating and inconsistent familial background. Compared with noncriminal children, the socialized delinquent has most often been raised in a family characterized by parental conflict, rejection, or neglect (Glueck & Glueck 1950). In such a family, the child finds that his elemental needs for self-esteem, security, and emotional warmth are frustrated. Not unnaturally, he searches for alternative ways of fulfilling his basic needs, and, if he lives in a delinquent neighborhood, the gang offers him a very "live" option. Typically, too, the socialized delinquent has been reared in a home characterized by a lack of supervision and erratic discipline. In consequence, he has not internalized the usual middle-class standards that could immunize him from delinquent influences in his broader social environment.

Such a child adopts the ethic and customs of the gang as a means of assuring himself the sense of importance and security denied him in other ways. The gang can offer him acceptance and guidance.

As socialized delinquents reach adulthood, the majority shed the pattern of criminal behavior: at least 60 per cent stop their criminal behavior by the age of 21 (McCord et al. 1959). This reformation is largely spontaneous and unaffected by society's conscious attempts to bring about change. It would seem to be due to the simple process of aging and entering new social roles. By adulthood, the socialized delinquent typically leaves his original home and neighborhood; he undertakes new responsibilities as a father, husband, and wage-earner. Thus, he escapes the influences that led him to delinquency and adopts new social roles that are inconsistent with membership in a juvenile gang.

Neurotic delinquency. The *neurotic delinquent* suffers from deep anxiety, intense insecurity, and, often, pervasive guilt. For such a boy, criminal behavior is a way of expressing an unresolved conflict and offers a release from anxiety. His behavior stems from deeply imbedded psychological causes rather than from a simple acceptance of a gang culture as a means of winning prestige. Unlike the socialized delinquent, the neurotic child often commits his crimes alone and usually commits only a single type of crime. His behavior exhibits a compulsive quality that is often absent in socialized delinquents. The juvenile arsonist, sexual offender, or narcotics addict usually comes from the ranks of neurotic delinquents. The motives behind the neurotic's crimes are varied and difficult to comprehend. The arsonist, for example, may set fires because of exhibitionistic desires; the neurotic burglar may commit his offenses because the act of burglary offers him sexual release (Abrahamsen 1960).

Although their specific characteristics and backgrounds differ markedly, neurotic delinquents generally emerge from a more middle-class, conventional environment than do socialized delinquents. Their families exhibit severe emotional strain, and their parents are usually neurotic or psychotic. Some studies have described the neurotic delinquent as possessing a "relatively weak ego" and as tending to isolate himself from other people, particularly other children (Hewitt & Jenkins 1947).

Because their reformation depends upon a profound reorientation in character, neurotic delinquents more often continue their criminal behavior into adulthood than do the typical gang delinquents.

Psychopathic delinquency. The *psychopathic delinquent* is relatively rare but, from society's point of view, perhaps the most dangerous of young criminals. The psychopath's distinguishing traits are (1) his inability to form a lasting emotional relationship with other human beings and (2) his almost total lack of guilt, remorse, or inhibition. Unlike the neurotic delinquent, the psychopath does not suffer from internal conflict or anxiety. Unlike the socialized delinquent, the psychopath does not find emotional satisfaction in gang membership. The psychopathic delinquent commits a wide gamut of crimes and has a remarkably high rate of recidivism. Almost all investigations of psychopaths' environments indicate that they have been raised in homes characterized by extreme parental brutality, neglect, discord, and intensely severe discipline. Many have come from foster homes or orphanages. They have seldom, if ever, experienced a warm, loving relationship with other human beings, and they seem to lack the capacity for affection. Quite often, the psychopath suffers from a neurological disorder, perhaps of a type that decreases his ability to inhibit impulses (McCord & McCord 1964). [See PSYCHOPATHIC PERSONALITY.]

Summary. Each of the above types of delinquent reacts to particular pressures operating in his environment: the socialized delinquent seeks guidance and security from the gang; the neurotic delinquent uses crime as a release from intolerable anxiety; the psychopathic delinquent fails to internalize the usual social norms, even those of a delinquent subculture. While it is difficult to specify the exact forces that produce each type of delinquent, social science has progressed to the point where one can propose some generalizations about causal forces.

Modern civilization and delinquency

As has been noted, all types of juvenile delinquency increase as industrialization and urbanization proceed. Industrial societies as a group greatly exceed "primitive" societies in their rate of crime. And within the class of economically affluent countries, the rate of delinquency correlates rather closely with the degree of industrialization. Thus, the United States, as the most economically advanced nation, leads all other countries in the commission of crimes by juveniles. What is there in the nature of modern civilization—particularly in North American culture—that creates this increasing criminal proclivity? Among the many explanations that have been offered, the following theories have gained prominence.

Depersonalization and anonymity. As urbanization increases, the "face-to-face" social controls of traditional society begin to lose their importance. In a rural, economically stagnant, village-based society, every person is subject to the scrutiny of his immediate community. In an urban environment, however, human relationships become more depersonalized and anonymous. The person feels, and is, freer to act as an individual rather than as a member of a closely knit community. One consequence of this greater freedom may well be that the individual feels less inhibition about experimenting with various forms of deviant behavior, including crime. [See ALIENATION.]

Increased mobility. Modern societies provide greater opportunities for social and geographical mobility. In the United States, for example, one out of every five families changes its place of residence each year. One obvious result of such mobility is that families in modern societies do not maintain the same continuous ties with their neighbors as do people in more traditional, stable societies. This depersonalization of communal relationships may also weaken the social controls exercised over children and thus contribute to a high incidence of delinquency. [See MIGRATION; SOCIAL MOBILITY.]

Increased family disorganization. The nature of family life apparently changes as industrialization goes forward. The extended kinship system gives way to a smaller "nuclear" family. For a variety of reasons, the stability of the family also seems to decline. In the United States in 1900, one divorce occurred for every fourteen marriages. In the contemporary period, one marriage in every five ends in divorce. Because of the well-established correlation between familial discord and juvenile delinquency, one would expect that the higher rate of familial disorganization in modern societies would be reflected in more juvenile crime.

Frustration of goal achievement. As Merton has suggested (1949), modern civilizations—particularly the United States—are characterized by an almost universal goal of individual achievement. Everyone is encouraged to seek material success, but society does not offer equal means to all for fulfilling this goal. The lower-class child, denied the chance of competing successfully, may turn to deviant channels for achieving his goals. According to this hypothesis, delinquency will be highest in societies that inculcate individualistic aspirations in all people but fail to provide equality of opportunity.

In modern industrialized civilizations, people live in a fast-moving, exciting atmosphere—in a society broken into atomized, mobile, and depersonalized groups. Traditional social controls lose their influence. The emphasis on competition puts extreme pressure on those individuals who have the least chance of success: for example, ethnic minority groups and members of the lower class. In consequence, an increasing proportion of youths turn to delinquent behavior.

Social factors

Within an industrialized civilization, the chance that a child will become delinquent varies considerably according to his particular social position. Among the more important of these variations, one should note the following contrasts.

Sex differences. Boys have a much higher rate of delinquency than do girls. In most modern societies, approximately five times as many males as females become juvenile offenders. Aside from the obvious differences in physical strength, several social factors account for this contrast.

Parsons (1949) has noted that boys in an industrialized society are traditionally reared by their mothers. Compared with children in peasant families, they have relatively little opportunity to identify with their fathers or to copy masculine forms of behavior. At the age of puberty, however, they are expected to become men and to shift their identification from the mother to the father. Parsons has hypothesized that this dislocation creates severe strain for boys. In an attempt to assert their masculinity, boys may well turn to delinquent behavior. In contrast, girls continue to identify with their mothers and do not suffer the same "crisis of identity" that boys do.

Further, it is clear that girls in our society do not normally achieve respect by participation in the "rough" activities characteristic of delinquents. For a girl who searches for warmth and recognition, the female role in our society encourages passivity rather than the masculine-oriented behavior of delinquents. Thus, a girl who experiences the same frustrations that produce a delinquent boy might well assert her femininity in promiscuous behavior but would be unlikely to turn to burglary or aggressive crimes.

It should be noted that as the female role in our society has more closely approximated that of the male, the incidence of female delinquency has increased and the gap in rates of crime between boys and girls has narrowed.

Minority groups. Minority groups, particularly in America, contribute disproportionately to the number of adjudicated delinquents. Formerly, in America sons of Irish or Italian immigrants became delinquent significantly more often than "native-born" children. As the immigrant groups have won middle-class status, however, their rate of delinquency has declined. Today, Negroes, Puerto Ricans, and Spanish-Americans most often find their way into the hands of police and courts. Many factors account for this. Police bias, particularly in the southern United States, undoubtedly has an influence. The inferior economic status of these groups, their high rate of familial disorganization, and their experience of cultural conflict also help to explain the differential rate of delinquency. Yet certain minority groups, most notably the Japanese, have not produced a high number of delinquents. While they, too, have suffered discrimination, their unusually tight familial organization has apparently insulated them from the usual delinquent patterns.

Rural and urban comparisons. Rural communities generally have about one-third the rate of delinquency of urban areas. The greater cohesiveness of rural communities, the closer social control, and the greater intimacy between the police and the citizens probably account for this contrast. Rural rates of delinquency have, however, gone up at the same pace as urban rates, and as urban patterns of life infiltrate even the remotest farming areas, the rural–urban difference becomes less striking.

Economic differences. Most importantly, delinquency has concentrated heavily in lower-class, deteriorated, slum areas. In such cities of the United States as Chicago and San Francisco, the incidence of delinquency in the most economically deprived areas is 55 times that in the privileged suburbs. This distinctive relationship cannot be dismissed as simply ephemeral or due to a tendency on the part of police to be more lenient with middle-class children. Since the investigations of the "Chicago school" of criminology, many theories have been proposed to explain this phenomenon (Shaw & Moore 1931). Today, the three most accepted explanations of delinquency's predominance in economically deprived areas have been presented by Cohen (1955), Cloward and Ohlin (1960), and Miller (1958).

Delinquent subculture. Following the work of Merton and Sutherland, Cohen has argued that the typical working-class youth has not been equipped by his family, school, or social environment for competition. A boy reared in a lower-class environment comes to realize his underprivileged status and the many obstacles that he faces in attempting to achieve self-respect in conventional ways. Because of his frustration, he rejects the usual ethic of society and accepts in its place a "delinquent subculture": a gang society that stresses negative, destructive, aggressive behavior. Since the typical lower-class boy cannot win status in the usual manner, he joins an "inverted" culture where he can express his spite against the larger society. His crimes are often nonutilitarian in nature—he steals or fights, not for material profit but for the glory of it. The most respected member of the subculture is the one who can best demonstrate his prowess, aggressiveness, and defiance of law-abiding standards.

Patterns of delinquent subcultures. Cloward and Ohlin accept Cohen's position that a delinquent subculture arises because of the frustrations experienced by members of the lower class, but they take the theory several steps further. They contend that there are several varieties of delinquent societies, each with its unique properties: the "criminalistic" pattern, where gang members accept organized crime as a distinctive way of life; the "conflict" pattern, where the gang turns to aggressive, destructive behavior, regardless of its material rewards; and the "retreatist" pattern, characterized by "beats" who use drugs or alcohol and maintain an attitude of nonchalant indifference to the ordinary world. Perhaps Cloward and Ohlin's most distinctive contribution is their belief that specific factors in a neighborhood determine which type of "delinquent adaptation" will take place. They emphasize, for example, the role of an adult system of criminal values. If adults in an area participate regularly in organized crime, Cloward and Ohlin assume that a "criminalistic," nonviolent pattern of delinquency will appear rather than another type.

Working-class norms. To some degree, Miller parts company with other sociologists concerned with the broad social base of delinquency, for he believes that lower-class culture itself generates a delinquent response among boys. He argues that delinquent subcultures do not have paramount importance, but rather that the entire environment of working-class people is one which supports an assertion of masculine "toughness," "smartness," and the ability to "con" other people.

General theoretical considerations. The variations between the different positions arouse dispute, but the basic contention appears similar: in an industrial society where all groups do not have equal access to power and privilege, the children of deprived economic groups will absorb an ethic that contradicts the society's usual values. For these theorists, delinquency represents a normal response to a particular social system.

Obviously, these theories do not explain all aspects of the problem of delinquency. They help to explain the actions of socialized delinquents but are of little aid in clarifying the nature of neurotic or psychopathic crime. Essentially, the theories are confined to explicating why certain areas within modern society produce a generally higher incidence of delinquency than do others. Nevertheless, even in the most deviant urban areas, the majority of boys do not develop a predominantly criminal pattern. To explain why one child chooses a delinquent adaptation and another does not, one must examine other aspects of the person's life, particularly his early familial environment.

Family experiences

Numerous studies have demonstrated that particular familial experiences are the crucial factors differentiating the delinquent from the nondelin-

quent child. Only certain types of families, clustered disproportionally in lower-class strata, create a delinquent child. Indeed, research in Minnesota and California estimates that only 5 per cent of American families account for all juvenile delinquency (Buell et al. 1952). The "delinquency-prone" family generally has the following features (Glueck & Glueck 1950; McCord et al. 1959; Healy & Bronner 1936).

Conflict. Delinquent families are rent with parental discord, bitterness, and even hatred. One of the first experiences of the potentially delinquent child is to see his parents engaged in acrimonious quarrels. Not unnaturally, he learns to suspect the motives and good will of people around him. Various studies have shown that a boy raised in a broken home in the United States has about twice the chance of becoming delinquent as a boy raised in a cohesive home. If the parents remain together but engage in constant conflict, the boy's chance of becoming delinquent is even further increased (McCord et al. 1959).

Paternal rejection. Fathers of delinquents tend to reject their sons or at best treat them with distant disdain. In one typical study of delinquents, 87 per cent came from families where the father was overtly cruel to the son, absent from the home, or severely neglectful—while only a small minority of noncriminal boys experienced paternal rejection (McCord et al. 1959).

Paternal delinquency. Fathers of delinquents are much more likely to have records of crime, alcoholism, or mental disorders (Glueck & Glueck 1950). Thus, to the degree that the child tends to copy his father's actions, the boy's chances of delinquency are increased.

Maternal behavior. Mothers of delinquents generally reject and neglect their sons. One study showed that seven times as many delinquents as nondelinquents had been reared by mothers who either felt indifferent toward their children or actively rejected them (Glueck & Glueck 1950). Another study demonstrated that a boy's chance of serving a sentence in a penal institution was increased by four times if his mother had neglected him in childhood (McCord et al. 1959). In addition, mothers of delinquents have a much higher rate of crime and other forms of social deviance.

Parental supervision. The parents of delinquents either fail to give their sons any supervision at all or tend to discipline them in a severe, often erratic fashion (Glueck & Glueck 1950). Contrary to the usual opinion, children raised under a regime of strict but inconsistent discipline have the highest incidence of delinquency.

General home environment. In general, delinquents come from homes that offer them a portrait of human relationships full of conflict and strife. They learn to view the world with suspicion and to conceive of other human beings as threatening, punitive, and aggressive. If the family resides in an area characterized by a delinquent subculture, the child not unnaturally turns to the gang as a cure for his frustrations. Although this general background characterizes most delinquents, the specific types emerge from somewhat different environments. The neurotic delinquent, for example, has more often been exposed to a highly religious background, where his sense of personal worthlessness has been reinforced by strict parental discipline. In contrast with the other varieties, the psychopathic child has suffered from almost total, continuous parental rejection and neglect.

Conclusions

Whether a child chooses delinquency as an adolescent mode of life depends upon a complex interaction of many factors in his background. It is improbable that social science will ever totally unweave the skein of influences that operate to produce delinquency. Nonetheless, studies have produced some generalizations concerning the interrelation of variables leading to delinquency (McCord et al. 1959):

(1) A cohesive, loving home tends to compensate for the influence of a delinquent subculture. The majority of children raised in a transitional slum area (but who live in a normal family) do not become delinquents.

(2) The effects of a father's absence, neglect, or cruelty on his son seem to depend largely upon the mother's attitude. If the mother is loving, the child is not likely to become delinquent.

(3) The nature of the parents' discipline does not affect criminality, but the consistency of its imposition does.

By considering the interaction of these factors (and others) in the person's background, it now appears probable that social science will be able to predict delinquency with a high degree of accuracy. Recent studies by the Gluecks (1959) have indicated that predictions made in early childhood and based on the nature of the child's family have an extraordinary degree of accuracy in later years. Because the psychological roots of delinquency are so deeply enmeshed in modern society and the family, it would be utopian to hope that delinquency can ever be totally eradicated. Nonetheless, our increasing knowledge of the varieties of delinquency and their sources offers hope that new techniques of prevention and rehabilitation may substantially reduce the toll of youthful crime.

WILLIAM MCCORD

[*Directly related are the entries* CRIME *and* PSYCHOPATHIC PERSONALITY. *Other relevant material may be found in* ADOLESCENCE *and* FAMILY.]

BIBLIOGRAPHY

ABRAHAMSEN, DAVID 1960 *The Psychology of Crime.* New York: Columbia Univ. Press.

BAKER, BELA O.; and SARBIN, THEODORE R. 1956 Differential Mediation of Social Perception as a Correlate of Social Adjustment. *Sociometry* 19:69–83.

BLOCH, HERBERT A.; and FLYNN, FRANK T. 1956 *Delinquency: The Juvenile Offender in America Today.* New York: Random House.

BLOCH, HERBERT A.; and GEIS, GILBERT 1962 *Man, Crime, and Society: The Forms of Criminal Behavior.* New York: Random House.

BOWLBY, JOHN (1944) 1946 *Forty-four Juvenile Thieves: Their Characters and Home-life.* London: Baillière.

BUELL, BRADLEY et al. 1952 *Community Planning for Human Services.* New York: Columbia Univ. Press.

CAPLAN, NATHAN S. 1965 Intellectual Functioning. Pages 100–138 in Herbert C. Quay (editor), *Juvenile Delinquency: Research and Theory.* Princeton, N.J.: Van Nostrand.

CLOWARD, RICHARD A.; and OHLIN, LLOYD E. 1960 *Delinquency and Opportunity: A Theory of Delinquent Gangs.* Glencoe, Ill.: Free Press.

COHEN, ALBERT K. 1955 *Delinquent Boys: The Culture of the Gang.* Glencoe, Ill.: Free Press.

DINITZ, SIMON; RECKLESS, WALTER C.; and KAY, BARBARA 1958 A Self Gradient Among Potential Delinquents. *Journal of Criminal Law, Criminology, and Police Science* 49:230–233.

GLUECK, SHELDON (editor) 1959 *The Problem of Delinquency.* Boston: Houghton Mifflin.

GLUECK, SHELDON; and GLUECK, ELEANOR 1950 *Unraveling Juvenile Delinquency.* Harvard Law School Studies in Criminology. New York: Commonwealth Fund; Oxford Univ. Press.

GLUECK, SHELDON; and GLUECK, ELEANOR 1959 *Predicting Delinquency and Crime.* Cambridge, Mass.: Harvard Univ. Press.

GODDARD, HENRY H. 1921 *Juvenile Delinquency.* New York: Dodd.

GORING, CHARLES B. 1913 *The English Convict: A Statistical Study.* London: H.M. Stationery Office.

HATHAWAY, STARKE R.; and MONACHESI, ELIO D. (editors) 1953 *Analyzing and Predicting Juvenile Delinquency With the MMPI.* Minneapolis: Univ. of Minnesota Press.

HEALY, WILLIAM; and BRONNER, AUGUSTA F. 1936 *New Light on Delinquency and Its Treatment.* New Haven: Yale Univ. Press.

HEWITT, LESTER E.; and JENKINS, RICHARD L. 1947 *Fundamental Patterns of Maladjustment: The Dynamics of Their Origin.* Springfield, Ill.: Thomas.

LINDNER, ROBERT M. 1942/1943 Experimental Studies in Constitutional Psychopathic Inferiority. *Journal of Criminal Psychopathology* 4:252–276; 484–503.

Lombroso, Cesare (1899) 1918 *Crime, Its Causes and Remedies.* Boston: Little. → First published in French.

McCord, William; and McCord, Joan 1964 *The Psychopath: An Essay on the Criminal Mind.* Princeton, N.J.: Van Nostrand.

McCord, William; McCord, Joan; and Zola, Irving 1959 *Origins of Crime.* New York: Columbia Univ. Press.

Mannheim, Hermann 1948 *Juvenile Delinquency in an English Middletown.* London: Routledge.

Mays, John B. 1963 *Crime and the Social Structure.* London: Faber.

Merton, Robert K. (1949) 1957 *Social Theory and Social Structure.* Rev. & enl. ed. Glencoe, Ill.: Free Press.

Miller, Walter B. 1958 Lower Class Culture as a Generating Milieu of Gang Delinquency. *Journal of Social Issues* 14, no. 3:5–19.

Ostrow, Mortimer; and Ostrow, Miriam 1946 Bilaterally Synchronous Paroxysmal Slow Activity in the Electroencephalograms of Non-epileptics. *Journal of Nervous and Mental Disease* 103:346–358.

Parsons, Talcott (1949) 1954 *Essays in Sociological Theory.* Rev. ed. Glencoe, Ill.: Free Press.

Powers, Edwin; and Witmer, Helen 1951 *An Experiment in the Prevention of Delinquency.* New York: Columbia Univ. Press; Oxford Univ. Press.

Quay, Herbert C. 1965 Personality and Delinquency. Pages 139–169 in Herbert C. Quay (editor), *Juvenile Delinquency: Research and Theory.* Princeton, N.J.: Van Nostrand.

Reckless, Walter C. 1940 *Criminal Behavior.* New York: McGraw-Hill.

Reiss, Albert J. Jr. 1952 Social Correlates of Psychological Types of Delinquency. *American Sociological Review* 17:710–718.

Rouček, Joseph S. (editor) 1958 *Juvenile Delinquency.* New York: Philosophical Library.

Schuessler, Karl F.; and Cressey, Donald R. 1950 Personality Characteristics of Criminals. *American Journal of Sociology* 55:476–484.

Shaw, Clifford R.; and Moore, M. E. 1931 *Natural History of a Delinquent Career.* Univ. of Chicago Press.

Sheldon, William H. 1949 *Varieties of Delinquent Youth.* New York: Harper.

Siebert, Lawrence A. 1962 Otis I.Q. Scores of Delinquents. *Journal of Clinical Psychology* 18:517 only.

Siegman, Aron W. 1961 The Relationship Between Future Time Perspective, Time Estimation, and Impulse Control in a Group of Young Offenders and in a Control Group. *Journal of Consulting Psychology* 25:470–475.

Stafford-Clark, D.; Pond, Desmond; and Lovett Doust, J. W. 1951 The Psychopath in Prison: A Preliminary Report of a Co-operative Research. *British Journal of Delinquency* 2:117–129.

Sutherland, Edwin H. 1931 Mental Deficiency and Crime. Pages 357–375 in Kimball Young (editor), *Social Attitudes.* New York: Holt.

Sutherland, Edwin H.; and Cressey, Donald R. (1924) 1960 *Principles of Criminology.* 6th ed. New York: Lippincott. → First published as *Criminology,* under the sole authorship of Edwin H. Sutherland.

Thrasher, Frederic (1927) 1963 *The Gang: A Study of 1,313 Gangs in Chicago.* Abridged and with an introduction by James F. Short. Univ. of Chicago Press.

Wechsler, David (1939) 1958 *The Measurement and Appraisal of Adult Intelligence.* 4th ed. Baltimore: Williams & Wilkins. → First published as *The Measurement of Adult Intelligence.*

Wootton, Barbara [Adam] 1959 *Social Science and Social Pathology.* London: Allen & Unwin; New York: Macmillan.

Yablonsky, Lewis 1962 *The Violent Gang.* New York: Macmillan.

IV
DELINQUENT GANGS

When the second United Nations Congress on the Prevention of Crime and the Treatment of Offenders met in London in 1960, delegates from most countries reported upsurges in adolescent delinquency, not only quantitatively greater than before but more violent and more likely to be group-based rather than individual in character (Middendorff 1960).

In more than a dozen countries, new words have been coined to describe adolescents, nondelinquent as well as delinquent, who wear distinctive clothing and hair styles, listen to special types of music, frequent amusement areas and other gathering places, and generally annoy adults: bar gangs (Argentina), *blousons noirs* (France), bodgies (Australia), *chimpira* (Japan), *Halbstarke* (West Germany), hooligans (Poland), *nozem* (Netherlands), *raggare* (Sweden), *stilyagi* (Soviet Union), *tapkaroschi* (Yugoslavia), *tau-pau* (Formosa), teddy boys (Great Britain), *vitelloni* (Italy). In short, adolescence has come to be regarded, by experts as well as by the general public, as a period of potential antisocial behavior. This is a recent image of adolescence; the turbulence traditionally associated with adolescence was an inner state resulting from sexual maturation and the search for an adult identity (Erikson 1962). In the context of this new perspective on adolescence, delinquent gangs tend to be interpreted as extreme manifestations of teen-age culture (Mays 1961), rather than as juvenile divisions of adult criminal gangs.

Comparability of findings. The term "delinquent gang" means different things to different people. An important reason for the confusion is that research reports on gangs in different cities and countries are not usually prepared with a view to rigorous comparisons. Since each investigator emphasizes those aspects of delinquent gangs in which he is most interested, readers of reports from different places cannot tell whether disparate phenomena are being included within the label "gang delinquency," or whether verbal habits differ.

For example, the widespread assumption of European criminologists that the delinquent gangs of American cities are larger, better organized, more violent, and more vicious than their European counterparts has not been tested by systematic comparisons (for one expression of this assumption, see Centre de Formation 1963, p. ix).

Gang characteristics—some unanswered questions. How large must a group be to constitute a gang? Should cliques of four or five boys be called gangs, or should the gang concept assume a membership of fifty or more? Size is, of course, related to internal differentiation. Must a gang have a recognized leader or leadership group, or can the leadership function shift from time to time and from activity to activity? How tightly integrated must members be with the group for the gang concept to be appropriate? One criminologist has suggested that delinquent gangs typically have moblike as well as grouplike characteristics (Yablonsky 1959). Perhaps the term "gang" suggests a higher degree of integration than is actually found. How delinquent must a gang be in order to be properly described as a "delinquent" gang? Some criminologists argue that a delinquent gang must require delinquent behavior of members, not merely permit or encourage it (Cloward & Ohlin 1960, p. 9). Other criminologists point out that actual gangs, even highly delinquent gangs in cities like Chicago, contain members who are fairly conventional in values and behavior (Matza 1964; Short & Strodtbeck 1965). This issue is related to that of specialization among delinquent gangs. Do fighting gangs differ strikingly from stealing gangs or drug-using gangs? Research suggests that most delinquent gangs engage in a wide variety of law-violative behavior rather than a few specialties (Cohen & Short 1958; Short et al. 1963).

Must a delinquent gang have some minimum continuity through time? The criminological literature contains accounts of gangs lasting a dozen or more years. Such continuity is usually the result of the simultaneous inclusion within the gang of a considerable age range. When 18-year-olds start dropping out, 11-year-olds are being recruited. However, all members of some gangs are about the same age. Not only does this give the gang a shorter life expectancy; it also means that gangs differ, one from the other, depending, for instance, on whether the members are mainly 14-year-olds or mainly 17-year-olds.

Without a precise description of what a delinquent gang is, criminologists can emphasize without fear of refutation one or another of a considerable array of causal factors: family disorganization, blighted neighborhoods, traditions of delinquency, early school leaving, employment problems, psychopathology. Each of these factors is capable of explaining the emergence of some of the phenomena included under the rubric "delinquent gangs."

Social upheaval and gang delinquency. The problem of explanation has been further confounded by factors associated with delinquent gangs, which may not be necessary conditions for gang formation. World War II is an example of such a factor. The conspicuousness of the problem of adolescent gangs following the war prompted some observers to infer a direct connection. It is possible, of course, that the violence of the war and the personal insecurity it engendered contributed directly to attitudes on the part of youth, which found expression in gang delinquency. More likely, the effect on delinquency was indirect—through disruption of family life and the resulting interferences with the socialization of children; through speeding up processes of urbanization and industrialization, thereby tearing people loose from their social moorings; and through inordinate material desires stimulated by increasing affluence.

Ethnic minorities and gang delinquency. Another confounding factor is ethnic status. Ethnic minorities serve as a catalyst for the development of gang delinquency and especially street fighting. Puerto Rican gangs in New York City, Negro gangs in Chicago, Mexican-American gangs in Los Angeles—like Irish gangs in Liverpool, Arab gangs in Paris, and Korean gangs in Tokyo—are community problems. Because they are marginally integrated in the host society, low-status minorities are in a weaker position than the majority to instill conventional motivations in preadolescents and to control adolescents informally. Thus ethnic cleavages reinforce and intensify the social forces making for gang delinquency.

But gangs form in urban industrial societies without war dislocations or ethnic minorities. The Swedish experience is instructive. Sweden was not a belligerent during World War II; the country has no appreciable minority population; welfare services are highly developed; and slums have been eliminated. Nevertheless, Swedish *raggare* gangs have been troublesome to the police, especially in Stockholm, Malmö, and Gothenburg. At one time *raggare* automobiles interfered with traffic in Stockholm to the extent that city officials invited *raggare* leaders to the Town Hall to discuss the problem.

If neither social upheaval nor ethnic discrimination is a primary factor in the development of delinquent gangs, what *is* responsible? Research is presently inconclusive, but the probability is that the social consequences of urbanism and industrialization can explain the conjunction of delinquency and affluence.

Gang formation and weak adult control. With the development of modern societies, control of adults over adolescents decreases. This weakness of adult control is most obvious under pathological circumstances such as slum neighborhoods or broken homes (McKay 1949; Toby 1957). Its ultimate source, however, is not pathology but the increasing social fluidity resulting from the allocation of education, recreation, work, and family life to separate institutional contexts. These changes in social organization affect everyone in contemporary societies, but their impact is especially great on adolescents because adolescence is a period of transition. Youngsters must disengage themselves from the family into which they were born and reared and establish themselves in a new family unit (Parsons 1942). They must eventually withdraw from the system of formal education and assume an occupational role.

While preparing to make these transitions and learning preparatory skills, many adolescents are socially adrift, except for such solidary relationships as they form with youngsters in their own situation (Cohen 1955). Delinquent gangs therefore represent an autonomous and antisocial development of adolescent solidarity, and they are, of course, less pleasing to adults than scouting or church-affiliated youth groups. Gang formation is always a possibility in contemporary societies because adolescents are not typically under effective adult supervision—although some adolescents are better controlled by adults than others. The automobile symbolizes the looseness of the ties between adults and adolescents because it is an instrument whereby adult supervision can be evaded.

Individualism. Decreasing control of adults over adolescents is reinforced by individualism. In contemporary societies, the unit of social participation is usually the individual rather than the family group or the community. The child is an individual in school and in the neighborhood play group. Later, he will participate in the political and economic systems as an individual. Besides this implicit principle of individualism embodied in the social organization of contemporary societies, there exists an explicit ideology of individual fulfillment. For example, the Declaration of Independence refers to the right to "life, liberty, and the pursuit of happiness." And contemporary motion pictures, television programs, and mass circulation maga-

zines suggest that thrilling entertainment, new clothes, cigarettes, automobiles, and liquor are necessary for happiness; such ideas are found even in societies where traditions emphasize collective goals (such as Japan). Some youngsters join delinquent gangs in order to satisfy these hedonistic desires.

Relative deprivation—a hypothesis. Although diminished adult control over adolescents and increased individualism may explain the increase in delinquency rates, the principle of *relative deprivation* is more useful in explaining recruitment into gangs. Some adolescents feel more at a disadvantage than others. It is among these alienated and uncommitted adolescents that delinquent gangs have their greatest appeal (Karacki & Toby 1962). Thus, the principle of relative deprivation helps account for the disproportionate representation of ethnic minorities in delinquent gangs. It also explains why school failures and those who withdraw from school before completing a course of study are more likely to become delinquents than students doing well in school. In contemporary societies, the system of formal education is an important mechanism for allocating youngsters to positions in the occupational system; students who do poorly at school have reason to grow discouraged about their futures. Such discouragement is often antecedent to rebellion (Stinchcombe 1964; Toby & Toby 1961).

However, the principle of relative deprivation does not help to explain the increasing rate of gang delinquency, unless one assumes that the sting of relative deprivation is increasing. A plausible argument can be made that it *is* increasing. In Sweden, for instance, where social and economic leveling has reduced poverty to a minimum, relatively few adolescents need feel hopeless about their chances for the future, but these few feel more deprived than Untouchable youths in India. Army studies during World War II have shown that the individual's expectations for himself—and therefore his feeling of deprivation or satisfaction—depend partly on the proportion of his reference group that is better off than he (Stouffer et al. 1949, pp. 250–258). The same reference group phenomenon may underlie adolescent delinquency in affluent societies [*see* REFERENCE GROUPS].

If factors related to urbanism and industrialization do indeed account for the proliferation of delinquent gangs in many large cities of the world, the problem will increase in seriousness in the years ahead. Countries like Italy and Spain, where adolescent gangs are still rare, will find that delinquency is part of the price industrial societies pay for their individualistic affluence and for the freedom of adolescents from close supervision by adults.

JACKSON TOBY

[*See also* ADOLESCENCE; COLLECTIVE BEHAVIOR.]

BIBLIOGRAPHY

BLOCH, HERBERT A.; and NIEDERHOFFER, ARTHUR 1958 *The Gang: A Study in Adolescent Behavior.* New York: Philosophical Library.

BORDUA, DAVID J. 1961 Delinquent Subcultures: Sociological Interpretations of Gang Delinquency. American Academy of Political and Social Science, *Annals* 338:119–136.

CENTRE DE FORMATION ET DE RECHERCHE DE L'ÉDUCATION SURVEILLÉE 1963 *La délinquance des jeunes en groupe: Contribution à l'étude de la société adolescente.* Paris: Éditions Cujas.

CLOWARD, RICHARD A.; and OHLIN, LLOYD E. 1960 *Delinquency and Opportunity: A Theory of Delinquent Gangs.* Glencoe, Ill.: Free Press.

COHEN, ALBERT K. (1955) 1963 *Delinquent Boys: The Culture of the Gang.* New York: Free Press.

COHEN, ALBERT K.; and SHORT, JAMES F., JR. 1958 Research in Delinquent Subcultures. *Journal of Social Issues* 14, no. 3:20–37.

EISENSTADT, SHMUEL N. 1956 *From Generation to Generation: Age Groups and Social Structure.* Glencoe, Ill.: Free Press.

ERIKSON, ERIK H. 1962 Youth: Fidelity and Diversity. *Dædalus* 91:5–27.

[FREEMAN, IRA H.] 1960 *Out of the Burning: The Story of a Boy Gang Leader,* by Carl Joyeaux, Jr. [pseud.]. New York: Crown.

KARACKI, LARRY; and TOBY, JACKSON 1962 The Uncommitted Adolescent: Candidate for Gang Socialization. *Sociological Inquiry* 32:203–215.

KOBRIN, SOLOMON 1959 The Chicago Area Project: A 25 Year Assessment. American Academy of Political and Social Science, *Annals* 322:19–25.

LEISSNER, ARYEH 1965 *Street-club Work in New York and Tel Aviv.* Tel-Aviv: Privately printed.

MCKAY, HENRY D. 1949 The Neighborhood and Child Conduct. American Academy of Political and Social Science, *Annals* 261:32–41.

MATZA, DAVID 1964 *Delinquency and Drift.* New York: Wiley.

MAYS, JOHN 1961 Teen-age Culture in Contemporary Britain and Europe. American Academy of Political and Social Science, *Annals* 338:22–32.

MIDDENDORFF, WOLF 1960 *New Forms of Juvenile Delinquency: Their Origin, Prevention and Treatment.* U.N. Congress on the Prevention of Crime and the Treatment of Offenders, Second. New York: U.N., Dept. of Economic and Social Affairs.

MORRIS, TERENCE 1958 *The Criminal Area: A Study in Social Ecology.* London: Routledge; New York: Humanities.

PARSONS, TALCOTT 1942 Age and Sex in the Social Structure of the United States. *American Sociological Review* 7:604–616.

SALISBURY, HARRISON E. 1958 *The Shook-up Generation.* New York: Harper.

SHAW, CLIFFORD R.; MCKAY, HENRY D.; and MCDONALD, JAMES F. 1938 *Brothers in Crime.* Univ. of Chicago Press.

SHAW, CLIFFORD R.; and MCKAY, HENRY D. 1942 *Juvenile Delinquency and Urban Areas: A Study of Rates of Delinquents in Relation to Differential Characteristics of Local Communities in American Cities.* Univ. of Chicago.

SHORT, JAMES F., JR., et al. 1963 Behavior Dimensions of Gang Delinquency. *American Sociological Review* 28:411–428.

SHORT, JAMES F., JR.; and STRODTBECK, FRED L. 1965 *Group Process and Gang Delinquency.* Univ. of Chicago Press.

STINCHCOMBE, ARTHUR L. 1960 Social Sources of Rebellion in a High School. Ph.D. dissertation, Univ. of California.

STOUFFER, SAMUEL A. et al. 1949 *The American Soldier.* Studies in Social Psychology in World War II. Vols. 1 and 2. Princeton Univ. Press; Oxford Univ. Press. → Volume 1: *Adjustment During Army Life.* Volume 2: *Combat and Its Aftermath.*

THRASHER, FREDERIC (1927) 1963 *The Gang: A Study of 1,313 Gangs in Chicago.* Abridged and with an introduction by James F. Short. Univ. of Chicago Press.

TOBY, JACKSON 1957 The Differential Impact of Family Disorganization. *American Sociological Review* 22:505–512.

TOBY, JACKSON; and TOBY, MARCIA L. 1961 Low School Status as a Predisposing Factor in Subcultural Delinquency. New Brunswick, N.J.: Rutgers State Univ. (mimeographed).

YABLONSKY, LEWIS 1959 The Delinquent Gang as a Near-group. *Social Problems* 7:108–117.

YABLONSKY, LEWIS 1962 *The Violent Gang.* New York: Macmillan.

DEMAND AND SUPPLY

I. GENERAL	*Kenneth E. Boulding*
II. ECONOMETRIC STUDIES	*Karl A. Fox*

I
GENERAL

The idea that prices are dependent in some way on demand and supply is very old. Long before the development of theoretical economics, it was understood that a large supply would cause a fall in price and a large demand would cause a rise in price. A good deal of economic theory revolves around the clarification and quantification of this simple idea.

Adam Smith distinguished carefully between *demand* and *desire* and defined effective demand essentially as the quantity that would be purchased at a given price. He had a clear conception of what today we would call "equilibrium," or "normal," price, which he called "natural price"—the price at which just enough would be forthcoming from the suppliers onto the market to equal the effective demand at that price. If the price in the market were above the natural price for a given commodity, there would be unusual incentives to produce this commodity and bring it to market, and the quantity offered for sale would increase. If the amount coming onto the market were larger than the effective demand, that is, the amount taken off the market, the price would fall. Similarly, if the price in the market were below the natural price, there would be a diminished incentive to produce the commodity and bring it to market; hence the amount coming onto the market would decline, and if this were less than the effective demand, the price would rise. Much of the development of the theory of demand and supply since Adam Smith can be regarded as a clarification and elaboration of the fundamental principles that he enunciated.

Functions and curves. The next major development in the theory of demand and supply was the development of the concept of demand and supply functions and curves, associated mainly with the name of Alfred Marshall, although a Scottish economist, Fleeming Jenkin, is usually credited with the first formulation of these concepts. In its simplest form the demand function is a function relating the quantity demanded to the price of the commodity. The supply function similarly relates the quantity supplied to the price. When only these two variables are involved, the functions can be expressed as demand and supply curves in a two-dimensional diagram, as in Figure 1. The quantity of the commodity demanded or supplied is measured along the horizontal axis and the price is measured along the vertical axis. DD' is the demand curve; SS' is the supply curve. Figure 1

shows the most typical forms of these curves. In the case of demand, there is some price OD at which nothing will be bought at all. At a zero price, a finite quantity OD' will be bought; this represents the point of satiation. The supply curve is drawn so that there is some price OS below which nothing will be offered and above which, as the price rises, a larger quantity will be supplied.

For many purposes it is convenient to describe the demand and supply curves in terms of parameters, that is, a set of numbers that is sufficient to identify each point on them. The simplest assumption is that of linearity, that is, that the demand and supply curves are straight lines. In this case the equations may be written:

$$(1) \qquad q_d = d + e_d p_d,$$
$$(2) \qquad q_s = s + e_s p_s,$$

where q_d is the quantity demanded, q_s is the quantity supplied, p_d is the price at which each quantity is demanded, and p_s is the price at which each quantity is supplied. Each curve or function can then be described by only two parameters. In the case of demand, d measures what might be called the height or extent of demand and is equal to OD in Figure 1; e_d may be called the absolute elasticity of demand, which in Figure 1 is negative. It measures the absolute change in the quantity demanded, which would result from a unit change in the price. In Figure 1 the slope or the gradient of the curve DD' at any point is the "inelasticity," $1/e_d$. Similarly the parameter s, equal to OS in Figure 1, is a measure of the height or extent of the supply, and the parameter e_s is the absolute elasticity of supply, which measures the change in the quantity supplied for each unit change in the price. Again, $1/e_s$ represents the slope of the curve SS'.

Elasticity. The term elasticity was introduced into economic analysis by Alfred Marshall, the analogy being the elasticity of a spring. In an elastic spring, a given increase in the weight exerted produces a large increase in the length of the spring; similarly, if either demand or supply is elastic, a given increase in the price produces a large increase in the quantity demanded or supplied. Another name that might be given to this concept is *responsiveness*, the quantity demanded or supplied being thought of as responding more or less eagerly to a change in the price. Marshall himself did not use the absolute elasticity concept but a concept of relative elasticity, defined as the proportionate change in quantity divided by the proportionate change in the price, or:

$$(3) \qquad \mathcal{E} = p\, dq / q\, dp.$$

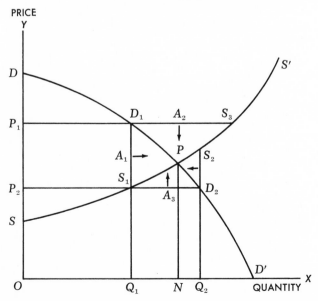

Figure 1 — Demand and supply: stable system

He apparently did this because it is a dimensionless parameter, that is, a number that is independent of the units in which the quantity or the price are measured. A demand or supply curve of constant relative elasticity would be a straight line on double-logarithmic paper. There is no reason to suppose in fact, however, that these functions are more likely to be logarithmic than linear in absolute terms, and for many purposes the absolute concepts are preferable. A logarithmically linear demand curve with constant relative elasticity, for instance, would not intersect either axis in Figure 1, implying that the price would have to be infinite before cutting off purchases altogether and that at a zero price an infinite quantity would be taken. This clearly is absurd. In practice, more than two parameters are often needed to describe demand and supply functions, but there are only a few problems in which the departure from linearity seems to have much economic significance. However, it is reasonable to suppose that there are eventual limitations on increasing the quantity supplied that cannot be overcome by a rise in price, so that the supply curve will become less elastic at high prices, as in Figure 1. It is possible also that a similar condition applies to demand. The simplest equation that can be used to express this condition is a quadratic form. [See ELASTICITY.]

Equilibrium. The equilibrium position of the system of Figure 1 is assumed to be the point P, where the demand and supply curves intersect and where PN is the equilibrium price and ON is the equilibrium quantity. Any equilibrium, however, must be seen as a special case of a dynamic system, and in this case there are at least two different dynamic systems that have this point of equilibrium. The first, associated particularly with Adam Smith and Alfred Marshall, is that in which the difference between the demand price and the supply price, leading to changes in quantity supplied, is the principal motivating factor of the dynamic system. The demand price of a given quantity is that price at which the quantity can be sold in the market; thus a point on the demand curve such as D_1 indicates that the quantity OQ_1 can be sold at the price Q_1P_1. The supply price is the price that will call forth a particular quantity. Thus, if S_1 is a point on the supply curve, Q_1S_1 is the price that could call forth an amount OQ_1. If then the quantity coming to market is OQ_1, when the demand price is in excess of the supply price by an amount D_1S_1, this means that the actual price received by the sellers, Q_1D_1, is greater than the price that would motivate them to produce the quantity involved, Q_1S_1. They are therefore receiv-

ing excessive returns, and the assumption is that this will motivate them to expand the quantity offered for sale, as indicated by the arrow A_1. Similarly, if the quantity coming on the market is OQ_2, which is larger than the equilibrium quantity ON, the demand price, which is the actual price received, will be below the supply price; the suppliers will receive less than is necessary to persuade them to put this quantity on the market, and the amount coming to market will decline. In the circumstances of Figure 1 it is clear that P is a stable equilibrium, for if the quantity is below ON it will increase; if it is above ON it will diminish.

Another approach to the problem of the equilibrium of demand and supply, associated typically with the names of Léon Walras and J. R. Hicks, interprets the demand curve as showing the quantity that will be bought at each price and the supply curve as indicating the quantity that will be sold at each price, with equilibrium achieved through price change. That is, at a price of P_1, the quantity that would be bought is P_1D_1, the quantity offered for sale is P_1S_3, and there is a "surplus," or excess supply, equal to D_1S_3. This is the amount that is being offered for sale but that can find no buyers. Under these circumstances it is supposed that some sellers will offer the commodity for sale at a lower price; and if the market is competitive, the prices in all transactions will correspondingly. If, therefore, there is a surplus, the price will fall in the direction of the arrow A_2. Similarly, if the price is below the equilibrium price, equal say to P_2, the quantity that the buyers wish to purchase, P_2D_2, is greater than the amount offered for sale, P_2S_1, and there is an excess demand equal to S_1D_2. Under these circumstances there are unsatisfied buyers who wish to buy at the price but who cannot find sellers; they will offer to buy at a higher price, causing the price to rise, as indicated by the arrow A_3. Here again the point P is an equilibrium price, for if the actual price is above NP it will fall; if it is below NP it will rise.

These different dynamic systems do not affect the position of stable equilibrium itself as long as the demand and supply curves have elasticities of opposite signs. However, if the two curves slope in the same direction, as in Figure 2, we are in serious trouble. Here we show a demand curve DD' and a negatively elastic supply curve SS' intersecting in three places, P_1, P_2, and P_3. In terms of the Smith–Marshall dynamics, P_1 and P_3 are stable positions of equilibrium; P_2 is unstable. At quantities smaller than implied by P_1, the demand price exceeds the supply price and hence the quantity will expand toward P_1. Between P_1 and P_2 the supply price exceeds the demand price and the quantity will contract toward P_1 again. Between P_2 and P_3 the demand price exceeds the supply price and the quantity will expand toward P_3. Thus any divergence around P_2 is extended in the initiated direction. At quantities larger than implied by P_3, the supply price exceeds the demand price and the quantity will contract toward P_3.

If, on the other hand, we look at the equilibrium from the Walras–Hicks point of view, we see that now P_2 is the stable position of equilibrium and P_1 and P_3 are unstable. At prices above P_1, there is excess demand and the price will rise still further. Between P_1 and P_2 there is excess supply, and the price will fall toward P_2. Between P_2 and P_3 there is again excess demand, and the price will rise toward P_2. Below P_3 there is excess supply and the price will fall away from P_3.

The full resolution of this problem requires an investigation of the dynamics of the price system that we cannot pursue here. In the real world, these dynamic factors, of course, operate simultaneously. Shortages create pressure for prices to rise, surpluses for prices to fall. Excess demand-prices create pressure for production to increase, excess supply-prices for production to diminish. Circumstances can be postulated in which there are no stable equilibrium sets of prices and quantities. These circumstances are fortunately somewhat unlikely. There have been occasions, such as in the depression of the 1930s or in hyperinflations, in which the relative price system seemed to suffer a real breakdown. These occasions, however, have always been associated with profound disturbances in the absolute level of money prices and incomes; there are no clear examples of the inability of a

relative price system to move toward an equilibrium in the absence of monetary breakdown.

The demand and supply functions have different meanings, depending on the period of time to which they refer and the nature of the system that they are intended to describe. They may be used either to describe the forces underlying the determination of a price in a market on a particular day, in which case they are usually called "market demand and supply curves," or they may be used to describe the forces determining a "normal" price, toward which the market price may tend.

Market curves. In the theory of market price, it is supposed that there is no production or consumption and the stocks of money and other exchangeables in the hands of the marketers remain constant during the "market day." The market demand and supply functions are then psychologically based, describing the state of mind of the people in the market. The market demand curve shows how much would be offered to purchase at each price; the market supply curve shows how much would be offered for sale at each price. In the course of the day in the market as a whole, the equilibrium market price is that at which the market is "cleared," that is, at which the quantity offered for sale is equal to the quantity offered to purchase. Here it is the shortage–surplus dynamic that clearly dominates the scene. The use of market demand and supply curves to describe the equilibrium of the market may be criticized on the grounds that in this case the two curves are not independent. For instance, a psychological change in the market that makes people more eager to buy will also make them less eager to sell. In other words, the same change will move the market demand curve to the right and the market supply curve to the left. If these moves are similar in extent, the price will rise without any change in the quantities exchanged. If on the other hand there is a decrease in the "divergence" in the market, that is, the degree to which the market is separated into buyers and sellers, people will be both more eager to buy and more eager to sell at each price. The market demand curve and the market supply curve will both move to the right, and the quantity of transactions will increase; the price will not change. Even though we recognize that market demand and supply curves are not independent, they still can be a very useful method, among others, of exposition and analysis of changes in the market.

Normal curves. Normal demand and supply curves refer not to the equilibrium of the market but to the equilibrium of production and consump-

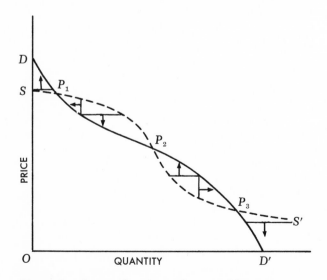

Figure 2 — Demand and supply: unstable system

tion. For each price, the normal demand curve shows what will be the amount consumed in the period under consideration. The normal supply curve likewise shows for each price what would be the quantity produced. At the point of intersection of the two curves, production is equal to consumption and also demand price is equal to supply price, that is, the production of the commodity is normally profitable. The position and shape of the curves will depend on the period of time that is considered. Generally speaking, the shorter the period of time under consideration, the more inelastic will be the demand and supply curves. In very short periods, a change in price will have little effect on the quantity produced, although it may have some effect on the quantity consumed. As we move to longer and longer periods, both production and consumption are more likely to make more adjustments, and the demand and supply curves will become more elastic.

Derivation of functions. A good deal of price theory is devoted to the derivation of demand and supply functions from the underlying functions that determine them. Supply functions are derived from the structure of cost functions, which in turn are derived from production functions. Demand functions are derived from preference functions. In the case of market demand and supply, both demand and supply curves are derived from the preferences of people in the market. Thus in Figure 3 we show the situation of a single marketer, let us say in the wheat market. In the upper part of the figure, we measure his stock of wheat along OW and his stock of money along OM. The point A represents his initial position, with a stock of wheat equal to ON and a stock of money equal to NA. The dashed lines are his indifference curves, each one showing a set of combinations of stocks of wheat and money to which he is indifferent. They may be thought of as the contours of a utility, or preference, "mountain" above the plane of the paper. In a perfect market, his exchange opportunity is represented by a straight line through A, the slope of which is equal to the price. Thus if the price of wheat is equal to OM_1/OW_1, his exchange opportunity is represented by the line M_1W_1 through A. He will look for the point on this exchange opportunity line that has the highest utility, which is the point at which it touches his highest attainable indifference curve, in this case at B_1. At this price, therefore, he will move from A to B_1, meaning that he will buy an amount of wheat equal to NN_1 for an amount of money equal to AC_1. At a higher price the exchange opportunity line would be M_2W_2 and he would move to

B_2, selling an amount of wheat equal to NN_2 for an amount of money equal to C_2B_2. At a price OM_0/OW_0, the exchange opportunity line is M_0W_0 and the marketer will neither buy nor sell. The locus of points such as B_1 and B_2 lies on the heavy curve through A, B_1, B_2. For each price, then, we can identify the quantity that the marketer will either buy or sell. This is shown in the lower part of Figure 3, in which price is measured on the vertical axis and quantity on the horizontal axis, reflecting the situation in the upper part. At a price equal to na, equal to OM_0/OW_0, the marketer will neither buy nor sell anything but will remain in his initial position. At a price equal to n_2b_2, equal to

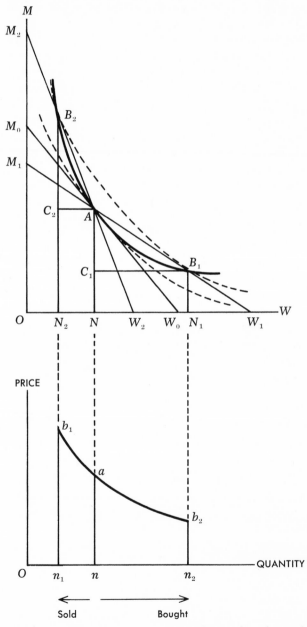

Figure 3 — The source of market demand and supply functions

DEMAND AND SUPPLY: General 101

OM_1/OW_1, he will buy an amount equal to nn_2. At a price equal to n_1b_1, equal to OM_2/OW_2, he will sell an amount equal to nn_1. The curve b_1ab_2 is then his market demand–supply curve, the section ab_2 being his market demand curve and section ab_1 being his market supply curve. If we summed these for all the marketers, we would get the total *market* demand and supply curves.

The problem of constructing *normal* demand and supply curves from the determining functions is more difficult. A simple model of normal supply can be derived if we suppose that we can identify the amount that will be produced at each level of average cost. Thus in the milk industry we might suppose that no milk is produced at an average cost below, say, 15 cents per gallon, that 10,000 gallons is produced at an average cost of 15 cents, 50,000 gallons at an average cost of 16 cents, 100,000 gallons at an average cost of 17 cents, and so on up the scale. If now the price is below 15 cents, no milk will be produced at all. At 15 cents, 10,000 gallons will be produced, at 16 cents, 60,000 gallons, at 17 cents, 160,000 gallons, and so again we go up the scale, cumulating the amounts that will be produced at all costs below the price in question. The supply curve is then seen to be the cumulative frequency distribution of those average costs that Marshall called "particular expenses." The situation is complicated by the fact that different firms produce different quantities at different average costs. Essentially, however, a point on the supply curve indicates the quantity that can be produced at costs equal to or below the price indicated. These cost functions in turn are determined by the production functions, which show how much of the commodity can be produced with given amounts of input. The total cost of producing a given quantity is equal to the sum of the values of the inputs needed to produce it, and the value of each input is equal to its quantity multiplied by its price. Demand is related in a complex way to the preferences and incomes of consumers and the prices of substitute or complementary commodities.

Use of functions. Demand and supply functions are useful mainly in problems involving comparative statics [see STATICS AND DYNAMICS IN ECONOMICS], that is, in the comparison of one position of equilibrium of the price system with another such position after change in the parameters that determine the equilibrium of the system.

Parametric change. Thus, suppose we have a "rise in demand," meaning by this a movement of the whole demand curve to the right, indicating that people are willing to buy more at each price

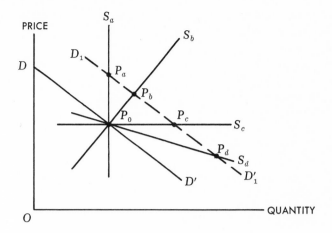

Figure 4 – Effect of a rise in demand

than they were before. The effect of this rise depends on the elasticity of supply, as shown in Figure 4. Here we suppose that DD' is the original demand curve and D_1D_1', the dashed line, is the new demand curve after the rise in demand. P_0 is the original equilibrium price. If the supply curve is perfectly inelastic, such as P_0S_a, there will be a rise in price to P_a but no change in the quantity. If the supply curve is perfectly elastic, such as P_0S_c, there will be an increase in the quantity from P_0 to P_c but no change in the price. In the intermediate situation, such as a supply curve P_0S_b, the new equilibrium will be P_b, where there is some increase in the quantity and some increase in the price. The more elastic the supply curve, the greater the increase in the quantity, the smaller the increase in the price. If the supply curve is negatively elastic, such as P_0S_d, there will be a decline in the price as a result of the increase in demand. Similarly we can show that the effect of an increase in supply, that is, a movement of the supply curve to the right, indicating that people will offer or produce larger quantities at a given price, depends on the elasticity of demand. The more elastic the demand, the greater the change in quantity and the less the change in price. These propositions, simple as they are, are of great importance in many branches of economics. They throw light, for instance, on the question as to why an increase in the money supply produces price and wage increases under some circumstances and produces increases in output and employment under other circumstances.

Tax and tariff incidence. Another important application of demand and supply curves is in the theory of the incidence of taxes and tariffs. The effect of a tax is shown in Figure 5. Suppose that DD' and SS' are the demand and supply curves, with an initial equilibrium at the point P. Suppose

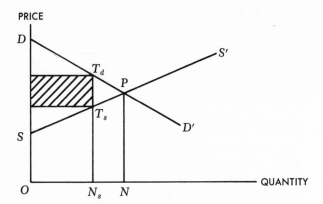

Figure 5 — Effect of a tax

now that a tax is imposed equal to T_dT_s. In equilibrium the demand price must now exceed the supply price by this amount, since a tax is, in effect, an addition to the cost of production. The output of the commodity will therefore decline from ON to ON_s, at which point the required condition is fulfilled. The more elastic the demand and supply curves, the greater the reduction in output. The more elastic the demand, the less the increase in the demand price; the more elastic the supply, the less the decline in the supply price. That is, the relative incidence of the tax as between demanders and suppliers depends on the relative elasticity of the two demand and supply functions. The yield of the tax is equal to the tax per unit of commodity, T_dT_s, multiplied by the total output, ON_s, that is, the shaded rectangle in the figure. This will clearly exhibit a maximum value at some point, so that if the tax is higher than at this point, a reduction in tax will actually increase the yield. The incidence of tariffs may be examined in like manner and be shown to depend on the elasticities of demand and supply curves in various countries.

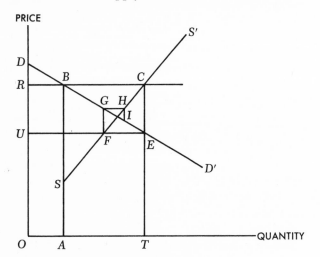

Figure 6 — The cobweb theorem

The general rule that emerges is that in any such situation the most adjustable variable adjusts. When supplies and demands are inelastic, this indicates that price is more adjustable than quantity, hence the major impact is made upon price. If demands and supplies are elastic, the major impact is made upon quantity.

Dynamic solutions.   Demand and supply curves can also be interpreted in such a way as to lead to certain dynamic solutions. The so-called cobweb theorem is a famous example. This is shown in Figure 6. Here DD', the demand curve, shows the price that a particular quantity, say the harvest of a crop, will fetch. The supply curve, SS', shows how much will be produced, let us say in the following year, in response to that price. Suppose then that we have a crop with the harvest equal to OA. The price is AB. As a result of this price, the harvest the following year is equal to RC, which makes the price that year equal to TE. In response to this, the harvest the following year is UF, and so we go on, following the path GHI, etc. If the demand curve is more elastic than the supply curve, the cycle will converge on the point of equilibrium, as in the figure. If the supply curve is more absolutely elastic than the demand curve, the cycle will explode. If the two elasticities are equal, the cycle will continue indefinitely with constant amplitude. There is some evidence of this phenomenon in agriculture, for instance in the so-called hog cycle and also in such crops as potatoes. These demand and supply curves are not stable over long periods, however, and we must be careful to avoid predictions from dynamic systems that are as simple as this, for the reality is always much more complex.

The demand and supply functions can easily be extended to include more variables, and for some purposes it is very important to do so. The demand and supply functions, for instance, may be written as functions of two or more commodities instead of one. We could, for instance, expand equations (1) and (2) into a two-commodity system as shown in equations (4) through (7),

$$(4) \qquad q_{ad} = d_a + e_{ad}p_a + f_{ad}p_b,$$
$$(5) \qquad q_{as} = s_a + e_{as}p_a + f_{as}p_b,$$
$$(6) \qquad q_{bd} = d_b + f_{bd}p_a + e_{bd}p_b,$$
$$(7) \qquad q_{bs} = s_b + f_{bs}p_a + e_{bs}p_b.$$

The notation is the same as for equations (1) and (2) except that the subscript a refers to commodity A and the subscript b refers to commodity B. The parameters f are the (absolute) cross-elasticities. For instance, f_{ad} shows by how much the quantity of A demanded changes per unit change in the price of B. Several types of relationships are possible. If the commodities are independent in demand or supply, the f parameters will be zero. If the f_d parameter is positive, it means that an increase in the price of B will raise the purchases of A, which means the two commodities are competitive in demand. If the f_d parameter is negative, a rise in the price of B, which presumably diminishes the purchases of B, also diminishes the purchases of A, suggesting that the commodities are complementary, such as knives and forks. Similarly in the case of supply, if the parameter f_{as} is positive, it means that an increase in the price of B raises the quantity of A supplied. This suggests that the commodities are complementary in production, such as beef and hides or wool and mutton. If f_{as} is negative, a rise in the price of B diminishes the quantity of A supplied, indicating that the commodities compete in production because, for instance, they use the same scarce resources. If we now add to equations (4) through (7) the two conditions of equilibrium, representing the equality of quantities demanded and supplied for both commodities, as in equations (8) and (9), we have a complete equilibrium system, with six equations and six unknowns, the four quantities and the two prices.

(8) $$q_{ad} = q_{as}$$
(9) $$q_{bd} = q_{bs}$$

The equations of course do not have to be restricted to the linear form.

We can easily extend this system to the general equilibrium of n commodities. In doing this, however, we have to be careful because there are certain constraints on the parameters of such a system imposed by the fact of scarcity. For instance, an increase in demand (or supply) for one commodity must almost always be counterbalanced by a decline in demand (or supply) for another. These constraints, however, are very complex, and it is virtually impossible to put them into simple mathematical form. It is possible, for instance, for the demand for all commodities to increase if the velocity of circulation of money increases. Similarly, it is possible for the supply of all commodities to increase if there is technological change and economic development.

The prices of factors of production, such as wages and rents, can be treated like any other prices in demand and supply analysis. They present, however, some interesting peculiarities. In the case of the supply of a factor such as labor, we have the possibility of what is called a backward-sloping supply curve. Thus, in Figure 7 we plot the wage on the vertical axis and the amount of labor offered on the horizontal axis. There is likely to be some wage, OA, that is so low that no labor will be offered at all, because at this wage the labor cannot subsist, or because there are better opportunities elsewhere. At the wage that will just induce labor to come into this occupation, there may be quite a large amount of labor offered, AB, because the laborer has to work long hours in order to make enough to live on. At higher wages, however, the amount of labor offered may be less, following the course BC, for if the laborer has a conventional standard of living and requires only a certain income to live on, the higher the wage the less he has to work in order to earn this fixed amount. It is also possible, however, that at a certain point, such as C, the laborer realizes that he can earn much more than subsistence if he works harder, and the elasticity of supply again becomes positive, from C to D. A similar phenomenon may sometimes be observed in the case of land, when a rise in rents causes the landowner to employ a larger area in parks and gardens for his own private pleasure because he can get an adequate income from a smaller amount of land rented out. Under these circumstances there may be quite serious breakdowns in the equilibrium of demand and supply, resulting, for instance, in inflation or in perpetual labor shortages in cases where custom prevents wages from rising. Some of the peculiarities of traditional societies may perhaps be explained in these terms.

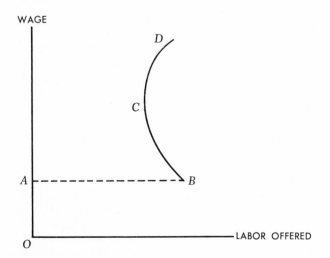

WAGE

Figure 7 — Backward-sloping supply curve

Demand and supply have emerged over the years as very useful tools of fairly rough analysis. They serve to break down the forces operating on prices and outputs into those that operate mainly on the side of the sellers and those that operate mainly on the side of the buyers. They should not be expected to answer all the problems of price theory. They remain, however, indispensable tools.

KENNETH E. BOULDING

[*See also the biographies of* MARSHALL; SMITH, ADAM; WALRAS.]

BIBLIOGRAPHY

BOULDING, KENNETH E. (1941) 1965 *Economic Analysis.* 4th ed. New York: Macmillan.

HENDERSON, H. D. (1922) 1958 *Supply and Demand.* Univ. of Chicago Press.

HICKS, JOHN R. (1939) 1946 *Value and Capital: An Inquiry Into Some Fundamental Principles of Economic Theory.* 2d ed. Oxford: Clarendon.

JENKIN, FLEEMING (1870) 1931 The Graphic Representation of the Laws of Supply and Demand, and Their Application to Labour. Volume 2, pages 76–106 in Fleeming Jenkin, *Papers: Literary, Scientific, etc.* London School of Economics and Political Science.

MARSHALL, ALFRED (1890) 1961 *Principles of Economics.* 9th ed. New York and London: Macmillan. → A variorum edition. The eighth edition is preferable for normal use.

SMITH, ADAM (1776) 1952 *An Inquiry Into the Nature and Causes of the Wealth of Nations.* Chicago: Encyclopedia Britannica. → See especially Book I, Chapter 7. A two-volume paperback edition was published in 1963 by Irwin.

WALRAS, LÉON (1874–1877) 1954 *Elements of Pure Economics: Or, the Theory of Social Wealth.* Translated by William Jaffé. Homewood, Ill.: Irwin; London: Allen & Unwin. → First published in French.

II
ECONOMETRIC STUDIES

Econometric studies of demand and supply are directed toward obtaining quantitative estimates of market demand and supply functions from empirical data. The principal data used have been time series of prices, quantities, incomes, and related variables; the traditional estimating technique has been regression analysis; and the interpretation of the resulting equations has been guided by the theory of consumer demand and the theory of the firm.

Concepts of demand and supply have occupied a prominent place in the development of economic theory. The pure theory of consumer demand reached a high level of refinement in the hands of Pareto, who portrayed the individual consumer as attempting to maximize a utility function that included the quantities of every good and service purchased by him. The quantities purchased were themselves functions of prices and of the consumer's income. The resulting demand functions of individual consumers were in principle measur-

able and could evidently be aggregated to yield market demand functions. Marshall and others specified the conditions of profit maximization for an individual firm and showed that the marginal cost curves of individual firms producing the same product could be aggregated to form an industry supply curve. Demand and supply functions for all commodities and services were included (conceptually) in the theory of general economic equilibrium formulated by Walras and Pareto.

Economic theory specified the *signs* of the coefficients relating prices and quantities in market demand and supply functions, but it could not specify the *magnitudes* of these coefficients for particular commodities. Yet major policy problems, for example, the effects of tariffs, bounties, and excise taxes, required quantitative knowledge. The policy interests of government agencies and the commercial interests of business firms began in the 1800s to generate time series data of an aggregative sort, including wholesale prices of staple commodities and quantities of imports, exports, production, and consumption of such commodities in various countries. The task confronting pioneers in the econometric analysis of demand and supply was to use market data of this kind as a basis for determining the required functions. When the task was first seriously taken up, after 1900, it was found to involve complex problems of statistical estimation and logical interpretation.

A sophisticated econometric analysis of the demand and supply relationships for particular commodities requires an analyst with many skills. He must be thoroughly grounded in economic theory. He must be well versed in the theory of statistical estimation (including the estimation of sets of simultaneous relationships) and in techniques for coping with the problems of autocorrelated disturbances and multicollinearity, which are frequently encountered in economic time series. He must acquaint himself very thoroughly with the conditions under which particular commodities are produced, marketed, and consumed, insofar as these conditions affect the decision processes of the relevant firms and consumers. He must take pains to determine the extent to which each of his economic time series corresponds to the variable called for by economic theory.

A person who has made the necessary investment in economic and statistical theory will ordinarily be tempted to slight the detailed study of data, institutions, and technology pertaining to a particular commodity. On the other hand, a person who because of predilection has made a major investment in learning the technological and institutional characteristics of an industry usually lacks sophistication in economic or statistical theory. This dilemma may sometimes be resolved by co-operation between the econometrician and the commodity or industry specialist.

The literature of demand analysis published prior to the late 1950s is much richer in volume and interest than that of supply analysis. The first and major part of this article will be devoted to studies of demand.

Studies of demand prior to 1939

The story of statistical demand analysis from its beginnings through 1938 can be told in terms of developments in economic theory, in statistical theory and techniques, and in published economic data.

Economic theory. The economic theory requisite for demand analysis was available at an early date. In 1838 Cournot stated the theory of demand in a form that lent itself to numerical application, and he suggested that it would be easy to learn, for all commodities for which statistics had been collected, whether current prices were above or below the value that would maximize the total value of the quantity sold during a given period. Marshall elaborated the concept of a market demand curve in a partial equilibrium context. Walras' general equilibrium theory, published in 1874, expressed the quantity demanded of any commodity as a function not only of its own price but of all other prices. In various articles and books from 1893 to 1911, Pareto extended Walras' theory and stated it with greater rigor.

Statistical theory and technique. Gauss's method of least squares was published early in the nineteenth century, but for several decades it was used primarily by physical scientists in dealing with errors of measurement. The first demand analysts were encouraged to adopt statistical methods as a result of the work of Galton, Pearson, and their fellow biometricians, very late in the century. The theory of correlation was elaborated during the 1890s by Pearson, Yule, and others; and several years elapsed before anyone tried to apply it to price–quantity relationships.

The early work on correlation emphasized bivariate or multivariate normal populations for which the simple, partial, and multiple correlation coefficients had structural significance [see MULTIVARIATE ANALYSIS, *article on* CORRELATION (1)]. This correlation emphasis, carried forward through various textbooks, was to prove quite misleading to the less sophisticated practitioners of statistical demand analysis during the 1920s and 1930s.

By the 1920s R. A. Fisher and others concerned with the design of experiments and the analysis of variance had arrived at a clear-cut distinction between the *correlation model*, emphasized by Galton and Pearson, and the *regression model*, in which values of the independent variables were predetermined by the investigator [see LINEAR HYPOTHESES, *article on* REGRESSION]. Ezekiel (1930), whose book was widely used by demand analysts in the United States, captured the new regression emphasis of Fisher but continued to use some of the older, correlation terminology.

In the 1930s the theory of statistical inference was further developed by J. Neyman and others. Frisch (1934) greatly illuminated the implications of multicollinearity (high intercorrelation) of the independent variables in regression analyses based on economic time series. The problem of autocorrelation in the residuals from time series regressions was largely ignored in empirical demand studies prior to the 1940s.

The problem of identifying a statistically estimated price–quantity relationship as a demand curve rather than a supply curve appears to have been recognized first by Lenoir, in 1913, and then, in 1914, by the critics of Moore's upward-sloping "demand curve" for pig iron [see STATISTICAL IDENTIFIABILITY]. It was very clearly stated by Working (1927), and its ready solution, in what would now be called *recursive models*, was noted by Ezekiel (1928). Statistical methods for dealing with the general simultaneous equation case were not available prior to 1943, although Wright (1934, pp. 196–201), in a paper relatively neglected by economists, successfully estimated what would now be called a just-identified model, by a method logically equivalent to that of reduced forms [see SIMULTANEOUS EQUATION ESTIMATION].

Economic data. The availability of data has been the most severely limiting factor in the estimation of demand functions, from Cournot's time to the present. The data resources of most countries have been greatly enriched since the 1930s, in connection with the development of national income accounts, index numbers of prices, production and consumption, input–output tables, and, in some cases, econometric models of their national economies. The price and quantity data available for empirical studies of demand prior to 1939 were much more limited in scope. Data on agricultural staples have been particularly accessible in the United States, and these commodities were used almost exclusively by Moore, Schultz, and others in their empirical work. Knowledge of data limitations fostered a pragmatic attitude on the part of some agricultural economists, whose applied work was highly useful for policy and forecasting purposes. Ignorance or disregard of data limitations often vitiated the empirical work of academic economists, who were mainly interested in "testing" theories or techniques.

Empirical studies.   At various times Cournot, Jevons, Marshall, and Pareto had all paid lip service to the idea of empirical studies of demand (Schultz 1938, pp. 657–658). Even earlier some businessmen and men of affairs (as well as economists) had no doubt formed judgments about price–quantity relationships of particular interest to them. Stigler (1954) reports some examples. These instances of casual empiricism had no cumulative effect. Benini (1907) computed a least squares multiple regression of coffee consumption on the price of coffee and the price of sugar—the first application to demand analysis of what came to be the dominant statistical technique.

Lenoir's book (1913) in some respects remained unsurpassed until the 1930s. Starting from Pareto's theory of consumer demand, Lenoir made an explicit transition to market demand curves. He made a similar derivation, based on Pareto, of market supply curves. A diagram showing three roughly parallel (nonlinear) demand functions intersecting two roughly parallel (nonlinear) supply curves was used to adumbrate, at least, what is now known as the identification problem. Lenoir then calculated multiple regression equations, involving as many as three independent variables, for a number of commodities, including coffee, wheat, and coal. His descriptions of the time series and the markets involved appear to reflect care and sound judgment. The book as a whole was a most promising integration of economic theory, statistical technique, and sophisticated attention to the data; but it was apparently unnoticed in the United States. It is not mentioned in later work by Moore. Schultz devotes part of one sentence to "Dr. Marcel Lenoir's important book" (1938, p. 64) but gives no description or appraisal of Lenoir's work.

Moore's work.   Schultz wrote, "The statistical study of demand is a new field in economics and may be said to be the creation of only one man—Professor Henry L. Moore" (1938, p. 63). Although recognizing that Moore had predecessors, Schultz commented that "none of these predecessors of Moore attracted much attention, none covered so wide a field, and none succeeded so well in wringing fresh knowledge from the accumulated masses of data" (p. 64).

Moore's books *Economic Cycles: Their Law and Cause* (1914) and *Forecasting the Yield and the Price of Cotton* (1917) furnished the inspiration for much of the statistical demand analysis that was carried on in the United States during the 1920s. Unlike most American economists of his generation, Moore was thoroughly familiar with the works of Cournot, Walras, and Pareto. He was personally acquainted with Walras and corresponded with him. In 1909 and 1913 he took courses in mathematical statistics, including correlation, with Karl Pearson (Stigler 1962, p. 2).

Despite his admiration for the general equilibrium theory of Walras, Moore was pleased to find that in practice he could obtain fairly good fits to his data (prices and production of farm crops) by using equations in two or three variables. His statistical procedures were simple, in keeping with the rather crude data that were available to him. He expressed his time series variables in terms of percentage changes from one year to the next or in terms of link relatives (the given year's value expressed as a ratio to the value in the preceding year) or as ratios to trend. The adjusted series on prices and production were then related by the method of least squares, using straight lines, second-degree parabolas, and in some cases third-degree parabolas. Moore derived statistical demand curves for corn, hay, oats, and potatoes in 1914 and a demand function for cotton in 1917. In subsequent articles, Moore introduced the concept of *the flexibility of price* (namely, the reciprocal of the elasticity of demand), estimated the response of cotton acreage to cotton prices in the preceding year, and described a moving equilibrium of demand and supply for potatoes in which the demand curve expressed current price as a function of current production and the supply curve expressed current production as a function of the preceding year's price. We have here the well-known *cobweb model*, the simplest member of a class of *recursive models*, which assume great importance in discussions of statistical techniques after 1943.

Moore's methods of data adjustment were chosen on a common-sense basis. Two of them, link relatives and per cent changes from year to year, were essentially first-difference transformations. Many years later it was shown that first-difference transformations not only reduced intercorrelation of the explanatory variables but also frequently eliminated significant autocorrelation in the residuals. Moore's third method, using ratios of actual observations to trends, largely eliminated the distorting effects of intercorrelated time trends, as did the quasi first-difference transformations. The constant term in a regression equation based on first differences of prices and quantities may be interpreted as a linear time trend in the level of the price–quantity relationship. [*See the biography of* MOORE, HENRY L.]

Other studies. The simplicity of Moore's statistical methods and his apparently successful applications of them to data for agricultural commodities excited great interest among agricultural economists in the United States. Some of them wished to provide farmers with dependable predictions of prices for the coming year, so that the farmers could adjust their production plans and increase their expected incomes. Some needed demand and supply functions to estimate the probable effects of alternative price support, supply control, tariff, or subsidy policies. Some of these men achieved a high level of sophistication in empirical demand analysis, notably Ezekiel, Waugh, H. Working, and E. J. Working, and a number of excellent studies were published by them between 1922 and 1929 (see the bibliography in Schultz 1938, pp. 779–803). Their work was distinguished by knowledge of data, technology, and institutions and by competent and in some cases highly creative use of economic and statistical theory. There were, also, some less competent "price analysts," whose work was empirical in the extreme and tended to discredit the whole field of statistical demand analysis. With the onset of the economic depression of the 1930s, several of those who had done significant demand studies were drawn into the action programs of the Department of Agriculture and other government agencies. Their unpublished analyses continued to be influential in the appraisal of programs and contemplated policies.

European econometricians did important work in the 1920s and the 1930s. Frisch in Norway estimated the marginal utility of money from a statistical analysis of the demand for sugar in Paris (1926). Hanau in Germany estimated the demand curve and the supply curve for hogs (1927). Leontief in Germany published a statistical analysis of demand and supply functions for several commodities, using a highly imaginative but statistically unreliable technique (1929). Tinbergen in the Netherlands published an important paper on supply curves, including a statistical measurement of the supply elasticity of potato meal (1929). Marschak in Germany made econometric studies of family budgets and argued that on certain assumptions these data would also yield estimates of demand elasticities with respect to price (1931). Roy in France published a collection of his econometric studies (1935), including measurements of demand elasticities for goods and services whose

prices change only infrequently—such as gas, postage stamps, trolley fares, and tobacco (a government monopoly in France). Some of these men had high creative potential in theory and methodology and are now well known for their important contributions to fields of econometrics other than demand analysis. Of those listed in this paragraph, Frisch had by far the greatest impact on econometric studies of demand, both before and after 1939.

Schultz's work. Henry Schultz was a student of H. L. Moore. Inspired by Moore, he studied the works of Cournot, Walras, and Pareto and during 1919 attended lectures on statistics by A. L. Bowley and Karl Pearson.

Schultz's monumental work *The Theory and Measurement of Demand* (1938) is the definitive statement on econometric analysis of demand prior to World War II. Schultz was the "complete demand analyst" of his generation, and his 24-page bibliography is still the best point of departure for a survey of the pre-1938 literature.

Schultz's life work is essentially summed up in his 1938 book (817 pages). Chapters 1, 18, and 19 together provide an excellent statement of the theory of consumer demand, incorporating the extensions of Pareto's basic formulation developed by J. R. Hicks, R. G. D. Allen, and E. Slutsky. Chapters 2 and 3 deal with the logic and theoretical validity of various proposed methods for deriving demand curves from time series and from family budget data. The empirical section (chapters 5–17) presents statistical demand analyses for ten major crops, along with summary comparisons and interpretations of the results for the various commodities, time periods, and functional forms investigated. Further empirical studies are presented in the chapters on related demands (chapters 18 and 19), and the 50-page appendix on elements of curve fitting and correlation provides an excellent guide to least squares regression methods. It would be difficult to name any econometric work of large scope in the 1930s that achieved a better integration of economic theory and statistics with painstaking and realistic attention to institutions, markets, and data. [*See the biography of* SCHULTZ.]

Summary of accomplishments to 1939. Success in empirical demand analysis was not held up by the need for further development in economic theory. Multiple regression analysis was the standard estimating technique from 1914 on, although a number of interesting experiments (weighted regression; regression analysis by short-cut graphic methods; confluence, or bunch-map, analysis) were tried.

The leading demand analysts of the 1920s and

1930s were more sophisticated about the identification problem than is often supposed. Most of the commodities with which Moore, Schultz, and the agricultural economists were concerned followed the cobweb, or recursive, model. As a result of biologically necessary time lags, the identification of a relation between the current production and the current price of a farm commodity, as a demand function, was straightforward; a relation between last year's price and this year's acreage or production could be readily identified as a supply function. E. J. Working made a clear statement of the identification problem, but Ezekiel pointed out that " 'correlated shifts in demand and supply' schedules, which Working feared might completely invalidate many price-analysis studies, are not so likely to cause trouble as he thought" (1928, p. 224). Only the "instantaneous" adjustment of supply to price within a given time unit could give rise to such trouble, and such adjustments (for farm products) were generally small, relative to those in subsequent time periods.

A few attempts were made in the 1930s to derive demand functions for consumer goods. In 1914 Moore found a positively sloping relationship between the price and production of pig iron and made the mistake of trying to rationalize it as a different kind of demand curve. Although it could be argued that the demand for iron, steel, and other producers' durable goods is *ultimately* derived from consumer demand, the empirical connection is tenuous and the subject is best treated in contexts other than that of demand analysis.

Studies of demand since 1939

Since 1939 there have been important developments in methods of estimation, in data networks, and in the objectives of demand studies.

Methods of estimation.   Tests for autocorrelation in the residuals from time series regressions were published in the early 1940s and became a standard feature of demand studies. Haavelmo's brilliant generalization of the identification problem (1943) created in the minds of theoretically oriented economists grave doubts concerning the validity of any demand function estimated by conventional least squares methods. Interestingly enough, the economists who were or had been most deeply involved in empirical demand analysis, including Wold, Stone, Fox, Waugh, and Ezekiel, were not impressed with the implications of Haavelmo's methods for their own work. Wold made the most creative response, and his articles on recursive models and causal chains did much to place the traditional single-equation methods and

the proposed simultaneous equation methods in a common perspective (1953 and articles noted therein). Fox (1958) used arrow diagrams, which can be readily interpreted as causal ordering diagrams, to express his hypotheses concerning the directions and relative magnitudes of the influences of each variable upon directly related variables in complete demand, supply, and price structures for farm and food products. Inspection of the arrow diagram for a given commodity frequently disclosed that the consumer demand function and certain other functions could be estimated appropriately by least squares. Debate concerning alternative estimators of simultaneous equation models, which was active in the early 1960s, has some implications for demand analysis as well as for other branches of econometrics.

Changes in data networks and objectives.   The Keynesian revolution in macroeconomic theory, by demonstrating the important analytical and policy uses of estimates of the national income and its components, stimulated many countries to develop comprehensive national income and product accounts. This interest reflected a growing recognition that governments must take a great deal of responsibility for economic stabilization and the avoidance of unemployment. Tinbergen's econometric models and Leontief's input–output models also required comprehensive coverage (at appropriate levels of aggregation) of all sectors of a national economy.

The prospective uses of economic data in comprehensive models have given a more analytical focus to the design of data systems in recent years than generally existed prior to World War II. At the same time, comprehensive models not only encourage but logically require certain restrictions upon the coefficients of demand functions for different commodities. These restrictions were generally disregarded in the pre-1939 tradition, except for a few studies (by Schultz, Waugh, and Ezekiel) of commodities closely related in demand, such as beef, pork, lamb, and chicken. Hence, empirical work in the 1960s has shown a much greater tendency to use "extraneous" or a priori information to supplement time series data and to rely on theoretical considerations in supplying coefficients that cannot be estimated directly from the data.

Major empirical works.   Wold (1953) published an excellent exposition of Paretian demand theory, of the theory of stationary random processes as it affects the analysis of economic time series, and of the theory of regression analysis. While the scope of Wold's theoretical chapters is similar to that of Schultz, Wold incorporates a number of major theoretical developments that had been made after 1938, by himself and others. Wold's book requires a higher level of mathematical and statistical competence on the part of its readers than does Schultz's, and in the 1950s it largely supplanted the latter as a graduate text and reference work. Wold's empirical chapters, however, were not particularly distinguished.

Stone's comprehensive book (1954) establishes him as a "complete demand analyst" in the Schultz tradition, and he had indeed been influenced by Schultz's writings. Stone explicitly covers those portions of economic theory and estimation procedures that are relevant to demand analysis. The mathematical level of his exposition is less demanding than Wold's, but the implications he draws for empirical work are equally authoritative. The volume and quality of the econometric results presented by Stone are also impressive. An interesting feature of his work is the use of income elasticities of demand, estimated from family budget data, to adjust time series of per capita consumption before regressing them on time series of prices.

Fox (1958 and articles noted therein) published the largest array of empirical demand functions that had so far been produced in the United States for farm products and foods, taking advantage of the many improvements achieved by the Bureau of Agricultural Economics between 1938 and 1950 in data on retail prices, per capita food consumption, disposable personal income, and food marketing margins. His demand studies covered both farm products and foods, whereas Wold and Stone dealt only with foods. Fox used logarithmic first-difference transformations and took explicit cognizance of identification problems.

Special adaptations of demand theory. Strotz (1957) put forward the concept of a "utility tree," which justified the aggregation of consumer goods into budget categories that were assumed to be *want independent* of one another. Cross elasticities of demand between individual commodities in two want-independent groups could then be ignored in applied work; nonzero cross elasticities might continue to exist and be recognized between groups of commodities. Strotz was motivated by a desire "to exchange some realism [in assumptions] for greater relevance [in applications]" (1957, p. 270) and stated that his hypothesis "implies certain empirically meaningful and interesting conditions on the price coefficients of the demand functions" (p. 269).

Frisch (1959) published a complete scheme for computing all direct and cross elasticities of demand in a model with many sectors. He noted that

it was easier to obtain estimates of budget proportions and Engel (income) elasticities than of elasticities with respect to price but that by making certain want-independence assumptions the price elasticities could be deduced from the knowledge of budget proportions and Engel elasticities. Frisch noted further that the direct elasticities with respect to price could, as a rule, be estimated more easily than the cross elasticities. If we are willing to assume that the behavior of the market can be described by the behavior of a *representative individual* and are also willing to make stipulated assumptions about want independence, all the cross elasticities of demand in a model including many commodities could be supplied in a reproducible way consistent with the other assumptions of demand theory.

Brandow (1961) followed Frisch's suggestions in specifying a complete matrix of price and income elasticities of demand at retail prices, for 24 foods or food groups and for the aggregate of all nonfood consumer goods and services. This matrix represented a careful synthesis of results obtained from United States data by other investigators, together with additional analyses of his own. He presented equations for converting each of his 24 consumer demand functions into demand functions at the farm price level and derived other equations for determining the internal balance of the livestock and feed economy. Brandow did not attempt to develop equations for forecasting acreages and supplies of crops, although adjustments of livestock supplies to quantities of feed available were endogenous in his model. As of 1965, Brandow's study was the most comprehensive and internally consistent application of demand analysis yet completed.

Apart from Schultz (who died in 1938), Waugh has been the most sophisticated of the American demand analysts in his command of economic theory and the most imaginative in his application of statistical techniques. His methodological and empirical contributions have extended from 1923 to 1964. His bulletin *Demand and Price Analysis* (1964), while written on an expository level, reports many methodological experiments, including a symmetric matrix of direct and cross elasticities of demand for three competing commodities; an empirically derived "indifference surface" for beef and pork; an orthogonal regression; an appendix on relationships between demand coefficients (along the lines of Frisch's 1959 article); and an appendix on the optimal allocation of commodity supplies among independent markets to maximize producer returns. Waugh's bulletin provides a brief, clear, and interesting survey of the theory and techniques of demand analysis, with many illustrations.

Smith (1964) applied linear programming to the electronic computation of human diets, drawing his data from time series of weekly purchases of some 600 food products by 176 families in Lansing, Michigan [*see* PROGRAMMING]. The retail prices of the products were also obtained. Smith showed that the solutions for least-cost diets meeting stated requirements for nutrients, specified complementarity restrictions, and "food-habit" or palatability stipulations could, under certain very special assumptions, be made to yield estimates of the marginal utilities of commodities and the marginal costs of the effective restraints. It remains to be seen whether this approach will converge with that of Frisch and Brandow. Ladd and Martin (1964) used the Lansing data to demonstrate the existence of distributed lags in the adjustment of consumer demand for some foods to price and income changes when the units of observation were four-week (and in some cases 13-week) periods [*see* DISTRIBUTED LAGS].

Econometric studies of supply

Prior to the late 1950s, econometric studies of supply were much less exciting to economists than were studies of demand. The theory of consumer demand embraces all consumer goods and services and embodies principles of rational choice applicable to consumers in general. But the technology (and geography) of supply may be highly specialized to particular commodities, and such conceptual unity as the field possesses may be submerged in these details.

In some countries and periods, agricultural production takes place under atomistic competition and provides data for econometric analysis. In the industrial sector, oligopoly and monopolistic competition are common; many firms operate at less than full capacity, and statistical studies suggest that their supply curves are nearly horizontal over the usual ranges of output. Data on the cost functions of individual firms are often closely held [*see* PRODUCTION AND COST ANALYSIS].

Published econometric studies of supply have for the most part dealt with agricultural commodities. Moore used least squares regression methods to estimate the response of potato yields in a given year to prices in the preceding year. Bean (1929) and other agricultural economists used regression techniques to estimate the responses of crop acreages to prices lagged one or two years and the responses of hog numbers to the lagged relative prices of hogs and corn.

In the United States, interest in econometric supply analysis was largely dissipated by the depression of the 1930s, by government programs to control acreages (after 1932), and by the severe droughts of 1934 and 1936. Some local interest continued in supply response studies for minor crops that were not subject to acreage allotments. In 1928 Schultz gave considerable attention to estimating the supply curve for sugar, in addition to the demand curve. It is significant that he had little to say about supply functions in his 1938 book.

Nerlove (1958) injected a new idea into the traditional type of supply response study. He hypothesized that farmers adjust their planted acreage of a crop in response to the difference between the most recently experienced actual price and their concept of the "long-run normal price" for the same year. The technique proposed for inferring the long-run normal price was ingenious, but it only momentarily dispelled the apathy of economists toward regression studies of acreage response in an era of government programs controlling acreage.

In the 1950s the popularization of linear programming methods among agricultural economists by Heady and others opened the way for a normative analysis of supply response. An individual farmer could be represented as adjusting his planted acreages of different crops in an effort to maximize net income, subject to his resource constraints and given his expectations concerning the prices at which the various crops would sell after harvest. The existence of support prices permitted accurate predictions in some cases.

Day (1963) applied recursive linear programming to a homogeneous eleven-county area in the Mississippi Delta, which he treated as though it were a single profit-maximizing unit. Day's model included nine possible outputs (counting cotton lint and cotton seed as separate products) and about 27 possible production inputs. He specified input and output vectors for a total of 97 different production processes, each process representing a particular crop grown on a particular soil type with a stated level of application of commercial fertilizer and a particular combination of machinery, labor, and pesticides.

Day applied his model *recursively*, year by year, from 1939 through 1958. New production activities, for example, mechanical cotton picking, were introduced into the profit-maximizing solution only when they had become more profitable than all previously existing activities on at least one soil type. The model generated time series for all outputs and inputs, as well as "shadow prices" for all the restrictions (including government acreage allotments) that were effective in each year's optimal solution.

In the early 1960s Heady and others applied linear programming to each farm in representative samples of farms to arrive at aggregative supply response functions. Heady and Egbert (1964) developed a linear programming model of agricultural production in the United States for more than 120 regions and for all major crops in each region. By 1965 plans were under way to include livestock production in the model and to increase the number of regions.

By 1965 the most ambitious econometric studies of demand and supply had achieved a (partly synthetic) comprehensiveness that would have astonished the early critics of Moore. But Moore himself would not have been astonished. In his last book, *Synthetic Economics* (1929), Moore had proposed an implementation of the general equilibrium model of Walras, the principal elements of which would be comprehensive sets of empirical demand and supply functions!

KARL A. FOX

BIBLIOGRAPHY

BEAN, L. H. 1929 The Farmers' Response to Price. *Journal of Farm Economics* 11:368–385.

BENINI, RODOLFO 1907 Sull'uso delle formole empiriche nell' economia applicata. *Giornale degli economisti* Series 2 35:1053–1063.

BRANDOW, G. E. 1961 *Interrelations Among Demands for Farm Products and Implications for Control of Market Supply.* Pennsylvania, Agricultural Experiment Station, University Park, Bulletin No. 680. University Park: The Station.

DAY, RICHARD H. 1963 *Recursive Programming and Production Response.* Contributions to Economic Analysis, No. 30. Amsterdam: North-Holland Publishing.

EZEKIEL, MORDECAI 1928 Statistical Analyses and the "Laws" of Price. *Quarterly Journal of Economics* 42: 199–227.

EZEKIEL, MORDECAI (1930) 1941 *Methods of Correlation Analysis.* 2d ed. New York: Wiley. → A third edition, with Karl A. Fox as co-author, was published in 1959 as *Methods of Correlation and Regression Analysis: Linear and Curvilinear.*

FOX, KARL A. 1958 *Econometric Analysis for Public Policy.* Ames: Iowa State College Press.

FRISCH, RAGNAR 1926 Sur un problème d'économie pure. *Norsk matematisk forenings skrifter* 1st Series 16: 1–40.

FRISCH, RAGNAR 1934 *Statistical Confluence Analysis by Means of Complete Regression Systems.* Oslo: Civiltryckeri. → Also published in the *Nordic Statistical Journal,* Volume 5.

FRISCH, RAGNAR 1959 A Complete Scheme for Computing All Direct and Cross Demand Elasticities in a Model With Many Sectors. *Econometrica* 27:177–196.

HAAVELMO, TRYGVE 1943 The Statistical Implications of a System of Simultaneous Equations. *Econometrica* 11:1–12.

HANAU, ARTHUR (1927) 1930 *Die Prognose der Schweinepreise.* 3d ed. Vierteljahrshefte zur Konjunkturforschung, Sonderheft 18. Berlin: Reimar Hobbing. → The first edition was issued as Sonderheft 2, the second as Sonderheft 7.

HEADY, EARL O.; and EGBERT, ALVIN C. 1964 Regional Programming of Efficient Agricultural Production Patterns. *Econometrica* 32:374–386.

LADD, GEORGE W.; and MARTIN, JAMES E. 1964 *Application of Distributed Lag and Autocorrelated Error Models to Short-run Demand Analysis.* Iowa Agricultural Experiment Station, Research Bulletin No. 526. Ames: The Station.

LENOIR, MARCEL 1913 *Études sur la formation et le mouvement des prix.* Paris: Girard & Brière.

LEONTIEF, WASSILY 1929 Ein Versuch zur statistischen Analyse von Angebot und Nachfrage. *Weltwirtschaftliches Archiv* 30:1*–53*. → The asterisks are a part of the pagination system of this volume.

MARSCHAK, JAKOB 1931 *Elastizität der Nachfrage.* Tübingen (Germany): Mohr.

MOORE, HENRY L. 1914 *Economic Cycles: Their Law and Cause.* New York: Macmillan.

MOORE, HENRY L. 1917 *Forecasting the Yield and the Price of Cotton.* New York: Macmillan.

MOORE, HENRY L. 1929 *Synthetic Economics.* New York: Macmillan.

NERLOVE, MARC 1958 *The Dynamics of Supply: Estimation of Farmers' Response to Price.* Studies in Historical and Political Science, Series 76, No. 2. Baltimore: Johns Hopkins Press.

ROY, RENÉ 1935 *Études économétriques.* Paris: Sirey.

SCHULTZ, HENRY 1938 *The Theory and Measurement of Demand.* Univ. of Chicago Press.

SMITH, VICTOR E. 1964 *Electronic Computation of Human Diets.* East Lansing: Michigan State Univ., Graduate School of Business Administration, Bureau of Business and Economic Research.

STIGLER, GEORGE J. 1954 The Early History of Empirical Studies of Consumer Behavior. *Journal of Political Economy* 62:95–113.

STIGLER, GEORGE J. 1962 Henry L. Moore and Statistical Economics. *Econometrica* 30:1–21.

STONE, RICHARD 1954 *The Measurement of Consumers' Expenditure and Behaviour in the United Kingdom: 1920–1938.* Cambridge Univ. Press.

STROTZ, ROBERT H. 1957 The Empirical Implications of a Utility Tree. *Econometrica* 25:269–280.

TINBERGEN, JAN 1929 Bestimmung und Deutung von Angebotskurven: Ein Beispiel. *Zeitschrift für Nationalökonomie* 1:669–679.

TUKEY, JOHN W. 1954 Causation, Regression, and Path Analysis. Pages 35–66 in Oscar Kempthorne et al. (editors), *Statistics and Mathematics in Biology.* Ames: Iowa State College Press.

WAUGH, FREDERICK V. 1964 *Demand and Price Analysis: Some Examples From Agriculture.* U.S. Department of Agriculture, Technical Bulletin No. 1316. Washington: U.S. Department of Agriculture, Economic and Statistical Analysis Division.

WOLD, HERMAN 1953 *Demand Analysis: A Study in Econometrics.* New York: Wiley.

WORKING, E. J. (1927) 1952 What Do Statistical "Demand Curves" Show? Pages 97–115 in American Economic Association, *Readings in Price Theory.* Edited by G. J. Stigler and K. E. Boulding. Homewood, Ill.: Irwin. → First published in Volume 41 of the *Quarterly Journal of Economics.*

WRIGHT, SEWALL 1934 The Method of Path Coefficients. *Annals of Mathematical Statistics* 5:161–215.

DEMOCRACY

The term democracy indicates both a set of ideals and a political system—a feature it shares with the terms communism and socialism. "Democracy" is harder to pin down, however, than either "socialism" or "communism"; for while the latter labels have found in Marxism an ideological matrix, or at least a point of reference, democracy has never become identified with a specific doctrinal source—it is rather a by-product of the entire development of Western civilization. No wonder, therefore, that the more "democracy" has come to be a universally accepted honorific term, the more it has undergone verbal stretching and has become the loosest label of its kind. Not every political system claims to be a socialist system, but even communist systems claim to be democracies. Since World War II, "democracy" encompasses everything; as stated by a UNESCO report: ". . . for the first time in the history of the world . . . practical politicians and political theorists agree in stressing the democratic element in the institutions they defend and in the theories they advocate" (United Nations . . . 1951, p. 522).

One reaction to this state of affairs has been to avoid using the term. As has been forcibly stated, ". . . discussions about democracy . . . are intellectually worthless because we do not know what we are talking about" (Jouvenel 1945, p. 338 in 1948 edition). The alternative is, of course, to dissect the term as analytically as possible.

Scope and meaning

Democratic legitimacy. Democracy is, to begin with, a principle of legitimacy [see also LEGITIMACY]. So conceived it is both the minimal and the sole common denominator of any and all democratic doctrine. From the democratic viewpoint nobody denies that power is legitimate only when it is derived from the authority of the people and based upon their consent. Nobody questions that democracy is the opposite of autocracy. But this agreement is short-lived and indeed rests on fragile foundations. For democracy as a legitimizing principle lends itself to two diverging interpretations: (1) that the consent of the people can be a mere presumption, an untested assumption; or (2) that there is no democratic consent unless it is verified through *ad hoc* procedures (which exclude, notably, consent by sheer acclamation). And these opposing views are related to an even more fundamental disagreement over the very meaning of the term people—a hazy notion indeed.

"The people" can be understood as a singular term (in fact, *peuple*, *Volk*, and *popolo* are singular nouns in French, German, and Italian) or as a plural, that is, as a single entity or as "everybody." And, clearly, it is only the latter notion that calls for a legitimacy ascertained by means of reliable procedures; for "the people" conceived as an entity, or as an organic whole, easily combines with a legitimacy assumed on the sole basis of acclamations and plebiscitary approbations. Therefore, on the grounds of democracy conceived merely as a principle of legitimacy, any and all governments can easily claim to be democracies simply by switching from verified consensus to presumed consensus. By itself, then, popular consent does not suffice to qualify any particular political system as a democracy. Such qualification is given only by the procedures of consent—and these are controversial.

The normative focus. From a normative standpoint the definition of democracy strictly derives from the literal meaning of the term—"power of the people." We may say that the *ought* of democracy amounts to the etymology of the term. There are, however, three different normative approaches: oppositional, realistic, and perfectionistic (or utopian). Used as an oppositional concept, democracy indicates what ought *not* to be; realistic normativism points to what *could* be; while utopian normativism presents the image of the perfect society that *must* be. Moreover, since the normative attitude is basically future-oriented, it is easily converted into "futurism" in the sense that "democracy" becomes a long-range projection unrelated to current deeds. The use of undemocratic means to achieve democratic ends finds its justification precisely in this attitude.

The descriptive focus. A descriptive standpoint leads to definitions that bear little resemblance, if any, to the normative definitions of democracy. A concern with what democracy *is* in the real world seldom, if ever, makes reference to the notion of people. As Dahl puts it, in actuality democracies are "poliarchies" (1956, pp. 63–89). And the standard definition provided by most authors describes democracy as a system based on competitive parties, in which the governing majority respects the rights of minorities. The discussion is focused on the concepts of representation, majority rule, opposition, competition, alternative government, control, and the like—hardly ever on the notion of a self-governing people. Even descriptively, however, the approaches can be quite different: structural, procedural, or behavioral. These are not clear-cut distinctions, for both the structures and the procedures of democracy are meant to elicit and to enforce a given behavior. Yet procedures are not necessarily related to institutional structures; and moreover the behavioral definition may be incompatible with the structural and procedural definitions, as we shall see.

The typological focus. Democracy is also one type of political system among others, and from this viewpoint the problem becomes to define the properties that distinguish it from nondemocratic polities. When the issue arises, the attempt is often made to qualify democracy with reference to an *ought* rather than to the *is*. Clearly, however, the identity of a political system cannot be ascertained on normative grounds. It can only be assessed on factual grounds, that is, with reference to the possibility of verification provided by a descriptive account.

Another source of confusion lies in the intermingling of three different standards. At times democracy is taken to include all the political systems falling short of outright dictatorships. This identification is purely negative; the standard is very low, and we are thus confronted with an *unspecific* type. However, since no political system has a definite form at the moment of its inception, this minimal standard of democracy may aptly indicate its "initial" type. In other instances the standards are higher, and democracy is identified positively by the existence of developed representative institutions and by the establishment of "constitutional government" [*see* CONSTITUTIONS AND CONSTITUTIONALISM; *see also* Friedrich 1937]. Since this is the more frequent case, as well as the meaning in which the term democracy is more frequently used, we may speak of it as the medium or *normal* type. Finally, when we use a high standard and refer to maximum achievement, we are confronted with a strict meaning of democracy, according to which the term denotes an *advanced* type.

According to the minimal standard, roughly half of the world may be included in the realm of democracy; according to the medium standard the number of democratic countries dwindles; and according to the high standard a mere dozen or so countries have achieved a satisfactory degree of democracy. And it requires little effort to imagine how easily the label "democratic" can be turned into "undemocratic," and vice versa, simply by switching from one standard to another.

The dimensional focus. A distinction must also be made between small-scale and large-scale operations, between microdimensions and macrodimensions. Microdemocracy applies to face-to-face relationships, i.e., to small groups. Macrodemocracy applies whenever a collectivity is too large and/or spatially too scattered to allow any direct interchange among its members and any kind of face-to-face relationships. The distinction implies that a macrodemocracy is not some kind of enlargement of a microprototype. Their respective properties have very little, if anything, in common, at least in the sense that voluntary associations and small political units provide no clues for understanding a modern political democracy. They are perhaps the most essential inner nourishment of a democratic political system, but they can neither replace it nor dispense with it. In particular, they provide no model for macrodemocracy. It may be argued that no definite line can be drawn between small and large, which are indeed relative concepts; nonetheless the fact remains that micro- and macrodemocracy are inversely correlated: the greater the geographical extension of democracy, the less its intensity as a real experience of shared decision making.

Secondary meanings

From the time the term *demokratía* was coined in the fifth century B.C. until roughly a century ago, democracy was used as a political concept. Tocqueville was struck, however, by the social aspect of American democracy, and we thus speak of "social democracy"; Marxism has popularized the expression "economic democracy"; and guild socialism, particularly the Webbs' book, *Industrial Democracy* (1897), has given currency to the label "industrial democracy." These are the major secondary usages of the term democracy; and since we shall be concerned mainly with the primary political usage, they will only be briefly considered.

Social democracy. "Social democracy" is generally conceived as an endogenous state and style of the society and should therefore not be confused with "socialist democracy," which is a policy enforced by the state upon the society. The expression social democracy usually points to the democratization of the society itself, as expressed by its manners and customs, and particularly by the belief in what Bryce called "equality of estimation," that is, equal treatment and equal respect for every man. Social democracy may thus be defined as an ethos and a way of life characterized by a general leveling of status differences. By implication it may also indicate a "multigroup society" in which a lively network of microdemocracies sustains and implements political macrodemocracy.

Economic democracy. Since political democracy is primarily concerned with political and juridical equality, and since the expression social democracy denotes equality of status, it follows that concern for the equalization of wealth may be called economic democracy. In this generic and obvious sense then, the label denotes a democracy whose primary policy goal is the redistribution of wealth and the equalization of economic opportunities. So conceived, economic democracy presupposes political democracy—indeed, it is meant to be the ultimate feedback of a democratic form of government.

However, in the Marxist sense—which is by far the prevalent association of the expression—"economic democracy" does not presuppose political democracy; it replaces it. This follows from the materialistic conception of history, i.e., from negation of the autonomy of politics. In the Marxist approach political democracy has no value in itself, for it is only a superstructure of bourgeois and capitalistic oppression, and "political" democracy is thus reduced to "capitalistic" democracy. But once the domain of politics disappears from our purview, there remains little, if anything, that one can say about democracy in constructive terms. One can oppose the "false" existing democracies, but what can one propose for the sake of rebuilding a "true" democracy? Therefore in the Marxist meaning "economic democracy" is only an oppositional concept, and a distorted one at that, for it is not really the obverse of capitalist *democracy* but merely the obverse of capitalist *economy*. In other terms, in this context, democracy only means an economic system, and one based on the assumption that politics can be taken out of politics.

Industrial democracy. "Industrial democracy" is a narrower but more constructive term for pinning down the problems associated with the idea of economic democracy. Basically, industrial democracy is democracy within industrial plants. In many ways it is an adaptation of the Greek formula to an industrial society: it is a microdemocracy in which the member of the political community, the *polítes*, is replaced by the member of an economic community, the worker. In its ultimate form, industrial democracy calls for self-government by the workers in a plant—a direct self-government which could or should be crowned at the national level by a "functional democracy," that is, by a political system based on functional representation [*see* REPRESENTATION]. In practice, the ideal of industrial democracy has materialized only at the microlevel in a number of schemes concerning the workers' participation in management: "codetermination" in Germany and Austria, workers' councils and "self-management" in Yugoslavia, and institu-

tionalized practices of joint consultation between management and trade unions in various other countries (reviewed, for example, in Clegg 1960).

To sum up, nobody will deny the importance of social democracy as a vital basis of a democratic polity; and it is usually conceded that economic equalization and industrial democracy are valuable goals. Nonetheless, all these conceptualizations are secondary in that they presuppose, explicitly or implicitly, a political democracy. In other words, these democracies are not *sovereign*. In particular, if the over-all political system is not a democratic system, economic equality has little meaning and industrial democracy can be eliminated overnight. This is the reason why democracy is first and foremost *political democracy*, with the understanding that "the importance of the democratic political method lies mainly in its nonpolitical by-products" (Frankel 1962, p. 167).

People's democracy. The labels "people's democracy," "progressive democracy," "Soviet democracy," and the like, pose a special problem. The difficulty is not simply that they point to a cluster of manifold elements but that the components of the cluster are so slippery that they defy analysis. A communist democracy is a "politico–economic" democracy, a "macro–micro" democracy, and a "supra–infra" democracy. It is almost impossible, therefore, to classify a people's democracy in terms of the distinction between the political and extrapolitical meanings of democracy. The notion is clearly derivative, however, and may be considered in this sense as another secondary meaning of democracy.

For one thing, the expression "people's democracy" was coined and launched only after World War II, as a transparent response to the "goodness" of the word democracy. The derivative nature of the notion is also revealed by its thinness. The range of any discourse about the communist-type democracy is basically confined to a normative context and leans particularly on normative–futuristic democracy. In any case, it remains refractory to empirical verification, since the communist theory bypasses both structural and procedural arguments and draws exclusively on a behavioral definition of democracy that cannot be disproved. It follows that the theory of communist democracy does not succeed in showing how this democracy is meaningfully related to the facts. All in all, by no criterion can the systems labeled "people's democracy," "Soviet democracy," etc., be differentiated from nondemocratic political systems [*see* COMMUNISM].

Democracy as a form of government

Greek and modern democracy. Greek democracy, as practiced in Athens during the fourth century B.C., was the closest approximation to the literal meaning of the term. One could argue, in effect, that the Athenian *demos* had more *kratos* (power) than any other people since. At the same time Greek democracy represents the maximum conceivable enlargement of a microdemocracy. When the *demos* gathered, the Athenian system actually operated as a "town-meeting" democracy in which some thousands of citizens expressed their ayes and nays.

To be sure, when the *demos* was assembled "democracy" consisted largely of decisions made by acclamation. But the town-meeting aspect was only the impressive part of the system. Its most effective part resided in the mechanism that made "all command each, and each in his turn all," as Aristotle concisely put it; i.e., the exercise of power was effectively and largely shared by means of a rapid turnover of officials. The sharing in the exercise of power was also effective in that it occurred at random, for most officials were chosen by lot. On both counts—the collective "self-governing" and the individual "governing in turn"—Greek democracy was a direct democracy based on the actual participation of the citizens in their government.

Modern democracy is entirely different. It is based not on participation but on representation; it presupposes not direct exercise of power but delegation of power; it is not, in short, a system of self-government but a system of *control* and *limitation* of government. While Greek democracy can be defined literally as a "government of the people over the people," modern democracy cannot, for the people who are governed are not the same people who govern. Therefore, we should not be misled into believing that present-day "electoral participation" resembles the real participation of the Greek citizen and even less that the devices we call "direct democracy" (referendum, initiative, etc.) can bridge the gap between the Greek and the modern formulas.

Greek and modern democracy are also entirely different in respect to political freedom. In fact, only the modern form can be called "liberal democracy." The vagueness of the term liberalism and the multifarious aspects of freedom make this a controversial topic, with some authors flatly denying that men of antiquity were free (for example, Fustel de Coulanges 1864) and other scholars (recently, Havelock 1957) affirming the contrary. Yet there is at least one sense, and a very real one, in which we can follow Benjamin Constant in contrasting ancient and modern liberty (1819). The freedom of the citizen of the *polis* consisted in his part of sovereignty. Moreover, his freedom was not conceived as liberty for each individual rooted in, and protected by, "personal rights." The individual as such, "each body," was absorbed in the collective "Allbody," that is, the *polítes* was called to exist for the *polis*; whereas we are likely to hold the opposite, that the state exists for the sake of the citizens. And while this does not imply that the Greeks called freedom what we consider oppression, it does point to the fact that their liberty was entirely dependent upon the existence of a diffuse and relatively small political community (hardly a "state" in our sense of the term) in which the liberty of the individual could still be entrusted to his share in the exercise of sovereignty [*see* Freedom].

It is fairly obvious that the Greek type of democracy is inapplicable to modern conditions. Modern political societies are large societies, and the greater the number of the people involved, the less their participation can be effective and meaningful. Furthermore, the modern nationwide state confronts us with spatial or extensional impossibility, for real self-government cannot occur among absentees; it requires a *demos* to be present in person on the spot. Finally, it should not escape our attention that the "directness" of a democracy is strictly related to political primitivism: the government of all in turn is, in effect, the counterpart of a low degree of distinctiveness, explicitness, and specialization of the political functions.

It would seem that we are confronted with a paradox. To the Greeks democracy, literally understood, was a *possible* form of government. To us, instead, literal democracy is an *impossible* form of government. The query is: Why did we reinstate—after two thousand years of oblivion and disrepute—a term whose original and literal meaning calls for a blatant impossibility?

It does not suffice to reply that we give the Greek term a different meaning. Names are important in themselves, and the fact is that all over the world the common man of the twentieth century understands the word democracy very much in the same way as did the citizen of ancient Athens: its utterance elicits similar behavior, similar expectations, and similar demands. Nor can the issue be evaded simply by saying that the choice of the term democracy was unfortunate. For the word has gained acceptance not despite but *because* of its utopian bent. It is not a coincidence that while the Greeks coined the term democracy to describe a possible form of government, we have revived a term that prescribes an impossible form. In the modern world, then, "democracy" is first and foremost a normative word: it does not *describe* a thing, it *prescribes* an ideal.

The ideal. Westerners have lived under democratic systems long enough to have reached the phase of democratic disillusionment. They are therefore likely to underestimate the impact of ideals and especially the force of the democratic "illusion"—no matter under which apocalyptic banner—in the rest of the world. Westerners are thus inclined to miss the peculiar temper of modern politics and—ironically enough—the fundamental change that Western rationalism has brought about in man's attitude toward history.

Until the Enlightenment political forms were not conceived as future-oriented paradigms; for the paradigm was in the past, in a lost paradise, or in a state of nature. For millennia political theorists have been concerned with what *could* be. But from the French Revolution onward we have become concerned with what *should* be. Classical liberalism still belonged to an age of reasonableness in which men were content with regulating the tide; democracy, socialism, and communism were born, instead, out of a Promethean attitude, out of the ambition to swim against the tide. The difference between the names liberalism and democracy is hardly descriptive; it is normative. The latter label has absorbed the former one in large part because "democracy" has a utopian potential that "liberalism" lacks [*see* LIBERALISM].

In fact, by any other criterion the term liberalism would have been a more advantageous choice. It was not associated with a memorable failure, an experiment that had rapidly degenerated into both sectional government—the "rule of the poor against the rich," as Aristotle realistically put it—and "mobocracy," a lawless rule of the mob. Moreover, the term liberalism pointed to the very crowning of the long-sought ideal of a mixed and balanced form of government. Thus the current success of the name democracy draws on the same reason that accounts for its previous abandonment, namely, that "democracy" points to an extreme ideal—no less extreme *qua* ideal than "communism," and so much so that in a purely normative context the two ideals can ultimately be joined.

This is not to say, of course, that "democracy" was deliberately reinstated because modern man has fallen into a utopian mood. The adoption of the name democracy was also a response to the entry into politics of ever-growing masses. The small literate elites of former times could well dispense with *miranda* and *credenda*, to use Charles Merriam's terms; but the more politics opens up to comparatively illiterate masses, the more *miranda* and *credenda* are needed to feed them no less than to mobilize and to manipulate them.

In a historical purview, then, it is the *ought*, the deontology of democracy, that comes to the fore. And a historical approach also helps to place the various forms of democratic normativism in perspective.

During the nineteenth century, the term democracy was mainly used in progressive circles as an oppositional ideal. As Louis Hartz points out, the image of democracy depicted by its early advocates was basically the negation of what they wanted to destroy (Chambers & Salisbury [1960] 1962, p. 27). Democracy so conceived is simply the reverse of absolutism, a polemical notion whose function is to oppose, not to propose. The utterance of "democracy" is a way of saying *no* to inequality, injustice, and coercion. But once the enemy is defeated the problem becomes to specify what *ought* to be, that is, to identify equality, justice, and freedom in a positive fashion. Faced with this problem democratic normativism splits: it can either adapt itself to the real world or consolidate itself into a future-oriented perfectionism.

Realistic normativism follows from awareness of the "opposite principle" (Herz 1951, pp. 168–189), or of the principle of the "opposite danger" (Sartori [1962] 1965, pp. 63–67). Its proponents realize that as an ideal is converted into reality, it must be continuously adjusted as it approaches fulfillment. Therefore, the more an actual democracy is maximized, the more its deontology must be minimized. If within an established democracy the democratic *ought* is maintained in its extreme form, it militates against the very system it has produced, that is, it produces "opposite" results.

Utopian normativism, on the other hand, maintains an oppositional attitude within an existing democracy. It refuses to admit that ideals have a countervailing function and will not allow the ideal to fade in victory. The normative attitude is to maximize ideals in their purity, in anticipation of a future in which the *ought* will finally overcome the *is*.

Theoretically, one can easily dismiss both oppositional and utopian normativism. But the fact remains that we live in a time of explosion of expectations and in which the high tide of democratic perfectionism has yet to come in most of Asia, Africa, and Latin America. We are thus faced with an apparently insoluble dilemma. In order to make democracy succeed in the real world we have adopted a realistic normativism; but a realistic image of democracy, and often a disillusioned one, can hardly compete on a world-wide scale against the appeal of Utopia. A realistic normativism loses the dimension of the future, and this suggests that Western democracies may well lose control over the explosive potentialities of the democratic ideal.

The reality. The *ought* and the *is* of democracy are inextricably intertwined. A democracy exists only insofar as its ideals and values bring it into being. Therefore, to deal separately with the norms and the facts is an analytical device. It is a necessary device, however, for while the name democracy is fitting for prescriptive purposes, it can be very misleading for descriptive purposes. Only in the Greek world did the name and the thing coincide. In our world the descriptive meaning of "democracy" cannot be explained and derived from its literal meaning.

When we come to the *how* of democracy, a democratic polity is usually identified by the manner of selection of its leaders and by the fact (which is also a corollary) that their power is checked and restrained. As Schumpeter puts it, in a democracy "the role of the people is to produce a government," and therefore "the democratic method is that institutional arrangement for arriving at political decisions in which individuals acquire the power to decide by means of a competitive struggle for the people's vote" ([1942] 1962, p. 269). The emphasis here is definitely procedural. It is also procedural in all the definitions concerned with majority rule and minority rights [see MAJORITY RULE]. On the other hand, when we deal with the institutional arrangements and agencies of "constitutional democracy" the emphasis tends to be structural. But in many cases the structural and procedural focuses are so tightly interlinked that we may well speak of a combined "structural–procedural" definition.

A neat distinction may be made instead between structural–procedural democracy, on the one hand, and the behavioral definition of democracy on the other. In this latter focus a democracy is identified by the activity of its leaders rather than by the manner of their selection. And the contention may follow that whenever one finds a "rule for the people" one finds a democracy.

No one denies that governing *for* the people is the very purpose of a democratic government; for nobody affirms that democratic structures and procedures are an end in themselves. The question is whether political altruism should be left to the gods or whether it should be secured precisely by structural and procedural means. Furthermore, the way in which the rulers happen to rule does not suffice to qualify a political system. A benevolent despotism remains a despotism no matter how benevolently the despot happens to behave. By the same token, ruling *for* the people is "demophily," not democracy. For democracy is not merely a manner of governing; it is a form of government, a political system.

The distinguishing mark of "real" democracy— i.e., of democracy in the real world—is provided, then, by the *means* that are conducive to the end of governing for the people. The step from demophily to democracy is indeed a long step. It occurs after endless deceptions and failures, and it occurs only when leaders are forced to respond to the people by means of structural and procedural safeguards [see REPRESENTATION, *article on* REPRESENTATIONAL SYSTEMS].

The standards. In order to define democracy as a type of political system it is essential to ascertain what democracy is *not*. This in turn presupposes clarification of the standards of democracy. For, depending on the standards, a political system may or may not be considered a democracy. Indeed, different standards have to be used, for democracy is not a static entity: democracy in the nineteenth century cannot be assessed like democracy in the twentieth, and a developed democracy is different from a developing democracy. The problem then is to make coherent use of the pertinent standard.

With reference to the developed and successful democracies of the Anglo–American or Scandinavian type, the standards are high. Here "democracy" denotes *more* than political machinery; it also denotes a way of living, a "social democracy." In particular, these democracies have gone a long way toward the maximization of equality—equality of status, of opportunity, and of starting points. We may thus speak of "full" or advanced democracy to denote the maximum current achievement of democracy in the real world. In this sense, then, democracy is a polar type, just as totalitarianism is the polar extreme of dictatorship.

In areas in which democracy has never been stable or effective—including a number of European countries—the standard is considerably lower. In this instance a polity qualifies as a democracy because of its machinery rather than its achievement and is more of a political arrangement than a state of the society. This more limited political character is revealed by the fact that emphasis is laid less on equality and more on liberty—as is only natural, for liberty has a procedural priority over equality. The test is provided by free elections, a competitive party system, and a representational system of government. It would be unfair to require a more exacting standard; for only the successful functioning of the machinery over time allows democracy to strike roots in the society. Aside from the United States, hardly any country was a full democracy before World War I, not even Great Britain; and even currently the existence of constitutional government, as opposed to arbitrary government, still represents the highest performance of democracy in most of the world. It is fair to say, therefore, that the standard provided by a constitutional government that secures political freedom, personal security, and impartial justice is the average standard, i.e., that this is what democracy "normally" means.

Up to this point we are able to specify what democracy *is:* the border between a democratic and a nondemocratic political system is still definite. But no sooner do we apply the word democracy to most of the Third World, and in particular to the so-called developing nations, than the standard becomes so low that one may well wonder whether the word democracy is still appropriate. At this point we speak of democracy simply to indicate that a given political system is not an overt dictatorship, that is, a dictatorship that allows no freedom, no opposition, and no independence to the courts. Some scholars are inclined to go even further. Shils speaks of "tutelary democracy" ([1959–1960] 1962, pp. 60–68), thereby implying that the standard can be reduced to the sole condition that the ruling elite earnestly profess democratic beliefs and pursue the goal of future establishment of some kind of democratic structure.

From the point of view of the classification of political systems it appears that the category of "initial" democracy cannot be stretched to include tutelary democracy. For promises are not deeds, and an authoritarian method of achieving democracy has to surmount the additional difficulty that the means shape the ends. A tutelary democracy may be even less than a mere "behavioral" democracy; it is only a possible future, only a futuristic democracy. Yet, the notion of tutelary democracy has its merits. For one thing, to profess democratic ideals is better than nothing at all; that is, the notion has the merit of singling out the importance of a belief system, in contrast to the somewhat deterministic and mechanical view that democracy follows from a set of socioeconomic conditions. In the second place, to raise the problem of democracy in the context of formless or transitional societies has the virtue of stimulating our imagination.

The question arises: When we speak of Western experience, is the key term "Western" or "experience"? In other words, can there be a non-Western path to democracy? But it would be premature to venture into these speculations without first discussing the conditions of democracy.

The conditions. Conditions are usually divided into necessary and/or sufficient. But we really know so little about the conditions of democracy that in most cases the best we can do is speak of facilitating conditions.

Economic development. Recently the trend has been to relate the conditions of democracy to a given stage of socioeconomic development. For example, Lipset argues that "the more well-to-do a nation, the greater the chances that it will sustain democracy." If the hypothesis is tested by the usual indexes of economic development, one finds that the average wealth, degree of industrialization and urbanization, and level of education is indeed much higher for the more democratic countries (Lipset 1960, pp. 45–76; Almond & Coleman 1960, pp. 538–544).

It has been pointed out, however, that if we look at specific cases rather than at over-all averages the correlation between democracy and economic development is weak, and that between the great extremes of wealth and sheer poverty is a large no man's land where apparently any political system can exist (Eckstein 1961, pp. 38–40). Moreover, a correlation is not a causal link. And even assuming that some sort of causal link does exist between welfare and democracy, we may still wonder whether a country became democratic because it was prosperous, or prosperous because it was democratic. If we abide by the low standard of initial democracy, then England surely became a democracy, i.e., a constitutional government, before the advent of industrialization, prosperity, and literacy. On the other hand, if we judge by the advanced type, it is fairly obvious that there can be no equalization of wealth until a people becomes wealthy. It would seem, therefore, that economic growth is a condition for the *growth* of democracy —not for its establishment [see ECONOMIC GROWTH, *article on* NONECONOMIC ASPECTS].

Two more specific caveats are also in order. First, much of the available evidence is statistically biased, in the sense that our findings are narrowly confined to the variables that are susceptible to quantification, and measurability is not a criterion of relevance. In this respect the objection could be that indexes of economic development correlate meaningfully only with the temperature of politics. Granted that prosperity is likely to moderate the tensions of the class struggle and the intensity of ideology, "cool" politics facilitates any regime, and therefore prosperity may help to stabilize a dictatorship as much as a democracy.

The second caution is that much of the available statistical evidence is gathered under categories that hopelessly lack discrimination. For instance, a strong positive correlation has been found between stable democracy and degree of literacy (with the perplexing exceptions of Germany and France), and it is often argued that the most important single factor in promoting democracy is the degree of education. In itself, however, literacy is only exposure to communications; and this implies that literacy can be conducive to mass manipulation no less than to individual self-realization. It appears, therefore, that our faith in education rests on the hidden premise that what we really mean is "liberal education," the kind that inculcates, among other things, liberal and democratic values. The problem is, then, whether a merely technological literacy, or a type of education that inculcates illiberal values, may not promote autocracy. And the statistical figures collected under the literacy category do not make the discrimination that we need most [see MODERNIZATION].

Intermediate structures.   The foregoing reservations remind us of the view held by Tocqueville (1856), followed by Durkheim and recently restated, for example, by Kornhauser, that democracy presupposes the backbone of an "intermediate structure" of independent groups and voluntary associations (1959, pp. 76–90). Unquestionably, the support of a vital and active "infrastructure" of self-governing organisms and institutions is of great help. One may say that political macrodemocracy is safer and more authentic the more it reflects and presupposes an "infrademocracy." Once again, however, one should be wary of considering this a necessary condition for any stage of democracy. The necessary condition (though in no way a sufficient one) should be stated in broader and less exacting terms, for example, by pointing to the fact that no modern democracy has yet succeeded until the development of a middle class bridges the gap between the populace and the state.

Leadership.   Furthermore, the fact that we have developed a keen interest in the socioeconomic preconditions of democracy should not lead us to underplay the strictly *political* conditions of democracy—as Aron has recently underlined (Aron et al. 1960). Since the current emphasis on the prepolitical requisites of democracy is partly due to a research bias (because of research facilities and the greater facility of the research), it is all the more necessary to stress the importance of leadership. Leadership is a disturbing variable in two senses: it disturbs the social scientist because of its "subjective" elusiveness, and it has a disturbing effect on the "objective" data. On the first count the social scientist should eliminate it; but on the second count he cannot. Prolonged effectiveness gives legitimacy to a political system, whereas in a modernizing society no legitimacy can withstand prolonged ineffectiveness (Lipset 1960, pp. 77–90). The effectiveness of democracy depends first and foremost on the efficiency and skill of its leadership. This becomes even truer the less favorable the objective conditions [see LEADERSHIP].

All in all, the conditions of democracy are still largely unknown. On the one hand, whenever our hypotheses can be tested empirically—as in the case of indexes of economic growth—the findings are somewhat circular, for we are told that the kind of soil that favors democracy is the soil that has been cultivated best. On the other hand, when we come to examine the specifically *political* conditions of democracy, our assumptions remain poorly verified. Although this follows from the intrinsic difficulties of the domain of politics, we surely could do better by formulating our queries with more precision.

Clearly the conditions of advanced democracy are not those of initial democracy, and the problem of implementing a political democracy is different from the problem of planting it. For instance, an open class system, an equalitarian value system, and an industrial society are necessary conditions neither for the take-off into democracy nor for normal democracy; in fact, these so-called conditions presuppose the successful performance of normal democracy and can be viewed, therefore, as consequences rather than antecedents. The rewarding query is, then, "which are the conditions for each standard?" and, conversely, "which level of democratization cannot be attained under given conditions?"

The point is not simply that there is no *one* factor crucially associated with the success of democracy; the point is also that the cluster of factors has a historical dimension, in the sense that all the relevant factors have to be considered in a *sequence*, with reference to their order of succession, their tempo, and their timing. It would seem, in fact, that "objective" factors are less important in initiating a democracy than (1) the will of an efficient and capable leadership, and (2) regulation of the flow of demands in such a way that the political system can process it without getting overloaded. For what throws a political system off balance—and particularly a democracy—is a sudden imbalance between an outburst of expectations and the capacity for meeting them.

Prospects and alternatives

The ways of history are not infinite, but they are varied. And the prospects for democracy in most of the world are related to the search for new solutions or, better said, to the search for adaptations and substitutions. If the question is whether there are "alternative forms of democracy," the reply can only be that this kind of new solution has not been discovered. But if the question is whether there are alternative ways of achieving democracy more quickly, this is surely pertinent and vital. In fact, the problem of the developing countries is to catch up, a matter of speed and short cuts. And there is no better evidence that economizing is possible and that elimination of steps is feasible than the evidence provided by the Western experience itself.

Let it be recalled that for a long time constitutional lawyers believed that bicameralism was an essential safety, and yet there are unicameral systems that do just as well. Likewise, we often claim that rotation in office is part and parcel of democracy; but there are political systems in which one predominant party competitively gains and keeps an absolute majority, thereby providing an instance of democracy without governmental turnover. In a similar vein we tend to think that the interplay between majority and opposition is the keystone of a democratic system, and only recently have we started to realize that the argument does not apply to any kind of opposition—indeed, the institutionalization of the opposition may not improve things at all, and an irresponsible and purely demagogic opposition is likely to wreck any democracy. This does not imply that there can be a democracy where dissent and contestation are impeded; it does suggest, however, that whenever the stakes are too high to allow a peaceful transmission of power to the opposer, we should explore the possibility of subsidiary forms and mechanisms of contest.

Finally, most people equate democracy with universal suffrage; and it is surprising how little attention is being paid to the tempo and sequence that enable a political system to process the entry into politics of hitherto excluded and far-removed masses, that is, to cope with the so-called crisis of participation. And this in spite of the evidence that a sudden, massive enfranchisement is either a sham or is likely to shatter any developing democracy. Universal suffrage, in fact, seems to be the one taboo that we are not prepared to break—again a confirmation of the extent to which we are fascinated by the word at the expense of the sub-

stance. To be sure, "people" means "all the people," and therefore in a literal sense there is no democracy until "everybody" is given the power to vote. But in our macrodemocracies the power of each amounts to a powerless fraction of power; and therefore the substance of the matter no longer is that everybody should be equally entitled to self-government (by virtue of his vote), but that as many people as possible should not be misgoverned. Thus, as long as free elections do occur, the size of the electorate matters far less than the essential goal, namely, the establishment of a political system that makes a government responsive and accountable.

The foregoing considerations are meant only to suggest that we need to cross-examine our dogmas and to acquire a fresh vision. In matters of polity building, genuine invention is very rare and very slow, and the successful innovations have usually been accidental. Before speculating about "new solutions" we should reduce to a minimum the requirements of the solutions that have been tested. Democracy, as Woodrow Wilson said, is the most difficult form of government. We cannot hope, therefore, to export the "complete" Western type. On the other hand, it is equally obvious that the new states and developing nations cannot pretend to start from the level of achievement at which the Western democracies have arrived. In fact, no democracy would ever have materialized if it had set for itself the advanced goals that a number of modernizing states currently claim to be pursuing. In a world-wide perspective, the problem is to minimize arbitrary and tyrannical rule and to maximize a pattern of civility rooted in respect and justice for each man—in short, to achieve a humane polity. Undue haste and overly ambitious goals are likely to lead to opposite results.

Giovanni Sartori

[*See also* Consensus; Constitutions and constitutionalism; Delegation of powers; Elections; Liberalism; Parties, political; Representation. *Other relevant material may be found in* Dictatorship; Political theory; Power.]

BIBLIOGRAPHY

Almond, Gabriel A.; and Coleman, James S. (editors) 1960 *The Politics of the Developing Areas.* Princeton Univ. Press.

Aron, Raymond 1965 *Démocratie et totalitarisme.* Paris: Gallimard.

Aron, Raymond et al. 1960 *La démocratie à l'épreuve du XX siècle.* Paris: Calmann-Lévy.

Bryce, James (1888) 1909 *The American Commonwealth.* 3d ed., 2 vols. New York and London: Macmillan. → An abridged edition was published in 1959 by Putnam.

BRYCE, JAMES 1921 *Modern Democracies.* 2 vols. New York: Macmillan.

CHAMBERS, WILLIAM N.; and SALISBURY, ROBERT H. (editors) (1960) 1962 *Democracy Today: Problems and Prospects.* 2d ed. New York: Collier. → See especially Eric A. Havelock's article.

CLEGG, HUGH A. 1960 *A New Approach to Industrial Democracy.* Oxford: Blackwell.

CONSTANT DE REBECQUE, HENRI BENJAMIN 1819 De la liberté des anciens comparée à celle des modernes. Volume 4, part 1, page 238 in Henri Benjamin Constant de Rebecque, *Collection complète des ouvrages publiés sur le gouvernement représentatif et la constitution actuelle de la France.* Paris: Plancher.

DAHL, ROBERT A. (1956) 1963 *A Preface to Democratic Theory.* Univ. of Chicago Press.

Democracy in the New States: Rhodes Seminar Papers. 1959 New Delhi: Congress for Cultural Freedom, Office for Asian Affairs.

DOWNS, ANTHONY 1957 *An Economic Theory of Democracy.* New York: Harper.

ECKSTEIN, HARRY 1961 *A Theory of Stable Democracy.* Center of International Studies Research Monograph No. 10. Princeton Univ., Woodrow Wilson School of Public and International Affairs.

FRANKEL, CHARLES 1962 *The Democratic Prospect.* New York: Harper.

FRIEDRICH, CARL J. (1937) 1950 *Constitutional Government and Democracy: Theory and Practice in Europe and America.* Rev. ed. Boston: Ginn. → First published as *Constitutional Government and Politics: Nature and Development.*

FUSTEL DE COULANGES, NUMA DENIS (1864) 1956 *The Ancient City: A Study on the Religion, Laws, and Institutions of Greece and Rome.* Garden City, N.Y.: Doubleday. → First published in French.

HARTZ, LOUIS (1960) 1962 Democracy: Image and Reality. Pages 13–29 in William N. Chambers and Robert H. Salisbury (editors), *Democracy Today: Problems and Prospects.* 2d ed. New York: Collier.

HAVELOCK, ERIC A. (1957) 1964 *The Liberal Temper in Greek Politics.* New Haven: Yale Univ. Press.

HERMENS, FERDINAND A. 1958 *The Representative Republic.* Univ. of Notre Dame (Ind.) Press.

HERZ, JOHN H. 1951 *Political Realism and Political Idealism: A Study in Theories and Realities.* Univ. of Chicago Press.

JOUVENEL, BERTRAND DE (1945) 1952 *Power: The Natural History of Its Growth.* Rev. ed. London: Batchworth. → First published in French.

KELSEN, HANS 1929 *Vom Wesen und Wert der Demokratie.* Tübingen (Germany): Mohr.

KELSEN, HANS 1955 Foundations of Democracy. *Ethics* 66, part 2:1–101.

KORNHAUSER, WILLIAM 1959 *The Politics of Mass Society.* Glencoe, Ill.: Free Press.

LINDSAY, A. D. (1943) 1959 *The Modern Democratic State.* Oxford Univ. Press.

LIPSET, SEYMOUR M. 1960 *Political Man: The Social Bases of Politics.* Garden City, N.Y.: Doubleday.

MAYO, HENRY B. 1960 *An Introduction to Democratic Theory.* New York: Oxford Univ. Press.

NAESS, ARNE 1956 *Democracy, Ideology and Objectivity.* Oxford: Blackwell.

PARAF, PIERRE 1962 *Les démocraties populaires.* Paris: Payot.

SARTORI, GIOVANNI (1962) 1965 *Democratic Theory.* New York: Praeger. → Based on the author's translation of his *Democrazia e definizione.*

SCHUMPETER, JOSEPH A. (1942) 1950 *Capitalism, Socialism, and Democracy.* 3d ed. New York: Harper; London: Allen & Unwin. → A paperback edition was published by Harper in 1962.

SHILS, EDWARD (1959–1960) 1962 *Political Development in the New States.* The Hague: Mouton.

TOCQUEVILLE, ALEXIS DE (1835) 1945 *Democracy in America.* 2 vols. New York: Knopf. → First published in French. Paperback editions were published in 1961 by Vintage and by Schocken.

TOCQUEVILLE, ALEXIS DE (1856) 1955 *The Old Regime and the French Revolution.* Garden City, N.Y.: Doubleday → First published in French.

UNITED NATIONS EDUCATIONAL, SCIENTIFIC AND CULTURAL ORGANIZATION 1951 *Democracy in a World of Tensions: A Symposium.* Edited by Richard McKeon. Univ. of Chicago Press.

WEBB, SIDNEY; and WEBB, BEATRICE (1897) 1920 *Industrial Democracy.* New ed., 2 vols. London and New York: Longmans.

DEMOGRAPHY

See under POPULATION.

DENOMINATIONALISM

See RELIGIOUS ORGANIZATION; SECTS AND CULTS; *and the biography of* TROELTSCH.

DEPENDENCE

See DRINKING AND ALCOHOLISM; DRUGS, *article on* DRUG ADDICTION; SMOKING.

DEPRESSION

See BUSINESS CYCLES.

DEPRESSIVE DISORDERS

The term "depressive disorders" refers to a large group of psychiatric conditions whose main characteristic is an abnormal feeling of depression. This classification is broad as well as vague; it implies a definition of depression and of abnormal depression. Moreover, the word "depression" refers sometimes to an ordinary emotion, at other times to a symptom, and still at other times to a given clinical entity.

This article will discuss depression as a normal and as an abnormal emotion, clinical pictures of depressions, psychodynamic and sociocultural aspects of depression, and treatment.

Depression as a normal emotion

Depression is a common emotion, second only to anxiety in psychiatric concern and study. Often depression is referred to by such terms as sadness, melancholy, despondency, dejection, low spirit, and anguish. Although practically all human beings have at some time experienced depression, this emotional state is among the most difficult to describe and to analyze. It is a pervading feeling of unpleasantness accompanied by such somatic conditions as numbness, paresthesias of the skin, alterations of muscle tone, and decreases in respiration, pulsation, and perspiration. The head of the depressed person has the tendency to bend; the legs flex; the trunk tilts forward. The face assumes a special expression because of increased wrinkles and decreased mimic play. There is also retardation of movements, rigidity in thinking, and a general feeling of weakness.

It is, however, at the mental rather than the somatic level that depression has more specific characteristics. Whereas anxiety is characterized by an expectancy of danger, depression is accompanied by a feeling that the dangerous event has already occurred, that the loss has already been sustained. For instance, the loved person has already died, the good position has been lost, the business venture has failed, a self-concept or an ideal can no longer be maintained. There is also a more or less marked sense of despair, of unpleasant finality, as the lost object is considered irreplaceable. The loss is deemed to have repercussions on the present as well as the future. From these examples it is evident that, at least in conditions considered normal, depression seems to be a reaction to psychological processes, such as evaluations and appraisals, that have occurred at a cognitive level. The person who becomes depressed must have been able to understand and to assess the significance of certain events. Thus, cognitive and, as we shall see later in detail, social factors (inasmuch as the latter enter into complicated cognitive processes) are very important in the engendering of depression.

Such considerations would make depression a uniquely human emotion, different from more primitive emotions such as fear, rage, and some forms of anxiety that occur also in much lower animals. This point, of course, is debatable. Inasmuch as animals cannot verbalize their feelings, it is an open question whether or not the belief that animals become depressed is an anthropomorphization. A dog, for instance, may appear depressed when his master is away, but it is doubtful that this is either a feeling involving the future or a sense of loss that transcends the immediate discomfort. A feeling of deprivation rather than despair seems to be involved here. On the other hand, these uncomfortable feelings of deprivation, which even infrahuman animals are capable of experiencing, may be the precursors of human depression.

According to Arieti (1959a), depression may have functional significance. If depression had

negative survival value, species capable of experiencing it probably would not have procreated themselves in the course of evolution. Other emotions have survival value; anxiety, for instance, is a warning of forthcoming danger. As with other unpleasant sensations and emotions, the function of depression is to urge the person who experiences it to alter his behavior, so that the factor engendering depression will disappear or be removed.

For example, an individual hears the news of the unexpected death of a person he loved. After he has understood and almost instantaneously evaluated what that death means to him, he experiences shock, then sadness. For a few days all thoughts connected with the deceased person will bring about a painful, almost unbearable feeling. Any group of thoughts even remotely connected with the dead person will elicit depression. The individual cannot adjust to the idea that the loved person does not live any more. And, since that person was so important to him, many of his thoughts or actions will be directly or indirectly connected with the dead person and therefore will elicit sad reactions.

Nevertheless, after a certain period of time, that individual adjusts to the idea that the person is dead. By being unpleasant, the depression seems to have a function—its own elimination. It will be removed only if the individual is forced to reorganize his thinking, to search for new ideas so that he can rearrange his life. He must rearrange especially those ideas that are connected with the departed, so that the departed will no longer be considered indispensable.

Depression as an abnormal emotion

Depression is deemed abnormal when it is excessive relative to the antecedent event or events that have elicited it; when it is inappropriate in relation to its known cause or precipitating factor; when it is a substitution for a more appropriate emotion, for instance, when it takes the place of hostility or anxiety; or, when it does not seem to have been caused by any antecedent factor of which the person is aware.

Both constitutional and psychological factors have been postulated to explain the occurrence of abnormal depressions. The constitutional factors have been studied particularly in connection with the depression that occurs in the course of manic–depressive psychosis. Slater (1936), for instance, believes that the inheritance of manic–depressive psychosis depends on a single dominant autosomal gene. To explain why the incidence of the psychosis is lower than would be expected from his hypothesis, he states that the dominant gene is a rare one. Kraines (1957) believes that the depression, as well as the manic state of manic–depressive psychosis, is due to a dysfunction (either increased or decreased function) of the diencephalon. Accordingly, the experience of depression is a "psychic response" to this diencephalic dysfunction. Elevated values for adrenal and thyroid functions, blood pressure, and pulse rate are reported frequently in depressed patients (Reiss 1954).

Arieti (1959a) has described what happens when the process of reorganizing ideas concomitant with normal depression fails. In such cases, depression, rather than forcing a reorganization of ideas, slows the thought processes that are carriers of mental pain. There appears to be a teleological or adaptational mechanism that seemingly acts with the goal of decreasing the quantity of thoughts in order to decrease the quantity of suffering. At times, the attempt to slow thought processes succeeds so well (as in the state called "stupor") that only a few thoughts of a general and vague nature remain. These are accompanied by an overpowering feeling of melancholy. Thus, the slowing down of thought processes that have an unpleasant emotional tone is a self-defeating mechanism and, in a vicious circle, aggravates the situation instead of alleviating it.

Often, abnormal depression defensively replaces seemingly more appropriate emotions, generally anxiety or hostility. The patient appears to be more capable of coping with a feeling of depression than with anxiety or hostility.

Clinical pictures of depressions

Depressive disorders have been known since ancient times. Some of the great physicians of antiquity, like Hippocrates and Aretaeus, wrote about the conditions that are now called "psychotic depressions." In spite of this long record in the history of medicine, no agreement has been reached about the various classifications of depressions or the nature of the various types. Following is a brief account of the different clinical pictures that have been recognized.

Reactive or psychoneurotic depression. Reactive or psychoneurotic depressions are characterized by relatively mild feelings of despondency, guilt, and self-depreciation; mild retardation and reduction of spontaneity; and the absence of hypochondrial preoccupations. These depressions seem to occur subsequent to, or as a reaction to, an unpleasant or tragic event in the life of the patient. The patient is aware of this connection. Some authors emphasize the fact that reactive depressions are not endog-

enous, that is, are not engendered by internal factors, such as organic or hereditary predispositions, but are consequent to external factors. In addition, the patient does not accept the depression as a way of living and, like all other psychoneurotic patients, would like to be relieved of his depressed condition.

Depressed type of manic–depressive psychosis. The depressive aspect of manic–depressive psychosis has generally received the most consideration. Although it was already recognized by Aretaeus, it was described more fully and clarified in some aspects by Kraepelin in the sixth edition of his *Psychiatrie: Lehrbuch für Studierende und Ärzte*, published in 1899 (see Kraepelin 1883).

This type of depression is characterized by a triad of symptoms: a pervading feeling of melancholia, disordered thought processes characterized by retardation and unusual content, and psychomotor retardation. In addition, there are, less typically and less frequently, some somatic dysfunctions.

This type of depression occurs much more frequently in women than in men. In the majority of cases it is periodic, not permanent. Attacks of depression are separated by normal intervals.

Feeling of melancholia. The onset of the pervading feeling of melancholia is sometimes quite acute and dramatic, at other times slow and insidious. At times, it is misunderstood or unrecognized at first. When an unpleasant event, such as the death of a close relative, has occurred, a certain amount of depression is justified. However, when a certain period of time has elapsed and the depression normally should have subsided, it becomes instead more intense. The patient has an unhappy, sad appearance. He looks older than his age, his forehead is wrinkled, and his face, although undergoing very little mimic play, reveals a despondent mood. In some cases the main fold of the upper eyelid at the edge of its inner third is contracted upward and a little backward (sign of Veraguth).

The patient is often unable to describe his feeling of intense unhappiness. He may say that "his eyes have consumed all the tears" and "his life is a torment." He experiences a desire to punish himself by destroying himself and, at the same time, to end his suffering. Suicidal ideas occur in about 75 per cent of patients, and actual suicide attempts are made by at least 10 to 15 per cent.

Disordered thought processes. The second important symptom concerns the content and type of thinking. Gloomy, morbid ideas leave little room for other thoughts. The patient convinces himself that he is hopeless; he has lost or will lose all his money, his family is in extreme poverty, he is incapable of working or even taking care of himself. There is no great variety in his thoughts. He gives the impression of selecting thoughts that have an unpleasant content so that his melancholic mood is retained. Quasi-delusional ideas or definite delusions may occur, often representing distortions of the body-image and hypochondriasis. The patient thinks, for example, that he has a tumor, syphilis, or tuberculosis, that he has lost his bowels, or that his brain is melting. The patient is often self-accusatory, in a delusional form. He believes that he has committed many crimes or that some crimes which have been committed by others are, indirectly, his responsibility. Especially in some Western subcultures that are permeated by intense religiosity, the ideas of guilt, sin, self-condemnation, and eternal damnation are prevalent. Hallucinations are rare in this condition and occur almost exclusively at night.

Psychomotor retardation. The third important sign of depression is retarded hypoactivity. The actions of the patient are reduced in number and are carried out at a slow pace. Talking is reduced to a minimum. Employment and household responsibilities are ignored, and appearances are neglected. When depression reaches a state of stupor, the patient cannot talk or move at all and may be mistaken for a catatonic patient.

Somatic dysfunctions. Frequent accessory symptoms are reduction in sleep, decrease in appetite, loss in weight, marked decrease in sexual desire, dryness of the mouth caused by decreased secretion of the parotid glands. A frequent subvariety of this condition, called "agitated depression," is characterized by motor restlessness rather than hypoactivity.

Manic episodes. Kraepelin emphasized that in many patients attacks of depression alternate with, or occasionally are followed by, other attacks that seem to have contrasting characteristics. These are the manic attacks, characterized by a state of elation or euphoria, a disorder of thought processes distinguished by flight of ideas and pleasant content, and an increased mobility. Kraepelin thought that when the illness manifests itself in a complete form, both the depressed and manic attacks occur, although in different sequences. Thus he conceived both forms of attack as part of a specific clinical entity, to which he gave the name "manic–depressive psychosis."

It was soon noticed that the manic attacks are much less frequent than the depressive ones. Perhaps the difference in frequency is not as marked as it seems. It could be, in fact, that mild attacks of mania are better tolerated or unrecognized by the patient or his relatives.

The intensity of the depression is not the only characteristic differentiating between psychotic and reactive depression. In a psychotic depression the patient accepts his depression as his way of life and feels justified in feeling as he does.

Psychotic depressions. Many depressions, even of psychotic proportions, are never preceded or followed by manic attacks. Many authors are reluctant to include such depressions in the manic–depressive syndrome. They feel that these depressions probably should have a classification unrelated to the Kraepelinian psychosis.

Except for the fact that it is not followed by manic attacks, psychotic depression is no different from the depression of the manic–depressive psychosis.

Involutional melancholia. Involutional melancholia (involutional psychosis, melancholic type) occurs in women at least three times as frequently as in men and is characterized by an intense feeling of depression that occurs around the "involutional" age. In women this age generally coincides with the menopause. However, involutional melancholia may precede or follow the menopause even by an interval of four to five years.

Involutional melancholia presents the same characteristics as the depression of the manic–depressive psychosis, with the following exceptions: (1) agitation and restlessness often substitute for, or are superimposed on, the hypoactivity, and (2) the prepsychotic personality differs from that of the manic–depressive. The patient is described as a quiet, retiring, worrisome, frugal, and rigid individual.

Kraepelin, who had originally excluded involutional melancholia from the manic–depressive category, reconsidered his views and finally included it in that group. Kraepelin thought that involutional melancholia had an unfavorable prognosis. However, as some of his contemporaries showed, this is not so. Electric shock treatment, devised by Ugo Cerletti and Lucio Bini in 1938 (Cerletti 1950), seems to be able to cure practically all cases, if by cure we mean a return to the prepsychotic level of adjustment, whatever it was.

Other types of depression. Depressions may also occur as parts of other syndromes or conditions. A depression occurring in old age is often referred to as "senile depression," and one occurring in schizophrenia as "schizophrenic depression." When a combination of schizophrenic and manic–depressive features occurs, the syndrome is often called "schizo–affective psychosis."

A type of depression that is often described in the French and Italian literatures is the one called "Cotard's syndrome," after the neurologist J. Cotard, who first described it. Cotard's syndrome is characterized by a depression accompanied by a delusional state of negation. Nothing exists; the world has disappeared. After the cosmic reality is denied, the physical reality of the patient himself is denied.

Spitz (1946) has described what he calls "anaclitical depression" in infants who have been separated from their mothers between the sixth and eighth months for an approximate period of three months. This type of depression seems more similar to a state or sense of deprivation, as it occurs in infrahuman animals, than to an emotional state that includes a sense of finality and despair.

Psychodynamic mechanisms of depression

Many authors feel that even if constitutional-hereditary facts are important in the etiology of depressive disorders, some experiential factors occuring in the early life of the patient have started psychodynamic patterns that have finally determined these conditions. Psychoanalytic studies have contributed greatly to the psychodynamic understanding of depressions. These psychodynamic mechanisms apply primarily to the depressions labeled as the depressed type of manic–depressive psychosis, psychotic depression, and involutional melancholia. It was Freud's pupil Abraham (1912), not Freud, who introduced manic–depressive psychosis to psychoanalytic conceptions through a comparison of abnormal depression with normal grief. Both conditions are at times elicited by a loss that the person has suffered; but, whereas the normal mourner is concerned about the lost person, the depressed patient is disturbed by guilt feelings. The unconscious hostility that he had for the lost object is now directed toward himself. Abraham also assumed a regression to an ambivalent pregenital stage of object-relationship, that is, a return to an anal-sadistic stage.

Freud (1917) accepted Abraham's idea that there is a relation between mourning and melancholia and pointed out that whereas in mourning the object was lost because of death, in melancholia there was an internal loss because the lost person had been incorporated (or introjected). The sadism present in the ambivalent relationship is then directed against the incorporated love-object.

Radó (1928) suggested that melancholia represents a desperate search for love. The ego tries to punish itself in order to prevent parental punishment.

According to Melanie Klein (1948), a "depressive position" is a normal event in the life of every child, generally at the time of weaning, that is, around the age of six months. The mother who before was seen by the child as two persons (one good and one bad), according to Klein, is at this time seen as one person; the mother continues, however, to be internalized as a good or bad object. The child is afraid that his instinctual aggressive impulses will destroy the good object, and he interprets the loss of his mother's breast and milk at the time of weaning as the result of the destructive impulses. The inability to solve adequately this "depressive position" may, according to Klein, lead later to a pathological depression.

Arieti (1959a) found the following mechanisms in the cases that came under his attention. Very early in the life of people who are prone to become psychotically depressed there is a period of intense gratification of needs. The mother or mother-substitute is motivated by a sense of duty to be as lavish as possible in her care and affection. This attitude predisposes the child to be very receptive to others, to introject the others, and later to be an extrovert and a conformist.

At a later period but still in early childhood, generally during the second or third year of life, although in some cases even much earlier, the family situation undergoes a drastic change. The mother now takes care of the child considerably less than before and makes many demands on him. This change in the mother's attitude may be due to the fact that in the meantime another sibling has been born, and the mother is now lavishing her care on the newborn with the same duty-bound generosity that she previously had for the patient. More often, however, the reason for the change is to be found in the personality of the mother, who believes that when a child is an infant, he has to be fully taken care of, but as soon as he shows the first signs of an independent personality, he should start to be given increasing responsibilities, a sense of duty, of obligation, and the like. No transitional stages are allowed. The child who experiences a drastic change from an atmosphere of receptivity from the others to an atmosphere of expectation by the others may undergo a trauma. He tries to find solutions or pseudosolutions. Generally he adopts one of the two following mechanisms, which he will repeat throughout his adult life. The first is an attempt to make himself even more babyish, more dependent, and aggressively dependent, so that the mother, or the important adult who later takes her place symbolically, will be forced to re-establish an atmosphere of babyhood and of early bliss. Another mechanism consists in trying to live up to the expectations of the mother, no matter how high the price, how heavy the burden. Love or the early bliss will be recaptured only by complying and working hard. If love is not obtained, the patient is at fault; he must atone or work harder.

The patient finds out later in life that these mechanisms do not work. No matter how aggressively dependent the individual becomes, he does not recapture the early bliss. No matter how compliant and hard working he is, he does not obtain what he wants. This realization brings about the depressed feeling. The actual manifest symptomatology of depression occurs when a symbolic reproduction of the early trauma takes place later in life. A loss has been sustained and the patient feels that his way of living has caused such a loss. The loss may be the death of a person important to the patient, the realization by the patient that an important interpersonal relationship has failed (generally with the spouse), or a severe disappointment in a relationship to an institution or work to which the patient has devoted his whole life. At times the loss is more difficult to evaluate; it may concern such abstract concepts as ideals, re-evaluation of the meaning of one's life, and personal significance.

Claiming and self-blaming depression. The psychological symptomatology of psychotic depressions has been divided by Arieti (1962) into two main types: the claiming depression and the self-blaming depression.

In the claiming depression, which has recently become more common at least in the United States, the symptomatology, although fundamentally one of depression, seems to be a gigantic claim. All the symptoms seem to have a message: "Help me; pity me. It is in your power to relieve me. If I suffer, it is because you don't relieve me of this suffering."

In the self-blaming type of depression the main emphasis is on self-accusation and self-depreciation. The patient feels he does not deserve help from others.

When the prepsychotic personality is of the aggressive–dependent type, the psychosis tends to be the claiming type of depression. When the prepsychotic personality is of the duty-bound, hard-worker type, the psychosis tends to be the self-blaming type.

The suicide attempt (often successful) made by patients affected by a psychotic depression has been the object of various psychodynamic interpretations. Several possibilities must be considered. (1) The suicide attempt may actually be a cry for help. The patient wants to convey this message to an important person in his life: "You have the power to prevent my death, if you wish to." (2) The patient wants relief from suffering. (3) The patient wants to punish himself, since he feels guilt-ridden and deserving of drastic punishment. (4) The patient does not really want to kill himself but the detested person whom he has incorporated. The last explanation is the one originally proposed by Freud (1917) and the one still accepted by the orthodox psychoanalytic school. It is actually based on little clinical evidence and is not unanimously accepted by other schools.

Sociocultural factors in depressions

Sociological and cultural factors may be important in facilitating those conditions which predispose to depression, especially those of the manic–depressive type. Some psychiatrists (Bellak et al. 1952; Arieti 1959b) have noted a decline in incidence of this psychosis. For instance, in a period of 20 years (from 1928 to 1947), the percentage of first admissions to hospitals of manic–depressive psychosis in New York State was reduced from 13.5 per cent of all admissions to 3.8 per cent. Relevant information has been gathered in other parts of the world. Gold (1951) has found a relatively higher incidence of manic–depressive than of schizophrenic psychoses in the lands of the Mediterranean Basin, as well as in Ireland. He reports that in Oriental countries, especially where Hinduism and Buddhism prevail, manic–depressive psychosis is less common, but in Fiji manic–depressive patients are numerous. Gold writes further that whereas in India the incidence of manic–depressive psychosis is low and that of schizophrenia higher, the reverse is true for the Indians who have immigrated to Fiji.

Recently, however, psychiatrists have noticed, at least in the United States, an increase in the number of depressive disorders. This increase has not yet been subjected to statistical study and seems to involve depressions not typically of the manic–depressive category.

In his attempts to understand the decline of manic–depressive psychosis Arieti (1959a; 1959b) drew upon the concepts of the sociologist Riesman (1950). Manic–depressive psychosis occurs more frequently in those cultures which Riesman has called "inner-directed" and tends to disappear where this orientation is also disappearing. It is thus possible to formulate the hypothesis that an inner-directed culture evokes or increases the manic–depressive propensity.

Inner-directed society. In the inner-directed society the mother feels duty-bound and therefore at the time of the birth of the child is very much concerned with his care, permitting the child to develop strong introjective tendencies. Soon, however, the mother will start to burden the child with responsibilities and with a sense of duty and guilt. This is often made necessary by the fact that the mother now has to devote herself to another child. The bliss of paradise is lost, and life becomes a purgatory. An inner-directed personality develops in the sense that this orientation is implanted early in life by the direct and definite influence of the significant adults. Family-life and child-rearing practices are established that seem to correspond to those found in the families of manic–depressive patients.

This hypothesis, suggesting the influence of inner-directed society upon manic–depressive psychosis, receives some validation from the research of Eaton and Weil (1955) on the mental health of the Hutterites. The Hutterites are a group of people of German ancestry who have settled in the Dakotas, Montana, and the prairie provinces of Canada. The Hutterite society seems to be an inner-directed one. In a population of 8,542 people, Eaton and Weil found only 9 persons who sometime in their lives suffered from schizophrenia and 39 with manic–depressive psychosis; that is, among the Hutterites manic–depressive psychosis occurred 4.33 times more frequently than schizophrenia, whereas in the general population of the United States the incidence of schizophrenia by far exceeds that of manic–depressive psychosis.

Treatment of depressions

Depressive disorders are generally treated with three types of therapy. (1) Psychotherapy (generally psychoanalytically oriented in the United States; in Europe, often existentially oriented) is generally administered to patients suffering from the reactive depressions, the various types of psychotic depressions provided they are of moderate intensity, and patients who are experiencing a symptom-free interval between psychotic attacks. (2) Drug therapy is employed in the treatment of moderately severe depressions. "Psychoanaleptic drugs," such as imipramine hydrochloride, and the large group of monoamine oxidase inhibitors are among those used. (3) Electric shock therapy, commonly used prior to the advent of drug therapy, is now reserved for the most recalcitrant and stuporous cases. It is still the most frequently used treatment in involutional melancholia.

SILVANO ARIETI

[*Other relevant material may be found in* ELECTROCONVULSIVE SHOCK; MENTAL DISORDERS; MENTAL DISORDERS, TREATMENT OF; PSYCHOANALYSIS; PSYCHOSIS; *and the biographies of* ABRAHAM; FREUD; KLEIN; KRAEPELIN.]

BIBLIOGRAPHY

ABRAHAM, KARL (1912) 1953 Notes on the Psychoanalytical Investigation and Treatment of Manic–Depressive Insanity and Allied Conditions. Pages 137–156 in Karl Abraham, *Selected Papers*. Volume 1: Selected Papers on Psychoanalysis. New York: Basic Books. → First published in German.

ARIETI, SILVANO 1959a Manic–Depressive Psychosis. Volume 1, pages 419–454 in *American Handbook of Psychiatry*. Edited by Silvano Arieti. New York: Basic Books.

ARIETI, SILVANO 1959b Some Socio-cultural Aspects of Manic–Depressive Psychosis and Schizophrenia. Volume 4, pages 140–152 in Jacob Moreno and Jules Masserman (editors), *Progress in Psychotherapy*. New York: Grune.

ARIETI, SILVANO 1962 The Psychotherapeutic Approach to Depression. *American Journal of Psychotherapy* 16: 397–406.

BELLAK, LEOPOLD et al. 1952 *Manic–Depressive Psychosis and Allied Conditions*. New York: Grune.

CERLETTI, UGO 1950 Old and New Information About Electroshock. *American Journal of Psychiatry* 107: 87–94.

EATON, JOSEPH W.; and WEIL, ROBERT J. 1955 The Mental Health of the Hutterites. Pages 223–239 in Arnold M. Rose (editor), *Mental Health and Mental Disorder: A Sociological Approach*. Prepared for a committee of the Society for the Study of Social Problems. New York: Norton.

FREUD, SIGMUND (1917) 1959 Mourning and Melancholia. Volume 4, pages 152–170 in Sigmund Freud, *Collected Papers*, International Psycho-analytic Library, No. 10. New York: Basic Books; London: Hogarth. → Authorized translation from the German.

GOLD, HENRY R. 1951 Observations on Cultural Psychiatry During a World Tour of Mental Hospitals. *American Journal of Psychiatry* 108:462–468.

KLEIN, MELANIE 1948 *Contributions to Psycho-analysis: 1921–1945*. International Psycho-analytic Library, No. 34. London: Hogarth.

KRAEPELIN, EMIL (1883) 1921 *Manic–Depressive Insanity and Paranoia*. Edited by George M. Robertson. Edinburgh: Livingstone. → Translated from Volumes 3 and 4 of the eighth German edition of *Psychiatrie*.

KRAINES, SAMUEL H. 1957 *Mental Depressions and Their Treatment*. New York: Macmillan.

RADÓ, SÁNDOR 1928 The Problem of Melancholia. *International Journal of Psycho-analysis* 9:420–438.

REISS, MAX 1954 Investigations of Hormone Equilibria During Depression. Pages 69–82 in American Psychopathological Association, Forty-second Annual Meeting, New York, June 1952, *Depression*. Edited by Paul H. Hoch and Joseph Zubin. New York: Grune.

RIESMAN, DAVID 1950 *The Lonely Crowd: A Study of the Changing American Character*. New Haven: Yale Univ. Press. → An abridged paperback edition was published in 1960.

SLATER, ELIOT 1936 The Inheritance of Manic–Depressive Insanity and Its Relation to Mental Defect. *Journal of Mental Science* 82:626–634.

SPITZ, RENÉ A. 1946 Anaclitical Depression. *Psychoanalytic Study of the Child* 2:313–342.

DEPTH PERCEPTION
See under PERCEPTION.

DESCARTES, RENÉ

René Descartes (1596–1650) was born at La Haye, in Touraine, near Poitou, into a family of merchants and lower civil servants aspiring to the *petite noblesse.* A second son, he was put to school with the Jesuits at the newly founded Collège Royale of La Flèche where, until he was sixteen, he studied, first, the trivium, then "philosophy"—that is, logic, physics, and metaphysics. Later in the curriculum, "morality" was added to logic and mathematics to physics; in mathematics his talent was at once evident. Two aspects of his education are notable: he received a thoroughly "modern" intellectual training, in which bodily fitness was valued, and Galileo's physics was early and naturally absorbed into Jesuit teaching.

Between 1612, when he left school, and 1618, when he took up the profession of arms, the events of Descartes's life are unclear. He was for a time in Paris and may then have come into contact with the scientific group around the Minim Father, Marin Mersenne, at the Place Royale. After some hesitation he evidently decided on a military career. As a soldier of fortune he took part in the Thirty Years' War, fighting with the Dutch, who in spite of their Protestantism allied with France against the Hapsburgs. During the night of November 10, 1619, Descartes had his famous dream of a universal and unified science; in his German *poêle* ("stove-heated room") that winter he worked out his "rules for thinking," finally published in 1637 as the *Discourse on Method.*

From 1620 until his death, Descartes led a life with neither a fixed profession nor a fixed abode. He was, simply, a thinker; his inherited income, his books, and his occasional patrons sufficed for his needs. He traveled through Europe, including Italy, before 1628, making Paris (and in Paris, Mersenne) his center; thereafter, until 1649, he lived chiefly in Holland, the first of a stream of immigrant visitors to profit from the freedom and stimulus of that country.

Descartes's fellowship was varied—the scientist Isaac Beeckman in Breda, who like him was deeply concerned with establishing a method for the new sciences; Claudius Salmasius, a French theologian at Leiden; the mathematicians Hortensius at Amsterdam and Golius and Van Schooten at Leiden; among doctors, the anatomist Plempius, with whom he studied; Plempius' disciples Heereboord and Heydanus, responsible for the introduction of "Cartesianism" into the academies; Étienne de Courcelles, who translated the *Discourse* into Latin; the polymath Constantijn Huygens, secretary to the prince of Orange (Descartes played a part in the education of his scientific son, Christiaan Huygens). His correspondence was enormous, and he maintained his connections with French scientists. He lived in Deventer, Leiden, Egmond, and Amsterdam, making several trips to France; in 1649 in the service of Queen Christina, he accepted an appointment to Stockholm, where he died in 1650.

Descartes's published work shows great consistency and care. In 1629 he was busy with a treatise in metaphysics, later expanded and published as the *Meditations* in 1641. From 1629 to 1633 he worked on his cosmological study, *Le monde* (1664), a book in two sections, one ostensibly on light (or action at a distance), the other on man; but, as he frankly reported in the *Discourse* of 1637, he was alarmed by the condemnation of Galileo's theories and did not publish the work (it was posthumously published in 1662 and 1664). At this point he evidently turned back to his dream and contemplations on method; in 1637 his vernacular *Discourse* appeared, written for ordinary thinking people, followed by long essays exemplifying its application to optics, meteorology, and geometry. Perhaps because of his nervousness over his discontinued cosmological speculation, Descartes made special efforts to secure approval for his book, sending a copy to the Jesuit Père Noel, rector of La Flèche, and seeking approval of the book, through Mersenne, from the French chancellor Pierre Séguier.

The *Discourse* was influential in many areas, from literary *explication de texte* to metaphysics. Appropriately, in a work in which human certainty is reduced to man's consciousness of his own thinking processes, Descartes described the etiology of the treatise itself—what sort of an instrument he himself was, how he was trained, where and under what conditions he got his idea of universal method, how he tested his method, how he came to write it. Throughout Descartes's work there are patches of autobiography, presented not as self-indulgence but as data relevant to the substance presented. Although the *Discourse* records his approval of his own training, it nonetheless, with its appendages, revised (or reformed) the Jesuits' philosophical curriculum, as it did the teaching of other groups. Logic, physics, and metaphysics all suffered reorganization at Descartes's hands, as did mathematics and morality (the last subject more fully developed with the appearance of *Les passions de l'âme* in 1649). In 1641 his *Meditations* came out, expansions both of the *Discourse* and his early metaphysical speculations and, in 1644, his *Principia philosophiae.* Though he was soon embroiled in methodological and theological polemic, particularly with Dutch Reformed divines, his social success was enhanced by a philosophical friendship with the bluestocking Princess Elizabeth, daughter of the dispossessed elector palatine, as well as by the patronage of Queen Christina.

Descartes made substantial contributions to

mathematics, physics, and psychology. In his own terms, his work in geometry and optics has remained viable: Cartesian geometry is still a legitimate entry to that discipline; his description of the operation of the eye, though since greatly refined, is the "correct" one. His "method," important for its influence in the social as well as in the natural sciences, has the following simple rules: (1) to accept nothing as true not clearly recognizable as such; (2) to divide up each difficulty into as many parts as possible; (3) to carry on reflections in due order, from the simplest part to the most complex combination; and (4) to make regular enumerations and reviews, in order to be certain of having made no omissions.

These regulations, striking for their common sense, involve two major presuppositions: the first, that ideas, fixed and reliable as numbers and mathematical ratios, build and follow as inexorably and securely upon one another as do mathematical processes; the second, that the proposition *cogito, ergo sum* ("I think, therefore I am") is radically true. Another way of stating the first is that Descartes believed in the truth of mathematics, and therefore used it as a model for his thinking about thinking, or that he was a thorough rationalist. Another way of stating the second is that Descartes used skepticism to establish an ontology based—again, in sharp break with the philosophical tradition—upon the self's irreducible recognition of the thinking self. From that conviction and by means of his own method, he constructed his (remarkably arrogant) ontological proof of God and his definitions of the existence of the material world and the laws of its nature.

Accompanying the crucial importance he attributed to mind is his notion of its separation from body, or matter; the sharp distinction he drew between mind and body resulted in part from his attempt to relate Galileo's mechanist physics—for him, in spite of the ban unassailably true—to the immaterial process of rationality and, through that process, to the immaterial deity in whose existence he believed. One result of that radical separation of mind and matter is his extremely abstract conception of deity (justifiably criticized as deist rather than Christian); another is his mechanist psychology. Animals, indeed, he concluded to be machines: man, endowed with soul and mind, is thereby no mere mechanism. *Les passions de l'âme* deals with psychological manifestations as functionally as possible, translating inward "passion" into outward "action" and discussing the sensible appearances of behavior rather than the *invisibilia* of man's inner life. Insofar as he could, relying heavily upon Harvey's work and his own ana-

tomical experience, Descartes provided a physiological explanation of behavior, one example of which (unfairly ridiculed) is his location of the soul in the pineal gland. Behavior was discussed in the "causal" terms of external stimuli and the passions classified as predictable reactions to certain situations and stimuli (e.g., wonder, desire, remorse, love and hatred, pride and shame). He was interested in such physiological manifestations of the passions as tears and flight. Psychology thus became a branch of "physics," or physiology, a hypothesis with great influence upon subsequent psychological experimentation. The Cartesian beast–machine became the model for animal study in the eighteenth century; inevitably, in spite of Descartes's precautions against such a step, La Mettrie presented the argument, firmly based in the Cartesian psychology, that man too is simply machine. In his effort to free thought and thinking from the debilitating influence of the mutable body and to exempt it, theoretically at least, from skewing by the passions, Descartes split inward life into two quite different and unrelated components, the rational and the emotional.

ROSALIE L. COLIE

[*Other relevant material may be found in* REASONING AND LOGIC; THINKING; VISION; *and in the biographies of* DURKHEIM *and* KANT.]

WORKS BY DESCARTES

(1637) 1954 *Discourse on Method.* Translated with an introduction by Laurence J. Lafleur. New York: Liberal Arts Press. → First published as *Discours de la méthode.* . . . A paperback edition was published in 1960 by Penguin.

(1641) 1961 *Meditations on First Philosophy.* 2d ed., rev. New York: Bobbs-Merrill. → First published as *Meditationes de prima philosophia,* . . .

1644 *Renati Des Cartes principia philosophiae.* Amsterdam: Elsevier.

1649 *Les passions de l'âme.* Paris: Legras.

1664 *Le monde de M. Descartes: Ou la traité de la lumière et des autres principaux objects des sens; Avec un discours de l'action des corps et un autre des fièvres, composez selon les principes du même auteur.* Paris: Bobin & Le Gras. → Published posthumously.

Oeuvres de Descartes. 12 vols. and index. Edited by Charles Adam and Paul Tannery. Paris: Cerf, 1897–1913.

SUPPLEMENTARY BIBLIOGRAPHY

ADAM, CHARLES 1937 *Descartes: Sa vie et son oeuvre.* Paris: Boivin.

BAILLET, ADRIEN (1691) 1946 *La vie de Monsieur Descartes.* Paris: Table Ronde.

BALZ, ALBERT G. A. 1951 *Cartesian Studies.* New York: Columbia Univ. Press.

BRUNSCHVICG, LÉON 1944 *Descartes et Pascal: Lecteurs de Montaigne.* New York and Paris: Brentano.

CRESSON, ANDRÉ 1962 *Descartes: Sa vie, son oeuvre.* Paris: Presses Universitaires de France.

Descartes et le cartésianisme hollandais. Edited by E. J. Dijksterhuis et al. 1950 Paris: Presses Universitaires de France.

GILSON, ÉTIENNE 1930 *Études sur le rôle de la pensée médiévale dans la formation du système cartésien.* Paris: Vrin.

JASPERS, KARL (1937) 1956 *Descartes und die Philosophie.* 3d ed. Berlin: de Gruyter.

KOYRÉ, ALEXANDRE 1922 *Essai sur l'idée de Dieu et les preuves de son existence chez Descartes.* Paris: Leroux.

MARITAIN, JACQUES 1944 *The Dream of Descartes.* New York: Philosophical Library.

PARIS, BIBLIOTHÈQUE NATIONALE 1937 *Descartes: Notices bibliographiques et iconographiques.* Edited by Thérèse d'Alverny. Paris: Bibliothèque Nationale.

SCOTT, J. F. 1952 *The Scientific Work of René Descartes.* London: Taylor & Francis.

SEBBA, G. 1964 *Bibliographia Cartesiana: A Critical Guide to the Descartes Literature, 1800–1960.* The Hague: Nijhoff.

SERRURIER, CORNELIA (1943) 1951 *Descartes: L'homme et le penseur.* Paris: Presses Universitaires de France.

DESCENT GROUPS
See under KINSHIP.

DESIGN OF EXPERIMENTS
See EXPERIMENTAL DESIGN.

DESPOTISM
See AUTOCRACY *and* DICTATORSHIP.

DETERMINISM, GEOGRAPHICAL
See ENVIRONMENTALISM; GEOGRAPHY; *and the biography of* HUNTINGTON.

DETERRENCE

As the release and utilization of energy from atomic nuclei have challenged and intrigued physical scientists, so behavioral and social scientists have been intrigued and challenged by the intrusion of this energy into the domain of their concern. Awareness of the potential destructiveness of weapons employing nuclear energy has prompted extensive consideration of their impact on international relations.

In its contemporary usage, the concept "deterrence" refers to hypothesized effects of nuclear weapons technology on the set of alternatives from which national policy makers choose their courses of action. By extension, these "effects" affect the conduct of international relations.

The set of alternatives from which national leaders make their choices has traditionally included among its elements the "resort to war" as an instrument of national policy; the hypothesized effects of nuclear weapons are relevant to this subset of foreign policy alternatives.

"Deterrence" refers to the attempt by decision makers in one nation or group of nations to restructure the set of alternatives available to decision makers in another nation or group of nations by posing a threat to their key values. The restructuring is an attempt to exclude armed aggression (resort to war), from consideration.

The fundamental deterrence hypothesis is: *If the threat to values is sufficiently large, the exclusion of armed aggression from consideration is probable.*

This hypothesis, taken together with a subsidiary hypothesis—*nuclear weapons pose a sufficiently large threat to values*—yields the deduction: *Nuclear weapons make probable the rejection of armed aggression as a potential policy alternative.*

The ubiquity of this syllogism in the deterrence literature (Brody 1960; Lefever 1962, pp. 313–332; Halperin 1963, pp. 133–184) argues for the examination of the postulates on which it is founded. Three central assumptions appear to underlie this syllogism; they may be classified under the following themes: (1) the rationality of decision makers; (2) the unidimensionality of threat and of response to threats; and (3) the constancy of sets of policy alternatives (see Deutsch 1963, pp. 71–72, for a critique of a somewhat different set of deterrence theory assumptions).

The assumption of rationality. The rationality of decision makers posited in the deterrence literature is both a norm against which behavior can be evaluated and a prescriptive guide to choice. The rational decision maker, in deterrence theory, is presumed to avoid the resort to war in those situations in which the cost anticipated from aggression is greater than the gain expected from such an action.

This notion of rationality concentrates on avoidance behavior; it predicts the rejection of alternatives where cost exceeds gain. Empirical studies on foreign policy decision making are not abundant, but those that have been done raise doubts about this characterization of the policy process (Snyder & Paige 1958; Holsti 1962). In the light of research on domestic and foreign policy making, this postulate of deterrence theory is of dubious validity.

Conceptions of threat. The fundamental deterrence syllogism contains implicit assumptions about the nature of threat and about the relationship of threat to deterrence.

Threat is presumed to be a simple function of

destructive capacity; the greater the destructive capability, the greater the threat. A more complex view of threat (for example, Singer 1958) calls this conception into question unless "destructive capacity" is construed very broadly—beyond numbers of weapons, warhead size (yield), and accuracy.

Experiments on the relationship of power to threat indicate that the ambiguity (or, conversely, the clarity) of the threat is closely related to the amount of threat experienced (Cohen 1959).

It has been suggested elsewhere (Brody 1963, pp. 696–697) that the threatening interaction can be conceived of as being determined by three factors: (1) perception by one party of the other party's hostile intentions; (2) perception of the other party's capability of inflicting damage to the perceiver; and (3) the credibility of the other party's declaratory policy. If threat inhered only in capability (and we ignored hostility and credibility), we would conclude that adversaries and allies are equally threatened by the same weapons systems.

Complex conceptions of threat call into question not only the proposition that threat varies uniformly with destructive power but also many of the assumptions about the relationship of threat to deterrence. The literature is replete with suggestions that the effectiveness of deterrence is a direct function of the amount of destructive capability. Wohlstetter (1959) has refined this conception by pointing out that deterrence is more properly conceived of as a function of the amount of capability potentially remaining after an attack has been absorbed. Both of these conceptions assume that the threatened decision maker will be "deterred," that is, that he will abandon even the consideration of the course of action that worried the threatener.

"Credibility" has received attention from deterrence theorists (Kaufmann 1956, pp. 12–38), but as a quality of weapons rather than of relations among nations. However, the possibility of an aggressive response to a credible threat receives much less attention (for example, Kahn 1963). Psychologists, on the other hand, have often found aggressive responses to threat (for example, McNeil 1959). This suggests at least the potential for such responses in threatening international situations.

Milburn, drawing on psychological research, proposes that we characterize threats on a number of dimensions (for example, symbolic–concrete and clear–vague); however, the relationship between types of threats, characterized on these dimensions, and the inhibition of behavior (deterrence) or excitation of behavior (provocation) is without empirical research, despite the salience of such knowledge for deterrence theory.

Availability of policy alternatives. Implicit also in much of the literature on deterrence is the assumption that alternatives to the resort to war are available to and perceived by decision makers, irrespective of the international situation.

The validity of this proposition is difficult to establish: the historical record is rich with examples of national leaders who, in intense crises, "saw no way out" and for whom war became the only viable alternative. On the other hand, despite extremely intense crises, decision makers in the nuclear-armed nations apparently have not felt that their policy alternatives were reduced to one—war.

Contradictory hypotheses can be entertained to resolve this paradox: Because of their destructiveness, nuclear weapons may have transformed the international system, thus making the prenuclear historical examples simply inapplicable. However, it is equally plausible that the international system has moved onto a plateau of high intensity (McClelland 1961)—the cold war—and that increases in tension (relative to this base), comparable to historical crises, have not yet been experienced by leaders in one nuclear nation when confronted by another. Which hypothesis will stand the test of research cannot be forejudged, but an answer is needed to strengthen the conceptual foundations of deterrence theory.

Deterrence strategies. Despite the lack of confirmation of the premises on which elemental deterrence theory is based, there is widespread a priori acceptance of them. The dialogue, which has produced a voluminous literature, has largely been concerned with how best to deter; thus, the debate has been primarily strategic rather than social scientific.

An important impetus to this debate has been the rapidly changing weapons technology; each new capability has found spokesmen arguing the necessity of including it in the considerations affecting strategic thought. Technology has tended to lead strategy, bringing an evanescent quality to the deterrence literature.

The debate among deterrence strategists can be characterized by examining the various positions along three dimensions: (1) the mission of the deterrent; (2) the means by which deterrence is to be accomplished; and (3) the values threatened and to be threatened.

There is little disagreement that a goal of foreign policy is the dissuasion of other nations from committing aggression of any kind—from strategic nuclear attack to guerrilla warfare. Debate arises over how much of this spectrum can be deterred with nuclear weapons.

Glenn Snyder (1961) provides a useful distinction between the missions of denying access to territory and of punishing aggression (that is, of retaliation); weapons appropriate to one mission may not be suited to the other. Thus, for example, the mission of denying western Europe to Soviet forces, it is argued, requires different weapons than does the mission of retaliating against the Soviet homeland, should the Soviet leaders choose to attack. The counter to this argument, stemming from the strategic doctrines of Douhet (Brodie 1959), asserts that the massive threat inherent in nuclear retaliatory capability will deter tactical as well as strategic aggression.

Those who argue for specific weapons for specific missions—the strategy usually called "graduated deterrence"—point to the ineffectiveness of strategic bombing as a deterrent in World War II (Blackett 1962) and to the reduced credibility of an all-purpose deterrent after the Soviet Union emerged as a nuclear power.

This debate overlaps the dialogue about the means by which deterrence can best be accomplished. The strategists who advocate graduated deterrence generally argue for the limitation of strategic capability at the minimum needed to deter (Morgenstern 1959). The logic of this position relies heavily on the invulnerability to attack of individual units of the deterrent force. The critics of minimum deterrence point out, however, that the continuation of this invulnerability in view of the growth of weapons technology is too uncertain for so fundamental an element of policy (Kahn 1960; 1963). The advocates of minimum deterrence argue that sustained effort in producing weapons beyond the minimum (in an attempt to guarantee at least "statistical invulnerability" of the force as a whole) is itself a stimulus to the search for countermeasures and to the uncontrolled stockpiling of arms, that is, to arms races.

Proponents of graduated deterrence argue that the absence of military capability to counter a particular lower-level or nonnuclear threat, for example, insufficient conventional forces to deny territory in western Europe to the Soviet Army, creates an unstable situation fraught with the danger of escalation to strategic nuclear war. It is in escalation, that is, in resort to weapons with much greater destructive capacity than the weapons employed by the attacking side, that deterrence theorists see the greatest likelihood of limited wars becoming general nuclear wars (Schelling 1960; Halperin

1963). Moreover, the expansion of limited conflicts is often seen as the most probable cause of general war.

Concentration on the deterrence of general war has led to a debate about what is the best object of threat: Is the threatened destruction of cities more effective than the threatened destruction of military targets in precluding resort to war?

The dual nature of weapons—they can be used to fight as well as to threaten—has brought an element of confusion to the debate. If a war is to be fought, response weapons capable of destroying military capability may be most effective in limiting damage to targets of high value to the responding nation (Kahn 1963). On the other hand, it is contended that producing this amount of weaponry (because there are many more well-defended military targets than civilian targets) could create an unstable arms race that would make war more likely.

The advocates of minimum deterrence have tended to opt for targeting population and industrial centers; the opposition to this point of view has tended to argue for preserving the option of retaliating against any target, civilian or military. The second policy seems to be characteristic of United States military posture; the first seems to have been adopted by the Soviet Union.

Deterrence and international relations. The lively debates among deterrence strategists has had a salutary effect on the field of international relations. Social scientists have expressed uncertainty about the validity of the principles on which deterrence theory rests and some skepticism about assertions concerning the way nations act and are likely to act; from this doubt and questioning, professional students of international politics have begun to think of the relationship of military technology to foreign policy as a significant area of research. Moreover, the subject matter has brought scholars from all the social sciences together and has forced interdisciplinary communication.

The strategic debates will continue as military technology continues to change, but the conceptual foundations laid by the work of concerned social scientists are the beginnings of the reintegration of military strategy into the study of international relations; in this context we can expect the patient development of an empirical theory of deterrence.

RICHARD A. BRODY

[See also NUCLEAR WAR; STRATEGY.]

BIBLIOGRAPHY

BLACKETT, PATRICK M. S. 1962 *Studies of War: Nuclear and Conventional.* New York: Hill & Wang.

Brodie, Bernard 1959 *Strategy in the Missile Age.* Princeton Univ. Press.

Brody, Richard A. 1960 Deterrence Strategies: An Annotated Bibliography. *Journal of Conflict Resolution* 4:443–457.

Brody, Richard A. 1963 Some Systemic Effects of the Spread of Nuclear Weapons Technology: A Study Through Simulation of a Multi-nuclear Future. *Journal of Conflict Resolution* 7:663–753.

Cohen, A. R. 1959 Situational Structure, Self-esteem, and Threat Oriented Reactions to Power. Pages 35–52 in Dorwin Cartwright (editor), *Studies in Social Power.* Ann Arbor: Univ. of Michigan, Institute for Social Research.

Deutsch, Karl W. 1963 *The Nerves of Government: Models of Political Communication and Control.* New York: Free Press.

Halperin, Morton H. 1963 *Limited War in the Nuclear Age.* New York: Wiley. → See especially the bibliography on pages 133–184.

Holsti, Ole R. 1962 The Belief System and National Images: A Case Study. *Journal of Conflict Resolution* 6:244–252.

Kahn, Herman (1960) 1961 *On Thermonuclear War.* 2d ed. Princeton Univ. Press.

Kahn, Herman 1963 Strategy, Foreign Policy, and Thermonuclear War. Pages 43–70 in Robert A. Goldwin (editor), *America Armed: Essays on United States Military Policy.* Chicago: Rand McNally.

Kaufmann, William W. (editor) 1956 *Military Policy and National Security.* Princeton Univ. Press.

Lefever, Ernest W. (editor) 1962 *Arms and Arms Control: A Symposium.* New York: Praeger. → See especially the bibliography on pages 313–332.

McClelland, Charles A. 1961 The Acute International Crisis. *World Politics* 14:182–204.

McNeil, Elton B. 1959 Psychology and Aggression. *Journal of Conflict Resolution* 3:195–293.

Milburn, Thomas W. 1959 What Constitutes Effective Deterrence? *Journal of Conflict Resolution* 3:138–145.

Morgenstern, Oskar 1959 *The Question of National Defense.* New York: Random House. → A paperback edition was published in 1961 by Vintage.

Schelling, Thomas C. 1960 *The Strategy of Conflict.* Cambridge, Mass.: Harvard Univ. Press.

Singer, J. David 1958 Threat-perception and the Armament-tension Dilemma. *Journal of Conflict Resolution* 2:90–105.

Singer, J. David 1962 *Deterrence, Arms Control, and Disarmament.* Columbus: Ohio State Univ. Press.

Snyder, Glenn H. 1961 *Deterrence and Defense: Toward a Theory of National Security.* Princeton Univ. Press.

Snyder, Richard C.; and Paige, Glenn D. 1958 The United States Decision to Resist Aggression in Korea: The Application of an Analytical Scheme. *Administrative Science Quarterly* 3:341–378.

Wohlstetter, Albert 1959 The Delicate Balance of Terror. *Foreign Affairs* 37:211–234.

DETRIBALIZATION

See Acculturation *and* Tribal society.

DEVALUATION

See International monetary economics, *article on* Exchange rates.

DEVELOPING COUNTRIES

See Economic growth; Industrialization; Modernization; Nationalism; Power transition; Stagnation; Technical assistance.

DEVELOPMENT BANKS

The label "development bank" attaches to a group of national financial institutions, in developing countries, that vary widely in size, source of funds, and scope of activity. Essentially, a development bank is a vehicle for mobilizing and channeling medium- and long-term capital into the productive sector of the economy; most are also a source of entrepreneurship and technical assistance. Some development banks create and finance public enterprises or plan or carry out national development programs, but these are the exception; typically, the term "development bank" describes an institution created to encourage the growth of the private sector. Although limitations of funds and of qualified personnel have led countries in an early stage of development to entrust to their development banks responsibilities in several fields—agriculture, industry, housing, mining—emphasis on a single field is more usual. Among these specialist institutions the greater and the growing number are concerned with industry, and it is these that best illustrate the possible range of a development bank's operations.

Among industrial financing institutions may be found not only public banks but a number of banks that are privately owned, wholly or predominantly. Banks that extend agricultural credit or are actively engaged in promotional work, however, are normally government owned. These activities are relatively risky, expensive, not immediately revenue producing, and hold little appeal for private investors. In countries with a low level of domestic savings and limited access to external sources of finance, any private participation in a development bank is likely to be no more than token, at least initially. Sometimes even in countries with a relatively high savings ratio, when government policy has called for support of the private industrial sector, the government will choose to create a public development bank as a vehicle for its assistance. In any event, a benevolent government interest is essential to a development bank's success, and most banks function in the context of a national development plan.

The antecedents of the modern development bank can be traced back some hundred years to industrial financing institutions in Europe and the

United States (Diamond 1957, pp. 19–37; Institut d'Études Bancaires et Financières 1964, pp. 49–66). Since the 1950s the number of development banks has increased rapidly, as developing countries have sought mechanisms to accelerate their economic growth and especially to stimulate industrialization. Tallies vary, depending on definition; moreover, they are soon outdated, as new banks come into operation; in 1964 there were well over one hundred, to be found in all parts of the less-developed world. The International Bank for Reconstruction and Development and its affiliates, the International Finance Corporation and the International Development Association, have encouraged the creation of private development banks in appropriate circumstances, extending both technical assistance in their establishment and operation (including recruitment of management and training of staff) and financial support (amounting to about $300 million by mid-1964) through loans or participation in share capital. Assistance has also been provided by the Inter-American Development Bank and through the aid programs of industrialized countries. The United States by mid-1964 had committed about $1,000 million to various types of development banks. The United Kingdom and France have a long history of extensive assistance to such institutions, the former concerned with banks in Commonwealth countries, the latter with those in former French Africa. Germany and Japan have entered the field more recently. The development bank has served as a means of retailing funds—often foreign exchange—to enterprises too small to be financed directly by these public sources.

Development banks are intended to fill a gap primarily, though not exclusively, financial. Commercial banks, traditionally, have not made available investment capital; they generally provide short-term money only, frequently at a high rate of interest, and tend to favor existing enterprises and the larger borrowers. Savers in the typical developing country prefer investments promising a quick return to those offering only the prospect of gradual growth; they would rather invest in commercial ventures or real estate or send funds abroad than participate in untried industrial enterprises. The financial institutions and capital market mechanisms that in more developed countries serve to transfer savings are absent, embryonic, or inefficient. Often the business community shows little inclination to look for new fields of activity or even to act when promising opportunities are called to its attention. Finally, the organizational and technical competence to launch and sustain a new enterprise is frequently lacking or in short supply.

A development bank appropriately capitalized, well managed and staffed, and free to reach investment decisions objectively on business and economic grounds can help to overcome these various difficulties. It can supply investment capital—loan or equity or some intermediate form—from its own resources and can recruit capital from other sources, domestic and foreign. It can encourage and facilitate direct investment in industrial securities and help to develop a capital market. It can spark industrial initiative, sponsor urgently needed new ventures, and provide advice at all stages of a project, from planning to operation.

Each bank is, or should be, designed with a particular country's needs and environment in view. In consequence, there is no model for a development bank, and no single description adequately fits them all.

Capitalization. Private development banks are organized as corporations, some with several hundred million dollars of initial capital, some with far less. The capitalization of any particular bank necessarily reflects a judgment concerning the amount that it appears feasible to raise from available sources. A second relevant consideration is the desirability of launching the bank with resources large enough to assure an impact on the economy and, assuming the bank is soundly run, earnings sufficient to cover operating costs, reserve and tax requirements and, before too long, payment of a modest dividend. Usually, institutional shareholders—commercial banks, insurance companies, investment houses—predominate. Many institutions in the industrialized countries have invested in development banks, primarily to obtain a window on events in a country to which they have some special tie or in the expectation that the bank will ultimately prove beneficial to their own interests. Foreign shareholders serve as a channel for the managerial skills and modern technology so scarce in developing countries and also help the bank to resist any undue local political pressure.

It has proved harder to attract individual shareholders, at least in the early stages of a bank's operations; they tend to have a greater concern for the probability of an adequate return on their investment. A successful development bank can be expected to earn moderate returns in time; none is likely to be highly profitable. Individual investors have, however, been attracted by the inducement of special government assistance in a bank's initial capitalization. The most effective device has been a long-term loan, interest-free or at low interest, subordinate to share capital in the event of the bank's liquidation. Earnings on the no-cost or low-cost funds enhance the return on equity; the subordination to equity provides shareholders with a cushion against losses. Some governments have permitted a development bank to manage public funds for a fee and without risk, or have extended special rediscount or borrowing privileges, granted preferential tax treatment for dividends, or guaranteed a minimum dividend. Development-bank loan capital has come primarily from public sources at home or abroad; a few banks have borrowed in the local capital market with a government guarantee.

Operation and policies. Normally, a development bank tries not to compete with other sources of funds, particularly the commercial banks. This is one reason why most development banks do not accept deposits and, in fixing their loan charges, take into account not only their own cost of capital but also the going rate of interest. Compared with commercial banks, the development bank gives greater weight in its investment decisions to growth potential and quality of management and places less emphasis on security and credit standing. As a development agency, the development bank is mindful of the needs and preferences of applicants and the potential benefit of a proposed investment to the economy. At the same time, if it is a shareholder-owned institution, it cannot ignore the source and cost of its own capital and the composition of its investment portfolio and must therefore take profitability into consideration (Boskey 1959, pp. 49–55).

Although development banks finance the modernization or expansion of established enterprises as well as the establishment of new enterprises, their characteristic willingness to take risks and to combine development and banking criteria in investment decisions makes them particularly useful to the latter; new enterprises cannot readily borrow in the market and have limited earnings to reinvest. Equity financing is frequently most appropriate for such enterprises: unlike a loan, it imposes no interest or repayment burden. But the bank is not always welcomed as a co-owner. Family-held enterprises are sometimes reluctant to admit outsiders to ownership; this may be particularly true where the bank is a government institution. Moreover, the banks take their own investment portfolios into account in determining the nature of their financing; they generally limit equity holdings to the equivalent of their own share capital plus reserves.

A development bank does not usually extend either very small or very large loans. Appraisal, administration, and follow-up of small loans is costly and time consuming; the loans themselves are risky. Unless the bank is a public institution

with no pressure to pay dividends or has special funds for assistance to small enterprises, it normally excludes such enterprises from its clientele by setting a minimum on the size of individual investments. For different reasons—to diversify its portfolio and avoid allocating an unreasonably large proportion of resources to a single project—the bank usually sets a ceiling on the amount of financing to any one client. Thus, development banks usually do not cater to very large projects either, except as partners or participants with other investors (such as the International Finance Corporation). Normally, a bank will supply no more than half of an applicant's financial requirements; this mobilizes capital in support of the bank's contribution and spreads the impact of its financing.

There are a number of ways open to a development bank to assist the growth of a capital market and to encourage the practice of industrial investment. When enterprises financed by the bank have "seasoned" and begun to show a profit, the bank may sell their securities from its portfolio. This adds to the supply of marketable securities in circulation and broadens industrial ownership and the base for future sales; in addition, it releases the bank's resources for new investments. The bank may underwrite new securities, normally only those issued by enterprises it has itself financed. It may offer participations in its investments and issue its own obligations. Each of these activities in effect invites investors to rely on the bank's appraisals and investment decisions. Consequently, the extent to which a development bank can be successful in these areas depends upon the extent to which it has been able to establish a reputation for sound business judgment. Finally, the bank may be an educator and innovator, introducing or making more familiar financial instruments and techniques employed in the capital markets of industrialized countries.

Role in stimulating investment. The development bank's promotional role—the stimulation of new industrial investment—is an important one. At the same time, since promotion is likely to be expensive and unlikely to produce immediate returns, private banks can afford only limited activity of this character unless they have special resources for the purpose. The possibilities are varied. Through its own staff or contacts available to it, the bank can help to translate an idea into a bankable project and a project into an operating enterprise. The bank's analysis, in the regular course of business, of proposals submitted to it may lead to suggestions for modifications in the financial, economic, technical, or managerial aspects, rendering the proposal more economic and technically sounder. The bank may find experienced industrial partners for new and complex undertakings. It will try to bring investment opportunities and private capital together. It may conduct a survey of a geographic region or an economic sector to find promising projects. It may actively sponsor, and establish in cooperation with other sources of capital and technology, new enterprises to meet specific needs of the economy. Once the bank has financed an enterprise, it provides continuing guidance to its clients on matters of operation and policy. By encouraging the adoption of good financial and managerial practices, it can help to create and maintain a sound industrial sector.

Although the development bank is a useful and versatile instrument of economic development, it is only one of many; it cannot by itself overcome the host of problems that developing countries encounter on the road to industrialization. Moreover, certain conditions are a prerequisite to the success of any development bank. Before a bank is created the needs it is to meet should be identified, to facilitate formation of an appropriate organization and financial design. For a private institution to be profitable, there must be within the country enough of the basic ingredients of industrialization to assure a continuing flow of a fair volume of business. There should be at the outset experienced management and a competent and sufficiently numerous staff; often this will mean some foreign personnel initially, a circumstance which developing countries, especially those newly independent, sometimes find hard to accept. Finally, realization of a development bank's potential requires government policies—fiscal, monetary, commercial—that support and facilitate the bank's activities and that, in particular, create a climate congenial to private enterprise. Experience indicates that it is a waste of scarce development resources, both of funds and personnel, to create a development bank where these conditions cannot be, or are not, met.

SHIRLEY BOSKEY

[*See also* ECONOMIC GROWTH.]

BIBLIOGRAPHY

ADLER, ROBERT W.; and MIKESELL, RAYMOND F. 1966 *Public External Financing of Development Banks in Developing Countries.* Eugene: Univ. of Oregon, Bureau of Business and Economic Research.

BOSKEY, SHIRLEY 1959 *Problems and Practices of Development Banks.* Published for the International Bank for Reconstruction and Development. Baltimore: Johns Hopkins Press.

DIAMOND, WILLIAM 1957 *Development Banks.* Published for the International Bank for Reconstruction and Development, Economic Development Institute. Baltimore: Johns Hopkins Press.

INSTITUT D'ÉTUDES BANCAIRES ET FINANCIÈRES 1964 *Les banques de développement dans le monde.* Volume 1. Paris: Dunod.

INTERNATIONAL FINANCE CORPORATION 1964 *Private Development Finance Companies.* Washington: The Corporation.

NYHART, J. D. 1964 Toward Professionalism in Development Banking. Unpublished manuscript, Massachusetts Institute of Technology.

DEVELOPMENT PLANNING
See under PLANNING, ECONOMIC.

DEVELOPMENTAL PSYCHOLOGY

I. THE FIELD   *Harold W. Stevenson*
II. A THEORY OF DEVELOPMENT   *Jean Piaget*

I
THE FIELD

Developmental psychology is concerned with the study of changes in behavior throughout the life span. Although, logically, equal emphasis should be placed on development during all stages of life, so far most research has dealt primarily with infants, children, and adolescents. Because of this emphasis the term "developmental psychology" is often used interchangeably with the older terms "child psychology," "adolescent psychology," and "genetic psychology." These areas are distinct from one another, but it is impractical to discuss them separately. Child and adolescent psychology traditionally include the investigation of behavior at, rather than across, particular periods of development, and genetic psychology involves a concern for ontogenetic as well as phylogenetic changes in behavior. Underlying all the terms, however, is a concern with the emergence of behavior in the human being, and, therefore, in this discussion no attempt is made to distinguish between the various approaches [*see* ADOLESCENCE; AGING; INFANCY].

In the growth of developmental psychology theoretical positions, practical needs, public awareness, and support of research have been closely interrelated. In various phases different forces have been dominant, depending on the psychological and social milieu of the time. The field, therefore, has been one of shifting emphases. It is necessary to review the historical background of developmental psychology in order to understand its current structure.

The early period (1880–1920)

Although for centuries parents and other adults had observed children and gathered much "common-sense" knowledge about them, the information was contaminated by the biases of the parent–child relationship and the goals and wishes of other observers. Interest in systematically investigating developmental changes in behavior is, in fact, relatively recent. Research in this area received its initial impetus from the late nineteenth-century work in evolutionary biology. Charles Darwin, Wilhelm T. Preyer, and other biologists observed the development of human infants as a means of gaining further understanding of human evolution. After the publication of these observations, many baby biographies were published. They gave some indications of the changes that occur in the infant's repertoire of behavior, although they were typically limited to a few cases and covered only a restricted age range.

The theory of evolution had a stimulating effect on other types of research, including that of the "founder" of developmental psychology, G. Stanley Hall. His belief in the theory that ontogeny recapitulates phylogeny resulted in his studying the behavior of the individual child as a source of insight into the behavior of man at earlier evolutionary periods. Many aspects of children's behavior were observed, including play and social relationships.

Hall introduced the questionnaire method, marking the end of a period in which observation was the primary method of obtaining data; questionnaires came to be widely used for studies of children's thoughts, interests, and wishes. Soon laboratory procedures were applied to children, but the early experiments tended to be little more than demonstrations that certain phenomena associated with lower animals or with adults also occur in children. These studies dealt with the traditional topics of experimental psychology, such as memory, learning, sensation, and perception. In many cases, studies originally using animals or college students were adapted so that children could be used as subjects.

Intelligence testing. By 1890 there was considerable emphasis on objective observation and laboratory methods. Society was faced with the growing number of problems related to children that accompanied increased urbanization and expansion of public education. When, for example, the question of how to handle mental defectives in schools and institutions arose, groups of individuals in Great Britain and France began studies of how to assess and deal with such children. One of the most significant outcomes of these investigations was the development by Alfred Binet of a scale to distinguish between individuals of normal and subnormal intelligence. Whereas previous efforts to assess intelligence had been unsatisfactory, Binet's work in constructing tests, which involved complex verbal and adaptive functions rather than simple sensory or motor functions, yielded a successful scale. It was soon obvious that such a scale had broader use than solely distinguishing between normal and defective children. Further work by Binet and others, such as Lewis M. Terman, resulted in useful tests for "measuring" children's intelligence and investigating the effects of variables potentially capable of influencing intellectual development [*see* INTELLIGENCE AND INTELLIGENCE TESTING].

Psychoanalysis. During this period Sigmund Freud was developing a theory of psychic functioning that emphasized the importance of childhood experiences as determinants of later behavior. Aspects of the theory were presented in 1909 to developmental psychologists and others at Clark University. Although Freud directed attention toward the early emotional life of children, his work had a minimal effect on early research in developmental psychology. Not until the 1930s, when developmental psychologists were no longer so strongly influenced by biological thinking, did the resistance to his views decrease and did serious investigations of his ideas concerning the effects of early experiences on psychological development begin.

The period of expansion (1920–1940)

Research during the first two decades of the 1900s was aimed at providing a clearer delineation and categorization of children's behavior. The research was highly empirical and not significantly influenced by theoretical analysis of psychological functioning. The work of this period, however, provided data necessary for the later development of systematic positions.

By the 1920s developmental psychology was rapidly becoming a visible and important area in psychology. The belief was widely held that the application of scientific methods to the study of children would lead to solutions of problems in education, pediatrics, child care, and treatment. Educators began lecturing parents on how to rear children. Clinics were organized to evaluate children's abilities and to advise parents on such matters as discipline, toilet training, and feeding. Nursery schools were established in most large universities and in many colleges and were quickly put to use as a source of subjects for psychological research. Most important, funds became available for the support of research. The most notable donor was the Laura Spelman Rockefeller Fund, under whose auspices institutes devoted to research with normal children were established or extended at the universities of California, Iowa, Minnesota, and Toronto, and at Columbia University. The Fels Research Institute and the Yale Child Study Center also became leading centers for the study of children's behavior in the United States. The Institut J.-J. Rousseau in Geneva and the Vienna Psychologische Institut were the most active European institutions for research in developmental psychology. The 1920s and 1930s were exciting and productive years at these institutes, but because the institutes were separated from departments of psychology, developmental psychologists tended to be isolated from psychologists interested in other aspects of behavior. Only during the past few years has the relationship with general psychology been firmly re-established.

Divergent viewpoints on how environmental and biological factors influence behavior resulted in a major controversy over the question of the contributions of nature and nurture to intellectual functioning. It was easy to take sides; it was much more difficult to accumulate information that withstood the tests of critical scrutiny. The controversy eventually ended in a stalemate, for although scores of studies were published, few survived the devastating attacks that were waged against their design, execution, and analysis. Solutions for the enormously complex issues that were being raised would have to await the time when developmental psychologists had more sophisticated tools and information at their disposal.

Behaviorism and its critics. The introduction of behaviorism into developmental psychology in the 1930s marked the beginning of an era in which schools of psychology, each with its own theories, problems, and preferred methods, polarized the field. Previous research had been aimed at providing information about children's behavior; now research was often directed toward establishing the validity of theories advanced by various schools. Behaviorism had an effective and vigorous advocate in John B. Watson. Edward L. Thorndike and Ivan P. Pavlov had provided a background of information and techniques in their studies of learning and conditioning in animals, which Watson was able to use to develop his approach to psychology. He espoused an extreme form of environmentalism and relied heavily on the use of conditioning as the means for modifying behavior. His studies of infant behavior and of the acquisition and extinction of fear responses in children became classics, and his belief that introspection should be superseded by objective observation and measurement of behavior exerted a healthy influence on developmental psychology. It was not long, however, before advocates of other views responded critically to Watson's position.

Among the most vocal schools of critics were gestalt psychologists and psychoanalysts. Although at the time neither group had a large influence on developmental psychology, their views provided the basis for later work. Another critic who took strong exception to the associationistic view of American behaviorists was Jean Piaget. As a result of his training in biology, Piaget emphasized the adaptive functions of behavior in maintaining an equilibrium between the individual and the environment. Piaget's views were elaborated into a comprehensive theory of cognitive development. The contrast between him and the behaviorists extended to all aspects of their work. Whereas the behaviorists utilized the experimental method in their investigations of simple forms of behavior and emphasized the role of controlled experiences in the modification of behavior, Piaget preferred the clinical method and chose to study the interaction of maturation and experience in the production of complex behavior and higher thought processes.

Normative and longitudinal studies. The charting of the development of behavior was not confined to cognitive development. Arnold Gesell at Yale and Charlotte Bühler in Vienna had begun extensive normative studies of child development. For nearly forty years Gesell maintained an active program of research in the exploration of motor, adaptive, language, and personal–social behavior from birth through adolescence. The normative information from these studies, along with the results of his investigations of feeding, sleep, and other topics, became a major source of guidance for mothers in many countries. Gesell, like Piaget, had a strong biological orientation. While other American psychologists were proclaiming the influence of the environment on behavior, Gesell continued to show how specific types of experiences may have differential effects on behavior, depending on the maturational level of the individual.

A series of longitudinal studies of child development was initiated in the early 1930s. The longitudinal method had not been employed extensively prior to this time, although such investigations as Terman's famous study of gifted individuals had demonstrated its productivity. At the University of California, Nancy Bayley began a study of the development of mental abilities in infants and children (1940), Herbert Stolz and Harold Jones began a study of somatic and psychological development during adolescence, and Jean Macfarlane began a study of personality development. At the Fels Research Institute, Lester Sontag and his associates began a comprehensive longitudinal study of growth and development. All these studies are still being conducted; data are being collected, and old data are being analyzed in new and interesting ways [see PERSONALITY, *article on* PERSONALITY DEVELOPMENT; *and* SENSORY AND MOTOR DEVELOPMENT].

Gestalt and field theories. Psychology began to be influenced significantly by the work of the gestalt psychologists, who, in turn, were influenced by field theory from physical science. The extension of the gestalt approach by Kurt Lewin had the greatest influence on research with children. During his years in Berlin and in the United States, Lewin directed a series of studies aimed at demonstrating the important role of situational factors in determining behavior. Lewin's preference for an ahistorical approach to the analysis of behavior led him and others to a careful consideration of the structure of the psychological field and the forces operating in it. [*See* FIELD THEORY; GESTALT THEORY; *and the biography of* LEWIN.]

Later developments (1940–1965)

The remarkable rate of growth in developmental psychology was seriously curtailed at the end of the 1930s. Many factors contributed to a temporary decline in activity. The normative, descriptive approach had lost its allure; it was no longer of interest to reaffirm the fact that behavior developed systematically. Other areas of psychology appeared to be more challenging, and the number of persons entering developmental psychology decreased. World War II disrupted research programs. Perhaps as important as any factor, however, was the withdrawal of supporting funds from the institutes and the general unavailability of new funds for research. For about fifteen years it became more and more difficult to initiate new research projects and, in many cases, to complete the analyses of data obtained from earlier studies. In 1938, for example, approximately 500 publications concerned with children's behavior appeared; by 1949 the number had dropped to approximately 250. The general level of the work also began to decline; writings became more speculative and less dependent on original observations or experiments (see Barker 1951). Fortunately, the field did not disintegrate; there was enough activity at an appropriately high level to maintain the interest in research with children during the critical years.

The period of decline came to a halt in the mid-1950s, when interest in developmental psychology was reactivated. Since then, interest has increased at a rapid pace and there has been a revitalization of the area of study. Research with children has been greatly stimulated by the rapid and sophisticated advances in psychological theories, methodology, and instrumentation. Many of the theoretical positions in general psychology have direct relevance to the discussion of the emergence of behavior and are readily applicable to developmental investigations. Funds became available at an unprecedented level to support research and training. In the United States, for example, in 1962, a national Institute of Child Health and Human Development was established to provide leadership in training of investigators and research in developmental sciences, including developmental psychology. More powerful statistical analyses have been adopted and developed. Computers have made possible many types of studies that could never have been carried out without rapid mechanical analyses of the data.

The descriptive approach in developmental psychology has been replaced by a variable-oriented approach. The adoption of systematic positions dealing with developmental changes in children's behavior has led to an increased interest in determining children's responses to particular specifiable or manipulable variables and to a decreased interest in describing behavior in naturalistic or controlled settings. There is a tendency for subsystems to be developed that deal with specific aspects rather than with whole domains of behavior. The level of conceptualization has increased; concepts and processes now dominate thinking in developmental psychology.

There has been a redistribution of emphases among the various methods used in studying children. The experimental method has gained in popularity, primarily because of the opportunity it allows for the control of both independent and dependent variables. An experiment is no longer conceived merely as a controlled situation yielding quantitative data but as a method that permits the manipulation of the variables under study. Few long-term longitudinal studies have been initiated; the problems involved in the selecting of appropriate measures at the beginning of the study, the maintaining of the sample of subjects over long periods of time, and the organizing of the large amounts of data accumulated in such studies have discouraged most investigators from undertaking more than four-year or five-year longitudinal investigations. Observations, interviews, and tests tend to be used less frequently than they were in earlier periods, but they are still employed when they are particularly applicable to the topic under investigation.

Although attention continues to be directed toward developmental changes in such areas as children's learning, motivation, perception, and language, new interests are developing. The rediscovery of Piaget's work and modifications in behavior theory have resulted in a rapid development of interest in research in cognitive processes. Research in socialization has been stimulated by psychoanalytic and social learning theories. Studies of personality development have concentrated on specific aspects of behavior, for example, anxiety, aggression, and dependence, rather than attempting to deal with such global problems as adjustment and emotional behavior. Interest has been reawakened in the study of neonates, especially in their sensory, perceptual, and adaptive behavior. Cross-cultural studies, once in the domain of social anthropology, have been undertaken to ascertain the effects of different child-rearing practices on children's later behavior. Studies of the ecology of behavior have resulted in detailed analyses of children's behavior in naturalistic settings.

It is doubtful that twenty years ago anyone could have anticipated the remarkable resurgence of interest in developmental psychology that has occurred in the past decade. More research on basic processes of behavior is being conducted than in any previous period. Programs designed to train psychologists for research in developmental problems are being initiated and expanded, both in departments of psychology and in research institutes. A strong interest in applied problems is not evident, perhaps as a reaction to the overcommitment to the solution of social problems that characterized earlier work in developmental psychology. There are indications, however, that the techniques and knowledge now being accumulated can be used effectively in attacking the practical problems of the developing child. As the interest in such problems increases, it may be expected that the gap in communication between developmental psychology and pediatrics, education, sociology, and other disciplines will begin to close.

HAROLD W. STEVENSON

[*Directly related are the entries* ADOLESCENCE; AGING; INFANCY; SENSORY AND MOTOR DEVELOPMENT; SOCIALIZATION. *Other relevant material may be found in* LEARNING, *article on* LEARNING IN CHILDREN; *and in the biographies of* GESELL *and* HALL.]

BIBLIOGRAPHY

Advances in Child Development and Behavior. Vols. 1–2. Edited by Lewis P. Lipsitt and Charles C. Spiker. 1963–1965 New York: Academic Press.

BARKER, ROGER G. 1951 Child Psychology. *Annual Review of Psychology* 2:1–22.
BAYLEY, NANCY 1940 *Studies in the Development of Young Children.* Berkeley: Univ. of California Press.
CARMICHAEL, LEONARD (editor) (1946) 1954 *Manual of Child Psychology.* 2d ed. New York: Wiley.
HOFFMAN, MARTIN L.; and HOFFMAN, LOIS W. (editors) 1964 *Review of Child Development Research.* Vol. 1. New York: Russell Sage Foundation.
KESSEN, WILLIAM 1965 *The Child.* New York: Wiley.
MUSSEN, PAUL H. (editor) 1960 *Handbook of Research Methods in Child Development.* New York: Wiley.
NATIONAL SOCIETY FOR THE STUDY OF EDUCATION, COMMITTEE ON CHILD PSYCHOLOGY 1963 *Child Psychology.* 62d Yearbook, part 1. Edited by Harold W. Stevenson. Univ. of Chicago Press.

II
A THEORY OF DEVELOPMENT

Most theories of development and of intelligence seek to explain new problem-solving or concept-formation behavior by the influence of acquired experience, that is, as a function of external reinforcements; and they seek to explain the formation of logical structures by the influence of language. In this double perspective, knowledge tends to be considered as a kind of "copy" of reality: either as a sensorimotor copy, because the "associations" on which the learning is based are seen to be in one-to-one correspondence with a series of relationships already existing in the external world, or as a verbal copy, because language simply describes a reality that is considered ready-made.

Without denying the fundamental importance of both acquired experience and language, I would include, in addition, the following three central notions:

(1) Knowledge of an object does not consist of having a static mental copy of the object but of effecting transformations on it and reaching some understanding of the mechanisms of these transformations. An intelligent act consists above all of coordinating operations, uniting, ordering (in the sense of introducing order), etc. These operations, which derive from the subject's internalization of his own actions, are the instruments of the transformations that knowledge is concerned with.

(2) Logical relationships are, first and above all, operational structures. Although their most advanced forms are certainly expressed by language, their origins are found in the coordination of the subject's own actions. Even at the sensorimotor, preverbal level, a child is involved in activities that include uniting, ordering, introducing correspondences, etc.; and these activities are the source of operations and logico-mathematical structures.

(3) Knowledge is not determined strictly by the knower, or by the objects known, but by exchanges

or interactions between the knower and the objects (between the organism and the environment). The fundamental relation is not one of simple association but of assimilation and accommodation; the knower assimilates objects to the structures of his actions (or of his operations), and at the same time he accommodates these structures (by differentiating them) to the unforeseen aspects of the reality he encounters.

It is with this emphasis on the subject's own activities and transformational operations that I look at the stages of mental development and the progressive formation of intelligence. In a word, a ready-made object knowledge is not assumed, because we must transform it in order to know it; nor is a fully formed knowing subject assumed, because the subject must elaborate his own structures through transforming objects.

Sensorimotor intelligence

Even at the sensorimotor level, before the emergence of language, we can see this two-sided development—the child's thought structures develop in the very process of his "construction of reality." Infants assimilate situations into their repertory of actions; they find out about new things by acting on them in the ways they are capable of, such as sucking and grasping. By repetition, coordination, and generalization, these actions engender a system of "schemas of assimilation." For example, a child who already pulls things and places things comes to coordinate these actions in the form of pulling a little rug toward himself in order to reach something placed on it. On the other hand, as part of this same development, this intelligence structures reality. For instance, at first, objects have no permanence; the universe is one of moving tableaux that appear and disappear and are without spatial localization once they have disappeared. But with the coordination of actions, a "schema of the permanent object" develops: an object is sought after it has disappeared, and it thus continues to exist in the sense of its having a spatial localization even when it is actually outside the field of perception and action.

Another basic schema, which, at the practical level, is closely tied to the schema of the permanent object, is that of the coordination of positions and changes of position, what geometers term "the displacement group"—the coordination of movements from positions with the possibility of a return to the point of departure and of the use of detours or alternate routes to get to the same point. There is even a sensorimotor schema of causality. First, this consists of attributing phenomena to the subject's own actions, without taking account of physi-

cal or spatial contact. Then, as causality is attributed to relations between objects themselves and some physical interaction is found necessary, there emerges progressive objectivation and spatialization of causal relations.

Sensorimotor intelligence thus makes two fundamental advances. (1) Actions are coordinated; and this is the source of later logic and operations, when these schemas will be internalized and restructured at the representational level. (2) From the point of view of structuring reality, the substructure is provided for certain fundamental concepts—object permanence, causality, space, and temporal succession. (For further elaboration on these ideas, see Piaget 1936; 1937.)

Figurative and operative symbolic functions

At about one and a half or two years of age, there emerge the beginnings of the symbolic function and representational evocation, or "thought" (or, again, internalized intelligence).

Knowing consists necessarily of a system of signification, and signification consists necessarily of a signifier and something signified. At the early sensorimotor level, the sensorimotor, perceptual, and postural actions upon objects—the schemas—are the things signified, and the signifiers are some aspect of these very schemas. Such signifiers are the cues or signals of conditioning, and at this early stage they are still relatively undifferentiated from what they signify.

By contrast, the symbolic function has its beginning (at around one and a half or two years) with the development of signifiers that are differentiated from the schemas that they signify; that is, something can be evoked or represented by something other than a part of itself. Such signifiers may be symbols that bear some resemblance to what they stand for or signs that are arbitrary conventions.

Language and imitation. The words of a language are signs. In children, at the same time the language sign system appears other aspects of functioning, which are based on symbols rather than signs, emerge: deferred imitation, symbolic (or fictional) play, and mental imagery (which is internalized imitation). All of these are alternate ways of evoking situations and objects in their absence.

Imitation is the medium by which the child progresses from sensorimotor to representational functions. A form of imitation is already present at the sensorimotor stage. This is a material, or active, representation and takes place only in the presence of the model being imitated. It is non-deferred imitation (even though it may keep going for a while after the model has disappeared). It does not imply any form of mental representation, and it does not necessarily result in any. On the other hand, deferred imitation (imitation that starts in the absence of the model) does lead to representation, as is clear in the case of symbolic play. It then becomes internalized as a mental image, which permits the acquisition of language. (Language is based on this deferred imitation, not only on conditioning; otherwise it would develop much earlier.)

Thought is made possible by the emergence of the symbolic function, through the internalization of sensorimotor actions and through the reconstruction of the early structures on the level of representational signification. But before looking more closely at this reconstruction, we must introduce an essential, although often overlooked, distinction. The recent research of Piaget and Inhelder reveals this distinction more and more clearly.

Figurative and operative aspects of thought. At the heart of cognitive processes are two aspects— not separated sectors, but different poles: the figurative aspect and the operative aspect.

The figurative aspect deals with static configurations of reality and provides adequate figural representations of these states. This aspect is predominant in perception, in imitation, and in mental imagery that is a form of internalized imitation.

The operative aspect, on the other hand, deals with transformations of these states. This aspect is predominant in actions in general and, in the special case of operations, in internalized actions that have become reversible. The operations of adding and subtracting, for instance, are products of the actions of uniting and separating. The term "operative" refers to both actions and operations, while the term "operational" refers to operations alone.

This distinction between the figurative and the operative aspects is an important one from the point of view of the development of intelligence. In adults, the figurative is subordinated to the operative; that is, states are seen as the result of one transformation and the starting point for another. However, in young children, especially in children who have not yet begun to think operationally, these two aspects remain uncoordinated; the children are not capable of certain elementary forms of reasoning because they focus too much on fixed states, without seeking to relate them operationally. For instance, the majority of four- to six-year-olds think that after a liquid is poured from a wide glass into a narrow one there is more of it, because they note only the fixed levels of the liquid and not the pouring action, which links the initial

and terminal states. (For further reference, see Piaget 1945; Piaget & Inhelder 1966.)

Preoperational thinking (two to seven years)

Operations are internalized, reversible actions, coordinated in total structures such as classifications, seriations, and multiplicative matrices. The psychological criterion for the existence of operational reversibility is the presence of the notion of conservation, a negative example of which is the children's reactions to the liquids, cited above.

Sensorimotor intelligence manifests the threshold of operativity, since the displacement group itself is a total structure characterized by reversibility, and there is an invariant, or a conservation schema, in the form of the schema of the permanent object. But internalization is missing here. These schemas consist merely of physical, successive actions and not yet of simultaneous representations.

One would be tempted to think that as soon as the symbolic function was formed, these sensorimotor structures would be internalized as operational structures. This is indeed what finally takes place but, because it is much more difficult to reproduce an action in thought than to execute it physically, it takes place much more slowly than one might suppose. This internalization requires a total reconstruction on a new plane; and during the course of this construction, the child must go through the same difficulties he did on the sensorimotor level. For example, the four- to six-year-olds we studied knew perfectly well the route they took from home to school but could, nonetheless, not represent this route on a sand table.

Egocentrism and decentering. The necessary condition for operational development at this age is a decentering from the child's own actions and own point of view. The phenomenon of the child's centering on his own point of view and on his own actions is what is called egocentrism (a term that has often been misunderstood because of confusion with affective egocentrism). By egocentrism, I mean nothing more than the absence of cognitive decentering. Already at the sensorimotor level the course of development is one of progressive decentering from an initial state of radical egocentrism. The newborn infant has no awareness at all of his own identity, precisely because of the fact that he does not distinguish his own point of view from other possible points of view. As a result, he lives in a universe without objects, centered spatially, causally, and temporally on his own body. The construction of object permanence, the displacement group, and objective causality are characterized, in general, by progressive decentering, to the point where he becomes one element in a universe of objects and of spatial and causal coordinations. This Copernican revolution, as it were, must be effected all over again in the realm of representational thought and in social relations; another decentering is necessary to liberate the child from his own point of view. One example, from the realm of spatial representation, involves a three-dimensional model containing three mountains; the child is given a series of drawings made from various positions and is asked to indicate the angle from which each of the drawings was made. Children at the preoperational stage cannot do this. A social example is the question of the number of brothers in a family. A child will say, for instance, that he has two brothers but that each of them has only one brother—because he doesn't count himself as a brother.

Absence of conservation in egocentrism. The main feature of egocentrism, however, is the absence of reversibility, and therefore of operations. None of the tests of conservation is successful at this level. We have already seen the example of the pouring of liquids. We get the same results using small beads instead of a liquid. Similarly, if ten blue tokens are lined up opposite a row of ten red tokens, the child will think that the number or quantity changes if you spread out or push together one of the rows. Again, if you give him two similar balls of Plasticine and then reshape one as a sausage or as a pancake, he will think that the quantity has changed. By about 7 or 8 years of age, he will affirm that the quantity has not been changed; but he will continue to think, until 9 or 10, that the weight has been changed; and only at 11 or 12 will he believe that the volume, as measured by water displacement, remains unchanged. These experiments, which were first conducted in Switzerland, have been replicated in other countries (for example, in the United States by Elkind 1961) with the same results.

In spatial conception at this age level, there is nonconservation of length. Two sticks of equal length will be judged equal by the child if they are placed side by side with their extremities aligned, but if one is moved so that it extends beyond the other, the child will now say that it is longer. Similarly, there is nonconservation of distance: the space between two points is considered smaller if an object is placed in the middle of it—empty space is not equated with filled space. Similarly, there is nonconservation of surfaces, volumes, etc. (For further reference, see Piaget & Inhelder 1941; 1948.)

The concrete operations

At seven or eight years of age, the first operational structures take form. These first operations are limited, dealing with manipulations of objects themselves and not with verbal hypotheses. They are limited to classes, relations, and number, dealing either with discontinuous elements or with spatial and temporal continuums. They do not attain the general level of propositional logic.

Moreover, these concrete operations do not cover the entire logic of classes and relations but only certain of the structures involved. These first operational structures, to which we have given the name of "groupings," relate to contiguous inclusions and relationships, without yet being generally combinatorial. They are only semilattices and incomplete groups, like seriations, classifications, multiplicative matrices, etc.

Seriation. Seriation, or succession of transitive asymmetrical relations, has its roots in early preoperational, even sensorimotor, schemas. Very young children can arrange a series of blocks in the order of their size. But at this level, it is done only by successive trial and error, with no use of deductive transitivity (knowing that $A < B$ and $B < C$ means that $A < C$). At seven or eight, there is a systematic method, consisting of finding the smallest of all, then the smallest of the remaining ones, etc., so that each element is understood as being bigger than all the preceding ones and smaller than all the following ones. This is the basis for an immediate deductive understanding of transitivity.

Classifications. Classifications, too, are present at the preoperational level, but in a form that remains elementary because it lacks operational reversibility. When small children, say four-year-olds, are asked to make classifications of objects, they make "figural collections," with them; that is, the spatial arrangement is made as if the class itself was dependent on a configuration in space. Slightly older children make nonfigural collections. The collections no longer have a significant shape, but they are still only material collections and not logical classes, because the children do not understand the intensive quantification of class inclusions. Suppose, for example, that we present seven primroses (class A) and three other flowers (class A'), which together make up a collection of ten flowers (class $B = A + A'$). The child will agree that all the primroses are flowers and that all the flowers are not primroses, but he does not conclude that there are fewer primroses than there are total flowers ($A < B$). He will say there are more primroses because there are only three others. He cannot reason at the same time with both the whole class and a subclass. In trying to compare A with B, he must split B into A and A', and then since A is already one term of the comparison, the child uses A' as the other term. At an advanced operational level, however, he will understand that $A = B - A'$ and $A' = B - A$. Therefore $A < (A + A')$, or $A < B$. In other words, understanding class inclusion presupposes operational reversibility.

The same sort of analysis can be made of children's notions of correspondences, multiplicative matrices, etc. However, the operational mechanisms involved in the construction of the notion of whole numbers deserve special attention. We have already seen that even though children may use number names, it is not until the age of seven, on the average, that they are convinced of the conservation of number if the spatial arrangement is changed. The operational concept of number is a synthesis of class inclusion and ordering. On the one hand, there are the inclusions $I < (I + I) < (I + I + I)$. On the other, since all the elements are equivalent, with all qualitative differences having been abstracted, the only way to distinguish one element, I, from another is by introducing order. This order may be a spatial array, a temporal array, or a logical enumerating order of the type $I \rightarrow I \rightarrow I$, where the sign $\rightarrow$ indicates any sort of transitive order. Bertrand Russell maintained that the cardinal number was based on one-to-one correspondence between classes of the same extension, without having to introduce order, whereas the ordinal number was based uniquely on ordering. But the one-to-one correspondence to which he referred is not the qualitative correspondence of the logic of classes, such as is found in multiplicative matrices, for example, where an element corresponds to another because of corresponding properties, but is rather a correspondence of one unity to another unity, with the qualities abstracted. And this already presupposes an arithmetical unity, that is, number. Cardinal and ordinal numbers can be neither understood nor formalized independently of one another. Only by seeing number as a synthesis of inclusion and seriation can we avoid the vicious circle inherent in Russell's formalization. This interpretation of number, as a synthesis of inclusion and seriation, was discovered purely through psychology and has since then been formalized by the logician J. B. Grize.

There is another whole area of operations at this level. So far, we have been discussing discontinuous elements, where the operations deal with likenesses and differences. There is also the area of infralogical or spatiotemporal operations, which deal with proximity and separation in a continuum.

Representative space.   Representative space (as opposed to sensorimotor and perceptual space) is based on the following operations: partition and addition of parts (corresponding to addition of classes), placement and displacement (corresponding to seriation), and measuring as a synthesis of partition and displacement (as number is a synthesis of inclusion and seriation). There is a point of interest here from the point of view of philosophy of science. These spatial operations apply equally to Euclidean (metric) projective, and topological space. In the historical development, Euclidean geometry is considered to have come first, followed much later by projective, and later still by topological, considerations. The psychological construction presented here is the contrary of this; topology is the most fundamental, with the other two being derived from it. We have found that in children, development follows this order. The first intuitions are topological, and from this come projective and Euclidean, or metric, representations.

Time.   The operations involved in the notion of time are again similar. There is the ordering of successive events; there is inclusion of time intervals; and the synthesis of these leads to time measurement. The notion of time is based on a primitive intuition of speed, which determines judgments of speed much before there is any metric notion of speed as a ratio of space to time. (Speed as a prerequisite to understanding time, rather than vice versa, is closer to relativity physics than to classical physics.) This primitive notion of speed is ordinal, based simply on the intuition that if one moving thing overtakes another on the same path, it is going faster. This judgment of speed is based on spatial order (behind and ahead) and temporal order (before and after) but does not require any evaluation of length of time or size of interval. [*For further reference, see* Piaget 1946a; 1946b; Piaget & Szeminska 1941; Piaget, Inhelder, & Szeminska 1948; *see also* TIME, *article on* PSYCHOLOGICAL ASPECTS.]

Formal, or hypothetico-deductive, operations

The period of formal, or hypothetico-deductive, operations begins at about 11 or 12 years of age. Children start to be able to reason not only about concrete objects but about verbal hypotheses. The operations of propositional logic, in a natural, nonaxiomatized form, of course, are added to the operational structures.

There are at least three types of external evidence of this new development. (1) Children are able to reason with verbal material alone, that is, without concrete referents. (2) In experimental problems they are able to make hypotheses about the possible factors and vary them systematically to test the hypotheses. (3) In general terms, they are now capable of "reflection," that is, of thinking about thinking or of operations on operations. Propositional logic is a kind of system of operations raised to the second power, since the contents of the propositions are class or relational operations and since new operations are involved in the inter-propositional structure (implications, disjunction, etc.). This is why adolescents can construct theories, naive though they may be, whereas children cannot.

These operations have two main characteristics. First of all, they are combinatorial, giving rise, for example, to a more complex lattice structure in place of the simpler "groupings." Second, the two forms of reversibility found at the concrete operational level are united in a single system known as the group of four transformations. These two types of reversibility are inversion, or negation (N), which characterizes classification structures, and reciprocity (R), which characterizes relational structures. The operations involved in the groups of four transformations then are N, R, I (identity), and C (correlativity); so that $NR = C$, $NC = R$, $RC = N$, and $NRC = I$. With these operations, 11- and 12-year-olds can develop new operational schemas, such as proportions, double reference systems, etc. (see Inhelder & Piaget 1955).

The mechanism of intellectual development

The classical factors that usually are called upon to account for intellectual development are biological maturation, environmental influence (experience), and social transmission (education). Each of the three does play an important role, but they are insufficient to completely account for intellectual development. Thus a fourth is necessary.

Biological maturation clearly needs to be supplemented when we see that the speed of development of operational structures is dependent upon cultural settings, individual experience, etc.

As for experience as a unique explanatory factor, it is indeed true that all notions need a basis in experience, even logical and mathematical notions. But there are two distinctly different types of experience, although they often go together. Physical experience consists of acting upon objects and drawing some knowledge about the objects themselves, for example, weighing things and finding

out that weight is not always proportional to volume. In logico-mathematical experience, on the other hand, the knowledge is drawn not from the objects that are acted upon but from the actions themselves. Arranging objects in various ways and finding out that the arrangement has no effect on the total number of objects is an example of this second type of experience. Physical experience certainly does not suffice to explain the development of intelligence. As for logico-mathematical experience, this is only a preparation for deductive thinking, which is based on the coordination of actions.

Finally, linguistic, educative, or social transmission, important though they are, can have an influence only to the extent that the child can assimilate what is offered to him into his own operational structures.

Progressive equilibration. Another factor thus becomes necessary—the progressive equilibration of actions as they become coordinated. There are two reasons why equilibrium is a satisfactory explanatory model. First, intellectual equilibrium derives from the subject's activities as they compensate for external disturbances. Since compensation leads to reversibility, this progressive equilibration of the operational structures takes the form of progress toward ever-increasing reversibility. Equilibration can thus be seen as a possible definition of intelligence, as well as an interpretation of its development. Second, an operational structure is equilibrated once it has achieved reversibility, but before then it passes through preoperational steps of successive equilibration. If we follow this progressive equilibration, we see that any given step, although not necessarily the most probable at the outset, becomes the most probable, once the preceding step has been reached. Equilibration thus includes a model of successive probabilities that is capable of dealing with factual detail, and which thus provides a learning theory based on internal reinforcement and not only on external or empirical reinforcement (see Apostel, Mandelbrot, & Piaget 1957).

Perception and mental imagery

The research on intellectual development is only a part of this line of developmental research. There is also work in the fields of perception and mental imagery.

Perceptual development. In the area of perceptual development, two groups of phenomena have been identified: (1) effects that diminish in intensity but whose structure remains unchanged and (2) activities that become more articulated with age.

The effects that are not structurally modified but whose intensity decreases with age can be interpreted by a common probabilistic model. About 15 classic opticogeometric illusions have been studied developmentally. Examples of these are the Delboeuf illusion, the Müller–Lyer illusion, and illusions of angles, rectangles, parallelograms, etc. Each one was studied in a variety of different proportions; and at every age, positive and negative maxima were established for the proportions. The maxima proportions were found to be the same for every illusion, which permitted the effects of all of the illusions to be reduced to a general law, that of a "centration" effect: the areas focused on are overestimated, and the peripheral areas are underestimated. A study of ocular movement, by Piaget, Vinh-Bang, and Matalon (1958), was able to support this interpretation in some of the simpler situations. For instance, vertical lines are overestimated in comparison with horizontal lines, and subjects were in fact found to focus during much of the exposure on the summit of the vertical line. [*See* PERCEPTION, *article on* ILLUSIONS AND AFTEREFFECTS; VISION, *article on* EYE MOVEMENTS.]

This centration effect was itself reduced to a probabilistic explanation based in part on the distribution of the points of "encounters" between elements of the figure and elements of the receptor organs and in part on the series of correspondences, or "couplings," established among these points of encounter. Studies were carried out to establish temporal maxima for each of the illusions, in both children and adults, for exposures ranging from .01 second to 1.0 second. These studies confirmed the duality of these two factors.

The second group of phenomena—activities that become more articulate with age—stems from exploration activities, such as comparing parts of the figure, structuring the figure by introducing perceptual coordinates, anticipating parts of the figure, etc. These activities give rise to certain systematic secondary illusions by exaggerating the deformation resulting from systematic centration. Once again, eye movement studies have confirmed this interpretation, showing, among other things, how much more systematic adult perceptual exploration is than that of children. This explains why these illusions become more pronounced with age.

These perceptual activities, then, come more and more under the influence and direction of intelligence. Intelligence has no effect on the primary perceptual illusions, but it does have an effect on perceptual activity, guiding exploration and introducing its own structure. It is important to note to what extent a figurative function like perception lacks independent development and to what extent it is subordinated to operative functions. It has its beginnings in early motor behavior, and its later development is directed by operational intelligence.

Mental imagery. Another figurative function whose development has been systematically studied is mental imagery, which has been relatively neglected in recent years but, indeed, was never much studied in children. Once again there are two problems to study: (1) to establish whether the evolution of imagery is autonomous or whether it is influenced by operational development and (2) to establish whether imagery paves the way for operations or whether, on the contrary, it is modified and structured by the operations.

As far as the first problem is concerned, two principal types of imagery have been distinguished. Besides reproductive, or "copying," imagery there is anticipatory imagery (which may be as simple as imagining the rotation of a stick as it pivots about one of its extremities). In children who are too young to engage in operations, reproductive imagery is adequate, but anticipatory imagery is far from adequate. The errors made are, in fact, reminiscent of the errors in preoperational thought. Anticipatory imagery does not, then, derive directly from reproductive imagery but depends on the intervention of operations. At the operational level, this imagery becomes more flexible and can serve as a useful symbolic auxiliary for operational thought.

The second problem is examined by going back to the various operational tests (conservation, for example) and having the children anticipate how the situation will be, after telling them what transformation is about to be carried out. For instance, for the conservation of number, 12 blue tokens are placed in a row 15–20 centimeters long. About 30 centimeters away, 12 red tokens are spread out in a row 30–40 centimeters long. Each blue token is coupled with a red token by means of a channel with walls 1 centimeter high, so that the tokens can move toward each other only along the channel and must ultimately meet. The children are asked, with the tokens in their original positions, whether there are as many blue as red, whether there will be as many if the blues are all moved up to where the reds are, whether there will be as many if they are moved up only halfway, etc. The findings are that small children are perfectly able to represent the displacement of the tokens, but before six and a half or seven years of age this does not lead them to assert that the number is the same. They report that the number increases as the row becomes longer, and decreases when the row is shorter. The anticipation remains transversal, focused on the length of the row. Later, at the operational level, it becomes longitudinal, focused on the paths traveled, and serves to verify the one-to-one correspondence. Other experiments support the same conclusion, namely, that adequate imagery in itself is not sufficient to bring about operational thinking but is structured and modified by the subject's operational level (see Piaget 1961).

Epistemological conclusion

This entire body of research bears witness to a single broad intention: to put to experimental test the principal epistemological hypotheses about the nature of empirical and logico-mathematical knowledge.

Above all, it reveals the insufficiency of empiricism as an epistemological theory: the development of empirical knowledge itself does not demand an empiricist interpretation. In point of fact, the study of this development in children reveals that experience is never simply "read," or passively registered. It is always assimilated by the subject into his own structured schemas. In other words, even physical knowledge (in its broadest sense) is always relative to a logico-mathematical framework brought to an experience by the subject himself. As for this framework, it is not simply a linguistic expression but is derived from the most general system of coordinations of the subject's own actions. In short, it is operational.

However, to say that the subject plays an active role in structuring the physical objects of knowledge does not mean that knowledge is rooted in the subject alone, as the a priori epistemological theories maintain. (The a priori influence is still alive in some forms of gestalt theory.) Knowledge derives neither from objects independent of a subject nor from a subject independent of objects; it derives from an indissociable interaction between subject and object or, in more general terms, between organism and environment. This interaction leads at first to a lack of differentiation, or confusion, between objective and subjective, as is evident in the child's egocentrism. Later, it takes two related developments. One is decentering, which results in the objectivity of experimental knowledge. (This objectivity is not a given of the knowing process but is a slow and laborious conquest.)

The other is reflective abstraction, which leads to the construction of logico-mathematical structures. (See Piaget 1950.)

JEAN PIAGET

[*Other relevant material may be found in* CONCEPT FORMATION; INFANCY; LEARNING, *especially articles on* DISCRIMINATION LEARNING *and* LEARNING IN CHILDREN; PERCEPTION, *article on* PERCEPTUAL DEVELOPMENT; PROBLEM SOLVING; REASONING AND LOGIC; THINKING.]

BIBLIOGRAPHY

APOSTEL, LÉO; MANDELBROT, B.; and PIAGET, J. 1957 *Logique et équilibre.* Paris: Presses Universitaires de France. → See especially Jean Piaget's contribution.

ELKIND, DAVID 1961 Children's Discovery of the Conservation of Mass, Weight and Volume: Piaget Replication Study II. *Journal of Genetic Psychology* 98: 219–227.

INHELDER, BÄRBEL; and PIAGET, JEAN (1955) 1958 *The Growth of Logical Thinking From Childhood to Adolescence.* New York: Basic Books. → First published as *De la logique de l'enfant à la logique de l'adolescent.*

PIAGET, JEAN (1936) 1952 *The Origins of Intelligence in Children.* New York: International Universities Press. → First published in French.

PIAGET, JEAN (1937) 1954 *The Construction of Reality in the Child.* New York: Basic Books. → First published in French. Also published by Routledge in 1955 as the *The Child's Construction of Reality.*

PIAGET, JEAN (1945) 1951 *Play, Dreams, and Imitation in Childhood.* New York: Norton; London: Heinemann. → First published in French.

PIAGET, JEAN 1946a *Les notions de mouvement et de vitesse chez l'enfant.* Paris: Presses Universitaires de France.

PIAGET, JEAN 1946b *Le développement de la notion du temps chez l'enfant.* Paris: Presses Universitaires de France.

PIAGET, JEAN 1950 *Introduction à l'épistémologie génétique.* 3 vols. Paris: Presses Universitaires de France.

PIAGET, JEAN 1961 *Les mécanismes perceptifs: Modèles probabilistes, analyse génétique, relations avec l'intelligence.* Paris: Presses Universitaires de France.

PIAGET, JEAN; and INHELDER, BÄRBEL 1941 *Le développement des quantités chez l'enfant.* Paris: Delachaux & Niestlé.

PIAGET, JEAN; and INHELDER, BÄRBEL (1948) 1956 *The Child's Conception of Space.* London: Routledge. → First published in French.

PIAGET, JEAN; and INHELDER, BÄRBEL 1966 *L'image mentale chez l'enfant.* Paris: Presses Universitaires de France.

PIAGET, JEAN; INHELDER, B.; and SZEMINSKA, A. (1948) 1960 *The Child's Conception of Geometry.* New York: Basic Books. → First published in French.

PIAGET, JEAN; and SZEMINSKA, ALINA (1941) 1952 *The Child's Conception of Number.* London: Routledge. → First published in French.

PIAGET, JEAN; VINH-BANG; and MATALON, B. 1958 Note on the Law of the Temporal Maximum of Some Optico–Geometric Illusions. *American Journal of Psychology* 71:277–282.

DEVIANT BEHAVIOR

Both "deviant behavior" and "social disorganization" have been variously defined, but there have been few efforts to distinguish between the two concepts. In fact, it has been suggested that they are not different, that along with "social problems" and the somewhat outmoded "social pathology," they signify only a potpourri of conditions that are considered undesirable from the standpoint of the observer's values, conditions that vary at different times and with different observers. According to this view, these terms have no scientific value and no legitimate status as sociological concepts.

Such nihilism and counsel of despair are not justified. True, there is no consensus on the meaning of these terms, and they are, indeed, burdened with value connotations. However, they point to a number of distinctions that sociology must take into account.

Concept of deviance. Turning first to the concept of deviant behavior, we must distinguish among the several definitions of the term, which are discussed below.

Behavior that violates norms. Deviant behavior is behavior that violates the normative rules, understandings, or expectations of social systems. This is the most common usage of the term and the sense in which it will be used here. Crime is the prototype of deviance in this sense, and theory and research in deviant behavior have been concerned overwhelmingly with crime. However, normative rules are inherent in the nature of all social systems, whether they be friendship groups, engaged couples, families, work teams, factories, or national societies. Legal norms are then but one type of norm whose violation constitutes deviant behavior. It is important to note that although deviance, in this sense, and conformity are "opposites," they represent the poles within the same dimension of variation; therefore, a general theory of the one must comprehend the other.

Statistical abnormality. There is fair consensus that "deviant behavior" does *not* mean departure from some statistical norm. However various the definitions and usages, they seem to have in common the notion of something that is, from *some* point of view, less "good" or "desirable," and not merely less frequent.

Psychopathology. For sociological purposes deviance is seldom defined exclusively in terms of psychopathology, mental illness, or personality disorganization, although it is commonly assumed that these phenomena are at least included within the scope of deviance. However, behavior is *deviant* in the first, or normative, sense because it departs from the normative rules of some social system, whereas behavior is *pathological* because it proceeds from a sick, damaged, or defective personality. It is probable that most deviant behavior in the normative sense is produced by personalities that are clinically normal and that most behavior that is symptomatic of personality defect or mental illness does not violate normative expectations. In short, the two are independently defined, and the relationship between them is a matter for empirical investigation. It seems preferable to keep them conceptually distinct, retaining for the one the term "deviant behavior" and for the other the established terminology of psychopathology.

It should be made clear that the distinction just drawn is not that between the psychological and the sociological levels of investigation. In viewing any human behavior we can ask, on the one hand, how it depends upon the history and structure of the personality that authors it. On the other hand, we can ask how it depends on the history and structure of the social system in which it is an event. Such questions can be asked about both mental illness and deviant behavior. However, inquiry on the psychological and sociological levels cannot proceed altogether independently, for each must make some assumptions about the other. Durkheim (1897), in his classic treatment of suicide, made clear the analytical independence of the sociological level by demonstrating that variations in rates of a given class of behavior within and between systems are a reality *sui generis* that cannot be explained simply in terms of the psychological properties of human beings but rather depend on the properties of the social system itself. However, he overstated his case and left the impression, whether it was his intention or not, that psychology has little to contribute to the understanding of suicide. In fact, Durkheim's own treatment of the sociology of suicide is interlarded with assumptions about human motivation and other considerations that are ordinarily considered "psychological" [see SUICIDE, *article on* SOCIAL ASPECTS].

Socially disvalued behavior and states. Deviant behavior may also be defined as socially disvalued behavior and states in general. This definition includes mental retardation, blindness, ugliness, other physical defects and handicaps, illness of all sorts, beggary, membership in ritually unclean castes and occupations, mental illness, criminality, and a "shameful past." What all these have in common is that, if known, they assign one to a socially disparaged role and constitute a blemish in the self. This blemish, or stigma, is an important constituent of all social encounters in which it is present. It poses problems to the stigmatized actor and his alters and has consequences for the development of personality and for social interaction. Goffman (1963) has demonstrated that it is possible to generalize about the phenomenon of stigma and its consequences on a level that abstracts from the diversity of its concrete manifestations.

Clearly, stigma is a legitimate and important object of investigation in its own right. Furthermore, it is ordinarily an attribute of normatively deviant behavior; it may play a part in its genesis and control. It must therefore figure in a theory of deviant behavior. However, the fact that behavior is stigmatized or disvalued is one thing; the fact that it violates normative rules is another. Not all disvalued behavior violates normative rules; nor is it certain that all behavior that violates normative rules is disvalued. Explaining stigma is not the same as explaining why people violate normative rules. In keeping with the more traditional and better established usage, it seems preferable to limit the reference of "deviant behavior" to the violation of normative rules.

Deviant behavior and deviant roles. It is necessary to distinguish between what a person has done and how he is publicly defined and categorized by members of his social world. It is mainly the latter—the social role attributed to him—that determines how others will respond to him. To steal is not necessarily to be defined as "a thief"; to have sexual relationships with one of the same sex is not necessarily to be defined as "a homosexual" (Reiss 1961). Behavior that violates social rules may or may not become visible and, if visible, may or may not result in attribution of a deviant role. Furthermore, deviant roles may be attributed even in the absence of violations of normative rules.

This distinction mirrors one of the perennial dilemmas of criminology. Is criminology concerned with all violations of criminal law or only with those violations that result in a legal adjudication of criminality? The former are infinitely more numerous than the latter, and data on their frequency and distribution are difficult to come by. The processes whereby some fraction of all violators come to be selected for legal stigmatization as "criminals" bear only a tenuous relationship to actual histories of criminal law violation. Furthermore, even legal attributions of criminality do not necessarily result in attributions of criminal roles in the world of everyday life. So, for example, "white-collar criminals" and income tax evaders,

even if legally convicted, are not likely to be defined as criminals in the world outside the courts and to experience the consequences of such definitions (Sutherland 1949).

The distinction between violating normative rules and being socially assigned to a deviant role is important. To explain one is not necessarily to explain the other. On the other hand, they interact in such ways that each must be taken into account in explaining the other. For example, to be adjudicated as an offender or even to be legally processed short of adjudication may have important effects on actual careers in criminal behavior (Tannenbaum 1938). It seems best to think of the field of deviant behavior as concerned with deviance in both these senses and with their interaction.

The relativity of deviant behavior. It is commonplace that normative rules vary enormously from one social system to another. It follows that no behavior is deviant in itself but only insofar as it violates the norms of some social system. This implies that the sociology of deviant behavior is not concerned with the encyclopedic study of prostitution, drug addiction, etc., but rather with the question: "How do we account for the occurrence of these and other behaviors in situations where they are interdicted or disvalued by normative rules?"

In fact, practical judgments of deviance in the world of everyday life take into account the collectivity membership of the actor. In general, a person comes under the jurisdiction of a system of normative rules when he is ascribed or successfully claims the role of member of a collectivity. This is equally true of subcollectivities—associations, cliques, academic institutions—within a larger collectivity. Indeed, to be subject to the normative rules of a collectivity comes very close to defining the social meaning of "membership" in a collectivity.

More generally, the same may be said of any role, not of collectivity roles alone. The expectations attaching to a role differentiate it from other roles and define the terms on which a person can be deviant. That this is true for such roles as husband and wife, doctor and patient, child and adult is elementary. It is equally true, but not so obvious, for such transient roles as those of the sick and the bereaved. To occupy either of these roles is to be exempted from some rules otherwise applicable, to be subjected to other rules, and to create special obligations for others in the role set of the sick or bereaved person. What it takes to be "sick" or "bereaved," that is, the criteria of the roles, depends on the culture of the system. In any case, however, membership in those roles must be validated in terms of *those* criteria. To successfully claim membership and then, in some manner, to betray oneself as "not really sick" or "not really bereaved," as these are defined in one's culture, is to lose the exemptions that go with that role, as well as to incur the special contumely of falsely claiming membership in a role for which one lacks the true credentials.

In speaking of deviance one must specify the system of reference. The same behavior may be both deviant and nondeviant, relative to different systems in which the actor is implicated. However, we are still left with the question: "For any given system, who is to say what is deviant? Whose notions of right and wrong define the rules of the system?" This has been one of the most troublesome issues in deviance theory. It is not entirely satisfactory to say that the rules of the system are those which are institutionalized—that is, agreed upon, internalized, and sanctioned (Johnson 1960, p. 20). This definition provides no criterion for a "cut-off point" defining the degree of institutionalization necessary to determine deviance; in fact, the criteria of institutionalization are themselves multiple, and to some degree they vary independently.

Alternative responses to normative rules. The difficulty may arise partly from a failure to recognize the importantly different ways in which people may be oriented to normative rules. People sometimes seem to violate rules without guilt and without even the necessity for some mechanism for neutralizing guilt. The inference is typically drawn that such people do not recognize the rules, that—as far as they are concerned—these are not the rules of the system, except, perhaps, in the sense of a probability that others will react in a hostile way to certain behavior. Then the question does indeed arise: "Who is to say what is deviant?" We have perhaps been too quick to assume that to "accept," "recognize," "internalize," "approve," and "feel bound by" normative rules all mean the same thing. We suggest, on the contrary, that one may recognize a rule and even insist upon its propriety and necessity; one may accept the legitimacy of efforts to enforce the rule, even against oneself; and one may appraise the "goodness" of people in terms of conformity to the rule—but see the job of securing compliance with the rule as essentially somebody else's job. One takes one's chances and either "wins" or "loses." It may be, for example, that "delinquent cultures" do not, in general, either "repudiate" (Cohen 1955) the rules of the "larger society," "deny their legitimacy" (Cloward & Ohlin 1960), or "neutralize" (Sykes & Matza 1957) them,

but somehow institutionalize this "gamester" attitude toward the rules.

Furthermore, it is necessary to distinguish between what may be called the attribution of "validity" to a rule and what might be called its "goodness" or "propriety." One may consider a rule stupid or unreasonable and yet recognize that it is *the rule* and therefore that it properly may or even ought to be enforced until it is changed. This would indicate that, within a given social system, there are criteria of what constitute the rules of the system that transcend individual differences about what the rule ought to be or differences with respect to depth of "internalization" of the rule. This distinction suggests a distinction made by Merton ([1949] 1957, pp. 359–368) with respect to two kinds of deviants: those who violate rules for any of a number of reasons but do not question the rules themselves; and those who violate rules in order to activate certain processes that, in that system, are necessary to effect "repeal" of a rule or to replace it with another. However, not all who would change a rule necessarily feel justified in doing so by violating it. In fact, it could be argued that the basis of social order is not consensus on what *ought to be* the rules, indeed that *dissensus* in this regard is the normal state, especially in modern society. Rather, the basis of order is agreement on the criteria of what the rules *are* and on the mechanisms for changing them. The intention of this discussion is to suggest that if we take account of these different ways of orienting to normative rules, disagreement on what the rules are is not so great as is commonly assumed.

The sociology of normative rules. Acts are deviant by virtue of normative rules that make them so. Therefore, the forms and rates of deviance change as the rules themselves change. In consequence of such changes, acts may move from normatively approved to forbidden; from one deviant category to another; from some category of deviance to the category of "sickness" or in the other direction. And some categories of deviance, such as "heresy," may become virtually extinct as part of the functioning conceptual equipment of a society. The study of such changes has been severely neglected, with some noteworthy exceptions in the sociology of law (Hall 1935). It should be stressed that changes in normative rules cannot be fruitfully investigated apart from the study of behavior oriented toward these normative rules. On the one hand, normative rules shape behavior; on the other hand, behavior is always testing, probing, and challenging normative rules, and in response to such behavior normative rules are continually being redefined, shored up, or abandoned (Mills 1959; Cohen 1965). The study of this interaction process is an integral part of the sociology of deviance.

Deviant behavior of collectivities. Whatever may be the metaphysical status of collectivities, for sociological purposes they are actors. They are social objects having names, public images, reputations, and statuses. They are publicly identified as authors of acts, and they are subject to rules. From the perspective of everyday life, collectivities, such as governments, corporations, fraternities, armies, labor unions, and churches, do things, and some of these things violate laws or other normative rules. Little is known about the cultural understandings on the basis of which acts (deviant and otherwise) are imputed to collectivities as distinct from their members severally, because the matter has received practically no systematic study except in the field of corporation law. It is true that the status of an event as the act of a collectivity is a definition imposed upon the situation by some public and depends upon a set of culturally given criteria for attributing acts to authors. However, this is equally true of the attribution of acts to individuals, and much of the law is concerned precisely with specifying and making explicit the criteria for such attribution.

All social acts are the outcomes of interaction processes. Whether they will be attributed to this concrete individual or that, or to a concrete individual or a collectivity, always depends on some culturally given schema through which action is viewed. Therefore, the neglect of deviant behavior of collectivities cannot be justified on sociological grounds. However, only in the area of "white-collar crime" (Sutherland 1949) has the subject even been approached.

Theories of deviant behavior. We will make no attempt here to inventory the theories bearing upon one or another variety of deviance, but will limit ourselves to identifying the main features of the two traditions that most closely approach a generalized theory of deviance. The discussion will deal with contrasting emphases. It does not intend to offer a rounded picture of either tradition or to suggest that they are incompatible.

The anomie tradition. The anomie tradition stems from the work of Durkheim (1897), especially his analysis of suicide. Its emphasis is *structural* and *comparative*, that is, it is concerned with explaining how variations in deviant behavior within and between societies depend on social structure. It is typically concerned with accounting for *rates* in contrast to individual differences. In Durkheim's work the system properties that figured most prominently were the degree of social integration (variations in this respect accounting for *suicide altruiste* and *suicide egoiste*) and system changes that create discrepancies between men's aspirations and the means for realizing them. The latter results in *dérégulation*, or anomie, that is, a breakdown in the power of social norms to regulate and discipline men's actions (variations in this respect accounting for *suicide anomique*). The elaboration of the anomie concept and the development of its implications constitute the anomie tradition.

Merton ([1949] 1957, pp. 131–194), in his seminal paper, "Social Structure and Anomie," made formal and explicit, and generalized to the field of deviant behavior, the model that was only partly explicit in Durkheim's analysis of *suicide anomique*. He emphasized the independent variability of both the culture goals and the accessibility of institutionalized means (i.e., means that are compatible with the regulative norms). The disjunction between goals and means, leading to strain and to anomie, depends on the values of both these variables. Adaptations to such strain involve either accepting or rejecting the culture goals and either accepting or rejecting the institutionalized means. Each adaptation therefore involves two dichotomous choices; the logically possible combinations of such choices yield a set of adaptations, one of which is conformity, and the others, varieties of deviance. This typology specifies the values of the dependent variable of the sociology of deviance–conformity. However, Merton's work is only a modest beginning toward specifying the conditions that determine choice among the logical possibilities.

The Chicago tradition. The other tradition, which may fittingly be called the Chicago tradition, begins with the work of Thomas and Znaniecki, especially in *The Polish Peasant* (1920). This remarkable work is strikingly similar to Durkheim's writings in many respects, especially in its concern with the breakdown in the regulative power of social norms. As the tradition has developed, however, it has taken on certain distinctive emphases. It has tended to focus not so much on deviance as an adaptation to strain as on deviance as culturally patterned behavior in its own right. It has emphasized the social–psychological problem of the process of socialization into deviant cultural patterns. This approach has been most systematically formulated by Clifford Shaw and Henry D. McKay (1942), by Edwin H. Sutherland in his theory of differential association (1942–1947), and most recently by Donald R. Cressey (1964).

Another development in the Chicago tradition stems from George Herbert Mead's (1934) conception of the self as an internalized object built up, in a process of communicative interaction, out of the social categories, or roles, available in the culture milieu. According to this conception, behavior, deviant or otherwise, is supportive or expressive of a social role. It is a way of validating one's claim to such a role by behavior that is culturally significant of membership in such a role. This approach has been most developed by Erving Goffman (1956; 1963) and Howard Becker (1963). In general, the Chicago tradition emphasizes the learned nature of deviant behavior, the role of association with others and of cultural models, the role of symbolism attaching to deviant behavior, and the gradual development of, and commitment to, deviant behavior in an extended interaction process (Short & Strodtbeck 1965).

Development of comprehensive theories. The most comprehensive single formulation in current theory of deviant behavior is that of Talcott Parsons (1951, chapter 7), which cannot be adequately subsumed under either tradition. It shares with the anomie tradition a stress on taxonomy, the concept "strain," and the structural sources of deviance. It shares with the Chicago tradition a deep concern with interaction process and a conception of deviance and conformity as commitments that develop in the course of such interaction. To a unique degree it integrates deviance theory with a more general theory of social systems.

Two recent developments point toward a fusion of the Chicago and anomie traditions. Cohen (1955), starting with the conception of socially structured strain, has emphasized the role of interaction process in the creation, as well as the transmission, of culturally supported deviant solutions or deviant subcultures. Cloward and Ohlin (1960), addressing themselves also to the determinants of choice among possible adaptations to strain, have emphasized the role of the availability, at the points of strain, of illegitimate or deviant opportunities, with special emphasis on the opportunity to learn and to perform deviant roles. However, the reconciliation or integration of the conception of deviant behavior as a way of dealing with a problem of ends and means, on the one hand, and as a way of communicating and validating a claim to a role, on the other, has not yet been achieved (Cohen 1965).

Social disorganization

When we say that a game, a plan, a committee, a family, an army, or a society has been "disorganized," we mean a number of closely related things: that it has been interrupted; that its identity is crumbling away; that its parts, although perhaps still recognizable, no longer hang together to constitute one thing; that it has disintegrated. In every case there is implied some criterion of sameness, wholeness, continuity, or *organization*. This criterion is the correspondence of something "out there" to some pattern, model, or cognitive map in the mind of the observer. It defines the essential attributes or "boundary conditions" of a given type of object; the term "disorganization" refers to a break in the correspondence of what is "out there" to such a pattern.

A social object, for example, a society or a family, is constructed of action. The pattern that defines such an object is a course of action or order of events. The same scene of action may be seen as containing several patterns: patterns that intersect and patterns within patterns. Whether a given object is disorganized depends on the pattern in terms of which it is defined.

It will be useful to distinguish several special senses of the term "disorganization" that are compatible with this more general definition.

From the perspectives of everyday life. This discussion will focus on the meanings of social events to the people who participate in them; indeed, this is the starting point of all sociological analysis. Crap games, corporations, political parties, and parades enter the sociologist's lexicon because the conceptual schemes of everyday life make it possible for people to envisage them as possibilities, to recognize their existence and demise, to orient their action toward them, to take part in them, and to wreck them.

One class of social objects may be called "activities": cleaning a rifle, preparing for battle, accomplishing a mission, carrying out the Normandy campaign. Each of these is a sequence of action that, from the standpoint of the actors, "hangs together" and constitutes "one thing." Each, in turn, is part of a larger, more extended activity. The sameness or continuity of an activity may depend, for the actor, on the correspondence of the flow of events to some *set of conventional rules* (Cohen 1959). The model here is the "game"; its constitutive order is defined by the rules of the game. There may be an infinite number of ways of continuing a game without "breaching its boundaries"; however, the set of possible events ("moves" or "plays") that will, at any juncture in the game, continue the game, are given in the rules. Many of the nongame activities of everyday life (for example, a party, a religious service, a judicial proceeding), or at least some of their essential components, are likewise defined by conventional rules. The sameness of the activity may also depend, for the actor, on the continued orientation of *action toward some goal.* Although the concrete action that goes into it may vary from moment to moment as the situation changes and although the act is literally built up out of bits of diverse action, it is seen and felt to be the same act so long as it is oriented to the same goal. Building a house would be an example. In either case, what has been going on, whether it is still going on, and the conditions that would constitute an interruption or disorganization of the activity depend on the pattern that defines that kind of activity for its participants.

Another class of social objects may be called "collectivities." Such are families, teams, corporations, nations, gangs. A collectivity exists when both a common identity and a capacity for action are attributed to the incumbents of a set of roles. In other words, the pragmatic tests of a collectivity are whether it has a socially defined membership and whether it is socially defined as an actor. The collectivity ceases to be a "going concern" and is destroyed or "disorganized" when the common identity is extinguished and it is no longer treated as an actor.

We have little systematic knowledge about the patterns to which structures of interaction must correspond in order to constitute collectivities in the world of everyday social life. However, if we are to talk about the "disorganization of collectivities," we must know what constitutes a breach of their boundaries; to do this we must determine what order of events defines a collectivity of a given sort for members of the society in question.

From the social scientist's perspective. Structures of action may exist as objects for the social scientist that are not social objects from the perspective of the "man in the street." A "market structure," a "substructure of goal attainment," a "homeostatic process," and an "ecological equilibrium"—all are orderings of events in terms of some pattern that is part of the conceptual equipment of the social scientist. If these patterns are precisely defined, they also imply a set of criteria for defining "disorganization" of the respective objects.

Disorganization as the spread of deviance. The definition of disorganization in terms of the spread of deviance has a long history in sociology. Thomas and Znaniecki defined social disorganization as a "decrease of the influence of existing social rules of behavior upon individual members of the group" and went on to say that "this decrease may present innumerable degrees, ranging from a single break

of some particular rule by one individual up to a general decay of all the institutions of the group" (1920, vol. 4, p. 20). The principal subject matter of most textbooks entitled "social disorganization" is deviant behavior. According to this view, disorganization may be reduced and the integrity of the system restored either by strengthening social controls or by redefining norms so that behavior defined as deviant becomes normatively acceptable (Thomas & Znaniecki 1920, vol. 4, p. 4; Mills 1959).

Whatever the merits of this conception of disorganization, it cannot provide a *general* definition of disorganization. Certainly there are many structures, visible from the specialized perspectives of the social scientist, that cannot be defined in terms of the conformity of action to normative rules. From the standpoint of the perspectives of everyday life as well, it seems important to distinguish between deviance and disorganization. "The rules of the game" *define* an activity or collectivity, that is, the pattern to which action must correspond if it is to constitute a certain sort of thing. The normative rules, departure from which is deviance, specify how people *ought* to behave; they are criteria for judging the moral status of an act. For example, there are "dirty" ways of playing a game, unethical ways of carrying on a business, and "inhuman" ways of fighting a war. Still, they are unequivocally recognizable as integral to the respective activities, as "moves" in the respective games; and the rules of the game typically define the "next moves" that would constitute the continuity of the game.

Precisely because deviance is so intimately related to disorganization but is not in general identical with it, it is necessary to distinguish them and treat the relationship between them as a problem for theory and empirical investigation.

One of the conditions of the survival of any social activity or collectivity is that people be *motivated* to "play the game," to take up their positions in the structure of interaction and contribute the moves that maintain the continuity of the structure in question. One of the general conditions of disorganization, then, is *breakdown of motivation,* and anything that undermines motivation contributes to disorganization. It is elementary that conformity to normative rules—to some degree that cannot be stated in general terms—is fundamental to the maintenance of motivation. When people elect to participate in any social structure, they subject themselves to a certain discipline; they commit resources; and they forgo alternatives. In other words, they pay a price.

Whatever the several reasons for which they join, their ends are attainable only if others "play the game," and play it according to certain restrictions defined by the normative rules. Violations of the normative understandings tend to erode trust and undermine motivation. A certain amount of deviance is expected. Although disappointing, it is not surprising; it is allowed for in advance, and does not seriously impair motivation. However, at *some* point the spread of deviance and the consequent erosion of trust will destroy motivation and precipitate disorganization.

On the other hand, deviance may contribute to stability and preservation of the common enterprise. Normative rules are usually adapted to typical, recurring situations and tend to produce results that enhance the viability of the enterprise. However, rules are categorical, and situations often arise in which conformity to the normative rules will thwart the attainment of the common objective and weaken or destroy the structure. In short, there are times when someone must violate the normative rules if the enterprise is to succeed and thrive. Sometimes there are implicit rules (patterns of "institutionalized evasion") that give flexibility to the normative rules so that the deviance is deviance only in an equivocal sense (Williams 1951). But this is not always so, and therefore the relationship between deviance and disorganization is rendered still more problematic.

Finally, it is probably true that some kinds of deviance, even if not motivated by collectivity concerns, create the conditions necessary for the stability of other substructures of the same system or of the system as a whole. Kingsley Davis (1937), for example, has made this argument relative to prostitution.

Disorganization theory. There has been relatively little attention to the explicit development of disorganization theory, as compared with deviance theory. However, the beginnings of such theory are implied in more general theories and conceptions of social systems, such as general systems theory, interaction process analysis, structural–functional theory, and the input–output, homeostatic, equilibrium, and cybernetic models. They tend to share the following ideas.

A social system is, from one point of view, a mechanism that operates for its own perpetuation. It is what it is because the participants are motivated to behave in certain ways characteristic of the system and because the situation of action makes possible these ways and restricts the alternatives. In order to preserve its structure (or so much of that structure as is constitutive of its

identity) that motivation and situation must somehow be reconstituted, or other motivations and situations must be created that will generate behavior coresponding to the same pattern. However, the system, as a product of its own functioning, tends to thwart the creation or re-creation of the conditions of its own survival For example, it tends to transform the environment to which it has become adapted; to use up or to lose its own human and nonhuman resources; to generate distance and distrust, resentment and alienation among its members; and to create new situations for which its culture provides no definitions or instructions. Various lists have been drawn up of conditions that must be met or tasks that must be performed if the system is not to fly apart in consequence of its own functioning (for example, see Aberle et al. 1950; Bales 1950; Parsons 1951, pp. 26–36).

Most systems do manage to preserve their identity. Therefore, the functioning of the system must also produce effects that correct or compensate for the centrifugal tendencies it produces. In particular, the structure of such systems must include mechanisms for picking up information about threatening changes in the environment or in the system itself and for communicating that information to positions in the system that are capable of taking corrective action. Such action, in turn, may consist of responses tending to reduce or eliminate the change or further modifications elsewhere in the system, enabling the system as a whole to maintain its boundaries or identity in the face of the change.

Systems do not always succeed. Some are wholly extinguished; others suffer radical disorganization of various substructures but cling to those minimal attributes that define their identity. Some have standby mechanisms that can be activated in time to do the job of some injured organ or to get about the work of reconstruction before the damage proves lethal to the system; and others do not. These differences have been most systematically studied in connection with disasters (Baker & Chapman 1962). In general, it is the task of a theory of social disorganization to account for variations in the ability of social structures to preserve their identity.

ALBERT K. COHEN

[*Directly related are the entries* CRIME; NORMS; SOCIAL PROBLEMS. *Other relevant material may be found in* DISASTERS; DRUGS, *article on* DRUG ADDICTION: SOCIAL ASPECTS; SOCIAL CONTROL; *and in the biography of* SUTHERLAND.]

BIBLIOGRAPHY

ABERLE, DAVID et al.   1950   The Functional Prerequisites of a Society. *Ethics* 60:100–111.

BAKER, GEORGE W.; and CHAPMAN, DWIGHT W. (editors)   1962   *Man and Society in Disaster.* New York: Basic Books.

BALES, ROBERT F.   1950   *Interaction Process Analysis: A Method for the Study of Small Groups.* Reading, Mass.: Addison-Wesley.

BECKER, HOWARD S.   1963   *Outsiders: Studies in the Sociology of Deviance.* New York: Free Press.

CLINARD, MARSHALL B. (editor)   1964   *Anomie and Deviant Behavior.* New York: Free Press.

CLOWARD, RICHARD A.; and OHLIN, LLOYD E.   1960   *Delinquency and Opportunity: A Theory of Delinquent Gangs.* Glencoe, Ill.: Free Press.

COHEN, ALBERT K.   (1955) 1963   *Delinquent Boys: The Culture of the Gang.* New York: Free Press.

COHEN, ALBERT K.   1959   The Study of Social Disorganization and Deviant Behavior. Pages 461–484 in Robert K. Merton et al. (editors), *Sociology Today.* New York: Basic Books.

COHEN, ALBERT K.   1965   The Sociology of the Deviant Act: Anomie Theory and Beyond. *American Sociological Review* 30:5–14.

CRESSEY, DONALD R.   1964   *Delinquency, Crime and Differential Association.* The Hague: Nijhoff.

DAVIS, KINGSLEY   1937   The Sociology of Prostitution. *American Sociological Review* 2:744–755.

DURKHEIM, ÉMILE   (1897) 1951   *Suicide: A Study in Sociology.* Glencoe, Ill.: Free Press. → First published in French.

GOFFMAN, ERVING   (1956) 1959   *The Presentation of Self in Everyday Life.* Garden City, N.Y.: Doubleday.

GOFFMAN, ERVING   1963   *Stigma: Notes on the Management of Spoiled Identity.* Englewood Cliffs, N.J.: Prentice-Hall.

HALL, JEROME   (1935) 1952   *Theft, Law and Society.* 2d ed. Indianapolis, Ind.: Bobbs-Merrill.

JOHNSON, HARRY M.   1960   *Sociology: A Systematic Introduction.* New York: Harcourt.

MATZA, DAVID   1964   *Delinquency and Drift.* New York: Wiley.

MEAD, GEORGE H.   1934   *Mind, Self and Society From the Standpoint of a Social Behaviorist.* Edited by Charles W. Morris. Univ. of Chicago Press.

MERTON, ROBERT K.   (1949) 1957   *Social Theory and Social Structure.* Rev. & enl. ed. Glencoe, Ill.: Free Press.

MILLS, THEODORE M.   1959   Equilibrium and the Processes of Deviance and Control. *American Sociological Review* 24:671–679.

PARSONS, TALCOTT   1951   *The Social System.* Glencoe, Ill.: Free Press.

REISS, ALBERT J.   1961   The Social Integration of Peers and Queers. *Social Problems* 9:102–120.

SHAW, CLIFFORD R.; and McKAY, HENRY D.   1942   *Juvenile Delinquency and Urban Areas: A Study of Rates of Delinquents in Relation to Differential Characteristics of Local Communities in American Cities.* Univ. of Chicago Press.

SHORT, JAMES F., JR.; and STRODTBECK, FRED   1965   *Group Process and Gang Delinquency.* Univ. of Chicago Press.

SUTHERLAND, EDWIN H.   (1942–1947) 1956   Differential Association. Part 1, pages 5–43 in Edwin H. Sutherland, *The Sutherland Papers.* Edited by Albert K. Cohen et al. Indiana University Publications, So-cial Science Series, No. 15. Bloomington: Indiana Univ. Press.

SUTHERLAND, EDWIN H.   (1949) 1961   *White Collar Crime.* New York: Holt.

SYKES, GRESHAM M.; and MATZA, DAVID   1957   Techniques of Neutralization: A Theory of Delinquency. *American Sociological Review* 22:664–670.

TANNENBAUM, FRANK   (1938) 1963   *Crime and the Community.* New York: Columbia Univ. Press.

THOMAS, WILLIAM I.; and ZNANIECKI, FLORIAN   (1920) 1958   *The Polish Peasant in Europe and America.* Volume 2. New York: Dover.

WILLIAMS, ROBIN M., JR.   (1951) 1960   Institutional Variation and the Evasion of Normative Patterns. Pages 372–396 in Robin M. Williams, Jr., *American Society.* 2d ed., rev. New York: Knopf.

DEWEY, JOHN

John Dewey (1859–1952), generally regarded as the most influential philosopher in American history, was born in Burlington, Vermont. After receiving his doctorate from Johns Hopkins University in 1884, he taught at the University of Michigan (except for a year spent at the University of Minnesota) until 1894, when he moved to the University of Chicago.

Dewey was attracted to Chicago because pedagogy there was included in one department with philosophy and psychology. At Chicago he established an experimental elementary school, wrote *The School and Society* (1899), and became involved with Jane Addams' Hull House. At this time Dewey was developing his pragmatic approach to the theory of mind and his "instrumentalist" theory of logic: his essay "The Reflex Arc Concept in Psychology," which had considerable influence on developments in psychology, appeared in 1896, and *Studies in Logical Theory*, a collection of essays by Dewey and some of his colleagues and students, appeared in 1903. The book was greeted by William James as the signal of the birth of a "Chicago school" of pragmatic philosophy.

In 1904 Dewey resigned his professorship at Chicago because he was displeased with the university administration's actions toward the experimental school he headed. He moved to Columbia University as professor of philosophy, with additional teaching responsibilities at Teachers College. Dewey taught at Columbia until his retirement in 1929. During the 1930s he produced some of the most ambitious philosophical works of his career. He also continued to take part in a wide assortment of civic and political activities, the most dramatic of which was his service in 1937 as chairman of the unofficial commission that held public hearings in Mexico and found Leon Trotsky innocent of the charges made against him in the Moscow trials.

Intellectual influences. Dewey's early intellectual attachments were to Hegel's philosophy. Dewey's New England upbringing had stressed the radical divisions that exist in man and the universe between body and soul, nature and God, the world and the self. He found these beliefs "an inward laceration." Hegel's philosophy, with its dialectical elimination of the presumed antitheses between matter and spirit, nature and the divine, and subject and object, offered release from these oppressive dualisms. Hegel's influence on Dewey can be seen in Dewey's lifelong polemic against all forms of dualism in philosophy, in his concept of individuality as a social product, in his tendency to identify freedom with rational self-realization, and in his view that logical and moral principles are not fixed, external standards to be imposed on human inquiry and conduct but are instead evolutionary phenomena that emerge within the actual course of human thinking and acting.

Over a period of fifteen years after leaving Johns Hopkins, however, Dewey drifted away from Hegel's philosophy and eventually renounced it altogether. The theme that came to seem increasingly important to him was what he called "the intellectual scandal" involved in the separation of science from morals. Hegel's abstract, metaphysical solution of this problem became increasingly uncongenial to Dewey, who desired to reformulate philosophical problems so that they implied clear alternative programs for social action. What Dewey described as his transition "from absolutism to experimentalism" was further aided by the pioneer work of Charles Sanders Peirce (1839–1914) in the development of a pragmatic theory of logic and by William James's *Psychology*. Dewey's own "pragmatism," or "instrumentalism," owes relatively little to James's pragmatism but much to James's biological approach to the problems of mind. The work of Dewey's friend George Herbert Mead (1863–1931) also had considerable influence on Dewey's philosophy. Dewey's conceptions of the self, and of the genesis and function of such phenomena as "consciousness" and "conscience," owe much to Mead's work in social psychology and philosophy. Finally, Dewey's thought is unintelligible except as a response to the Darwinian theory of evolution by natural selection. Dewey's theory of mind, his translation of Hegel's categories into biological and cultural terms, his views on logic and morals, and his conception of the task of philosophy are all efforts to trace the implications of Darwin's mode of thought.

With respect to the question of intellectual influences on him, Dewey's own judgment, however, should be emphasized. He believed that most of the significant influences on his intellectual development came not from books but from personal associations and practical experience, particularly in education.

Instrumentalism. Throughout his career Dewey's central interest was to repair moral and social beliefs and practices by encouraging the application of scientific methods and critical intelligence to them. Dewey believed that one of the principal obstacles to this was the traditional notion, embedded in common sense and defended and enshrined by philosophy, that "theory" is contemplative, passive, and unmarked by practical concerns and that "practice" is by its very nature not susceptible to intellectual formulation or control. The development of a logic of human inquiry that would reveal the underlying unity of "theory" and "practice" was therefore Dewey's central intellectual enterprise.

According to Dewey the advent of modern experimental science had shown that theory and practice, far from being opposed, are in fact interdependent in successful scientific inquiry. Using such inquiry as a model, he formulated the view that general ideas are instruments for reconstructing "problematic situations." An idea, in other words, is what is sometimes known as a "leading principle" or an "inference ticket"—a rule directing and regulating the movement of an inquiry or argument from one set of observations to another. The truth of an idea lies in its capacity to reorganize the materials of experience so that the problem that originally provoked reflection is resolved in accordance with the canons of disciplined inquiry. The power of an idea is measured by the novelty and significance for further inquiry of the questions it leads us to ask. Dewey thus rejected, or seemed to reject, the traditional "correspondence theory of truth," according to which the truth of an idea is simply a matter of its correspondence to the external, independent reality to which it refers.

Dewey's "instrumentalism" appears to involve, at the least, an overstatement, for if all ideas are simply rules for making inferences, then we are forced to the paradoxical conclusion that there are no general statements in the sciences that refer to anything external to human habits of thought. The emphasis of Dewey's instrumentalism, nonetheless, was extremely useful in enhancing critical understanding of science. It presented inquiry as a phase in the continuing readaptation of a social animal to its environment and portrayed general ideas as prescriptions for behavior, mental or physical, and as directives for action on the environment. It thus cast doubt on classic distinctions between theory and practice.

Theory of moral judgment.   To establish still further the continuity of science and morals Dewey also undertook to show that moral judgments are subject to the same essential logic of inquiry as that of the sciences. Dewey's argument, as developed, for example, in *Logical Conditions of a Scientific Treatment of Morality* (1903*b*) and *Theory of Valuation* (1939*a*), is that moral ideals are properly interpreted as hypotheses proposing that certain courses of action will resolve specified sets of difficulties. Moral ideals, therefore, like the general ideas of the sciences, are instruments for the solution of problems, and their validity is to be determined by a matter-of-fact examination of the consequences of acting on them, analogous to the procedure by which general ideas in the sciences achieve acceptance.

Dewey's position is frequently criticized on the ground that he erased the distinction between factual statements and value judgments, a distinction on which the very conception of an objective science depends. The force of these accusations is weakened when it is seen that Dewey's argument entails the denial of the normally accepted view that there is a hard and fast distinction between means and ends. Critics of Dewey frequently ask how, in Dewey's terms, instrumental moral value can be ascribed to a course of action when he denied that there are in the last analysis any ends that have value for themselves. Dewey, however, rejected this question as irrelevant to the actual conditions under which moral choice takes place, for he believed that moral perplexities arise in specific contexts where certain established values are imperiled but where a host of other values, which might be questioned in other contexts, are not in fact in question. The problem of infinite regress is therefore not relevant to the practical contexts in which moral judgments are made; it implicitly introduces standards of demonstrative certainty that are not appropriate to this domain of thought.

The analyses of moral judgments that Dewey offered in different works were, however, not entirely consistent, and in the eyes of many critics he never successfully refuted the charge that he confused descriptive and prescriptive statements.

Critique of philosophy.   Much of Dewey's work consisted of polemics against "the classic tradition" in philosophy. The major effort of classic philosophy, he argued in such books as *Reconstruction in Philosophy* (1920) and *The Quest for Certainty* (1929), had been to give men a sense of surcease from surrounding perils they were helpless to overcome. Accordingly, the usual message of classic philosophy was that behind the everyday world of change and irrationality there is an unchanging and rational world, in the contemplation of which men may gain understanding and serenity. Thus, in Dewey's view, philosophical "dualism" was essentially an instrument of conservatism and retreat. It was also, he argued, an expression of such aristocratic social prejudices as the distaste for manual labor. Although relatively few scholars accept Dewey's picture of the history of philosophy, his placing of that history within a social context has been the source of a considerable reappraisal of the Western philosophical inheritance.

Philosophy of education.   For Dewey the principal object of education was to instill in students the attitudes and habits conducive to the development of their capacity to solve problems. As he argued in *Democracy and Education* (1916*a*), this required that classroom emphasis be placed not on arrays of factual information or on inherited ideas presented as settled and accepted but on the intellectual methods by which such factual information or such ideas are discovered and reliably established. This view was further fortified by Dewey's belief that objective attitudes toward moral and social questions require the rejection of absolutes and the cultivation of flexibility and tolerance. Moreover, Dewey argued that a democratic culture requires from its members a capacity to adapt to diverse circumstances and to cooperate as equals with men and women of many different sorts. Schools responsive to these democratic imperatives would therefore aim at training students in habits of free and constant inquiry, in capacities to learn quickly, and in attitudes of social fellow feeling and cooperation. In spelling out this prescription, Dewey laid great stress on the atmosphere of the classroom: he opposed rote learning, stressing instead the pedagogical desirability of "learning by doing" and of connecting the materials of formal school instruction with the child's experiences outside the classroom.

Dewey's theories of education came to be widely adopted, and they were given a variety of interpretations by ardent disciples. In his short book *Experience and Education* (1938*a*), written toward the end of his life, Dewey took account of some of the varieties of "progressive education" that had been associated with his name and expressed his serious misgivings about them.

Conception of the social sciences.   Dewey provided intellectual support for the view that the logic of inquiry in the natural sciences is applicable in its major features to the study of human affairs. However, although he argued that the social sciences could and should offer objective descriptions of facts, he also stressed that their progress as intellectual disciplines depended on the importance of the subjects they chose for study and on the refusal of social scientists to dodge controversial issues. He argued that adequate social inquiry, like physical inquiry, requires the experimental manipulation of existential conditions. Accordingly, the removal of taboos against social planning, he believed, would greatly aid the progress of man's social knowledge.

Social outlook.   Dewey's social views, in general, may be characterized as reasonably typical of the so-called progressive era of American thought. His special contributions to progressive thought consisted in his critique of ivory-tower ideals of scholarship, his attacks on such intellectual absolutes as the doctrine of natural rights, and his enlargement of the concept of freedom to include the dimension of personal self-realization, beyond the mere absence of external restraints. Closely connected with this was Dewey's restatement of the relation of the growth of individuality to environing cultural conditions, a view that led to the emphasis on the role of the school in social reconstruction. In such essays as "Logical Method and Law" (1924), Dewey also applied his instrumentalist approach to questions of jurisprudence, influencing the evolution of American "legal realism"; in *The Public and Its Problems* (1927), he applied a similar approach to problems of political science, contributing to the progress of "interest group" theory.

The broad ideal behind his social outlook was articulated in several works, most notably, perhaps, in *Art as Experience* (1934). His critique of the industrial society of his day was based mainly on his conviction that this society reduced men to a state of passive acquiescence in external routines laid down for them. His image of a good society was one in which men are active agents, intelligently setting their own standards and participating freely and equally in the making of their common destiny.

Influence.   Dewey's impact on American philosophy before World War II was massive, and his impact on educational theory and practice was even greater. His influence on psychology, jurisprudence, political science, and styles of thought in history and economics was also considerable. Even more important, perhaps, was his general influence on the atmosphere of American scholarship. He helped free that scholarship from sub-

servience to genteel conventions and theological modes of thought, and he was one of those principally responsible for the acceptance of the view that the study of human affairs is properly a task of empirical science. By the example of his life, by his activities as a leader of such organizations as the American Association of University Professors, and most of all by his courageous articulation of his conception of philosophy, he contributed as much as any man to the spread of the idea in America that free scientific inquiry, recognizing no limits to the questions it might ask, is the linchpin of a sound society and of all responsible social action.

CHARLES FRANKEL

[*For the historical context of Dewey's work, see the biographies of* DARWIN; HEGEL; JAMES; MEAD; PEIRCE. *For discussion of the subsequent development of his ideas, see* EDUCATION; EDUCATIONAL PSYCHOLOGY; LEARNING; *and the biographies of* ANGELL; BEARD; BENTLEY; MERRIAM; ROBINSON.]

WORKS BY DEWEY

1896   The Reflex Arc Concept in Psychology. *Psychological Review* 3:357–370.

(1899) 1961   *The School and Society.* Rev. ed. Univ. of Chicago Press.

1903*a*   *Studies in Logical Theory.* Univ. of Chicago Press.

1903*b*   *Logical Conditions of a Scientific Treatment of Morality.* Univ. of Chicago Press.

(1916*a*) 1953   *Democracy and Education: An Introduction to the Philosophy of Education.* New York: Macmillan.

(1916*b*) 1953   *Essays in Experimental Logic.* New York: Dover.

(1920) 1948   *Reconstruction in Philosophy.* Enl. ed. Boston: Beacon.

1924   Logical Method and Law. *Philosophical Review* 33: 560–572.

(1925) 1958   *Experience and Nature.* 2d ed. La Salle, Ill.: Open Court.

(1927) 1957   *The Public and Its Problems.* Denver, Colo.: Swallow.

(1929) 1960   *The Quest for Certainty: A Study of the Relation of Knowledge and Action.* New York: Putnam.

1934   *Art as Experience.* New York: Putnam. → A paperback edition was published in 1959.

1938*a*   *Experience and Education.* New York: Macmillan.

(1938*b*) 1960   *Logic: The Theory of Inquiry.* New York: Holt.

1939*a*   *Theory of Valuation.* International Encyclopedia of Unified Science, Vol. 2, No. 4. Univ. of Chicago Press.

1939*b*   *Freedom and Culture.* New York: Putnam.

SUPPLEMENTARY BIBLIOGRAPHY

BERKSON, ISAAC B.   1958   *The Ideal and the Community: A Philosophy of Education.* New York: Harper.

CREMIN, LAWRENCE A.   1961   *The Transformation of the School: Progressivism in American Education, 1876–1957.* New York: Knopf.

Geiger, George R. 1958 *John Dewey in Perspective.* New York: Oxford Univ. Press.

Hook, Sidney 1939 *John Dewey: An Intellectual Portrait.* New York: Day.

Schilpp, Paul A. (editor) (1939) 1951 *The Philosophy of John Dewey.* 2d ed. New York: Tudor. → Contains an extensive bibliography.

Thayer, Horace S. 1952 *The Logic of Pragmatism: An Examination of John Dewey's Logic.* London: Routledge; New York: Humanities.

White, Morton G. 1943 *The Origin of Dewey's Instrumentalism.* New York: Columbia Univ. Press.

DIALECTICAL MATERIALISM

See History, *article on* the philosophy of history; Knowledge, sociology of; Marxist sociology; *and the biographies of* Hegel *and* Marx.

DICEY, ALBERT VENN

Albert Venn Dicey (1835–1922), British constitutional lawyer and political theorist, was given his middle name in honor of John Venn, leader of the Clapham evangelists. On his mother's side he was related both to the Venns and to the Stephens— Sir Leslie Stephen, philosopher, literary critic, and author of *The English Utilitarians,* and Sir James Fitzjames Stephen, a judge and the author of a celebrated history of English criminal law. Dicey was educated at Balliol College, Oxford, where one of his friends and contemporaries was James (later Viscount) Bryce, author of *The American Commonwealth.* Later Dicey became a fellow of Trinity and in 1882 was elected to the Vinerian professorship of English law at All Souls College, Oxford, the chair first occupied by Sir William Blackstone. Dicey's two major works were his *Introduction to the Study of the Law of the Constitution* (1885) and *Lectures on the Relation Between Law and Opinion in England, During the Nineteenth Century* (1905). Both books are masterpieces of compression, and the *Law of the Constitution* still commands attention for its exposition of three major principles of the British system of government. These principles, as Dicey saw them, were (1) the close relationship between formal legal rules and informal conventions of constitutional behavior, (2) the legislative supremacy of Parliament, and (3) the rule of law.

Each of these principles has provoked criticism and debate in the twentieth century. Thus, Dicey insisted that conventions (for example, that governments resign if defeated on an issue of confidence in the House of Commons) were obeyed because of the existence of an ultimate legal sanction; a government that defied the convention about resignation, he argued, would find that the Commons would refuse to appropriate taxes or pass the Army Act, and administration could not thereafter be carried on legally. The explanation is not convincing. It does not tell us why conventions are obeyed when governments have solid majorities in the House of Commons; or why the majority respects the rights of the opposition (and pays its leader a salary); or why the Queen assents automatically to legislation; or why the legal powers of the crown and of Parliament are not exercised over territories to which only *de facto* independence has been given.

About the "sovereignty of Parliament" Dicey had much to say. It meant, he pointed out, the legal supremacy, or absolutism, of the "queen-in-Parliament." In the eyes of the English lawyer and the English courts, the queen-in-Parliament is capable of making or unmaking any law, and no body or person or court can set aside this sovereign and omnicompetent will. Fundamental laws and judicial review are unknown to the law of England. The only legal impossibility is that of binding or restricting the powers of future Parliaments; for what one Parliament can do, another can undo.

The inconvenient practical implications of this common-law doctrine become evident when proposals are made, as they have been in Canada and other Commonwealth countries, to insert into the legal system a body of enforceable legal rights. If each successive English Parliament is sovereign in Dicey's sense, such proposals cannot in legal principle be carried out. As a matter of political practice, however, Britain's "sovereign" Parliament did bind itself irrevocably, and its successors as well, when in 1931 (and since then with increasing frequency) it relinquished the power to legislate for formerly dependent territories. And the United States is a monument to the futility of the English principle of legislative omnipotence, whether exercised by George iii's Parliament or any other.

From the jurisprudential point of view, there have developed in recent times some differences on a problem that Dicey did not foresee, namely, whether Parliament is prohibited by the sovereignty principle from altering the legislative process in such a way that it prevents future Parliaments from repealing or amending, by simple majority vote, laws deemed to be of constitutional importance. There is disagreement about what the probable attitude of the courts would be if Parliament were to attempt to bind itself or its successors procedurally by requiring a special majority for the repeal of certain "entrenched" laws. This question is of great potential importance in new constitutional systems deriving from the British parliamentary model, though it remains a theoretical issue in the United Kingdom.

Dicey saw his third principle, the rule of law, as one that precludes not only arbitrary acts but even the existence of any wide discretion on the part of government officials. The rule of law makes possible the single jurisdiction, admired by Dicey, in which both citizens and state servants are subject to the same set of courts. He preferred the rule of law (thus defined) to the Continental system, in which administrative courts for the adjudication of disputes between the citizen and the administration exist alongside of the ordinary courts. Under the common-law principle, he believed, the state and the individual are treated as equals.

Critics have suggested that Dicey's view is politically and administratively conservative and that it underrates the need for administrative discretion at the same time that it disregards substantial inequalities that may arise between citizens and officials as a result of executive privileges. A system of *droit administratif* may, by contrast, overcome these deficiencies. Dicey was not, however, in his later writing entirely insensitive either to the merits of the Continental system of control or to the need for discretionary powers on the part of government departments (Dicey 1915; also, Lawson 1959). Furthermore, Dicey's strictures on official arbitrariness and discretion in matters of civil, as distinct from economic, liberties and in regard to the powers of policemen, if not those of civil servants, are today widely accepted. Indeed, Dicey's views on free speech and the right of public assembly sound very modern, in contrast to his statements on economic welfare and state intervention. Since similar comments could be made about other contemporaries of Dicey's, notably John Stuart Mill, it would be worth investigating why the economic principles of Victorian England should have proved so ephemeral and the political ones so durable.

Dicey's social and economic views were those of a Whig and a free trader. On the Irish question he was a Unionist and supported his opinion with a vigorous tract, *England's Case Against Home Rule* (1886). Although his *Law and Opinion* is primarily historical and descriptive, his dislike of collectivist legislation can be divined in it without difficulty. In dealing with the relation between legislation and English thought and opinion, he refers to "opinion" primarily in the sense of organized juristic, political, and economic theory rather than in the sense of "public opinion." In linking legal development

to intellectual movements, he saw a period of "Old Toryism" linked to Blackstonian optimism, followed by a period of Benthamite reform linked with the utilitarian philosophy, and finally a period of collectivism, which he thought reflected "a sentiment rather than a doctrine."

Collectivism, he believed, owes a direct debt to Benthamism, which by providing precedents for centralized governmental intervention of a limited kind, had forged the instruments for more extensive collectivist measures. The first form of intervention he styled "negative," the latter "positive." The contrast was an unclear one, since any "positive" state purpose can be reformulated in terms of some social or economic impediment to freedom of access (to opportunity or happiness), which it is necessary to remove by collective restrictions. In 1860, Dicey thought, there was a widespread belief in Mill's "simple principle" of individual liberty. But by 1914 there was collective provision for old age pensions, national health insurance, and school meals. Dicey doubted whether these measures could be justified on the principles set out in the essay *On Liberty*. He was surprised that the recipients of pensions from the state were allowed to continue to vote.

One interesting question raised in *Law and Opinion* is why English society has absorbed major legislative changes without resistance or obstruction from those whose interests are adversely affected. (The same question was posed by many after World War II.) One of the answers suggested by Dicey is the misleading English belief that legislation changes little and in the end leaves most things in society much as they were. Dicey himself sometimes seemed to accept this view, which may explain his faith in social change through an enlightened public opinion.

GEOFFREY MARSHALL

[*For discussion of the history and subsequent development of Dicey's ideas, see* ADMINISTRATIVE LAW; CONSTITUTIONS AND CONSTITUTIONALISM; JUDICIAL PROCESS, *article on* JUDICIAL REVIEW; LEGAL SYSTEMS; LEGISLATION; PARLIAMENTARY GOVERNMENT.]

WORKS BY DICEY

(1885) 1961 *Introduction to the Study of the Law of the Constitution.* 10th ed. With an Introduction by E. C. S. Wade. London: Macmillan; New York: St. Martins.
1886 *England's Case Against Home Rule.* London: Murray.
(1905) 1962 *Lectures on the Relation Between Law and Public Opinion in England, During the Nineteenth Century.* 2d ed. With a preface by E. C. S. Wade. London: Macmillan. → A paperback edition was published in 1962 by Macmillan.

1915 The Development of Administrative Law in England. *Law Quarterly Review* 31:148–153.

1925 *Memorials of Albert Venn Dicey: Being Chiefly Letters and Diaries.* Edited by Robert S. Rait. London: Macmillan.

SUPPLEMENTARY BIBLIOGRAPHY

HANBURY, HAROLD G. 1958 *The Vinerian Chair and Legal Education.* Oxford: Blackwell. → See especially pages 131–163, on "A Prophet of the Constitution."

HART, HERBERT L. A. 1961 *The Concept of Law.* Oxford: Clarendon. → See especially pages 49–76, on "Sovereign and Subject"; and pages 97–120, on "The Foundations of a Legal System."

HEUSTON, ROBERT F. (1961) 1964 *Essays in Constitutional Law.* 2d ed. London: Stevens. → See especially pages 1–29, on "Sovereignty."

JENNINGS, WILLIAM I. (1933) 1959 *The Law and the Constitution.* 5th ed. Univ. of London Press. → See especially Appendix II on "Dicey's Theory of the Rule of Law."

JENNINGS, WILLIAM I. 1935 In Praise of Dicey: 1885–1935. *Public Administration* 13:123.

LAWSON, FREDERICK H. 1959 Dicey Revisited. *Political Studies* 7:109–126; 207–221.

MARSH, NORMAN S. 1961 The Rule of Law as a Supranational Concept. Pages 223–264 in Anthony G. Guest (editor), *Oxford Essays in Jurisprudence: A Collaborative Work.* Oxford Univ. Press.

MARSHALL, GEOFFREY 1957 *Parliamentary Sovereignty and the Commonwealth.* Oxford: Clarendon.

RAIT, ROBERT S. 1937 Albert Venn Dicey. Pages 259–261 in *Dictionary of National Biography, 1922–1930.* London: Oxford Univ. Press.

WADE, H. W. R. 1955 The Basis of Legal Sovereignty. *Cambridge Law Journal* [1955]: 172–197.

DICTATORSHIP

In contemporary usage "dictatorship" refers to the unrestricted domination of the state by an individual, a clique, or a small group. Instances of dictatorial rule are found in all epochs and in all civilizations. The term "dictatorship" may signify not only the governing principle of a political system but also an ideology underlying a way of life and a normative expression of political behavior. Several expressions have been used to characterize the historical phenomenon of dictatorial rule: tyranny, despotism, autocracy, Caesarism, *Führerstaat*, authoritarianism, totalitarianism.

Apart from constitutional dictatorships established to deal with governmental emergencies, all forms of dictatorship share the following features:

(1) *Exclusivity and arbitrariness in the exercise of power.* Dictatorships are characterized by the absence of a division of power, the suppression of competing, legitimate political and social groups and institutions, the concentration of political power in the hands of a dictator or of an autocratically governing group of leaders (elite), and the utilization of an autocratically guided and manipulated ruling apparatus to develop a monopoly of power.

(2) *Abolition or loosening of the juridical bonds of political power.* The constitutional state is eliminated, or a new revolutionary or counterrevolutionary law created, merely as an instrument of rule. Related to this feature is the difficulty or impossibility of regulating the succession of the dictator in a lawful fashion.

(3) *Elimination or substantial restriction of civil liberties.* Instead of voluntary cooperation of socially and politically autonomous groups and associations in the erection of the commonwealth, emphasis is placed on the citizens' obligation to perform compulsory labor or collective services.

(4) *The predominantly aggressive, impulsive form of decision making.* The domestic and foreign policies followed by the dictator and/or the leading political elite are usually made impulsively and are inspired by a dynamic political activism, often based upon an ideological Messianism and aimed at transforming or disciplining the society.

(5) *Employment of despotic methods of political and social control.* Such methods range from intimidation to propaganda, from imposing the duty of obedience to methods of terror.

These characteristics of dictatorship are to be found in various combinations and modifications in different historical configurations: in the Greek and Sicilian tyrannies described by Plato and Aristotle and in the postconstitutional Caesarist dictatorship of the Roman Empire, from Sulla and Caesar to the imperial despots; in the many manifestations of the tyranny of the noble families and the urban oligarchies in the early and late Renaissance, whose problems were condensed in classic form by Machiavelli in *The Prince*; in the English absolute monarchy and the hesitant despotism of its revolutionary opponent, Oliver Cromwell; in the terroristic Jacobin dictatorship of the French Revolution and the social-revolutionary communist states; in the short-lived, counterrevolutionary fascist and National Socialist states; in the earlier forms of Latin American military dictatorships; and, since World War I, in numerous completely or partially totalitarian structures patterned on the sociopolitical models of fascism or communism (e.g., Falangist Spain, Peronist Argentina, communist Cuba, and the states of such leaders as Nasser and Nkrumah).

The concept of dictatorship, in its origin and evolution, may be understood both as a complementary and protective constitutional device and as a complete antithesis to the democratic constitutional state. Thus, Carl J. Friedrich (1937), in referring to the ancient Roman model, makes a distinction between constitutional and unrestricted dictatorship. Franz L. Neumann (1957, p. 248) comments that dictatorship may arise and function as "implementation of democracy," "preparation for democracy," or the "very negation of democracy." Plato and Aristotle saw the origin of tyranny in the weaknesses and degeneration of democracy, and political theory has been based on the polarity of democracy and dictatorship ever since. However, the view that a revolutionary dictatorship necessarily presupposes the existence or the counterpart of a democratic constitution is disputed. Answers may be provided by the recent sociological and political research into the historical process of transition from a constitutional, restricted dictatorship to an unrestricted, total dictatorship. It has also been held that the communist "totalitarianism of the left" has evolved from the rudiments of egalitarian, messianic democracy of the French Revolution (Talmon 1952).

The inability to function and the internal weakness of democracy are undoubtedly among the main causes of the establishment of dictatorial rule. The totalitarian communist system of the Soviet Union arose in consequence of the crumbling away of tsarist autocracy, hastened along by a mass movement. In general it can be shown that unresolved social tensions and economic crises, together with the undermining of constitutional order and the development of undemocratic power aggregates, are among the conditions that give rise to dictatorial regimes.

Types of dictatorship

Differences in origin, legitimation, organization of rule, and goals, as well as in political style, have led scholars to isolate types of dictatorship and to differentiate among them.

Both Plato (*Republic* VIII and IX) and Aristotle (*Politics* book III) dealt mainly with the structure and methods of tyranny and provided initial insight into the nature of dictatorial rule. Machiavelli was the first to distinguish between dictatorship as a constitutional institution of the republic and as a despotic form of government, which he recommended to the ruler as a means of restoring political order. Absolute monarchies are generally not regarded as dictatorships, since the exercise of power is clothed in traditional legitimacy. Yet whenever an absolute sovereign actually rules despotically, violating the customary standards of

monarchical authority, his rule must be termed a dictatorship (e.g., Louis XI, Richard III, Henry VIII, Philip II).

The well-known distinction between provisional dictatorship (*kommissarische Diktatur*—the grant of special full powers in the event of state emergencies) and sovereign dictatorship (aimed at a revolutionary change of the entire political and social order) made by Carl Schmitt (1921) is hardly fruitful sociologically in view of the historical and cultural variations in dictatorial rule.

The three ideal types developed by Franz L. Neumann (1957, p. 256 ff.), which use as a criterion the instruments of rule employed or required by dictators, are far better suited for classifying the various historical phenomena and systems of dictatorship. Neumann distinguishes "simple dictatorship" (the ruler exercises absolute control of the traditional instruments of state power), "Caesaristic dictatorship" (to gain power and to consolidate it, the ruler requires the support of broad masses of the people and the execution of social–economic reforms), and "totalitarian dictatorship" (rule is exercised through a differentiated power apparatus controlled by a governing party and a "social movement").

Some authors assume that the process of transforming a constitutional dictatorship into a revolutionary dictatorship leads, in modern industrial societies, either to authoritarianism, a form of dictatorship based upon the prevailing values in the society, or to totalitarianism, the form of dictatorship that is able to force through a new system of values in society (cf. Drath 1958). This distinction is worthy of note because it makes allowance for the fundamental importance of the different sociocultural presuppositions and sociopolitical goals of dictatorships.

Indeed, in any endeavor to set up a political–sociological typology of dictatorial systems the sociocultural factors must be regarded as the primary differentiating criteria, in addition to the specific governmental structures and the means of safeguarding the monopoly of power.

The summary below of certain ideal types of dictatorship attempts to make allowance for the interaction of the cultural, social, political, and psychological factors, which is characteristic of the different historical manifestations of these systems of rule. At the same time, these types show how different are the intensity of this interaction and the stability of the political–social relationships within the several systems.

Despotic one-man rule. Despotic one-man rule is historically represented by the many forms of tyranny in ancient Greece and Sicily and in Renaissance Italy, by some instances of Oriental monarchic despotism, and by certain cases of one-man rule in the developing countries. Political power is seized, usually by a palace revolution or *coup d'état,* when a state or a society is in a critical situation; it is usually exercised only for a short time by a despot without moral scruples but capable of bold decisions. This distinctly arbitrary rule is particularly unstable, because it is not supported by a strong organization; as a rule, it is backed only by some conspiratorial groups, small coteries, political bands or factions, camarillas, or military cliques. Usually the motive for the seizure of power is not concern for the commonweal, but personal gain, the suppression of opponents, or the conquest of foreign territory. The wielders of power are aristocratic conspirators, plebeian demagogues and "tribunes of the people," or war leaders (*condottieri*). Sometimes these leaders have the political regime they usurped confirmed by plebiscites or try to consolidate it by victorious military campaigns.

This type is related to Neumann's "simple dictatorship" but differs from it in that here the traditional instruments of state power are played off against one another, rather than being meaningfully coordinated and utilized to consolidate the *ad hoc* rule. The premises of such rule are the insecurity of social conditions, class conflicts, crises phenomena in existing democratic systems, military threats from foreign countries, as during the period of tyranny in ancient Sicily, and the meeting of different civilizations. In some instances (e.g., Cola de Rienzi) this form of rule has social-revolutionary traits, but it usually endeavors to consolidate *ad hoc* an existing or vanishing social *status quo.* Despotic one-man rule has an unmistakable Machiavellian appearance: a pragmatic will for the exercise of raw power through the manipulation of all the available social and technological means.

Elite-related rule. The most important feature of elite-related rule, whether by one man or by a group, is the development of a pyramid of power in an authoritarian state. The dictator controls the decisive key positions at the head of a combination of social elites and power aggregates consisting of such elements as the army, the police, the bureaucracy, the nobility, the propertied class, and/or the dominant groups in a parliament. He endeavors to achieve a balance of power among these elites or else to range the groups that support him against others. Recognition of the fact that the more stable the foundations of this rule, the greater the likelihood of continuous exercise of power, places limitations on the arbitrariness of the dictator. In many instances such rulers have attempted to provide constitutional guarantees for their regimes. This trend may be found in the various stages of Cromwell's dictatorship as well as in the period of Jacobin rule.

This form of rule is constantly subject to the hazard that its terroristic nature will be exacerbated by rivalries among the leading elites or by foreign military threats. In an elite-related dictatorship a division of political functions exists almost by definition. The rulers surround themselves with revolutionary councils, advisory committees, and paramilitary organizations. Ambitious aides or competitors of the dictator demand their share of political power (e.g., Danton, Barras, Hébert, Fouché during the rule of the Jacobins; or Abbé Sieyès and Talleyrand under Napoleon I).

Governmental systems of this type may in certain cases serve to maintain a sociopolitical *status quo,* to overcome a crisis, to prevent a revolution. Yet, as a rule, the measures taken by dictators and their advisory committees in a given socioeconomic situation are based on a particular sociopolitical concept of planning. The revolutionary or reform or restoration policies they advocate require popularity among the masses of the people. Consequently, this type often resembles Franz Neumann's definition of Caesarist rule.

Historical examples of this type are: the later Roman dictatorships (Sulla, Caesar, Augustus) with their Senate cliques and civil war factions, their triumvirates, rival armies, and provincial bureaucracies; the regime of Cosimo and Lorenzo di Medici (urban oligarchy, Council of Seventy, organization of the city's poor); Oliver Cromwell's rise from a radical speaker in Parliament and political leader of the Ironsides to Lord Protector (manipulation of Parliament's rule, supported by the army and by a newly established, rudimentary bureaucracy); the dictatorships of the Reign of Terror in the French Revolution (Robespierre, the club of the Jacobins, the Committee of Public Safety, and the Commune); the consulate and empire of Napoleon Bonaparte, founded on the prestige of his victorious army; the plebiscitarian, adventurous regime of Louis Bonaparte; the older South American dictatorships of the nineteenth and early twentieth centuries, established by corrupt generals through pronunciamento and based upon the power of the army; and finally, some of the more recent authoritarian forms of rule in the developing countries.

These dictatorships exhibit the rudiments of ideological justification of authoritarian rule (a "political formula" in Gaetano Mosca's sense) and the beginnings of ideologically oriented social movements (in the English revolution the independentism of the parliamentary Left and of Cromwell's army; in the French Revolution the tendency toward an egalitarian socialist democracy). The means of social control employed are primarily aimed at the core of the power organization or at the elites emerging from the ruling class. The masses of the people are constrained to admire or revere the personality of the leader. The social and political activities of such dictatorships are partly revolutionary and partly restorative—especially when the powers of the different social classes are balanced. Thus, Sulla's exercise of power, and that of many South American dictators, were counterrevolutionary or restorative, since they arrogated to themselves the function of "preserving law and order" in times of crisis and thereby prevented thoroughgoing social reforms. On the other hand, Cromwell's rule, like that of the Jacobins, bore revolutionary traits; both were pacemakers of that bourgeois revolution in whose name Napoleon I later waged his campaigns.

Oriental despotism. The concept of an Oriental or Asian society, including primarily the ancient civilizations of China, India, the Near East, and Tatar and tsarist Russia, but also the Eastern Roman and Byzantine empires, was known to the early political economists, as well as to Karl Marx and Max Weber. Recently K. A. Wittfogel (1957) has explored anew the socioeconomic, cultural, and political factors that characterized it. He finds that Oriental despotism differs in essential features from the dictatorships of antiquity, the Middle Ages, and modern Europe, although it is akin in some ways to the elite-related as well as the totalitarian types.

A "hydraulic" society, based on extensive systems of waterworks, evolved a widespread bureaucratic network that directed the organization and planning of *corvée* (forced labor) for irrigation projects. According to Wittfogel, this brought forth an absolutist "managerial state." The principal economic, administrative, and political functions lay in the hands of a ruling class consisting of bureaucratic landowners and land managers, officers, and an influential priesthood. The person of the ruler enjoyed the highest secular and, in part, religious authority. His despotic regime was based on the state's bureaucracy and on the army, but it was not totalitarian. Although the ruler did demand obedience and complete submissiveness from his servants, he respected the human rights of social groups in areas outside the purview of the state.

Most political conflicts occurred within the ruling class; social conflicts and insubordination outside the ruling stratum were prevented by customary techniques of terror [see ASIAN SOCIETY, *article on* SOUTHEAST ASIA].

Totalitarian rule. Examples of totalitarian rule fall into two groups. First there are the sociopolitical systems of fascist Italy, Nazi Germany, and the semifascist dictatorships of Peron in Argentina and Franco in Spain; second, there is the communist system in its various historical versions (above all, the Soviet Union and China) and similar political structures in the developing countries.

Dictatorships of the Western fascist type arose as "crisis products" of the capitalist economic and social systems. Basically counterrevolutionary, they were characterized by an activist, militant social movement, which employed the *Führer* principle and methods of social discipline and control to mobilize and organize social and political forces, especially members of the middle classes who felt socially threatened. The Soviet communist system, on the other hand, was born of the class antagonisms of bourgeois society, with the aid of an originally democratic mass movement based on a revolutionary theory of society. Yet this movement is not itself a dictatorship, even in the sense of the concept "dictatorship of the proletariat." (This term, seldom used today, implies that all political power stems from the organized working class; but the dictatorship of the proletariat has a utopian character and does not fall within the meaning of dictatorship as defined at the outset of this article; see Lenin 1917.)

Notwithstanding resemblances and parallels in social structure, in the use of political ideology for legitimizing and maintaining the regime, and in the application of modern scientific and technological means of organizing the economy and controlling men, there are striking differences between the communist and fascist systems. Fascism and National Socialism proceeded from counterrevolutionary concepts of society. Communism, however, has a revolutionary model of social development and evolved rational, bureaucratic forms of policy making that have maintained the system through many generations and have helped to consolidate the political structure despite domestic and external perils. Some of these differences involve the historical conditions under which the movements developed and the structure and the special functions of the political ideologies and values that determine the actions of the leadership and mass behavior.

Every fully developed totalitarian rule involves not only the political structure, the position and function of the monopoly party and its organizational satellites, and the relations among the state, the social movement, and the society. The concept of totalitarianism also includes the entire social structure and all the measures taken to transform it, a centrally directed economy, as well as the political ideology and legal system developed to justify and maintain the regime. In sum, we can speak of totalitarian rule only where a centralistically oriented mass movement, led by a militant political minority in an authoritarian manner, relying on the monopoly of power, and with the aid of a dictatorially ruled state, builds an apparatus of power which bears upon all parts of the society.

This multidimensionality, and the diversity of the various historical systems making up the phenomenon of totalitarianism, makes it difficult to elaborate a politically and sociologically fruitful concept of totalitarian rule, as is shown by the existing literature, in which the concept of totalitarianism has become increasingly subject to scientific criticism. Some scholars maintain that there are no significant differences between the older dictatorships and modern mass despotisms except, say, in the art of mass domination (Hallgarten 1954; 1957, p. 176 ff.). Others deny that totalitarianism is merely a product of industrial society and point to totalitarian features that may be found, for example, in ancient Sparta and in the tyranny of Diocletian (Neumann 1957, p. 246). Several younger scholars believe that general concepts of ideal types and static, classificatory methods are of little use in the historical–empirical analysis of the various totalitarian power structures [*see* TOTALITARIANISM].

Constitutional dictatorship. Unlike the revolutionary and counterrevolutionary types of dictatorship, in which the legality of the exercise of power is dubious and in many cases represents a break with the political evolution of the state, constitutional dictatorship respects the limits fixed by the constitution. Its function is to protect or restore the traditional, legal order in crisis situations or in domestic or foreign emergencies. Such an emergency (*Staatsnotstand*) can be defined as a serious disturbance or endangering of public safety and order, which cannot be overcome in normal, constitutional ways but can only be eliminated by the use of exceptional means (Hesse 1962).

A constitutional dictatorship exists when martial law or a state of siege is proclaimed, and the executive, specifically the military commanders, can limit civil rights and liberties. A tendency toward this form of dictatorship can also be seen, however, in the so-called emergency decree legislation.

Some constitutions of democratic states (article 48 of Germany's Weimar constitution, article 16 of the French constitution of 1958, article 77 of the Italian constitution of 1947) grant full powers to the executive to take temporary measures to restore law and order in the event of an emergency [*see* DELEGATION OF POWERS].

The problem of assuring respect for the limits of constitutional dictatorship is a very difficult one and has been exhaustively debated in politics and in scholarly literature. A limited emergency dictatorship may turn into a counterrevolutionary dictatorship whenever the conditions of political power are favorable, as shown by the exploitation of article 48 of the Weimar constitution by the National Socialists. A constitutional dictatorship has no revolutionary objectives with regard to sociopolitical change, although it may fulfill counterrevolutionary functions if class conflicts or disputes between social and political elites become widespread. The restoration of constitutional conditions, which is the objective of emergency legislation, often signifies the hardening of a socioeconomic *status quo* and may encourage revolutionary forces within a country to intensify their attacks upon the existing political and social order.

The following historical instances of constitutional dictatorship are often cited. First, the classical legal dictatorship of the early Roman Republic in which one of the consuls appointed the dictator, upon the motion of the Senate, for a term of no more than six months and entrusted him with the task of defending or restoring constitutional order. He became, in effect, an extraordinary constitutional organ and remained bound by the laws. Second, the exercise of power by the medieval Italian commissioners, who were appointed by a sovereign prince in conformity with the constitutional order and were given extraordinary powers to act on his behalf. (For the first use of the term "commissionary dictatorship," see Schmitt 1921, p. 6 ff.) Third, the "educational dictatorship" of Kemal Atatürk in Turkey, in which the dictator himself established constitutional rules for his exercise of power [*see* CRISIS GOVERNMENT].

Research interests and problems

Legitimacy. The issue of the legitimacy of dictatorial systems has often been discussed in terms of the relation of the dictatorship to tradition, to law, and to the constitution [*see* LEGITIMACY]. Practically every historical dictatorship has tried to justify its existence, its methods, and its measures. In many cases where the dictatorship tried to secure legitimation by appealing to a law that it created, the attempt failed, because the leadership, the state organs, and the administration always succumbed to the impulsive element in decision making. Whenever they have been unable to appeal to tradition, to natural law, to customary or existing law, they have endeavored to legitimize the despotic exercise of power either, in an existential, Machiavellian vein, as the exalted art of building a state and directing society; or else, on a more pretentious ideological plane, as the expression of a communal order predestined by providence or by historical evolution. In so doing, they have appealed to "national interest" and "reason of state," to "the common welfare," to "the welfare of the people," to the interests and vital rights of a social class, as well as to the idea of a revolution and the laws of social development.

The charismatic element has always been a major factor in efforts to legitimize dictatorship. Dictators and their aides have time and again managed to achieve an identification of broad strata of the population with the rulers, especially whenever they have manipulated the democratic means for the expression of public opinion (popular assemblies, plebiscites, and parliamentary elections). In the process they have imposed extraordinary restrictions on the freedoms of the citizens. Civil rights are occasionally set forth in the written constitution, but in everyday life they are constantly imperiled by the regime's claim to total control of the formation of political will and the conduct of social life. The development of "islands of freedom" and the progress of "liberalization" in dictatorships are, therefore, always highly problematic.

Social structure and mobility. The problems of the interdependence of the political and social orders found in the various dictatorships are another subject of lively contemporary discussion. Researchers are studying the social and economic prerequisites of such systems and the influence that such a regime and its policies have on a country's social structure, economic system, and elite formation.

It is widely recognized that dictatorships are able to change social structure, provided they have sociopolitical ambitions and approach the solution of social and economic problems with progressive goals and programs. This applies not only to the various systems of modern mass dictatorship in which, as under Soviet rule, some social classes (workers, peasants, and the working intellectuals) have an economically and politically dominant function, while others (the petty bourgeoisie) are assigned a tributary function, and still others disappear completely (the nobility, the upper class);

it also applies to the systems of elite-dominated, authoritarian dictatorship. The very formation of a new political and economic ruling class from the leading elites, bureaucrats, and political functionaries that are needed to run the state apparatus can serve as an index of social-class formation in these systems of government. But little research has been done thus far on the specific forms of social mobility in societies that are dictatorially manipulated. The rise from the lower classes may be due to advancement within the political organization as well as to active participation in solving the economic problems of these achievement-oriented societies. Many dictatorships evolve systems of social incentives and rewards for conformist behavior, thus manipulating the social prestige of the "fellow travelers," "careerists," and "parvenus" of a political upheaval.

Political sociology is interested in ascertaining the social and political composition of the ruling class and of the larger groupings from which members of the elite are drawn; in determining how change in this composition is effected; and in discovering the causes of conflicts within the elite and how they are resolved.

The conquest of a foreign country or its political penetration—a common occurrence of the last fifty years—may place large sections of the conquered population in the role of an oppressed class. The only way to maintain such a situation is by the use of adequate military, police, and administrative instruments of power. Otherwise, the social structure and the national consciousness of the conquered country must be transformed by political–ideological infiltration in the image of the conquering society. The establishment of satellite states and political satrapies and their relationship to the respective autocratic or totalitarian central state is, therefore, an interesting problem for research. Supranational social movements and elites develop, whose revolutionary or counterrevolutionary aims try to affect foreign societies (Lenin, Stalin, and Mao Tse-tung, on the one hand; Mussolini and Hitler, on the other). Rudiments of such developments are to be found even in the imperial Roman dictatorship and in Oriental despotism.

Political ideology. The ideological components of various forms of dictatorship are also an interesting subject of study. Totalitarian regimes in industrial society are inconceivable without the force of a political ideology that moves both the masses and the elites. Even in the older forms of dictatorship the "political formula" was a rather important instrument of rule. Tyrants and mass leaders have always made use of myths, utopias, doctrines of salvation, and, especially in modern times, social theories and *Weltanschauungen* in order to establish the charisma of a leading personality, the historical mission of a ruling elite, or the necessity of a revolution. Alongside the despotic perfectionism of pure power politics can be found the cult of the leader, hero worship, and collective delusions, and also sociopolitical concepts with specific programs and claims upon the behavior of the citizens and the wielders of power.

The structure and the sociopolitical functions of ideology differ widely under various dictatorships. Comparison of the ideologies of fascism, National Socialism, and Bolshevism, clearly shows the purely instrumental nature of the fascist and National Socialist ideologies, which are very vague and largely based on irrational, poorly formulated theoretical premises. In contrast, Soviet communist ideology is nourished by the rational core of a dogmatized theory; it has been able to furnish the foundation for extensive social and economic planning and has proved able to cope with changing conditions.

Behavior and techniques of dictators. Various attempts have been made to study the psychological and social-psychological peculiarities of dictatorship (e.g., Milosz 1953; Neumann 1957, p. 270; Lange 1954). Studies of the psychopathology of the personalities of dictators evoke much interest, as do the behavior, cooperation, and conflicts of members of the inner circle and of lesser aides and functionaries of the dictatorship. The clearer the sociopolitical ambitions of a dictatorship, the more emphasis is placed on methods of manipulating social and cultural activities, the more regard is paid to the desired image of man in the educational system, and the more attention is paid to the attitudes of the individual and the masses toward superiors, organizations, and the state.

The extent to which anxieties and fears govern the behavior of men under tyrannies is in dispute. Readiness to subordinate oneself "voluntarily" and to cooperate in building up the state can often be found and examined in modern mass dictatorships, although in many cases mimicry and political "schizophrenia" are also prevalent.

Plato and Aristotle long ago described the behavior and methods of tyrants, and much of what they wrote applies to dictatorships that are more fully developed than the city-state despotisms of their day. The principal instruments employed by the tyrant are force, oppression, threats, and espionage, and, even today, the common weapons are terror, persecution, and intimidation. Yet it is often overlooked that modern mass dictatorships have also been able to achieve successes by such methods as deception, corruption, and social rewards. Massive propaganda and the whole educational system are geared to breeding a conforming man, toward whom a benevolent attitude is then displayed. Modern mass leaders demand admiration and devotion; propaganda sees to it that they obtain them. Wittfogel (1957, p. 181) refers to the "myth of a benevolent despotism." In fact, however, the motivating principle of "the carrot and the stick" prevails in many dictatorships. Terror is aimed primarily at nonconformists of all kinds, although it may also be used against the supporters of the system when factional fights break out or when there is a change of leadership.

In order to facilitate identification with the *Führer* and the prevailing system, many dictatorships also create an "adversary type" (the Jews for National Socialism, the "imperialists" for communism), to which the blames for all problems can then be shifted.

In modern dictatorships an important instrument of control is the compulsion to join state organizations. Only such affiliation guarantees social status, social recognition, and job security. Even Aristotle pointed out that a sort of "occupational therapy" is advantageous to tyranny. And today we find that individuals, organizations, and the masses are kept in constant activity in dictatorial states.

Dictatorship in new nations. In conclusion, a word should be said about the susceptibility of the developing countries to dictatorship. "Strong man" regimes are evolving in Asia and Africa, either in the form of military states or of presidential regimes. Whether these forms of authoritarian rule are primarily products of the colonial era or inevitable types of transition to constitutional systems with political parties is currently being debated. This question is complicated by the fact that countries with such different cultural, social, and political backgrounds as Burma, Indonesia, Egypt, and Ghana have all proved susceptible to dictatorship. (It has been suggested that the difficulties of analyzing such diverse sociopolitical systems may be surmounted by a comparative "developmental approach" to political systems—Almond 1965, pp. 183 ff.; Almond & Coleman 1960.) Effective democracy is only possible in countries where there is a broad, stable middle class anchored in the population, a social and political ethos, and adequate two-way communication between the leadership and the masses. In most developing areas these prerequisites did not exist. Consequently the forms of parliamentary democracy imported from the colonizing powers could hardly take root; instead they proved to be structurally alien to native cultures. Actually, in most of these countries the traditional feudal institutions were strengthened, and only a small minority of native intellectuals capable of political thought and action evolved.

According to some scholars, the belief of these intellectuals in progress, especially their strong urge to accomplish rapid, radical industrialization and to establish the welfare state at once, can be realized only by an authoritarian government (Newman 1963, p. 16). Substitution of a one-party system, supported by the military and the bureaucracy, for a multiparty system is the rule in many countries. Powerful military, monarchic, and autocratic state traditions facilitate authoritarian measures, whether under the banner of military dictatorship or of the one-party state with a charismatic leadership. The problems arising from the opposition of the old elites to the new ones, the transformation of the new elites into oligarchies, and the distance between them and the masses—all play an important role in the growth of authoritarian political systems in the developing countries. Behrendt (1965; see also Lewis 1965) warns against the notion that "developmental dictatorships" are necessary to the socioeconomic development of these countries and concludes that such a dictatorship merely signifies a postponement of the process of social self-education but can never be a substitute for it.

OTTO STAMMER

[See also AUTOCRACY; CAUDILLISMO; COMMUNISM; DEMOCRACY; FASCISM; NATIONAL SOCIALISM; TOTALITARIANISM.]

BIBLIOGRAPHY

ADORNO, THEODOR W. et al. 1950 *The Authoritarian Personality.* American Jewish Committee, Social Studies Series, No. 3. New York: Harper.

ALMOND, GABRIEL A. 1965 A Developmental Approach to Political Systems. *World Politics* 17:183–214.

ALMOND, GABRIEL A.; and COLEMAN, JAMES S. (editors) 1960 *The Politics of the Developing Areas.* Princeton Univ. Press.

ARENDT, HANNAH (1951) 1958 *The Origins of Totalitarianism.* 2d ed., enl. New York: Meridian.

BEHRENDT, RICHARD F. 1965 *Soziale Strategie für Entwicklungsländer: Entwurf einer Entwicklungssoziologie.* Frankfurt am Main (Germany): Fischer.

BRACHER, KARL D. (1955) 1964 *Die Auflösung der Weimarer Republik: Eine Studie zum Problem des Machtverfalls in der Demokratie.* 4th ed. Villingen (Germany): Ring.

BRACHER, KARL D.; SAUER, WOLFGANG; and SCHULZ, GERHARD (1960) 1962 *Die nationalsozialistische Machtergreifung: Studien zur Errichtung des totalitären Herrschaftssystems in Deutschland 1933–1934.* 2d ed. Cologne (Germany): Westdeutscher Verlag.

BRZEZINSKI, ZBIGNIEW K. 1956 *The Permanent Purge.* Cambridge, Mass.: Harvard Univ. Press.

DEUTSCH, JULIUS (1953) 1963 *Wesen und Wandlung der Diktaturen.* 2d ed., rev. & enl. Munich: Humboldt.

DRATH, MARTIN (1958) 1963 Totalitarismus in der Volksdemokratie. Introduction in Ernst Richert, *Macht ohne Mandat: Der Staatsapparat in der sowjetischen Besätzungszone Deutschlands.* 2d ed., rev. & enl. Cologne (Germany): Westdeutscher Verlag.

DUVERGER, MAURICE 1961 *De la dictature.* Paris: Julliard.

FERRERO, GUGLIELMO (1923) 1924 *Four Years of Fascism.* London: King. → First published as *Da Fiume a Roma: 1919–1923.*

FERRERO, GUGLIELMO 1942 *The Principles of Power: The Great Political Crises of History.* New York: Putnam. → First published in the same year as *Pouvoir: Les génies invisibles de la cité.*

FORSTHOFF, ERNST 1933 *Der totale Staat.* Hamburg (Germany): Hanseatische Verlagsanstalt.

FRIEDRICH, CARL J. (1937) 1950 *Constitutional Government and Democracy: Theory and Practice in Europe and America.* Rev. ed. Boston: Ginn. → First published as *Constitutional Government and Politics: Nature and Development.*

FRIEDRICH, CARL J.; and BRZEZINSKI, ZBIGNIEW K. (1956) 1965 *Totalitarian Dictatorship and Autocracy.* 2d ed., rev. Cambridge, Mass.: Harvard Univ. Press.

GROTH, ALEXANDER J. 1964 The "Isms" in Totalitarianism. *American Political Science Review* 58:888–901.

HALLGARTEN, GEORGE W. F. 1954 *Why Dictators? The Causes and Forms of Tyrannical Rule Since 600 B.C.* New York: Macmillan.

HALLGARTEN, GEORGE W. F. (1957) 1960 *Devils or Saviours: A History of Dictatorship Since 600 B.C.* London: Wolff. → First published as *Dämonen oder Retter?*

HEBERLE, RUDOLF 1951 *Social Movements: An Introduction to Political Sociology.* New York: Appleton.

HELLER, HERMANN (1929) 1931 *Europa und der Fascismus.* 2d ed. Berlin and Leipzig: De Gruyter.

HESSE, KONRAD 1962 Staatsnotstand und Staatsnotrecht. Volume 7, columns 607–613 in *Staatslexikon: Recht, Wirtschaft, Gesellschaft.* 6th ed. Freiburg (Germany): Herder.

LANGE, MAX G. 1954 *Totalitäre Erziehung: Das Erziehungssystem der Sowjet-zone Deutschlands.* Frankfurt am Main (Germany): Frankfurter Hefte.

LENIN, VLADIMIR I. (1917) 1964 The State and Revolution: The Marxist Theory of the State and the Tasks of the Proletariat in the Revolution. Volume 25, pages 381–492 in Vladimir I. Lenin, *Collected Works.* 4th ed. Moscow: Progress. → First published in Russian.

LEWIS, W. ARTHUR 1965 Beyond African Dictatorships: The Crisis of the One-party State. *Encounter* 25, no. 2:3–18.

LUDZ, PETER C. 1964 Theoretischer Bezugsrahmen. Pages 11–58 in Peter C. Ludz (editor), *Studien und Materialien zur Soziologie der DDR.* Cologne (Germany): Westdeutscher Verlag.

MILOSZ, CZESLAW (1953) 1955 *The Captive Mind.* New York: Vintage. → First published in Polish as *Zniewolony umysł.*

MONNEROT, JULES (1949) 1960 *The Sociology and Psychology of Communism.* Boston: Beacon. → First published as *Sociologie du communisme.*

MOSCA, GAETANO (1896) 1939 *The Ruling Class.* New York: McGraw-Hill. → First published as *Elementi di scienza politica.*

Neumann, Franz L. 1957 *The Democratic and the Authoritarian State: Essays in Political and Legal Theory.* Edited by Herbert Marcuse. Glencoe, Ill.: Free Press. → See especially pages 270–300 on "Anxiety and Politics" and pages 233–256 on "Notes on the Theory of Dictatorship."

Neumann, Sigmund (1942) 1965 *Permanent Revolution: Totalitarianism in the Age of International Civil War.* 2d ed. New York: Harper.

Newman, Karl J. 1963 *Die Entwicklungsdiktatur und der Verfassungsstaat.* Frankfurt am Main and Bonn: Athenäum.

Schmitt, Carl (1921) 1928 *Die Diktatur.* 2d ed. Munich and Leipzig: Duncker & Humblot.

Spencer, Henry R. 1931 Dictatorship. Volume 5, pages 133–136 in *Encyclopaedia of the Social Sciences.* New York: Macmillan.

Stammer, Otto 1955 *Demokratie und Diktatur.* Berlin: Gehlen.

Stammer, Otto 1961 Aspekte der Totalitarismusforschung. *Soziale Welt* 12:97–111.

Stammer, Otto 1965 *Politische Soziologie und Demokratieforschung: Ausgewählte Reden und Aufsätze zur Soziologie und Politik.* Berlin: Duncker & Humblot.

Talmon, Jacob L. (1952) 1965 *The Origins of Totalitarian Democracy.* 2d ed. New York: Praeger.

Wittfogel, Karl A. 1957 *Oriental Despotism: A Comparative Study of Total Power.* New Haven: Yale Univ. Press. → A paperback edition was published in 1963.

DIET

See Famine; Food; Obesity.

DIFFERENTIAL PSYCHOLOGY

See Individual differences.

DIFFERENTIATION, SOCIAL

See Population, *article on* population composition; Social differentiation; Stratification, social, *article on* the structure of stratification systems.

DIFFUSION

i. Cultural Diffusion   *Robert Heine-Geldern*
ii. The Diffusion of
     Innovations   *Torsten Hägerstrand*
iii. Interpersonal Influence   *Elihu Katz*

I
CULTURAL DIFFUSION

Diffusion means the spread of culture from one ethnic group or area to another. Various definitions have been proposed in order to distinguish between diffusion and acculturation; the difference is one of continuity and intensity of contact. Acculturation generally involves prolonged contact of whole culture complexes and may be unilateral or bilateral.

Diffusionism in ethnological theory. As early as the fifth century B.C., Herodotus noted examples of diffusion, but it was the discovery of America that stirred intellectual discussion and speculation. Had the cultures of the New World developed independently, or had they been imported from the Old World? From the sixteenth to the eighteenth century numerous authors supported the diffusionist view, but their more or less naive writings, based on totally insufficient data, did not carry conviction. The prevailing trend in European science favored a theory of natural laws, which were thought to govern human progress and to produce similar results in the various regions of the earth. These ideas were clearly formulated in the eighteenth century and culminated in the nineteenth century in the evolutionist school of anthropology. At the same time truly scientific treatises on the diffusion of culture traits began to appear. One of the first was Alexander von Humboldt's brilliant attempt to prove the Asiatic origin of the Mesoamerican calendric systems. Even the evolutionists did not deny that diffusion had played a certain role in the development of culture, although they minimized its importance. One of the most prominent, Edward Tylor, wrote several excellent papers in which he demonstrated the diffusion of various culture traits.

Diffusion studies. Around 1890 a reaction appeared in Europe and America against the logical inconsistencies of the evolutionist theory. Franz Boas in the United States, Gabriel Tarde in France, and Friedrich Ratzel in Germany stood up as its critics, all of them stressing the importance of diffusion. Scandinavian archeologists showed that the development of the Bronze Age in Europe was influenced by cultures of the Near East and the Mediterranean regions. They thus started a trend which ever since has been important in prehistoric research. Fritz Graebner (1911) wrote the first systematic treatise on the theory of diffusion, and many important studies were made tracing the diffusion of single traits, such as the plow, whole complexes of metallurgical technique, and the spread of basic cosmological ideas and corresponding religious practices. The most important studies of the processes of diffusion, however, were made by American anthropologists. It is to them, even more than to Graebner, that we owe the theoretical foundations for the appraisal of diffusion in its various aspects.

The processes of diffusion. Although whole cultures may spread as a result of the migration of their bearers, a culture is practically never adopted by other ethnic groups without considerable change and selection of traits. This applies also to diffusion on a minor scale. Whether a particular trait is accepted depends not only on its utility to the borrowers but even more on whether or not it can be integrated into the receiving culture. The borrowing of more elaborate utensils and techniques and of sophisticated ideas presupposes a complex sociocultural level on the part of the borrowing people. Nomadic hunters may turn with relative ease to some kind of primitive shifting agriculture but will hardly be inclined to prepare permanent fields with all that this implies with regard to change in mode of life. The diffusion of elements of social structure encounters greater difficulties than that of material or religious traits. Among some peoples of southeast Asia and among the Tuareg of the Sahara, matrilineal forms of society, although unorthodox from the point of view of Islamic law, survived even conversion of these people to Islam. In general, however, the conversion to one of the higher religions is invariably accompanied by the acceptance of numerous other culture traits—such as script, types of behavior, modes of dressing and housing, laws, and forms of government—and is one of the most potent factors in diffusion. Prestige, too, plays an important role. Traits have been borrowed merely for the sake of prestige, even though they are detrimental to the borrowers' hygiene or economy. The adoption of European clothing by peoples in the tropics is a case in point.

Negative selection, i.e., the rejection of certain cultural items, may be due to their incompatibility with firmly established customs, with the prevailing social structure, or with religious tenets and usages. Mere habit and the addiction to the traditional way of doing things are no less powerful sources of resistance to innovations. Frequently, however, no particular reason can be detected that could explain why one foreign trait was accepted and another not. In many instances "traits spread erratically and unpredictably" (Dixon 1928, p. 120).

The more traits a people has already borrowed from another, the easier will be the acceptance of additional traits. Traits that at first were rejected may then be adopted since they no longer conflict with those of the receiving culture, which has already been modified. Occasionally, the diffusion of even a single culture trait may have far-reaching consequences. The introduction of firearms, for instance, necessitated a change in the type of warfare, and this, in turn, affected the social structure of Europe. When the Tanala in Madagascar borrowed from their neighbors the trait of planting rice on irrigated terraces and abandoned the slash-and-burn type of shifting agriculture, a complete transformation took place, not only of their rules of land tenure, but of their social and political organization (Linton 1936, pp. 348–354).

Borrowed elements of culture usually undergo some kind of change or adaptation. We need only think of the innumerable variations, from tribe to tribe, when techniques of pottery-making, metallurgy, and weaving have been diffused. Gothic art was not the same in Germany and Italy as in France, nor was the Hindu and Buddhist art of Java identical with that of India from which it was derived. When the Greeks adopted the old Semitic alphabet, they adapted it to their own language, and new changes took place when the alphabet was transferred to the various peoples of Europe. When a myth spreads from one area to another, details may be lost and new ones may be added to or substituted for the original ones.

Stimulus diffusion. In many instances it is not the actual culture trait that is adopted by the borrowing people but merely the principle on which it is based. This process has been termed "stimulus diffusion." It must have played an important role in the spread of agriculture and animal domestication. The domestication of the reindeer by Siberian tribes, for instance, was almost certainly due to some aquaintance with the horse and cattle breeding of their southern neighbors. Members of illiterate tribes in Africa, Asia, and America who knew of the existence of the European or Arabic alphabets created new systems of writing for their respective languages. The development of Egyptian hieroglyphics probably resulted from some knowledge of the Babylonian script of the Jemdet Nasr period, even though the actual characters of each script are completely different.

Agents of diffusion. The kind of traits transferred from one people to another depends largely on the agents of diffusion—those giving and those taking. The traits will differ according to whether the agents are priests, medicine men, traders or artisans, men or women. Men's societies and rituals, weapons, methods of hunting and warfare with the concomitant religious and magical practices, such as scalping or head-hunting, can, of course, be disseminated only from men to men. Very often the relative conservatism of women has contributed considerably to cultural diffusion. Where intergroup marriage is practiced, the women hold on to their native customs and will transmit them to their children. This is bound to further the diffusion of techniques of pottery and weaving, of ornamental designs, of myths, etc., occasionally even of languages. In some instances the acceptance of new culture traits has been due to the initiative of one prestigious person.

Diffusion may be the result of deliberate actions on the part of the donors. This applies to missionaries of whatever religion and to the founders and promoters of nativistic cults and movements. Conquerors and colonial powers furthered, or even enforced, the adoption of their laws, customs, and techniques. However, even in such cases diffusion was frequently reciprocal. We need only cite the adoption of maize, tobacco, rubber, etc., by the Europeans in America or the flood of Oriental influences that reached Europe as the result of the British occupation of India. If the conquerors were relatively few in number and the culture of the conquered superior to that of the conquerors, the rate of diffusion was occasionally reversed, with the result that the conquerors were more readily assimilated by the conquered, abandoning even their own language and eventually losing their ethnic identity. This happened, for instance, to the Langobards in Italy.

The deliberate initiative of the borrowers may be no less important than that of the donors. In the mid-twentieth century Asians and Africans who study in Europe or America and take home their acquired knowledge are among the principal agents of diffusion. Similar processes have no doubt contributed to the spread of ancient civilizations, even though literary evidence of this is scarce. The visits of Romans to Greece in order to study Greek philosophy and rhetoric, and the pilgrimages of Chinese scholars to India to study the tenets and monastic rules of Buddhism, are cases in point.

Diffusion versus independent invention. Whether the occurrence of similar culture traits among different peoples is due to diffusion or to independent invention and parallel development has been a perennial subject of anthropological discussions. In the past, anthropologists who favored the argument for parallelism referred to the "psychic unity of mankind" and to those natural laws thought to produce similar effects.

Where literate civilizations are concerned, the role of diffusion can usually be determined by historical research. There are still some moot cases—such as the question whether gunpowder and printing were invented independently in Europe or as the result of stimuli derived from China—but wherever we stand on firm ground it is apparent that the independent repetition of inventions has been exceedingly rare, particularly when compared to the enormous effects of diffusion.

Where written sources are not available, the solution of problems of diffusion is frequently more difficult. Independent invention can be proved only rarely, and perhaps never with regard to immaterial culture traits or where perishable materials are concerned. We can be sure that the fine pressure-flaking of stone tools was invented independently in northwestern Australia and not derived from that of the Solutrean culture, since nothing of the kind has been found in the intermediate areas. Cases like this are exceptions. In general we can only try to demonstrate the probability of diffusion, and if this proves impossible, leave the question unanswered. The following criteria of diffusion, first formulated by Graebner (1911), are still applied, with only minor variations, by most anthropologists interested in the subject: the more complex a culture trait is, the more secondary traits it contains that are not essential to its function (*criterion of form*), and the more similar the traits (*criterion of quantity*) shared by two areas, the more likely it is that the presence of these traits is due to diffusion.

Loss of traits. In Graebner's opinion these principles were valid also in the case of discontinuous distribution of traits. Boas and others were reluctant to admit diffusion except where contiguous areas were concerned. There are, however, numerous explanations that can easily account for gaps in the distribution of related culture traits. We need not even refer to those famous and frequently cited cases—the disappearance of the bow, of pottery, and of boatbuilding on several Oceanic islands. These were isolated incidents and of little importance. Of greater significance is the fact that any major culture change, whether due to internal development or to diffusion, is not only bound to add new culture traits but to result in the elimination of others. We need only think of all the appliances, customs, and types of behavior that within a lifetime are replaced by others and become obsolete, but which still survive in marginal areas. This process of elimination has been occurring since the Paleolithic. Above all, it was the spread of the higher civilizations, and of Christianity, Buddhism, and Islam, that ripped apart formerly uninterrupted areas of archaic culture traits.

Head-hunting may serve as an illustration. In the Old World during the nineteenth century head-hunting was largely restricted to southeast Asia and Oceania and to some tribes in Africa. Here was a case that clearly seemed to warrant the assumption of independent parallel development. The picture changes, however, when we consult the archeological record, or ancient literature. We shall find that head-hunting was practiced in vast regions of Europe, from the Iberian Peninsula to southern Russia. There are many indications of its having been practiced by tribes in central Asia, and if we extend our research further back in time, we shall find traces of head-hunting in predynastic Egypt and in the ancient Near East. Obviously, the two regions in which head-hunting was found in modern times, even though thousands of miles apart, were mere remnants of an area stretching from the Atlantic Ocean eastward to the Pacific where head-hunting was practiced.

Closing the gaps in distribution. Occasionally, archeology helps to bridge gaps between widely separated areas. For example, a special type of harp, with a boat-shaped body, is found in west and central Africa, in Burma, and in Siberia. This puzzling distribution would seem to defy any attempt to explain it as the result of diffusion had not archeological discoveries shown that the same type existed in ancient Babylonia, Egypt, and India.

In considering the possibility of diffusion the time factor should never be forgotten. Such a custom as that of perforating the lower lip and inserting a plug, found among some tribes in Africa and the Americas, may very well have spread from continent to continent and then disappeared from most of its former area with the passage of time. On the other hand, gaps in the distribution of traits may occasionally be due to rapid migrations. When, in the sixteenth century, a group of the Tupi-Guarani covered the thousands of miles from the Atlantic coast of Brazil to the Andes in ten years and, in the eighteenth century, a Kalmuk horde took nine months for its migration from the Volga to Mongolia, they cannot have left many traces on their way. Such rapid migrations have frequently been observed in historic times. There is no reason why this should not have occurred in prehistoric periods as well. Finally, we must not forget that wherever boatbuilding and navigation were sufficiently developed arts, peoples separated by the sea were in a certain respect neighbors. Given the necessary means of transportation, the same applies to peoples separated by deserts.

Complex traits. In summary, we may conclude that the geographical distance between two similar culture traits, be it ever so great, does not in itself suffice to disprove diffusion, and that in such instances, too, we must rely primarily on the criterion of form. Very simple inventions may, of course, have been made more than once. However, inventions of weaving, of the various metallurgical processes, or of intricate calendrical systems were not single events but the results of whole series of innovations and improvements. The probability of such a series having been repeated in more or less the same order and with similar results is practically nil.

Some reservations must be made with regard to social phenomena, such as sib and kinship systems, marriage rules, totemism, chieftainship, priesthood, etc. There can be no doubt that in these respects, too, diffusion played an important role, but we do not yet know to what extent social trends and psychological factors may occasionally have produced similar, but unconnected, results. The subject has not yet been studied sufficiently on a world-wide basis. Therefore caution in asserting or denying the diffusion of specific social traits is advisable.

Selected problems. The following examples may serve to illustrate some kinds of major problems concerning diffusion that are of anthropological interest.

Megaliths. The widespread distribution of megalithic monuments in the Old World stimulated many fantastic and unsound speculations. In recent times, however, the relevant problems of diffusion have been carefully studied, particularly with regard to areas in Africa, Asia, and Oceania where such monuments are still raised and where their religious and social basis survives. It now appears certain that the custom of erecting megaliths belongs to a socioreligious complex characterized by emphasis on an ancestor cult and genealogy, by wealth and fertility rites, animal sacrifice, and rank-conferring rituals that are thought to ensure for the souls of the performers or recipients a better lot in the hereafter. The original center from which this complex spread has not yet been determined. It lay probably in the Mediterranean area, possibly in Palestine and the surrounding regions, where megalithic monuments have been dated to the fourth millennium B.C. In some instances the megalithic complex spread as a result of migrations, in others by slow diffusion from tribe to tribe. In studying its various aspects, we are dealing with a prehistoric religious and social movement, which over thousands of years spread throughout an area reaching from the Atlantic coast of Europe to Oceania.

Trans-Pacific diffusion. More than any other problem of diffusion, the question of trans-Pacific relations between the Old World and the New agitates anthropologists. It is crucial to all of anthropological thought. The proof of parallel development could lie in determining whether or not similar textile and metallurgical techniques, calendrical systems, art styles, etc., originated independently in Asia and America. The inescapable conclusion would be that what happened this one time could have taken place in other instances as well. The results of everything written since Ratzel and Boas in order to disprove independent parallel development would be jeopardized. We cannot base our theories on two contradictory sets of principles.

In recent years the problem has been studied systematically by comparing whole archeological complexes, circumscribed by area and date, both in the New World and in the Old. It is now known that art styles appeared in America not only in the same sequence as comparable ones in Asia, but even at approximately the same dates, and that other correspondences, such as those in calendrical and cosmological systems or in metallurgy, fit into this chronological pattern. This cannot be accidental. There were no movements of whole populations from Asia to America, nor colonial settlements like those of the Europeans after Columbus. Arguments in favor of the independent development of ancient American civilizations that were based on the absence of Old World crops and various aspects of technology are thus less compelling. Chinese records make it clear that at the periods in question ocean-going vessels were available both in eastern and southern Asia, vessels that could not have encountered greater difficulties in crossing the North Pacific than the clumsy Manila galleons of the sixteenth and seventeenth centuries. In summary, we are justified in stating that as matters stand America offers no exception to the rule according to which close similarities between complex cultural phenomena are the results of diffusion.

The historic role of diffusion. Diffusion has always had a catalytic function in sociocultural development. "The comparatively rapid growth of human culture as a whole has been due to the ability of all societies to borrow elements from other cultures and to incorporate them into their own" (Linton 1936, p. 324). Moreover, the necessity of integrating newly acquired elements into one's cultural heritage creates new problems, which demand new solutions and thereby engender new ideas. It was the opportunity for relatively rapid interchange of inventions and ideas between a number of local cultures that made possible the birth of the oldest civilizations in the Near East. It was stimuli emanating from these oldest civilizations which started the chain reaction that eventually resulted in the emergence of one civilization after the other through the whole of world history (Heine-Geldern 1956). Obviously, the cultures of marginal peoples least exposed to diffusion, such as the Australians, Tasmanians, and Fuegians, have remained the most primitive known in modern times.

Robert Heine-Geldern

[*Directly related are the entries* Ethnology; History, *article on* culture history. *Other relevant material may be found in the biographies of* Graebner; Schmidt.]

BIBLIOGRAPHY

Boas, Franz (1887–1936) 1949 *Race, Language and Culture.* New York: Macmillan.

Dixon, Roland B. 1928 *The Building of Cultures.* New York: Scribner.

Ekholm, Gordon F. 1964 Transpacific Contacts. Pages 489–510 in Jesse D. Jennings and Edward Norbeck (editors), *Prehistoric Man in the New World.* Univ. of Chicago Press.

Goldenweiser, Alexander 1937 *Anthropology: An Introduction to Primitive Culture.* New York: Crofts.

Graebner, Fritz 1911 *Methode der Ethnologie.* Heidelberg (Germany): Carl Winter.

Heine-Geldern, Robert 1956 The Origin of Ancient Civilizations and Toynbee's Theories. *Diogenes* 13: 81–99.

Herskovits, Melville J. 1948 *Man and His Works: The Science of Cultural Anthropology.* New York: Knopf.

Hodgen, Margaret T. 1952 *Change and History: A Study of the Dated Distributions of Technological Innovations in England.* Viking Fund Publications in Anthropology, No. 18. New York: Wenner-Gren Foundation for Anthropological Research.

Koppers, Wilhelm 1955 Diffusion: Transmission and Acceptance. Pages 169–181 in William L. Thomas, Jr. (editor), *Yearbook of Anthropology.* New York: Wenner-Gren Foundation for Anthropological Research.

Kroeber, A. L. (1923) 1948 *Anthropology: Race, Language, Culture, Psychology, Pre-history.* New rev. ed. New York: Harcourt.

Linton, Ralph 1936 *The Study of Man: An Introduction.* New York: Appleton.

Lowie, Robert H. (1920) 1947 *Primitive Society.* Rev. ed. New York: Liveright.

Lowie, Robert H. (1934) 1940 *An Introduction to Cultural Anthropology.* Rev. ed. New York: Farrar & Rinehart.

Lowie, Robert H. 1937 *The History of Ethnological Theory.* New York: Farrar & Rinehart.

Sapir, Edward A. (1910–1944) 1949 *Selected Writings in Language, Culture, and Personality.* Edited by David G. Mandelbaum. Berkeley: Univ. of California Press.

Smith, Marian W. (editor) 1953 Asia and North America: Transpacific Contacts. *American Antiquity* 18, no. 3, part 2. → Published also as Memoir No. 9 of the Society for American Archaeology.

Wallis, Wilson D. 1929 Magnitude of Distribution, Centrifugal Spread, and Centripetal Elaboration of Culture Traits. *American Anthropologist* New Series 31:755–771.

Wissler, Clark 1923 *Man and Culture.* New York: Crowell.

II
THE DIFFUSION OF INNOVATIONS

Any society can be looked upon as forming an ordered system in which all individuals and all pieces of material equipment, including land, are component parts, linked together in a multitude of ways. Such a system may quite possibly remain in a stable state for a long period of time, in the sense that economic, social, and cultural activities are carried on over days, seasons, and years according to a fixed rhythmical pattern with an invariable structure and a stereotyped distribution of roles. Changes take place only as quantitative adjustments owing to changes in size of population.

If in a subregion of the system a hitherto unknown element is introduced, say, for example, a new technical device, a new way of allotting social roles, or a new cultural manifestation, this event constitutes a perturbation that under certain conditions may be transmitted out into the surrounding regions and propagate itself until eventually the whole system has become permeated and at the same time to some degree transformed. A permeation of this kind, either partial or total, is known as a diffusion of innovation.

In some parts of the world and in certain prehistoric or historic periods, more sweeping instances of diffusion of innovation obviously have been rather unusual occurrences. On the other hand, in present-day Western societies, diffusion of innovation is in the regular course of things, and the whole social system is oriented toward constant change.

Diffusion of innovation as a social phenomenon has been noted by scholars and other observers since antiquity, and a large amount of information on specific cases is available. More is, however, known of the results of diffusional processes than of the processes in action, for the obvious reason that processes of this kind are extremely hard to observe. Since the time of Friedrich Ratzel the traditional way of studying diffusion, from the large-scale point of view, has been to compare the spatial distribution of cultural traits by the aid of maps. As a result of research work in this tradition, a set of national atlases of folk culture has been produced in Europe, each containing a wealth of suggestive information on preindustrial cultural relationships.

In recent decades there has been a growing interest in the study of modern instances of diffusion, and scholars have increasingly taken advantage of the fuller supply of quantitative data and the possibilities of immediate observation of ongoing processes. No doubt such studies can lead to results that also throw light on how diffusion took place earlier in history. One approach toward the diffusion process focuses on the characteristics of the acting individual and his reactions to his immediate environment. Another approach is more concerned with the social system as a whole. In the tradition of cultural history and cultural geography various macroconcepts come into the foreground, such as growth curves, centers of innovation and centers of spread, channels of diffusion, barriers to diffusion, cultural boundaries, and regional differences in receptivity. The diffusion of innovations will be discussed in terms of these organizing concepts.

Growth patterns

Diffusion of innovation, as seen in its system-wide context, undoubtedly tends to show a series of recurring traits. The most easily observed pattern, when statistical information is at hand, is *the curve of cumulative growth* (Pemberton 1936; Sorokin 1937–1941). If the number of individual adopters of innovations—or in some cases such more relevant units as villages, cities, and firms—are measured over time, an S-shaped curve normally appears. This curve shows a slow take-off stage of varying length, an intermediate stage of more rapid development, and a final stage of declining growth, which seems to approach a ceiling asymptotically. Different innovations run through this process with very different speed, and various degrees of symmetry and irregularity are noted. In particular, the initial stage may vary considerably in length.

The three stages of the growth curve can normally be shown to have recurring counterparts in the way the spatial distribution of adopters develops (Hägerstrand 1965a). In the initial stage, adopters are usually concentrated in a small cluster or a small set of clusters. In the intermediate stage, expansion likewise takes place in a pattern that indicates that a new adoption is more likely to occur in the vicinity of existing adoptions than farther away; sometimes a jump of unexpected length comes about, and with it a new center of dispersal may begin to function (Kniffen 1951a). The "neighborhood effect" creates an outward movement along a more or less sharply defined frontier (as ripples on the water), while at the same time the general density of adoption behind the frontier is continuously growing. A saturation stage may be reached in the central area of dispersal while the frontier is still advancing. Statistically, therefore, the total growth curve can be divided into a set of subcurves, showing time lags between them and also different rates of growth (Griliches 1957; Jones 1963).

Urban–rural comparison. The neighborhood effect, together with the total pattern of spatial growth, shows itself on many different scales. It is perhaps most clearly seen when the spreading trait concerns the rural population (Hägerstrand 1953; Griliches 1960). In such cases the diffusion tends to proceed in small steps, almost from farm to farm and from village to village. However, the extent of the neighborhood effect seems to be rather different in the United States in comparison with Europe, even for rural areas.

If the innovation under observation belongs to the modern urban scene, the process has to be viewed on a nationwide or even international scale before the same fundamental patterns of change are evident. The most important cities are usually strongly reflected in the initial stages of urban or general innovations; this means that the national capitals are usually early adopters, followed by metropolitan centers next in rank. In the following stages the neighborhood effect seems to become gradually dominating over hierarchical rank (Bowers 1937; Pemberton 1938). It must be stressed that there are still very few thoroughly analyzed cases of urban innovations; the picture just given refers to ongoing investigations and may have to be revised as information is accumulated.

Centers of innovation and diffusion

Not much is known either about the factors at work behind the appearance and persistence of *centers of innovation* and *centers of spread*. It seems to hold true that certain areas or points may function as such centers over very long periods of time, emitting wave after wave in a manner that is repetitious in the main lines even if details differ. As far as the "true" centers of innovation are concerned, it might be assumed that the cumulative principle of cultural development always is more easily at work in a few restricted areas than randomly throughout a population (Sauer 1952; Edmonson 1961). It might also be hypothesized that innovative individuals are continuously attracted to areas that seem to be able to make use of their talents. Paris as a center of fashion over a long period of time is an obvious example.

The cumulative principle of development. An innovation most often consists of a new combination of some pre-existing elements, and so it cannot come into being until these elements are at hand either as ideas or as hardware. The cumulative principle is most easily appreciated in the realm of material culture, but undoubtedly it also exists in immaterial culture. The gradual development of scientific theory is a case in point, but so also is the growing richness through time in modes of expression in the visual arts and music. Because of this principle, it did not help very much in practice that Leonardo da Vinci invented an aircraft or Charles Babbage a computer; the actual realization of these things as working innovations had to await the appearance of basic component parts before production and spread were possible. However, this combination of more basic elements into more advanced ones certainly does not take place everywhere with equal ease, and the incentive to make such combinations is also affected by spatial variables.

Choice of solution. Although a certain spectrum of simpler parts must exist and be known in order to allow a new step forward, it is by no means self-evident that more advanced tasks can be undertaken only in one way. Many solutions may be possible, and a selection may be made just randomly or because of certain conditions in a steering environment. As technological diversity increases, so also do the opportunities for choice between alternative technologies or between different permutations of technological elements.

The existence of a wide range of alternative technologies asserts itself in the various cultures, within which approximately the same basic tasks have been solved differently and with varying degrees of success. It is probably not correct to think of these alternative solutions as conscious selections from a known full set of possibilities, but rather as an unsystematic trial-and-error use of elements at hand. As seen in this perspective, a center of innovation is, then, a place or area where an unusual amount of technological elements or "building blocks"—for the time and area—are available, as well as a felt need for new combinations. It would, however, be an exaggeration to claim that very much is known about these problems.

Channels of spread

Centers of spread represent a somewhat different concept. These may be original centers of innovation, but more often they are only points where already existing innovations coming from the outside first begin to penetrate a new region. In urban or general innovational movements, the larger cities tend to take on this function. Innovation in agriculture or industry shows various different systems of centers. In general, centers of spread remain stable over long periods of time, fulfilling a normative function for their surroundings.

Centers of spread are parts of the channels of spread. The nature of these channels is relatively well known, both through historical studies and modern quantitative analysis. Even today, when the sheer quantity of information pouring forth from the mass media may seem to make everything known equally well everywhere without much delay, the fact is that personal communication between pairs of individuals and direct observation are still the basic instruments for the diffusion of innovation. On second thought this is not so surprising, if one realizes that new things and ideas often look complicated to the novice and that therefore people have to be able to ask questions, take things in their hands, try them, and get a feeling for them in order to fully understand and adopt.

The exchange of information between individuals is a never-ending process; it is perhaps the most important ingredient in molding a society (or one might even say the whole human race) into one system of connected links. Everyone functions in that system as a sender, a receiver, and an amplifier. The influence that reaches an individual and the influence he can exert are both a function of his particular position in the network, a position that he is born into and subsequently can extend or change only to a certain degree. Most of the time the influences that travel through the links only reinforce the stable set of cultural traits that prevails in a particular subregion of the system; but occasionally—and today more and more often —an innovational flow will pass through and, if adopted, change the patterns of traits.

Spatial range of contacts. For most individuals, it seems that the links of personal communication are heavily restricted by distance. Few actual investigations of the spatial range of regular social contacts have been carried through. However, the few that exist indicate that among farming populations in Europe and Asia the probabilities of contact decrease at a rate steeper than the square of the distance (Hägerstrand 1953; 1965a). A minority of the population may be assumed to have wider contacts, but most of these are confined to the national area; very few have links with the international field. The reason for this is not so much the difficulty of movement as the existence of linguistic barriers. As the ability to understand and use different languages varies from country to country, so inevitably the flows of influences tend to show corresponding asymmetries.

The fact that in general the links of communication tend to be a decreasing function of distance accounts for the neighborhood effect noted in the diffusion of innovation. It also means that in any local area a growing pressure on nonadopters of an innovation builds up very quickly as the number of adopters grows. This is a process that can be simulated quantitatively and to a certain extent predicted, if the parameters of the links of social communication can be estimated (Hägerstrand 1965b).

Changes in the network. The observation that the spread of innovations from certain centers tends to follow repeatedly the same spatial course seems to indicate that the communication network has a very stable configuration over time. The frequency of contacts between areas and places remains very much the same through time, even though the individuals involved change. The structure of this network, which now can be seen only vaguely, deserves close study as to morphology and ways of change. That some change takes place is obvious. In the more developed parts of the world, the distances over which regular contacts occur is gradually increasing as the means of transportation improve. This change makes the neighborhood effect more diffuse today, in the pure spatial sense, as compared to the pattern observed in earlier times, when an innovation sometimes moved along a sharper front.

The observation that the speed of diffusion of innovation is accelerating should not be explained only in terms of spatially increasing links of communication. The growing diversification in the occupational composition of populations also has to be taken into account as an explanatory variable (Edmonson 1961). Many innovations, although important for the whole society in which they become introduced, nevertheless are of immediate concern only for a fraction of the total population. This situation may mean a very fast diffusion over a wide geographical area among those professionally engaged in the application of the innovation. At the same time the spread, in terms of the numbers of adopters, need not take place differently from a corresponding development in a larger population.

Cultural boundaries. The notion of a rather stable network of communication links between individuals, and especially between populations in places and areas, makes it possible to explain the existence of cultural boundaries in at least two meaningful ways. The first and classic case is the cultural boundary that follows a barrier in the communication system, caused, for example, by physiography or gaps in the continuity of settlement. The second and more interesting case is the following. Influences that step by step move out from two different centers of spread located at a distance from each other are bound to meet along a line or zone in between. If the elements are mutually exclusive, as in religious affiliation or in the use of a certain dialect, then the flows will arrest each other. A cultural boundary will appear, remain in a fixed position, and become reinforced as long as the two competing centers retain the same position and strength (Weiss 1952).

Receptivity factors

If influences channeled through the links of social communication were the only determinants of the course of diffusion and the distribution of culture elements, then the cultural map would not be as complicated as it actually is. We also have to consider a quite different group of factors, which explain the differentials in resistance and receptivity toward innovational influences.

An aggregate of complicated circumstances causes keenness, hesitation, delay, or refusal to adopt innovations suggested by signals through the communication network. Part of the picture is, of course, the personal characteristics of individuals. Another part is the necessity for various time-consuming adjustments and preparations before an adoption can be fitted into pre-existing procedures, habits, and value systems. Also, the cost involved in adoption of an innovation may slow down adoption, or the revenue expected from adoption may cause the opposite reaction (Griliches 1957; 1960).

Again, not much is known in any systematic way. One can observe, however, how resistance factors work when a spreading trait suddenly stops along a religious borderline or when the spread of a new crop dies off where soil is less suitable. A similar killing effect on the spread of new types of production has also resulted from the existence of a limitation on the market. When the market cannot absorb more, it becomes gradually more difficult for new producers to enter the business and take up the innovation; several instances of outward growth that came to a halt because of marketing difficulties can be cited for Europe. Cases in point that have been analyzed in some detail are the agglomeration of nursery gardens in Holstein, Germany (Brüggemann 1953) and of glass-making factories in Smaland, Sweden (Nordström 1962).

If a diffusional process fails to break through some area of resistance, this fact may sometimes create a shadow effect over a wider region, because the nonreceptive area does not send out a stimulus for further adoption in the way it could have if the innovation had moved straight through.

Reducing resistance to change. Diffusion of innovation is an all-important part of the economic growth in all countries but particularly so in those that need development. Thus a significant question is to find out how diffusion of innovation can be encouraged. Two methods of intervention present themselves; one refers to the pattern of communication and the other to the distribution of resistance to change.

It is probably not possible to influence the structure of communication in a society through outside action, and therefore the channels of spread must be taken as given. But knowledge about the pre-existing matrix of links would be useful, because it would make it possible to choose points of introduction of desirable innovations at the most efficient centers of spread. One method for locating such centers is to try to follow the course of some earlier innovations.

The receptivity factors are perhaps more open to moderately successful manipulation, at least as far as innovations in the economic field are concerned. It is well known that economic rewards can help to break down resistance to change. The notion of a stable and given network of social communication suggests that a response to subsidies or similar devices should be most powerful where the knowledge of the innovation is most widespread, that is, just outside the areas where it has already been adopted.

TORSTEN HÄGERSTRAND

[See also CULTURE, *article on* CULTURE CHANGE; EVOLUTION, *article on* SOCIAL EVOLUTION; INNOVATION; *and the biography of* RATZEL.]

BIBLIOGRAPHY

BARNETT, HOMER G. 1953 *Innovation: The Basis of Cultural Change.* New York: McGraw-Hill.

BOWERS, RAYMOND V. 1937 The Direction of Intra-societal Diffusion. *American Sociological Review* 2:826–836.

BRÜGGEMANN, GÜNTER 1953 *Die holsteinische Baumschulenlandschaft.* Schriften des Geographischen Instituts der Universität Kiel, Vol. 14, Part 4. Kiel (Germany): Hirt.

EDMONSON, MUNRO S. 1961 Neolithic Diffusion Rates. *Current Anthropology* 2:71–102.

GEIGER, PAUL; and WEISS, RICHARD 1950–1963 *Atlas der schweizerischen Volkskunde.* 2 vols. Basel: Schweizerische Gesellschaft für Volkskunde.

GINI, CORRADO 1949 Aree e centri culturali. *Genus* 6/8: 1–103.

GRILICHES, ZVI 1957 Hybrid Corn: An Exploration in the Economics of Technological Change. *Econometrica* 25:501–522.

GRILICHES, ZVI 1960 Hybrid Corn and the Economics of Innovation. *Science* New Series 132:275–280.

HÄGERSTRAND, TORSTEN 1953 *Innovationsførloppet ur korologisk synpunkt.* Lund (Sweden): Gleerupska Universitetsbokhandeln.

HÄGERSTRAND, TORSTEN 1965a Quantitative Techniques for Analysis of the Spread of Information and Technology. Pages 244–280 in C. Arnold Anderson and Mary J. Bowman (editors), *Education and Economic Development.* Chicago: Aldine.

HÄGERSTRAND, TORSTEN 1965b A Monte Carlo Approach to Diffusion. *Archives européennes de sociologie* 6: 43–67.

JONES, GWYN E. 1963 The Diffusion of Agricultural Innovations. *Journal of Agricultural Economics* 15: 387–409. → Contains four pages of discussion.

KNIFFEN, FRED B. 1951a The American Covered Bridge. *Geographical Review* 41:114–123.

KNIFFEN, FRED B. 1951b The American Agricultural Fair: Time and Place. Association of American Geographers, *Annals* 41:42–57.

KNIFFEN, FRED B. 1965 Folk Housing: Key to Diffusion. Association of American Geographers, *Annals* 55:549–577.

McVOY, E. C. 1940 Patterns of Diffusion in the United States. *American Sociological Review* 5:219–227.

NORDSTRÖM, OLOF 1962 *Svensk glasindustri, 1550–1960: Lokaliserings- och arbetskraftsproblem.* Meddelanden från Lunds Universitets Geografiska Institution, Avhandlingar 41. Lund (Sweden): Gleerup.

PEMBERTON, H. EARL 1936 The Curve of Culture Diffusion Rate. *American Sociological Review* 1:547–556.

PEMBERTON, H. EARL 1938 The Spatial Order of Culture Diffusion. *Sociology and Social Research* 22:246–251.

ROGERS, EVERETT M. 1962 *Diffusion of Innovations.* New York: Free Press.

SAUER, CARL O. 1952 *Agricultural Origins and Dispersals.* New York: American Geographical Society.

SOROKIN, PITIRIM A. (1937–1941) 1962 *Social and Cultural Dynamics.* 4 vols. Englewood Cliffs, N.J.: Bedminster Press. → Volume 1: *Fluctuation of Forms of Art.* Volume 2: *Fluctuation of Systems of Truth, Ethics, and Law.* Volume 3: *Fluctuation of Social Relationships, War, and Revolution.* Volume 4: *Basic Problems, Principles, and Methods.*

SVENSSON, SIGFRID 1942 *Bygd och yttervärld.* Nordiska Museets Handlingar, No. 15. Stockholm: Fritzes.

WEISS, RICHARD 1952 Kulturgrenzen und ihre Bestimmung durch volkskundliche Karten. *Studium Generale* 5:363–373.

III

INTERPERSONAL INFLUENCE

Interpersonal influence is a term used by sociologists to refer to the role of intimate, interpersonal relations in the communication of information, influence, and innovation. Students of interpersonal influence have concerned themselves primarily with describing the ways in which networks of interpersonal communication intercept messages that originate in the mass media or elsewhere and the consequent effect on the formation of public opinion, the diffusion of innovation, and the like.

Some effort has been made to compare the workings of oral communication systems in traditional societies with the flow of interpersonal influence in modern society. These investigations have emphasized, relative to modern society, the formal situations in which influence is transmitted; the elite status, often based on ascription, which gives communicators their authority; the multiple spheres over which the same communicators exert influence; and, correlatively, the hierarchical and asymmetrical flow of such influence (Lerner 1958; Eisenstadt 1955). It follows that the flow of innovation is not very rapid in such societies and that acceptors of change are often deviant or marginal members, although the successful conversion of a formal leader is often sufficient to accomplish the conversion of an entire group (Barnett 1953, chapter 14). The rate of change is also limited by intergroup relations, since acceptance of an innovation across group boundaries is dependent on the character of social relations between the groups and on more mundane things, such as distance and physical barriers. The success of such professional advocates of change as traders, missionaries, colonial administrators, and, more recently, agents of technical assistance appears to be strongly determined by their personal relations with the target group, by their ability to understand and harness existing communications channels in an acceptable way, and by the compatibility of their message with extant values and vested interests. Alternatively, some professional agents of change have succeeded only by breaking apart the traditional structure or capturing and caring for groups of deviant souls. Altogether, though, the role of informal communication has probably been underemphasized in the study of traditional societies (Gluckman 1963).

The rise of egalitarian structures of interpersonal influence in modern societies has interested students of public opinion. Tarde (1901) went so far as to argue that conversation itself is essentially a modern phenomenon, and he described the way in which the intellectual salons of his day were able to effect changes in the art, politics, and general culture of French society. Speier (1950) has shown that the middle-class coffeehouses of seventeenth-century England were similarly influential. Contemporary equivalents of these institutions will readily suggest themselves; but the communication processes that they embody have not been much studied by sociologists [*see* CREATIVITY, *article on* SOCIAL ASPECTS].

Interpersonal influence and mass communication. Indeed, interpersonal influence seemed irrelevant at first to students of the media of mass communication. At the time empirical research on the effects of radio was begun, in the 1930s, it was widely thought that the mass media would exert a powerful and direct influence on thought and practice, the more so because society was conceived as a mass of atomized individuals alienated both from traditional institutions, such as church and guild, and from intimate contact with other people. Yet, empirical research has revealed that, at least in a democratic society, the mass media are far less potent than had been thought and, in themselves, are quite unable to effect radical changes of opinions, attitudes, and actions on subjects that "matter" (Klapper 1960). At the same time, one of the major discoveries of research on mass communications (just as it is one of the major discoveries of research on mass production) is the enduring and powerful influence of interpersonal relations, even in "mass society." However, the role of interpersonal relations in transmitting (or retarding) the flow of influence and innovation is not the same now as it was in the past. While there are some kinds of messages that apparently travel with startling speed through interpersonal networks alone (Opie & Opie 1960), the central problem of communication and diffusion in modern society has to do with the nature of the linkages between networks of interpersonal relations, on the one hand, and the media of mass communication, on the other.

The two-step flow of communication. The discovery that "people" play a part in the mass communications process is, in a sense, a by-product of a study of the decisions made by voters during the U.S. presidential election campaign of 1940 (Lazarsfeld, Berelson, & Gaudet 1944). Employing the panel method of repeated interviews with the same people, the authors found that, despite the barrage of mass communications, there were remarkably few voters who had changed their minds during the course of the campaign. Those who *did* change their vote intentions, however, reported that other people, rather than the mass media, had influenced them.

An attempt was then made to locate people who had been influential on others. Study of these "opinion leaders" revealed that they had few personal or social traits that distinguished them from others. This suggested that such influence goes on in the course of everyday contacts among like-minded people who share similar characteristics.

The influentials were different, however, in their greater exposure to the mass media. A "two-step flow of communication" was therefore hypothesized; the media were held to reach widely dispersed opinion leaders, who then passed on what they had learned to those for whom they were influential.

This hypothesis inspired a series of studies of the influence of different channels of communication, including interpersonal influence, on the purchase of consumer goods, the communication of political ideas, the adoption of a new drug by physicians, and the like. Taken together, these studies suggested that conversation with other people is generally more influential than the mass media in decisions to accept some new idea or practice; that people who influence others are typically close associates; that influentials "specialize," for example, a woman who influences another in the decision to try a new food product will probably not be influential in the field of fashion; and that both partners to an influence transaction have to have a minimum level of interest in the subject before any influence is exchanged, but that the influential person is probably somewhat more interested. It also appeared that influentials are more exposed to "outside" sources, generally, but particularly to those sources—mass media, or particular institutions, or other people—that have direct bearing on their spheres of influence; that, despite this greater exposure, it is unusual even for an influential to report that one of the media of mass communication has been the major source of influence on his own decision; and that the function of interpersonal relations is not only to transmit information but to "legitimate" decisions (or to veto them), as well as to provide the kind of social support necessary for taking innovative risks (Katz 1957).

Respecification of the two-step flow hypothesis. Thus the studies mentioned above contributed to the specification of the two-step flow hypothesis by, on the one hand, exposing it as overly simple, but, on the other hand, confirming the validity of approaching the flow of influence and innovation via the interaction of mass media and interpersonal communication. As a direct result, two other things were also accomplished. First, there was effected a kind of convergence, or, at least, a growing mutual interest, among various traditions of study of the diffusion and acceptance of innovation that previously had not recognized any kinship. In particular, in departments of sociology and, to a certain extent, in schools of journalism, students of mass communication discovered, to everybody's surprise, that they shared a set of problems with rural sociologists studying the diffusion and acceptance of new farm practices, with anthropologists studying the spread of culture and technology, and with folklorists, researchers in education, archeologists, geographers, and others (Katz, Levin, & Hamilton 1963). Second, this series of studies gradually led to the realization that the design of research on the diffusion of innovation needed revision.

The design of diffusion research

The 1940 voting study had departed from the traditional design of mass communications research in that it did not seek to locate the effect of a given message in a given population but, instead, sought to "reconstruct," with the help of the respondent, the sources of information and influence that had gone into the making of a decision. It was this research procedure that made possible the discovery that interpersonal influence had a substantial part in the process of decision making. As the role of interpersonal influence became clearer, methods were developed for locating and studying influentials (Katz & Lazarsfeld 1955). And, gradually, the focus of research shifted from a concern with interpersonal influence as simply a channel of communication bearing on individual decisions, to a conception of interpersonal relations as networks of communication through which influence and innovation spread through society.

Diffusion, acceptance, and influence. With this conception in mind, a study was carried out of the diffusion of a new drug among physicians. This study employed the methods of sociometry to map the potential channels of interpersonal communication; in this way, it was possible to explore the extent to which the channels were actually utilized in the transmission of an innovation over time and to locate those points at which they were linked to "outside" sources of influence (Coleman, Katz, & Menzel 1957). Note that this concern with the process of "diffusion" (as distinct from a concern with the effects of mass communications or with the interlocking roles of mass media and interpersonal communication in the making of individual decisions) led also to the choice of a specific item for study (a new drug) and to a method for dating the acceptance of the item by each adopter [*see* SCIENCE, *article on* SCIENTIFIC COMMUNICATION].

The components of the process called diffusion thus came into better focus. Diffusion could then be defined as the acceptance of some specific item, over time, by adopting units—individuals, groups, communities—that are linked both to external channels of communication and to each other by means of both a structure of social relations and a system of values, or culture. Rural sociologists studying the diffusion and acceptance of new farm practices arrived at much the same conceptions (Lionberger 1960), and it is noteworthy that the design of a study of the diffusion of hybrid seed corn (Ryan & Gross 1943) parallels, in a number of important respects, the just described, much later study.

This definition of the diffusion process makes it possible to point out some of the methodological problems in designing research on the role of interpersonal influence in diffusion and in discussing some of its findings. It is evident, first of all, that one must specify the *kind* of item one has selected for study. While the original formulation of the two-step flow hypothesis referred only vaguely to the flow of ideas, it is altogether clear, by now, that items of information must be distinguished from items that require changes of attitude (influence) or action (innovation). Various proposals have been made for classifying innovations in terms of such concepts as their communicability (how easily can their working be described), their pervasiveness (how many of the adopters' roles are implicated), the amount of risk involved, and the like. The familiar distinction between "material" and "nonmaterial" items may be redefined in these terms (Menzel 1960). The important point, in the present context, is that different kinds of items are transmitted over different kinds of channels.

Second, the concept of "acceptance" must be given operational definition. Distinctions have been made between such concepts as "external conformity" and "internalized acceptance," or between "compartmentalized acceptance" and "full fusion with previous values." There is a noteworthy convergence here between students of acculturation and social psychologists concerned with change of opinions and attitudes (Spicer 1954; Kelman 1958). A related emphasis is to be found in recent writings in the field of rural sociology, where the process of acceptance is divided into stages, beginning with the stage of "awareness" of the innovation, and continuing through "interest," "evaluation," "trial," and finally "acceptance" (Lionberger 1960; Rogers 1962). While there is debate over the names and the number of stages, whether the stages are sequential in time and prerequisite to each other (thus constituting degrees, or levels, of acceptance), or whether they are simply different dimensions of decision making, which may be ordered differently or even concurrently (Mason 1964), it is now well established that the several media are differentially appropriate to different stages.

After characterizing the item selected for study, and giving an operational definition to what constitutes its acceptance, there remains the task of determining whether or not influence has taken place, and, if so, by what means. Most diffusion studies have relied on the respondent's recall, aided by a detailed interview, of how (and perhaps when) he first heard of the item and what other sources he consulted prior to adopting it. In an attempt to obtain more valid data, other studies have preferred variations on this basic method. Thus, many studies have attempted to infer causal relationships from observed correlations between a respondent's (usually self-reported) communications behavior and his innovative behavior. A typical finding is that farmers who have more frequent contact with the extension agent adopt new practices earlier (see, for instance, Emery & Oeser 1958). Another major set of studies is based on tracing the flow of "planted" messages, rather than relying on more nearly natural events (Dodd 1958).

Particularly problematic is the methodology of taking account of interpersonal influence within the design of the sample survey. In small communities, such as those of physicians or farmers, complete enumeration is possible; and sociometric methods can be readily adapted. To trace the spread of some new fashion in a metropolis, on the other hand, networks of interacting individuals must somehow be sampled. One way to do this is to select the usual kind of representative sample and then to build up a social "molecule" around each respondent.

Some functions of interpersonal influence

As for the functions, or the impact, of interpersonal communication, the first thing that must be said is that it is *not* a major source for the diffusion of noteworthy information. The function of the mass media is to provide a direct link between the public and the makers of news, the creators of fashion, or the producers of new products; interpersonal communication cannot compete with the mass media in this respect. The two-step flow hypothesis was understood as implying that opinion leaders relay information to others who are not exposed to the media, and, as a result, several studies were undertaken to prove that the vast majority of the American public learns about major news events directly from the mass media (Deutschmann & Danielson 1960). Interestingly, when an event is of such magnitude that early hearers run to tell others what they have heard, interpersonal channels do serve as a major source of information; the assassination of President Kennedy was such an event, and it is likely that upward of 50

per cent of the population first heard the news from other people (Greenberg 1964). Interpersonal communication may also play an informational role when an event is of importance to a small group of people, or where the mass media are under strict official control (Bauer & Gleicher 1953), or where the mass media are not yet fully accessible. Indeed, it appears that the two-step flow hypothesis, as applied to the diffusion of information, best fits developing areas, where some of those who are exposed to the mass media pass on what they have learned to "less active sections of the population," who are otherwise unexposed and who do not relay the message further (Abu-Lughod 1963).

What is true for information about news events is also true for first information about technical innovations. Rural sociologists and others have found that the channel that makes for awareness of an innovation is typically a formal one—generally one of the mass media, or an institutionalized source such as a dealer or salesman, whose job it is to spread news of the innovation as quickly as possible to as many people as possible. But extremely few people adopt an innovation on the basis of awareness alone. At the stages of interest and evaluation, more personal sources, both formal and informal, take over; and the impersonal media become quite unimportant. The mass media "inform" decisions; interpersonal contacts "support" and "legitimate" them.

Effectiveness of interpersonal influence. Many writers have speculated about the reasons for the greater effectiveness of interpersonal influence. Interpersonal influence, it has been pointed out, is two-way communication; the audience can talk back and convince itself. It is flexible, in the sense that the communication can be adapted to the recipient's particular situation. It is more trustworthy, because it is assumed to be motivated by the recipient's interest rather than the personal or professional interest of the influential; one rarely gets advice *not* to do something from a professional agent of change, whereas friends and neighbors frequently give such advice. Interpersonal influence is typically embedded in casual conversation and is often a by-product of such conversations (which are gratifying in themselves), compared with the more "purposive" communications of formal sources of influence. Interpersonal influence is generally "local" and thus is more likely to be both instrumentally and normatively appropriate, under local community conditions; and, what is more, a local influential can be held directly accountable for his advice. By the same token, a person seeking to influence another can provide immediate reward or punishment for acceptance or the lack of it, whereas other communication media can rarely provide immediate reward or punishment.

Some of these attributes also characterize more formal and purposive interpersonal communicators, such as agricultural extension agents, salesmen, or community health workers. Or, to put the matter another way, formal sources of influence (particularly when these are also personal) may be perceived by some people as sufficiently trustworthy, sufficiently accessible, sufficiently normative (although these norms may be at odds with those of the local community), or sufficiently gratifying in themselves to motivate the acceptance of influence. This would seem to be the case for early adopters of technical innovation, in particular, but also for marginal members of a community who embrace the agent of change as a welcome companion. For most people, however, the word of a trusted friend or a respected colleague is a prerequisite to action.

Interpersonal influence and social change. It is incorrect, however, to infer from the role of interpersonal influence in the acceptance of social and technical change, whether in the field of diffusion or, say, in a field like group dynamics (Lewin 1947), that interpersonal influence is a channel that functions primarily in the service of change. Indeed, rural studies have shown that, under certain conditions, the more farmers one talks to the later one is likely to accept an innovation; and the same thing is true if one uses interpersonal channels to learn about an innovation for the first time (Wilkening, Tully, & Presser 1962; Copp, Sill, & Brown 1958). Studies of political communication have shown that while the mass media may motivate someone to change his political intentions, it is conversation that *prevents* the change (Deutschmann 1962). In fact, the mass media may be said to be most effective when interpersonal communication is inoperative for some reason, as when a topic is not sufficiently interesting or important to motivate discussion, when one finds oneself among others whom one prefers not to hear, when a topic is taboo, or when a totalitarian regime suppresses personal contacts (Klapper 1960). Otherwise, it may safely be said that the tendency of interpersonal influence is a conservative one. Since a person who is motivated by the mass media on a given subject is also more likely to discuss it with others, and since these others typically share his prior sentiments, interpersonal communication probably reduces the pace of change. Only when a communication or a proposed innovation is deemed compatible with group norms, particularly if the group

has an over-all norm of "progressiveness" or "openness to change," or when one's consultant has already been won over, does interpersonal influence reinforce the message of change. In other words, whether interpersonal communication will result in a change of attitude or behavior depends partly on whom one talks with. But it should be borne in mind that the influential members of a group are also bound by group norms; while influentials in progressive groups have a higher rate of innovation, influentials in conservative groups lead in resisting change (Marsh & Coleman 1954).

The flow of interpersonal influence

In discussions of the flow of interpersonal influence, the central figure appears to be the natural leader or the opinion leader, in other words, the individuals to whom others look for advice. It is evident, from many studies, that such people exist; and while sociometric techniques are probably the most appropriate means for locating them, there is also some reason to believe in the validity of a self-designating technique whereby respondents are asked (in effect) whether they have recently influenced another person in some matter, or whether anyone has come to them for advice. Experience has shown that it is rare for more than 30 per cent of a population to answer such questions in the affirmative.

Characteristics of influentials. Whether influence is accepted from an influential who is precisely like the seeker, or from one who is different in some way, apparently depends on a number of factors. In modern societies, at any rate, influentials are more similar to those whom they influence and more specialized in the areas over which they are influential; influentiality is also less likely to be synonymous with the holding of formal office. The early studies of decision making in the realms of marketing, fashion, politics, and the like emphasized the fact that influentials were hardly distinguishable from those whom they influenced, at least as far as attributes of social status were concerned. Studies in the field of rural sociology have emphasized that farmers who are actively seeking information reach out beyond their own neighborhood and status levels to consult other farmers who are more competent than they, even though their access to the farmers they consider "best" may be limited by status disparities and clique boundaries. This behavior is characteristic of "progressive" communities, and particularly communities of professionals. Where the need for information and advice is less keenly felt, the source is likely to be found much closer to home (Blanckenburg 1964).

Competence and accessibility are not the only attributes of influentials; strategic location, with respect to some relevant outside source, is another, as is the case with drivers of buses and trucks who bring news of the outside world to outlying villages in underdeveloped areas, or even up-to-the-minute market news in modern agricultural settings. This, of course, is simply a version of the two-step flow of communication that in more sophisticated guise takes the form of propositions such as the one that finds rates of diffusion in different communities related to the extent to which farmers in each community talk about farming with respected others who have more extensive contacts with the communications media than themselves (Coughenour 1964). In other words, communities in which interpersonal and mass media networks are more closely integrated are characterized by a more rapid rate of diffusion. In such communities, interpersonal networks are organized hierarchically in terms of competence and range of outside connections, although probably less so in terms of social class. The diffusion of a new fashion, to take a different example, probably proceeds through even more homogeneous channels, although this does not preclude the possibility that the chains of interpersonal contact link up, at key points, with those of a higher social class. The fact that most individuals follow the lead of their closest associates does not necessarily contradict the hypothesis (Tarde 1890) that fashion "trickles down" through society.

Chains of communication. It is important to emphasize that influentials and influences are not usually very different from each other, nor do they constitute isolated dyads. Instead, they are better conceived as part of a long chain of interpersonal connections that embraces large segments of a community, or even a nation. In fact, it is very likely that the concepts of "opinion leader" and "influential" have been overstressed—the more so because it is almost impossible to single them out as a distinguishable target audience. The more basic stress should be placed on intimate interpersonal relationships and their function as channels of communication and as anchorage points for group norms.

For instance, given an undifferentiated population, communicating freely and continually with one another, it is possible to specify mathematically the properties of the growth curve that would describe the flow of innovation. Deviations from the expected curve may result from differentiation, and thus from the restricted access of certain people to each other; or they may reflect external

sources of influence (such as the mass media) impinging on the network at more than one point. Such mathematical models have long been of interest to diffusion researchers (Tarde 1890; Chapin 1928; Dodd 1958; Coleman 1964; Hägerstrand 1965). It has even been suggested that the neolithic era must have been characterized by this kind of homogeneous population and, consequently, that there was an essentially uninterrupted, world-wide spread of innovations moving at a constant rate (Edmonson 1961).

Differential activation of communication networks. It should also be noted that a social structure of interacting individuals typically includes many different networks of communication that are differentially activated by different topics. For example, the drug study referred to earlier found that the network of professional relations among physicians was particularly active early in the history of the new drug, whereas the network of friendship relations among physicians began to transmit information and influence only after the drug was better established (Coleman, Katz, & Menzel 1957). An attempt to replicate the same study in a large city suggested that only the professional network, but not the friendship network, was active; this implies that the size of a community may affect the degree of overlap and specialization, as well as the different functions, of different networks of interpersonal relations. A parallel example may be found in the fact that different social classes employ different kinds of networks for transmitting similar communication content; this is the case with lay networks of referral and advice giving in the seeking of medical help (Freidson 1961). By the same token, the culture of a community defines the differential appropriateness of different interpersonal channels for the different sorts of communication; in a traditional society, for example, channels reserved for sacred communications are violated by the transmission of secular communications (Eisenstadt 1955).

Creation of new networks. Sometimes people go outside their interpersonal networks to send or receive influence. One way of looking at revolutionary change, for example, as compared with changes in fashion or technology, is to examine the extent to which new networks are created for the transmission of influence. Each successive fashion tends to travel through the same networks, simply succeeding the fashion that came before. Revolutionary change, on the other hand, may often be characterized as both a disruption of the traditional networks in which individuals have been embedded and as the creation of new channels of communication. Another occasion on which individuals may go beyond their traditional networks of communication is during disasters or other types of major catastrophe. The death of President Kennedy, for example, found people telling the news to total strangers on the street—and discussing it with them (Greenberg 1964; Greenberg & Parker 1965). It is a good illustration of the latent functions of interpersonal communication to think of how much more than mere information was being conveyed in these conversations.

ELIHU KATZ

[*See also* COMMUNICATION, MASS; DISASTERS; MASS SOCIETY; SOCIOMETRY.]

BIBLIOGRAPHY

ABU-LUGHOD, IBRAHIM 1963 The Mass Media and Egyptian Village Life. *Social Forces* 42:97–104.

BARNETT, HOMER G. 1953 *Innovation: The Basis of Cultural Change.* New York: McGraw-Hill.

BAUER, RAYMOND A.; and GLEICHER, DAVID B. 1953 Word of Mouth Communication in the Soviet Union. *Public Opinion Quarterly* 17:297–310.

BLANCKENBURG, P. VON 1964 [A Book Review of] Ban, A. W. van den, *Boer en landbouwvoorlichting* (1963). *Sociologia ruralis* 4:83–84.

CHAPIN, FRANCIS S. 1928 *Cultural Change.* New York: Appleton.

COLEMAN, JAMES S. 1964 *An Introduction to Mathematical Sociology.* New York: Free Press.

COLEMAN, JAMES S.; KATZ, ELIHU; and MENZEL, HERBERT 1957 The Diffusion of an Innovation Among Physicians. *Sociometry* 20:253–270.

COPP, JAMES H.; SILL, MAURICE L.; and BROWN, EMORY J. 1958 The Function of Information Sources in the Farm Practice Adoption Process. *Rural Sociology* 23: 146–157.

COUGHENOUR, CHARLES M. 1964 The Rate of Technological Diffusion Among Locality Groups. *American Journal of Sociology* 69:325–339.

DEFLEUR, MELVIN; and LARSEN, OTTO N. 1958 *The Flow of Information: An Experiment in Mass Communication.* New York: Harper.

DEUTSCHMANN, PAUL J. 1962 Viewing, Conversation, and Voting Intentions. Pages 232–252 in Sidney Kraus (editor), *The Great Debates: Background, Perspective, Effects.* Bloomington: Univ. of Indiana Press.

DEUTSCHMANN, PAUL J.; and DANIELSON, WAYNE A. 1960 Diffusion of Knowledge of the Major News Story. *Journalism Quarterly* 37:345–355.

DODD, STUART C. 1958 Formulas for Spreading Opinions. *Public Opinion Quarterly* 22:537–554.

EDMONSON, MUNRO S. 1961 Neolithic Diffusion Rates. *Current Anthropology* 2:71–102.

EISENSTADT, S. N. 1955 Communication Systems and Social Structure: An Exploratory Comparative Study. *Public Opinion Quarterly* 19:153–167.

EMERY, FREDERICK E.; and OESER, O. A. 1958 *Information, Decision and Action: A Study of the Psychological Determinants of Changes in Farming Techniques.* Carlton (Australia): Melbourne Univ. Press.

FREIDSON, ELIOT 1961 *Patients' Views of Medical Practice: A Study of Subscribers to a Prepaid Medical Plan in the Bronx.* Monograph No. 6. New York: Russell Sage Foundation.

GLUCKMAN, MAX 1963 Gossip and Scandal. *Current Anthropology* 4:307–316.

GREENBERG, BRADLEY S. 1964 Diffusion of News of the Kennedy Assassination. *Public Opinion Quarterly* 28: 225–232.

GREENBERG, BRADLEY S.; and PARKER, E. B. (editors) 1965 *The Kennedy Assassination and the American Public: Social Communication in Crisis.* Stanford (Calif.) Univ. Press.

HÄGERSTRAND, TORSTEN 1965 Quantitative Techniques for Analysis of the Spread of Information and Technology. Pages 244–280 in C. Arnold Anderson and Mary J. Bowman (editors), *Education and Economic Development.* Chicago: Aldine.

KATZ, ELIHU 1957 The Two-step Flow of Communication: An Up-to-date Report on an Hypothesis. *Public Opinion Quarterly* 21:61–78.

KATZ, ELIHU; and LAZARSFELD, PAUL F. 1955 *Personal Influence: The Part Played by People in the Flow of Mass Communications.* Glencoe, Ill.: Free Press. → A paperback edition was published in 1964.

KATZ, ELIHU; LEVIN, MARTIN L.; and HAMILTON, HERBERT 1963 Traditions of Research on the Diffusion of Innovation. *American Sociological Review* 28:237–252.

KELMAN, HERBERT C. 1958 Compliance, Identification, and Internalization: Three Processes of Attitude Change. *Journal of Conflict Resolution* 2:51–60.

KLAPPER, JOSEPH T. 1960 *The Effects of Mass Communication.* Glencoe, Ill.: Free Press.

LAZARSFELD, PAUL F.; BERELSON, BERNARD; and GAUDET, HAZEL (1944) 1960 *The People's Choice: How the Voter Makes Up His Mind in a Presidential Campaign.* 2d ed. New York: Columbia Univ. Press.

LERNER, DANIEL 1958 *The Passing of Traditional Society: Modernizing the Middle East.* Glencoe, Ill.: Free Press.

LEWIN, KURT (1947) 1958 Group Decision and Social Change. Pages 197–211 in Society for the Psychological Study of Social Issues, *Readings in Social Psychology.* 3d ed. New York: Holt.

LIONBERGER, HERBERT F. 1960 *Adoption of New Ideas and Practices.* Ames: Iowa State Univ. Press.

MARSH, C. PAUL; and COLEMAN, A. LEE 1954 Farmers' Practice-adoption Rates in Relation to Adoption Rates of "Leaders." *Rural Sociology* 19:180–181.

MASON, ROBERT G. 1964 The Use of Information Sources in the Process of Adoption. *Rural Sociology* 29:40–52.

MENZEL, HERBERT 1960 Innovation, Integration, and Marginality: A Survey of Physicians. *American Sociological Review* 25:704–713.

OPIE, IONA; and OPIE, PETER 1960 *The Lore and Language of School Children.* Oxford: Clarendon.

ROGERS, EVERETT M. 1962 *Diffusion of Innovations.* New York: Free Press.

RYAN, BRYCE; and GROSS, NEAL C. 1943 The Diffusion of Hybrid Seed Corn in Two Iowa Communities. *Rural Sociology* 8:15–24.

SPEIER, HANS 1950 Historical Development of Public Opinion. *American Journal of Sociology* 55:376–388.

SPICER, EDWARD H. 1954 Spanish–Indian Acculturation in the Southwest. *American Anthropologist* New Series 56:663–678.

TARDE, GABRIEL (1890) 1903 *The Laws of Imitation.* New York: Holt. → Translated from the second French edition, 1895.

TARDE, GABRIEL 1901 *L'opinion et la foule*. Paris: Alcan.
→ See especially Chapter 2.
WILKENING, EUGENE A.; TULLY, JOAN; and PRESSER, HARTLEY 1962 Communication and Acceptance of Recommended Farm Practices Among Dairy Farmers of Northern Victoria. *Rural Sociology* 27:116–197.

DILTHEY, WILHELM

Wilhelm Dilthey (1833–1911), German philosopher, historian, literary critic, and biographer, was professor of philosophy at Basel in 1867, at Kiel from 1868 to 1870, at Breslau from 1871 to 1881, and at Berlin, where he succeeded Hermann Lotze in 1882. He had studied philosophy at Heidelberg under Kuno Fischer and at Berlin under Friedrich Trendelenburg; while at Berlin he had also been deeply influenced by such leading historians as August Böckh, Jacob Grimm, and, above all, Leopold von Ranke. His chief interest as a philosopher was in the logic and methodology of the historical and social studies (*Geisteswissenschaften*). His conclusions are set forth in the *Einleitung in die Geisteswissenschaften* (see *Gesammelte Schriften*, vol. 1) and in the unfinished "Entwürfe zur Kritik der historischen Vernunft" (*ibid.*, vol. 7, pp. 189–291).

The "Geisteswissenschaften"

Dilthey agreed with Kant and the positivists in their rejection of metaphysics but differed from the positivists in that he did not accept natural science as a model that the *Geisteswissenschaften* should follow. Natural science can do no more than explain (*erklären*) observed events by relating them to other events in accordance with natural laws. These laws tell us nothing of the inner nature of the things and processes that we study. But with human beings there is a sense in which it is possible to go behind observable actions to something internal: we may understand (*verstehen*) their actions in terms of their thoughts, feelings, and desires. We can know not merely what a man does but the experiences (*Erlebnisse*), the thoughts, memories, value judgments, and purposes that have led him to do it.

Knowledge in this field is not, as in natural science, merely phenomenal and external. We have direct insight into the transitions whereby perceptions lead to thoughts, these to feelings, and these again to desires and acts of will. Such connections constitute the "structure" of the individual personality, and the understanding of them is also the key to a wider understanding of historical processes. Because men can communicate with one another, one man's experiences can arouse thoughts and feelings and lead to actions on the part of other men as well as himself, and thus the individual "structural" pattern ramifies and becomes the life pattern of social groups, of nations and civilizations. The historical life of mankind is a continual process of interactions of this kind, and to understand a particular event or action or utterance, we must see it in this kind of context.

Dilthey's *Geisteswissenschaften* are a somewhat heterogeneous group of subjects. They include an experimental and generalizing science (psychology), a study of individual persons and societies in the concrete particularity of their lives and actions (history, biography, autobiography), and normative and valuational studies (jurisprudence, moral theory, political theory, literary criticism, etc.). What all these have in common, according to Dilthey, is that they are all aspects of the study of human life and experience and that that study is not complete unless they are all brought in. Taken together, the *Geisteswissenschaften* show that men do live under conditions that can to some extent be formulated in general laws, whether of the individual psyche or of social groupings. Men are intelligible to us as individuals and interesting to us precisely because of their individuality and uniqueness. And all human experience and activity are shot through with choices, preferences, value judgments. Because human life as known to us is in itself more complex and many-sided than the phenomena of nature, the *Geisteswissenschaften* must also be a more various and many-sided body of disciplines, and no one method or principle can govern them all. They are all, however, dependent on our ability to understand the "structural" pattern of experience and thereby to see human behavior from within.

In the *Einleitung in die Geisteswissenschaften* Dilthey also argued that psychology has a fundamental place among these studies. He was not thinking of the experimental science of psychology as we know it today but of a descriptive and comparative kind of psychology that would culminate in a theory of personality types. Such a theory would be a useful tool in all the *Geisteswissenschaften*. While the *Einleitung* endorsed psychology, it was critical of sociology, which Dilthey considered to be a pseudo science. He was thinking of sociology in the grand manner, as conceived by Auguste Comte and Herbert Spencer, a study embracing all forms of cultural as well as social life and comparable in the vastness of its range to a philosophy of history such as Hegel's. Such a grand synthesis, Dilthey held, would not give unity to the

Geisteswissenschaften; they would achieve this unity only if world history were written in a way that made use of all the *detailed* insights that the *Geisteswissenschaften* can offer. Years later, in some notes made with a view to a revision of the *Einleitung*, Dilthey made it clear that he had no objection to sociology if it meant merely a comparative study of different forms of social groupings and stratifications.

Historiography

In the "Entwürfe zur Kritik der historischen Vernunft" and elsewhere in his later writings, Dilthey laid less emphasis on the role of psychology and turned his attention to a philosophical analysis of the process by which one mind becomes aware of what goes on in another. The process may be summed up in the words experience, expression, understanding (*Erlebnis, Ausdruck, Verstehen*). We understand an expression by re-experiencing (*nacherleben*) in our own consciousness the experience from which the expression arose. This re-experiencing is, of course, not a perfect reproduction of the original experience; it is schematic, telescoped, incomplete, fallible. Dilthey distinguished different types of expression and different degrees of accuracy and confidence with which they can be interpreted. His particular approach to the problem of understanding led him to an interest in hermeneutics, that is, in the possibility of laying down principles and working rules for the guidance of those whose work is the interpretation of written texts. He showed how a theory of hermeneutics arose in patristic times out of the needs of scriptural exegesis, how it was developed under the influence of Reformation controversies and the beginnings of Biblical criticism, and how it was generalized and made into a philosophical discipline in the nineteenth century by Friedrich Schleiermacher. And taking the art of understanding expressions as the underlying factor common to all the *Geisteswissenschaften*, he showed that there is an easy transition from personal experience to autobiography, thence to biographical and historical writings, thence to the more abstract and generalizing studies and the sectional disciplines, and finally to the grand synthesis in world history.

Dilthey's doctrine of understanding as re-experiencing is open to question. Some may feel that it is too intense, too intimate and personal, and that he expects of the historian and social scientist too much of the poet's or novelist's gift. But by raising the question in the way he did, Dilthey touched off a lively and fruitful discussion, both among philosophers interested in the theory of knowledge and among those historians and social scientists who are interested in the aims and methods of their disciplines but are not satisfied with a statistical and behavioristic approach.

Dilthey's interest in historical method was shared by Wilhelm Windelband and Heinrich Rickert; but these, while better equipped than Dilthey in the logical techniques of philosophy, had no comparable experience of the actual work of historical writing. Dilthey was himself a biographer (*Das Leben Schleiermachers* 1870; "Die Jugendgeschichte Hegels," *Gesammelte Schriften*, vol. 4, pp. 1–187); a historian of ideas ("Auffassung und Analyse des Menschen im 15. und 16. Jahrhundert," *ibid.*, vol. 2, pp. 1–89); and a literary historian and critic (*Das Erlebnis und die Dichtung . . .* 1905).

Relativism

Dilthey was one of the proponents of the doctrine known as historicism, which insists that all human customs, institutions, and ideas are conditioned by the historical circumstances in which they arise and flourish and that although every society and every individual thinker professes to be in possession of objective truth, an outside observer can always see how this "truth" is conditioned by social and historical factors. Applied uncritically in the theory of knowledge, this view can lead to a historical relativism, that is, to the doctrine that all "truth" is relative to time and place and that objective knowledge is impossible. Dilthey's view can also lead to a psychological relativism. He believed that a man's *Weltanschauung*, the complex of his beliefs and judgments concerning ultimate questions, is determined as much by his psychological structure and basic attitudes as by valid reasoning from sound premises. He developed a typology of *Weltanschauungen*; the basic types are naturalism, the idealism of freedom, and objective idealism. Naturalism means that one is impressed chiefly by the impersonal order of nature; idealism of freedom, that one gives priority to the unique status of man as a free agent; and objective idealism, that one conceives of the universe as an organic whole. Schools of art, and religious and philosophical systems, can be classified by their conformity to and expression of one of the three main types of attitude or, as may happen, of any combination of these.

Views such as these seem to verge on an ultimate skepticism. Controversy has arisen both about the merits of Dilthey's argument in itself and about the degree to which he personally drew skeptical conclusions. He was in fact no skeptic and did not believe that his principles must lead to skepticism; he believed rather that in those spheres where empirical methods can be applied, which include some sections of the *Geisteswissenschaften* as well as the natural sciences, real discoveries and real progress can be made, and there is objective knowledge. It is in the realm of value judgments and life attitudes that he felt that relativity is inescapable, but also that proper acceptance of it can lead to an enrichment of life rather than to frustration (Hodges 1952, pp. 310–314). Karl Jaspers, for instance, who in his early work was influenced by Dilthey's typology of *Weltanschauungen* (see 1931), has moved on to a form of existentialist philosophy, and this is another possible outcome of Dilthey's teaching.

H. A. HODGES

[*See also* HISTORY, *article on* THE PHILOSOPHY OF HISTORY; KNOWLEDGE, SOCIOLOGY OF; *and the biographies of* MANNHEIM; MEINECKE; ORTEGA Y GASSET.]

WORKS BY DILTHEY

(1870) 1922 *Das Leben Schleiermachers.* 2d ed. Berlin and Leipzig: Gruyter.
1894 Ideen über eine beschreibende und zergliedernde Psychologie. Akademie der Wissenschaften, Berlin, *Sitzungsberichte* 2:1309–1407.
(1905) 1957 *Das Erlebnis und die Dichtung: Lessing, Goethe, Novalis, Hölderlin.* Stuttgart (Germany): Teubner.
(1905–1910) 1961 *Meaning in History: W. Dilthey's Thoughts on History and Society.* Edited with an introduction by H. P. Rickman. London: Allen & Unwin. → A partial translation of Wilhelm Dilthey's, *Der Aufbau der geschichtlichen Welt in den Geisteswissenschaften.* A paperback edition was published by Harper in 1961 as *Pattern and Meaning in History.*
(1907) 1954 *The Essence of Philosophy.* Chapel Hill: Univ. of North Carolina Press. → First published as *Das Wesen der Philosophie.*
(1931) 1957 *Philosophy of Existence: Introduction to Weltanschauungslehre.* New York: Bookman Associates. → A translation of "Die Typen der Weltanschauung und ihre Ausbildung in dem metaphysischen System," pages 75–118 in Dilthey's *Weltanschauungslehre.*
Gesammelte Schriften. 12 vols. Leipzig: Teubner, 1914–1958. → Volume 1: *Einleitung in die Geisteswissenschaften,* (1883) 1923. Volume 2: *Weltanschauung und Analyse des Menschen seit Renaissance und Reformation,* (1889–1904) 1921. Volume 3: *Studien zur Geschichte des deutschen Geistes,* 1927. Volume 4: *Die Jugendgeschichte Hegels und andere Abhandlungen zur Geschichte des deutschen Idealismus,* (1864–1906) 1921. Volume 5–6: *Die geistige Welt,* (1867–1907) 1924. Volume 7: *Der Aufbau der geschichtlichen Welt in den Geisteswissenschaften,* (1905–1910) 1927. Volume 8: *Weltanschauungslehre,* 1931. Volume 9: *Pädagogik,* 1934. Volume 10: *System der Ethik,* 1958. Volume 11: *Von Aufgang des geschichtlichen Bewusstseins,* 1936. Volume 12: *Zur preussischen Geschichte,* (1861–1872) 1936. Volume 12 contains a comprehensive bibliography of Dilthey's writings.

SUPPLEMENTARY BIBLIOGRAPHY

GARDINER, PATRICK (editor) 1959 *Theories of History: Readings From Classical and Contemporary Sources.* Glencoe, Ill.: Free Press. → Contains a previously untranslated extract from Dilthey's writings.
HODGES, H. A. 1944 *Wilhelm Dilthey: An Introduction.* London: Trubner.
HODGES, H. A. 1952 *The Philosophy of Wilhelm Dilthey.* London: Routledge.
KLUBACK, WILLIAM 1956 *Wilhelm Dilthey's Philosophy of History.* New York: Columbia Univ. Press.

DIPLOMACY

There are at least two senses in which the term "diplomacy" is used: the first and more narrowly defined refers to the process by which governments, acting through official agents, communicate with one another; the second, of broader scope, refers to modes or techniques of foreign policy affecting the international system (Nicolson [1939] 1964, pp. 13–14).

In the past it was believed that the narrower notion of diplomacy embraced all official contacts and connections of a peaceful nature between state units (Satow [1917] 1962, p. 1). It is now clear that it does not do so: governments have means of communicating officially that could scarcely be called diplomatic. In 1962, during the Cuban missile crisis, official messages were broadcast to save time and the protagonists negotiated in a number of other unorthodox ways (Schlesinger 1965). More generally, public statements of policy, speeches by influential leaders, and revelations to the press have served as means of direct contact with foreign states. In its restricted definition, then, diplomacy refers specifically to the use of accredited officials for intergovernmental communication, not simply to communications links between states.

Origin and development of diplomacy. Employment of diplomatic envoys is as ancient as polities themselves (C. D. Burns 1931), but not until the fifteenth century were the first permanent legations established. The Italian states inaugurated the ambassadorial system, which rapidly spread to the rest of Europe. Until the beginning of the nineteenth century two classes of diplomatic representatives were utilized: ambassadors, who were obliged to vie for precedence in the capital to which they were assigned; and semiofficial agents, who, though less involved in court functions, did not have access to fully authoritative sources of information. At the Congress of Vienna in 1815, four categories of representatives were established: (1) ambassadors, papal legates, and nuncios; (2) envoys extraordinary and ministers plenipotentiary; (3) ministers resident; and (4) chargés d'affaires. Precedence was to be based on the rank of the appointment conferred by the home government and on seniority of service in the particular capital. Thus were enunciated the basic diplomatic conventions as we know them today (Nicolson [1939] 1964, pp. 28, 31–33).

Until the twentieth century, members of the diplomatic corps were recruited from the wealthy classes (C. D. Burns 1931). Those selected were generally amateurs, whose rank and social position entitled them to consideration for diplomatic appointment. Examinations, when required, placed inordinate emphasis upon linguistic competence, and a degree of financial independence was a prerequisite. By World War II an appreciable democratization and professionalization of foreign services had occurred (Ilchman 1961). Competitive substantive examinations requiring high educational attainment had been instituted in most major countries (Nicolson [1939] 1964, pp. 208–218). Independent means was no longer a requirement for entry into the diplomatic corps, and women became eligible for appointment.

Impact of technology on diplomacy.   With the technological revolution of the twentieth century, the role of the diplomatist has changed appreciably. In the 1920s diplomatic officials were still given a certain latitude by their controlling agencies on questions of secondary importance; only in a crisis did they act merely as messengers (C. D. Burns 1931). Today the reporting function has become virtually all-encompassing; negotiations are largely conducted by foreign offices, and diplomatic representatives are utilized only for transmission of requests and responses. The daily traffic of United States messages alone totals more than 400,000 words (U.S. Congress . . . [1964] 1965, p. 584). Rewards in the American Foreign Service are distributed partly on the basis of the variety and quality of cables sent to Washington. We are now far removed from Jefferson's complaint in 1791 to William Carmichael, American chargé in Spain, that he had received only one dispatch from him in 2½ years (*ibid.*, p. 584). This is not to say that ambassadors exercising their independent judgment do not occasionally make determinations of very great importance (Rusk [1964] 1965, p. 582; Merchant 1964, pp. 123–124). At the time of the

Dominican crisis in 1965, Ambassador Bennett made assessments of crucial significance concerning the need for United States military intervention; these were heeded and acted upon in Washington. Once information and interpretation have been provided, however, decisions are taken in national capitals. Even on fairly minor matters the local ambassador possesses little power (Kennan [1964] 1965, pp. 589–590).

Diplomatic proliferation.   The decline in decision-making authority of the individual diplomatist is partly correlated with the vast expansion of diplomatic missions since World War II. In 1930 the London diplomatic corps totalled 56 embassies and legations, the *largest* including only 17 staff members (C. D. Burns 1931). In 1964 London had 96 foreign missions, with an *average* of 13.6 diplomats each. The United States housed diplomatic establishments from 107 countries. If each of the almost three thousand American diplomats abroad in 1964 had been allotted independent negotiating tasks, the foreign relations of the United States would soon have been in disorder (Brams 1966, pp. 39, 42). Even communications with overseas missions posed great difficulties. Of the 1,300 incoming daily cables, the secretary of state saw only twenty to thirty; of the one thousand outgoing cables, he read about six. Increasingly, lesser officials and desk officers have become responsible for the information on which policy determinations are made (Rusk [1964] 1965, p. 578).

Another important feature of present-day diplomacy is its multilateral character. In 1963 the United States belonged to intergovernmental organizations having a gross membership of 1,141; 103 states were represented in this total. France held an even larger number of common memberships (Brams 1966, p. 49). In the same year the United States attended over 400 international conferences and participated in more than 10,000 votes (Merchant 1964, p. 128). As a consequence, much of the organization of foreign ministries has been determined by the need to prepare for and develop positions in multilateral bodies (Beloff 1961). The result has probably been to influence in some measure the content of foreign policy (E. Haas 1958; 1964).

Changing diplomatic techniques.   The second and more broadly defined meaning of "diplomacy" applies to modes or techniques of foreign policy affecting the international system. In this extended sense diplomatic techniques have undergone a considerable metamorphosis since the eighteenth century (Rosecrance 1963). The extensive use of propaganda, subversion on a wide scale, and the manipulation of national economic instruments for foreign policy purposes have greatly enlarged the range of multilateral dealings on the world scene. Now even cultural and educational exchange may be seen as a tool in the cold war (Coombs 1964). To be sure, a plentiful armory of diplomatic weapons has been the stock in trade of state action since the time of Machiavelli. The most vigorous use of these implements, however, awaited the French Revolution and the fruition of nationalism (Rosecrance 1963). And it was not until the 1930s and World War II that the "old diplomacy" was transformed (Craig 1961, pp. 23–25).

The evolution of techniques was, at the same time, an alteration of the boundary between domestic and external politics. While domestic affairs during the eighteenth century had remained largely unaffected by wars, in the twentieth violence came to be expressed internally, as well as externally (Scott 1964). Subversion, propaganda manipulation, and economic pressure combined to sap the sinews of domestic strength.

Of equivalent importance, new systems of action appeared in international diplomacy. The totalitarians inaugurated a new form of diplomacy, consisting of bluff, bluster, and intemperate attack. They did not hesitate to sign agreements with democratic powers, knowing that they could violate them later with impunity.

After World War II the emergence of a large number of new nations added a new dimension to the practice of diplomacy. In 1914 approximately twenty states had abiding interests in foreign relations, and of these all but two or three were European (Craig 1961). A generation after World War II there were more than 115 states engaged in world politics and more than half were Afro–Asian. These new nations operated on behalf of divergent objectives, and the techniques they employed were often distinct (Binder 1958). The hypothesis could be entertained that the new nations represented a separate subsystem of international relations. In the twenty years following World War II an essentially European system of international relations had been transformed into a world system. The world system was not fundamentally European: it consisted of a congeries of separate regional subsystems, unified only at the topmost level of interaction. Under the circumstances it was not surprising that nations should follow different "rules of the game." Perhaps the most characteristic difference between European and Afro–Asian systems was illustrated in attitudes toward the balance of power. Even minor shifts in Europe brought forth a countervailing powerful coalition to prevent fur-

ther imbalance; in Asia even fundamental alterations in the power balance did not stimulate formation of an opposing bloc (Rosecrance 1956).

Diplomatic patterns. Diplomatic techniques are, of course, related to diplomatic patterns. Twenty years after the close of World War II it was still difficult to discern the direction in which international constellations were moving. In the immediate postwar era, bipolarity was an accepted general description of the state of the international system. As a range of new nations attained independence and refused to align with either of the two major blocs, however, multipolarity was hailed as the emergent system of the future (Rostow 1960). Some authors found a mixed system most realistic, with bipolarity characteristic of military matters and multipolarity of political matters (Liska 1963). Still others declared the two major alliance systems to be incidents of the balance of power process; alliance patterns would be reshaped as new threats emerged, and the world would revert to the combinations and procedures of the nineteenth century (Bull 1964).

Part of the debate revolved around the nature of dynamic processes: international politics could be seen as a sociological process, with political outcomes dependent upon the balance and intensity of communications flows (Deutsch 1953); it could be seen as a power process, with political outcomes dependent upon the external impact of other actors (Hinsley 1963). If diplomacy depended partly upon cultural communications and political, economic, and historical ties, some degree of North Atlantic cohesion might survive after cooperation was no longer strictly necessary on grounds of threats to the peace. If diplomacy was a product of military–political factors only, the quiescence of Russia and the resurgence of China should produce entirely new constellations of force.

Material considerations were also relevant. In economic and technological terms the Soviet Union and the United States were likely to remain the dominant international powers until at least the beginning of the 21st century (Waltz 1964). Their rate of industrial development, as compared to that of the new nations, was likely to increase their preeminence. The challenges to technological bipolarity were to be found within or on the fringes of major-power alliance systems. Japan, western Europe, and China would be independent power centers, in economic–technological terms, at some point in the future. These powers, if they pursued separate international courses, could create an oligopolistic international order, partially akin to the five-power confraternity of the eighteenth and nineteenth centuries. For a considerable period of time, however, western Europe seemed destined to remain disunited: the relaxation of cold war hostilities, if it diminished the need for Atlantic cohesion, also reduced the momentum behind European integration. And as long as western Europe was divided, it would remain a tempting prize in the cold war and a reason for continued, if limited, hostility between the Western and the Soviet camps. In the circumstances, it was interesting that the divergence of interests between the haves and have-nots led to so little conflict along North–South lines. East–West disputes continued to be controlling (Russett 1965; Alker 1964). Such patterns, if perpetuated, suggested the projection of a modified bipolarity well into the future.

Determinants of diplomacy. Future patterns of diplomatic action depend, of course, on the same basic factors that underlie international order. Some writers have viewed these as primarily domestic and sociopsychological, arguing that wars are caused by internal tensions and that domestic conflicts, explicit or latent, spill over into the international arena (Freud 1930; M. Haas 1964; and Rosecrance 1963). There has been some historical evidence for this proposition in the period since the French Revolution: the working out of domestic revolutionary issues often had consequences for the international system; patterns of external peace often were correlated with periods of internal stability (Rosecrance 1963). And yet this was not always the case: military power could be either a facilitative or a restraining influence (Hinsley 1963).

It was possible even to advance contrary hypotheses: that domestic change might be caused by international factors (Liska 1963) or, at the least, that domestic conflict was not clearly related to foreign conflict in certain recent periods (Rummel 1963). Such approaches led directly to claims that the form of the international system—specifically the lack of a strong supranational framework, capable of regulating international conflict—ensured the continuance of war (Waltz 1959). Whatever the validity of such contentions (and some evidence pointed in another direction: Deutsch et al. 1957), they could not be fully tested in the absence of international government. World government, moreover, was, as nearly everyone admitted, unobtainable, and theorists of diplomacy were forced back on less fundamental remedies for international strife. At this level no particular relationship was found between specific alliance patterns and the existence of war (Singer & Small 1965*a*, p. 35).

Some writers, however, observed a connection between the levels of international threat and a conflict spiral ending in war. The argument was that if threats (or the perception of injury) reach a certain magnitude, a state is tempted to go to war regardless of the military consequences. This theory was intended as an explicit refutation of the deterrent hypothesis, i.e., that states never attack when they believe their opponent is stronger at the time they must make the decision. Its advocates claimed that political threats overbore military threats (Zinnes et al. 1961).

This argument is based upon a partial misunderstanding of deterrent mechanisms that was developed by military writers (Ellsberg 1960). Deterrence is not simply a matter of respective military proportions; it is inextricably connected with the probability that military forces might be used. If a state was sure that its opponent was going to attack it anyway, that state might decide to attack first, despite an unfavorable balance of military force, in order to reap the advantages of the initiative. If the *status quo* had worsened decisively from the point of view of one state, it might wish to attack (even though the probability of its winning was very small) in order to avoid the disastrous consequences of the situation. In the theory of deterrence, the risks of not striking had to be assessed alongside the risks that striking entailed (Wohlstetter 1959). Deterrence calculations, then, did not rest solely or even primarily on the balance of military postures. Nor did it follow that military deterrence analyses prescribed in crisis situations an increased military threat against an opponent in order to forestall his possible decision for war.

Because of the threat posed by nuclear weapons, it was generally believed that their acquisition by additional countries would raise the risks of war. Such an impact could not be discounted (Beaton & Maddox 1962); neither, however, on the basis of available evidence, could it be confirmed. There remained the possibility that nuclear weapons might turn out to be an expensive detour, useful for prestige purposes but irrelevant for war. As smaller states opted for nuclear capabilities, larger ones were concentrating on conventional and counterinsurgency postures. The very success of deterrence in preventing nuclear war raised the stakes and possible rewards of internal violence and warfare (Huntington 1962). In the longer run deterrent stability seemed likely to focus attention on conventional arenas, in which middle powers might contend much more equally with the great states for position and influence than they would be able to do in a nuclear arms race. Under such conditions the spread of nuclear weapons would merely divert resources from those types of conflicts in which major political and military gains would be likely and enhanced bipolarity could actually result [*see* DETERRENCE].

The prospects for diplomacy. Different international constellations would require different diplomatic methods to attain desired outcomes. A bipolar order places major emphasis upon military competition between two great blocs. Intrabloc diplomacy becomes coalition management, in the face of exterior threat. As long as the danger of war between blocs is not negligible, individual interests are submerged in a common opposition to the external foe. In such circumstances diplomacy proceeds by military reassurance of allies and military deterrence of enemies. Integrated or quasi-supranational military–political mechanisms may be set up within blocs. Between blocs only the most tenuous diplomatic connections need be maintained. In other words, a bipolar world largely substitutes military for diplomatic skills and operates within clearly distinguished arenas of common and opposed objectives.

In a multipolar order, on the other hand, enemies and allies are no longer clearly differentiated and different standards of diplomatic competence and practice are therefore required. International outcomes will be determined as much by diplomatic skill as by military force. As long as no single, salient threat to the international system emerges, alliances and antagonisms will be tentative and short-lived. Since the major powers will by and large be able to fend for themselves, military arrangements with other states will be less necessary. Increments to national position will accrue more from diplomatic than from military feats. A truly multipolar order will require a vastly increased diplomatic corps and enhanced diplomatic prescience. Since political combinations will be hard to predict and the number of significant actors very large, diplomatic intelligence and research will be all-important.

In the intermediate case, that of an oligopolar order, military arts would continue to exert an important influence, while the number of crucial national actors would rise to five or six. Major military capacities would be confined to the international oligopoly; other states would not play a significant military role. Relations between the large powers would require a delicate balancing of military and diplomatic techniques. Changes in combinations among the ruling powers might have a decisive impact upon the security of one of their number. Diplomatic virtuosity akin to that practiced in the eighteenth century would be a necessary supplement to nuclear deterrence. A united oligarchy would have theoretical supremacy over the rest of the world; its internal divisions, however, would be likely to sanction diplomatic contests for the allegiance of smaller states. Again military and diplomatic variables would contend for influence.

A tentative assessment of these possibilities would stress the growing influence of diplomacy. If hostilities are focused and raised to peak intensity, military factors are dominant; if they are diffused and lessened, diplomacy becomes preeminent. Even in a bipolar order, diplomacy has played an important part: nations might have wished for war or an overturn of past patterns of international outcomes; if they used coercion to achieve their objectives, however, its expression had to be disciplined and restrained. Negotiation was as essential an ingredient as proportionate force. In the 1960s it remains possible that there will be in the future a revival of historic diplomacy: if unlimited violence cannot be tolerated, diplomacy may flourish anew.

R. N. ROSECRANCE

[*See also* ALLIANCES; COMMUNISM, *article on* THE INTERNATIONAL SYSTEM; FOREIGN POLICY; INTERNATIONAL POLITICS; NEGOTIATION; SYSTEMS ANALYSIS, *article on* INTERNATIONAL SYSTEMS. *Guides to other relevant material may be found under* INTERNATIONAL RELATIONS *and* WAR.]

BIBLIOGRAPHY

ALKER, HAYWARD R. JR. 1964 Dimensions of Conflict in the General Assembly. *American Political Science Review* 58:642–657.

BEATON, LEONARD; and MADDOX, JOHN R. 1962 *The Spread of Nuclear Weapons.* New York: Praeger.

BELOFF, MAX 1961 *New Dimensions in Foreign Policy: A Study in British Administrative Experience, 1947–1959.* New York: Macmillan.

BINDER, LEONARD 1958 The Middle East as a Subordinate International System. *World Politics* 10:408–429.

BRAMS, STEVEN J. 1966 Flow and Form in the International System. Ph.D. dissertation, Northwestern Univ.

BULL, HEDLEY 1964 *Strategy and the Atlantic Alliance: A Critique of United States Doctrine.* Policy Memorandum No. 29. Princeton Univ., Center of International Studies.

BURNS, ARTHUR L. 1957 From Balance to Deterrence: A Theoretical Analysis. *World Politics* 9:494–529.

BURNS, C. DELISLE 1931 Diplomacy. Volume 5, pages 147–153 in *Encyclopaedia of the Social Sciences.* New York: Macmillan.

COOMBS, PHILIP 1964 *The Fourth Dimension of Foreign Policy: Educational and Cultural Affairs.* New York: Harper.

CRAIG, GORDON 1961 *On the Diplomatic Revolution of Our Times.* Haynes Foundation Lectures, 1961. Riverside: Univ. of California Press.

DEUTSCH, KARL W. 1953 *Nationalism and Social Communication: An Inquiry Into the Foundations of Na-*

tionality. Cambridge, Mass.: M.I.T. Press; New York: Wiley.

DEUTSCH, KARL W. et al. 1957 *Political Community and the North Atlantic Area: International Organization in the Light of Historical Experience.* Princeton Univ. Press.

ELLSBERG, DANIEL 1960 *The Crude Analysis of Strategic Choices.* RAND Corporation Paper 2183. Santa Monica, Calif.: The Corporation.

FREUD, SIGMUND (1930) 1958 *Civilization and Its Discontents.* Garden City, N.Y.: Doubleday. → First published as *Das Unbehagen in der Kultur.*

HAAS, ERNST B. 1958 *The Uniting of Europe: Political, Social, and Economic Forces, 1950–1957.* Stanford Univ. Press.

HAAS, ERNST B. 1964 *Beyond the Nation-state: Functionism and International Organization.* Stanford Univ. Press.

HAAS, MICHAEL 1964 Some Societal Correlates of International Political Behavior. Ph.D. dissertation, Stanford Univ.

HINSLEY, FRANCIS H. 1963 *Power and the Pursuit of Peace: Theory and Practice in the History of Relations Between States.* Cambridge Univ. Press.

HUNTINGTON, SAMUEL P. 1962 Patterns of Violence in World Politics. Pages 17–50 in Samuel P. Huntington (editor), *Changing Patterns of Military Politics.* New York: Free Press.

ILCHMAN, WARREN F. 1961 *Professional Diplomacy in the United States, 1779–1939: A Study in Administrative History.* Univ. of Chicago Press.

KENNAN, GEORGE F. (1964) 1965 Impressions of a Recent Ambassadorial Experience. Pages 587–594 in Harry Howe Ransom (editor), *An American Foreign Policy Reader.* New York: Crowell.

LISKA, GEORGE 1963 Continuity and Change in International Systems. *World Politics* 16:118–136.

MERCHANT, LIVINGSTON 1964 New Techniques in Diplomacy. Pages 117–135 in Edgar A. J. Johnson (editor), *The Dimensions of Diplomacy.* Baltimore: Johns Hopkins Press.

NICOLSON, HAROLD (1939) 1964 *Diplomacy.* 3d ed. New York: Oxford Univ. Press.

ROSECRANCE, RICHARD N. 1956 The Aims and Methods of American Policy in Asia. *Public Policy: A Yearbook of the Graduate School of Public Administration* (Harvard University) 7:3–24.

ROSECRANCE, RICHARD N. 1963 *Action and Reaction in World Politics: International Systems in Perspective.* Boston: Little.

ROSTOW, WALT W. 1960 *U.S. in the World Arena: An Essay in Recent History.* New York: Harper.

RUMMEL, RUDOLPH J. 1963 Dimensions of Conflict Behavior Within and Between Nations. *General Systems* 8:1–50.

RUSK, DEAN (1964) 1965 Diplomacy as an Instrument. Pages 576–583 in Harry Howe Ransom (editor), *An American Foreign Policy Reader.* New York: Crowell.

RUSSETT, BRUCE M. 1965 *Trends in World Politics.* New York: Macmillan.

SATOW, ERNEST M. (1917) 1962 *A Guide to Diplomatic Practice.* 4th ed. Edited by Nevile Bland. London: Longmans.

SCHLESINGER, ARTHUR M. JR. 1965 *A Thousand Days.* Boston: Houghton Mifflin.

SCOTT, ANDREW M. 1964 International Violence as an Instrument of Cold Warfare. Pages 154–169 in James N. Rosenau (editor), *International Aspects of Civil Strife.* Princeton Univ. Press.

SINGER, J. DAVID; and SMALL, MELVIN 1965a Formal Alliances, 1915–1939: Quantitative Description. Unpublished manuscript, Univ. of Michigan, Mental Health Research Institute.

SINGER, J. DAVID; and SMALL, MELVIN 1965b The Composition and Status Ordering of the International System: 1815–1940. Unpublished manuscript, Univ. of Michigan, Mental Health Research Institute.

U.S. CONGRESS, SENATE, COMMITTEE ON GOVERNMENT OPERATIONS, SUBCOMMITTEE ON NATIONAL SECURITY STAFFING AND OPERATIONS (1964) 1965 *The American Ambassador.* Pages 584–587 in Harry Howe Ransom (editor), *An American Foreign Policy Reader.* New York: Crowell.

WALTZ, KENNETH N. 1959 *Man, the State and War.* New York: Columbia Univ. Press.

WALTZ, KENNETH N. 1964 The Stability of a Bipolar World. *Dædalus* 93:881–909.

WOHLSTETTER, ALBERT 1959 The Delicate Balance of Terror. *Foreign Affairs* 37:211–234.

ZINNES, DINA A.; NORTH, ROBERT C.; and KOCH, HOWARD E. 1961 Capability, Threat and the Outbreak of War. Pages 469–482 in James N. Rosenau (editor), *International Politics and Foreign Policy: A Reader in Research and Theory.* New York: Free Press.

DISARMAMENT

From the time that men first organized themselves into exclusive social groupings, they have relied upon the threat or use of physical violence as a major means of influencing the behavior of neighboring groups. As the size of the group controlling the tools of violence increased, so did the destructiveness of these tools; thus, by the mid-twentieth century, that group was the national state, and its tools included nuclear warheads, intercontinental missiles, and biochemical weapons. However, the acquisition and maintenance of national armaments is never a wholly attractive enterprise, and some incentives for the absence, reduction, or elimination of such capabilities always exist. Since the considerations affecting decisions to arm and disarm are highly interdependent, it might be useful to examine them in sequence at the outset.

Incentives to arm. First, the traditions of the international community make it clear that armed forces are the most tangible evidence of a nation's independence and sovereignty. Second, armed forces at the disposal of the governing elites can be, and often are, used to impose and maintain domestic order. Third, their establishment provides jobs (and training) for otherwise underemployed people and legitimate economic activity for the nation's industry and technology (Benoit & Boulding 1963).

In addition to these symbolic and domestic considerations, political elites may arm their nations in order to secure and enhance the nation's position in the still ungoverned international community. Legal norms, moral restraints, and political institutions at the international level may all impinge on such efforts, but a nation's power remains the most effective basis for pursuing its self-defined interests. And though there is increasing evidence that other components are beginning to replace military capability in a nation's power equation, arms are still the primary component. Thus, national leaders will seek to develop and maintain military capability not only in order to use it but to threaten to use it. The actual employment of such capability could be for the purpose of weakening or destroying another nation, or of defending or counterattacking if such action were undertaken in the first place. More often, however, military capability exists in order to be brandished or alluded to in the normal processes of diplomatic confrontation and bargaining; the objective is to back up demands and requests or to resist those made by others. Finally, armed forces may be used or kept in readiness for such disparate purposes as carrying out enforcement obligations under international organizations, such as the League of Nations or the United Nations, or for occupying the territory of a defeated nation.

Incentives to disarm. Normally, there is a sharp discrepancy between the number of weapons and men that nations retain in peacetime and the numbers deployed in wartime. Since the diplomatic and military effectiveness of a country's armed forces is a function of the size and quality of one's allies and one's adversaries, there is little incentive for a nation that supports the *status quo* to arm up to full capacity unless the potential adversaries are doing so or are expected to do so. This tendency toward modest levels of military preparedness is reinforced by two essentially domestic considerations. First, voluntary enlistments in most societies are relatively low, and conscription is usually unpopular in peacetime. Second, the designing, testing, building, and maintaining of military hardware are quite costly, and unless it is acquired from outside, under a military aid program, the money must be raised by some form of public or corporate taxation. Lower taxes are always preferable to the public, and if taxation is relatively high, the general preference is for its application to services of a more socially useful nature. Finally, in many societies there is a deep suspicion of, and hostility to, the military establishment on ideological grounds.

Given this combination of incentives and disincentives, it becomes clear that the size and quality of a nation's armed force represent a compromise between the two sets of pressures. Only within the context of these two types of pressure can a nation's tendency to arm or disarm be understood. Even in periods of extreme diplomatic tranquillity, there will be serious pressures toward an increase in capability even in nations having no aggressive designs; likewise, pressures for arms reduction often exist even in nations at, or over, the brink of war. It is in response to these contrasting external and internal forces that nations get caught up in both armament and disarmament "races."

Arms races. The cost and danger of an arms race, or the actual consequences of one, usually produce the incentives for disarmament. If we bear in mind the contrasting economic, political, and military considerations at work, it becomes evident that an arms race is a highly reciprocal social process, involving interaction not only between the governments of the nations involved but also conflicting factions within and across the national boundaries. In the absence of effective international government, nations have no real source of security other than their own power. In seeking to maximize such power vis-à-vis others that might threaten their security, nations compete with one another for prestige, markets, raw materials, waterways, territory, allies, and spheres of influence. The pursuit of such goals by one nation is often detrimental to the interests of another, which can resist by using various diplomatic, economic, and psychological techniques. Most often, these clashes of interest are temporarily resolved by tacit or negotiated compromise, but occasionally both parties commit themselves to goals that are clearly incompatible and not susceptible to such settlement. The goal seems important enough to one to justify an abnormal allocation of its resources to military capabilities, and thwarting that effort seems equally important to the other. At this point, the normal level of internation competition is exceeded, and one or both parties try to improve their bargaining position by seeking temporary allies, by increasing their individual capabilities, or by some combination of the two. Once either party does this, the other must either make serious concessions or try to counteract by increasing its own bargaining power. As each invests further in its own strength, its decision makers feel justified in increasing their demands, making the cost of capitulation that much higher for the other. If that cost then seems prohibitive, its decision makers must improve *their* capacity to resist or to win.

Whether increases in power are sought in arms or in allies, the domestic sector must be increasingly mobilized. In order to produce the manpower, money, and material for such bargaining, the population must be persuaded that its vital interests or its very survival are at stake. Gradually, this propaganda program succeeds in associating compromise with treason and conciliation with capitulation.

Thus, even while there is still time to turn back, the policy makers seldom can afford to do so; the public—or at least the political opposition—would raise the cry of treason. At this point, the process is largely out of the hands of those who initiated the arms race in the first place, and serious diplomatic bargaining becomes increasingly difficult. While the conflict *may* terminate in a gradual deceleration of weapons procurement, eventual public disenchantment, the appearance of new and more pressing conflicts, or negotiated settlement, the odds increasingly favor war as the likely outcome.

The above is a highly simplified and abstract treatment of what seems to have been the pattern of arms races over the past two centuries or so. Unfortunately, no scholar has yet attempted a comprehensive and comparative study of arms races in the modern international system. But some useful studies do exist and could provide a solid basis from which to proceed. *A Study of War* (Wright 1942, appendix 22) provides data for the major powers from 1820 to 1937, and "A Mathematical Study of the Present Arms Race" (Smoker 1963) covers the 1949–1960 period. A less quantitative but more theoretical effort is "Arms Races: Prerequisites and Results" (Huntington 1958), which offers a penetrating verbal analysis from the Franco–British naval race of 1840–1846 to the post-World War II race between the United States and the Soviet Union. In *Arms and Insecurity* (Richardson 1960) we find the nearest approximation to a comparative, quantitative analysis, but it covers only the races preceding both world wars [*see* RICHARDSON]. Finally, there are studies of individual arms races (Hirst 1937; Sloutzki 1941). Thus the interpretation offered here must be recognized as tentative and prescientific, resting as it largely does on incomplete data, anecdotal recollection, and theoretical deduction.

Types of disarmament

No formal definition of disarmament has been offered here since the phenomenon may take many forms. In the light of historical experience as well as logical possibilities, it is useful to classify the types of disarmament along two particular dimensions. One such dimension is the *degree* of arms reduction, and the other may be called the *reciprocity* dimension. The first refers to the quantitative and qualitative extent of a nation's military reductions, the second to the extent to which its reductions are matched, or in some fashion reciprocated, by other nations.

Degree of arms reduction. The "degree of disarmament" continuum is not, in fact, limited to *dis*armament measures in the literal sense. In accord with diplomatic custom and scholarly usage, we include arms *control* as well as a number of intermediate restraints that fall well short of *reduction.*

Total disarmament. At the upper end of the continuum is total or complete disarmament, involving the elimination of all military capability beyond that defined as necessary for the maintenance of domestic order. That minimal level may include local and national police, border guards, or perhaps even a modest paramilitary force for antiriot types of duty, depending on the treaty provisions, the requirements imposed by other nations, or the unilateral decision of the disarming nation itself. Complete disarmament has been proposed frequently (most recently in the partially compatible Soviet and American draft treaties on general and complete disarmament of March 22 and April 18, 1962, respectively) but it has never been achieved by formal negotiations among the major powers. It has, however, been imposed on defeated nations by victorious ones at the close of war, but seldom with lasting effect. As commitments shift according to the vagaries of international alignments, the victors either acquiesce in gradual rearmament, as after World War I, or even encourage it, as did the United States and the Soviet Union soon after World War II.

Arms control. At the opposite and lowest end of the degree continuum are arms control measures. These are provisions that may not call for reduction or prohibition of any weapons, yet have the effect of inhibiting a nation's full development of a given weapon category. Arms control measures do not directly prohibit the *production* or *possession* of that weapon type but rather seek to work indirectly by limitations or prohibitions on the *testing, deployment,* or *use* of it. Leaving out the last (once weapons are made and deployed, any commitment not to use them is unlikely to survive even the mildest temptation after hostilities begin), we note that limits or prohibitions on testing may well prevent, retard, or diminish the quality of the weapon's production. Or, for a variety of political, military, or technological reasons, it may be desirable to permit production (and thereafter possession) but to restrict or ban their deployment within a given geographical region. One of the rare successes in negotiating a reciprocal ban on testing was the August 5, 1963, Treaty of Moscow, which prohibited the signatories from experimental detonations of nuclear weapons in outer space, in the atmosphere, or under water. Although a number of demilitarized frontiers have been arranged in the past, today's major powers have been unable to negotiate any regional deployment prohibitions.

Arms control also may be applied to certain less obvious measures having no effect at all on the quantity or quality of a nation's armed forces. Normally, they deal with *information about* military capability rather than the capability itself and generally require more information than is available through normal military intelligence channels. In the past, much emphasis of this sort was on publishing military budgets, war college curricula, manning and organization tables, results of weapon experiments, inventories, and war plans; often observers were invited to attend maneuvers or to verify published information. As the advance of military technology enhanced the offense at the expense of the defense, however, surprise attack became an increasingly serious concern for the defenders of the *status quo*. As a consequence, much of the information exchanged (or proposed for exchange) in earlier days has become a potential aid to the aggressor; the types of information exchange proposed in the post-1945 era are intended to redress that imbalance and to aid the defender (more accurately, the *retaliator*, since effective strategic defense has become nearly impossible). For example, it has been proposed that information regarding the location of land-based or sea-borne retaliatory weapons be kept secret and that the potential adversary commit himself not to seek out such information. In a similar vein, but tending toward more information, foreign observation posts and limited aerial inspection within a nation's boundaries have been discussed as a means of improving the early-warning system of its neighbors.

Closely related to such techniques for reducing the advantage of the attacker are those intended for crisis control. In 1963 the Soviet Union and the United States installed a direct communication line between their two capitals, so that prompt and reliable information might be sought and transmitted during crises; the objective here was to mitigate the ever-increasing probability of accidental war because of erroneous reading of intelligence reports or radar and sonar displays. As in prior periods, the intent is to reduce the incentive to attack by reducing the fear of being attacked,

and the objective remains one of preserving the relative military *status quo*.

A final form of arms control (liberally defined) is neutralization. In such a case, the neutralized nation or region is not necessarily prohibited from acquiring or maintaining armed forces but is prohibited from joining a military alliance. Generally, the neutralized region is either outside the sphere of influence of two potential enemy coalitions or in an area in which they overlap; hence such an arrangement usually requires formal or tacit negotiation between major powers. Although the enforcement of neutralization may be assigned to an international organization or an *ad hoc* multinational commission, its continuance depends on the major powers' willingness to merely deny the region to the other rather than acquire it for themselves [see DISENGAGEMENT].

Partial disarmament.   In the middle of the continuum are those measures known as partial disarmament. They may cover (*a*) incomplete reductions in *all* weapon categories or (*b*) complete reductions in *some* categories, or (*c*) some combination of the two. In the first case, the tendency has been to seek across-the-board cuts or limits based on a budgetary or a manpower ceiling, the idea being that adherence to such a ceiling will compel nations to keep their armaments down. Normally, the plan is to permit each nation to allocate its military resources, within the budgetary restriction, to whichever weapon types it sees fit. The monetary maximum for any given year or period may, in turn, be based on average expenditures during a prior period, on the highest expenditure during a given prior period, or on some ratios among the signatories, to preserve their relative power positions. If a mobilized manpower ceiling is contemplated, similar baselines or else a percentage of each nations' total of male population or of males in a given age bracket, may be used. Normally, a manpower ceiling prescribes numerical and age limits not only upon active duty personnel but on reserves of different categories, and it will also set minimum periods of active duty in order to prevent the rapid training of many reserves by high turnover in a relatively small active force.

Another version of the across-the-board, but partial, measure is that based on real or hypothetical war-making units. A German periodical in 1909 proposed, for example, that each nation be allotted one unit for each 700 in its population and that 10 army men or 50 tons of ship be thought of as one unit. Thus, under this scheme the 63 million Germans would have been entitled to 90,000 units and the 45 million British to 64,300, to be allocated among ships and men as the decision makers of each country thought best.

When the second type of partial reduction—complete prohibitions in a few categories—is attempted, the prospective signatories are left free to arm fully in the nonproscribed categories; such partial provisions are also referred to as *qualitative* disarmament. This type may be negotiated, imposed, or unilaterally undertaken in order to (1) avoid the expenditure for more elaborate or costly weapons, (2) eliminate the more inhuman ones if war occurs, (3) make the soldier's burden lighter in weight, (4) strengthen the defense vis-à-vis the offense in order to make aggression less attractive, or (5) compensate for the asymmetries arising out of the different geographical or technological security needs of particular nations. All of the above considerations have been explicitly noted either in formal proposals or in actual agreements. Qualitative measures might embrace the prohibition, elimination, or a ceiling upon mobile artillery, rifles above a certain caliber, bullets under a certain weight, railroads within a certain distance of a border, ships above a certain length or tonnage, ships capable of submerging, armor plates of a given thickness or hardness, aircraft capable of carrying bombs, chemical weapons, nuclear weapons on board space satellites, delivery vehicles of given range, and so forth; they may also embrace certain classes of trained personnel. The incentives may not be completely pacifistic, and the results may actually be to increase a nation's over-all military capability, but these partial measures clearly belong under the rubric of disarmament.

Reciprocity of disarmament measures. Turning to the second dimension—reciprocity—the major question is whether a given nation disarms unilaterally and unconditionally or receives (or expects) reciprocal behavior from one or more other nations as a condition of its own limitations or reductions. There are many possible positions on this continuum, five of which will serve to explore and define it.

Unilateral disarmament. At one end is a nation's elimination of its armaments and demobilization of its military personnel without any *quid pro quo* at all. Such a unilateral move might be prompted by the decision makers' conviction that: (1) the maintenance, threat, or use of armed force is morally wrong; (2) the domestic economy cannot afford the cost of the military establishment; (3) public opinion strongly favors such a move; (4) war is extremely unlikely in the relevant future; (5) diplomacy does not require the threat of

force behind it; (6) alternative sources of influence, such as wealth, skill, or prestige, are more effective; (7) other relevant nations are, or have finished, disarming unilaterally; (8) others will probably follow this example; (9) others will not exploit a disarming or disarmed nation; (10) third parties will intervene to prevent any attempted diplomatic exploitation of the disarmed nation; (11) others will defend it in case of attack; or (12) alternative responses to invasion, such as nonviolent resistance or noncooperation, will be more effective than military resistance. Although not exhaustive, this list suggests the possible attractions of unilateral disarmament, even in a largely ungoverned world. When and if the political and military efficacy of global organization increases, such incentives would tend to be magnified.

Multilateral disarmament. At the opposite end of the reciprocity continuum would be the disarmament agreement embodied in a bilateral or multilateral treaty, following *formal negotiations*. In such a situation, every reduction undertaken by one nation is conditional upon the reductions accepted by others. The primary objective here is to assure the preservation (or, if possible, the improvement) of one's relative military power position vis-à-vis the other signatories, both during and at the end of the disarmament process. Normally, such negotiations involve nations of approximate military parity which are already in partial conflict with one another, and although some or all of the unilateral incentives may be motivating the negotiators, the inevitable lack of trust between some of the parties creates serious domestic and international inhibitions to success. The propensity to compromise is generally low, the bargaining is hard, and the treaty (if ever concluded) tends to be full of detailed procedures, contingencies, and exceptions.

Somewhere between the pure unilateral and the pure reciprocal type of disarmament is *imposed* disarmament. Although usually the consequence of formal negotiation, it is negotiation between nations of extremely disparate power, however impermanent that disparity may be. And although it may be nearly unilateral in its effects, the dominant bargainer normally accepts certain limited restrictions on its own armed forces. The extreme form of imposed disarmament is the one accepted by the defeated nation following a war whose conclusion is close to unconditional surrender, such as the disarmament of the Axis powers after World War II. In its milder version, it is a form of demilitarization that is demanded by one or more major powers and acquiesced in by minor ones.

At an intermediate point between the unilateral and the imposed forms is a semivoluntary process, undertaken on the premise that failure to do so voluntarily might require the nation to disarm later under duress. This usually occurs in minor powers which are clearly within a major power's sphere of influence. At the other intermediate position, between the multilateral and the imposed forms, is the *tacitly negotiated* arrangement, in which the political realities make it mutually evident that the nations are overarmed for their security purposes. As the perceived need for armed forces diminishes, one nation may express that perception by some minor reductions, and others may respond in kind, thus setting in motion a reciprocal process of apparently voluntary disarmament. However, if one party levels off at a certain state of preparedness or reverses the process and begins to rearm the others are likely to follow suit.

The negotiating process

Of the five degrees of reciprocity outlined above, the one that is most frequently attempted, most frequently unsuccessful, and yet most relevant to the search for international stability and peace is the formally negotiated, highly reciprocal agreement; hence this article's emphasis on it at the expense of the other forms. Before turning to certain other considerations in, and obstacles to, negotiated disarmament, let us examine the effects of the forum or setting within which these negotiations might take place. Two dimensions are most relevant here: (*a*) which nations participate and (*b*) under whose auspices?

Since reference here is not to an imposed arrangement, it is understood that at least two of the negotiating nations are powerful enough to resist dictation by one another but are not sufficiently in agreement to dictate to third parties. Consequently, the locale and composition of the negotiations is itself a subject for bargaining. The party whose position is most likely to be politically attractive to third parties or who wants to bring extra pressure to bear on the negotiating partner will tend to advocate a larger number of participants and may urge that the sessions be held at the seat of, or under the auspices of, the relevant international organization, such as the League of Nations or the United Nations. On the other hand, preference for smaller, isolated sessions may reflect either a nation's unwillingness to bargain seriously or a conviction that the technicalities and sensitivities of disarmament require private negotiation among

the major powers only. During the post-World War II period, the Soviet Union and many of the nonaligned nations have favored the large and open conference, while the United States and its allies have tended to prefer private negotiations among a small number of major powers. As a consequence, both approaches have been used, but with equally limited success.

Despite the advantages of quiet and privacy that the smaller session affords, the larger forum is generally to be preferred. First, when the key nations *are* ready to parley in earnest, their representatives can easily meet in private. Second, the sharp bilateral cleavages become blurred by the involvement of third and other parties, with the key protagonists under pressure to satisfy their demands. Third, while some of these pressures will be purely nationalistic ones, many will create new incentives for compromise on the part of the major protagonists. Fourth, relations between the representative and his home government become more complicated by the injection of unexpected people, and he may be given more bargaining latitude. Finally, even if one side is more interested in propaganda than diplomacy, the other side has an opportunity for face-to-face education of those third parties who might otherwise be easily misled at a distance.

A final point in regard to the negotiation of disarmament concerns the composition and latitude of the separate delegations. Generally speaking, if they arrive with rigid instructions and are required to clear all departures from them with the foreign office or defense ministry, the prospects for success will not be good. It is equally unsatisfactory for a negotiator to be sent under quite flexible conditions only to discover that the bargains he has struck will not be honored by his government, owing to his lack of effective support at home. In this same vein, a government can easily paralyze negotiations by sending delegates who may have considerable bargaining freedom but whose personal interests and associates are opposed to a treaty. At the first Hague conference, for example, the United States was represented by Admiral Mahan, the British by Admiral Fisher, Germany by Colonel von Schwarzhoff, and so on; such men could not be expected to bargain away the basis of their careers and prestige, and they were quite adept at discovering and articulating technical and tactical reasons for rejecting the tsar's proposals. It is one thing to have military experts on hand and quite another to give them a dominant role in the negotiations. More recently, the difficulty has been compounded by assigning engineers and physical scientists to the delegations (or to the groups responsible for instructing the delegations)—the careers and prestige of these men are often dependent upon the very weapon programs whose termination the delegates are allegedly trying to negotiate.

Studies of almost all conferences and negotiations have been made by historians, political scientists, and lawyers. Perhaps the two most useful general analyses of the several interwar negotiations are Madariaga (1929) and Tate (1942). Among those concentrating on the post-World War II efforts are Bechhoefer (1961), Spanier and Nogee (1962), and Jacobson and Stein (1966). [*See* NEGOTIATION.]

Direction and phasing

Up to this point we have made two simplifying assumptions. One is that there is no essential difference between reducing armament levels *down* to some specified level and permitting increases *up* to such a level. The fact that in one case a nation begins with more than the agreed capability and must therefore come down to it and that in the other case the nation begins with less than the ceiling and is free to go up to it must obviously have some important implications. The other simplification is that the *rate* at which a nation moves up or down to a given threshold in a given weapon category need not be a source of concern and that the nature of the limit or prohibition is of major, if not sole, concern. It is equally evident that phasing can be profoundly important to both the disarmament process and its outcome.

With regard to the matter of *direction*, experience and logic both point to the advantage of negotiating or deciding upon a ceiling or prohibition *before* it is breached, rather than after. First, for every weapon developed and produced, national decision makers have had to invest a certain amount of money, national prestige, and their own personal reputations. Thus, these weapons have a high symbolic as well as security value and they will not be given up without a high price. Second, the technicians who developed the weapons, the manufacturers and laborers who produce them, and the military personnel who maintain them have profited financially and psychologically in the process; they are not only interested in continuing such profits, but they are likely to have more political influence after performing these roles than they had before. Third, due to the inspection problem, there is less certainty that the potential adversary is *reducing* his weapons than *not adding* to them, creating serious risks in the security realm. Fourth, the decision makers will be uncer-

tain how many of a given weapon type the others have and will therefore be reluctant to engage in reductions that possibly increase the others' numerical advantage.

Conversely, negotiations are likely to be more successful when material and psychic investments are low, the antireduction lobby has not yet been created or strengthened, the military risks are lower, and the inspection requirements are minimal. To put it another way, it is less difficult *not* to arm than to *disarm*.

Closely related to the direction of arms limitation is its *phasing*, or the relative speed with which all or certain classes of weapons are to be limited, reduced, or eliminated. The critical nature of this problem is manifested when we recall that no two nations have precisely the same security requirements, even if neither is interested in aggression. From the first Hague conference of 1898 through the pre-World War II negotiations, for example, Britain's heavy reliance on sea power posed certain difficulties quite distinct from those facing France, Germany, Russia, and other land-oriented powers. Likewise, in the Soviet–American negotiations of the post-1945 period, the discrepancies in the two powers' needs and capabilities made successful bargaining especially difficult. There is not only the hoary problem of quantitatively equating battalions and battleships, tanks and submarines, bombers and missiles, but the fact that even successful equating of them can be dangerous to one party or the other. Thus, if one side is superior in long-range strategic forces and the other in localized conventional forces because of differing location, technology, demography, and military doctrine, it may feel justified in demanding the elimination of all or most of the other's forces before proceeding to any reduction of its own. Or one may require overseas bases more than the other, making negotiation about bases nearly impossible.

But even if these were not such complicating qualitative differences, the phasing problem would pose awkward obstacles to negotiated disarmament. On the one hand is the necessity to reduce personnel, budgetary, or weapon levels fast enough to (*a*) make it clear that there *is* a disarmament process under way; (*b*) escape from the instability of a heavily armed world; and (*c*) take advantage of and perpetuate the temporary period of mutual confidence that would probably accompany the signing and ratification of the treaty or convention. On the other hand are the fears of reducing one's capabilities before (*a*) there is assurance that others are doing likewise; (*b*) there is evidence that the others have given up their "aggressive" designs; and (c) alternate modes of national protection have been developed. Further complicating the timing and phasing problem is the likelihood that some signatories, seeking revision of the global distribution of influence, will have developed and are prepared to use nonmilitary or other indirect techniques of waging international conflict; the nations that support the *status quo* may, therefore, insist on a very gradual and prolonged disarmament schedule. Finally, all parties will have some fear that whatever inspection and control agencies are created will be unduly influenced or dominated by the others.

It is probably safe to say, on the basis of the few available analyses of disarmament negotiations, that the issue of phasing has been as much a historical obstacle to success as has the question of which weapons should be reduced or limited to what levels.

Inspection

Given the likelihood that disarmament negotiations will generally take place, if at all, within an atmosphere of moderate to high distrust and fear, it is reasonable to expect suspicion regarding compliance of whatever agreements might be reached. To weaken one's major source of security without some assurance that the others are doing likewise is so unattractive a prospect that inspection is generally considered an essential adjunct of arms reduction or limitation.

Such inspection may be carried out by other signatories, by *ad hoc* international commissions, or by international organizations, and the objects of such inspection may be budgets, war plans, training facilities, weapon installations, factories, transport junctions, or entire regions, depending upon the activities proscribed by the agreement. Just as in the reduction schedule itself, the problem of phasing in inspection is often a major source of failure: how much inspection is necessary and safe at which stages of reduction? In order of increasing intrusiveness, inspection may focus upon (a) the destruction or dismantling process to ensure that the reduction schedule is being followed; (b) test or production facilities to inhibit or prevent the acquisition of a weapon type; or (c) present inventories (or a sample thereof) to ensure that a given ceiling has not been exceeded.

Often the negotiations reveal a marked difference in attitude toward the rate at which inspection should be introduced, and its intensiveness or extensiveness, once established. The dilemma is

dramatized when we consider that a nation may refuse to consider any reductions or limitations until it knows the size and quality of the other's inventories, while inspection for such purposes would be the most far-ranging, onerous, and costly. Yet the demand for even a modest form of pre-reduction surveillance, before any arms reduction, may well be interpreted by another nation as motivated by espionage intentions only. These basic difficulties can be mitigated if the negotiations and early reductions occur in an environment of moderate trust, permitting each side to tolerate more inspection and demand less. Or high inspection requirements can be mitigated by remote surveillance techniques, made increasingly possible by such advanced technology as intercontinental radar and orbiting camera satellites, or modern computer-based analysis of full production, inventory, and cost records.

Although the above principles of inspection may continue to hold, the rapidity of technological innovation produces constant change in both the problems encountered and the techniques available. There is already a rich literature covering inspection and its technological aspects (Melman 1958), legal aspects (Henkin 1958), and psychological aspects (Milburn et al. 1961); many anthologies deal with the interplay of politics, strategy, and technology (Brennan 1961; Frisch 1961; The American Assembly 1961; and Singer 1963). The many hearings and reports of the United States Senate Subcommittee on Disarmament, the Congressional Joint Committee on Atomic Energy, and reports of the various United Nations conferences are highly informative and detailed.

Enforcement and protection

Whether a disarmament agreement provides for on-site or remote, human or machine, or adversary or international inspection, one problem always remains: how to respond to suspected or verified evasions?

At one extreme is the emphasis on unilateral abrogation, and at the other is the demand for punishment by some international or supranational agency. Neither seems feasible. In all past, present, and future processes of arms reduction or limitation, many evasions can be expected; some will be intentional, some will be accidental, and many more will merely be suspicions of an evasion. If the purpose of inspection is to generate mutual confidence, responses must be graduated and appropriate. Thus, suspected violations should produce increased inspection, not a renewed arms race or premature punishment; extreme sanctions would be relevant only as evasions become patently intentional and serious. When such a situation develops, of course, the signatories are at a critical turning point, the outcome of which will depend on the intentions and fears of the respective decision makers, the distance already traveled toward fulfillment of the agreement, and the strength of the international institutions established in conjunction with the arms arrangements.

Considerations of enforcement, of course, go to the very heart of the disarmament problem. Recalling the earlier discussion of the incentives affecting a nation's armament policy, we note that the major source of national security has been and largely remains that of military capability relative to potential enemies. If the decision is to limit or reduce such capability, it is usually on the assumption of reciprocal measures by other nations. But even if reciprocal reductions were to carry most of the world's nations down to complete disarmament levels without any upset by violation—and this has so far never occurred—there would still remain not only the problem of inspection and enforcement in a disarming world, but also that of conflict control and protection in a disarming and a disarmed world. Put another way, nations require supranational agencies both to help in carrying through any disarmament process and to protect them at the end of the process. Incompatibilities among nations might well be as serious and dangerous *after* disarmament as during it, and conflicts all along the way are inevitable. Without supranational institutions, no disarmament process of any significance is likely to be completed, and without them in a world of already disarmed nations, the *re*armament process would be nearly inevitable.

If and when nations disarm, therefore, they need to arrange, in a cautious and gradual manner, both the diminution of their own capabilities and the accretion of the international organization's capabilities. These shifts of relative capability must, of course, embrace both the military and the political realm, requiring the gradual build-up of supranational peace-keeping facilities. Implicit in such shifts is an inevitable modification, however slow and imperceptible, in the structure and the culture of the international system, and although all the specifics need not be negotiated in advance, the major powers and many of the minor ones must be quite aware of the transition they are setting in motion. Therefore, there must be agreement on the rules by which the rules will be made

and modified, even though the concrete future is only dimly perceived.

There may be less radical paths to disarmament, but they are unlikely to be irreversible ones. Historically, nothing approximating global disarmament has been successfully negotiated, and the more restricted attempts have tended to be short-lived. With no alternative means of self-protection and conflict resolution, the nations have consistently returned to armament, regardless of their peaceful intentions.

Research and policy

Although much of the analysis presented here may convey an impression of certainty, such an impression would be misleading; the above discussion is based almost entirely on "trained intuition" and impression. The same must be said of almost all the writing on the subject: whether the study is by university scholars, governmental or intergovernmental agencies, journalists, or private research organizations, the results fall well short of the most modest scientific criteria. Where hard comparative evidence, gathered by visible and replicable observational procedures, is called for, we find haphazard impressions or highly selective recollections. Where an explicit and disciplined theoretical framework is called for, we find inconsistent and incompatible arguments based all too often on the immediate demands of a highly ephemeral political "reality." Because few of those who conduct research bearing on disarmament and national security are trained in or committed to social science methods, most of the writing on the subject cannot be taken as a reliable guide to policy. In no nation of the world today (as far as can be ascertained) is any significant amount of rigorous research on the political, social, or psychological aspects of disarmament under way. As indicated above, however, some high quality work on economic obstacles to, and consequences of, disarmament, has been completed, and on the technological side some excellent research has been and continues to be undertaken. Under the U.S. Arms Control and Disarmament Agency—which in general has shown little scientific competence or political courage in the social science research it has conducted or supported—several dozen studies of high quality on inspection and verification have been completed to date.

Part of the difficulty lies in the fact that most of the political and strategic problems fall in the domain of political scientists and lawyers, and neither field has a strong tradition of scientific method. And when scholars from the more rigorous social sciences (such as psychology and sociology) or from the physical sciences and engineering move into this research realm, they tend to leave their methodological norms behind, while responding more to their ethical values or the demands of role and career.

Admittedly the research problems are difficult and complex, given the lack of historical precedents and parallels to the contemporary situation, but several options are nevertheless available. One would be the systematic examination of those aspects of diplomatic and military history which *are* comparable to the present, and there are many such partial parallels waiting to be identified and described. Another would be the search for basic principles in governmental decision making, public opinion formation and its change, internation bargaining, etc. A third might be the systematic examination of analogous situations in such other empirical domains as *intra*national politics, labor-management relations, racial conflict, small group experiments, and the like. Finally, there is the possibility of rigorous simulation of real world situations using role-playing human subjects, more formal computer simulations, or some combination of men and machines for the replication and analysis of present and projected situations. Some progress in the application of this latter strategy has been made, but the validity of such simulations is highly dependent upon inputs derived from the other three approaches, and they have not yet been provided in the quantity and quality that is necessary. [*See* SIMULATION, *article on* POLITICAL PROCESSES.]

The prospects for disarmament are not promising. The combination of domestic and foreign incentives and constraints tends to inhibit political elites that might want to negotiate arms reduction agreements. National citizens, propagandized as they are by the elites, lack the information and motivation that might permit them to modify the domestic incentives of the elites. And even if these obstacles could be overcome, the policy makers themselves have so weak a research base upon which to make their political judgments that they are unlikely to make the correct decisions even if they want to. An effective combination of good will, courage, knowledge, and luck is required if the nations are to move toward meaningful disarmament, and at this writing we seem to be considerably short of achieving that combination.

J. DAVID SINGER

[*See also* DIPLOMACY; PEACE; WAR. *Other relevant material may be found in* INTERNATIONAL RELATIONS; MILITARY.]

BIBLIOGRAPHY

THE AMERICAN ASSEMBLY 1961 *Arms Control: Issues for the Public.* Edited by Louis Henkin. Englewood Cliffs, N.J.: Prentice-Hall.

BECHHOEFER, BERNARD G. 1961 *Postwar Negotiations for Arms Controls.* Washington: Brookings Institution.

BENOIT, EMILE; and BOULDING, KENNETH E. (editors) 1963 *Disarmament and the Economy.* New York: Harper.

BRENNAN, DONALD G. (editor) 1961 *Arms Control, Disarmament and National Security.* New York: Braziller.

CLARK, GRENVILLE; and SOHN, LOUIS B. (1958) 1960 *World Peace Through World Law.* 2d ed., rev. Cambridge, Mass.: Harvard Univ. Press.

FRISCH, DAVID H. (editor) 1961 *Arms Reduction: Program and Issues.* New York: Twentieth Century Fund.

HENKIN, LOUIS 1958 *Arms Control and Inspection in American Law.* New York: Columbia Univ. Press.

HIRST, FRANCIS W. 1937 *Armaments: The Race and the Crisis.* London: Cobden-Sanderson.

HUNTINGTON, SAMUEL P. 1958 Arms Races: Prerequisites and Results. *Public Policy: A Yearbook of the Graduate School of Public Administration* (Harvard University) 8:41–86.

JACOBSON, HAROLD K.; and STEIN, ERIC 1966 *Diplomats, Scientists and Politicians: The United States and the Nuclear Test Ban Negotiations.* Ann Arbor: Univ. of Michigan Press.

MADARIAGA, SALVADOR DE 1929 *Disarmament.* New York: Coward-McCann.

MELMAN, SEYMOUR (editor) 1958 *Inspection for Disarmament.* New York: Columbia Univ. Press.

MILBURN, THOMAS W. et al. (editors) 1961 *Non-physical Inspection Techniques.* Boston, Mass.: American Academy of Arts and Sciences.

NOEL-BAKER, PHILIP 1958 *The Arms Race: A Programme for World Disarmament.* London: Stevens; Dobbs Ferry, N.Y.: Oceana.

RICHARDSON, LEWIS FRY 1960 *Arms and Insecurity: A Mathematical Study of the Causes and Origins of War.* Edited by Nicolas Rashevsky and Ernesto Trucco. Pittsburgh: Boxwood; Chicago: Quadrangle Books. → Published posthumously.

SCHELLING, THOMAS C.; and HALPERIN, MORTON H. 1961 *Strategy and Arms Control.* New York: Twentieth Century Fund.

SINGER, J. DAVID 1962 *Deterrence, Arms Control, and Disarmament.* Columbus: Ohio State Univ. Press.

SINGER, J. DAVID (editor) 1963 Weapons Management in World Politics. *Journal of Conflict Resolution* 7, no. 3. → Also published as a special issue of the *Journal of Arms Control.*

SLOUTZKI, NOKHIM M. 1941 *The World Armaments Race: 1919–1939.* Geneva Studies, Vol. 12, No. 1. Geneva Research Centre.

SMOKER, PAUL 1963 A Mathematical Study of the Present Arms Race. *General Systems: Yearbook of the Society for General Systems Research* 8:51–59.

SPANIER, JOHN W.; and NOGEE, JOSEPH L. 1962 *The Politics of Disarmament: A Study in Soviet–American Gamesmanship.* New York: Praeger.

TATE, MERZE 1942 *The Disarmament Illusion: The Movement for a Limitation of Armaments to 1907.* New York: Macmillan.

U.S. DEPARTMENT OF STATE 1960 *Documents on Disarmament, 1945–1959.* Publication No. 7008. Washington: Government Printing Office.

U.S. DEPARTMENT OF STATE 1961 *Documents on Disarmament, 1960.* Publication No. 7172. Washington: Government Printing Office.

WRIGHT, QUINCY (1942) 1965 *A Study of War.* 2d ed. Univ. of Chicago Press.

DISASTERS

The word "disaster" evokes many different mental images and is used in diverse ways. In popular speech, the term is often used loosely to refer to any sudden, unexpected, or extraordinary misfortune, regardless of whether it occurs to an individual, a family or other small group, a community, a region, a nation, or the entire world.

Social scientific interest tends to center on relatively large-scale community or societal disasters—the sudden or rapidly developing events that disrupt the prevailing order of life and produce danger, injury, illness, death, loss of property, or other severe privations to large numbers of people residing within a common geographic area. Such events are produced by a variety of natural and man-made destructive agents, including earthquakes, epidemics, floods, hurricanes, tidal waves, tornadoes, volcanic eruptions, explosions, fires, and wartime bombing attacks.

In formal sociological terms, a disaster may be defined as "an event, concentrated in time and space, in which a society, or a relatively self-sufficient subdivision of a society, undergoes severe danger and incurs such losses to its members and physical appurtenances that the social structure is disrupted and the fulfillment of all or some of the essential functions of the society is prevented" (Fritz 1961, p. 655). Viewed in this way, a disaster is an event that disturbs the vital functioning of a society. It affects the system of *biological survival* (subsistence, shelter, health, reproduction), the system of *order* (division of labor, authority patterns, cultural norms, social roles), the system of *meaning* (values, shared definitions of reality, communication mechanisms), and the *motivation* of the actors within all of these systems.

Disasters differ in various ways: in the nature of the precipitating agent (earthquake, explosion, etc.); in their source of origin (natural forces or human actions); in their degree of predictability, probability, and controllability; in their speed of onset (instantaneous, progressive); in their scope (focalized, diffused); and in their destructive effects on people, physical objects, and the natural environment. Human behavior differs somewhat in relation to each of these features of disaster, and also within a given disaster by spatial zones, time periods, type of involvement, nature and degree of prior preparation and training, frequency and recentness of previous disaster experience, and by differences in culture and personality. The behavioral responses of disaster survivors also vary in relation to the type of protective actions taken by responsible political authorities in the predisaster and postdisaster periods, and in accordance with the human management techniques used by the organized disaster warning, control, relief, and rehabilitation agencies. Detailed and specific comparisons of disaster behavior must take these and other distinctions into account. This article reviews the typical forms of behavior that have been discovered in a wide variety of disaster research studies.

Significance of disaster studies. Disasters provide a realistic laboratory for testing the integration, stamina, and recuperative power of large-scale social systems. They provide the social scientist with advantages that cannot be matched in the study of human behavior under more normal or stable conditions. Disasters compress vital activities into a brief time span and bring normally private behavior under public observation; social processes and linkages between social and personal characteristics thus become much more visible. Cycles and patterns of human behavior that usually span many years are enacted in a matter of hours, days, or months. Because disasters disrupt and undermine social distinctions and force people to make critical choices under similar conditions, they also provide the social scientist with a unique opportunity to study human nature and the basic processes of social interaction.

The findings of disaster research have obvious practical applications. They provide foreknowledge of the social and psychological conditions brought about by disaster: in other words they enable us to know in advance what the survivors would know afterward. Thus they provide a basis for developing more realistic and effective preparations for disaster warning, control, relief, and recovery.

Historical review of disaster research. Although there is nothing novel or modern about man's desire to know what happens in disasters, the social scientific study of human and organizational behavior in disaster is relatively new. The first attempt to apply systematic social science concepts to the study of disaster was Samuel H. Prince's investigation of the munitions ship explosion in the harbor of Halifax, Nova Scotia, in 1917. His pioneering study of the social effects of disaster has provided a major source of stimulating ideas and hypotheses for subsequent investigators (Prince 1920). During the period between this study and World War II, empirical studies of disaster were conducted sporadically, primarily by single investigators using personal observation techniques or small interview and questionnaire samples. Representative examples of the research conducted during this period are Prasad's study (1935) of rumor in the Indian earthquake of 1934, Kutak's study (1938) of the social effects of the flood of 1937 in Louisville, Kentucky, and Mira's psychiatric observations (1939) of the effects of bombing attacks on civilians during the Spanish Civil War.

World War II and postwar research. The World War II bombing of British cities stimulated a large number of useful observations and individual studies by psychologists and psychiatrists. Many of these studies, together with government-sponsored research on the problems encountered in evacuating civilians from London during the blitz, have been reviewed by Titmuss (1950).

Immediately following World War II, the United States conducted large-scale sample surveys of German and Japanese cities that had been subjected to bombing attacks (U.S. Strategic Bombing Survey 1947a; 1947b). These retrospective studies were concerned primarily with indicators of morale rather than disaster behavior. Janis later reanalyzed these data, summarized the findings of other wartime studies, and developed a more systematic psychological interpretation of disaster behavior (1951).

In the 1950s, a planned program of disaster research studies emerged, stimulated and supported by various government agencies charged with responsibility for handling the hazards involved in the new arsenal of nuclear, chemical, and biological weapons. The devastating power of these new weapons dramatized, as never before, the need for developing more adequate, systematic knowledge of the social and psychological consequences of widespread disasters. In Canada, Tyhurst (1951) conducted immediate postimpact studies of individual reactions to several disasters. In 1950, the National Opinion Research Center began a four-year program of disaster field studies in various disaster-struck communities throughout the United States (Marks & Fritz 1954). Similar field study programs were undertaken by the University of Oklahoma Research Institute (Logan &

Killian 1952), by the University of Maryland Psychiatric Institute (Powell 1954), and by the University of Texas (Moore 1958).

In 1952, the National Academy of Sciences–National Research Council appointed the Committee on Disaster Studies (reorganized in 1957 as the Disaster Research Group). This group supported a wide-ranging program of disaster studies in the United States and several other countries. Its 19 "Disaster Study Series" publications (1956–1963), together with numerous unpublished materials, constitute a major contribution to the social scientific literature on disasters.

The Disaster Research Group was dissolved in 1962, but its extensive bibliography and library were transferred in 1963 to the Disaster Research Center at Ohio State University, which serves as a centralized repository for disaster research information. This center has conducted numerous field studies of disasters throughout the world, including the Vaiont Dam flood of 1963 in northern Italy, the Alaskan and Japanese earthquakes of 1964, and the Chilean and San Salvador earthquakes of 1965. Particular attention has been given in these studies to organizational responses to disaster.

The volume of social scientific research studies on disaster has thus grown to large proportions. In 1961, an inventory of disaster field studies revealed a total of 114 studies of 103 different events (National Research Council 1961); these studies, together with the U.S. bombing surveys, produced nearly 22,000 interviews and questionnaires—about 15,000 obtained from individuals exposed to peacetime disasters and about 7,000 from Germans and Japanese affected by World War II bombings. By 1965, these totals had been augmented by over 25 additional field studies and by several thousand interviews.

Common misconceptions of disaster behavior. One of the first tasks of systematic disaster research involved an act of intellectual debris clearance: the accumulated myths and distorted ideas of many centuries had to be cleared from the conceptual attic before more fundamental studies of human and organizational behavior in disasters could be made.

The traditional picture of disaster behavior consists of lurid scenes of society and human nature in the process of disintegration. Most of these simple stereotypes have not stood the test of critical research scrutiny. Contrary to the commonly held notions, disaster field studies have shown that panic is a comparatively rare form of behavior in disasters. Stricken populations do not, on the whole, become hysterical but help themselves and perform most of their own rescue and relief tasks. Only a few cases of looting have been reported. The major problem of crowd control is not so much the flight of victims from the disaster scene as the convergence of vast numbers of people from outside the disaster area. There are only isolated examples of the breakdown of moral codes. Emotional aftereffects are widespread but relatively transitory. Morale and optimism are quickly restored; indeed, the morale of the survivors may be abnormally high in some respects. Abatement of the usual social conflicts greatly strengthens social integration, and most of the social and personal behavioral pathologies of everyday life either fail to increase significantly or actually decline under disaster conditions.

Disasters do indeed pose many serious problems of human planning and management, but the actual problems discovered by research rarely coincide with those envisaged by the usual notions of disaster behavior. Moreover, the traditional stereotypes have obscured the fact that disasters produce not only disruptive and disorganizing effects but also reconstructive and regenerative human responses. Both of these perspectives must be kept in mind in any balanced treatment of the social aspects of disaster.

Disaster preparations.   The minimization of social disruption requires highly organized preparations for disasters before they occur. It is difficult, however, to establish and maintain an adequate state of preparation under normal conditions, especially if there has been no recent disaster experience. Programs designed to prepare people for an uncertain future threat must compete with immediate and pressing human concerns: the day-to-day problems of earning a livelihood, protecting oneself and family from the daily dangers to life and health, and securing recognition, response, and status in relations with members of one's personal community. Most people are not vitally concerned with problems outside the orbit of their immediate personal lives, even when there is threat of war or other disaster.

Disaster preparedness programs relying on individual initiative for developing protective measures have always failed because they ignore this overwhelming preoccupation with daily concerns and the universal human tendency to err on the side of normalcy by assuming that everything is all right until events clearly prove otherwise. As a consequence, the recognition of danger and preparation for disaster are usually postponed until it is too late to prepare well-organized precautionary and protective measures.

Warning and threat.   The common tendency to deny that danger is at hand is illustrated in studies of disaster warning. Difficulties in public warning often start with the persons or agencies responsible for detecting the danger and issuing the warnings. They are usually reluctant to issue a specific warning until they are reasonably certain that danger will actually materialize. Waiting for this degree of certainty has sometimes delayed the dissemination of the warning until it is too late.

Even where the existence, nature, and time of the danger can be adequately forecast, it is difficult to secure public acceptance of warning messages. People tend to seize on any vagueness, ambiguity, or incompatibility in the warning message that enables them to interpret the situation optimistically. They search for more information that will confirm, deny, or clarify the warning message, and often they continue to interpret signs of danger as familiar, normal events until it is too late to take effective precautions.

Disaster impact.   When danger is recognized as imminent and personal, people seek safety or escape, and their behavior is generally adaptive. Rather than engaging in irrational acts, which increase the danger, they usually take action to protect themselves and their associates. The success of their actions depends to a large extent upon the possibilities available in the situation and the adequacy and accuracy of information that they possess.

Flight is one means of escaping danger, but it should not be equated with panic. It is more often orderly and goal-directed than disorderly or panic-stricken, and it is often the only rational choice if one is to survive.

Even during violent impacts, most people continue to be concerned about the safety of other people in their immediate surroundings and the welfare of their family members. The family group is a central object of orientation during the impact period and throughout all phases of the emergency.

During and immediately after impact, people tend to define the situation in terms of what is happening to themselves and their immediate surroundings and to think of it as something happening only there. This tendency to underestimate the scope and destructiveness of the disaster makes for considerable variability in the initial behavior of disaster-struck populations; and it helps to account for the seemingly chaotic, confused, and conflicting behavioral patterns that the outside observer witnesses in the immediate postimpact period.

Postimpact emergency.   The most significant problems of behavior in the immediate postimpact period derive from social disorganization and uncoordinated action rather than from irrational individual behavior or helplessness of the survivors. Many, if not most, of the immediate tasks of rescue and relief are handled informally by the disaster survivors before the arrival of outside aid. However, much of this informal activity is sporadic and unsystematic. The separate and independent actions of many thousands of people and small groups, each trying to cope with the disaster in its own way, often produces duplication of effort or conflicting patterns of action. They constitute a "mass assault" on the problems of disaster that frequently accomplishes the essential tasks but with considerable inefficiency of effort.

A persistent source of uncoordinated activity found in all disasters arises from anxiety over missing family members and friends. Within moments after impact, survivors who are separated from family members or other intimates begin a desperate search for them. These independent and separate search activities by large numbers of people produce conflicting patterns of action and often interfere with the performance of community-oriented tasks.

Separation anxiety is sometimes an important problem for personnel who have important official disaster responsibilities. As Killian (1952) has noted, people are confronted with "role conflicts" in choosing between family duties and their more formal social roles. Most people quickly resolve the conflict in favor of loyalty first to intimates, and only then turn their attention to larger social-group loyalties. For people with clearly defined disaster jobs, however, the conflict may persist and cause considerable personal stress unless special provisions are made to assure them of the location and condition of their families.

Convergence behavior. A central problem of coordination and control in disasters derives not from the victim population but from the informal, spontaneous "convergence behavior" (Fritz & Mathewson 1957) of persons living outside the disaster area. Shortly after impact, thousands of persons begin to converge on the disaster area and on first-aid stations, hospitals, relief centers, and communication centers near the area. Along with this movement of persons, incoming messages of anxious inquiry and offers of help from all parts of the nation and from foreign countries overload communication facilities; and tons of unsolicited equipment and supplies of clothing, food, bedding, and other materials begin to arrive.

This convergence action, which continues for days and weeks following a disaster, seriously con-

gests transportation and communication facilities and hampers the administration of organized rescue, medical, emergency relief, and rehabilitation programs. It graphically demonstrates that the people affected by disaster are not confined to the immediate geographical area of destruction, death, or injury. All persons who are related to, or who identify themselves with, persons and organizations in the stricken area are also affected. Thus the effective unit of disaster management is usually national in scope, even when the primary sufferers are in a single community.

Problems of disaster agencies. Various problems of coordination and control stem not from public responses to disaster but from inadequacies in the plans, organization, and operations of formal disaster agencies. Disaster plans are often too limited in scope, both functionally and geographically, to provide the requisite coordination and integration of organizational actions. Conflicts in authority sometimes arise because there is an absence of an agreed-upon, understood division of labor among different groups and agencies concerning which official or agency has the authority to make decisions. Duplicating or conflicting agency actions frequently occur because the disaster management authorities have failed to establish centralized mechanisms for coordinating requests for equipment and supplies; distributing patients among hospitals; pooling casualty and survivor information; or for screening, organizing, and using large numbers of untrained volunteers.

Much of the confusion and lack of coordination in the rescue, relief, and rehabilitation efforts results from the lack of systematic procedures for maintaining a central strategic overview of the disaster, so that leadership, controls, and resources can be applied in the places where they are most critically needed. Lack of coordination also stems from the natural human tendency to feel a great sense of urgency to get something done to help the victims, which makes taking time to communicate and coordinate decisions seem a luxury. Under stress it is also difficult to exercise the more complex intellectual processes such as looking ahead and thinking about the indirect consequences of a decision.

Communication is often inadequate, partly because of the destruction of communication facilities but more generally because of improper use of these facilities. Finally, many of the problems of disaster management result from insensitivity to the changes in the structure, values, and prevailing climate of opinion among the victims during the various postdisaster phases, resulting in a lack of fit between the rather different conceptions of need held by relief organizations and by those whom they are trying to help.

Social adaptations to disaster

The great significance of behavioral problems in disaster has, understandably, caused many observers to overlook the fact that disasters produce many therapeutic effects on social systems. The sharing of a common threat to survival and the widespread suffering produced by disaster usually result in a dramatic increase in social solidarity and a temporary breakdown of pre-existing social and economic distinctions. This newly developed solidarity is of major significance in facilitating both social and personal recuperation. It resolves pre-existing personal and social conflicts; prevents or ameliorates the usual disorganized responses to trauma, loss, and privation; reduces the amount of self-aggressive and antisocial behavior; and motivates people to devote their energies to socially regenerative tasks.

Evidence supporting the existence of these therapeutic results during the integrative phase of disaster may be found in many different accounts and reports, both past and present, wartime and peacetime. In general, the findings can be summarized as follows: (1) injured disaster victims and their families are unusually calm, quiet, undemanding, and thoughtful of other people; (2) ethnic and minority group differences tend to disappear; (3) families tend to develop greater internal solidarity; (4) social relationships tend to be strengthened, not only with kin and extended family but with all survivors; (5) disaster sufferers report a relatively low sense of deprivation when comparing their losses with others; (6) there are frequent cases of remission of pre-existing neurotic and psychosomatic symptoms; (7) there is a decrease in admissions to mental hospitals and to psychological outpatient clinics; (8) the suicide rate declines; (9) homicides and crimes against the person show a downward trend; and (10) the verified cases of theft, looting, profiteering, and other forms of exploitation and antisocial behavior are quantitatively insignificant when compared with actions aimed at mutual aid, restoration, and reintegration.

These integrative effects of disaster apparently provide a major stimulus for rapid restoration and social reconstruction. Virtually all modern disaster-struck communities and nations have not only been quickly restored, but in many cases they have experienced an "amplified rebound," in which the society is carried far beyond its predisaster levels of solidarity, productivity, and capacity for growth. Likewise, historical analyses of wars and other large disasters usually have emphasized their legacy of positive social change.

It is obvious that most disasters produce some types of relatively persistent social change. However, the exact nature of these long-run changes, and the process by which they occur in various societies (both developed and underdeveloped), under varying disaster conditions, is still imperfectly understood. The study of the long-term effects of disaster is a major area for future systematic research.

General implications of research findings. Disasters produce a new and different referential framework within which people perceive and judge their experiences. The recurrent crises and accidents of everyday life tend to be isolated, random events that produce private human troubles and suffering but do not induce changes in the organization of society. In contrast, disasters are sufficiently concentrated in time and place to pose a clear, easily perceivable threat to social survival. They affect all persons indiscriminately, and thereby produce a temporary breakdown in hierarchical status distinctions. The reference changes from "Only I have suffered" to "All of us have suffered; we are all in it together." Danger, loss, and suffering become public, rather than private, phenomena. Disasters thus lead to social remedy and social change, rather than requiring the individual or small group to bear the burden of readjustment to an intact, unchanged society.

The social disorganization that occurs in disaster is essentially a disruption of the complex structure of social differentiations and culturally defined communication networks of secondary group life. Except momentarily, disaster does not disorganize primary group life. On the contrary, this is strengthened, becomes more pristine, and is more widely based than in ordinary social life. The quality of interaction throughout the entire community of sufferers approximates more closely the characteristics of intimate, informal interaction set forth in the concept of the primary group.

This capacity of human societies under severe stress to contract from a highly elaborated set of secondary group organizations to a kind of universal primary group existence is probably their central, built-in protective mechanism. It helps to account for the fact that nations and communities typically demonstrate amazing toughness and resiliency in coping with the destructive effects of disaster and unusual speed in restoring and regenerating more complex forms of social life.

If disaster studies have demonstrated nothing else, they have shown that man is a highly adaptive social animal when he is directly confronted with clear challenges to his continued existence. He has survived every conceivable form of disaster in the past, and, short of total annihilation, he is likely to do so in the future.

CHARLES E. FRITZ

[*See also* COLLECTIVE BEHAVIOR; MASS PHENOMENA.]

BIBLIOGRAPHY

BAKER, GEORGE W.; and CHAPMAN, DWIGHT W. (editors) 1962 *Man and Society in Disaster.* New York: Basic Books.

BARTON, ALLEN H. 1963 *Social Organization Under Stress: A Sociological Review of Disaster Studies.* Disaster Research Group, Disaster Study No. 17. Washington: National Academy of Sciences–National Research Council.

BROWNLEE, ALETA 1931 Disasters and Disaster Relief. Volume 5, pages 161–166 in *Encyclopaedia of the Social Sciences.* New York: Macmillan.

Disasters and Disaster Relief. 1957 American Academy of Political and Social Science, *Annals* 309:1–228. → The entire issue is devoted to disasters.

FORM, WILLIAM H.; and NOSOW, SIGMUND N. 1958 *Community in Disaster.* New York: Harper.

FRITZ, CHARLES E. 1960 Some Implications From Disaster Research for a National Shelter Program. Pages 139–156 in National Research Council, Disaster Research Group, *Symposium on Human Problems in the Utilization of Fallout Shelters.* Disaster Study No. 12. Washington: National Academy of Sciences–National Research Council.

FRITZ, CHARLES E. 1961 Disaster. Pages 651–694 in Robert K. Merton and Robert A. Nisbet (editors), *Contemporary Social Problems.* New York: Harcourt.

FRITZ, CHARLES E.; and MARKS, E. S. 1954 The NORC Studies of Human Behavior in Disaster. *Journal of Social Issues* 10, no. 3:26–41.

FRITZ, CHARLES E.; and MATHEWSON, J. H. 1957 *Convergence Behavior in Disasters: A Problem in Social Control.* Committee on Disaster Studies, Disaster Study No. 9. Washington: National Academy of Sciences–National Research Council.

FRITZ, CHARLES E.; and WILLIAMS, HARRY B. 1957 The Human Being in Disasters: A Research Prospective. American Academy of Political and Social Science, *Annals* 309:42–51.

Human Adaptation to Disaster. 1957 *Human Organization* 16, no. 2. → The entire issue is devoted to disaster research.

Human Behavior in Disaster: A New Field of Social Research. 1954 *Journal of Social Issues* 10, no. 3. → The entire issue is devoted to disaster research.

IKLÉ, FRED C. 1958 *The Social Impact of Bomb Destruction.* Norman: Univ. of Oklahoma Press.

INSTITUUT VOOR SOCIAAL ONDERZOEK VAN HET NEDERLANDSE VOLK 1955 *Studies in Holland Flood Disaster 1953.* 4 vols. Amsterdam: The Institute; Washington: Committee on Disaster Studies of the National Academy of Sciences–National Research Council.

JAMES, WILLIAM 1911 On Some Mental Effects of the Earthquake. Pages 207–226 in William James, *Memories and Studies.* New York: Longmans.

JANIS, IRVING L. 1951 *Air War and Emotional Stress: Psychological Studies of Bombing and Civilian Defense.* New York: McGraw-Hill.

KILLIAN, LEWIS M. 1952 The Significance of Multiple-group Membership in Disaster. *American Journal of Sociology* 57:309–314.

KILLIAN, LEWIS M. 1956 *An Introduction to Methodological Problems of Field Studies in Disasters.* Committee on Disaster Studies, Disaster Study No. 8. Washington: National Academy of Sciences–National Research Council.

KUTAK, ROBERT I. 1938 Sociology of Crises: The Louisville Flood of 1937. *Social Forces* 17:66–72.

LOGAN, LEONARD; and KILLIAN, LEWIS M. 1952 A Study of the Effect of Catastrophe on Social Disorganization. Technical Memorandum No. ORO-T-194. Unpublished, mimeographed manuscript, Operations Research Office, Chevy Chase, Md.

MARKS, E. S.; and FRITZ, CHARLES E. 1954 Human Reactions in Disaster Situations. 3 vols. Unpublished report, National Opinion Research Center, Univ. of Chicago. → Available as U.S. Armed Services Technical Information Agency Document No. AD-107594.

MIRA, E. 1939 Psychiatric Experiences in the Spanish War. *British Medical Journal* 1:1217–1220.

MOORE, HARRY E. 1958 *Tornadoes Over Texas: A Study of Waco and San Angelo in Disaster.* Austin: Univ. of Texas Press.

MOORE, HARRY E. et al. 1963 *Before the Wind: A Study of the Response to Hurricane Carla.* Disaster Research Group, Disaster Study No. 19. Washington: National Academy of Sciences–National Research Council.

NATIONAL RESEARCH COUNCIL, DISASTER RESEARCH GROUP 1961 *Field Studies of Disaster Behavior: An Inventory.* Disaster Study No. 14. Washington: National Academy of Sciences–National Research Council.

POWELL, JOHN W. 1954 An Introduction to the Natural History of Disaster. Unpublished manuscript, Univ. of Maryland Psychiatric Institute (Baltimore).

PRASAD, JAMUNA 1935 The Psychology of Rumour: A Study Relating to the Great Indian Earthquake of 1934. *British Journal of Psychology* 26:1–15.

PRINCE, SAMUEL H. 1920 *Catastrophe and Social Change: Based Upon a Sociological Study of the Halifax Disaster.* New York: Columbia Univ. Press.

QUARANTELLI, E. L. 1954 The Nature and Conditions of Panic. *American Journal of Sociology* 60:267–275.

RAYNER, JEANNETTE F. 1957 Studies of Disasters and Other Extreme Situations: An Annotated Selected Bibliography. *Human Organization* 16, no. 2:30–40.

SCHELSKY, HELMUT (1953) 1955 *Wandlungen der deutschen Familie in der Gegenwart.* 3d enl. ed. Stuttgart (Germany): Enke.

TITMUSS, RICHARD M. 1950 *Problems of Social Policy.* London: Longmans; H.M. Stationery Office.

TYHURST, J. S. 1951 Individual Reactions to Community Disaster: The Natural History of Psychiatric Phenomena. *American Journal of Psychiatry* 107:764–769.

U.S. STRATEGIC BOMBING SURVEY 1947a *The Effects of Strategic Bombing on German Morale.* 2 vols. Washington: Government Printing Office.

U.S. STRATEGIC BOMBING SURVEY 1947b *The Effects of Strategic Bombing on Japanese Morale.* Washington: Government Printing Office.

WOLFENSTEIN, MARTHA 1957 *Disaster: A Psychological Essay.* Glencoe, Ill.: Free Press.

DISCOVERY

See Creativity; Innovation; Research and development; Technology; *and the biography of* Ogburn.

DISCRETE DISTRIBUTIONS

See under Distributions, statistical.

DISCRIMINANT FUNCTIONS

See Multivariate analysis, *article on* classification and discrimination.

DISCRIMINATION, ECONOMIC

As a general and somewhat loose statement, economic discrimination can be said to occur against members of a group whenever their earnings fall short of the amount "warranted" by their abilities. Public interest has usually been centered on groups that are either numerical minorities (such as Negroes in the United States, Untouchables in India, Jews in the Soviet Union, Laplanders in Sweden, and Chinese in Indonesia) or are political, social, or economic minorities (such as the Blacks in South Africa, immigrants from Africa in Israel, and women in most countries). Until recent years, economic discrimination was generally seen as evidence of exploitation of minorities by majorities. This interpretation is clearest in writings with Marxist sympathies (Aptheker 1946), although it is also found in weaker form in much of the literature (Allport 1954, p. 210).

In the past, economists tended to neglect the study of discrimination against minorities, primarily because they were reluctant to interpret any appreciable economic phenomena in terms of "exploitation," which stems from what is technically called monopsony power [see Monopoly]. The growing interest of economists in discrimination during the last decade has been stimulated by an approach that is not based as much on exploitation as on considerations that may involve even a sharper break with traditional economic theory. In this approach, members of a group earn less than their abilities warrant if other persons are willing to "pay" (that is, give up resources) in order to avoid employing, working with, lending to, training, or educating these members.

Discrimination in the market place. Further discussion is facilitated by distinguishing discrimination affecting the talents that are brought to the market place from discrimination in the market place itself. Since the latter is taken to mean that less is earned than is warranted by productivity, such discrimination would not exist *if all persons maximized money incomes* and if all markets were competitive. For, under these circumstances, the increased money incomes of employers, employees, or consumers, resulting from associating with members of a group receiving less than their productivity, would stimulate a demand for such members that would continue until their earnings rose sufficiently to cover their productivity.

Accordingly, discrimination in competitive markets is said to occur because some participants have *tastes for discrimination*, more loosely called "prejudice." Because of these tastes, they are willing to forfeit money income or other resources in order to avoid employing, working with, or buying from members of a particular group. Indeed, the intensity of their prejudice is measured by how much they are willing to forfeit (Becker 1957, chapter 1). The measuring rod of money provides an operational and quantifiable concept of prejudice that is consistent with the economist's concept of tastes and the statistician's concept of subjective probabilities (Savage 1954). Objections to such a behavioristic concept of prejudice and hatred might be tempered upon reflecting that a hatred cannot be very strong, in any meaningful sense, if there is a reluctance to satisfy it by parting with some resources. This approach to discrimination not only incorporates common notions about prejudice much more fully than does one based on exploitation, but also is more consistent with the general prevalence of workably competitive markets.

Although the extent of market discrimination depends, of course, on the intensity of the average taste for discrimination, it by no means depends on this alone. Also very relevant are any differences among participants in the desire to discriminate, the relative number and occupational distribution of minority members, the extent of competition in product markets, and the degree of substitution between different groups (Becker 1957). For example, consider discrimination by employers against a group working in a competitive industry. Even if the employers' average taste for discrimination were large, market discrimination could be negligible if the group were a small fraction of the total labor force in the industry and if some employers' tastes for discrimination were weak (or even negative). For then, members of the group could be fully employed by these employers. An increase in the size of the group or a decline in the fraction of employers with weak tastes for discrimination would tend to increase market discrimination, perhaps substantially, because members could no longer be fully employed by these employers, and some members would have to find employment among those employers with stronger tastes for discrimination. However, the latter would employ these members only if the cost of discriminating were sufficiently large—that is, the earnings of members sufficiently low—to offset their tastes.

Even the market form in which the discrimination manifests itself can be very important. If the result were simply lower hourly earnings, discriminators would have to balance the gain from discriminating—satisfying their prejudice—against the cost of discriminating—their loss in income from not associating with persons receiving less than their productivity. If, however, because of market imperfections, trade union behavior, or minimum wage or "equal pay" legislation (Alchian & Kessel 1962), hourly earnings of minorities were prevented from falling, the cost of discrimination would be eliminated because no resources would be forfeited by not hiring minorities; and discriminators would be encouraged to discriminate still more. The result would be greater unemployment of minorities, and discrimination would take the market form of, say, lower annual earnings rather than lower hourly earnings.

Quantitative evidence on the extent of market discrimination against different minorities is surprisingly limited; the most extensive evidence relates to Negroes in the United States. Significant market discrimination against them is suggested by the much lower earnings of urban male Negroes than of urban male whites of the same age, years of schooling, and region, and the somewhat greater unemployment of Negro males, even when occupation is held constant. The absolute occupational position of Negroes has risen substantially in both the North and South during the last hundred years. Since, however, the position of whites has risen at about the same rate, the relative position of Negroes has changed surprisingly little, the greatest change (a rise) coming after 1940. One of the most striking findings is that market discrimination is apparently relatively slight against young new entrants into the labor force, but it increases significantly with age. This finding is presumably explained by a combination of inadequate preparation of Negroes for occupational advance and greater market prejudice against more advanced Negroes. Similar findings would probably apply to other minority groups in the world. (For evidence on the economic position of Negroes, see Becker 1957, chapters 7–10;

Dewey 1952; Gilman 1963; and Ginzberg et al. 1956.)

Deficiencies brought to the market place.   Perhaps more than half the total difference between the earnings and abilities of Negroes in the United States results from deficiencies brought to the market place, rather than from market discrimination itself; again, a similar relation would probably be found for other minorities. These deficiencies include poor health, low morale and motivation, and limited information about opportunities. The most pervasive force, however, is insufficient and inferior education and training. For example, in 1960, Negro males aged 25–64 averaged less than 8 years of schooling, while whites averaged more than 10.5 years; and Negro schooling has clearly been inferior in quality.

An important cause of deficiencies in education and training are the limitations imposed by poverty itself, especially when combined with the usual difficulties in financing large expenditures. Of course, poverty may in part result from either past discrimination, as exemplified by Negro slavery, or current discrimination, thus leading to the so-called vicious circle of discrimination (Myrdal 1944). Discrimination by governments and private institutions in charge of education and training facilities has been common, as illustrated by the government restrictions on the education of Blacks in South Africa and (at least in the past) Jews in eastern Europe, the quotas applied by certain private universities in the United States, or the racial (and even religious) restrictions on admission to apprenticeship and other training programs administered by trade unions in many countries.

Role of government.   Undoubtedly, some of the worst economic discrimination, as well as other kinds, is directly traceable to government action. One need only note the restrictions placed on the economic advance of Blacks in South Africa, the harassment of the Chinese in Indonesia and other parts of Asia, or the virtual confiscation of some of the property of Japanese Americans in the United States during World War II. On the other hand, government action is often a force in widening opportunities and thus breaking down economic discrimination: of greatest influence is the enforcement of equality before the law, although the provision of free or subsidized education has also been important. Legislation of the "fair employment" kind, prohibiting racial, ethnic, religious, and other forms of discrimination in employment, can have some effect too. Very little scholarly analysis has been made of the economic effects resulting from this kind of legislation. In the United States, the evidence provided by the states with such legislation suggests that it somewhat increases both the earnings and unemployment of minorities (Landes 1966).

A few of the more extreme nineteenth-century advocates of a competitive market economy believed that eventually its extension and development would eliminate most economic discrimination and hatred. Unfortunately, this has not yet taken place; discrimination exists, and at times even flourishes, in competitive economies, the position of Negroes in the United States being a clear example. At the same time, one must realize that the pressures of competition, the emphasis on material goods, the impersonality of and the cost accounting in a market economy often help mitigate, and sometimes even eliminate, the effects of prejudice. Indeed, in desperation, market participants in the United States, South Africa, Great Britain, Indonesia, and elsewhere have (successfully) appealed to their governments for protection from the "unfair" competition of various minorities.

In spite of the widespread public interest in economic discrimination throughout the world, relatively little is known about its quantitative importance and socioeconomic determinants. Much greater understanding of the formation of prejudice is necessary, although economists are unlikely to be of great value here. Their comparative advantage lies in analyzing how prejudices combine with various institutional arrangements to produce actual discrimination. It has already been mentioned that the degree of competition, the size of minority groups, and many other factors as yet insufficiently studied also affect the amount of market discrimination.

Likewise, the effect of prejudice, by the electorate, trade union members, or directors of educational institutions, on the extent of nonmarket discrimination is determined by whether different political issues are effectively tied together, whether the costs of discriminating or the gains from not discriminating are hidden, and on many other institutional arrangements (Becker 1957, chapter 5; 1959). Consider, for example, the election by majority rule of representatives to decide on two issues, one dealing with discrimination against a minority. Assume that the minority is more concerned about discrimination while the majority, although more concerned about the other issue, does not agree on how to resolve it. A successful campaign could be conducted by promising to satisfy the minority on discrimination and a segment of the majority on the other issue. The decision on discrimination could, therefore, be more favorable to the minority than if each issue were decided separately (by, say, referendum), or if the majority were less split on the other issue, or if the majority attached greater importance to discrimination. Considerably more study of institutional arrangements is required in order to know more about the factors determining the talents that minorities are permitted to bring to the market place.

GARY S. BECKER

BIBLIOGRAPHY

ALCHIAN, ARMEN A.; and KESSEL, REUBEN A. 1962 Competition, Monopoly, and the Pursuit of Pecuniary Gain. Pages 156–183 in Universities–National Bureau Committee for Economic Research Conference, Princeton, N.J., 1960, *Aspects of Labor Economics.* Princeton Univ. Press. → Includes a discussion by Gary S. Becker and Martin Bronfenbrenner.

ALLPORT, GORDON W. 1954 *The Nature of Prejudice.* Reading, Mass.: Addison-Wesley. → An abridged paperback edition was published in 1958 by Doubleday.

APTHEKER, HERBERT 1946 *The Negro People in America: A Critique of Gunnar Myrdal's* An American Dilemma. New York: International Publishers.

BECKER, GARY S. 1957 *The Economics of Discrimination.* Univ. of Chicago Press.

BECKER, GARY S. 1959 Union Restrictions on Entry. Pages 209–224 in Philip D. Bradley (editor), *The Public Stake in Union Power.* Charlottesville: Univ. of Virginia Press.

DEWEY, DONALD J. 1952 Negro Employment in Southern Industry. *Journal of Political Economy* 60:279–293.

GILMAN, HARRY J. 1963 The White/Non-white Unemployment Differential. Pages 75–113 in Mark Perlman (editor), *Human Resources in the Urban Economy.* Washington: Resources for the Future.

GINZBERG, ELI et al. 1956 *The Negro Potential.* New York: Columbia Univ. Press. → A paperback edition was published in 1963.

LANDES, WILLIAM 1966 An Economic Analysis of Fair Employment Practice Laws. Ph.D. dissertation, Columbia Univ.

MYRDAL, GUNNAR (1944) 1962 *An American Dilemma: The Negro Problem and Modern Democracy.* New York: Harper. → A paperback edition was published in 1964 by McGraw-Hill.

SAVAGE, LEONARD J. 1954 *The Foundations of Statistics.* New York: Wiley.

DISCRIMINATION, SOCIAL

See ASSIMILATION; MINORITIES; PREJUDICE; RACE RELATIONS; SEGREGATION.

DISCRIMINATION LEARNING

See under LEARNING.

DISEASE, CONCEPTS OF

See EPIDEMIOLOGY; HEALTH; HYSTERIA; ILLNESS; MENTAL DISORDERS; MENTAL HEALTH; NEUROSIS; PSYCHOSIS; PSYCHOSOMATIC ILLNESS; PUBLIC HEALTH.

DISENGAGEMENT

Disengagement became part of the vocabulary of international politics after World War II. It was offered as an alternative policy prescription to the perilous face-to-face confrontation, especially in central Europe, of opposing political systems and armed forces equipped with nuclear weapons capable of total destruction. The essence of disengagement is the separation of the contending forces and the creation, in the intervening territory, of a nonaligned state (or states) with political, social, and economic systems equally acceptable (or unacceptable) to both adjacent powers, including a level of military forces that by itself does not constitute a significant threat to either side.

A second, but less common, definition of disengagement pertains to areas where a variety of powers contend for dominant influence and where, as in the Middle East during the post-1945 epoch, there is great political instability but not a direct military confrontation of major powers. Here disengagement describes a national policy characterized by aloofness and watchful nonintervention, rather than the withdrawal of two forces pitted face to face.

This article will deal with disengagement primarily in its first, more usual, sense.

The term distinguished. Disengagement policies must be distinguished from three antecedent practices of interstate relations in the period between the World Wars: the policy of *cordon sanitaire*; the creation of buffer states; and the existence of corridors.

A *cordon sanitaire* is a territory separating two powers who if they combined in a single land mass might constitute a threat to other nations. Thus the principal victor powers in World War I sought to keep Germany and Russia apart by creating between them a belt of nations consisting of the Baltic states, Poland, and Czechoslovakia, whose sovereignty was to be guaranteed by the major Western powers.

Buffer states are weak states existing by leave of their preponderant neighbor, whose military, political, and economic interests they serve. An example is Belgium, which owed its independent existence, from 1831 to World War II, to its chief neighboring powers, Great Britain and France, who used it to establish a balance of power favorable to them.

A *corridor* is a strip of territory giving a state access to a remote component part across the sovereign territory of a neighboring state. Pomerania constituted the link between East Prussia and the rest of Germany until 1919. The Versailles Treaty gave Pomerania to Poland, in order to allow it access to the Baltic Sea, thereby separating East Prussia from the rest of Germany and creating the so-called corridor across Poland, which became a major source of tension between the two countries.

Disengagement policies seek to separate two mutually antagonistic powers, unlike the *cordon sanitaire*, which was employed to keep potential allies apart. The states from which foreign troops are withdrawn—or disengaged—would not favor the policy interests of any one neighbor; buffer states, on the other hand, exist by sufferance of neighbors whose interests they serve. Disengagement policies aim to eliminate the impediments to direct contact between people of a given nationality instead of perpetuating the uncertainties of access that result from the establishment of corridors.

These distinctions can be further clarified by citing the circumstances of central European politics following World War II. While no effort to create a *cordon sanitaire* has been made in Europe since 1945, East and West Germany have been kept divided because of the fear that a reunified Germany might constitute a new international danger. Most disengagement policies aim at the reunification of Germany to eliminate the tensions resulting from continued partition. The nations of the Warsaw Pact, stretching along the western and southwestern frontiers of the Soviet Union from Finland to Bulgaria, are in effect buffer states serving Russia's security interests. A principal aim of Western disengagement proposals is withdrawal of the U.S.S.R.'s forces and the reduction of its influence in eastern Europe, so as to reinstate a balance of power in that area. A corridor in fact exists linking West Germany with Berlin across the territory of the East German state. Disengagement proposals aim at the elimination of the barriers to free air, road, rail, and canal connections with Berlin. Thus the concept of disengagement is not only distinguishable from the practices of *cordon sanitaire*, buffer state, and corridor, but disengagement proposals aim at eliminating vestiges of these historically antecedent practices to be found in Europe today as part of the cold war *status quo*.

Plans for disengagement. Since 1945 the concept of disengagement has been implicit in a variety of plans evolved to meet the situation in central Europe, where the two supernuclear powers, the Soviet Union and the United States, who feared only each other, failed to agree on the future of Germany as a whole and refused to withdraw their military forces, which enforced their political interests in East and West Germany.

Through 1964 more than a hundred different plans for the disengagement of East and West military forces in central Europe had been put forward by national governments, individual statesmen, prominent ex-leaders, and private individuals and groups. (For a listing, see Hinterhoff 1959, pp. 414–442.) A distinguishing feature of these plans is that all concern the future of Germany. Solutions for the divided state of Germany range from U.S. Secretary of State James F. Byrnes's 1946 proposal for a 25-year four-power treaty guarantee against further aggression from a united, disarmed Germany to Soviet Premier Nikita Khrushchev's 1959 plan for withdrawal of foreign troops from all of Europe, creation of an atom-free zone in central Europe, and retention of the *status quo* of a divided Germany. Over the years, the concept of disengagement evolved from taking measures to deal with renewed threats of German aggression to creating broad neutral zones in Europe. These zones would require dismantling of nonindigenous military installations and either retaining the political *status quo* or providing for the reunification of Germany under changed circumstances. This evolution of plans, none of which received support from both East and West, was marked by specific proposals of the Polish foreign minister, Adam Rapacki; the leader of the British Labour party, Hugh Gaitskell; and the chairman of the U.S. State Department's Policy Planning Staff, George F. Kennan. Each of these statesmen proposed major changes in the stance and policies of the major powers in Europe; the essential common denominator of the three proposals was the disengagement of American and Russian forces.

The first version of the Rapacki plan, in October 1957, provided for an atom-free zone covering Poland, Czechoslovakia, East Germany, and West Germany, with a four-power guarantee but no withdrawal of foreign forces or changes in the alliances of the powers. The second version, in November 1958, and a later revision added provisions for reducing and eventually withdrawing foreign forces from the zone, with appropriate control measures. The Gaitskell plan was publicized in lectures at Harvard University in January 1957 and differed from the Rapacki plans in that it provided for the reunification of East and West Germany in the context of a restricted armaments zone from which foreign troops were to be gradually withdrawn, the zone to include, in addition to Germany, Poland, Czechoslovakia, Hungary, and possibly Rumania. This arrangement was to be guaranteed by a European security pact, which both the Soviet Union and the United States would sign. The Rapacki plans, which appeared to have support from the Soviet government, were rejected by the major NATO powers. The Gaitskell plan was unacceptable to the Soviet bloc and was also rejected by the West German government of Konrad Adenauer.

Ambassador Kennan's disengagement policy proposals were in some ways the best thought out, and their elaboration in the Reith lectures over the BBC in the autumn of 1957 (later published as *Russia, the Atom and the West*, 1958) provoked widespread public discussion and controversy involving high political leaders of the major powers. Kennan had gained an international reputation for framing and defining the West's policy of containment (1947). For Kennan, disengagement was a logical successor policy to containment, which by the mid-1950s had pitted effectively equal powers hard against one another, creating an inflexible situation in which either an incident or a misinterpretation of intentions could unleash world-wide nuclear destruction. He held that this danger could only be reduced through the separation of military forces and the reuniting of Europe through a negotiated settlement of the German problem. Specifically, Kennan proposed reunifying Germany and joining it with Poland, Czechoslovakia, and Hungary in a zone from which NATO and Soviet troops would be withdrawn. The balance of power in the zone would be maintained by national armed forces and militia. Germany's freedom to associate with NATO or the East would be restricted, while Germany and the other states constituting the zone would receive guarantees from NATO and the Warsaw Pact powers who would join in a European security pact.

Criticisms of disengagement. In the heated debate stirred up by Kennan's proposals, the entire concept of disengagement was sharply criticized. Some critics took issue with the concept because it was diametrically opposed to the idea of forcing a unilateral withdrawal of the Russian army and liberating eastern Europe from communist domination. Other critics, including some of Kennan's former colleagues, such as Dean Acheson (1958), opposed and ridiculed disengagement on a variety of other grounds. Foremost among these was the charge that the idea of disengagement rested on a fundamental misunderstanding of national and international power. According to this view, a classic imperialist power such as the U.S.S.R. could not realistically be expected to keep from disrupting the precarious balance in a relatively weak territory from which forces of the major powers had been withdrawn. A parallel criticism was that a disengagement in Europe would be inherently unequal. Soviet Russia's forces would withdraw several hundred miles, whereas U.S. forces would be pulled back thousands of miles across the Atlantic. Another major criticism was that disengagement could not achieve any positive result because the essential danger is in the confrontation of missiles poised thousands of miles apart. Indeed, some argued that disengagement would create a vacuum in central Europe and increase the danger that the missiles would be used because they would be the only resort in the event of an incident (Acheson 1958).

These criticisms were eloquently refuted by Kennan in an article, "Disengagement Revisited" (1959), in which he accused opponents of disengagement of seeking the ideal military posture, which "is simply the enemy of every political *détente* or compromise." This article and other writings by proponents of disengagement focused on the problems of Germany's partition which, they argued, could not continue indefinitely. Unless reunification were achieved through East–West negotiations resulting in disengagement, direct West German dealings with Moscow would become a constant threat that could disrupt NATO, while eastern Europe remained under communist domination.

The future of disengagement. Research and writing on disengagement falls into the general field of international political research, chiefly pertaining to Europe. Theoretically the concept could be applied to situations in other parts of the world; for example, to the confrontation between Arab and Israeli forces. The term has in fact been applied to United States policy of the 1960s in the Middle East, adopting the second and less common definition of disengagement, described above, as a policy of watchful nonintervention (Nolte 1964). But it is understandable that the focus of disengagement proposals and research has been on the critical European situation, where the principal nuclear powers confront one another. Recent scholarly efforts to deal with this situation fall into two categories: (1) proposals, plans, and formulas for the achievement of disengagement; and (2) discussions of its feasibility in the context of evolving East and West strategies and goals. Apart from Hinterhoff's book, only Michael Howard's *Disengagement in Europe* (1958) concerns itself exclusively and explicitly with evaluating the prospects of these policy prescriptions. In Howard's opinion, the adoption of any disengagement proposal is un-

likely as long as German reunification on terms acceptable to a West German government is to be a primary result. This result remains inimical to the stated aims of the Soviet government. In addition, West Germany's territory and its armed forces play a central role in NATO's defense against possible aggression; a scheme in which West Germany is excluded from NATO is, therefore, likely to require too great a sacrifice in terms of present Western strategy. Beyond these considerations, it needs to be noted that most proposals for disengagement are characteristically all-inclusive formulas providing for instant resolution of a complex of problems. Although the problems of Berlin, Germany, eastern Europe, nuclear strategy, and disarmament may be inextricably interrelated, any sharp or wholesale change in this delicate structure poses even greater dangers than its continuance; formulas for radical change are, therefore, likely to remain unacceptable to both sides. Possibly the only practical disengagement proposals that can be implemented are those of George Kennan and the few others who do not prescribe formulas for salvation but rather encourage the adoption of new attitudes and aims. The West will have to recognize the existence of Soviet Russia's influence in central Europe for the foreseeable future, while Russia will have to realize that hegemony in Europe can be achieved only at a catastrophic price. These new attitudes may then lead to compromises by both sides and to the gradual unraveling of the network of conflicts.

GERALD FREUND

[*See also* CONTAINMENT; INTERNATIONAL POLITICS.]

BIBLIOGRAPHY

ACHESON, DEAN 1958 The Illusion of Disengagement. *Foreign Affairs* 36:371–382.
GAITSKELL, HUGH 1957 *The Challenge of Coexistence.* Cambridge, Mass.: Harvard Univ. Press.
HINTERHOFF, EUGENE 1959 *Disengagement.* With a foreword by John Slessor. London: Stevens.
HOWARD, MICHAEL 1958 *Disengagement in Europe.* Harmondsworth, Middlesex (England) and Baltimore: Penguin.
KENNAN, GEORGE F. 1947 The Sources of Soviet Conduct. *Foreign Affairs* 25:566–582. → This article was written under the pseudonym X.
KENNAN, GEORGE F. 1958 *Russia, the Atom and the West.* New York: Harper.
KENNAN, GEORGE F. 1959 Disengagement Revisited. *Foreign Affairs* 37:187–210.
NOLTE, RICHARD H. 1964 United States Policy and the Middle East. Pages 148–182 in American Assembly, *The United States and the Middle East.* Edited by Georgiana G. Stevens. Englewood Cliffs, N.J.: Prentice-Hall.

DISHONESTY

See MORAL DEVELOPMENT.

DISORGANIZATION, SOCIAL

See COMMUNITY, *article on* COMMUNITY DISORGANIZATION; DEVIANT BEHAVIOR; DISASTERS; SOCIAL PROBLEMS.

DISPERSION

See STATISTICS, DESCRIPTIVE, *article on* LOCATION AND DISPERSION; VARIANCES, STATISTICAL STUDY OF.

DISPLAY

See EXCHANGE AND DISPLAY.

DISTRIBUTED LAGS

In theory, distributed lags arise when any economic cause, such as a price change or an income change, produces its effect (for example, on the quantity demanded) only after some lag in time, so that the effect is not felt all at once at a single point in time but is distributed over a period of time. Thus, when we say that the quantity of cigarettes demanded is a function of the price of cigarettes taken with a distributed lag, we mean essentially that the full effects of a change in the price of cigarettes is not felt immediately, and only after some passage of time does the quantity of cigarettes demanded show the full effect of the change in the price of cigarettes.

To consider the matter more concretely, let q_t be the quantity of cigarettes, say, demanded per unit time, and let p_t be the price per unit of cigarettes during time period t. Other things remaining constant, such as income, population, and the price of cough drops, we may express q_t as a function of current and past prices:

$$(1) \qquad q_t = f(p_t, p_{t-1}, p_{t-2}, \cdots).$$

In particular, let us assume the demand function f to be linear with constant coefficients $a, b_0, b_1, \cdots$,

$$(2) \qquad q_t = a + b_0 p_t + b_1 p_{t-1} + b_2 p_{t-2} + \cdots.$$

Suppose the price of cigarettes has been constant for a long time at a level p, so that $p = p_t = p_{t-1} = p_{t-2} = \cdots$. Then the quantity of cigarettes demanded per unit time will also be a constant:

$$(3) \qquad q = a + b_0 p + b_1 p + b_2 p + \cdots = a + p \sum_{i=0}^{\infty} b_i.$$

Now let the price of cigarettes change from p to $p + \Delta p$ in period $t + 1$ and remain at this new level indefinitely. The effect of the change in period $t + 1$ will be to change the quantity demanded from q to $q + b_0 \Delta p$. But the effects of the price change do not stop here; in the next period, $t + 2$, the quantity demanded is further altered to $q + b_0 \Delta p + b_1 \Delta p$. In general, after θ periods, the change in q will be $\Delta p \sum_{i=0}^{\theta} b_i$. Thus, the effect of the change in price on demand is distributed over time: $b_0 \Delta p$ the first period, $b_0 \Delta p + b_1 \Delta p$ the second, and so on.

The example used to illustrate the concept of a distributed lag is taken from demand analysis, but the use of distributed lags is not restricted to analysis of problems of consumer demand. The wide application of distributed lags in econometrics may be indicated by a few examples: import demand (Tinbergen 1949); hyperinflation (Cagan 1956); investment (Koyck 1954; Jorgenson 1963; Eisner 1960); demand for chemical fertilizers in the United States (Griliches 1959); advertising of oranges by the two major U.S. orange grower cooperatives (Nerlove & Waugh 1961).

The causes of distributed lags in economic relationships are as varied as the variables entering such relationships. To illustrate, the cigarette example may be used again. When the price is increased, we expect, other things being equal and if cigarettes are not an inferior good, that the demand will fall off. *How* it falls off, that is, the time path that demand follows, is not discussed in the ordinary static theory of demand. At first, a price rise may induce many people to stop smoking, but the tenacity of the habit being what it is, some will return to it. Others may either temporarily or permanently reduce consumption. It is also conceivable that those who do not regard the price increase as permanent, and who do not react at first, may come eventually to believe in the permanence of the price change as it persists and be willing to go through the painful process of adjustment. Finally, some who are nonsmokers, but who might have begun smoking when prices were lower (for example, adolescents), may now never begin. Thus, we see that there are three general types of factors that cause the effects of the price change to be distributed over time: (1) habit persistence, (2) expectational rigidities, and (3) a semitechnological factor related to the age distribution of the population and the conventional time at which a person begins to smoke.

We could just as well deal with an income change or with the effects of a change in the price of a factor of production upon its employment in a certain branch of manufacturing. The exact causes and pattern of the distribution of lag would, of course, depend on the particular circumstances studied. The pattern (and causes) could be different for changes in one direction than for those in another. Indeed, as F. M. Fisher has pointed out (1962, p. 29), there is no need in theory even to assume, as we implicitly have, "that when a decision is made at given time, *t*, the events of a certain fixed period previous are given a certain weight, regardless of what those events were or of what happened before or since their occurrence." One can imagine the effect if a government report condemning smoking were issued just after the price of cigarettes declined. Nonetheless, for most practical purposes of econometrics, drastic simplifications must be made and the results can be regarded only as approximate.

History and forms. Irving Fisher (1925) was the first to use and discuss the concept of a distributed lag. In a later paper (1937, p. 323), he stated that the basic problem in applying the theory of distributed lags "is to find the 'best' distribution of lag, by which is meant the distribution such that . . . the total combined effect [of the lagged values of the variables taken with a distributed lag has] . . . the highest possible correlation with the actual statistical series . . . with which we wish to compare it." Thus, we wish to find the distribution of lag that maximizes the explanation of "effect" by "cause" in a statistical sense. There are unsophisticated, almost mechanical, approaches to this problem; and there are more sophisticated approaches involving considerable use of economic theory to develop underlying models of dynamic adjustment that in turn generate the distributed lags observed. There are also both more sophisticated and less sophisticated approaches to estimation.

No assumption may be made about the form of the distribution of lag, i.e., the relationships among the *b*'s in an equation such as (2). This is the approach adopted by Tinbergen (1949) and Alt (1942). The procedure is then to estimate an equation such as (2), for example, by least squares. Since the number of observations is limited, only a finite number of lag terms may be included. Indeed, the coefficients of the lagged values may quickly become quite erratic because of the presence of strong serial correlation in most economic time series. Such difficulties led Alt, Irving Fisher (1925; 1937), and others to suggest that the parameters of a relationship such as (2) be constrained by specifying the form of the distribution of lag. Fisher (1937) suggests, for example, that

all *b*'s, after a certain point *θ*, are proportional to an arithmetical progression up to a certain maximal lag, *θ′*. Thus,

$$(4) \qquad b_i = b\left(1 - \frac{i - \theta}{\theta' - 1}\right), \qquad \theta \leqslant i \leqslant \theta'.$$

Fisher (1925) earlier had suggested that the weights of the distribution might plausibly be assumed to follow a logarithmic normal probability density function (with appropriate modification for the measurement of time in discrete units). Alt recommends a number of exponential forms. Koyck (1954) suggests weights that decline geometrically. Theil and Stern (1960) consider weights proportional to what are essentially approximations to the densities given by a gamma distribution with mean 2. Solow (1960) presents perhaps the ultimate flexibility and sophistication obtainable by a purely formal approach in suggesting the two-parameter family of unimodal lag distributions generated by the Pascal distribution. Thus, the weights are

$$(5) \qquad b_i = b\binom{r + i - 1}{i} (1 - \lambda)^r \lambda^i.$$

This family provides the discrete analogue of the exponential and gamma distributions. It represents a natural generalization of the geometrically declining weights of Koyck and may be thought of as *r* simple Koyck lags cascaded in series. The case *r* = 1 is the original Koyck lag. The distribution of lag is skewed; the larger the value of *λ* and the smaller the value of *r*, the greater is the degree of skewness. Both the center of gravity and the spread of the distribution increase with *λ* and *r*. This distribution offers a considerable gain in flexibility as compared with earlier suggestions.

A more complete review of the literature up to 1958 and some additional suggestions are contained in Nerlove (1958*a*, pp. 1–25).

Rather than directly specify the form of the lag, an alternative approach is to develop a dynamic model that leads to a distributed lag or lags in the observed relationships. This may be done at varying levels of generality, either by dealing with broad classes of causes in an attempt to derive models of wide applicability or by attempting to isolate dynamic features of a particular problem and show that these lead to certain forms of lag structure. Brown (1952) and Friedman (1957) develop different dynamic models designed to explain the behavior of total consumption expenditures. As Nerlove (1958*a*; 1958*c*) shows, both models lead essentially to a Koyck distribution of lag in the relation between income and consumption. The two models are examples of the two general classes of models leading to distributed lags extensively discussed by Nerlove (1958a; 1958b; 1958c): expectational models and dynamic adjustment models. Both classes in their simplest forms lead to Koyck distributions of lag but have quite different implications for estimation and are not at all the same in more complicated cases. Friedman's model is a member of the class of expectational models; and Brown's model is a member of the class of dynamic adjustment. The two models, however, were designed to be quite general and to apply to a variety of problems. Examples taken from the area of agricultural supply analysis are used here to illustrate each model (Nerlove 1958b, pp. 25–26).

An expectational model of supply response. Suppose that the quantity supplied in year t, x_t, is a linear function not of the current price p_t but of the price expected for year t in year $t-1$, p_t^* (for example, many agricultural crops are planted or planned far ahead):

$$(6) \qquad x_t = a + b p_t^* + u_t,$$

where u_t is a stochastic residual. Suppose further that price forecasts are corrected each period by farmers in proportion to the error made:

$$(7) \qquad p_t^* - p_{t-1}^* = \beta(p_{t-1} - p_{t-1}^*), \qquad 0 < \beta \leqslant 1,$$

where β is called the coefficient of expectations. A similar model is used explicitly by Cagan (1956) to generate expectations of changes in the general price level during hyperinflations. After some manipulation, it may be shown that

$$(8) \qquad \begin{aligned} x_t = a\beta &+ b\beta p_{t-1} \\ &+ (1-\beta)x_{t-1} + u_t - (1-\beta)u_{t-1}. \end{aligned}$$

A dynamic adjustment model of supply response. In contrast, suppose that the desired or equilibrium quantity supplied, x_t^*, is linearly related to the price at the time of decision, p_{t-1}:

$$(9) \qquad x_t^* = a + b p_{t-1} + u_t.$$

However, for a variety of technological and economic reasons (including plain habit), only a fraction, γ, of adjustment occurs each period:

$$(10) \qquad x_t - x_{t-1} = \gamma(x_t^* - x_{t-1}), \qquad 0 < \gamma \leqslant 1,$$

hence

$$(11) \qquad x_t = a\gamma + b\gamma p_{t-1} + (1-\gamma)x_{t-1} + u_t.$$

Apart from the residual terms, which differ in

the two relations, both equations imply:

$$(12) \qquad \begin{aligned} x_t = a + b\alpha\,[p_{t-1} &+ (1-\alpha)p_{t-2} \\ &+ (1-\alpha)^2 p_{t-3} + \cdots] + v_t, \end{aligned}$$

where α equals β for the expectational model, and α equals γ for the adjustment model. Equation (12) represents supply as a function of price taken with a Koyck distribution lag. In multiple-equation systems, however, the expectational and dynamic adjustment models do not lead to such similar results; in particular, in expectational models one can make use of the fact that the distribution of lag for the same variable in different equations should be the same (Nerlove 1958a, pp. 31–39).

Examples of further extension toward developing distributed lag relationships incidental to a more fundamental dynamic model of behavior are given by Jorgenson (1963) and Muth (1961). Jorgenson gives a model of investment behavior based on a theory of the demand for capital goods over time and on a theory of the relation between such demand and its translation into realized investment, which in turn rests on a distribution of times-to-completion of new investment projects. This model results in a case of a very general distribution of lag. Jorgenson calls the general case the "rational power series distribution"; the Pascal distribution discussed above is a member of this class. Jorgenson's distribution of lag, although general in form, results in fact from a highly particularized model of dynamic adjustment in the investment decision-and-realization process.

Muth elaborates on a model of expectation formation. In the highly simplified case of a single market with a nonstochastic demand function in which the quantity supplied is a linear function of expected price plus a residual generated by shocks of a permanent and transitory nature, the "rational expectations" that Muth develops can be shown to satisfy (7). Hence, the model leads to a distributed lag of the Koyck form. However, in more realistic models the rational expectations are no longer so simple.

Estimation problems. If one examines equations (8) or (11)—those that one might attempt to estimate by least-squares methods if one sought to determine both the distribution of lag and the long-run supply response—it can be seen that the presence of serial correlation in the residual terms will cause serious trouble. For example, least-squares estimates of autoregressions with serially correlated residual terms are known to be statistically inconsistent. Indeed, from (8) it appears that serially correlated residuals will be the rule. This is a subject that is too technical and complex for discussion here. The reader is referred to Koyck (1954, pp. 32–39); Griliches (1961); Klein (1958); Liviatan (1963); Malinvaud (1964); Phillips (1956); and especially Hannan (1964), who gives the most complete and fundamental discussion of this problem and its solution. While Hannan's results refer primarily to Koyck lags, they can be generalized.

MARC NERLOVE

BIBLIOGRAPHY

ALT, FRANZ L. 1942 Distributed Lags. *Econometrica* 10: 113–128.

BROWN, TILLMAN M. 1952 Habit Persistence and Lags in Consumer Behavior. *Econometrica* 20:355–371.

CAGAN, PHILLIP 1956 The Monetary Dynamics of Hyperinflation. Pages 23–117 in Milton Friedman (editor), *Studies in the Quantity Theory of Money.* Univ. of Chicago Press.

EISNER, ROBERT 1960 A Distributed Lag Investment Function. *Econometrica* 28:1–29.

FISHER, FRANKLIN M. 1962 Rigid Lags and the Estimation of "Long-run" Economic Reactions. Pages 21–47 in Franklin M. Fisher, *A Priori Information and Time Series Analysis: Essays in Economic Theory and Measurement.* Amsterdam: North-Holland Publishing.

FISHER, IRVING 1925 Our Unstable Dollar and the So-called Business Cycle. *Journal of the American Statistical Association* 20:179–202.

FISHER, IRVING 1937 Note on a Short-cut Method for Calculating Distributed Lags. International Statistical Institute, *Bulletin* 29, no. 3:323–328.

FRIEDMAN, MILTON 1957 *A Theory of the Consumption Function.* National Bureau of Economic Research, General Series, No. 63. Princeton Univ. Press.

GRILICHES, ZVI 1959 Distributed Lags, Disaggregation, and Regional Demand Functions for Fertilizer. *Journal of Farm Economics* 41:90–102.

GRILICHES, ZVI 1961 Note on Serial Correlation Bias in Estimates of Distributed Lags. *Econometrica* 29:65–73.

HANNAN, E. J. 1964 Estimation of Relationships Involving Distributed Lags. *Econometrica* 33:206–224.

JORGENSON, DALE W. 1963 Capital Theory and Investment Behavior. *American Economic Review* 53:247–259.

KLEIN, LAWRENCE R. 1958 The Estimation of Distributed Lags. *Econometrica* 26:553–565.

KOYCK, LEENDERT M. 1954 *Distributed Lags and Investment Analysis.* Amsterdam: North-Holland Publishing.

LIVIATAN, NISSAN 1963 Consistent Estimation of Distributed Lags. *International Economic Review* 4:44–52.

MALINVAUD, EDMOND 1964 Modèles à retards échelonnés. Pages 478–499 in Edmond Malinvaud, *Méthodes statistiques de l'économétrie.* Paris: Dunod.

MUTH, JOHN F. 1961 Rational Expectations and the Theory of Price Movements. *Econometrica* 29:315–335.

NERLOVE, MARC 1958a *Distributed Lags and Demand Analysis for Agricultural and Other Commodities.* U.S. Dept. of Agriculture, Handbook No. 141. Washington: Government Printing Office.

NERLOVE, MARC 1958b *The Dynamics of Supply: Estimation of Farmers' Response to Price.* Studies in Historical and Political Science, Series 76, No. 2. Baltimore: Johns Hopkins Press.

NERLOVE, MARC 1958c The Implications of Friedman's Permanent Income Hypothesis for Demand Analysis. *Agricultural Economics Research* 10:1–14.

NERLOVE, MARC; and WAUGH, FREDERICK V. 1961 Advertising Without Supply Control: Some Implications of a Study of the Advertising of Oranges. *Journal of Farm Economics* 43:813–837.

PHILLIPS, A. W. 1956 Some Notes on the Estimation of Time-forms of Reactions in Interdependent Dynamic Systems. *Economica* New Series 23:99–113.

SOLOW, ROBERT M. 1960 On a Family of Lag Distributions. *Econometrica* 28:393–406.

THEIL, H.; and STERN, ROBERT M. 1960 A Simple Unimodal Lag Distribution. *Metroeconomica* 12:111–119.

TINBERGEN, JAN 1949 Long-term Foreign Trade Elasticities. *Metroeconomica* 1:174–185.

DISTRIBUTION

See INTERNAL TRADE; TRADE AND MARKETS.

DISTRIBUTION OF POWERS

See under CONSTITUTIONAL LAW.

DISTRIBUTION PROCESSES

See SIZE DISTRIBUTIONS IN ECONOMICS. *Related material may be found in* INCOME DISTRIBUTION, *article on* SIZE; RANK–SIZE RELATIONS.

DISTRIBUTION-FREE STATISTICS

See NONPARAMETRIC STATISTICS.

DISTRIBUTIONS, STATISTICAL

I. SPECIAL DISCRETE DISTRIBUTIONS   *Frank A. Haight*
II. SPECIAL CONTINUOUS DISTRIBUTIONS *Donald B. Owen*
III. APPROXIMATIONS TO DISTRIBUTIONS   *N. L. Johnson*
IV. MIXTURES OF DISTRIBUTIONS   *Wallace R. Blischke*

I

SPECIAL DISCRETE DISTRIBUTIONS

The continuous distributions mentioned in this article, together with others, are described in detail in the companion article on SPECIAL CONTINUOUS DISTRIBUTIONS.

A discrete probability distribution gives the probability of every possible outcome of a discrete experiment, trial, or observation. By "discrete" it is meant that the possible outcomes are finite (or countably infinite) in number. As an illustration of the ideas involved, consider the act of throwing three coins onto a table. Before trying to assess the probability of various outcomes, it is necessary first to decide (as part of the definition of the experiment) what outcomes are possible. From the point of view of the dynamics of the falling coins, no two throws are exactly identical, and there are thus infinitely many possible outcomes; but if the experimenter is interested only in the heads and tails shown, he may wish to reduce the number of outcomes to the eight shown in Table 1.

Table 1 — Possible outcomes of the experiment of tossing three coins

Coin 1	Coin 2	Coin 3
Head	Head	Head
Head	Head	Tail
Head	Tail	Head
Head	Tail	Tail
Tail	Head	Head
Tail	Head	Tail
Tail	Tail	Head
Tail	Tail	Tail

If the coins are *fair*, that is, equally likely to show a head or tail, and if they behave independently, the eight possibilities are also all equally probable, and each would have assigned probability $\frac{1}{8}$. The list of eight $\frac{1}{8}$'s assigned to the eight outcomes is a discrete probability distribution that is exactly equivalent to the probabilistic content of the verbal description of the defining experiment.

The same physical activity (throwing three coins on a table) can be used to define another experiment. If the experimenter is interested only in the *number* of heads showing and not in which particular coins show the heads, he may define the possible outcomes to be only four in number: 0, 1, 2, 3. Since of the eight equally probable outcomes of the first experiment, one yields zero heads and one yields three heads while three yield one head and three yield two heads, the discrete probability distribution defined by the second experiment is

probability of no heads $= \frac{1}{8}$;
probability of one head $= \frac{3}{8}$;
probability of two heads $= \frac{3}{8}$;
probability of three heads $= \frac{1}{8}$.

It is frequently convenient to write such a list in more compact form by using mathematical symbols. If p_n means the probability of n heads, the second experiment leads to the formula

$$(1) \qquad p_n = \frac{1}{8}\binom{3}{n}, \qquad n = 0, 1, 2, 3,$$

where $\binom{N}{n}$, the binomial coefficient, is the mathematical symbol for the number of combinations of N things taken n at a time,

$$\binom{N}{n} = \frac{N!}{n!(N-n)!},$$

$n!$ (which is read "n-factorial") being equal to $n(n-1)(n-2)\cdots 3\cdot 2\cdot 1$. Note that in (1) the form is given for the probabilities and then the domain of definition is stated.

A domain of definition of a probability distribution is merely a list of the possible outcomes of the experiment. In nearly every case, the experimenter finds it convenient to define the experiment so that the domain is numerical, as in the second experiment above. However, there is no reason why the domain should not be nonnumerical. In the first experiment above, the domain could be written (HHH), (HHT), (HTH), (HTT), (THH), (THT), (TTH), (TTT), where T means tails and H means heads.

An expression for p_n like the above needs only two properties to describe a valid discrete probability distribution. It must be nonnegative and the sum over all possible outcomes must be unity: $p_n \geqslant 0$, $\sum p_n = 1$. It is therefore possible to invent any number of discrete probability distributions simply by choosing some function p_n satisfying these simple conditions. In both theory and applications, it is more important to study certain probability distributions that correspond to basic probability experiments than to attempt a systematic classification of all functions satisfying these conditions. In the following list of important discrete distributions, the corresponding experiment is stated in very general terms, accompanied in many cases by concrete interpretations.

Discrete distributions

Binomial distribution. Suppose an experiment can have only two possible outcomes, conventionally called *success* and *failure*, and suppose the probability of success is p. If the experiment is repeated independently N times under exactly the same conditions, the number of successes, n, can be 0, 1, $\cdots$, N. A composite experiment consisting of observing the number of successes in the N performances of the individual experiment can therefore have one of the following outcomes: 0, 1, 2, $\cdots$, N. The probability of observing exactly n successes forms the binomial distribution:

$$(2) \qquad p_n = \binom{N}{n}p^n(1-p)^{N-n}, \qquad n = 0, 1, \cdots, N.$$

The second experiment mentioned in the introduction is of this form, where $N = 3$ and $p = \frac{1}{2}$.

The mean value of the binomial distribution is Np and its variance is $Np(1 - p)$. The tails of the binomial distribution (and of the negative binomial discussed below) may be expressed as incomplete beta functions.

The following list of interpretations for the abstract words *success* and *failure* will indicate the breadth of application of the binomial distribution: male–female; infected–not infected; working–broken; pass–fail; alive–dead; head–tail; right–wrong. If a common test is known to give the right answer (using the last pair as an example) nine times out of ten on the average, and if it is performed ten times, what is the probability that it will give exactly nine right answers and one wrong one?

$$p_9 = \binom{10}{9} (.9)^9 (.1)^1 = .38742.$$

In using the binomial distribution for this purpose, it is important to remember that the probability of a success must be constant. For example, if each of 30 students took an examination composed of 3 equally difficult parts and each separate part was graded pass or fail, the number of fails out of the 90 grades would not have a binomial distribution since the probability of failure varies from student to student.

If, for the binomial distribution, N is large and p is small, then the simpler Poisson distribution (see next section) often forms a good approximation. The sense of this approximation is a limiting one, with $N \to \infty$ and Np having a finite limit.

The normal distribution is often a good approximation to the binomial, especially when N is large and p not too close to 0 or 1. The limiting sense of the normal approximation is in terms of the *standardized* variable, n less its mean and divided by its standard deviation.

Poisson distribution. Imagine a machine turning out a continuous roll of wire or thread. Minor defects occur from time to time; their frequency and their statistical behavior are of interest. If the defects occur independently and if the risk of a defect is constant (that is, if the probability of a defect in a very small interval of the wire is a constant, λ, times the length of the interval), then the average number of defects per unit length is λ and the probability that a unit length contains exactly n defects is

$$(3) \qquad p_n = \frac{\lambda^n e^{-\lambda}}{n!}, \qquad n = 0, 1, 2, \cdots.$$

This distribution, named for the French mathematician Poisson, is an important example of a distribution defined over an infinite set of integers. Any value of n is possible, although large values (compared with λ) are unlikely. The mean and variance of the Poisson distribution are both λ. If the segment of unit length is replaced by a segment of length L, this is only a change in scale and one need only substitute $L\lambda$ for λ in (3) and in the moments. The tails of the Poisson distribution are incomplete gamma functions.

The Poisson distribution has a very wide range of application, not only because of its mathematical simplicity but because it represents one important concept of true randomness. In addition, the Poisson distribution, as has been noted, is useful as an approximation.

The most important interpretations of the Poisson distribution occur when the line is considered to be the axis of real time and the points to be times at which certain events take place. The following is a partial list of events that have been compared with the Poisson distribution: deaths by horse kick, radioactive particles entering a Geiger–Müller counter, arrival of patients into a doctor's waiting room, declarations of war, strikes of lightning, registration of vehicles over a road tape, demands for service at a telephone switchboard, demands for parking space, occurrence of accidents, demands for electric power, instants of nerve excitation, occurrence of suicide, etc. [*for a discussion of some of these applications, see* QUEUES].

On the other hand, the interpretation of the Poisson distribution as a criterion of perfect disorder remains valid in space of any number of dimensions, provided only that L is interpreted as length, area, or volume as the case may require. Space examples are perhaps not as numerous, but the following can be noted: one dimension, misprints per line, cars per mile; two dimensions, bomb bursts per square mile, weeds per square yard, stars per square unit of photographic plate; three dimensions, raisins per loaf of raisin bread, bacteria per cubic centimeter of fluid.

Morse distribution. The Poisson distribution is an example of a counting distribution. In a single dimension (whether time or space) it is characterized by the fact that the continuous density function (the gap distribution) of distance between consecutive points is negative exponential (with $\lambda = 1/\theta$). If the gap distribution is more general (for example, the Pearson Type III, with $\lambda = 1/\theta$), the counting distribution may be very complicated indeed. With Pearson Type III gaps, the counting probabilities are

$$p_n = (1 + n) [\Gamma_{nr+r} - \Gamma_{nr}] + (1 - n) [\Gamma_{nr} - \Gamma_{nr-r}]$$
$$+ (\lambda L/r) [- \Gamma_{nr+r-1} + 2\Gamma_{nr-1} - \Gamma_{nr-r-1}],$$

where

$$\Gamma_n = \frac{1}{(n-1)!} \int_{\lambda L}^{\infty} e^{-x} x^{n-1} \, dx.$$

This distribution takes its name from Philip Morse (1958), and reduces to the Poisson for $r = 1$. In data that fitted such a function, one would have a mixture of randomness and regularity, suggesting two factors at work.

Negative binomial distribution. There are two traditional important probability models leading to the negative binomial distribution, although others have been suggested. (i) If each member of a population experiences Poisson events (for example, accidents) but with the mean value λ varying statistically from member to member according to the Pearson Type III distribution, then the probability that n events occur in time T among all members of the population is

$$p_n = \binom{n + r - 1}{r - 1} p^r (1 - p)^n, \qquad n = 0, 1, \cdots,$$

where $p = \theta/(T + \theta)$ and r and θ are the parameters of the Pearson Type III distribution. (ii) If experiments are performed in sequence with a fixed probability p of success (as for the binomial distribution), then the negative binomial distribution gives the probability that exactly n failures will precede the rth success. This is particularly useful for $r = 1$, since in many applications one calls a halt after the first "success," for example, in repeated dialings of a telephone that may be busy. The negative binomial distribution takes its name from its formal similarity to the binomial distribution.

The mean of the negative binomial distribution is $(1 - p)r/p$ and its variance is $(1 - p)r/p^2$. It is an example of a mixed distribution, obtained by assuming a parameter in one distribution to be itself subject to statistical fluctuation. [*Many other such distributions, including those called "contagious," are discussed in* DISTRIBUTIONS, STATISTICAL, *article on* MIXTURES OF DISTRIBUTIONS.]

Geometric distribution. In certain types of waiting lines, the probability of n persons in the queue is

$$p_n = \left(1 - \frac{\lambda}{\mu}\right)\left(\frac{\lambda}{\mu}\right)^n, \qquad n = 0, 1, 2, \cdots,$$

where λ is the mean arrival rate and μ is the mean service rate and $\lambda < \mu$. The mean value of the geo-

metric distribution is $\lambda/(\mu - \lambda)$, and the variance is $\lambda\mu/(\mu - \lambda)^2$. The geometric distribution is a special case of the negative binomial distribution with $r = 1$ and $p = (\mu/\lambda) - 1$. [*These waiting line problems are discussed in* QUEUES.]

Hypergeometric distribution. Suppose a collection of N objects contains k of one kind and $N - k$ of another kind—for example, any of the dichotomies of the binomial distribution model. If exactly r objects are taken at random from the collection, the probability that n of them will be of the first kind is

$$(4) \quad p_n = \frac{\binom{k}{n}\binom{N - k}{r - n}}{\binom{N}{r}}, \quad n = 0, 1, \cdots, \min(r, k).$$

The mean of this distribution is kr/N and the variance is $kr(N - k)(N - r)/N^2$.

The binomial distribution and the hypergeometric distribution can be regarded as arising from analogous experiments, the former by sampling "with replacement" and the latter by sampling "without replacement." This can be seen from either of two facts: (i) if, in the probability experiment described for the hypergeometric distribution, each of the r objects is put back before the next one is chosen, the probability model leading to the binomial distribution would result; (ii) if $N \to \infty$ in equation (4), with $(N - k)/N$ replaced by p, the resulting limit is equation (2). Thus, if the total number of objects is very large and the proportions of the two types remain fixed, the hypergeometric model approaches the binomial model. If the number of objects of the first kind is very small in comparison with the total number of objects, the hypergeometric distribution will approach the Poisson. The hypergeometric distribution has important statistical application in Fisher's so-called exact test in a 2×2 table [*see* COUNTED DATA].

It is possible to obtain many other distributions, both discrete and continuous, as special or limiting cases of the hypergeometric. Karl Pearson used the probability model leading to the hypergeometric distribution as the basis for his analysis of density functions and obtained 12 separate types as special limiting cases. Of these, only the Pearson Type III is still frequently called by his designation, although many of the most common continuous densities (including the normal) fit into his classification system [*see* DISTRIBUTIONS, STATISTICAL, *article on* APPROXIMATIONS TO DISTRIBUTIONS].

Negative hypergeometric distribution. If the parameter p in a binomial distribution is itself beta distributed, then the unconditional distribution of the discrete variate is

$$p_n = \binom{N}{n} \frac{B(n+p, N+q-n)}{B(p, q)}, \quad n = 0, 1, \cdots, N,$$

where p and q are the parameters of the beta distribution and

$$B(p, q) = \int_0^1 x^{p-1} (1-x)^{q-1}\, dx.$$

This model is the discrete time analog of the first interpretation of the negative binomial distribution; the events (such as accidents) would be counted in short time periods so that only a success or failure would be recorded.

Occupancy distribution. If each of k objects is thrown at random into one of N boxes, the probability that a given box contains n objects is

$$p_n = \binom{k}{n} \frac{(N-1)^{k-n}}{N^k}, \quad n = 0, 1, \cdots, k.$$

This distribution has mean k/N and variance $(k/N)(1 - 1/N)$. Problems of this type are called occupancy problems and are important in statistical mechanics.

Busy period distributions. A box contains r objects, and additional objects are thrown into the box at random instants, that is, in accordance with a Poisson distribution (mean λ). If one object is removed in every time interval of length $1/\mu$, then the probability that exactly n objects will pass through the box before it first becomes empty is

$$p_n = \frac{r}{(n-r)!} n^{n-r-1} e^{-\lambda n/\mu} (\lambda/\mu)^{n-r},$$
$$n = r, r+1, r+2, \cdots.$$

This is the Borel–Tanner distribution, with mean $r/(1 - \lambda/\mu)$ and variance $(\lambda r/\mu)/(1 - \lambda/\mu)^3$. If the objects are removed also in accordance with a Poisson distribution (mean μ), then the probability that n will pass through before the box first becomes empty is

$$p_n = \frac{r}{n} \binom{2n-r-1}{n-1} \frac{(\lambda/\mu)^{n-r}}{(1+\lambda/\mu)^{2n-r}},$$
$$n = r, r+1, \cdots,$$

which is called the Narayana distribution. This distribution has mean $r/(1 - \lambda/\mu)$ and variance $[(\lambda r/\mu)(1 - \lambda/\mu)]/(1 - \lambda/\mu)^3$.

Such distributions are important in the theory of queues, where the box represents the collection of people waiting. Then the number n, which has probability p_n, is the length of a busy period for the service mechanism, beginning with r in the system [*see* QUEUES].

Uniform distribution. An experiment with N equally likely outcomes corresponds to the discrete uniform (or discrete rectangular) distribution:

$$p_n = \frac{1}{N}, \quad n = 1, 2, \cdots, N.$$

For a single throw of a die, $N = 6$. This distribution has mean $\frac{1}{2}(N+1)$ and variance $\frac{1}{12}(N^2 - 1)$.

Yule distribution. Some experimental data suggest that in a long list of names (for example, a telephone book) the probability that a randomly chosen name occurs n times is

$$p_n = \frac{k}{n} \binom{n+k}{k}^{-1}, \quad n = 1, 2, \cdots.$$

Fisher distribution. In the distribution of frequency of plant species, the distribution

$$p_n = \frac{1}{n} a p^n, \quad n = 1, 2, \cdots,$$

occurs, where $1/a = -\log_e(1-p)$. The Fisher distribution has mean $ap/(1-p)$ and variance $ap(1-ap)/(1-p)^2$. This distribution has also been called the logarithmic distribution because of its close relationship to the Taylor series for $-\log_e(1-p)$. Fisher's distribution can be obtained from the negative binomial by truncating the zero category and letting r approach zero.

Formation of distributions from others

The most important families of secondary distributions are the so-called mixed distributions, in which the parameter in a given distribution is itself subject to statistical fluctuation [*see* DISTRIBUTIONS, STATISTICAL, *article on* MIXTURES OF DISTRIBUTIONS]. Two examples above (the first case of the negative binomial and the negative hypergeometric) are also mixed. In addition, the following paragraphs illustrate other methods of obtaining secondary distributions.

Truncated distributions. It may happen that the domain of definition of a distribution does not exactly agree with some data, either for theoretical reasons or because part of the data is unobtainable, although the model is in other respects quite satisfactory. The most famous example of this is concerned with albinism. The Poisson distribution gives a satisfactory fit to the number of albino children born to parents genetically capable of producing albinos, except for the value of p_0, the probability of no albino children. This frequency cannot be observed, since such parents with no albino children are ordinarily indistinguishable from normal parents. Therefore, a new distribution is formed from the Poisson by removing the zero category, and dividing each probability by $1 - p_0$ so that the total sum remains one:

$$p_n = \frac{e^{-\lambda} \lambda^n}{n! \, (1 - e^{-\lambda})}, \qquad n = 1, 2, 3, \cdots.$$

In certain applications, it has been useful to truncate similarly the binomial distribution. [*The practice, which has also been applied to continuous density functions, is discussed in* STATISTICAL ANALYSIS, SPECIAL PROBLEMS OF, *article on* TRUNCATION AND CENSORSHIP.]

Bissinger's system. In connection with an inventory problem, the distribution q_n, formed from a given distribution p_n by the transformation

$$q_n = \frac{1}{1 - p_0} \sum_{j=n+1}^{\infty} \frac{p_j}{j}, \qquad n = 0, 1, \cdots,$$

has been useful. A more general transformation of this type is

$$q_n = \frac{\displaystyle\sum_{j=n+k}^{\infty} \frac{p_j}{j - k + 1}}{\displaystyle\sum_{j=k}^{\infty} p_j}, \qquad n = 0, 1, 2, \cdots,$$

which reduces to the simpler form for $k = 1$. This transformation is discussed by Bissinger in Patil (1965).

Joint occupancy. Let p_n be the probability of an object of type I in a box, and let β be the probability that an object of type I brings an object of type II with it into the box. Then the probability q_n of a total of n objects in the box is

$$q_n = \sum_{i=0}^{[\frac{1}{2}n]} \binom{n - i}{i} p_{n-i} \, (1 - \beta)^{n-2i} \, \beta^i,$$
$$n = 0, 1, 2, \cdots,$$

where $[k]$ represents the integer part of k. This form of distribution has been applied to the number of persons in an automobile and to the number of persons in a group buying a railway ticket. The two types of objects might be male–female or adult–child.

Analogy with density functions. It is only necessary to adjust a constant in order to convert a continuous distribution into a discrete one. For example, the negative exponential density $\lambda e^{-\lambda x}$, usually defined over $0 < x < \infty$, can be applied to the domain $n = 0, 1, 2, \cdots$. However, since

$$\sum_{n=0}^{\infty} \lambda e^{-\lambda n} = \frac{\lambda}{1 - e^{-\lambda}},$$

the discrete probability distribution will be

$$p_n = (1 - e^{-\lambda}) \, e^{-\lambda n}, \qquad n = 0, 1, \cdots.$$

Several such discrete analogs, including the normal, have appeared in the literature.

Alternative descriptions of distributions

A probability distribution p_n can be transformed in many ways, and, provided the transformation is one-to-one, the result will characterize the distribution equally well. Some of the principal auxiliary functions are

$$P_n = \sum_{i=0}^{n} p_i, \text{ the cumulative distribution, or left tail;}$$

$$Q_n = \sum_{i=n+1}^{\infty} p_i = 1 - P_n, \text{ the right tail of the distribution;}$$

$$\phi(s) = \sum_{i=0}^{\infty} p_i s^i, \text{ the generating function;}$$

$$\alpha(s) = \sum_{i=0}^{\infty} p_i s^i / i!, \text{ the exponential generating function;}$$

$$\beta(s) = \sum_{i=0}^{\infty} e^{is} p_i, \text{ the moment generating function;}$$

$$\sigma(s) = \sum_{i=0}^{\infty} (1 + s)^i p_i, \text{ the factorial moment generating function.}$$

The last two functions are so named because in the corresponding power series expansion the coefficients involve, respectively, the central moments and the factorial moments.

For certain mathematical operations on discrete probability distributions, such as the calculation of moments, generating functions are extremely useful. In many cases the best way to obtain p_n from a defining experiment is to calculate $\phi(s)$ first. Many examples of this type of argument can be found in Riordan (1958).

Multivariate distributions

There have been a few discrete multivariate distributions proposed, but only one, the multinomial, has been very widely applied.

Multinomial distribution. If an experiment can have r possible outcomes, with probabilities p_1, p_2, $\cdots$, p_r and if it is repeated under the same conditions N times, the probability that the jth outcome will occur n_j times, $j = 1, 2, \cdots, r$, is

$$\frac{N!}{n_1! \, n_2! \cdots n_r!} \, p_1^{n_1} p_2^{n_2} \cdots p_r^{n_r},$$

which reduces to the binomial for $r = 2$.

Negative multinomial distribution. If, in the scheme given above, trials stop after the rth outcome has been observed exactly k times, the joint probability that the jth outcome will be observed n_j times ($j = 1, \cdots, r - 1$) is called the negative multinomial distribution.

Bivariate Poisson distribution. The joint probability

$$p_{n_1, n_2} = \exp\left[-(\lambda + \mu + \rho)\right] \cdot$$

$$\lambda^{n_1}\mu^{n_2} \sum_{j=0}^{\min(n_1, n_2)} \frac{\rho^j}{(n_1 - j)!\,(n_2 - j)!\,j!}$$

has been proposed as a generalization of the Poisson; when $\rho = 0$, n_1 and n_2 are independently Poisson.

FRANK A. HAIGHT

[*Other relevant material may be found in* PROBABILITY *and in the biographies of* FISHER, R. A.; PEARSON; POISSON.]

BIBLIOGRAPHY

By far the best textbook on the theory and application of discrete distributions is Feller 1950. Busy period distributions and other distributions arising from queueing theory will be found in Takács 1962. Riordan 1958 explains the various auxiliary functions and the relationships between them. An index to all distributions with complete references to the literature is given in Haight 1961. The most complete and useful volume of statistical tables is Owen 1962. Further references to tables may be found in Greenwood & Hartley 1962. Computer programs for generating tables are distributed on a cooperative basis by SHARE Distribution Agency, International Business Machines Corporation. Patil 1965 contains several research and expository papers discussing the probabilistic models, structural relations, statistical theory, and methods for many of the discrete distributions mentioned in the list above, together with a bibliography on the subject by the editor.

FELLER, WILLIAM 1950–1966 *An Introduction to Probability Theory and Its Applications.* 2 vols. New York: Wiley. → A second edition of Volume I was published in 1957.

GREENWOOD, JOSEPH A.; and HARTLEY, H. O. 1962 *Guide to Tables in Mathematical Statistics.* Princeton Univ. Press.

HAIGHT, FRANK A. 1961 Index to the Distributions of Mathematical Statistics. U.S. National Bureau of Standards, *Journal of Research* Series B: Mathematics and Mathematical Physics 65B:23–60.

MORSE, PHILIP M. 1958 *Queues, Inventories and Maintenance: The Analysis of Operational Systems With Variable Demand and Supply.* New York: Wiley.

OWEN, DONALD B. 1962 *Handbook of Statistical Tables.* Reading, Mass.: Addison-Wesley. → A list of addenda and errata is available from the author.

PATIL, GANAPATI P. (editor) 1965 *Classical and Contagious Discrete Distributions.* Proceedings of the International Symposium held at McGill University, Montreal, Canada, August 15–August 20, 1963. Calcutta (India): Statistical Publishing Society; distributed by Pergamon Press. → See especially pages 15–17 on "A Type-resisting Distribution Generated From Considerations of an Inventory Decision Model" by Bernard H. Bissinger.

RIORDAN, JOHN 1958 *An Introduction to Combinatorial Analysis.* New York: Wiley.

TAKÁCS, LAJOS 1962 *Introduction to the Theory of Queues.* New York: Oxford Univ. Press.

II
SPECIAL CONTINUOUS DISTRIBUTIONS

This article describes, and gives the more important properties of, the major continuous distributions that arise in statistics. It is intended as both an overview for the reader generally interested in distributions and as a reference for a reader seeking the form of a particular distribution.

Technical terms, such as "density function," "cumulative distribution function," etc., are explained elsewhere [*see* PROBABILITY].

The present article is, with a few exceptions, restricted to univariate distributions. Further specific references to numerical tabulations of distributions are not generally given here; most of the distributions are tabulated in Owen (1962) or in Pearson and Hartley (1954), and full references to other tabulations are given in Greenwood and Hartley (1962). Tables of many functions discussed here and an extensive reference list to tables are given in Zelen and Severo (1964). An index to properties of distributions is given in Haight (1961).

Normal distributions. The most important family of continuous distributions is that of the normal (or Gaussian) probability distributions. [*See* PROBABILITY, *article on* FORMAL PROBABILITY, *for more of the many properties of the normal distributions.*]

The normal probability density function is

$$\frac{1}{\sigma\sqrt{2\pi}} \exp\left[-\tfrac{1}{2}\left(\frac{x - \mu}{\sigma}\right)^2\right], \quad -\infty < x < +\infty,$$

where μ is the mean (and also here the median and the mode) and σ is the standard deviation. Figure 1 shows the shape of this density. Note that it is symmetric about μ, that is, $f(\mu + x) = f(\mu - x)$, and that the density is essentially zero for $x > \mu + 3\sigma$ and $x < \mu - 3\sigma$. The normal distribution is sometimes said to be "bell-shaped," but note that there are many nonnormal bell-shaped distributions. The normal distribution is "standardized" or "normalized" by the transformation $z = (x - \mu)/\sigma$, which gives the standard–normal density,

$$\frac{1}{\sqrt{2\pi}} \exp(-\tfrac{1}{2} z^2).$$

A standardized normal random variable is also referred to as a "unit" normal since the mean of the standardized form is zero and the variance is one. The cumulative distribution function for the normal distribution in standardized form is

$$\frac{1}{\sqrt{2\pi}} \int_{-\infty}^{z} \exp(-\tfrac{1}{2} y^2)\,dy.$$

Thus, to find the probability that a normal random variable with mean μ and standard deviation σ is

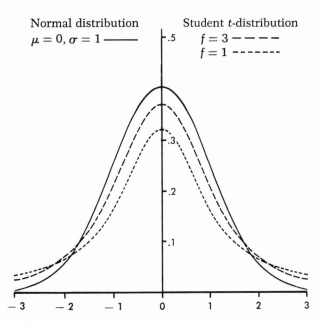

Figure 1 — Standard normal distribution and Student t-distribution showing density on the vertical scale corresponding to argument on the horizontal scale

less than x, first compute the number of standard deviations x is away from μ, that is, let $z = (x - \mu)/\sigma$. Probabilities associated with x then may be read from tables of the standardized distribution. Care must be exercised to determine what is tabulated in any particular table. Various tables give the following: the cumulative probability; the probability in the right-hand tail only; the sum of the probabilities in the two tails; the central probability, that is, the probability that the absolute value of the random variable is less than the argument; and others.

A great many probability distributions are derived from the normal distribution; see Eisenhart and Zelen (1958); Kendall and Stuart ([1943–1946] 1958–1961); Korn and Korn (1961); Zelen and Severo (1964). These references also list additional continuous distributions not covered here.

Normal distributions are sometimes called Gaussian, sometimes Laplace–Gauss distributions, and sometimes distributions following Laplace's second law. This terminology reflects a tangled and often misstated history [see Walker 1929, chapter 2; see also GAUSS; LAPLACE].

Chi-square distributions. If X is unit normally distributed, X^2 has a chi-square distribution with one degree of freedom. If $X_1, X_2, \cdots, X_f$ are all unit normally distributed and independent, then the sum of squares $X_1^2 + X_2^2 + \cdots + X_f^2$ has a chi-square distribution with f degrees of freedom.

The probability density function for a chi-square random variable is

$$\frac{1}{2^{\frac{1}{2}f}\Gamma(\frac{1}{2}f)} x^{\frac{1}{2}(f-2)}e^{-\frac{1}{2}x}, \qquad 0 \leqslant x < \infty.$$

This is also a probability density function when f is positive, but not integral, and a chi-square distribution with fractional degrees of freedom is simply defined via the density function.

The mean of a chi-square distribution is f, and its variance is $2f$. For $f > 2$, the chi-square distributions have their mode at $f - 2$. For $0 < f \leqslant 2$, the densities are J-shaped and are maximum at the origin. Figure 2 shows the shape of the chi-square distributions.

If Y_1, Y_2 are independent and chi-square distributed with f_1, f_2 degrees of freedom, then $Y_1 + Y_2$ is chi-square with $f_1 + f_2$ degrees of freedom. This additivity property extends to any finite number of independent, chi-square summands.

If Y has a chi-square distribution with f degrees of freedom, then Y/f has a *mean-square distribution*, or a chi-square divided by degrees of freedom distribution.

The cumulative distribution function for the chi-square random variable with an even number of degrees of freedom (equal to $2a$) is related to the Poisson cumulative distribution function with mean λ as follows:

$$\sum_{j=0}^{a-1} \frac{e^{-\lambda}\lambda^j}{j!} = \frac{1}{2^{\frac{1}{2}f}\Gamma(\frac{1}{2}f)} \int_{2\lambda}^{\infty} x^{\frac{1}{2}(f-2)}e^{-\frac{1}{2}x}\,dx,$$

where $f = 2a$.

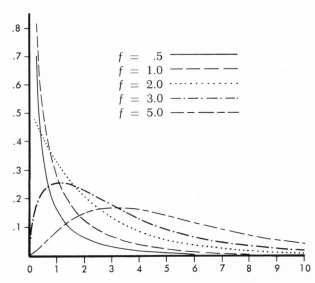

Figure 2 — Chi-square distributions showing density on the vertical scale corresponding to argument on the horizontal scale

Gamma or Pearson Type III distributions. The gamma distribution, a generalization of the chi-square distribution, has probability density function

$$\frac{1}{\theta\Gamma(r)}\left(\frac{x}{\theta}\right)^{r-1}\exp\left(-\frac{x}{\theta}\right),$$

where $0 < \theta < \infty$, $0 < r < \infty$, and $0 < x < \infty$. Note that r does not have to be an integer. The mean of this distribution is $r\theta$, and the variance is $r\theta^2$. A simple modification permits shifting the left end-point from zero to any other value in this distribution and in several others discussed below. If $r = \frac{1}{2}f$ and $\theta = 2$, the gamma distribution reduces to a chi-square distribution. If X has a chi-square distribution with f degrees of freedom, then $Y = \frac{1}{2}\theta X$ has a gamma distribution with parameters θ, $\frac{1}{2}f$. If Y has a gamma distribution with parameters θ, r, then $2\theta^{-1}Y$ has a chi-square distribution with $2r$ degrees of freedom.

Negative exponential distributions. Negative exponential distributions are special cases of gamma distributions with $r = 1$. The probability density is $(1/\theta)\exp(-x/\theta)$ for $0 \leqslant x < \infty$, $0 < \theta < \infty$; the mean is θ and the variance is θ^2. If $\theta = 2$, the negative exponential distribution reduces to a chi-square distribution with 2 degrees of freedom.

The cumulative distribution is

$$1 - \exp(-x/\theta), \qquad 0 \leqslant x < \infty, 0 < \theta < \infty.$$

This distribution has been widely used to represent the distribution of lives of certain manufactured goods, for example, light bulbs, radio tubes, etc. [see QUALITY CONTROL, STATISTICAL *article on* RELIABILITY AND LIFE TESTING].

Suppose that the probability that an item will function over the time period t to $t + \Delta t$ is independent of t, given that the item is functioning at time t. In other words, suppose that the age of an item does not affect the probability that it continues to function over any specified length of future time provided the item is operating at present. In still other terms, if X is a random variable denoting length of life for an item, suppose that

$$Pr\{X \geqslant x \mid X \geqslant \xi\} = Pr\{X \geqslant x - \xi\}$$

for all ξ and $x > \xi$. This "constant risk property" obtains if, and only if, X has a negative exponential distribution. The underlying temporal process is called a stationary Poisson process; and, for a Poisson process, the number of failures (or deaths) in any given interval of time has a Poisson distribution [see QUEUES *and the biography of* POISSON].

Noncentral chi-square distributions. If X_1, X_2, $\cdots$, X_f are all normally distributed and independent, and if X_i has mean μ_i and variance one, then the sum $X_1^2 + X_2^2 + \cdots + X_f^2$ has a noncentral chi-square distribution with f degrees of freedom and noncentrality parameter $\lambda = \mu_1^2 + \mu_2^2 + \cdots + \mu_f^2$. This family of distributions can be extended to nonintegral values of f by noting that the density function (not given here) obtained for integral values of f is still a density function for the non-integral values of f. The mean of the noncentral chi-square distribution is $f + \lambda$ and the variance is $2(f + 2\lambda)$.

Perhaps the main statistical use of the noncentral chi-square distribution is in connection with the power of standard tests for counted data [see COUNTED DATA].

The distribution also arises in bombing studies. For example, the proportion of a circular target destroyed by a bomb with a circular effects region may be obtained from the noncentral chi-square distribution with two degrees of freedom if the aiming errors follow a circular normal distribution. (A circular normal distribution is a bivariate normal distribution, discussed below, with $\rho = 0$ and $\sigma_X = \sigma_Y$.)

Noncentral chi-square distributions have an additivity property similar to that of (central) chi-square distributions.

Weibull distributions. A random variable X has a Weibull distribution if its probability density function is of the form

$$\frac{r}{\theta}\left(\frac{x}{\theta}\right)^{r-1}\exp\left(-\frac{x}{\theta}\right)^r,$$

where $0 \leqslant x < \infty$, $0 < \theta < \infty$ and $r \geqslant 1$. This means that random variables with Weibull distributions can be obtained by starting with negative exponential random variables and raising them to powers $\geqslant 1$. If in particular $r = 1$, the Weibull distribution reduces to a negative exponential distribution. The Weibull distributions are widely used to represent the distribution of lives of various manufactured products. The mean of X is $\theta\Gamma[(r + 1)/r]$, and $\theta^2\{\Gamma[(r + 2)/r] - \Gamma^2[(r + 1)/r]\}$ is the variance of X.

Student (or t-) distributions. If X has a unit normal distribution and if Y is distributed independently of X according to a chi-square distribution with f degrees of freedom, then $X/\sqrt{Y/f}$ has a Student (or t-) distribution with f degrees of freedom. Note that f need not be an integer since the degrees of freedom for chi-square need not be integral. The only restriction is $0 < f < \infty$. The density for a random variable having the Student distribution is

$$\frac{\Gamma(\frac{1}{2}f + \frac{1}{2})}{\sqrt{f\pi}\,\Gamma(\frac{1}{2}f)}\left(1 + \frac{x^2}{f}\right)^{-\frac{1}{2}(f+1)},$$

where $-\infty < x < +\infty$. A graph of the density functions for $f = 1$ and $f = 3$ is shown in Figure 1. Note that the density is symmetric about zero. As f approaches ∞, the Student density approaches the unit normal density.

The rth moment of the Student distribution exists if and only if $r < f$. Thus for $f \geq 2$, the mean is zero; and for $f \geq 3$, the variance is $f/(f-2)$. The median and the mode are zero for all f.

The Student distribution is named after W. S. Gosset, who wrote under the pseudonym Student. Gosset's development of the t-distribution, as it arises in dealing with normal means, is often considered to be the start of modern "small sample" mathematical statistics [see GOSSET].

The sample correlation coefficient, r, based on n pairs of observations from a bivariate normal population, may be reduced to a Student t-statistic with $n - 2$ degrees of freedom, when the population correlation coefficient is zero, by the transformation $t = (r\sqrt{n-2})/\sqrt{1-r^2}$ [see MULTIVARIATE ANALYSIS, articles on CORRELATION].

Cauchy distributions. The Cauchy distribution is an example of a distribution for which no moments exist. The probability density function is

$$\frac{1}{\pi\beta} \cdot \frac{1}{1 + [(x-\lambda)/\beta]^2},$$

where $-\infty < x < +\infty$, $\beta > 0$, and $-\infty < \lambda < +\infty$. The cumulative probability distribution is

$$Pr\{X \leq x\} = \frac{1}{\pi}\arctan\left(\frac{x-\lambda}{\beta}\right) + \frac{1}{2}.$$

The median and the mode of this distribution are at $x = \lambda$. For $\beta = 1$ and $\lambda = 0$, the Cauchy distribution is also a Student t-distribution with $f = 1$ degree of freedom.

Noncentral t-distributions. If X is a unit normal random variable and if Y is distributed independently of X according to a chi-square distribution with f degrees of freedom, then $(X + \delta)/\sqrt{Y/f}$ has a noncentral t-distribution with f degrees of freedom and noncentrality parameter δ where $0 < f < \infty$ and $-\infty < \delta < \infty$. The mean for $f \geq 2$ of this distribution is $c_{11}\delta$ and the variance for $f \geq 3$ is $c_{22}\delta^2 + c_{20}$, where $c_{11} = \sqrt{f/2}\, \Gamma(\frac{1}{2}f - \frac{1}{2})/\Gamma(\frac{1}{2}f)$, $c_{22} = [f/(f-2)] - c_{11}^2$, and $c_{20} = f/(f-2)$. If $\delta = 0$, the noncentral t-distribution reduces to the Student t-distribution. Note that the moments do not exist for $f = 1$; despite this similarity, the noncentral t-distribution with $\delta \neq 0$ is not a Cauchy distribution. The noncentral t-distribution arises when considering one-sided tolerance limits on a normal distribution and in power computations for the Student t-test.

F-distributions. If Y_1 has a chi-square distribution with f_1 degrees of freedom and Y_2 has a chi-square distribution with f_2 degrees of freedom, and Y_1 and Y_2 are independent, then $(Y_1/f_1)/(Y_2/f_2)$ has an F-distribution with f_1 degrees of freedom for the numerator and f_2 degrees of freedom for the denominator. The F-distributions are also known as Snedecor's F-distributions and variance ratio distributions. They arise as the distributions of the ratios of many of the mean squares in the analysis of variance [see LINEAR HYPOTHESES, article on ANALYSIS OF VARIANCE].

The density of F is

$$\frac{\Gamma(\frac{1}{2}f_1 + \frac{1}{2}f_2)f_1^{\frac{1}{2}f_1}f_2^{\frac{1}{2}f_2}}{\Gamma(\frac{1}{2}f_1)\Gamma(\frac{1}{2}f_2)} \cdot \frac{x^{(\frac{1}{2}f_1-1)}}{(f_2 + f_1 x)^{\frac{1}{2}(f_1+f_2)}},$$

where $0 < x < \infty$, $0 < f_1 < \infty$ and $0 < f_2 < \infty$. Figure 3 shows a plot of this density for four cases: $f_1 = f_2 = 1$, $f_1 = f_2 = 2$, $f_1 = 3$, $f_2 = 5$, and $f_1 = f_2 = 10$. Of these the cases of $f_1 = 3$, $f_2 = 5$, and $f_1 = f_2 = 10$ are most typical of F-distributions.

The mean of this distribution is $f_2/(f_2 - 2)$ for $f_2 > 2$; for $f_2 > 4$ the variance is given by $2f_2^2(f_1 + f_2 - 2)/[f_1(f_2 - 2)^2(f_2 - 4)]$; and the mode is $f_2(f_1 - 2)/[f_1(f_2 + 2)]$ for $f_1 > 2$. The F-distribution is J-shaped if $f_1 \leq 2$. When f_1 and f_2 are greater than 2, the F-distribution has its mode below $x = 1$ and its mean above $x = 1$ and, hence, is positively skew.

Let F_{f_1, f_2} represent a random variable having an F-distribution with f_1 degrees of freedom for the

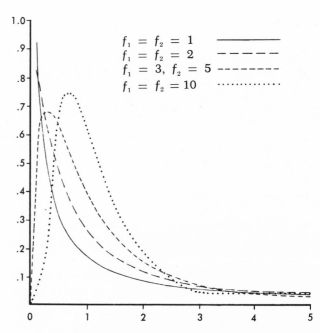

Figure 3 — F-distributions showing density on the vertical scale corresponding to argument on the horizontal scale

numerator and f_2 degrees of freedom for the denominator. Then $Pr\{F_{f_1, f_2} \leqslant c\} = 1 - Pr\{F_{f_2, f_1} \leqslant 1/c\}$. Hence the F-distribution is usually tabulated for one tail (usually the upper tail), as the other tail is easily obtained from the one tabulated.

The chi-square and t-distributions are related to the F-distributions as follows: $f_2/F_{\infty, f_2}$ has a chi-square distribution with f_2 degrees of freedom; $f_1 F_{f_1, \infty}$ has a chi-square distribution with f_1 degrees of freedom; F_{1, f_2} is distributed as the *square* of a Student-distributed random variable with f_2 degrees of freedom; $1/F_{f_1, \infty}$ is distributed as the square of a Student-distributed random variable with f_1 degrees of freedom.

Let $E(n, r, p) = \sum_{i=r}^{n} \binom{n}{i} p^i (1-p)^{n-i}$, that is, let $E(n, r, p)$ be the probability of r or more successes for a binomial probability distribution where p is the probability of success of a single trial [see DISTRIBUTIONS, STATISTICAL, *article on* SPECIAL DISCRETE DISTRIBUTIONS]. Let c_{v, f_1, f_2} be defined by $Pr\{F_{f_1, f_2} \leqslant c_{v, f_1, f_2}\} = v$. Then the following relationship exists between the binomial and F-distributions. If $E(n, r, p) = v$ then

$$p = \frac{r}{r + (n - r + 1)c_{1-v, 2(n-r+1), 2r}}.$$

A slight variation on the F-distribution obtained by the change of variable $Y = [f_1/f_2]X$ is often referred to as the inverted beta distribution, the beta distribution of the second kind, or the beta prime distribution. These names are also occasionally applied to the F-distribution itself. Another variation on the F-distribution is Fisher's z-distribution, which is that of $\frac{1}{2} \ln F$.

Beta distributions. A random variable, X, has a beta distribution with parameters p and q if its density is of the form

$$\frac{\Gamma(p + q)}{\Gamma(p)\Gamma(q)} x^{p-1}(1-x)^{q-1},$$

where $0 < x < 1$; $p, q > 0$. If the transformation $X = f_1 F_{f_1, f_2}/(f_2 + f_1 F_{f_1, f_2})$ is made, then X has a beta distribution with $p = \frac{1}{2}f_1$ and $q = \frac{1}{2}f_2$.

The cumulative beta distribution is known as the incomplete beta function,

$$I_x(p, q) = \frac{\Gamma(p + q)}{\Gamma(p)\Gamma(q)} \int_0^x u^{p-1}(1-u)^{q-1} \, du.$$

The incomplete beta function has been tabulated by Karl Pearson (see Pearson 1934). The relationship $I_x(p, q) = 1 - I_{1-x}(q, p)$ is often useful. The mean of the beta distribution is $p/(p + q)$, and the variance is $pq/[(p + q)^2(p + q + 1)]$.

The mode for $p \geqslant 1$ and $q \geqslant 1$, but p and q not both equal to 1, is $(p - 1)/(p + q - 2)$. For $p \leqslant 1$ and $q > 1$, the density is in the shape of a reversed

J; for $p > 1$ and $q \leqslant 1$ the density is J-shaped; and for $p < 1$ and $q < 1$, the density is U-shaped. For both p and $q = 1$, the density takes the form of the density of the rectangular distributions with $a = 0$ and $b = 1$. The beta distribution is also known as the beta distribution of the first kind or the incomplete beta distribution.

Let $E(n, r, x) = \sum_{i=r}^{n} \binom{n}{i} x^i (1-x)^{n-i}$, that is, let $E(n, r, x)$ be the probability of r or more successes in n trials for a binomial probability distribution where x is the probability of success of a single trial. Then $I_x(p, q) = E(p + q - 1, p, x)$. In other words, partial binomial sums are expressible directly in terms of the incomplete beta function. To solve $I_x(p, q) = \gamma$ for x, with γ, p, and q fixed, find x from $x = p/[p + qc_{1-\gamma, 2q, 2p}]$ where c_{γ, f_1, f_2} is defined by $Pr\{F_{f_1, f_2} \leqslant c_{\gamma, f_1, f_2}\} = \gamma$, that is, c_{γ, f_1, f_2} is a percentage point of the F-distribution.

If Y_1 and Y_2 are independent random variables having gamma distributions with equal values of θ, $r = n_1$ for Y_1, and $r = n_2$ for Y_2, then the variable $X = Y_1/(Y_1 + Y_2)$ has a beta distribution with $p = n_1$ and $q = n_2$.

Bivariate beta distributions. The random variables X and Y are said to have a joint bivariate beta distribution if the joint probability density function for X and Y is given by

$$\frac{\Gamma(f_1 + f_2 + f_3)}{\Gamma(f_1)\Gamma(f_2)\Gamma(f_3)} x^{f_1-1} y^{f_2-1}(1 - x - y)^{f_3-1}$$

for $x, y > 0$ and $x + y < 1$, $0 < f_1 < \infty$, $0 < f_2 < \infty$, and $0 < f_3 < \infty$. This distribution is also known as the bivariate Dirichlet distribution. The mean of X is given by f_1/f_+, and the mean of Y by f_2/f_+, where f_+ represents $(f_1 + f_2 + f_3)$. The variance of X is $f_1(f_2 + f_3)/f_+^2(f_+ + 1)$; the variance of Y is $f_2(f_1 + f_3)/f_+^2(f_+ + 1)$; the correlation between X and Y is $-f_1 f_2/\sqrt{f_1 f_2 (f_2 + f_3)(f_1 + f_3)}$. The conditional distribution of $X/(1 - Y)$, given Y, is a beta distribution with $p = f_1$ and $q = f_3$. The sum $X + Y$ has a beta distribution with $p = f_1 + f_2$ and $q = f_3$.

Noncentral F-distributions. If Y_1 has a noncentral chi-square distribution with f_1 degrees of freedom and noncentrality parameter λ, and if Y_2 has a (central) chi-square distribution with f_2 degrees of freedom and is independent of Y_1, then $(Y_1/f_1)/(Y_2/f_2)$ has a noncentral F-distribution with f_1 degrees of freedom for the numerator and f_2 degrees of freedom for the denominator and noncentrality parameter λ. The cumulative distribution function of noncentral F may be closely approximated by a central F cumulative distribution function as follows:

$$Pr\{F_{f_1, f_2, \lambda}^N \leqslant c\} \cong Pr\left\{F_{f^*, f_2} \leqslant \frac{f_1 c}{f_1 + \lambda}\right\},$$

where $F^N_{f_1, f_2, \lambda}$ has a noncentral F-distribution and F_{f^*, f_2} has a central F-distribution and f^* denotes $(f_1 + \lambda)^2/(f_1 + 2\lambda)$. The mean of the noncentral F-distribution is $f_2(f_1 + \lambda)/[(f_2 - 2)f_1]$ for $f_2 > 2$, and the variance is

$$\frac{2f_2^2[(f_1 + \lambda)^2 + (f_1 + 2\lambda)(f_2 - 2)]}{(f_2 - 2)^2 f_1^2 (f_2 - 4)}$$

for $f_2 > 4$. The means do not exist if $f_2 \leqslant 2$ and the variances do not exist if $f_2 \leqslant 4$.

The ratio of two noncentral chi-square random variables also arises occasionally. This distribution has not yet been given a specific name. The noncentral F-distribution is, of course, a special case of the distribution of this ratio. The noncentral F-distribution arises in considering the power of analysis of variance tests.

Bivariate normal distributions. To say that X and Y have a joint (nonsingular) normal distribution with means μ_X and μ_Y, variances σ_X^2 and σ_Y^2, and correlation ρ is to say that the joint probability density function for X and Y is

$$\frac{1}{2\pi\sigma_X\sigma_Y\sqrt{1 - \rho^2}} \cdot$$

$$\exp\left[\frac{\left(\frac{x-\mu_X}{\sigma_X}\right)^2 - 2\rho\left(\frac{x-\mu_X}{\sigma_X}\right)\left(\frac{y-\mu_Y}{\sigma_Y}\right) + \left(\frac{y-\mu_Y}{\sigma_Y}\right)^2}{-2(1 - \rho^2)}\right].$$

The cumulative distribution function occurs in many problems; it is a special case (two-dimensional) of the multivariate normal distribution. A fundamental fact is that X and Y are jointly normal if and only if $aX + bY$ is normal for every a and b [see MULTIVARIATE ANALYSIS].

Distributions of the sum of normal variables. Let $X_1, X_2, \cdots, X_n$ be jointly normally distributed random variables so that X_i has mean μ_i and variance σ_i^2 and the correlation between X_i and X_j is ρ_{ij}. Then the distribution of the weighted sum, $a_1 X_1 + a_2 X_2 + \cdots + a_n X_n$, where $a_1, a_2, \cdots, a_n$ are any real constants (positive, negative, or zero), is normal with mean $a_1\mu_1 + a_2\mu_2 + \cdots + a_n\mu_n$ and variance

$$\sum_{i=1}^n a_i^2 \sigma_i^2 + 2 \sum_{i=1}^n \sum_{j=i+1}^n a_i a_j \sigma_i \sigma_j \rho_{ij} .$$

If the normality assumption is dropped, then the means and variances remain as stated, but the form of the distribution of the sum $a_1 X_1 + a_2 X_2 + \cdots + a_n X_n$ is often different from the distribution of the X's. If a linear function, $\sum_{i=1}^n a_i X_i$, $a_i \neq 0$, of a finite number of independent random variables is normally distributed, then each of the random variables $X_1, X_2, \cdots, X_n$ is also normally distributed.

Note that in this instance independence of the random variables is required.

In particular, if X_1 and X_2 are jointly normally distributed, the sum $X_1 + X_2$ is normally distributed with mean $\mu_1 + \mu_2$ and variance $\sigma_1^2 + \sigma_2^2 + 2\rho_{12}\sigma_1\sigma_2$. The difference $X_1 - X_2$ is normally distributed with mean $\mu_1 - \mu_2$ and variance $\sigma_1^2 + \sigma_2^2 - 2\rho_{12}\sigma_1\sigma_2$. If $X_1, X_2, \cdots, X_n$ are jointly normally distributed with common mean μ and variance σ^2 and are independent, then the mean of the X's, that is, $\bar{X} = (1/n)\sum_{i=1}^n X_i$, is normally distributed with mean μ variance σ^2/n.

Rectangular distributions. The rectangular (or uniform) distribution has the following density: it is zero for $x < a$; it is $1/(b - a)$ for $a \leqslant x \leqslant b$; and it is zero for $x > b$, where a and b are real constants. In other words, it has a graph that is a rectangle with base of length $b - a$ and height of $1/(b - a)$. The cumulative distribution function is zero for $x < a$; it is $(x - a)/(b - a)$ for $a \leqslant x \leqslant b$; and it is one for $x > b$. The mean and the median of this distribution are both $\frac{1}{2}(a + b)$, and the variance is $(b - a)^2/12$.

One of the principal applications of the rectangular distribution occurs in conjunction with the probability integral transformation. This is the transformation $Y = F(X)$, where $F(X)$ is the cumulative distribution function for a continuous random variable X. Then Y is rectangularly distributed with $a = 0$ and $b = 1$. Many distribution-free tests of fit have been derived starting with this transformation [see GOODNESS OF FIT; NONPARAMETRIC STATISTICS].

If Y has the rectangular distribution with $a = 0$, $b = 1$, then $-2 \ln Y$ has the chi-square distribution with 2 degrees of freedom. It follows, from the additivity of chi-square distributions, that if $Y_1, Y_2, \cdots, Y_n$ are jointly and independently distributed according to rectangular distributions with $a = 0$ and $b = 1$, then the sum, $-2 \sum_{i=1}^n \ln Y_i$, has a chi-square distribution with $2n$ degrees of freedom.

There is also a discrete form of the rectangular distribution.

Pareto distributions. The density functions for Pareto distributions take the form: zero for $x < b$; $(a/b)(b/x)^{a+1}$ for $b \leqslant x < \infty$, where a and b are positive real constants (not zero). The cumulative distribution function is zero for $x < b$ and is equal to $1 - (b/x)^a$ for $b \leqslant x < \infty$. For $a > 1$, the mean of the Pareto distribution is $ab/(a - 1)$, and for $a > 2$ the variance is $(ab^2)/[(a - 1)^2(a - 2)]$. The median for $a > 0$ is at $x = 2^{1/a}b$, and the mode is at $x = b$. The Pareto distribution is related to the negative exponential distribution by the transformation $Y = \theta a \ln (X/b)$ where Y has the negative exponential distribution and X has the Pareto distribution.

Pareto distributions have been employed in the study of income distribution [see INCOME DISTRIBUTION].

Laplace distributions. A random variable X has the Laplace distribution if its probability density function takes the form

$$\frac{1}{2\theta} \exp\left(-\left|\frac{x-\lambda}{\theta}\right|\right),$$

where $-\infty < \lambda < +\infty$, $0 < \theta < \infty$ and $-\infty < x < +\infty$. The mean of this distribution is λ, and the variance is $2\theta^2$. This distribution is also known as the double exponential, since the graph has the shape of an exponential function for $x > \lambda$ and it is a reflection (about the line $x = \lambda$) of the same exponential function for $x < \lambda$. The Laplace distribution is sometimes called Laplace's first law of error, the second being the normal distribution.

Lognormal distributions. A random variable X is said to have a logarithmic normal distribution (or lognormal distribution) if the logarithm of the variate is normally distributed. Let $Y = \ln X$ be normally distributed with mean μ and variance σ^2. The mean of X is $\exp(\mu + \frac{1}{2}\sigma^2)$ and the variance of X is $(\exp\sigma^2 - 1)\exp(2\mu + \sigma^2)$. Note that $0 < X < \infty$, while $-\infty < Y < +\infty$. The base of the logarithm may be any number greater than one (or between zero and one), and the bases 2 and 10 are often used. If the base a is used, then the mean of X is $a^{\mu + \frac{1}{2}(\ln a)\sigma^2}$, and the variance of X is $(a^{\sigma^2 \ln a} - 1)a^{2\mu + (\ln a)\sigma^2}$.

Logistic distributions. The logistic curve $y = \lambda/[1 + \gamma e^{-\kappa x}]$ is used frequently to represent the growth of populations. It may also be used as a cumulative probability distribution function. A random variable, X, is said to have the logistic probability distribution if the density of X is given by

$$\frac{\pi}{4\sigma\sqrt{3}} \operatorname{sech}^2\left[\left(\frac{x-\mu}{\sigma}\right)\frac{\pi}{2\sqrt{3}}\right],$$

where $-\infty < x < +\infty$; μ is the mean of X and σ^2 is the variance of X. As with the normal distribution, the transformation $z = (x - \mu)/\sigma$ gives a standardized form to the distribution. The cumulative distribution function for the standardized variable is

$$1/[1 + \exp(-\pi z/\sqrt{3})],$$

where $-\infty < z < +\infty$. The shape of this cumulative distribution so nearly resembles the normal distribution that samples from normal and logistic distributions are difficult to distinguish from one another.

The exponential family of distributions. The one-parameter, single-variate, *exponential density functions* are those of the form

$$c(\theta) \exp[\theta A(x) + B(x)],$$

where c, A, and B are functions usually taken to satisfy regularity conditions. If there are several parameters, $\theta_1, \cdots, \theta_r$, the exponential form is

$$c(\theta_1, \cdots, \theta_r) \exp\left[\sum \theta_i A_i(x) + B(x)\right].$$

Analogous forms may be considered for the multivariate case and for discrete distributions. Most of the standard distributions (normal, binomial, and so on) are exponential, but reparameterization may be required to express them in the above form.

The exponential distributions are important in theoretical statistics, and they arise naturally in discussions of sufficiency. Under rather stringent regularity conditions, an interesting sufficient statistic exists if, and only if, sampling is from an exponential distribution; this relationship was first explored by Koopman (1936), Darmois (1935), and Pitman (1936), so that the exponential distributions are sometimes eponymously called the Koopman–Darmois or Koopman–Pitman distributions [see SUFFICIENCY].

A discussion of the exponential family of distributions, and its relation to hypothesis testing, is given by Lehmann (1959, especially pp. 50–54).

It is important to distinguish between the family of exponential distributions and that of negative exponential distributions. The latter is a very special, although important, subfamily of the former.

DONALD B. OWEN

BIBLIOGRAPHY

DARMOIS, GEORGES 1935 Sur les lois de probabilité à estimation exhaustive. Académie des Sciences, Paris, *Comptes rendus hebdomadaires* 200:1265–1266.

EISENHART, CHURCHILL; and ZELEN, MARVIN 1958 Elements of Probability. Pages 134–164 in E. U. Condon and Hugh Odishaw (editors), *Handbook of Physics.* New York: McGraw-Hill.

GREENWOOD, JOSEPH A.; and HARTLEY, H. O. 1962 *Guide to Tables in Mathematical Statistics.* Princeton Univ. Press.

HAIGHT, FRANK A. 1961 Index to the Distributions of Mathematical Statistics. U.S. National Bureau of Standards, *Journal of Research* Series B: Mathematics and Mathematical Physics 65B:23–60.

KENDALL, MAURICE G.; and STUART, ALAN (1943–1946) 1958–1966 *The Advanced Theory of Statistics.* 3 vols. New ed. New York: Hafner; London: Griffin. → The first edition was written by Kendall alone.

KOOPMAN, B. O. 1936 On Distributions Admitting a Sufficient Statistic. *American Mathematical Society, Transactions* 39:399–409.

KORN, GRANIO A.; and KORN, THERESA M. 1961 *Mathematical Handbook for Scientists and Engineers: Definitions, Theorems, and Formulas for Reference and Review.* New York: McGraw-Hill. → See especially pages 521–586 on "Probability Theory and Random Processes" and pages 587–626 on "Mathematical Statistics."

LEHMANN, ERICH L. 1959 *Testing Statistical Hypotheses.* New York: Wiley.

OWEN, DONALD B. 1962 *Handbook of Statistical Tables.* Reading, Mass.: Addison-Wesley. → A list of addenda and errata is available from the author.

PEARSON, EGON S.; and HARTLEY, H. O. (editors), (1954) 1958 *Biometrika Tables for Statisticians.* 2 vols., 2d ed. Cambridge Univ. Press. → See especially Volume 1.

PEARSON, KARL (editor) (1922) 1951 *Tables of the Incomplete Γ-function.* London: Office of Biometrika.

PEARSON, KARL (editor) 1934 *Tables of the Incomplete Beta-function.* London: Office of Biometrika.

PITMAN, E. J. G. 1936 Sufficient Statistics and Intrinsic Accuracy. *Cambridge Philosophical Society, Proceedings* 32:567–579.

U.S. NATIONAL BUREAU OF STANDARDS 1953 *Tables of Normal Probability Functions.* Applied Mathematics Series, No. 23. Washington: The Bureau.

U.S. NATIONAL BUREAU OF STANDARDS 1959 *Tables of the Bivariate Normal Distribution Function and Related Functions.* Applied Mathematics Series, No. 50. Washington: The Bureau.

WALKER, HELEN M. 1929 *Studies in the History of Statistical Method, With Special Reference to Certain Educational Problems.* Baltimore: Williams & Wilkins.

ZELEN, MARVIN; and SEVERO, NORMAN C. (1964) 1965 Probability Functions. Chapter 26 in Milton Abramowitz and I. A. Stegun (editors), *Handbook of Mathematical Functions: With Formulas, Graphs, and Mathematical Tables.* New York: Dover. → First published as National Bureau of Standards, Applied Mathematics Series, No. 55. A list of errata is available from the National Bureau of Standards.

III
APPROXIMATIONS TO DISTRIBUTIONS

The term *approximation* refers, in general, to the representation of "something" by "something else" that is expected to be a useful replacement for the "something." Approximations are sometimes needed because it is not possible to obtain an exact representation of the "something"; even when an exact representation is possible, approximations may simplify analytical treatment.

In scientific work, approximations are in constant use. For example, much scientific argument, and nearly all statistical analysis, is based on mathematical models that are essentially approximations. This article, however, is restricted to approximations to distributions of empirical data and to theoretical probability distributions.

When approximating empirically observed distributions—for example, a histogram of frequencies of different words in a sample of speech—the primary objectives are those of compact description and smoothing. These are also the primary objectives of much approximation in demographic and actuarial work [see LIFE TABLES].

On the other hand, approximation to a theoretical distribution is often needed when exact treatment is too complicated to be practicable. For example, an econometrician who has developed a new estimator of price elasticity may well find the exact distribution of his estimator quite intractable; he will probably resort to large-sample (asymptotic) methods to find an approximate distribution.

It may also happen that a distribution arising not from statistical considerations, but from another kind of mathematical model, requires approximation to improve understanding. For example, a psychologist may use a probabilistic model of the learning process, a model that leads to a theoretical distribution for the number of trials needed to reach a specified level of performance. This distribution may be so complicated that an approximate form will markedly increase appreciation of its meaning.

The final section of this article discusses a general requirement, the measurement of the goodness of any particular approximation; this is especially important in the comparison of different approximations.

Approximation to empirical distributions. This section deals with approximations to distributions of numerical data representing measurements on each of a group of individuals. (Usually the group is a sample of some kind.) Among important techniques not discussed here are those that are purely mathematical (such as numerical quadrature and iterative solutions of equations) and those associated with the analysis of time series (such as trend fitting and periodogram and correlogram analysis) [see TIME SERIES].

As a specific example, data on the distributions of diseases by frequency of diagnosis (for males) in the teaching hospitals of England and Wales for the year 1949 (based on Herdan 1957) are presented in Table 1. The figures mean, for example, that out of 718 different diseases of males reported during the year, 120 occurred between one and five times each, while two were reported between 4,000 and 5,000 times each.

The figures shown in the table have already been grouped but present a rather irregular appearance; it would be useful to summarize the data in a more readily comprehensible form. A quick way to do

Table 1 — Diseases by frequency of diagnosis in the teaching hospitals of England and Wales for 1949

FREQUENCY OF DIAGNOSIS	NUMBER OF DISEASES	
	Observed	Fitted
1–5	120	103
6–10	55	74
11–15	44	54
16–20	31	43
21–25	28	34
26–30	32	28
31–40	45	45
41–50	37	35
51–60	33	28
61–70	22	23
71–80	23	19
81–90	22	17
91–100	15	14
101–119	21	22
120–139	18	19
140–159	19	15
160–179	19	13
180–199	12	11
200–239	19	17
240–279	24	13
280–319	13	11
320–359	4	8.5
360–399	9	7.0
400–499	15	13.1
500–599	13	9.1
600–699	5	6.7
700–799	6	5.0
800–899	2	4.0
900–999	2	3.1
1,000–1,999	6	14.0
2,000–2,999	1	4.1
3,000–3,999	1	1.9
4,000–4,999	2	1.0
≥ 5,000	–	2.25
Total	718	717.75

Source: Herdan 1957.

this is to group further and to form a histogram (as in Figure 1). [*Further information on this method is presented in* GRAPHIC PRESENTATION; STATISTICAL ANALYSIS, SPECIAL PROBLEMS OF, *article on* GROUPED OBSERVATIONS.]

Grouping is in itself a kind of approximation, since it does not reproduce *all* features of the original data. For concise description, however, representation by a formula can be more useful. This is effected by fitting a frequency curve. If the fitted curve is simple enough and the effectiveness of approximation ("goodness of fit") is adequate, considerable benefit can be derived by replacing a large accumulation of data, with its inevitable irregularities, with a simple formula that can be handled with some facility and is a conveniently brief way of summarizing the data.

The present-day decline in the importance of fitting observed frequency distributions may well be only a temporary phenomenon. In the years

1890 to 1915 (roughly) there was a need to demonstrate that statistical methods did apply to real physical situations. The χ^2 test developed by Karl Pearson (1900) demonstrated clearly that the normal distribution, which had previously been assumed to be of rather general application, was not applicable to much observed data. It was desirable, therefore, to show, if possible, that some reasonably simple mathematical formula could give an adequate fit to the data.

Subsequent development of the theory of mathematical statistics has, on the one hand, been very much concerned with clarification of the logical principles underlying statistical method (assuming that there is some fairly well-established mathematical representation of the distributions involved); and on the other hand it has produced "distribution free" procedures, particularly significance tests, that eliminate the need for considering the actual form of distribution (to any but the broadest detail) [*see* NONPARAMETRIC STATISTICS].

Both these lines of work tend to reduce interest in description of actual distributions in as precise detail as the data allow. However, from the more general viewpoint of scientific inquiry, the neglect of systematic study of distributional form in favor of application of formal techniques to arbitrarily hypothetical situations can represent a wasteful use of the data.

In the data of the example, the frequency of occurrences is naturally discrete—it takes only integer values—and, therefore, prime consideration should be given to formulas appropriate to discrete variables. In view of the wide range of variation of frequency, however, formulas appropriate to continuous variables may also give good approximations, and they are worth considering if they offer substantially simpler results.

A number of families of frequency curves have been found effective in approximating observed sets of data. Provided that a suitable form of curve has been chosen, fitting a maximum of *four* parameters gives a reasonably effective approximation. Fitting the curve is equivalent to estimating these parameters; this may be effected in various ways, among which are (*i*) the method of *maximum likelihood;* (*ii*) the method of *moments,* in which certain lower moments of the fitted curve are made to agree with the corresponding values calculated from the observed data; and (*iii*) the method of *percentile points,* in which the fitted curve is made to give cumulative proportions agreeing with those for the observed data at certain points (7%, 25%, 75%, and 93% are often recommended) [*see* ESTIMATION, *article on* POINT ESTIMATION].

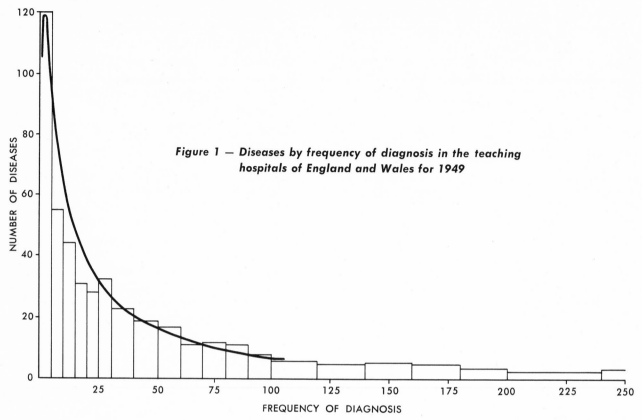

Figure 1 — Diseases by frequency of diagnosis in the teaching hospitals of England and Wales for 1949

Source: Herdan 1957.

In cases where a clear probabilistic model can be established, there is usually good reason to prefer the method of maximum likelihood. When it is not possible to establish such a model, another method is required.

Fitting is sometimes facilitated by using appropriately designed "probability paper," with the ordinate and abscissa scales such that if cumulative frequency (ordinate) is plotted against variable values (abscissa), a straight line relationship should be obtained [see GRAPHIC PRESENTATION].

Among the more commonly used families of frequency curves are those representing the normal, exponential and gamma distributions. These specify the proportion less than, or equal to, a fixed number x (the cumulative distribution function, often denoted by the symbol $F(x)$) as a function depending on two or three parameters (and also, of course, on x) [see DISTRIBUTIONS, STATISTICAL, *article on* SPECIAL CONTINUOUS DISTRIBUTIONS]. The best-known system of curves is the *Pearson* system (Elderton 1906), which is derived from solutions of the differential equation

$$\frac{d^2F}{dx^2} = -\frac{dF}{dx}\left[\frac{c(x + a_0)}{x^2 + a_1 x + a_2}\right].$$

Originally (Pearson 1895) this equation was ar-

rived at by (*i*) considering limiting cases of sampling from a finite population and (*ii*) requiring the curve $y = dF/dx$ to satisfy certain natural conditions of unimodality, smoothness, etc. (Note that there are *four* parameters, c, a_0, a_1, a_2, in this equation.)

Methods have been worked out (Elderton 1906) for estimating the values of these parameters from the first four moments of the distributions. In certain cases, the procedures can be much facilitated by using Table 42 of the *Biometrika* tables (Pearson & Hartley 1954) or the considerably extended version of these tables in Johnson et al. (1963). Entering these tables with the values of the moment ratios ($\sqrt{\beta_1}$ and β_2) it is possible to read directly standardized percentage points (X'_P) for a number of values of P. The percentage points X_P (such that $\hat{F}(X_P) = P$) are then calculated as Mean $+ X'_P \times$ (Standard Deviation).

Other systems are based on "transformation to normality" with $z = a_1 + a_2 g[c(x + a_0)]$, where z is a normal variable with zero mean and unit standard deviation, and $g[\ ]$ is a fairly simple explicit function. Here, c, a_0, a_1, and a_2 are again parameters. If $g[y] = \log y$, one gets a *lognormal* curve. Such a curve has been fitted to the distribution of frequency of diagnosis in Figure 1 (for clarity, up to frequency 100 only). Since $z = a_1 + a_2 \log [c(x + a_0)]$ can be written as $z = a_1' + a_2 \log (x + a_0)$, where now $a_1' = a_1 + a_2 \log c$, there are in fact only *three* separate parameters in this case. In fitting the curve in Figure 1, a_0 has been taken equal to -0.5, leaving only a_1 and a_2 to be estimated. This has been done by the method of percentile points (making the fitted frequencies less than 11 and less than 200 agree with the observed frequencies—175 and 596 respectively). The fitted formula is (rounded)

Number less than, or equal to, x (an integer)
$$= 718 \, \Phi(.55 \ln x - 1.95),$$

where Φ is the cumulative distribution function of the unit-normal distribution [see DISTRIBUTIONS, STATISTICAL, *article on* SPECIAL CONTINUOUS DISTRIBUTIONS]. Numerical values of the fitted frequencies are shown in the last column of Table 1.

While a reasonable fit is obtained in the center of the distribution, the fit is poor for the larger frequencies of diagnosis. As has been noted, although the data are discrete, a continuous curve has been fitted; however, this is not in itself reason for obtaining a poor fit. Indeed many standard approximations—such as the approximation to a binomial distribution by a normal distribution—are of this kind.

Another system of curves is obtained by taking the approximate value of $F(x)$ to be

$$\hat{F}(x) = \sum_{j=0}^{k} a_j \, \Phi^{(j)}\left(\frac{x - \xi}{\sigma}\right),$$

where $\Phi^{(j)}$ is the jth derivative of Φ, and where the parameters are $a_0, a_1, \cdots, a_k, \xi$, and $\sigma > 0$. The number of parameters depends on the value of k, which is usually not taken to be greater than 3 or 4. This system of curves is known as the Gram–Charlier system; a modified form is known as the Edgeworth system (Kendall & Stuart 1943–1946, chapter 6). If all a's after a_0 are zero (and a_0 is equal to one) then $F(x)$ is simply the normal cumulative distribution. The terms after the first can be regarded as "corrections" to the simple normal approximation. It should not automatically be assumed, however, that the more corrections added the better. If a high value of k is used, the curve may present a wavy appearance; even with a small value of k it is possible to obtain *negative* values of fitted frequencies (Barton & Dennis 1952).

Similar expansions can be constructed replacing $\Phi(x)$ by other standard cumulative distribution (see Cramér 1945, sec. 20.6). If the $\Phi^{(j)}$'s are replaced by cumulative distribution functions $\Phi_j(x)$, (with, of course, $a_0 + a_1 + a_2 + \cdots + a_k = 1$), then $F(x)$ is represented by a "mixture" of these distributions [see DISTRIBUTIONS, STATISTICAL, *article on*

MIXTURES OF DISTRIBUTIONS]. When joint distributions of two or more variates are to be fitted, the variety of possible functional forms can be an embarrassment. A convenient mode of attack is to search for an effective normalizing transformation for each variate separately. If such a transformation can be found for each variate, then a joint multinormal distribution can be fitted to the set of transformed variates, using the means, variances, and correlations of the transformed variates. A discussion of some possibilities, in the case of two variates, will be found in Johnson (1949).

Approximation to one theoretical distribution by another. Approximation is also useful even when it is not necessary to deal with observed data. An important field of application is the replacement of complicated formulas for the theoretical distributions of statistics by simpler (or more thoroughly investigated) distributions. Just as when approximating to observed data, it is essential that the approximation be sufficiently effective to give useful results. In this case, however, the problem is more definitely expressible in purely mathematical terms; there are a number of results in the mathematical theory of probability that are often used in constructing approximations of this kind.

Among these results, the "Central Limit" group of theorems has the broadest range of applicability. The theorems in this group state that, under appropriate conditions, the limiting distribution of certain statistics, T_n, based on a number, n, of random variables, as n tends to infinity, is a normal distribution. [See PROBABILITY *for a discussion of the Central Limit theorems*.]

If the conditions of a Central Limit theorem are satisfied, then the distribution of the statistic $T_n' = [T_n - E(T_n)][\sigma(T_n)]^{-1}$, where $E(T_n)$ is the mean and $\sigma(T_n)$ the standard deviation of T_n, may be approximated by a "unit normal distribution." Then the probability $Pr[T_n \leqslant \tau]$ may be approximated by using tables of the normal integral with argument $[\tau - E(T_n)]/\sigma(T_n)$.

There are many different Central Limit theorems; the most generally useful of these relate to the special case when the X's are mutually independent and $T_n = X_1 + X_2 + \cdots + X_n$. The simplest set of conditions is that each X should have the *same* distribution (with finite expected value and standard deviation), but weaker sets of conditions can replace the requirement that the distributions be identical. These conditions, roughly speaking, ensure that none of the variables X_i have such large standard deviations that they dominate the distribution of T_n.

Central Limit results are used to approximate distributions of test criteria calculated from a "large" number of sample values. The meaning of "large" depends on the way in which the effectiveness of the approximation is measured and the accuracy of representation required. In turn, these factors depend on the use that is to be made of the results. Some of the problems arising in the measurement of effectiveness of approximation will be described in the next section.

Very often there is a choice of quantities to which Central Limit type results can be applied. For example, any power of a chi-square random variable tends to normality as the number of degrees of freedom increases. For many purposes, the one-third power (cube root) gives the most rapid convergence to normality (see Moore 1957), although it may not always be the best power to use. While many useful approximations can be suggested by skillful use of probability theory, it should always be remembered that sufficient numerical accuracy is an essential requirement. In some cases (for example, Mallows 1956; Gnedenko et al. 1961; Wallace 1959), theoretical considerations may provide satisfactory evidence of accuracy; in other cases, *ad hoc* investigations, possibly using Monte Carlo methods, may be desirable. Interesting examples of these kinds of investigation are described by Goodman and Kruskal (1963) and Pearson (1963). [*A discussion of Monte Carlo methods may be found in* RANDOM NUMBERS.]

Another type of result (Cramér 1945, sec. 20.6) useful in approximating theoretical distributions and, in particular, in extending the field of Central Limit results, may be stated formally: "if $\lim_{n \to \infty} Pr[X_n < \xi] = F(\xi)$ and Y_n tends to η in probability, then $\lim_{n \to \infty} Pr[X_n + Y_n < \xi] = F(\xi - \eta)$," or less formally, "the limiting distribution of $X_n + Y_n$ is the same as that of $X_n + \eta$." Similar statements hold for multiplication, and this kind of useful result may be considerably generalized. A fuller discussion is given in the Appendix of Goodman and Kruskal (1963).

A classic and important example of approximation of one theoretical distribution by another is that of approximating a binomial distribution by a normal one. If the random variable X has a binomial distribution with parameters p, n, then the simplest form of the approximation is to take $Pr\{X \leqslant c\}$ as about equal to

$$\Phi\left\{\frac{c - np}{[np(1 - p)]^{\frac{1}{2}}}\right\},$$

where $c = 0, 1, 2, \cdots, n$. One partial justification for this approximation is that the mean and standard deviation of X are, respectively, np and $[np(1 - p)]^{\frac{1}{2}}$; the asymptotic validity of the approximation follows from the simplest Central Limit theorem.

The approximation may be generally improved by replacing $c - np$, in the numerator of the argument of Φ, with $c - np + \frac{1}{2}$. This modification, which has no asymptotic effect, is called the "continuity correction." Together with similar modifications, continuity corrections may often be used effectively to improve approximations at little extra computational cost.

The methods described in the section on approximating numerical data can also be used, with appropriate modification, in approximating theoretical distributions. Different considerations may arise, however, in deciding on the adequacy of an approximation in the two different situations.

Measuring the effectiveness of an approximation. The effectiveness of an approximation is its suitability for the purpose for which it is used. With sufficiently exhaustive knowledge of the properties of each of a number of approximations, it would be possible to choose the best one to use in any given situation, with little risk of making a bad choice. However, in the majority of cases, the attainment of such knowledge (even if possible) would entail such excessively time-consuming labor that a main purpose for the use of approximations —the saving of effort—would be defeated. Considerable insight into the properties of approximations can, however, be gained by the careful use of certain representative figures, or indexes, for their effectiveness. Such an index summarizes one aspect of the accuracy of an approximation.

Since a single form of approximation may be used in many different ways, it is likely that different indexes will be needed for different types of application. For example, the approximation obtained by representing the distribution of a statistic by a normal distribution may be used, *inter alia*, (*a*) for calculating approximate significance levels for the statistic, (*b*) for designing an experiment to have specified sensitivity, and (*c*) for combining the results of several experiments. In case (*a*), effectiveness will be related particularly to accuracy of representation of probabilities in the tail(s) of the distribution, but this will not be so clearly the case in (*b*) and (*c*). It is important to bear in mind the necessity for care in choosing an appropriate index for a particular application.

This article has been concerned with approximations to theoretical or empirical distribution functions. The primary purpose of such approximations is to obtain a useful representation, say $\hat{F}(x)$, of the actual cumulative distribution function $F(x)$. It is natural to base an index of accuracy on some function of the difference $\hat{F}(x) - F(x)$. Here are some examples of indexes that might be used:

$$(1) \quad \max_x |\hat{F}(x) - F(x)|$$

$$(2) \quad \max_{x_1, x_2} |\{\hat{F}(x_1) - \hat{F}(x_2)\} - \{F(x_1) - F(x_2)\}|$$

$$(3) \quad \max_x \frac{|\hat{F}(x) - F(x)|}{F(x)\{1 - F(x)\}}$$

$$(4) \quad \max_{x_1, x_2} \frac{|\{\hat{F}(x_1) - \hat{F}(x_2)\} - \{F(x_1) - F(x_2)\}|}{\{F(x_1) - F(x_2)\}[1 - \{F(x_1) - F(x_2)\}]}$$

The third and fourth of these indexes are modifications of the first and second indexes respectively. A further pair of definitions could be obtained by replacing the intervals (x_1, x_2) in (2) and (4) by sets, ω, of possible values, replacing $|\hat{F}(x_1) - \hat{F}(x_2)|$ and $|F(x_1) - F(x_2)|$ by the approximate and actual values of $Pr[X \text{ in } \omega]$, and replacing $\max_{x_1, x_2}$ by $\max_\omega$. Indexes of type (3) and (4) are based on the *proportional* error in the approximation, while indexes of type (1) and (2) are based on *absolute* error in the approximation. While the former are the more generally useful, it should be remembered that they may take infinite values. Very often, in such cases, the difficulty may be removed by choosing ω to exclude extreme values of x.

In particular instances ω may be quite severely restricted. For example, the 5% and 1% levels may be regarded as of paramount importance. In such a case, comparison of $F(x)$ and $\hat{F}(x)$ in the neighborhood of these values may be all that is needed. It has been suggested in such cases that actual values between 0.04 and 0.06, corresponding to a nominal 0.05, and between 0.007 and 0.013, corresponding to a nominal 0.01, can be regarded as satisfactory for practical purposes.

In measuring the accuracy of approximation to empirical distributions, it is quite common to calculate χ^2. This is, of course, a function of the differences $\hat{F}(x) - F(x)$. Even when circumstances are such that no probabilistic interpretation of the statistic is possible, indexes of relative accuracy of approximation have been based on the magnitude of χ^2. A similar index for measuring accuracy of approximations to theoretical distributions can be constructed. Such indexes are based on more or less elaborate forms of average (as opposed to maximum) size of error in approximation.

N. L. JOHNSON

[*See also* GOODNESS OF FIT.]

BIBLIOGRAPHY

BARTON, D. E.; and DENNIS, K. E. 1952 The Conditions Under Which Gram–Charlier and Edgeworth Curves Are Positive Definite and Unimodal. *Biometrika* 39: 425–427.

CRAMÉR, HAROLD (1945) 1951 *Mathematical Methods of Statistics.* Princeton Mathematical Series, No. 9. Princeton Univ. Press.

ELDERTON, W. PALIN (1906) 1953 *Frequency Curves and Correlation.* 4th ed. Washington: Harren.

GNEDENKO, B. V. et al. 1961 Asymptotic Expansions in Probability Theory. Volume 2, pages 153–170 in Berkeley Symposium on Mathematical Statistics and Probability, Fourth, University of California, 1960, *Proceedings.* Berkeley: Univ. of California Press.

GOODMAN, LEO A.; and KRUSKAL, WILLIAM H. 1963 Measures of Association for Cross-classifications: III. Approximate Sampling Theory. *Journal of the American Statistical Association* 58:310–364.

HERDAN, G. 1957 The Mathematical Relation Between the Number of Diseases and the Number of Patients in a Community. *Journal of the Royal Statistical Society* Series A 120:320–330.

JOHNSON, NORMAN L. 1949 Bivariate Distributions Based on Simple Translation Systems. *Biometrika* 36:297–304.

JOHNSON, NORMAN L.; NIXON, ERIC; AMOS, D. E.; and PEARSON, EGON S. 1963 Table of Percentage Points of Pearson Curves, for Given $\sqrt{\beta_1}$ and β_2, Expressed in Standard Measure. *Biometrika* 50:459–498.

KENDALL, MAURICE G.; and STUART, ALAN (1943–1946) 1958–1961 *The Advanced Theory of Statistics.* 2 vols. New ed. New York: Hafner; London: Griffin. → Volume 1: *Distribution Theory,* 1958. Volume 2: *Inference and Relationship,* 1961. Third volume in preparation.

MALLOWS, C. L. 1956 Generalizations of Tchebycheff's Inequalities. *Journal of the Royal Statistical Society* Series B 18:139–168.

MOORE, P. G. 1957 Transformations to Normality Using Fractional Powers of the Variable. *Journal of the American Statistical Association* 52:237–246.

PEARSON, EGON S. 1963 Some Problems Arising in Approximating to Probability Distributions, Using Moments. *Biometrika* 50:95–112.

PEARSON, EGON S.; and HARTLEY, H. O. (editors) (1954) 1958 *Biometrika Tables for Statisticians.* 2d ed., 2 vols. Cambridge Univ. Press.

PEARSON, KARL 1895 Contributions to the Mathematical Theory of Evolution: II. Skew Variations in Homogeneous Material. Royal Society of London, *Philosophical Transactions* Series A 186:343–414.

PEARSON, KARL 1900 On the Criterion That a Given System of Deviations From the Probable in the Case of a Correlated System of Variables Is Such That It Can Be Reasonably Supposed to Have Arisen From Random Sampling. *Philosophical Magazine* 5th Series 50:157–175.

WALLACE, DAVID L. 1959 Bounds on Normal Approximations to Student's and the Chi-square Distributions. *Annals of Mathematical Statistics* 30:1121–1130.

IV

MIXTURES OF DISTRIBUTIONS

A mixture of distributions is a weighted average of probability distributions with positive weights that sum to one. The distributions thus mixed are called the *components* of the mixture. The weights themselves comprise a probability distribution called the *mixing distribution.* Because of this property of the weights, a mixture is, in particular, again a probability distribution.

As an example, suppose that the probability distribution of heights of 30-year-old men in New York is approximately a normal distribution, while that of 30-year-old women in New York is another approximately normal distribution. Then the probability distribution of heights of 30-year-old people in New York will be, to the same degree of approximation, a mixture of the two normal distributions. The two separate normal distributions are the components, and the mixing distribution is the simple one on the dichotomy male–female, with the weights given by the relative frequencies of men and women in New York.

Probability distributions of this type arise when observed phenomena can be the consequence of two or more related, but usually unobserved, phenomena, each of which leads to a different probability distribution. Mixtures and related structures often arise in the construction of probabilistic models; for example, models for factor analysis. Mixtures also arise in a number of statistical contexts. A general problem is that of "decomposing" a mixture on the basis of a sample, that is, of estimating the parameters of the mixing distribution and those of the components.

Mixtures occur most commonly when the parameter, θ, of a family of distributions, given, say, by the density or frequency functions $f(x; \theta)$, is itself subject to chance variation. The mixing distribution, say $g(\theta)$, is then a probability distribution on the parameter of the distributions $f(x; \theta)$.

The components of a mixture may be discrete, continuous, or some of each type. Mixtures are classified, in accordance with the number of their components, as *finite*, *countable*, or *noncountably infinite*.

The generic formula for the most common form of finite mixture is

$$(1) \qquad \sum_{i=1}^{k} f(x; \theta_i) g(\theta_i);$$

the infinite analogue (in which g is a density function) is

$$(2) \qquad \int f(x; \theta) g(\theta) \, d\theta.$$

As an illustration of the above ideas, consider the following simple example. Two machines produce pennies, which are fed into a common bin. The pennies are identical except that those produced by machine 1 have probability θ_1 of showing a head when tossed, while those produced by machine 2 have probability $\theta_2 \neq \theta_1$ of showing a head. Let α be the proportion of coins produced by ma-

chine 1, and $1 - \alpha$ the proportion produced by machine 2.

A coin chosen at random from the bin is tossed n times. By the basic rules of probability theory, the probability of observing x heads is

$$
\begin{aligned}
Pr\{x \text{ heads out of } n \text{ tosses}\} & \\
= Pr\{&\text{penny from machine 1}\} Pr\{x \text{ heads} \\
&\text{given machine 1}\} \\
(3) \qquad + Pr\{&\text{penny from machine 2}\} Pr\{x \text{ heads} \\
&\text{given machine 2}\} \\
= \alpha \binom{n}{x}& \theta_1^x (1 - \theta_1)^{n-x} \\
+ (1 - \alpha)& \binom{n}{x} \theta_2^x (1 - \theta_2)^{n-x}.
\end{aligned}
$$

This is a mixture of two binomial distributions (the components) with mixing distribution $g(\theta_1) = \alpha$, $g(\theta_2) = 1 - \alpha$. [See PROBABILITY, *article on* FORMAL PROBABILITY, *for a discussion of the rules giving rise to* (3).]

By contrast, if $\theta_1 = \theta_2 = \theta$, that is to say if the two machines produce exactly identical coins, then

$$Pr\{x \text{ heads out of } n \text{ tosses}\} = \binom{n}{x} \theta^x (1 - \theta)^{n-x},$$

which is the simple binomial. Similarly if the experimenter selected a coin from a particular machine, say machine 2, rather than choosing a coin at random, the distribution of outcomes would be a binomial with parameter θ_2. A simple binomial also results if n distinct coins are chosen and each is tossed a single time. In this case, however, the binomial parameter is $\alpha\theta_1 + (1 - \alpha)\theta_2$.

A generalization of the above example is a mixture of two trinomial distributions. It is applicable to description of the sex distribution of twins (cf. Goodman & Kruskal 1959, p. 134; Strandskov & Edelen 1946). Twin pairs fall into three classes: *MM*, *MF*, and *FF*, where *M* denotes male and *F* female. This leads to the trinomial distribution. Since, in addition, twins may be dizygotic or monozygotic, a mixture of trinomials results. Because the sexes of individual dizygotic twins are independent, the corresponding trinomial has parameters p^2, $2p(1 - p)$, and $(1 - p)^2$, where p is the probability of a male. Monozygotic twins, however, are genetically identical, so that the corresponding trinomial has parameters p, 0, and q. The mixing distribution is determined by the relative frequencies of monozygotic and dizygotic twin births.

Some properties of mixtures. Mixtures are themselves probability distributions, and hence their density or frequency functions are nonnegative and sum or integrate to unity.

While the definitions (1) and (2) are given in

terms of the density or frequency functions, precisely the same relationships hold with regard to the corresponding cumulative distribution functions. Similarly, the moments (about zero) of a mixture are weighted averages (that is, mixtures) of the moments of the component distributions. Thus, for a finite mixture, if $\mu'_r(\theta_i)$ is the rth moment about zero of the ith component, then the rth moment about zero of the mixture is

$$\sum_{i=1}^{k} g(\theta_i)\mu'_r(\theta_i).$$

The same is true of the factorial moments. A similar, although slightly more complicated, relationship holds for moments about the mean.

An important property of many common mixtures of discrete distributions is the relationship imposed upon the generating functions: if $\phi_1(s)$ and $\phi_2(s)$ are the generating functions of the mixing distribution and the component distributions, respectively, then $\phi_1(\phi_2(s))$ is the generating function of the mixture. This greatly simplifies certain calculations. [See DISTRIBUTIONS, STATISTICAL, *article on* SPECIAL DISCRETE DISTRIBUTIONS, *for a discussion of generating functions.*]

Mixtures of standard distributions may possess interesting geometric properties. They may be bimodal or multimodal and are ordinarily more dispersed than are the components. Properties such as these account, at least in part, for the fact that mixtures frequently fit data more satisfactorily than do standard distributions.

Conditionality. The concept of conditionality underlies the definitions (1) and (2), for the function $f(x; \theta)$ is the conditional probability distribution given the value of θ, while the product of $f(x; \theta)$ and $g(\theta)$ is the joint probability distribution of x and θ, and the sum (or integral) is the unconditional distribution of x.

The importance of conditionality in applications can be seen in the coin example: the machine on which the randomly chosen coin was produced may be thought of as an auxiliary chance variable (taking on the values 1 and 2 with respective probabilities α and $1 - \alpha$); conditional on the value of the auxiliary chance variable, the distribution of heads is a simple binomial.

The auxiliary chance variable is usually unobservable and hence cannot play a direct role in data analysis. The merit of introducing the auxiliary chance variable in this context is, therefore, *not* that it results in simpler data analyses but that it yields a proper understanding of the *underlying mathematical structure* and simplifies the *derivation of the probability distribution.*

This situation is typical; the conditional distribution of the chance variable under investigation, given the value of a related unobservable chance variable, is either known exactly or is of a relatively simple form. Because of the inability to observe the related chance variable, however, the unconditional distribution is a mixture and is usually much more complex.

Some applications. Because of the immense complexity of living organisms, variables that the investigator can neither control nor observe frequently arise in investigations of natural phenomena. Some examples are attitude, emotional stability, skills, genotype, resistance to disease, etc. Since mixtures of distributions result when such variables are related to the variable under investigation, mixtures have many applications in the social and biological sciences.

Mixtures have played an important role in the construction of so-called contagious distributions. These distributions are deduced from models in which the occurrence of an event has the effect of changing the probability of additional such occurrences. An early example of a contagious distribution was given by Greenwood and Yule (1920) in an analysis of accident data. Greenwood and Yule derived the classical negative binomial distribution as a mixture of distributions. Other contagious distributions that are mixtures are given by Neyman (1939, the Neyman types A, B, and C) and Gurland (1958).

Mixtures of distributions also arise in dealing with unusual observations or outliers. One approach to the problem of outliers is predicated upon writing the underlying probability distribution as a mixture of distributions (see Dixon 1953). [*For further discussion, see* STATISTICAL ANALYSIS, SPECIAL PROBLEMS OF, *article on* OUTLIERS.]

Mixtures of distributions also arise in the Bayesian approach to statistical analysis. *Bayes' Procedures* are constructed under the assumption that the parameters of the underlying probability distribution are themselves chance variables. In this context, the mixing distribution is called the a priori distribution [*see* BAYESIAN INFERENCE].

The following are a few additional applications of mixtures:

(1) Life testing of equipment subject to sudden and delayed failures (Kao 1959).

(2) Acceptance testing, when the proportion of defectives varies from batch to batch (Vagholkar 1959).

(3) Latent stucture analysis based on mixtures of multivariate distributions with independence be-

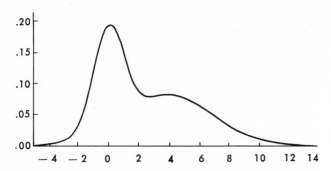

Figure 1 — A mixture of two normal distributions with $\mu_1 = 0$, $\mu_2 = 4$, $\sigma_1^2 = 1$, $\sigma_2^2 = 9$, and $\alpha_1 = 0.4$, showing f(x) on the vertical axis corresponding to x on the horizontal axis

tween the variates within each component (Lazarsfeld 1950; Green 1952). Factor analysis also comes under this general description. [See FACTOR ANALYSIS; LATENT STRUCTURE.]

(4) Construction of a learning model as a weighted average of two simpler such models (Sternberg 1959).

(5) A model for spatial configurations in map analysis (Dacey 1964).

Special mixed distributions. Using the definitions (1) and (2), it is easy to generate large numbers of probability distributions. Furthermore, the process of mixing of distributions may be repeated; that is, new mixtures, in which the components are themselves mixtures of distributions, may be formed by repeated application of (1) and (2). Thus, it is possible to form an unlimited number of probability distributions by this relatively simple process. In addition, many classical probability distributions can be represented nontrivially as mixtures. Teicher (1960) gives two representations of the normal distribution as a mixture of distributions. [See DISTRIBUTIONS, STATISTICAL, *article on* SPECIAL DISCRETE DISTRIBUTIONS, *for both classical and mixture representations of the negative binomial distribution.*]

It is customary, when both component and mixing distribution are well known, to call the mixture by the names of the distributions involved.

The following are a few specific examples of mixtures:

Mixture of two normal distributions. The density function of a mixture of two normal distributions is

$$f(x) = \frac{1}{\sqrt{2\pi}}\left[\frac{\alpha_1}{\sigma_1}\exp\left\{-\frac{(x-\mu_1)^2}{2\sigma_1^2}\right\}\right.$$
$$\left. + \frac{\alpha_2}{\sigma_2}\exp\left\{-\frac{(x-\mu_2)^2}{2\sigma_2^2}\right\}\right],$$

where $-\infty < x < \infty$, $0 < \alpha_1 < 1$, $0 < \alpha_2 < 1$, $\alpha_1 + \alpha_2 = 1$, and μ_1, μ_2 and σ_1^2, σ_2^2 are the respective means and variances of the component normal distributions. This example is due to Pearson (1894). The distribution has mean $\alpha_1\mu_1 + \alpha_2\mu_2$ and variance $\alpha_1\sigma_1^2 + \alpha_2\sigma_2^2 + \alpha_1\alpha_2(\mu_1 - \mu_2)^2$. An example of this mixture with $\mu_1 = 0$, $\mu_2 = 4$, $\sigma_1^2 = 1$, $\sigma_2^2 = 9$, and $\alpha_1 = 0.4$ is given in Figure 1.

Mixture of two Poisson distributions. The frequency function of a mixture of two Poisson distributions is

$$p(x) = \frac{1}{x!}\left[\alpha_1\lambda_1^x e^{-\lambda_1} + \alpha_2\lambda_2^x e^{-\lambda_2}\right], \quad x = 0, 1, 2, \cdots,$$

where α_1 and α_2 are as before and $\lambda_1 \neq \lambda_2$ are the parameters of the components. This distribution has mean $\alpha_1\lambda_1 + \alpha_2\lambda_2$ and variance $\alpha_1\lambda_1 + \alpha_2\lambda_2 + \alpha_1\alpha_2(\lambda_1 - \lambda_2)^2$. An example of this discrete mixed distribution with $\lambda_1 = 1$, $\lambda_2 = 8$, and $\alpha_1 = 0.5$ is given in Figure 2.

Poisson–binomial distribution. The frequency function of the Poisson–binomial distribution is

$$p(x) = e^{-\lambda}\sum_{i=0}^{\infty}\frac{\lambda^i}{i!}\binom{ni}{x}\theta^x(1-\theta)^{ni-x},$$
$$x = 0, 1, 2, \cdots,$$

where $0 < \theta < 1$, $0 < \lambda < \infty$, and n is an integer. The components are binomial distributions; the mixing distribution is Poisson. The probabilities can also be obtained by successive differentiation of the generating function

$$\phi(s) = \exp\{\lambda[(1 - \theta + \theta s)^n - 1]\},$$

or from the recursion formulas

$$p(0) = \exp\{\lambda[(1 - \theta)^n - 1]\},$$
$$p(x + 1) = \frac{\lambda n(1-\theta)^n}{x+1}\sum_{i=0}^{x}\binom{n-1}{x-i}\left(\frac{\theta}{1-\theta}\right)^{x+1-i}p(i).$$

The mean is $n\theta\lambda$; the variance is $n\theta\lambda[1 + (n-1)\theta]$.

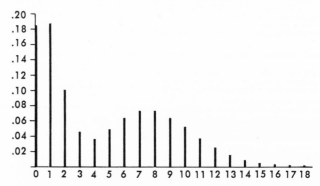

Figure 2 — A mixture of two Poisson distributions with $\lambda_1 = 1$, $\lambda_2 = 8$, and $\alpha_1 = 0.5$, showing p(x) on the vertical axis corresponding to x on the horizontal axis

Poisson–negative binomial distribution. The frequency function of the Poisson–negative binomial distribution is

$$p(x) = e^{-\lambda} \sum_{i=0}^{\infty} \frac{\lambda^i}{i!} \binom{ni+x-1}{x-1} \theta^{ni}(1-\theta)^x,$$
$$x = 0, 1, 2, \cdots,$$

where $0 < \theta < 1$, $0 < \lambda < \infty$, and $0 < n < \infty$. This is a Poisson mixture of negative binomial distributions. Here

$$\phi(s) = \exp\{\lambda[\theta^n(1 - s + s\theta)^{-n} - 1]\};$$

the recursion formulas are

$$p(0) = \exp[-\lambda(1 - \theta^n)],$$

$$p(x+1) = \frac{\lambda}{x+1} \sum_{i=0}^{x} \left[\binom{n+x-1}{x}\right.$$
$$\left. (x+1-i)\theta^n(1-\theta)^x - ip(i)\right].$$

The mean and variance are $n\lambda(1-\theta)/\theta$ and $n\lambda(1-\theta)(n-n\theta+1)/\theta^2$, respectively.

Neyman Type A contagious distribution. The frequency function of the Neyman Type A distribution is

$$p(x) = e^{-\lambda_1} \frac{\lambda_2^x}{x!} \sum_{i=0}^{\infty} \frac{i^x}{i!} e^{-i\lambda_2}\lambda_1^i,$$

where $0 < \lambda_1 < \infty$ and $0 < \lambda_2 < \infty$. The Neyman Type A is a Poisson–Poisson. The generating function is

$$\phi(s) = \exp\{\lambda_1[e^{\lambda_2(s-1)} - 1]\};$$

the recursion formulas are

$$p(0) = \exp[\lambda_1(e^{-\lambda_2} - 1)],$$

$$p(x+1) = \frac{\lambda_1\lambda_2}{x+1} e^{-\lambda_2} \sum_{i=0}^{x} \frac{\lambda_2^i}{i!} p(x-i).$$

The mean is $\lambda_1\lambda_2$, and $\lambda_1\lambda_2(1-\lambda_2)$ is the variance.

Point probability–negative exponential. An example of a mixture of a discrete and a continuous distribution is written in terms of its cumulative distribution function,

$$\begin{aligned} F(x) &= 0 && \text{if } x < 0 \\ &= \alpha_1 && \text{if } x = 0 \\ &= \alpha_1 + \alpha_2(1 - e^{-x/\theta}) && \text{if } x > 0, \end{aligned}$$

where $\theta > 0$ and α_1 and α_2 are as in previous examples. An application in economics is given by Aitchison (1955). The distribution has mean $\alpha_2\theta$ and variance $\alpha_1(1 + \alpha_2)\theta^2$.

Identifiability. The subject of identifiability, that is, of unique characterization, is of concern on two levels. On both levels, identifiability, or lack thereof, has very important practical implications.

The first level is in model construction. Here the question revolves around the existence of a one-to-one correspondence between phenomena observed in nature and their corresponding mathematical models. That such one-to-one correspondences need not exist is apparent in the application of contagious distributions to accident data. Greenwood and Yule (1920) devised two models, *proneness* and *apparent proneness*, for accidents. Both lead to the negative binomial distribution. As noted by Feller (1943), even complete knowledge of the underlying negative binomial distribution therefore would not enable the experimenter to distinguish between proneness and apparent proneness as the cause of accidents.

The question of identifiability is an important consideration in mathematical modeling generally. It is particularly crucial in attempting to distinguish between competing theories. Such distinctions *can* be made through properly designed experiments. For example, proneness and apparent proneness can be distinguished in follow-up studies or by sampling in several time periods.

The question of identifiability also arises in a purely mathematical context. A mixture is called identifiable if there exists a one-to-one correspondence between the mixing distribution and the resulting mixture. Mixtures that are not identifiable cannot be expressed uniquely as functions of component and mixing distributions. This is true, for example, of a mixture of two binomials when $n = 2$. For example, both $\alpha_1 = .4$, $p_1 = .3$, $p_2 = .6$ and $\alpha_1 = .6$, $p_1 = .36$, $p_2 = .66$ result in identical mixed distributions.

The derivation of conditions under which mixtures are identifiable in this sense is difficult. Teicher (1963) derives some such conditions and discusses identifiability for many common mixtures. Identifiability in this sense has important statistical implications in that it is not possible to estimate or test hypotheses about the parameters of unidentifiable mixtures. [*For further discussion, see* STATISTICAL IDENTIFIABILITY.]

All of the mixtures listed in the section on "Special mixed distributions" are identifiable. The mixture of two binomial distributions given in equation (3) is identifiable if, and only if, $n \geq 3$.

Estimation. The construction of estimates for the parameters of mixtures of distributions is difficult. Procedures such as maximum likelihood and minimum χ^2, which are known to be optimal, at least for large sample sizes, require the solution of systems of equations that are typically intractable for mixtures. The problem has been somewhat alleviated with the advent of high-speed electronic computers, but it is by no means resolved. In any case the distributions of the estimators are likely to be difficult to work with. [*For further discussion, see* ESTIMATION.]

Because of this complexity, it is not uncommon to choose estimation procedures almost solely on the basis of computational simplicity. Moment estimators are often used even though they may be inefficient in that they require larger sample sizes to attain a given degree of accuracy than do maximum likelihood estimators. Moment estimators are constructed by equating sample moments to population moments, the latter being written in terms of the parameters of the underlying distribution, then solving the resulting system of equations for the parameters. For example, for the Poisson–binomial distribution the moment estimators based on the sample mean, $\bar{x}$, and variance, s^2, are

$$\hat{\lambda} = \frac{(n-1)\bar{x}^2}{n(s^2 - \bar{x})}, \qquad \hat{\theta} = \frac{s^2 - \bar{x}}{(n-1)\bar{x}}.$$

Even moment estimators can become quite complex. Moment estimates for mixtures of binomial distributions can require formidable calculations (see Blischke 1964). Pearson's (1894) solution for a mixture of two normal distributions requires extraction of the roots of a ninth-degree equation. In the normal case, the problem is greatly simplified if the two normal components are assumed to have the same variance (see Rao 1952, section 8*b*.6).

Moment estimators and/or maximum likelihood estimators for the distributions mentioned above are given in the references. For a summarization of these results and some additional comments on the estimation problem, see Blischke (1963).

Another aspect of the estimation problem that can be troublesome in practice occurs if two components of a finite mixture are nearly identical. If this is the case, extremely large sample sizes are required to estimate the parameters of the mixture with any degree of accuracy. Such mixtures are, for all practical purposes, unidentifiable (cf. Chiang 1951).

Nomenclature. It is important to distinguish between the concepts of mixing of distributions and the distribution of a sum of random variables. The latter distribution is called a *convolution* and, except for special cases or particular notational conventions, is not a mixture of distributions.

There are, however, several additional terms sometimes used as synonyms for "mixture of distributions." These include "compound distribution," "mixed distribution," "probability mixture," "superposition," "composite distribution," and "sum of distributions." The most common terms are "mixture," "mixed distribution," and "compound distribution." In addition, certain "generalized distributions" are mixtures of some specific structure (cf. Feller 1943).

The terms "dissection" and "decomposition" are sometimes used in connection with estimation for finite mixtures. These terms are descriptive since the estimates give information about the components from observations on the composite.

WALLACE R. BLISCHKE

BIBLIOGRAPHY

AITCHISON, JOHN 1955 On the Distribution of a Positive Random Variable Having a Discrete Probability Mass at the Origin. *Journal of the American Statistical Association* 50:901–908.

BLISCHKE, WALLACE R. (1963) 1965 Mixtures of Discrete Distributions. Pages 351–372 in Ganapati P. Patil (editor), *Classical and Contagious Discrete Distributions.* Proceedings of the International Symposium held at McGill University, Montreal, Canada, August 15–20, 1963. Calcutta: Statistical Publishing Society; Distributed by Pergamon Press.

BLISCHKE, WALLACE R. 1964 Estimating the Parameters of Mixtures of Binomial Distributions. *Journal of the American Statistical Association* 59:510–528.

CHIANG, CHIN LONG 1951 On the Design of Mass Medical Surveys. *Human Biology* 23:242–271.

DACEY, MICHAEL F. 1964 Modified Poisson Probability Law for a Point Pattern More Regular Than Random. Association of American Geographers, *Annals* 54:559–565.

DIXON, W. J. 1953 Processing Data for Outliers. *Biometrics* 9:74–89.

FELLER, W. 1943 On a General Class of "Contagious" Distributions. *Annals of Mathematical Statistics* 14:389–400.

GOODMAN, LEO A.; and KRUSKAL, WILLIAM H. 1959 Measures of Association for Cross Classifications: II. Further Discussion and References. *Journal of the American Statistical Association* 54:123–163.

GREEN, BERT F. JR. 1952 Latent Structure Analysis and Its Relation to Factor Analysis. *Journal of the American Statistical Association* 47:71–76.

GREENWOOD, MAJOR; and YULE, G. UDNY 1920 An Inquiry Into the Nature of Frequency Distributions Representative of Multiple Happenings With Particular Reference to the Occurrence of Multiple Attacks of Disease or of Repeated Accidents. *Journal of the Royal Statistical Society* 83:255–279.

GURLAND, JOHN 1958 A Generalized Class of Contagious Distributions. *Biometrics* 14:229–249.

KAO, JOHN H. K. 1959 A Graphical Estimation of Mixed Weibull Parameters in Life-testing of Electron Tubes. *Technometrics* 1:389–407.

LAZARSFELD, PAUL F. 1950 The Logical and Mathematical Foundation of Latent Structure Analysis. Pages 362–412 in Samuel A. Stouffer et al., *Measurement and Prediction.* Studies in Social Psychology in World War II, Vol. 4. Princeton Univ. Press.

NEYMAN, J.   1939   On a New Class of "Contagious" Distributions, Applicable in Entomology and Bacteriology. *Annals of Mathematical Statistics* 10:35–57.

PEARSON, KARL   1894   Contributions to the Mathematical Theory of Evolution. Royal Society of London, *Philosophical Transactions* Series A 185:71–110.

RAO, C. RADHAKRISHNA   1952   *Advanced Statistical Methods in Biometric Research.* New York: Wiley.

STERNBERG, SAUL H.   1959   A Path-dependent Linear Model. Pages 308–339 in Robert R. Bush and William K. Estes (editors), *Studies in Mathematical Learning Theory.* Stanford Univ. Press.

STRANDSKOV, HERLUF H.; and EDELEN, EARL W.   1946   Monozygotic and Dizygotic Twin Birth Frequencies in the Total, the "White" and the "Colored" U.S. Populations. *Genetics* 31:438–446.

TEICHER, HENRY   1960   On the Mixture of Distributions. *Annals of Mathematical Statistics* 31:55–73.

TEICHER, HENRY   1963   Identifiability of Finite Mixtures. *Annals of Mathematical Statistics* 34:1265–1269.

VAGHOLKAR, M. K.   1959   The Process Curve and the Equivalent Mixed Binomial With Two Components. *Journal of the Royal Statistical Society* Series B 21:63–66.

DISTRICTING

See APPORTIONMENT.

DIVINATION

See MAGIC.

DIVISIA, FRANÇOIS

François Divisia (1889–1964), was born at Tizi-Ouzou, the principal town in the Great Kabylia region of northern Algeria. His family had been established for three generations on both the French and Algerian shores of the Mediterranean. He was awarded baccalaureates in mathematics and philosophy at the Algiers *lycée*. In 1910 he won admission to both the École Normale Supérieure and the École Polytechnique and chose to attend the latter. After two years at the École Polytechnique, he entered the government department of civil engineering (Ponts et Chaussées). In 1913 he became a graduate student at the École Nationale des Ponts et Chaussées, and at the outbreak of World War I he was mobilized as a lieutenant in the engineering corps. Promoted to the rank of captain in 1916 and wounded in 1917, he was commended in dispatches and named chevalier of the Légion d'Honneur. Having completed his engineering studies in 1919, he pursued his career as a government engineer for about ten years and was then transferred to the Ministry of National Education to devote himself entirely to research and teaching in economics, a subject that had previously absorbed his spare time. It was the influence of Clément Colson that was decisive in turning Divisia toward economics; eventually he was to succeed Colson as professor of applied economics and finance at the École Nationale des Ponts et Chaussées. (This was in 1932, after he had also taught for brief periods at the École Libre des Sciences Politiques, the Conservatoire National des Arts et Métiers, and the École Polytechnique.)

Divisia was to remain strongly influenced by the training, both practical and scientific, that he had received as an engineer. It played an important role in his contributions to mathematical economics, where statistical data are constantly used, and it led him quite naturally to take an active part first in the creation and then in the development of econometrics. A founding member and vice-president of the Société d'Économétrie in 1931, he was elected president of the society in 1935. In the meantime he was also elected to the Institut International de Statistique in 1933, and he became president of the Société de Statistique de Paris in 1939.

At the outbreak of World War II, he was asked to administer the seaports for the Ministry of Public Works. There he was one of the first to appreciate the problem of determining optimum transportation routes. Confronted by the mathematical difficulties that this problem involved, he called upon the mathematician Maurice Fréchet. Fréchet turned the problem over to two of his students, one of whom, Nachman Aronszajn, submitted a solution, published only much later. In this way, Divisia contributed to the genesis of linear programming, which was soon to be one of the most productive branches of operations research [*see* OPERATIONS RESEARCH; PROGRAMMING]. In his work *Technique et statistique* (1941), he was also one of the first, perhaps the very first, in France to envisage and advocate the application of statistics to technical problems.

Divisia resumed his many teaching activities during the occupation and in the years following France's liberation. He participated in an increasing number of scientific organizations, particularly on an international level. In 1951 he became a foreign member of the Accademia Nazionale dei Lincei. In 1950 he resigned from his professorship at the École Nationale des Ponts et Chaussées and was then able to give more of his time to work in the laboratories he had set up at the Conservatoire National des Arts et Métiers in 1943 and at the École Polytechnique in 1950. The laboratory at the latter institution concentrated its research on the relationships between the French economy and national defense; that at the Conservatoire focused on the collection and interpretation of statistics relevant to the state of the economy: rates of return, price indexes, and characteristics of industrial, commercial, and banking activity, as they are related to international commerce. Divisia valued this kind of research very highly and devoted considerable time to it.

Major contributions. The earliest of Divisia's important contributions to economics is contained in his book *L'indice monétaire et la théorie de la monnaie* (1926). The monetary index, commonly known as the "Divisia index," is related to a general equation of exchange, known mainly through the work of Irving Fisher but independently developed by Divisia [see MONEY, *article on* QUANTITY THEORY]. Using this equation, Divisia, by differentiation, distinguished two indexes whose product is always proportional to the total payments, expressed in money, of the period to which the equation applies. These two indexes are a monetary or price index, expressing the general level of prices for the totality of monetary transactions, and an index of exchange activity (a quantity index), measuring the volume of transactions for the period involved.

The first of these is a weighted price index, with weights that vary from period to period, each period being treated as sufficiently short for the weights to be regarded as constant within the period. Price level comparisons between periods further separated in time are effected by the chain index method, which in contrast to a fixed-base method compounds the price index changes of successive (intermediate) periods, each with its own set of weights. Consequently, it is not possible to compare the price levels of nonadjacent time periods that link together the extremities of the chain of prices. The Divisia monetary index therefore involves more information about prices and quantities than do fixed-base indexes.

Divisia's *Économique rationnelle* (1928*a*) is without doubt his masterpiece: witness its favorable reception by mathematical economists as well as by economists of the traditional school. Essentially devoted to the classical interrelationships, it is a didactic account, both synthetic and concise, and its conclusions are drawn from concrete and objective observations. The work also advances an original view of the role of money in the theory of value and of economic equilibrium. Divisia's reputation in the scientific world was enlarged by this book; in France the work was awarded prizes by the Académie des Sciences and by the Académie des Sciences Morales et Politiques.

The questions that Divisia raised in his *L'épargne et la richesse collective* (1928*b*) in many instances anticipated aggregative problem areas that have since become very important in the writings of economists.

Since Divisia addressed himself in his teaching to practitioners in business and in industry and to students of engineering with a scientific background, he was able, while at the École Nationale des Ponts et Chaussées, to maintain close contact with the problems faced by nonacademic economists, especially problems related to technological change. In his courses he discussed, with great care and originality, problems concerning money, credit, the establishment and management of public works, and the operation of transportation facilities.

Divisia's last important work, *Traitement économétrique de la monnaie, l'intérêt, l'emploi* (1962), is a kind of summing up of his opinions on some of the most important problems in economics. It is necessary to remember that Divisia was moved to write it primarily because of his dissatisfaction with the lack of precision in Keynes's general theory. To highlight Keynes's deficiencies, Divisia used mathematics for logical sequence and statistics for handling evidence.

Reacting against Keynes's methods and faithful, instead, to classical traditions, Divisia stressed the danger of macroeconomic studies. He based his own model on the analysis of individual behavior, i.e., on microeconomics. In his opinion this is the only approach that offers sufficient reliability for the analysis of the permanent motives in decision.

The most original characteristic of his model is its distinction between three kinds of flow: (*a*) the technical flow of the circulation of goods, meaning physical units; (*b*) the monetary flow, expressed in nominal value and fed by payments correlative to the transactions involving the goods of the technical flow; and (*c*) the flow of credits and claims arising from these transactions and expressed in monetary terms. These three circuits do not overlap. They are interrelated, however, in that claims originating on the technical level are established on the contractual level and are liquidated by the circulation of money.

This analysis of economic behavior is highly aggregative, since it introduces only four types of economic agents: the household, the business enterprise, the state, and the bank. Even with this limitation, the model generates a great many equations dealing with the categories that are usually considered in presentations of this kind.

Divisia then attempted to discover the "degree of freedom" possessed by the economy, given a system of relationships that contains seven mathematical unknowns. He subtracted what are now called "policy variables," that is, the behavioral data reflecting the policies of the economic agents. (After extensive research he had decided that there are five such variables, corresponding to policies with respect to the floating of shares, loans, self-financing, production, and the issuing of currency.) The number of unknowns is thus reduced to two, and these must be identified with the rates of flow in the technical and monetary circuits, i.e., the total flow of goods and the total flow of money —in other words, the real and nominal manifestations of national income. In terms of equations, the two unknowns are the flow of the labor force employed and the general price level governed by the monetary unit chosen.

This leads to conclusions sharply opposed to the theories of Keynes. Here is how Divisia put it: "Full employment is possible provided that we accept the real wages that follow from it; or, if real wages are fixed, in any way, at a higher level, the necessary outcome is a certain amount of unemployment" (1962, p. 179). The model on which Divisia essentially based his critique of Keynes is a revised version of Walras' concept of equilibrium. To be sure, it differs considerably from the latter, for it is in no way static or timeless; it can be applied to a trend and also to cyclical fluctuations. It is well suited to economic calculations because of its high degree of aggregation.

Divisia therefore confidently expressed his judgment of Keynesian theories: ". . . both the concept of a general, long-term equilibrium that establishes endemic underemployment without any reaction from the economic agents, and a theory of interest rates that is based solely on a preference for liquidity and excludes the productivity of capital, seem indefensible" (1962, p. 195). At best, he felt Keynes's propositions may be used to explain relative changes over short periods of time. Construed in this way, they do not even differ fundamentally from other explanations of the particular relationships that constitute the framework of the general equilibrium. A necessary further step is to account for all the factors involved and for their various interrelationships.

RENÉ ROY

[For the historical context of Divisia's work, see the biography of KEYNES, JOHN MAYNARD. For discussion of the subsequent development of Divisia's ideas, see ECONOMETRIC MODELS, AGGREGATE; ECONOMIC EQUILIBRIUM; INDEX NUMBERS; PROGRAMMING.]

WORKS BY DIVISIA

1926   L'indice monétaire et la théorie de la monnaie. Paris: Sirey.
1928a   Économique rationnelle. Paris: Doin.
(1928b) 1931   L'épargne et la richesse collective. Paris: Sirey.
(1941) 1943   Technique et statistique. Privately published. → First published in the Annales des ponts et chaussées.
1950   Aspects de la technique des sondages statistiques dans le domaine social. International Statistical Institute, Bulletin 32, no. 2:240–244.
1951–1965   Exposés d'économique. 3 vols. Paris: Dunod. → Volume 1. Introduction générale: L'apport des ingénieurs français aux sciences économiques. Volume 2: Assise pour les études et techniques monétaires. Volume 3: Assise pour les études et techniques monétaires d'économique.
1954   Sur un avantage de la statistique graphique. International Statistical Institute, Bulletin 34, no. 2:268–273.
1954–1957   DIVISIA, FRANÇOIS; DUPIN, JEAN; and ROY, RENÉ À la recherche du franc perdu. 3 vols. Paris: Société d'Édition de Revues et de Publications.
1957   Corrélation ou régression? Un exemple instructif de statistique inductive: La hausse des prix 1913–1953 en France. International Statistical Institute, Bulletin 35, no. 4:231–239. → Contains a summary in English.
1962   Traitement économétrique de la monnaie, l'intérêt, l'emploi. Paris: Dunod.

DIVISION OF LABOR

For the origins of the concept of division of labor, see the biographies of PLATO *and* ARISTOTLE; *for the development of the modern tradition of thought into which the concept enters, see the biographies of* BÜCHER; DURKHEIM; MARX; SMITH, ADAM; WEBER, MAX. *The economic concept is discussed in* SPECIALIZATION AND EXCHANGE. *Some sociological aspects of the division of labor are discussed in* ECONOMY AND SOCIETY; MEDICAL PERSONNEL; OCCUPATIONS AND CAREERS; PROFESSIONS. *For anthropological thought, see* SOCIAL STRUCTURE, *article on* THE HISTORY OF THE CONCEPT. *Material on the effects of technological change on the division of labor will be found in* AGRICULTURE, *article on* SOCIAL ORGANIZATION; AUTOMATION; MODERNIZATION; TECHNOLOGY.

DIVISION OF POWERS

See CONSTITUTIONAL LAW, *article on* DISTRIBUTION OF POWERS; DELEGATION OF POWERS; FEDERALISM.

DIVORCE

See FAMILY, *article on* DISORGANIZATION AND DISSOLUTION.

DIXON, ROLAND B.

Roland Burrage Dixon was born in Worcester, Massachusetts, in 1875 and died at his bachelor home in Harvard, Massachusetts, in 1934. He was appointed assistant in anthropology in the Peabody Museum at Harvard upon his graduation from that institution in 1897, thereupon beginning a career of anthropological teaching and research at his alma mater that continued until his death. While a graduate student there he engaged in archeological field work in Ohio and later, as a member of the Jesup North Pacific Expedition of the American Museum of Natural History, in ethnological field work among the Indians of British Columbia. In 1899 he spent the first of six field seasons among the California Indians. The following year, upon completion of his thesis dealing with the language of the Maidu Indians, he was awarded the PH.D. degree. Thus, Dixon became one of the first Americans to receive a doctor's degree in the emerging discipline of anthropology. Interestingly enough, Harvard's other doctorate in anthropology in 1900 went to John R. Swanton, a man whose anthropological orientation was very similar to Dixon's. Following a year spent in research and travel in Germany, Siberia, and Mongolia, Dixon returned to Harvard in 1901 as an instructor in anthropology. He advanced through the various academic grades to full professor and was for a long period chairman of the division of anthropology. His Harvard service was briefly interrupted during World War I, when he did special work in Washington, D.C.; he was sent to Paris with the American Commission to Negotiate the Peace.

Dixon brought to anthropology a marked natural-history orientation. He enjoyed outdoor life, and his early interest in geography was deepened by intensive reading combined with travel and research in New Zealand, Australia, Tasmania, the Himalayas, Burma, Malaysia, Indonesia, China, Japan, and Central America. No student ever took a course with Dixon without becoming aware of the interrelationship between culture and the natural environment. This geographic interest was combined with a historical approach. Dixon was well-read in French, Italian, German, and Russian and in the Scandinavian languages. The range and depth of his anthropological knowledge were reflected in his writings and his classroom lectures.

Dixon was a generalist at a time when such virtuosity was still possible in anthropology. Following his brief introduction to mound archeology, he concentrated for some years on California ethnology, and his many publications on this culture area cover the fields of descriptive ethnography, folklore, and linguistics. Although he was not a trained linguist, his work on California languages provided the guidelines for future work in this field.

Some of his California publications were done jointly with Alfred L. Kroeber. The linking of the names of these two men is appropriate, since they not only were contemporaries (Kroeber received his PH.D. from Columbia in 1901), but both also did extensive ethnographic work in California and took a basically historical approach to anthropology. Dixon lacked Kroeber's philosophical overview and theoretical interests, but the two were similar in the range and depth of their scholarship. They held each other in mutual esteem, and Kroeber's obituary of Dixon is unusually perceptive (Tozzer & Kroeber 1936).

After completing his California work, Dixon turned from ethnography to a wide range of other problems. In connection with the thirteenth census of the United States he compiled the most complete and accurate enumeration of the Indian population by stocks and tribes, and after tabulating the sterility and fecundity of pure Indian marriages in comparison with mixed marriages, he concluded that the latter produced both more and healthier offspring (U.S. Bureau of the Census 1915). Some years later he published his most ambitious work, *The Racial History of Man* (1923). Utilizing three basic indices, Dixon analyzed all the anthropometric data then available and classified men into racial types. Although this methodology was criticized by physical anthropologists, the book did demonstrate the morphological diversity of many populations, particularly the American Indians and Polynesians. In *The Building of Cultures* (1928) Dixon attempted to deal with theory and with cultural dynamics. The real contribution of the book, however, lay in its meticulous discussion of the diffusion process.

In the final analysis, Dixon was not so much a theoretician as a culture historian who combined vigorous scholarship with geographic understanding. His study of the early migrations of the New England Indians (1914), for instance, illustrates his interest in movements of peoples, reinforced by an understanding of ecological factors and a mastery of ethnohistorical sources—all features that came increasingly to characterize his later writings. Insofar as it was possible for one man to do so, Dixon mastered the ethnography of the world, particularly in the field of material culture. He was less interested in details of social organization.

During most of his years at Harvard, Dixon served as librarian of the Peabody Museum. He brought to this task the same bibliographic expertise that characterized his scholarship, with the result that the library catalogue eventually became an index of all anthropological literature, listed not only by author but also by geographical area and by topic. This great research tool, invaluable to generations of Harvard graduate students, has since been updated and made available to institutions all over the world (1963).

Dixon's greatest contribution to American anthropology may well have been the building up of an outstanding program at Harvard—broad in scope and designed for both the undergraduate and the graduate student. Dixon's work at Harvard is in some ways comparable to that of Boas at Columbia and Kroeber at California, the three institutions that trained the bulk of American anthropologists during the first third of the twentieth century. Dixon founded no "school" and left no disciples; but his students gained from him a tremendous body of carefully organized ethnographic information and a training in rigorous scholarship. Many of these students in turn became professional anthropologists, including such early Viking Medalists as A. V. Kidder, J. O. Brew, Hallam Movius, Ralph Linton, I. H. H. Roberts, Carleton Coon, W. W. Howells, and S. K. Lothrop, together with many other eminent teachers and researchers active in anthropology throughout the world.

ROBERT A. McKENNAN

[For the historical context of Dixon's work, see the biography of KROEBER. For discussion of the subsequent development of his ideas, see RACE and the biography of KIDDER.]

WORKS BY DIXON

(1900) 1911   Maidu: An Illustrative Sketch. Part 1, pages 679–734 in Franz Boas (editor), *Handbook of American Indian Languages.* U.S. Bureau of American Ethnology, Bulletin No. 40. Washington: Government Printing Office.

1914   The Early Migrations of the Indians of New England and the Maritime Provinces. American Antiquarian Society, *Proceedings* New Series 24:65–76.

1916   *Oceanic* [*Mythology*]. Boston: Marshall Jones. → Volume 9 of *Mythology of All Races.*

1923   *The Racial History of Man.* New York: Scribner.

1928   *The Building of Cultures.* New York: Scribner.

SUPPLEMENTARY BIBLIOGRAPHY

HARVARD UNIVERSITY, PEABODY MUSEUM OF ARCHAEOLOGY AND ETHNOLOGY, LIBRARY   1963   *Catalogue.* 53 vols. Boston: Hall. → Part 1: *Authors.* Part 2: *Subjects.*

TOZZER, ALFRED M.; and KROEBER, ALFRED L.   1936   Roland Burrage Dixon. *American Anthropologist* New Series 38:291–300. → Contains a comprehensive bibliography of Dixon's writings.

U.S. BUREAU OF THE CENSUS   1915   *Indian Population in the United States and Alaska: 1910.* Washington: Government Printing Office. → Prepared under the supervision of William C. Hunt, Roland B. Dixon, and F. A. McKenzie.

DOMESTICATION

I.   THE FOOD-PRODUCING
     REVOLUTION   *Robert J. Braidwood*
II. ANIMAL DOMESTICATION   *Robert H. Dyson, Jr.*

I

THE FOOD-PRODUCING REVOLUTION

The domestication of plants and animals marked the beginnings of effective food production by man, a stage in human sociocultural development that has frequently been called the Neolithic.

Usages of the word "Neolithic."   There have been a number of confusing usages of the word "Neolithic" (a term this author does *not* normally employ in his own writing), and it is clear that the confusion is not yet resolved.

Earliest usages.   Neolithic has prehistoric archeological connotations: the word is a Neo-Grecism for "New Stone Age," coined a century ago by Sir John Lubbock, along with "Paleolithic," or "Old Stone Age." The contrast between the two ages was seen to depend upon the fact that various inventories of archeological materials from western European ice-age contexts yielded stone tools with forms and cutting edges prepared only by chipping, whereas certain archeological inventories from early postglacial contexts also included stone tools whose outlines or cutting edges were prepared by grinding or polishing. The end of the "Neolithic" was seen as marked by the appearance of archeological inventories with at least some metal tools, usually of copper or bronze; hence, the "Bronze Age" followed the "Neolithic." Moreover, it was soon sensed that "traits" other than ground-stone tools might be used to characterize the general range of "neolithic" inventories or assemblages. Traces of crude pottery vessels, weaving, architecture, and the bow, as well as traces of ground-stone artifacts other than cutting tools, came to be included as characteristic "traits" of the "Neolithic," provided that items of metal or of other more sophisticated substances or manufacturing procedures did not appear in the same assemblage.

Both the nomenclature (i.e., "Paleolithic," "Neolithic," "Bronze Age," and "Iron Age") and its rationale reflect an early period of evidence collection and of scholarly thought about European prehistory, during which a kind of world-wide evolutionary chronological and cultural uniformitarianism was assumed to have been the ordering principle of things. During this early period in the development of prehistoric scholarship it was thought, for the most part, that at a given time in the past, generally similar cultures were producing generally similar types of artifacts. At first, the consequences of this assumption were not too serious, but as the twentieth century opened and more came to be learned of prehistory beyond the classic western European area and of ethnology in general, it became increasingly clear to perceptive prehistorians that the uniformitarian image was a vastly oversimplified one.

In the meantime, however, the word "Neolithic" has come to be used as an adjective or as a noun and may denote either (1) the chronological age, (2) the developmental level or stage, or (3) the typological appearance or description of an archeological site or of an artifact or assemblage of artifacts. Thus, in a given piece of writing, the author may hop at will between the chronological, developmental, and typological connotations, his lack of precision in meaning neatly camouflaged behind the learned-looking Neo-Grecism.

Techno–economic usage. V. Gordon Childe's presidential address to the Prehistoric Society in 1935 marked the crystallization of a new meaning for "Neolithic" as "a self-sufficing food-producing economy" (Childe 1953, p. 193). It should be noted that Childe credited Elliot Smith, Harold J. E. Peake, and others with the original notion of ". . . the revolutionary contrast between food-gatherers and food-producers." The importance of the achievement of food production was hardly a new idea, even to archeologists (e.g., Mortillet 1882, p. 576). What interests us here is Childe's selection of a developmental factor—the techno–economic factor —as the most meaningful sense for "Neolithic," if this was to remain a useful term for prehistorians and culture historians. Owing to the deservedly wide popularity of Childe's general writings, his viewpoint that the "Neolithic" began with the appearance of effective ("self-sufficing") food production is now usually followed, at least in western European prehistoric thought. This means that "neolithicness" commenced *wherever* and *whenever* effective food production was assured, regardless of the typological descriptions of the associated artifacts. In fact, Childe's Huxley lecture (1944) shows his own firm grasp of the principle of homotaxis—that the same techno–economic stage may appear in the record of different regions at quite different times in a real chronological sense.

There is still no very new or clear thought on what marks the end of the "Neolithic" stage or era.

Usage relating to regions outside Europe. Probably the greatest confusion with the usage "Neolithic" has occurred in writings concerning the prehistory of regions other than those in Europe.

Fortunately, the usage of "Neolithic" has not appealed to Americanist archeologists (Ehrich 1963), although effective food production certainly did appear in the prehistoric New World. It seems probable that, in the Old World, confusion increases as prehistorians deal with paleoenvironments different from those of Europe, especially if the prehistorians have had European training and if they retain a European image of the way things *ought* to have worked. However, we need not expect that the three factors in the important equation— chronology, developmental level, and typological description—were always the same everywhere in the world.

Thus, the exact timing of the sequences in extra-European regions may be quite different from those of Europe (factor of chronology). Food production appears to have reached Europe with the diffusion of a southwestern Asiatic complex of domesticated food-plants and animals and to have become effective in Europe with the acceptance of this complex by indigenous European peoples already at an intensified or "mesolithic" level of food collection. It is certainly not clear that what happened in Europe was a universal pattern for the first appearance of food production (factor of developmental level). When we view artifacts and characteristic assemblages of artifacts as a manifestation of man's cultural means of adaptation to environments and their natural resources, it is not surprising that both the artifacts themselves and also significant constellations of artifacts should look, and be, quite different in non-European paleoenvironmental situations (factor of typological description).

Since most prehistorians' impressions of the meaning of "Neolithic" seem to have been cast in a European image, one of two things appear to follow the farther we move from Europe. Either the word "Neolithic" is qualified with a bewildering variety of prefixes (e.g., "pre-Neolithic," "proto-Neolithic," "preceramic-Neolithic") which have little or no bearing on the Childean usage (i.e., effective food production), or the Childean usage is implicitly (Arkell 1959, p. 237) or explicitly (Okladnikov 1962, p. 273) denied. In fact, Okladnikov believes that Childe's ". . . so-called 'neolithic revolution' in the Near East should be assigned to the mesolithic" and, on the basis of his own Siberian materials, holds ". . . to the older view that neolithic culture, in contradistinction to the mesolithic and paleolithic, is founded on the appearance of ground axes and pottery as well as of the bow and arrow tipped with a bifacially worked point."

Following Okladnikov, then, food production did not appear in Siberia until long after the beginning of the "Neolithic."

In the opinion of the writer, the word "Neolithic" has completely outlived its usefulness. What follows is a brief consideration of present knowledge about the earliest levels of the stage of effective food production.

The earliest levels of the food-producing stage

The appearance of effective food production. Three trends in the over-all pattern of human biological and cultural evolution have been particularly notable: increasing group size, increasing sociocultural complexity, and increasing permanency of settlement. Little reflection is needed to realize the direct bearing that the availability of a stable food supply and the artifactual means of assuring it have on these trends. Except under highly specialized environmental circumstances, moreover, man has seldom been a very efficient food gatherer or even intensive collector. Also, except under such highly specialized (and hence, relatively rare) environmental circumstances, food gatherers or collectors have not achieved any degree of what are normally referred to as "higher" sociocultural forms. With the appearance of a produced food supply, based upon effective domestication of plants and sometimes of animals, the situation may be otherwise.

In fact, the record of man's past is sufficiently clear to allow the generalization that human evolution (at least on its cultural side) may be divided into at least three grand techno–economic stages: a very long food-gathering and collecting stage, a relatively recent food-producing stage, and the present-day industrial stage. (There is also some tendency to consider a dawning stage of nuclear energy.) Passage from the first to the second stage was achieved independently more than once in different parts of the world, but in neither of the two instances for which we now have any degree of understanding did the event take place before approximately 10,000 B.C.

The two instances of which we have some fair notion were centered in southwestern Asia and in Mesoamerica, and the independent appearances of food production in these two foci depended on the domestication of two quite peculiar and separate complexes of (1) plant-and-animal elements or (2) primarily plant elements, and upon the development of artifactual adaptations to a life based on these complexes. It is also completely evident that both the southwest Asian and the Mesoameri-

can foci of appearance of food production immediately served as centers of diffusion, from which the primary plant-and-animal or plant elements, and the respective artifactual responses to them, moved outward into regions still inhabited by food collectors. The exact cultural mechanics of these "movements" are not yet understood in either case, nor are the mechanics by which indigenous outlying food collectors accepted or rejected portions of the new way of life.

Without doubt, there was at least one or more other independent or semi-independent appearances of food production. Sub-Saharan Africa, southern or southeastern Asia, China, the Andean slopes, and Amazonia have all been named (cf. Braidwood & Willey 1962) as likely areas, but there is as yet far less surety of evidence or agreement among authorities in these cases.

It is also quite clear that there has been no achievement of an urban and civilized way of life, in any meaningful sense of these words, save upon the basis of an effective level of food production. The appearances of the known ancient urban civilizations each followed several thousand years after the earliest appearances of effective food production. In fact, it is quite impossible to conceive of the sociocultural dimensions of urban civilization based solely upon food-gathering or collection.

The background for food production. We are not concerned here with the over-all length of Pleistocene time and of man's early appearance toward the beginning of this time. We need only note that by about 40,000 years ago, if not earlier, our fully modern single species, *Homo sapiens*, was spreading into all parts of the world where human inhabitation was possible. This spread depended largely upon man's increasing capacity for culture, including the acceleration of a long trend toward increasing dependence upon artifactual (i.e., cultural) rather than immediately biological means of adapting to ever greater varieties of environmental circumstances. A probable concomitant of this trend seems often to have been an increasing tendency toward sedentism, or "in-settling," and more experimentation with an increasing number of elements in the total resource spectrum of any given environmental niche (cf. Braidwood 1960*a*; 1960*b*).

Following about 15,000 B.C., the most spectacular known responses to this general trend—still within the general stage of food-gathering, but at a rather highly intensified level of specialized hunting and collecting—are those of the French Dordogne and of Franco-Cantabria. In these regions appeared the brilliant "upper paleolithic" cave art, one cultural manifestation of peoples whose ways of life were based upon their highly successful procedures for hunting the great gregarious animals of that particular paleoenvironment. Another type of adaptation had appeared at least as early in central eastern Europe and beyond, and involved open-air "in-settling" based on mammoth hunting (cf. Klima 1962).

On the same time horizon, however, we may select for contrast the far less spectacular assemblages from the Zagros mountain flanks in southwestern Asia. The animals hunted here were far smaller and more elusive than those pictorialized in the Franco-Cantabrian art: they included wild sheep, goat, and pig, all species that were potentially domesticable. Although the animals were undoubtedly still wild following about 15,000 B.C. and were clearly the objects of hunting pursuits alone, the archeological sites indicate a considerable increase in the proportions of the bones of these particular animals (in contrast to those of deer, bear, onager, and other available, but persistently wild, forms). Moreover, from what the immediately following phases show in several subregions of southwestern Asia, it would appear that certain wild cereal grains must also have been attracting men's (or women's?) attentions at this time.

Natural habitat zones.   We appear to be dealing with the following situation. Certain regions of the world seem to have served as "natural habitat zones" for certain clusters of potentially domesticable plant-and-animal or primarily plant forms while these were still in their wild states. It is certainly possible that more such "natural habitat zones" existed than man took advantage of. To become an effective "natural habitat zone" for our purposes, the "potential domesticates" of a region would have had to be domesticated. This did happen in southwestern Asia and quite separately in Mesoamerica and, as noted above, may also have happened independently or semi-independently in several other regions.

It has always been exasperatingly difficult, archeologically, to point to the very beginnings of food production. The moment of beginning—of the first manipulation of a plant or animal form in a direction that would lead specifically to domestication—would hardly be apparent to us either in the morphologies of the plant or animal forms (if by great fortune traces of these should be recovered), or by an artifactual response to domestication. Also, unfortunately, beginning artifactual "responses" are seldom exclusive or specific; a hoe-like tool was easy to devise, but might it not have been devised for collecting edible roots rather than for conscious *planting*? A very efficient flint blade for a sickle was easily knapped, but was it necessarily used on plants that were consciously *planted* and *cultivated*, or simply on wild ones?

The level of incipience.   Following an explicit suggestion made by Julian Steward (1949), the notion of a level of incipient cultivation and domestication has come into some use and is seen as the first level or phase of the food-producing stage (Braidwood 1960a). It is not supposed that this level resulted in "self-sufficiency" based on produced food; in fact, the great bulk of the diet of people living at this level must have resulted from intensified hunting and collecting. The idea of a level of incipient cultivation and domestication has been applied in considerations of both the southwest Asian and Mesoamerican evidence, as well as of the bits of evidence that are available from other natural habitat zones. It is maintained (Braidwood & Willey 1962, especially pp. 342 ff.) that the presently available evidence suggests that:

(1) The important natural habitat zones seem to have been in semiarid regions (of temperate to tropical latitudes) of some subregional diversity and without an overabundance of collectible foods. However, the possibility that there were independent or semi-independent beginnings of tropical forest "vegeculture" is not ruled out.

(2) There is no binding reason to see the incipience of food production as the result of marked degrees of climatic or environmental change.

(3) The incipient level of food production was probably bound to the environment of its particular natural habitat zone, with neither its domesticates nor the preliminary artifactual responses to them seen as viable elements for extrazonal diffusion.

(4) Incipience seems to have appeared within a context of some degree of pre-existing "in-settling."

(5) The trend from generalized food-collecting to incipient cultivation and domestication appears to have been a slow process.

(6) Incipience does not seem to have been attended by sudden or marked changes in culture.

Diversity within the natural habitat zones.   As field work progresses, it is probable that the matter of subregional diversity within a given natural habitat zone will be seen as increasing in importance. Braidwood's (1952) older notion of the "hilly flanks of the Crescent," as a unitary locale of *the* natural habitat zone in southwestern Asia, has needed revision and expansion (Braidwood 1962), and the desiccation and oasis–riverine propinquity theory of the origins of food production (cf. Childe 1936, p. 86; Toynbee [1934–1939] 1947, p. 69) is now suspect. The sheep–goat–pig, emmer-einkorn wheat, two-row barley complex in the Zagros flanks subregion was certainly present long before approximately 7000 B.C., when we first know it from archeological context. There is a suggestion that sheep may have been domesticated two thousand years earlier, although claims for cultivated cereals on the basis of a restricted pollen count (Solecki 1963) are not so widely accepted. The Natufian culture of Palestine, which on artifactual grounds "looks as if" it ought to have been based upon incipient food production, has as yet yielded no primary evidence of domesticated plant or animal elements, and Perrot rejects his earlier claims (1962) that they should have been there. The domesticated goat is only questionably evidenced in the so-called "Pre-Pottery Neolithic B" of Tell es Sultan (Jericho), but despite the size and artifactual complexity of this site, there is an opinion (Zeuner 1958) that cultivation did not yet obtain in its earliest levels.

It is likewise becoming clear that consideration will have to be given to subregional diversities in Mesoamerica. Willey's (1962, p. 88) useful résumé of the long development of incipient cultivation following about 7000 B.C. in Tamaulipas must now be supplemented with MacNeish's report of work in the Tehuacán valley (Phillips Academy 1962). In Tamaulipas plant-food collection was gradually replaced by increasing dependence on domesticated pumpkin, pepper, and beans, with a small type of maize (similar to that from Bat Cave, New Mexico), appearing about 2000 B.C. In Tehuacán, a more primitive variety of maize seems to have appeared almost two thousand years earlier in a complex that already included squash and pepper, gourds, amaranth, and possibly beans. MacNeish is of the opinion that full-time agriculture with semipermanent village settlements was present in Tehuacán after 3000 B.C.

The primary village–farming community level. Unfortunately, it is not yet possible to point to a clear and uninterrupted sequence, on a single site, in which a progression from the developing phases of incipience into those of "self-sufficing" food production may be seen. In this sense, Mesoamerica (on present archeological evidence) appears to have proceeded somewhat more slowly and evenly than did southwestern Asia. In both regions, however, with a modest degree of typological extrapolation from one generalized assemblage to a next succeeding one, we arrive at a broad picture of a second level of early food production. Direct and ample evidence of the plant-and-animal or primarily plant domesticates is associated with an increasingly impressive inventory of artifacts, which reasonably imply means and procedures adapted to producing food.

It would be within the development of successive phases of this primary village–farming community level that we sense quite new sociocultural dimensions. With a more stable food supply, population growth is indicated by architectural evidence of further increase in size and number of sedentary communities. Specialized artifacts, indicating efforts at carpentry, boatbuilding, housebuilding, weaving, and the pyrotechnics of pottery production, hint at (1) the gradual rise of specialized crafts, (2) some increasing degree of division of labor, and (3) freedom of some of the community from the immediate activities of the quest for food. A gradual shift in religious focus is implied by items reasonably interpreted as having some role in assuring, among other things, the increase of fertility. It would be impossible, however, in the present state of our knowledge, to generalize on the details of the expanding sociocultural complexity of the level, but it is also quite apparent that a marked expansion must have obtained.

The spread of primary food production. There is ample evidence to indicate that the advancing phases of the primary food-production level served as viable planes from which extraregional diffusion might take place. It may be that a critical factor here was the appearance of mutant forms of the plant-and-animal or primarily plant domesticates that would tolerate new environmental circumstances. As noted above, the exact mechanics of such diffusion of either the primary plant and/or animal domesticates, and of the artifacts and procedures necessary to make them effective, are not yet fully understood. Childe's (1953) account of the spread of food production into Europe may be supplemented by the accounts given by several authors in the *Courses Toward Urban Life* symposium (Braidwood & Willey 1962). The latter also contains résumés of present knowledge regarding domestication in sub-Saharan Africa, India, China, and the New World.

It would probably be fair to say that by about 4000 B.C. on the alluvial plain of classic southern Mesopotamia, and perhaps by about 1000 B.C. in Mesoamerica, the primary level of food production was superseded by a further level of at least incipient urbanization. On the other hand, a few remote groups of even present-day peoples in their pristine conditions, such as the Eskimo or the Kalahari Bushmen, have not yet entered the level of primary food production. It is anticipated that future research on the origins and early development of food production will expand its concerns to include the other possibilities of independent or semi-independent achievement of the stage. Further, what were the mechanics of cultural diffusion, mixing, and change, and of acceptance and rejection, as the stage proceeded? Only through archeological means can problems bearing on long-range socio-cultural development and change be approached.

ROBERT J. BRAIDWOOD

BIBLIOGRAPHY

ARKELL, A. J. 1959 The Editor of *Kush*. *Kush: Journal of the Sudan Antiquities Service* 7:237–238. → A letter to the editor.

BRAIDWOOD, ROBERT J. 1952 *The Near East and the Foundations for Civilization: An Essay in Appraisal of the General Evidence.* Eugene: Oregon State System for Higher Education.

BRAIDWOOD, ROBERT J. 1960a Levels in Prehistory: A Model for the Consideration of the Evidence. Pages 143–151 in Sol Tax (editor), *The Evolution of Man: Man, Culture, and Society.* Volume 2: Evolution After Darwin. Univ. of Chicago Press.

BRAIDWOOD, ROBERT J. 1960b Prelude to Civilization. Pages 297–313 in Symposium on Urbanization and Cultural Development in the Ancient Near East, University of Chicago, 1958, *City Invincible.* Univ. of Chicago Press.

BRAIDWOOD, ROBERT J. 1962 The Earliest Village Communities of Southwestern Asia Reconsidered. International Congress of Prehistoric and Protohistoric Sciences, *Proceedings* 1:115–126.

BRAIDWOOD, ROBERT J.; and WILLEY, GORDON R. (editors) 1962 *Courses Toward Urban Life: Archeological Considerations of Some Cultural Alternates.* Viking Fund Publications in Anthropology, Vol. 32. Chicago: Aldine.

CHILDE, V. GORDON (1925) 1958 *The Dawn of European Civilization.* 6th ed., rev. & enl. New York: Knopf.

CHILDE, V. GORDON (1936) 1965 *Man Makes Himself.* 4th ed. London: Watts.

CHILDE, V. GORDON 1944 Archaeological Ages as Technological Stages. *Journal of the Royal Anthropological Institute of Great Britain and Ireland* 74:4–24.

CHILDE, V. GORDON 1953 Old World Prehistory: Neolithic. Pages 193–210 in International Symposium on Anthropology, New York, 1952, *Anthropology Today: An Encyclopedic Inventory.* Edited by A. L. Kroeber. Univ. of Chicago Press.

EHRICH, ROBERT W. 1963 Further Reflections on Archeological Interpretation. *American Anthropologist* New Series 65:16–31.

HELBAEK, HANS 1963 Textiles From Çatal Hüyük. *Archaeology* 16:39–46.

KLIMA, BOHUSLAV 1962 The First Ground-plan of an Upper Paleolithic Loess Settlement in Middle Europe and Its Meaning. Pages 193–210 in Robert J. Braidwood and Gordon R. Willey (editors), *Courses Toward Urban Life.* Chicago: Aldine.

MORTILLET, GABRIEL DE 1882 *Le préhistorique, antiquité de l'homme.* Paris: Reinwald.

OKLADNIKOV, A. P. 1962 The Temperate Zone of Continental Asia. Pages 267–287 in Robert J. Braidwood and Gordon R. Willey (editors), *Courses Toward Urban Life.* Chicago: Aldine.

PERROT, JEAN 1962 Palestine–Syria–Cilicia. Pages 147–164 in Robert J. Braidwood and Gordon R. Willey (editors), *Courses Toward Urban Life.* Chicago: Aldine.

PHILLIPS ACADEMY, ROBERT S. PEABODY FOUNDATION FOR ARCHAEOLOGY 1962 *Tehuacán Archaeological–Botanical Project, Second Annual Report,* by Richard S. MacNeish. Andover, Mass.: The Foundation.

SOLECKI, RALPH S. 1963 Prehistory in Shanidar Valley, Northern Iraq. *Science* 139:179–193.

STEWARD, JULIAN H. 1949 Cultural Causality and Law: A Trial Formulation of the Development of Early Civilization. *American Anthropologist* New Series 51:1–27, 669–671.

TOYNBEE, ARNOLD J. (1934–1939) 1947 *A Study of History.* Abridgment of Vols. 1–6 by D. C. Somervell. Issued under the auspices of the Royal Institute of International Affairs. New York: Oxford Univ. Press.

WILLEY, GORDON R. 1962 Mesoamerica. Pages 84–105 in Robert J. Braidwood and Gordon R. Willey (editors), *Courses Toward Urban Life.* Chicago: Aldine.

ZEUNER, F. E. 1958 Dog and Cat in the Neolithic [Levels of the Tell] of Jericho. *Palestine Exploration Quarterly* [1958]: Jan.–June, 52–55.

II
ANIMAL DOMESTICATION

The term "domestication" as applied to the animal kingdom is commonly defined as that condition in which animals of one species continue to breed freely under conditions of captivity by another. Domestication involves the establishment of a symbiotic relationship from which both species derive some benefit. As practiced by man domestication profoundly affects the ecology and social habits of the animal species as well as man's own cultural patterns.

From a zoological viewpoint, domestication by *Homo sapiens* is viewed as "that condition wherein the breeding, care and feeding of animals are, to some degree, subject to continuous control by man" (Hale 1962, p. 21). Such control, whether loosely or intensively exercised, induces changes in the morphology, physiology, and behavior of the animals concerned. The nature of these changes has been the subject of study since the time of Darwin in the middle nineteenth century, with an emphasis first on skeletal morphology and, more recently, on behavior (Hafez 1962). Such studies make it clear that the cumulative changes brought about by domestication "serve to shift the species to a new adaptive peak, characterized by the domestic habitat, and make it unsuitable for independent existence in nature" (Hale 1962, p. 50). Reed concludes that "in a very important sense, then, domestic animals (as well as plants) are a type of human artifact, since they exist in a form changed by man" (1959, p. 1638, note 7).

On the other hand, from the viewpoint of social

science, the establishment and practice of domestication are significant for human society. The successful performance of the activities of domestication imposes requirements upon a society which affect both its social and economic structure and its system of symbols and values. At the same time the impact of the community upon the landscape is greatly intensified through the destruction of natural vegetation by grazing, through the opening up of new areas for pastoral exploitation, and because of the increased ability to travel and transport goods. Maintenance of human control over an animal species for several generations usually leads to dependence upon the animals for cultural well-being. The animals frequently become an integral part of the human habitation area, at least for part of the time. Such intimate accommodation and control are justified by the fact that the animals fulfill one or more roles in the cultural pattern. Most commonly these roles include serving as a source of food, fuel, power, or raw materials. Equally important, however, are the roles the animals play as symbols of wealth, prestige, or religious belief, as sources of aesthetic pleasure, and as a means of aggression and defense. Dependent upon the specific role or roles a given species plays in a particular society are multiple secondary effects concerning settlement pattern, architecture, and equipment, as well as the value placed on the animals and the elaboration of rules governing property rights concerning them. In addition, there is the important role that animals play in the verbal symbolism expressed in myths, songs, and the vocabulary of the society possessing them.

In spite of the fundamental importance of animal domestication to societies based upon food-producing economies, the study of the initial stages of domestication has lagged. During the early twentieth century the problem was discussed more or less independently by zoologists studying morphology without benefit of population genetics and by ethnologists working largely without supporting archeological data. The latter tried to reconstruct prehistoric events from observation of contemporary nonliterate peoples. The best known of these efforts is probably the *Hirtenkulturkreis* hypothesis formulated by Wilhelm Schmidt of the Vienna school. According to this hypothesis domestication of the horse and reindeer preceded that of other animals, thus permitting pastoral nomads to provide the organizational impetus leading to the higher civilizations. With more intensive archeological field work and the growth of genetic studies in zoology, these earlier theoretical formulations have been largely discredited. Since 1950 there has

been a reassessment of the available evidence and the initiation by archeologists and zoologists of cooperative research aimed at the recovery of evidence specifically relating to the question of early domestication (Fürer-Haimendorf 1955; Hale 1962; Reed 1960; Zeuner 1963).

Archeological evidence

Archeological data concerning domestication have been limited and difficult to interpret. The evidence is both direct and indirect, consisting of animal bones and artifacts. Of the latter, representational art is a major category of information and has been studied in the Near East and north Africa. Such art is often difficult to date, and its conventionalized style often makes specific identification of the animals portrayed almost impossible. There is also the question of whether the animal depicted is wild or domestic. Indirect evidence—such as harnesses, bits, rein rings, or similar kinds of equipment, and refuse such as animal dung and straw used in plaster or to temper pottery, and ash from dung fires—may occasionally shed light on the question of domestication.

Animal bones themselves, with their altered morphology, provide a better source of evidence. But the use of this evidence raises complicated problems of identification and interpretation. First and foremost is the problem posed by the lack of adequate comparative collections of bones of the wild ancestors. Second, there is the mass of poorly documented and misidentified materials from older archeological excavations. This mass has been critically reviewed for the Near East (Reed 1960) and reduced to a small residue of reliable identifications. In most instances these latter materials date from several thousand years after domestication must have taken place and after extensive morphological changes had had time to establish themselves. Such changes often have not occurred to any extent in the earliest remains, and the study of morphology alone is unable therefore to establish the fact of domestication. Before an interpretation can be made for these earliest periods, a combination of morphological and statistical evidence (such as the relative abundance of species, the relative number of animals of different age groups within a species, and the degree of variability between populations) must be taken into account, along with stratigraphic position and general cultural level. This approach attempts to establish the presence of domestication by demonstrating a statistical shift from a general paleolithic hunting pattern, exhibiting a random killing of individuals of various ages in a variety of species, to patterns of selective killing of yearlings within one or two species. It is inferred that the ability to select a single age group from a single species, almost to the exclusion of other animals, reflects sufficient human control over the animal population to warrant use of the term "domestication" (Reed 1962). Preliminary application of this approach to materials from several sites in the Near East suggests that the final results will prove highly significant.

Origins. Theoretical considerations dealing with the problem of how domestication began have focused on the environment (Childe 1928), conscious human behavior (Sauer 1952), or unconscious human behavior and animal behavior (Zeuner 1963) as the major factors. The environmental argument has sometimes been called the "riverine–oasis" or "propinquity" theory. It presupposes a continuous period of desiccation in southwest Asia and northern Africa from the end of the Pleistocene to the present. According to this theory, human and animal inhabitants of these areas were gradually forced together in river valleys and oases, the end result being domestication. The theory may be discounted on both ecological and paleoclimatological grounds. Recent studies by geologists in the Near East show that snow lines and floral zones, depressed during the height of the last glaciation, have gradually shifted upward to their present locations. Since animals occupy specific habitat niches, they either move where those habitats move or they become extinct; they do not cross over into other niches and crowd together. In Africa, where desiccation has occurred, many of these niches undoubtedly became extinct, along with the animals which occupied them, but there is no evidence that they ever crowded into oases. It should be noted that desiccation in Africa was interrupted by periods of wetter conditions and was not a single event. According to present evidence the appearance of domestic animals in the area seems to have occurred during one of these wet rather than dry phases.

Arguments purporting to identify a human motive for domestication are more difficult to deal with, since they are largely logical inferences which are not susceptible to scientific proof. They remain, therefore, always in the realm of speculation. It seems probable that domestication occurs as a result of human and animal behavioral interaction. It is apparent that all hunting-and-gathering peoples of the present day possess extensive knowledge of the habits of wild animals as a necessity for, as well as a by-product of, their hunting activities. It is reasonable to infer that similar knowledge was available to late paleolithic hunters. Given this knowledge, there is general agreement between ethnologists and zoologists that, whether or not it was consciously aimed at domestication, the act of *taming* (that is, the elimination of the tendency to flee from man) must have been the initial mechanism by which animals were brought into the human cultural environment. Since taming can be achieved most effectively with young animals during their critical periods of socialization or imprinting, it is thought that the raising of such young animals by human beings produced domesticated adults. In some instances it is possible that certain wild adults with short flight distances relative to man may have become partially self-domesticated when tolerated in the area by human beings. Otherwise it would have been necessary to feed infant animals. The custom of using a human wet nurse, observed among some contemporary nonliterate groups, suggests itself as a possible method. Sauer (1952) has suggested a religious motivation involving totemic animals in this process, but there is no agreement that such is the case and no evidence either for or against such an assertion. Aside from arguments attributing domestication to religious or other purposeful behavior on the part of man, there is a widely shared belief that agriculture was a necessary precondition to domestication (Childe 1951; Reed 1959; Sauer 1952; Zeuner 1963). The idea has long been suggested in relation to cattle and is accepted in that context by Zeuner (1963). Reed (1959) extends the thesis to cover all four of the basic food animals—sheep, goats, pigs, and cattle—pointing out that they occur only in the context of more or less settled agricultural villages. His point is that such villages would have reached a level of organization complex enough to meet the requirements imposed by the keeping of animals. It must be stressed, however, that it was still uncertain in the mid-1960s that the very earliest context proposed for domestic sheep, Zawi Chemi Shanidar in northern Iraq, was in fact an agricultural settlement.

Biological considerations

Certain biological factors have been stressed as fundamental to the establishment of domestication. Only those animals exhibiting characteristics favorable to domestication were potentially adaptable. These factors include patterns of sexual behavior, social structure, parent–young interaction, response to man, and characteristic foods and habitat. Ability to satisfy dietary needs while in man's environment, or to live on the by-products of his agriculture, was essential to complete domestication. Domestication became possible only because the animals involved were already preadapted socially and psychologically to being tamed without loss of reproductive ability. Observable changes in the behavior of animals that have become domesticated are nevertheless profound. Reed (1959) points out that while conscious selection probably occurred rather late, unconscious selection must have previously led to the establishment of desirable characteristics, such as submissiveness.

Since the domestication of animals can have taken place only in those areas in which the ancestors of the domesticated animals lived, large areas of the earth's surface are automatically eliminated from consideration. Thus, large areas of southern Africa, northern Asia, Australia, and Oceania are ruled out. Significantly, the major centers of domestication seem to correspond to the more important centers of agriculture: the Near East and Egypt (seed cultivation—domestication of dogs, sheep, goats, pigs, cattle); southeast Asia (vegetative planting—chickens, ducks, geese, dogs, pigs, certain types of cattle); Peru (vegetative planting—llamas, alpacas, guinea pigs, muscovy ducks); Mexico (seed cultivation—turkeys). The failure to domesticate any of the herd animals of North America may have been due to the lateness of the development of agriculture in that area. In no world area is there evidence of the domestication of any animal before the end of the Pleistocene around 10,000 B.C. It is important to bear in mind that while we are able to discuss the domestication of specific animals in the Near East at a very early date, this fact does not rule out the probability that animals of the same or related species were domesticated at different times in other areas. Zeuner is of the opinion that wherever socially preadapted animals lived near a human society that had reached a certain degree of cultural complexity, domestication would have followed "almost automatically." In no case, however, is it thought that any purposeful behavior by primitive man occurred with the aim of domesticating an animal, except in very late times, where the idea was copied from existing practices—as perhaps in the case of the reindeer. Least of all would such action have been taken to obtain products such as wool or fat, which are largely secondary products of domestication itself.

Zeuner hypothesizes a progressive order through feeding, taming, and domestication. In the Near East, where the record is most clear, archeological evidence suggests that the scavenger dog was the first to be domesticated; second, the nomadic sheep and goat; third, the scavenger pig; and fourth and finally, cattle, domesticated only when culture was effectively established. The position of the dog at the head of the list is based largely on theory, since its earliest-known remains are in fact found only in the seventh millennium B.C. in pre-pottery neolithic Jericho (the Natufian dog having been identified as a wolf) and in the Maglemosian culture of northern Europe at about the same time.

History of domestication

The oldest animal of a domestic status for which there is actual evidence seems to be the domestic sheep, which is descended from the wild sheep, *Ovis orientalis*, found in the mountains of Turkey and Iran. Perkins (Reed 1962), on the basis of statistics, thinks it probable that the sheep was already domesticated around 9000 B.C. at Zawi Chemi Shanidar in northern Iraq. At this site roughly 60 per cent of the sheep bones were from yearlings, and the majority of bones found were of sheep; this is in contrast to nearby Shanidar Cave in which, in the late paleolithic levels, the bones of yearling sheep made up only about 25 per cent of the total number of sheep bones, which in turn made up only about 33 per cent of the total number of animal bones. Thus a dramatic shift occurred with the settlement of the open-air site of Zawi Chemi Shanidar, a shift which suggests an early stage of domestication. Somewhat later, around 6500 B.C., domestic goats descended from the wild *Capra hircus aegagrus*, found in the same general area, make their appearance. Bones of the domestic goat, identified as such largely by the flattened medial surface of the horn cores, have been found at Jericho (Jordan), Jarmo (Iraq), and Guran and Ali Kosh (Iran) from about this time. The goat seems to have been the first domestic food animal to have become widespread, moving from the highlands into the lowlands of Mesopotamia and Egypt and on into Africa, Asia, and Europe. Several centuries later, perhaps around 6000 B.C., the domestic pig was introduced to Jarmo from some as yet unidentified area. The domestic status of the pig has been established through the morphology of its teeth, which differ from those of wild species presently in the area. While the pigs of southeast Asia generally are descendants of *Sus vittatus*, the native wild pig of those areas, the Near Eastern and European animals appear to be descended from *Sus scrofa*, the local wild boar. The appearance of domestic cattle, on present evidence, occurs somewhat later, around 5500 B.C., at Tepe Sabz in southwestern Iran (Hole et al. 1965) and at Halafian sites such as Banahilk in Iraq. It is perhaps significant that these sites occur in the Assyrian steppe zone bordering the Fertile Crescent.

It may be noted that at this period ox horns were in general use at Çatal Hüyük (south-central Turkey) in religious shrines, but as yet there is no evidence that they were obtained from domestic animals. At an even later date in Mesopotamia an attempt was made to domesticate the local wild onager (as documented in bones found at Tell Asmar); but by 2000 B.C., when the true horse was introduced from southern Russia, this attempt had been given up. The horse appears to have been domesticated in Russia about a millennium earlier. Fragmentary evidence suggests that it was at about this time that the dromedary camel was domesticated in Arabia. The ass or donkey, previously the main beast of burden, appears to have originated in Egypt in predynastic times.

The four major food animals, together with wheat and barley, formed the basic economic complex underlying the higher civilizations of the Near East. From here various selected elements of this complex diffused to cultural groups in adjacent temperate grassland regions. Adoption of the techniques of domestication meant the constant crossbreeding of animal stock with local wild relatives of the same species, and with the occasional substitution of other local species. In general, before domestication of the horse facilitated the development of full pastoral nomadism, these cultural groups probably practiced a mixed economy with a few upland districts specializing in local animal herding. In the first millennium B.C. there is some evidence that the practice of domestication may have been borrowed from sheep and cattle raisers and applied to reindeer in the Minusinsk and Altai highlands. Thus, transport animals appear to have been domesticated generally later than food animals, and animals in marginal nonagricultural areas later still.

A number of other animals have been domesticated for special uses, such as the elephant, the ferret, etc., but little is known about them archeologically. Zeuner (1963) gives the best summary in English with an extensive bibliography.

ROBERT H. DYSON, JR.

[See also PASTORALISM.]

BIBLIOGRAPHY

ANGRESS, SHIMON; and REED, CHARLES A. 1962 An Annotated Bibliography on the Origin and Descent of Domestic Mammals: 1900–1955. Chicago Natural History Museum, *Fieldiana: Anthropology* 54, no. 1.

CHILDE, V. GORDON 1928 *The Most Ancient East*. London: Routledge. → A revised edition was published in 1934 as *New Light on the Most Ancient East*. A fourth edition of the revised work was published in 1952.

CHILDE, V. GORDON 1951 *Social Evolution*. New York: Schumann.

DYSON, ROBERT H. JR. 1953 Archaeology and the Domestication of Animals in the Old World. *American Anthropologist* New Series 55:661–673.

FÜRER-HAIMENDORF, C. VON 1955 Culture History and Cultural Development. Pages 149–168 in *Yearbook of Anthropology, 1955*. Edited by W. L. Thomas, Jr. New York: Wenner-Gren Foundation for Anthropological Research.

HAFEZ, E. S. (editor) 1962 *The Behaviour of Domestic Animals*. Baltimore: Williams & Wilkins.

HALE, E. B. 1962 Domestication and the Evolution of Behaviour. Pages 21–53 in E. S. Hafez (editor), *The Behaviour of Domestic Animals*. Baltimore: Williams & Wilkins.

HANČAR, FRANZ 1955 *Das Pferd in prähistorischer und früher historischer Zeit*. Vienna: Herold.

HOLE, FRANK; FLANNERY, KENT; and NEELY, JAMES 1965 Early Agriculture and Animal Husbandry in Deh Luran, Iran. *Current Anthropology* 6, no. 1:105–106.

JETTMAR, KARL 1954 Les plus anciennes civilisations d'éleveurs des steppes d'Asie Centrale. *Cahiers d'histoire mondiale* 1, no. 4:760–782.

POHLHAUSEN, H. 1954 *Das Wanderhirtentum und seine Vorstufen*. Brunswick (Germany): Limbach.

REED, CHARLES A. 1959 Animal Domestication in the Prehistoric Near East. *Science* 130:1629–1639.

REED, CHARLES A. 1960 A Review of the Archaeological Evidence on Animal Domestication in the Prehistoric Near East. Pages 119–145 in Robert J. Braidwood and Bruce Howe, *Prehistoric Investigations in Iraqi Kurdistan*. Univ. of Chicago Press.

REED, CHARLES A. 1962 Osteological Evidences for Prehistoric Domestication in Southwestern Asia. *Zeitschrift für Tierzüchtung und Züchtungsbiologie* 76, no. 1:31–38.

SAUER, CARL O. 1952 *Agricultural Origins and Dispersals*. New York: American Geographical Society.

SCHMIDT, WILHELM; and KOPPERS, WILHELM 1924 *Völker und Kulturen*. Regensburg (Germany): Habbel.

ZEUNER, FREDERICK E. 1963 *A History of Domesticated Animals*. New York: Harper.

DOMINANCE

See AGGRESSION, *article on* PSYCHOLOGICAL ASPECTS; SOCIAL BEHAVIOR, ANIMAL, *article on* THE FIELD.

DOUHET, GIULIO

General Giulio Douhet, Italian military theorist, was born in Caserta in 1869 and died in Rome in 1930. While he was a young career officer he studied the application of physics—especially electricity and low-temperature physics—to military problems. He wrote essays on these subjects, on the problems arising from the motorization of the army, and on the tactical lessons to be drawn from the Russo–Japanese War.

From 1908 on, he devoted himself, as a student of strategy, to the study of the military implications of developments in aeronautics. As an active officer in the Italian army, he hoped to make his influence felt in the arming of the Italian forces, and after his appointment as commanding officer of the air battalion in Turin, it seemed that Douhet might have an opportunity to put his ideas into practice. He was convinced by his studies and by his experience in the Italo–Turkish War of 1911–1912 that the airplane was far superior to the dirigible as an offensive weapon. This idea was reinforced by his work with Gianni Caproni, the aeronautical engineer who designed and built the first biplane.

Douhet's vigorously expressed views led to disagreement with the military establishment and with the Italian general staff. He was removed from his command and received an assignment unrelated to his professional specialization. He was even subjected to two official investigations, which concluded quite favorably for him, but he was so embittered that he thought of resigning from active service. He retracted this decision only because of the outbreak of World War I.

During the war he frequently criticized the Italian high command and the Allied direction of the war. His dissent was mainly centered upon the value of offensive actions, and he continued to advocate use of the airplane. The nucleus of his criticism (which he put in writing at the time, but which was not, of course, printed until after the war) was that the strategy of the Western Allies was basically wrong because it insisted on partial offensives, which are exceedingly costly in men and weapons and cannot produce a strategic success. He maintained that in land warfare the defensive side is in a far stronger position than the attacking side because of the progress in defensive weapons and ground defense systems. Thus, the Allied powers should conduct the war defensively, with a minimal consumption of men, and should launch an offensive only after having built up the overwhelming armed strength that their superior industrial capacity permitted them. This offensive action should be carried out by airplanes, and Douhet insisted again and again that a powerful fleet of bombers be built and used autonomously. This air force should have as its targets not the enemy forces but the supply centers and the lines of communication in order to paralyze the enemy military system.

On the demand of a member of the Italian Cabinet he summarized his criticism of the Italian high command in a memorandum. The document was discovered by the military authorities, and Douhet was court-martialed and condemned to a year of confinement. After he served the sentence,

the new Italian commander in chief, General Armando Diaz, appointed him director of aeronautics in the defense ministry. In this capacity he was, toward the end of the war, again able to devote himself to his chosen field of action. After his full rehabilitation, which did not take place until 1920, Douhet tried to find employment again, even in a subordinate capacity, in the air force. He was unsuccessful and felt doomed to uselessness.

Douhet's theories, although to a degree based on his experiences in World War I, had already been outlined in some of his prewar writings (e.g., 1910). In these articles Douhet insisted on the autonomous role of the air force, then considered as a mere auxiliary of the army and the navy.

The main argument of Douhet's theory is that the offensive power of an air fleet of bombers is the most formidable instrument of war a country can have; that against such a force fighters are ineffectual, so that it is preferable to build bombers, which also have fighting capability; and that the very first aim of a fleet of bombers is to destroy the enemy air force on the ground in order to achieve air supremacy. Once this has been achieved, a country has to make every effort to strike the severest possible blow against the enemy and to inflict upon him the greatest possible damage. Road junctions, supply and production centers, indeed the cities of the enemy, should be the targets, so that the people will be panic-stricken and ask for an end to the war. Therefore it is more important to inflict destruction on the enemy than to try to avoid devastation of one's own territory.

Douhet's thinking was original and bore no relationship to any previous strategic conception. Indeed, it very often contradicted well-established doctrines; this fact and the zeal of Douhet—a man of great intellectual and moral probity—repeatedly led him into trouble.

Douhet made a major contribution to the theory of air warfare. In the United States, his ideas undoubtedly influenced General "Billy" Mitchell. It has been remarked that during World War II, the very war envisaged in one of Douhet's works, "The War of 19—" (1930), some of his assumptions were proved wrong. Bombers had no decisive effect, fighters proved to be a very effective war instrument, especially in the Battle of Britain, and land forces were able to penetrate deeply into the enemy's territory and possessed a very real offensive capability. This criticism is certainly justified as far as World War II is concerned. In particular, it has been correctly observed that Douhet exaggerated the power of conventional explosives. On the other hand, there is no doubt that many of his ideas seem to be more applicable to our nuclear age: one may detect a first outline, in his theories, of the counter-force and counter-city strategy. It may be of some interest to add that, in a passage in his main work, *The Command of the Air* (1921), Douhet envisaged the possibility that such a formidable instrument of war as an air force might serve an international authority in enforcing the observance of existing treaties.

Fausto Bacchetti

[*For the historical context of Douhet's work, see* Strategy; War; *and the biographies of* Clausewitz; Mahan.]

WORKS BY DOUHET

1910   La possibilità dell'aereonavigazione. *Rivista delle communicazioni* [1910]:1303–1319.
(1921) 1942   The Command of the Air. New York: Coward-McCann. → First published as *Il dominio dell'aria*.
1921–1922   *Diario critico di guerra*. 2 vols. Turin (Italy): Paravia.
(1930) 1942   The War of 19—. Pages 293–394 in Giulio Douhet, *The Command of the Air*. New York: Coward-McCann. → First published in the *Rivista aeronautica* as "La guerra aerea del 19—."
1951   *Scritti inediti*. Edited by Antonio Monti. Florence (Italy): Scuola di Guerro Aerea. → Published posthumously.

SUPPLEMENTARY BIBLIOGRAPHY

Brodie, Bernard 1959   The Heritage of Douhet. Pages 71–106 in Bernard Brodie, *Strategy in the Missile Age*. Princeton Univ. Press.
Earle, Edward M. 1943   Douhet, Mitchell, Seversky: Theories of Air Warfare. Pages 485–503 in Edward M. Earle, *Makers of Modern Strategy: Military Thought From Machiavelli to Hitler*. Princeton Univ. Press.
Sigaud, Louis A. 1941   *Douhet and Aerial Warfare*. New York: Putnam.
Vauthier, Arsène Marie Paul 1935   *La doctrine de guerre du Général Douhet*. Paris: Berger-Levrault.

DRAMA

There is a curious contradiction within theater arts: nothing of man originates from deeper or more hidden sources, and nothing surfaces to a more flamboyantly exposed and lasting arena for observation. Refracted as art may be through the prisms of a nation's culture, customs, habits, and manners, still and all a vital pulse of universality beats. This is theater's potential for evoking emotional response. Dance and drama depict moods and ideas, instincts even, of so private and yet so public a nature that no other aspect of civilized life seems as revelatory or explanatory. Artifacts and art works, of course, visually record the details of an ancient civilization. For example, the poses of the dance figurines excavated from the site of the Indus civilization of three thousand

years ago demonstrate graphically the stylistic continuities between the pre-Vedic and present-day Indian dance, but the life of the past returns only when theater preserves it, no matter how faintly. Recorded history tells of vanished events, but in the drama, history becomes a living representation. The workings of the inner mind that created the past and breathed in its very atmosphere emerge clear and true. Poetic truth, rather than logic, determines men's actions. Our attention is held by considering how man feels in the midst of events without requiring the dry dispassion of a scholar's interest. Indeed, for all its license, theater gives us true value, as well as face value, because it deals with impelling forces, not surfaces. It is not without reason that science to a greater or lesser extent has always followed, rather than preceded, the artist's intuitive dictate or that, so often, the scientist is the artist.

The dramas of ancient Greece are now in desuetude: the language dead, the choral declamation unknown, the music lost, and the dance gestures forgotten. Still, when remaining texts are staged they tell the story of the Greek past that transcends time. They give thoughts to cold marble statues; they inhabit the ruins with meaning and motive, with living yet dead people. The validity of theater lies in its power to span distances of time and space and to bridge the gaps in understanding between peoples who may be either strangers or neighbors. Theater is and is not life. It embraces man's fantasy. If man cannot live without fantasy, and yet if he must remain loyal to reality, then theater satisfies a human need.

Freud, oddly enough, was the first interpretative critic to pinpoint the secret eternity of the Greek drama. By disclosing Oedipus' double realization of father destruction and mother possession, Freud exposed more to drama than psychiatric content. He defined the potent wellspring within the human psyche without which art must appear as false. Before psychology, it was the artist who intuitively tapped these sources.

When dealing with the theater arts of antiquity one touches even deeper *ur* memories of man. One mystery is the permanent hold mudra, or gesture language, has kept over India's dances and formerly over Sanskrit drama. To the outsider seeing and hearing an Indian performance laden with song-words performed by the musicians and the dancer–actor, the language seems sufficiently expressive of meaning. However, the performer simultaneously acts with his or her hands. Sometimes the hands illustrate the words of the song. At other times, in a linguistic counterpoint, the hands enlarge its sense or tell a different story.

At still other times, the hands in a visual paronomasia will pun and countermand the musical words. Mudras are not limited to India. They spread from there throughout Asia, where they may still be seen, attenuated sometimes to little more than heightened gesture but never altogether absent. It is a general principle of Asian theater arts that hands speak while the body dances the mood of what the music suggests. Socrates, it is claimed, said to his pupils, "Speak so that I may see you." An Asian artist might say, "Dance so that I may hear you." Such is the linguistic interdependence between hand-formed words and sung words.

Why have mudras figured so prominently in Indian art and, by extension, in Asian art? What is their hold, at once so redundant and duplicative? Of course, the gesture of hands forming patterns in the air and spinning meanings in space is a highly delectable aspect of aesthetics. Certainly, it arouses pleasing responses. But it is the specific precision of the mudras that is so startling and so enduring. Mudras can be used by a deaf-mute. The mudras, in their very nature as symbolic communication, perform the functions of art.

Theater arts have more tangible and instantly comprehensible importance as well. At the risk of sounding pretentious, one may say with fairness that theater houses its nation's soul. Think, for a moment, of Chekhov and late nineteenth-century Russia, or of Shakespeare's England, or further afield from our experience, perhaps, of Japan's *kabuki*, where the noblest and most vicious attitudes of the past are enshrined. *Chushingura*, the tale of the 47 lordless knights, is a case in point. Not only is it a national theater piece in the sense of actual history embodying ideals through its dramatizations (its eleven acts take two days to perform), but it combines the realism and fantasy of grand theater. The drama is based on a sensational event that happened in 1701: 47 loyal retainers bided one year before avenging the unjust self-immolation of their lord and then committed mass hara-kiri. Versions of the story appeared on the *kabuki* and puppet stages within weeks. The dramatic masterpiece, which endures to this day, appeared a few decades later, after the astonishment and the dust of controversy had settled. The annual revival of the drama, with its magnificent recital of patience, hardships endured, difficulties surmounted, and loyalty and duty opposed to heart and affection, perpetuates many of the values and attitudes of Japanese culture.

The modern Japanese are not warriors, nor are they full of vengeance. They do not believe in eighteenth-century morality, and present society could not conceivably permit the events immortalized in the play of *Chushingura*. Stomachs are tenderer. But just as Americans in New York City weep as *Chushingura* unfolds its story, so do Japanese at their *kabuki* and puppet theaters. Why? Because a common chord of understanding is struck by such themes as human suffering and the righting of flagrant wrong. Thus, if one wishes to learn about another country, the theater serves to characterize cultural patterns.

One historical axiom of drama seems to be that early theater portrayed the gods; then, in a later period, the theater portrayed kings and persons of high rank. Finally and lastly, it touched on the life of the common man. The theory behind this is clear. If theater enlarges life so as to appeal to large numbers rather than to few individuals, then surely it must deal with the most exalted themes —the gods. As time sometimes proves gods less than omnipotent, and the strong power of temporal rulers is keenly felt, it follows that relationships between rulers and men have greater consequence. For instance, the fall of a king or a kingdom is more significant than the collapse of the blacksmith in the next village. It is a real mark of theatrical evolution, however, when audiences perceive that depth of feeling does not and should not depend on the importance of the character or his station in life. Drama which treated the sorrows and sufferings of common ordinary men with the same dignity as that of gods and kings and portrayed plights other than lost thrones, abandoned queens, or vengeful gods, replaced earlier drama.

In Asia, the progression from gods to kings to men is still present in its near-original state. India reflects in its theater the burden that religion presently imposes on other aspects of its culture. Many Indians have never seen a theatrical representation of anything other than the holy books *Ramayana* or *Mahabharata*. Granted that these are also epics and adventure stories, their intent as theater is spiritual elevation. An even greater number of Indians have never heard a piece of music that was not a devotional song to God, even though they have seen modern Indian movies with their songs and dances. In China, that most irreligious of countries, the classical theater is caught in its history of kings and generals of the past. In the Peking operas, they vie and contend, intrigue and counterplot, all in dark tragedy and high bright humor and to the accompaniment of raucously beautiful orchestration.

In the theatrically happier countries of China and Japan, it is possible to see the life of gods, kings, and the common man of the past as well as the present, depending on which theater is selected. One of the marvels of Asia's theatrical world is Japan. There a wise spectator can see dances 1,500 years old. He can attend elaborately staged performances (the Japanese invented the revolving stage and the trap door) by actors whose lineage and names go back 350 years. The play in which they appear may be an adaptation of a novel a thousand years old. Age, in itself and despite the cult of antiquity so fashionable in the West, proves nothing. But in the theater it does reveal the infinitely lasting values of morality and humanity glowing in the fires of aesthetic transmutation. A foreigner can weep with sincerity at a *nō* play in which the pivotal point of conflict is the murder of a bird. He responds to the truth, in this instance, of pity.

In Japan, where modern theater was inspired and trained by Soviet Russia, one may see reactionary plays extolling the past even at the expense of modern progress. Theatrical politics is, of course, like a football kicked toward a variety of goals.

For example, a good amount of the communist-encouraged modern theater in China deals with the abuses of the past, such as those of widowhood or landlord cruelty. But there are also plays that express the turmoils and difficulties within the minds and hearts of present-day Chinese, as they come into conflict or agreement with communist ideals.

One surprising fact appears. Society's immediate problems are not always to be found on the contemporary stage. For example, the postwar difficulties between the Japanese and the American occupation forces were never revealed in the theater. At the same time, the Japanese theater has reached to the core of the social problems posed by Westernization without getting lost in transient details. A somewhat similar problem was dealt with in a different way in India before its independence. There, for lack of a genuinely thriving modern theater, dramatists turned to ancient history to find the reflections or resonances that could convey the urgent message of anticolonialism.

FAUBION BOWERS

BIBLIOGRAPHY

BARNOUW, ERIK; and KRISHNASWAMY, S. 1963 *Indian Film.* New York: Columbia Univ. Press.

BOWERS, FAUBION 1952 *Japanese Theatre.* New York: Hermitage.

BOWERS, FAUBION 1953 *Dance in India.* New York: Columbia Univ. Press.

BOWERS, FAUBION 1956 *Theatre in the East.* New York: Nelson.

BOWERS, FAUBION 1959 *Broadway: USSR.* New York: Nelson.

CHIKAMATSU, MONZAEMON *Four Major Plays of Chikamatsu.* Translated by Donald Keene. New York: Columbia Univ. Press, 1961.

ERNST, EARLE 1956 *The Kabuki Theatre.* New York: Grove; Oxford Univ. Press.

GARGI, BALWANT 1962 *Theatre in India.* New York: Theatre Arts Books.

KAWATAKE, SHIGETOSHI 1960 *History of Japanese Theatre.* Tokyo: Iwanami Shoten.

RAGHAVAN, V. 1963 *Bhoja's Śṛṅgāra Prakāśa.* Madras (India): Punarvasu.

DRAMATISM
See under INTERACTION.

DREAMS

Dreaming is a unique form of behavior. It ordinarily occurs only during sleep and may be the only psychological activity that does occur during sleep. It is involuntary and unintentional in the usual meaning of these words. Customarily, it is not accompanied by, and does not eventuate in, appropriate, relevant, or purposeful overt activity. Dreaming is expressed in the form of hallucinatory imagery that is predominantly visual and is often very vivid and lifelike in nature. It is this hallucinatory experience that constitutes the dream. No other human experience seems to have excited so much interest or so much speculation regarding its cause.

Until recently, the process of dreaming was not directly accessible to scientific investigation; no one knew how to tell when a person was dreaming. Nevertheless, one could study the product of dreaming—the dream—when it was reported or described by the dreamer upon his awakening. Today, we can tell with almost complete certainty when a person is dreaming. The dream itself, however, still remains virtually inaccessible to direct investigation and will remain inaccessible until the invention of some means of transcribing the dream as it is taking place. Until that time, investigators must depend upon the dreamer to communicate his dream verbally or through some other medium. Studies of dreams, therefore, are actually studies of reported dreams. How much correspondence there is between the dream as reported and the dream as dreamed cannot, as yet, be determined. We know now that failure to recall a dream does not mean that the person has had a dreamless sleep. In fact, except under certain abnormal conditions, everyone dreams every night, having from four to six separate dreams.

The process of dreaming

Objective study of eye movements. The process of dreaming, as distinguished from the product, was made available for scientific study by the discovery of objective indicators of dreaming. The first of these was reported in 1953 by E. Aserinsky and N. Kleitman, who noted while observing sleeping subjects that bursts of rapid eye movements (REMs) occurred periodically during sleep. Kleitman later described this fruitful discovery:

In our laboratory at the University of Chicago we literally stumbled on an objective method of studying dreaming while exploring eye motility in adults, after we found that in infants eye movements persisted for a time when all discernible body motility ceased. Instead of direct inspection, as was done for infant eye movements, those of adult sleepers were recorded indirectly, to insure undisturbed sleep in the dark. By leads from two skin spots straddling the eye to an EEG machine, located in an adjacent room, it was possible to register potential differences whenever the eye moved in its socket. . . . By this method . . . slow eye movements were found to be related to general body motility. In addition, jerky rapid eye movements . . . , executed in only a fraction of a second and binocularly symmetrical, tended to occur in clusters for 5 to 60 minutes several times during a single night's sleep. In order to correlate the REMs with other concomitants, simultaneous recordings were made of changes in the sleepers' EEG, pulse, and respiration. It was soon apparent that the REMs were associated with a typical low-voltage EEG pattern and statistically significant increases in the heart and respiratory rates . . . though occasionally the pulse was slowed. These changes suggested some sort of emotional disturbance, such as might be caused by dreaming. To test this supposition, sleepers were aroused and interrogated during, or shortly after the termination of, REMs and they almost invariably reported having dreamed. If awakened in the absence of REMs, . . . they seldom recalled dreaming.   (Kleitman 1963, pp. 93–94)

Like most discoveries, the correlation of eye movements with dreaming was not unanticipated. In 1892, G. T. Ladd tentatively concluded on the basis of introspective studies that the eyes move during dreaming, and many years later, E. Jacobson (1938) corroborated Ladd's introspections by actually observing that the eyes do move during dreaming. Despite these historical antecedents, it was the findings of Aserinsky and Kleitman that launched the modern era of dream research, just as half a century earlier it had been Freud's book *The Interpretation of Dreams* (1900) that established the dream as the main vehicle for studying the operations and products of unconscious processes.

Why do the eyes move during dreaming? The best answer seems to be that the eyes are scanning the dream scene, just as the eyes of a person who is awake scan the visual field. There is some evidence to support this scanning hypothesis. Dreams that involve much action are reported after a REM period in which there are many large eye movements, whereas more passive dreams are correlated with smaller eye movements (Berger & Oswald 1962). In some instances, the direction of the eye movement has been shown to correspond with the direction of the movements in the reported dream (Dement & Wolpert 1958). For example, following a REM period in which only vertical eye movements were recorded, the subject reported a dream of looking alternately down at the sidewalk and up toward the top of a flight of stairs.

Dreaming and sleep cycles.   Not only is dreaming a unique form of behavior, but it also occurs during a unique stage of sleep. Unlike any of the other stages, the one during which dreaming occurs is characterized not only by bursts of rapid, conjugate movements of both eyes and by a low-voltage EEG pattern but also by other physiological and behavioral concomitants. Breathing and heart rate tend to be irregular, and the muscles of the throat adjacent to the larynx become flaccid, although, interestingly, the penis becomes more erect. The electrical resistance of the skin, which is ordinarily high during sleep, is reported to be even higher during so-called dreaming sleep. All of this evidence suggests that the stage during which dreaming occurs may be, as one authority has stated, "a separate organismic state, different from both 'nondreaming' sleeping and from waking" (Snyder 1963).

Dreaming is cyclical throughout the sleep period, with from four to six such cycles occurring during the night. The first cycle appears approximately an hour after a person falls asleep, and succeeding ones occur about every 90 minutes. The length of successive REM periods increases from 5 to 10 minutes for the first one to 30 minutes or longer for the last one. This finding revokes the common belief that a dream lasts for only a few seconds. In fact, some recent evidence suggests that what transpires in a dream occupies approximately the same length of time as it would were the same events to occur in waking life.

Although a hallucinatory dream experience is rarely reported if a person is awakened when eye movements are lacking, some investigators have obtained thoughtlike reports from persons who were awakened during non-REM periods. In one such study the subjects compared their reports of non-REM periods with those obtained from dreaming sleep. They found that their reports of non-REM periods were more difficult to recall, were more plausible and less emotional, were more concerned with contemporary events, and, generally speaking, resembled thinking more than dreaming (Rechtschaffen et al. 1963.) It has been suggested that the thinking the subject reports on being awakened from a non-REM period occurs while the sleeper is being awakened and does not reflect mental activity during sleep itself.

Universality. By employing the objective indicators of dreaming in studies involving numerous subjects, investigators in the United States and abroad have established that everyone dreams every night. Exceptions to this have been noted when the subject is in an abnormal state, such as during a high fever or when certain drugs have been administered. Even people who say they have never dreamed or who rarely remember a dream will report dreams when they are awakened during a rapid-eye-movement period (Goodenough et al. 1959).

A young adult spends about one-fifth of the sleep period dreaming, babies considerably more, and older people less. Rapid eye movements have been observed in blind people whose blindness is not of long standing. In those who have been blind for several years, low-voltage EEG waves still occur and a nonvisual type of dream is reported when the blind person is awakened (Berger et al. 1962). Other animals besides man show cyclical periods of rapid eye movements during sleep.

Biological necessity? One of the most interesting findings resulting from the use of objective indicators of dreaming is that when a person's dreaming is reduced by awakening him every time his eyes begin to move, there is a significant increase in REM time when he is finally permitted to sleep undisturbed (Dement 1960). Moreover, if a person is deprived of dreaming for a number of nights, his waking behavior appears to be adversely affected. He manifests various aberrant "symptoms" that border on being pathological, and it has been conjectured that if he were deprived of dreams long enough, he might become psychotic. These results seem to indicate a "need to dream," comparable in its psychobiological insistence to any of the other basic needs of the individual.

One authority believes, however, it may be the kind of sleep and not the dreaming itself that is the biological necessity (Snyder 1963). Support for this hypothesis is found in the work of the French investigator Jouvet, who has observed periods of eye movements and low-voltage waves in decorticate cats (Jouvet 1961) and in decorticate humans (Jouvet et al. 1961). It is considered unlikely that either a decorticate cat or a decorticate person is capable of having dreams, yet the physiological concomitants of dreaming persist in the decorticate state. It is these physiological processes and not the dreaming that Snyder considers to be the biological necessity.

External events. The availability of indicators of dreaming will enable investigators to observe the effects of certain stimuli upon dreaming. Studies made prior to the discovery of objective indicators showed that experimentally introduced discrete stimuli had, for the most part, very little influence upon the dream (Ramsey 1953). They may appear either directly or in distorted form in the dream, but they do not instigate, control, or shape the substance of the dream. Preliminary studies using the objective indicators have produced similar results, namely, that such external stimuli as sounds, pressures, and temperature changes have little influence on the dream. It is believed, however, that more complex forms of stimulation, such as movies shown to a person before he retires, will influence dreams. It is an established fact that the experimental situation for monitoring sleep becomes represented in dreams, especially during the subject's initial nights in the laboratory. It will now be possible also to determine whether the sleeping person is more sensitive to telepathic or clairvoyant influences, as some authorities believe, by noting the appearance of subliminal stimuli in his dreams.

One question that is being investigated is whether the dreams obtained from persons whose sleep is monitored can be compared with dreams remembered by them upon awakening from non-monitored sleep. Preliminary findings indicate that the two samples are not comparable. A related question is whether the dreams of a person throughout the night show any consistent pattern of thematic material. Again preliminary findings suggest that there are minimal correspondences among a person's dreams of the same night.

Dream interpretation

Interpretation before Freud. Although Freud was not the first person to assume that the dream has a "deeper" meaning—such an assumption seems always to have existed—he was the first to develop an empirical method for "interpreting" a dream. Dream interpreters before Freud—men like Artemidorus, who is credited with being the first compiler of a dream book, and Joseph, whose exploits are recounted in the Bible—depended upon intuition, wisdom, and a scholarly knowledge of dream lore for deriving significance from the dream. Elements in a dream were assumed by these ancient dream interpreters to have a fixed meaning. It is this assumption that underlies dream books. Although dream books, with their prophecies of good and bad fortune, have fallen into disrepute among educated people, they are still published and purchased in large quantities and influence the decisions of many people (Weiss 1944). Among societies lacking books, dream interpreters still flourish and enjoy great prestige for their knowledge of a phenomenon deemed to be steeped in personal and even social relevance. There are societies like the Senoi in which people tell each other their dreams for the express purpose of reducing interpersonal tensions (Steward 1951).

That the dream among all the cognitive activities of man should be singled out as possessing special and mysterious properties, and requiring as a consequence special and often supernatural explanations, is not surprising when one considers how unique the dream is. For example, the ancient theory that the dream is a record of the experiences of a soul that leaves the body during sleep is based upon the fact that many dreams are so vivid and lifelike that they are mistaken for real perceptions.

Also, in view of the fact that the dream appears as an alien visitation without warning and without intention during the dead of sleep, a condition that is itself charged with mystery, it is not difficult to comprehend why many people construe the dream as a prophetic message from supernatural beings, from the sleeping person's ancestors, or, in the present age of science fiction, from people living on other planets. Other prescientific theories that purport to explain dreaming are based upon other equally singular features of the dream.

Freud's theory. Freud's empirical method for interpreting a dream involves free association. After a person reports a dream to his analyst, he is instructed to say everything that comes into his mind when each successive element of the dream is presented back to him. By using the method of free association with his patients' dreams, Freud (1900) was able to formulate a comprehensive theory of the dream. The dream has two kinds of content: the manifest (conscious) content, which is the dream as experienced and remembered by the dreamer, and the latent (unconscious) content, which is discovered through free association. Dream interpretation involves replacing the manifest with the latent content. The nucleus of the latent content is an unconscious infantile wish with which later experiences have become implicated. The ultimate task of interpretation is to unearth the nuclear infantile wish through free association. Much of the latent content consists, however, of "day residue," that is, memories of experiences and

thoughts that the dreamer has had on the day previous to the dream. Day residue alone is not sufficient to create a dream; it must be charged by an infantile wish in order to transform it into the conscious imagery of a dream.

When the dream thoughts (latent content) are transformed into the manifest content of the recalled dream, they are altered in certain ways. They are subject to condensation; an element in the manifest dream may be a compression of several dream thoughts. They are subject to displacement; feeling associated with a particular dream thought is transferred to an otherwise neutral element in the manifest dream. Latent thoughts may also be represented in the experienced dream by symbols. The interpretation of a dream requires, then, that all of the condensed manifest elements be expanded into their constituent dream thoughts, that all displaced affects be traced to their proper sources in the latent content, and that referents be found for all symbols. This is a formidable undertaking, the result of which is an interpreted version that is many times longer than the text of the manifest dream. The practicability of this method of interpreting dreams appears to be restricted to long-term psychotherapy.

Freud hypothesized that the dream work, which consists of the operations for transforming latent into manifest content is governed by two aims: regard for representability and disguise. Regard for representability refers to the transformation of abstract dream thoughts into concrete dream imagery. The aim of disguise is protection, based on the assumption that the undisguised latent thoughts would evoke so much anxiety that the dreamer would awaken. Many dreams do, in fact, awaken the sleeper because they are not sufficiently disguised. The sleep-protection hypothesis is a biological one, for it explains not what we dream but why we dream.

Dreams, then, according to Freud's theory, are useful in establishing the contents of the unconscious. Since the foundation of the unconscious is laid down early in life, before the age of five or six, and contains repressed material from the psychosexual stages, the analysis of dreams constitutes one of the few methods for studying early psychological development. That the unconscious may also contain material from the racial past was discussed by Freud, but he neither strongly affirmed nor denied the notion, although he seems to have been sympathetic to it.

Jung's theory. It remained for one of Freud's early associates (later an apostate), Carl Jung, to examine dreams for evidence of a racial unconscious that all men share (Jung 1960). Jung was convinced that there was sufficient evidence in dreams and other types of material, e.g., myths and religion, to validate the concept of a collective unconscious. He called the contents of this unconscious "archetypes" and identified a number of them: the anima, the shadow, the earth mother, the wise old man, and, most important of all, the archetype of personal unity symbolically represented in dreams and elsewhere by the form of the mandala. Whereas Freud used dreams to explore the formative years of a person's life, Jung used them to explore the psychological development of the race.

Jung also thought, in contradistinction to Freud, that dreams are oriented to the future as well as to the past. They mark out for the individual the proper path to a more complete actualization of personality and help reveal poorly developed parts of the personality.

Other theories. In addition to the theories of Freud and Jung, there are a number of other theories, for example, those of Hall (1953), French (1954), Hadfield (1954), Boss (1953), Ullman (1955; 1958; 1959), and Jones (1962). These have several features in common. They deal more with the manifest than with the latent content, and they are more concerned with the dream as an expression having adaptive significance for the dreamer than as a disguise for infantile wishes. Hall, for example, regards the dream as a concrete representation of the dreamer's conception of himself, of others, and of his world. The dream reveals more than it conceals. French stresses the integrative role played by the dream. The dreamer is attempting to solve his emotional problems. Hadfield also sees the dream as problem-solving activity, and Ullman emphasizes the dream's adaptive function. For Boss, an existential–phenomenological therapist, the dream is a confrontation experience in which the dreamer faces directly his own questions of existence as a unique experiencing self. In the most recent of these theoretical formulations, Jones describes the synthesizing function of the dream within the context of a developmental sequence of critical phases through which a person passes in growing up.

It would seem from these theories that the dream was a complex, multidimensional, multileveled phenomenon capable of supporting diverse theoretical superstructures. The dream may, in fact, be just such a complex phenomenon, although the ratio of research to speculation is still so small that it is difficult to draw any firm conclusions regarding the validity of these speculations. Although research is

scanty, the usefulness of dream analysis in psychoanalytic and other forms of psychotherapy seems to be generally acknowledged by psychotherapists (Bonime 1962).

Experimental studies of dreams

The dream as a projective device. It is not possible to say just how much research on dreams has been deterred by Freud's distinction between manifest and latent content and by the complex set of operations that must be carried out under a very special type of relationship between the observer and the subject before the operations can be successful. There are indications that these methodological obstacles are being bypassed by treating the manifest dream as significant material in its own right (Hall 1947; Eggan 1952; Jones 1962). This approach regards the dream, or preferably a series of dreams, as a projective device similar to those of the Rorschach and story-telling techniques. It may be argued that the dream is almost a pure form of projection, since external stimuli seem to have so little to do with its formation or its content.

The projective approach may be illustrated by a study made by Hall and Van de Castle (1965). Following Freud's theory of sex differences in psychosexual development, they hypothesized that there would be a greater frequency of castration anxiety in dreams reported by males and that there would be a greater incidence of castration wish and penis envy in dreams reported by females. Scales for identifying castration anxiety, castration wish, and penis envy in dream reports were developed, and a large number of male and female dream series were scored using these scales. The hypotheses were confirmed at a high level of significance.

Another study employing the same methodology was conducted by Beck and Hurvich (1959). They predicted that depressed patients would show a greater incidence of manifest dreams with masochistic content than would nondepressed patients. A collection of dreams secured from depressed and nondepressed patients was scored, and the hypothesis was confirmed at an appropriate level of significance.

This method of dream analysis has much to recommend it. Dream reports can easily be collected in large numbers from groups of people living under different cultural, economic, social, educational, and geographical conditions. They can be subjected to quantification, and the same set of dreams can be analyzed in many ways to serve different empirical and theoretical purposes. Norms for different populations can be established so that an individual's deviation from the norms for the group may be accurately described. The influence of experimental manipulation of variables can be assessed by comparing a treated group with a control one.

Of particular significance for the social sciences is the comparison of dreams obtained from people living in different cultures. Dorothy Eggan's pioneering efforts in studying the dreams of Hopi Indians show what can be done by correlating the themes of reported dreams with culturally relevant material (1961).

The objective method of analyzing dreams. It is to be expected that the availability of objective indicators of dreaming will prove a stimulant to research and increase our knowledge of dreams and dreaming in the future. The physiological emphasis so far in research probably reflects the fact that rapid eye movements and brain waves were discovered by physiologists and that their measurement employs apparatus that is more familiar to physiologists than to social and behavioral scientists.

CALVIN HALL

[*Other relevant material may be found in* ANALYTICAL PSYCHOLOGY; NERVOUS SYSTEM, *article on* ELECTROENCEPHALOGRAPHY; PROJECTIVE METHODS; PSYCHOANALYSIS; SLEEP; *and in the biography of* JUNG.]

BIBLIOGRAPHY

ASERINSKY, EUGENE; and KLEITMAN, NATHANIEL 1953 Regularly Occurring Periods of Eye Motility, and Concomitant Phenomena During Sleep. *Science* 118:273–274.

BECK, AARON T.; and HURVICH, MARVIN S. 1959 Psychological Correlates of Depression: 1. Frequency of "Masochistic" Dream Content in a Private Practice Sample. *Psychosomatic Medicine* 21:50–55.

BERGER, RALPH J.; OLLEY, P.; and OSWALD, IAN 1962 The EEG, Eye-movements and Dreams of the Blind. *Quarterly Journal of Experimental Psychology* 14: 183–186.

BERGER, RALPH J.; and OSWALD, IAN 1962 Eye Movements During Active and Passive Dreams. *Science* 137:601 only.

BONIME, WALTER 1962 *The Clinical Use of Dreams.* New York: Basic Books.

BOSS, MEDARD (1953) 1958 *The Analysis of Dreams.* New York: Philosophical Library. → First published as *Der Traum und seine Auslegung.*

DEMENT, WILLIAM 1960 The Effect of Dream Deprivation. *Science* 131:1705–1707.

DEMENT, WILLIAM; and WOLPERT, EDWARD A. 1958 The Relation of Eye Movements, Body Motility, and External Stimuli to Dream Content. *Journal of Experimental Psychology* 55:543–553.

DIAMOND, EDWIN 1962 *The Science of Dreams.* Garden City, N.Y.: Doubleday. → This book, written by the science editor of *Newsweek,* is a popularized account of recent dream studies.

EGGAN, DOROTHY 1952 The Manifest Content of Dreams:

A Challenge to Social Science. *American Anthropologist* New Series 54:469–485.

EGGAN, DOROTHY 1961 Dream Analysis. Pages 550–577 in Bert Kaplan (editor), *Studying Personality Crossculturally.* Evanston, Ill.: Row, Peterson.

FRENCH, THOMAS M. 1954 *The Integration of Behavior.* Volume 2: The Integrative Process in Dreams. Univ. of Chicago Press.

FREUD, SIGMUND (1900) 1953 *The Interpretation of Dreams.* 2 vols. New York: Macmillan; London: Hogarth. → Constitutes Volumes 4 and 5 of *The Standard Edition of the Complete Psychological Works of Sigmund Freud.*

FROMM, ERICH 1951 *The Forgotten Language: An Introduction to the Understanding of Dreams, Fairy Tales and Myths.* New York: Holt.

GOODENOUGH, DONALD A. et al. 1959 A Comparison of "Dreamers" and "Nondreamers": Eye Movements, Electroencephalograms, and the Recall of Dreams. *Journal of Abnormal and Social Psychology* 59:295–302.

HADFIELD, JAMES A. 1954 *Dreams and Nightmares.* Baltimore: Penguin.

HALL, CALVIN S. 1947 Diagnosing Personality by the Analysis of Dreams. *Journal of Abnormal and Social Psychology* 42:68–79.

HALL, CALVIN S. 1953 *The Meaning of Dreams.* New York: Harper.

HALL, CALVIN S.; and VAN DE CASTLE, R. L. 1965 An Empirical Investigation of the Castration Complex in Dreams. *Journal of Personality* 33:22–29.

JACOBSON, EDMUND 1938 *You Can Sleep Well: The ABC's of Restful Sleep for the Average Person.* New York: McGraw-Hill.

JONES, RICHARD M. 1962 *Ego Synthesis in Dreams.* Cambridge, Mass.: Schenkman.

JOUVET, M. 1961 Telencephalic and Rhombencephalic Sleep in the Cat. Pages 188–208 in Ciba Foundation, *Symposium on the Nature of Sleep.* Edited by G. E. W. Wolstenholme and Maeve O'Connor. Boston: Little.

JOUVET, M.; PELLIN, B.; and MOUNIER, D. 1961 Étude polygraphique des différentes phases du sommeil au cours des troubles de conscience chronique (comas prolongés). *Revue neurologique* 105:181–186.

JUNG, CARL G. 1960 *Collected Works.* Volume 8: The Structure and Dynamics of the Psyche. New York: Pantheon. → Contains works first published between 1916 and 1954.

KLEITMAN, NATHANIEL 1963 *Sleep and Wakefulness.* Rev. & enl. ed. Univ. of Chicago Press. → Extracted matter is reproduced by permission. © 1939, 1963 by the University of Chicago.

LADD, GEORGE T. 1892 Contribution to the Psychology of Visual Dreams. *Mind* New Series 1:299–304.

RAMSEY, GLENN V. 1953 Studies of Dreaming. *Psychological Bulletin* 50:432–455.

RECHTSCHAFFEN, ALLAN; VERDONE, PAUL; and WHEATON, JOY 1963 Reports of Mental Activity During Sleep. *Canadian Psychiatric Association Journal* 8:409–414.

SNYDER, FREDERICK 1963 The New Biology of Dreaming. *Archives of General Psychiatry* 8:381–391.

STEWARD, KILTON 1951 Dream Theory in Malaya. *Complex: The Magazine of Psychoanalysis and Related Matters* 6:21–33.

ULLMAN, MONTAGUE (1955) 1958 The Dream Process. *American Journal of Psychotherapy* 12:671–690. → This paper was originally published in expanded form in *Psychotherapy,* Vol. 1, No. 1, 1955.

ULLMAN, MONTAGUE 1958 Dreams and Arousal. *American Journal of Psychotherapy* 12:222–242.

ULLMAN, MONTAGUE 1959 The Adaptive Significance of the Dream. *Journal of Nervous and Mental Disease* 129:144–149.

WEISS, HARRY B. 1944 Oneirocritica americana. New York Public Library, *Bulletin* 48:519–541.

DRINKING AND ALCOHOLISM

I. PSYCHOLOGICAL ASPECTS   *Edith S. Lisansky*
II. SOCIAL ASPECTS   *Charles R. Snyder*
                                   and David J. Pittman

I

PSYCHOLOGICAL ASPECTS

Drinking and alcoholism will be considered as related but distinct phenomena. The use of alcoholic beverages by almost all societies over recorded history as a stimulant, anesthetic, social lubricant, and ceremonial substance is well known. Ingestion of alcohol may be normal or pathological; here the problem of definition begins. There is *moderate* drinking, acceptable in many (but not all) human groups; there is *excessive* drinking, for example, intoxication; there are behavior problems *associated* with drinking; and there is *alcoholism*. A recent definition of alcoholism states that "alcoholism is a psychogenic dependence on or a physiological addiction to ethanol, manifested by the inability of the alcoholic consistently to control either the start of drinking or its termination once started . . ." (Keller 1962, p. 312). Loss of control is the pathognomic symptom here, and the definition specifies for the epidemiologist those behaviors that will permit him to define the alcoholic—marked and repetitive drinking—as well as the ill effects on the drinker's health or on his social or economic functioning.

Drinking behavior has been interpreted in terms of different theoretical systems in psychology: for example, drinking has been viewed as a reducer of fear and conflict, by behaviorists, or as a dissolver of the superego, by psychoanalysts. Studies of the influence of alcohol on human behavior may be viewed as a wedge into related areas of knowledge: knowledge of the effects of alcohol on learning efficiency or motor coordination may be considered data about learning efficiency or motor coordination per se, about general drug effects, or about individual differences in response. The relation of deviant drinking behavior to human misery, personal and social, gives some insight into the dynamics of psychic pain and how ways of coping are passed on and learned. Alcohol studies in social anthropology may suggest usable hypotheses about the relationship of individual maladjustment and social organization in different societies. There are some groups in which drinking is virtually universal, where the lone drinker or abstainer is unknown, and where frequent intoxication and spree drinking is not the symptomatic, deviant behavior of a relatively few, for example, the fiesta drinking of Central American and South American Indian groups. In some social groups and societies, such as nineteenth-century European Jewish communities, alcohol may serve to reinforce social organization. In other groups, alcohol may hasten processes of disorganization and deculturation; the example of many North American Indian tribes is well known. Alcohol has been used occasionally as an instrument to achieve the submission of and control over others.

Drinking

The term "drinking" seems simple enough: an organism ingests an alcoholic beverage. But as a behavioral term, it includes many related aspects: in describing drinking behavior, one needs to know the kind and amount of beverage ingested and the circumstances of ingestion, such as where it is drunk, how rapidly, with whom, how diluted, whether before or during meals, etc. The term "drinking" encompasses the determination of the blood-alcohol level produced by the drinking; the effects on efficiency, mood, and social interaction; the past experiences of the drinker; and the drinking customs of the social group.

Organic and psychological aspects. The physiological aspects of drinking have been summarized in an excellent review that includes much of the recent physiological and biochemical research on alcohol (Kalant 1962, pp. 52–93).

The psychological aspects of drinking will be narrowed here to a review of research on the behavioral effects of alcohol on individual organisms.

There is a vast literature involving animal subjects and the effects of alcohol on their behavior. Often, these are studies of alcohol effects in classical or operant conditioning procedures, reaction time and maze behavior, but there have also been many laboratory reports demonstrating increased voluntary consumption of alcohol under different experimental conditions, such as vitamin deficiency or stress, as well as some reports of laboratory work demonstrating genetic strain differences in alcohol preference. The term "experimental alcoholism" to describe these studies was criticized by the World Health Organization, Expert Committee on Alcohol

(1954), which expressed the opinion that the phenomenon of alcoholism was closer to experiments dealing with "the relief by alcohol of experimentally induced neurotic manifestations in animals." Such experiments include studies of experimenter-induced conflicts and stress and of "experimental neurosis." Whether such experiments relate to alcoholism or to the relief afforded by alcohol in everyday, nonpathological social drinking may be a legitimate question, but there is another caveat: not to go too far in generalizing from the responses to alcohol of the animal in laboratory-generated stress to the complex, socially patterned drinking behavior of the human subject.

There was a sizable amount of laboratory experimentation during the first four decades of this century on the effects of alcohol on different psychological variables. These have been summarized and evaluated in a monograph by Jellinek and McFarland (1940). Experiments were grouped under these headings: chronaxy, reflexes, sensations, perception and attention, simple reaction time, muscular strength and coordination, miscellaneous tests of dexterity and skill, learning and simple learned performances, memory, the associative functions, judgment, reasoning and intelligence, volition, emotion and personality. The generalization made from the authors' analysis of the experiments was that "alcohol has a depressing effect on all psychological functions yet measured, and . . . such stimulation as has been reported for some psychological variables is a pseudostimulation" (ibid., p. 362–363). The reviewers also concluded that "the simple psychological functions are less affected by alcohol than the complex ones" (ibid., p. 363).

These conclusions are now under critical reexamination and challenge. There is some evidence that small amounts of alcohol may in some task situations have a facilitating effect. It turns out, too, that inferences about "pseudostimulation" are based on a melange of psychology and neurology: if behavior or performance *improves* with alcohol, the argument is that such improvement occurs because cortical inhibitions are disinhibited by the alcohol. But studies of behavior need to be described in behavioral and not in neurological terms (particularly not in oversimplified neurological terms that have been superseded by newer concepts of cerebral activity). As it appears now, alcohol in small and moderate amounts is frequently a behavioral depressant, but may—under some conditions, for some tasks, for some individuals—act as a facilitator (Lisansky 1964, pp. 104–121).

The issue of simple versus complex psychological functions has also been critically re-evaluated: "The traditional idea that intellectual functions are particularly susceptible to deterioration by alcohol is questioned . . . a reevaluation of the idea that intellectual functions are a 'complex' or 'higher' or 'fragile' activity is necessary . . ." (Carpenter 1962, p. 310).

Experimental study of the effects of alcohol on emotional behavior and the relationship of such effects to personality variables is in its infancy. There is some research suggesting that individual characteristics related to the effects of alcohol may be a subject's general adjustment, his introversive or extroversive tendencies, his past experience with alcohol, and his familiarity with a task. Interestingly enough, when people are asked to report their subjective feelings about how alcohol affects them, they almost invariably reply in terms of *stimulating* effects; this is true whether the people are laboratory subjects or participants in surveys. Experiments involving groups and the effects of alcohol on the emotional behavior of individuals drinking together have been conducted by the Finnish Foundation for Alcohol Studies. The limited number of group studies to date report increases in aggressive behavior, in the sexual content of fantasies, and in emotionality of behavior generally.

Drinking practices in the United States, in some Central American and South American communities, among several African peoples, in many countries of Europe and Asia, and in preliterate primitive societies have been described (McCarthy 1959; Pittman & Snyder 1962). Jellinek (1960) has reported on attitudes toward intoxication and alcoholism in the different countries of Europe and the Americas.

Alcoholism

Any discussion of alcoholism must begin by distinguishing between "drinking related misbehaviors" (Keller 1962, p. 310) or "intoxication-caused problems" (Tongue 1962) on the one hand and alcoholism on the other. Jellinek commented: "International experience leads to the conclusion that in many countries more serious problems of national magnitude arise from other types of drinkers than from those who are termed 'alcoholics' in America" (1960, p. 15). Other types of drinking, like occasional excessive drinking, may lead to behaviors that present a problem to society; examples of these would be "explosive drinking" in Finland, or "fiesta drinking" in Spain, Portugal, Brazil, and Argentina. Jellinek (1960) described the so-called "inveterate drinker" in France, who may consume two or even three liters of wine daily, rarely becoming intoxicated yet frequently presenting the medical symptoms of the diseases of chronic alcoholism.

European state programs have concerned themselves with both alcoholism *and* alcohol-related problems; most of the programs in the United States have dealt more or less exclusively with the treatment and rehabilitation of alcoholics. This difference does not seem to be related to the severity of the alcoholism problem. It is more likely related to differing national attitudes toward social legislation and government responsibility.

Etiology.   When we refer to "etiology" or "treatment," we are speaking of alcoholism per se as it presents itself in the industrialized, urbanized countries. Alcoholism is viewed by many in these countries as a disease or a symptom of a disease process, and the concepts of etiology and treatment relate to this view. To perceive the most extreme of alcohol problems, alcoholism, as a disease requires a kind of mental-health viewpoint not universal in the medical profession or welfare agencies, to say nothing of the lay public. It is a deviant behavior, and as such it is seen by many as immorality, weakness of will, perversity, or a bad habit.

Physiopathological theories.   Etiological theories have been primarily physiopathological or psychopathological. Among physiopathological theories, there are explanations in terms of allergy, brain pathology, biochemical substances, nutritional deficiencies, and glandular disorder. These theories have not gained more than limited acceptance; one of the major problems has been the difficulty of demonstrating that the particular physiopathological condition offered as the cause actually predated the onset of alcoholism. Generally, evidence has been based on the condition of patients with long-standing alcoholism.

The World Health Organization, Expert Committee on Alcohol (1954) placed alcohol "in a category of its own, intermediate between addiction-producing and habit-forming drugs." The questions of alcohol and physical dependence or craving, alcohol and withdrawal, and alcohol and tolerance changes (craving, withdrawal, and tolerance changes being the criteria of addiction) have not been solved and are still in debate.

Psychopathological theories.   Psychopathological theories were divided by Jellinek (1960) into those viewing alcoholism as the illness per se and those viewing it as a symptom of illness. Overriding this distinction is the common view that some personality deviation or difficulty in social–emotional development is a necessary condition of alcoholism. The psychoanalytic view emphasized "the oral and narcissistic premorbid personality," and various writers, theorizing from clinical data, have written of passivity, self-destruction, guilt, infantile traits, anxiety, and oral regression. There has been debate as to whether there is a single psychological predisposition, several such predispositions, or whether, indeed, any personality is vulnerable. Psychological test research has failed to turn up a single "alcoholic type." Psychological clinical research with emphasis on social as well as psychological data about subjects and on behavioral criteria for differentiating among alcoholics might yet make a contribution. There has been some speculation by psychologists about how alcoholism is learned, for instance, whether it is a result of the reinforcement involved in reduction of fear, conflict, and tension. A little has been written about the function alcohol serves in solving conscious and unconscious emotional needs. This literature has been reviewed (Zwerling & Rosenbaum 1959; Lisansky 1960).

There would probably be agreement by most who work with alcoholic patients in the United States that the alcoholic is an individual with low tolerance for frustration and stress, that he has not developed much by way of ego defenses other than denial, and that he has weak sexual drives, his affectional bind being largely with alcohol.

The weakness of psychopathological theories standing alone as an explanation of alcoholism is the difficulty of answering this question: If, as seems to be the case, there is no absolutely unique set of predispositional psychological circumstances, why do some people become alcoholic while others do not? There is, for example, no absence of neurotic problems or depression or guilt among the Jews, who maintain an extremely low rate of alcoholism. Psychopathology may be a necessary but not a sufficient causal explanation of alcoholism.

Sociopsychological theories.   The most promise lies in a sociopsychological theory of etiology. One needs to know not only about individual tensions and frustrations but also about the group's methods of coping and its attitudes toward and perception of alcohol. Jellinek (1960), for example, has offered a hypothesis relating a society's degree of acceptance of "large daily alcohol consumption" and the psychological vulnerability of individuals. It is a start. In the United States, different normative orientations toward drinking (Pittman & Snyder 1962) appear in different ethnic and religious subcultures, the Irish-American orientation producing higher rates of alcoholism than the Jewish-American. The question remains: Why do some Irish-Americans become alcoholics and not others? Perhaps the same psychological vulnerability that predisposes toward alcoholism in the Irish-American group predisposes toward other psychopathologies in the Jewish-American group.

In several European and South American viticultural countries, there is widespread belief in the "economic origin" of alcoholism. This may refer to economic deprivation of individuals or of the country, and the view that intoxication and alcoholism are related to want and economic misery may be valid for certain times and groups and parts of the world. The "economic origin" theory also refers to pressure from a national economy in which viticultural interests loom large, but the oversimplification of such an explanation is manifest in the differences in alcohol consumption and the rates of alcoholism in France and in Italy, both viticultural countries.

There is no all-embracing explanation of alcoholism in sight, but if one begins with a distinction between alcoholism and problems related to alcohol, if one is aware of the need for a classification of variants within the diagnosis of alcoholism, and if one is willing to include physiological, psychological, and social variables in an explanation of etiology, some ground is cleared. Probably no theory can ever account for all the problems men have with alcohol.

Treatment.   In spite of the lack of solutions to questions about alcoholism, there has been a great proliferation of state programs in Europe and the Americas since World War II. The emphasis has been primarily on the treatment and rehabilitation of alcoholics, with secondary emphasis on educational programs and, in a few places, some support for a research program. With pressure coming from a variety of sources—the government itself, welfare workers and physicians, temperance organizations, or those concerned with the relationships between alcohol and acting-out crimes—some attempt has been made to offer treatment.

Treatment programs fall into three major categories:

(1) *Residential* treatments place the alcoholic in (a) a hospital or a ward in a general or psychiatric hospital, (b) rehabilitation living quarters, like a halfway house, for chronic drunkenness offenders or, relatively new, day-or-night-care centers.

(2) Among *psychological and rehabilitative* treatments are (a) individual and group psychotherapy, frequently psychoanalytically oriented, (b) a special form of group help, Alcoholics Anonymous (a brotherhood of former alcoholics that has taken hold in many countries other than the United States, for instance, the "Ring i Ring" in Denmark), (c) groups of religious and quasi-religious organizations, including the churches and the Salvation Army, (d) the use of hypnosis and its variations, and (e) the use of conditioned-reflex treatment.

(3) *Drug* treatments include (a) ataractic and antidepressant drugs in current use as the sole treatment or as adjunct to other forms of treatment and (b) the administration of disulfiram (Antabuse), discovered by Dr. Erik Jacobsen of Denmark, very widely used in alcoholism treatment.

A particular treatment program is organized, hopefully, in terms of the needs of the patients it seeks to reach. Where the patients are physically ill or debilitated or homeless, more than outpatient service is needed. There are some countries, for example, Sweden and Norway, in which the supervision and rehabilitation of alcoholics is compulsory under law. In most countries treatment is more or less voluntarily undertaken.

Research and problems

Research activity has been most fruitful at those interdisciplinary centers designed for research in alcohol studies. These centers, which combine the efforts of physiologists, physicians, and biochemists, psychiatrists, psychologists, and social workers, sociologists, anthropologists, and economists, demonstrate the usefulness of a multidisciplined research approach to problems like drinking and alcoholism. The Alcohol and Drug Addiction Research Foundation of Ontario in Canada, the Finnish Foundation for Alcohol Studies, the Department of Alcohol Research of the Karolinska Institutet in Sweden, and the Rutgers (formerly Yale) Center of Alcohol Studies in New Jersey have been outstanding. These centers have produced research results over a wide range of problems: physiological and biochemical action of alcohol, the effects of alcohol on behavior and performance, alcohol usage in different cultural and social groups, attitudes, prevalence of alcoholism, the effectiveness of various drug treatments, drinking and driving, governmental policy and social controls—the gamut of alcohol-related problems.

There are many unanswered questions, but the most pressing problems in the psychological aspects of drinking and alcoholism, those which should have priority in research development, are: first, basic research on the effects of alcohol on mood, feelings, emotional response, and group behavior and, second, a meaningful classification of the alcoholisms, probably in behavioral terms objectively defined, which can be used internationally and which will, hopefully, lead to an understanding of the different etiologies and most effective treatments.

EDITH S. LISANSKY

[*Other relevant material may be found in* DRUGS; SMOKING.]

BIBLIOGRAPHY

ALCOHOLISM AND DRUG ADDICTION RESEARCH FOUNDATION OF ONTARIO 1962 *A Decade of Alcoholism Research: A Review of the Research Activities of the Alcoholism and Drug Addiction Research Foundation of Ontario, 1951–1961.* Univ. of Toronto Press.

BACON, MARGARET K. et al. 1965 A Cross-cultural Study of Drinking. *Quarterly Journal of Studies on Alcohol* Supplement No. 3.

CARPENTER, JOHN A. 1962 Effects of Alcohol on Some Psychological Processes: A Critical Review With Special Reference to Automobile Driving Skill. *Quarterly Journal of Studies on Alcohol* 23:274–314.

JELLINEK, ELVIN M. 1960 *The Disease Concept of Alcoholism.* New Haven: Hillhouse.

JELLINEK, ELVIN M.; and MCFARLAND, ROSS A. 1940 Analysis of Psychological Experiments on the Effects of Alcohol. *Quarterly Journal of Studies on Alcohol* 1:272–371.

KALANT, HAROLD 1962 Some Recent Physiological and Biochemical Investigations on Alcohol and Alcoholism: A Review. *Quarterly Journal of Studies on Alcohol* 23:52–93.

KELLER, MARK 1962 The Definition of Alcoholism and the Estimation of Its Prevalence. Pages 310–329 in David J. Pittman and Charles R. Snyder (editors), *Society, Culture, and Drinking Patterns.* New York: Wiley.

LISANSKY, EDITH S. 1960 The Etiology of Alcoholism: The Role of Psychological Predisposition. *Quarterly Journal of Studies on Alcohol* 21:314–343.

LISANSKY, EDITH S. 1964 The Psychological Effects of Alcohol. Pages 104–121 in Raymond G. McCarthy (editor), *Alcohol Education for Classroom and Community.* New York: McGraw-Hill.

MCCARTHY, RAYMOND G. (editor) 1959 *Drinking and Intoxication: Selected Readings in Social Attitudes and Controls.* New Haven: Yale Center of Alcohol Studies.

PITTMAN, DAVID J.; and SNYDER, CHARLES R. (editors) 1962 *Society, Culture, and Drinking Patterns.* New York: Wiley.

Selected Statistical Tables on the Consumption of Alcohol, 1850–1962, and on Alcoholism, 1930–1960. Prepared by Vera Efron and Mark Keller. 1963 New Brunswick, N.J.: Rutgers (Univ.) Center of Alcohol Studies.

TONGUE, ARCHER 1962 What the State Does About Alcohol and Alcoholism: An International Survey. Pages 594–600 in David J. Pittman and Charles R. Snyder (editors), *Society, Culture, and Drinking Patterns.* New York: Wiley.

VÄKI JUOMAKYSYMYKSEN TUTKIMUSSÄÄTIÖ (FINNISH FOUNDATION FOR ALCOHOL STUDIES) 1964 *Report on Activities, 1958–1963.* Helsinki: Maalaiskuntien Lilton Kirjapamno.

WASHBURNE, CHANDLER 1961 *Primitive Drinking: A Study of the Uses and Functions of Alcohol in Preliterate Societies.* New Haven: College & Universities Press.

WORLD HEALTH ORGANIZATION, EXPERT COMMITTEE ON ALCOHOL 1954 First Report. World Health Organization, *Technical Report Series* [1954], No. 84.

ZWERLING, ISRAEL; and ROSENBAUM, MILTON 1959 Alcoholic Addiction and Personality (Nonpsychotic Conditions). Volume 1, pages 623–644 in *American Handbook of Psychiatry.* Edited by Silvano Arieti. New York: Basic Books.

II
SOCIAL ASPECTS

A generation ago Donald Horton (1943) pioneered the first systematic cross-cultural study of drinking patterns in a report on the functions of alcohol in primitive societies. In this work he offered an eloquent plea for intensifying systematic research on drinking behavior and for moving toward the goal of incorporating empirical findings into a general theory of the social and psychological functions of alcohol. Since then, the systematic study of drinking behavior has proceeded at an accelerated pace in various branches of social science. Yet it cannot be said that the research of the past two decades has produced the general theory which Horton had in mind. At best it has yielded new facts, questions, and hypotheses suggestive of the directions that synthesis may eventually take. Here we shall first consider some of the more general findings of comparative studies of drinking in primitive societies and of sociological and related studies of drinking in complex societies. Attention will then be given to the nature of alcoholism; to its prevalence, patterning, and genesis; and to social responses to alcoholism.

Drinking in primitive societies

Alcohol and anxiety reduction. Central to Horton's research was the view that patterns of drinking behavior are determined by the interrelations of psychological and cultural variables and, more specifically, the proposition that the primary function of alcoholic beverages in all societies is the reduction of anxiety. Horton recognized other functions of alcohol as well as the seeming paradox that drinking, in net balance, may not be anxiety-reducing where social controls give rise to powerful and inhibiting counteranxieties. Yet, weaving the basic notion of anxiety reduction into a larger complex of psychocultural assumptions, he derived some important theorems, enabling indirect tests of his basic proposition on a sample of 56 culturally distinct societies thought to represent a cross section of primitive societies throughout the world (Horton 1943).

It was reasoned, for instance, that drinking tends generally to be accompanied by the release of aggressive and sexual impulses; all societies must to some extent inhibit expression of these impulses, and to reduce impulse-anxiety through alcohol is, in effect, to release the inhibition. Moreover, the strength of the drinking response, which Horton indexed by "the degree of insobriety," was thought to vary inversely with the occurrence of painful social experiences associated with the release of these impulses—experiences which, in turn, might vary from culture to culture. The ethnographic data reviewed by Horton corroborated the hypothesis that aggressive behavior tends to be associated with drinking, although a marked range of variation became apparent. To explain this variation, he proposed, with some supporting evidence, that societies characterized by high levels of inhibited aggression (indexed by the prevalence of sorcery) and coordinate systems of social control, as contrasted with superordinate systems capable of effectively punishing aggression, exhibit a maximum of drunken aggression. With regard to sexuality, the results were not, on the whole, what had been expected, although the suggestion of an inverse relation between premarital sexual restrictions and the degree of insobriety highlighted the possible role of counteranxiety in restraining drinking.

The most dramatic of Horton's findings, however, related to the deduction that the strength of the drinking response ("insobriety") varies directly with the general level of anxiety, which is an expression of the state of the total social structure and especially of the economy. As a clue to this, Horton referred to "subsistence anxiety" or insecurity, which he indexed by the type of economy (scaled from hunting through higher agriculture) and by specific subsistence hazards, including the hazards of acculturation. As Horton himself put it, the statistical findings supported the conclusion that "insobriety varies directly with anxiety as measured indirectly in terms of the anxiety-provoking conditions of subsistence insecurity and acculturation" (1943, p. 294).

Patterns of drinking behavior. Because his method of analysis treated variables in isolation from one another, Horton also offered a generalized qualitative sketch of three distinctive drinking patterns, found in different parts of the world, which are expressions of the similarity in the crucial psychocultural variables seen as systems. The first pattern is associated with societies having high sub-

sistence anxiety, strong belief in sorcery, weak sexual restraints, and coordinate social control. Here inebriety is extreme and, because of the vacuum in social power capable of restraining it, is almost always accompanied by extreme aggression. Cultural adaptation to this condition typically involves precautions of various kinds that are usually entrusted to the women, who drink less than the men. The second pattern occurs where the belief in sorcery is absent or relatively unimportant but where subsistence anxiety is also high and the anxiety motive too strong to be countered by sexual anxieties. Horton made no attempt to characterize the control of aggression in these societies but assumed from the unimportance of sorcery a minimum of motivation and thus little need for control. In any event, in the second pattern insobrietry is seen as invariably excessive but as accompanied by only moderate aggression in most cases. Finally, in the third pattern, fear and restraint in drinking are predominant, sometimes even extending to a complete taboo on alcoholic beverages. This sketch of patterns was not intended as exhaustive, but it offers the nucleus of a typology of patterns that have recurred with some frequency in primitive societies on a world-wide basis. Regrettably, little has been done to verify or modify this sketch, although it would seem to offer a fruitful point of departure for research.

Social organization. A note of challenge to Horton's basic proposition on anxiety reduction was sounded in a cross-cultural study by Field (1962), who used Horton's original sample of primitive societies but extended the investigation to include variables not previously considered. Noting the highly inferential nature of Horton's measures of anxiety, Field introduced new indexes of "fear," which were thought to be more direct reflections of levels of anxiety, and found no consistent correlation with "extent of drunkenness." In his reconsideration, the relation between subsistence insecurity and extent of drunkenness seemed more indicative of differences in economy, and hence in social organization, than of strikingly different levels of anxiety. Consequently, Field abandoned Horton's anxiety-reduction view in favor of exploring further the relations between social organization and drunkenness in primitive societies. Although, for reasons given elsewhere (Snyder 1964), we do not share Field's apparent dismissal of the role of anxiety in drinking, important relations between drunkenness and social organization are suggested by his research. For instance, he found that societies with strong corporate kin groups (organized on unilineal principles, exhibiting continuity in time, capable of concerted social action, and having elaborate collective ceremonial and symbolism) seemed markedly sober, whereas those structured bilaterally, with amorphous, fragmented, and loosely organized social relationships, appeared marked by extensive drunkenness. Generalizing his findings, Field proposed a distinction between "corporate" and "personal" types of social organization as the principal determinant of sobriety or drunkenness in primitive societies.

In a later large-scale research study of drinking in primitive society, Margaret Bacon and others (1965) offered an important commentary on parts of Horton's and Field's earlier work and another hypothesis to account for part of the cultural variation in drinking and drunkenness. Their research has advantages over previous work since it virtually doubled the societies sampled (to 110), increased the number of key variables, developed a factor analysis of dimensions of drinking, and employed independent ratings of variables and more sensitive measures of association. The findings corroborate Horton's linkage of type of economy and drunkenness, call into question certain other aspects of his work, and diminish the significance of the findings reported by Field. Yet, because the relevant variables are treated singly rather than in combination, it cannot be said that the configurations of psychocultural factors and drinking patterns suggested by Horton are without substance. Also, the pattern of correlations established by Field remains, by and large, in the predicted direction, suggesting some validity to his conclusions on drunkenness and social organization.

Socialization and dependency needs. The study by Bacon and others took as its starting point the repeated clinical observation that persons with drinking problems exhibit marked conflict over the expression of dependency needs and the fact that, while the helplessness of the infant is a universal aspect of the human situation and the socialization of dependence a universal cultural imperative, there are pronounced differences among societies in the attention paid to and indulgence of infants; in the cultural pressures toward achievement, self-reliance, and general independence in childhood; and in the extent to which cultural attitudes prescribe, tolerate, or enjoin the expression of dependency needs in adult life. These initial observations were expanded into the hypothesis that amounts and patterns of alcohol consumption have their roots partly in the degree of nurturing in infancy, the extent of demands for self-reliance and achievement in childhood, and the extent to which the

expression of dependent needs is permitted in adult life. It was assumed further that alcohol would be especially rewarding where dependency conflict is acute, because of its triple function of reducing anxiety and tension, permitting the satisfaction of dependency needs, and facilitating uncritical indulgence of unrealistic achievement fantasies. As a test of this view, various indexes bearing on the indulgence of dependency and pressures toward independent behavior were correlated with independently rated measures of alcohol consumption and frequency of drunkenness, and the statistical results support the hypothesis with consistency. Thus, the conclusion that "frequent drunkenness or high consumption, or both, tend to occur in cultures where needs for dependence are deprived or punished, both in childhood and in adult life, and where a high degree of responsible independent and achieving behavior are required" (M. Bacon et al. 1965, p. 43) seems warranted by the facts.

Ceremonial usage and solidarity. The extensive ceremonial usage of alcohol among primitive peoples has been explored by Klausner (1964) in a comparative study of 48 societies. He classified ceremonies in terms of their underlying meaning and characteristic form, according to the basic problems on which they center and the means employed, whether exorcism, scapegoating, sacrifice, prayer, or other. Like M. Bacon and her associates, Klausner found no regular bond between ceremonial usage and sobriety but even noted a tendency, at the cultural level, for usage in religious ceremonies to be associated with heavy drinking in nonreligious situations. The findings also pointed up a connection between heavy drinking in nonreligious situations and the use of alcohol in sacrifice (relative to other religious means), especially when religious ceremonies were oriented toward "moral integration and control of the human world." And regardless of the ceremonial orientation, alcohol was more likely to be used in conjunction with sacrifice than with any other religious means. To account for cultural cases in which there was virtually no drinking beyond the boundaries of ceremonial situations, Klausner suggested—in the light of the ancient symbolic equation of life-giving power, blood, and alcohol—that when blood is considered holy, its symbolic equivalent, alcohol, will not be drunk heavily in secular situations.

Sacrifice as a ceremonial means is, as Klausner has noted, closely linked to the establishment of social solidarity, enabling worshipers to transcend barriers when their solidarity is threatened by sin and guilt. Broadly, then, he sees the widespread use of alcohol in the sacrificial ritual of primitive peoples as suggesting a link between its use and coping with the problem of evil in man's relationship to man (and God) and proposes that this stamp of meaning most frequently extends to secular drinking situations. Indeed, it is suggested that the modern "cocktail party" exhibits (in its group nature, normative prescriptions, sentiments of betrayal for failure to participate, removal of social distinctions among participants) formal similarities to ancient sacrificial ritual and serves a "guilt-ridding" and integrating function equivalent to that formerly met through these rituals. The proliferation of cocktail parties and related social drinking in contemporary society may be thus viewed as an integrating response to structural breakdowns in society that have left individuals in socially and normatively ambiguous situations with consequent high anxiety.

Interrelationships of factors. Although the comparative studies of drinking in primitive societies touched upon here hardly display the richness of anthropological investigations of particular cultures, they highlight the importance of sociocultural factors in shaping drinking behavior and, without offering a total explanation, are indicative of crucial factors in variation. Moreover, there is reason to think that significant interrelationships exist among the variables brought to light by these studies. For instance, socialization maximizing conflict over dependency needs, as described by Margaret Bacon and her associates, may be functionally linked to the characterological requirements of the kinds of economies identified by Horton as associated with extensive drunkenness. Or, again, the amorphous social organization depicted by Field may intensify dependency conflict and engender acute problems in sustaining the social solidarity emphasized by Klausner. However, substantiation of these probable interrelationships awaits research that treats systematically the interaction of variables provisionally identified as crucially affecting patterns of drinking behavior.

Drinking and alcoholism in complex society

Bold attempts to portray the functions of drinking in complex society have been rare in the writings of social scientists. An exception is Selden Bacon's (1945) essay depicting large, highly specialized society as broadly "anomic"—characterized by rapid change, lack of normative integration, compartmentalized social controls, the paradox of heightened individualism and functional interdependence, intense competition, mobility, and impersonality. The social value of alcohol is presumably enhanced in this context not only because it

affords relief for tension-ridden individuals but also because it offers a needed mechanism of social integration, and the absence of generally held drinking norms is conducive to extremes of drinking. This is a setting that also seems likely to precipitate rapid deterioration and isolation of the person who is prone to excessive drinking and to lend drinking a greater individualistic significance than it is likely to have in better integrated societies.

Although such a portrait is admittedly speculative, there are a number of empirical investigations which have yielded findings consonant with it. Studies in the United States and Canada by E. M. Jellinek (1947) and John R. Seeley (1962), for example, have demonstrated a relationship, within broad cultural limits, between concentration of population, on the one hand, and alcohol consumption and alleged rates of alcoholism, on the other. The research of Richard Jessor and others (1963) has established connections between extreme drinking and peaks of "anomie"—both in the sense of dissociation of cultural goals and means (after Robert K. Merton) and in terms of simple breakdown in normative consensus. Excessive drinkers have also been found, in a scattering of studies, to exhibit signs of anomie and alienation. And alcoholics and incipient alcoholics, as studied by Ralph G. Connor (1962) and Peter Park (1962), evidenced difficulty in structuring their social roles in accordance with the role requirements of an impersonal complex society.

From a historical standpoint, there is evidence of the increasingly widespread use of alcohol in rapidly urbanizing societies such as the United States, although this does not necessarily imply an increase in per capita consumption among drinkers. The United States, like several European countries, experienced a strong temperance movement during the nineteenth and early twentieth centuries. Joseph Gusfield (1962) has suggested that the relative dominance of the abstinence orientation in the United States signified the ascendance in the status structure of a middle class whose values were congruent with the needs of small-scale capitalism and were generally hostile to the expression of emotional impulses. Abstinence was important as a criterion for acceptance in the middle class, and membership in the Woman's Christian Temperance Union was an important symbol of status in small-town and rural America in the nineteenth century. Yet, even prior to the repeal of prohibition in the United States in 1933 there had been a decay in the abstinence tradition that reflected deeper shifts in the styles of life and the organization of society. The cosmopolitanism of the new middle classes

(Stone 1962) apparently supports a relatively permissive drinking norm, and thus abstinence has undergone devaluation in its status connotations.

At the bottom of the modern urban social structure lies "Skid Row," which is increasingly an object of study and concern on the part of social scientists (for example, Jackson & Connor 1953; Pittman & Gordon 1958; Rubington 1958; Bogue 1963). In broad sociological perspective, Skid Row may be viewed as embracing varieties of the retreatist mode of adaptation to the anomie of modern society. For several decades its population appears to have been declining, becoming less geographically mobile, and undergoing other demographic changes, although it is still almost exclusively male in composition. A significant proportion of these men are permanent residents—living in the cheap hotels, flophouses, and missions indigenous to the area—and a majority of them are characterized by casual labor, poverty, and homelessness. Although it must be emphasized that only a small fraction of all alcoholics are inhabitants of Skid Row, the incidence of alcoholism and related drinking pathologies, and of other psychiatric and physical disease as well, is unquestionably high among habitués, even though comprehensive statistics are unavailable. While men on Skid Row are largely alienated from the mainstream of social life, popular imagery of complete social isolation needs to be corrected by awareness that Skid Row constitutes a subcultural system, binding men in a complex network of social relationships with distinctive norms and values. This has now been recognized among the better informed as having an important bearing on the outcome of ameliorative approaches to Skid Row—a matter in which the policies and programs of several European nations are in advance of those prevailing in the United States [see HOMELESSNESS].

Group rates of alcoholism. For the most part, recent sociological investigation of drinking in complex society has focused on diverse, fragmentary problems, such as the examination of drinking patterns and pathologies of ethnic groups, age and sex categories, and socioeconomic strata, or has aimed at delimiting the parameters and gross social correlates of drinking through surveys of drinking behavior and attitude among state, regional, or national populations (for example, Gadourek 1963; Lawrence & Maxwell 1962; Mulford & Miller 1960). Although the scope of this article does not allow summarization of the varied findings of these studies, some of them have, potentially, a broader relevance for understanding alcohol problems than

might be supposed at first glance. This is because marked differences in rates of alcoholism have unequivocally been established for various subgroups and categories of contemporary society. Although absolute rates of alcoholism are not known with certainty, it has been established, for instance, that there are sex differences in rates (and that sex ratios vary from one social milieu to another) and that there are marked differences in alcoholism rates among ethnic groups. These facts pose problems for social scientists analogous to the problem which Durkheim saw in varying group rates of suicide and likewise seem to call for explanation, in part at least, at the sociocultural level.

An illustration of the broader relevance of specific sociological studies to understanding alcohol problems may be seen in research on the Jews, whose traditional drinking patterns were studied in contrast to those of the Irish by Robert F. Bales (1944) and in the aspect of change by Charles R. Snyder (1958). The case is instructive because alcoholism is rare among Jews, although virtually everyone in the group is exposed to alcohol, and there is no absence of psychic tensions of the sort that may play a role in alcoholism. Moreover, there is sufficient heterogeneity of physical type to make biological immunity implausible. Careful study of the drinking patterns, cultural settings, and incidence of psychic disorders led Bales to the conclusion that the distinctive normative orientation to drinking in traditional Jewish culture accounted for much of the difference in rates of alcoholism between the Jews and groups like the Irish. More generally, it led to the formulation that group rates of alcoholism may be thought of as resultants of the interaction of three major sets of factors: dynamic factors, or the group incidence of acute psychic tensions or needs for adjustment sufficient to provide the driving force in drinking pathologies; alternative factors, or culturally defined possibilities of adopting behavior patterns that are functional equivalents of excessive drinking from the standpoint of relieving acute psychic tensions; and orienting factors, or the kinds of normative attitudes toward drinking itself carried in the cultures of different groups. Although this scheme poses methodological difficulties in application, it offers, heuristically, a more satisfactory provisional framework for analyzing the etiology of alcoholism than do one-sided schemes which neglect either the psychological or the sociocultural dimension.

Predominant type of alcoholism. The important problem of the definition of alcoholism will not be treated in this article; here we will simply note that alcoholism should be distinguished from drinking and even from excessive drinking, and that this matter of definition is very complex.

The extent of alcoholism in primitive societies remains largely unknown. In complex societies, such as the United States and several countries of northern Europe, what Jellinek (1960, p. 37) has referred to as "gamma" alcoholism is the predominant type, "in which (1) acquired increased tissue tolerance to alcohol, (2) adaptive cell metabolism . . . (3) withdrawal symptoms and 'cravings' . . . and (4) loss of control are involved." Gamma alcoholism is patterned in terms of a definite progression of symptoms (phases), moving from psychological to apparent physical dependence and entailing marked behavioral changes. Jellinek's research on the drinking of male alcohol addicts found that the symptoms associated with gamma alcoholism could be sequentially arranged into four phases: the *prealcoholic symptomatic phase*, associated with the relief of personal tension in drinking situations; the *prodromal phase*, characterized by, among other symptoms, the appearance of repeated blackouts; the *crucial phase*, identified by the drinker's loss of control; and the *chronic phase*, marked by prolonged bouts of intoxication. This view of the phasic development of gamma alcoholism has received some support in other research (Trice & Wahl 1958; Park 1962) and seems to be in accord with typical drinking histories of members of Alcoholics Anonymous. It has certainly colored the thinking of much social science research bearing upon alcoholism and has led not only to the construction of indexes of incipient alcoholism, enabling study of the illness at its inception, but also to the possibility of therapeutic intervention before alcoholism has run its course.

Personality factors.   The sociological and related literature on alcoholism runs the gamut of assumptions regarding the relevance of personality factors to the etiology of alcoholism and about their variable or unitary nature, aside from speculation as to the specific factors involved. Moreover, critical reviews by sociologists such as Edwin H. Sutherland and others (1950) and Leonard Syme (1957), who focused on the methodological inadequacies of a host of investigations purporting to identify personality factors in alcoholism, serve to reinforce an attitude of caution in this regard. Nevertheless, recent longitudinal and quasi-longitudinal research that avoids the pitfall of confusing possible consequences of alcoholism with conditions at or prior to its inception (for example, Park 1962; McCord & McCord 1962; Robins et al. 1962) tends, in our

judgment, to support the view that disturbances in socialization experience and personality prior to alcoholism are the rule rather than the exception (at least in so-called "Anglo-Saxon" cultures). Taken together with a growing body of retrospective analyses of life histories of alcoholics, these studies strengthen the impression that, without viewing alcoholism as the invariable outcome of a single personality type, certain types of personality under certain environmental stresses are particularly prone to alcoholism as a means of adjustment. Howard Jones's (1963) diagnostic grouping of alcoholics into types characterized by acute adjustment needs centering on maternal dependence, ego need, social inadequacy, social dependence, escapism, latent homosexuality, and Oedipal fixation is suggestive in this connection. Rather typically, current studies of alcoholism are, like Jones's, replete with allusions to socialization experiences and personality dynamics in relation to the root problems of early emotional deprivation and dependency conflict.

Prevalence of alcoholism.   While there are a variety of ways of estimating the extent of alcoholism in small, circumscribed populations (for example, field studies, analyses of hospital admissions, arrest records), the Jellinek Estimation Formula has been widely used in estimating the prevalence of alcoholism in large populations. This formula is $A = (PD/K)R$, where A signifies all alcoholics, D reported deaths from cirrhosis of the liver in a given year, P an assumed constant percentage of such deaths attributable to alcoholism (different for men and women), K a constant representing the percentage of all alcoholics-with-complications who die of cirrhosis, and R a presumed ratio of all alcoholics to alcoholics-with-complications in the given time and place. This formula has been criticized (Seeley 1959; Brenner 1959), but Mark Keller (1962) has maintained that the underlying theory of the formula is sound. From statistical data on alcohol consumption and numbers of drinkers, Keller has contended that current alcoholic rate estimates have approximate validity. Although the available data are insufficient to permit exact international comparisons, alcoholism rates for a dozen countries estimated by means of the Jellinek formula for various years in the decade following World War II show the following rank order (from higher to lower): France, United States, Chile, Sweden, Switzerland, Denmark, Canada, Norway, Finland, Australia, England and Wales, Italy (Alcoholism Research Foundation of Ontario 1958). Keller (1962) has concluded that there were approximately 4,470,000 alcoholics in the United States in 1960. This figure is suggestive of the magnitude of the alcoholism problem, but the costs of alcoholism in all its ramifications from the standpoint of human values are not amenable to precise calculation, although they are certainly enormous.

Social responses to alcoholism. Legislation in the Netherlands and Norway aimed at treating alcoholism dates back to the turn of the century (for accounts of the development of national programs on alcoholism and alcohol problems in Europe, see Tongue 1962; Pittman & Tongue 1963). However, it was not until the 1930s in the United States that a large-scale movement with a treatment orientation toward alcoholism first took shape, with the appearance of Alcoholics Anonymous in 1934 and the establishment of an American Research Council on Alcoholism four years later. In 1940 the first issue of the *Quarterly Journal of Studies on Alcohol*, a scientific journal dealing with such problems as the physiological, psychosocial, and cultural ramifications of alcohol and alcohol usage, was published at Yale University's Laboratory of Applied Physiology by the Journal of Studies on Alcohol, Inc. In 1943 the Yale Summer School of Alcohol Studies was established to train persons interested in this field, and in 1945 the National Council on Alcoholism was organized to disseminate information to the general public. This new approach focused on removing the stigma from alcoholism and on making it the object of scientific investigation. In the past the state and local governments had conceived of their roles as controlling the sale of alcohol and punishing the alcoholic offender, whereas the new emphasis predicated alcoholism as a problem of public health. In accordance with this outlook, Oregon, in 1943, became the first state to institute a public health program aimed at alcoholism. By 1965, 42 American states, the District of Columbia, and seven Canadian provinces had official agencies on alcoholism.

It would be a mistake, however, to imply that the public health approach to alcoholism was widespread and always accepted with little or no resistance. Although the repeal of prohibition in 1933 dealt a serious blow to the older "moralistic" view of alcoholism, attitudes which had predominated for generations were not easily discarded. Resistance to the treatment of the alcoholic is indicated by the slow acceptance by many professional health and social welfare personnel of the proposition that alcoholism is a disease requiring their special knowledge and skills. It was not until 1956 that the American Medical Association expressed the opinion that alcoholism should come under the scope of medical practice, that hospitals should make provisions for the care of alcoholics, and that medical interns should be trained in the treatment of alcoholics. In 1957 the association finally gave its official approval to the statement that alcoholism is a disease, and the American Hospital Association also urged that each case of alcoholism be examined individually to determine whether or not the condition was amenable to medical treatment. This represents a notable change from the situation prevailing a generation ago.

CHARLES R. SNYDER AND DAVID J. PITTMAN

[*See also* ANXIETY; DRUGS.]

BIBLIOGRAPHY

A representative bibliography, indicating the growing number of anthropological studies with a special focus on drinking patterns, may be found in Heath 1958, and an overview of systematic work, particularly in sociology, may be gained from Pittman & Snyder 1962.

ALCOHOLISM RESEARCH FOUNDATION OF ONTARIO 1958 *Statistics of Alcohol Use and Alcohol in Canada: 1871–1956.* Compiled by Robert E. Popham and Wolfgang Schmidt. Univ. of Toronto Press.

BACON, MARGARET K. et al. 1965 A Cross-cultural Study of Drinking. *Quarterly Journal of Studies on Alcohol* Supplement no. 3.

BACON, SELDEN D. 1945 Alcohol and Complex Society. Pages 179–200 in Yale University, Laboratory of Applied Psychology, School of Alcohol Studies, *Alcohol, Science and Society.* New Haven: Quarterly Journal of Studies on Alcohol.

BALES, ROBERT F. 1944 The "Fixation Factor" in Alcohol Addiction: An Hypothesis Derived From a Comparative Study of Irish and Jewish Social Norms. Ph.D. dissertation, Harvard Univ.

BOGUE, DONALD J. 1963 *Skid Row in American Cities.* Univ. of Chicago, Community and Family Study Center.

BRENNER, BERTHOLD 1959 Estimating the Prevalence of Alcoholism: Toward a Modification of the Jellinek Formula. *Quarterly Journal of Studies on Alcohol* 20: 255–260.

CONNOR, RALPH G. 1962 The Self-concepts of Alcoholics. Pages 455–467 in David J. Pittman and Charles R. Snyder (editors), *Society, Culture, and Drinking Patterns.* New York and London: Wiley.

FIELD, PETER B. 1962 A New Cross-cultural Study of Drunkenness. Pages 48–74 in David J. Pittman and Charles R. Snyder (editors), *Society, Culture, and Drinking Patterns.* New York and London: Wiley.

GADOUREK, IVAN 1963 *Riskante gewoonten en zorg voor eigen welzijn* (Hazardous Habits and Human Wellbeing). Groningen (Netherlands): Wolters. → Contains a summary in English.

GUSFIELD, JOSEPH R. 1962 Status Conflicts and the Changing Ideologies of the American Temperance Movement. Pages 101–120 in David J. Pittman and Charles R. Snyder (editors), *Society, Culture, and Drinking Patterns.* New York and London: Wiley.

HEATH, DWIGHT B. 1958 Drinking Patterns of the Bolivian Camba. *Quarterly Journal of Studies on Alcohol* 19:491–508.

HORTON, DONALD 1943 The Functions of Alcohol in Primitive Societies: A Cross-cultural Study. *Quarterly Journal of Studies on Alcohol* 4:199–320.

JACKSON, JOAN K.; and CONNOR, RALPH 1953 The Skid Road Alcoholic. *Quarterly Journal of Studies on Alcohol* 14:468–486.

JELLINEK, ELVIN M. 1947 Recent Trends in Alcoholism and in Alcohol Consumption. *Quarterly Journal of Studies on Alcohol* 8:1–42.

JELLINEK, ELVIN M. 1960 *The Disease Concept of Alcoholism.* New Haven: Hillhouse Press.

JESSOR, RICHARD et al. 1963 Tri-ethnic Research Project. Research Report No. 25. Unpublished manuscript, Univ. of Colorado.

JONES, HOWARD 1963 *Alcohol Addiction: A Psycho–Social Approach to Abnormal Drinking.* London: Tavistock.

KELLER, MARK 1962 The Definition of Alcoholism and the Estimation of Its Prevalence. Pages 310–329 in David J. Pittman and Charles R. Snyder (editors), *Society, Culture, and Drinking Patterns.* New York and London: Wiley.

KLAUSNER, SAMUEL Z. 1964 Sacred and Profane Meanings of Blood and Alcohol. *Journal of Social Psychology* 64:27–43.

LAWRENCE, JOSEPH J.; and MAXWELL, MILTON A. 1962 Drinking and Socio-economic Status. Pages 141–145 in David J. Pittman and Charles R. Snyder (editors), *Society, Culture, and Drinking Patterns.* New York and London: Wiley.

MCCORD, WILLIAM; and MCCORD, JOAN 1962 A Longitudinal Study of the Personality of Alcoholics. Pages 413–430 in David J. Pittman and Charles R. Snyder (editors), *Society, Culture, and Drinking Patterns.* New York and London: Wiley.

MULFORD, HAROLD A.; and MILLER, DONALD E. 1960 Drinking in Iowa. II: The Extent of Drinking and Selected Sociocultural Categories. *Quarterly Journal of Studies on Alcohol* 21:26–39.

PARK, PETER 1962 Problem Drinking and Role Deviation: A Study in Incipient Alcoholism. Pages 431–454 in David J. Pittman and Charles R. Snyder (editors), *Society, Culture, and Drinking Patterns.* New York and London: Wiley.

PITTMAN, DAVID J.; and GORDON, C. WAYNE 1958 *Revolving Door: A Study of the Chronic Police Case Inebriate.* Glencoe, Ill.: Free Press.

PITTMAN, DAVID J.; and SNYDER, CHARLES R. (editors) 1962 *Society, Culture, and Drinking Patterns.* New York and London: Wiley.

PITTMAN, DAVID J.; and TONGUE, ARCHER (editors) 1963 *Handbook of Organizations for Research on Alcohol and Alcoholism Problems.* Lausanne (Switzerland): International Bureau Against Alcoholism.

ROBINS, LEE N.; BATES, WILLIAM M.; and O'NEAL, PATRICIA 1962 Adult Drinking Patterns of Former Problem Children. Pages 395–412 in David J. Pittman and Charles R. Snyder (editors), *Society, Culture, and Drinking Patterns.* New York and London: Wiley.

RUBINGTON, EARL 1958 The Chronic Drunkenness Offender. American Academy of Political and Social Sciences, *Annals* 315:65–72.

SEELEY, JOHN R. 1959 Estimating the Prevalence of Alcoholism: A Critical Analysis of the Jellinek Formula. *Quarterly Journal of Studies on Alcohol* 20: 245–254.

SEELEY, JOHN R. 1962 The Ecology of Alcoholism: A Beginning. Pages 330–344 in David J. Pittman and

Charles R. Snyder (editors), *Society, Culture, and Drinking Patterns.* New York and London: Wiley.

SNYDER, CHARLES R. 1958 *Alcohol and the Jews.* Glencoe, Ill.: Free Press.

SNYDER, CHARLES R. 1964 Inebriety, Alcoholism, and Anomie. Pages 189–212 in Marshall E. Clinard (editor), *Anomie and Deviant Behavior: A Discussion and Critique.* New York: Free Press.

STONE, GREGORY P. 1962 Drinking Styles and Status Arrangements. Pages 121–140 in David J. Pittman and Charles R. Snyder (editors), *Society, Culture, and Drinking Patterns.* New York and London: Wiley.

SUTHERLAND, EDWIN H.; SHROEDER, H. G.; and TORDELLA, C. L. 1950 Personality Traits and the Alcoholic: A Critique of Existing Studies. *Quarterly Journal of Studies on Alcohol* 11:547–561.

SYME, LEONARD 1957 Personality Characteristics and the Alcoholic: A Critique of Current Studies. *Quarterly Journal of Studies on Alcohol* 18:288–302.

TONGUE, ARCHER 1962 What the State Does About Alcohol and Alcoholism: An International Survey. Pages 594–600 in David J. Pittman and Charles R. Snyder (editors), *Society, Culture, and Drinking Patterns.* New York and London: Wiley.

TRICE, HARRISON M.; and WAHL, J. RICHARD 1958 A Rank Order Analysis of the Symptoms of Alcoholism. *Quarterly Journal of Studies on Alcohol* 19:636–648.

DRIVES

I. PHYSIOLOGICAL DRIVES · · · · · · *Paul Thomas Young*
II. ACQUIRED DRIVES · · · · · · · · · · *Judson S. Brown*

I
PHYSIOLOGICAL DRIVES

Physiological drives are regarded as persisting, organic motivations: conditions that arouse, sustain, and regulate human and animal behavior. Insofar as drives are based upon metabolic conditions they are common to all men in all societies and to many animals. Examples of drives originating in metabolic conditions are: general hunger, specific food appetites, thirst, air hunger, the urges to urinate and defecate, the urge to maintain a constant internal temperature and to sleep, to rest when fatigued, to be active when rested.

Carl J. Warden defined "drive" empirically as persisting goal-oriented behavior, and he measured the strength of hunger, thirst, sex, maternal, and exploratory drives by observing the frequency with which a rat approached and crossed a charged grille to reach an incentive object: food, water, mate, etc. Most psychologists, however, regard drive as an explanatory concept. Behavior is *driven* by certain internal conditions called *drives;* drive is a hypothetical construct employed to explain activity.

Physiological drives must be distinguished from external determinants, including the whole gamut of social goals, interests, values, attitudes, and personality traits. When, for example, Buddhist monks in Vietnam committed suicide by burning, their motivation was derived from their complex social situation and not from physiological drives.

Drive versus drives.   The term "drive" was introduced to American psychology by Robert S. Woodworth in 1918. He derived the term from mechanics rather than biology. A machine, he claimed, is a mechanism that can accomplish work only if there are energy transformations within its parts. The *drive* of a machine is the physical energy that makes it go.

Following Woodworth, other psychologists (Fred A. Moss, John F. Dashiell, Edward C. Tolman, Curt P. Richter, Carl J. Warden, Calvin P. Stone, and others) adopted the term but began experimenting with drives (in the plural), such as the hunger, thirst, and sex drives. These drives were not distinguished as forms of physical energy (mechanical, thermal, electrical, chemical, photic) but, rather, in terms of the external and bodily conditions that underlie and regulate behavior.

Energizing and regulating functions.   Some psychologists restrict the concept of drive to the energetic aspect of motivation. Judson S. Brown (1961) clearly distinguished drive as an energizing function from the functions of directing and regulating behavior. Regulation is thought to be accomplished by associative bonds, habit systems, innate structures. Drive stimuli originate in tissue conditions and as stimuli they have a common energizing function. Brown wrote of different sources of drive rather than of different drives. Again, Elizabeth Duffy distinguished between the activating and directing aspects of motivation. She identified drive with activation and defined it in terms of energy potentially available for behavior (1962, p. 17).

The distinction between energizing and regulating functions is of prime importance in any definition of the drive concept. But since energy transformations always occur within bodily mechanisms and since these mechanisms regulate the pattern and direction of activity, it is difficult, if not impossible, to consider energizing apart from bodily structures.

The stimulation theory of drive.   In the writings of Clark L. Hull, drive (D) is a nonspecific energizing factor that can raise the excitatory potential of various habits (1943). In addition to D, Hull postulated various specific drive stimuli (symbolized by S_d or D_s) arising from tissue needs. S_d strengthens only those responses that are relevant to satisfying a specific need, but D strengthens all responses that happen to be aroused when D is present [see HULL].

Some behavior theorists, for example, Neal

Miller and Kenneth W. Spence, have staunchly supported Hull's postulate of two drive factors—general drive and specific drives—but others have questioned the need for a nonspecific drive factor. Thus, Edwin R. Guthrie argued that the concept of stimulus is fully adequate to account for all drives. A persisting stimulus from a tense bladder, he wrote, is adequately described as a stimulus and nothing is gained by designating it a drive. William K. Estes (1958) wrote that drive stimuli are similar to all other stimuli, and he suggested that selective behavior can be explained without the benefit of a nonspecific, energizing drive factor. Robert C. Bolles (1958), after reviewing the positions taken by behavior theorists, questioned the utility of the drive concept. Use of the drive concept, he wrote, reflects an ignorance of the stimulus; if more were known about the stimuli associated with each specific drive, one could dispense with a general nonspecific drive factor [see GUTHRIE].

Despite these views, there is sound physiological evidence, as Donald O. Hebb has pointed out (1955), for the existence of a general, nonspecific factor of arousal or activation. The evidence will be considered below [see STIMULATION DRIVES].

Chemical motivation.   Every theory of drive must take account of persisting chemical sensitizers, excitants, inhibitors, and tranquilizers that act directly upon neural centers. A single example of hormonal control will illustrate the nature of chemical motivation:

In a series of studies upon male sexual behavior, Frank A. Beach demonstrated a positive relation between the rat's sexual reaction to an estrous female and his speed of locomotion to the goal box in which she is held. The active males, after demonstrating normal sexual activity, were castrated. Following the operation there was a gradual loss of sexual ability, shown by decrease in the intensity, completeness, and frequency of mating responses and by a steady lengthening of the time required to traverse a runway to reach a mate. Copulatory responses were finally abolished, and many males remained in the starting box, failing to enter the runway. At this stage of the experiment the inactive males were given daily injections of testosterone propionate. While injections continued there was an increase in sexual reactions to the estrous female and a steady decrease in the time required to reach the goal box. The experiment (Beach 1956, p. 12) clearly demonstrated the importance of hormonal factors in maintaining sexual responsiveness.

Homeostatic needs and drives.   Claude Bernard pointed out that the cells of the body can survive only if the fluid matrix within which they exist remains relatively stable in its physical and chemical constitution. Following Bernard, Walter B. Cannon coined the term "homeostasis" to designate the steady physical state essential to life. Within the blood, for example, there are homeostases of oxygen content, water content, temperature, acidity, glucose, fat, proteins, and calcium, sodium, and other minerals.

The principle of homeostasis provides an important basis for defining objectively the metabolic needs of men and animals. To maintain homeostasis an organism *needs* (requires) certain nutritive substances: oxygen, water, proteins, fat, carbohydrate, minerals, and vitamins. Also, an organism *needs* to maintain a constant internal temperature despite wide variations in external temperature [*see* HOMEOSTASIS].

Some psychologists have equated needs and drives, but the concepts are distinct. Homeostatic needs may affect growth, reproduction, metabolism, and health with little or no influence upon behavior.

Curt P. Richter extended the homeostatic doctrine by showing ways in which behavior aids the organism in maintaining homeostasis (1943). When homeostasis is disturbed, he pointed out, behavior compensates to restore a steady state. To illustrate: If the adrenal glands of rats are surgically removed, the adrenalectomized animals die in 10 to 15 days as a result of loss of sodium chloride through the urine. But if the operated rats are given free access to a 3 per cent sodium chloride solution, they ingest several times the normal amount of salty fluid and survive indefinitely in seemingly good health. The increased appetite for salt serves to maintain homeostasis and to preserve life. Richter (1943) believed that the effort to maintain homeostasis is one of the most universal and powerful of all behavioral urges, or drives, in animals and human beings.

Other psychologists have extended the homeostatic doctrine far beyond its physiological limits. Attempts have been made to extend the doctrine to the maintenance of stability within the social order, to the perceptual constancies of the physical and social worlds, to constancies in personality, and to psychophysical judgments. It seems preferable, however, to hold to the original physiological meaning of homeostasis and to use some other concept, for example, adjustment, in considering the dynamic relations between an organism and its environment. [*See* PERCEPTION, *article on* PERCEPTUAL CONSTANCY.]

The homeostatic doctrine has met with a good many criticisms. For example, in a review of the literature on thirst, Lawrence I. O'Kelly (1963) pointed out that the homeostatic doctrine does not greatly help a physiologist who is dealing with the specific processes that regulate body water. It is difficult to identify thirst with any one specific bodily event. What is needed is patient collection of empirical data rather than speculation about a homeostatic thirst drive.

Motivation and functional capacity. Robert S. Woodworth (1958) argued that when an active organism is dealing with its environment, no extrinsic drive is required to explain activity. The organism observes, explores, manipulates, and studies its environmental surroundings with intrinsic motivation.

Behavior manifests the innate capacities of the creature. The bird is hatched with an innate capacity to fly. From this fact one can safely predict that the bird will fly. The young bird, in fact, makes considerable progress in mastering its mode of locomotion before using this skill in hunting food. The creature exercises its capacity to fly first for its own sake and later in the service of food seeking. Again, the chimpanzee has considerable inclination to climb trees and to brachiate—a performance for which he has considerable talent thanks to his bodily proportions and lever systems, bones, tendons, and muscular and nervous structures.

Henry W. Nissen (1954), Robert W. White (1959), Daniel E. Berlyne (1960), and others argued that human sense organs, muscles, and brain have the functional capacity to observe, explore, manipulate, test, reflect, think. These innate structures require activity for health and growth. No extrinsic motivation is needed to explain the functioning of an active human brain. Man, in fact, seeks stimulation. He rides a roller coaster, engages in dangerous sports, plays games that involve risk and suspense, works endlessly to solve puzzles. The motivation is *neurogenic*, and the patterns of behavior are regulated according to a structure–function principle.

White emphasized the human tendency to acquire competence in dealing with the environment. Underlying this tendency is a form of motivation he labeled effectance. Effectance motivation is selective, directed, persistent. Its energies are neurogenic, being the energies of the living, active cells that make up the nervous system.

Similar views have been expressed by Harry F. Harlow, who demonstrated that manipulative and exploratory behavior does not depend on homeostatic drives, and by Gordon W. Allport in his doctrine of the functional autonomy of motives [*see* PERSONALITY: CONTEMPORARY VIEWPOINTS].

Neurogenic drive. Under the influence of classical associationism and the stimulus–response formula an organism was regarded as a passive structure aroused to action by hunger, thirst, pain, sexual stimulation, and other primary drives and, secondarily, by acquired drives associated with these primary motivations. This view has proved to be inadequate because the fact that the nerve cell is not inert has become increasingly evident; the nerve cell does not have to be excited from the outside in order to discharge. The cells of the brain are spontaneously active even during deep sleep. It is not necessary to postulate an extrinsic stimulus or drive to activate them.

In his outstanding book *The Organization of Behavior* (1949), Hebb did not use the term "drive." He believed that the main problem of motivational psychology was to account for the *direction* of behavior and that this could be done in terms of his physiological theories. He changed his opinion, however, when it became clear that there exists an anatomical and physiological basis for a nonspecific drive (1955). The evidence for neurogenic drive rests upon several lines of investigation, particularly upon work in the field of electroencephalography, as well as studies of the reticular activating system.

Brain waves and levels of activation.   Donald B. Lindsley (1957) distinguished different levels of activation, or arousal, in terms of brain wave characteristics. When the subject is calm his brain waves reveal a smooth, rhythmic pattern of about ten oscillations per second, known as the alpha rhythm. When the subject is excited, as by the bang of a gun or by pain or anxiety, the alpha rhythm is inhibited and instead there are fast waves of low amplitude. This change of rhythm is known as the activation pattern.

Figure 1 — Continuum showing levels of activation
Source: Based on Lindsley 1957.

Different levels of activation are revealed in behavior and in awareness, as well as in the pattern of brain waves. Figure 1 represents some of these levels of activation [*see* NERVOUS SYSTEM].

The reticular activating system.   The reticular activating system is a network of fibers and synapses located at the levels of the medulla, hypothalamus, and subthalamus. It consists of two main parts: (1) the brain stem reticular formation, a network with many synapses and neural subsystems; and (2) a system of fibers that project diffusely from the thalamic nuclei to many regions of the cerebral cortex.

It is known that every sensory stimulation has two kinds of effects upon the cerebral cortex: impulses are discharged through thalamic nuclei directly to the cortical areas where they provide sensory information; and impulses are sent through collaterals into the reticular activating system and are conducted over diffuse multisynaptic pathways to all parts of the cortex—to both sensory and nonsensory areas—where they have a nonspecific activating effect.

The reticular activating system is not limited to one-way conduction—from sensory nerves to cortex. The system is excited by cerebral action, which in turn produces motor effects over efferent pathways. It is likely that when one anticipates misfortune, as in anxiety, the cerebral cortex excites the reticulum. The motor effects are general, such as increasing muscle tonus in widespread regions.

The feedback from all reactions has a dual effect. When, for example, the organism maintains a set of attention or when effort is expended, as in driving an automobile against a blinding light, there is a sensory feedback from the proprioceptors. This feedback conveys sensory information and also has a nonspecific activating influence.

Cue function and arousal function.   Hebb distinguished between cue function and arousal, or vigilance, function. Cue function exists when sensory stimulation transmits information directly and efficiently to the cerebral cortex over the great sensory projection systems: from sensory nerve to sensory tract, thence to the corresponding sensory nucleus of the thalamus, and thence directly to one of the projection areas of the cortex. Arousal function is different. Collaterals from sensory nerves feed excitations into the reticular activating system. These excitations trickle through a tangled thicket of fibers and synapses. There is mixing of messages, and the scrambled messages are delivered indiscriminately to wide areas of the cortex. In fact, the excitations are no longer messages. Instead of conveying information they serve to tone up the cortex with supporting excitations that are necessary if the messages are to have their effect. Without the arousal system, the sensory impulses over the direct and quick routes would reach the sensory cortex and go no further; the rest of the cortex would be unaffected; learned associations would be unavailable for behavior [*see* ATTENTION].

The arousal function implies a nonspecific, neurogenic drive. This drive is an energizer, not a guide; an activator, not a steering mechanism. Hebb (1955) claimed that direction and regulation are dependent upon cue function, but cue function is useless and impotent apart from arousal, or drive.

This view is important because it points to a source of motivation underlying observant, manipulative, exploratory, playful, and other forms of behavior. One does not have to look outside the nervous system for sources of physiological drive.

Affective arousals. A complete theory of physiological drives must take account of affective arousals associated with stimulation, frustration, play, rewards bestowed, and punishments inflicted.

Traditionally, the affective processes have been regarded as conscious experiences of pleasantness and unpleasantness that are present in simple feelings, emotions, moods, and sentiments. The affective processes vary in sign (positive or negative), intensity, and temporal course. Sign and intensity can be represented on a bipolar continuum as in Figure 2.

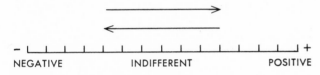

Figure 2 — The hedonic continuum

Source: Young 1961, p. 153.

The hedonic continuum extends from the extreme of negative affectivity (distress) to the extreme of positive affectivity (delight), with indifferent processes at the midpoint. Different intensities of affective arousal are represented by arbitrary units marked off upon the continuum. Arrows indicate two important directions of hedonic change: toward the positive pole and toward the negative pole.

Young and others have shown that affective processes can be studied objectively and quantitatively with need-free rats. As a single example, consider a study by Young and Madsen (1963). Using a brief-exposure preference technique, they obtained data for plotting a curve that showed the hedonic equivalence of simple solutions of sucrose and saccharin. Using compound solutions, they plotted isohedonic contour lines on a surface defined by the concentrations of sucrose and saccharin. The contour lines showed the hedonic equivalence of simple sucrose standards and compound sucrose–saccharin solutions.

The affective arousals are in the nervous system. They energize behavioral patterns that lead to approach and withdrawal and that influence choice and the development of preferences. The physiology of affective processes is under extensive investigation.

James Olds (1955) demonstrated that if bipolar needle electrodes are implanted within the limbic system of a rat's brain, electrical stimulation of subcortical points may be either rewarding or punishing. When stimulated in the septal area, the rats acted as if they liked the internal excitation. For example, if a hungry rat was stimulated in the septal area while he approached food, he would stop at the place where internal stimulation occurred rather than proceed to the food. Again, an apparatus was arranged so that pressing a bar stimulated points within the septal area. Rats repeatedly pressed the bar, but bar pressing ceased promptly when the circuit was broken and there was no longer septal stimulation. The stimulation of other points was punishing. For example, if the needle electrode was implanted in the medial lemniscus, a rat acted as if stimulation hurt him. In the absence of internal stimulation a rat pressed the bar in about 2 to 10 per cent of the total time during a two-hour test, but with self-stimulation in the medial lemniscus the bar-pressing score dropped to zero. The rat avoided the lever. Self-stimulation at other subcortical points was neutral—neither rewarding nor punishing.

Similar results have been obtained by other workers and with cats, monkeys, and other subjects. There can be no doubt that affective arousals have an objective existence within subcortical centers [*see* NERVOUS SYSTEM, *article on* BRAIN STIMULATION].

Physiological drives and reinforcement. Major research problems center on the relation between physiological drives and learning. It should be clear from this discussion that a psychologist must consider the nature of drive when exploring problems of learning and development.

From the point of view of stimulation theory the major emphasis has been upon conditioning. Thus, John F. Dashiell hypothesized that when an external stimulus frequently occurs with a drive stimulus, the external stimulus becomes a substitute for the drive stimulus and tends to elicit the same responses. Again, Edward E. Anderson argued that in the early stages of learning, behavior is controlled by internal drives, but as learning progresses there is increasing environmental control of behavior—a transition that he called the *externalization* of drive.

From the point of view of homeostatic need the

emphasis has been upon need and drive reduction. Thus, Clark L. Hull argued that responses are reinforced when they lead to drive reduction and the meeting of a need; and secondary drive is acquired through association with primary drive reduction.

The neurogenic theory of drive implies that drive reduction is not necessary to learning. And the affective arousal theory implies that behavioral patterns are organized in a way that leads to hedonic change toward the positive pole of the bipolar continuum (Figure 2), independently of drive reduction. A hedonic principle is presupposed by Edward L. Thorndike's well-known law of effect.

PAUL THOMAS YOUNG

[*See also* MOTIVATION. *Other relevant material may be found in* EMOTION; LEARNING; *and in the biographies of* CANNON; THORNDIKE; WOODWORTH.]

BIBLIOGRAPHY

The study of physiological drives can be pursued in the texts by Berlyne 1960; Bindra 1959; Brown 1961; Cofer & Appley 1964; Hall 1961; and Young 1961.

BEACH, FRANK A. 1956 Characteristics of Masculine "Sex Drive." Volume 4, pages 1–32 in Marshall R. Jones (editor), *Nebraska Symposium on Motivation.* Lincoln: Univ. of Nebraska Press.

BERLYNE, D. E. 1960 *Conflict, Arousal, and Curiosity.* New York: McGraw-Hill.

BINDRA, DALBIR 1959 *Motivation: A Systematic Reinterpretation.* New York: Ronald Press.

BOLLES, ROBERT C. 1958 The Usefulness of the Drive Concept. Volume 6, pages 1–33 in Marshall R. Jones (editor), *Nebraska Symposium on Motivation.* Lincoln: Univ. of Nebraska Press.

BROWN, JUDSON S. 1961 *The Motivation of Behavior.* New York: McGraw-Hill.

COFER, CHARLES N.; and APPLEY, MORTIMER H. 1964 *Motivation: Theory and Research.* New York: Wiley.

DUFFY, ELIZABETH 1962 *Activation and Behavior.* New York: Wiley.

ESTES, WILLIAM K. 1958 Stimulus–Response Theory of Drive. Volume 6, pages 35–69 in Marshall R. Jones (editor), *Nebraska Symposium on Motivation.* Lincoln: Univ. of Nebraska Press.

HALL, JOHN F. 1961 *Psychology of Motivation.* New York: Lippincott.

HEBB, DONALD O. 1949 *The Organization of Behavior: A Neuropsychological Theory.* New York: Wiley.

HEBB, DONALD O. 1955 Drives and the C.N.S. (Conceptual Nervous System). *Psychological Review* 62: 243–254.

HULL, CLARK L. 1943 *Principles of Behavior: An Introduction to Behavior Theory.* New York: Appleton.

LINDSLEY, DONALD B. 1957 Psychophysiology and Motivation. Volume 5, pages 44–105 in Marshall R. Jones (editor), *Nebraska Symposium on Motivation.* Lincoln: Univ. of Nebraska Press.

NISSEN, HENRY W. 1954 The Nature of the Drive as Innate Determinant of Behavioral Organization. Volume 2, pages 281–321 in Marshall R. Jones (editor), *Nebraska Symposium on Motivation.* Lincoln: Univ. of Nebraska Press.

O'KELLY, LAWRENCE I. 1963 The Psychophysiology of Motivation. *Annual Review of Psychology* 14:57–92.

OLDS, JAMES 1955 Physiological Mechanisms of Reward. Volume 3, pages 73–139 in Marshall R. Jones (editor), *Nebraska Symposium on Motivation.* Lincoln: Univ. of Nebraska Press.

RICHTER, CURT P. 1943 Total Self Regulatory Functions in Animal and Human Beings. Harvey Society, New York, *Harvey Lectures* 38:63–103.

WHITE, ROBERT W. 1959 Motivation Reconsidered: The Concept of Competence. *Psychological Review* 66: 297–333.

WOODWORTH, ROBERT S. 1918 *Dynamic Psychology.* New York: Columbia Univ. Press.

WOODWORTH, ROBERT S. 1958 *Dynamics of Behavior.* New York: Holt.

YOUNG, PAUL T. 1961 *Motivation and Emotions: A Survey of the Determinants of Human and Animal Activity.* New York: Wiley.

YOUNG, PAUL T.; and MADSEN, CHARLES H. JR. 1963 Individual Isohedons in Sucrose–Sodium Chloride and Sucrose–Saccharin Gustatory Areas. *Journal of Comparative and Physiological Psychology* 56:903–909.

II
ACQUIRED DRIVES

As used by contemporary behavioral scientists, the term "acquired drive" (synonyms: secondary motive, psychogenic drive or need, acquirable or learnable drive, and sociogenic need) refers to a motive, need, or source of motivation (rarely defined) that is a product of learning. In principle, animals as well as man can acquire drives, but man's opportunities for such learning during the process of socialization are held to be far more numerous, and the complexity and diversity of his activities are thought more urgently to demand an acquired-drive interpretation.

Typically, some form of learned drive is invoked in accounting for such behavior as working for money; seeking power, affection, status, or security; and striving for artistic creativity or other "higher" goals. Behavioral phenomena involving the motivational consequences of incentives and the acquisition by neutral objects of rewarding power are closely linked with those subsumed under the heading of acquired drives.

Precise, carefully worded definitions of the phrase "acquired drive" are not often encountered in the writings of behavior scientists, nor is it customary to find clear descriptions of exactly what is being learned or of how behavior is affected "motivationally" thereby. This looseness of conception and expression permeates writing in this field, and the multiplicity of different views resulting therefrom suggest that acquired-drive concepts are still in primitive stages of development.

Historical notes. Philosophical, literary, and religious writings from the earliest times contain references to the desires, strivings, wishes, and motives that have been said to govern man's behavior. And from the Middle Ages onward, references to the will and to conation became increasingly common in the theories of the famous philosophers. But it was not until the latter part of the nineteenth century that the concept of motivation entered boldly and systematically into science-oriented psychological concepts of behavior. Many factors exerted an effect at that time. Darwin's views advanced the growing tendency to regard unlearned predispositions as the most important sources of motivation, a tendency strengthened by William James's insistence on the multiplicity of man's instincts and by William McDougall's emphasis on innate propensities and their correlated emotional qualities. Freudian theory likewise underscored the importance of unlearned primitive motivational forces and may have been the first to emphasize a nonspecific driving agency, the libido. Students of animal learning, notably Edward L. Thorndike, found the primary drives and rewards of tremendous practical importance in teaching animals to make new responses, and the "law of effect" emerged as the conceptual counterpart of efficient training procedures.

During the first two decades of the twentieth century, Watsonian doctrine was accompanied by a decline of interest in the introspectionistic emphasis on the will as the precursor and cause of action, a shift that was reflected in the rather widespread substitution of the term "reaction" for "action." Robert S. Woodworth, in 1918, was apparently the first in America to use the specific term "drive." He distinguished drive, as the energy that moves the organism, from the other mechanisms that direct and control reactions, a distinction that has been widely adopted. Moreover, his notion that habits can be converted into drives may constitute a historically memorable reference to acquired-drive phenomena.

Although O. H. Mowrer's classic paper on the motivating effects of learned anxieties appeared in 1939 and Henry A. Murray published his list of psychogenic needs in 1938 (*Explorations . . . 1938*), Neal E. Miller was apparently the first to make use of the term "acquired drives," in the title of a paper published in 1941. Moreover, the chapter on acquired drives in Miller and Dollard's *Social Learning and Imitation* (1941) looms large as the first general theoretical treatment of such drives. The recent emphasis upon secondary drives reflects, in part, the intermingling of Freudian and stimulus–response doctrines, a growing confidence in the idea that intervening variables could be given pre-

cise operational meanings, and an increasing tendency to extrapolate to humans theories based on animal behavior. Whereas experimental studies of learned drives have burgeoned during the past decade, systematic theoretical analyses have not. Such cogitations will have to wait upon further developments in the broad field of motivation in general; there are strong signs that cherished conceptions in the latter area are being seriously challenged. Prominent theories of motivation have been expertly summarized by Madsen (1959) and the University of Nebraska Symposia on Motivation, published yearly since 1953, provide an excellent over-all view of the thinking of American psychologists on the general topic of motivation.

Current trends and basic problems.   The present-day tendency to appeal to a concept of acquired drives can be ascribed to a variety of factors. Some champions of the acquired-drive view justify their stand on the ground that learned human motives are manifestly visible "on the face of behavior." This attitude may mirror the fact that the language to which most of us have been exposed during the early years of life is not the language of science, particularly behavioral science, but that of the arts, literature, and religion. This nontechnical lexical heritage, which we learn first and best, contains a wide variety of such "motivational" synonyms as needs, wishes, impulses, desires, motives, aspirations, and hopes. Having matured within this linguistic environment, the student of behavior is almost certain to believe that these well-worn words, like other words learned at the parental knee, denote existential realities. He is also quite likely to feel that each of these "entities" is an important determinant of behavior and that his task as a scientist is simply to find ways of identifying and quantifying them.

A second reason for the widespread acceptance of the acquired-drive notion is the general conviction that biological drives, although capable of explaining certain instances of animal behavior, are inapplicable to human activities. Homeostatic regulatory mechanisms and biological deficiency states are deemed impotent in accounting for the alleged fact that man is motivated to work for praise, power, and recognition. It is considered self-evident, therefore, that man is driven by nobler, more intellective, more spiritual tendencies. Perhaps this is why acquired-drive concepts are never invoked to explain the persistence of morally or socially undesirable behavior. The activities of theologians, musicians, and scientists are held to reveal the power of sociogenic motives but the actions of dope peddlers, prostitutes, or garbage collectors are not.

A third reason for stressing the role of learning in motivation is that individuals are seen to vary among themselves to a surprising degree. This variation, both within a single society and from one society or culture to another, exceeds expectations based solely on genetic mechanisms. Attention is drawn, therefore, to what the individual learns during the course of his development when multitudes of objects and varieties of behavior are allegedly acquiring value. It is a sensible next step, some maintain, to assume that as values are being acquired, needs or drives for objects or for courses of action are also being learned.

Reappraisal. Although these arguments carry some conviction, there is a growing body of opinion favoring the conclusion that learned-drive constructs may not be essential to adequate theories of human behavior. For example, Estes (1958), Brown (1961), and others have seriously considered the possibility that motivational constructs, at least those of the traditional biogenic variety, may be superfluous and that adequate interpretations of alleged motivational phenomena may in some cases be based solely upon associative learning concepts. These views have not been extended, as yet, to secondary-drive manifestations, but there is no reason, in principle, why this could not be done.

The central theme, of course, is simply that complex human behavior is learned and that its acquisition is governed by known learning processes. If power-seeking behavior, for instance, were under scrutiny, one would aver that reinforcement (as yet largely unspecifiable) is responsible for the acquisition and maintenance of the actions. Instances in which motivational processes seemed to be operative would be termed illusory, the illusion being laid to the fact that some of the variables of which behavior is a function have been erroneously dubbed "motivational" by uncritical precursors. The known capacity of such variables to affect the organism would be put down to altered stimulation, a stratagem that reduces all so-called motivational variables to stimulus variables. According to this view, in a word, man learns to react but not to be motivated. Neither the artist, nor the novelist, nor the office secretary need be regarded as having, respectively, drives to paint, write, and type. Each has learned to perform certain acts because these have been repeatedly reinforced by the complex societal machinery in which they are embedded.

Actually, a theorist would not be required to abandon the concept of motivation altogether. He might maintain, for example, that a theory should include primary but not secondary sources of drive. Thus, whatever motivational process the theory de-

mands could be provided by primary sources of drive, such as mild hunger, thirst, or sexual needs. These and other biogenic sources of drive, operating in conjunction with learned reactions, could easily give one the impression that persisting behavior reflects a learned drive *for* a goal object of some sort.

Those who accept, as a working hypothesis, the view that some kind of learned-drive concept is desirable or necessary must wrestle with many subsidiary problems. Chief among these is the issue of whether a learned drive, or for that matter any drive, should be conceived as having both energizing (activating) and behavior-directing functions. Hull (1943), Spence (1956), and Duffy (1951) may be seen as representing those who have, in part or in whole, regarded drive as a unitary, nonspecific, energizing agency and have attributed the directionality or specificity of behavior to associative tendencies or habit strengths. The fact that such variables as food deprivation seem to affect the direction of behavior is handled by assuming that such variables influence not only drive level but also the intensity, quality, or number of deprivation-generated stimuli.

Many other writers, of course (*Explorations . . .* 1938; Young 1961), are insistent that drives (sometimes motives) must be directing, response-selecting agents, as well as activators. Young states repeatedly that motivation "is the process of arousing action, sustaining the activity in progress, and regulating the pattern of activity" (1961, pp. 23–24). Moreover, he adds that he would broadly define the study of motivation as "*a search for the determinants (all determinants) of human and animal activity*" (*ibid.*, p. 24). To adopt such a view, of course, is to rob the term "motivation" of all unique characteristics. As a search for *all* the determinants of activity, motivation becomes coextensive not only with all of psychology, but with all other sciences, natural or social, that contribute to the understanding of behavior.

Closely allied with the question of whether a drive or motive can guide or steer behavior is the problem of whether the drive itself can properly be said to have direction. Here again those who embrace such broad definitions as the foregoing tend also to say that one has drives *for* particular goal objects or conditions. This view may well be a carry-over from purposive conceptions of behavior and appears to be plagued with many of the ancillary difficulties that teleological notions must surmount. For example, how can one decide, unequivocally, that one particular object or bit of behavior, rather than something else, is *the* goal?

Consider the man who works hard in his office, is praised by his boss, gets a raise in salary, buys a new car, gets a date because of the car, and consequently is able to frustrate a rival suitor. In this case, the praise, the raise, the car, the date, or the satisfaction of thwarting the rival might each be described as a goal. But it would make little sense to say that the man had acquired a drive for each of these goals or a drive for one to the exclusion of all others. Actually, advocates of the position that one may have a drive *for* a specific goal object have never defended this concept on systematic or theoretical grounds. The only support has been of the "we know this is true" variety. Nor has the attribute of "having a drive for something" ever been assigned specific action-determining properties within a formal behavior system.

Drive as dissatisfaction with status quo. Interestingly enough, although fear is widely regarded as a good example of an acquired drive, one never says that fear is a drive *for* anything specific. Such an assertion would make sense only if one were to argue that the drive of fear is a drive *for* a nonfearful status. Since many different actions may be equally effective in getting an organism away from fear-arousing stimuli, the "goals" of the fear drive, if this manner of speaking is permissible, are incredibly numerous. But in the same way, of course, one may say that the drive for food is a drive to get away from hunger. Apparently all so-called drives or sources of drive share the property of being states or conditions from which the organism would prefer to escape. Even the emotion of hope, regarded by some as a "positive" drive, may be seen as indicating a lack of the thing hoped for and, hence, as essentially unpleasant. Hope, to be sure, may involve pleasant anticipations, but since it is always characteristic of the pregoal attainment periods, it is undesirable relative to the actual goal. Perhaps, therefore, the only meaningful sense in which a drive may be said to be a drive *for* something is in the sense in which it must be a drive to be anything but what it is at the time it is functioning as a drive. This holds for the drive to be an artist, to convert the heathen, or whatever. All involve dissatisfaction with the *status quo*. Every assertion to the effect that behavior is activated by positive, future goals can thus be transformed into the counterproposition that the behavior is driven by a contemporary state of unrest or imbalance. Such a translation is, it will be seen, consistent with the view that empirical variables can be identified as motivational provided (1) they serve as relatively nonspecific energizers, (2) their elimination following a response is reinforcing, and (3) their

appearance following a reaction is punishing. Conditions that are inherently "positive" would not meet the second and third of these rather widely accepted criteria for identifying motivational variables.

The incentive–motivation construct. An interesting example of what appears, at first sight, to be an acquired drive *for* a specific goal is provided by the Hull–Spence construct of incentive–motivation. Suppose that one has been fed at a given region in space and is now situated at a point from which a food reward is invisible. At such a time the visual stimuli provided by food can serve no incentive function and cannot elevate drive level directly. Hidden rewards cannot affect an organism's prereward behavior save through the agency of a stimulus-evoked anticipatory response. According to Spence, when a subject is rewarded, a consummatory goal response becomes classically conditioned to the cues provided by the food and to the surrounding environmental stimuli. Similar stimuli at a distance evoke fractional parts of the goal response, and these components of the total goal reaction are held to contribute in some measure to total drive level. Thus, even prior to reaching the reward, the subject reacts anticipatorily and appropriately with respect to it, and these reactions are said to increase drive. Inasmuch as these components of the total goal response are uniquely relevant to the particular reward experienced on previous trials, it might be tempting to speak of an acquired drive *for* that rewarding object. Nonetheless, whereas the anticipatory responses of salivating, chewing, and the like are appropriate to food, the increment in drive level, or incentive–motivation, that they are postulated to generate is not. Within the Hull–Spence theory, incentive-motivation, like drive, is a multiplier of habit strengths and contains no integral label directing it toward or away from any particular goal object [*see* HULL].

What is learned in acquired drives. Little can be said that is definitive in reply to the general question, "What does one learn when one learns to be motivated?" Typically, phasic or rhythmical skeletal movements have rarely been nominated for positions of central importance in secondary-drive theory. Such reactions are not specifically excluded; the Miller–Dollard view suggests that any learned reaction capable of producing strong internal stimuli qualifies as an acquired drive. Emotional reactions are most frequently cast in the role of drives, with the accent placed on learned expectations of pleasant events (hopes) and anticipations of noxious events (fears or anxieties). Emotional systems are favored because they are relatively diffuse (as is also the case with such primary motivating conditions as hunger), they can be conditioned readily and, if the unconditioned stimulus is strong, resist extinction remarkably well. Verbal reactions, particularly those involving self-directed, "try hard" instructions have only recently been suggested for consideration as learned responses potentially capable of functioning as sources of drive. Provided these responses can be woven securely into well-established learning theories, they may serve a valuable function as contributors to drive.

Inadequacies of theoretical formulations. We terminate this section by noting again that acquired-drive theorists have been gravely remiss in formulating specific theoretical presuppositions and details. Few have wrestled with the question of whether it is profitable to postulate the existence of more than one acquired drive and, should this question be answered in the affirmative, in what ways the drives resemble or differ from one another and from primary sources of drive. Similarly, little attention has been paid to the puzzles of whether drives should be treated as having directing as well as activating functions, whether whatever is learned in the process of acquiring drives is similar to other learned behaviors, how such new learnings are brought about, and how an acquired drive functions when it is alleged to be operating "motivationally." Some of the solutions proposed as answers to these queries are noted in the following review of research and theory in the field of conditioned emotionality.

Conditioned emotional responses. This discussion begins with, and concentrates on, an examination of the acquired drive of *fear* (sometimes termed "anxiety") because this exemplifies the most tightly reasoned theory and the most convincing experimental buttressing in the acquired-drive literature.

Whereas Freud clearly saw that a learned anxiety might have motivating properties and that its reduction would be rewarding, Mowrer (1939) crystallized these notions by translating them into the newly developing stimulus–response–reinforcement language of the 1930s. Linking Freud's conception with Pavlovian conditioning principles, Mowrer proposed, in brief, that the repeated paired presentation of a neutral and a noxious stimulus would result in the conditioning of anxiety to the neutral cue. After a few such trials, presentations of the neutral stimulus alone should evoke the learned emotional state. Moreover, this state ought to serve as a drive, because its presence should exert a dynamogenic effect upon other responses and its

diminution, following a response, should be reinforcing.

Experimental data from a variety of sources indicate that conditioned fear exhibits these motivation-like properties. The conclusion, therefore, seems firmly established that reactions leading to the cessation of fear-arousing cues will be strengthened. Fear has also been shown to have an energizing or activating effect under rather specialized circumstances; the augmentation of startle reactions to auditory stimuli provide the clearest example. Ample support for the view that fear also manifests dramatic inhibiting properties comes from studies showing that lever-pressing reactions in the rat cease almost entirely in the presence of stimuli formerly paired with shock. This response-suppressing function, taken at face value, does not seem to square with the concept of fear as an acquired drive, but one might assume in these instances that the onset of fear has followed and has blocked bar pressing because of a punishing property characteristic of all drive states [see EMOTION; PHOBIAS].

Generalization to human behavior. Extensions of these experimentally demonstrated principles to human behavior have been common. Usually the accent has been placed on the position that anxieties are probably entirely acquired and that anxiety-reducing behavior tends to be perpetuated. Moreover, it has been argued that many human activities that appear to reflect acquired drives for particular goals are actually motivated by anxiety. Thus, for example, behavior suggesting a secondary drive for money has been reinterpreted as reflecting a learned tendency to be anxious in the absence of money. The receipt of money necessarily reduces this "deficiency anxiety," which, in turn, reinforces money-obtaining actions, such as working. Comparably, the gregarious reactions of both humans and animals have been regarded as reflecting an anxiety-like state produced by physical isolation and reduced by companionship [see ANXIETY].

Perhaps the most successful application of the conditioned fear paradigm has been its use in the interpretation of behavior that repeatedly succeeds in enabling one to avoid an impending traumatic event. The problem to be surmounted here is that each anticipatory avoidance reaction prevents the noxious stimulus from impinging on the subject and, hence, constitutes an extinction trial. Avoidance reactions, however, are sometimes remarkably resistant to extinction, and it is this observation that is explained by saying (Mowrer 1939) that avoidance responses are strengthened by virtue of their own anxiety-reducing function. The conditioned anxiety hypothesis also has furthered our understanding of guilt reactions. Here it is assumed that the emotional reaction becomes conditioned to internal, response-produced cues as well as to external ones. Therefore, when the first elements of a punished response sequence are evoked, the cues generated by these reactions evoke conditioned fear, guilt, or apprehension. Interrupting the chain by doing something else eliminates the guilt and thereby reinforces the competing "virtuous" responses.

Variables contributing to fear.   Concerning the variables of which fear is believed to be a function, there appears to be rather general agreement that fear increases with the intensity of the noxious stimulus; with the number of conditioning trials, for a time at least; and perhaps also with lengthened intertrial intervals and with the strength of an appetitive source of drive such as hunger. The principal procedure for eliminating or reducing fear is that of the Pavlovian extinction trial, on which the conditioned stimulus is presented without the unconditioned stimulus. Extinction may be accelerated by massing trials and by structuring the situation to permit competing activities, for example, when one eats in the presence of the conditioned stimulus. Incidentally, the empirical finding that learned fears are extremely resistant to extinction when very noxious stimuli have been used has stilled the earlier criticism that acquired anxieties are too transitory to provide a stable base for persisting human reactions. Indeed, it has been suggested by Solomon and Wynne (1954) that anxieties acquired under these "traumatic" conditions may never be extinguished completely, because the changes produced by the learning process may be irreversible.

Need for achievement.   In recent years an ambitious theoretical and experimental program concerned with the psychogenic drive, "need for achievement," and other motives from Murray's list has been carried out by D. C. McClelland, J. W. Atkinson, R. A. Clark, and E. L. Lowell (1953). The conceptions of these investigators are included here inasmuch as their theory gives central staging to an affective arousal model of motivation. Two kinds of affective conditions are described. One, a negative state (anxiety), differs in no discernible way from the conditioned fear concepts of motivation discussed above. The other, a positive state (appetite), is essentially an anticipatory reaction to the coming of a pleasant stimulus and is the consequence of the pairing of neutral cues with pleasant ones. A motive, for these investigators, is the arousal of either a positive or negative affect by

the presentation of a conditioned stimulus. Thus all motives are necessarily learned, but it is not clear whether the primary affective reactions that serve as the basis for the conditioning of motives are, or are not, motivating. Part of the difficulty here arises from a failure to spell out precisely the effects of motives on behavior in general. Apparently, a motive (the affective expectancy) operates as a selective facilitator of actions appropriate to the motive. These motives thus seem to function as though they provided cues appropriate to the criterion reactions rather than as general activators. This has led to the suggestion that the term motivation may be inappropriate to this work, although obviously so long as the study of motivation is as broadly defined as it often is, hardly any usage can be pegged as inappropriate [*see* ACHIEVEMENT MOTIVATION; FIELD THEORY].

This review has presented only the barest outline of the acquired-drive problem in all its complexity. Contemporary conceptions stress the view that an acquired drive is, in essence, a learned response, often an operationally definable emotion, such as fear, hope, or anxiety, capable of affecting other responses "motivationally." Because the functions most commonly described as "motivational" are those of energization, reinforcement, and punishment, a learned response seems to qualify as a motivational variable and, hence, as a secondary source of drive, provided it displays these functions with respect to other responses. Contemporary writers, however, also seriously entertain the notion that acquired-drive concepts are not required even when complex human behavior is being interpreted. For these theorists, the principles of associative learning theory are adequate to explain phenomena that, to others, are patently motivational.

JUDSON S. BROWN

[*Directly related are the entries* LEARNING, *article on* REINFORCEMENT; MOTIVATION, *article on* HUMAN MOTIVATION. *Other relevant material may be found in* LEARNING THEORY; MOTIVATION; PERSONALITY: CONTEMPORARY VIEWPOINTS, *article on* A UNIQUE AND OPEN SYSTEM; STIMULATION DRIVES; *and the biographies of* THORNDIKE *and* WOODWORTH.]

BIBLIOGRAPHY

BROWN, JUDSON S. 1961   *The Motivation of Behavior.* New York: McGraw-Hill.

DUFFY, ELIZABETH 1951   The Concept of Energy Mobilization. *Psychological Review* 58:30–40.

ESTES, WILLIAM K. 1958   Stimulus–Response Theory of Drive. Volume 6, pages 35–69 in Marshall R. Jones (editor), *Nebraska Symposium on Motivation.* Lincoln: Univ. of Nebraska Press.

Explorations in Personality: A Clinical and Experimental Study of Fifty Men of College Age, by Henry A. Murray et al.   1938   London and New York: Oxford Univ. Press.

HULL, CLARK L.   1943   *Principles of Behavior: An Introduction to Behavior Theory.* New York: Appleton.

MCCLELLAND, DAVID C. et al.   1953   *The Achievement Motive.* New York: Appleton.

MADSEN, K. B.   1959   *Theories of Motivation.* Copenhagen: Munksgaard.

MILLER, NEAL E.   1941   An Experimental Investigation of Acquired Drives. *Psychological Bulletin* 38:534–535.

MILLER, NEAL E.; and DOLLARD, JOHN   1941   *Social Learning and Imitation.* New Haven: Yale Univ. Press.

MOWRER, ORVAL H.   1939   A Stimulus–Response Analysis of Anxiety and Its Role as a Reinforcing Agent. *Psychological Review* 46:553–565.

SOLOMON, RICHARD L.; and WYNNE, LYMAN C.   1954   Traumatic Avoidance Learning: The Principles of Anxiety Conservation and Partial Irreversibility. *Psychological Review* 61:353–385.

SPENCE, KENNETH W.   1956   *Behavior Theory and Conditioning.* New Haven: Yale Univ. Press.

YOUNG, PAUL T.   1961   *Motivation and Emotions: A Survey of the Determinants of Human and Animal Activity.* New York: Wiley.

DRUGS

I. PSYCHOPHARMACOLOGY   *Sherman Ross*
II. DRUG ADDICTION: ORGANIC
   AND PSYCHOLOGICAL ASPECTS   *Abraham Wikler*
III. DRUG ADDICTION: SOCIAL
   ASPECTS   *John A. Clausen*

I

PSYCHOPHARMACOLOGY

Although psychopharmacology is a relatively new scientific word, the interactive effects of drugs and behavior are perhaps as old as man himself. This presentation will describe contemporary interest in psychopharmacology and will emphasize the social research frontiers. It will not attempt to describe the emerging body of human and animal research results or the treatment aspects of drugs.

Although there are clearly a number of focuses for discussion, the individual human has been selected as the center of analysis; this article will deal with a number of individual and social factors relating to the effects of drugs. These factors are complex and generally poorly identified and weakly conceptualized. The ramifications of the questions lead one to consideration of the pathways of activity in the nervous system, the complexities of biochemical analysis, the assessment of human performance in laboratory or simulated situations, the management of patients, and the social matrix in which all of human behavior is embedded.

Historical considerations.   Drug utilization for health, religious, or individual purposes is one of the many primary characteristics of human behavior in a wide variety of cultures. Drugs thus constitute an almost universally present element in human social behavior, and one to which individual reinforcement, social training, and private meaning are attached. One of the world's oldest professionals, the medicine man, has long made use of a variety of chemical substances in the technology of his affairs.

Although the term "psychopharmacology" has been used with increasing frequency over the past few years, the concept is by no means new to psychology. Studies of the effects of drugs on the behavior of animals were undertaken in the nineteenth century, and the classic investigations of the effects of caffeine on human behavior were carried out by Hollingworth (1912) in the first decade of the twentieth century. This series of studies embodied many of the aspects of good design and may still have value as a model for analysis of the effects of drugs on human behavior.

The current dramatic expansion of interest in psychopharmacology as a special area dates from the early 1950s. In its early phases it was a product of the joint action of pharmacologist and psychiatrist in their attempts at modification of the behavior of psychiatric patients.

Since the early 1950s, when drugs such as reserpine and chlorpromazine were introduced, the list of compounds has grown, although some central questions surround these drugs and their utilization.

Problems.   Any real understanding of drugs that affect behavior depends upon the development of adequate theory relating biochemical or pharmacological events to behavioral events. Callaway and Stone (1960) have examined the nature of theory in this area and find that an integrating theory is still to be developed. On the biochemical side they find that the problem is formidable and aggravated by the lack of appropriate behavioral referents. Theories proposed by behavioral scientists may greatly oversimplify the underlying biological complexities. On the other hand, theories constructed by biochemists and pharmacologists may be naive about the behavioral complexities. No available theory is consistent with the available data, and many approaches use ambiguous and subjective terms. Callaway and Stone express the hope that the new psychotropic drugs can serve as a valuable class of independent variables in an integrated theory of behavior.

The task of analyzing the specific pharmacological effects of a drug is confounded by the history, learned expectations, and social roles of the individuals involved. Poffenberger (1942, pp. 200–202) discussed several major sources of error in drug investigations. He expressed serious concern about the "suggestibility of people who have a knowledge of the effects to be expected," the lack of control subjects, the difficulties in the selection of appropriate measures of drug effects, the short duration of drug studies, and, finally, the facts of interindividual and intraindividual differences [see SUGGESTION].

Modell has recently reviewed the problem of experimental controls in clinical pharmacology. He writes:

It may surprise some laboratory workers as well as a large number of clinicians that the pharmacologic experiment in man is really far more difficult than in the animal. The training and the orientation of the physician, as well as his relationship to the patient, make him an interested and purposive observer rather than a precise and objective one. Also realistic restrictions on the techniques that may be used in making observations on man make the clinical experiment difficult to perform and limit the depths which can be proved directly. Then there is the subject, whose human mind, human culture, human society, and human frailties make it uniquely difficult to experiment on him. All of these factors make the establishment of controls in a human experiment quite a different kettle of fish from the laboratory procedure of dividing littermates into two equal groups.   (1963, p. 372)

Methodological developments

Experimenter and subject bias are presumably dealt with by the *double-blind control*, in which both *E* and *S* are prevented from knowing who has been assigned to a specific experimental group. The *placebo* presumably is utilized to deal with the implications of medication, and *randomization* of other variables permits dealing with extraneous factors. The advantages and liabilities of the double-blind procedure have been discussed by Nash (1962) and need not be pursued here [see EXPERIMENTAL DESIGN].

Placebo effects and research design.   The placebo issue has also been of much interest and has been reviewed by Wolf (1959) and by Roueché (1960, pp. 85–98). Beecher (1955) has stressed the importance of the placebo concept, distinguishing between the effects of suggestion and the direct pharmacological effect. Wolf defines placebo effect as "any effect attributable to a pill, potion, or procedure, but not to its pharmacodynamic or specific properties" (1959, p. 689).

An experimental design involving an extra group of subjects in addition to the usual drug, placebo, and untreated groups has been developed (Ross

Table 1

	DRUG	NO DRUG
PILL	Drug	Placebo
NO PILL	Drug disguised	Nothing

et al. 1962; Lyerly et al. 1964). This extra group, called the "drug disguised group," receives the drug in a disguised form. Table 1 outlines this fourfold design.

The main question to which this design is directed is the analysis of drug effects. Most studies are based on a drug group–placebo group design or, less frequently, a drug group–placebo group–untreated control group design. In the typical drug–placebo experiment, both drug and placebo groups are given pills with the same instructions. The effects observed in the drug Ss are generally attributed to the pharmacological properties of the agent after subtraction of the effects found in the placebo Ss. But these "drug" effects may be partly a function of Ss' expectations or of the experimental or therapeutic setting. When a nontreatment group is added to the design, however, the differences between the untreated and the placebo groups can be attributed to the placebo effect. The special advantage of the four-group design is that it permits direct assessment of drug and placebo effects. In a typical experiment the drugs and placebos were given to the Ss in capsules, and all Ss received orange juice, which was also the vehicle for the disguised medication. The untreated group received orange juice only.

One experiment has been reported on the effects of d-amphetamine sulfate. The results of this experiment, carried out with neutral instructions, indicated a positive pill effect on mood, that is, the S felt more "comfortable," and a negative effect of the drug when administered in the disguised condition. The untreated group provided results similar to those of the group that received the drug as a pill. Motor performances of both the drug and the drug-disguised groups were significantly poorer than those of the placebo and untreated groups.

Effects of expectancies.   A second experiment was designed to determine the specific effects of *direct* and *conflicting* instructions and the effects of two drugs (amphetamine sulfate and chloral hydrate) that might be expected to produce different pharmacological and perceptual effects. Two sets of instructions were developed to lead Ss to expect that the capsules they swallowed would yield the specific effects of one of the two drugs. Groups similar to those in the previous experiment were used.

Instructions alone affected motor performance but had little or no effect on mood. Direct instructions, appropriate to the presumed drug effects, produced performance deterioration with the simple motor tasks used. Conflicting instructions, inappropriate to the presumed drug effects, counteracted much of the drug-produced decrement. A slight decrement in performance was found in the placebo group which received instructions appropriate to the effects of amphetamine. Amphetamine produced reports of greater comfort on the "mood index" than did chloral hydrate. On the other hand, the chloral hydrate instructions resulted in greater comfort than the amphetamine instructions. There was no interaction between drug effects and instructional effects. The two placebo groups did not differ significantly on the mood index. The effects of instructions on mood were found only when the drug was present.

The general problem of placebos has been analyzed from a variety of viewpoints (Fisher 1962; Gorham & Sherman 1961; Hawkins et al. 1961; Kast 1961; Wilson & Huby 1961) and is far from settled.

Personality and social aspects

Increased sophistication has been emerging in the field of human experimentation, stimulated by analyses of the social psychology of the psychological experiment (Orne 1962; Rosenthal 1963). The issue of ecological validity and the appropriate generalization from the laboratory to nonexperimental situations were treated by Brunswik (1947). Perhaps it is fair to say that the problem has not received its appropriate emphasis to date. Orne has suggested that the subject must be recognized as an active participant in any experiment and that it may be fruitful to view the psychological experiment as a special form of social interaction. He has proposed that the behavior of the subject is a function of the total situation, which includes the experimental variables being studied and at least another set of variables. The latter group has to be put under the heading of "demand characteristics" of the experimental situation. Rosenthal has described a program of research dealing with experimenter bias. It is shown that the expectation of the experimenter was a partial determinant of the results of behavioral research. The issues in these studies are vital ones for psychopharmacology, and it is hoped that future research will attend to these problems.

Drug therapy. A recent analysis of psychopharmacology and personality takes stock of personality measurement in relation to drugs. It reports the rather meager progress in psychopathology and

deduces a static plateau in personality measurement "cushioned by factor analysis on the one hand and by psychodynamics on the other" (Zubin & Katz 1964).

In the specific domain of the treatment of hospitalized psychiatric patients, additional aspects of the effects of drugs become of interest to the social scientist. Klerman (1961) states that before the 1930s major interest lay in such disorders as general paresis or epilepsy. Metrazol, electroconvulsive therapy, insulin coma, and lobotomy made their appearance at this time. It was in the decade before World War II that schizophrenia became the center of attention. Psychotherapeutic innovation also appeared under the leadership of Harry Stack Sullivan, Jacob Moreno, Frieda Fromm-Reichmann, and others. Klerman indicates that it is unfortunate for drug evaluation that the advent of the newer tranquilizing agents in the 1950s coincided with a wave of hospital reforms and innovations in the treatment of psychotic patients. This interaction is a complex one, and it is difficult to assess the effects of "drugs" on hospital admission, readmission, and other rates.

In addition to affecting the individual patient or subject the psychotropic drugs also affect the hospital milieu and functional organization. Elkes has described this interaction as follows:

In an age of revolutions, one is apt to get used to revolutions. In considering the impact of the pharmacotherapies on the management of the psychoses in a mental hospital, one is apt to be reminded of the violent changes brought about in the past by the introduction of other somatic therapies, such as deep insulin coma, electroplexy, and the lobotomies. Each of these has wielded changes, based essentially upon relatively short-term results; only in recent years could these be viewed against the perspectives of long-term follow-up studies. The changes in management, and the attendant changes in attitude, however, have stayed and become cumulative. It is quite possible that a similar fate may befall the pharmacotherapies of mental disorder, though three important differences distinguish them from earlier treatments and encourage a more hopeful view. The first is the fact that these therapies can be graded and made individual in a way which was quite impossible with the less variable and massive procedures used in the past. Secondly, they can be used on a scale far larger than the earlier therapies. Thirdly, whereas in the past systematic studies of mode of action followed essential empirical findings and measures, the empirical findings of the pharmacotherapies are being increasingly related to a growing body of modern theoretical neuropharmacology and neurochemistry. Theories are thus likely to keep abreast of clinical findings in a way never before witnessed in psychiatry, and are likely to make these ever more precise, discriminate and long-term.

The impact of the drug therapies on mental hospital

population is essentially threefold. They have altered the immediate management and treatment of certain types of acutely disturbed psychotic patients; they have mobilized large chronic populations hitherto secluded in the continued-treatment units of the average mental hospital; and, in individual cases, have made possible measures of rehabilitation which would have been very difficult to achieve in their absence. Lastly, they have increased and made more urgent the contacts between the mental hospital and the community. In terms of all these effects the drugs are wielding profound changes in staff attitudes at all professional levels. The precise pattern of these changes at present is far from clear, and for the moment can only be discussed in the broadest terms.   (1961, pp. 91–92)

With respect to the clinical treatment of the chronically hospitalized patient, there has long been evidence that increases in staff attention alone will produce symptomatic improvement (Galioni et al. 1953). A recent study by Bullard, Hoffman, and Havens (1960) indicates that drugs may be more important than environment in producing changes in chronic patients. An excellent review of this problem by Hordern and Hamilton (1963) indicates its complexities and the lack of clarity regarding the contributions to patient response of drugs and special nondrug treatments and of staff and patient attitudes. It is unfortunate but true that the effects of the drug and/or environment found in any single study represent only a single case in the larger sense, since it is almost impossible at present to measure or even meaningfully hypothesize what aspects of the staff–patient–milieu–drug context are responsible for the effects produced.

The introduction to a recent volume on specific and nonspecific factors in psychopharmacology states the central issue cogently: "The concept of specificity of drug action is at the heart of all pharmacological enquiry and speculation, and the stated hope of chemotherapy. Yet, in the unfamiliar terrain now extending between biochemistry and behavior, the term is assuming new and unexpected meaning. The interaction between the somatic and the symbolic compels a revision of premises, a recalibration of tools, and a reassessment of rules" (Elkes 1963, p. v). In this revision, recalibration, and reassessment, all of the sciences of man are involved. The social sciences have their special assignment and central contribution.

SHERMAN ROSS

[*Directly related are the entries* MENTAL DISORDERS, *article on* BIOLOGICAL ASPECTS, *and* MENTAL DISORDERS, TREATMENT OF, *article on* SOMATIC TREATMENT. *Other relevant material may be found in* DRINKING AND ALCOHOLISM.]

BIBLIOGRAPHY

BEECHER, HENRY K. 1955 The Powerful Placebo. *Journal of the American Medical Association* 159:1602–1606.

BRUNSWIK, EGON 1947 *Systematic and Representative Design of Psychological Experiments: With Results in Physical and Social Perception.* Berkeley: Univ. of California Press.

BULLARD, DEXTER M.; HOFFMAN, BARBARA R.; and HAVENS, LESTON L. 1960 The Relative Value of Tranquilizing Drugs and Social and Psychological Therapies in Chronic Schizophrenia. *Psychiatric Quarterly* 34:293–306.

CALLAWAY, ENOCH; and STONE, GEORGE C. 1960 Psychopharmacologic Theories: A Critical Review. *Clinical Pharmacology and Therapeutics* 1:247–267.

ELKES, JOEL J. 1961 Psychotropic Drugs: Observations on Current Views and Future Problems. Pages 65–114 in Conference on Experimental Psychiatry, Western Psychiatric Institute and Clinic, 1959, *Lectures on Experimental Psychiatry.* Univ. of Pittsburgh Press.

ELKES, JOEL J. 1963 Introduction. In Symposium on Specific and Non-specific Factors in Psychopharmacology, Montreal, 1961, *Specific and Non-specific Factors in Psychopharmacology: Proceedings.* Edited by Max Rinkel. New York: Philosophical Library.

FISHER, SEYMOUR 1962 On the Relationship Between Expectations and Drug Response. *Clinical Pharmacology and Therapeutics* 3:125–126.

GALIONI, E. F.; ADAMS, F. H.; and TALLMAN, F. F. 1953 Intensive Treatment of Backward Patients: A Controlled Pilot Study. *American Journal of Psychiatry* 109:576–583.

GOODMAN, LOUIS S.; and GILMAN, ALFRED Z. (1941) 1965 *The Pharmacological Basis of Therapeutics.* 3d ed. New York: Macmillan. → Covers literature on the effects of drugs on human behavior, from a pharmacological viewpoint.

GORHAM, DONALD R.; and SHERMAN, LEWIS J. 1961 The Relation of Attitude Toward Medication to Treatment Outcomes in Chemotherapy. *American Journal of Psychiatry* 117:830–832.

HAWKINS, DAVID R. et al. 1961 A Multivariant Psychopharmacologic Study in Normals. *Psychosomatic Medicine* 23:1–17.

HOLLINGWORTH, H. L. 1912 The Influence of Caffeine on Mental and Motor Efficiency. *Archives of Psychology* No. 22.

HORDERN, ANTHONY; and HAMILTON, MAX 1963 Drugs and "Moral Treatment." *British Journal of Psychiatry* 109:500–509.

KAST, ERIC C. 1961 Alpha-Ethyltrytamine Acetate in the Treatment of Depression: A Study of the Methodology of Drug Evaluation. *Journal of Neuropsychiatry* 2 (Supplement) no. 1:114–118.

KLERMAN, GERALD L. 1961 Historical Baselines for the Evaluation of Maintenance Drug Therapy of Discharged Psychiatric Patients. Pages 287–301 in Milton Greenblatt, David T. Levinson, and Gerald L. Klerman (editors), *Mental Patients in Transition.* Springfield, Ill.: Thomas.

KRANTZ, JOHN C. JR.; and CARR, C. JELLEFF (1949) 1965 *The Pharmacologic Principles of Medical Practice.* 6th ed. Baltimore: Williams & Wilkins. → Contains a major section on psychopharmacology: "The Use of Drugs in the Treatment of the Mentally Ill."

LYERLY, SAMUEL B. et al. 1964 Drugs and Placebos: The Effects of Instructions Upon Performance and Mood Under Amphetamine Sulfate and Chloral Hydrate. *Journal of Abnormal and Social Psychology* 68: 321–327.

MODELL, WALTER 1963 The Protean Control of Clinical Pharmacology. *Clinical Pharmacology and Therapeutics* 3:371–380.

NASH, HARVEY 1962 The Double-blind Procedure: Rationale and Empirical Evaluation. *Journal of Nervous and Mental Disease* 134:34–47.

ORNE, MARTIN T. 1962 On the Social Psychology of the Psychological Experiment: With Particular Reference to Demand Characteristics and Their Implications. *American Psychologist* 17:776–783.

POFFENBERGER, ALBERT T. 1942 *Principles of Applied Psychology.* New York: Appleton.

ROSENTHAL, ROBERT 1963 On the Social Psychology of the Psychological Experiment: The Experimenter's Hypothesis as Unintended Determinant of Experimental Results. *American Scientist* 51:268–283.

ROSS, SHERMAN; and COLE, JONATHAN O. 1960 Psychopharmacology. *Annual Review of Psychology* 11:415–438. → An analysis of the major literature.

ROSS, SHERMAN et al. 1962 Drugs and Placebos: A Model Design. *Psychological Reports* 10:383–392.

ROUECHÉ, BERTON 1960 Placebo. *New Yorker* October 15:85–86, 88, 90–92, 97–98, 100, 102–103.

UHR, LEONARD; and MILLER, JAMES G. (editors) 1960 *Drugs and Behavior.* New York: Wiley. → A general reference book.

WILSON, CEDRIC W. M.; and HUBY, PAMELA M. 1961 An Assessment of the Responses to Drugs Acting on the Central Nervous System. *Clinical Pharmacology and Therapeutics* 2:587–598.

WOLF, STEWART 1959 The Pharmacology of Placebos. *Pharmacological Reviews* 11:689–704.

ZUBIN, JOSEPH; and KATZ, MARTIN M. 1964 Psychopharmacology and Personality. Pages 367–395 in Symposium on Personality Change, University of Texas, *Personality Change.* Edited by Philip Worchel and Donn Byrne. New York: Wiley.

II
DRUG ADDICTION:
ORGANIC AND PSYCHOLOGICAL ASPECTS

Common to all of the conditions to which the term "drug addiction" has been applied is the criterion of habitual use of chemical agents (natural or synthetic) in spite of harmful consequences to the individual, society, or both. The present article deals mainly with the organic (pharmacological and physiological) and psychological aspects of the problem, particularly with reference to the opioids.

In part, harmful consequences may arise from the pharmacological and toxicological properties of the drug employed. These vary greatly, depending on the class of drug, the dose, and regularity and frequency of administration. Thus the toxic states induced by opioids (all chemical substances with morphinelike properties, including morphine itself) are characterized by respiratory depression, stupor, or coma; barbiturates, certain nonbarbiturate sedatives, and alcohol can produce mental confusion, incoordination, and coma; cannabis products (marijuana, hashish), amphetamine and allied "stimulant amines," and cocaine, as well as a number of "psychosomimetic" agents (mescaline, d-lysergic acid diethylamide), can give rise to psychoses of various sorts.

Repeated administration of opioids, barbiturates and allied drugs, or alcohol can give rise to a state of "pharmacogenic" (or "physical") dependence—i.e., a state such that abrupt withdrawal of the drug is followed by physiological and psychological disturbances ("abstinence syndromes"), which are usually transient but may be fatal. These also differ, depending on the class of drug involved—for example, predominantly autonomic disturbances in the case of the opioids, and convulsions and delirium in the case of barbiturates, nonbarbiturate sedatives, or alcohol. Associated in varying degrees with the development of pharmacogenic dependence is the acquisition of "tolerance"—i.e., progressive decline in degree of effect produced by a given dose of the drug—which can be almost complete in opioid users but is achieved only partially by regular use of the barbiturate and allied drugs or alcohol. With the acquisition of tolerance, the user is impelled to increase progressively the dosage and/or frequency of administration in striving for the original effects, thereby incurring the risk of inducing toxic reactions and intensifying still further the degree of pharmacogenic dependence—a state that in itself has disastrous consequences for the psychological as well as the physical functioning of the user.

Social consequences. In part, the harmful consequences of habitual drug use are social in nature. Even at subtoxic dose levels the effects of a given drug may impair the user's usefulness to the society in which he lives or may otherwise modify his behavior in unacceptable ways. In addition, harmful consequences may result from the user's attendant neglect of the welfare of his dependents, through either indifference to them, diversion of income for purchase of drugs, or adverse effects on his own health caused by inattention to proper nutrition, hygiene, and treatment of disease. Since in most societies it has been found necessary to place legal restrictions on the manufacture and distribution of many drugs of abuse, criminalism constitutes another of the consequences of this practice.

Clinical features of opioid addiction

The more commonly abused opioids include opium itself (containing 10 per cent morphine); morphine and certain of its derivatives, such as codeine, diacetylmorphine (heroin), dihydromorphinone (Dilaudid), dihydrohydroxycodeinone (eucodal); and a number of synthetic analgesics, such as meperidine (pethidine, Demerol, dolantin), ketobemidone, methadone (Dolophine, Amidone), and dextromoramide (Palfium). Heroin is the most common opioid purveyed illicitly throughout the world, although opium is still widely used in the Orient. Important variations occur, depending upon the particular opioid and the mode of utilization (smoking, sniffing, ingestion, injection), but the effects of morphine under experimental conditions are quite illustrative of the specific patterns of chronic intoxication, tolerance, and pharmacogenic dependence that develop with repeated use of opioids in general.

In nontolerant persons a single injection of a "therapeutic" dose of morphine (e.g., 15 milligrams) commonly produces a state of drowsiness from which the subject can be readily aroused. Pain, if present, is relieved and anxiety allayed. The sensorium remains intact, although some subjects may report that they feel "mentally clouded." Contrary to popular notions, lurid fantasies are rare, and sexual desires are not increased, although in the male potency may be enhanced by delay of orgasm. Particularly if injected intravenously, morphine may produce transient sensations in the abdomen that are sometimes described as akin to orgasms. Flushing of the skin and itching, as well as giddiness and vomiting, are also common effects. Characteristically, the pupils are constricted, respiratory rate is depressed, the pulse is slowed, and body temperature is lowered slightly. These effects, which last four to six hours, may be evaluated in different ways by different subjects, depending upon circumstances, but even among future habitués the effects of the first injection of morphine (or heroin) are often judged as unpleasant.

With further experience, however, some individuals come to evaluate the constellation of effects more positively, and their observers describe the subjects as "euphoric." With more frequent repetition, however, tolerance develops, albeit at different rates for various effects. Thus, the degree and duration of drowsiness, relief of pain and anxiety, depression of respiration, slowing of the pulse, nausea, and vomiting decrease progressively, whereas pupillary constriction and lowering of the body temperature decline at less rapid rates, and spasm of smooth muscle continues to be very pronounced with the resultant production of severe constipation. In the tolerant state, secretion of adrenocorticotrophic hormone (ACTH) by the pituitary gland is reduced, sexual interest is lost,

males become impotent, and females cease to menstruate. In attempts to regain "euphoria" addicts have been known to increase the daily dose to 5,000 mg. or more, with only partial and transitory success. If the accustomed dose of morphine is then withheld, a fairly stereotyped abstinence syndrome ensues. Beginning 12–16 hours after the last dose, restlessness, anxiety, frequent yawning, rhinorrhea, lacrimation, pupillary dilation, sweating, and piloerection are noted first. In addition, muscular aches and twitches, abdominal cramps, vomiting and diarrhea, elevated blood pressure, insomnia, agitation, weight loss, spontaneous ejaculations in the male, and profuse menstrual bleeding in the female supervene later, developing maximally during the next two or three days and then subsiding gradually, although physiological normality may not be achieved for six months or longer. Such abstinence phenomena are quickly alleviated by injection of the accustomed dose of morphine (or an equivalent dose of another opioid), only to reappear some hours later. The untreated morphine abstinence syndrome is rarely fatal, except in patients with cardiac disease, active tuberculosis, or other debilitating illness.

Of clinical importance are some special features of addiction to a number of other opioids. In the case of meperidine (Demerol), myoclonic jerks or generalized convulsions (with characteristic electroencephalographic abnormalities) may occur if the total daily dose level attained in the tolerant state is over 2,000 mg. Although the over-all effects of methadone are practically identical with those of morphine, the duration of action of methadone is somewhat longer, and therefore cumulative depressant effects on the central nervous system may occur if the drug is administered several times daily. The methadone abstinence syndrome is slower in onset and milder in degree (with respect to autonomic disturbances) than that observed after withdrawal of morphine. For these reasons methadone may be substituted for morphine and other opioids of addiction in the management of drug withdrawal. Despite widespread assumptions to the contrary, neither the intensity of "euphoric" effects, the rate of development of tolerance, nor the peak intensity of the abstinence syndrome is greater for heroin than for morphine when these two drugs are administered in equipotent doses (1.80 to 2.66 mg. of morphine sulfate is equal to 1 mg. of heroin), although some opioid addicts can distinguish morphine from heroin by their subjective effects when these drugs are administered intravenously.

The diagnosis of pharmacogenic dependence on

opioids can be made in two ways: (*a*) by observation of the abstinence syndrome that ensues when the drug is withheld; and (*b*) by subcutaneous injection of a specific morphine antagonist, such as nalorphine (3–15 mg. in divided doses). With the latter procedure an "acute abstinence syndrome" may be precipitated within minutes after injection in persons addicted to any of the opioids (except possibly meperidine), the severity of which depends upon the daily dose level and duration of addiction. Experimentally it has been shown that mild abstinence phenomena, such as yawning, lacrimation, rhinorrhea, piloerection, sweating, and pupillary dilatation, can be precipitated by subcutaneous injection of 15 mg. of nalorphine in persons who have been receiving as little as 15 mg. of morphine four times daily for two or three days or equivalent doses of heroin or methadone on the same schedule.

Treatment.   Wikler (1962) provides the details of treatment. Evaluation of the results of treatment has been extremely difficult. The best evidence available, that of a large group of addicts returning to New York after treatment at the U.S. Public Health Service Hospital in Lexington, Kentucky, indicates that over 90 per cent of the patients became addicted again, more than 90 per cent of these within six months after their discharge (Hunt & Odoroff 1962, p. 53). On the other hand, there is some evidence suggesting that opioid addiction may run a self-limiting course after a number of years. Thus, it has been found that at the end of five years of follow-up, 25 per cent of a sample of the group described above were "voluntarily abstinent," and attention has been directed to the "35–40 age drop-off" in names of "active addicts" in the files of the Bureau of Narcotics. This phenomenon requires further evaluation.

Organic aspects of opioid addiction

Physical characteristics of addicts.   In a study of four hundred opioid addicts (Caucasian) at the U.S. Public Health Service Hospital, Lexington, Brown (1940) found them to be of average or slightly superior height and weight, with normal distribution of body build, although there was a trend toward the pyknic habitus. Electroencephalographic studies by Andrews (1941) on fifty addicts (one year after drug withdrawal) revealed only that the groups differed from published data on "normals," in that among the addicts, individuals with occipital alpha indices either of 90–100 per cent or of 0–10 per cent were more common. These deviations from "normal" have no known clinical significance. In the personal experience of

the author, there are no physical traits or diseases among opioid addicts in the United States that distinguish them from nonaddicts except for those consequent to drug abuse, such as cutaneous scars and pigmentations, phlebosclerosis, and a relatively high incidence of systemic infectious diseases (malaria, bacterial or mycotic endocarditis) resulting from use of contaminated needles and more common diseases allowed to progress through neglect. No irreversible organic damage to the nervous system or viscera is known to occur as a result of opioids per se.

Effects of single doses of opioids.   Since one of the major actions of morphine and other opioids is the production of analgesia, it might be supposed that these drugs block transmission or otherwise exert depressant effects somewhere in the direct sensory pathways presumed to mediate pain. However, the evidence bearing on this supposition is far from conclusive. In the cat morphine prolongs recovery time of interneurons in the thalamic "relay" nuclei (responding to electrical stimulation of the sciatic nerve), but in the dog morphine does not depress amplitude or latency of responses, evoked by electrical stimulation of the tooth pulp, in the contralateral coronal gyrus, the contralateral nucleus ventralis posteromedialis, or the medial lemniscus. Apart from the question of species differences, resolution of this problem is complicated by uncertainty about the specific modalities of sensation that are activated by the stimuli used in animal research on pain and analgesia. In this regard, electrical stimulation of the tooth pulp would seem to be the least ambiguous. Tentatively, therefore, it may be assumed that actions on the direct pain pathways cannot account for the analgesic effects of these drugs.

Insofar as the "indirect" sensory pathways are concerned, a depressant action of morphine on the ascending midbrain reticular "arousal" mechanism has been found in the rat and the rabbit, but in the case of the cat the evidence is conflicting. In both the rabbit and the dog morphine enhances recruiting responses evoked by stimulation of thalamic intralaminar nuclei, but in the cat such responses are said to be depressed. These discrepancies may perhaps be related to the differences in general behavioral effects of morphine in the rabbit and dog (depression) on the one hand and the cat (excitation) on the other. In the dog, however, the effects of morphine on potentials evoked in the "indirect" pathways by stimulation of tooth pulp were found to be exceedingly complex, augmentation as well as depression or no effect being observed in different components of this system.

In any case, the relevance of these data to the problem of morphine analgesia is open to question because the "indirect" pathways are selectively affected by small doses of barbiturates and other drugs that are not classified as analgesics.

Effects on reflex activity.   More consistent, and perhaps more relevant to the problem of analgesia, are the effects of morphine on certain reflex activities at various segments of the neuraxis. Thus, in adequate doses, morphine depresses "sham rage" in decorticated cats and dogs, flexor and crossed extensor reflexes in spinal cats and dogs, the flexor reflex in spinal man, and mandibular response to stimulation of the tooth pulp in dogs. In addition, morphine exerts depressant actions on the "skin-twitch" in the dog and the "tail-flick" in the rat, both of which have been used successfully in the screening of drugs for analgesic properties in man. In part, morphine affects these reflexes by a direct depressant action of spinal interneurons, but a major component of its action in the intact animal appears to be augmentation of supraspinal inhibition. From the neurophysiological standpoint, therefore, it would appear that morphine alters the "reaction" to noxious stimulation at several levels of the neuraxis rather than affecting propagation of impulses generated by such stimuli from the periphery to the cerebral cortex. However, there is no reason to assume that the selective actions of morphine on nociceptive reflexes are related solely to the analgesic actions of this drug. In fact, it may be that what is termed "morphine analgesia" merely refers to the component of the total pattern of effect produced by this drug (indifference to ordinarily painful conditions, drowsiness, "euphoria") that interests the clinician under a given set of circumstances. As Schaumann (1954) has pointed out, the analgesic action of morphine is but part of its "antiprotective" spectrum of effects —quite similar to the concept "primary-need reducing," which has also been applied in this connection (Wikler 1952).

Sites of morphine action.   Much research has also been devoted to the problem of accounting for the selectivity that characterizes the sites of action of morphine in the central nervous system. In isolated smooth muscle preparations, morphine has been shown to reduce both the resting output of acetylcholine and the output from postganglionic cholinergic nerve endings when they are stimulated, and to inhibit the release of sympathetic transmitter substance from postganglionic nerve endings in rats. It was found that single doses of morphine decrease the brain concentrations of norepinephrine, but repeated administration of mor-

phine increases these concentrations. The possible significance of this finding will be discussed further in connection with the mechanisms of pharmacogenic dependence.

Chronic effects.   Not only have abstinence phenomena been observed in babies born of mothers addicted to opioids, but tolerance to many of the effects of opioids after repeated administration of these drugs and clear-cut abstinence phenomena following their abrupt withdrawal have been demonstrated in intact monkeys, dogs, and rats, in long-surviving decorticated dogs, in chronic spinal dogs, in a chronic spinal man, and even in unicellular organisms and tissue cultures. It has also been reported that in vitro, cortical slices from brains of rats treated with morphine daily for one week exhibit tolerance to the depressant effects of morphine on respiration (oxygen consumption) stimulated by potassium chloride. Since there is no evidence that the development of tolerance to opioids is associated with an increased capacity of the organism to destroy the drug (Woods 1954) or that "immune" or "antimorphine" circulating substances are formed during chronic morphine intoxication, these findings suggest a cellular site of origin for both tolerance and pharmacogenic dependence. Presumably, such cellular processes involve changes in enzymatic activity, but the identity of the enzymes concerned is not yet known.

Axelrod (1956*a*; 1956*b*) found that in rats the development of tolerance to morphine is associated with progressive decrease in the capacity of the liver to N-demethylate this drug, as well as other agents with morphinelike actions, and that chronic administration of N-allylnormorphine with morphine reduces both the rate of development of tolerance to morphine and the decrease in N-demethylating capacity of the liver in this species. Using the hepatic N-demethylating enzyme system as a model for the study of tolerance, it was suggested that a decreased response to narcotic drugs on repeated administration may develop as a result of unavailability of receptor sites, due to deactivation of these sites through continuous interaction with opioids. Other data suggest that enzyme systems concerned with the metabolism of catecholamines may be critically involved in the genesis of the abstinence syndrome. In the rat brain concentration of catecholamines is supranormal during chronic morphine intoxication. It has also been reported that in both the dog and the rat urinary excretion of catecholamines is markedly increased during the acute abstinence period. At the present time the precise manner in which these changes are related to pharmacogenic dependence is difficult to establish because of some differences in regard to details that depend on the species used and the techniques employed by different investigators.

Although the phenomena of tolerance and pharmacogenic dependence appear to be due to changes at the cellular level, it is quite likely that certain features of the clinical opioid abstinence syndrome are modulated by "counteradaptive" changes involving systems not directly affected, or only slightly affected, by this class of drugs.

Electroencephalograms of addicts "stabilized" on morphine are characterized by abnormally high alpha output, with marked slowing in some cases, but the electroencephalogram returns to the control (normal or high alpha index) pattern promptly after abrupt withdrawal of the drug (Andrews 1941)—a surprising finding in view of the intense autonomic and emotional disturbances that occur during the early abstinence period. In man, bilateral prefrontal lobotomy has little effect on the "nonpurposive" features of the morphine abstinence syndrome (preponderantly autonomic) but does attenuate "purposive" abstinence phenomena, such as "craving" and drug-seeking behavior (Wikler et al. 1952). In monkeys experimentally addicted to morphine, bilateral section of the cingulum (a fiber bundle connecting the frontal cortex with the limbic system) does attenuate the morphine abstinence syndrome (Foltz & White 1957), but certain details of the findings (White 1953) suggest that in this species also the "attenuating" effects of the operative procedure were exerted mainly upon withdrawal signs analogous to human "purposive" abstinence phenomena. Removal of facilitatory frontal cortical influences on subcortical autonomic centers may also have contributed to the "attenuation" of the simian morphine abstinence syndrome as a whole. In addition, it appears that at least in man the hypothalamic–pituitary system is depressed during maintained morphine addiction and becomes hyperactive during the acute phase of the abstinence syndrome, Eisenman, Fraser, Sloan, and Isbell (Eisenman et al. 1958) having shown that during chronic morphine intoxication, urinary excretion of 17-ketosteroids is significantly depressed although the adrenal glands remain responsive to ACTH. In contrast, both plasma levels and urinary excretion of 17-ketosteroids increase far above control values after abrupt withdrawal of morphine, along a time course roughly parallel to that of the acute abstinence syndrome. Further studies on animals are needed to determine whether these endocrinal changes are consequent to changes in neural activity during chronic morphine intoxication and during the abstinence period, or whether the reverse is the case.

Of special importance to theories of opioid addiction and relapse are data acquired with the use of N-allylnormorphine (nalorphine), a specific morphine antagonist. As has already been noted, this agent is capable of precipitating clear-cut abstinence phenomena in man after four-times-daily administration of "therapeutic" doses of morphine, heroin, or methadone for as brief a period as two or three consecutive days. Martin and Eades (1961) have shown that in dogs nalorphine can precipitate fairly severe abstinence phenomena when given in a single subcutaneous dose (20 mg./kg.) within 15 minutes after termination of a single continuous intravenous infusion of morphine at the rate of 3 mg./kg. per hour for 7.5 to 8 hours. In addition, it was demonstrated that such animals had developed a considerable degree of tolerance to several of the effects of morphine during the single continuous infusion of the drug. It is probable, therefore, that the processes of tolerance and pharmacogenic dependence begin to develop in man with the first dose of morphine even though these changes may not be clinically detectable. Also, evidence is accumulating that full recovery from the morphine abstinence syndrome may require much longer periods of time than has heretofore been believed. As has already been noted, minor but persistent deviations from normal have been detected in man for as long as six months after withdrawal from morphine following a period of addiction (Himmelsbach 1942). Martin, Wikler, Eades, and Pescor (Martin et al. 1963) have demonstrated that in the rat an early "primary" phase of the morphine abstinence syndrome is succeeded by a "secondary" phase, lasting over six months, during which the morphine-abstinent rat continues to display mild but definite signs of hyperirritability in comparison with concurrently observed control rats.

Psychological aspects of opioid addiction

Personality characteristics of addicts. The most extensive studies on the personality characteristics of opioid addicts are those which have been conducted over a period of about twenty years on the population of the U.S. Public Health Service Hospital in Lexington. Although other characteristics of this population have undergone changes in the course of two decades (shift in racial distribution from predominantly white to predominantly Negro, increase in proportion of patients from large metropolitan centers, and decrease in median age), the large majority of individuals that constitute this population have consistently been classified as "psychopathic." Thus, on the basis of their study with the Minnesota Multiphasic Personality Inventory (MMPI) on 270 subjects, Hill, Haertzen, and Glaser (1960) concluded that narcotic addicts are often psychopathic, that hospitalized adolescent and adult addicts do not differ in their MMPI profiles, that great similarities exist between adolescent addicts and delinquent nonaddicts, and that psychopathology is an important etiological element in addiction (p. 138).

However, very similar MMPI profiles have also been found by this group of investigators to characterize not only juvenile delinquents but also hospitalized chronic alcoholics (Hill, Haertzen, & Davis 1962). Speculating on the commonness of elevated scores for psychopathy in the MMPI among narcotic (opioid) and alcoholic subjects, Hill (1962) has suggested that the "social deviant" does not engage in the daily activities that are ordinarily reinforced by and satisfy the larger society. Counteranxieties and inhibitions that deter unusual behavior in the mature adult do not do so in the social deviant. Thus, he is particularly vulnerable to short-term satisfactions and can readily manipulate his personal affairs if drugs are available (p. 573). The deviant who is immature and inadequate and is unable to solve problems of adult life independently may find temporary freedom from frustration and problems in alcohol or complete elimination of such problems in opiates (p. 578).

Other investigators have stressed "passive dependency" as a dominant trait among opioid addicts, and Wikler and Rasor (1953) have suggested that such individuals choose opioids for repeated use from among a number of other drugs, including alcohol, with which they have had experience precisely because the opioids facilitate their preferred mode of dealing with frustrating and anxiety-arousing situations—namely, by promoting "indifference" to them rather than by increasing aggressiveness, as would the use of alcohol. However, a major difficulty in relating personality characteristics found in opioid addicts to the addiction process is the paucity of suitable control data. Gerard and Kornetsky (1955) compared the personalities of 32 young addicts treated at the Lexington Hospital with those of 23 nonaddict acquaintances named by addicts who were undergoing treatment at another hospital. They concluded that although the addicts were more disturbed (with a high incidence of overt or incipient schizophrenia), about half of the control group also showed evidence of significant psychiatric disorder. Further research

in this area, especially on the personality characteristics of parents and siblings of opioid addicts, may help clarify many questions about the relation between personality characteristics and addiction that are still unanswered.

Single doses of opioids. Whether the nontolerant opioid addict is more susceptible to morphine "euphoria" than the nonaddict individual is a question of considerable importance for the dynamics of addiction. Lasagna, Von Felsinger, and Beecher (1955) compared the effects on mood of single doses of placebo, amphetamine, pentobarbital, morphine, and heroin in a group of "postaddict" prisoners and a group of normal volunteers, as well as another group of chronically ill patients. As expected, these investigators found that heroin produced the greatest incidence of "euphoric" effects in the postaddicts, but only a few individuals in the other groups responded to either morphine or heroin in this manner. In another study on the volunteer group alone, Von Felsinger, Lasagna, and Beecher (1955) obtained data on personality dynamics indicating that typical or atypical reactions to the drugs used in the previous study could be correlated with differences in mature controls and emotionality (p. 1119). However, it is difficult to evaluate the significance of these findings for the addiction process because the postaddict and nonaddict groups in the study of Lasagna, Von Felsinger, and Beecher (1955) differed in ways other than presumed personality structures (prior experience with drugs, sociolegal status). In further studies on normal subjects, Smith and Beecher (1959) found that morphine (10 mg./70 kg.) produced a variety of unpleasant subjective effects, among which "mental clouding" was especially prominent.

As judged by objective performance tests, however, the mental impairment produced by small single doses of opioids would seem to be much less than is implied by the term "mental clouding." Bauer and Pearson (1956) studied the performance of 96 nonaddict male subjects on a difficult perceptual–motor task involving manipulation of throttle, stick, and rudder controls to compensate random movements of four instrument pointers from the null position and found that the effects of 8 mg. of morphine could not be differentiated from those of placebo (saline) injections. Kornetsky, Humphries, and Evarts (1957) reported that 100 mg. of meperidine produced only a slight and nonsignificant impairment of performance on a variety of mental tests of nonaddict individuals. Smith, Semke, and Beecher (1962) did find that single doses of morphine (10 mg./70 kg.) or heroin (4 mg./70 kg.) produced significant impairment of performance on a number of tests of mental function but noted that the impairment was primarily one of speed rather than accuracy. Studies with comparable techniques have not been made in postaddicts, but the earlier studies of Brown (1946) suggest that the effects of opioids relevant to the addiction process lie in the "emotional" area rather than in "cognitive" functioning. Thus, in a long-term study on two postaddicts during experimental readdiction to morphine, he found that although this drug did produce a mild degree of impairment of performance on code learning, continuous subtraction, and immediate and delayed recall of nonsense syllables, as well as on the speed of voice and hand responses to word stimuli, the most striking effect was the reduction of differences in speed between voice responses to "indifferent" word stimuli and those to "disturbing" word stimuli (drugs, sex, and crime), suggesting the possibility that morphine might alleviate the disturbances of personal and social conflicts. Such circumstances might be the reason for morphine addiction and relapse after periods of abstinence (p. 52). In addition, Brown (1943) found that Rorschach responses of postaddicts were generally "constricted" and immature; single doses of morphine reduced the degree of constriction and increased the occurrence of fantasy and human movement responses.

Other data on the "emotional" effects of morphine have been obtained by Hill and others in a series of studies on "anxiety associated with the anticipation of pain" in postaddicts. Noting that the effects of single doses of morphine on the so-called pain threshold are unpredictable (Andrews 1943; Denton & Beecher 1949), these investigators hypothesized that one important action of morphine in the production of analgesia is dissociation of "anxiety" from perception of the noxious stimulus. In agreement with this hypothesis, others found that morphine (15 mg.) had no significant effect on the ability of postaddicts to estimate intensities of brief but painful electric shocks under "nonanxious" conditions; under "anxious" conditions untreated subjects overestimated the intensity of such stimuli, whereas after injection of morphine the estimated and actual intensities of these stimuli did not differ significantly. Likewise, it has been reported that single doses of morphine (15 mg.) significantly reduced the disruption of performance on a visual–manual reaction time test, produced by repeated self-inflicted electric shock penalties for "slow" reaction times—an action not shared by pentobarbital (250 mg.). Further evidence of the effectiveness of morphine in reducing "anxiety associated with anticipation of pain" was obtained by Kornetsky (1954) in a study on postaddicts, employing radiant heat stimuli instead of electric shocks. In addition to measurement of "stronger or weaker than standard" judgments of the noxious stimulus, several measures of "anticipation" were included, under both "anxious" and "nonanxious" conditions. It was found that morphine decreased significantly the number of "stronger" responses, as well as anticipatory psychogalvanic responses, only under "anxious" conditions.

That reduction of "anxiety associated with anticipation of pain" may be but one example of a more general effect of morphine on "motivation" is suggested by the results of another study by Hill, Belleville, and Wikler (1957) on postaddicts. In this study, visual–manual reaction times were measured under four different incentive conditions (defined as such in terms of different schedules of morphine rewards for participation in the experiments) in untreated subjects, one hour after administration of morphine (15 mg.), and after intramuscular injection of 250 mg. of pentobarbital. In untreated subjects mean reaction times varied from "slow" to "fast," depending upon the incentive condition under which they were measured. Morphine significantly reduced the "range of change," while pentobarbital had the opposite effect. It would thus appear that, at least in postaddicts, single doses of morphine reduce responsivity to a variety of stimuli that have in common the property of producing "emotional" arousal.

Chronic effects. Although morphine-produced "euphoria" would seem to be a decisive factor in reinforcing repeated use of this drug, the rapid development of tolerance to this effect results in marked changes in the behavior of the addict. Thus, Brown (1946), in his long-term study on experimental readdiction in two subjects, noted that there was seldom a level of dosage that maintained satisfaction for a period longer than three weeks. There were no signs that morphine had increased the general sense of pleasantness, although there were short periods of euphoria. The general mood level during the period of addiction was one of unpleasantness (p. 42). Similar observations were made by Wikler (1952) in a study on self-regulated experimental readdiction to morphine in a single postaddict. Over a period of three and a half months this subject progressively increased the size of each dose and the frequency of self-injections (intravenous) to a total daily dose level of about 1,350 mg. of morphine taken in 12 divided doses throughout the day and night. Nevertheless, he was unable to regain the euphoric effects he had experienced initially after a single dose of 30 mg. of morphine, and his prevailing mood was one of dejection, remorse, guilt, and anxiety, which were also reflected in his dream material. The experimental arrangements provided for self-reduction of the dose of morphine and eventual withdrawal by the methadone substitution method whenever the subject might request such treatment, but he gave no evidence of entertaining such an idea at any time before the date of the termination of the study, of which, by prior agreement, he received one month's notice. In the absence of "euphoria," the subject's persistence in self-administration of morphine was difficult to explain, but a striking feature of his "free associations" was the frequency with which he compared craving for morphine with hunger and the relief of craving with satiation. It appeared, therefore, that instead of being a deterrent, the physical dependence brought about by repeated morphine injections seems to be one of the drug's attractive attributes, since it is a new source of gratification. The new pharmacogenic need may in some cases become strong enough to displace other primary needs.

In terms of instrumental conditioning theory, this inference can be restated as the proposition that in the state of pharmacogenic dependence, drug-acquisitory behavior is reinforced by the efficacy of opioids in reducing the drive engendered by early abstinence phenomena following the last previous dose of the drug. There is evidence that such, indeed, may be the case and also that reinforcement resulting from reduction of abstinence phenomena may outlast the acute ("primary") abstinence period. However, as Martin, Wikler, Eades, and Pescor (Martin et al. 1963) have demonstrated, the "primary," or acute, abstinence syndrome is succeeded by a long-enduring "secondary" abstinence syndrome (six months or more) in the rat, and therefore the possibility cannot be excluded that such evidence of "relapse" is based upon persistence of "unconditioned" abstinence phenomena that are relieved by morphine.

To account for "late" relapse, Wikler (1948) suggested that under certain circumstances morphine abstinence phenomena may become conditioned in the classical manner during periods of pharmacogenic dependence and may therefore reappear as conditioned responses long after complete subsidence of the abstinence syndrome following withdrawal of the drug. Some experimental evidence that such conditioning is possible has been acquired in studies on the rat, and Wikler

(1961; 1965) has proposed a "two-factor learning theory" of relapse, in which classical conditioning of the abstinence syndrome is postulated as the basis for recurrence of a drive state similar to that operating during previous episodes of addiction, and operant conditioning, also taking place during previous episodes of pharmacogenic dependence, is postulated as the basis for renewed drug-acquisitory behavior long after "cure." In addition, Wikler has suggested (1955) that an important factor in relapse may be "the need for continuous activity directed toward attainable, but recurring goals" (p. 567), which, in the case of the addict, is furnished by pharmacogenic dependence on opioids. That such "hustling" activity is highly valued by opioid addicts is suggested by their preoccupation with this topic even when confined in an institution. Viewed as an "effort" variable, "hustling" may increase resistance to extinction of drug-acquisitory behavior.

Although the various roles assigned to pharmacogenic dependence are still highly speculative, they would seem to deserve intensive research, since one obvious fact about "drug addiction" in general is that the drugs which create the most persistent degrees of "habitual use with harmful consequences" are precisely those which engender pharmacogenic dependence.

ABRAHAM WIKLER

[*Other relevant material may be found in* DRINKING AND ALCOHOLISM *and* SMOKING.]

BIBLIOGRAPHY

ANDREWS, H. L. 1941 Brain Potentials and Morphine Addiction. *Psychosomatic Medicine* 3:399–409.

ANDREWS, H. L. 1943 The Effects of Opiates on the Pain Thresholds in Post-addicts. *Journal of Clinical Investigation* 22:511–516.

AXELROD, JULIUS 1956a The Enzymatic N-Demethylation of Narcotic Drugs. *Journal of Pharmacology and Experimental Therapeutics* 117:322–330.

AXELROD, JULIUS 1956b Possible Mechanism of Tolerance to Narcotic Drugs. *Science* New Series 124:263–264.

BAUER, ROBERT O.; and PEARSON, RICHARD G. 1956 The Effects of Morphine–Nalorphine Mixtures on Psychomotor Performance. *Journal of Pharmacology and Experimental Therapeutics* 117:258–264.

BROWN, R. R. 1940 The Relation of Body Build to Drug Addiction. *Public Health Reports* 55:1954–1963.

BROWN, R. R. 1943 The Effect of Morphine Upon the Rorschach Response Pattern in Post-addicts. *American Journal of Orthopsychiatry* 13:339–342.

BROWN, R. R. 1946 A Cycle of Morphine Addiction: Biological and Psychological Studies. Part 2: Psychological Investigations. *Public Health Reports* 61:37–53.

DENTON, JANE E.; and BEECHER, HENRY K. 1949 New Analgesics. *Journal of the American Medical Association* 141:1051–1057; 1146–1153.

EISENMAN, ANNA J. et al. 1958 Urinary 17-Ketosteroid Excretion During a Cycle of Addiction to Morphine. *Journal of Pharmacology and Experimental Therapeutics* 124:305–311.

FOLTZ, ELDON L.; and WHITE, LOWELL E. 1957 Experimental Cingulumotomy and Modification of Morphine Withdrawal. *Journal of Neurosurgery* 14:655–673.

GERARD, DONALD L.; and KORNETSKY, CONAN 1955 Adolescent Opiate Addiction: A Study of Control and Addict Subjects. *Psychiatric Quarterly* 29:457–486.

HILL, HARRIS E. 1962 The Social Deviant and Initial Addiction to Narcotics and Alcohol. *Quarterly Journal of Studies on Alcohol* 23:562–582.

HILL, HARRIS E.; BELLEVILLE, R. E.; and WIKLER, ABRAHAM 1957 Motivational Determinants in the Modification of Behavior by Morphine and Pentobarbital. *A.M.A. Archives of Neurology and Psychiatry* 77:28–35.

HILL, HARRIS E.; HAERTZEN, CHARLES A.; and DAVIS, HOWARD 1962 An MMPI Factor Analytic Study of Alcoholics, Narcotic Addicts and Criminals. *Quarterly Journal of Studies on Alcohol* 23:411–431.

HILL, HARRIS E.; HAERTZEN, CHARLES A.; and GLASER, ROBERT 1960 Personality Characteristics of Narcotic Addicts as Indicated by the MMPI. *Journal of General Psychology* 62:127–139.

HIMMELSBACH, C. K. 1942 Clinical Studies of Drug Addiction: Physical Dependence, Withdrawal and Recovery. *Archives of Internal Medicine* 69:766–772.

HUNT, G. HALSEY; and ODOROFF, MAURICE E. 1962 Followup Study of Narcotic Drug Addicts After Hospitalization. U.S. Public Health Service, *Public Health Reports* 77:41–54.

KORNETSKY, CONAN 1954 Effects of Anxiety and Morphine on the Anticipation and Perception of Painful Radiant Thermal Stimuli. *Journal of Comparative and Physiological Psychology* 47:130–132.

KORNETSKY, CONAN; HUMPHRIES, OGRETTA; and EVARTS, EDWARD V. 1957 Comparison of Psychological Effects of Certain Centrally Acting Drugs in Man. *A.M.A. Archives of Neurology and Psychiatry* 77:318–324.

LASAGNA, LOUIS; VON FELSINGER, JOHN M.; and BEECHER, HENRY K. 1955 Drug-induced Changes in Man: 1. Observations on Healthy Subjects, Chronically Ill Patients and "Postaddicts." *Journal of the American Medical Association* 157:1006–1020.

MARTIN, W. R.; and EADES, C. G. 1961 Demonstration of Tolerance and Physical Dependence in the Dog Following a Short-term Infusion of Morphine. *Journal of Pharmacology and Experimental Therapeutics* 133:262–270.

MARTIN, W. R. et al. 1963 Tolerance to and Physical Dependence on Morphine in Rats. *Psychopharmacologia* 4:247–260.

SCHAUMANN, O. 1954 Analgetika und protektives System. *Deutsche medizinische Wochenschrift* 79:1571–1573.

SMITH, GENE M.; and BEECHER, HENRY K. 1959 Measurement of "Mental Clouding" and Other Subjective Effects of Morphine. *Journal of Pharmacology and Experimental Therapeutics* 126:50–62

SMITH, GENE M.; SEMKE, CHARLES W.; and BEECHER, HENRY K. 1962 Objective Evidence of Mental Effects of Heroin, Morphine and Placebo in Normal Subjects. *Journal of Pharmacology and Experimental Therapeutics* 136:53–58.

VON FELSINGER, JOHN M.; LASAGNA, LOUIS; and BEECHER, HENRY K. 1955 Drug-induced Changes in Man: 2. Personality and Reactions to Drugs. *Journal of the American Medical Association* 157:1113–1119.

WHITE, L. E. JR. 1953 Attenuation of the Morphine Abstinence Syndrome of the Addicted Monkey (Macaca Mulatta) by Lesions in the Anterior Cingulate Gyrus. Ph.D. dissertation, Univ. of Washington (Seattle).

WIKLER, ABRAHAM 1948 Recent Progress in Research on the Neurophysiologic Basis of Morphine Addiction. *American Journal of Psychiatry* 105:329–338.

WIKLER, ABRAHAM 1952 A Psychodynamic Study of a Patient During Experimental Self-regulated Re-addiction to Morphine. *Psychiatric Quarterly* 26:270–293.

WIKLER, ABRAHAM 1955 Rationale of the Diagnosis and Treatment of Addictions. *Connecticut State Medical Journal* 19:560–568.

WIKLER, ABRAHAM 1961 On the Nature of Addiction and Habituation. *British Journal of Addiction* 57:73–79.

WIKLER, ABRAHAM 1962 Drug Addiction. Volume 8, pages 17–58 in Frederick Tice (editor), *Practice of Medicine.* Hagerstown, Md.: Prior.

WIKLER, ABRAHAM 1965 Conditioning Factors in Opiate Addiction and Relapse. Pages 85–100 in D. Wilner and G. G. Kassebaum (editors), *Narcotics.* New York: McGraw-Hill.

WIKLER, ABRAHAM et al. 1952 The Effects of Frontal Lobotomy on the Morphine Abstinence Syndrome in Man: An Experimental Study. *A.M.A. Archives of Neurology and Psychiatry* 67:510–521.

WIKLER, ABRAHAM; and RASOR, ROBERT W. 1953 Psychiatric Aspects of Drug Addiction. *American Journal of Medicine* 14:566–570.

WOODS, L. A. 1954 Distribution and Fate of Morphine in Non-tolerant and Tolerant Dogs and Rats. *Journal of Pharmacology and Experimental Therapeutics* 112:158–175.

III

DRUG ADDICTION: SOCIAL ASPECTS

The taking of drugs is culturally patterned behavior. Both the prevalence and the consequences of drug use in any society depend as much upon social norms as upon physiological responses to drugs or general psychological characteristics of drug users. The ends sought through use of drugs are varied: relief from pain, fatigue, or anxiety, the celebration of social solidarity, "kicks," and enhanced mystical experience. Beliefs about the effects of the substances used and the specific ends sought through such use are closely linked with more general cultural goals and orientations. A particular drug—for example, marijuana (also called hashish and bhang)—may be accepted as an appropriate adjunct to sociability in one society, used as an invaluable ingredient in religious contemplation in another, and banned by law as dangerous in a third.

There is no evidence that *addiction* to drugs is favorably regarded in any society or culture, but the status accorded the addict varies markedly. In the United States he has been defined as a criminal and stereotyped as a "dope fiend." In much of Europe, on the other hand, the addict is regarded as an unfortunate person whose problem is primarily psychological and medical. Having stated that great differences exist in cultural orientations to specific drugs or drug effects, we are, however, far from being able to explain them. Opium and hashish have been widely used without extreme devaluation in Muslim society, although the Koran proscribes the use of substances that alter the state of consciousness. In traditional interpretations, it appears that the Koran's injunction has been limited to alcohol.

To cite another example, a student of culture and personality has suggested that opium smoking was prevalent in China because it afforded a means of achieving the cultural goal of individual harmony with the environment. But opium smoking did not exist in China until it was introduced by European traders in the seventeenth century (Sonnedecker 1963, p. 16). Opium was subsequently forced upon the Chinese by the East India Company, despite protests by the Chinese government. An adequate understanding of drug use within a given culture requires a knowledge of historical facts that is seldom available.

To the extent that the beliefs and practices surrounding drug use reflect different perspectives and value orientations, the social correlates and the consequences of drug use will themselves vary substantially from one country to another and from time to time within any given country. Coffee and tobacco have, in various societies, been proscribed as debilitating or debauching; the smoking of tobacco was a crime punishable by death in Russia, Persia, Turkey, and parts of Germany (Lewin 1924). The term "drug" refers to a wide variety of chemical substances consumed by man, not merely to narcotics or "dangerous drugs." When applied to substances consumed outside of medical channels, however, "drug" tends to connote something negatively valued. Hence, we do not normally apply the term "drug habit" to the smoking of tobacco, but we do to the smoking of marijuana (a non-addicting drug produced from the hemp plant), even though many more persons may be psychologically habituated to tobacco smoking than to marijuana. Because of common usage, this article is primarily concerned with narcotics addiction.

Historical background

From the earliest record in antiquity through the Middle Ages, it appears that the primary use of opium was medical. The letters and records of European travelers in the Orient during the Middle Ages occasionally refer to opium as a drug used by the people to overcome fatigue, but they do not mention chronic intoxication or indicate recognition of the phenomena of tolerance and dependency (Sonnedecker 1963, p. 16). Available records suggest that opium consumption was not a widespread practice or problem anywhere until the beginning of the seventeenth century, when opium smoking was introduced into China. Although the pleasures of opium smoking and opium eating were extolled by writers like De Quincey and Coleridge in the nineteenth century, in general neither the British nor other Europeans were drawn to opium; it was primarily an article for trade with alien peoples.

Drug use in the United States. Attitudes were in general no more favorable in the United States than in Europe, but for several reasons opiate addiction was a more frequent occurrence in the former (Terry & Pellens 1928, pp. 66–90). Among these was the reliance on patent medicines containing opium and its derivatives. Such medicines were widely used in nineteenth-century America to combat a variety of ailments, especially "female disorders." Another source of addiction in the United States was the excessive use of hypodermically administered morphine in medical practice. Many soldiers wounded in the Civil War became addicts. Of quite a different nature was the third general influence, the introduction of opium smoking by devotees of the sporting world on the west coast in the last quarter of the nineteenth century. In this instance, opium was used purely for pleasure.

Although strongly disapproved of by the conventional citizenry (local legislation against opium dens became widespread), the practice was taken up by many persons on the fringes of polite society, and it flourished among prostitutes and underworld characters. Imports of smoking opium generally exceeded 100,000 pounds a year between 1880 and 1909, when they were finally cut off. As a consequence of these influences, opium consumption tripled in the period from 1870 to 1909. Simultaneously, the image of the addict changed rapidly as opium use became more widespread in the underworld (Eldridge 1962, pp. 9–10). Prior to the enactment of the Harrison Act, most users of narcotics were, however, conventional members of society.

The Harrison Act, passed by Congress in 1914, was basically designed to eliminate the nonmedical use of narcotics by providing controls and a careful system of accounting for and taxing all drugs defined as addicting that were produced or imported into the United States. With the enforcement of this act, as interpreted by the narcotics section of the Treasury Department, an addict could no longer secure drugs legally. In the first two decades after passage of the Harrison Act, the number of addicts in the United States markedly declined. Since then, however, a persistent problem of somewhat changing character has emerged in the United States.

Extent of drug addiction

The extent of drug use and drug addiction, historically or currently, is known only in very general terms. Since the use of opiates and of marijuana and the so-called "dangerous drugs" is devalued by the great mass of the population in Western society, and since the possession of these drugs is illegal in many countries, it is not possible to get a direct count of drug users but only an indication of those who come to official attention in one way or another. An *ad hoc* panel on drug abuse reported in 1962 that discrepancies between estimates provided by federal, state, and local enforcement agencies and other sources of data were so great that they precluded any adequate estimate of the number of addicts in the United States (White House Conference 1963, pp. 290–292).

The Federal Bureau of Narcotics, which has attempted to maintain a register of "active addicts," listed therein nearly fifty thousand names. There is no way, however, of knowing how many of the persons so listed are actively addicted at any given time or, indeed, how many are still living. From various fragments of available data, it appears that the number of persons in the United States actively addicted to opiates within the past decade is almost certainly not less than 50,000 and probably not more than 100,000. By contrast, it does not appear that any other Western country has as many as five thousand opiate addicts, according to a review of foreign experience by the Joint Committee on Narcotics of the American Bar Association and the American Medical Association (Joint Committee 1961, pp. 121–153).

Great Britain has long reported an addict population of between three hundred and four hundred. None of the Scandinavian countries has more than a few hundred addicts, nor does France or Italy. Only in West Germany does the number of known addicts go much higher, and even there the estimate is well under five thousand (Joint Committee 1961, p. 151).

Among Western countries, a significant fraction of all addicts is found among physicians and other medical personnel. Beyond this fact, very little is known about the social characteristics of drug users and addicts except for the United States. Because the problem is more prevalent in the United States than in any other Western country, and because in recent years detailed studies have been undertaken to establish the characteristics of drug users, the following discussion of patterns of drug use and of characteristics of drug users will be confined almost entirely to the United States.

Changing character of drug use. When the Harrison Act was passed, drug addicts were widely dispersed in American society. Impressions of the dominant characteristics of the addict population varied according to the segment of the population seen in treatment—highly successful individuals, middle-class neurotics, criminals, and degenerates (Terry & Pellens 1928, pp. 513–516). It seems probable that female addicts outnumbered male addicts at the turn of the century. Moreover, the large majority of addicts were native-born whites of mature years. In the following two decades, the new addicts were largely white males. Most of them were introduced to drug use as young adults already somewhat detached from conventional society. They tended to frequent or to take up residence in areas in which illegal drugs could be purchased, chiefly the most disorganized areas of the largest cities (Dai 1937). These were areas characterized by overcrowding, high rates of crime, and other social problems; they were areas that afforded anonymity in the pursuit of illicit activity.

Drug use and minority group status. By the early 1950s, many of the areas in which illicit narcotics had long been available were occupied by new waves of migration from the southeast section of the United States, from Puerto Rico, and from Mexico. The new residents were at a considerable disadvantage economically and were poorly equipped to cope with the demands of an industrial society. Many adolescents and young adults were exposed to the availability of marijuana and heroin in their home neighborhoods. Opportunities for drug use were afforded, whether or not the individual was favorably oriented toward drug use. In some neighborhoods, as many as 10 per cent of all males in late adolescence were officially recorded as drug users (Chein et al. 1964, pp. 40–41).

In recent years nearly three-fourths of all addicts recorded on the register of the Bureau of Narcotics have been Negro, Puerto Rican, or Mexican-American in extraction. One-third of these recent drug users have been under 25 years of age. Thus there has been a marked shift in the character of the problem of drug addiction in the United States in recent years; it is now entwined with minority group status. While the psychological needs and frustrations of minority group members undoubtedly contribute to the attractiveness of drugs, addiction among them cannot be adequately explained or dealt with in terms of individual psychology.

Becoming a drug user

It is obvious that narcotics must be available before there can be narcotics users; it is perhaps less obvious that an individual must learn the techniques of drug use and to some degree the proper way to perceive and enjoy drug effects before he becomes a regular drug user. The process of becoming a user is closely related to patterns of association and access to drugs.

In the period between initial enforcement of the Harrison Act and World War II, most persons who became addicted to opiates through nonmedical channels probably did so either by virtue of close affiliation with another addict or in the course of thrill-seeking behavior (Dai 1937, p. 173). Following World War II, however, a high proportion of those who became drug users had been introduced to the use of narcotics in the slum areas in which their families lived. These recent addicts have tended to come from family backgrounds and life circumstances conducive to the production of psychopathy. There is much evidence, however, that psychological difficulties are far more widespread than is illicit drug use. Recent research in New York City and Chicago suggests that the use of heroin and other opiates, in most instances, is learned through association with peers in the subculture of "street-corner society." The norms of this subculture are generally inconsistent with and often openly hostile to those of conventional society. The orientation on the part of substantial numbers of adolescents is manifested in delinquency and in the search for and exploitation of "kicks" (Finestone 1957a).

In general, the prevailing sentiment toward drug use, even on the part of residents of slum areas, is decidedly negative. Most children learn that heroin and marijuana are considered "bad" by most adults. In areas of highest drug use, however, rejection of the standards of conventional society, distrust of policemen, and relatively favorable attitudes toward drugs tend to be much more widely prevalent, even among a cross section of school children, than in other areas of the city (Chein et al. 1964, p. 102). A substantial proportion of young people are likely to have friends or associates who use marijuana or heroin.

The subculture of addiction.   Many young people have their initial drug experience with marijuana reefers provided by older companions. The neophyte who likes the experience and wishes to move toward regular use must have a more stable source of supply than can be provided by chance encounters with other users. He is likely to spend more time with persons who use marijuana and to avoid those who strongly disapprove (Becker [1953b] 1963, pp. 62–72). This reduces the need for secrecy in smoking marijuana and enhances the pleasures of use. Simultaneously, changing contacts help to negate the popular stereotype of the marijuana "addict." It becomes apparent that marijuana does not completely transform the personality; the new user learns a series of positive beliefs about the beneficial effects of marijuana, beliefs constantly being reinforced by their verbalization within the group (Becker [1953b] 1963, pp. 72–78).

The use of heroin is a step further along the path of alienation from conventional values. Here the prevailing attitudes, even in delinquent subcultures, are much more negative. Here there is the promise of a bigger kick but also at much greater cost. Most of those who try heroin for the first time, however, are aware that addiction does not come from a single or an occasional trial. It is likely that few anticipate that they will be "hooked." Some—no one knows what proportion—manage to use the drug for a time on an occasional basis and then stop altogether without ever becoming addicts (Chein 1964, p. 159). Others, especially those for whom heroin use leads to a marked increase in feelings of adequacy, move quickly to the subculture of the addict, where "connections" can be made and where the drug itself becomes the central fact of existence.

Lindesmith (1947, chapter 4) has noted the critical importance of the individual's recognition that withdrawal sickness can be warded off by use of the drug. It is at this time that he becomes fully aware of the nature of addiction and of his dependency upon the opiates. Both his patterns of association and his self-image change markedly as he becomes assimilated into the subculture of addict society.

Social backgrounds, personality, and drug use. Certain personality characteristics of narcotics addicts are markedly different from those of normal middle-class persons, and to a lesser degree they are different from those of nonaddicted persons coming from the same social backgrounds as the addicts. One major expression of the personality differences is in attitude. Addicts are characterized by attitudes of pessimism and futility on the one hand and of distrust and rejection of the standards and representatives of middle-class society on the other. These attitudes do not merely characterize addicts, however. As indicated above, Chein found them to be rife among eighth-grade pupils in schools located in areas of high drug use. To a substantial degree, then, they would seem to be prevalent social orientations which are conducive to drug use.

Another major aspect of personality difference between the addict and the nonaddict is the low self-esteem and high degree of social immobilization of the narcotics user by virtue of anxiety. A major appeal of the opiates is that they permit the constricted ego greater scope and freedom (Chein 1964, chapter 9). But again the personality attributes appear to reflect aspects of the social environment in which the addict has been nurtured, particularly the devaluation and deprivation that are experienced by residents, especially minority group members, of urban slums. The same terms relating to personality characteristics have been used to describe slum dwellers elsewhere who were not involved in drug use (Clausen 1957, pp. 263–266). Within the areas of highest rates of drug use, users tend to come from families lacking a stable father figure, lacking warmth between parents, and characterized by vague or inconsistent standards (Chein 1964, chapter 10). All of these factors would tend to contribute to psychopathy in the child; families with such characteristics are in part a product of migration to and life in the urban slum.

The world of addiction

Criminality and drug use. Although narcotics use has long been prevalent in the underworld, prior to the passage of the Harrison Act the great majority of opiate users and addicts in the United States were law-abiding citizens. Thereafter, addiction or occasional use of opiates for nonmedical reasons could be maintained only by criminal means—either the illegal purchase of smuggled drugs or the theft of drugs. Moreover, few addicts could afford the high cost of illegal drugs without resorting to theft or other criminal activities.

In general, addiction to narcotics reduces the inclination toward aggressive or violent behavior (Joint Committee 1961, p. 68). In this respect, heroin is far less likely to lead to violence than is alcohol. It is the lack of the drug, rather than its consumption, that is most closely linked with criminal activities on the part of the addict. Larceny,

or theft for money to buy drugs, is the dominant crime of the narcotics offender (Finestone 1957b, p. 71).

At the same time, drug use provides one type of adjustment within a delinquent milieu. Many, perhaps most, of the young drug users growing up in the worst urban slums are involved in delinquency long before they try marijuana or heroin. There is some evidence that those whose drug use is part of a subcultural pattern that begins with delinquency may be psychologically more sound than those whose delinquent behavior did not start until they had become drug users and needed money in order to support the habit (Chein 1964, chapter 6).

The important point to be made is that drug effects, even when harmful, are not the primary cause of criminal behavior. British opiate addicts are not criminals to any significant degree (Schur 1962, pp. 135–140). The meaning of drug use and its linkage with crime depends largely on the laws relating to narcotics and on public attitudes toward addiction.

Employment and drug use. To the extent that narcotics or other drugs become the central preoccupation of an individual, as is true of an addict, that individual is likely to be an undependable employee. A substantial proportion of physician addicts are reported to have functioned adequately for long periods while addicted to narcotics, but the great majority of addicts are, at best, irregularly employed (Schur 1962, p. 131). Except for entertainers and physicians, the population from which addicts are drawn in the United States tends to be relatively disadvantaged in the job market. Since possession of a drug calls for more serious penalties than do most forms of theft, there is little incentive for the active addict to work. Even in Britain, however, where addiction and drug possession are not defined as crimes, most addicts have unsatisfactory work records (Schur 1962, p. 134). It is not possible to state to what degree their poor work records reflect the personality problems that gave rise to their addiction or that are a direct consequence of the use of drugs.

Contextual supports. By virtue of his alienation from conventional norms and his stigmatization, the narcotics addict tends, even when he is not using drugs, to have his closest associations with persons who speak his argot and accept him without regard for his criminal record. Many addicts voluntarily undertake "cures" in one of the hospitals established to provide for drug withdrawal and treatment in a drug-free environment. Few appear to be content with continual addiction (Lindesmith 1947, chapter 6; Ray 1961, p. 134), but the rate of relapse to drug use is exceedingly high. Follow-up studies suggest that relapses tend to occur very soon after discharge from a treatment center. Of patients returned to New York City from the Public Health Service Hospital at Lexington, Kentucky, during the period from July 1952 to December 1955, only 9 per cent were voluntarily abstinent six months later and less than 3 per cent were abstinent for a full five years (Duvall et al. 1963). Yet at the end of the five-year period, nearly 25 per cent of the study group had been voluntarily abstinent for three months or more.

Ray (1961) notes that the abstinent former addict is likely to be viewed with distrust by relatives and representatives of conventional society. Even though not using drugs, he may be periodically picked up by the police for questioning. Under such circumstances, he is likely to turn again to his association with other addicts.

Narcotics control

The primary objective of efforts in the United States to control drug use has been to stamp out the trade in illicit drugs. Efforts to mobilize public sentiment against drug addicts and the drug traffic have often relied on the dissemination of markedly distorted information and on attempts to suppress consideration of alternative points of view (Eldridge 1962, pp. 39–40, 78–80). Legislation has provided severe penalties for the sale or possession of drugs, but this approach has neither eliminated illicit drug use nor contributed to the rehabilitation of addicts.

Most addicts engage in small-scale peddling of drugs on those occasions when they are able to purchase more than enough for their own needs. They are then subject to the same penalties for drug sale and possession as are the nonaddicted distributors of narcotics. As a consequence of longer prison sentences, the number and proportion of narcotics offenders, chiefly addicts, in prison populations has more than doubled. Increasingly, professional groups have called attention to the lack of success of punitive measures (Joint Committee 1961; Eldridge 1962; White House Conference 1963).

It is too soon to predict the effect of such re-evaluations, but attention has been focused on alternative approaches. One such approach is the so-called British system of control (Schur 1962). The basic legislation relating to narcotics use in England is not markedly different from that in the United States, except that penalties are far less stringent. Moreover, in interpretation of the law, the medical profession has been left free to deal with addiction as a medical problem. The addict has neither been stigmatized nor forced into criminal activity.

Hallucinogenic and other "new" drugs

In recent years a new group of drugs, the hallucinogens (also called psychedelic or psychotomimetic drugs), has come increasingly into attention and use, especially among young intellectuals interested in deepening their psychic experiences (Barron et al. 1964). In the case of these drugs, as with alcohol, it appears that the effects are markedly influenced not only by the nature and amount of the drug taken but by the personality and current mood of the subject and by the context in which the drug is used and the expectations held. In a few places, cults have arisen around the use of the hallucinogens. Where this has occurred, some of the opprobrium directed toward illegal drug use has been noted.

More closely linked with the orientation toward thrill-seeking and deviant behavior that characterizes much opiate addiction in the United States has been the increasing use of amphetamine and other stimulants (White House Conference 1963, pp. 286–289). Although many of the new drugs are not addicting, their use is to a high degree expressive of rebellion and problematic behavior. It is not unlikely that experience with an ever-increasing number of new drugs will in time force a reconsideration of both the criteria and the standards underlying legislation for the control of drugs.

JOHN A. CLAUSEN

BIBLIOGRAPHY

BARRON, FRANK; JARVIK, M. E.; and BUNNELL, S. 1964 The Hallucinogenic Drugs. *Scientific American* 210, April: 29–37. → A general review of effects and points of view regarding a new class of drugs.

BECKER, HOWARD S. (1953a) 1963 Becoming a Marihuana User. Pages 41–58 in Howard S. Becker, *Outsiders: Studies in the Sociology of Deviance.* New York: Free Press.

BECKER, HOWARD S. (1953b) 1963 Marihuana Use and Social Control. Pages 59–78 in Howard S. Becker, *Outsiders: Studies in the Sociology of Deviance.* New York: Free Press.

CHEIN, ISIDOR et al. 1964 *The Road to H: Narcotics, Delinquency and Social Policy.* New York: Basic Books. → Part I describes a comprehensive program of research on adolescent drug use.

CLAUSEN, JOHN A. 1957 Social Patterns, Personality, and Adolescent Drug Use. Pages 232–272 in Alexander H. Leighton et al. (editors), *Explorations in Social Psychiatry.* New York: Basic Books.

DAI, BINGHAM 1937 *Opium Addiction in Chicago.* Shanghai (China): Commercial Press.

DUVALL, HENRIETTA J. et al. 1963 Followup Study of Narcotic Drug Addicts Five Years After Hospitalization. U.S. Public Health Service, *Public Health Reports* 78:185–193.

ELDRIDGE, WILLIAM B. 1962 *Narcotics and the Law: A Critique of the American Experiment in Narcotic Drug Control.* New York: American Bar Foundation.

FINESTONE, HAROLD 1957a Cats, Kicks and Color. *Social Problems* 5:3–13.

FINESTONE, HAROLD 1957b Narcotics and Criminality. *Law and Contemporary Problems* 22:69–85.

JOINT COMMITTEE OF THE AMERICAN BAR ASSOCIATION AND THE AMERICAN MEDICAL ASSOCIATION ON NARCOTIC DRUGS 1961 *Drug Addiction: Crime or Disease?* Bloomington: Indiana Univ. Press.

KOLB, LAWRENCE 1963 Factors That Have Influenced the Management and Treatment of Drug Addicts. Pages 23–33 in *Symposium on the History of Narcotic Drug Addiction Problems: Proceedings.* Edited by Robert B. Livingston. U.S. Public Health Service, Publication No. 1050. Washington: Government Printing Office.

LEWIN, LOUIS (1924) 1931 *Phantastica: Narcotic and Stimulating Drugs; Their Use and Abuse.* New York: Dutton; London: Routledge. → First published in German. Reissued as *Drugs: Their Use and Abuse* in 1938.

LINDESMITH, ALFRED R. 1947 *Opiate Addiction.* Evanston, Ill.: Principia Press.

LINDESMITH, ALFRED R. 1965 *The Addict and the Law.* Bloomington: Indiana Univ. Press.

Narcotics. 1957 *Law and Contemporary Problems* 22: 3–154. → Contains review articles on various aspects of drug addiction in the United States.

RAY, MARSH B. 1961 The Cycle of Abstinence and Relapse Among Heroin Addicts. *Social Problems* 9:132–140.

SCHUR, EDWIN M. 1962 *Narcotic Addiction in Britain and America: The Impact of Public Policy.* Bloomington: Indiana Univ. Press.

SONNEDECKER, GLENN 1963 Emergence and Concept of the Problem of Addiction. Pages 14–22 in *Symposium on the History of Narcotic Drug Addiction Problems: Proceedings.* Edited by Robert B. Livingston. U.S. Public Health Service, Publication No. 1050. Washington: Government Printing Office. → A brief historical overview.

TERRY, CHARLES E.; and PELLENS, MILDRED 1928 *The Opium Problem.* New York: Bureau of Social Hygiene. → The most comprehensive compilation of historical and scientific knowledge available up to 1928.

UNITED NATIONS, ECONOMIC AND SOCIAL COUNCIL, COMMISSION ON NARCOTIC DRUGS *Summary of the Annual Reports of Governments Relating to Opium and Other Dangerous Drugs.* → Began publication with the 1944 Summary. Contains information relating to many aspects of narcotics production and abuse within member nations.

WHITE HOUSE CONFERENCE ON NARCOTIC AND DRUG ABUSE 1963 *Proceedings.* Washington: Government Printing Office. → The Appendix, by an *ad hoc* panel on drug abuse, provides an excellent summary of the nature of drug use in the United States.

DUAL ECONOMY

See ECONOMY, DUAL.

DuBOIS, W. E. B.

William Edward Burghardt DuBois (1868–1963), American Negro leader and sociologist, was born in Great Barrington, Massachusetts. He was trained at Fisk University, at Harvard, where he received a PH.D. in 1895, and at the University of Berlin. DuBois turned from history to sociology in the hope of providing accurate information as the basis for public policy on Negro rights.

He set himself against the enigmatic abstractions, the "verbal jugglery," of Herbert Spencer. In *The Philadelphia Negro* (1899), his finest scholarly work, he used the technique of Charles Booth's *Life and Labour of the People in London* to yield a pioneering door-to-door survey of the occupations, values, political influence, social intercourse, and family life of the 45,000 Negroes in the seventh ward of Philadelphia. With the research for this book, he tried to uncover information to replace the "fantastic theories, ungrounded assumptions, or metaphysical subleties" that passed among white men for knowledge about the Negro.

As professor of economics and sociology at Atlanta University, from 1897 to 1910, he edited the Atlanta University Publications, a series of yearly pamphlets on different aspects of Negro life—artisans, college graduates, schools, groups organized for social betterment, criminals, etc. The volumes were partly hortatory, partly factual. The factual section summarized DuBois' year-long research, generally based on questionnaires distributed in Negro communities throughout the country. His results, although fragmentary, contained valuable data not available elsewhere. DuBois was the first student of Negro life to make empiricism the core of his work. For years he stood almost alone.

The failure of scholarly research to budge the prejudices of white Americans moved him to more active agitation. Contemptuous of the gradualism advocated by Booker T. Washington, DuBois called for full equality as the immediate demand of justice. To lead the Negro's fight he looked to a college-trained Negro elite, which he called the "talented tenth" (1903a), and in 1905 organized the Niagara movement, consisting of a handful of educated northern Negroes committed to his program. The National Association for the Advancement of Colored People (NAACP), a biracial group, absorbed most of these men and the lean, aloof DuBois became director of research and editor of its monthly magazine, *Crisis.* He spoke from this podium during the 24 years from 1910 to 1934, making himself, after Washington's death in 1915, the most significant spokesman for Negro rights in America and the greatest single influence on the generation of leaders that followed. DuBois supported the association's program of organization, publicity, and legal action; at the same time, he urged Negroes to free themselves from the white man—create their own ideals and assert control over their own organizations. He broke with the NAACP in 1934, when under the pressure of the great depression he argued for voluntary segregation in a self-sufficient Negro community within America. He again became a professor at Atlanta, where he completed *Black Reconstruction* (1935), an eccentric blend of racial chauvinism, unassimilated Marxist terminology, and melodramatic fantasy, that nevertheless summarized for the first time the striking achievements of black-and-white governments in the South after the Civil War.

DuBois felt a special kinship with nonwhite peoples, especially black men in Africa, whom he regarded as victims of Western capitalism and white prejudice. To publicize their needs he organized Pan-African congresses, the first of which met in Paris in 1919. DuBois nursed the movement through the 1920s, but it went into eclipse until 1945, when, again at his call, the sixth congress met as Asian and African peoples were breaking out of European colonial systems. Jubilant, DuBois found himself the intellectual "father of Pan-Africanism." He drew away from the United States. Unsympathetic to American policies and despairing of the Negro leadership of the time, he looked upon the Soviet Union's campaigns for peace and for world socialism as the most promising paths to the future.

In his later years DuBois traveled widely in China and in eastern Europe, where he was cordially acclaimed at a time when his reputation at home had faded. He was awarded a Lenin peace prize in 1959. The following year he went to Ghana to fulfill a half-century-old dream of editing the first African encyclopedia. Late in 1961, DuBois joined the American Communist party. Finally, caught in the movement of African nationalism, he became a Ghanaian citizen just before his death, in Accra, Ghana, in 1963.

FRANCIS L. BRODERICK

[*For the historical context of DuBois' work, see the biography of* BOOTH. *For discussion of the subsequent development of his ideas, see* RACE RELATIONS.]

WORKS BY DUBOIS

(1896) 1954   *The Suppression of the African Slave-trade to the United States of America, 1638–1870.* New York: Social Science Press.

1898   The Study of the Negro Problems. American Academy of Political and Social Science, *Annals* 11:1–23.

1899   *The Philadelphia Negro: A Social Study, Together With a Special Report on Domestic Service by Isabel Eaton.* Series in Political Economy and Public Law, No. 14. Philadelphia: Univ. of Pennsylvania.

1903a   The Talented Tenth. Pages 31–75 in *The Negro Problem: A Series of Articles by Representative American Negroes of Today.* New York: Pott.

(1903b) 1963   *The Souls of Black Folk: Essays and Sketches.* Gloucester, Mass.: Peter Smith.

1920   *Darkwater: Voices From Within the Veil.* New York: Harcourt.

(1935) 1956   *Black Reconstruction: An Essay Toward a History of the Part Which Black Folk Played in the Attempt to Reconstruct Democracy in America, 1860–1880.* New York: Russell. → A paperback edition was published in 1964 by Meridian Books.

1940   *Dusk of Dawn: An Essay Toward an Autobiography of a Race Concept.* New York: Harcourt.

(1947) 1964   *The World and Africa: An Inquiry Into the Part Which Africa Has Played in World History.* Rev. ed. New York: International Publishers.

SUPPLEMENTARY BIBLIOGRAPHY

BRODERICK, FRANCIS L. 1959   *W. E. B. DuBois, Negro Leader in a Time of Crisis.* Stanford (Calif.) Univ. Press.

ISAACS, HAROLD R. 1960   DuBois and Africa. *Race* 7: 3:23.

RUDWICK, ELLIOT M. 1960   *W. E. B. DuBois: A Study in Minority Group Leadership.* Philadelphia: Univ. of Pennsylvania Press.

DUE PROCESS
See the articles under CONSTITUTIONAL LAW.

DUGUIT, LÉON

Léon Duguit (1859–1928) was a professor in the Faculté de Droit at Bordeaux from 1886 until his death. The portion of his work that is relevant to social science in general is contained essentially in two major works: one is the two-volume *Études de droit public* (1901–1902); the other is *Traité de droit constitutionnel* (1911).

Duguit's predominant concern was to discover the rules that should "control, direct [and] limit" the actions of those who govern. He sought to ascertain how those who hold political power and the force to compel compliance should use that power and that force—given that they hold them not as their personal right but merely as a means of performing a social function. They should not, therefore, use them arbitrarily but solely according to the interests of society; otherwise their actions would be unlawful, and hence invalid.

In the modern state, political power is primarily exerted through legislation—that is, by the establishment of rules of conduct for the governed.

Consequently, to determine "the norm for government action" means, in the first place, to establish what laws the political authority should and should not lay down. This is, then, a much larger and more general task than Duguit implied when he wrote in traditional liberal terms of "limiting the State," of "limitation of the power of those who govern." Actually, what is involved is nothing less than determining the entire juridical order that those in power shall create: all the rules of law that go to make it up, whatever their object, whether it be relations among private persons (private law) or between those who govern—or their agents—and private persons (public law).

Duguit did make a basic distinction, however, between two sorts of legal rules, the "normative rules of law," or "legal norms properly so called," and the "constructive or technical rules of law." The former rules constitute prohibitions or commands; in particular, injunctions on individuals to act or abstain from acting—e.g., not to commit murder, to pay taxes, to respect property. The latter rules enact measures to ensure that the former are respected and enforced, defining the authority entrusted with applying a sanction to persons breaking them. There is no doubt that Duguit intended to determine only what normative rules control the actions of those who govern.

For Duguit the "constructive rules of law," as their name indicates, are consciously made by man, whereas the "legal norms properly so called" are quite different. Another fundamental element of his theories on law is the distinction (in a way more basic than the previous one) between "objective law" and "positive law." It is not difficult to define positive law: it is those rules of law laid down, applied, and enforced by "the public power" or state. But what did Duguit mean by "objective law"?

On some occasions, he defined it by a sociological criterion: a juridical norm is a social norm in that the bulk of the members of a group accepts as legitimate its regular enforcement by those in power. A rule of law obtains if the conscience of the bulk of the people desires and demands this sanction as necessary to the maintenance of social solidarity. In short, "objective law" consists of the rules of law that in the opinion of the majority should have an organized sanction. Thus, juridical norms are a spontaneous product of mass conscience.

On other occasions, however, Duguit gave a genuinely objective definition of objective law: a legal rule is one that is derived from the current and changing conditions of the life of a given society and determined by observation and rational analysis, and that prescribes certain actions and prohibits others to all the members of the society. Viewed in this way, objective law is contingent on social fact, is in fact a spontaneous creation of social life.

Regardless of his uncertainty about the exact nature of positive law, Duguit considered the task of operating with these notions of law as belonging to the science of law, in cooperation, to be sure, with other social sciences. In fact, he regarded this as the chief mission and *raison d'être* of the social sciences; if they fail to perform this task, they convict themselves of futility: "Social research has reason for existing and value only insofar as it can draw up rules of conduct that gain the respect of those who govern" (Duguit 1902, p. xxiii). "[All] juridical speculations are vain unless they succeed in determining . . . the solid basis of a juridical limitation on the action of those who govern" ([1911] 1921–1925, vol. 1, p. 65). Duguit further admitted that it is possible to establish these rules of objective law by observation alone, by "direct determination of facts" perceived by the senses, i.e., by the scientific method. Bent on being a positivist and realist, he rejected, in the tradition of Auguste Comte, all theological or metaphysical speculation. He insisted that the legal rules are present in social reality and that the role of the jurist consists in "discovering them beneath the social facts" and in noting them, rather than in any way promulgating them because he happens to believe that they are good.

This scientific task will by no means produce "higher principles," but rather rules that vary from one society to another and, over time, in the same society. Duguit categorically rejected the idea that there are rules of law that are valid absolutely, eternally, and universally. He asserted that all that we observe are rules that are diverse, relative, and contingent. In a word, he rejected the idea of natural law. The higher principle or principles posited by its advocates are posited a priori; they may indeed be "objects of metaphysical or religious belief," but there is "nothing scientific" about them.

Given these two kinds of law—objective and positive—how did Duguit conceive of their normative relationships? His position is very explicit: only the rules of objective law (which alone are "legal norms properly so called") have an obligatory force of their own, i.e., validity for those whose conduct they claim to determine. The rules of positive law (what we would call, basically, the law), on the other hand, are not binding in and of themselves, but only if, and hence because, they sanction a rule of objective law. When a legislative rule is not backed up by a rule of objective law, it is invalid, has no obligatory force, and is not juridically binding on the citizens, or on the courts, for that matter. "Obedience is due not to legislation as such, but only to legislation as expressing and executing a juridical norm. . . . Legislation can only be obligatory if it expresses a juridical norm that is prior to it, created by the very conscience of those to whom it is addressed, i.e., spontaneous" (*ibid.*, vol. 1, p. 153). Logically, then, it is the duty of the state "when it makes a law, to formulate an already existing rule of law that is binding in and of itself, or to take constructive measures to assure its enforcement" (*ibid.*, vol. 3, p. 555) and never to set itself up in opposition to objective law, the "higher law," which is rigorously binding on it, even if that higher law has not been sanctioned by a source of positive law. Thus, objective law is higher than positive law and is the condition of its validity, its obligatory character, its very character as a rule or norm. At bottom, it alone is truly law or, in any event, original law. The "sources of positive law"—legislation, jurisprudence, custom—are not as such sources of rules of law; they only become that on the condition that the rules they profess to lay down conform to the rules of objective law, which is the supreme principle of all juridical validity.

As Duguit saw it, his theory of the state and his theory of law were positivistic, realistic, and sociological. It was a "sociological–juridical doctrine" that he had "tried to base on pure observation of social facts," sticking to "the observable facts" and therefore rejecting "metaphysics and all a priori concepts." He liked to call himself a "sociological jurist." The two thinkers who influenced him most were Auguste Comte, the positivist philosopher and precursor of sociology, and Émile Durkheim, the great French sociologist of the early twentieth century. These influences can be noted in some of his general views on law and government.

He rejected the idea of natural law and refused to idealize a fortiori or to deify the state and its rulers. He rejected all systems that present the state as an organic unity or even as an ideal unity, and he declared that the state is merely a society in which there is a differentiation between the governed and the governors (i.e., those who hold political power). The state is nothing more or less than "a fact of greater force." He constantly repeated that "those who govern are individuals like the others," that they are not higher in nature or qualities than those who are governed, that their will is not higher in essence or virtue than the will of the latter. The only constant difference between those who govern and those who are governed is that the former control the force of constraint.

Duguit's system did not succeed in establishing scientifically the proper juridical order. Rather than a theory of positive science (whether juridical or sociological), Duguit presented a doctrine of political philosophy or political ethics. His central theses clearly are meant to act on people's minds, to help anchor in them certain beliefs that will determine their behavior. The absolute intellectual acceptance of facts that he advocated has come off second best. Duguit himself went so far as to admit that the statement that the state is limited by objective law is only an academic formula and that this limitation cannot in fact exist at all, "for there is no law without a material sanction and there can be no sanction against the state" (*ibid.*, vol. 3, p. 549). But he nonetheless advocated that "we should never tire of energetically asserting the subordination of the state to a higher law, chiefly in order to impress that idea more deeply into the consciousness of the collectivity, so that those who hold power will hesitate to oppose [this law] openly" (*ibid.*, vol. 3, p. 550). These dogmatic assertions patently contradict nearly all the basic principles of positive law. Duguit acknowledged this explicitly.

Duguit also failed to found "objective law," that is, positive law supported by scientific method. He never even provided examples that might indicate how this could be done. He confined himself to propositions just as formal and dialectical as those of the traditional theorists of the "common weal": social law, which is binding on all, is that law that governs the formation and development of the group; the members of the group, and the governors first of all, should strive to maintain and develop their interdependence, their solidarity with the group, by promoting justice and welfare. At best, these are theoretical principles from which no concrete rules can be deduced, with the possible exception of a few rules that are self-evident in any society.

The great error that vitiates this system is Duguit's belief in the possibility of establishing, as a scientific truth, that individuals are bound by conscience to observe social rules emerging directly from social facts or, at a deeper level perhaps, the belief that rules of conduct exist in social facts—i.e., that they can in some way be read there, discovered there, and that men, or rather the "learned," need only declare their obligatory force. He acknowledged these beliefs; they contain in embryo the failure of his enterprise, and the weakness of the major part of his theory of law and the state.

Although many of Duguit's theories have been criticized, there is no doubt whatever that they exerted a considerable influence on several generations of professors in French law faculties, from the time of their first publication early in the twentieth century. He not only gained wide acceptance among legal scholars for methods of juridical analysis, but he also won adherents among the politically oriented for his realistic approach to the state and for his assertion that the power of those who govern is to be considered simply a social function, existing only in the interest of the nation and to be exercised only in that interest. (This position was the very antithesis of the Hegelian or Prussian tradition that dominated German theories of public law, with their metaphysical or political exaltation of the power of the state.) Duguit's best-known follower in the theory of international law was Georges Scelle; in the field of administrative law, his most important intellectual descendants were Gaston Jèze, Roger Bonnard, and Louis Rolland. If Duguit's doctrine as a whole, then, no longer has the impact it once had, his name is nevertheless a great one in the history of French juridical thought.

CHARLES EISENMANN

[*For the historical context of Duguit's work, see the biographies of* COMTE; DURKHEIM. *For discussion of similar ideas, see* JURISPRUDENCE; LAW, *article on* THE SOCIOLOGY OF LAW; *and the biographies of* BRECHT; EHRLICH; HAURIOU; HELLER; JELLINEK; KANTOROWICZ; KELSEN; LLEWELLYN; POUND.]

WORKS BY DUGUIT

1901–1902 *Études de droit public.* 2 vols. Paris: Fontemoing. → Volume 1: *L'état, le droit objectif et la loi positive.* Volume 2: *L'état, les gouvernants et les agents.*

1902 Preface. In Volume 1, Woodrow Wilson, *L'état: Éléments d'histoire et de practique politique.* Paris: Giard & Brière.

(1911) 1921–1925 *Traité de droit constitutionnel.* 2d ed., 5 vols. Paris: Boccard. → Volume 1: *La règle de droit —Le problème de l'état.* Volumes 2–3: *La théorie générale de l'état.* Volume 4: *L'organisation politique de la France.* Volume 5: *Les libertés publiques.*

(1913) 1919 *Law in the Modern State.* Translated by Frida Laski and Harold J. Laski. New York: Huebsch. → First published as *Les transformations du droit public.*

WORKS ABOUT DUGUIT

BONNARD, ROGER 1928–1929 Léon Duguit: 1859–1928. *Revue internationale de la théorie du droit* 3:58–70. → Contains a bibliography on pages 68–70.

BONNECASE, JULIEN 1928–1929 La science juridique française: Quelques aspects fondamentaux de l'oeuvre

de Léon Duguit. *Revue générale du droit, de la législation et de la jurisprudence en France et à l'étranger* 52:281–288; 53:60–67, 123–131, 205–215.

EISENMANN, CHARLES 1930 Deux théoriciens du droit: Duguit et Hauriou. *Revue philosophique de la France et de l'étranger* 110:231–279.

DUOPOLY

See OLIGOPOLY.

DUPUIT, JULES

Arsène Jules Étienne Juvénal Dupuit (1804–1866), usually subscribed J. Dupuit, was a French civil engineer and economist; he is known today chiefly for his development of the concept later termed "consumer's surplus."

Dupuit was born in Fossano, in the Piedmont, and moved with his family to France in 1814. He studied at the *collèges* of Versailles, Louis le Grand, and Saint Louis, at the École Polytechnique, and at the École des Ponts et Chaussées. After serving in the Corps des Ponts et Chaussées in various outlying departments, he became chief engineer for the city of Paris in 1850 and inspector-general of the Corps des Ponts et Chaussées in 1885.

Early in his career he became interested in the problem of determining under what conditions the construction of bridges or other public works could be justified, becoming probably the first person to pursue what is now known as cost–benefit analysis on a rigorous basis. In the course of this analysis he developed the concept that the benefits are to be measured not by what is actually paid but by the amount that might be paid under conditions of perfect discrimination—as measured by the area under the demand curve. He seems to have developed the concept of the demand curve independently of Cournot. [*See the biography of* COURNOT.] His measure of the "utility" of a facility was the excess of the benefits so measured over the costs or tolls paid by the user, later called "consumer's surplus" by Marshall.

Dupuit was highly critical of attempts to justify public works by reference to vague "secondary benefits"; he reiterated that "Il n'y a d'utilité que celle qu'on consent à payer," by which he meant that unless a benefit is somehow reflected in the demand curve, it is illusory. He was undoubtedly correct in his criticism of the double counting often found in justifications for some of the more grandiose schemes of his contemporaries. His formulation did, however, exclude "neighborhood effects" from his evaluation, which would be justifiable either on the ground that they were, in this context, negligible, or that they could, in principle, be charged for, even though not includable in the usual type of demand curve.

These concepts were first published in 1844 in "De la mesure de l'utilité des travaux publics" ([1844–1854] 1933, pp. 29–65) and in 1849 elaborated in "De l'influence des péages sur l'utilité des voies de communication" (*ibid.*, pp. 97–162) and in 1853 in "De l'utilité et de sa mesure" (*ibid.*, pp. 165–181). This last was apparently prepared as an article for Coquelin and Guillaumin's *Dictionnaire d'économie politique* (1852–1853), which included articles by Dupuit on "Eau," "Poids et mesures," "Ponts et chaussées," "Routes et chemins," "Voies de communication," and an article on "Péage," which contains cross references to an omitted article on "Utilité"; it is somewhat ironical that this article, which contains the ideas for which Dupuit is best remembered, was omitted in favor of a relatively conventional one by H. Passy.

Beginning about 1850 Dupuit became increasingly interested in economics, and his name, which had since 1838 been appearing fairly regularly as contributor to the *Annales des ponts et chaussées*, began appearing in the *Journal des économistes*, while his engineering articles became less frequent. Dupuit became an ardent advocate of laissez-faire. He wrote a vigorous tract, "La liberté commerciale," in defense of free trade, which was published in parts in the *Revue européenne* in 1860 and as a separate volume in 1861. He was a staunch Malthusian, arguing that standards of living were observably higher in areas with low density of population and low rates of population growth and even going so far as to condemn charitable distributions in times of famine on the ground that while the direct objects of charity were helped, such activities, since they would drive up food prices, would be primarily at the expense of the nourishment of the remaining poor classes.

True to his engineering background, however, Dupuit remained essentially a pragmatist. He did not let his antagonism toward government interference in general inhibit his recognition that in the case of natural monopolies a government would be likely to set a price more conducive to economical utilization of the facility than would a private monopoly. He did not go so far as to advocate pricing at marginal cost, as A. P. Lerner and Harold Hotelling later did, and indeed at points he seems to suggest that on occasion private enterprise, since it has greater incentive to ferret out more profitable schemes of discrimination, might produce a better utilization of the facility than would a government agency. He vigorously attacked the natural law

theory of property rights, asserting that the particular forms that property rights took, particularly in relation to mineral rights and the rights of authors and inventors, were the result of man-made law that could and should decide in favor of those forms of property tenure that would be most conducive to economic efficiency. While he was reluctant, in many cases, to specify in detail what pattern of property rights this principle called for, he did indicate that patents should have a shorter term than copyrights and that discoverers of minerals should have some (not very clearly indicated) rights vis-à-vis the landlord. On the other hand, he considered that property rights legitimized by contract or created by government sanction must be respected, even if such rights were plainly of a sort leading to inefficiency and even if the contract was only implicit. Postmasters, having enjoyed the right to a toll on all traffic over their route whether or not the post relay facilities were used, could not be deprived of this right without compensation; on the other hand, their claim to a similar toll on the growing traffic on parallel railroads should not be allowed. Unlimited freedom of contract was not, however, desirable in all cases; in particular, freedom of bequest was undesirable in that parents should not be allowed to bring children into the world and then disinherit them and cause them to become a burden to the rest of the community. Indeed, Dupuit at one point suggested that parents of uneducated children should be required to pay a special tax. Dupuit's pragmatism showed itself again in his attitude toward the tobacco tax; while he regarded this tax as essentially unjust in singling out a particular taste for a special burden, and doubly so in that the grades consumed by the poor were taxed most heavily, ad valorem, the tax was nevertheless a good one in that it did not impair productivity.

During his later years Dupuit was an active member of the Société d'Économie Politique, and he often engaged in vigorous disputation at its meetings. He argued that economics was attaining the status of a science, by which he meant that there was a growing body of universally accepted principles, a penumbra of matters still under debate and investigation, and a vast domain of unexplored matters. He regarded free trade as one of the universally accepted principles and went so far as to take editor Henri Baudrillat to task (1863) for stooping to include in the *Journal des économistes* such "unscientific" articles as the review by R. de Fontenay of a French translation of Henry Carey's *Principles of Social Science*, in which free trade and Malthusian doctrines were strongly attacked.

On other occasions he spoke out vigorously against controls over banks and dealers in foreign exchange, against licensing of doctors, against the promotion of workers' cooperatives and labor unions, against child labor laws, government crop predictions, and property transfer taxes. While he felt that woman's place is in the home, he opposed legal barriers to the employment of women that existed in certain occupations. However, he expressed himself in favor of government ownership of railroads. He considered the premature redemption of bonds as inequitable if not clearly provided for in the indenture and preferred that government bonds take the form of nonredeemable perpetuals or "consols," arguing that to provide explicitly for redemption was unduly costly. He objected to the state monopoly of education, holding that it made it impossible to teach economic doctrines that implied criticism of state action, and he felt, moreover, that too much time is wasted in higher education as compared with apprenticeship.

Dupuit was no less a center of controversy in his engineering role. In 1842 he published the results of a series of experiments on friction in wagon wheels, in which he came to the conclusion, backed by theoretical analysis, that the rolling component of the friction varied inversely as the square root of the radius of the wheel, contradicting both the relation inherited from the eminent Coulomb and the empirical work of his contemporaries, who claimed the component varied inversely as the radius itself. Over the next decade he actively advocated more liberal traffic rules, particularly those relating to maximum loads on vehicles, on the basis that road maintenance, consisting in those days mainly in the replacement of material ground into dust by passing traffic, varied very nearly in proportion to the gross weight of the traffic and hence that heavy vehicles would not be uneconomical for the nation as a whole if they were profitable to the operator. This effort met with only limited success. In 1850 he published the results of an investigation of the collapse of a suspension bridge at Angers. During the crossing of an army detachment in a heavy storm, 226 lives were lost; Dupuit blamed the failure on the ineffectiveness of measures taken to protect the suspension cables from rust as they passed through the anchorages, which were subject to flooding. Since the same methods had been fairly widely used elsewhere, his findings were attacked with some vigor.

With regard to his economic activities, it is his work on utility and consumer's surplus that constitutes his lasting contribution. While there is no mention of Dupuit in the first edition of Jevons' *Theory of Political Economy* (1871), the second edition contains an extensive discussion of Dupuit's contribution in the preface, and full references in the bibliographical appendix. That Jevons highly respected Dupuit's contribution is shown further by the extensive comments interpolated by H. S. Jevons from his father's manuscript notes in the bibliographical appendix for the fourth edition. Maffeo Pantaleoni refers frequently to Dupuit in his *Principles of Pure Economy*, but he is concerned primarily with the concept of utility as an element of value theory and makes little prescriptive use of Dupuit's concepts. Marshall also refers to Dupuit but indicates that both he and Jevons originally arrived at their own formulations independently of Dupuit. And while Marshall does discuss the possibility that it might be desirable to subsidize decreasing cost industries, his exposition lacks the incisiveness of that of Dupuit. It remained for Pigou in 1912 in his *Wealth and Welfare* and in 1920 in his *Economics of Welfare* to elaborate the prescriptions to which Dupuit pointed. Pigou, however, does not refer to Dupuit as a source, nor do most of the writers on the theme of marginal cost pricing or subsidy to decreasing cost industries throughout the 1920s and 1930s until Hotelling, in 1938, possibly stimulated by the republication of Dupuit's salient works by Mario de Bernardi in 1933, based his mathematical analysis of the case for marginal cost pricing squarely on Dupuit as a precursor. Thus, although Dupuit must clearly be given priority in the formulation of some of the fundamental concepts of modern welfare economics, his work appears to have had singularly little actual influence on the way economic thought developed over the next century.

WILLIAM S. VICKREY

[*For discussion of the subsequent development of Dupuit's ideas, see* CONSUMER'S SURPLUS; UTILITY; WELFARE ECONOMICS.]

WORKS BY DUPUIT

1842 Mémoire sur le tirage des voitures et sur le frottement de roulement. *Annales des ponts et chaussées* Part 2 3:261–335.

(1844–1854) 1933 *De l'utilité et de sa mesure: Écrits choisis et republiés par Mario de Bernardi.* Turin (Italy): La Riforma Sociale. → Contains a bibliography of Dupuit's works.

1850 Rapport de la commission d'enquête nommée . . . pour rechercher les causes et les circonstances qui ont amené la chute du pont suspendu de la Basse-Chaîne. *Annales des ponts et chaussées* Part 2 20:394–411.

(1860) 1861 *La liberté commerciale: Son principe et ses conséquences.* Paris: Guillaumin.

1863   Réponse de M. Dupuit à M. Baudrillat au sujet de l'article "L'économie est elle une science ou une étude?" *Journal des économistes* Series 2 37:474–482.

SUPPLEMENTARY BIBLIOGRAPHY

COQUELIN, CHARLES; and GUILLAUMIN, GILBERT U. (editors) (1852–1853) 1874 *Dictionnaire d'économie politique.* 2 vols. Paris: Guillaumin.

HOTELLING, HAROLD 1938 The General Welfare in Relation to Problems of Taxation and of Railway and Utility Rates. *Econometrica* 6:242–269.

JEVONS, WILLIAM S. (1871) 1965 *The Theory of Political Economy.* 5th ed. New York: Kelley. → Pages xi–lii contain the "Preface" to the second edition by Jevons.

DURKHEIM, ÉMILE

Émile Durkheim (1858–1917) may be called one of the two principal founders of the modern phase of sociological theory, the other being his somewhat younger contemporary Max Weber. In his four major works, starting with *The Division of Labor in Society* of 1893 and ending with *The Elementary Forms of the Religious Life* of 1912, and in a large number of articles, monographs, and carefully worked out courses of lectures (several of which have been published posthumously), Durkheim established a broad framework for the analysis of social systems that has remained central to sociology and a number of related disciplines, particularly anthropology, ever since. Even those who basically disagree with it take it as a major point of reference. This frame of analysis underwent substantial development in the course of Durkheim's own career, but it focused continually on the nature of the social system and the relation of that system to the personality of the individual.

Durkheim was born in the town of Épinal in the Vosges, not far from Strasbourg. He was of Jewish parentage, and some of his forebears were rabbis. Indeed he was expected to be a rabbi himself until he became an agnostic. He attended the famous École Normale Supérieure in Paris, together with such luminaries as Henri Bergson, Jean Jaurès, and Pierre Janet. His primary focus was on philosophy, but he already had the strong concern with political and social applications that he retained throughout his life. He was too rebellious to rank high among the *agrégés* of his year, and his first academic appointments were as teacher of philosophy in several provincial *lycées*.

In 1885–1886 Durkheim took a year's leave of absence to study in Germany, where he was par-

ticularly impressed by the work of the psychologist Wilhelm Wundt. A professorship of sociology (combined with education), the first in France, was created for him in 1887 at Bordeaux, and he remained there until, in 1902, he realized the ambition of all French academics: he was called to a professorship in sociology and education at the Sorbonne in Paris. There he gathered round himself a distinguished group of younger men, including Henri Berr, Marcel Granet, François Simiand, Maurice Halbwachs, and, not least, his own nephew, Marcel Mauss. In the most intimate relationship to his own work, Durkheim founded and edited the very important journal, *L'année sociologique.* On two significant occasions he became very much involved in political affairs: during the Dreyfus case and during World War I. And over a considerable period he was actively concerned with applied sociology, most notably perhaps in the field of education.

The first three of Durkheim's four books, the *Division of Labor,* the *Rules of Sociological Method,* and *Suicide,* were all published during his Bordeaux period, in 1893, 1895, and 1897 respectively. Then there was an interval of 15 years before the *Elementary Forms* (1912) appeared. After the move to Paris, Durkheim was deeply involved both with his teaching and with the group discussions and activities centering on *L'année sociologique.* It is clear, however, that his thought was developing very rapidly and continuously during this period: witness such fundamentally important articles as "The Determination of Moral Facts" (1906) and "Primitive Classification" (Durkheim & Mauss 1903). The great book on religion, then, was the ripe harvest of a long process of intensive cultivation.

There is evidence that the war was a very great blow and strain to Durkheim. Not only was the cost to France high indeed: Peyre tells us (1960) that over half the class that entered the École Normale in 1913 was killed before the war ended; but Durkheim also lost his only son in 1916. These strains may well have helped to cause his own death from a heart attack, on November 15, 1917, at the age of 59.

Intellectual background. Despite some controversy about the influence of his stay in Germany, the evidence shows that Durkheim's thought was rooted overwhelmingly in French intellectual history. In the remoter background, Descartes and Rousseau were the most important, although in quite different ways. Much closer to him were Saint-Simon, Auguste Comte, and his own teacher,

Fustel de Coulanges, as well as such others as Émile Boutroux.

Durkheim's deep concern with the prominent contemporary intellectual currents of other countries, especially England and Germany, was authentically French: it is no disparagement of the originality of French thought on problems of man and society to say that it filled a mediating position between the two wings of the main European trends of thought, British empiricism and utilitarianism and German idealism. In a crucial sense, modern sociology is a product of the synthesis of elements that have figured most prominently in these two traditions, and it seems to have been the mediating character of his French background that gave Durkheim a distinctive "place to stand," from which he contributed so effectively to this synthesis. Hence a brief sketch of both "wings" will help in the understanding of Durkheim's own orientation and statement of problems (see also Parsons 1937; 1965).

As both these traditions developed, perhaps the crucial problem was what happened as the Cartesian approach to the problem of knowledge was adapted to the analysis of *action*. The British position is clearest in the economic branch of utilitarian thought, although it dates from the earliest utilitarian formulation by Hobbes: man is conceived as having not only "sensations" or "ideas," in the epistemological sense of Locke, but also what the economists called "wants" (and what Hobbes, speaking in a political context, went so far as to call "passions"). The wants define the goals of action, whereas knowledge of the situation in which action takes place provides guidance for the instrumental use of resources (including the individual's own capacities) toward the satisfaction of these wants. Mere knowledge of the situation clearly does not suffice to satisfy wants; the situation must be changed in desired ways and prevented from changing in undesirable ways. Throughout, the point of reference is the conception of an individual acting in pursuit of his own "interests."

This frame of reference provided the background for a most important development in the analysis of action, namely, a first technical analysis of the structuring of social means for the satisfaction of wants. The economists, by considering how a plurality of individuals, as producers and consumers, interact in the division of labor and exchange, ingeniously extended Hobbes's formulation—of men interdependent in their interest in "power"—to a conception of *social systems of action* coordinated by the market and the monetary mechanism rather than of action by discrete individuals. As far

as it went in classical economics, this conceptual venture was brilliantly successful; but its exceedingly limited scope gradually became evident in two borderline contexts.

One concerned the analysis of the bases of action of the individual. The inadequacy of classical economics here lay not only in its tendency to assume "wants" as given but also in its lack of a clear-cut way of establishing relationships among the different wants of a single individual, to say nothing of the different wants of several persons interacting in the same social system. Without concepts to establish these relationships, the treatment of wants as given easily shaded over into the assumption of their randomness. Likewise, shaky assumptions were made with respect to the problem of "rationality," that is, of the relation between means and wants conceived as ends. In this context, the empiricist–utilitarian tradition tended to a reductionism that is still very much with us: it moves from consideration of the characteristics of the social system (in the economic case, a market system) to the consideration of the properties of constituent units (i.e., individuals rationally engaged in want-satisfaction), then to the wants, next to the psychological determinants of the wants, and eventually to their biological conditions.

The second problematic context bordering on classical economic analysis concerned what we now call the problem of order. How could the relational structure of a market economy be expected to have even a minimum level of stability when the individual participants were in the first instance bound to that structure only by "self-interest," i.e., by their interest in the effective satisfaction of their several wants? Hobbes had presented a radical solution to this problem—the establishment of an absolute sovereign authority—in *Leviathan*, but, as Halévy made clear (Halévy 1901–1904), Hobbes's influence was pushed aside by that of the Lockean wing of the utilitarian tradition, which assumed a "natural identity of interests." The Lockean tradition did not really attempt to solve the problem of order but instead tried to justify the refusal to consider it. Although the Lockean approach facilitated certain valuable developments in economic analysis and in some forms of political analysis, it failed to provide that solution to the problem of order which was needed before a generalized interpretation of modern "economic individualism" could be developed. A notable version of the problem, which greatly influenced Ricardo and indirectly influenced Marx, was advanced by Malthus, but it remained for Durkheim to make a fundamental direct attack on the problem. In terms of substantive sociology, this is the main starting point of his more technical theory.

Before taking this up, however, a few words must be said about the other current of thought converging on the French "middle ground," namely German idealism and the movements stemming from it.

The problems that social science must explain, in Durkheim's view, lie on the subjective side of the Cartesian dichotomy, since the entire main tradition of epistemology, of which Descartes's work was the focal point, virtually limited the external world to the world of objects as understood in terms of the new physical science. (It was, of course, possible—witness biologically based psychology and anthropology—to move into social science from the base of the object world, but this path was relatively unimportant to Durkheim.) Whereas the empiricist utilitarians had used this "subjective" element merely as a reference point for the study of behavior, failing conspicuously to structure it on its own terms, the idealists increasingly focused upon it and tended to treat it as a category of objects. In this respect Kant's philosophy seems to have been transitional, while the Hegelian "objective spirit" (*objektiver Geist*) is the focal idealistic conception relevant here. This conception of *Geist* was primarily cultural, somewhat in the tradition of Platonic Ideas. As such it was *transindividual*, on quite a different level from the discrete wants of utilitarianism.

The Hegelian conception underwent various changes, only two aspects of which require mention here. One was the abandonment of the grandiose Hegelian *Weltgeist* in favor of the more restricted "spirits" of what many late nineteenth-century German scholars called discrete "historical individuals," such as particular cultures or civilizations in particular epochs. This modification was perhaps most consistently expounded by Wilhelm Dilthey. The other was that developed by Marx. As the one who "set Hegel on his head," Marx was ostensibly a materialist rather than an idealist. Nevertheless, his materialism belongs to the idealist tradition in that it treats human culture and motivated action as objects, and it tends to be "historical" in the special sense of handling "history" as a series of ideographic exemptions from treatment in terms of generalized analytical categories.

Durkheim accepted the crucial Cartesian statement of the problem of knowledge in terms of the relation between the knowing subject and the known world of external objects. In his initial orientation he was a Cartesian "rationalist," in the sense that he approached the sociological problem

as a problem of knowing "social facts" in terms of their place in the object world. However, as he shifted from the problem of knowledge to that of action, he became *concurrently* concerned with social facts as both the social scientist and the actor in society, as subjects, know them. The problem of the relation between the two references was the core problem of Durkheim's scheme. Thus, although basically Cartesian, this scheme could not be developed without going beyond a Cartesian position in several respects.

Rousseau, as the primary philosopher of "democratic individualism" in his time, influenced Durkheim by his special point of view about the characteristics of social phenomena. While Rousseau shared the frame of reference of natural law and natural rights that was so prominent in the seventeenth and eighteenth centuries (and which, in important respects, came to France from England through Locke), he handled the problem of the social integration of those "born free" into a society without invoking the predominantly coercive sovereign of Hobbes or assuming the natural identity of interests, as did Locke. Rather, he postulated a resolution of interests at the level of integrative action processes in terms of the concept of "will." More than any other, Rousseau's famous concept of the *volonté générale* provided a conception of social solidarity that was neither economic in the sense of classical economics nor political in the sense of Hobbes or Austin. It was not a given "identity" of interests, but one achieved and institutionalized in the course of social process. Comte's concept of "consensus," which stood more immediately in Durkheim's background and was explicitly defined as sociological, was transitional between Rousseau's "general will" and Durkheim's conception of solidarity, which lay at the core of his sociology.

The problem of order.   Durkheim's initial orientation to the study of society was twofold. The substantive aspect was developed in the *Division of Labor* and concerned the problem of order in a type of system we might call economic individualism. The methodological frame of reference was developed more fully in the *Rules of Sociological Method*, published two years later.

The critical starting point of the *Division of Labor* is its discussion of Herbert Spencer's conception of a system of contractual relations (*Division of Labor*, book I, chapter 7). Durkheim clearly understood that *order* in a concrete system of contractual relations—in which the market figured prominently—could not be accounted for in the terms set forth by Spencer, whom Durkheim treated as a representative utilitarian. Unless controlled by other factors, a society dominated by the pure pursuit of self-interest would dissolve into a Hobbesian state of nature, a complete breakdown of order. The other factor or set of factors Durkheim formulated in two different ways, and on different levels. Closest to Spencer's analysis was the conception of the "non-contractual elements of contract," the important idea that contracts, i.e., the *ad hoc* agreements between parties, are always subject to generalized norms. These norms are not open to negotiation between parties; they exist prior to any such agreements, having evolved over time. In more comprehensive systems, these rules or norms are part of the formal law and are enforced by the legal sanctions of public authority. Their subject matter is the definition of the interests for which contracts may be entered into (for example, a man may not contract away his basic civil rights), the means by which such interests may legitimately be pursued (in general terms, coercion and fraud are excluded), and the bearing on contracts of interests other than those of the contracting parties (both the public interest and those of third private parties must be protected).

As noted, at one level the institution of contract is a prominent part of the legal system. Durkheim, however, wanted to go behind the establishment of norms by political authority to societal structures that may be said to "underlie" the mobilization of political authority for the enforcement of contracts. He introduced the concept of organic solidarity essentially to designate the capacity of a social system to integrate the diverse interests inherent in qualitative structural differentiation. Durkheim related solidarity, in turn, to a conception of its underlying ground, which he called *conscience collective*—translatable as either collective conscience or collective consciousness. The normative emphasis of the first translation was important to Durkheim himself: the *conscience collective* was a "system of beliefs and sentiments" held in common by the members of a society and defining what their mutual relations ought to be.

Clearly the *conscience collective* is a derivative of Rousseau's "general will" and Comte's "consensus." Equally clearly, it is not purely cognitive in reference. The most important step that Durkheim took beyond his predecessors, however, was to treat solidarity and with it, presumably, the *conscience collective*, not simply as given, but as variable entities. He made a distinction, therefore, between organic solidarity and mechanical solidarity. Organic solidarity is the analytical type characterized by the structural differentiation of the division of labor; modern society represents a case of predominantly organic solidarity. Mechanical solidarity, by contrast, is characterized by uniformity and lack of differentiation. With this distinction, Durkheim from the beginning built both historical—indeed, evolutionary—and comparative dimensions into his sociological analysis (Bellah 1959).

There is an initial difficulty in interpreting the relation between Durkheim's two types of solidarity, on the one hand, and the concept of the *conscience collective*, on the other. Since the *conscience collective* stresses the commonness of the beliefs and sentiments that constitute it, this seems to identify it with mechanical solidarity and suggests that organic solidarity, associated as it is with differentiation in the social structure, must develop at the expense of the *conscience collective*. The broad solution to this difficulty, which becomes clearer in Durkheim's later work, hinges on the functions attributed to values and norms in social systems of different degrees of differentiation. The focus of the *conscience collective* seems to be what we have come to call the values common to the members of any relatively well integrated social system; the sharing of common values is a constant feature of all such systems—at whatever level of differentiation. In the case of mechanical solidarity, these values are not clearly differentiated from the norms through which they are implemented, but in the organic case the norms come to have independent salience. In the relatively less differentiated social systems characterized by mechanical solidarity, common, in the sense of uniform, sentiments tend to be implemented *directly* in collective action, while in the case of organic solidarity the common element lies at a more general level and must be implemented in relation to different functions in the system through norms that are not identical for different sections of the collectivity.

Sociological method. The second main line of development of Durkheim's analysis has to do with the fitting of these broad empirical considerations into what I have called his Cartesian frame of reference. The starting point is the conception of the *actor* as member of a social system and as oriented to the environment in which he acts. This actor, conceived on the model of the philosopher–scientist, observes and interprets the facts of the external world: the distinctive problem is not their status as facts (of the environment), but as *social* facts. Here Durkheim self-consciously and explicitly denied the physical environment its unique "reality." The *milieu social*—for him the relevant environment—is, as part of society, a "reality *sui generis*," to be studied in its own right. The central problem concerns the properties of this category of "reality."

This problem in turn has two principal aspects. From the viewpoint of the scientific observer, this reality is clearly factual, or as we would say, empirical. But what was it from the viewpoint of the actor, in the second sense in which Durkheim was using the Cartesian scheme? A society is a given reality (it has "exteriority") from the point of view of its own members, but it also regulates ("constrains") their action. This it does not only in the sense in which the physical environment sets conditions that action must take into account but also by defining goals and normative standards for action. Durkheim quite early conceived of this constraint as more than a matter of given conditions; he saw it rather as a system of rules enforced by humanly imposed sanctions. In this theoretical development, Durkheim was evidently following up his previous analysis of the law (in the *Division of Labor*) as both an index of the structure of the society (e.g., of the nature and extent of its differentiation) and, when it is considered together with the beliefs and sentiments of the *conscience collective*, as a very important normative component of all societies.

There is, however, a still deeper aspect of the problem. A scientific observer of physical events is not in quite the same sense a "member" of the system he observes as is the social actor, although it is not acceptable to suggest that there is *no* sense in which they are similarly "members." It was necessary, therefore, to relativize the sense in which the system that Durkheim calls society constitutes *only* an environment to the individual actor-members that compose it. This problem, then, came to be intertwined with that of the status of the normative aspects of a society.

The essential conclusion of Durkheim's thinking is that for the sociologist the boundary between "individual" and "society" cannot be that of common sense. If we interpret the former concept as something like the human personality, it must *include* a sector of the social system, most specifically, the normative aspect of that system, the *shared* beliefs and sentiments that constitute the *conscience collective*. By this path Durkheim arrived at the crucially important view that essential elements of culture and social structure are *internalized* as part of the personality of the individual. In this he converged notably with Freud and with the movement in American social psychology from Charles H. Cooley to George Herbert Mead and W. I. Thomas. Durkheim's quite revolutionary conclusion now seems to follow more or less inevitably

from his premises, once he tried seriously to fit into the Cartesian frame of reference a distinctive normative level of the social system both as a "reality *sui generis*," for the actor as well as for the observer, and as an environment that is much more than just an environment.

This meant a radical reinterpretation of Durkheim's original criteria of social facts—constraint and exteriority. The concept of social facts was developed, then, through three phases: first, exteriority, or the givenness of empirical existence, as in the case of the physical environment; second, constraint, or the effect of a normative rule to which sanctions are attached; and now, third, what Durkheim called the "moral authority" of internalized values and norms, which "constrain" the individual to conform by arousing guilt in his own conscience if he does not conform. An element of exteriority is involved in moral authority because, although internalized, the normative system must also objectively be part of a system extending beyond the individual. It is not "subjective" in the sense of being purely private to the individual, for it is also a "cultural object" in a sense relevant to the idealistic tradition.

The theoretical development at this highest level of generality—Durkheim's decisively new conception of individuals interacting in a social system—did not fully crystallize until the early years of the present century, when Durkheim gave primary attention to the relations between moral norms and the process of education (1902–1906). Some of its roots in the more empirical emphases of the *Division of Labor* have already been indicated. Certainly the most notable transitional formulation of the concept of social fact is in his study of suicide. Durkheim's sensitivity to the major problems of suicide went back to the *Division of Labor* and its critique of utilitarianism, more specifically the utilitarian claim that an increasing division of labor and the resultant economic progress would be accompanied by increasing "happiness." Durkheim was struck by the fact that the economic progress of newly industrialized societies was everywhere accompanied by a rise in suicide rates. This was clearly an anomaly from the point of view of utilitarian theory and stimulated Durkheim to a major, if not complete, theoretical reconstruction in his classic monograph *Suicide* (1897).

Very advanced for its time as an empirical study, *Suicide* established a most important link between Durkheim's theoretical work and the traditions of empirical research that have since become prominent, especially in the United States. Durkheim's essential method was systematically to mobilize available statistical information on suicide rates and to relate their variations to a whole series of characteristics of the populations involved. In the nature of the case, he was limited to the modern Western world, which alone provided the kind of information he sought. With this limitation, he studied nationality, religion, age, sex, marital status, family size, place of residence, economic status, and variations in economic conditions, as well as the seasons of the year and even the times of day when suicides occurred. He showed great ingenuity and a capacity to take pains—for example, in breaking down the data published for France by *départements* into *arrondissements*, in order to reveal important variations masked in the larger units. As Bellah points out (Bellah 1959), Durkheim brought together what information he could find from the broadest possible comparative range, even when it could not be stated quantitatively. For instance, he cited voluntary self-immolation on the part of Buddhist zealots as an example of what he called "altruistic" suicide.

Durkheim found the conventional classification of the "causes" of suicide, in terms of which the data were generally reported, quite unhelpful for his purposes. He introduced a highly original scheme of his own, built about the problem of the individual's relations to the normative structuring of the social system in which he is involved. This scheme embodies two pairs of polar extremes, at which suicide rates are relatively high, and median continua between the poles, in which suicide rates are relatively low. The first pair of poles has *altruisme* and *égoïsme* at the extremes, the second *anomie* and *fatalisme*.

That Durkheim was no mere extoller of the virtues of solidarity (as is sometimes alleged) is shown by his conception of the first polar pair in general and of the concept of "altruistic" suicide in particular. In this type the claims of the collectivity are so strong that there is a repeated tendency to subordinate personal interests to them to the extent of sacrificing life, even when there does not appear to be a practical emergency that requires such sacrifice. Durkheim found military officers most prone to this in modern societies, but adduced numerous other examples from other societies. The antithesis of this type is "egoistic" suicide, which, for example, results in a higher rate of suicide among Protestants than among Catholics. This Durkheim explained by the social pressure inherent in Protestant norms toward a higher order of individual religious responsibility. It is a remarkable interpretation, both in itself and because it converges with

the theme developed a few years later by Max Weber concerning the importance of the Protestant ethic in modern society. There is also, interestingly, an echo of Rousseau, in that Durkheim seemed to be citing an instance of the famous paradoxical formula about a man being "forced to be free," adding that this enforced freedom may become too hard to bear.

The second pair of polar concepts that Durkheim advanced in this connection was that of *anomie* and *fatalisme* (the latter concept not being developed). Anomie has become one of the small number of truly central concepts of contemporary social science. It is best interpreted in terms of Durkheim's Cartesian reference. The observer as actor is naturally concerned with the definiteness of the "reality" with which he is confronted. In a purely cognitive context, this is a matter of the adequacy of his information and analysis. Insofar, however, as the "reality" is man-made and, in one aspect, is normative *for* the actor, the problem of definiteness becomes that of "definition of the situation" in the sense established by W. I. Thomas and by reference-group theory more generally [*see* REFERENCE GROUPS].

The focus, then, is on what is *expected* of the actor and on the problem of the definiteness of expectations. In the case of the physical conditions of, for example, technological procedures, expectations can reasonably be defined in terms of the goals of the actors; they do not pertain to the external processes and technically defined probabilities concerning the environment itself, since it does not "act." In a system of social interaction, on the other hand, "success" cannot simply be a function of "control" over the environment, but necessarily involves also the "sense" it makes to exert effort and, generally, to expend resources, unless the outcome to which the actor is committed is clearly desirable. The sense to ego of his goal-striving is thus a function both of alter's action and of ego's expectation concerning it. The meaning of success cannot be established without understanding the interplay between the motivation of the actor and the normative claims impinging upon him from his social environment. At the same time, the social environment of any *given* actor of reference is composed of *other* actors whose action must be analyzed in the same terms as the first. In this interactive framework anomie may be considered that state of a social system which makes a particular class of members consider exertion for success meaningless, not because they lack capacity or opportunity to achieve what is wanted, but because they lack a clear definition of what is desirable. It is a "pathology" not of the instrumental system but of the collective normative system.

Spelling out this concept leads to many refinements. In more contemporary terms, what is ill-defined may be ultimate beliefs, values, norms, or goals. Anomic uncertainty may affect either very generalized orientations or relatively specific goals; or the difficulties may arise from conflicting expectations, as in the classic instance of "cross-pressures."

The two concepts of *égoïsme* and *anomie* epitomize Durkheim's concern over the state of modern society. Because of the current preoccupation with problems of "meaning" in contemporary life, it is not surprising that *anomie* has attracted far more attention than *égoïsme*. It is my own view that the balance is in need of being redressed. *Égoïsme*, in Durkheim's special sense, is a designation for one aspect of a prominent feature of modern social structure that can be called, more generally, "institutionalized individualism." Another context in which Durkheim emphasized *égoïsme* was his discussion of the "cult of individual personality" (Neyer 1960). At least some aspects of the subject of "alienation" (discussed so often and with so much confusion) may also be interpreted in terms of *égoïsme* and *altruisme*. Thus, alienation appears to be the pathological extreme (anomic in certain aspects, cf. Tiryakian 1962) of institutionalized individualism at which "conformism" becomes associated with the altruistic tendencies, in Durkheim's sense. The alienated person, then, is under such pressure to establish his independence from pressures to conform that he becomes unable to accept the essential normative conditions of a stable *system* of organized individual freedom.

Theory of culture.   In the last major phase of his intellectual career, Durkheim dealt mainly with another set of themes that grew out of, but were distinct from, those outlined so far. These concerned religion, symbolic systems, and his somewhat new conception, "collective representations." In short, he emphasized the theory of culture in relation to that of the social system. As early as the Preface to Volume 2 of *L'année sociologique* (1899), Durkheim acknowledged the strong emphasis on religion in that publication and outlined his conception of religion as the primordial "matrix," out of which the principal elements of culture emerged by the process of differentiation. His concern with primitive religion, as well as with an articulated evolutionary perspective, was already clear in this statement. It is important for these later developments in Durkheim's thought that the relatively new science of anthropology had arisen as a kind of mediator between utilitarianism and Darwinian biology. Anthropology became the "study of man" as part of the organic world, concerned especially with primitive societies, particularly with their magic and religion.

We have noted that Durkheim's conception of society as a "reality *sui generis*" steadily changed; he placed an increasing emphasis on the normative components. While the legal norms constituted his initial prototype, he gradually focused upon more general aspects, moving toward the conception of what we would now call institutionalized values. He particularly stressed the attitude of moral respect as a component of internalized norms.

What is perhaps Durkheim's most important single step in extending this perspective was stated as one of the primary orienting perspectives of the *Elementary Forms*. This was a double proposition: first, that the attitudinal distinction between treating things as sacred and as profane is basically the same as that between moral obligations and expediency or utility; and second, that the quality of sacredness does not reside in the intrinsic properties of the object treated as sacred, but in its properties as a *symbol*. From this it was a short step to relate sacred physical and social objects to the whole world of "cultural" objects, which, although very close to Durkheim's early category of beliefs and sentiments, he increasingly formulated as "representations." We may certainly interpret them as symbolic systems, leaving open the question of the meaning references of various categories of symbols.

Durkheim was greatly impressed by the closeness of integration between the religious system of representations and the structure of the society itself, the attitude of moral respect being, as noted, the main connecting link. This integration seems particularly close in the case of primitive religion but it also exists in others. It justifies Durkheim's emphasis on collective representations. Indeed, we can say that any symbolic system that can justifiably be called "cultural" must have a collective aspect; symbolization that is autistic—in the sense of being wholly private to one individual (the limiting case)—is no longer cultural, if indeed it can be truly symbolic. Language is perhaps the prototype here.

It seems to have been Durkheim's view, a strongly defensible one, that the more primitive the society and the culture, the less differentiated they are from each other. He extensively analyzed the case of the Australian aborigines on the strength of this theory: the phenomena of the integration of culture and society could be seen there in their "elementary forms." But his interest in these elementary forms does not mean that Durkheim did not have a broad understanding of the possibility and importance of differentiating conceptually between cultural and social systems, even though, as Bellah points out (Bellah 1959) he somewhat obscured this vital point by using the term "social" for both. Unfortunately, he never worked out a thorough analysis of the place of religion in a highly differentiated society—a task that might well have led him to clarify his conception of the relations between "representations" and social structure.

The problem of integration also arises internally to the system of collective representations, to culture itself. Durkheim presented the broad perspective on this problem several years before *Elementary Forms* in the monograph on primitive classification written in collaboration with Mauss (1903), although he developed it further in his book. His main point is that in primitive systems all culture is at the same time both religious and social, in a sense not true of more advanced systems. A particularly telling example is the categorization of physical space in terms directly corresponding to the arrangement of kinship groups in the camp.

This conception of twofold integration, between a cultural and a social system and among the different elements of a cultural system, is particularly significant for the broad problem area we now generally call the sociology of knowledge. Undoubtedly Durkheim was at least as important a founder of this discipline as was Karl Mannheim, and in many respects his views were the clearer and better analyzed.

Durkheim's combined interest in cultural problems, religion, and evolutionary origins had a series of implications for the development of social science theory. Both the utilitarian tradition and that stemming from the French Enlightenment had tended not only to disparage traditional religion but even to deny its substantive importance. Evolutionary perspectives, however, focused attention on religion, partly because of the sheer empirical prominence of religion and magic in nonliterate societies, which were becoming increasingly well-known. The early Tylor–Spencer phase of social science tended strongly to consider these phenomena characteristic of the early stages of sociocultural evolution and destined to disappear with advancement—a position shared by Marx. Durkheim's position established a quite new order of

functional significance for religion in society. Durkheim made it clear that even at the later stages of sociocultural development, every society would require the "functional equivalent" of a religious system (whether or not it is called "religion" is primarily a semantic issue).

Beyond this, Durkheim established the groundwork for an exceedingly valuable conception of the morphology of social development—the conception of processes of structural differentiation and of attendant new, more general levels of integration. The conception of religion as the original matrix of both society and culture suggests further that society and culture themselves tend to become more completely differentiated from each other and that "secular" elements develop from this matrix on both the social and cultural levels. An important semantic point is that just because a relatively undifferentiated complex is called "religion" for an earlier stage of development and only one of its two or more differentiated derivatives retains that name for a later stage, it is not legitimate to assert that "religion has declined." Thus, Durkheim viewed the secularization of education as an imperative of the stage of social differentiation that France had reached in his time, but he denied that this meant that the function of religion in French society had therefore been downgraded.

Durkheim's combination of a comparative and evolutionary perspective with a special concern for cultural–symbolic systems should have been connected with a theoretical analysis of the processes of social and cultural change. Durkheim did not, to be sure, give this as much explicit attention as he did problems of social morphology, but the contributions he did make to an understanding of the process of change seem not to have been understood as fully as his more "static" analysis. In any case, it is clear that Durkheim provided the groundwork for a major theory of developmental change in societies and that he made important direct contributions to it himself.

His later work, in particular, tended to stress the importance of cultural creativity as a factor in change; one of the clearest statements is in his late essay "Value Judgments and Judgments of Reality" (1911), which stresses the incidence and salience of "effervescence" in periods of crisis in the development of the sociocultural system. At the same time, Durkheim was quite clearly a "multifactor" theorist of social change.

Conclusion. Durkheim contributed substantially —and very eminently for the time in which he worked—to relatively specific empirical problems in sociology. To this day, analyses of the nature of contractual systems, of suicide rates, and of primitive religions cannot ignore his contributions. Equally, he was a highly effective entrepreneur of sociology—as teacher, as editor of a distinguished periodical, and as leader of a highly talented and creative group of research scholars.

These are not, however, the achievements that place him in the top rank among the founders of a scientific discipline. This higher eminence stems from the fact that Durkheim used the framework of solidly established intellectual traditions—those of English utilitarianism, in certain respects of German idealism, and of his own French background—to formulate a theoretical framework that was both solidly grounded in those traditions and yet highly original. As grounded in tradition, it was capable of taking full account of established knowledge; but it also went far beyond this. It was precise and clear in its logical structures and imaginative in opening up new ways of considering social phenomena, defining problems, and developing patterns of interpretation. In his special conception of the nature of "social reality," which emphasized the involvement of *normative components* in both social reality and, through internalization, the personality of the individual, Durkheim was following, along with a few others, the major line of the theoretical development of social science. But he went even beyond this to link the social and personality systems thus conceived with a highly sophisticated analysis of cultural symbolic systems and to set the whole action structure in a comprehensive evolutionary framework. The resulting enrichment of the theoretical resources of the field of social science, of its insight into significant problems and its capacity to deal determinately with them, is incalculable. Only a very select few among the figures in intellectual history have contributed so crucially—at such a significant juncture—to the development of scientific culture.

Talcott Parsons

[*For the historical context of Durkheim's work, see* Knowledge, sociology of; Law, *article on* the legal system; Religion; Sociology, *article on* the development of sociological thought; Suicide, *article on* social aspects; Survey analysis, *article on* methods of survey analysis; Utilitarianism; *and the biographies of* Comte; Descartes; Fustel de Coulanges; Hegel; Hobbes; Locke; Rousseau; Saint-Simon. *For discussion of the subsequent development of Durkheim's ideas, see* Community–society continua; Integration; Interaction, *article on* social interaction; Punishment; Systems analysis, *article on* social systems; *and the biographies of* Granet; Halbwachs; Mauss; Simiand.]

WORKS BY DURKHEIM

(1893) 1960 *The Division of Labor in Society.* Glencoe, Ill.: Free Press. → First published as *De la division du travail social.*

(1895) 1958 *The Rules of Sociological Method.* 8th ed. Edited by George E. G. Catlin. Glencoe, Ill.: Free Press. → First published in French.

(1897) 1951 *Suicide: A Study in Sociology.* Glencoe, Ill.: Free Press. → First published in French.

(1898–1911) 1953 *Sociology and Philosophy.* Glencoe, Ill.: Free Press. → Written between 1898–1911. First published in French in 1924.

(1899) 1960 *Prefaces to L'année sociologique:* Preface to Volume 2. Pages 347–353 in Kurt H. Wolff (editor), *Émile Durkheim, 1858–1917: A Collection of Essays With Translations and a Bibliography.* Columbus: Ohio State Univ. Press.

(1902–1906) 1961 *Moral Education: A Study in the Theory and Application of the Sociology of Education.* New York: Free Press. → Lectures first published in French.

(1903) 1963 Durkheim, Émile; and Mauss, Marcel. *Primitive Classification.* Translated and edited by Rodney Needham. Univ. of Chicago Press. → First published as "De quelques formes primitives de classification" in *L'année sociologique.*

(1906) 1953 The Determination of Moral Facts. Pages 35–62 in Émile Durkheim, *Sociology and Philosophy.* Glencoe, Ill.: Free Press. → First published in French.

(1911) 1953 Value Judgments and Judgments of Reality. Pages 80–97 in Émile Durkheim, *Sociology and Philosophy.* Glencoe, Ill.: Free Press. → First published in French.

(1912) 1954 *The Elementary Forms of the Religious Life.* London: Allen & Unwin; New York: Macmillan. → First published as *Les formes élémentaires de la vie religieuse, le système totémique en Australie.* A paperback edition was published in 1961 by Collier.

WORKS ABOUT DURKHEIM

Alpert, Harry (1939) 1961 *Émile Durkheim and His Sociology.* New York: Russell.

Barnes, Harry E.; and Becker, Howard (1938) 1961 *Social Thought From Lore to Science.* 3d ed., rev. & enl. New York: Dover. → See especially Volume 2, Chapter 12.

Bellah, Robert N. 1959 Durkheim and History. *American Sociological Review* 24:447–461.

Davy, Georges 1960 Émile Durkheim. *Revue française de sociologie* 1:3–24.

Gehlke, Charles E. 1915 *Émile Durkheim's Contributions to Sociological Theory.* New York: Columbia Univ. Press.

Gurvitch, Georges 1937 La science des faits moraux et la morale théoretique chez E. Durkheim. *Archives de philosophie du droit et de sociologie juridique* [1937], no. 1/2:18–44.

Gurvitch, Georges (1950) 1957–1963 *La vocation actuelle de la sociologie.* 2d ed., 2 vols. Paris: Presses Universitaires de France. → Volume 1: *Vers la sociologie différentielle.* Volume 2: *Antécédents et perspectives.*

HALBWACHS, MAURICE 1918 La doctrine d'Émile Durkheim. *Revue philosophique de la France et de l'étranger* 85:353–411.

HALÉVY, ÉLIE (1901–1904) 1952 *The Growth of Philosophic Radicalism.* New ed. London: Faber. → First published in French.

HUGHES, HENRY STUART 1958 *Consciousness and Society: The Reorientation of European Social Thought, 1890–1930.* New York: Knopf.

LÉVI-STRAUSS, CLAUDE 1945 French Sociology. Pages 503–537 in Georges Gurvitch and Wilbert E. Moore (editors), *Twentieth Century Sociology.* New York: Philosophical Library.

MALINOWSKI, BRONISLAW (1916–1941) 1948 *Magic, Science and Religion, and Other Essays.* Glencoe, Ill.: Free Press. → A paperback edition was published in 1954 by Doubleday.

MERTON, ROBERT K. 1934 Durkheim's *Division of Labor in Society. American Journal of Sociology* 40:319–328.

MERTON, ROBERT K. (1938) 1957 Social Structure and Anomie. Pages 131–160 in Robert K. Merton, *Social Theory and Social Structure.* Rev. & enl. ed. Glencoe, Ill.: Free Press.

NEYER, JOSEPH 1960 Individualism and Socialism in Durkheim. Pages 32–76 in Kurt H. Wolff (editor), *Émile Durkheim, 1858–1917: A Collection of Essays With Translations and a Bibliography.* Columbus: Ohio State Univ. Press.

PARSONS, TALCOTT 1937 *The Structure of Social Action.* New York: McGraw-Hill.

PARSONS, TALCOTT 1965 Unity and Diversity in the Modern Intellectual Disciplines: The Role of the Social Sciences. *Dædalus* 94:39–65.

PEYRE, HENRI 1960 Durkheim: The Man, His Time, and His Intellectual Background. Pages 3–31 in Kurt H. Wolff (editor), *Émile Durkheim, 1858–1917: A Collection of Essays With Translations and a Bibliography.* Columbus: Ohio State Univ. Press.

SIMPSON, GEORGE 1933 Émile Durkheim's Social Realism. *Sociology and Social Research* 18:2–11.

SOROKIN, PITIRIM A. 1928 *Contemporary Sociological Theories.* New York: Harper. → A paperback edition was published in 1964 as *Contemporary Sociological Theories Through the First Quarter of the Twentieth Century.*

TIRYAKIAN, EDWARD A. 1962 *Sociologism and Existentialism: Two Perspectives on the Individual and Society.* Englewood Cliffs, N.J.: Prentice-Hall.

WOLFF, KURT H. (editor) 1960 *Émile Durkheim, 1858–1917: A Collection of Essays With Translations and a Bibliography.* Columbus: Ohio State Univ. Press. → A paperback edition was published in 1964 by Harper as *Essays on Sociology and Philosophy, With Appraisals of Durkheim's Life and Thought.*

DUTY

"Duty is a thing which may be *exacted* from a person, as one exacts a debt. Unless we think that it may be exacted from him, we do not call it his duty" (Mill [1861] 1957, p. 60). The word "duty" is derived through the French *devoir* from Latin *debitum*, which means what is owed by or due from one person to another, and as Mill saw, analogy with a debt is still a most important feature in the various legal, moral, and other social phenomena which are referred to as duties. Yet notwithstanding this apparently unifying analogy, there has been much dispute as to whether or not there really is a single generic concept of duty with specific applications in the different fields of law, morality, and so on, and also much controversy over the analysis of the notion within these fields. Since these issues and other problematic features of the notion of duty have received the clearest and most detailed attention from legal theorists, legal duties are first considered here.

Legal duties

Whenever legal rules require or prohibit certain conduct, the notion of duty has application. The plainest examples of such requirements and prohibitions are the duties created by the criminal law when it provides for the punishment of certain forms of conduct. The duties it thus creates may be either negative (e.g., to abstain from murder or theft) or positive (e.g., to report for military service or pay taxes). Most legal theorists, however, extend the notion of duty to cases where the law provides for compensation to be paid to those who have suffered damage through the failure of another either to perform a contract or to abstain from any of the variety of civil (as distinguished from criminal) wrongs, which are called torts. Here conventional jurisprudence distinguishes the primary duty (e.g., to perform the contract or to abstain from the tort) from the secondary or "sanctioning" duty to pay compensation for the breach of the primary duty.

Though the word "duty" refers to a constantly recurring situation created by the existence of legal rules, it is in fact rarely used in the authoritative text of legal codes or statutes. Thus, English and American criminal codes and statutes create duties, not by the use of the expression "duty," but by such formulas as "whosoever shall . . . shall be guilty of an offense . . ." or "whosoever shall . . . shall be liable to a penalty of. . . ." Similar formulas avoiding the equivalent of the word "duty" are commonly used in Continental legal codes. "Duty" therefore is primarily part of the language used in the exposition and theoretical discussion of the law to designate a specific type of effect or situation created by the existence of legal rules. In the wording of these rules, however, the expression "duty" does not usually appear.

Obligation and duty. By jurists of some systems, mainly those descended from Roman law, a distinction is drawn between obligation and duty, the former being reserved for cases such as those where a determinate person is bound as a result of some past transaction or relationship to pay or render some service to another determinate individual who has a corresponding legal right to such payment or service. Obligations are typically "incurred" or created by a man for himself, whereas duties "arise" from his position under the law without any act on his part. Typical examples of obligation in this sense are cases where a person is bound by his contract to pay or render services to another or is bound as the result of some tort to pay compensation to another. Some jurists distinguish between the requirements of the criminal law or the primary duties arising under the law of tort and obligations, since the first two cannot be incurred by the person under the duty. Though there are still traces of this distinction in Anglo–American jurisprudence, it has very largely disappeared and is generally ignored in philosophical or jurisprudential discussions concerning the general nature of law. It is however still of importance in the classification of other nonlegal social norms.

The notion of duty is generally considered by jurists to be both essential and fundamental. Some (e.g., Austin and Kelsen) treat it as essential in a strong sense of insisting that *every* legal rule creates a duty; other jurists insist only that every legal system includes *some* rules which create duties. Duty can be considered fundamental as well as essential, because other notions, such as legal rights, powers, crimes, and torts, require in their analysis the use of the notion of duty. Thus, to have a legal right is (in one important sense) to be free from some specific duty to act in certain ways or (in a second important sense) to have the option of insisting on the performance by another person of his duty or releasing him from it.

Some jurists (e.g., Oliver Wendell Holmes) have looked upon the idea of duty as a potent source of confusion tending to obscure the radical differences between the requirements of legal and moral rules. Holmes at one time proposed to dispense with "all talk of duties and rights" and to substitute for it simply "a statement of the circumstances in which the public force will be brought to bear upon a man through the Courts" (Holmes & Pollock [1874–1932] 1961, p. 307). Many legal theorists of the positivist tradition (e.g., Bentham and Austin as well as Holmes himself) have put forward similar views in the form of analysis of the notion of duty rather than a proposal to dispense with it. Bentham ([1789] 1948; [1843] 1962) defined legal obligation or duty to do or abstain from some action as a chance or likelihood of suffering at the hands of officials in the event of failing to do so. Holmes similarly defined a statement of duty as a prophecy that if a man does certain things, he will be subject to disagreeable consequences by way of imprisonment or compulsory payment of money ([1897] 1952, p. 173).

The predictive analysis of duty. The form of analysis favored by Holmes and Bentham has commended itself to many jurists and some sociologists. It is, however, open to the following objections:

(1) The statement that a man has a legal duty to do a particular action may without any contradiction or absurdity be conjoined with the statement that he is *not* likely to suffer at the hands of officials in the event of his failing to do the action. Indeed there will be frequent occasions—especially in a system such as English law, where there are no minimum penalties but only prescribed maxima—for asserting just this conjunction of statements. This is so when, for example, it is known or thought likely that someone who proposes to disobey the criminal law will not be caught or if caught will not be convicted (perhaps because of lack of relevant evidence) or if convicted will not in fact be punished (perhaps because of the clemency or corruption of the court).

(2) Similarly, there is no redundancy in conjoining with the statement that a man has a legal duty to do a particular action the statement that he is likely to suffer at the hands of officials in the event of his failing to do it.

(3) If it is allowed that a statement that a man has a legal duty to do a particular action may be assessed as either true or false, we can summarize the above two criticisms by saying that Bentham's analysis fails to state even a necessary condition for the truth of such a statement. But the following considerations show that it also fails to state a sufficient condition for the truth of such a statement. This is so because the notion "of suffering at the hands of officials in the event of doing (or failing to do) a particular action" has no specific connection with the idea of duty unless it is conceived or interpreted in a restricted way. Such suffering is wholly irrelevant to the idea of duty unless the suffering is conceived of as punishment or compulsory compensation supporting or securing conformity with legal standards of conduct, that is, as a means for discouraging or preventing actions of a certain sort or restoring (so far as compensa-

tion can) the *status quo* disturbed by such actions. Hence suffering, in the form of compulsory payment of money, though provided for by legal rule, is irrelevant to the idea of legal duty if it is interpreted as a tax on certain conduct (and not as a punishment by way of fine or as compensation for injury done) and does not render abstention from that conduct a duty.

The normative analysis of duty. The principal rival to the predictive analysis may be termed normative. This approach, without identifying moral and legal duties by insisting on any common content, stresses certain formal features which these duties share as forms of rule-guided conduct involving the idea of what "ought to be done." From this point of view an act is called a legal duty not merely because failure to do it renders likely sanctions or suffering at the hands of officials but because, owing to the existence of the relevant rules of law, it is also an act which like a debt may be correctly or justifiably *demanded* of those concerned as something which ought to be done. Similarly, failure to do the act required is significant because punishment or compulsory compensation is properly applicable or justified according to the legal rule even if predictions that it will in fact follow are falsified. The normative analysis therefore reproduces the point of view of those who, though they may not regard the law as the moral or final arbiter of conduct, in general accept the existence of legal rules as a guide to conduct and as legally justifying demands for conformity, punishment, or enforced compensation. Attention to these normative features of the idea of legal duty seems essential for understanding the way in which law in fact operates in a modern legal system.

The predictive analysis of duty has found favor among positivist writers for a variety of theoretical and practical reasons. On the one hand, it has seemed to free the idea of legal duty both from metaphysical obscurities and irrelevant associations with morals and, on the other hand, to provide a realistic guide to life under law. For it isolates what for some men is the only important fact about the operation of a legal system and what for all men is always one important fact: the occasions and ways in which the law may work adversely to them. This is of paramount importance not only to the malefactor—"if you want to know the law and nothing else, you must look at it as a bad man [would]" (Holmes [1897] 1952, p. 171)—but also to the utilitarian critic and reformer of the law who is concerned to balance the costs of the law in terms of human suffering against the benefits which it brings. A reconciliation between the two types of theory is, however, possible, though exclusive correctness has often been attributed to one or the other. The normative account might be said to give correctly the standard *meaning* of the statement that a person has a legal duty to do a certain action, and the predictive theory may be taken as stating the *point* or *purpose* of making a statement of duty (i.e., to warn that suffering is likely to follow upon disobedience). This distinction between the meaning of a statement and what is implied by the making of it in different contexts is of general importance in legal philosophy.

Duties and sanctions. Many, perhaps most, legal theorists have argued that legal and moral duties can only be distinguished by the provision made by legal rules for coercive sanctions. However, this argument seems mistaken, since there are other important features which may be used to distinguish between them. It is conceptually impossible to hold (1) that moral duties may be extinguished by legislative repeal or fiat, as legal duties can, (2) that moral duties may relate to activities which are not considered in any way important as some legal duties may be, and (3) that general moral duties could be expressly created simply for the purpose of advancing some specific objective or social aim as general legal duties frequently are. Furthermore, lawyers and jurists sometimes use the expression "duty" of actions where no sanction is provided. These considerations suggest that it is mistaken to define the idea of duty in terms of coercive sanctions but that a wider notion of social demand, pressure for conformity, and the liability of the lawbreaker to different forms of adverse criticism and treatment should be used instead. The coercive sanctions of the law may then be more illuminatingly regarded as the characteristic, but not invariant, legal form of this wider notion.

Moral duties

In considering moral duties it is important to distinguish the accepted or conventional positive morality of an actual social group from the moral principles and ideals which may govern an individual's life but which do not exist as a shared code of a social group. The duties of positive morality are those forms of conduct (negative or positive) which like a debt are, according to the rules of the accepted moral code, held to be justifiably exacted or demanded from individuals. Though organized coercive sanctions may not be used to enforce conformity or to punish deviation, various distinctively moral forms of pressure are available. In the case of actual or threatened breach of the moral code, appeal will usually be made to the sense of respect for the rules as important in themselves, and reminders are given of the moral character of the action. These reminders assume that respect for the rules is shared by those addressed, and it is also assumed that they will excite in those addressed a sense of shame or guilt. Deviations from the positive moral code may lead to many different forms of hostile reaction, ranging from expressions of blame and contempt to severance of social relations. But reminders of what the rules demand and appeals to "conscience" and reliance on the operation of a sense of guilt and shame are the characteristic forms of pressure used in the support of conventional moral duties.

In spite of the differences noted above between moral and legal duties, there are still certain striking similarities between them. Both are supported by serious social pressure for conformity, though this pressure characteristically takes different forms. Compliance with both legal and moral duties is generally taken as a matter of course and not as a matter for praise except when marked by exceptional difficulties or efforts, since performance is thought of as a minimum contribution to social life. Further, legal and moral duties relate to actions the opportunities for which constantly recur throughout life and not only on special occasions. Although legal rules and conventional moralities may include much that is peculiar to different societies, both make demands which must obviously be satisfied if any considerable number of human beings are to succeed in living together. Hence in almost all societies where a legal system can be distinguished from a moral code, there are both legal and moral duties to abstain from violence and theft and to show some minimum forms of honesty and truthfulness in social intercourse.

When we turn from the positive morality of social groups to morality in the sense of the rules, or principles, or ideals of individuals to which they subscribe on religious or theoretical grounds, the scope of the notion of duty appears a matter of more philosophical controversy. Some philosophers extend it so as to include not only the minimum demands of an individual's morality, which may be formulated in general rules, but any action which for any moral reason "ought" to be done. Thus extended, it includes both the action which is held to be "the best on the whole" in cases of a conflict of duties or otherwise problematic situations and also works of supererogation or the satisfaction of ideals (e.g., of heroism or saintliness). This extension of the idea of duty is no doubt guided by the analogy between legal punishment and other forms of social pressure and the experience of guilt and remorse which follow on deviation from individual morality. This extension seems confusing, since the minimum demands of a morality that can be formulated in general rules referring to constantly recurring situations in daily life must always present important features different from the requirements of individual morality.

Duty in other social contexts

Legal and moral rules are of course not an exhaustive dichotomy, and the notion of duty also refers to the requirements of rules which fall into neither of these two categories (e.g., the rules of voluntary associations like clubs or business organizations, rules governing activities for which there are only intermittent opportunities such as ceremonies, or activities like games which are held to be voluntary and from which withdrawal is permitted).

Broadly speaking, the notion of duty or, sometimes, obligation may be used where there is a relatively enduring office or social role in which the occupant performs a specific function calling for specific forms of behavior. Thus, it is common to speak of the duties of a host or of the captain of a team or the chairman of a committee, where rules which are neither legal nor moral specify the forms of behavior required. Sometimes however such duties attached to roles or offices may be supported by specifically moral pressure, as in the case of the duties of a father or husband. In all such cases the analogy of a debt is still present, for the duties attached to such roles or offices are those actions which it is held may be demanded from the occupant, even though neither legal sanctions nor moral pressure is available to support the demand.

Finally, it is salutary to remember that even in these wider social contexts there is no simple equivalence between the notion of duty and of what ought to be done according to social rules. This is evident from the fact that there are many rules, such as those of etiquette or correct speech, where it would be misleading to refer to duties. In such cases the correct action or mode of speech is not conceived of as something which may be peremptorily demanded, no doubt because of the lesser importance to others or to social life of the activities in question.

H. L. A. HART

[*See also* POLITICAL THEORY; RESPONSIBILITY; *and the biographies of* AUSTIN; BENTHAM; HOLMES; KELSEN. *A guide to other relevant material may be found under* LAW.]

BIBLIOGRAPHY

BENTHAM, JEREMY (1789) 1948 *An Introduction to the Principles of Morals and Legislation.* New ed., corrected by the author. New York: Hafner.

BENTHAM, JEREMY (1843) 1962 *Essay on Logic.* Volume 8, pages 213–293 in Jeremy Bentham, *The Works of Jeremy Bentham.* Edited by John Bowring. New York: Russell. → First published posthumously.

DIAS, R. W. M. 1959 The Unenforceable Duty. *Tulane Law Review* 33:473–490.

HOLMES, OLIVER WENDELL (1897) 1952 The Path of the Law. Pages 167–202 in Oliver Wendell Holmes, *Collected Legal Papers.* New York: Smith.

HOLMES, OLIVER WENDELL; and POLLOCK, FREDERICK (1874–1932) 1961 *Holmes–Pollock Letters: The Correspondence of Mr. Justice Holmes and Sir Frederick Pollock, 1874–1932.* 2d ed., 2 vols. Edited by Mark DeWolfe Howe. Cambridge, Mass.: Belknap Press.

MILL, JOHN STUART (1861) 1957 *Utilitarianism.* Indianapolis, Ind.: Bobbs-Merrill.

WEBER, MAX (1922) 1956 *Wirtschaft und Gesellschaft: Grundriss der verstehenden Soziologie.* 4th ed., 2 vols. Tübingen (Germany): Mohr.

DYNAMICS IN ECONOMICS

See STATICS AND DYNAMICS IN ECONOMICS.

E

EARLY EXPERIENCE

See INFANCY. *Related material may be found under* DEVELOPMENTAL PSYCHOLOGY.

EBBINGHAUS, HERMANN

Hermann Ebbinghaus, German psychologist, was born on January 24, 1850. He was the son of Carl Ebbinghaus, a merchant in the town of Barmen near Bonn, Germany. Of his infancy and childhood it is known only that he was brought up in the Lutheran faith and was a pupil at the town Gymnasium until he was 17. In 1867 he went to the University of Bonn and somewhat later to Berlin and Halle. Although his initial interest was in history and philology, he was gradually drawn to philosophy. When the Franco–Prussian War broke out in 1870 he joined the Prussian Army. In the spring of 1871, however, he left the army to continue his philosophical studies at Bonn. He completed his dissertation, *Über die Hartmannsche Philosophie des Unbewussten* (1873), and received his PH.D. on August 16, 1873, passing his examination with distinction.

In 1880 he received his habilitation at Berlin. In 1885 he published *Memory: A Contribution to Experimental Psychology.* He was made a professor in the same year, probably in recognition of this publication. While at Berlin he founded the psychological laboratory, and in 1890, in association with Arthur König, he founded the *Zeitschrift für Psychologie und Physiologie der Sinnesorgane.*

He was called to Breslau in 1894 to become a full professor in the chair left vacant by Theodor Lipps' departure for Munich. (Lipps replaced Stumpf, who, in turn, was bound for Berlin.) At Breslau, Ebbinghaus again founded a psychological laboratory. In 1905 he moved to Halle to succeed Alois Riehl, who was going to Berlin. He remained there as professor of philosophy until his death from pneumonia on February 26, 1909.

Ebbinghaus found his own way to psychology. None of his instructors determined in any marked way the direction of his thinking, even though they included such eminent persons as Johann E. Erdmann, Friedrich A. Trendelenburg, and Jürgen B. Meyer. A major influence, however, was the combination of philosophical and scientific points of view that he found in Fechner, a copy of whose *Elemente der Psychophysik* he picked up in a Parisian secondhand bookstall. He acknowledged his debt in the *Grundzüge* (1897–1908), which he dedicated to the memory of Fechner.

One *leitmotiv* runs through his work: psychology is *Naturwissenschaft.* The very first thesis in his dissertation sets forth the proposition that psychology (in the broadest sense) belongs no more to philosophy than does natural science (1873, p. 2). His goal was the establishment of psychology on a quantitative and experimental basis. This focus is well brought out in the short historical sketch that introduces his *Abriss der Psychologie.* "When Weber in 1828 had the seemingly petty curiosity to want to know at what distances apart two touches on the skin could be just perceived as two, and later, with what accuracy he could distinguish between two weights laid on the hand . . . his curiosity resulted in more real progress in psychology than all the combined distinctions, definitions, and classifications of the time from Aristotle to Hobbes (inclusive)" (1908, p. 17). Ebbinghaus' desire to bring into psychology clear and exact methods resulted in his extreme carefulness in experimental technique and his considerable interest in apparatus.

Ebbinghaus was an unusually good lecturer. His buoyancy, his humor, and the unusual clarity and ease of his presentation assured him of large audiences. Another outstanding trait, especially valuable for a journal editor, was his Jamesian tolerance (Boring [1929] 1950, p. 390). This capacity led him to publish widely diverse opinions—a policy vital to a young science. In contacts with his students, he invariably showed great interest in their problems.

It may seem surprising that Ebbinghaus had so few disciples. In his obituary of Ebbinghaus, Jaensch attributed this to Ebbinghaus' lack of interest in developing them (1909). He never urged others to undertake investigations; in fact, to work with him one had to obtrude oneself upon him with determination. Some of his better known students are Arthur Wreschner, Louis W. Stern, and Otto Lipmann.

Ebbinghaus did psychology a great service in founding and editing the *Zeitschrift für Psychologie*. The 50 volumes published up to his death present a practically complete portrait of psychology in the two decades from 1890 to 1910. A brief selection of names from the index—Hermann von Helmholtz, Carl Stumpf, Georg E. Müller, Friedrich Schumann, Theodor Lipps, Johannes von Kries—is convincing evidence that the *Zeitschrift* was the most important psychological organ in Germany and therefore in the world.

Ebbinghaus published relatively little. His own point of view with regard to print is expressed in a passage quoted by Woodworth (1909, p. 255) to the effect that "the individual has to make innumerable studies for his own sake. He tests and rejects, tests once more and once more rejects. For certainly not every happy thought, bolstered up perhaps by a few rough and ready experiments, should be brought before the public. But sometimes the individual reaches a point where he is permanently clear and satisfied with his interpretation. Then the matter belongs to the scientific public for their further judgment." The seriousness of Ebbinghaus' attitude in this regard is shown by his memory experiments. Although they were completed in 1880, he did not report the results until 1885, after having repeated them in their entirety in 1883.

The interest aroused by Edward von Hartmann's *Philosophie des Unbewussten*, which appeared in 1869, testifies to the general interest in the uncon-

scious at that time. The unconscious was a popular dissertation subject among doctoral candidates. Ebbinghaus' treatment of it in his own dissertation was very critical, in line with his views concerning the essential similarity of psychology and the natural sciences and the excessively abstract and verbal nature of the then existing psychology. Two of his verdicts on contemporary psychology were: "Wherever the structure is touched, it falls apart" (1873, p. 57); and "What is true is alas not new, the new not true" (*ibid.*, p. 67).

It is unfortunate that Ebbinghaus left no record of the work he did before he began his work on memory, which was published in 1885. In the introduction to the section on nonsense syllables he made the bare statement, "In order to test practically, although only for a limited field, a way of penetrating more deeply into memory processes . . . I have hit upon the following method" ([1885] 1964, p. 22), and he went on to discuss the nature and mechanics of nonsense syllables. As nearly as we can tell, he conceived of nonsense syllables for the investigation of the nature of memory between 1875 and 1879.

Before the publication of *Memory*, exact work on the mind had been limited to problems of predominantly physiological affinities. Not that interest in more strictly psychological phenomena had been lacking; rather, the means for their study had not been easily available. Now, however, a fundamental central function had been subjected to experimental investigation. This must have meant a good deal to the young science, although comparatively little of the contemporary effect can be discovered in print. James ([1890] 1962, p. 443) was impressed with the "heroic" nature of the experiment, as was Tanzi (1885, p. 598), who characterized it as "truly worthy of a Carthusian monk." A later opinion was expressed by Titchener: "It is not too much to say that the recourse to nonsense syllables, as means to the study of association, marks the most considerable advance, in this chapter of psychology, since the time of Aristotle" ([1909] 1928, pp. 380–381). However, Titchener also thought that the "introduction of nonsense syllables . . . has nevertheless done psychology a certain disservice. It has tended to place the emphasis rather upon organism than upon mind" (*ibid.*, p. 414). Murphy later described this investigation as "one of the greatest triumphs of original genius in experimental psychology" ([1929] 1949, p. 174).

In 1894, Dilthey's "Ideen über eine beschreibende und zergliedernde Psychologie" appeared.

This amounted to an attack on the very keystone of Ebbinghaus' faith. Dilthey claimed that the new psychology could never be more than descriptive and that attempts to make it explanatory and constructive were wrong in principle and led to nothing but confusion of opinion and fact. He asserted that we "explain nature, but we understand psychic life," and that any psychology which is modeled after atomistic physics—as is that of Ebbinghaus—can never "understand," for in the final analysis the process of "understanding" has to be experienced (*erlebt*) and cannot be inferred logically (*erschlossen*).

Although Ebbinghaus was reluctant to enter into controversy, he did undertake to defend psychology as he understood it. In an article in the *Zeitschrift* for 1896, "Über erklärende und beschreibende Psychologie," he justified the use of hypothesis and causal explanation in psychology. He claimed that, insofar as Dilthey was attacking explanatory psychology, he was attacking the old associationists, who had indeed failed. He felt their difficulty had arisen because they had analogized psychology to the fields of chemistry and physics rather than to biology. Dilthey, as Ebbinghaus saw it, was not actually discussing modern psychology; what he identified with explanatory psychology was actually only the work of Johann Herbart—and Herbart was no longer read, even in Germany. To Ebbinghaus, Dilthey's point that explanatory psychology works, like physics, on the principle that cause is exactly equal to effect was incorrect; rather, all that psychology can and does say, according to Ebbinghaus, is that "the contiguity of two sensations is considered as causal relationship because later a representation of one sensation results in a *Vorstellung* of the other" (1896, p. 186). This controversy has yet to be settled.

In 1895 the school authorities of Breslau were interested in the advisability of holding longer school sessions. Ebbinghaus was appointed to a commission that was created to investigate this problem. His contribution was the *Kombinationsmethode,* a form of completion test (1897, pp. 401–459) designed to measure intellectual fatigue. Although it did not serve its original purpose, it proved very valuable as a measure of general intellectual capacity, since scores on it correlated highly with the rank and scholarship of the pupils. There are many current adaptations of the test's principle.

When Ebbinghaus died in 1909, the systematic treatise—the *Grundzüge*—that he had begun early in the 1890s was only a little more than half completed. The first half of Volume 1 had come out in 1897. This volume was published as a whole only in 1902, and a second edition of it followed in 1905. In 1908 the first section of Volume 2 (96 pages) appeared. On Ebbinghaus' death Ernst Dürr took over the editing of his works and completed Volume 2. The major virtues of the *Grundzüge* lie in its readableness and convenient format rather than in any radical approach to psychology, but these, together with its comprehensiveness and its minor innovations, were sufficient to produce an enthusiastic reception.

Abriss der Psychologie (1908), an elementary textbook of psychology, achieved considerable success, as is evidenced by the fact that on the average more than one new edition appeared every two years until 1922. Additionally, an English translation by Max Meyer appeared in 1908, and French editions were published in 1910 and 1912—all of which attests to the value and appeal of the volume. The introduction consists of an admirable short history of psychology and begins with the well-known statement, "Psychology has a long past, yet its real history is short."

Ebbinghaus' influence on psychology, great as it was, has been mostly indirect. *Memory* is undoubtedly his outstanding contribution. His work on memory was the starting point not only for practically all the studies that have followed in this field but probably also for much of the work on the acquisition of skill. His *Grundzüge* is next in importance, not for its new system (which is very much like that of his contemporaries) but for its clear and concise treatment of the literature and its experimental emphasis. His *Kombinationsmethode* has been valuable to the field of mental testing. His editing of the *Zeitschrift* did much to advance psychology during a very productive period. His emphasis on experiment and his faith in the laboratory approach led to his personally establishing at least two laboratories and developing a third. His qualities as a lecturer and writer helped to spread a knowledge of orthodox psychology.

Despite an early training in philosophy, he was one of the leaders in the movement to emancipate psychology from philosophy. He belongs fundamentally in the tradition that leads from prepsychological science, to physiology and the work of Helmholtz and Fechner, to Wundt and "content psychology." Dunlap (1927) would give him, together with Aristotle and Binet, the credit for making psychology "behavioristic," but that is probably going too far. His psychology does, however, have a functional emphasis, as suggested by his constant reference to the biological affinity of psychology, his nativism in the matter of general attributes of sensation, and his contribution to the problem of individual differences.

As Boring (1929) has pointed out, the history of general experimental psychology has passed through three successive phases: (1) sensation and perception; (2) learning; and (3) motivation. The landmark for the first is Fechner's *Elemente der Psychophysik* of 1860 and for the last is Freud's *Die Traumdeutung* of 1900. Ebbinghaus' *Über das Gedächtnis* of 1885 stands as the middle-phase landmark. If he had produced nothing else, this work would assure Ebbinghaus an important place in the history of psychology.

DAVID SHAKOW

[*For the historical context of Ebbinghaus' work, see the biographies of* DILTHEY; FECHNER. *For discussion of the subsequent development of Ebbinghaus' ideas, see* FORGETTING; LEARNING, *article on* TRANSFER; PSYCHOPHYSICS.]

WORKS BY EBBINGHAUS

1873 *Über die Hartmannsche Philosophie des Unbewussten*. Düsseldorf (Germany): Dietz. → Translation of extract in text provided by David Shakow.

(1885) 1964 *Memory: A Contribution to Experimental Psychology*. Gloucester, Mass.: Smith; New York: Dover. → First published as *Über das Gedächtnis: Untersuchungen zur experimentellen Psychologie*.

1896 *Über erklärende und beschreibende Psychologie*. *Zeitschrift für Psychologie und Physiologie der Sinnesorgane* 9:161–205. → Translation of extract in text provided by David Shakow.

1897 *Über eine neue Methode zur Prüfung geistiger Fähigkeiten und ihre Anwendung bei Schulkindern*. *Zeitschrift für Psychologie und Physiologie der Sinnesorgane* 13:401–459.

(1897–1908) 1911–1913 *Grundzüge der Psychologie*. 3d ed. 2 vols. Leipzig (Germany): Veit.

1901 *Die Psychologie jetzt und vor hundert Jahren*. Pages 49–60 in International Congress of Psychology, Fourth, Paris, 1900, *Compte rendu des séances et texte des mémoires, publiés par les soins du Dr. Pierre Janet*. Paris: Alcan.

1908 *Psychology: An Elementary Text-book*. Translated and edited by Max Meyer. Boston: Heath. → First published in the same year as *Abriss der Psychologie*.

SUPPLEMENTARY BIBLIOGRAPHY

BORING, EDWIN G. (1929) 1950 *A History of Experimental Psychology*. 2d ed. New York: Appleton.

DILTHEY, WILHELM 1894 Ideen über eine beschreibende und zergliedernde Psychologie. Akademie der Wissenschaften, Berlin, *Sitzungsberichte* 2:1309–1407.

DUNLAP, KNIGHT 1927 Use and Abuse of Abstractions in Psychology. *Philosophical Review* 36:462–487. → See especially page 477.

JAENSCH, E. 1909 Hermann Ebbinghaus. *Zeitschrift für Psychologie und Physiologie der Sinnesorgane* 51:i–viii.

JAMES, WILLIAM (1890) 1962 *Principles of Psychology*. New York: Smith.

MURPHY, GARDNER (1929) 1949 *Historical Introduction to Modern Psychology*. Rev. ed. New York: Harcourt.

SHAKOW, DAVID 1930 Hermann Ebbinghaus. *American Journal of Psychology* 42:505–518.

TANZI, EUGENIO 1885 *Über das Gedächtnis*: Untersuchungen zur experimentellen Psychologie von W. [H.] Ebbinghaus. *Rivista di filosofia scientifica* 4:598–600. → Translation of extract in text provided by David Shakow.

TITCHENER, EDWARD B. (1909) 1928 *A Textbook of Psychology*. New York: Macmillan.

TITCHENER, EDWARD B. 1910 The Past Decade in Experimental Psychology. *American Journal of Psychology* 21:404–421.

WOODWORTH, R. S. 1909 Hermann Ebbinghaus. *Journal of Philosophy, Psychology and Scientific Methods* 6:253–256.

ECOLOGICAL ASSOCIATION

See ECOLOGY; FALLACIES, STATISTICAL; MULTIVARIATE ANALYSIS; STATISTICS, DESCRIPTIVE.

ECOLOGY

I. HUMAN ECOLOGY   Amos H. Hawley

II. CULTURAL ECOLOGY   Julian H. Steward

I
HUMAN ECOLOGY

The term "ecology," which has its root in the Greek word *oikos* (household or living place), came into use in the latter part of the nineteenth century in the works of zoologists and botanists to describe the study of the ways in which organisms live in their environments. Soon two branches of ecology were distinguished: *autecology*, the study of the individual organism's interaction with environment, and *synecology*, the study of the correlations between the organisms engaged with a given unit of environment. The latter study has prevailed, however, and has become the principal connotation of ecology, since it became evident in numerous field studies that organisms, whether plant or animal, establish viable relationships with environment, not independently but collectively, through the mechanism of a system of relationships. Bioecologists were thus led to employ a set of concepts and techniques of investigation that imparted a markedly sociological coloration to their work.

Origins and history

The ecological approach was introduced as human ecology into the field of sociology at a critical period in the development of the latter discipline.

In the 1920s the reformistic phase of sociology was drawing to a close, and the subject was gaining acceptance as a respected discipline in the curricula of American universities. That the transition would have been effected so quickly without the aid of a theoretical framework lending itself to empirical research seems doubtful. Ecology opportunely provided the necessary theory. A period of vigorous research followed that was to prove instrumental in launching sociology on its career as a social science.

Sociologists made free use of analogy as they borrowed heavily from the concepts of plant and animal ecology. The Darwinian notion of animate nature as a web of life became at once a general orienting concept and a basic postulate; it directed attention to the necessary interdependence among men as well as among lower forms of life. A second concept, the balance of nature, denoting a tendency toward stabilization of the relative numbers of diverse organisms within the web of life and of their several claims on the environment, provided human ecology with its characteristic equilibrium position. The more or less balanced web of relationships, when viewed in a specific local area, presented the aspect of community, a concept with obvious appeal for students of human social life.

According to plant and animal ecologists, the community, or ecosystem, is a population comprising a set of species whose reactions to the habitat and coactions between each other constitute an integrated system having some degree of unit character. Coactions involve members behaving both with reference to their similarities in an *intra*specific relationship known as commensalism and with reference to their differences in what is called symbiosis, an *inter*specific relationship. The community develops from simple to more complex forms through a sequence of stages described as succession. Each stage in the sequence is marked by an invasion of a new species or association of species, the series culminating in a climax stage in which a *dominant* species appears. The dominant species is related to the environment in such a way that it is able to control and maintain the community indefinitely. The community, then, tends to approximate a self-maintaining, or "closed," system.

Community and environment.   The application of the concepts from plant and animal ecology to the human community carried with it the implication that the community was essentially a natural phenomenon, which meant that it had developed independently of plan or deliberation. From this it was a short, though uncritical, step to the interpretation of human ecology as a study of the biotic or subsocial aspect of human social organization (Park 1936), a view that was elaborated at some length by Quinn (1950). Not only did the subsocial characterization convey an excessively narrow concept of social organization, but it posed an operational problem for which there was no workable solution.

A somewhat different definition of human ecology, which ignored any reference to the cognitive level of events, was enunciated by McKenzie ([1924] 1925, pp. 63–64), whose formulation of the subject as a study of the spatial and temporal relations of human beings, affected by the selective, distributive, and accommodative forces of the environment, was widely accepted as authoritative. Although McKenzie's definition inspired a large amount of fruitful research effort, it had the unfortunate effect of concentrating attention almost exclusively on spatial distributions and correlations. In consequence, many promising implications of ecological assumptions were neglected.

Hawley, in attempting to restore a conceptual continuity with plant and animal ecologies, advanced the view of human ecology as the study of the form and development of the human community (1950, p. 68). Community, in this connection, is construed as a territorially localized system of relationships among functionally differentiated parts; human ecology, then, is concerned with the general problem of organization conceived as an attribute of a population—a point of view that has been shown to be consistent with a long-standing sociological tradition (Schnore 1958). Although the emphasis is centered on the functional system that develops in a population, it is not intended to exclude concern with spatial and temporal aspects; rather, these aspects are regarded as useful dimensions for the measurement of organization.

A further step in making the orientation of human ecology explicit within the larger context of general ecological theory was made by Duncan (1959, pp. 683–684), who described four principal variables of human ecology—population, organization, environment, and technology—that constitute an ecosystem. In other words, while any one of the four may be treated as a dependent variable for certain purposes, it is also reciprocally connected with each of the other variables. The virtue of this perspective lies in the range of problems it opens to the student of human ecology. Yet it seems unlikely that that advantage can be fully enjoyed without a clear notion of how organization is constituted.

Other applications. While sociologists were at work defining human ecology for their purposes and pursuing many of its research leads, the concept spread into various other fields of inquiry. Human geographers wondered if the term "human ecology" was not a more apt characterization of their discipline; but their historic preoccupation with the landscape and their general addiction to a macroscopic treatment of occupance led them to discard this notion. Archeologists, in their efforts to reconstruct population distributions, have made use of ecological concepts and techniques, but without attempting to give formal statement to the approach.

Studies of human evolution by anthropologists involved questions of the man–environment relationship, which, in turn, led them to describe their work as human ecology; indeed, social or cultural anthropologists have long engaged in various ecological studies, although not until recently have they so defined their activity. One definition by an anthropologist is that of Steward (1955), for whom human ecology is the study of the adaptation of specific items of culture to particular environments. This conception, which reduces ecology to something akin to a research technique, is shared by a number of Steward's contemporaries.

The language of human ecology has also made its appearance in economics, psychology, epidemiology, and other fields. In some instances, the term is used merely as a label for an environmental emphasis; in others, it is put forward in an effort to broaden the purview of a discipline.

But in spite of the widespread diffusion of ecological concepts, responsibility for systematic development of human ecology has been left to sociologists, who have drawn heavily on related fields for both theoretical and technical aid. The writings on real estate, finance, public administration, demography, planning, history, and other areas of inquiry, in addition to the literature of the fields previously mentioned, have at one time or another been exploited in the interest of human ecology. The reason for that catholicity of taste is not hard to find; human ecology is concerned with sociological problems in their fullest breadth. It overlaps, therefore, all the spheres of learning that concern the social life of man.

Distinctive features of human ecology

As human ecology has moved toward a major concern with the general problem of social organization and thus closer to the central concern of sociology, it has retained certain distinctive features. Foremost among these is the importance attributed to environment.

The broad, positional hypothesis is that organization arises from the interaction of population and environment. Environment, however, defined as whatever is external to and potentially or actually influential on a phenomenon under investigation, has no fixed content and must be defined anew for each different object of investigation. Environment is seen both as presenting the problem of life and as providing the means for its resolution; to adopt this position is to place the problem in a time–space context.

A second distinguishing characteristic is the emphasis on population as the point of reference; organization, it is contended, is exclusively the property of a population taken as a whole and not of an assemblage of individuals. Obvious as this position may be, it has profound methodological and theoretical implications for the manner in which the ecological problem is put, the variables employed, and the data to be observed. The concreteness of population, however, in contrast with the seemingly ephemeral nature of organization, tends to beguile the student to a view of population as the independent variable in all things pertaining to organization. It is obviously more convenient to proceed from the more accessible to the less accessible by asking how a population makes a unitary response to its environment; yet that is merely a common-sense way of approaching the problem, and investigation soon makes it apparent that population is for many purposes better regarded as the dependent variable, delimited and regulated by organization.

A third characteristic is the treatment of organization as a more or less complete and self-sustaining whole. The interaction of population and environment is seen as culminating in a system of relationships between differentiated parts which gives the population unit character and enables it to maintain its identity. As the property of a population, organization lends itself most readily to a morphological, or structural, analysis. The parts are the units—individuals or clusters of individuals—that perform functions and the relationships by which these units are linked. Differing configurations of unit functions and relationships are expected to occur with differences in relationship to environment and at different stages in development.

A morphological concern does not exclude the problem of development. Presumably, any given form of organization had an earlier form and is capable of having a later form. Every organization has a history, perhaps a natural history, the knowledge of which may shed light on the nature of organizations by indicating, for example, at what points they are vulnerable to change and how change spreads through them.

Related to the conception of organization is a fourth distinctive, although by no means unique, attribute of human ecology: the central position given to an equilibrium assumption. Morphological change is assumed to be a movement toward an equilibrium state, whether through a succession-like sequence of stages or through a process of continuous modification. Unlike the equilibrium notion in some of its other applications, such as in functionalist theory, the ecological usage of the term harbors no teleological overtones; on the contrary, this usage merely implies that as an organization attains completeness, it acquires the capacity for controlling change and for retaining its form through time, although the interval need not be specified. To put it differently, to the extent that an organization possesses unit character, an approximation to equilibrium obtains.

There is a further implication that a stable relationship with environment is contingent on relative stability in the relationships between the parts of an organization. A population always remains open to environment, but the formation of organizations canalizes environmental influences and makes for increasing selectivity of response.

The term "community" has commonly been used to denote the unit of organization for ecological purposes. Operationally defined as that population which carries on its daily life through a given system of relationships, the community is regarded as the smallest microcosm in which all the parameters of society are to be found. For reasons that were largely fortuitous, human ecologists at first focused their attention on the city and its tributary area as the prototype of community; later, in an effort to encompass the antecedents of cities, they broadened their consideration to include all forms of nucleated settlement. The term "community," however, has the disadvantage of referring to the organization of a more or less localized settlement unit that does not always approximate a self-maintaining whole. For example, in an extensively urbanized society, local settlement units are usually components of more inclusive systems; in that event, the entire system must be treated as the object of study. But the difference between a simple, compact organization and a large, diffuse one is primarily a difference in scale; accordingly, the principles of organization should be the same in

each. Since the designation of both simple and complex systems as communities threatens confusion, a more neutral term, such as "social system," is to be preferred.

Principles of ecological organization

Inasmuch as principles of organization hinge on what is meant by population, it is imperative that the concept be developed more fully.

A human population is an aggregate of individuals who possess the following characteristics. As a living organism, every individual must have access to environment, for that is the only possible source of sustenance. Moreover, the interdependence of individuals is necessary; this condition, which obtains for all forms of life, holds true to an exceptional degree in the case of man, because of the naked state in which he comes into the world and his long period of postnatal maturation. Interdependence is the irreducible connotation of sociality.

The human being also possesses an inherent tendency to preserve and expand his life to the maximum permitted by prevailing circumstances; this is a general motive of which all other motives are special cases. In its most elementary sense, expansion of life refers to the multiplication of man-years through either the leaving of progeny or the extension of longevity; but it also includes all that is involved in the realization of that objective. Another important characteristic is the indeterminacy of the human being's capacity to adapt; there is no known restriction on the kind or extent of refinement of activity in which he can engage. Finally, the human individual, again like other organisms, is time-bound; the recurring needs for food and rest fix the fundamental rhythm of life and regulate the allocation of time to all other activities. Accordingly, the time available for movement is limited and, in consequence, the space over which activities can be distributed is correspondingly limited.

These several attributes of individuals not only define the kind of population with which human ecology deals, but they also constitute a cardinal set of assumptions from which principles of ecological organization may be deduced. The following are some of the more salient of these principles of organization.

Principle of interdependence. Interdependence develops between units on each of two axes: the symbiotic (on the basis of their complementary differences) and the commensal (on the basis of their supplementary similarities). That is, units that combine in a symbiotic union may also enter into other combinations of a commensal character; the effect of each type of union is to raise the power of action above what it would be were the units to remain apart.

The effect, however, is not the same in each case. The symbiotic union enhances the efficiency of production or creative effort; the commensal union, since its parts are homogeneous, can only react and is suited, therefore, only to protective or conservative actions. Although commensalism is an elemental form of union, it is applicable to a wide array of situations. The point of importance at present is that a population tends to be knit together through an interwoven set of symbiotic and commensal relationships.

It should be evident that interdependence has temporal and spatial implications for the units involved. Relations of functional complementation and supplementation require mutual accessibility among units; since this is contingent on the time available for movement, the distance separating related units is always subject to some limitation. In general, for every set of related units, there should be, other things being equal, an appropriate pattern of distribution in the temporal and spatial dimensions.

Principle of the key function. A second principle may be described as the principle of the key function. That is, in every system of relationships among diverse functions, the connection of the system to its environment is mediated primarily by one or a relatively small number of functions, the latter being known as the key function or functions. To the extent that the principle of the key function does not obtain, the system will be tenuous and incoherent; in the extreme case, in which no system exists, every function has the same relationship to environment. Given a functional system, then, there are always some functions or functional units directly involved with environment and others that secure access to the environment indirectly, through the agency of the key function.

The notion of key function invokes the question of how to define the notion of environment, which can refer to many different kinds of things. For present purposes, these things may be classified in two broad categories: the natural and the social. Although every organized aggregate must contend with both, the relative importance of each may vary over a wide range. In some instances, because of the inaccessibility of the settlement, activities of necessity center on the exploitation of the local natural environment, while influences from the social field are relatively infrequent or of no great consequence. In this event, the key function is the

activity that extracts the principal sustenance supply from local resources. But where the product from local resources, or a substantial part of it, is exchanged for other sustenance materials, whether through trade or other distributive mechanisms, the key function is determined by the comparative importance of production and of trade as sources of sustenance.

In many such instances, no distinction is necessary because the producer is also the trader—two functions combined in one functionary. But even before the two functions appear as separate specialties, the requisites of trade or distribution begin to regulate the uses of local resources. As the reliance on exchange advances, the social environment actually displaces the natural environment as the critical set of influences. A population is never emancipated from its dependence on physical and animate matters, but the importance of locale declines with increasing involvement in a network of intersystem relations; the natural environment is extended and diffused, and contacts with it are mediated through a variety of social mechanisms. Hence, the functions that link the local system to the social environment come to occupy the key position.

Principle of differentiation. The extent of functional differentiation varies with the productivity of the key function or functions; this is the principle of differentiation. A corollary is that the size of population supportable by the system varies with the productivity of the key function. For given the simplifying assumption that each unit is fully occupied, the number of people is determined by the number of functions to be performed.

In a hunting and gathering community, for instance, productivity is usually low, even though the physical environment is richly endowed; hence, there is little time or opportunity available for the cultivation of more than a few specialized functions. Nor is it possible to support enough people to staff even a moderate extent of specialization. By contrast, where the key function is devoted to stable agriculture, the range of possibilities is much greater, while in an industrial system productivity is so great that there are no known upper limits on either the number of specializations or the size of the population that can be supported.

The productivity of the key function, then, constitutes the principal limiting condition on the extent to which a system can be elaborated, on the size of population that can be sustained in the system, and on the area or space the system can occupy.

A question of some importance has to do with

the relative number of units engaged in each of several interrelated functions. That question remains unanswered at present. It may be suggested, however, that the number of units engaged in any given function is inversely proportional to the productivity of the function and directly proportional to the number of units that utilize the product of the function.

It follows, of course, that functional differentiation involves a differentiation of environmental requirements. As the materials and conditions used by diversely specialized units differ, so also will their needs for location in space and time. In general, units performing key functions have the highest priority of claim on location. Other units tend to distribute themselves about the key function units, their distances away corresponding to the number of degrees of removal separating their functions from direct relation with the key functions. The temporal spacing may be expected to reveal a similar pattern. Special location requirements, however, as for type of soil or other resource, may obscure the tendency to a symmetrical arrangement of functions by degree of indirectness of relationship with key functions.

An important implication of the principles of the key function and of differentiation is that of transitivity in the relation among functional units. Relations with environment are necessarily transitive for some units. By the same token, relations among many units are transitive. The advance of specialization increases transitive relations more than proportionally and lengthens the transitive sequences. Thus, it is possible for functional units widely removed from one another so far as direct encounters are concerned to be inextricably linked through their respective linkages with one or more units performing intervening functions. All functions, regardless of kind, are subject to the environmental nexus. They differ only in the immediacy with which influences reach them. Those which operate at or near the ends of chains of relationships may appear to have large degrees of independence of environment. The appearance is illusory, however. It is due, rather, to the time required for effects to reach them and, in complex systems, to their having positions in two or more relational sequences which expose them to countervailing influences.

Principle of dominance. Given the principles stated above, it is a simple inferential step to a principle of dominance. According to this principle, functional units having direct relations with environment, and thus performing the key function, determine or regulate the conditions essential to the functions of units having indirect relations with environment. Dominance, in other words, is an attribute of function.

But while the power inherent in a system is unevenly distributed, it is not confined to the key function unit. Power is held in varying degrees by all other units, in measures that vary inversely with the number of steps of removal from direct relation with the unit performing the key function. A single power gradient running through all the units involved in a system assumes a very simple situation, of course, one in which a single unit occupies a key function position. Before introducing complications into this overly simplified conception, it is opportune to note some further implications of the dominance principle.

Where the progress of differentiation has distinguished a relatively large number of units, they tend to form clusters or complex units. A corollary to the dominance principle sheds light on how that comes about: the greater the extent to which variously specialized units are subject to the environmental conditions mediated by some one unit, the greater their tendency to coalesce in a corporate body. The interdependence among such units is manifestly close, and their requirements for mutual accessibility are correspondingly acute. A hierarchic pattern emerges in which the number of strata corresponds to the number of degrees that the parts are removed from direct relations with the key function; thus, symbiotic subsystems appear as components of a parent system. The nuclear family, although its origins are obscure, fits this principle. But instances with more proximate origins are found in the combinations of specialists to form producing enterprises, welfare agencies, governing bodies, etc., and again in the combinations of producing enterprises, retail establishments, or governments to constitute larger, more complex units. There is no restriction of scale or complexity in the formation of symbiotic or corporate units.

On the other hand, units that are of a given functional type and therefore occupy equivalent positions in the power hierarchy may raise their power potential by the formation of categoric unions. Any threat to a function or to the conditions of its performance can provoke such a response; groups of elders, the medieval guilds, labor unions, professional associations, councils of churches, retail associations, and associations of manufacturers are examples of categoric units. A social class is at most a loose form of categoric unit.

As with the corporate union, the categoric union may be composed of units of any size or kind. It may appear as a federation of categoric units or as an association of corporate units. So long as it retains its pure categoric form, however, such a unit can do little more than react to circumstances affecting it. Nor can it have more than a transitory existence, since in order to engage in positive action of any kind and to attain some measure of permanence, it must develop at least a core of specialists. Although the categoric unit tends to assume the characteristics of the corporate unit, it remains distinctive as long as its criterion for membership is possession of a given, common characteristic. In any event, the categoric unit is a source of rigidity in a social system, and once formed, its effect is to preserve the position of a functional category in the system.

The concept of dominance has been widely employed for the purpose of delimiting the boundaries of systems. It is argued that centers of settlement, such as cities, exercise dominance over their surrounding areas, in diminishing degrees as the distance from the center increases; the margin of influence marks the boundary of the system. Empirical support for this proposition is provided by the evidence of nonrandom distribution of related functions and by the gradient pattern that appears in the frequencies with which outlying functions are involved with central functions.

Two qualifications of this conclusion are needed; first, dominance is exercised from and not by centers, since it resides in functional units rather than in the places where they are located. Further, the apparent decline of dominance results less from an effect of distance in reducing control over related functions than from the increased difficulty of establishing dominance uniformly over an exponentially widening area.

Isomorphism. A principle of isomorphism has been implied in much that has been said and needs now to be stated. Units subject to the same environmental conditions, or to environmental conditions as mediated through a given key unit, acquire a similar form of organization. They must submit to standard terms of communication and to standard procedures in consequence of which they develop similar internal arrangements within limits imposed by their respective sizes. Each unit, then, tends to become a replica of every other unit and of the parent system in which it is a subsystem.

Since small units cannot acquire the elaborate organizations of which large units are capable, they jointly support specialized functions that complement their meager organizations. For example, whereas a large unit may include among its functionaries accountants, lawyers, engineers, public relations experts, and other specialists, the small unit must purchase comparable services from units specializing in each of the relevant functions. The principle of isomorphism also applies to the size of units, at least as a tendency; that is, all units tend toward a size that enables them to maintain contact with all relevant sectors of the parent system.

Closure and social change

Operation of the several principles mentioned thus far moves a system toward a state of closure. This term must be employed here with circumspection, for it cannot have its usual connotation of independence of environment. Closure can only mean that development has terminated in a more or less complete system that is capable of sustaining a given relationship to environment indefinitely. For closure to be realized, it is required not only that the differentiation of function supportable by the productivity of the key function has attained its maximum but also that the various functions have been gathered into corporate and categoric subsystems; moreover, the performance of the key function should have been reduced to one unit or to a number of units united in a categoric federation. Then a system is highly selective of its membership and capable of exercising some control over factors that threaten change in the system.

Under these circumstances, certain conditions of equilibrium are held to obtain: the functions involved are mutually complementary and collectively provide the conditions essential to the continuation of each; the number of individuals engaged in each function is just sufficient to maintain the relations of the functions to each other and to all other functions; and the various units are arranged in time and space so that the accessibility of one to others bears a direct relation to the frequency of exchanges between them. Needless to say, equilibrium as thus defined is a logical construct; the conditions express an expected outcome if the principles of organization are allowed to operate without any external disturbances.

Origins and effects of change. Every social system is continuously subject to change, for since the environment is always in some state of flux, the equilibrium that can be attained is seldom more than partial. A system founded on nonreplaceable resources is faced with "immanent change"; sooner or later it will either pass into decline or shift perforce to a different resource base. Such, for instance, has been the experience of innumerable mining communities; in a similar manner agricultural communities often alter the soil composition of their lands by the uses they practice, with the ultimate result that the lands will no longer support the systems as they are constituted. Instances of maladaptation, such as the reliance of the Irish on the potato as a food staple in the nineteenth century, can lead to catastrophic consequences.

In general, however, change has an external origin, a proposition that follows by definition from an equilibrium position. Some influences emanate from the physical or biotic environment, such as variations in the growing season or invasion by parasites. To the extent that episodic occurrences of that order fail to modify one or more functions comprised in the system, their effects are transitory; the system returns to its original form. But where a function, particularly a key function, is substantially modified, the system must be reconstituted. The disappearance of a game supply, the silting of an estuary, or the eruption of a volcano may render a key function inoperative in its usual location. The population must relocate and work out a new system of activities. Unless there is an increase of productivity, new ways of acting will merely displace old ways, and the change will not be cumulative.

Cumulative change. Cumulative change, or growth of the system, presupposes an increase in the productivity of a key function. Only in this way is it possible to multiply specialization, to employ a greater variety of techniques, and to support a larger population. The probability of the occurrence of disturbances having that effect rises with the number of points of contact with a social environment; location, therefore, is an important factor. A site on a traveled route is more exposed to external influences than one situated at a distance from an avenue of movement; a site at a conflux of routes is much more vulnerable to disturbances from without. Any location that fosters frequent meetings of people from diverse backgrounds is a gateway for the infusion of alien experiences and techniques into the social system centered there. Whether change is released through a deposit of numerous small additions to the culture or through a simple, dramatic innovation is immaterial.

The process of cumulative change may be generalized as a principle of expansion. Expansion is a twofold process involving, on the one hand, the growth of a center of activity from which dominance is exercised and, on the other hand, an enlargement of the scope of the center's influence. The process entails the absorption and redistribution of the functions formerly carried on in outlying areas, a centralization of mediating and control functions, an increase in the number and variety of territorially extended relationships, a growth of

population to man a more elaborate set of activities, and an accumulation of culture together with a leveling of cultural differences over the expanding domain. After the revival of trade in Europe, from the tenth century onward, the favorably situated village with its narrow vicinage grew into a market town that served as a center of an enlarged territorial organization. That gave way, in turn, to the emergent city capable of exercising an integrating influence over an area of regional scope. Most recently, the metropolis has superseded the city and has brought under its dominion a vast interregional territory. Although the process is as old as recorded history, it has not advanced in a simple linear progression. It has moved and then stalled in one place, only to surge ahead in another; it has faltered and even on occasion has seemed to turn back upon itself, but it has always resumed its course with renewed vigor.

The limits to expansion are sometimes fixed by the facility of movement between center and periphery—by the maximum distance over which the exercise of dominance is feasible. More often than not, however, the limits are drawn at the points of juncture with the expanding domains of social systems in neighboring regions. As a system encounters its limits, however they are fixed, it loses capacity to absorb further change, and equilibrium tendencies begin to assert themselves once more.

Under conditions of closure, environmental effects, and particularly cultural innovations, would be expected to enter a system through the key function, for the obvious reason that it has the most direct connection with environment. And, presumably, change would spread through the system by affecting units successively in the order in which they are removed from direct relation with a key function. But in a system centered on a convergence of routes, many units may have direct, although not equal, access to the outside world. Change may therefore enter the system at many points, at least until its structure is fully developed with the parts systematically arrayed relative to a key unit. An expanding system, in other words, is an open system, and it remains so until the limits to expansion are reached.

In many instances, however, the first symptoms of change are experienced at the periphery of a system. Since the effects of dominance grow more uneven with increased distance from a center, boundaries are apt to be permeable at many points. Yet, in the degree to which a system is integrated, events at the boundary are transmitted directly to the key unit, from which they are communicated to ancillary units; it is always at the boundary that one system begins its absorption of another. Expansion may be resumed at any moment and in any of the systems that hem in one another. An innovation, even though it might present itself to all systems about the same time, gains admission to one or another by virtue of a more favorable location for its use, a more appropriate organization for its acceptance, or some other local advantage. The renewed expansion encroaches upon the territories of adjoining systems, sometimes reducing them to mere components of a single, greatly enlarged system.

Burgess' hypothesis of city growth. A hypothesis of city growth, stated by E. W. Burgess ([1925] 1961, pp. 37–44), pertains to a special case of the more general principle. According to that proposal, city growth takes the form of expansion from a zone centered on a highly accessible location. Growth involves increasing density of occupance of the central zone and, at the same time, a redistribution of activities or land uses scattered around the center to conform to a gradient pattern of variation of intensity of land use according to distances from the center. Redistribution results from increasing pressure at the center and a consequent encroachment by high-intensity uses into the spaces occupied by lower-intensity uses in a succession-like manner. Alternating periods of redistribution and stabilization of distribution, and those of growth and partial equilibrium, create a wavelike effect more or less visible in a set of concentric zones. By venturing to describe, in rather specific terms, the content of the zones and by thus reifying a set of statistical constructs, Burgess diverted attention from a growth process and caused it to be fixed on a specious distribution pattern. His argument, therefore, seemed to acquire a historical limitation that it need not have had.

The miscarriage of the import of the Burgess hypothesis is evident in criticisms that have opposed the preindustrial city to the industrial city as a qualitatively different phenomenon. Whereas Burgess suggested that the social–economic status of residents is higher in each successive concentric zone, critics have shown that in the preindustrial city the social–economic gradient runs in the opposite direction. Useful as that finding may be, it misses the essential point. That is, the significant gradient is one of dominance; units tend to distribute themselves over space in a way that reflects their relationships to the dominant unit. In this respect, both industrial and preindustrial cities are similar. The qualitative difference lies in the kinds of units that exercise dominance. In the preindus-

trial city, all functions are carried in familial or household units, and power is unevenly distributed among them. But in the industrial society, the household unit has been relegated to a minor position; specialized functions are performed by extra-familial units, and the separation of functions from the household has involved a spatial separation as well.

Furthermore, the notion of a monocentered system is applicable only to the simplest instances. All others include a constellation of settlement nuclei, that is to say, subsidiary service centers within cities, and villages, towns, or cities within hinterlands. Each serves as a locus of influence over a localized area, varying in scope with the types of functions centered in the nucleus. Thus, as Christaller observed, the constellation of nuclei forms a hierarchy by size and number of places and by order of functions performed (1933). Small places provide low-order, or ubiquitous, functions, whereas each larger place performs, in addition to low-order functions, higher-order functions for broader domains. At the apogee of the hierarchy is the metropolis, in which the integrating and coordinating functions for the entire system are domiciled. Thus, dominance is exercised downward and outward through nested sets of subsidiary centers [*see* CENTRAL PLACE].

The least satisfactory aspect of the theory of change concerns its temporal incidence. The idea of succession, borrowed initially from bioecology, lingers in the dictionary of human ecology. Change as cyclical in form, consisting in movements between equilibrium stages, is clearly the most intelligible conception. Nevertheless, apart from the difficulty in empirically identifying an equilibrium stage, there are unsolved conceptual problems of the spacing of stages, and of the factors governing the intervals between stages. Thus far, succession has been applied only in retrospect. Its utility will remain uncertain until it can be projected into prediction. Quite possibly, that may have to wait for more extensive work on social system taxonomy.

The limits of human ecology

Human ecology has progressed since its inception from an effort to apply the concepts of plant and animal ecology to human collective life, through an extended period of preoccupation with spatial configurations, to an increasing concern with the form and development of territorially based social systems. In the last phase, human ecologists have sought to clarify the assumptions of ecology and to draw out their implications for organization. Although the results of that work are far from complete, it seems clear that they indicate the direction in which human ecology will continue to develop.

As with most approaches in social science, human ecology has limited objectives. It seeks knowledge about the structure of a social system and the manner in which the structure develops. Hence, it is not prepared to provide explanations for all of the manifold interactions, frictions, and collisions that occur within the bounds of a social system. The findings of human ecology, however, define the context in which all such phenomena take place, and which is therefore pertinent to their full understanding.

Human ecology is not qualified to deal with the normative order in a social system. Yet consistent with its position is the expectation that a normative order corresponds to and reflects the functional order. The two are different abstractions from the same reality.

AMOS H. HAWLEY

[See also CITY, article on COMPARATIVE URBAN STRUCTURE; ENVIRONMENT; ENVIRONMENTALISM; GEOGRAPHY; and the biographies of BURGESS; DARWIN; PARK.]

BIBLIOGRAPHY

BURGESS, ERNEST W. (1925) 1961 The Growth of the City: An Introduction to a Research Project. Pages 37–44 in George A. Theodorson (editor), *Studies in Human Ecology.* Evanston, Ill.: Row, Peterson.

CHRISTALLER, WALTER 1933 *Die zentralen Orte in Süddeutschland: Eine ökonomisch-geographische Untersuchung über die Gesetzmässigkeit der Verbreitung und Entwicklung der Siedlungen mit städtischen Funktionen.* Jena (Germany): Fischer.

DUNCAN, OTIS DUDLEY 1959 Human Ecology and Population Studies. Pages 678–716 in Philip M. Hauser and Otis Dudley Duncan (editors), *The Study of Population: An Inventory and Appraisal.* Univ. of Chicago Press.

HAWLEY, AMOS H. 1950 *Human Ecology: A Theory of Community Structure.* New York: Ronald.

McKENZIE, RODERICK D. (1924) 1925 The Ecological Approach to the Study of the Human Community. Pages 63–79 in Robert E. Park, Ernest W. Burgess, and Roderick D. McKenzie, *The City.* Univ. of Chicago Press. → First published in Volume 30 of the *American Journal of Sociology.*

PARK, ROBERT E. (1936) 1952 Human Ecology. Pages 145–158 in Robert E. Park, *Human Communities: The City and Human Ecology.* Collected Papers, Vol. 2. Glencoe, Ill.: Free Press. → First published in Volume 42 of the *American Journal of Sociology.*

QUINN, JAMES A. 1950 *Human Ecology.* Englewood Cliffs, N.J.: Prentice-Hall.

SCHNORE, LEO F. 1958 Social Morphology and Human Ecology. *American Journal of Sociology* 63:620–634.

STEWARD, JULIAN H. 1955 *Theory of Culture Change: The Methodology of Multilinear Evolution.* Urbana: Univ. of Illinois Press.

II
CULTURAL ECOLOGY

Cultural ecology is the study of the processes by which a society adapts to its environment. Its principal problem is to determine whether these adaptations initiate internal social transformations or evolutionary change. It analyzes these adaptations, however, in conjunction with other processes of change. Its method requires examination of the interaction of societies and social institutions with one another and with the natural environment.

Cultural ecology is distinguishable from but does not necessarily exclude other approaches to the ecological study of social phenomena. These approaches have viewed their special problems—for example, settlement patterns, the development of agriculture, and land use—in the broad context of the complexly interacting phenomena within a defined geographical area. Explanatory formulations have even included the incidence of disease, which is related to social phenomena and in turn affects societies in their adaptations. This modern concept of ecology has largely superseded other concepts, such as "urban," "social," and "human" ecology, which employed the biological analogy of viewing social institutions in terms of competition, climax areas, and zones.

Cultural ecology is broadly similar to biological ecology in its method of examining the interactions of all social and natural phenomena within an area, but it does not equate social features with biological species or assume that competition is the major process. It distinguishes different kinds of sociocultural systems and institutions, it recognizes both cooperation and competition as processes of interaction, and it postulates that environmental adaptations depend on the technology, needs, and structure of the society and on the nature of the environment. It includes analysis of adaptations to the social environment, because an independent tribe is influenced in its environmental adaptations by such interactions with its neighbors as peaceful trading, intermarriage, cooperation, and warfare and other kinds of competition, in the same way a specialized, dependent segment of a larger sociocultural system may be strongly influenced by external institutions in the way it utilizes its environment.

The cultural ecological method of analyzing culture change or evolution differs from that based on the superorganic or culturological concept. The latter assumes that only phenomena of a cultural level are relevant and admissible, and it repudiates "reductionism," that is, consideration of processes induced by factors of a psychological, biological, or environmental level. The evolutionary hypotheses based upon this method deal with culture in a generic or global sense rather than with individual cultures in a substantive sense, and they postulate universal processes. Cultural ecology, on the other hand, recognizes the substantive dissimilarities of cultures that are caused by the particular adaptive processes by which any society interacts with its environment.

Cultural ecology does not assume that each case is unique. Its method, however, requires an empirical analysis of each society before broader generalizations of cross-cultural similarities in processes and substantive effects may be made. Cultural ecologists study highly diversified cultures and environments and can prescribe neither specific analytic formulas nor theoretical or ideal models of culture change; there can be no a priori conclusions or generalizations concerning evolution. The heuristic value of the ecological viewpoint is to conceptualize noncultural phenomena that are relevant to processes of cultural evolution.

Empirical studies disclose that among the simpler and earlier societies of mankind, to whom physical survival was the major concern, different social systems were fairly direct responses to the exploitation of particular environments by special techniques. As technological innovations improved man's ability to control and adjust to environments, and as historically derived patterns of behavior were introduced, the significance of both the environment and the culture was altered and the adaptive processes not only became more complex but also acquired new qualities.

The ecological concept of interacting phenomena draws attention to certain general categories of relevant data. The resources, flora, fauna, climate, local diseases and their vectors of occurrence and many other features of the environment constitute potential factors in one part of the interacting system. The nature of the culture, especially its exploitative and adaptive technology but also features of the internal and external social environment, constitutes the other part. The interaction involves the social arrangements that are required in land exploitation; population density, distribution, and nucleation; permanence and composition of population aggregates; territoriality of societies; intersocietal relationships; and cultural values. In each case the empirical problem is whether the adaptation is so inflexible as to permit only a certain pattern or whether there is latitude for variation which may allow different patterns to be developed or borrowed.

Explanations in terms of cultural ecology require certain conceptual distinctions about the nature of culture. First, the various components of a culture, such as technology, language, society, and stylistic features, respond very differently to adaptive processes. Second, sociocultural systems of different levels of integration profoundly affect the interaction of biological, cultural, and environmental factors. Societies having supracommunity (state or national) institutions and the technological ability to expand the effective environment beyond that of the local or primary group can utilize resources within and outside the area controlled by the larger society. The adaptive responses of complex societies are thus very unlike those of a tribal society, which adapts predominantly to its own environment.

Culture history and ecological adaptations

The historical processes by which a society acquires many of its basic traits are complementary to studies of adaptive processes. The historical processes include the extensive borrowing of many cultural traits and trait complexes from diverse sources; the migrations of people; the transmission of cultural heritages to successive generations; and local innovations or inventions. Recognition of these historical processes, however, does not relegate environment to the circumscribed role of merely permitting or prohibiting certain cultural practices so that all origins must be explained by such history. It is obvious that fishing will have minor importance in desert areas and that agriculture is impossible in arctic regions. It is equally clear that abundant fishing resources cannot be exploited without appropriate techniques and that agricultural potentials cannot be utilized without domesticated plants. The presence of gold, oil, and uranium is unimportant until the society has demands for them and means of extracting them.

The Indians of the Southwest had at one time been predominantly food collectors, but the introduction of food crops, largely from Mesoamerica, provided the basis for the development of the more complex Pueblo village culture. Many details of this culture, such as ritual elements, were borrowed from the south, but the development of Pueblo sociocultural patterns are comprehensible only in terms of the processes of population growth, extension of biological families into lineages, eventual consolidation of lineages into larger settlements, and the appearance of many village institutions that cut across kinship groups.

Dissimilar ecological adaptations may also occur among societies that have been subjected to similar historical influences. The Indians of California and of the semiarid steppes and deserts of the Great Basin shared substantially the same devices for collecting wild foods and for hunting, but the vastly greater abundance of flora and fauna in California supported a population thirty times that of the Great Basin. The California Indians lived in fairly permanent villages which had developed some social elaborations, whereas the Great Basin Indians were divided into independent family units which foraged over large territories during most of the year and assembled only seasonally in encampments that did not always consist of the same families.

The investigation of cultural ecological processes must consider the possibility that basic sociocultural patterns may have diffused or been carried by migrations from one kind of environment to another, but it also must examine whether these patterns have been modified. Assessment of modifications requires a distinction between the outer embellishments of the culture, such as ritual elements, art styles, and kinds of architecture, and those social patterns which are human arrangements for self-perpetuation.

Biological factors.   Man's adaptations to his natural environment cannot be comprehended in purely culturological terms because man not only shares basic biological needs with all animals but also has distinctively human characteristics. All activities are culturally conditioned, but ecological factors cannot be wholly distinguished from inherent biological and psychological factors which are the basis of behavior. Analyses that ascribe importance to inherent human qualities bear directly upon the validity of common hypotheses and raise new problems.

It has generally been assumed that the nuclear family consisting of parents and children has always been the irreducible social structure because the sexes serve complementary functions in meeting procreational and subsistence needs and in caring for and training the young during their long period of dependency. This assumption is generally valid for all ethnographically known societies, especially for primitive societies, among whom there is a clear sexual division of labor in subsistence, maintenance of the household, and child rearing. In contemporary industrial societies, however, the biological family has surrendered many of its functions, and cultural differences between sex roles have been diminished. Conceivably, the nuclear family might be reduced to little more than a procreational unit if its cultural functions are lost.

In primitive societies, larger suprafamilial bands or other groups that developed in response to cooperative needs, especially in subsistence activities, had a biological basis, especially through lineages. The patrilineages of hunting bands, for example, had the advantage that particular skills, knowledge of the environment, and obedience to authority were transmitted from father to son in a male-dominated group. Biological relationships have so long been fundamentally important in culture history that they may be ascribed excessive importance, as when the position of head of a family or even kingship is transmitted through primogeniture. The biological basis survived because of the lack of patterned alternatives.

Another basic biological factor in cultural ecological adaptations is the prolonged period of human growth. The factors of age and environment interact in many ways to affect behavior patterns. The Shoshoni child may help in rabbit drives but not in big game hunting; the east African boy may herd cattle but not go to war; modern American youths attend school for a required number of years; in areas of precarious subsistence the aged may be abandoned to die, while in other areas they may be accorded special consideration; and everywhere the marriage age group is determined by biological development, culture, and adaptations to the environment.

There are, however, many problems concerning the interaction of biological and cultural ecological factors. One of these arises from the assumption that the nuclear or biological family is a basic part of every human society. This assumption might rest on the obvious biological nature of the family or upon the universal cultural functions the family is believed to serve. The higher primates usually live in fairly small bands that consist of females and their dependent offspring, a single powerful male, and subordinate adult males. In certain depressed segments of modern society, however, the matrifocal family or kin group, which consists of women and dependent children and somewhat subordinate males who are loosely attached to the family, appears to be the irreducible social unit. This family represents an adaptive response to restricted territoriality, low income, and lack of opportunity for improvement.

Although the transition from a precultural primate society to the nuclear family has not been explained, the contemporary existence of the matrifocal kin group raises the question of origin. How did the nuclear family develop from an early kind of society which may have lacked the cultural ecological processes that created and have subsequently supported it?

Speculation about the origin of the family must be based on what is known archeologically about the origins of technology and on ethnographic evidence. In all ethnographic cases of prefarming societies the nuclear family is based on clear complementarity of the sexes in subsistence activities. Women are food collectors because they must not leave their children, who are their inescapable responsibility, whereas men may spend long periods away from their families hunting large game or fishing, if the technology makes this possible. Prior to the invention of such distinctly male-associated hunting devices as spears, bows, nets, and traps, both sexes may have collected food in so similar a way that they were no more differentiated than were the higher primates. If so, there may have been a long transitional stage when some type of matrifocal kin group persisted. The hand ax, which was long the principal weapon, may attest to men's role in protecting the group but not specialization in hunting, for its use was in close combat.

Settlement patterns and the adaptive process. A culture that is introduced into a wholly new environment must adapt in some ways to local conditions, but only empirical research can determine whether the adaptations are unalterably fixed or whether there is latitude for variations. In some instances, the case for narrow limits of variation seems clear. Simple societies that exploit only sparse and scattered resources obtained by food collecting must obviously fragment into small groups, for members of the society are in competition with one another. More abundant resources, such as rich areas of vegetable foods, large game herds, fisheries, or intensive farming, may permit variation in some features and thus allow latitude for borrowing or for local innovations.

There can, however, be no a priori conclusions: whether a society is dispersed over its land or clustered in large settlements may result from adaptive factors, from historical patterns, or from both. The Indians of California and the Northwest Coast had very similar native population densities, but the dispersed acorns and game in California led to considerable dispersal of the villages, whereas the rich salmon fisheries of British Columbia and Alaska required the people to concentrate on the main streams in fairly large settlements. Similarly, agricultural areas dependent upon irrigation concentrated the population within the network of canals. On the rainless and barren deserts of coastal Peru,

the people had to live in dense settlements along or near the rivers. The large communities on the coasts of British Columbia and Peru, however, were parts of unlike sociocultural systems. Each developed from a different historical background, and each had a distinctive local adaptation; there were fisheries on the Northwest Coast and intensive, irrigation farming together with ocean resources in Peru.

A dense population supported by a rich economy is not always concentrated in large centers. The native agricultural peoples of the northern Andes of Colombia and the Araucanian Indians of the central valley of Chile had very similar population densities, but the northern Andean peoples were organized in strong, class-structured chiefdoms with communities of five hundred persons or more, whereas the Araucanians were dispersed in many closely spaced villages, each a patrilineage of no more than one hundred persons. This contrast is not explained by farm productivity or other technological factors involved in maintaining large communities. The northern Andean chiefdoms were the result of a diffused cult-complex of temples, priests, warriors, and human sacrifice, which may have originated in Mesoamerica but was readapted to the diversified environment of high mountains and deep valleys. Presumably, the Araucanians could have supported chiefdoms, but the nucleating factors were absent. A limited pastoral nomadism based on llama herding may have been an ecological deterrent to community growth, although this factor did not inhibit the development of states and empires in Peru.

Nontechnological features of culture may also affect the adaptive arrangements through the external social environment of the society. Peaceful interaction of societies through marriage, trade, visiting, and participation in ceremonies, games, and other activities may take various patterns within the limits imposed by the environment. Intergroup hostilities, however, may have a decisive influence, because fear of warfare often causes peoples to cluster in compact settlements that are not required by subsistence patterns and sometimes do not give optimum access to resources. Thus, the palisaded villages of parts of the Amazon somewhat inhibited farming of the frequently shifting slash-and-burn farm plots. To judge by the prehistory of the Pueblo Indians, the nature of farming permitted considerable variation. Early settlements were small and widely scattered, but in later periods the population declined as the settlements became large and tightly nucleated. This was the result of increased precariousness of farming in an area that had frequent droughts and was inhabited by marauders. In Tanganyika, people did not dare disperse along the fertile lands near the waterways until colonialism largely eliminated warfare. Throughout much of history, warfare has been a major factor in the interaction of culture and environment.

Exploitation of an environment by means of certain cultural devices may also drastically affect the environment, which again reacts upon the culture. In native California, as in many other areas, the Indians deliberately fired the grass in order to kill seedlings of brush and trees and thus increase the grazing land for game. Deforestation, overgrazing with concomitant soil erosion, the damming and rechanneling of rivers, drainage of swamps, and conversion of rural areas to urban or suburban land-use patterns also alter the environment. In such instances as the firing of grasslands, the development of irrigation works, or reclamation of swamps, the culture increases its basic resources. In others, such as overgrazing, lack of conservation, or the exhaustion of basic minerals, the culture destroys or impairs certain aspects of its local foundations.

Cultural variables versus holism

Although the culture of any society constitutes a holistic system in which technology, economics, social and political structure, religion, language, values, and other features are closely interrelated, the different components of a culture are not similarly affected by ecological adaptations. Technology, which exemplifies progress in man's control of nature, tends to be cumulative. A language, unless replaced by another one, slowly but continuously evolves into divergent groups of languages. Humanistic and stylistic cultural manifestations may retain their formal aspects during social transformations but acquire new functions. Societies change through a series of structural and functional transformations.

Social structures respond most clearly to environmental requirements. This basic structuring is related most immediately to cooperative productive activity, and it is manifest in community and band organization and in essential kinship systems. Among simple societies, any interpersonal or interfamilial arrangements necessary for survival in particular areas are virtually synonymous with social organization. Because food collecting, such as in the case of seed gathering, is competitive, societies in unproductive environments tend to become fragmented into nuclear family units. Societies of hunters are more productive under cooperative arrangements and attain various patterns of cohesion. Societies that depend primarily upon farming tend to have permanent community organization, whether in dispersed or nucleated settlements, because cooperation in such activities as clearing plots and irrigation projects facilitates production. Increase in productivity is delimited by the environmental potentials, crops, and farm methods, but it may lead to larger communities and to internal specialization of role and status.

Productive increases achieved by social cooperation and improvements in exploitative technology became the bases of the transformation of small, homogeneous societies into larger societies that were internally specialized by occupational role and social status. Structural aspects of cooperation are reasonably well known, but quantitative statements of productivity, potential and actual surpluses, manpower hours that might be available for pursuits other than production of basic necessities, numbers of persons engaged in special occupations, and other measurable activities are rarely available. These serious lacunae in our data leave open the question of the part that sheer quantities of people and things played in the transformations from simple to complex societies.

Even within the category of culture subsumed under social patterns, it cannot be assumed that all features are equally fixed by a given ecological pattern. Among simple societies, residence, kinship, and subsistence patterns are more fundamental and less alterable or variable than clans, moieties, religious and secular associations, and other elaborations which are secondary embroideries on the basic social fabric. Distributional evidence in many parts of the world clearly shows that such elaborations have diffused widely across different kinds of environments and to fundamentally different social structures adapted to use of the environments. In the Southwest, for example, matrilineal clans occurred among the western Pueblo farm villages and the seminomadic pastoral Navajo, and moieties were a secondary adjunct of the patrilineal hunting bands in southern California and some of the eastern Pueblo agriculturalists.

A final problem concerning the response of different aspects or components of culture to adaptive processes is whether old or traditional forms may acquire new functions. Among the Sonjo of Tanganyika, the men's age-group that served as warriors in precolonial times now spends several years performing wage labor in the new nonmilitaristic, cash-oriented context. Clan-owned or lineage-owned land and traditional types of ownership and inheritance of herds may persist under production for an outside market. Although traditional structures and trait-complexes tend to perpetuate themselves in all stages of cultural development, the evidence seems clearly to indicate that the new functions of the changing context eventually alter old forms beyond recognition, or that these forms wither and are replaced by new ones.

Levels of sociocultural integration

The adaptations of a complex or highly developed society differ in many ways from those of a simple society. The internal specialization that developed after the agricultural revolution and more so after the industrial revolution has affected the adaptive processes of the local segments of states and nations. Land use has increasingly reflected the importance of external economic institutions rather than local subsistence goals. Trade, improved transportation, mechanization, and other factors related to industrialization have made each local social group a more highly specialized and dependent part of the larger sociocultural system. There is a tendency toward monocropping in areas best suited to production of crops for external markets and toward specialization of local extractive industries, such as mining, oil, and timber, which have little intrinsic value to the local subsociety. Larger sociocultural systems have also created metropolitan and industrial centers and set aside special recreational areas.

Owing to technological achievements, the impact or conditioning effects of nature upon society are far less direct and compelling in a complex society than in a simple one. Culture increasingly creates its own environment. Foods and other necessities can be transported, water diverted, and electric power transmitted great distances. Reasonable comfort can be provided even for those who live for a time in Antarctica.

In a more fundamental sense, however, the distinction between primitive and developed societies is not merely one of social complexity or of technological knowledge. Among primitive peoples, the family, extended kin group, or fairly small village or band adapts directly to its own territory. Among more complex societies, there are suprafamilial and supracommunity institutions that are impersonal in that they do not involve the total cultural behavior of the people connected with them. State economic institutions—corporations, for example, that extract new materials and manufacture and distribute the products—serve the varied needs of the many subcultural groups within the state. They also extend the interaction of culture and environment far beyond state boundaries through the ex-

ploitation of distant resources and through extensive commerce. These vast economic extensions of the more developed societies penetrate local societies, and by creating new uses for land and other resources and imposing outside political and economic patterns, they fundamentally transform the local societies.

Within a modern, complex state, there is increasing specialization of land use within environmental potentials, but distinctiveness of local subcultures is partly leveled by the impact of national influences. The subcultures of ranchers in Nevada, sugarcane workers in Puerto Rico, tea-plantation workers in Kenya, and other subsocieties who live on the land are shaped by the outside economic institutions to which they are linked, as well as by the local environment. As technology develops and subsocieties become more dependent upon the larger society, direct adaptation to the local environment decreases. The way of life, or subculture, of business executives of New York City, for example, has become dichotomized: in part it is derived from their highly specialized occupational role in a city and in part from their residence in suburbia, where the family and neighborhood culture differs from that of their profession and neither is closely adapted to the local environment. Even more remote from direct environmental impact are certain urban institutions found in contemporary Nevada, where the divorce, gambling, and entertainment complexes are linked to special aspects of the total national culture rather than to the semideserts of the Great Basin.

Some substantive applications

The concept of cultural ecology may be clarified by a number of substantive applications. These cases range from simple to complex societies, from the most elementary level of sociocultural integration to higher levels.

The precursors of man lacked culturally derived devices for killing game and for gathering, storing, and preparing food. They were food scavengers, and any food they collected was preserved without culturally prescribed techniques. Because animals can best forage a known habitat, they may have lived in groups or bands that were somewhat territorially delimited. Any social structuring was probably biologically oriented around the male's dominance and protection of the group and the female's role of caring for the young.

When culture provided more efficient techniques for survival, the essential human biological facts of sex, age, and kinship continued to affect the nature of society but were patterned in various ways by cultural ecological adaptations. Where the principal resource was seeds, roots, fruits, insects, small mammals, or shellfish, which occur sparsely, food gathering was necessarily competitive rather than cooperative because the yield decreases with the number of families that exploit the same site. If the local occurrence of principal resources varied each year, as it did among the Shoshoni Indians of Nevada, a multifamily society of permanent composition was not possible. Each Shoshoni family was linked with other families through intermarriage, through largely fortuitous association at a winter campsite, and through brief cooperation during antelope and rabbit hunts wherever there happened to be game. There were no bands of constant membership and no claims to territory or to resource areas. These families were not free wanderers, however, for any human society more effectively exploits a territory familiar to it.

The Chilean archipelago is completely unlike the Great Basin, but the erratic occurrence of shellfish, which was the principal food of the Alacaluf Indians, was functionally similar to Great Basin resources in preventing the formation of permanent social units larger than the nuclear family. That the nomadic, food-collecting family was the irreducible social unit in both cases is a function of the biological factors underlying marriage, division of labor, and child rearing. The independent nuclear family, however, is rarely reported ethnographically, and its occurrence in history is an empirical question rather than a matter of deduction from evolutionary principles.

Many societies fragment seasonally into family units of food collectors, but if the resources are sufficiently abundant and their whereabouts is predictable, the same families maintain contact with one another in loose groups that associate for suprafamilial activities. Examples are the Indians of California, who subsisted on acorns, and the Indians of Lake Superior and the upper Paraguay River, who gathered wild rice. It appears that such groups tended to consist of extended families or lineages, although the evidence is not clear on this point.

Hunting generally requires cooperation, but there are various kinds of hunting societies, each reflecting special ecological adaptations. The Central Eskimo, whose population density was one person to 250 square miles or more, lived in small, somewhat isolated family clusters. Since some cooperation was necessary in arctic hunting, nuclear families could not well have survived alone.

In societies that hunted large herds of bison, the concentrated resources supported bands of several hundred persons that exceeded the size of traceable lineages and consisted of many unrelated kin groups. The clans among certain Plains Indians were fictitious kinship extensions and an embellishment of the basic subsistence group. The Plains bands were more tightly integrated than the hunting bands of Canada, because game herds were larger, cooperative hunts were more highly developed, and warfare, especially after horses were acquired, became a major factor. By contrast, hunters of small and less-migratory game herds cooperated in bands of thirty to sixty persons who constituted a patrilineal lineage that controlled territorial resources, married outside the band, and brought wives to the husband's band.

The basic social structure of these types of bands is essentially an interfamilial arrangement that is a necessary—or an optimum—organization for survival, depending on the conditions. A historical explanation that they originated elsewhere and were introduced to the areas through diffusion or migration is not credible, especially in the case of the patrilineal hunting bands that occurred in South Africa, Australia, Tasmania, southern California, and Tierra del Fuego. Each is a special kind of evolutionary development.

Societies of early farmers seem also to have been small, except where intercommunity warfare forced the people to concentrate in protected villages, and each probably consisted of lineages that tended to bud off as long as land was available. Although few analyses of the ecological adaptations of such farmers have been made, several types are suggested. In tropical rain forests such as the Amazon basin, where root crops were staples, slash-and-burn cultivation together with rapid soil exhaustion required the frequent shift of plots and sometimes villages. In addition, dietary needs made riverine protein foods of major importance, and canoe transportation facilitated the concentration of the population along rivers. In temperate areas, such as the United States, there was a marked contrast between the small villages of woodland farmers, who contended with prairie sods or forests, and the river-bottom farmers, as in the Mississippi system, whose fertile soils, once cleared of vegetation, supported large communities that were able to adopt the temple-mound complex from Mesoamerica.

In several temperate, arid areas, early farming was restricted to flood plains or to the rainy highlands. Increased population density in the valleys—made possible by irrigation in such cases as Peru—led to theocratic and militaristic states, whose power extended over wide areas, and to urban centers, which were the containers of civilization. It is not now clear to what extent trade, based upon increasingly specialized local production in adjoining areas, religious cults, and militaristic controls regimented the people to achieve maximum production and fill special statuses and roles.

Animal domestication entailed other kinds of ecological adaptations. Herds require more land for subsistence purposes than farming, have to be tended and moved about, and may be subject to theft. Claims to exclusive grazing areas were difficult to enforce until barbed wire was mass-produced in the last century. Cattle stealing and consequent intergroup hostility could therefore develop, as they did among many cattle breeders of east Africa. Free-roaming livestock, moreover, is a threat to crops, and until recently, farmers had to fence out the animals.

When societies became mounted, for example, the horse or camel nomads, other special adaptations occurred. They became more efficient hunters or herders and could transport foods a greater distance, thus extending their areas of exploitation and permitting larger social aggregates to remain together. They could also engage in predatory activities against one another and their settled neighbors. Mounted predators even created several ruling dynasties in the empires of the Middle East, China, and India.

After the agricultural revolution, the development of supracommunity state- or imperial-level institutions extended the areas of resource exploitation beyond those occupied by any of the subsocieties that were welded into the larger sociopolitical unit. Each local subsociety, although adapted in some measure to its terrain, became a specialized part of a new kind of whole to which it contributed different foods, raw materials, products, and even people—all for state purposes.

The industrial revolution enormously expanded the areas of exploitation through its improved transportation, mass manufacturing, communications, and economic and political controls. Its technology also gave importance to many latent resources. Modern nations and empires embrace highly diversified environments and draw upon areas beyond their political boundaries. Their technology may modify environments to meet their cultural needs, and, above all, any localized subsociety reacts to a complex set of state institutions, to a diversified social environment, and to a large number of goals other than survival. Although people necessarily live in particular places, members of highly industrialized nations must be viewed as increasingly nonlocalized to the extent that their behavior is determined by a great overlay or elaboration of cultural patterns that are only remotely connected

with particular environments and are even minimizing some of the child-rearing and economically complementary functions of members of the nuclear family. It can be imagined that nuclear power, hydroponic and synthetic food production, and other technological developments might create wholly artificial environments, as in a permanent space station.

JULIAN H. STEWARD

[See also CULTURE, *article on* CULTURAL ADAPTATION; EVOLUTION, *articles on* HUMAN EVOLUTION *and* CULTURAL EVOLUTION. *Other relevant material may be found in* HUNTING AND GATHERING *and* KINSHIP.]

BIBLIOGRAPHY

BARTH, FREDERIK 1956 Ecologic Relationships of Ethnic Groups in Swat, North Pakistan. *American Anthropologist* New Series 58:1079–1089.
HELM, JUNE 1962 Ecological Approach in Anthropology. *American Journal of Sociology* 67:630–639. → Includes a review of the literature of cultural ecology.
LATTIMORE, OWEN (1940) 1951 *Inner Asian Frontiers of China.* 2d ed. Irvington-on-Hudson, N.Y.: Capital.
SAHLINS, MARSHALL D.; and SERVICE, ELMAN R. (editors) 1960 *Evolution and Culture.* Ann Arbor: Univ. of Michigan Press.
STEWARD, JULIAN H. 1955 *Theory of Culture Change: The Methodology of Multilinear Evolution.* Urbana: Univ. of Illinois Press.
WASHBURN, SHERWOOD L. (editor) 1961 *Social Life of Early Man.* Viking Fund Publications in Anthropology, No. 31. Chicago: Aldine.

ECONOMETRIC MODELS, AGGREGATE

An *econometric model* is a set of equations designed to provide a quantitative explanation of the behavior of economic variables. This article discusses models that focus on the behavior of an economy in the *aggregate*, especially on the time paths of variables such as national income and product, consumption, investment, employment, the price level, the interest rate, etc. The pioneering model of this type was constructed by Jan Tinbergen (1939). The leading aggregate model builder for some years has been Lawrence R. Klein.

Aggregate econometric models grew out of a blend of several different streams of work. One is the mathematical stream springing from the work of Léon Walras, which represents the economy by a system of simultaneous equations. Another is the work of Ragnar Frisch and others in the theory of economic dynamics. A third is the work in statistical inference associated with Karl Pearson and his successors, showing how to estimate the value of unknown parameters with the aid of prior information and observed data. A fourth is the development by Willford King and Simon Kuznets and others of numerical estimates of national income and expenditure and their components [*see* NATIONAL INCOME AND PRODUCT ACCOUNTS]. A fifth is the formulation of aggregative economic theories of income and employment, by R. F. Kahn, John Maynard Keynes, and others.

General features.   The general characteristics of aggregate econometric models are described in the following sections. Then a very simple example is given, and contemporary models are discussed.

Definitional equations (identities).   In any aggregate model some of the equations are *definitions* (usually called *identities*), of the type arising in national accounting; they are supposed to hold exactly and contain no unknown parameters. Examples are, "Consumption plus net investment plus government purchases plus exports minus imports equals net national product," and "Total money wage bill equals average money wage rate times quantity of labor input."

Stochastic equations.   The remaining equations are stochastic. They are supposed to hold only approximately, and they contain disturbances that are assumed to be unobservable, small, and random, with expected values of zero. An example is, "Consumption during any period equals a constant proportion of that period's disposable income plus a constant proportion of the preceding period's consumption plus a third constant plus a random disturbance." In some models the disturbances take the form of random errors in the measurement of the variables. The assumption of *random* disturbances is very convenient for statistical estimation of the values of the unknown constants, called parameters. It is sometimes justifiable even if the disturbances have systematic components; for if those components are small and numerous and independent of each other, their total effect behaves approximately as if it were random. In formulating a model of this kind, one hopes to include explicitly in each equation all the important systematic influences that are present, so that the disturbances will be small and at least approximately random.

Structural equations.   Some of the stochastic equations describe the *behavior* of a group in the economy, such as consumers (as in the foregoing example), investors in real capital goods, etc. Some describe institutional or technological *restraints*, such as the tax laws or the so-called production function, which indicates the maximum output that can be produced with any given quantities of inputs. Some describe *adjustment* processes that

take place in particular markets (e.g., for labor or goods) when there is excess demand or supply. (A special case of an adjustment equation is an equilibrium condition asserting that demand equals supply.) These four types of equations (definitional, behavior, restraint, and adjustment) are called *structural* equations, for each is supposed to describe some more or less well-defined part of the structure of the economy.

Types of variables.   In addition to constant parameters and unobservable random disturbances, the equations contain observable variables, usually more than there are equations in the model. Some of the variables are supposed to be determined by forces completely outside the model, and their values are assumed to be given; these are called *exogenous*. Variables often regarded as exogenous are government policy variables, population, foreign countries' actions, etc. The other variables, whose values are determined by the system when parameters, disturbances, and exogenous variables are given, are called *endogenous*. Typically, in a complete model there are just as many equations as endogenous variables. In many cases the equations for a given period will contain both current and lagged (i.e., past) values of the endogenous variables. The current endogenous variables are known as *jointly dependent* variables. The exogenous variables and lagged endogenous variables together are known as *predetermined* variables, for their values are determined as of any time period (either outside the system or by the past operation of the system) when the system goes to work to determine the jointly dependent variables for that time period.

The reduced form—forecasting.   Suppose that the system of structural equations is solved for the jointly dependent variables, each being expressed as a function of structural-equation parameters, predetermined variables, and disturbances. The result is called the *reduced form* of the model. It could be used to forecast future values of the jointly dependent variables if its parameters and the future values of disturbances and predetermined variables were known in advance. In practice these are unknown, so that parameters must be estimated, future disturbances must be approximated by estimates of their expected values (zero is often used for these estimates, since the disturbances are assumed to have zero expected values), and future values of predetermined variables must be assumed. Thus, forecasts made from the reduced form are necessarily approximate.

When the exogenous and lagged endogenous variables are taken as given, reduced-form forecasts based on them are said to be *conditional* upon the values of the exogenous and lagged endogenous variables. For example, a model might forecast that *if* tax rates are cut 10 per cent at the end of this year and other predetermined variables are unchanged, then national income next year will be 7 per cent higher than this year; whereas *if* tax rates are not changed, other things being the same, then national income next year will be only 4 per cent higher than this year. When the unknown future values of predetermined variables are forecast in some way (for exogenous variables this involves using information from outside the model), reduced-form forecasts of jointly dependent variables are said to be *unconditional*. For example, one might forecast that tax rates *will* be cut by 10 per cent at the end of this year, and then use a model to forecast that next year's national income will be 7 per cent higher than this year's.

Dynamic features. If a model contains lagged endogenous variables, it has a dynamic character, for its jointly dependent variables are affected not only by parameters, disturbances, and exogenous variables but also by the past history of the system. Simple systems containing lagged values or year-to-year changes of endogenous variables can generate cycles and/or long-term growth or decline, even with no changes in parameters, disturbances, or exogenous variables. There are other devices for introducing dynamic effects, e.g., time-trend variables, derivatives with respect to time, and cumulative variables such as capital stock that is the sum of past net investments. [See TIME SERIES.]

Linearity versus nonlinearity. If the structural equations are linear in the jointly dependent variables and if the matrix of parameters of those variables is nonsingular, then the solution (the reduced form) is linear in the jointly dependent variables and is unique. If the structural equations contain nonlinearities in the jointly dependent variables, their solution will be nonlinear and may fail to be unique. In that case, one may use additional information to rule out the spurious solutions and find the one that represents the behavior of the economy (for example, any solution giving a negative national income would be spurious). Alternatively, a nonlinear model may be approximated by a linear one, with results that are acceptable as long as the range of variation of the variables being studied is small relative to their extreme values (this is likely to be so over short periods, but not over long periods). A model thus linearized has a linear reduced form. While models nonlinear in *variables* are fairly common, almost all models are

built to be linear in unknown *parameters*, because that makes estimation of the parameters vastly simpler.

Model building and estimation. Numerical estimates of the unknown and supposedly constant parameters of reduced-form or structural equations are obtained by statistically fitting the equations to past data for the jointly dependent and predetermined variables, provided that the parameters have the property of *identifiability* [see SIMULTANEOUS EQUATION ESTIMATION; STATISTICAL IDENTIFIABILITY].

In this estimation process, one uses specifications indicating what variables appear in the model; which are endogenous and which are exogenous; what lags appear, if any; which variables appear in each of the structural equations; what the mathematical form of each structural equation is; and what properties the probability distribution of the random disturbances is assumed to have. In principle, these specifications are supposed to represent the model builder's prior knowledge of the economy—prior in the sense of arising from sources other than the observed data that are to be used in estimating the parameters. In practice, the model builder is often uncertain about some of the specifications of the model, and so he may try fitting several differently specified theoretically plausible models to the data and then choose the one that offers the best combination of (*a*) goodness of fit to the data and (*b*) consistency with any knowledge that may not have been incorporated into the formal specifications of the models. Such knowledge may come from economic theory, cross-section studies, results obtained for other countries or time periods, or other sources. Recently developed methods of Bayesian inference are suitable for incorporating probabilistic prior knowledge into the estimation process [see BAYESIAN INFERENCE].

Forecasting and model testing in practice. Conditional forecasts can be expected to be quite accurate if (*a*) the specification of the model is substantially correct for both the sample period and the forecast period; (*b*) the data sample and estimation technique used are such as to give approximately correct estimates of the reduced-form parameters under assumption (*a*); and (*c*) a highly accurate explanation of the sample-period jointly dependent variables is provided by the estimated reduced-form equations, in the sense that when the observed values of the predetermined variables are substituted into the reduced form to get calculated sample-period values of the jointly dependent variables, the calculated values are close to the observed values. Conditional forecasts can be expected to have substantial errors if the foregoing conditions are not met.

Condition (c), above, can readily be tested by substituting sample-period data into the estimated reduced form. Condition (b) can be tested in a probabilistic sense, with the aid of statistical inference techniques that reveal the degree of confidence one should have in the estimated parameters, on the assumption that the model is correctly specified. Condition (a), the correct specification of the model, is more difficult to test. Economic theory provides some information concerning the adequacy of a model's specifications, but the most powerful test is the indirect one based on the quality of forecasts that a model makes when conditions (b) and (c) are reasonably well satisfied. Individual *structural* equations can also be usefully tested by similar procedures, although the typical structural equation contains more than one jointly dependent variable and hence is not capable of making forecasts in the same sense as is the reduced form.

Unconditional forecasts, of course, can go wrong if the three foregoing conditions are not met, and also if the values of the predetermined variables used in the forecasts are not substantially correct.

A simple example. A very simple three-equation model will illustrate many of the foregoing points. Equation (1), below, is the accounting definition mentioned earlier: net national product (NNP) equals consumption plus net private domestic investment plus government purchases plus exports minus imports. Equation (2), below, is the consumer behavior equation mentioned earlier, specifying that consumption is a linear function of disposable income and lagged consumption plus a random disturbance. A third equation is needed to relate disposable income to NNP. Assume an economy in which (a) the whole of government revenue is raised by an income tax whose yield is a linear function of NNP; (b) there are no transfer payments; and (c) all business income is paid out to individuals, so that disposable income is also a linear function of NNP. Equation (3), below, expresses this. The three structural equations of this model are as follows (the notation and units are explained below:

(1) $y = c + i + g$,
(2) $c = \alpha + \beta d + \gamma c_{-1} + u \cong 5.7 + .69d + .25c_{-1}$,
(3) $d = y(1 - m) - h$.

This model specifies further that there are three endogenous variables (c = consumption, d = disposable income, and y = NNP); and that there are

four exogenous variables (i = net private domestic investment, g = government purchases plus exports less imports, h = the fixed part of tax revenues independent of NNP, and m = the marginal tax rate on NNP). Lagged consumption is denoted by c_{t-1} or in brief by c_{-1}; α, β, and γ are three unknown parameters; and u is a random disturbance with zero mean. All these quantities are expressed in billions of real (i.e., deflated) dollars per year, except for m, β, and γ, which are pure numbers between 0 and 1.

The approximate numerical estimate of the consumption equation (2), above, was obtained by the two-stage least squares estimation method, from United States data (expressed in billions of 1954 dollars per year) for the years 1929–1941 and 1946–1959. The ratios of the three estimated parameters to their estimated standard errors are respectively 1.8, 12, and 3.5; and the standard error of estimate is 2.7 billion 1954 dollars per year (as compared with the maximum and minimum observed consumption values of 288.9 and 103.5 billion respectively).

The tax variable h may be negative if the income tax allows for a fixed total exemption. If equation (3) were to be applied to the United States economy, it would have to include a disturbance, for the United States tax structure is only *very roughly* described by a linear function of NNP.

The reduced form of this model is obtained by solving the three structural equations for y, d, and c, thus:

$$y = \frac{\alpha + \gamma c_{-1} + u + i + g - \beta h}{1 - \beta(1 - m)},$$

$$d = \frac{(1 - m)(\alpha + \gamma c_{-1} + u + i + g) - h}{1 - \beta(1 - m)},$$

$$c = \frac{\alpha + \gamma c_{-1} + u + \beta(1 - m)(i + g) - \beta h}{1 - \beta(1 - m)}.$$

Note that the model and its reduced form are linear in *endogenous* variables, but not in *all* variables because of the term containing ym in equation (3). If in the reduced form one substitutes estimated values for the three structural parameters, zero for the disturbance u, and numerical values for the five predetermined variables for a certain year, one obtains estimates of the expected values of the three jointly dependent variables y, d, and c for that year, conditional on the chosen values of the predetermined variables.

Medium-scale models. Most of the medium-scale aggregate econometric models published so far have from 14 to 48 equations and accordingly are much more detailed and complex than the simple example just given, although, of course, they still involve great simplifications of reality. These models differ from each other in significant ways, but the following features are typical of most of the medium-scale models listed in the bibliography.

There is an identity, substantially like equation (1), above, stating that national product equals consumption plus investment plus government purchases plus imports minus exports. Consumption, private investment, and imports (and in some cases exports) are endogenous variables, and there are behavior equations to explain them or their components. Consumption is sometimes divided into parts, with one equation for each—such as consumer durable goods, nondurable goods, and services—and is explained in terms of variables such as disposable income, past consumption, liquid asset holdings, consumer credit conditions, and income distribution. Investment is commonly separated into plant and equipment purchases and inventory investment, and in some models residential construction is treated in one or more separate equations. Plant and equipment investment is explained in terms of accelerator variables, such as output and capital stock, or profits or both. Inventory investment is usually specified to depend on lagged inventory holdings, sales or output, and other variables. Most import functions depend on income and exogenous import prices. If exports are not exogenous, they are a function of exogenous variables such as world income and world prices. Government purchases are regarded as exogenous. [See Consumption function; Inventories; Investment, *article on* the aggregate investment function.]

In the early models tax revenues and government transfer payments (such as social security benefits, unemployment compensation, and interest on the national debt) were specified as exogenous, but in more recent models the tax and transfer *schedules* are specified as exogenous and equations are provided to explain tax and transfer payments as endogenous variables depending upon national income, the number of retired persons, unemployment, the national debt, and so on, according to the exogenous schedules.

There is a production function, to explain the output of goods and services in terms of inputs of labor and capital. There is a demand-for-labor equation, in many cases expressing total real labor income in terms of total real output. There is an identity expressing property income as the difference between total income and labor income. In many cases there is an equation explaining the

allocation of property income between retained income (which is not part of disposable income) and payments to individuals (including interest and dividends).

There is a wage-rate adjustment equation, commonly expressing the change in the money wage rate in terms of the unemployment rate and the rate of inflation. (But see Netherlands 1961 for a model in which the wage rate is exogenous, since it has been a policy variable in the Netherlands in recent years.) Unemployment of course is the difference between the labor force, typically exogenous, and employment.

The general price level is endogenous in most of these models; and in some cases other prices appear that, when endogenous, are usually expressed as functions of the general price level. Typically, real output and the price level can be thought of as determined by a pair of equations containing only these two variables plus predetermined variables, the equations being obtained by substituting into two important identities all the other equations of the model. One of these identities is that equating output to the sum of all expenditure components; the other expresses the total real wage bill as employment multiplied by the real wage rate.

Among the more commonly used exogenous policy variables are government purchases, government transfer payments, and tax revenues or tax rates. In some models there are few or no variables or equations describing interest rates and the supply and demand for money, and where they do appear, they are commonly rather loosely tied to the rest of the model. Thus, most models built so far are much better suited to an analysis of effects of fiscal policy (government purchases, taxes, and transfer payments) than the effects of monetary policy.

Among the more commonly used exogenous nonpolicy variables are population and its distribution (and sometimes labor force), import prices, exports (or world income and world prices), and time. In certain more recent models there are variables measuring attitudes or anticipations, obtained from surveys.

Behavior equations, in most cases, contain variables in real (deflated) terms rather than in money terms, to reflect the theoretical postulate that real economic behavior depends upon real tastes and real opportunities, unaffected by price changes that leave these things the same. Some consumer behavior equations are stated in per capita terms, to allow for the possibility that an increase in aggregate income may have different effects, depending upon how it is distributed between increases in population and in per capita income; but most behavior equations are stated in aggregate terms.

Nearly all models contain some nonlinearities, especially where identities of the form "value equals price times quantity" are involved; but nonlinearities in unknown parameters are rare in stochastic equations whose parameters have to be estimated. Tinbergen's models (1939, 1951) and the model of the Netherlands (1961) have had all their nonlinear equations linearized.

First differences (i.e., year-to-year changes) of the data are used occasionally (e.g., Suits 1962), but most models use ordinary data, without this transformation. Early models used annual data, but quarterly models are becoming more common as quarterly data become available. Time trends, lags, and cumulated variables are the main devices used for dynamic effects, although occasionally a ratchet-type variable is used for this purpose. An example of a ratchet-type variable is the value of disposable income at its previous peak, which is sometimes included in the consumption function.

Parameters of structural equations are estimated by a variety of methods. Least squares is common, in spite of its asymptotic bias in a simultaneous equations context. With the advent of electronic computers, consistent estimating methods have become cheap and are increasingly used, especially the limited-information and the two-stage least squares methods [see SIMULTANEOUS EQUATION ESTIMATION].

Large-scale models. Two large-scale models have appeared. One, dealing with the United States and having 219 equations, is sponsored by the Social Science Research Council (SSRC) and the Brookings Institution (Duesenberry et al. 1965). The other, dealing with Japan and having 164 equations, is the work of a group at Osaka University (Ichimura et al. 1964). In essential conception these models are similar to the medium-scale models discussed above; they innovate chiefly in providing a more detailed treatment of certain markets and sectors of the economy. The SSRC–Brookings model goes into detail particularly regarding consumption, housing, fixed and inventory investment, new orders, six nonagricultural production sectors, agriculture, government, and population and labor force. The Osaka model is particularly detailed regarding fixed and inventory investment, eight production sectors (including agriculture), foreign trade, and the monetary and financial sector. The SSRC–Brookings model contains a seven-by-seven input–output model corresponding to its seven production sectors, and plans are under way for a more detailed model to contain about 32 production sectors [see INPUT–OUTPUT ANALYSIS].

Application and evaluation. Econometric model forecasts and their comparison with subsequent actual events have been all too uncommon but are becoming accepted as one important means of evaluating models. Some recent results have been quite good. The Klein–Goldberger model (1955) and its successors under Suits (1962) have been used each November since 1952 to make annual unconditional forecasts of real United States gross national product (GNP) for the following year. The percentage errors for the years 1953 to 1962 have been as follows (where, for example, -0.7 means that the model's forecast of GNP was too low by 0.7 per cent of the subsequently observed value, $+0.5$ means that it was 0.5 per cent too high, etc.): $-0.7, +0.5, -6.4, +0.2, +0.5, +0.05, -4.0, -1.6, +0.7, -0.1$.

Such models may also be used for simulation studies of the economy's stability and long-term behavior, as in Adelman and Adelman (1959), or of its reaction to policy changes. Simulation studies, as well as forecasts, acquire practical value to the extent that the models used can be shown to be accurate representations of the relevant aspects of economic behavior and not merely systems of equations that fit past data well. [See SIMULATION, *article on* ECONOMIC PROCESSES.]

CARL F. CHRIST

[*Directly related are the entries* AGGREGATION; BUSINESS CYCLES, *article on* MATHEMATICAL MODELS; PREDICTION AND FORECASTING, ECONOMIC; INCOME AND EMPLOYMENT THEORY.]

BIBLIOGRAPHY

Following most of the entries is a notation giving the time period fitted, the number of equations, and the number of exogenous variables.

ADELMAN, IRMA; and ADELMAN, FRANK L. 1959 The Dynamic Properties of the Klein–Goldberger Model. *Econometrica* 27:596–625.

BROWN, T. M. 1964 A Forecast Determination of National Product, Employment, and Price Level in Canada, From an Econometric Model. Pages 59–86 in Conference on Research in Income and Wealth, *Models of Income Determination.* Studies in Income and Wealth, No. 28. Princeton Univ. Press. → 1926–1941 and 1946–1956 annually; 40 equations, 47 exogenous variables.

CHRIST, CARL F. 1951 A Test of an Econometric Model for the United States: 1921–1947. Pages 35–107 in *Conference on Business Cycles, New York, 1949.* New York: National Bureau of Economic Research. → 1921–

1941 and 1946–1947 annually; 14 equations, 16 exogenous variables.

CHRIST, CARL F. 1956 Aggregate Econometric Models: A Review Article. *American Economic Review* 46, no. 3:385–408.

DUESENBERRY, JAMES S.; ECKSTEIN, OTTO; and FROMM, GARY 1960 A Simulation of the United States Economy in Recession. *Econometrica* 28:749–809.

DUESENBERRY, JAMES S., et al. (editors) 1965 *The Brookings Quarterly Econometric Model of the United States.* Chicago: Rand McNally; Amsterdam: North-Holland Publishing. → 1948–1962 quarterly; 219 independent equations (including about 150 estimated equations), over 100 exogenous variables.

ICHIMURA, SHINICHI et al. 1964 A Quarterly Econometric Model of Japan: 1952–1959. *Osaka Economic Papers* 12, no. 2:19–44. → 1952–1959 quarterly; 164 equations, about 130 exogenous variables. This paper presents only the equations and definitions of symbols; a book describing the model is scheduled to appear.

KLEIN, LAWRENCE R. 1950 *Economic Fluctuations in the United States: 1921–1941.* New York: Wiley. → 1921–1941 annually; 16 equations, 13 exogenous variables.

KLEIN, LAWRENCE R. 1961 A Model of Japanese Economic Growth: 1878–1937. *Econometrica* 29:277–292. → 1878–1937 quinquennially; 10 equations, 3 exogenous variables.

KLEIN, LAWRENCE R. 1964 A Postwar Quarterly Model: Description and Applications. Pages 11–36 in Conference on Research in Income and Wealth, *Models of Income Determination.* Studies in Income and Wealth, No. 28. Princeton Univ. Press. → A model of the United States. 1948–1958 quarterly; 34 equations, 19 exogenous variables.

KLEIN, LAWRENCE R.; and GOLDBERGER, A. S. 1955 *An Econometric Model of the United States: 1929–1952.* Amsterdam: North-Holland Publishing. → 1929–1941 and 1946–1952 annually; 20 or 25 equations, 20 exogenous variables.

KLEIN, LAWRENCE R.; and SHINKAI, Y. 1963 An Econometric Model of Japan: 1930–1959. *International Economic Review* 4:1–28. → 1930–1936 and 1951–1958 annually; 22 equations, 15 exogenous variables.

KLEIN, LAWRENCE R. et al. 1961 *An Econometric Model of the United Kingdom.* Oxford: Blackwell. → 1948–1956 quarterly; 37 equations, 34 exogenous variables.

LIEBENBERG, MAURICE; HIRSCH, ALBERT A.; and POPKIN, JOEL 1966 A Quarterly Econometric Model of the United States: A Progress Report. *Survey of Current Business* 46, no. 5:13–39. → 1953–1964 quarterly; 49 equations, 32 exogenous variables.

LIU, TA-CHUNG 1963 An Exploratory Quarterly Econometric Model of Effective Demand in the Postwar U.S. Economy. *Econometrica* 31:301–348. → 1947–1959 quarterly; 36 equations, 16 exogenous variables.

NARASIMHAN, NUTI V. A. 1956 *A Short-term Planning Model for India.* Amsterdam: North-Holland Publishing. → 1923–1948 annually; 18 equations, 13 exogenous variables.

NERLOVE, MARC 1962 A Quarterly Econometric Model for the United Kingdom: A Review Article. *American Economic Review* 52, no. 1:154–176.

NERLOVE, MARC 1966 A Tabular Survey of Macro-econometric Models. *International Economic Review* 7:127–175.

NETHERLANDS, CENTRAL PLANBUREAU 1961 *Central Economic Plan 1961.* The Hague: The Bureau. → 1923–1938 and 1949–1957 annually; 30 equations, 20 exogenous variables.

SMITH, PAUL E. 1963 An Econometric Growth Model of the United States. *American Economic Review* 53, no. 4:682–693. → 1910–1959 annually; 10 equations, 1 exogenous variable.

SUITS, DANIEL B. 1962 Forecasting and Analysis With an Econometric Model. *American Economic Review* 52, no. 1:104–132. → 1947–1960 annually; 32 equations, 21 exogenous variables.

TINBERGEN, JAN 1939 *Statistical Testing of Business-cycle Theories.* Volume 2: Business Cycles in the United States of America: 1919–1932. Geneva: Economic Intelligence Service, League of Nations. → 1919–1932 annually; 48 equations, 22 exogenous variables.

TINBERGEN, JAN 1951 *Business Cycles in the United Kingdom: 1870–1914.* Amsterdam: North-Holland Publishing. → 1870–1914 annually; 45 equations, 9 exogenous variables.

UENO, HIROYA 1963 A Long-term Model of the Japanese Economy, 1920–1958. *International Economic Review* 4:171–193. → 1920–1936 and 1952–1958 annually; 38 equations, 35 exogenous variables.

VALAVANIS-VAIL, STEFAN 1955 An Econometric Model of Growth: USA 1869–1953. *American Economic Review* 45, no. 2:208–221. → 1869–1948 quinquennially; 20 equations, 7 exogenous variables.

ECONOMETRICS

Succinctly defined, econometrics is the study of economic theory in its relations to statistics and mathematics. The essential premise is that economic theory lends itself to mathematical formulation, usually as a system of relationships which may include random variables. Economic observations are generally regarded as a sample drawn from a universe described by the theory. Using these observations and the methods of statistical inference, the econometrician tries to estimate the relationships that constitute the theory. Next, these estimates may be assessed in terms of their statistical properties and their capacity to predict further observations. The quality of the estimates and the nature of the prediction errors may in turn feed back into a revision of the very theory by which the observations were organized and on the basis of which the numerical characteristics of the universe postulated were inferred. Thus, there is a reciprocating relationship between the formulation of theory and empirical estimation and testing. The salient feature is the explicit use of mathematics and statistical inference. Nonmathematical theorizing and purely descriptive statistics are not part of econometrics.

The union of economic theory, mathematics, and statistics has been more an aspiration of the econometrician than a daily achievement. Much of what is commonly known as econometrics is mathematical economic theory that stops short of empirical work; and some of what is known as econometrics is the statistical estimation of *ad hoc* relationships that have only a frail basis in economic theory. That achievement falls short of aspiration, however, ought not to be discouraging. It is part of the developmental process of science that theories may be advanced untested and that the search for empirical regularities may precede the systematic development of a theoretical framework. A consequence of this, however, is that although the word "econometrics" clearly implies measurement, much abstract mathematical theorizing that may or may not ultimately lend itself to empirical validation is often referred to as part of econometrics. The meaning of the word has frequently been stretched to apply to mathematical economics as well as statistical economics; and in common parlance the "econometrician" is the economist skilled and interested in the application of mathematics, be it mathematical statistics or not. In this article I shall accept this extended definition and consider both econometrics in its narrow sense and mathematical economic theory.

A brief history

The use of mathematics and statistics in economics is not of recent origin. In the latter part of the seventeenth century Sir William Petty wrote his essays on "political arithmetik" [*see the biography of* PETTY]. This fledgling work, remarkable for its time, was econometric in its methodological framework, even from the modern point of view. Despite the fact that it was not referred to by Adam Smith, it had a discernible influence on later writers. In 1711 Giovanni Ceva, an Italian engineer, urged the adoption of the mathematical method in economic theory. Although many statistical studies appeared during the intervening years, the revolutionary impact of the mathematical method did not occur until the latter part of the nineteenth century. More than any other man, Léon Walras, professor at the University of Lausanne, is acknowledged to be the originator of general equilibrium economics, which is the basic framework of modern mathematical economics [*see the biography of* WALRAS]. His work, removed from any immediate statistical application, developed a comprehensive system of relationships between economic variables, including money, in order to explain the mutual determination of prices and quantities of commodities and capital goods produced and exchanged. Walras conceived of the economy as operating along the lines of classical

mechanics, the state of the economy being determined by a balancing of forces between all market participants. His general equilibrium system was, however, essentially static because the values of the economic variables did not themselves determine their own time rates of change. For that reason the term "equilibrium" is something of a misnomer because, since Walras' general system was not explicitly dynamic, its solution cannot be described as an equilibrium state. Nevertheless, as is still true in much of economic theorizing, there were side discussions of the adjustment properties of the economy, and so, in a wider context, the solution can be regarded as the result of a balancing of dynamic forces of adjustment.

The significant combination of mathematical theory and statistical estimation first occurred in the work of Henry Luddell Moore, a professor at Columbia University during the early part of the twentieth century [*see the biography of* MOORE, HENRY L.]. Moore did genuine econometric work on business cycles, on the determination of wage rates, and on the demand for certain commodities. His major publication, culminating some three decades of labor, was *Synthetic Economics*, which appeared in 1929. Incredibly, this work, of such seminal importance for the later development of a significant area of social science, sold only 873 copies (Stigler 1962).

Econometrics came to acquire its identity as a distinct approach to the study of economics during the 1920s. The number of persons dedicated to this infant field grew steadily, and, on December 29, 1930, they established an international association called the Econometric Society. This was achieved in large measure through the energy and persistence of Ragnar Frisch of the University of Oslo, with the assistance and support of the distinguished American economist, Irving Fisher, a professor at Yale University [*see the biography of* FISHER, IRVING]. To call this small minority of economists a cult would impute to them too parochial and evangelical a view; nevertheless, they had a sense of mission "to promote studies that aim at a unification of the theoretical-quantitative and the empirical-quantitative approach to economic problems and that are penetrated by constructive and rigorous thinking similar to that which has come to dominate in the natural sciences" (Frisch 1933).

Their insights and ambitions were well founded. During the following years and through many a methodological controversy about the role of mathematics in economics (a topic now rather passé) their numbers grew and their influence within the wider profession of economics was steadily extended. Today all major university departments of economics in the Western world, including most recently those in the Soviet-bloc countries, offer work in econometrics, and many place considerable stress upon it. Specific courses in econometrics have been introduced even at the undergraduate level; textbooks have been written; the younger generation of economists entering graduate schools arrive with improved training in mathematics and statistical methods, gravitate in what appear to be increasing proportions toward specialization in econometrics, and soon excel their teachers in their command of econometric techniques. Membership in the Econometric Society increased from 163 in 1931 to over 2,500 in 1966. The society's journal, *Econometrica*, has virtually doubled in size over these years, and nearly all other scholarly journals in economics publish a regular fare of articles whose mathematical and statistical sophistication would have dazzled the movement's founders in the 1920s and 1930s.

Areas of application of econometrics within economics have been steadily widened. There is now scarcely a field of applied economics into which mathematical and statistical theory has not penetrated, including economic history. With the increasing interest and concentration in econometrics on the part of the economics profession, the very notion of specialization has become blurred. With its success as a major intellectual movement within economics, econometrics is losing its identity and is disappearing as a special branch of the discipline, becoming now nearly conterminous with the entire field of economics. These remarks must not be misunderstood, however. There remain many problems and much research in economics that is neither mathematical nor statistical, and although the modern economist's general level of training and interest in mathematics and statistics far exceeds that of his predecessors, a quite proper gradation of these skills and interests inevitably continues to exist. Moreover, to repeat, much of what is known as econometrics still falls short of the interrelating of the mathematical-theoretical and the statistical, which is the aspiration contained in the field's definition.

A survey of econometrics

Since econometrics is no longer a small enclave within economics, a survey of its subject matter must cover much of economics itself.

General equilibrium. Pursuing Walras' conception of a general economic equilibrium, mathematical economists have in recent years been engaged in a far more thorough analysis of the problem than Walras offered [*see* ECONOMIC EQUILIBRIUM]. In the earlier work a general economic equilibrium was described by a system of equalities involving an indefinitely large number of economic variables, but a number equal to the number of independent equations. It was presumed that a system of simultaneous equations with the same number of unknowns as independent equations would have an "equilibrium" solution. This is loose mathematics, and in recent times economic theorists have been concerned to redevelop the earlier theory with greater rigor. Equality of equations and unknowns is neither a necessary nor a sufficient condition for either the existence or the uniqueness of a solution. Consequently, one cannot be sure that the early theory is adequate to explain the general equilibrium state to which the economy is postulated to converge. This might be because the theory does not impose conditions necessary to assure the existence of a general equilibrium state or because the theory might be indeterminate in that several different solutions are implied by it. The modern equilibrium theorist has therefore tried to nail down the necessary and sufficient conditions for the existence and uniqueness of the general economic equilibrium.

The concept of an *equilibrium* is that of a state in which no forces within the model, operating over time, tend to unbalance the system. Even if such a state can be demonstrated to exist within the framework of some general equilibrium model, there remains the question of whether it is stable or unstable, that is, whether, for any departure of the system from it, forces tend to restore the original equilibrium or to move the system further away. An analysis of these questions, which are rather more involved than suggested here, requires the explicit introduction of dynamical adjustment relationships.

Questions of the existence, uniqueness, and stability of an equilibrium are, in the present context, not questions about the actual economy, but questions regarding the properties of a theoretical model asserted to describe an actual economy. In this sense, their examination is oriented toward an improved understanding of the implications of alternate specifications of the theory itself rather than toward an improved empirical understanding of how our economy works.

Most of this work, moreover, has been restricted to an examination of the general equilibrium model of a *competitive* economy, which is a special case indeed. It is a case of particular interest, however, because, under idealized assumptions, welfare economists have imputed features to a competitive equilibrium that satisfy criteria which are regarded as interesting for a social evaluation of economic performance [*see* WELFARE ECONOMICS]. According to a concept of Pareto's, a state of the economy (not to be thought of as unique) is said to be optimal if there is no other state that is technologically feasible in which some individual would be in a position he prefers while no individual would be in a position that he finds worse [*see the biography of* PARETO]. The conditions under which a general economic equilibrium would be optimal in this sense have therefore been subject to rigid scrutiny. Thus, Pareto welfare economics is intimately involved in the modern examination of general equilibrium systems, but it is not well developed as an empirical study.

The positive economist, concerned with prediction, has also been concerned with general equilibrium systems in principle, but from a different point of view. His central question is, How does a change in an economic parameter (a coefficient or perhaps the value of some autonomous variable not itself determined by the system) induce a change in the equilibrium value of one or more other variables that are determined by the system? In short, How does the equilibrium solution depend upon the parameters? This is a problem in *comparative statics* which contrasts two different equilibria defined by a difference in the values of one or more parameters.

Comparative statics—partial equilibrium. It is in the problem of comparative statics—the comparison of alternative equilibrium states—that we can most ably distinguish between general equilibrium economics and *partial equilibrium economics*, a familiar contrast in the literature.

Suppose that, in the neighborhood of an equilibrium, a general system of simultaneous economic relationships is differentiated totally with respect to the change in a particular parameter, so that all direct and indirect effects of that change are accounted for. One might then hope to ascertain the direction of change of a particular economic variable with respect to that parameter. For example, if a certain tax rate is increased or if consumer preferences shift in favor of a particular commodity, will the quantity demanded of some other commodity increase, diminish, or stay the same? This question can sometimes be answered on the basis of the constellation of signs (plus, minus, zero) of many or all of the partial derivatives of the functions constituting the system (assuming here that they are continuously differentiable). Theoretical considerations or common

sense may enable one to specify a priori the signs of these partial derivatives, for example, to assert that an elasticity of demand is negative or that a cross elasticity of demand is positive. In some cases, however, the theorist is not comfortable in making such assertions about a derivative, and hence some signs may be left unspecified. The question is whether the restrictions that the theorist is willing to impose a priori suffice to determine whether the total derivative of the economic variable of interest wtih respect to a given parameter is positive, negative, or zero. The formal consideration of the necessary and sufficient restrictions needed to resolve this question unambiguously constitutes the study of qualitative economics and presents a mathematical problem in its own right (Samuelson 1947; Lancaster 1965). In some situations it may be critical to know not only the signs of various partial derivatives but also their relative algebraic magnitudes. This points to the need for the statistical estimation of these derivatives, a task belonging to econometrics in its most narrow meaning.

At times it is also useful to know that certain derivatives are sufficiently close to zero that if they are assumed equal to zero the conclusion about the sign of the total derivative being investigated would not be affected. The trick or art of deciding when to regard certain partial derivatives as zero, that is, of deciding that certain economic variables do not enter in any significant way into certain relationships, is the essence of partial equilibrium analysis, so called because it tends to isolate a portion of the general system from other portions that have little interaction with it. Partial equilibrium analysis is, thus, a special case of general equilibrium analysis, in which more daring a priori restrictions have been introduced with the object of deducing more specific and meaningful results in comparative statics. Just as general equilibrium economics has been commonly associated with the name of Walras, so partial equilibrium economics has been associated with the work of Alfred Marshall [*see the biography of* MARSHALL].

In qualitative economics some light is shed upon the signs of the partial derivatives of the system by considering the dynamic stability of the model. With assumptions about the nature of the dynamic adjustment relationships, correspondences might be found between the conditions necessary for an equilibrium to be stable and the signs of the partial derivatives. Thus, just as stability depends upon assumptions about whether different variables enter a given relationship positively or negatively, so, also, the way in which those variables enter a given relationship may sometimes be inferred from the assumption that an equilibrium is stable. This is the famous correspondence principle, due to Samuelson. [See STATICS AND DYNAMICS IN ECONOMICS.]

Spatial models. Most general equilibrium models have conceived of the economy as existing at a single point in space, thereby ignoring transportation costs, the regional specialization of resources, and locational preferences. Some studies, however, explicitly introduce the spatial dimension in which a general equilibrium occurs. This provides a framework for the study of interregional location, specialization, and interdependency in exchange. [See SPATIAL ECONOMICS, article on THE GENERAL EQUILIBRIUM APPROACH.] These models, because of their greater complexity, generally involve more special assumptions, such as linearity of relationships and the absence of opportunities for substitution among factor services in production. They have also, however, lent themselves more directly to empirical work.

In the application of partial equilibrium analysis to problems of spatial economics, it is assumed, moreover, that the locations of certain economic activities are determined independently of the location decisions regarding other economic activities, and therefore the former can be regarded as fixed in the analysis of the latter. [For a discussion of this line of inquiry, see SPATIAL ECONOMICS, article on THE PARTIAL EQUILIBRIUM APPROACH.]

Aggregation and aggregative models. Since general equilibrium systems are conceived of as embracing millions of individual relationships, they obviously do not lend themselves to quantitative estimation. Much interest, therefore, inheres in reducing the dimensionality of the system, so that there is some possibility of econometric estimation. This means that relations of a common type, such as those describing the behavior of firms in a given industry or households of a certain character, need to be *aggregated* into a single relationship describing the behavior of a collectivity of comparable economic agents. The conditions needed to make such aggregation possible and the methods to be used are still in a rather preliminary stage of exploration. But a literature is developing on this subject. [See AGGREGATION.]

An older problem is simply that of aggregating into a single variable a multiplicity of similar variables. This is the familiar problem of "index numbers"—for example, how best to represent the prices of a great variety of different commodities by a single price index. The index number problem, therefore, has its theoretical aspects [see INDEX NUMBERS, *article on* THEORETICAL ASPECTS] as well as its statistical aspects [see INDEX NUMBERS, *articles on* PRACTICAL APPLICATIONS *and* SAMPLING]. The theory has been useful in guiding the interpretation of alternative statistical formulas.

The major efforts in the empirical study of general equilibrium systems that have to some limited degree been aggregated come under the heading *input–output analysis*. This approach, originated by Wassily Leontief in the late 1930s, consists essentially in considering the economy as a system of simultaneous *linear* relationships and regarding as constant the relative magnitudes of the inputs into a production process that are necessary to produce the process's output. These inputs may, of course, be the outputs of other processes. Thus, with fixity of coefficients relating the inputs and outputs of an integrated production structure, it is possible to determine what "bill of goods" can be produced, given an itemization of the quantities of various "primary" nonproduced inputs that are available. Alternatively, the quantities of primary inputs necessary to produce a given bill of goods can also be determined. The coefficients of such a system can be estimated by observing the ratios of inputs to outputs for various processes in a given year or by averaging these ratios over a sequence of years or by using engineering estimates. This may be done for an economy divided into a large number of different sectors (a hundred or more), or it may be done for portions of an economy, such as a metropolitan area. Moreover, the sectoring of the economy may be by regions as well as by industries, and the former makes the method applicable to the study of interregional or international trading relations. A great deal of empirical research has been done on input–output models, tables of coefficients having now been developed for over forty countries. The quantitative analysis of the workings of these models has, as one may readily surmise, required the availability of large-scale computers. [See INPUT–OUTPUT ANALYSIS.]

Aggregative models in economics may be of either the partial or the general equilibrium type. Those of a partial equilibrium type deal with a single sector of the economy in isolation, under the assumption that the external economic variables that have an important impact on that sector are not in turn influenced by its behavior. Thus, for example, a market model of demand and supply for a particular commodity may regard the total income of consumers and its distribution as determined independently of the price and output of the particular commodity being studied. Yet, the market demand and supply functions are aggregates of the demand and supply functions of many individuals and firms. Aggregative models of the general equilibrium type may explain the mutual determination of many major economic variables that are aggregates of vast numbers of individual variables. Examples of the aggregate variables are total employment, total imports, total inventory investment, etc. These models are generally called *macroeconomic* models, in contrast to *microeconomic* models, which deal, in a partial equilibrium sense, with the individual household, firm, trade union, etc. Many macroeconomic models treat not only so-called *real* variables, which are physical stocks and flows of goods and productive services, but also *monetary* variables, such as price levels, the quantity of money, the value of total output, and the interest rate. Models of this sort have been especially common since 1936, having been stimulated by John Maynard Keynes's *General Theory of Employment, Interest and Money* and by the literature that devolved therefrom.

One type of aggregative, macroeconomic model is that which distinguishes a few important sectors of the economy or which relates macroeconomic variables of two or more economies interrelated in trade. Much of the theory of international trade deals with models of this sort [*see* INTERNATIONAL TRADE, *article on* MATHEMATICAL THEORY]. In fact, since this has been a natural mode for the analysis of international economic problems, international trade theory has historically been one of the liveliest areas for the development of economic theory, both mathematical and otherwise. More-narrowly econometric studies in this area have focused on estimates of import demand elasticities.

Moreover, macroeconomic models have lent themselves to the study of economic change, and it is with these models that the most significant work in economic dynamics has occurred. Dynamical systems in economics are those in which the values of the economic variables at a given point in time determine either their own rates of change (continuous, differential equation models) or their values at a subsequent point in time (discrete, difference equation models). [*For a general discussion of dynamic models see* STATICS AND DYNAMICS IN ECONOMICS.] Thus, dynamic models involve both variables and a measure of their changes over time. The former often occur as "stocks," and the latter as "flows." When both stocks and flows enter into a given model, there are complexities in reconciling the desired quantities of each. These problems become especially important when monetary variables are introduced, for example, when we consider the desire of individuals both to hold a

certain value of monetary assets and to save (add to assets) at a certain rate. [*Specific problems of stock–flow models are discussed in* STOCK–FLOW ANALYSIS.]

Dynamic models arise both in the theory of long-run economic growth [*see* ECONOMIC GROWTH, *article on* MATHEMATICAL THEORY], where both macroeconomic and completely disaggregated general equilibrium models have been employed, and in the theory of business fluctuations or business cycles [*see* BUSINESS CYCLES, *article on* MATHEMATICAL MODELS], where macroeconomic models are most common. Not all models intended to explain the level of business activity need be cyclical in character. The modern emphasis is more on macroeconomic models, cyclical or not, that explain the level of business activity and its change by a dynamical system that responds to external variables. These include variables of economic policy (government deficit, central bank policy, etc.) and other variables that, while having an important impact on the economy, have their explanation outside the bounds of the theory, for example, population growth and the rate of technological change. Thus, outside variables, known as exogenous or autonomous variables, play upon the dynamical economic system and generate fluctuations over time that need not be periodic. These models lend themselves to empirical investigation, and a great deal of work has been done in estimating them [*see* ECONOMETRIC MODELS, AGGREGATE]. The structure of these models has been refined and developed as a consequence of the empirical work.

The great advantage of aggregative models, of course, is that they substantially reduce the vast number of variables and equations that appear in general equilibrium systems and thereby make estimation possible. Even so, these models can be quite complex, either because they still contain a large number of variables and equations or because of nonlinearities in their functional forms. The modern computer makes it possible to estimate systems of this degree of complexity, however. But if one is interested in analyzing the dynamical behavior of these systems, the difficulties often transcend our capabilities in mathematical analysis. The computer once again comes to the rescue. It is possible, with the computer, to simulate complex systems of the type being considered, to drive them with exogenous variables, and to shock them with random disturbances drawn from defined probability distributions. In that way the performance of these systems under a variety of assumptions regarding the behavior of the exogenous variables and for a large sample of random variables can be surveyed.

[*Simulation studies of this sort are discussed in* SIMULATION, *article on* ECONOMIC PROCESSES.]

Variables that commonly arise in macroeconomic models are aggregate consumer expenditure, inventory investment, and plant and equipment investment. Aggregate consumer expenditure, or consumption, reflects the behavior of households in deciding how much to spend on consumer goods, which in some studies may be further broken down into categories such as consumer durables, nondurables, and services. Using regression techniques, consumer expenditure is made to depend upon other variables, some of which are economic in character (consumer income, change in income, highest past income, the consumer price level and its rate of change, interest rates and terms of consumer credit, liquid assets, etc.) and some of which are demographic (race, family size, urban–rural residence, etc.). The empirical study of the dependency of consumer expenditure on variables of these kinds has been intensive during the past twenty years. [*For a survey of this work, see* CONSUMPTION FUNCTION.]

The behavior of inventory investment has likewise been the object of intensive study, both in terms of how inventories have varied over time relative to the general level of business activity and in terms of how inventory investment has responded to such variables as the interest rate, sales changes, unfilled orders, etc. [*This work is reviewed in* INVENTORIES, *article on* INVENTORY BEHAVIOR.] There are some subtle issues involved in formulating an inventory investment function. Sometimes inventories accumulate when firms intend they should, and other times they accumulate despite the desire of firms to reduce them, for example, when sales fall off rapidly relative to the capability of firms to alter their rates of output. Theoretical work concerned with the optimum behavior of firms in matters of inventory policy can therefore provide some underpinning to the selection and interpretation of the role of different variables in an inventory investment function. [*See* INVENTORIES, *article on* INVENTORY CONTROL THEORY.]

The dependency of plant and equipment investment upon such variables as business sales, sales changes, business profits, liquidity, etc., may also be studied by econometric techniques, and different theories have been advanced to support notions about the relative importance of these different variables. As with the consumption function and the determination of inventory investment, the plant and equipment investment function has also been the subject of intensive empirical research over the past couple of decades. [*This work is re-*viewed *in* INVESTMENT, *article on* THE AGGREGATE INVESTMENT FUNCTION.]

Decision making. Though it is methodologically proper for the economist to postulate *ad hoc* relationships between macroeconomic variables (Peston 1959), it is more gratifying, more unifying of economic theory, if the behavior of the macrovariables can be derived from elementary propositions regarding the behavior of the microvariables whose aggregates they are. This is the aggregation problem, referred to earlier. The aspiration is that an axiomatic theory of the behavior of the individual economic decision maker, most importantly the individual (or household) and the firm, can serve as a fundament to theories of the interaction of the aggregated macrovariables. Most of the behavioral theory of firms and households, however, is in the context of partial equilibrium analysis, because the individual economic agent does not bother to take account of the very slight influence that his own decisions exert on the market or on the economy as a whole. Thus, each household and each competitive (but not monopolistic) firm regards market prices as fixed and unaffected by its own choices. But in linking together such partial equilibrium models of the behavior of vast multitudes of individual households and firms, one cannot ignore the impact of their combined behavior on the very market variables they regard as constants. Thus, the partial equilibrium micromodels must be reorganized into more general models allowing for these individually unperceived but collectively important interactions.

Microeconomic theory is largely deductive, proceeding systematically from axioms regarding preference and choice to theorems regarding economic behavior. To proceed carefully through the logical intricacies of this deductive theory, formal mathematics is heavily invoked. Market decisions of economic agents are usually hypothesized to be prudent or rational decisions, by which is meant that they conform by and large to certain basic criteria of decision making that are thought to have wide intuitive appeal as precepts of prudent or rational choice. The situations in which a decision maker may be called upon to choose can be formulated in a variety of ways. There are "static" situations, where the decision is not assumed to have a temporal or sequential character. There are "dynamic" situations, in which a sequence of decisions must be made and in some consistent way. The decision problem may also be categorized according to the knowledge the decision maker believes he has about the consequences of his decisions. At one extreme is the case of complete certainty, where the consequences are thought to be completely known in advance. Other cases involve risk and arise when the decision maker is assumed to know only the probability distribution of the various outcomes that can result from the decision he makes. Finally, at the other extreme, the decision problem may be conceived of as involving almost complete uncertainty, in which case the decision maker knows what the possible outcomes are but has no a priori information about their probabilities. [*For a discussion of various criteria proposed for these different situations, see* DECISION MAKING, *article on* ECONOMIC ASPECTS.] Fundamental, however, is the notion that the decision maker has preferences and that he exercises these within the range of choice available to him. An index giving his preferences is commonly called *utility* and is conceived of as a function of the objects of his choice. In particular, where an individual with a fixed income is choosing among various "market baskets" of commodities, utility is commonly postulated to be a function of the components of the market basket. Axiomatic systems that are necessary and sufficient for the existence of such a function have been the object of intensive study by mathematical economists. [*This central problem and many subtle aspects of it are considered in* UTILITY.] Great effort, with perhaps little benefit for empirical economics, has gone into the refinement of the axiomatics of utility theory or of the theory of consumer choice; unfortunately, much less work has been done to strengthen the assumptions of the theory so as to increase its empirical content. From the theory of consumer behavior comes the concept of the demand function of the consumer for a particular commodity, depending characteristically on all prices and on income.

As for the theory of the firm, prudent, purposeful behavior is also assumed, and in the theory's most common formulation it is supposed that the firm wishes to maximize some measure of its preference among streams of future profits. This must be done subject to the prices that the firm must pay for factor services, the market opportunities it confronts when selling its products, and its internal technology of production. From this analysis comes the theory of production and of supply. [*For the theory of production of the firm, see* PRODUCTION; *for econometric studies of production relationships and of the cost of production, see* PRODUCTION AND COST ANALYSIS; *and for econometric studies of demand and supply, see* DEMAND AND SUPPLY, *article on* ECONOMETRIC STUDIES.]

In the derivation of the theory of consumer behavior and the theory of the firm, purposeful and prudent behavior has characteristically been associated with the notion that the decision maker attempts to maximize some function subject to market and technological constraints. Thus, the mathematics of constrained maximization has served the economist as the most important tool of his trade. In an effort to develop models of maximizing behavior that would lend themselves better to quantitative formulation and solution, interest came to focus on problems where the function being maximized is linear and the constraints constitute a set of linear inequalities. Methods for solving such problems became known as linear programming. With further advances, nonlinearities and random elements were introduced, and the method came to be applied, as well, to problems of sequential decision making. The entire area is now known as mathematical programming [*see* PROGRAMMING]. Because of their practical usefulness, these methods lent themselves to the analysis of various specific planning and optimization problems, especially to problems internal to the operation of the firm. Stimulated by the availability of these techniques, as well as by advances in probability theory and some wartime experience in systems analysis, there has come to flourish a modern quantitative approach to the problems of production and business management. This is known as management science or operations research [*see* OPERATIONS RESEARCH]. This development is a case of fission, management science now being regarded as distinct from econometrics, although both fields have much in common and share many a professor and practitioner.

The most complex problems in the area of prudent decision making are those that involve strategical considerations. In its essence this means that the consequence of a decision or action taken by one participant depends upon the actions taken by others; but their actions in turn depend upon the actions of each of the other participants. Thus, the structure of the problem is not that of simple maximizing, even in the face of risk or uncertainty, but is that of the strategical game. [*See* GAME THEORY, *article on* THEORETICAL ASPECTS.] Based upon considerations of the prudent strategy of the individual participant and of the incentives for subsets of participants to form coalitions, the theory of games can be presented as a general equilibrium problem and has become intimately associated with the modern work in general equilibrium economics. In a more partial context, game theory has appeared applicable to the decision problems of firms in oligopolistic and bilateral monopoly situations. These are characterized by the fact that each firm, in choosing its best course of action, must take into account the effect of its action on the actions of other firms, which also perform in a prudent way. In general, the early enthusiasm for the application of game theory to these problems of industrial behavior has thus far been confirmed in only limited degree. [*For a review of the applications of game theory to business behavior, see* GAME THEORY, *article on* ECONOMIC APPLICATIONS.]

Distribution processes. A concern of long standing in economics has been the size distribution of economic variables. What determines the distribution of family incomes or the distribution of the assets or sales of firms in a given industry? In past years these problems have been dealt with descriptively by fitting frequency distributions to the data of different countries, different years, or different industries. A good fit to data from different sources could be declared an empirical "law"; thus, the Pareto law of income distribution. In more recent years the size distribution problem has been redefined. Econometricians now regard it as one of formulating a dynamic process of growth or decay with random elements. The task is to estimate the parameters of the process and to determine whether there is an equilibrium distribution of the size of units and what that distribution is. A good fit can thus have a theoretical mechanism behind it, and the parameters can be made to depend upon other economic variables that may change or may be controlled. [*In this connection, see* SIZE DISTRIBUTIONS IN ECONOMICS *and* MARKOV CHAINS.]

Statistical methods. In the natural sciences the investigator must make his own measurements. In economics, however, the economy itself generates data in vast quantities. Taxpayers, business firms, banks, etc., all record their operations, and in many cases these records are available to the economist. Unfortunately, these data are not always precisely the kind the economist wants, and they must frequently be adjusted for scientific purposes. In recent decades the government has been engaged increasingly in the accumulation and processing of economic data. This has been of tremendous help in the development of econometrics. Not only is this the case for the United States and western European governments but data are also accumulated in the planned economies, where they are of critical importance in the planning operation. [*See* ECONOMIC DATA.] The absence of adequate data is felt most severely in the study of the underdeveloped economies, although, through the United Nations and other organizations, an increasing amount of data for those parts of the world is being gathered and collated.

A major form in which economic data occur is that of successive recordings of economic observations over time. Thus, there may be many years of price data for particular commodities, of employment data, etc. The econometrician, therefore, has traditionally been heavily concerned with time series analysis [*see* TIME SERIES] and especially with the use of regression methods, where the various observations are ordered in a temporal sequence. This has lent itself to the development of dynamical regression equations attempting to explain the observation of a particular date as a function not only of other variables but also of one or more past values of the same variable. Thus, the dynamic regression relationship is a difference equation incorporating a random term. When many past values of the variable are introduced into the difference equation, so that it is one of very high order, it becomes difficult to estimate the coefficients of these past variables without losing many degrees of freedom. As a result, the econometrician has tried to impose some pattern of relationship on these coefficients, so that they may all be estimated as functions of relatively few parameters. This is the technique of distributed lag regressions. [*See* DISTRIBUTED LAGS.]

The techniques just described have largely come to replace the older methods of time series decomposition, whereby a time series is split up into such components as trend, cycles of various lengths, a seasonal pattern of variation, and a random component. These methods implied the interaction of recurrent influences of regular periodicity and amplitude. With the move toward the difference equation and regression approach, exogenous variables have been introduced and random disturbances made cumulative in their effects. The temporal performance of a time series is thereby described less in terms of some inherent law of periodicity and more in terms of a succession of responses to random influences and to the temporal variation of other causal variables. Forecasting is not, therefore, the inexorable extrapolation of rhythms but is the revised projection, period by period, of an incremental relationship depending on present and past values, on exogenous variables, and on random elements. [*See* PREDICTION AND FORECASTING, ECONOMIC.]

Nevertheless, it has always been sensible to assume a rather strict periodicity for the seasonal component because of the recurrent nature of seasons, holidays, etc. As a result, when studying time series where the observations are daily, weekly, or monthly, it is customary first to estimate and remove the seasonal influence. [*Techniques for doing this are discussed in* TIME SERIES, *article on* SEASONAL ADJUSTMENT.]

The other kind of data that the economist uses is cross-sectional. For example, he may use a sample of observations, all made at approximately the same time, of assets, income, and expenditures of different households, firms, or industries. [*See* CROSS-SECTION ANALYSIS.] By observing differences in the behavior of the individuals in the sample and, again usually through regression analysis, ascribing these differences to differences in other variables beyond the control of these individuals, the econometrician attempts to infer how the behavior of similar economic units would change over time if the values of the independent variables were to alter. There are many pitfalls in this process of inferring change over time for a given firm or household on the basis of differences among firms and households at a given point of time. What becomes especially useful are data that are both cross sectional and time series in character, as, for example, when the budgets of a sample of households are observed, each over a number of successive years. To obtain usable information of a cross-section or of a cross-section and time-series sort commonly requires the design of a sample survey. [*The application of survey methods in economics is discussed in* SURVEY ANALYSIS, *article on* APPLICATIONS IN ECONOMICS.]

A very common problem in econometrics arises when different variables are related in different ways. For example, aggregate investment depends on national income, but national income depends, in a different way, on aggregate investment. In demand and supply analysis, equilibrium quantity exchanged and market price must satisfy both a demand and a supply function simultaneously. This simultaneity of multiple relationships between the same variables presents special problems in the application of regression methods. These problems have been much studied over the past twenty years, and various devices for dealing with them are now available. These methods are often quite complex, but with advances in statistical theory and in the availability of data and with the use of the large-scale computer they have come into common use in estimating both partial equilibrium and macro-economic models, sometimes of quite large dimension. Although touched upon only briefly here, this commanding problem in statistical methodology is perhaps the most central feature of econometric analysis and is the subject of a number of texts and treatises. It is also probably the largest block

of material covered in most special courses in econometrics. [*See* SIMULTANEOUS EQUATION ESTIMATION.]

To those engaged in research at the frontiers of any science, progress seems always to be exceedingly slow; but a review of the accomplishments of econometricians both in the development of economic theory and in its quantitative estimation and testing over the past two or three decades gives one the feeling of great achievement. But as old problems are solved, new ones are invented. Thus, the advance of econometrics continues unabated.

ROBERT H. STROTZ

BIBLIOGRAPHY

Works dealing with the nature and history of econometrics are Divisia 1953; Frisch 1933; Tintner 1953; 1954. *Basic works in the field are* Allen 1956; Malinvaud 1964; Samuelson 1947.

ALLEN, R. G. D. (1956) 1963 *Mathematical Economics.* 2d ed. New York: St. Martins; London: Macmillan.
DIVISIA, FRANÇOIS 1953 La Société d'Économétrie a atteint sa majorité. *Econometrica* 21:1–30.
[FRISCH, RAGNAR] 1933 Editorial. *Econometrica* 1:1–4.
LANCASTER, K. J. 1965 The Theory of Qualitative Linear Systems. *Econometrica* 33:395–408.
MALINVAUD, EDMOND (1964) 1966 *Statistical Methods in Econometrics.* Chicago: Rand McNally. → First published in French.
PESTON, M. H. 1959 A View of the Aggregation Problem. *Review of Economic Studies* 27, no. 1:58–64.
SAMUELSON, PAUL A. (1947) 1958 *Foundations of Economic Analysis.* Harvard Economic Studies, Vol. 80. Cambridge, Mass.: Harvard Univ. Press. → A paperback edition was published in 1965 by Atheneum.
STIGLER, GEORGE J. 1962 Henry L. Moore and Statistical Economics. *Econometrica* 30:1–21.
TINTNER, GERHARD 1953 The Definition of Econometrics. *Econometrica* 21:31–40.
TINTNER, GERHARD 1954 The Teaching of Econometrics. *Econometrica* 22:77–100.

ECONOMIC ANTHROPOLOGY

Economic anthropology is the analysis of economic life as a subsystem of society. The facts of economic anthropology are arrived at through field observations, either as a by-product of the ethnographer's investigation of the total culture or as the focus of his attention. The small-scale society was the hearth on which the methods and theories of economic anthropology were forged, but modern interests have expanded as anthropologists have begun to study complex, industrialized, and modern societies. As anthropologists extend their interests they come into contact with the discipline of economics, which has a highly developed body of theory. This confrontation between economists, who are reaching toward what they have professionally considered the "backwashes and underworlds" of economics, and anthropologists, who are moving toward the complex monetized systems, has generated some fruitful interchange, particularly regarding economic change and development.

The methods of economic anthropology are the basic methods of social and cultural anthropology; they are designed to discover social regularities in an alien social setting and to attribute meaning to these regularities.

The problems of getting the basic facts of economic life in a small-scale nonmonetary or partially monetized economy are often tests of methodological ingenuity. Taking household censuses, plotting landholdings, collecting data on income and expenditure patterns from representative social units, observing the contexts of exchange and valuation, and calculating the output of productive units are now standard field procedures. Methodological innovations like the construction of subsistence–exchange ratios for the extended household in northern Nigeria (Smith 1955), the development of annual output indices for artisan communities (Nash 1961), and the critical ratio of labor export for Rhodesian tribal societies (Watson 1958) are some examples of attempts to quantify available economic data.

Peasant and primitive economies appear to have some startling and pervasive organizational differences from the monetized, market-directed or state-directed, and industrialized society of the Western world. Interpreting and explaining these differences is a major task of economic anthropology. Early evolutionary interpretations (Bücher 1893; Buxton 1924; Hoyt 1926) and those of more recent years that are based on some field observation (Thurnwald 1932; Viljoen 1936) view primitive economies as polar opposites to market economies. These interpretations, however, have fallen under the weight of modern field work, which has revealed a host of variables that the crude classification by stages could not contain, and the dynamics of economic change have turned out to be vastly more varied and complex than the evolutionary schematics allowed.

Attempts to import wholesale the techniques of economics (Goodfellow 1939) have proved of as little use in handling the anthropological data as the programs to build a specific "economics" to handle premarket (Polanyi et al. 1957) or non-Western societies (Boeke 1947).

The arguments about the economic rationality of peasants and primitives—whether or not they respond to economic incentives, whether or not they maximize, whether or not they have habits of mind about advantage—have turned out to be sham encounters or semantic confusions. The real issue is not that of the presence or absence of economic rationality in economic life, our own or other; rather, it is a matter of discovering what patterns of rationality, of choice, of action, are appropriate to varying social and cultural arrangements. This research perspective sees any and all social and cultural structures that define and channel the patterns of economic choice and activity. There are no economic motives, only motives relevant to the economic sphere. Debate over concepts of maximization and rationality thus dissolves into the construction of models of social and economic choice in various cultural and social structures. Recognition of the social necessity of bringing scarce means into relation with competing ends along some culturally determined axes of valuation makes the search for the empirical patterns actually governing allocation in varyingly constituted societies the most fruitful line of analysis.

Peasant and primitive economies

Information about peasant and primitive economies appears at first to be a heterogeneous mass impervious to analysis. A four-dimensional model, however, seems to provide the axes along which a classification can be built and also to provide initial hypotheses for the understanding of the form, function, and dynamics of peasant and primitive economies.

Technology and division of labor. In societies with a relatively simple technology the number of different tasks involved in any productive act are few. Usually it is the skill of a single or a few producers that carries production from beginning to end. Many primitive and peasant technologies are ingenious, marvelously fitted to a particular environment, requiring high levels of skill and performance, but still very simple. The Bemba of Rhodesia (Gluckman 1945) wrest a living from poor soil with uncertain water supply by an intricate method of cultivation requiring tree pollarding. They climb the tall trees, cut several branches, burn them, and use the ash for fertilizer on hoed ground. With good rains and luck they harvest their crop of finger millet. The system is one of balance in a precarious ecological niche, but the task structure is simple and the tools involved require only human energy to operate. The specialized operations involved are not the kind that make an interrelated web of occupations. Men do most of the agricultural work of the Bemba, and one man is virtually as good as another in agricultural skill. The division of labor follows lines of sex and age. An occupational list in a peasant and primitive society is not a long one. Persons tend to learn their productive skills in the ordinary business of growing up, and within age and sex categories there is high substitutability of productive workers. Work and tasks are apportioned to the appropriate persons without much regard to functional differences in skill or productivity. The technology also sets limits on the size of combined working parties. Except at peak periods—planting or harvesting in agricultural communities, an organized hunt at the height of the animal running season, or gathering clay in a pottery-making community—large working parties are not found. Effort and work are closely fitted to the annual and ceremonial cycle.

Structure of productive units. Peasant and primitive societies do not have organizations whose only tasks are those of production, and there are no durable social units based solely on productive activities. The unit of production—that is, the social organization carrying out the making of goods—is dependent on and derived from other forms of social interaction. The bonds of kinship within and between families, clans, and kindreds often provide the structure for economic activities. The political structure, especially in societies with hereditary nobilities, is often a mechanism for forming productive units. Territorial bonds also serve to create local producing organizations. Economic units are thus dependent on prior kinds of social relations. Productive units in peasant and primitive societies are multipurposed; their economic activities are but one aspect of the things done by the unit. These productive units are limited in the sorts of personnel they are able to recruit, the capital they are able to command, and the ways in which a product may be distributed. Usually there is no labor market, or capital market, or system of distribution to factors of production. A striking example of reduplicative productive units based on relations derived from the organization of social groups only partially oriented to economic activity is an Indian pottery-making community in southeastern Mexico. This community is composed of 278 households. Each household engaged in the production of pottery for sale has virtually the same technology (Nash 1961). Among the people of Tepoztlán, also in Mexico, many make their living by the sale of services at a wage. Yet people must be sought out for employment, and hiring a fellow member of the community is a delicate social job: an individual's social position may not be im-

pugned, nor can the transaction appear strictly economic (Lewis 1951). Use of the capital accumulated by a multipurposed productive unit based on noneconomic criteria for membership is constrained by the whole task structure of the social unit, not just its economic dimension.

This kind of economy is relatively inflexible. Possibilities of technical advance, of innovation in organization, or of extended risk taking are not only often precluded by poverty but also cut off by the social constitution of the productive unit. But all economies need some flexibility, and this is often provided by resident strangers. The role of the resident stranger highlights the ways in which social and cultural features channel economic activity. Resident strangers come to other societies for business reasons. They lend money, they bring commodities, or they tie communities into larger networks of exchange. The resident strangers are not morally bound to the people of the community; they stand outside the social structure. The Chinese of southeast Asia, the Lebanese of the West Indies, the Muslims and Hindus in sub-Saharan Africa, and the Jews of medieval Europe are all examples of resident strangers who played the role of providing flexibility to economies not organized for exclusively economic ends.

The system and media of exchange. In primitive and peasant economies the close calculation of costs is often impossible or merely irrelevant. The advantages of a change in the use of time, resources, and personnel are arrived at through the logic of social structure, through a calculus of relative values, and not in terms of the increase of a single magnitude such as productivity. The inability to estimate closely costs and benefits is aggravated by the absence of money as *the* medium of exchange. Most of the world now has some familiarity with the use of a monetary medium of exchange. In fact, some societies developed complete, all-purpose monetary systems prior to contact with the industrial and commercial West (Davenport 1961). Many societies have other standards of exchange, like the Polynesian shell currencies, the tusked pigs of Melanesia, the salt currency of the Horn of Africa, or the cocoa beans of the Aztecs. But money, in the sense of measure of the value of goods and services with derived attributes of demand convertibility, futurity, and anonymity of source and indifference to who holds it, is much less frequent. When quasi money, or special-purpose money, exists, it is merely the standard with the widest sphere of exchange. Special-purpose money is confined to a particular circuit of exchange, and the circuits of exchange in the economy are only partially articulated. Among the Siane of New Guinea (Salisbury 1962) there are different kinds of exchange goods, and each kind of goods is limited to its particular circuit of exchange. Some goods can be exchanged only for subsistence items, others only for luxury items, and others only for items that confer status and prestige. The Tiv of Nigeria (Bohannan 1955) have a similar multi-centered exchange system, with media appropriate to each sphere of exchange. Food is exchanged for food and can be exchanged for brass rods; brass rods exchange for the highest valued goods, women and slaves. A reverse or downward movement of exchange items is severely resisted and considered illogical and unfortunate among the Tiv.

The media of exchange and the circuits of exchange are set into various kinds of systems of exchange. The most common systems of exchange are markets, redistribution, reciprocity, and mobilization. The market system is widespread among peasants, and, as in Mesoamerica, tends to be free, open, and self-regulating (Tax 1953). Sometimes, as in Haiti (Mintz 1961), special bonds of personal attachment grow up between some buyers and some sellers that cut down some of the risk and uncertainty involved in small-scale peasant trading. Rotating market centers, with a central market and several subsidiary markets, are a fairly common feature in Burma among the Shans and the Chins, in several parts of Africa north and south of the Sahara, and in many places in the Near East. These market systems usually operate without the presence of firms and do not have expensive facilities for the spread of information or other activities. The complex of markets, firms, capital investments, entrepreneurs, deliberate technical investment, and property rules to facilitate accumulation and exchange is apparently historically peculiar to the West. In the ethnographic record it does not appear as a necessary bundle or sequence of events.

Reciprocity is a form of exchange exemplified by the practices of gift giving (Mauss 1925) and tends to lack much bargaining between trading partners. It involves fixed sets of trading partners and occurs between equivalent units of the social structure. Thus, clans exchange with clans; barrios or wards with wards; households with households; communities with communities. The exchanges are for near equivalences in goods and services and approach fixed rates.

Redistributive trade takes place in societies with marked systems of social stratification but lacking market exchange. An African paramount chief may collect tribute in the form of goods and redistribute it down the social hierarchy through his clients and kinsmen. Or a political center may administer trade at fixed prices, exchanging with its peripheries (Polanyi et al. 1957). The effect of redistributive exchanges is to keep a differentiated political and status system operating without great gaps in wealth between the different status levels. A mobilization system of exchange (Smelser 1959) concentrates goods and services in the hands of an elite for the broad political aims of the society. The irrigation empires of the early civilizations apparently had these sorts of exchange systems, and some of the new nations of Asia and Africa control capital in this manner, in conjunction with some aspects of market, redistributive, and reciprocal exchange.

The control of wealth and capital. Generally, investment takes the form of using resources and services to support or expand existing social arrangements. The chief capital goods in peasant and primitive societies are land and men. Tools, machines, terraces, livestock, and other improvements in productive resources are controlled in a manner derived from the conventions of control and allocation of land and human beings. Land tenure is an expression of the social structure of a peasant and primitive society, and the allocation of land results from the operation of the system of kinship, inheritance, and marriage, rather than through contracts or transactions between economic units. Even in those societies where corporate kin groups (clans) do not exist as the land-holding bodies, special devices like titles obtained through kinship bonds or kindred-based land-holding corporations, as on Truk (Goodenough 1951), may be established. Manpower, like land, is also organized to flow in terms of given social forms, rather than according to abstract concepts of maximization.

For peasants and primitives to maintain their societies, capital or property rules or economic chance may not be permitted to work in ways disruptive of the values and norms of the society. A fairly ubiquitous device for ensuring that accumulated resources are used for social ends is a leveling mechanism. The leveling mechanism is a means of forcing the expenditure of accumulated resources or capital in ways that are not economic or productive. The leveling mechanism may take the form of forced loans to relatives or coresidents; a large feast following economic success; a rivalry of expenditure, like the potlatch of the Northwest Coast Indians, in which large amounts of valuable goods were destroyed; the ritual levies consequent on office holding in civil and religious hierarchies, as in Mesoamerica; or the giveaways of horses and goods that characterized Plains Indian culture. This institutionalized means of scrambling wealth inhibits reinvestment in technical advance and prevents crystallization of class lines on an economic base.

This schematic presentation of the major features of peasant and primitive economies serves to emphasize the range of social contexts for comparative economic analysis. An alternative model can be found in Meillassoux (1960). Forde (1956) and Firth (1951) also give descriptive summaries of the major features of small-scale economic systems. But charting the range and diversity of economic systems is only a part of the task of anthropology. How economic systems relate to the total social system is a question of major theoretical importance in social science.

Relations of economy and society

The value system of a society defines and grades the ends actors seek. The ends sought in the economic sphere must be consonant with, or complementary to, goals in other spheres. Economic activity derives its meaning from the norms of the society, and people engage in economic activity for rewards often extrinsic to the economy itself. In peasant and primitive societies the norms and values used to define a resource, a commodity, control over certain goods and services, the distributive process, and standards of economic behavior are norms governing most social interaction. The economy is not so structurally differentiated that one set of values holds there and other sets hold in other contexts. In the language of social science, the economy is "embedded" in other social systems and does not exhibit an ethic counterposed to the regnant value system.

The functional interdependence of economy and society (Parsons & Smelser 1956) stems from the fact that the same persons are actors in the economic, the kinship, the political, and the religious spheres. Thus, among the Tallensi (Fortes 1949) the role of father must fit in some way with the role of farmer, and these must fit with the role of believer in the ancestor cult, and these must fit with authority position in the lineage. The interdependence of parts of a society means that there are limits to the sorts of economies and societies that may coexist in one time-and-space continuum. But it is patent that a system of reciprocal exchange rests on social units that are nearly equivalent in status, power, and size. Similarly, an economy forbidding the performance of any economic role by its religious specialists, as in some Theravada Buddhist countries, will not have funded clerical estates. The marriage and descent system of the Nayar (where husbands were warriors who lived away from wives and where descent was matrilineal) is an instance of the functional compatibility of an occupational and status system with a marriage and descent system.

The causal interaction of economy and society pivots on the provision of facilities. For given forms of social structure a given variety and volume of goods and services are required, and if there are shifts in facilities available there will be shifts in the rest of society. The converse is also logically true; shifts in the social structure will change the volume and variety of goods and services a society produces. To discover the causal interactions of these processes, we study peasant and primitive societies undergoing change. The facts of change are the only sure guides to generalizing on the sequences, forms, and processes of economic and social interaction. Much of the change in the economic life of peasants and primitives comes from the expansion and spread of the Western forms of economic activity. This may occur through the export of goods and labor services by the peasants and primitives or through the introduction of complex industrial and commercial organizations in the midst of peasant and primitive societies.

The expansion of the economic frontier can be seen in places like Orissa, a hilly tribal region in India (Bailey 1957). Here economic opportunity in the wake of the spread of the money economy has allowed some castes to move quickly up the status ladder and forced some traditionally high status castes downward. The economic frontier in the form of money and new opportunities tends to change the role of corporate kin groups and place more emphasis on smaller familial units (Worsley 1956), to introduce a re-evaluation of the goods of a society (Bohannan 1959), and to put pressures on traditional authority systems.

The chief way that peasants and primitives get involved in the world economy is by entering a wage labor force or by producing something that can sell in international trade. Entering a wage labor force (Watson 1958) often generates conflict between generations, raises problems about the control of income, and sometimes depopulates the society, so that its social structure collapses. A rural proletariat may replace a tribal society. Income from entrepreneurial activity by peasants poses larger problems for the social system (Firth 1954). It may result in greater wealth differences, in modifications of the conventional use of capital, in loosening the normative integration of the society, and in restructuring the political and authority patterns. The boom involved in peasant agriculture (Belshaw 1955) often involves a change in religious and ethical concepts and an increase in the importance of economic activity relative to other forms of social activity.

The introduction of factories to peasant and primitive societies (Nash 1958) provides, in theory, the widest possibilities for transformation. The change induced by a factory may be akin to that induced by the increased monetization from wage labor or the expansion of the economic frontier, but it tends to tie the community more closely to a national and international economic network, to provide the context for political change, to lay the basis for new voluntary groupings, and to exert great pressures on extended familial networks and on traditional patterns of respect and authority, and to demand of persons and institutions a type of flexibility and mobility usually not found in traditional societies (Moore & Feldman 1960).

Studies of economic change have shown that modifications in economic activity set up a series of pressures and tensions in the society and culture and that there are limited possibilities for their resolution. There is no generally agreed upon sequence of change, and hardly more consensus on final forms, but the evidence seems to indicate that economic systems are among the most dynamic parts of a society and that economic activity, in the sense of providing facilities for the organization of the rest of social life, is one of the most pervasive and determinative aspects of social life. It sets the limits within which social structures and cultural patterns may fall.

The challenge and potential of economic anthropology is the fashioning of a theory encompassing both economic and noneconomic variables in a single explanatory system. It may then provide a framework for a truly comparative study of the form, function, and dynamics of economic systems.

MANNING NASH

[*Directly related are the entries* ECONOMY AND SOCIETY; EXCHANGE AND DISPLAY; PEASANTRY; TECHNOLOGY. *Other relevant material may be found in* ANTHROPOLOGY, *article on* SOCIAL ANTHROPOLOGY; *and in the biographies of* MAUSS *and* POLANYI.]

BIBLIOGRAPHY

BAILEY, FREDERICK G. 1957 *Caste and the Economic Frontier: A Village in Highland Orissa.* Manchester (England) Univ. Press.

BELSHAW, CYRIL S. 1955 *In Search of Wealth: A Study of the Emergence of Commercial Operations in the Melanesian Society of Southeastern Papua.* Menasha, Wis.: American Anthropological Association.

BERLINER, JOSEPH S. 1962 The Feet of the Natives Are Large: An Essay on Anthropology by an Economist.

Current Anthropology 3:47–61. → A discussion appears on pages 61–77.

BOEKE, JULIUS H. 1947 *Oriental Economics.* New York: Institute of Pacific Relations, International Secretariat.

BOHANNAN, PAUL 1955 Some Principles of Exchange and Investment Among the Tiv. *American Anthropologist* New Series 57:60–70.

BOHANNAN, PAUL 1959 Impact of Money on an African Subsistence Economy. *Journal of Economic History* 19:491–503.

BÜCHER, KARL (1893) 1912 *Industrial Evolution.* New York: Holt. → First published in German.

BURLING, ROBBINS 1962 Maximization Theories and the Study of Economic Anthropology. *American Anthropologist* New Series 64:802–821.

BUXTON, LEONARD H. D. 1924 *Primitive Labour.* London: Methuen.

DALTON, GEORGE 1961 Economic Theory and Primitive Society. *American Anthropologist* New Series 63:1–25.

DAVENPORT, WILLIAM H. 1961 Primitive and Civilized Money in the Santa Cruz Islands. Pages 64–88 in American Ethnological Society, Spring Meeting, Columbus, Ohio, 1961, *Symposium: Patterns of Land Utilization, and Other Papers.* Seattle, Wash.: American Ethnological Society.

FIRTH, RAYMOND W. (1939) 1965 *Primitive Polynesian Economy.* 2d ed. Hamden, Conn.: Shoe String Press.

FIRTH, RAYMOND W. 1951 *Elements of Social Organization.* London: Watts. → A paperback edition was published in 1963 by Beacon.

FIRTH, RAYMOND W. 1954 Money, Work and Social Change in Indo-Pacific Economic Systems. *International Social Science Bulletin* 4:400–410.

FORDE, DARYLL 1956 Primitive Economics. Pages 330–344 in Harry L. Shapiro (editor), *Man, Culture, and Society.* Oxford Univ. Press.

FORTES, MEYER 1949 *The Web of Kinship Among the Tallensi: The Second Part of an Analysis of the Social Structure of a Trans-Volta Tribe.* Oxford Univ. Press.

GLUCKMAN, MAX 1945 How the Bemba Make Their Living: An Appreciation of Richards' *Land, Labour and Diet in Northern Rhodesia. Rhodes–Livingstone Journal* no. 3:55–67.

GOODENOUGH, WARD H. 1951 *Property, Kin and Community on Truk.* Yale University Publications in Anthropology, No. 46. New Haven: Yale Univ. Press.

GOODFELLOW, DAVID M. 1939 *Principles of Economic Sociology: The Economics of Primitive Life as Illustrated From Bantu Peoples of South and East Africa.* London: Routledge.

HERSKOVITS, MELVILLE J. (1940) 1952 *Economic Anthropology: A Study in Comparative Economics.* 2d ed., rev. & enl. New York: Knopf. → First published as *The Economic Life of Primitive Peoples.*

HOYT, ELIZABETH E. 1926 *Primitive Trade: Its Psychology and Economics.* London: Routledge.

LEWIS, OSCAR 1951 *Life in a Mexican Village: Tepoztlán Restudied.* Urbana: Univ. of Illinois Press.

MAUSS, MARCEL (1925) 1954 *The Gift: Forms and Functions of Exchange in Archaic Societies.* Glencoe, Ill.: Free Press. → First published as *Essai sur le don: Forme et raison de l'échange dans les sociétés archaïques.*

MEILLASSOUX, CLAUDE 1960 Essai d'interprétation du phénomène économique dans les sociétés traditionelles d'auto-subsistance. *Cahiers d'études africaines* 1, no. 4:38–67.

MINTZ, SIDNEY W. 1961 Pratik: Haitian Personal Economic Relationships. Pages 54–63 in American Ethnological Society, Spring Meeting, Columbus, Ohio, 1961, *Symposium: Patterns of Land Utilization, and Other Papers*. Seattle, Wash.: American Ethnological Society.

MOORE, WILBERT E.; and FELDMAN, ARNOLD S. (editors) 1960 *Labor Commitment and Social Change in Developing Areas*. New York: Social Science Research Council.

NASH, MANNING 1958 *Machine Age Maya: The Industrialization of a Guatemalan Community*. Memoir, No. 87. Menasha, Wis.: American Anthropological Society.

NASH, MANNING 1961 The Social Context of Economic Choice in a Small Society. *Man* 61:186–191.

PARSONS, TALCOTT; and SMELSER, NEIL J. 1956 *Economy and Society: A Study in the Integration of Economic and Social Theory*. Glencoe, Ill.: Free Press.

POLANYI, KARL; ARENSBERG, CONRAD M.; and PEARSON, HARRY W. (editors) 1957 *Trade and Market in the Early Empires*. Glencoe, Ill.: Free Press.

SALISBURY, RICHARD F. 1962 *From Stone to Steel: Economic Consequences of a Technological Change in New Guinea*. London and New York: Melbourne Univ. Press; Cambridge Univ. Press.

SMELSER, NEIL J. 1959 A Comparative View of Exchange Systems. *Economic Development and Cultural Change* 7:173–182.

SMITH, MICHAEL G. 1955 *The Economy of Hausa Communities of Zaria: A Report to the Colonial Social Science Research Council*. Great Britain, Dept. of Technical Co-operation, Colonial Research Studies, No. 16. London: H.M. Stationery Office.

TAX, SOL (1953) 1963 *Penny Capitalism: A Guatemalan Indian Economy*. Univ. of Chicago Press.

THURNWALD, RICHARD 1932 *Economics in Primitive Communities*. Oxford Univ. Press.

VILJOEN, STEPHAN 1936 *The Economics of Primitive Peoples*. London: King.

WATSON, WILLIAM 1958 *Tribal Cohesion in a Money Economy: A Study of the Mambwe People of Northern Rhodesia*. Published for the Rhodes–Livingstone Institute. Manchester (England) Univ. Press.

WORSLEY, P. M. 1956 The Kinship System of the Tallensi: A Reevaluation. *Journal of the Royal Anthropological Institute of Great Britain and Ireland* 86:37–75.

ECONOMIC DATA

I. GENERAL   *Richard Ruggles*
II. THE SOVIET UNION AND
   EASTERN EUROPE   *Nicolas Spulber*
III. MAINLAND CHINA   *Ta-Chung Liu*

I
GENERAL

During the first half of the twentieth century there was considerable evolution in the scope and content of economic data. At the turn of the century, statistical abstracts of economic data generally contained only information relating to the production and prices of specific agricultural and mineral commodities, the value of imports and exports, and, in some cases, information on tax revenues and outlays by central governments. The

financial crises of the late nineteenth century and early twentieth century stimulated an increase of interest in banking and financial statistics, and as central banks were set up and systems of reporting regularized, data on the operation of the banking system emerged as another type of basic economic data.

Economists as such did not play an important role in fashioning economic data prior to World War I. In the 1920s, however, the situation changed rather dramatically. One of the first areas of data in which the activities of economists became important was that of index number construction. Irving Fisher and Warren Persons did much to advance index number theory and to foster the development of price and output measurements. Fisher not only developed the measurement of index number formula (1922) but he also pioneered in the development of what later became known as econometrics —the advancement of economic theory in its relation to statistics and mathematics. Warren Persons' work and, later, that of Wesley C. Mitchell gave impetus to the analysis of economic time series; they concentrated on the task of separating trends and seasonal and cyclical factors from one another. Mitchell was the founder of the National Bureau of Economic Research, an institution in the United States that has continued to be in the forefront in the development and analysis of economic data. In England during this period, work on economic data was concerned somewhat more with the development of statistical theory. Bowley and Stamp were particularly influential in the development of statistical techniques and techniques for the analysis of economic data.

In spite of the rapid development during the 1920s, however, it is fair to state that prior to the great depression of the 1930s economic data remained highly fragmented, and there was no unifying framework to integrate the large number of independent series. Economists had been preoccupied with the search for a few key economic indicators that would solve all their problems, revealing the true economic cycle and showing the level of prices and industrial activity.

A completely different view of the functioning of the economic system was introduced by John Maynard Keynes in *The General Theory of Employment, Interest and Money* (1936). By emphasizing the basic idea that the functioning of the economy depended upon the interaction of its parts, Lord Keynes fostered the concept of economic data as a systematic body of interrelated information. For the first time a comprehensive set of economic data covering all production, consumption, saving, and investment for the economy as a whole was introduced in the context of an operational economic model. The pioneering work in the field of national income measurement that had been done by Willford I. King (1930), Simon Kuznets (1941), and Erik Lindahl (see Stockholm, Universitetet 1933–1937) was developed into a social accounting framework by Richard Stone (1951). Simultaneously, Wassily Leontief (1941) was developing another operational economic model involving the interrelation of inputs and outputs of specific industrial sectors of the economy.

The development of national income accounting and input–output analysis thus introduced the idea that economic data are a set of systematically interrelated pieces of information that can be utilized to show the functioning of the various parts of the economy. However, this concept of a framework for economic data did not supplant interest in the growing body of partial data in almost every area of economic analysis. Data in such fields as agriculture, labor, manufacturing, trade, etc., continued to expand. The significance of the more systematic approach to economic data lay partly in its ability to digest, integrate, and put order into the massive increase in information about specific sectors of the economy.

World War II provided a further impetus to the expansion of economic data. The mobilization of the war economy required vast amounts of information about the productive capabilities of various industries and their supply requirements. The suppression of inflation through taxation and price control required the further development of national income accounts. In almost all countries considerable advances were made in the development of systematic bodies of economic data, and in the immediate postwar period these advances continued. Programs of economic recovery were instituted, and international organizations such as the Organization for European Economic Cooperation and the United Nations stimulated countries to make basic improvements in their statistical reporting systems.

The trend toward the utilization of more comprehensive bodies of economic data in econometric models is continuing. Prior to World War II econometric models were generally quite aggregative, but in recent years these models have become considerably less so. For example, the model Lawrence Klein developed for the United States economy in 1950 contained 16 equations; the 1959 Klein–Goldberger model contained 32 equations; and the 1963 Social Science Research Council model contains over two hundred equations. Similarly, the research studies by Jan Tinbergen in the

Netherlands and by Richard Stone in England have been moving toward disaggregated econometric models involving complex interrelations among the variables. [See ECONOMETRIC MODELS, AGGREGATE.]

Recently a somewhat different approach has been developed, utilizing computer simulation techniques in order to project economic behavior over a future period or to analyze how an economic system behaves under specific conditions. Basically, simulation utilizes economic models in such a way that major pieces or segments of the model are treated as probability samples for which behavioral characteristics are taken from sample surveys or masses of detailed data observations at the microeconomic level. By utilizing a building-block approach, simulation techniques can handle many different levels of aggregation simultaneously and therefore are capable of utilizing both highly detailed microeconomic data and more aggregated macroeconomic data. The recent advances in computer technology have thus made feasible the utilization of economic data in a manner that was previously not thought possible. [See SIMULATION.]

Types of economic data available. It is obvious that the content of economic data is undergoing profound change and that at the present time we are in the middle of these changes. Nevertheless, it will be useful to identify what are the main types of economic data currently available and to discuss the ways these bodies of data are changing.

National income accounts. Within the past decade national income accounts have come to be recognized as one of the most basic types of information about a nation's economic activity. In a number of countries the government is required to present, along with its budget, a forecast of the national income accounts for the coming period, showing how the proposed government budget relates to anticipated economic developments.

National income accounts today generally cover five sectors of the economy. (1) The gross national income and product account shows who purchases the final output of the economy and how the income generated by such economic activity flows to individuals as income, to governments as taxes, or to corporations as profits. (2) The personal income account shows the income received by individuals, whether in their role as participants in the productive process or as recipients of social security benefits or other transfers from government. The personal income account also shows how people dispose of their income, i.e., how much of their income goes for consumer expenditures and personal taxes and how much is saved. (3) The public sector account, which has become considerably more important in recent years, shows, on the receipts side, what the government receives from taxes on individuals or on businesses and how much it receives as property income, such as the surplus of government enterprises. The expenditure side of the government account shows the outlays of the government in terms of the functions which it undertakes, such as education, health, defense, general administration, and economic development. (4) The balance of payments account shows the foreign trade of an economy in terms of imports and exports and transfers to and from abroad. This account shows whether a nation is running down its reserves of foreign exchange or acquiring a surplus. (5) The final account, the saving and investment account, on one side brings together the excess of income over expenditure in each of the other sectors, and on the other side shows the capital formation by government and by public and private enterprises.

These five sector accounts are so set up that an expenditure in one account corresponds to a receipt in some other account. Thus, for example, the amount of consumer expenditures in the personal income account corresponds exactly to the sale of goods to consumers appearing in the gross national product account. [See NATIONAL INCOME AND PRODUCT ACCOUNTS.]

Flow-of-funds data.   The national income accounts cover only current income and expenditure transactions; they exclude those financial transactions that merely alter the assets and liabilities of the various sectors of the economy. Because this type of financial information is important in any analysis of fiscal and monetary policy, sets of information on the sources and uses of funds by the different sectors of the economy have been developed in many countries. In the United States information on the flow of funds is published by the Federal Reserve Board. This information is generally consistent with the national income accounting data, but the two sets of data are not fully integrated. In some other countries—for example, Canada, the Netherlands, and France—the flow-of-funds data have been integrated with national income data to produce one consistent set of data interrelating the income accounts with the financial transactions of each sector.

Input–output data.   Input–output data showing the purchase of inputs and sale of outputs by industrial sectors of the economy are also becoming available for many countries, but unlike national income and flow-of-funds data, this information rarely appears on an annual basis. The statistical requirements of a complete input–output system are very considerable, and it is usually possible to obtain such a body of data only for periods for which economic censuses are available. Again, however, there is an increasing tendency toward integration of national income accounting data and input–output data. For example, the gross product originating by industrial sector has come to be a common breakdown in the national income accounts, and this often matches the industrial breakdown provided in the input–output matrix. [See INPUT–OUTPUT ANALYSIS.]

National wealth.   The development of flow-of-funds accounts and input–output matrices has fostered increased interest in balance sheets for various sectors of the economy. Data on the financial transactions of each sector and on capital formation make possible, via a perpetual-inventory approach, the development of national wealth and sector balance sheets. This work, however, is still in its early stages, and few countries at present publish official current data on national wealth. [See NATIONAL WEALTH.]

Data coverage, collection, and processing.   One of the major characteristics of economic data systems at the present time is increasing detail, both in terms of time coverage and in terms of disaggregation. For example, today most of the industrial economies publish quarterly data on national income accounts; and for some components, such as personal income, they may even publish monthly data. There is also increasing interest in regional breakdowns of information within nations. In large part this is due to the fact that the different regions of a nation develop differently, and economic development must recognize differences in regional patterns, for the consideration of problems of location of new industries and for dealing explicitly with problems of regional poverty. [See REGIONAL SCIENCE.]

In developing these new bodies of data, governments have made use of two new tools which have made possible the development of much more reliable data at lower cost: (1) the use of sample surveys and (2) the development of electronic data processing. Since World War II there has been a considerable increase in the use of sample surveys that are specifically designed to obtain desired information. Many of these sample surveys have been very successful in providing data which heretofore were completely unavailable. Private groups as well as governments have been able to develop important bodies of data. For example, in the United States the Survey Research Center at the University of Michigan has developed an important body of information on consumer expenditures, and the McGraw-Hill Publishing Company has developed an interesting and useful survey of investment plans of industrial firms.

The development of electronic data processing techniques has permitted governments to make use of existing bodies of information in ways which were previously impossible because of the extremely high cost of processing. The increased use of high-speed computers to process and edit data has meant that major bodies of data that are collected for other purposes, e.g., income taxes and social security, can be utilized for statistical purposes. Furthermore, bodies of information, such as census data, can be made available in a space of a few months rather than the several years which used to be required before final tabulations were available.

Problems of measurement and reliability. There can be little doubt that the quality as well as the quantity of economic data has shown substantial improvement in recent years. In part this improvement has been due to increasing knowledge of sample design with resulting improvements in the ability to measure biases and to take into account errors in reporting. It is generally true that careful sampling in any given area can produce much-higher-quality data at very much lower cost than can complete reporting. The flexibility of sampling techniques permits the analysis of a large number of different factors in a way that would not be possible if complete and uniform reporting were required of each responding unit.

Furthermore, the reliability of data is not determined purely at the point of collection. Careful editing is very important if the final results are to be meaningful and consistent, and great strides have been made in recent years in this area. The computer is especially valuable in this context. It is now possible to carry out many internal checks within a body of data to reveal inconsistencies and to resolve such inconsistencies in an optimal manner. Perhaps even more important, however, is the increasing possibility of bringing together information from a number of different sources for comparisons and consistency checking. For example, matching census data with income tax data provides some overlapping information which, when compared on a case by-case basis, may reveal unexpected weaknesses in one or both sets of data. Awareness of problems is the first step toward the improvement of the quality of data.

The problem of reliability of data and the measurement of error in empirical work in economics is complex. In the simplest case the concept of sampling error is not too difficult to comprehend or measure. One is essentially asking how much

variance can be expected to occur on repeated sampling of a given type of information. In point of fact, however, a given piece of economic data is never used in isolation; it is always related to other pieces of economic data, which also have sampling or reporting errors. The problem of measurement of error, therefore, comes down to the joint error distribution of the different pieces of data that are used in conjunction with each other. For example, data on the volume of consumer expenditures in a particular period may have a certain sampling error, but it does not follow that the error in the change in consumer expenditures from one period to another can be calculated on the basis of sampling errors. The reason for this is rather simple. The sampling errors in the consumer expenditure data in different periods may be expected to be somewhat correlated with each other, and to the extent that this is true the error in the change in consumer expenditures will be affected. It would be quite possible, for example, for the error in the level of consumer expenditures to be quite substantial; but as long as the error is relatively constant, the change in consumer expenditures may be quite accurate.

Validity of measurement and operationalism. For economic data as a whole, the problem of the validity of measurement is often considerably more important than that of reliability. It is, of course, quite proper that economists approach empirical information with a framework that embodies preconceptions as to the nature of the data. To do otherwise would result in a chaotic mass of information without any principles for organizing the data. Nevertheless, the economists' preconceptions often represent an oversimplification of the actual situation.

In the field of price measurement, for example, economists reasoning from a static model envisage an economy where all transactions can be expressed as the product of a price and a quantity, and the quantity of output of the system as a whole can be measured in terms of a properly constructed index. This basic concept of price and output underlies our measurement of the gross national product in constant prices. Unfortunately, there are impediments to making this simple theoretical model operational. Few products remain unchanged over time, and there is no satisfactory way to evaluate whether changes in price do or do not correspond to changes in quality. Furthermore, one of the most common features of economic development is that new products are developed to replace old products. Unfortunately, the newly developed products seldom bear a one-to-one relationship with the old products. Thus, central heating may replace heavy wool clothes, and telephone communications may replace travel and mail correspondence. These substitutions are very subtle and cannot be perfectly measured.

The statistician must make tremendously oversimplifying assumptions in order to make data about the real world fit into the theoretical economic models. For example, price statisticians usually assume implicitly that new products are exactly equivalent in utility and cost to the products they replace and that old products improve in quality only in a few, rigidly specified ways. The problem with such a solution, however, is that the results of measurement in a given situation are often dictated by the assumptions that are made rather than by what has actually happened. In measuring output in such areas as construction and services, for instance, the statistician is often forced to substitute the measurement of inputs for the measurement of the output, thus, by definition, assuming that there is no change in productivity in these sectors.

Similar problems have arisen in many other areas of economics where the statistician has attempted to implement concepts developed by the theorist. For example, in the development of the concept of capital, theorists have been vague as to the definition and meaning of real capital over time. Statisticians have dealt with the problem by adopting certain conventions, such as formal rates of obsolescence and depreciation, but in doing so they have in part determined by assumption the answer to the question of how much the growth in real capital contributes to the expansion of output.

In view of these limitations, economics is still far from being able to answer such interesting questions as how much better off we are now than at some previous time or how much productivity in various sectors has advanced. But such questions, interesting as they are, may not be the most important or productive questions that might be asked. Perhaps it is more important to find out how the economy functions, what parts are growing relative to other parts, and how the change comes about. Questions of this sort are much more likely to be answered by the growing body of economic data now becoming available. It is much easier to describe and analyze economic change than to evaluate the welfare or productivity effects of such change.

RICHARD RUGGLES

[*Directly related are the entries* COMPUTATION; GOVERNMENT STATISTICS; INDEX NUMBERS; SAMPLE SURVEYS; SURVEY ANALYSIS.]

BIBLIOGRAPHY

COPELAND, MORRIS A. 1952 *A Study of Moneyflows in the United States.* Publication No. 54. New York: National Bureau of Economic Research.

FISHER, IRVING (1922) 1927 *The Making of Index Numbers: A Study of Their Varieties, Tests, and Reliability.* 3d ed. Boston: Houghton Mifflin.

GOLDSMITH, RAYMOND W. 1955–1956 *A Study of Saving in the United States.* 3 vols. Princeton Univ. Press.

GOLDSMITH, RAYMOND W. 1962 *The National Wealth of the United States in the Post War Period.* National Bureau of Economic Research Studies in Capital Formation and Financing, No. 10. Princeton Univ. Press.

KEYNES, JOHN MAYNARD 1936 *The General Theory of Employment, Interest and Money.* London: Macmillan. → A paperback edition was published in 1965 by Harcourt.

KING, WILLFORD I. 1930 *The National Income and Its Purchasing Power.* Publication No. 15. New York: National Bureau of Economic Research.

KLEIN, LAWRENCE R.; and GOLDBERGER, A. S. 1955 *An Econometric Model of the United States: 1929–1952.* Amsterdam: North-Holland Publishing.

KUZNETS, SIMON 1941 *National Income and Its Composition: 1919–1938.* Publication No. 40. New York: National Bureau of Economic Research.

LEONTIEF, WASSILY W. (1941) 1951 *The Structure of the American Economy; 1919–1929: An Empirical Application of Equilibrium Analysis.* 2d ed. New York: Oxford Univ. Press.

McGRAW-HILL PUBLISHING COMPANY, INCORPORATED, DEPARTMENT OF ECONOMICS *Business Plans for New Plants and Equipment.* → Published annually.

MICHIGAN, UNIVERSITY OF, SURVEY RESEARCH CENTER *Survey of Consumer Finances.* → Published since 1945/1946.

MITCHELL, W. C. (1915) 1938 *The Making and Using of Index Numbers.* 3d ed. U.S. Bureau of Labor Statistics, Bulletin No. 656. Washington: Government Printing Office.

OHLSSON, INGVAR 1953 *On National Accounting.* Stockholm: Konjunkturinstitutet.

ORCUTT, GUY H. et al. 1960 Simulation: A Symposium. *American Economic Review* 50:893–932.

ORCUTT, GUY H. et al. 1961 *Microanalysis of Socioeconomic Systems: A Simulation Study.* New York: Harper.

RUGGLES, RICHARD; and RUGGLES, NANCY (1949) 1956 *National Income Accounts and Income Analysis.* 2d ed. New York: McGraw-Hill. → First published as *Introduction to National Income and Income Analysis.*

STOCKHOLM, UNIVERSITETET, SOCIALVETENSKAPLIGA INSTITUTET 1933–1937 *Wages, Cost of Living and National Income in Sweden: 1860–1930.* Volume 3: *National Income of Sweden: 1861–1930,* by Erik Lindhal, Einar Dahlgren, and Karin Kock. London: King.

STONE, RICHARD 1951 *The Role of Measurement in Economics.* Department of Applied Economics Monographs, No. 3. Cambridge Univ. Press.

TINBERGEN, JAN 1938–1939 *Statistical Testing of Business-cycle Theories.* 2 vols. Geneva: League of Nations, Economic Intelligence Service. → Volume 1: *A Method and Its Application to Investment Activity.* Volume 2: *Business Cycles in the United States of America: 1919–1932.*

UNITED NATIONS, STATISTICAL OFFICE (1953) 1964 *A System of National Accounts and Supporting Tables.* Studies in Methods, Series F, No. 2, Rev. 2. New York: United Nations.

II
THE SOVIET UNION AND EASTERN EUROPE

Adequate collection of economic information, rapid transmission and processing of the data, and proper utilization of scientific procedures for drawing conclusions from the data are vital for any modern society—a fortiori, for centrally planned economies. The Soviet Union and the communist-ruled east European countries are *socialist planned economies*, that is, economies whose "commanding heights" (banking, industry, transport, etc.) are in the hands of the state. From these commanding positions the communist leadership attempts to guide the main economic processes of each country within the framework of comprehensive plans that set specific goals for the economy as a whole and for its main sectors and branches. Resources are channeled by a variety of means toward fulfilling these goals, and performance of each production unit is systematically followed up as plan implementation unfolds.

Industrial and nonindustrial data. For planning purposes a vast and comprehensive amount of information is needed. The statistical organization must reach deeply into the economic and social system and must have access to all the relevant data. Systematic collection of data on many facets of economic life, adequate condensation of information at various levels, feeding of the appropriate information to planning and management organs, methodic follow-up of the operational aspects of plan implementation, and manifold analyses of the developmental aspects of the economy are permanent tasks in continuous planning. These tasks raise complicated problems with respect to methods of aggregation and disaggregation of the data, accuracy in record keeping, comprehensiveness and timeliness in reporting, effectiveness and speed in auditing and processing and, above all, boldness and freedom in analyzing the results obtained.

In the Soviet Union and in each east European country, the backbone of statistical apparatus is the Central Statistical Administration (CSA)—in Yugoslavia, the Federal Institute of Statistics. The CSA handles all the statistical data, that collected by itself as well as that collected by all other agencies involved in statistical operations (banks, ministries, etc.). The main stream of information flowing to the statistical offices comes from the producing enterprises. The producers report daily, weekly, monthly, etc., so-called *operating–technical* data, in which inputs and outputs are expressed in physical terms. A second basic stream of information, furnished in value terms, flows to the CSA from the producers and from the banking and financial system, particularly the national and investment banks and, in Yugoslavia, the Social Auditing and Accounting Agency. On the basis of the data processed by the CSA and the information collected by their own organs and consolidated at local, regional, or ministerial levels, the planning organs elaborate the operational (short-term) and "perspective" (long-term) plans within the framework laid down by the directives of the policy makers.

There are avowedly numerous deficiencies in the producers' input–output data used in preparing the planning statistics. The deficiencies are due primarily to the following: (*a*) performance is judged on the basis of reported data; (*b*) operating–technical and value data are not well coordinated; (*c*) far too heavy demands are continuously placed on the producers for data on all aspects of their activity.

Since plan fulfillment is evaluated and managerial rewards are assigned on the basis of reported data, managers are tempted to manipulate and misreport statistics in a variety of ways.

Further, the Soviet and east European enterprises (excepting the Yugoslav) obey numerous, often conflicting, commands and have to keep a variety of overlapping and poorly integrated accounts: *operating–technical* records of physical flows; *accounting* records in value terms; *controlling* records of plan fulfillment. The flow of materials organized on the basis of specified norms of uses of inputs and outputs is not well coordinated with the value aspects of production either at the level of the plant or at higher levels. There are no unified balance sheets at the level of the enterprise on the basis of which the over-all situation could be easily and rapidly appraised, and there is lack of integration between recorded material flows and value indicators at the level of the economy as a whole.

Finally, the enterprises are called upon to produce an enormous volume of statistical reports, often overlapping and superfluous, in response to the urgent requests of statistical, banking, or planning organs at local or regional levels. Swamped by innumerable forms which they must complete for a variety of purposes, the enterprises deliver a vast but low-quality output of data. The fight against paperwork (the *Kampf gegen die Papierflut* as the East Germans call it) has long been a continuous but losing battle in all the east European economies except Yugoslavia.

At the heart of almost all of these problems is the limited opportunity for decision making granted to the managers of producing enterprises, that is, the centralization of economic management and decision making. The greater the volume of commands from above, the greater the volume of norms to be complied with from below; the broader the decentralization in decision making, the better the incentive system—as in Yugoslavia since the early 1950s—and the smaller the needs for specifications, norms, and continuous checking from above.

The deficiencies of the *non*industrial statistics are even more glaring than the deficiencies of the industrial statistics. Agriculture, for instance, furnishes notoriously poor information because of its over-all low level of development, its type of organization, its system of statistical reporting, and the poorly trained personnel used for record keeping, particularly on the collective farms.

Social accounting.   The principal responsibility of the CSA is to compile output indexes by branches, sectors, or regions, in physical or value terms, and feed them to the appropriate planning and management organs. (The efforts of these organs depend in effect upon the completeness, rapidity, and accuracy of the data collected by the central statistical offices.) Moreover, the CSA is charged with the elaboration of social accounts. The accounts deal with production, consumption, and investment, with transfers and "redistributions" of the social product, and with labor resources. Integration and aggregation of data are achieved by the CSA following the Marxian definitions of production. According to these definitions, production includes services directly connected with the processing and distribution of goods and excludes all other services.

Publication.   Only a relatively small portion of the information available to the CSA is published. What is published is still in some cases annoyingly incomplete, of questionable quality, or of little relevance for assessing the true performance of these economies. During the Stalin era—1928 to 1952—concealment, bizarre manipulations, and outright distortions became the trademarks of Soviet statistics. A cloak of secrecy was cast over most of the key domestic economic data. This secrecy has been appreciably lifted since the mid-1950s, but even now many economic aspects of the Stalin period for the Soviet Union, and of the early postwar decade—1945 to 1955—for all the area, remain unclear; further, some crucial data are still withheld.

The Soviet and east European policy makers have a high stake in the performance of their planned economies. Hence, they are always sensitive about some troublesome indicators, such as the rate of growth of agricultural output or the rate of growth of the economy as a whole in certain years. Generally, however, ample statistical materials are currently released on industrial outputs, manpower, investment, state budgets, etc. Much of this data is not readily comparable to the Western data. The differences are due not only to dissimilarities in underlying statistical methodologies and frames of reference but also to underlying discrepancies between East and West concerning taxation and pricing systems. The Soviet-type tax system blurs the line between requited and unrequited factor returns, and administrative price manipulation raises complex problems concerning the valuation of output. The severe limitations in the nature of the underlying ruble prices and of the definitional frameworks used, along with the various other deficiencies mentioned, hamper the usefulness of Soviet social account and of Soviet income indexes. A systematic effort has been made in the West to eliminate the distortions of the available Soviet statistical materials and to recompute the Soviet national income series for the whole of the planning era opened in 1928. A similar effort of recomputation has been made for various east European countries.

During the late 1950s and early 1960s, Soviet and east European statistical recording, processing, and publishing have increasingly improved. Early in 1945, the fledgling east European statistical administrations achieved the necessary shift in focus from the prewar type of social statistics to the type of economic statistics needed for planning purposes. After centering their attention on the compilation of industrial or agricultural inventories, statistical administrations made a serious effort to progress from the collection of "photographic" inventory-type data to the collection of "cinematic" production-type data that would be valuable for planning and forecasting. During the 1950s the CSAs solved in part the problems of following up the plan performance and of elaborating output measurements by branches, sectors, planning controls, etc. During that period the first complete postwar population censuses were published in eastern Europe. Since then, the energies of the statistical machines have been turned toward the complex problems of social accounting. In some countries—for example, the Soviet Union, Yugoslavia, Hungary, Poland, and East Germany—relatively successful steps have been taken toward the elaboration of input–output tables. The volume and quality of statistical information published have notably increased, and the publication of detailed and informative statistical yearbooks has been undertaken by all these countries. Statistical and economic journals are published regularly.

Concepts and methods.   All this activity has been highly dependent in the area as a whole, except Yugoslavia, on statistical concepts and methods elaborated during the Stalin era. Severe doctrinaire limitations have existed in regard to the use of probability theory and to the use of mathematical methods in general in the social sciences. The key contention that dominated Soviet statistical thought under Stalin was that socioeconomic statistics form a special "social science" based on Marxian dialectics; the body of methods known as mathematical statistics based on probability and the law of large numbers—to which, incidentally, many great Soviet scientists contributed—was considered applicable only to the natural sciences.

Since 1960, however, sustained efforts have been made in all these countries to break away from the specious Stalinist concepts and methods. Mathematical methods are increasingly being introduced into economics and statistics. Throughout the area, there is growing interest in Western theories of decision making under uncertainty, Western techniques of sampling, planning, social accounting, and activity analysis, and Western concepts of efficiency and optimality. These influences will play a crucial role in the late 1960s and beyond, when Soviet and east European statistics will have to tackle new and more complex tasks. Hopefully, they will result in better training of statisticians, new points of view in statistical elaboration, and less high-handedness in the publication of data.

Improvements in the general quality of the data will require several reforms and innovations. Reporting demands on producing enterprises must be reduced, and the output indicators now compiled should be supplemented with quality indicators. Automating the collection and transmission of data would significantly increase speed and efficiency in the performance of these tasks.

Developing an optimal system of unified accounting for economic planning and control is an ambitious task. Further progress toward this goal will necessitate a vast amount of research, not only in mathematics and statistics but also in economics, cybernetics, and sociology. Complex multistaged programming models must be formulated, and methods must be developed to solve short-term and long-term planning control problems at various levels. To implement these models and methods, an integrated network of computational centers is indispensable.

The prospects for improvement and progress also depend very much on reorganizations of the economies themselves. The volume of centralized commands will probably decrease as the market mechanism is increasingly relied on to determine resource allocation. This should lead to an overhauling of incentive systems and should produce price systems that indicate relative scarcities and production costs of goods more accurately than present price systems. If such reorganizations take place, serious progress in the elaboration and dissemination of economic data may be expected. Statistical theory and experimentation have a long tradition in these countries; however, the basic challenge now is not so much renewing ties with the past but successfully meeting the new tasks and problems that a developing economy poses to economists and statisticians.

NICOLAS SPULBER

[See also COMMUNISM, ECONOMIC ORGANIZATION OF; PLANNING, ECONOMIC, *article on* EASTERN EUROPE.]

BIBLIOGRAPHY

Statistical yearbooks have been published regularly by all the communist-ruled countries of the area since the mid-1950s. After World War II, only Yugoslavia and Poland published yearbooks before the mid-1950s. Nearly all the countries publish a bulletin (usually monthly) of current statistics and a journal covering theoretical or methodological problems. The bibliographical items below discuss the concepts and problems of information in historical perspective.

BERGSON, ABRAM 1961 *The Real National Income of Soviet Russia Since 1928.* Cambridge, Mass.: Harvard Univ. Press.

CAMPBELL, ROBERT W. 1963 *Accounting in Soviet Planning and Management.* Russian Research Center Studies, No. 45. Cambridge, Mass.: Harvard Univ. Press.

EGERMAYER, FRANTIŠEK 1959 The Evolution of Soviet Views on Statistics. *Czechoslovak Economic Papers* 1:229–265. → Also published in 1959 in Czech.

FEDORENKO, N. P. 1965 *Devising Methods of Managing the National Economy.* Washington: Joint Publications Research Service. → Also published in 1965 in Russian.

FESHBACH, MURRAY 1960 *The Soviet Statistical System: Labor Force Recordkeeping and Reporting.* U.S. Bureau of the Census, International Population Statistics Reports Series P-90, No. 12. Washington: U.S. Bureau of the Census.

GROSSMAN, GREGORY 1960 *Soviet Statistics of Physical Output of Industrial Commodities: Their Compilation and Quality.* National Bureau of Economic Research, General Series, No. 69. Princeton Univ. Press.

JASNY, NAUM 1962 *Essays on the Soviet Economy.* New York: Praeger.

KASER, MICHAEL 1960 Economic Development in the Soviet Union and Eastern Europe: With Special Reference to Statistics. *Statsøkonomisk tiddskrift* 74:284–295.

KOTZ, SAMUEL 1965 Statistics in the USSR. *Survey: A Journal of Soviet and East European Studies* [1965], no. 57:132–141.

NEMCHINOV, V. S. 1963 The Use of Statistical and Mathematical Methods in Soviet Planning. Pages 171–188 in International Conference on Input–Output Techniques, Geneva, 1961, *Structural Interdependence and Economic Development: Proceedings.* New York: St. Martins.

SCIENTIFIC CONFERENCE ON STATISTICAL PROBLEMS, BUDAPEST, *1961* 1962 *Input–Output Tables: Their Compilation and Use.* Edited by O. Lukács et al. Budapest: Akadémiai Kiadó.

III
MAINLAND CHINA

The communist regime was established on the Chinese mainland in October 1949. A substantial amount of economic statistics was published by the regime during the period 1949–1960. While poor in quality, the statistics for 1952–1957 could, with proper caution and careful evaluation, serve as a reference for understanding the performance of the economy. The data for the earlier years, 1949–1951, are less reliable and those for the "great leap forward" years, 1958–1959, are extremely untrustworthy. No significant economic statistics have been released by the regime since 1960.

There is no clear evidence of intentional falsification of statistics at the level of the central government prior to 1958. The poor quality of the data was primarily due to the underdeveloped nature of a large sector of the economy. The collection of reliable statistics from hundreds of millions of old-fashioned producing units was inherently difficult; and the numerous drives to fulfill targets, often unreasonable even before the "great leap forward" in 1958, induced and compelled local units to file exaggerated reports of achievement.

Development of a statistical network. There was no effective national statistical reporting system until the establishment of the State Statistical Bureau on August 8, 1952. By the end of 1953 roughly 160 local statistical offices had been established at the provincial level for the relatively large cities. During 1955 and 1956 efforts were made to extend this network to smaller towns and rural units, but even as late as the end of 1957 the difficult task of establishing perhaps a quarter of a million local statistical offices had not been completed. Without an effective organization to collect them, the data cannot be expected to be reliable (Li 1962).

Major statistical undertakings completed from 1952 to 1957 include the population census of 1953, the unification of statistical reports on state-managed enterprises and construction in 1954, the 1954 census of private industry and individual handicraftsmen, the 1955 census of private trade and restaurants, and the 1955 census of workers and employees in the socialist sectors. Reporting on agriculture had to be entrusted to the regular local government units. "Model surveys" of questionable quality were carried out mainly for food crops and cotton in 1953 and 1954, the choice of the sample being left to the judgment of the individual investigators. A survey of the income distribution of agricultural producer cooperatives was carried out in 1955 and 1956. Sample surveys of the incomes of farm households and of urban workers and employees were conducted in 1956. A study of the age and sex distribution and the educational and political background of workers and employees of all industrial, construction, and transportation enterprises, as of February 1957, was reported to have been made.

The effort toward improving the statistical system was abruptly shattered by the "great leap forward" in 1958. The collection and reporting of statistics were in effect taken over by the Communist party mechanism and were integrated into emulative drives to increase production. This led to the unprecedented statistical fiasco of 1958, from which the regime learned a sober lesson. A serious effort was made in 1960 to rehabilitate and strengthen the statistical system. With this effort, however, the publication of national economic statistics practically stopped.

Important data for 1952–1957. For 1952–1957, a period of relatively good statistics, the best data are those on government budgets and such homogeneous products as steel and electric power, produced by large industrial enterprises. Poor as it is, the population count of 1953 must be considered better than the reports on agricultural and handicraft production. A substantial amount of retail trade was transacted by small private traders, for whom no reliable information was available. Estimates of national income had to be made with these basic data of varying degrees of unreliability. Only a brief review of some of the available data will be given.

Population. Table 1 presents the U.S. Census Bureau's summary of the regime's 1953 population census. This census has been criticized by scholars both inside and outside mainland China. The census was not obtained by house-to-house canvassing. Instead, heads of households were required

Table 1 — Population of mainland China, by age and sex, June 30, 1953

Age	Male	Female	Total
		(In millions)	
All ages	302.1	280.5	582.6
		(In per cent)	
0–4 years	15.5	15.7	15.6
5–14 years	21.0	19.7	20.3
15–24 years	17.5	17.1	17.3
25–34 years	15.0	14.2	14.6
35–44 years	12.0	12.0	12.0
45 years and over	19.0	21.3	20.2

Source: Aird 1961, pp. 81, 83.

to report to registration stations set up for this purpose. Since the census was taken primarily for registering voters for the national election of 1953–1954, it is doubtful that political undesirables would have come to register. Inadequate preparation and insufficient pilot surveys, the prolonged period of enumeration, the highly inaccurate "pencil stroke system of tallying," the troublesome problem of temporary residents (supposedly reported by families or neighbors at place of permanent residence), and the tradition of underreporting of females must have resulted in substantial inaccuracy. The high degree of social control in Communist China, the one factor favorable to an accurate count, was not sufficient to counterbalance all the unfavorable factors.

Further doubts were cast on the accuracy of the census on the basis of demographic analysis. Aird (1961) found a marked deficiency of persons 5 to 14 years of age and an excess of persons 45 and over. The former, however, could have been the result of the Sino–Japanese and the nationalist–communist conflicts from 1937 to 1949, which were unprecedentedly violent even for China. The latter could have been the result of the relative absence of large-scale wars during the last two decades of the Ching dynasty. Aird also constructed theoretical models of population dynamics for mainland China and found the vital rates implicit in the age distribution of the reported 1953 population to be incompatible with the demographic history of China. Conversely, using the vital rates reported for the years near 1953, Aird could not derive the reported 1953 population. These analyses, while interesting, are inconclusive. It is doubtful that vital rates were constant in China during any reasonably long period of time, an assumption made in these analyses. The vital rates reported for the years near 1953 were not a part of the 1953 census and are even less reliable than the 1953 population count. Thus, they should not be used to invalidate the census itself.

The 1953 census is certainly not comparable in accuracy to censuses of the more developed countries. It was, nevertheless, collected by a systematic and comprehensive effort, however poorly designed. Comparable efforts have never been made to obtain statistics for the output of agriculture and the small producing units in the underdeveloped sectors of industry and transportation or for the incomes and expenditures in these sectors. These other statistics must be considered inferior to the population data for 1953.

Industrial production. Modeled on the Soviet concept of gross value of industrial production, the official data on this important item are aggregates of the gross value of production of the reporting enterprises. With some important exceptions, double counting was not permitted within an enterprise; raw materials produced and used by the same enterprise in making its own output were excluded from its value of production. Purchases from other enterprises, however, were not excluded. It is known that managers of individual enterprises went as far as purchasing one another's intermediate products in an attempt to increase their respective gross values of production and to fulfill or overfulfill quotas.

Prices for the third quarter of 1952 were used as weights in computing the official gross values of production for years prior to 1957. Prices of consumer goods were depressed in the fall of 1952 because of the "Five Anti" campaign against private enterprises (a movement outwardly directed against (1) bribery; (2) tax evasion; (3) theft of public assets; (4) fraud in fulfilling government contracts; and (5) theft of government information), but prices of producer goods were little affected. Thus, producer goods were overvalued relative to consumer goods. Since output of producer goods increased faster than output of consumer goods after 1952, the official rates of growth of industrial production were upward biased. The valuation of new products at trial-manufacturing expenses (deflated by 1952 prices) also exaggerated the increasing trend.

Table 2 — Indexes of industrial production of mainland China

Year	Official I[a]	Official II[b]	Chao[c]	Liu–Yeh[b]
1952	100	100	100	100
1953	132	134	125	128
1954	154	157	142	149
1955	166	169	147	161
1956	217	243	182	225
1957	241	268	196	248

a. Gross value of factory output.
b. Net value added in factory production.
c. Factory production.

Sources: Official I index from China 1960, p. 16; Official II index from Liu & Yeh 1965, p. 150; Chao index from Chao 1965, p. 88; Liu-Yeh index from Liu & Yeh 1965, p. 66.

Attempts were made by scholars in the United States to correct some of the biases. Since the concepts used in the different studies are not the same, only the rates of change are roughly comparable. The different estimates are therefore presented as index numbers in Table 2.

Agricultural production. There is a consensus among Western scholars that the official data on production of food crops underestimated output in earlier years, so the rate of growth for the 1952–1957 period was overstated (Eckstein 1962, p. 32; Hollister 1958, pp. 19, 29; Li 1959, p. 65; Liu & Yeh 1965, pp. 43–46; Wu et al. 1963, p. 185). The official data and the other estimates are given in Table 3.

Table 3 — Food crops production of mainland China (millions of metric tons)

Year	Official	Liu–Yeh	Wu
1952	154	177	184
1953	157	180	180
1954	161	185	177
1955	175	186	184
1956	183	184	183
1957	185	185	185

Sources: Official data from China 1960, p. 119; Liu–Yeh data from Liu & Yeh 1965, p. 132; Wu data from Wu et al. 1963, p. 185.

National income. The concept used by the regime in computing national income is the net material product, that is, the net value produced by agriculture, industry, construction, freight transportation, the part of communications serving other productive sectors, trade, and restaurants. Income originating in government administration (including armed forces), cultural and educational organizations, and personal services is excluded.

Table 4 — National income of mainland China (billions of 1952 yuan*)

Year	Official	Eckstein	Hollister	Li	Liu–Yeh	Wu
1952	61.13	71.26	67.86	72.9	71.41	72.4
1953	70.04		77.06	80.2	75.33	75.4
1954	73.88		81.92	86.6	79.28	78.3
1955	78.80		85.41	93.8	82.30	82.0
1956	88.75		97.21	107.3	92.08	91.7
1957	93.53		102.42	111.8	95.34	94.8

* Official rate of exchange: 1 U.S. dollar equals 2.343 yuan in 1952. For well-known reasons, the yuan figures should not be converted into U.S. dollars at the official exchange rate for the purpose of comparing them with the national income of the United States or of other countries.

Sources: Official data from Liu & Yeh 1965, p. 220; Eckstein data from Eckstein 1962, p. 56; Hollister data from Hollister 1958, p. 2; Li data from Li 1959, p. 106; Liu–Yeh data from Liu & Yeh 1965, p. 66; Wu data from Wu et al. 1963, p. 241.

Scholars in the United States have attempted to construct independent estimates following standard Western concepts. Eckstein (1962) estimated the gross national product of 1952 by using the value-added approach for agriculture and the factor shares method for other sectors. Hollister (1958) applied the final-expenditure method to estimate gross national product. Li (1959) adjusted the official estimate of net domestic product to derive

an estimate of net national product but cautioned that the implied rate of growth in his estimates was excessively high. Liu and Yeh (1965) used the value-added approach to estimate net domestic product. Wu and associates (1963) used the Liu–Yeh framework but modified the estimates in several respects.

The official data and the independent estimates are presented in Table 4. Because of the different concepts of national income used, only the rates of growth can be even roughly compared. The average annual rates of growth for the 1952–1957 period are as follows: official, 9.0 per cent; Hollister, 8.6 per cent; Li, 8.8 per cent (an overestimate, according to Li); Liu and Yeh, 6.0 per cent; and Wu, 5.6 per cent.

The 1958 fiasco and its aftermath. The production targets set for 1958 during the "great leap forward" were extremely ambitious and completely unrealistic. The statistical reporting system gradually developed since 1952 was cast aside, and the local cadres dutifully reported unprecedented but impossible achievements. In April 1959 the regime announced 100 per cent increases in the output of food crops, cotton, and steel in 1958 alone. A drastic downward revision of the claims, however, was announced in August 1959, reducing the estimated production of food crops and cotton by one-third. The claimed increase in iron and steel production was also scaled down substantially but in a more subtle way. Official economic statistics published for 1958 and 1959 (China 1960) are of much lower quality than those of 1952–1957, and the several independent Western estimates made for 1958 and later years can be considered only as conjectures.

The disruptive economic policies undertaken during the "great leap forward," together with severe floods and droughts in 1959 and 1960, resulted in a serious agricultural crisis and a sharp reduction in output in the ensuing years. The rest of the economy also suffered setbacks, resulting from the shrinking supply of raw materials from the agricultural sector, the withdrawal of Soviet technicians in 1960, and the generally lower morale and efficiency of workers because of food shortages. The almost complete blackout of economic statistics from the Chinese mainland since 1960 makes it exceedingly difficult if not impossible to give any quantitative evaluation of the performance of the economy from 1960 to 1964. There are some indications that by 1964 the 1957 level of production may have been regained in most sectors of the economy.

TA-CHUNG LIU

BIBLIOGRAPHY

AIRD, JOHN S. 1961 *The Size, Composition and Growth of the Population of Mainland China.* Washington: U.S. Department of Commerce, Bureau of the Census.

CHAO, KANG 1965 *The Rate and Pattern of Industrial Growth in Communist China.* Ann Arbor: Univ. of Michigan Press.

CHEN, NAI-RUENN 1963 *The Economy of Mainland China, 1949–1963: A Bibliography of Materials in English.* Berkeley: Social Science Research Council, Committee on the Economy of China.

CHEN, NAI-RUENN 1966 *Chinese Economic Statistics: A Handbook.* Chicago: Aldine.

CHINA (PEOPLE'S REPUBLIC), KUO CHIA T'UNG CHI CHŪ (STATE STATISTICAL BUREAU) 1960 *Ten Great Years: Statistics of the Economic and Cultural Achievements of the People's Republic of China.* Peking: Foreign Languages Press.

ECKSTEIN, A. 1962 *The National Income of Communist China.* New York: Free Press.

EMERSON, JOHN P. 1965 *Nonagricultural Employment in Mainland China: 1949–1958.* Washington: U.S. Department of Commerce, Bureau of the Census.

HOLLISTER, WILLIAM W. 1958 *China's Gross National Product and Social Accounts: 1950–1957.* Glencoe, Ill.: Free Press.

LI, CHOH-MING 1959 *Economic Development of Communist China: An Appraisal of the First Five Years of Industrialization.* Berkeley and Los Angeles: Univ. of California Press.

LI, CHOH-MING 1962 *The Statistical System of Communist China.* Berkeley: Univ. of California Press.

LI, CHOH-MING (editor) 1964 *Industrial Development in Communist China.* New York: Praeger.

LIU, TA-CHUNG; and YEH, K. C. 1965 *The Economy of the Chinese Mainland: National Income and Economic Development, 1933–1959.* Princeton Univ. Press. → Data in tables, reproduced by permission. Copyright © 1965 by The RAND Corporation.

ORLEANS, LEO A. 1961 *Professional Manpower and Education in Communist China.* Washington: Government Printing Office.

WU, Y. L.; HOEBER, F. P.; and ROCKWELL, M. M. 1963 *The Economic Potential of Communist China.* Unpublished manuscript, Stanford Research Institute.

ECONOMIC DEMOCRACY

See DEMOCRACY.

ECONOMIC DEVELOPMENT

See ECONOMIC GROWTH *and* STAGNATION.

ECONOMIC DISCRIMINATION

See DISCRIMINATION, ECONOMIC.

ECONOMIC EQUILIBRIUM

There are perhaps two basic, though incompletely separable, aspects of the notion of general equilibrium as it has been used in economics: (1) the simple notion of determinateness—that is, the relations that describe the economic system must form a system sufficiently complete to determine the values of its variables—and (2) the more specific notion that each relation represents a balance of forces. The last usually, though not always, is taken to mean that a violation of any one relation sets in motion forces tending to restore the balance (as will be seen below, this is not the same as the stability of the entire system). In a sense, therefore, almost any attempt to give a theory of the whole economic system implies the acceptance of the first part of the equilibrium notion, and Adam Smith's "invisible hand" is a poetic expression of the most fundamental of economic balance relations, the equalization of rates of return, as enforced by the tendency of factors to move from low to high returns.

The notion of equilibrium ("equal weight," referring to the condition for balancing a lever pivoted at its center) and with it the notion that the effects of a force may annihilate the force (for example, water finding its own level) had been familiar in mechanics long before the appearance of Smith's *Wealth of Nations* in 1776, but there is no obvious evidence that Smith drew his ideas from any analogy with mechanics. Whatever the source of the concept, the notion that through the workings of an entire system effects may be very different from, and even opposed to, intentions is surely the most important intellectual contribution that economic thought has made to the general understanding of social processes.

1. History of the concept

It can be maintained that Smith was a creator of general equilibrium theory, although the coherence and consistency of his work can be questioned. A fortiori, later systematic expositors of the classical system, such as Ricardo, J. S. Mill, and Marx, in whose work some of Smith's logical gaps were filled, can all be regarded as early expositors of general equilibrium theory. Marx, in his scheme of simple reproduction, read in combination with his development of relative price theory in Volumes 1 and 3 of *Das Kapital*, has indeed come in some ways closer in form to modern theory than any other classical economist, though of course everything is confused by his attempt to maintain simultaneously a pure labor theory of value and an equalization of rates of return on capital. The view that the classical economists had a form of the general equilibrium principle is further bolstered by modern reconstructions (see, e.g., Samuelson 1957; 1959).

There is, however, a very important sense in which none of the classical economists had a true general equilibrium theory: none had an explicit role for demand conditions. No doubt the more systematic thinkers, most particularly Mill and Cournot, gave verbal homage to the role of demand and the influence of prices on it, but there was no genuine integration of demand with the essentially supply-oriented nature of classical theory. The neglect of demand was facilitated by the special simplifying assumptions made about supply. A general equilibrium theory, from the modern point of view, is a theory about both the quantities and the prices of all economic goods and services. However, the classical authors found that prices appeared to be determined by a system of relations not involving quantities, derived from the zero-profit condition. This is clear enough with fixed production coefficients and a single primary factor, labor, as in Smith's famous exchange of deer and beaver, and it was the great accomplishment of Malthus and Ricardo to show that land could be brought into the system. If, finally, Malthusian assumptions about population implied that the supply price of labor was fixed in terms of goods, then even the price of capital could be determined (although the presence of capital as a productive factor and recipient of rewards was clearly an embarrassment to the classical authors, as it remains to some extent today).

Thus, in a certain definite sense the classicists had no true theory of resource allocation, since the influence of prices on quantities was not studied and the reciprocal influence was denied. But the classical theory could solve neither the logical problem of explaining relative wages of heterogeneous types of labor nor the empirical problem of accounting for wages that were rising steadily above the subsistence level. It is in this context that the neoclassical theories emerged, with all primary resources having the role that land alone had before.

(In all fairness to the classical writers, it should be remarked that the theory of foreign trade, especially in the form that Mill gave it, was a genuine general equilibrium theory. But, of course, the assumptions that were made, particularly factor immobility, were very restrictive.)

Cournot (1838), and after him Jenkin (1870) and the neoclassical economists, employed extensively the partial equilibrium analysis of a single market. In such an analysis, the demand and supply of a single commodity are conceived of as functions of the price of that commodity alone; the equilibrium price is that for which demand and supply are equal. This form of analysis must be viewed either as a pedagogical device that takes advantage of the ease of graphical representation of one-variable relations or as a first approximation to general equilibrium analysis in which repercussions through other markets are neglected.

The contributions of Walras.   The full recognition of the general equilibrium concept can unmistakably be attributed to Walras (1874–1877), although many of the elements of the neoclassical system were worked out independently by W. Stanley Jevons and by Carl Menger. In Walras' analysis, the economic system is made up of households and firms. Each household owns a set of resources, commodities useful in production or consumption, including different kinds of labor. For any given set of prices a household has an income from the sale of its resources, and with this income it can choose among all alternative bundles of consumers' goods whose cost, at the given prices, does not exceed its income. Thus, Walras saw the demand by households for any consumers' good as a function of the prices of both consumers' goods and resources. The firms were—at least in the earlier versions—assumed to be operating under fixed coefficients. Then the demand for consumers' goods determined the demand for resources; and the combined assumptions of fixed coefficients and zero profits for a competitive system implied relations between the prices of consumers' goods and of resources. An *equilibrium* set of prices, then, was a set such that supply and demand were equated on each market; under the assumption of fixed coefficients of production, or more generally of constant returns to scale, this amounted to equating supply and demand on the resource markets, with prices constrained to satisfy the zero-profit conditions for firms. Subsequent work of Walras, J. B. Clark, Wicksteed, and others generalized the assumptions about production to include alternative methods of production, as expressed in a production function. In this context, the prices of resources were determined by marginal productivity considerations. [*See* PRODUCTION.]

That there existed an equilibrium set of prices was argued from the equality of the number of prices to be determined with the number of equations expressing the equality of supply and demand on various markets. Both are equal to the number of commodities, say n. In this counting, Walras recognized that there were two offsetting complications: (1) Only relative prices affected the behavior of households and firms, hence the system of equations had only $n-1$ variables, a point which Walras expressed by selecting one commodity to serve as *numéraire*, with the prices of all commodities being measured relative to it. (2) The budgetary balance of each household between income and the value of consumption and the zero-profit condition for firms together imply what has come to be known as Walras' law, that the market value of supply equals that of demand for any set of prices, not merely the equilibrium set; hence, the supply–demand relations are not independent. If supply equals demand on $n - 1$ markets, then the equality must hold on the nth.

Walras wished to go further and discussed the stability of equilibrium essentially for the first time (that is, apart from some brief discussions by Mill in the context of foreign trade) in his famous but rather clumsy theory of *tâtonnements* (literally, "gropings" or "tentative proceedings"). He starts by supposing a set of prices fixed arbitrarily; then supply may exceed demand on some markets and fall below on others (unless the initial set is in fact the equilibrium set, there must, by Walras' law, be at least one case of each). Suppose the markets are considered in some definite order. On the first market, adjust the price so that supply and demand are equal, given all other prices; this will normally require raising the price if demand initially exceeded supply, decreasing it in the opposite case. The change in the first price will, of course, change supply and demand on all other markets. Repeat the process with the second and subsequent markets. At the end of one round, the last market will be in equilibrium, but none of the others need be, since the adjustments on subsequent markets will destroy the equilibrium achieved on any one. However, Walras argues, the supply and demand functions for any given commodity will be affected more by the changes in its own price than by the changes in other prices; hence, after one round the markets should be more nearly in equilibrium than they were to begin with, and with successive rounds the supplies and demands on all markets will tend to equality.

It seems clear that Walras did not literally suppose that the markets came into equilibrium in some definite order. Rather, the story was a convenient way of showing how the market system could in fact solve the system of equilibrium relations. The dynamic system, more properly expressed, asserted that the price on any market rose when demand exceeded supply and fell in the opposite case; the price changes on the different markets were to be thought of as occurring simultaneously.

Finally, Walras had a still higher aim for general equilibrium analysis: to study what is now called *comparative statics*, that is, the laws by which the equilibrium prices and quantities vary with the underlying data (resources, production conditions, or utility functions). But little was actu-

ally done in this direction. [*See the biography of* WALRAS.]

Important contributions were made by Walras' contemporaries, Edgeworth, Pareto, and Irving Fisher. One contribution perhaps calls for special mention, since it has again become the subject of significant research, the *contract curve* (Edgeworth 1881), known in modern terminology as the *core* (see section 3 below and Debreu & Scarf 1963).

Developments during and after the 1930s. The next truly major advances did not come until the 1930s. There were two distinct streams of thought, one beginning in German-language literature and dealing primarily with the existence and uniqueness of equilibrium, the other primarily in English and dealing with stability and comparative statics. The former started with a thorough examination of Cassel's simplification (1918) of Walras' system, an interesting case of work which had no significance in itself and yet whose study turned out to be extraordinarily fruitful. Cassel assumed two kinds of goods: commodities which entered into the demand functions of consumers, and factors which were used to produce commodities (intermediate goods were not considered). Each commodity was produced from factors with constant input–output coefficients. Factor supplies were supposed totally inelastic. Let a_{ij} be the amount of factor i used in the production of one unit of commodity j; x_j the total output of commodity j; v_i the total initial supply of factor i; p_j the price of commodity j; and r_i the price of factor i. Then the condition that demand equal supply for all factors reads

$$(1) \qquad \sum_j a_{ij} x_j = v_i, \qquad \text{for all } i,$$

while the condition that each commodity be produced with zero profits reads

$$(2) \qquad \sum_i a_{ij} r_i = p_j, \qquad \text{for all } j.$$

The system is completed by the equations relating the demand for commodities to their prices and to total income from the sale of factors. In total, there are as many equations as unknowns. But three virtually simultaneous papers by Zeuthen (1932), Neisser (1932), and von Stackelberg (1933) showed in different ways that the problem of existence of meaningful equilibrium was deeper than equality of equations and unknowns. Neisser noted that even with perfectly plausible values of the input–output coefficients, a_{ij}, the prices or quantities which satisfied (1) and (2) might well be negative. Von Stackelberg noted that (1) constituted a complete system of equations in the outputs, x_j, since the factor supplies, v_i, were data; but nothing had been assumed about the numbers of distinct factors or distinct commodities. If, in particular, the number of commodities were less than that of factors, equations (1) would in general have no solutions.

Zeuthen reconsidered the meaning of equations (1). He noted that economists, at least since Carl Menger, had recognized that some factors (for example, air) were so abundant that there would be no price charged for them. These would not enter into the list of factors in Cassel's system. But, Zeuthen argued, the division of factors into free and scarce should not be taken as given a priori. Hence, all that can be said is that the use of a factor should not exceed its supply; but if it falls short, then the factor is free. In symbols, (1) is replaced by

$$(1') \qquad \sum_j a_{ij} x_j \leqslant v_i \, ;$$

if the strict inequality holds, then $r_i = 0$. To a later generation of economists, to whom linear programming and its generalizations are familiar, the crucial significance of this step will need no elaboration; equalities are replaced by inequalities, and the vital notion of the complementary slackness of quantities and prices is introduced. [*See* PROGRAMMING.]

Independently of Zeuthen, the Viennese banker and amateur economist K. Schlesinger came to the same conclusion. But he went much further and intuitively grasped the essential point that replacement of equalities by inequalities also resolved the problems raised by Neisser and von Stackelberg. Schlesinger realized the mathematical complexity of a rigorous treatment, and, at his request, Oskar Morgenstern put him in touch with a young mathematician, Abraham Wald. The result was the first rigorous analysis of general competitive equilibrium. In a series of papers (see Wald 1936 for a summary), Wald demonstrated the existence of competitive equilibrium in a series of alternative models, including the Cassel model and a model of pure exchange. Competitive equilibrium was defined in the Zeuthen sense, and the essential role of that definition in the justification of existence is made clear in the mathematics. Wald also initiated the study of uniqueness. Indeed, both of his alternative sufficient conditions for the uniqueness of competitive equilibrium have since become major themes of the literature: (1) that the weak axiom of revealed preference hold for the market demand functions (the sums of the demand functions of

all individuals), or (2) that all commodities be gross substitutes (see definitions below).

Wald's papers were of forbidding mathematical depth, not only in the use of sophisticated tools but also in the complexity of the argument. As they gradually came to be known among mathematical economists, they probably served as much to inhibit further research by their difficulty as to stimulate it. Help finally come from the development of a related line of research, John von Neumann's theory of games (first basic paper published in 1928; see von Neumann & Morgenstern 1944). The historical relation between game theory and economic equilibrium theory is paradoxical. In principle, game theory is a very general notion of equilibrium which should either replace the principle of competitive equilibrium or include it as a special case. In fact, while game theory has turned out to be extraordinarily stimulating to equilibrium theory, it has been through the use of mathematical tools developed in the former and used in the latter with entirely different interpretations. It was von Neumann himself who made the first such application in his celebrated paper on balanced economic growth (1937). In this model, there were no demand functions, only production. The markets had to be in equilibrium in the Zeuthen sense. But beyond this, there was equilibrium in a second sense, which may be termed *stationary equilibrium* (see section 8 below). To prove the existence of equilibrium, von Neumann demonstrated that a certain ratio of bilinear forms has a saddle point, a generalization of the theorem which shows the existence of equilibrium in two-person zero-sum games. But in game theory the variables of the problem are probabilities (of choosing alternative strategies), while in the application to equilibrium theory one set of variables is prices and the other is the levels at which productive activities are carried on.

Von Neumann deduced his saddle-point theorem from a generalization of Brouwer's fixed-point theorem, a famous proposition in the branch of mathematics known as topology. A simplified version of von Neumann's theorem was presented a few years later by the mathematician Shizuo Kakutani, and Kakutani's theorem has been the basic tool in virtually all subsequent work. With this foundation, and the influence of the rapid development of linear programming on both the mathematical—again closely related to saddle-point theorems—and economic sides (the work of George B. Dantzig, Albert W. Tucker, Harold W. Kuhn, Tjalling C. Koopmans, and others, collected for the most part in an influential volume [Cowles Commission . . . 1951]) and the work of John F. Nash, Jr. (1950), it was perceived independently by a number of scholars that existence theorems of greater simplicity and generality than Wald's were possible. The first papers were those of McKenzie (1954) and Arrow and Debreu (1954). Subsequent developments were due to Hukukane Nikaidô, Hirofumi Uzawa, Debreu, and McKenzie. (The most complete systematic account of the existence conditions is in Debreu 1959; the most general version of the existence theorem is in Debreu 1962.)

Independently of this development of the existence conditions for equilibrium, the Anglo–American literature contained an intensive study of the comparative statics and stability of general competitive equilibrium. Historically, it was closely related to analyses of the second-order conditions for maximization of profits by firms and of utility by consumers; the most important contributors were John R. Hicks, Harold Hotelling, Paul Samuelson, and R. G. D. Allen. In particular, Hicks (1939) introduced the argument that the stability of equilibrium carried with it some implications for the shapes of the supply and demand functions in the neighborhood of equilibrium; hence, the effects of small shifts in any one behavior relation may be predicted, at least as to sign. Hicks's definition of stability has been replaced in subsequent work by Samuelson's (1941–1942); however, Hicks showed that (locally) stability in his sense was equivalent to a condition which has played a considerable role in subsequent research. Let X_i be the excess demand (demand less supply) for the ith commodity; it is in general a function of $p_1, \cdots, p_n$, the prices of all n commodities. Then Hicks's definition of stability was equivalent to the condition that the principal minors of the matrix whose elements were $\partial X_i / \partial p_j$ had determinants which were positive or negative according as the number of rows or columns included was even or odd. Such matrices will be referred to as *Hicksian*. Hicks also sought to derive comparative-statics conclusions about the response of prices to changes in demand functions. Presently accepted theorems derive the same conclusions but from somewhat different premises (see section 6).

Samuelson formulated the presently accepted definition of stability. It must be based, he argued, on an explicit dynamic model concerning the behavior of prices when the system is out of equilibrium. He formalized the implicit assumption of Walras and most of his successors: the price of each commodity increases at a rate proportional to excess demand for that commodity. This assumption defined a system of differential equations; if every path satisfying the system and starting sufficiently close to equilibrium converged to it, then the system was stable. Samuelson was able to demonstrate that Hicks's definition was neither necessary nor sufficient for his and that the economic system was stable if the income effects on consumption were sufficiently small. He enunciated a general *correspondence principle*: that all meaningful theorems in comparative statics were derived either from the second-order conditions on maximization of profits by firms or of utility by consumers or from the assumption that the observed equilibrium was stable.

The current period of work in comparative statics and stability dates from the work of Mosak (1944) and Metzler (1945). The emphasis has tended to be a little different from Samuelson's correspondence principle; rather, the tendency has been to formulate hypotheses about the excess demand functions which imply both stability and certain results in comparative statics. [*See the biographies of* CASSEL; SCHLESINGER; VON NEUMANN; *and* WALD.]

2. The existence of competitive equilibrium

Consider a system with n commodities, with prices $p_1, \cdots, p_n$, respectively. Let us first suppose that at each set of prices, each economic agent (firm or household) has a single chosen demand or supply. If supplies are treated as negative demands, then for each commodity the net total excess demand (excess of demand over supply) by all economic agents is obtained by summing the excess demands for the individual agents and this is a function of all prices; let $X_i(p_1, \cdots, p_n)$ be the excess demand function for the ith commodity. At an equilibrium, excess demand cannot be positive since there is no way of meeting it. Further, if the excess demand is negative (that is, there is an excess of supply over demand), the good is free and should have a zero price. Formally, a set of nonnegative prices $\bar{p}_1, \cdots, \bar{p}_n$ constitutes an *equilibrium* if

$$(3) \qquad X_i(\bar{p}_1, \cdots, \bar{p}_n) \leqslant 0 \qquad \text{for all } i,$$

$$(4) \qquad \bar{p}_i = 0 \qquad \text{for all } i \text{ such that} \\ X_i(\bar{p}_1, \cdots, \bar{p}_n) < 0.$$

With this definition, the following assumptions are sufficient for the existence of equilibrium:

(H) The functions $X_i(p_1, \cdots, p_n)$ are (positively) homogeneous of degree zero, that is, $X_i(\lambda p_1, \cdots, \lambda p_n) = X_i(p_1, \cdots, p_n)$ for all $\lambda > 0$ and all $p_1, \cdots, p_n$.

(W) $\sum_i p_i X_i(p_1, \cdots, p_n) = 0$ for all sets of prices.

(C) The functions $X_i(p_1, \cdots, p_n)$ are continuous.

(B) The functions $X_i(p_1, \cdots, p_n)$ are bounded from below (that is, supply is always limited).

Assumption (H) is standard in consumers' demand theory; (W) is Walras' law referred to above. Assumption (C) is the type usually made in any applied work, although, as will be seen later, it is closely related to assumptions of convexity of preferences and production. Assumption (B) is trivially valid in a pure exchange economy, since each individual has a finite stock of goods to trade. In an economy where production takes place, the matter is less clear. At an arbitrarily given set of prices, a producer may find it profitable to offer an infinite supply; the realization of his plans will, of course, require him to demand at the same time an infinite amount of some factor of production. Such situations are of course incompatible with equilibrium, but since the existence of equilibrium is itself in question here, the analysis is necessarily delicate.

The current proofs that the assumptions listed above imply the existence of competitive equilibrium require the use of Brouwer's fixed-point theorem, a mathematical theorem which asserts that a continuous transformation of a triangle or similar figure in higher-dimensional spaces into itself must leave at least one point unaltered. The argument may be sketched as follows: From (H), an equilibrium is unaltered if all prices are multiplied by the same positive constant; hence, without loss of generality we can assume that the sum of the prices is one. The set of all price vectors with nonnegative components summing to one is clearly a generalized triangle (technically called a *simplex*). For each set of prices, compute the excess demands (positive or negative) and then form a new price vector in which those components with positive excess demands are increased and the others decreased (but not below zero). These new prices are then adjusted so that the sum is again one. This process defines a continuous transformation of the simplex into itself and thus has a fixed point, a price vector which remains unaltered under the adjustment process. It is easy to see that this price vector must be an equilibrium.

The point of view just sketched is not sufficiently general for most purposes. We have already seen that the boundedness assumption appears artificial in the case where production is possible. Closely related to this is a second issue; the assumption that supplies and demands are single-valued ap-

pears unduly restrictive. Consider the simplest case of production: one input and one output which is proportional to the input. The behavior of the profit-maximizing entrepreneur depends on the ratio of the input price to the output price. If the price ratio is greater than the output–input ratio, then the firm will lose money if it engages in any production; hence, the profit-maximizing point is zero output and zero input, which is indeed single-valued. If the two ratios are equal, however, all output levels make zero profit; hence, the profit-maximizing entrepreneur is indifferent among them, and the supply function of the output and the demand function for the input must be taken to be multivalued. If the price ratio is less than the output–input ratio, then the entrepreneur will make increasing profits as he increases the scale of activity. There is *no* finite level which could be described as profit-maximizing.

To state a general definition of competitive equilibrium more precisely, the following model can be formulated: there are presumed to exist a set of households and a set of firms; all production is carried on in the latter. Each household has a collection of initial assets (here assumed to include the ability to supply different kinds of labor) and also a claim to a given portion (possibly zero, of course) of the profits of each firm; it is assumed that for each firm there are claims for exactly the entire profits (these claims are interpretable as equities or partnership shares). For given prices and given production decisions of the firms, the profits of the firms and the value of each individual's initial assets are determined and, hence, so is the individual's total income. The commodity bundles available are those whose value, at the given prices, does not exceed income and whose individual components are nonnegative (or satisfy some still stronger condition independent of prices). It is further assumed that the household can express preferences among commodity bundles and that these preferences have suitable continuity properties. The aim of the household is taken to be selection of the most preferred bundle among those available.

The behavior of the firms is more simply described. Each firm has available to it a set of possible production bundles; conventionally, the components are taken to be positive for outputs and negative for inputs. For a fixed set of prices, the profits for each possible production bundle are determined; then the firm chooses the (or a) bundle which maximizes profits. Notice that the profit-maximizing bundle need not be unique. Indeed, under constant returns to scale, it is never unique unless the firm's best policy is to shut down completely. (Under constant returns, if any bundle is possible, the bundle obtained by doubling all components, inputs and outputs alike, is also possible. Then if any bundle makes positive profits, doubling the bundle will double the profits; hence, there can be no profit-maximizing bundle. The existence of a profit-maximizing bundle thus entails that maximum profits be nonpositive. Since zero profits are always possible by zero activity level, we must have zero profits at the maximum. Either profits are negative for all nonzero bundles, in which case shutting down is the unique optimal policy, or profits are zero for some nonzero bundle, in which case any nonnegative multiple also achieves zero and therefore maximum profits.)

In this terminology, a "firm" may actually be producing zero output and therefore may not be statistically observable; the firm is potentially capable of producing outputs and would find it profitable to do so at different sets of prices than those prevailing.

A *competitive equilibrium*, then, is a designation of nonnegative prices for all commodities, of a bundle for consumption for each household, and of a production bundle for each firm satisfying the following conditions:

(*a*) for each household, the designated bundle maximizes utility among all available bundles;

(*b*) for each firm, the designated bundle maximizes profit among all technically possible bundles;

(*c*) for each commodity, the total consumed by all households does not exceed the total initially available plus the net total produced by all firms ("net" here means that input uses by some firms are subtracted from outputs of others);

(*d*) for those commodities for which total consumed is strictly less than total initially available plus total produced, the price is zero.

The adjective "competitive" refers to the assumption that each household or firm takes prices as given and independent of its decision.

The following assumptions are sufficient to ensure the existence of competitive equilibrium:

(I) The preference ordering of each household is continuous (a strict preference between two bundles continues to hold if either is slightly altered), admits of no saturation (for each bundle, there is another preferred to it), and is convex (if a bundle is varied along a line segment in the commodity space, one of the end points is least preferred).

(II) The set of possible production bundles for each firm is convex (any weighted combination of two possible production bundles is possible) and closed (any bundle that can be approximated by

possible bundles is itself possible); further, it is always possible to produce no outputs and use no inputs.

(III) No production bundle possible to society as a whole (a bundle is possible for society as a whole if it is the algebraic sum of production bundles, one chosen among those possible for each firm) can contain outputs but not inputs; there is at least one bundle possible for society that contains a positive net output of all commodities not possessed initially by any household.

(IV) The economy is irreducible—a concept developed by Gale (1960) and McKenzie (1959)—in the sense that no matter how the households are divided into two groups, an increase in the initial assets held by the members of one group can be used to make feasible an allocation which will make no one worse off and at least one individual in the second group better off.

It is perhaps interesting to observe that "atomistic" assumptions concerning individual households and firms are not sufficient to establish the existence of equilibrium; "global" assumptions III and IV are also needed (though they are surely unexceptionable). Thus, a limit is set to the tendency implicit in price theory, particularly in its mathematical versions, to deduce all properties of aggregate behavior from assumptions about individual economic agents.

The hypotheses of convexity in household preferences and in production are the empirically most vulnerable parts of the above assumptions. In production, convexity excludes indivisibilities or increasing returns to scale. In consumption, convexity excludes cases in which mixed bundles are inferior to extremes; for example, in the very short run, a mixture of whiskey and gin is regarded by many as inferior to either alone, or living part time in each of two distant cities may be inferior to living in either one alone. It is of interest to know how far these assumptions may be relaxed.

Convexity does play an essential role in the proof. This may be illustrated by considering the simplest case—one input and one output proportional to it. As noted earlier, there will be one ratio of output to input prices at which the entrepreneur will be indifferent among all levels of output. If the supply of the input is given, then the equilibrium levels of input and output, as well as price, are determined. Now suppose that production is possible only at integer-valued levels of input, so that the production possibility set is not convex. If the supply of the input is not an integer, there is no way of equating demand and supply for it. It should be noted, though, that the input (and output) level can be so chosen that the difference between supply and demand does not exceed one half. In effect, convexity ensures that supply and demand are, in a suitable sense, continuous and thus can be adjusted to varying levels of initial assets.

The assumption of convexity cannot be dispensed with in general theorems concerning the existence of equilibrium strictly defined. However, a line of thought begun by Farrell (1959) and developed by Rothenberg (1960) and Aumann (1966) suggests that the gap between supply and demand does not tend to increase with the size of the economy. More explicitly, if each agent (household or firm) is small compared with the total economy, then by suitable choice of prices and of consumption and production bundles, the discrepancy between supply and demand can be made small relative to the economy. Each household is certainly small relative to the economy, so that nonconvexities in individual preferences have no significant effect on the existence of equilibrium. However, increasing returns to scale over a sufficiently wide range may mean that a competitive profit-maximizing firm will be large at a given set of prices if it produces at all; hence, there is a real possibility that equilibrium may not exist.

3. Optimality and the core

Although the view that competitive equilibria have some special optimality properties is at least as old as Adam Smith's invisible hand, a clarification of the relation is fairly recent. Since the subject belongs to the field of welfare economics, only a brief statement is given here. An allocation (designation of bundles for all households and all firms) is *feasible* if each bundle is possible for the corresponding agent and if, in the aggregate, the net output of each commodity (including quantities initially available) is at least as great as the demand by consumers. Each allocation, then, determines the utility level of the consumption of each household. One allocation is *dominated* by a second if the latter is feasible and if each individual has a higher utility under the second than under the first (more frequently, in the literature, the condition is put in the more complicated form of having each individual at least as well off and one individual better off, but the difference is trifling). Then an allocation is said to be optimal if it is feasible but not dominated by any other (a definition due to Pareto).

There are two theorems relating competitive equilibrium and optimal allocations, one concerning sufficiency and the other concerning necessity; the two have not always been distinguished in the literature. They are stated here without some minor qualifications.

Sufficiency.   Any competitive equilibrium is necessarily optimal.

Necessity.   Given any optimal allocation, there is some assignment of society's initial assets among individuals such that the optimal allocation is a competitive equilibrium corresponding to that distribution, provided that the assumptions of section 2 which ensure the existence of equilibrium hold.

It is useful to note that the sufficiency theorem is valid even if the assumptions of section 2 do not hold.

The concept of optimality is defined without regard to a price system or any prescribed set of markets. The optimality theorems assert that even though prices do not enter into the definition of optimality, there happens to be an identity between optima and competitive equilibria (under suitable conditions). This relation has been brought into still sharper relief with the modern theory of the core (Debreu & Scarf 1963), which also, however, serves to emphasize the special role of large numbers of economic agents in the theory of perfect competition.

We start with essentially the same model of the production and consumption structure as in section 2, deleting, of course, all references to prices and to income. However, the analyses of the core have so far made one significant restriction on the relation between producers and consumers. It is assumed that any coalition of households has access to the same set of possible production vectors, which is further assumed to display constant returns to scale. Consider now any feasible allocation. It is said to be *blocked* by a coalition S (a set of households) if there is another allocation among the members of S feasible for them (using only the assets they collectively started with) which makes each of them better off. Notice that the coalition might consist of all households in the society; for that coalition, blocking reduces to domination in the sense used earlier. A coalition might also consist of one individual; then he can block an allocation if, with only his own resources and the universally accessible technological knowledge, he can produce a bundle whose utility is higher than that of the bundle allocated to him.

The *core*, then, consists of all allocations that are not blocked by any coalition. The first theorem concerning the core generalizes the sufficiency theorem for optimality: *Any competitive equilibrium belongs to the core.* More interesting is a sort of converse proposition, which may be loosely stated as follows: *If the hypotheses of section 2 which ensure the existence of equilibrium hold, and if each individual is small compared with the economy, then the allocations in the core are all approximately competitive equilibria.* (The words "small" and "approximately" are rigorously interpreted as referring to suitably chosen limiting processes.)

Some interpretive remarks are in order here. First, the natural interpretation of the core is that if any sort of bargains are permitted by the rules of the economic game, the allocation finally arrived at should be in the core, since otherwise some coalition would have both the power and the desire to prevent it. Hence, it would follow, very strikingly, that for large numbers of participants the outcome would be the competitive equilibrium, provided the assumptions of section 2 were satisfied. Even under nonconvexity some scattered results of L. S. Shapley and M. Shubik (unpublished) suggest that the same holds approximately (that is, there may be no core in the precise definition, but there is a set of allocations that can be blocked but only with very small preference on the part of the blocking coalition). Hence, the existence of monopoly must depend on one of the three factors: (1) specialized abilities that are scarce relative to the economy; (2) increasing returns on a scale comparable to that of the economy; or (3) costs of coalition formation that are relatively low among producers of the same good and high for coalitions involving consumers and producers.

Second, the assumption that the production possibilities are the same for all coalitions is one that has been used by McKenzie and, with suitable interpretation, is not as drastic as it seems. We can assume that some or all productive processes require as inputs "entrepreneurial skills" or special talents of some kind. The commodity space is enlarged to include these skills, which may be distributed very unequally in the population. It can then be argued that diminishing returns to scale in the observable variables really results from a combination of constant returns in all variables, including entrepreneurial skills and a fixed supply of the latter. Further, different coalitions will really have very different access to production possibilities because of their very different endowments of skills. [*See* WELFARE ECONOMICS.]

4. Uniqueness of competitive equilibrium

Results concerning the uniqueness and stability of competitive equilibrium have been stated only for the case where the excess demand functions are single-valued, as at the beginning of section 2. It will then be assumed that assumptions (H), (W),

and (B) hold; in fact, (C) will be strengthened to require differentiability of the excess demand functions.

Without further assumptions, there is no need that equilibrium be unique, and examples of nonuniqueness have been known since Marshall. The mathematical basis for a fairly general uniqueness theorem has only recently been worked out by Gale and Nikaidô (1965), and the most appropriate economic theorem has not been fully explored. However, one theorem along these lines can be stated. Suppose there is one commodity for which the excess demand is positive whenever its price is zero, regardless of the prices of all other commodities. Such a commodity is an eminent candidate for Walras' role of *numéraire*, and we may choose its price to be 1, since it cannot be zero (and therefore will be positive) in any equilibrium, and, from the homogeneity of excess demand functions, multiplying any equilibrium set of prices by a positive number leads to a new equilibrium (uniqueness of price equilibrium is, of course, defined only up to positive multiples). Call this the nth commodity, and consider the excess demands for commodities $1, \cdots, n - 1$ as functions of $p_1, \cdots, p_{n-1}$, with p_n held constant at 1. The Jacobian of this set of functions is defined in mathematics as the matrix with components $(\partial X_i / \partial p_j)$, where i and j range from 1 to $n - 1$. As noted in section 1, a matrix is termed *Hicksian* if the determinant of a principal minor is positive when it has an even number of rows and negative otherwise.

Uniqueness theorem 1. If the Jacobian of the excess demand functions, omitting a *numéraire* and holding its price constant, is Hicksian for all sets of prices, then the equilibrium is unique.

A special case of this theorem originated in effect with Wald (1936). Commodity i will be said to be a *gross substitute* for commodity j if an increase in p_j, holding all other prices constant, increases X_i. It follows from (H) that if all commodities are gross substitutes, the Jacobian of the excess demand functions, omitting a *numéraire*, is Hicksian. Then a consequence of uniqueness theorem 1 is: *If all commodities are gross substitutes, then equilibrium is unique.*

Finally, an entirely different sufficient condition was also stated by Wald:

Uniqueness theorem 2. If the weak axiom of revealed preference holds for consumers as a whole, then equilibrium is unique.

What is now termed the weak axiom of revealed preference—developed independently by Samuelson (1938)—states that if the commodity bundle chosen at prices prevailing in situation 1 are no more expensive at the prices prevailing in situation 0 than the bundle chosen in situation 0, then the latter bundle must be more expensive than the former at the prices in situation 1. For an individual, this axiom is a simple consequence of rational behavior; both bundles were available to him in situation 0, and the bundle he chose in that situation must therefore have been preferred. If both bundles had also been available in situation 1, then the less preferred bundle could never have been chosen; hence, the bundle chosen in situation 0 must have been unavailable because of cost in situation 1. However, the statement that the axiom holds for the demand functions of the market as a whole is not a consequence of rational behavior but is an additional assumption that is valid, in effect, when income effects are not too large in the aggregate.

5. Stability

The stability problem, as formalized by Samuelson, can be stated as follows: Suppose that an arbitrary (in general, nonequilibrium) set of prices is given so that there are nonzero excess demands, some of which are positive. It is assumed that prices adjust under the influence of the excess demands, specifically rising when excess demand is positive and falling in the opposite case. This suggests the following dynamic system:

$$(5) \qquad dp_i/dt = k_i X_i(p_1, \cdots, p_n), \qquad i = 1, \cdots, n,$$

that is, the changes in prices (t denoting time) are proportional to the excess demands. Notice that allowing for "speeds of adjustment," k_i, that are different from 1 and from each other is not merely due to a desire for generality but is virtually a logical necessity, for a careful dimensional analysis shows that k_i will change with changes in the units of measurement of commodity i. More general (nonlinear) adjustment models have been studied, for example, a model in which dp_i/dt has merely the same sign as X_i.

A variation of this system, which has often been studied, distinguishes one commodity as *numéraire* and assumes that its price is held fixed, say at 1:

$$(6) \quad dp_i/dt = k_i X_i(p_1, \cdots, p_n), \quad i = 1, \cdots, n-1,$$
$$p_n = 1.$$

One difficulty arises in either system when the rules call for a price to become negative, which can happen if, for some i, $X_i(p_1, \cdots, p_n) < 0$ with $p_i = 0$. Since the excess demand functions are not even defined for negative prices, the rules must be altered. It has become customary to modify (5) and (6) by requiring that a price remain at zero

under these conditions; but whether the rules remain consistent is a difficult mathematical question, which has been studied only by Uzawa (1958) and Morishima (1960a) and then only for very special cases.

The systems (5) or (6) are systems of differential equations; their solutions are time paths of prices, which are determined by the specification of initial conditions as well as by the system. The stability question is whether or not the resulting time path converges to an equilibrium. Global stability means that convergence occurs for any initial conditions; local stability that the path converges for initial conditions sufficiently close to an equilibrium. However, at the present time the most interesting results are sufficient for global as well as local stability, so we need not distinguish the two.

It should first be noted that neither of the systems is necessarily stable even if all the hypotheses which ensure the existence of equilibrium are satisfied; examples have been supplied by Scarf (1960) and Gale (1963). Gale's example is particularly simple: Suppose there are two individuals and three commodities, and there is no production. Individual 1 starts with a supply of good 1 and individual 2 with supplies of goods 2 and 3. Individual 1 has a utility function involving only goods 2 and 3, while individual 2 wishes only good 1. It is easy to see that there is a unique equilibrium. Now suppose that Giffen's paradox holds with regard to good 2 for individual 1 (that is, a rise in the price of good 2, holding other prices constant, raises individual 1's demand). Then it is possible to show that, for suitably chosen adjustment speeds, the solution of system (5) or (6) remains away from the equilibrium.

There are three different conditions, due to Arrow, Block, and Hurwicz (1959), any one of which is sufficient for the stability of the system.

Stability theorem 1. If all commodities are gross substitutes, then systems (5) and (6) are both stable.

Stability theorem 2. If the market satisfies the weak axiom of revealed preference, then systems (5) and (6) are both stable.

To state the third theorem we have to introduce the mathematical concept of a matrix with dominant diagonal. A matrix (a_{ij}) is said to have a dominant diagonal if $|a_{ii}| > \sum_{j \neq i} |a_{ij}|$ for all i. (The diagonal element is more important than all others in the same row.)

Stability theorem 3. If the Jacobian of the excess demand functions (excluding a *numéraire*) has a dominant diagonal, all elements of which are negative, then system (6) is stable.

Whether the Jacobian has a dominant diagonal may depend on the units in which the commodities are measured; stability theorem 3 asserts stability if there is *any* way of choosing the units so as to achieve diagonal dominance.

Stability theorem 2 can be interpreted as meaning that the transfers of income which take place during the course of the time path produce broadly offsetting results on demand; income effects are not too asymmetrical. Stability theorem 3 is perhaps closest to Walras' initial concepts; stability holds when the excess demand for a commodity is much more affected by a change in its own price than by any other price change (holding the price of a *numéraire* constant).

In all discussion of stability so far it has been implicitly assumed that no transactions take place at nonequilibrium prices, for if they did the excess demand functions would shift. (An alternative interpretation is that all commodities are completely perishable and that utilities and production are independent as between time periods. Then any transactions occurring in one period will have no effect on transactions occurring in the next period.) This assumption is the classical one of "recontracting," in Edgeworth's terminology, and was made by him and by Walras. The problem raised by transactions at nonequilibrium prices was immediately recognized, but little analysis took place. Several recent writers, particularly Negishi (1961), Hahn and Negishi (1962), and Uzawa (1962), have considered this problem under the rather awkward title of "non-*tâtonnement* stability." The system, to be complete, has to specify the nature of the transactions; since the system is not at equilibrium there will have to be rationing of sellers or of buyers. If it is simply assumed that any transactions that do take place cannot change the value of any individual's holdings, then gross substitutability is again a sufficient condition for stability. Under more specific assumptions about transactions, stability can be shown in much wider classes of cases.

6. Comparative statics

The question raised in comparative statics is, What can be said of the effect of a shift in the excess demand functions on the price system? As might be supposed from the nature of the question, answers can only be given in a limited range of cases. Suppose that a *binary* shift has occurred —that is, the excess demand for one commodity, say 1, has decreased at every set of prices; the excess demand for another commodity, say 2, has

increased correspondingly (the money value of the increased demand for 2 exactly equals the decrease in money value of demand for 1 at any given set of prices); and the excess demand functions for all other commodities have remained unchanged. Then the only general result in the literature is the following (Morishima 1960b): *If all commodities are gross substitutes and there has occurred a binary shift in demand from commodity 1 to commodity 2, then all prices of commodities other than 1 rise relative to the price of 1 or do not fall, and no relative price rise is greater than that of commodity 2.*

7. Partial equilibrium

A great deal of economic analysis has been concerned with equilibrium of a single market. Demand and supply for a commodity are regarded as functions of a single price, and equilibrium is interpreted as equality of supply and demand or as an excess of supply over demand at zero price.

Partial equilibrium analysis is to be regarded as a special case of general equilibrium analysis. The existence of one market presupposes that there must be at least one commodity beyond that traded on that market, for a price must be stated as the rate at which an individual gives up something else for the commodity in question. If there were really only one commodity in the world, there would be no exchange and no market.

Suppose for the moment that there are only two commodities, say 1 and 2. Because of homogeneity, demand and supply (which may, as before, be multivalued) are determined by the ratio of the price of commodity 1 to that of commodity 2, that is, the price of commodity 1 with commodity 2 as *numéraire*. From Walras' law, equilibrium on market 1 ensures equilibrium on market 2. Partial equilibrium analysis of market 1 is, in the case of two commodities, fully equivalent to general equilibrium analysis. All the previous theorems hold, and one more theorem on stability may be stated (Arrow & Hurwicz 1958): For two commodities, equilibrium is always globally stable in the sense that for any initial price or prices systems (5) and (6) of section 5 always converge to some set of equilibrium prices (if the equilibrium price set is not unique up to positive multiples, the prices to which the system converges will depend on the starting point). This theorem has not always been recognized in discussions of stability of equilibrium in foreign trade, where the analysis has frequently been confined to two commodities.

Analysis of a two-commodity world may have

considerable didactic usefulness as a way of studying general equilibrium through a special case admitting of simple diagrammatic representation, but it may be asked if partial equilibrium analysis has any empirical interest for a world of many commodities. An answer is provided by the following theorem, due independently to Hicks (1939) and Leontief (1936): If the relative prices of some set of commodities remain constant, then for all analytical purposes the set can be regarded as a single composite commodity, the price of which can be regarded as proportional to the price of any member of the set and the quantity of which is then defined so that expenditure (price times quantity) on the composite commodity is equal to the sum of the expenditures on the individual commodities in the set. In symbols, if the prices $p_1, \cdots, p_m$ of a set of commodities $1, \cdots, m$ satisfy the conditions $p_i = \rho \bar{p}_i$ ($\bar{p}_i$ a constant for each i while ρ may vary), then we can take ρ to be the price of the composite commodity and $\sum_{i=1}^{m} \bar{p}_i q_i$ to be the quantity, where q_i is the quantity of the ith good.

The Hicks–Leontief aggregation theorem can be used to justify partial equilibrium analysis. Suppose that a change in the price of commodity 1 leaves the relative prices of all others unchanged. Then insofar as we are considering only disturbances to equilibrium from causes peculiar to the market for commodity 1, the remaining commodities can be regarded as a single composite commodity, and partial equilibrium analysis is valid.

The assumption of strict constancy of relative prices of the other commodities will not usually be valid, of course, but it may hold approximately in many cases of practical interest. It is sufficient for the purpose that the changes in the relative prices of other commodities induced by a change in the price of the commodity being studied do not in turn induce a significant shift in supply or demand conditions on the market for that commodity.

8. Equilibrium over time

While the above summarizes the central part of the literature on general economic equilibrium, there is a related conceptual question that deserves brief mention. Consider an economy extending over time, with dated inputs and outputs and household plans that run into the future. What can be said about the equilibrium of such an economy and, indeed, what is meant by the term?

One straightforward answer is that originally due to Hicks. We may simply date all commodity transactions and regard the same physically defined commodity at two different times as being two different commodities. Then the formal model of section 2 remains, with reinterpretation, and we can still argue that there is an equilibrium over time. Planned supplies and demands are equated in the usual way.

This is a legitimate and indeed important interpretation. Problems of optimality, the core, uniqueness, and comparative statics (perhaps to be renamed "comparative dynamics") are restatable with no difficulty. Stability theory faces a more serious challenge, since time now enters in two different ways—in the underlying model and in the adjustment process. If all markets are taken to be futures markets, so that all adjustments take place simultaneously, there is no difficulty, but otherwise there is a new range of problems which have been approached only in the most fragmentary way.

However, the simple redating has the important implication of perfect foresight (possibly achieved through having all future economic transactions determined in currently existing futures markets). This seems empirically most unsatisfactory and involves significant logical problems of knowledge (Morgenstern 1935). An alternative is to assume that each individual has expectations about the future that are continuous functions of present observed variables. Then in each period there will be an equilibrium, although each individual's plans for the future generally will not in fact be carried out.

From either point of view, considerable interest has attached to another meaning of equilibrium, which we may term *stationary equilibrium*. The equilibrium over time in the case of perfect foresight defines a set of prices and quantities for each period. The same is true of the succession of short-run equilibria defined by individuals acting under expectations. The question is, Does this time sequence have a stationary or equilibrium value? Is there a set of prices and quantities such that, if they governed in the initial period, they would remain equilibrium values for all subsequent periods? Or, in a growing economy, would at least the relative prices and quantities remain constant if the appropriate values held in the initial period? This might be termed the question of existence of stationary equilibrium, frequently termed the *balanced growth path*. The distinction between equilibrium in general and the stationary state, implicit in classical economics, was first clarified by Frisch (1935–1936).

The stability of stationary equilibrium is a different problem from that of stability in the sense used in section 5. Suppose we have an arbitrary initial quantity configuration. The question then arises, Will the equilibrium values of the successive periods tend to converge to the stationary equilibrium? The study of this problem has been a major preoccupation of modern growth and capital theory, and it will not be enlarged on here.

KENNETH J. ARROW

[*Directly related are the entries* BUSINESS CYCLES, *article on* MATHEMATICAL MODELS; ECONOMIC GROWTH, *article on* MATHEMATICAL THEORY; GAME THEORY; INPUT–OUTPUT ANALYSIS; INTERNATIONAL TRADE, *article on* MATHEMATICAL THEORY; SPATIAL ECONOMICS, *article on* THE GENERAL EQUILIBRIUM APPROACH; STATICS AND DYNAMICS IN ECONOMICS; STOCK–FLOW ANALYSIS.]

BIBLIOGRAPHY

ARROW, KENNETH J.; BLOCK, HENRY D.; and HURWICZ, LEONID 1959 On the Stability of the Competitive Equilibrium. Part 2. *Econometrica* 27:82–109.

ARROW, KENNETH J.; and DEBREU, GERARD 1954 Existence of an Equilibrium for a Competitive Economy. *Econometrica* 22:265–290.

ARROW, KENNETH J.; and HURWICZ, LEONID 1958 On the Stability of the Competitive Equilibrium. Part 1. *Econometrica* 26:522–552.

AUMANN, ROBERT J. 1966 Existence of Competitive Equilibria in Markets With a Continuum of Traders. *Econometrica* 34:1–17.

CASSEL, GUSTAV (1918) 1932 *The Theory of Social Economy.* New rev. ed. New York: Harcourt. → Translated from the fifth edition of *Theoretische Sozialökonomie.*

COURNOT, ANTOINE AUGUSTIN (1838) 1960 *Researches Into the Mathematical Principles of the Theory of Wealth.* New York: Kelley. → First published in French.

COWLES COMMISSION FOR RESEARCH IN ECONOMICS 1951 *Activity Analysis of Production and Allocation: Proceedings of a Conference.* Edited by Tjalling C. Koopmans. New York: Wiley.

DEBREU, GERARD 1959 *Theory of Value: An Axiomatic Analysis of Economic Equilibrium.* New York: Wiley.

DEBREU, GERARD 1962 New Concepts and Techniques for Equilibrium Analysis. *International Economic Review* 3:257–273.

DEBREU, GERARD; and SCARF, HERBERT 1963 A Limit Theorem on the Core of an Economy. *International Economic Review* 4:235–246.

EDGEWORTH, FRANCIS Y. (1881) 1953 *Mathematical Psychics: An Essay on the Application of Mathematics to the Moral Sciences.* New York: Kelley.

FARRELL, M. J. 1959 The Convexity Assumption in the Theory of Competitive Markets. *Journal of Political Economy* 67:377–391.

FRISCH, RAGNAR 1935–1936 On the Notion of Equilibrium and Disequilibrium. *Review of Economic Studies* 3:100–105.

GALE, DAVID 1960 *The Theory of Linear Economic Models.* New York: McGraw-Hill.

GALE, DAVID 1963 A Note on Global Instability of Competitive Equilibrium. *Naval Research Logistics Quarterly* 10:81–87.

GALE, DAVID; and NIKAIDÔ, HUKUKANE 1965 The Jacob-ian Matrix and Global Univalence of Mappings. *Mathematische Annalen* 159:81–93.

HAHN, FRANK H.; and NEGISHI, TAKASHI 1962 A Theorem on Non-*tâtonnement* Stability. *Econometrica* 30:463–469.

HICKS, JOHN R. (1939) 1946 *Value and Capital: An Inquiry Into Some Fundamental Principles of Economic Theory.* 2d ed. Oxford: Clarendon.

JENKIN, FLEEMING (1870) 1931 The Graphic Representation of the Laws of Supply and Demand, and Their Application to Labour. Volume 2, pages 76–106 in Fleeming Jenkin, *Papers: Literary, Scientific, etc.* London School of Economics and Political Science.

KUENNE, ROBERT E. 1963 *The Theory of General Economic Equilibrium.* Princeton Univ. Press.

LEONTIEF, WASSILY W. 1936 Composite Commodities and the Problem of Index Numbers. *Econometrica* 4:39–59.

MCKENZIE, LIONEL W. 1954 On Equilibrium in Graham's Model of World Trade and Other Competitive Systems. *Econometrica* 22:147–161.

MCKENZIE, LIONEL W. 1959 On the Existence of General Equilibrium for a Competitive Market. *Econometrica* 27:54–71.

METZLER, LLOYD A. 1945 The Stability of Multiple Markets: The Hicks Conditions. *Econometrica* 13:277–292.

MORGENSTERN, OSKAR 1935 Vollkommene Voraussicht und wirtschaftliches Gleichgewicht. *Zeitschrift für Nationalökonomie* 6:337–357.

MORISHIMA, MICHIO 1960a A Reconsideration of the Walras–Cassel–Leontief Model of General Equilibrium. Pages 63–76 in Stanford Symposium on Mathematical Methods in the Social Sciences, Stanford University, 1959, *Mathematical Methods in the Social Sciences.* Edited by Kenneth J. Arrow, Samuel Karlin, and Patrick Suppes. Stanford Univ. Press.

MORISHIMA, MICHIO 1960b On the Three Hicksian Laws of Comparative Statics. *Review of Economic Studies* 27:195–201.

MOSAK, JACOB L. 1944 *General Equilibrium Theory in International Trade.* Bloomington, Ind.: Principia.

NASH, JOHN F., Jr. 1950 Equilibrium in *n*-Person Games. National Academy of Sciences, *Proceedings* 36:48–49.

NEGISHI, TAKASHI 1961 On the Formation of Prices. *International Economic Review* 2:122–126.

NEGISHI, TAKASHI 1962 The Stability of a Competitive Economy: A Survey Article. *Econometrica* 30:635–669.

NEISSER, HANS 1932 Lohnhöhe und Beschäftigungsgrad im Marktgleichgewicht. *Weltwirtschaftliches Archiv* 36:415–455.

ROTHENBERG, JEROME 1960 Non-convexity, Aggregation, and Pareto Optimality. *Journal of Political Economy* 68:435–468.

SAMUELSON, PAUL A. 1938 A Note on the Pure Theory of Consumer's Behavior. *Economica* New Series 5:61–71.

SAMUELSON, PAUL A. 1941–1942 The Stability of Equilibrium. *Econometrica* 9:97–120; 10:1–25.

SAMUELSON, PAUL A. 1957 Wages and Interest: A Modern Dissection of Marxian Economic Models. *American Economic Review* 47:884–912.

SAMUELSON, PAUL A. 1959 A Modern Treatment of the Ricardian Economy. *Quarterly Journal of Economics* 73:1–35, 217–231.

SCARF, HERBERT 1960 Some Examples of Global Instability of the Competitive Equilibrium. *International Economic Review* 1:157–172.

STACKELBERG, HEINRICH VON 1933 Zwei kritische Bemerkungen zur Preistheorie Gustav Cassels. *Zeitschrift für Nationalökonomie* 4:456–472.

UZAWA, HIROFUMI 1958 Gradient Method for Concave Programming. Pages 117–126 in Kenneth J. Arrow, Leonid Hurwicz, and Hirofumi Uzawa, *Studies in Linear and Non-linear Programming.* Stanford Univ. Press.

UZAWA, HIROFUMI 1962 On the Stability of Edgeworth's Barter Process. *International Economic Review* 3:218–232.

VON NEUMANN, JOHN (1937) 1945 A Model of General Economic Equilibrium. *Review of Economic Studies* 13:1–9. → First published in German in Volume 8 of *Ergebnisse eines mathematischen Kolloquiums.*

VON NEUMANN, JOHN; and MORGENSTERN, OSKAR (1944) 1964 *Theory of Games and Economic Behavior.* 3d ed. New York: Wiley.

WALD, ABRAHAM (1936) 1951 On Some Systems of Equations of Mathematical Economics. *Econometrica* 19:368–403. → First published in German in Volume 7 of *Zeitschrift für Nationalökonomie.*

WALRAS, LÉON (1874–1877) 1954 *Elements of Pure Economics: Or, the Theory of Social Wealth.* Translated by William Jaffé. Homewood, Ill.: Irwin; London: Allen & Unwin. → First published in French as *Éléments d'économie politique pure.*

ZEUTHEN, F. 1932 Das Prinzip der Knappheit, technische Kombination und ökonomische Qualität. *Zeitschrift für Nationalökonomie* 4:1–24.

ECONOMIC EXPECTATIONS

Economic actions are chosen with a view to imagined consequences assigned to some more or less distant future date or stretch of time. Such imagined and temporally projected consequences are what we mean by economic expectations. The decision maker, choosing among the rival schemes he has in mind for using his resources, must find some principle and basis for assigning to each such scheme a statement of its meaning to him in possible outcomes. The outcomes that he connects with any one scheme may be plural and mutually exclusive. In this case, he is *uncertain* what will be the outcome of the scheme. He must then adopt some procedure for valuing (in a general and not necessarily monetary sense) as a whole the array of rival conceived outcomes. This valuation has as its purpose, which governs the choice of the basis and method of valuation, a comparison of the rival schemes in order to choose one of them and act upon it.

The principal matters that have to be considered by a theory of economic expectations are the following:

(1) What kinds of evidence or data play a part in the decision maker's task of conceiving the outcomes he connects with any specified scheme of action?

(2) Can a set of rules be found that are, or that ought to be, invariably used by any decision maker in this task?

(3) Is this task a process of pure reasoning, capable, if correctly performed, of logical justification; or do elements of judgment, of invention or inspiration, or of *ex nihilo* creative origination enter into it?

(4) When the outcomes imagined for any action scheme are plural and mutually exclusive, what procedure of valuation of the scheme and its array of rival conjectured outcomes as a whole is employed for the purpose of ordering the schemes or of selecting the best?

(5) Is the choice of such a procedure made independently of the evidence available for forming the expectations, or does this evidence influence or govern it?

(6) The array of imagined outcomes that the decision maker connects with any contemplated scheme of action will influence his valuation of that action in two ways: by the character of each such outcome individually and by the structure composed by all these hypotheses taken together. What are the relative strengths and respective effects of these influences, and what is the nature of their interaction?

(7) If any such expectation structure is the outgrowth of fragmentary, enigmatic, elusive, or self-contradictory evidence; if, as must be the case when several rival hypotheses are entertained concerning the result of any one action, the evidence is insufficient to determine a unique outcome; and if, in consequence, the evidence possessed by the decision maker at any moment is liable to be supplemented, canceled, differently illuminated, partly contradicted, or reinterpreted, what effect upon his valuations of different action schemes will this inherent and recognized fragility of his expectations have?

Logical teeth, however sharp, do nothing toward the nourishment and development of the body of practical knowledge until they have bitten upon fact. Some classification and cross classification of impressions reaching the mind from outside, some sorting of records and measurements, some emergence of repetitive associations and configurations are indispensable to the formation of tools for coping with the environment. The knowledge of "fact" that is appropriate for expectation forming is of two sorts. First, there must be knowledge of pervasive, repeated *stereotypes of structure.* These are answers to the following questions: How, by the ineluctable testimony of nature (including human nature), do things hang together? What things do we constantly find in association, either at one moment or in temporal sequence? How do things work? What *can* happen? These are statements of the principles of the world we live in, not the logical but the factual principles. Given such facts, logic, especially mathematics, may reveal a vast body of entailments that then assume the rank of fact without having been actually observed. Second, when we have some idea of where the state of affairs can go from a *given* situation, we need to know what situation, at the moment of seeking to form expectations, *is* given. This is the other sort of fact.

Historical determinism. The most fundamental question, on which the expectation-former determined to start from first principles would need some opinion, is whether the course of world history, in detail as well as in the large, is at each moment the uniquely inevitable sequel of the past. There are at least two hypotheses, either of which if true would require a negative answer to the foregoing question. One is an essential randomness in the origin of events at subatomic levels, or at the level of genetic mutation. The other is the non-existence of any necessitating link between circumstance, past and present, and the thoughts that a man may have. If a thought can be in some sense, as to some part of its character, "uncaused," we have plainly the possibility that history from time to time and from place to place makes a fresh start. One further feature would need to be true of the world if randomness in nature, or essential novelty of thought in man, were to defeat that statistical determinacy, which, for example, makes possible the laws of thermodynamics. This extra feature is the principle of self-reinforcing processes, by which a "small" event (such as a "favorable" genetic mutation) releases larger forces, such as the rise of a species adapted to a hitherto barren environment, and so leads to biological events on the largest terrestrial scale. Having, for the sake of completeness, tried to suggest the nature of these ultimate questions, we have to admit their virtual irrelevance for the practical business of forming expectations. This irrelevance arises from the fact that, whether or not it is in the nature of things (and, in principle, possible) to predict the future from the past, it is plainly inconceivable that the requisite information about the past could be possessed and processed by any individual, more especially since the time available for such processing, if it were to give any useful answer, would be strictly limited.

Expectations that reach beyond the immediate threshold of the future or that concern themselves with any but the most direct physical effects of the proposed action must accordingly always be uncertain. This uncertainty is responsible for the whole difficulty that expectations bring into economic analysis; and it is the source of much the greater part of the difficulty arising in economics from considerations about *time*, under any of its aspects. Uncertainty of expectation gives rise to agreeable or disagreeable states of mind, and can thus have an economic valuation and enter directly into the play of economic influences. Indeed, it is itself one of the most powerful of such influences and explains the possibility of large-scale unemployment in a world of omnipresent scarcity. It is the chief explanation of the existence of rates of interest. A service is rendered to society by those who, by embarking their resources in enterprises looking to a distant future, expose themselves to uncertainty to an especial degree; and if, on the whole, the rendering of this service entails discomfort, some compensating hope of profit will be needed to elicit this service. Such a hope might not sustain itself in the minds of those concerned unless there were a record of some degree of fulfillment of these hopes.

The stereotype. The venture of forming economic expectations depends upon an extension of the stereotype from the plane of the physical and technical to that of the psychical, social, and historical. By "stereotype," we mean a fixed and stable pattern or configuration, composed of specific antecedent circumstances, or kinds of circumstance, and a specific sequel or end situation, or a specific train of consequences. By calling it stable, we mean that it occurs repetitively and can be frequently observed, or may even appear to be a universal and infrangible aspect of the natural order. It is upon such stereotypes (whether or not they have been combined into a larger, more general, and comprehensive system of knowledge) that all applied science or technology depends. When such stereotypes are used in isolation, they are rules of thumb. When combined into a great structure of interlocking ideas, they constitute a science or an art. In a bridge, the conformation, scantlings, and materials are together the source of strength; in a chemical process, the reaction is the consequence of juxtaposing certain substances under certain conditions of temperature and pressure; in biology a crossing of certain breeds may yield a predictable kind of offspring. When we look at events on a cosmical scale, the idea of the stereotype takes on a somewhat different aspect. If astronomers agree that the outer galaxies are receding from us, what is repeated is not their positions, as of planets in their orbits, but the recession at a given acceleration, that is, at a speed proportional to distance attained. Thus even an evolutionary, irreversible transformation can exhibit repetitiveness and the essence of the notion of the stereotype. It is when we come to events in the human and social sphere that the application of this tool, although still inescapable, becomes altogether more difficult and hazardous. Although Spengler (1918–1922), Toynbee (1934–1961), and Rostow (1960) have sought to demonstrate repetitiveness in history (as the only hope of making history a predictive science), still there are immense difficulties, dangers, and a widespread skepticism even (or perhaps especially) among historians.

These difficulties lead the businessman to distinguish two types of questions (Keirstead 1953): First, how will the general posture of affairs, describable by large aggregative statistical measurements such as the general level of prices, the monthly or annual expenditure of the community on all retail goods together or on goods of particular types, the percentage of the labor force unemployed, the rate of income tax or profits tax, and so on develop over the coming months or years? Second, what are the prospects for a particular enterprise—exactly specified as to the nature of its product; the type, design, and scale of its equipment; its location, marketing policy, research policy, management recruitment policy, and so on —given the particular industry's record of fast or slow innovation, its composition of many small or a few large firms, etc.? For his answer to the first of these questions, he may rely on a particularly simple form of that permanence or stability in the world of nature and of man upon which all possibility of prognostication depends—namely, on what we can alternatively call inertia or momentum in affairs. Cataclysmic change can occur: a crucial battle can be lost; a revolution can break out. But, save for such upheavals, some of the great public aggregates cannot change very abruptly. Governments and political parties are committed to certain policies and programs and could not abandon them without electoral disaster; thus, the budget may leave little room for choice. To a lesser degree, the same may apply, although for different reasons, to the investment policies of large firms and publicly owned industries. Government expenditure and the investment expenditure of business enterprises together account for a large part of the Keynesian multiplicand, which, with a Keynesian multiplier deriving its numerical value and its stability from the habitual or conventional behavior of large masses of people in electing what proportions of their incomes to spend and what to save, largely determines national prosperity or depression. Alongside such reliance on the present as an image of the near future, businessmen pay great heed to each other's opinions (Keynes 1937) without caring to explain to themselves how these can be better founded than their own.

Keynes (1936) has suggested the extreme mutability, fragility, and instability, with possible explosive or cumulative self-reinforcing consequences, that characterize such "conventional" opinions or assumptions about the future. Indeed, he paints a picture of the businessman's suppressed and latent desperation, his urge to clutch at straws, and thus, finally, to swing in behind any apparent coalescence of opinion or hint of leadership and turn it into a mass movement. The bear and bull markets of the stock exchanges have their rationale but can partake also of hysteria. Since it matters nothing to the speculator whether or not a rise in share prices has any basis in the genuine situation of the firm concerned, he needs only to know that bulls of the shares are more numerous, wealthy, or convinced than the bears; then he can safely join the bulls in their self-justifying operation, which itself drives up the price. The game of trying to guess what the other man is guessing, what he is guessing that you are guessing, and so on to the nth degree, is plainly unrelated to accounting facts or the real state of the economy and leads therefore to inherently restless markets, which generate movements out of nothing or next to nothing. Moreover, no speculative profit can be made in any market unless there is a *change* of opinion, bringing about a change of price; and there exists at all times, therefore, a motive for some speculators to set afloat ideas that will cause such changes of opinion. Genuine investment decisions in the economist's sense, that is, decisions by firms to order plant and equipment, are somewhat insulated from such speculative markets. But it is still true, as Keynes (1936, p. 151) indicates, that a firm that can acquire another firm as a going concern at a depressed stock exchange price may find this a more profitable use of its reserve funds than establishing a mint-new plant of its own. Such a choice tends, of course, to depress employment, unless the sellers of the shares use the proceeds themselves to order newly made equipment.

It was, at one time, common to speak of the "business cycle," meaning by this a repetition of alternate phases of increasing and decreasing prosperity, as measured by national general output or income, employment, the general level of prices, and so on. The record of the nineteenth century and early twentieth century seemed to show a length, from crest to crest or from trough to trough, of from 7 to 11 years. The amplitude of these fluctuations seemed to increase greatly after World War I and to disappear completely after World War II, being then replaced in the United States and Great Britain by a much shorter and milder cycle. At no time, however, could any such pattern have offered a sure guide to general business conditions for a number of years ahead. If there is a cyclical mechanism, its effect can be transformed or obliterated by the kind of extreme political and social upheavals that have occurred in our time. It has not been the experience of our generation that general history, in the large, can be foreseen.

It is in seeking an answer to the second type of question, concerning the prospects of a closely specified projected enterprise, that the businessman can more plausibly have recourse to stereotypes of business and investment situations. Such stereotypes will be quite distinct from case studies, although possibly founded on them. The stereotype will need to select and combine features from many such studies. The information a stereotype affords will be like that derived by a yachtsman about the likely performance of a sailing boat in a race, from a knowledge of the boat's design. This knowledge may tell him how the boat will perform in this set of conditions or in that set, but can, of course, tell him nothing as to which set will in fact prevail. Such stereotypes may be derived by what we may call a clinical method, that is, by so close an examination of a few particular instances, recorded or observed, that insight is gained into the precise interplay of policy and circumstance and a grasp of the reasons for success or failure in each case obtained; or they may be derived by a statistical method, where only the probabilities of success, in this and that degree, of each given design of enterprise is studied and no attempt is made to penetrate the mechanism or rationale of this success. Naturally, these methods can be combined.

Probability.   For an enterprise of given design, it will be natural to suppose that each distinct hypothetical degree of success will be associated with a different degree of probability. The pattern of association of these two variables, if statistically derived, will be expressed in a frequency table. If derived by some procedure of intuitive judgment, it will be expressed as a subjective probability distribution. We have to ask whether these two kinds of expression can, in practice, be so sharply distinguished. Many meanings have been proposed for the word "probability"; but these, for the most part, converge on the idea of recorded, or else po-

tential, relative frequency, that is to say, on the notion of the counting of cases. To say that a given outcome Q has a probability of $\frac{1}{6}$ is to say that if a trial or performance, the nature and circumstances of which lie within strictly stated bounds, is many times repeated, the result will be Q in approximately $\frac{1}{6}$ of the instances. Now when this trial or performance consists in tossing a coin or throwing dice, it may be easy to specify that the coin or dice must preserve their physical character exactly throughout the series of tosses and that each of these must be made by hand, in still air, etc. But what of the proposed setting-up of a business enterprise? The nature of the product; the type, design, and scale of the physical equipment; the location; and even the particular persons composing the initial cadre of directors and managers can no doubt be specified. The policy of the enterprise can be laid down in broad terms. But who can guarantee that the political, fiscal, social, commercial, fashionable, technological, and epistemic circumstances within which the enterprise will have to operate will remain unchanged? And if they change, what becomes of the meaning of probability? The relevance and applicability of any given statistical record of the past to the future experience of a new firm can be only a matter of judgment, that is, of conjecture, on the part of the enterpriser, since this relevance involves a double stretch of time in which the circumstances have evolved and will evolve further. Thus, in our context, there is no clear dividing line between statistical and subjective probability. But there are deeper questions.

Frequency ratios give us knowledge, namely, knowledge of the proportions in which the total list of individual results—one result for each of many repetitions of some kind of trial, a kind of trial exactly specified as to the range of permitted variation of its circumstances—have fallen under this or that head, or into this or that range of the variable whose values are the form taken by the results. This knowledge is applicable also to contemplated further repetitions of the same kind of trial, specified precisely as before. Let us call the complete list of contemplated further trials, considered as one whole, a *divisible experiment*. Then, a properly derived frequency table gives us knowledge of what will be the outcome of a divisible experiment, provided that experiment can in fact be performed. With a tossed coin or thrown dice, with any game sufficiently constrained by explicit rules, there is no question but that it can in fact be performed. But what of the establishment of a new business or a new plant? Here the tide of history itself is, willy nilly, changing some highly relevant circumstances all the time, rapidly or slowly. The question is whether the establishment of precisely this kind of business, in a given location and facing given conditions in the market for its product and in the market for its factors of production, can conceivably be repeated enough times before the whole scene has changed. If not, the statistical frequency table ceases to provide knowledge of what will happen and merely offers a tipster's suggestion of which horse is the most promising, on past form.

Potential surprise.   The enterpriser who tries to go beyond statistics and to gain insight into the conditions of success still needs a means of expressing a degree of solidity, of seriousness, which he adjudges to this and to that imagined (hypothetical) degree of success or of misfortune of some given project. The rival (mutually exclusive) suppositions that he makes concerning the degree of success of some project, when these suppositions are treated as values of one variable, need to be associated with values of a second variable that measures the strength of the claim of each supposition to be taken seriously. Such a measure is afforded by the notion of *subjective probability*, which is the formal husk of statistical probability filled with quite different content; or it is afforded, alternatively, by a concept differing essentially from that of probability not only in meaning but in form, namely, a measure of possibility. The actual occurrence of something that we had supposed impossible causes us surprise. Some surprise is caused by an occurrence that we had only with difficulty been able to think of as feasible. Thus, a measure of adjudged possibility, or rather of degree of difficulty in supposing a given outcome possible, is provided by the potential surprise (Shackle 1949; 1955; 1958; 1961) to which the individual is exposed by his attitude to that outcome. Subjective probability, on one hand, and possibility or potential surprise, on the other, may each be called an uncertainty variable. They differ radically in nature. Probabilities must be assigned, in effect, to a list of contingencies looked on as exhaustive and complete; or, if probability is expressed as probability density, the function connecting these densities with values of the outcome variable must be supposed to rest on exhaustive and stable analysis of the underlying conceivable outcome situations. Since the exhaustiveness of the list implies that the factual outcome, when it shall emerge, will necessarily be found in one or another of the contingencies of the list, the probability to be assigned to the list as a unified whole is the equivalent of *certainty*, represented by the

number 1. This probability is distributed over the listed contingencies in fractions that, therefore, sum to unity; and so the present writer calls subjective probability a distributional uncertainty variable. Possibility, or potential surprise, by contrast, can be assigned in mutually independent degrees to an indeterminate number of contingencies, the list of which, therefore, has no need to be looked on at any moment as complete. Potential surprise, measuring adjudged imperfection of possibility, is a nondistributional uncertainty variable. Methods of applying the two sorts of uncertainty variables must, like the nature of the variables themselves, differ radically.

Whereas a statistical frequency table can be applied directly, as it stands, to express the result of a divisible experiment, subjective probability, on the other hand, being concerned essentially with the outcome of a single, special, and nondivisible experiment, needs to be summarized to yield any usable message. This summary will take the form of a mathematical expectation, the result of multiplying each contingency (for example, each hypothetical amount of monetary profit) by its adjudged probability and adding together the results. Other moments of the distribution may also be used. The second moment, for example, indicates the dispersion of those "frequencies" that, although meaning little in the application of subjective probability as a guide to policy, are nonetheless the form in which the subjective probability judgments are expressed. The dispersion may be looked upon as a measure of the relevance, or lack of it, of the mathematical expectation. The doubtful relevance of any measure that seeks to average a collection of rival and mutually exclusive (that is, mutually contradictory) hypotheses is a chief reason for adopting the other type of uncertainty variable and using it as a basis of *focus values*. These are the two constrained maxima of a function that increases with the numerical size of supposed gain or loss and decreases with increase of the potential surprise associated with the various hypotheses. Such a function, or surface, may be visualized as follows. Imagine a seacoast where the straight shore line represents that degree of potential surprise corresponding to absolute rejection of hypotheses as impossible, while somewhat inland a line parallel to the shore represents zero potential surprise, the judgment that hypotheses are *perfectly* possible. A straight arm of the sea runs inland at right angles to the shore; and on either side of it near the sea, the sloping hillsides swing away to merge with those that front the sea. Sea level, along the shore edge and the central fiord, now stands for zero *ascendancy*, a zero degree of the "interestingness" of hypotheses, the power of any one imagined or hypothetical outcome of a contemplated action to arrest attention. Ascendancy will be nil for hypotheses adjudged impossible, and it will be nil, we are supposing, for those that mean no change in the decision maker's situation, these being the hypotheses represented by points along the central fiord. The greater the improvement or deterioration represented by any hypothetical outcome (the greater the distance from the central fiord), the more interesting, the more ascendant, or attention commanding, the hypothesis will be. But the more nearly impossible (the nearer the sea) it is, the *less* will be its ascendancy over the decision maker's mind. Now upon this landscape is superimposed a hill path, crossing the central fiord at its inland end, where potential surprise is nil, climbing on either hand across the bluffs where they swing round from the fiord to the sea, and descending again to sea level some little way along the coast. This path, in its shape in the *horizontal* plane, represents the adjudgment of potential surprise to diverse hypotheses of the outcome of some specified action. The highest altitudes attainable without quitting this path are the two constrained maxima of the ascendancy function, the *focus points* or, looked upon as purely scalar quantities of gain or loss, the *focus values* referred to above. A pair of focus values may be held to reconcile, as far as may be, the conflicting needs of the enterprisers' situation: to settle upon *one* policy or course of action in face of an essentially *plural* or uncertain vision of the consequences.

Uncertainty of expectation is not a contingent, curable disability from which human beings will some day be rescued by the advance of science. To suppose it would be like supposing that the physical horizon of the ocean can be brought nearer by sailing toward it. Frank Knight has said that consciousness itself involves uncertainty. This surely must be so. Consciousness is the continual apprehension of subjectively new things, circumstances, and conjunctures that were hitherto not known to exist or to be imminent. To know the future would destroy the possibility of this stream of continually fresh perceptions. But at a somewhat less basic level, we may say that uncertainty is the price of hope, and hope is the sustaining force of human endeavor. Who would exert himself if the result were a foregone conclusion? How could the result be a foregone conclusion if no one exerted himself? Uncertainty is the price of hope, for only by exposing ourselves to possible loss can we expose ourselves to possible gain. The practical question

is, How can this price be most explicitly, incisively, unmistakably expressed? How can it be made easy to judge and to grasp, so that a comparison can be made between what is paid in anxiety and what is gained in imagination of success? Can this best be done by throwing into the cauldron all the mutually contradictory hypotheses that the individual can think of, each multiplied by some subjective probability that apes the gestures but altogether lacks the meaning of statistical probability? Or can it be done in a more clear-cut fashion by setting clearly in view what the decision maker stands to lose by each given available choice of action? Both methods involve a judgment, a judgment, moreover, that by its nature quite escapes the categories, in P. W. Bridgman's sense, of "operational" or "nonoperational." If *measurement* were possible, there would be no need for judgment; moreover, each method involves giving some weight to two or more possibilities, only one of which can come true. We are here concerned with a once-for-all, nondivisible, experiment.

G. L. S. SHACKLE

[*See also* DECISION MAKING, *article on* ECONOMIC ASPECTS; PROBABILITY, *article on* INTERPRETATIONS.]

BIBLIOGRAPHY

ARROW, KENNETH J. 1951 Alternative Approaches to the Theory of Choice in Risk-taking Situations. *Econometrica* 19:404–437.
BOWMAN, MARY JEAN 1958 Introduction. Pages 1–10 in Social Science Research Council, Committee on Business Enterprise Research, *Expectations, Uncertainty and Business Behavior.* Edited by Mary Jean Bowman. New York: The Council.
CARTER, CHARLES F. 1950 Expectation in Economics. *Economic Journal* 60:92–105.
CARTER, CHARLES F. (1953) 1957 A Revised Theory of Expectations. Pages 50–59 in Charles F. Carter, G. P. Meredith, and G. L. S. Shackle (editors), *Uncertainty and Business Decisions.* 2d ed. Liverpool Univ. Press. → First published in Volume 63 of the *Economic Journal.*
CARTER, CHARLES F. 1957 The Present State of the Theory of Decisions Under Uncertainty. Pages 142–152 in Charles F. Carter, G. P. Meredith, and G. L. S. Shackle (editors), *Uncertainty and Business Decisions.* 2d ed. Liverpool Univ. Press.
COHEN, JOHN 1960 *Chance, Skill and Luck.* Harmondsworth (England): Penguin.
EDWARDS, WARD 1954 The Theory of Decision-making. *Psychological Bulletin* 51:380–417.
EGERTON, R. A. D. 1960 *Investment Decisions Under Uncertainty.* Liverpool Univ. Press.
GEORGESCU-ROEGEN, NICHOLAS 1958 The Nature of Expectation and Uncertainty. Pages 11–29 in Social Science Research Council, Committee on Business Enterprise Research, *Expectations, Uncertainty and Business Behavior.* Edited by Mary Jean Bowman. New York: The Council.
HART, ALBERT G. (1940) 1951 *Anticipations, Uncertainty and Dynamic Planning.* New York: Kelley.

JOUVENEL, BERTRAND DE 1964 *L'art de la conjecture.* Monaco: Editions du Rocher.

KEIRSTEAD, BURTON S. 1953 *An Essay in the Theory of Profits and Income Distribution.* Oxford: Blackwell.

KEYNES, JOHN MAYNARD 1936 *The General Theory of Employment, Interest and Money.* London: Macmillan. → A paperback edition was published in 1965 by Harcourt.

KEYNES, JOHN MAYNARD 1937 The General Theory of Employment. *Quarterly Journal of Economics* 51:209–223.

LACHMANN, LUDWIG M. 1959 Professor Shackle on the Economic Significance of Time. *Metroeconomica* 11:64–73.

MARSCHAK, JACOB 1950 Rational Behavior, Uncertain Prospects and Measurable Utility. *Econometrica* 18:111–141.

MEREDITH, G. PATRICK 1957 Methodological Considerations in the Study of Human Anticipation. Pages 37–49 in Charles F. Carter, G. P. Meredith, and G. L. S. Shackle (editors), *Uncertainty and Business Decisions.* 2d ed. Liverpool Univ. Press.

NIEHANS, JÜRG 1959 Reflections on Shackle, Probability and Our Uncertainty About Uncertainty. *Metroeconomica* 11:74–88.

ROSTOW, WALT W. (1960) 1963 *The Stages of Economic Growth: A Non-Communist Manifesto.* Cambridge Univ. Press.

SHACKLE, G. L. S. (1949) 1952 *Expectation in Economics.* 2d ed. Cambridge Univ. Press.

SHACKLE, G. L. S. 1955 *Uncertainty in Economics and Other Reflections.* Cambridge Univ. Press.

SHACKLE, G. L. S. 1958 *Time in Economics.* Amsterdam: North-Holland Publishing.

SHACKLE, G. L. S. 1961 *Decision, Order and Time in Human Affairs.* Cambridge Univ. Press.

SPENGLER, OSWALD (1918–1922) 1926–1928 *The Decline of the West.* 2 vols. Authorized translation with notes by Charles F. Atkinson. New York: Knopf. → Volume 1: *Form and Actuality.* Volume 2: *Perspectives of World History.* First published as *Der Untergang des Abendlandes.*

TOYNBEE, ARNOLD J. 1934–1961 *A Study of History.* 12 vols. Oxford Univ. Press.

WATKINS, J. W. N. (1955) 1957 Decisions and Uncertainty. Pages 107–121 in Charles F. Carter, G. P. Meredith, and G. L. S. Shackle (editors), *Uncertainty and Business Decisions.* 2d ed. Liverpool Univ. Press.

WECKSTEIN, RICHARD S. 1952–1953 On the Use of the Theory of Probability in Economics. *Review of Economic Studies* 20:191–198.

ECONOMIC FORECASTING

See PREDICTION AND FORECASTING, ECONOMIC. *Related material may be found under* TIME SERIES.

ECONOMIC GROWTH

The articles under this heading give several views of the process of economic growth as a whole. For the role of specific factors in economic growth, see CAPITAL; CAPITAL, HUMAN; CAPITAL, SOCIAL OVERHEAD; *and* INNOVATION. *On the role of productivity in economic growth, see* PRODUCTIVITY *and* AGRICULTURE, *article on* PRODUCTIVITY AND TECHNOLOGY. *Related material may be found under* DEVELOPMENT BANKS; ECONOMY, DUAL; FOREIGN AID, *article on* ECONOMIC ASPECTS; INDUSTRIALIZATION; INDUSTRY, SMALL; MODERNIZATION; *and* PLANNING, ECONOMIC, *article on* DEVELOPMENT PLANNING.

I. OVERVIEW   *Richard A. Easterlin*
II. THEORY   *Gustav Ranis*
III. MATHEMATICAL THEORY   *Michio Morishima*
IV. NONECONOMIC ASPECTS   *Bert F. Hoselitz*

I

OVERVIEW

As a distinctive epoch in economic organization, modern economic growth, or development, dates from the eighteenth century, when its beginnings in western Europe can first clearly be discerned. It may be defined as a rapid and sustained rise in real output per head and attendant shifts in the technological, economic, and demographic characteristics of a society. Together with the more recent concepts of social development and political development, it forms the phenomenon historians designate "modernization," which embraces innovation in numerous aspects of individual behavior and social organization. Although not a revolution in the literal sense of the word, modern economic growth merits recognition as a distinctive epoch by virtue of the scope of the changes associated with it, the irreversible nature of many of them, and the unprecedented rate at which they have occurred. It seems safe to say that in those economies now characterized as "developed," most of the population has experienced in the last one hundred years a greater advance in material well-being and a more sweeping change in way of life than occurred in any previous century of human history.

This transformation encompasses wide-ranging changes in techniques of producing, transporting, and distributing goods, in the scale and organization of productive activities, and in types of outputs and inputs. It embraces major shifts in the industrial, occupational, and spatial distribution of productive resources and in the degree of exchange basis and monetization of the economy. On the social and demographic side it involves significant alterations in fertility, mortality, and migration, in place of residence, in family size and structure, in the educational system, and in provision for public health. Its influence extends into the areas of income distribution, class structure, government organization, and political structure.

Compared with previous epochs, modern economic growth has involved marked acceleration in the rate of social change generally—so great that it frequently creates a significant difference in the experience of only two successive generations. The rate of growth has varied substantially, however, among different economies undergoing development at a given time and within a given economy over time. Attempts to distinguish phases of modern economic growth, to classify types, and to identify sequences between economic and non-economic characteristics or among different economic aspects are still at at an early stage, but some suggestive generalizations have been advanced.

From the viewpoint of the world as a whole, the international spread of modern economic growth has so far been limited, although few parts of the world have remained untouched. While the pattern of diffusion in time and space has yet to be established with quantitative precision and partly depends on how widely the process is conceived, the picture in broad outline is as follows. Elements of the transformation become increasingly apparent when one examines parts of northwestern Europe in the eighteenth century, especially, on a fairly extensive scale, in Great Britain. In the course of the nineteenth century, as the process gathered increasing headway in the area of origin, its gradual diffusion southward and eastward throughout Europe occurred. By the end of the century, aspects of its beginnings could be identified in easternmost Europe, including Russia, and also in Japan. A somewhat similar development had been taking place concurrently in overseas areas settled by Europeans, mirroring to some extent the diffusion pattern within Europe. It was apparent first in areas initially settled chiefly by migrants from northwestern Europe—the United States in the first part of the nineteenth century, followed by Canada, Australia, and New Zealand—and subsequently in parts of Latin America, where migration from southern and eastern Europe was especially important. In the twentieth century, and increasingly since World War II, the initial signs have become more widespread in parts of Asia and, to a smaller extent, Africa—perhaps most noticeably in areas with the longest and fullest contact with some of the original centers. However, by the middle of the twentieth century, for only about a fourth of the world's population has the transformation proceeded far enough for them to qualify as "developed" by most of the usual indicators.

The appearance and spread of modern economic development sharply accelerated the trend toward wider international contacts, which had been set in motion several centuries earlier by the great voyages of discovery. The peoples of the world have come increasingly to be linked together in a mutually interdependent system of economic and political relations and through new communications networks furthering the flow of information. At the same time, the piecemeal character of the diffusion process has sharply aggravated international differences in economic, social, and political conditions, has repeatedly disturbed the balance of political power both between developing and underdeveloped areas and within the developing group, and has become a major factor in modern wars. In a fundamental sense, modern economic growth is a creature of the scientific revolution, for it reflects man's growing knowledge of natural phenomena and the power thereby attained to mold his environment to his needs. Whether it will prove possible to contain the disruptive effects of its spread within a framework of nation-states would seem ultimately to depend on whether progress in social science can match that in natural science.

Characteristics of modern economic growth

It is possible to identify a number of recurrent features of modern economic growth if one draws on both the historical experience of now-developed nations and comparisons of countries at different levels of development at a given time. However, the latter comparisons, which are frequently resorted to in lieu of sufficient historical data or research, are not always trustworthy guides to changes over time. The "nation" is adopted here as the unit of economic growth because although there are significant growth differentials among regions within a nation, they are substantially less than those among nations. Moreover, the central government plays an important role in decisions affecting secular growth. The present summary emphasizes similarities, both between countries with different institutional conditions, such as the degree of central planning, and between the current experience of today's less-developed nations and the earlier experience of the now-developed countries. It emphasizes further the contrast between premodern conditions and those characterizing modern economic growth. Only brief reference will be possible to differences in the experience of individual nations and variations in trends from one period to another within a given country, although such differences are sometimes substantial.

Production. From the viewpoint of the economic system as a whole, the central feature of modern economic growth is an immense and continuous rise in the yield from human economic activity. This is reflected in the long-term growth rates of output per head of the total population shown in Table 1. For most of the countries listed, the rate has averaged from 13 to 19 per cent per decade. Such rates, continued throughout a century, imply an expansion of product per capita between 3.4-fold and 5.7-fold. For Sweden, Japan, and the Soviet Union, which have sustained average rates on the order of 26 to 28 per cent per decade for five decades or more, the multiplication in a century would exceed 10-fold.

Table 1 — *Average rate of growth of real product per capita in developed countries for long periods up to about 1960*

	Period (in years)*	Per cent change in real product per capita per decade
England and Wales (later U.K.)		
1780 to 1881	101	13.4
1855–1859 to 1957–1959	101	14.1
France		
1841–1850 to 1960–1962	105.5	17.9
Germany (later F.R.G.)		
1871–1875 to 1960–1962	88	17.9
Netherlands		
1900–1904 to 1960–1962	59	13.5
Belgium		
1880 to 1960–1962	81	14.8
Switzerland		
1890–1899 to 1957–1959	63.5	16.1
Denmark		
1870–1874 to 1960–1962	89	19.4
Norway		
1865–1874 to 1960–1962	91.5	19.0
Sweden		
1861–1865 to 1960–1962	98	28.3
Italy		
1898–1902 to 1960–1962	61	18.7
United States		
1839 to 1960–1962	122	17.2
Canada		
1870–1874 to 1960–1962	89	18.1
Australia		
1861–1865 to 1959/1960–1961/1962	97.5	8.0
Japan		
1879–1881 to 1959–1961	80	26.4
European Russia (later U.S.S.R.)		
1860–1913	53	14.4
1913–1958	45	27.4

* Calculated from midpoints.

Source: Kuznets 1966.

It should be recognized that any summary measure, such as real national product per capita, reflects certain value judgments and that, consequently, levels or rates of development cannot be measured with the scientific precision of, say, steel output. For example, centrally planned economies would confine such a measure of aggregate output to material production. The concept of economic growth is itself a subjective one to some extent. However, almost any reasonably comprehensive measure would show comparably immense productivity growth, largely because requirements for such elementary goods as food, clothing, and shelter continue to take up such a large proportion of economic endeavor.

The rates shown are averages for half a century or more. For shorter periods much higher and also much lower rates have prevailed; this reflects a second characteristic of modern economic growth, significant variability in the growth rate over time. Wide fluctuations in output growth also occur in premodern economies, primarily in connection with the vagaries of agricultural conditions. In developing economies, however, the nonagricultural sector becomes increasingly responsible for fluctuations. The movements in centrally planned economies have so far received relatively little study. In noncentrally planned economies the most fully analyzed movement is the "business cycle," which has typically averaged 3 to 4 years in duration. Longer-term movements for which some regularity is said to exist are "major cycles" (Juglar cycles), of approximately 7 years' duration; "long swings" (Kuznets cycles), ranging from approximately 10 to 30 years in duration; and "long waves" (Kondratieff cycles), of approximately 50 years in duration. Although these longer-term movements have not found general acceptance among economists, they serve to emphasize the high variability that has been observed in growth rates over periods of a decade or two, making inferences regarding secular trends from data confined to such limited periods quite hazardous.

The trend in output per head cannot be attributed to a corresponding rise in labor input per head of the population. It is generally true that in now-developed nations the proportion of the population in the labor force is higher than in the premodern period, chiefly because the proportion of the population of working age has risen as fertility has declined. But this has been more than offset by a decline in the average hours worked per year, so that, on balance, the man-hour input per head of the total population has usually declined somewhat.

More plausible factors in the rise of output per head are capital input and average education per worker. Certainly the rises in these are among the most striking trends in modern economic growth. Although precise evidence is lacking, the expansion in the per-worker stock of reproducible capital (primarily structures and equipment) has involved orders of magnitude comparable to that of expansion in output per worker. With regard to education, modern economic growth has been accompanied by the virtual elimination of illiteracy, a trend toward universal primary and, subsequently, secondary school education, and a rise in college enrollments. The quality of the labor input has been further enhanced by substantial advances in the nutrition and health of the labor force.

Nevertheless, when one considers the nature of premodern methods of production, it seems doubtful that greater capital, education, and other quality inputs per worker, within the framework of that rudimentary technology, would have yielded the immense and continuing rates of productivity improvement characterizing modern growth.

Technological innovation. The fundamental basis for this productivity growth has been technological innovation on a widespread and continuous scale. Indeed, the concrete nature of the technological developments helps explain the changing nature of the economic inputs, as well as a number of other trends accompanying modern economic growth.

Although the great variety of these innovations makes a summary description difficult, it is possible, nevertheless, to identify a few general features that usually distinguish modern from premodern methods. Specifically, the use of methods involving mechanization and high-energy inputs per worker and the associated shift toward a mineral-based economy especially set off many modern techniques. Large and carefully controlled volumes of energy are applied to productive processes, drawing on mineral sources such as coal, petroleum, and natural gas; in contrast, premodern energy inputs, deriving largely from human, animal, wood, wind, and water sources, are much smaller and more erratic. Intimately associated with the energy changes are the shift from hand tools to machine processes and wider use of physical-structure materials derived from ferrous and nonferrous minerals rather than forests or agriculture. With the resort to machine production, final products become more standardized; labor becomes much more specialized, both by industry and, within enterprises in an industry, by process. A corresponding proliferation of detailed industrial and occupational classifications occurs.

Effective use of modern techniques entails a number of corollaries. Because of technological indivisibilities, optimum scales of production become greater. In manufacturing, this means that production tends to be organized in factory establishments, employing large numbers of workers and producing far in excess of local requirements,

rather than in small shops involving few hands and producing largely for local consumption.

Optimal locations too are affected by the more advanced techniques. With regard to raw materials, minerals are substantially less ubiquitously distributed than forest and agricultural materials, and differentials with regard to the efficiency of different locations, particularly with regard to energy materials, are thereby heightened. On the side of markets, because production so greatly exceeds the needs of those immediately engaged, existing population centers offering concentrated markets become increasingly attractive. Transport junctions providing ready access to markets and/or materials also become more advantageous. The resulting differential advantage of certain locations, where one or more such factors is particularly favorable, leads to geographic concentration of production and urbanization. This tendency is reinforced up to a point by external, or "agglomeration," economies.

Even these limited observations clarify some of the trends in the industrial and occupational characteristics of the labor force during modern economic growth. Associated with the growth in specialization of labor by industry, task, and location in the production of commodities is an increasing need for transportation of these commodities and for internal trade generally—and, in turn, for increasing monetization of the economy to facilitate the manifold growth of transactions. A rise is observed in the proportion of the labor force specialized, not in the direct production of tangible commodities or final services but in ancillary activities, such as moving, storing, and distributing goods. Associated with the growth of scale is a growing need for labor in control functions—in administrative and clerical jobs—as problems of coordination of processes and of plant layout multiply. (Even in direct production itself, the worker's function increasingly becomes one of control, the tending of a machine.) A premodern economy could not spare such a large proportion of specialized workers for continuous employment outside direct production; a developing economy not only can, but apparently must, at least to a substantial extent. Thus the trends in industrial and occupational structure of a developing economy testify both to the distinctiveness and immense productivity of the underlying technological innovations, for they show that the methods employed both require and permit a substantial proportion of labor to be engaged in activities other than direct production. [*See* INDUSTRIALIZATION.]

The nature of the underlying technological developments also helps explain the previously mentioned trends in economic inputs. The growth of machine production and scale calls for much more capital investment per worker, both in equipment and (particularly) structures to house production. Transportation and power needs have major capital requirements, as does the need for workers' accommodations where new locations are developed. Similarly, the much greater complexity of production requires a better educated labor force to learn and execute the new techniques. The continuous change characterizing modern economic growth (in techniques, locations, types of goods and jobs) calls for qualities of adaptability and adjustment on the part of labor which education facilitates.

These brief remarks on energy and mechanization as leading technological features of a developed economy do not do justice to the immense number of detailed changes implied by such characteristics or to the variety of other technological advances that have taken place, such as scientific hybridization, chemicals and plastics, electronic communications and controls, scientific management, and the supermarket, to mention only a few. Nevertheless, they do suggest the underlying logic of some of the principal trends in economic organization characterizing modern economic development.

Consumption.   The rise in output per man-hour implies a similar trend in real income per member of the population, although in part, as was noted, the benefits of higher productivity are taken in the form of more leisure per worker. The specific implications of this rise in real income for the condition of the population would best be revealed by level of living indicators, if they were available, such as per capita calorie consumption, the starchy-staple ratio, persons per room, per cent of dwellings with piped water and flush toilets, various household electrical appliances per capita, physicians and hospital beds per capita, school enrollment ratios, and newspaper circulation and cinema attendance per capita. Suffice it to say that modern economic development in general has meant an unprecedented advance for most of the population in food, clothing, shelter, household furnishings, and health, education, and recreational services—to the extent that dire conditions such as malnutrition have virtually been eliminated.

The foregoing statement refers to absolute levels. When one turns to relative magnitudes, to the proportionate distribution of the end product of the economy, the trends are less clear-cut. This is partly because variations among countries in the institutional conditions governing resource allocation cause differences in the uses to which the

higher productivity accompanying modern economic growth is put. One well-established allocative trend is a rise in the share of the gross national product devoted to gross capital formation, attributable to the capital requirements of modern growth. A second is a decline in the proportion of consumption expenditure devoted to food. This development, rooted in the structure of consumer preferences, plays an important part in the decline in the relative importance of agriculture during economic growth, one of the most characteristic and pervasive trends. A third is a rise in the proportionate importance of new or modern goods relative to that of traditional items of consumption, reflecting the impact of technological progress in the consumption sphere. It is an interesting speculation that whereas much of the substantive increase in the early phases of modern economic growth takes the form of food, clothing, and shelter, at a more advanced phase much of the change is connected with the automobile and the way of life associated with it.

Income distribution.   It is obvious that such massive changes in industrial, occupational, and spatial distribution, and in the relative proportions of factor inputs must leave their imprint on the income distribution of a society, for not all segments of the population would be equally motivated or equipped to pursue the new opportunities. Generalizations about trends, however, are frustrated by a serious lack of data and the fact that institutional differences intervene in this area to such an extent that even the concept of income shares sometimes differs among countries. Two statements, based almost entirely on fragmentary data for a few noncentrally planned economies in this century, may be ventured. One is that the return per unit of labor has risen relative to that of capital, offsetting a contrary movement in the relative factor quantities. As a result, changes in the relative income shares of labor and property have been confined within fairly small limits. The second is that income inequality has on balance tended to lessen. This is suggested both by direct observations on the size distribution of income and by scattered data on income-per-worker differences by industry, occupation, and/or region. There is some indication that this trend has chiefly involved an increase in the share of middle-income groups at the expense of upper and thus is partly bound up with the growing importance of a "middle class" during modern economic growth. [*See* INCOME DISTRIBUTION.]

External trade.   Modern economic growth has brought with it a vast expansion in the absolute volume of a nation's international trade. Indeed, for most developed nations it has involved a greater relative rise in international trade than of GNP, despite the unprecedented growth rate of the latter (although this trend has been somewhat reversed in the twentieth century). Economies not experiencing a relative rise in international trade are those centrally planned economies which have sharply restricted participation in international trade through autarkic policies and some of the overseas countries settled by Europe where trade played a major role even in the premodern period.

Social and political changes. The movement from relatively high to low levels in mortality and fertility associated with modern economic growth has been so pronounced that it merits the distinctive title "demographic transition." The mortality decline, which typically precedes that in fertility, has been most marked among (although not confined to) younger age groups, particularly infants. Life expectancy at birth in developed nations is now in the vicinity of seventy years, compared with a premodern figure of thirty to forty years. The major pestilential diseases (smallpox, the plague, cholera, yellow fever, typhoid, and typhus) have largely been eliminated, and, more recently, mortality from infectious and parasitic diseases, such as tuberculosis, pneumonia, and dysentery, has been drastically reduced. The principal causes of death in developed economies today are chronic and degenerative illnesses (heart disease, cancer, accidents, and so on). The mortality movement is bound up in part with the improved living levels of the population, for example, improved nutrition, which strengthens resistance to disease. It is due also and increasingly, however, to important advances in medical knowledge and significant innovations in the sphere of public health.

In a developed economy women usually marry later and bear fewer children—typically those surviving to the end of childbearing age will have averaged two to three births versus four to six for women in the premodern period. The reduction in the birth rate appears partly attributable to the decline in infant mortality, since to achieve a given number of surviving children, a smaller number of births is needed. From the viewpoint of females' time required in childbearing and care, reproduction, in the significant sense of surviving descendants, becomes, like economic production, a more efficient process during modern economic growth.

The "dependency burden," the ratio of dependent children and elderly persons to those in prime working ages (say, from 15 to 59 years) usually declines in the course of development. This is due to

a reduction in the proportion of children in the population as fertility declines; the proportion of elderly persons actually rises somewhat. The number of persons per household also declines. In part this reflects the lower ratio of children to adults; in part it is due to the progressive decline of two-generation or three-generation family units during economic growth.

As has already been noted, economic growth is marked by a progressive shift of population from rural to urban areas. The basic impetus for this arises from the impact of technological change on the spatial distribution of given industries, but it is significantly reinforced by the shift in final consumption patterns which favors the growth of non-agricultural industry relative to agriculture. The growth of urban centers necessitates a substantial redistribution of population through internal migration. [See LABOR FORCE, *article on* MARKETS AND MOBILITY.]

These changes in population characteristics have, in turn, influenced the trends in final products. The reduction in household size and the aging of the population have altered final demands. The effect of the shift to urban locations is apparent in the upward trend in consumer expenditures on a number of predominantly urban services—transportation, communication, personal services, and recreation.

In addition, the trend toward urbanization, and the consequent need for public municipal services, is one of the factors responsible for an increase in the relative size of government during modern economic growth, even in noncentrally planned economies. More generally, in these economies an expansion tends to occur in public expenditure on "social" purposes (education, health, social security, housing, recreation) and "economic" purposes (agriculture, mineral resources, fuel and power, transport, roads, and so on). The size of the central government usually tends to rise relative to that of local governments, partly because of the growing complexity and integration of the economy. With regard to revenue sources, direct taxes, particularly individual income taxes, usually grow in importance relative to indirect levies, such as excise taxes and foreign trade duties. [See TAXATION.]

The trends characterizing modern economic growth significantly alter the economic bases of class differences and political power. In noncentrally planned economies, for example, there has been a marked rise in the proportion of employees in the labor force and a diminution of self-employed workers. In part this is associated with the shift in the industrial structure of the labor force toward nonagricultural activity, since the latter is characterized by a substantially higher proportion of employees to self-employed workers than is agriculture. In part, however, it reflects a trend within the nonagricultural sector in favor of employees, due to the growth of factory relative to handicraft operations. Another pertinent change has been the rise in white-collar employment relative to manual labor, an influence strengthening "middle class" tendencies. Still another has been the drastic decline in the relative economic importance of agriculture, which has weakened the political importance of this sector. Such "noneconomic" repercussions of modern economic growth have, in turn, had feedback effects on the growth process through the types of social attitudes and political measures that have ensued.

Patterns and types of economic growth. The time shape of these various trends is by no means uniform among the different characteristics. Moreover, shorter-run changes through time may show significant departures from the underlying trend over lengthy intervals, because of fluctuations such as those mentioned earlier or other factors.

A number of the changes are, however, subject to a distinct upper or lower limit, such as the rise in urbanization, literacy, and nonagricultural activity. As might be expected, for such characteristics the basic secular trend exhibits a logistic pattern, that is, initially change occurs at a slow rate, then at an accelerating one, and finally, as it approaches the limit more closely, at a decelerating one. Even with regard to narrowly defined categories of commodities or industries, where no comparable logical limit exists, evidence has been advanced to show the existence of a secular pattern of acceleration followed by retardation. Among other factors, the nature of technological change has been accorded an important role in accounting for this—in part because technological progress within a narrowly defined industry appears to slow down after a time, in part because technological developments in new commodities and industries create opportunities competing with the older ones. The latter point helps to reconcile the seemingly contradictory observation that growth in the economy-wide level of output per man-hour does not show retardation.

It has already been suggested that noticeable differences between countries sometimes exist in the pattern for a given variable or in the relationships among two or more variables. This may be illustrated by reference to demographic phenomena, where the currently available documentation is in some respects fullest, especially for the premodern period. A shift from early to late marriage occurred in many western European areas well before the eighteenth century, and in a number of these a mild reversal, a decline in age at marriage, occurred in conjunction with economic advance in the nineteenth and twentieth centuries. In eastern Europe, on the other hand, early marriage persisted in many areas through the 1930s despite other developmental changes. With reference to the demographic transition, it appears that fertility began to decline in some European areas prior to or simultaneously with the mortality decline. Recent declines in mortality appear typically to be sharper and more rapid than earlier ones. An important issue, which can only be noted here, is to what extent differences such as these tend to vary systematically between early comers and late comers to the growth process.

To turn from individual aspects of modern economic growth to the process viewed as a whole, we must examine whether it is possible to distinguish regular phases or periods in the process and whether the experience of various countries can be classified in terms of different growth "types." For example, one stage-scheme that has been proposed identifies five phases: traditional society, preconditions for take-off, take-off, drive to maturity, and age of high mass consumption (Rostow 1963). Another recent typology, proposed by Hoselitz, employs a threefold classification of growth: (1) expansionist versus intrinsic, depending on the degree to which unused land and other resources are available; (2) dominant versus satellitic, depending on the importance of foreign trade in the economy; and (3) autonomous versus induced, based on the degree of central planning (Conference . . . 1959). One advantage of the proposed stage conception is that it highlights the fact that modern economic growth is characterized by a substantial acceleration in the pace of social change. Moreover, its emphasis on the take-off as a point of transition to "self-sustaining" growth underscores a fundamental aspect of some of the changes, namely, that they are largely irreversible. Similarly, the suggested typology brings to the fore certain factors—the absolute size of the economy, the nature of the decision-making processes—influencing the growth process. On the other hand, attempts to apply such schemes in their specific form to interpretation of actual experience have encountered important difficulties. Although they are suggestive with regard to some of the causal mechanisms or factors underlying modern economic growth, the use of such concepts as valid generalizations about stages or types of growth seems premature in view of the

Table 2 — Crude death rate per thousand of total population, selected areas, since 1750 or earliest known date thereafter

	England and Wales	United States	Germany (later F.R.G.)	Italy	Russia (later U.S.S.R.)	Japan	Chile	India	Africa
About 1750	32								
About 1800	25	25							
About 1850	23	23[a]	27	31[b]	40		35		
1900–1909	15	16	19	22	30	21[d]	32	43	
1930–1939	12	11	11	14	18[c]	18	24	31	30–35[c]
1955–1959	12	9	11	10	8	8	14	20	27

a. 1870–1880.
b. 1861–1870.
c. 1937.
d. 1905–1909; probably an underestimate.

Principal sources: Demographic Yearbook; Population Bulletin of the United Nations; Kuznets 1966.

limited extent to which the facts of growth have so far been established and runs the danger of tending to strait-jacket thinking on the subject.

International spread of economic growth

Ideally, a description of the world-wide diffusion process would be built on a number of time series of growth characteristics for each of the countries of the world since around 1750. Lacking this, principal reliance is placed here on a few characteristics of what are taken as fairly representative situations in different parts of the world—although availability of data has played a part too in the choice of series and areas. In keeping with the approach adopted here, economic growth is viewed as one facet of modernization more generally conceived. Two indicators of social development are used, the crude death rate and school enrollment rate, and two of economic development, nonagricultural share of the labor force and the growth rate of GNP per capita. Although the measures are crude—for example, variations in the age distribution of population in time and space impair the comparability of death or school enrollment rates—as a whole they produce a reasonably consistent picture.

Typically, economic historians trace the origin of modern economic development to eighteenth-century England, and in particular to the industrial revolution. By the latter is meant, in part, the commercial application of Watt's steam engine and certain innovations in the iron and textile industries over the period from around 1730 to 1820, especially the latter half. From England, the industrial revolution is viewed as having diffused gradually, first to neighboring European nations and England's overseas descendants and then to some further nations, although the latter aspect of the picture becomes increasingly blurred. The description presented is qualitative in nature, although approximate periods of an industrial revolution are identified for some of the now-developed nations.

Indicators of modernization provide a broader picture, of which the economic forms a reasonably consistent part. Tables 2, 3, and 4 reflect, respectively, the diffusion of modern mortality conditions, education, and industrialization; each tells a fairly similar story. For this purpose, a useful way of forming impressions is to compare the dates at which countries reach a crude death rate of 30 per thousand, a school enrollment rate of 10 per cent

Table 3 — Estimated percentage of total population of all ages enrolled in school, selected areas, since 1818 or earliest known date thereafter

	England and Wales	United States	Germany (later F.R.G.)	Italy	Russia (later U.S.S.R.)	Japan	Chile	India	Nigeria
1818	6								
1830	9	15	17	3					
1850	12	18	16	b	2	4[c]			
1887	16	22	18	11	3	7	4	2	
1928[a]	16	24	17	11	12	13	15[d]	4	1[d]
1954[a]	15	22	13	13	15	23	18	7	5

a. Values for 1954 (and, to some extent, for 1928) for the most-developed countries are biased downward relative to those for other times and places, because of decline in ratio of school age to total population.
b. Not available.
c. Around 1870.
d. 1938.

Source: Easterlin 1965.

Table 4 — Percentage of labor force in nonagricultural activity, selected areas, since 1700 or earliest known date thereafter

	England and Wales	United States	Germany (later F.R.G.)	Italy	Russia (later U.S.S.R.)	Japan	Chile	India	Africa
1700–1775	55–60[a]								
1801	65 (68[a])	28[b]							
1841	77	31							
About 1870–1880	85	50	58	38		17			
About 1900	91	63	65	41	25	30		28	
About 1925	93	76	70	48	29	49	61	25	
About 1935	94	80	72	52	c	54	63	c	
About 1950–1960	95	91	77	59	60	67	70	27	26

a. Share of nonagricultural activity in national product.
b. 1820.
c. Not available.

Principal sources: Kuznets 1957; 1966.

of the population, and a percentage of labor force in nonagricultural industry of around 30. England tended to be the leader, with major changes usually discernible in the eighteenth century. Within Europe, Germany, a representative of northern and western Europe, was well on the road by the middle of the nineteenth century, followed with some lag by Italy, a representative of southern Europe, and, somewhat later still, Russia, a representative of eastern Europe.

In the overseas areas settled by Europe, modernization was well under way in the United States in the first half of the nineteenth century. Canada, Australia, and New Zealand, if data were shown, would probably lag somewhat, although not a great deal. The series for Chile show signs of modernization in the early twentieth century. As a representative of Latin America, Chile has been in the vanguard, rather than near the average, and has been at least several decades ahead of Latin American nations with substantial Indian populations. (Also, Chile's position with regard to the share of the labor force in nonagricultural activity has been disproportionately high compared to most countries in this area.) In general, modernization in overseas countries populated chiefly by settlers from north-

ern and western Europe preceded that in Latin America, whose settlers originated primarily in southern Europe. Thus the New World pattern reflects to some extent the diffusion pattern within Europe itself.

In Asia and Africa, indications of modernization were apparent in Japan in the latter part of the nineteenth century and in the Union of South Africa in the early twentieth; but these are noticeable exceptions, at least as far as indexes of economic development are concerned. Typically, these indexes show relatively little evidence of modern economic growth in these continents. With regard to social development, however, the indicators for India, a country reasonably representative of changes in Asia, do suggest that elements of modernization have been occurring in the course of the twentieth century, and even the fragmentary data for Africa show some signs of this since the 1930s. Nations of northern Africa would probably tend to be somewhat ahead of the sub-Saharan countries and more like India in timing.

A table in a form comparable to the preceding ones, showing levels of real product per capita at various dates, would shed valuable light on trends in the relative standing of nations and the extent

Table 5 — Per cent per decade growth rate of real gross national product per capita, selected areas, since 1700 or earliest known period thereafter

	England and Wales	United States	Germany (later F.R.G.)	Italy	Russia (later U.S.S.R.)	Japan	Latin America	India[a]
1700–1780	2.0							
1780–1841	13.5							
1841–1881	13.3	16.2	9.2[b]	−0.8[c]				
1881–1913	17.4	16.9	18.1	9.1	14.4[d]	24.3		4
1913–1960	15.5	18.0	17.4	17.4	27.4	27.9		5
1927–1960	14.1	17.3	23.7	22.1	e	26.0	18.8	5

a. Periods are, in order, 1857–1863 to 1896–1904, 1896–1904 to 1946–1954, and 1937–1940 to 1959–1962.
b. 1851–1855 to 1871–1875.
c. 1862–1868 to 1874–1883.
d. 1860 to 1913.
e. Not available.

Principal sources: Kuznets 1964a; 1966.

of the gaps between them. Although sufficient data are not presently available for this, enough information can be secured on rates of growth to at least check some of the impressions so far obtained (Table 5). For those developed nations where rates are available over a long enough period, a noticeable rise to modern growth-rate levels is usually apparent at a time consistent with the previous tables. On the other hand, for India, the one less-developed area shown here with a reasonably long time series, the growth rate remains at a relatively low level, a picture consistent with that relating to the nonagricultural share of the labor force.

Since the social development indicators do suggest the gradual spread in the twentieth century of elements of modernization to less-developed areas in Asia and Africa, it is of interest to look at their most recent experience. Estimates of the rates of change, converted to a per decade basis, of product per capita in these areas (available only for noncommunist countries) for 1957/1958 to 1963/1964 are given in Table 6. There is perhaps a suggestion here of an increase in the rates for these areas compared to experience prior to World War II, although the earlier observation regarding variability of growth rates over time cautions against placing excessive confidence in interpretation of such rates as secular ones. Some support for this inference, however, is provided by data on capital formation, which show a noticeable rise since the pre-World War II period in the proportion of resources devoted to this purpose in underdeveloped countries.

Table 6

	Per cent
All noncommunist countries	25
Less-developed areas only	23
India	21
Africa*	11

* Not including Algeria, Congo (Leopoldville), and Republic of South Africa.

Source: U.S. Agency for International Development.

Effect on international disparities. One consequence of the uneven spread of modernization has been the creation of wide differences in various economic and social conditions among nations at any given time. Tables 2 through 5 shed light on the size and trend of such differences. The pattern for mortality and school enrollment rates is rather similar. In the century or so up to, say, World War I, international differences widened markedly as rapid improvement occurred in Europe, northern America, and Oceania, and relatively little in Asia, Africa, and Latin America. Since then, and particu-

larly after World War II, as advances in the former group slowed down and those in the latter accelerated, differences have narrowed noticeably, most markedly in mortality conditions.

There is little indication in the economic development indicators, however, of a lessening of differences. On the contrary, Table 4 suggests that the gap in the percentage of labor force in nonagricultural activity has continued to widen. With regard to GNP per capita, it can also be inferred, despite the limited data, that relative levels have continued to diverge. Today's developed countries, considered as a bloc, account for approximately one-quarter of the world's population; four less-developed nations (mainland China, India, Indonesia, and Pakistan) account for about four-tenths. To judge from the indicators for the latter part of the nineteenth century, the developed group was well ahead of these four less-developed countries at that time. Since then, the developed group grew at a rate on the order of 15 per cent per decade, enough to double income in five decades. On the other hand, the four less-developed countries had such low income levels as of 1950 that to assume a growth rate over this preceding period of even the same magnitude would imply improbably low income levels for them in the late nineteenth century. This is supported by the figures for the only one of the four for which an estimate is available, India, where the estimated growth rate averaged only around 5 per cent per decade.

Table 7 provides a summary view of the current state of international differences in GNP per capita produced by these historical trends. Although defects of the measure tend on balance to exaggerate differences, there is little question that to date the spread of modern economic development has created an unprecedented disparity in economic condition between, on the one hand, a small though sizable segment of the world's population, chiefly resident in Europe and its overseas descendants, and, on the other, the vast majority, primarily concentrated in Asia and Africa. (Table 7, in which populations are classified according to the national average GNP per capita, may exaggerate somewhat the relative position of the mass of the people in Latin America, since there is some evidence that income inequality there may be disproportionately high.) The disparity portrayed, which reinforces (and in part has arisen from) an already existing cultural division, itself becomes, via its political and other repercussions, a factor bearing on the prospect for continued long-term growth of now-developed nations and the further spread of modern economic growth to less-developed ones.

Table 7 — Per cent of world population distributed by national average GNP per capita and geographic area, about 1958

GNP per capita (1958 U.S. dollars)	World total	Northwestern Europe*	Southern and eastern Europe*	Northern America and Oceania	Latin America	Asia	Africa
Total	100.0	6.7	15.0	7.1	7.0	57.1	7.1
1,000 and over	13.3	6.2	0	7.1	0	0	0
575–999	8.9	0.4	8.1	0	0.3	0.1	0
350–574	6.1	0.1	3.9	0	1.4	0.1	0.6
200–349	13.3	0	2.9	0	4.3	5.7	0.5
100–199	6.6	0	0.1	0	0.8	3.8	1.9
Below 100	51.7	0	0	0	0.1	47.4	4.1

* Northwestern Europe comprises the U.K., France, F.R.G., Eire, the Low Countries, Scandinavia, and Switzerland; southern and eastern Europe, all the rest of Europe including all of Russia.

Sources: Demographic Yearbook for 1963; United Nations 1952–1963; Kuznets 1964b.

Consequences for world population. The spread of modernization has brought major consequences for the size, distribution, and condition of the population of the world, viewed as a whole. The progressive diffusion of improved mortality conditions has led to a noticeable rise in the rate of increase of the world's population. Between 1000 and 1750 A.D. growth occurred at a rate that on the average would not quite have doubled population every 500 years. (This is, of course, an average; there were wide variations over time and in space.) In the modern period world population doubled between 1750 and 1900, and in the twentieth century it has almost doubled again in the first 60 years.

The uneven spread of modern mortality conditions has noticeably altered the international distribution of population, particularly between Europe, northern America, and Oceania, on the one hand, and Asia (excluding Asiatic Russia) and Africa, on the other. The lead of the former area in the mortality decline raised population growth rates there relative to Asia and Africa, so that by 1930 its share in the world total had risen from a fifth to a third. Since then, with the spread of reduced mortality conditions to Asia and Africa and with the continued transition to lower fertility in the West, this trend has been somewhat reversed. The share in the world total of Latin America, although small, has risen, at first gradually and then in the twentieth century with increasing rapidity as mortality declined sharply. The first line of Table 7 shows the approximate distribution of world population by region in the late 1950s.

By 1960 the world population exceeded three billion—more than four times the 1750 level. Despite this great and accelerating growth, it is probably true that if one considers absolute rather than relative levels, most persons throughout the world at that date were better off with regard to health conditions and formal education than was true in the past, although much of this change has been fairly recent. Whether economic conditions, in absolute terms, have generally improved is more debatable. Recent estimates of world per capita food production by region show, in general, fairly little difference for better or worse in the situation of those in less-developed areas between the late 1930s and early 1960s.

Effect on international relations. In 1750 the fortunes of those in any one area of the world were usually but tenuously connected with those of persons in other parts; in many respects individuals and nations were isolated from one another. A major consequence of the appearance and spread of modern economic growth has been a vast expansion in international contacts and an increasing degree of interdependence among the peoples of the world. The obstacles imposed by physical distance have been drastically reduced by technological developments in transport and communication. The speed of international travel has been cut to less than one per cent of what it was at the beginning of the nineteenth century, and the international transmission of messages is virtually instantaneous. At the same time, the uneven spread of economic development has altered the international configuration of economic costs and political power in a way that contributes to the rapid expansion of contacts.

Economic relations. In the area of economic relations, the physical volume of international trade rose almost sixfold from 1750 to 1850 and more than twentyfold in the next hundred years. This meant a growth in trade per capita of almost fourfold in the first period and tenfold in the second. Even though world GNP per capita rose over this period it was in a substantially smaller proportion; hence it is clear that world trade rose greatly relative to world production. Moreover, all major areas of the world participated. A rough estimate for the share in world trade of Asia, Africa, and Latin America would run on the order of a fifth to a quarter both in the early nineteenth century and in the middle of the twentieth century. External indebtedness and international migration rose too at an unprecedented rate. At the peak of their growth, roughly between 1870 and 1914, the constant-price volume of foreign debts outstanding expanded around sevenfold and the volume of intercontinental migration was three times that in the preceding half-century. The international distribution of investment and migration differed noticeably, however. In 1914, Asia and Africa accounted for perhaps one-quarter of the debt outstanding, but almost all intercontinental migration was confined to the European culture area and involved the settlement of overseas areas. The expansion of all three economic flows—trade, investment, and migration—was sharply curtailed in the interwar period, but since World War II it has resumed, although at a more moderate rate than before World War I.

The international flow of information, partly abetted by development of the international economy, has expanded immensely too. Indications of this would be provided by such data as international mail flows per capita, exports and imports of foreign publications, and the number of international periodicals and scholarly organizations.

Political relations. Measures relating to international political relations are scarce, but again there can be no doubt that the trend has been toward vastly expanded contacts—simple series on the number of personnel in consulates and diplomatic organizations would reflect this.

Since productive capacity is more closely related to military potential than is population, the spread of modern economic development has had major implications for the distribution of political power. The impression created by the population distribution as to the relative power of areas is virtually reversed when one looks at production. Although Asia, Africa, and Latin America outnumber the rest of the world by almost three to one, the rest of the world outproduces the former areas by more than three to one. Such differences are obviously pertinent to understanding why in 1914 Great Britain, France, and Germany, which together accounted for only about one-twelfth of the world's population, counted as political dependencies areas embracing another one-quarter. But the spread of modern economic development altered the power balance not only between developed and less-developed areas but also among the various developed nations themselves. The hegemony of Great Britain in much of the nineteenth century and the subsequent appearance of rivals such as Germany, the United States, Japan, and the Soviet Union show a timing pattern corresponding closely to the spread of modern economic development. The eruption in the twentieth century of the deadliest wars in the history of mankind, in which the developed nations were the leading antagonists, is also clearly related. Rough estimates of the world-wide total of deaths from all wars involving 500 or more deaths show the following trend: 1820–1863, 1.5 million; 1863–1907, 4.0 million; 1907–1950, 41.0 million.

In the international political realm, then, as in the case of economic relations, the long-term record, broadly conceived, shows an immense expansion of contacts, marred by serious disruption in this century. As this has occurred, so too have efforts at international cooperation on economic and political matters, as might be shown by data on the growing number of international conferences, administrative agencies, and arbitral tribunals. The establishment of world economic and political organizations can itself be conceived in part as a response to the pressing problems caused by the international diffusion of modern economic development within a world political framework of nation-states.

Origins of modern economic development. The reasons for treating modern economic development as a distinctive epoch should be clear. In those nations now most developed there has occurred a radical change in the way of life of the average individual. At the same time, the diffusion of this new form of economic organization throughout the world has drastically altered international relations and created interdependence on an unprecedented scale. Although it is true that the majority of the world's population has so far only begun to be touched, the rate of diffusion, compared with previous epochs, such as that of settled agriculture, has been very rapid.

How can one account for the appearance on the world scene of this phenomenon? The answer would appear to lie in the virtual explosion in the stock of knowledge, and particularly in scientifically established knowledge, which has occurred in the past three centuries. Efforts to conceptualize this development in quantitative terms are only now in their beginning stages. One indication (but no more than that) is provided by the number of scientific periodicals at various dates: 1 in 1665; 10 in 1750; 1,000 in 1850; and 80,000 in 1950. These figures, which represent only approximate orders of magnitude, suggest around a tenfold expansion in each of the two successive centuries after 1650 and only a slightly lower expansion in the most recent century.

In the developments of the seventeenth century now described as the scientific revolution, the dividing line between "pure" science and technology was vague. As man mastered procedures for establishing the "laws of nature," it is understandable that among the problems which both stimulated such inquiry and attracted applications of the new knowledge, those of production of commodities and services should rank high. Thus, progress in the scientific comprehension of natural phenomena went hand in hand with the use of such knowledge to direct and control man's physical environment in line with material needs. [See SCIENCE, *article on* THE HISTORY OF SCIENCE.]

The scientific revolution helps account not only for the appearance of modern economic development as a distinctive epoch but also for the broad geographic pattern of its spread. Modern economic development makes its appearance in the Western world where the scientific revolution is occurring and spreads most rapidly to those areas where educational development has made the transfer of new knowledge most feasible. The gains to be had from modern technology are not costless, however. As has been shown, major changes are involved which often require painful adjustments on the part of individuals or groups—in family life, economic activity, social status, or political power—and, therefore, call forth resistances to adoption of modern technology and more generally to change. It is understandable that typically the societies having so far found such adjustments most feasible (although nevertheless difficult) are those in which the same intellectual movement that had fomented the scientific revolution was promoting rational examination and discussion of social institutions as well. [See TECHNOLOGY.]

Viewed in these terms, modern economic growth is the manifestation in production of the growth and diffusion of the stock of knowledge stemming from the scientific revolution or, more generally, from the intellectual revolution, which began with the Renaissance. The increasingly urgent problems to which the spread of modern economic development has given rise are, at a remove, a reflection of the uneven development of this knowledge itself. However slow the diffusion of modern economic growth may appear to those interested in the wel-

fare of mankind as a whole, it has been rapid enough to produce serious social disruption within countries and major crises in international affairs. The capacity to cope with these problems has been limited by man's inadequate grasp of social phenomena—indeed, by the limited awareness that such phenomena are even subject to scientific study and generalization. Moreover, the spread of economic development within a framework of nation-states may itself have impeded the growth of social science by promoting national ideologies that pose as science. If, therefore, one turns from the question of the origins of modern economic development, which lie in the growth of natural science, to that of the future outlook, much would seem to turn on the prospect for comparable progress in social science.

RICHARD A. EASTERLIN

BIBLIOGRAPHY

Valuable surveys and bibliographies are provided by Ashworth 1962; The Cambridge Economic History . . . 1965; Kuznets 1966; Woytinsky & Woytinsky 1953 *and* 1955, *with the first two emphasizing economic history, the others, quantitative material. For current developments,* United Nations . . . 1952–1963 *and* United Nations . . . 1945— *are good starting points. Quantitative international comparisons are stressed in* Clark 1957; Ginsburg 1961; Kuznets 1966; Woytinsky & Woytinsky 1953 *and* 1955. *Of particular interest for noneconomic aspects are* Banks & Textor 1963 *and* Russett et al. 1964 *as well as the annual lists of publications in* Social Science Research Council. Dewhurst et al. 1961; Kirk 1946; Maddison 1964; Svennilson 1954 *are major sources on particular aspects or periods of Western experience. Recent discussions of typologies and periodization are* Conference on the State . . . 1959 *and* Rostow 1963.

ASHWORTH, WILLIAM 1962 *A Short History of the International Economy Since 1850.* 2d ed. London: Longmans. → First published in 1952.

BANKS, ARTHUR; and TEXTOR, ROBERT 1963 *A Cross-polity Survey.* Cambridge, Mass.: M.I.T. Press.

The Cambridge Economic History of Europe From the Decline of the Roman Empire. Volume 6: The Industrial Revolutions and After: Incomes, Population and Technological Change. Edited by H. J. Habakkuk and M. Postan. 1965 Cambridge Univ. Press.

CLARK, COLIN 1957 *The Conditions of Economic Progress.* 3d ed. London: Macmillan. → First published in 1940.

CONFERENCE ON THE STATE AND ECONOMIC GROWTH, NEW YORK, *1956* 1959 *The State and Economic Growth.* Edited by Hugh G. J. Aitken. New York: Social Science Research Council.

Demographic Yearbook. → Published annually by the United Nations since 1948. Data in tables, copyright United Nations 1963. Reproduced by permission.

DEWHURST, J. FREDERIC et al. 1961 *Europe's Needs and Resources: Trends and Prospects in Eighteen Countries.* New York: Twentieth Century Fund.

EASTERLIN, RICHARD A. 1965 A Note on the Evidence of History. Pages 422–429 in C. Arnold Anderson and Mary J. Bowman (editors), *Educational and Economic Development.* Chicago: Aldine.

GINSBURG, NORTON S. (editor) 1961 *Atlas of Economic Development.* Univ. of Chicago Press.

KIRK, DUDLEY 1946 *Europe's Population in the Interwar Years.* Geneva: League of Nations.

KUZNETS, SIMON 1957 Quantitative Aspects of the Economic Growth of Nations: 2. Industrial Distribution of National Product and Labor Force. *Economic Development and Cultural Change* 5, no. 4, part 2.

KUZNETS, SIMON 1964a *Postwar Economic Growth: Four Lectures.* Cambridge, Mass.: Belknap.

KUZNETS, SIMON 1964b Quantitative Aspects of the Economic Growth of Nations. 9. Level and Structure of Foreign Trade: Comparisons for Recent Years. *Economic Development and Cultural Change* 13, no. 1, part 2.

KUZNETS, SIMON 1966 *Modern Economic Growth: Rate, Structure, and Spread.* New Haven: Yale Univ. Press.

MADDISON, ANGUS 1964 *Economic Growth in the West: Comparative Experience in Europe and North America.* New York: Twentieth Century Fund.

Population Bulletin of the United Nations. [1962] No. 6.

ROSTOW, WALT W. (editor) 1963 *The Economics of Take-off Into Sustained Growth: Proceedings of a Conference Held by the International Economic Association.* London: Macmillan; New York: St. Martins.

RUSSETT, BRUCE et al. 1964 *World Handbook of Political and Social Indicators.* New Haven: Yale Univ. Press.

SOCIAL SCIENCE RESEARCH COUNCIL *Annual Report.* → Published by the Council since 1926/1927.

SVENNILSON, INGVAR 1954 *Growth and Stagnation in the European Economy.* Geneva: United Nations Economic Commission for Europe.

UNITED NATIONS, BUREAU OF ECONOMIC AFFAIRS 1945— *World Economic Survey.* New York: United Nations.

UNITED NATIONS, BUREAU OF SOCIAL AFFAIRS 1952–1963 *Report on the World Social Situation.* New York: United Nations.

U.S. AGENCY FOR INTERNATIONAL DEVELOPMENT, STATISTICS AND REPORTS DIVISION 1966 Estimated Annual Growth Rates of Developed and Less Developed Countries. R. C. W-138. Unpublished manuscript.

WOYTINSKY, WLADIMIR S.; and WOYTINSKY, EMMA S. 1953 *World Population and Production: Trends and Outlook.* New York: Twentieth Century Fund.

WOYTINSKY, WLADIMIR S.; and WOYTINSKY, EMMA S. 1955 *World Commerce and Governments: Trends and Outlook.* New York: Twentieth Century Fund.

II

THEORY

Perhaps no subject has more fully engaged the minds and energies of economists from the very beginning than the search for a satisfactory explanation of economic growth. This was, in fact, the main focus of the work of Adam Smith and the classicists endeavoring to explain industrialization in eighteenth- and nineteenth-century England, of Marx and Schumpeter in the long neoclassical eclipse of interest, and, most recently, of the post–World War II revival by those concerned with growth both in the mature industrial and in the less developed nonindustrial societies.

While there is by no means unanimity on how to define growth, it is convenient to adhere to the convention that real per capita national income or output represents the most reliable indicator of a system's economic achievement at any point in time and that any change in real per capita income over time connotes economic growth. Statesmen and philosophers have joined economists in recognizing that economic growth defined in this way represents the most objective indicator of a society's welfare. It reflects changes in its ability to attain any socially agreed-upon set of goals, whether consumption, capital formation, national defense or, for that matter, leisure.

Any viable theory of economic growth must thus be able to explain both the level of per capita income of a given economic system at a point in time and the determinants of changes in that per capita income from one period to the next. With respect to the former task, it is generally agreed that the determination of the level of per capita income at any particular historical moment depends in part on the quantity and quality of the economy's human resources; in part on the available stock of material resources; in part on how efficiently people organize themselves for productive activity; and, finally, in part on the institutional environment in which the society finds itself. Similarly, changes in income per head from one period to the next must be explained in terms of changes in the above four dimensions. All growth theories must thus take into account, in one fashion or another, at least the following: the initial characteristics of and changes in the stock of material agents, i.e., the capital stock and changes in it; the initial characteristics of and changes in the society's stock of human agents, i.e., population or labor force and population growth; the initial characteristics of and changes in the quality or efficiency of the production process, i.e., technological change; and, finally, the evolution of the society's organizational or institutional milieu.

The first of the above dimensions relates to the initial material wealth or capital stock per head and to the size of the economy's saving, i.e., that portion of output not consumed in the current period. Under the standard full employment assumptions we shall adhere to, all such savings are automatically invested and thus come to represent additions to the economy's capital stock in the next period. Since the size of the capital stock per head of the population is a principal determinant of output per head (or per capita income), the annual magnitude of the surplus per head is of the greatest importance. The second dimension, population and population growth, must be viewed as a two-edged sword. On the one side it provides the economy with the labor force necessary for productive activity, but on the other it requires consumption for its maintenance, thus diminishing the surplus available to enhance the per capita capital stock in the next period. The third dimension, technological change, really is a shorthand way of referring to changes in the quality of the economy's human agents, in the quality of the economy's material agents, and in the over-all efficiency with which these factors are combined to produce output. Finally, changes in the way a society organizes itself with respect to its dominant social and political institutions, e.g., between markets and direct controls as organizational devices, may have a profound impact on the more narrowly conceived economic performance of the society in question.

Virtually all growth theory may thus be viewed as an elaboration of one or another of the above four essential facets, with each particular theory emphasizing what is considered most essential given the inductive evidence under consideration and the deductive reasoning being employed. Keeping this in mind, we shall first present the basic outlines of some of the more relevant growth theories of an earlier day and then examine, again in necessarily broad terms, the status of the present-day theory of growth.

The classical theory. The classicists—though there exist considerable differences as between Smith, Ricardo, Malthus, and Mill—thought in terms of the three factors of production—land, labor, and capital—cooperating to produce national output; and growth, consequently, was seen as determined by what happens to land, labor, and capital over time. While in the classical theory land is viewed as fixed in supply, the population, following Malthusian notions, is seen to be a function of the real wage (more exactly, of the gap between the market wage and a long-run subsistence norm). Capital formation, made possible by the society's saving, provides the main engine of growth. More precisely, the total output generated at any given time is distributed to the various agents who exercise control over the three factors, i.e., the society's workers, landlords, and capitalists, according to certain rules. Each class of owners then makes its own decision as to what proportion of income to consume and what proportion to save. To understand what happens to the stock of material wealth available for production in the next period, we must thus first understand the underlying classical theory of distribution and the classical theory of saving.

The classical theory of distribution is inextricably intertwined with the concept of diminishing returns to increased dosages of labor (and capital)

on the fixed land. As acreage that is less and less productive is brought under cultivation, the incremental output declines and the incremental return on the least productive land determines the return to land, or rent. The portion of total output left after rents have been paid is then distributed between workers and capitalists, with workers paid at or near the institutionally determined subsistence wage level. Over time, as more and more labor (and associated capital) is expended on the land and diminishing returns become more pronounced, the landlord's return (rent) increases and the capitalist's return (profit) declines, with the worker's wage retaining its long-run constancy (as population growth erases any temporary gaps between the market wage and the subsistence wage). Since the classicists assume that workers, being inherently poor, are not able to save and that landlords, being inherently wastrel, do not choose to save, the entire burden of saving and investing falls on capitalists and their profits. With declining profits, capital accumulation is increasingly squeezed, finally culminating in the cessation of further growth. Implicitly, if not explicitly, this prediction is based on the assumption that diminishing returns in the preponderant agricultural sector will swamp constant or possibly even increasing returns in industry—and that improvements in the quality of the factors of production, or in the efficiency with which they can be organized, are unlikely to be sufficiently important to change the outcome. [*See the biographies of* MALTHUS; MILL; RICARDO; SMITH, ADAM.]

Marx's theory. Marx, in *Capital: A Critique of Political Economy* (1867–1879), sees capital and labor combining in fixed proportions to produce output, with the accumulation of new capital resulting from the economy's surplus over consumption requirements in one period providing the motive force for carrying the system forward to higher levels of per capita output in the next. The size of the saving fund automatically converted into investment is once again determined by a distribution theory and a saving theory. Marx's distribution theory is based on the inequality of bargaining power between capitalists and laborers in the market place, forcing wages down near subsistence levels. In his world, as in the classical, workers do not save and capitalists do not consume; thus, once again, investment is equal to total profits.

Unlike his predecessors, however, Marx is much concerned with changes in technology altering the proportions in which capital and labor are combined to produce output. It is his view that all innovations are by nature very laborsaving, in the sense that they raise the capital–labor ratio and displace employed labor. It is this, plus exogenously determined population growth (Marx rejected Malthusian population theory), which contributes to the creation of the "reserve army of the unemployed," which, in turn, deprives workers of all bargaining power. Meanwhile, as the capital stock per employed worker continues to increase, capital begins to lose its scarcity value, and its rate of return begins to fall. Capitalists will try to rescue the profit rate by using their dominant bargaining strength in the labor market to make employees work harder and further to reduce the wage, but the drive for capital accumulation finally reduces the rate of profit to a level which brings the capitalist system to a halt. [*See the guide to related articles under* MARXISM.]

Schumpeter's theory. Perhaps Marx's greatest contribution to growth theory was his emphasis on the importance of technological change in the production process. This emphasis was carried forward by Joseph Schumpeter in *The Theory of Economic Development* (1912). Schumpeter expanded the concept of innovation to include not only changes in technique but also changes in quality, in markets, and in supply sources. He was, moreover, the first really to focus on the human agent, the entrepreneur, who was capable of perceiving the potentiality of such changes and of doing something about them.

Schumpeter's theory attempted to analyze the economy's long-run progress by way of an explanation of its cyclical behavior as the system continuously departs from various quasi-equilibrium stationary states, only to return to others at ever higher levels of per capita income. A Schumpeterian stationary state is characterized by the fact that only enough net investment is being made to equip additions to the labor force at the capital–labor ratio applying to the already existing labor force. The economy is thus moving sideways: labor, capital, and output are all growing at the same rate and per capita income remains constant. This quasi-equilibrium state is then upset by the appearance—for reasons unclear but related to changes in the "climate"—of numbers of gifted individuals capable of perceiving additional attractive investment opportunities. These entrepreneurs appeal to the banking system for the creation of credit, which forces additional savings out of the public's hands (through inflation) and into their own. Subsequently, pioneering entrepreneurs are followed by large numbers of less gifted imitators who tend to excess, and the system experiences overproduction and recession. But the new Schumpeterian stationary state is reached

at a higher level of material wealth per person and a consequently higher level of per capita income. The growth process thus occurs as the consequence of discontinuous bursts of creative entrepreneurial activity. It finally comes to a halt only because of a change in the institutional setting as the "climate" for entrepreneurship deteriorates secularly with the increasing bureaucratization of corporate enterprise. [*See the biography of* SCHUMPETER.]

Modern theory

Where contemporary growth theory also is concerned with the performance of the mature industrial society, it differs from the earlier attempts in that it is both less ambitious and more precise. Postwar growth theorists have been content to relegate theories of population growth, of changes in the organizational or institutional framework, sometimes even of technological change, to other disciplines or to accept changes in these rather crucial dimensions as given, rather than to be explained within the framework of the growth theory itself. At the same time there is a conscious attempt to be more rigorous, to lean more heavily on modern methods of model construction, i.e., structural relationships supplemented by behavioristic relationships.

Harrod–Domar model. Modern growth theory, moreover, is not content to hypothesize certain reasonable behavioristic relationships based on casual observation but insists increasingly on statistical verification, including the estimation of the key parameters involved. It is thus greatly indebted both to the development of the national income accounting system during the 1930s and to Keynes (1936), who, while himself primarily concerned with other, short-run stability matters, employed this system for more general theory construction and statistical implementation. [*See* NATIONAL INCOME AND PRODUCT ACCOUNTS.] This can perhaps best be demonstrated by examining a particular view of growth, the so-called Harrod–Domar model (Harrod 1939; Domar 1946), as a prototype of post-Keynesian growth theory. While it represents a rather early and relatively simple formulation of the problem, much of contemporary growth theory which follows can be said to represent departures from the basic theme presented here, e.g., using more realistic behavioristic assumptions.

The basic ingredients of the Harrod–Domar view of long-run growth are as follows:

(1) A production function which relates the generation of total output, Q, to the available capital stock, K, via the capital–output ratio, v, that

is, $Q = K/v$. The theory assumes the constancy of the capital–output ratio, i.e., the number of units of capital it takes to produce a unit of output.

(2) A theory of saving based on the Keynesian propensity to save, which stipulates that total savings, S, in any one period is a given fraction, s, of total income or output, Q, of that period: $S = sQ$.

(3) Adherence to the full employment of capital hypothesis, i.e., all savings are automatically invested and become additions to the capital stock: $S \equiv I \equiv \Delta K$.

Capital is the only factor of production explicitly considered in the Harrod–Domar system. Labor combines with capital in fixed proportions, but there is no attempt to reconcile exogenously determined increases in the population or labor force with changes in the derived demand for labor as a factor input as capital accumulation proceeds.

Table 1 — Harrod–Domar growth model

t	K	Q	$S \equiv I$	C	L	Q/L
1	30	10	2	8	100	.1000
2	32	10.67	2.13	8.54	102	.1046
3	34.13	11.38	2.28	9.10	104	.1094
4	36.41	12.14	2.43	9.71	106	.1145
5	38.84	12.95	2.59	10.36	108	.1199

Table 1 may help give a clearer picture of how the Harrod–Domar system operates. Let us assume that it requires 3 units of capital to produce each unit of output, i.e., the capital–output ratio is 3, and that the economy's saving propensity is .2, i.e., the various income recipients decide to consume 80 per cent of their income in each period and to put away 20 per cent in the form of savings. If such an economy starts with, say, a capital stock (K) of 30 in period (t) 1, it produces an output (Q) of 10. Out of this income 8 units are consumed (C) and 2 are saved ($S \equiv I$), leading to an increase of 2 in the capital stock of the next period. The new capital stock of 32 units is capable of producing 10.67 units of output in period 2. This new and higher level of income is once again allocated in proportions of 80 and 20 between consumption and savings; the latter yields a further increment in the capital stock, and thus the economy continues to grow from one period to the next. The exogenous growth of the population or labor force (L), say at the rate of approximately 2 per cent a year, has no consequence for the productive capacity of the system, but affects its measured performance only in terms of per capita income growth as indicated in the last column of the table (Q/L).

The rate of growth of capital can then be quickly determined by dividing each year's increment, or the investment during that period, $I \equiv S = sQ$, by the already existing capital stock: $I/K = sQ/K = s/v$. In our example with $s = .2$ and $v = 3$, capital will be growing at an annual rate of 6.7 per cent. Moreover, since $v \equiv K/Q$ (the capital–output ratio) is a constant, the rate of growth of output or income over time must equal the rate of growth of capital. Whether or not per capita income increases or decreases in the course of the growth process will then depend on the relative speed with which the population is growing. If the rate of growth of population, g, is less than the rate of growth of income, s/v, per capita income will be rising at the rate $(s/v) - g$, etc. In the example, in other words, with population growing at a rate of approximately 2 per cent, per capita income is rising, i.e., growth is occurring, at a rate of about 4.7 per cent annually.

While we may raise a series of questions about its realism, this Harrod–Domar view of the world serves as a point of departure for much modern growth theory, not only as applied to the developed but also to the less developed world. The departures take the form of a series of modifications—sometimes quite sweeping—of the stipulated rules governing the way in which factors are combined to produce output, of how output is distributed, and of how technological and institutional change occurs. What follows will first trace some of the major modifications in modern growth theory as applied to the mature economy and then summarize the state of contemporary growth theory as applied to the underdeveloped world.

Substitutable inputs models. A first and major modification of the Harrod–Domar world results from the explicit recognition (or better, a return to the recognition) that there exists more than one factor of production and that there is a strong possibility not only of joint inputs of labor and capital but of their substitutability in producing a given output. This is the view typical of the so-called neoclassical growth theory represented by Solow (1956) and Swan (1956). Like Harrod–Domar, Solow accepts a proportional saving function, $S = sQ$, but unlike his predecessors, he conceives of a production process in which both capital and labor appear as substitutable inputs. The production function meets the usual conditions of constant returns to scale, i.e., if we double the amount of both labor and capital inputs, we double output. With the growth of the capital stock determined by the constant saving propensity and the now variable capital–output ratio [$\Delta K/K = (I/Q)/(K/Q) = s/v$] and with the growth of the other input, labor, determined exogenously at the rate g [$\Delta L/L = g$] we have all the necessary ingredients to trace the performance of the system as a whole from one period to the next.

If, for example, the rate of growth of capital, s/v, exceeds the rate of growth of population or labor, g, the economy's capital–labor ratio rises, i.e., each worker is equipped with a larger stock of material resources. According to the law of diminishing returns, as each worker cooperates with more and more capital, the *extra* output due to each unit of capital declines, i.e., the capital–output ratio rises. As the capital–output ratio, v, rises, the rate of growth of capital, s/v, declines, and this process will continue in the long run until the rate of growth of capital falls to the level g, the rate of growth of labor. At this point the rate of growth of human and material resources is the same, and no further increases in the capital–labor ratio result. Consequently, the capital–output ratio also ceases to rise, and so we have arrived at a so-called "steady state" growth, in which capital, labor, and output are all growing at the same rate. Alternatively, if initially the rate of growth of labor, g, exceeds the rate of growth of capital, s/v, as the capital–labor ratio falls, the economy reaps more and more extra output per unit of extra capital: the capital–output ratio falls, and, by an argument entirely symmetrical, the rate of growth of capital rises until it reaches the level of the rate of growth of population. We again achieve a steady state, if now from the opposite "direction." Output per person, our index of growth, is, of course, constant in the steady state; but it will have reached that particular level by increasing toward it continuously in the case of the increasing capital–labor ratio regime and by falling toward it continuously in the case of the decreasing capital–labor ratio regime. Moreover, the permanently maintainable level of per capita income toward which the economy is tending in this very long run will differ, depending on the production function, the saving rate, and the rate of population growth.

Prevalence of distribution theories. A second major modification of the Harrod–Domar world questions the implied irrelevance for aggregate savings of how income is distributed among the various economic agents. Robinson (1956) and Kaldor (1961), for example, point out that profit recipients and wage earners are likely to save different proportions of their income, and since their relative shares in the total are bound to change over time, they challenge the constancy of the aggregate savings ratio, s, in the course of the growth process. In the extreme case they assume, like Marx and the classicists, that workers do not save and that profit recipients do not consume. In that case the savings rate, s, is equal to the profit share, $\pi K/Q$, and the rate of growth of capital, $I/K = sQ/K$, is equal to the profit rate, π.

In this general context two major types of distribution theory have been advanced. One—often called the neoclassical theory of distribution, since it depends on the possibility of continuous factor substitution—stipulates that market forces ensure that all human and material agents participating in the production process are compensated according to their marginal contribution to output. The smooth neoclassical production function, with constant returns to scale, permits us to "attribute" the total output of the economy, Q, to the quantities of the factors of production, say K and L, weighted by their productive contribution at the margin, i.e., their marginal productivities, MPP_K and MPP_L, respectively. Thus $Q = MPP_K K + MPP_L L$, with $MPP_K K/Q$ representing the portion of total output attributable to capital and $MPP_L L/Q$ the portion of total output attributable to labor. Alternatively put, a given percentage rate of growth of output between any two periods can be decomposed into two portions: (1) a "capital contribution," which is the percentage increase in the capital stock multiplied by the capital elasticity of output (i.e., the measure of how much output increased due to each percentage point increase in the capital stock), and (2) a "labor contribution," which is the percentage rate of growth of the labor force multiplied by the labor elasticity of output (i.e., the measure of how much output increased due to each percentage point increase in the labor force). Hence $\Delta Q/Q = (\Delta K/K)(MPP_K K/Q) + (\Delta L/L)(MPP_L L/Q)$. The neoclassical theory of income distribution then states that competitive market conditions force the wage rate, w, to equality with the marginal product of labor, MPP_L, and the profit rate, π, into equality with the marginal product of capital, MPP_K. Consequently labor's relative share in total income, wL/Q, is equal to its relative contribution to total output, $MPP_L L/Q$; and similarly for the equality between $\pi K/Q$ and $MPP_K K/Q$.

A second theory, sometimes called the Marxian theory of distribution, insists, on the other hand, on the noncompetitive nature of markets and shifts from a functional or impersonal determination of rates of return to labor and capital to a determination through the interplay of personal forces related to the relative bargaining strengths of contending groups. Since there is no need to assume equality between various factors' contributions and their income shares, this view is perfectly consistent with a belief in smooth neoclassical production functions. It is, however, true that many of its modern adherents, e.g., Kaldor and Robinson, view production in terms of fixed proportion processes and thus have no choice but to abandon marginal productivity. Unless the extreme case of subsistence wages is accepted, the distribution of income —and thus the aggregate savings ratio—in such models can be determined only in the sense that they must somehow be brought into line with an otherwise determined investment demand. We shall not, however, concern ourselves here with views of growth which abandon the notion that the system is "pushed forward" by the automatic investment of full employment savings and is instead "pulled ahead" by investment opportunities, animal spirits, and the like.

Technological change theories.   The discussion of contemporary growth theory has thus far been concerned only with the consequences of larger quantities of inputs participating, perhaps in different combinations, in the production process. As was pointed out earlier, however, it is not merely the stock of material agents per capita but also changes in the efficiency with which they are deployed which may matter a great deal—not to speak of changes in the quality of the inputs or in the institutional framework within which the system is operating. Thus, a third and major modification of the simple Harrod–Domar formulation must be the reintroduction of technological change. Kaldor (1957), for example, has introduced a so-called technical progress function intended to summarize the twin impact of a larger stock of capital per capita (capital deepening) and favorable changes in productive techniques (technological change) on the index of growth, per capita income. In the same year, Solow (1957), using a three-factor production function with constant returns to scale, the third factor being "time" or technological change, found that only 15 per cent of recent per capita output growth in the United States can be explained by increases in the capital stock; 85 per cent must be ascribed to technological change. Whether or not we accept these statistical findings matters less than the growing realization that growth cannot be explained simply in terms of larger quantities of constant quality inputs combining in known ways to produce output. Economists are reaching a real consensus that the as yet unexplained residual which Abramovitz has aptly labeled "a measure of our ignorance" (1956) is large; consequently, much recent growth-theoretic effort has been directed at this problem. This effort has been twofold: on the one hand, to define more rigorously what is really meant by technological change, and, on the other,

to work toward meaningful behavioristic relationships which may tell how and why such changes in production functions occur. [*See* AGRICULTURE, *article on* PRODUCTIVITY AND TECHNOLOGY; PRODUCTIVITY.]

As has been noted, the growth performance of any system in terms of the rate of increase of its per capita income invariably depends on the *amount* of material agents that collaborate with labor, i.e., the capital stock per capita, and on the *quality* of the economic agents and the efficiency with which they are used in the production process. "Technological change" is a semantic umbrella extended over all the latter; that is to say, all increases in output while the quantity of capital and labor is kept constant. At any point in time, then, technological change will raise the productivity of the existing quantities of capital and labor. Just how the introduction of a particular new method affects the productivity of the existing human and material agents provides the basis for Hicks's attempt to classify innovations (1932). Hicks defines neutral technological change as one which raises the marginal productivity of labor and of capital at the same rate; a labor-saving technological change as one which increases the marginal productivity of capital more than that of labor; and symmetrically for a capital-saving technological change. Harrod (1948) provides a somewhat different definition of technological change. Here there is neutrality if, after the innovation has occurred, the capital–output ratio remains unchanged at a constant rate of profit. If the capital–output ratio rises, it is a labor-saving innovation; if it falls, capital-saving. For reasons that cannot be dwelt on here, a Harrod-neutral innovation is equivalent to a labor-augmenting innovation, i.e., one which converts natural units of labor into better or more efficient units over time. It is the only type of technological change which still permits the system to move toward steady-state growth in the long run. Finally, and quite symmetrically to Harrod, Solow (1963) and Fei and Ranis (1965) propose a third definition of neutrality: constancy of the labor–output ratio, or per capita income, in the presence of a constant wage rate. Such an innovation may also be called capital-augmenting.

An equally important classification of technical change for purposes of advancing growth theory proper is the differentiation between "embodied" and "disembodied" technological change—between innovations which have to be incorporated or embedded in new capital goods or in the labor force and those which do not and can, rather, be viewed as an independent or third factor of production. Another question revolves around whether innovations should be viewed as exogenous and costless, falling in unpredictable quantity, like manna, from heaven, or endogenously related, perhaps to some specific economic activity, e.g., expenditures on education or on research and development, in the past.

The early Solow and Abramovitz view of innovations as an unexplained residual really implies that technological change is disembodied and exogenous. But this must be viewed as only a first step on the road to probing deeper into the nature of the changes which actually occur in the real world and into how they are produced. His prima facie implausible statistical results led Solow himself, as well as others, to search for a so-called new view of investment (1960), in which technological change is embodied in the latest vintage of capital, i.e., the current year's investment. One model is essentially neoclassical, with labor allocated to the various heterogeneous qualities of capital stock (the younger the vintage, the more productive) according to the usual competitive assumptions. Other so-called putty-to-clay models (Johansen 1959; Phelps 1963) accept the neoclassical smooth production assumptions for the latest vintage of capital but assume it becomes "frozen" thereafter, i.e., it is transformed into a Harrod–Domar fixed-proportions type of production process. Arrow (1962) uses a somewhat different version of the vintage approach by linking a continuous reduction in the labor requirements per unit of output on new machines to "experience," which is in turn related to cumulative past investment activity in the economy.

Finally, other models focus attention on changes in the quality of the labor force affecting either all vintages or only the latest entrants. Denison (1962) includes elements of both approaches. Moreover, there remains the question whether technological change, embodied or disembodied, is to be treated exogenously—perhaps as a free good—or endogenously, i.e., springing from some action of the system in the previous period. Improvements in the quality of machinery and of the labor force can, for example, be attributed either to the sheer passage of time or experience, or to previous expenditures, e.g., on research and development and on health and education. Emphasis on the latter type of theory has been growing of late [see, for example, CAPITAL, HUMAN *and* Schultz 1961].

It should be noted that there exists a large range for choice among the various innovation-theoretic hypotheses sketched in here. It is possible, for example, that all kinds of technological change are occurring simultaneously, from fully embodied (or factor quality-enhancing) innovations to fully disembodied (or organizational efficiency-raising) technological change, in one dimension; and from fully endogenous to fully exogenous, in the other. Unfortunately, the ability to advance reasonable hypotheses has run considerably ahead of the ability to test them rigorously in a statistical or econometric sense. Moreover, even if we could precisely relate improvements in physical capital to research and development expenditures, and improvements in human capital to educational expenditures, a really satisfactory theory of innovations must also be able to incorporate a plausible inducement or motivational mechanism at the level of the individual entrepreneur. In spite of some attempts in this direction (Fellner 1961), we still do not have a satisfactory explanation of just how the profit-maximizing entrepreneur is motivated to select one available type of innovation over another. In summary, the as yet inadequate understanding of the manifold possible interactions between the economy's surplus over consumption, technological change, and the passage of time provides the biggest obstacle at this time to a really satisfactory theory of economic growth, i.e., one which is not only *sufficient* to explain the historical record but is also *necessary*, and thus is ready for the ultimate predictive test.

But if contemporary growth theory as applied to the mature economy has not yet given a completely satisfactory understanding of the sources of economic growth, a consensus seems to be emerging to the effect that conventional growth in the quantity of human and physical resources is of less importance than changes in the quality of the inputs and in the efficiency with which they are combined in the production process. By experimenting with different types of production functions and applying theoretical as well as econometric ingenuity to the problem of "explaining" the residual growth in productivity, we are making steady, if slow, progress in the attempt to recapture some of the magnificence of the explanatory apparatus of an earlier day—while keeping our feet on firm, i.e., empirically testable, ground.

Underdeveloped economies

Thus far we have dealt mainly with the theory of growth in the mature or industrial economy. A second, and no less important, component of the post-World War II revival of interest in growth is the concern with economic progress, or the absence of such progress, in the so-called underdeveloped or nonindustrial economies. The attempt to formulate a theory of growth applicable to such countries essentially may be viewed as another strand from the same basic framework of inquiry identified here as the post-Keynesian theory of growth. Patently there must exist a large measure of transferability in the way economic progress is viewed among contexts. Everywhere it requires, at a minimum, abstention from consumption, i.e., capital accumulation; and everywhere it is governed by certain technological constraints, i.e., the state of the arts. Thus the basic Harrod–Domar formulation can again be viewed as a point of departure; but now in modifying the simplified view of how the world operates, we must take into account not only more realistic notions of the role of labor, factor substitutability, and technological change but also of the heretofore neglected changes in the institutional milieu within which an economy operates. No longer is it possible to view organizational change as *de minimis* and to be neglected; in fact, changes in the environment and in the way a society chooses to organize itself in various markets may have a major impact on the growth performance of the system as a whole. For example, an understanding of the changing legal framework required to initiate and sustain growth, of the changing role of markets and administrative controls as allocative devices, and of the transition from extended to nuclear family concepts may be required along with an understanding of the more narrowly conceived interactions between the society's human and material resources. Any approach to a really useful theory of economic growth is thus likely to require a broadening of the customary analytical framework.

The typical less-developed economy is characterized by an extremely low ratio of material to human resources and a backward technology, together yielding extremely low levels of per capita income, frequently barely above subsistence. Often a substantial proportion of the labor force is openly or disguisedly unemployed. Substantial growth is likely to be ruled out by the low level of saving possible at extremely low levels of per capita income, plus the customary stagnant levels of domestic entrepreneurship and technology. Often even the most elementary preconditions for sustained growth, e.g., geographic or political cohesiveness, absence of internal market barriers, a unified currency and postal system—all essential for welding a conglomeration of resources into a national economy in the first place—are absent. And even where the environment is more conducive, attempts to move such an economy off dead center must overcome the formidable gravitational pull of accelerating population growth.

One difficulty standing in the way of a viable theory of growth for the less developed world is that most of the considerable post-World War II efforts—by practitioner and academic economist alike—have been directed toward meeting the pressing problems of improved decision making in the immediate present and heavily tinged with the flavor of a country's, or a region's, particular economic and institutional characteristics. Few attempts to generalize from such specific country experience have been forthcoming. One of the notable exceptions is Rostow's stages theory (1960), which moves directly from an interpretation of the history of the now advanced countries to a general theory of growth in terms of sequential stages, including the famous "take-off" into self-sustained growth. While it may provide insights and direct the attention of others to more analytical inquiry, it also does some disservice in terms of its casual marshaling of evidence and its disregard of the need to isolate key behavioristic relationships which determine the path of the system. However, most of the body of what may be called the theory of development evolving over the past several decades is of a more modest character and may, in fact, be characterized as a series of useful theoretical insights, as yet falling short of being fitted together into any more general theoretical framework.

Most of these insights start with the premise that the underdeveloped system initially finds itself in some sort of "trap," escape from which requires a major effort or considerable structural change. Rosenstein-Rodan (1961), for instance, emphasizes the importance of externalities and economies of scale, and thus the need for a large nonincremental development effort where only a small industrial base exists. Leibenstein (1957) points to the need to overcome the gravitational pull of stagnation, mainly the forces of accelerated population growth, as the system departs from quasi equilibrium. Nurkse (1953) sees the need for balanced growth between industries and sectors to ensure the simultaneous creation of markets and sources of supply for a sufficient number of hesitant entrepreneurs to move forward together. Hirschman (1958), on the other hand, hopes to solve the same decision-making bottleneck via imbalance between direct private and social overhead activity, a strategy which forces expansion on the system.

While such ideas are essentially policy-focused, they patently cannot be divorced from some underlying view of how the typical underdeveloped system behaves. Formulations which recognize, implicitly or explicitly, the prevalence of a structural condition called dualism in many of these economies are especially helpful in this respect. Dualism in this context means that the economy is composed of at least two sectors: one relatively small, capitalistic, and mainly industrial, behaving like the mature competitive economy; the other relatively large, traditional, and mainly agricultural, in which the material resources available, land in particular, are insufficient to employ productively the existing supply of labor at prevailing rates of remuneration, i.e., in which there exists substantial overt and disguised unemployment. [*See* ECONOMY, DUAL.]

Quite early Rosenstein-Rodan (1943) and Nurkse (1953) recognized that the disguised unemployed in the subsistence or agricultural sector, sharing equally in the extended family's produce but contributing little or nothing to it, represent a form of "hidden saving," or surplus, which can be mobilized through its reallocation to productive activity elsewhere. W. Arthur Lewis (1954) advances the notion that growth in this sort of dualistic economy is a function of the rate at which the "unlimited supply" of low (or zero) productivity agricultural workers in one sector can be reallocated to higher productivity, commercialized activities in the other. With real wages in agriculture institutionally anchored, Lewis' attention is focused largely on the creation of employment opportunities in the industrial sector, which would exercise a demand for the released agricultural workers at the same (or a slightly higher) constant level of real wages. Jorgenson (1961) and Fei and Ranis (1964) follow this up by examining the developmental process in terms of the interaction between the two sectors over time. The latter, for example, emphasize the requirements for balanced intersectoral growth as increases in agricultural labor productivity—a function mainly of technological improvements—release agricultural workers and generate agricultural surpluses. These surpluses, together with the reinvestment of industrial profits, increase the quantity and quality of the industrial sector's capital stock and thus its demand for the simultaneous absorption of such workers. As long as this balanced reallocation process pulls people out of the noncommercialized and into the commercialized sector at a rate in excess of population growth (population growth may be viewed as simultaneously adding to the pool of the underemployed) the economy is gradually divesting itself of its labor surplus characteristics. Once the twin forces of capital accumulation and technological change, raising productivity in both sectors in a balanced fashion,

have achieved this objective, labor, like capital, becomes a scarce factor, bid for by landlords and industrial entrepreneurs alike, and the entire economy has become commercialized. The economic calculus in the familiar one-sector world context then comes into operation, participation of all economic agents in the system's productive and innovative processes becomes possible, and the transition to the mature economy is achieved.

It should, of course, be recognized that the labor surplus economy, while representing a common species of underdevelopment, is by no means typical of all such systems. Some underdeveloped economies, for instance, still have exploitable free land and experience year-round labor shortages. Others have no large traditional sectors but suffer from a colonial pattern of trade. There can, in short, be little doubt that the search for any really general theory of development has been severely handicapped by the heterogeneity in initial resource endowment, in the rules of behavior, and in the institutional framework among the countries loosely bearing the underdeveloped label. In the face of this, economists presumably will continue to seek elements of transferability in the experience of particular types of economic systems. The evolution of a meaningful typology of less-developed economies may thus constitute a first step in the direction of a more generally applicable theory of development.

GUSTAV RANIS

BIBLIOGRAPHY

ABRAMOVITZ, MOSES 1956 Resource and Output Trends in the United States Since 1870. *American Economic Review* 46, no. 2:5–23.

ARROW, KENNETH J. 1962 The Economic Implications of Learning by Doing. *Review of Economic Studies* 29:155–173.

DENISON, EDWARD F. 1962 *The Sources of Economic Growth in the United States and the Alternatives Before Us.* New York: Committee for Economic Development.

DOMAR, EVSEY D. 1946 Capital Expansion, Rate of Growth, and Employment. *Econometrica* 14:137–147.

FEI, JOHN C. H.; and RANIS, GUSTAV 1964 *Development of the Labor Surplus Economy: Theory and Policy.* Homewood, Ill.: Irwin.

FEI, JOHN C. H.; and RANIS, GUSTAV 1965 Innovational Intensity and Factor Bias in the Theory of Growth. *International Economic Review* 6:182–198.

FELLNER, WILLIAM J. 1961 Two Propositions in the Theory of Induced Innovations. *Economic Journal* 71:305–308.

HARROD, ROY F. 1939 An Essay in Dynamic Theory. *Economic Journal* 49:14–33.

HARROD, ROY F. (1948) 1960 *Towards a Dynamic Economics: Some Recent Developments of Economic Theory and Their Application to Policy.* London: Macmillan; New York: St. Martins.

HICKS, JOHN R. (1932) 1964 *The Theory of Wages.* New York: St. Martins.

HIRSCHMAN, ALBERT O. 1958 *The Strategy of Economic Development.* Yale Studies in Economics, No. 10. New Haven: Yale Univ. Press.

JOHANSEN, LEIF 1959 Substitution Versus Fixed Production Coefficients in the Theory of Economic Growth: A Synthesis. *Econometrica* 27:157–176.

JORGENSON, DALE W. 1961 The Development of a Dual Economy. *Economic Journal* 71:309–334.

KALDOR, NICHOLAS 1957 A Model of Economic Growth. *Economic Journal* 67:591–624.

KALDOR, NICHOLAS 1961 Capital Accumulation and Economic Growth. Pages 177–222 in International Economic Association, *The Theory of Capital: Proceedings.* New York: St. Martins.

KEYNES, JOHN MAYNARD 1936 *The General Theory of Employment, Interest and Money.* London: Macmillan. → A paperback edition was published in 1965 by Harcourt.

LEIBENSTEIN, HARVEY (1957) 1963 *Economic Backwardness and Economic Growth: Studies in the Theory of Economic Development.* New York: Science Editions.

LEWIS, W. ARTHUR 1954 Economic Development With Unlimited Supplies of Labour. *Manchester School of Economics and Social Studies* 22:139–191.

MARX, KARL (1867–1879) 1925–1926 *Capital: A Critique of Political Economy.* 3 vols. Chicago: Kerr. → Volume 1: *The Process of Capitalist Production.* Volume 2: *The Process of Circulation of Capital.* Volume 3: *The Process of Capitalist Production as a Whole.* Volume 1 was published in 1867. The manuscripts of Volumes 2 and 3 were written between 1867 and 1879. They were first published posthumously in German in 1885 and 1894.

NURKSE, RAGNAR (1953) 1962 *Problems of Capital Formation in Under-developed Countries.* New York: Oxford Univ. Press.

PHELPS, EDMUND S. 1963 Substitution, Fixed Proportions, Growth and Distribution. *International Economic Review* 4:265–288.

ROBINSON, JOAN 1956 *The Accumulation of Capital.* Homewood, Ill.: Irwin; London: Macmillan.

ROSENSTEIN-RODAN, PAUL N. 1943 Problems of Industrialization of Eastern and Southeastern Europe. *Economic Journal* 53:202–211.

ROSENSTEIN-RODAN, PAUL N. 1961 Notes on the Theory of the "Big Push." Pages 57–67 in International Economic Association, *Economic Development for Latin America: Proceedings of a Conference Held by the International Economic Association.* New York: St. Martins.

ROSTOW, WALT W. (1960) 1963 *The Stages of Economic Growth: A Non-Communist Manifesto.* Cambridge Univ. Press.

SCHULTZ, THEODORE W. 1961 Investment in Human Capital. *American Economic Review* 51:1–17.

SCHUMPETER, JOSEPH A. (1912) 1934 *The Theory of Economic Development: An Inquiry Into Profits, Capital, Credit, Interest, and the Business Cycle.* Harvard Economic Studies, Vol. 46. Cambridge, Mass.: Harvard Univ. Press. → First published as *Theorie der wirtschaftlichen Entwicklung.*

SOLOW, ROBERT M. 1956 A Contribution to the Theory of Economic Growth. *Quarterly Journal of Economics* 70:65–94.

SOLOW, ROBERT M. 1957 Technical Change and the Aggregate Production Function. *Review of Economics and Statistics* 39:312–320.

SOLOW, ROBERT M. 1960 Investment and Technical Progress. Pages 89–104 in Stanford Symposium on Mathematical Methods in the Social Sciences, Stanford University, 1959, *Mathematical Methods in the Social Sciences, 1959: Proceedings.* Edited by Kenneth J. Arrow, Samuel Karlin, and Patrick Suppes. Stanford Univ. Press.

SOLOW, ROBERT M. 1963 *Capital Theory and the Rate of Return.* Amsterdam: North-Holland Publishing.

SWAN, T. W. 1956 Economic Growth and Capital Accumulation. *Economic Record* 32:334–361.

III
MATHEMATICAL THEORY

Long-run economic growth, like short-run economic equilibrium, is studied from both the microeconomic and macroeconomic points of view. The microeconomic or multisector theory of growth, which can be thought of as a dynamic extension of the general equilibrium theory of exchange and production, has received considerable mathematical attention in recent decades. Golden equilibrium growth (defined below) is the theory's central concept, and the mathematical analyses deal with the existence, optimality, and stability of golden equilibrium growth paths.

The roles of monetary phenomena, international trade, and technological change have so far received little attention in the analyses. These factors may have important influences on actual processes of economic growth, and neglect of them may be the source of serious shortcomings in the microtheory. But the microtheory is still in its early stages of development, and the study of these factors must as yet be left to macroeconomic analysis.

The Walrasian model. The prototype of contemporary growth models was formulated by Walras (1874–1877). A description of the Walrasian model in its simplest form follows.

It is assumed that there are two groups of citizens—workers and capitalists—and two industries—one producing a consumption good and the other producing a capital good. Assume for the moment that the capital good is not subject to depreciation. A number of basic manufacturing processes are available to firms in both industries, and the capital-input and labor-input coefficients of each process are assumed constant. If perfect competition prevails among firms, no firm will gain supernormal profits. Thus, in an equilibrium state,

(1) the price of the consumption good is less than or equal to the cost per unit of out-

put of any process of the consumption good industry,

and

(2) the price of the capital good is less than or equal to the cost per unit of output of any process of the capital good industry.

Cost per unit of output is the sum of the capital-input coefficient multiplied by the price of the capital service and the labor-input coefficient multiplied by the wage rate. Conditions (1) and (2) must hold with equality for some processes, and those processes for which the conditions hold with strict inequality are not used in equilibrium.

Demand for the consumption good is assumed to depend on the price of the consumption good, the price of the capital good, and total money income. If prices and money income change by the same proportion, demand is assumed to remain unchanged. Furthermore, the elasticity of demand with respect to total money income is assumed to be unity. In view of the definition of savings as the excess of income over consumption,

(3) total income is identically equal to consumption plus savings.

The amount of capital used in the economy is the sum over all processes of the output produced by each process multiplied by the corresponding capital-input coefficient. The range of summation covers the entire economy, that is, the consumption good industry as well as the capital good industry. Since the amount of capital utilized at any point of time cannot exceed the amount available,

(4) the amount of capital utilized must be less than or equal to the amount of capital in existence.

Similar conditions must hold for labor, the consumption good, and the capital good, namely,

(5) the amount of labor utilized must be less than or equal to the amount of labor available,

(6) demand for the consumption good must be less than or equal to total output of the consumption good,

(7) demand for the capital good must be less than or equal to total output of the capital good.

The rule of free goods prevails in the markets, so that if one of the conditions (4) to (7) holds with strict inequality, then the corresponding price, say the price of the capital service in the case of (4),

is set at zero. Conditions (1) to (7) are then found to imply the equality of savings and investment.

Existence of a golden growth equilibrium. We now examine the Walrasian model for the existence of a golden growth equilibrium, defined as a state in which outputs of all goods grow at a rate equal to the rate of growth of the labor force and in which all prices remain unchanged forever. The argument proceeds in terms of the warranted and natural rates of growth, the most fundamental concepts of growth economics originally due to Harrod (1948).

Harrod defined the warranted rate of growth as "that over-all rate of advance which, if executed, will leave entrepreneurs in a state of mind in which they are prepared to carry on a similar advance" (1948, p. 82). Some preliminary analysis is required to establish the warranted rate, for it is a concept that results from a combination of the so-called factor–price frontiers (Morishima 1964, pp. 76–83; Samuelson 1962) and Kahn's interindustrial multiplier (Kahn 1931).

Suppose that prices are normalized so that the price of the consumption good is unity. Then the normalized wage rate gives the real wage. Conditions (1) and (2) now contain three variables—the price of the capital good, the price of the capital service, and the real wage rate. Therefore, two of these prices, say the first two, can be expressed as functions of the third. We can then obtain a relation between the rate of return on capital, that is, the ratio of the price of the capital service to the price of the capital good, and the real wage rate. This relation is referred to as the envelope of the factor–price frontiers, or simply the factor–price frontier. The rate of return on capital can be shown to decrease when the real wage rate increases in an interval permitted by technology.

It follows from (1) and (2) that there exist positive prices corresponding to any preassigned nonnegative value of the real wage rate, provided the value of the real wage does not exceed the maximum permitted by technology. This implies that (4), (6), and (7) hold as equalities. Since demand for the consumption good equals total income multiplied by the average propensity to consume (denoted by c),

(8) consumption equals c times the sum of consumption and savings.

If ξ denotes the output of the consumption good, x the output of the capital good, and p the price of the capital good in terms of the consumption good, then conditions (6) and (7), together with other equilibrium conditions, imply that consumption equals ξ and that savings equals px. Substituting (6) and (7) into (8), we obtain the Kahn multiplier,

$$(9) \qquad \xi/x = pc/(1-c).$$

From the factor–price frontier, prices depend on the real wage rate. Since c is assumed to depend only on prices, it is seen that the real wage rate is the ultimate determinant of the relative outputs of the two industries.

The warranted rate of growth can easily be established now. Dividing condition (4) by the output of the capital good, we obtain to the right of the equality the reciprocal of the rate of growth of the capital stock. Since the processes for which (1) or (2) hold with strict inequality are not adopted, and since the choice of other processes is subject to (9), the rate of growth of the capital stock depends on the real wage rate. Hence, there is a relation between the growth rate of the capital stock and the real wage rate in the entire interval permitted by technology. This relation is called the warranted growth rate curve. Suppose w is the real wage rate arbitrarily set in the technologically permitted interval. Entrepreneurs will increase the stock of capital at the rate corresponding to the given value of w, and all the equilibrium conditions except (5) will be fulfilled. Entrepreneurs will wish to maintain this growth rate, and it will persist if the supply of labor adapts itself to the demand for labor.

In the absence of technological change, the natural rate of growth is equal to the rate of growth of the labor force. The rate of growth of the labor force is often assumed to be constant (independent of the values of economic variables) but may more realistically be considered a function of the real wage rate. Suppose that the growth rate of the labor force is positive, zero, or negative depending on whether the real wage is above, equal to, or below the subsistence level. This relation between the natural growth rate (the growth rate of the labor force) and the real wage rate is called the natural growth rate curve.

The warranted and natural growth rate curves will generally have at least one point of intersection, and at that point the stock of capital and the labor force grow at a common rate. Suppose $\bar{w}$ is a real wage rate at which the stock of capital, K, and the labor force, L, increase at the same rate $\bar{g}$. Let the values of the other variables that satisfy the equilibrium conditions (1) to (7) be denoted by corresponding letters with bars above them. A proportional increase in K and L gives rise to an increase of the same proportion in total income, provided

prices remain constant. Since the income elasticity of demand for the consumption good is unity, the increase in total income gives rise to an increase of the same proportion in the demand for the consumption good. Therefore, if prices remain constant over time, equilibrium at any point of time t is established when

$$\bar{\xi}_t = e^{\bar{g}t}\bar{\xi}_0,$$
$$\bar{x}_t = e^{\bar{g}t}\bar{x}_0,$$
$$\bar{K}_t = e^{\bar{g}t}\bar{K}_0,$$
$$\bar{L}_t = e^{\bar{g}t}\bar{L}_0,$$

where subscripts indicate time; that is to say, when the real wage rate $\bar{w}$ prevails, the stock of capital, the labor force, and the outputs of the two industries grow forever at the common rate $\bar{g}$, and prices remain unchanged. Such a state is called a state of golden growth equilibrium (Robinson 1956, p. 9; Morishima 1964, p. 78).

The von Neumann model.   The two-sector model examined so far assumes, among other things, (a) that firms can be classified into two industries producing distinct outputs, (b) that factors of production are instantaneously transformed into products, (c) that the capital good does not suffer wear and tear, and (d) that the capital stock and the supply of labor are freely transferable from one firm to another. All these assumptions are unrealistic, and they crucially affect the analytical properties of the model.

First, it is clear from actual input–output tables of various countries that many goods are both consumed and used as inputs in many industries in the economy; there is no clear demarcation between consumption goods and capital goods. Second, a certain length of time generally must elapse between the original input of factors and the final output of a product. The period of production usually differs from one good to another, but we may justify the assumption of uniform production lags by introducing as many fictitious intermediate products at each point of time as required.

Third, according to the neoclassical treatment of depreciation, capital goods that were produced several years ago and have been subject to wear and tear are considered to be physically equivalent to some smaller amounts of new capital goods of the same kind. But it is generally impossible to find *quantitative* equivalents, in terms of new capital goods, of capital goods damaged in various degrees from past use. In fact, if an entrepreneur has a certain amount of a capital good that is in its final stage of wear and tear, he will have no capital equipment at the beginning of the next year; while if he has a certain amount, however small, of a new capital good, he may use it for production throughout its whole lifetime. Only by treating capital goods at different stages of depreciation as *qualitatively* different goods can we adequately deal with the age structure of the capital stock. Von Neumann (1937) suggested that used capital goods appearing simultaneously with products at the end of the production period be treated as by-products of the manufacturing process. A process that uses capital equipment is regarded as a process that converts a bundle of "inputs" into a bundle of "outputs," where inputs are defined to include capital goods left over from the preceding period and outputs are defined to include qualitatively different capital goods left over at the end of the current period.

This treatment of capital goods enables us to discard the final assumption of perfect transferability of capital equipment. In addition to being more productive, a new capital good is generally more transferable than a used one. A new machine will be sold to any factory that demands it, while a machine that has already been set up in a factory usually will not be transferred to another factory, even if the factory that owns the machine is overequipped and some other factory is underequipped. This asymmetry in the transferability of capital goods can readily be incorporated in the growth model if we permit joint production in the sense von Neumann suggested and treat capital goods at different dates as different goods.

From these considerations, it is clear that the growth model, if it is not to be trivial, must not only be multisectoral but must also be capable of dealing successfully with joint production. A model fulfilling these requirements was first proposed by von Neumann. He assumed the following: (*a*) there are constant returns to scale in production of all goods; (*b*) the supply of labor can be expanded indefinitely; (*c*) the wage rate is fixed at a level at which workers can only purchase the minimum amounts of goods biologically required to subsist; and (*d*) the whole of capitalists' income is invested in new capital goods. It is evident that the model ignores the role played by consumers' choice in the determination of the rate of growth; workers are like farm animals, and capitalists are simply self-service stands of capital.

Consumers' choice has been introduced into the model by relaxing the classical assumption that workers only consume and capitalists only save. Morishima (1964) studied models where (1) although workers still consume their entire income, their demand for consumption goods allows substitution in response to price changes, and (2) capitalists spend a portion of their income on consumption goods in such a way that their demand for each good depends not only on relative prices but also on their income—the income elasticity of demand being unity. Morishima also replaced von Neumann's unrealistic assumption of an indefinitely expandable labor force with a more plausible assumption of a labor force growing at a rate that depends on the real wage rate.

Perfect transferability of capital goods is not a necessary condition for the existence of golden growth equilibrium; but the assumption of *unitary* income elasticities of demand, which is very stringent and unrealistic, is an indispensable condition. Aside from uneven effects of technological change on various industries, the only obstacle to golden growth is the existence of *different* income elasticities of demand for different consumption goods.

In an economy where wages are paid at the end of each period, the golden equilibrium growth rate equals the product of the capitalists' average propensity to save and the rate of profit on fixed capital. On the other hand, if wages are advanced at the beginning of each period, they earn profit during the period, and the golden equilibrium growth rate equals the capitalists' propensity to save multiplied by the rate of profit on total capital, which is the sum of fixed capital and the wages fund (Morishima 1964, pp. 145–151).

Stability of a golden growth equilibrium. In examining the stability of a golden growth equilibrium, a problem posed is whether the maintenance of full employment of labor and capital along a path starting from arbitrarily or historically given endowments of capital and labor will eventually lead to a state of golden equilibrium growth. Various writers have studied this problem and have found that a large class of two-sector models have a stable golden equilibrium if certain plausible restrictions are imposed on technology or on the consumption function. For example, in the case of the Walrasian two-sector model, stability is ensured if a constant proportion of income is devoted to consumption.

However, in more realistic multisector models, the tendencies toward a golden growth equilibrium may not exist. It has been argued that the stability of outputs in a multisector model implies the instability of prices, and vice versa. Jorgenson (1960) proved that this is the case for a *closed* dynamic Leontief input–output system. However, for an *open* system, he showed that stability of outputs implies stability of prices, except under rather implausible circumstances. Since examples of both stability and instability of golden equilibrium growth can be found, the maintenance of full employment of labor and capital is not a sufficient condition for the attainment of a golden growth state.

A growth path is called efficient if there is no other path along which more of some goods can be produced without reducing the output of another good. A growth path is called optimal if there is no other path that can make the society better off. Full employment of labor and capital is a characteristic of an efficient or optimal growth path if labor and capital are always scarce. Whether or not these factors are scarce, however, depends on the amounts of goods to be produced. In a planned economy, a certain amount of the capital stock may not be used at some point of time if the existing capital stock exceeds the amount required by a long-run growth plan designed to attain either efficiency in production or maximum satisfaction of the citizenry. Similarly, a portion of the labor force may not be used. Hence, rather than examining the convergence of a full employment growth path to the golden equilibrium path, we might examine the convergence of efficient growth paths to the golden equilibrium path.

The turnpike theorems. The turnpike growth path (or, more briefly, the turnpike) is defined as the golden equilibrium growth path (there may be many such paths) that gives the maximum rate of growth. The study of convergence of efficient growth paths to the turnpike has produced the so-called turnpike theorems.

Adopting von Neumann's assumptions presented above, the basic turnpike theorem may be stated as follows: Let the stocks of goods that the economy intends to have at the end of a planning period be specified in their proportions (but not in their absolute values) by the planning authorities. Consider efficient paths in the set of all feasible growth paths. In this instance, a feasible growth path is one leading from the historically given present state to the prescribed end. There is a long-run tendency for such efficient paths to approximate the turnpike as the planning period becomes longer and longer. In other words, the long-run efficient paths run along the turnpike for most of the planning period, although they will have to leave the turnpike in the final part of the planning period in order to reach the objective (Dorfman et al. 1958, pp. 326–345).

This theorem would be especially useful in formulating a seven-year or ten-year growth plan for underdeveloped or socialist economies. Mathematical economists have provided rigorous statements and proofs of the theorem (Radner 1961; McKenzie 1963) and have found that there are exceptions to the theorem. Unless the technology available to the economy satisfies some special conditions, efficient paths will trace out undamped oscillations around the turnpike (Morishima 1964, pp. 171–173; Hicks 1965, pp. 224–225, 327–331).

The theorem can be modified or extended in several directions. For example, it has been shown that the stocks of goods discounted by one plus the turnpike rate of growth and averaged along efficient paths over the whole planning period are very close to the turnpike stock vector if the length of the planning period is sufficiently long. Such a convergence theorem may be termed the mean turnpike theorem. There is no cyclic exception to the mean turnpike theorem; even though efficient paths may fluctuate around the turnpike regularly or irregularly, the average of the discounted values of deviations from the turnpike always approaches zero in the limit (Morishima 1965).

The turnpike theorems discussed so far are based on the assumption that the labor force can be expanded at any rate. This assumption can be replaced by the more general assumption that the production and reproduction of workers is part of the over-all process of production. Workers cannot choose goods according to their own tastes but are fed by the dictator or planning authorities just as farm animals are. When there is a shortage of workers, they will be fed well to increase the birth rate; in a period of excess supply of workers, they will be underfed. Obviously, the model describes a shameless society such as a slave economy, although this is not very far from the state of affairs in some countries. The turnpike (mean turnpike) theorem for such an economy asserts that all efficient paths converge to the turnpike in the sense that output of each good per worker (the average discounted output per worker) approximates the turnpike output per worker when the planning period is very long.

In the models just described, the planning authorities specified only terminal stocks of goods. Outputs of goods at any intermediate date were simply inputs for the immediately succeeding date, and there was no consumption at intermediate dates. (Feeding the workers was necessary to *produce* workers; the food they ate was an *input* for the process that produced workers who, in turn, were inputs for other production processes.) Hence, a growth path was feasible if it merely satisfied the final-state conditions, and the turnpike theorems stated may be called final-state turnpike theorems. They hold when the sole objective is to bequeath certain stocks of goods to a remote future generation, for example, to our great-grandchildren. But if the welfare of children and grandchildren is to be taken into account, their consumption should also be part of the desiderata in the growth plan. Intermediate states as well as the final state must be evaluated according to some measure of welfare.

This can be accomplished by introducing a utility function that depicts the preference orderings (by the workers or by the ministry of welfare) of different streams of consumption and of amounts of work over the planning period. In particular, suppose we discount consumption and the amount of work at each future date by a subjective time-preference factor that does not exceed the turnpike growth rate. It is assumed that utility depends on the averages over all dates in the planning period of these discounted values. An optimal growth path is one that maximizes this utility function.

With the aid of some additional assumptions, we can establish the following consumption turnpike theorem: As the length of the planning period tends to infinity, any optimal path converges to the turnpike. As in the case of the final-state turnpike theorem, there will be cyclic exceptions to this consumption turnpike theorem if technology does not satisfy some restrictive conditions. Optimal paths may oscillate around the turnpike forever. However, a consumption *mean* turnpike theorem that is similar to the final-state mean turnpike theorem discussed above can be established, and there is no cyclic exception to the mean theorem.

The consumption turnpike theorem, unlike the final-state turnpike theorems, could avoid cyclic exceptions if it were assumed that society has an aversion to fluctuations. Of two consumption streams having the same average discounted values but having different fluctuations over the planning period, society may prefer the stream with the lesser fluctuations. An optimal growth path would then be one that maximizes a utility function that depends upon the average discounted values of consumption and of amounts of work *and* upon some measure of the variances of these streams. When the society's aversion to fluctuations is very strong, its optimal growth path will be a feasible path that has no fluctuations in consumption per capita, so that the convergence of consumption per capita to the turnpike is secured.

Even in this case, however, it is still possible to have fluctuations of outputs around the turnpike; in fact, people would be prepared to accept fluctuations of outputs if fluctuations are required for an optimum steady stream of consumption. Hence,

the introduction of very strong aversion to fluctuations will eliminate cycles in the per capita consumption of goods but not in per capita outputs.

Michio Morishima

[*See also* Economic equilibrium; Interest; Statics and dynamics in economics; *and the biographies of* von Neumann; Walras.]

BIBLIOGRAPHY

Dorfman, Robert; Samuelson, Paul A.; and Solow, Robert M. 1958 *Linear Programming and Economic Analysis.* New York: McGraw-Hill.

Hahn, F. H.; and Matthews, R. C. O. 1964 The Theory of Economic Growth: A Survey. *Economic Journal* 74:779–902.

Harrod, Roy F. (1948) 1960 *Towards a Dynamic Economics: Some Recent Developments of Economic Theory and Their Application to Policy.* London: Macmillan; New York: St. Martins.

Hicks, John R. 1965 *Capital and Growth.* New York: Oxford Univ. Press; Oxford: Clarendon.

Jorgenson, Dale W. 1960 A Dual Stability Theorem. *Econometrica* 28:892–899.

Kahn, R. F. 1931 The Relation of Home Investment to Unemployment. *Economic Journal* 41:173–198.

McKenzie, Lionel W. 1963 Turnpike Theorems for a Generalized Leontief Model. *Econometrica* 31:165–180.

Morishima, Michio 1964 *Equilibrium, Stability and Growth: A Multi-sectoral Analysis.* Oxford: Clarendon.

Morishima, Michio 1965 On the Two Theorems of Growth Economics: A Mathematical Exercise. *Econometrica* 33:829–840.

Radner, Roy 1961 Paths of Economic Growth That Are Optimal With Regard Only to Final States: A Turnpike Theorem. *Review of Economic Studies* 28:98–104.

Robinson, Joan 1956 *The Accumulation of Capital.* Homewood, Ill.: Irwin; London: Macmillan.

Samuelson, Paul A. 1962 Parable and Realism in Capital Theory: The Surrogate Production Function. *Review of Economic Studies* 29:193–206.

von Neumann, John (1937) 1945 A Model of General Economic Equilibrium. *Review of Economic Studies* 13:1–9. → First published in German in Volume 8 of *Ergebnisse eines mathematischen Kolloquiums.*

Walras, Léon (1874–1877) 1954 *Elements of Pure Economics: Or, the Theory of Social Wealth.* Translated by William Jaffé. Homewood, Ill.: Irwin; London: Allen & Unwin. → First published in French as *Éléments d'économie politique pure.*

IV

NONECONOMIC ASPECTS

The concept of underdevelopment which has become quite popular since the end of World War II applies primarily to societies which are inferior to the principal Western nations in terms of economic performance and technological sophistication. In previous periods these societies were customarily referred to as "backward" or "arrested," but these terms have fallen into disuse, and in their stead "underdeveloped" or "developing" is used. In even more recent times, and with special regard to countries emerging from colonialism, the concept of "new nations" is being employed.

Although the condition of "underdevelopment" therefore is primarily an economic and technological feature of certain societies, it appears to have important sociological concomitants, and it is these social and cultural aspects of the condition of underdevelopment, as well as the variables which appear important in analyzing the gradual emergence of these societies from a condition of economic and technological underdevelopment to a level of higher economic and technical performance, which will be stressed in the subsequent paragraphs.

The description of underdevelopment and the identification of processes and policies which will lead out of it to higher levels of performance is primarily undertaken by economists. But economists realize that in performing this task they have to take account of noneconomic, i.e., primarily social and cultural, factors which strongly influence patterns of development. In fact, it may be argued that on the purely analytical level the economic problems of economic development are relatively simple, whereas the social and political aspects of the process are much more complex and elusive.

It is generally acknowledged that the main path to higher levels of economic performance is through the rational organization of production, and this rational organization in turn depends primarily on the introduction of industry. Thus, in terms of occupational structure, underdevelopment is characterized by the absolute prevalence of agriculture as the main source of livelihood; and economically more advanced societies usually show an increasing proportion of their labor force in secondary (manufacturing and mining) and tertiary (service) occupations. All societies which are in a state of underdevelopment, therefore, are nonindustrialized or little industrialized, and the process of economic development may in a rough way be equated with the progress of industry and associated forms of economic activity.

Classical approaches. We do not lack descriptions of nonindustrial societies, beginning with the ethnographic reports of "savages," "barbarians," or "exotic peoples." But these accounts are of little analytical value. The first useful attempts to come to grips with the analysis of the social system of nonindustrial societies begin with the work of scholars who sought to describe entire social systems associated with different levels of economic performance. Among the most famous attempts at holistic descriptions of differentiated social systems are the well-known dichotomies of Ferdinand Tönnies (1887) between *Gemeinschaft* and *Gesellschaft*, of Robert Redfield (1941; 1950) between folk and urban society, and of authors following Max Weber (1919–1920) between traditional and rational patterns of social action. This last contrast has received a great deal of attention, and we find not infrequently that action and behavior patterns in technologically and economically little developed societies are described as "traditional" and that this concept implies that these action patterns are inefficient, technologically noncomplex, and strongly resistant to innovation.

Redfield's "folk society."   Before entering into a more detailed analysis of the concept of tradition-oriented behavior, it would be useful to draw attention to two features of nonindustrialized societies which have received extensive treatment in the work of Redfield and Tönnies and their followers. One point often reiterated by Redfield is the fact that social acts in a folk society typically are not "single-interest" but "multiple-interest" actions. Productive activity, for example, not only has an economic purpose but also is conceived by the members of folk societies as containing ritual elements, elements pertaining to social cohesion or structure, "political goals," and others. This very "multidimensionality" of all social behavior in folk societies is at the bottom of some of the difficulties in bringing about changes in behavior. If social behavior were unidimensional, change would be relatively easy. Since in addition to meeting one specific objective, a given action is conceived of as simultaneously meeting other objectives, change is possible only if the new way of acting can be interpreted as comprising all these associated objectives also. In brief, some such behavior as planting, or harvesting, or engaging in exchange is conceived of not merely as productive activity but also as behavior maintaining the stability and relational adequacy of a person's position in his culture. Hence, if different forms of productive activity are proposed, they will prove acceptable (without strong external compulsion) only if they also meet in some form or another all or most of the other objectives which were met by the activity to be replaced.

Tönnies' "small community."   The emphasis placed by Tönnies and his disciples on the significance of community also has played an important role in the study of conditions surrounding technological change and economic innovation. The point to be emphasized in this context is that for many nonindustrialized societies, the small group is the relevant unit of social cohesion. This small community often has its origin in tribal or kinship relations, but what is important about it is that its membership is usually strictly circumscribed, limited to persons who have either long-standing face-to-face relationships or some other form of close common identification. All outsiders, i.e., all persons who do not belong to the small community, are strangers and are often regarded with suspicion.

In many underdeveloped societies these highly particularistic groups still exist, and in some instances they have considerable strength. They often appear as tribal groups, but also may constitute village communities, castes, or other associations based on kinship or quasi-kinship ties or joint occupancy of a small area. Usually the group lives in a compact area. Geography and familiarity thus reinforce one another, and the small community may be considered in some cultural contexts as a hard-shelled unit whose main forms of social interaction occur only within the community and whose relations to the outside are tenuous and often associated with suspicion and fear. In the development process, strong tendencies are set in motion to break up this isolation of the community and to enmesh its members in different forms of social relations with the outside. Moreover, it is often those persons who have low status within the community who most easily penetrate the wall built around it and who tend to interact most frequently with the remainder of the society.

Thus the significance of the small community is its resistance against absorption into the "great society" and the conflicts which arise on the social and personal level in the absorption process, in which primary loyalties to the small group gradually tend to be replaced by loyalties to the larger society. Moreover, many of the institutions which have meaning within the context of the small community lose this meaning in the framework of the larger society. The family as a productive unit that yields economic security loses its place in a society in which industrialization has occurred and in which the economic ties are with persons outside the kinship group and economic security is obtained through governmental or other insurance schemes. Similarly, the intimate relation with tribal or village deities loses its full significance for those who enter the larger society, and the patterns of deference and authority within the small community have no force outside it. All this tends to produce conflicts within and beyond the small community. One may notice them in India, where they manifest themselves in conflicts within and between castes; in Africa, where they appear as struggles between centralized authorities and tribal chieftains; and elsewhere, where they take on still different forms.

The strong nationalism which permeates many industrializing countries is the chief ideological underpinning for a process of social change which leads from the ubiquity of small, particularistic communities to a more uniform, structurally diversified but more highly interdependent society. Other processes associated with industrial development and less subject to manipulation by agitators and intellectuals support this trend. Among these are urbanization and bureaucratization of governmental and productive procedures. The onslaught on the small community thus comes from all sides, and it is not likely that it can withstand the combined impact of these forces.

From the description of the small community and the folk society, with its multifaceted features of social interaction, we can see that these two concepts are mainly different descriptions of the same social type. A third, and on the whole more popular, way of describing this type of society is to point to its traditionalism or, perhaps more correctly, to describe it as a society in which traditional forms of action predominate. As we have seen, the concept of traditional social action ultimately goes back to Max Weber (1922), who juxtaposed it to different forms of rational action. Since the concept of traditional or tradition-oriented action has gained such wide popularity, it must be considered in somewhat more detail.

Weber's "traditional behavior." Although Max Weber did not explicitly make the important distinction between *traditional action* and *traditionalistic action*, it is implicit in his work. Traditional or tradition-oriented social action is found in all societies. Weber described it as action based upon the psychic attitude set for the habitual workaday and the belief in the everyday routine as an inviolable norm of conduct (1922). But beyond this, the concept of traditional action may be widened by including forms of social behavior which have been taken over from ancestors and forebears, because all populations have a sense of their historical past and a need for continuity of behavioral norms and because these forms of social action can appropriately be fitted into the action schema of a society. This does not mean that traditional action excludes change. Many practices in modern, highly industrial societies are based on tradition and traditional norms. This is true of such everyday behavior patterns as forms of greeting and rules of personal conduct, but it is also true of more complex behavior in the political and economic spheres. It would be difficult to separate societies at different levels of economic performance by the relative "quantity" of tradition-oriented behavior that their members show.

Traditionalistic action, on the other hand, may be defined as action based upon the self-conscious, deliberate affirmation of traditional norms in full awareness of their traditional nature and alleging that their merit derives from that traditional transmission from a sacred orientation (Weber 1919–1920). In other words, traditionalistic action is a conscious revival of a past glorious age or past sacred lore, an ideology which looks to the past as providing a set of norms whose revival would again lead to splendor and greatness. In the nationalisms of many industrializing countries, especially those whose roots go deep into a great past—such as India and the Islamic countries—we can find strong traditionalistic admixtures. These ideologies consist not merely in the rejection of Western values; the revival and revitalization of old values, often long dead, is demanded, and external behavior is approved which is thought to be in conformance with these norms.

Traditional action, though it may sometimes conflict with the demands of modernization and technological change, usually is an important reinforcing element in the preservation of stability in a period of rapid change. On the whole, the permanence of manifold traditions in social behavior may be an important factor mitigating the many dislocations and disorganizations which tend to accompany rapid industrialization and technical change. Traditionalistic action, on the other hand, since it tries to elevate outdated practices and values to the level of current behavioral norms, usually has a reactionary character and tends to retard economic change. [*See the biographies of* REDFIELD; TÖNNIES; *and* WEBER, MAX.]

Parsons' pattern variables approach. One attempt to elaborate further the characteristics of tradition-oriented societies and, in fact, to break into its components the rationalism–tradition dichotomy, is the description of societies at different levels of economic performance by means of the pattern variables developed by Talcott Parsons (1951).

Of the five pairs of pattern alternatives stated by Parsons, three are immediately applicable: the choice between modalities of the social object (achievement versus ascription), the choice between types of value orientation (universalism versus particularism), and the definition of scope of interest in the object (specificity versus diffuseness). In applying these three pattern variables to the distinctions between industrialized and pre-

dominantly nonindustrial societies, we find that industrialized societies are characterized by the predominance of achievement standards in the distribution of economic roles and objects, that they employ universalistic criteria in this distribution process, and that economic roles in these societies are typically functionally specific. Underdeveloped societies, on the other hand, predominantly exhibit features of ascription, particularism, and functional diffuseness in the corresponding fields of social action. It should be emphasized that we are considering norms of social behavior. In other words, the complex of pattern variables present in any society constitutes an ideal type.

Achievement–ascription. The achievement–ascription dichotomy is closely related to, though not identical with, the contrast between status-oriented and contract-oriented societies first stressed by Henry Sumner Maine (1861). If we apply this dichotomy to economic objects, we find that in a society in which ascription is the norm, economic roles are distributed ideally on the basis of who a person is rather than what he can do. A practical example of a society based on ascription would be an "ideal" caste system, in which each caste is associated with a certain occupation and in which only members of a given caste are admitted to that occupation. The caste system, however, although it may have come close to this ideal in some localities at certain times, never, as a whole, exhibited fully ascriptive features [*see* CASTE]. But it is quite clear, from the example given, that in a society in which economic roles are assigned on the basis of status or ascription, social mobility is made difficult and social change, to the extent to which it depends upon mobility, is severely impeded.

In contrast, the predominance of an achievement norm with respect to the distribution of economic roles means that the primary criterion for attaining a certain occupation is based on a person's capacity to perform the required tasks. In practice, an actual test may be involved in the process of allocating economic roles, or, lacking this, certain objective criteria, such as successful completion of a certain number of years of school, or the obtaining of a degree, may be prescribed. Again, it is well known that pure performance criteria are not applied everywhere in industrialized countries, but the ideal of an achievement norm is strong enough so that even where economic roles are actually allocated on the basis of ascription, the pretense is made that the performance requirement has been met.

Universalism–particularism. The next pair of pattern alternatives, universalism–particularism, is related to the first pair. They do not prescribe norms concerning who is to perform a given role but stipulate whether the same rules apply to everyone. A good example of the application of particularistic norms with respect to economic action is the case of European medieval society, in which specific rules applied to peasants and burghers, to nobles and commoners. In many underdeveloped societies, certain markets and certain transactions are reserved to certain groups, and only the admission of an outsider to an otherwise closed group permits him to perform the functions reserved for this group. The principle of universalism, on the contrary, makes no such distinctions. The same rules apply to all, the principle of formal equality being elevated to a general norm of social behavior.

Specificity–diffuseness. It almost follows logically that in a society in which economic roles are distributed on the basis of universalistic performance criteria, the roles themselves are functionally highly specific. This requirement is an outflow of the rigorous application of the principle of achievement, which is of little value unless a role can be clearly defined and circumscribed. Functional specificity is, moreover, an outflow of the increasing division of labor. Adam Smith, in his famous example of the manufacture of pins, clearly demonstrates its economic advantage. For, as he points out, "the improvement of the dexterity of the workman necessarily increases the quantity of work he can perform; and the division of labour, by reducing every man's business to some one simple operation, and by making this operation the sole employment of his life, necessarily increases very much the dexterity of the workman" (Smith [1776] 1937, p. 7). There are other advantages, in Adam Smith's view, to the division of labor, but he quite accurately places the development of a high degree of functional specificity first.

Functional diffuseness stands in direct contrast with specificity. The simple peasant in a nonindustrial society is a characteristic representative of the functionally diffuse. He not only performs all work connected with producing a crop but he also builds his house, makes his implements, and often produces his own clothes and other final consumption goods. As in the cases of the ascription–achievement duality and the particularism–universalism duality, we find noncharacteristic cases which seem to contradict the generalization that diffuseness is normally associated with underdeveloped societies. For example, in India the system of social division of labor under the predominance of caste has led, even in a nonindustrial society, to a high degree of

functional specificity. On the other hand, certain occupations, especially on the highest managerial level, are functionally diffuse, even in highly industrialized societies. In general, functional specificity has been instituted more widely for the simpler and less complex tasks, but the progressive specialization in business management, and even in scientific pursuits, is a sign that this process of occupational differentiation is ubiquitous and strong in modern advanced societies.

The use of pattern variables has the advantage of bringing into sharper focus some of the strategic mechanisms of social change associated with industrialization and technical progress. Although universalistic norms need not generally replace particularistic ones, the transition from a system of ascription to one based on achievement in the allocation of economic roles and the replacement of functionally diffuse by functionally specific norms for the definition of economic tasks appear to have taken place in all cases of successful economic development. It is, therefore, useful to relate the description of industrial and nonindustrial societies which uses the pattern variables to the earlier descriptions which used the folk–urban continuum and the community–society dichotomy.

Integration of approaches. We have seen earlier that the folk society is characterized by a multidimensional meaning of economic acts, i.e., their relevance not merely as acts of production or exchange but also as acts of ritual, assertion of associative values, and so on. Alternatively, this fact can be described by pointing to the high degree of functional diffuseness of economic acts in the folk society. If a particular form of social behavior has meaning in several spheres of social action, it must, by necessity, be diffuse. It has many meanings, and although the actual manipulations demanded in its performance may be rigidly prescribed, its "multidimensionality" gives it the character of functional diffuseness, which, incidentally, also makes it so resistant to change.

Similarly, we may conceive of the small community as a set of institutionalized interpersonal relationships based primarily on ascriptive characteristics. The cohesion and compactness of the small community are enhanced because economic roles are tied to ascriptive status and because even where there is a considerable degree of specificity in different economic roles, as in the Indian village, ascriptive norms provide a stability and internal rigidity which makes change from within exceedingly difficult. It is only the breakup of the small community or its infiltration from the outside which tends to reduce the significance of ascription in the distribution of economic (and other, e.g., political or deference) roles.

The gradual destruction of the traditional folk-like small community thus is accompanied in the economic and technological spheres by a process of differentiation of economic roles and a relaxation of the rules assigning those roles to particular actors. But the process is not a smooth one; it proceeds in spurts and jolts. In this process new institutions develop, and as each new institution becomes established, it provides a pivotal point around which further changes gather momentum. If the juxtaposition of societies on different levels of economic modernization provides a classic case of the comparative analysis of social institutions, the analysis of the transformation from one to the next level of economic performance may be regarded as a study of the dynamics of institutional change.

Social deviance. This is not the place to discuss in an exhaustive manner the process of institutional change, which is a much broader process than merely overcoming a state of economic underdevelopment. But it may be useful to discuss the phenomena of *social deviance* and *social marginality*, because they have been applied quite commonly in the analysis of the social concomitants of industrialization and economic development.

Deviance. Let us first turn to a brief consideration of social deviance. As already stated, we are concerned here primarily with those forms of deviant behavior which are relevant for economic activity and organization. If the concept of deviance is to have operational meaning, it cannot be interpreted simply as signifying behavior which is new; it must imply that this set of innovating acts is opposed in some way to existing social norms or approved forms of behavior. In other words, a deviant always engages in behavior which constitutes a breach of the existing order and which is either contrary to, or at least not positively weighted in, the hierarchy of existing social values. If we apply this concept to the behavior displayed by businessmen and merchants in the course of the economic history of western Europe, we find that we can speak of genuine deviance in those periods and societies in which entrepreneurial behavior did not belong to the category of social actions which were considered as constituting the "good life." As late as the fifteenth century, this was true of certain kinds of financial entrepreneurship, which was always tainted by the official opposition of the church against usury. And later, when financial entrepreneurship became fully respectable, indus-

trial entrepreneurship came to be regarded with some disdain because it "dirtied one's hands." These sentiments toward business or industrial activity as not quite proper for a gentleman are familiar in many underdeveloped countries today.

If deviance implies some breach with existing social norms, it is interesting to investigate further from what social classes or groups persons come who engage in various forms of deviant behavior. Clearly, the expected rewards of this behavior must be attractive, and persons engaged in this behavior are likely to feel a strong urge to rise in the social scale (perhaps a strong motivation for achievement) or to have resentments against some aspects of the existing order. It is in these terms that the rise of the western European bourgeoisie or even of the lower samurai groups in Japan have been explained. In the view of some, this reshuffling of social positions is the result of class struggles; in the view of others, it is a gradual evolutionary process.

Marginality. An alternative hypothesis is that persons engaging in deviant behavior are at the margin of a given culture or are in a social or cultural position in which they straddle more than one culture. We may identify cases in which deviance coincides with social marginality. For example, in medieval Europe the earliest money-lenders were often foreigners. In Italy at the time of Gothic and Langobard rule, they were Syrians, Byzantines, and Jews. Later, when Italians turned to financial entrepreneurship on a large scale, the Genoese and Pisans, Sienese and Florentines, who were all lumped together under the name "Lombards," became the financial entrepreneurs north of the Alps.

The role of marginal individuals in various economic pursuits in many economically underdeveloped countries is eminently manifest today. One could cite the Chinese in various southeast Asian countries, the Indians in east Africa, and the widely scattered Lebanese and Syrians who make their appearance as businessmen in west Africa, Latin America, and elsewhere in poor societies.

What is the mechanism which allows marginal individuals to perform the roles they apparently have so widely accepted? As Robert E. Park (1913–1944), the inventor of the concept and of the significance of social marginality, has stressed, marginal men are—precisely because of their ambiguous position from a cultural, ethnic, linguistic, or sociostructural standpoint—strongly motivated to make creative adjustments in situations of change and, in the course of this adjustment process, to develop innovations in social behavior. Although many of Park's very general propositions have been refined by subsequent researchers, the theory of social marginality has not advanced sufficiently to supply convincing evidence for the role marginal individuals may play in all episodes of social change. Even if it is admitted that marginal persons tend to make creative adjustments more often than to relapse into old orthodoxies or to embrace new ones, the record is not at all clear, and there are some students who warn us that marginal individuals may be more prone than others to succumb to anomie and thus to become carriers of trends leading toward social disorganization rather than to creative innovations. [*See the biography of* PARK.]

Institutionalization of deviance. In circumstances in which a certain amount of deviant behavior has been displayed, the anchoring of this behavior in a new institution is of strategic significance. Originally a form of deviance, it becomes routinized and may display all the characteristics of some highly approved form of social behavior. Thus the institutions in which deviant action is anchored form an advance post from which further deviance becomes possible. For example, the institutions which arose in western Europe before the industrial revolution and in Japan before the Meiji period were already the end products of a process of social change which had begun with deviant behavior; these institutions, in turn, by their very existence made possible further economic and technological change.

Sanctions. Whether or not any given form of deviance will lead to the elaboration of new social institutions and ultimate routinization of this pattern of social action will depend upon several factors, among which the system of sanctions existing in a society may be the most important. These sanctions may be internalized, i.e., they may reside in the values and beliefs of a population; or they may be externalized, i.e., they may be imposed by persons in power, by the elite, against actual or would-be deviants. It appears that in some societies, e.g., imperial China, both these types of sanctions were very strong. In pre-Meiji Japan, internal sanctions had partially broken down, and the power of the shogunate had become increasingly weak, so as to soften external sanctions to a point at which they were inadequate to prevent the formation of new institutions, or at least the beginnings of these innovations.

Strategic groups. Thus the analysis of social change may be couched largely in terms of considering the impact of deviance, whether exercised by marginal men or not, the gradual institutionalization and routinization of deviance, and the range of sanctions opposed to deviant behavior. This analysis may be carried out, initially, on the "aggregate level," i.e., it may take into account an entire society at once. But our insights into social change may be sharpened if we disaggregate the variables in our analysis, i.e., if in a complex society, we take account not of changes affecting the society as a whole but of those affecting specialized sections or classes in the society. For deviance, sanctions, and the process of institutionalization have a different place and impact among different groups. Take sanctions as an example. Clearly, in societies in which ascriptive norms are strong, different individuals, depending upon their status positions, will be subject to different internalized sanctions; and in a society with extensive particularism, even external sanctions will be imposed and enforced to a very different degree on persons belonging to different groups or classes.

Elites. Thus, we are likely to discover in any society certain strategic groups which become the carriers of innovations. In some instances these groups may be composed of marginal individuals, especially if the innovations are transmitted from the outside. The role of marginal individuals in the acculturation or culture contact process has as yet been insufficiently explored, but their prominent participation in this process follows almost as a matter of definition. Another group which often plays a strategic role is the elite of a society. Although considerable attention has been given to the role of the elite in preserving a *status quo*, its impact on the introduction of organizational and technological innovations has perhaps been underestimated. In general, social change has been seen as being accompanied by a "circulation of elites," rather than as a process in which existing elites are capable of reorienting the systemic goals which they attempt to implement. Yet in the present economically underdeveloped countries, in which so much economic change is managed by the holders of political power, the role of the existing elites as innovators must be acknowledged. The entrepreneurial functions, which in Western countries were displayed predominantly by independent businessmen often belonging to a not fully enfranchised and politically impotent bourgeoisie, have been taken over by bureaucrats who operate with the blessing and under the protection of the political power apparatus. [*See* ELITES; ENTREPRENEURSHIP.]

Role of the state. In part, the intervention of the state in the industrialization process is certainly an outcome of the greater pressures, of the greater distance between reality and aspirations, which exist in the present. We may list several general factors which tend to enhance the role of the state in the process of economic growth. The urge for massive state intervention in the process of economic and industrial growth will be the stronger: (1) the greater the range of ends and the higher the level of attainment sought; (2) the shorter the time horizon within which the ends are to be attained, that is, the more rapid the rate of economic growth desired; (3) the more unfavorable the factor and resource endowments; (4) the greater the institutional barriers to economic change and industrialization; and (5) the more backward the economy in relative terms. As time progresses without development, the fifth condition is bound to obtain, simply because the later the onset of industrialization, the more backward a country will be in relative terms. But if this condition holds, it is also likely that the first, second, and fourth conditions will obtain, and thus we may conclude from this empirically derived set of conditions that in the course of time incentives and urges for state intervention in the industrialization process are constantly on the increase. But this means that industrialization as a goal progressively becomes an objective of over-all social policy and that existing elites, whatever their primary ends may have been in the past, have reoriented the hierarchy of the systemic goals by assigning an increasingly important place to economic development. But the increased interest of governments in economic growth and industrialization means not merely that they are capable of exercising control over the total resources of a society to be applied to its economic buildup, but also that, more effectively than any other agency, they can influence the forms of social behavior by altering patterns of rewards and sanctions and otherwise intervening in the social structure. This shows again that, in spite of the strong impact of ideological considerations in present-day developing nations, the conditions of social structure and the state of relative retardation and underdevelopment exert, in turn, an important influence upon the ideological forms as well as the socioeconomic relations under which the development process takes place.

BERT F. HOSELITZ

BIBLIOGRAPHY

ALMOND, GABRIEL A.; and COLEMAN, JAMES S. (editors) 1960 *The Politics of the Developing Areas.* Princeton Univ. Press.

BANFIELD, EDWARD C. 1958 *The Moral Basis of a Backward Society.* Glencoe, Ill.: Free Press.

BOEKE, JULIUS H. 1953 *Economics and Economic Policy of Dual Societies as Exemplified by Indonesia.* New York: Institute of Pacific Relations. → Revision of the author's two earlier studies: *The Structure of the Netherlands Indian Economy,* 1942, and *The Evolution of the Netherlands Indies Economy,* 1946.

HAGEN, EVERETT E. 1962 *On the Theory of Social Change.* Homewood, Ill.: Dorsey.

HOSELITZ, BERT F. (editor) 1952 *The Progress of Underdeveloped Areas.* Univ. of Chicago Press.

HOSELITZ, BERT F. 1960 *Sociological Aspects of Economic Growth.* Glencoe, Ill.: Free Press.

KUZNETS, SIMON S. 1959 *Six Lectures on Economic Growth.* New York: Free Press.

MAINE, HENRY J. S. (1861) 1960 *Ancient Law: Its Connection With the Early History of Society, and Its Relations to Modern Ideas.* Rev. ed. New York: Dutton; London and Toronto: Dent. → A paperback edition was published in 1963 by Beacon.

MEIER, RICHARD L. 1956 *Science and Economic Development: New Patterns of Living.* Cambridge, Mass.: M.I.T. Press.

NORTH AMERICAN CONFERENCE ON THE SOCIAL IMPLICATIONS OF INDUSTRIALIZATION AND TECHNOLOGICAL CHANGE, CHICAGO, *1960* 1963 *Industrialization and Society: Proceedings.* Edited by Bert F. Hoselitz and Wilbert E. Moore. Paris: UNESCO.

PARK, ROBERT E. (1913–1944) 1950 *Collected Papers of Robert Ezra Park.* Volume 1: Race and Culture. Glencoe, Ill.: Free Press.

PARSONS, TALCOTT 1951 *The Social System.* Glencoe, Ill.: Free Press.

REDFIELD, ROBERT 1941 *The Folk Culture of Yucatan.* Univ. of Chicago Press.

REDFIELD, ROBERT 1950 *A Village That Chose Progress: Chan Kom Revisited.* Univ. of Chicago Press. → A paperback edition was published in 1962.

ROSTOW, WALT W. (1952) 1960 *The Process of Economic Growth.* 2d ed. Oxford: Clarendon.

SHANNON, LYLE W. 1957 *Underdeveloped Areas.* New York: Harper.

SLOTKIN, JAMES S. 1960 *From Fields to Factory: New Industrial Employees.* New York: Free Press.

SMITH, ADAM (1776) 1937 *An Inquiry Into the Nature and Causes of the Wealth of Nations.* New York: Modern Library.

TÖNNIES, FERDINAND (1887) 1957 *Community and Society (Gemeinschaft und Gesellschaft).* Translated and edited by Charles P. Loomis. East Lansing: Michigan State Univ. Press. → First published in German. A paperback edition was published in 1963 by Harper.

WEBER, MAX (1919–1920) 1961 *General Economic History.* Translated by Frank H. Knight. New York: Collier. → Lectures delivered 1919–1920.

WEBER, MAX (1922) 1957 *The Theory of Social and Economic Organization.* Edited by Talcott Parsons. Glencoe, Ill.: Free Press. → First published as Part 1 of *Wirtschaft und Gesellschaft.*

ECONOMIC HISTORY
See under HISTORY.

ECONOMIC INTEGRATION
See INTERNATIONAL INTEGRATION, *article on* ECONOMIC UNIONS.

ECONOMIC MAN

See DECISION MAKING, *article on* ECONOMIC ASPECTS.

ECONOMIC PLANNING

See PLANNING, ECONOMIC.

ECONOMIC SOCIOLOGY

See ECONOMY AND SOCIETY.

ECONOMIC THOUGHT

This entry includes articles on the major schools of economic thought other than those which now constitute the main body of academic thought in the Western world and their most direct antecedents. For discussion of the English classical school, see the biographies of SMITH, ADAM; RICARDO; MILL; HUME; McCULLOCH; SENIOR. *For the English and American neoclassical economists, see the biographies of* MARSHALL; JEVONS; PIGOU; CLARK, JOHN BATES; FISHER, IRVING; KNIGHT. *For discussion of the influence of Keynes, see* KEYNES, JOHN MAYNARD; HANSEN; *and the articles* INCOME AND EMPLOYMENT THEORY *and* LIQUIDITY PREFERENCE.

I. ANCIENT AND MEDIEVAL THOUGHT   *Raymond de Roover*
II. MERCANTILIST THOUGHT   *Jacob Viner*
III. PHYSIOCRATIC THOUGHT   *Joseph J. Spengler*
IV. SOCIALIST THOUGHT   *Maurice Dobb*
V. THE HISTORICAL SCHOOL   *Theo Surányi-Unger*
VI. THE AUSTRIAN SCHOOL   *Friedrich A. von Hayek*
VII. THE INSTITUTIONAL SCHOOL   *Allan G. Gruchy*

I
ANCIENT AND MEDIEVAL THOUGHT

Ancient period

Greek thought. In ancient Greece, "economics" did not mean what it means today; rather, it embraced everything pertaining to household management. (It kept this meaning until the eighteenth century.) Political economy, or economics in the present sense of the word, was not regarded as an independent discipline but was an integral part of ethics or politics. Socioeconomic questions were the province of ethics insofar as they dealt with private business contracts and of politics insofar as they touched upon public policy and affected social arrangements. It is not surprising, therefore, that Aristotle discusses economics in his books *Nicomachean Ethics* and *Politics*.

The Greek philosophers did not go beyond fundamentals and trite observations. Yet, their contributions are important because, as Joseph A. Schumpeter (1954) remarks, their economics is the fountainhead of practically all further work. They raised all the crucial questions, from value and price to economic organization, with which economists are still concerned at the present time.

Plato. Plato (427–347 B.C.) started in his *Dialogues* from the premise that no individual is self-sufficient and stated that cooperation and mutual intercourse are therefore the basis of the state as well as of the economy. Division of labor creates efficiency because, according to Plato, diversity of innate talents prompts individuals to specialize in what they are best fitted for, a fact that is sometimes overlooked or even denied—for example, by Adam Smith. States also are not self-sufficient, and rarely do they possess such a variety of resources that they can get along without commerce. The existence of an exchange economy is taken for granted, since Plato stated that each community will need a market place and a token money for purposes of exchange. Contrary to what is often asserted, Plato was not really an advocate of communism. In his scheme, communism was limited to the warrior class, whose members were forbidden to own property and were expected to share common meals and to live together like soldiers in a camp. Nevertheless, Plato was taunted by his pupil Aristotle for making this impractical proposal.

Aristotle. Like Plato, Aristotle (384–322 B.C.) assumed from the outset the existence of an exchange economy based on the division of labor and the institution of private property. He justified the latter on grounds of efficiency—people take better care of what is their own than of what is held in common. Money is necessary to obviate the inconveniences of barter. Besides being a medium of exchange, money is a measure of all things and "a guarantee of exchange in the future," since it can be stored until needed. Although money, Aristotle recognized, varies in purchasing power, its value tends to be rather constant and more stable than that of other commodities. Therefore, Aristotle, unlike Plato, did not favor a token currency, but required money to be made of a substance, such as silver, that is "really valuable itself" as well as easy to carry.

According to Aristotle, the source of value is *need*, for no exchange will take place without need; and the basis of exchange will differ as needs differ. Although in his *Topica* Aristotle referred to the marginal principle, there is no evidence that he ever thought of applying it to demand theory. Instead, he developed the concept of *value in use* and *value in exchange*, which much later involved Adam Smith in inextricable difficulties. Medieval and later commentators have tried in vain to elucidate the obscure passages that Aristotle devoted to price determination in Book V of his *Nicomachean Ethics*. While remaining silent about the virtues of competition, he mentioned monopoly as a device for exploiting the public.

Aristotle was definitely of the opinion that economic relations ought to be ruled by justice, of which there were two kinds: corrective, or commutative, justice, which applied to such private transactions as buying and selling; and distributive justice, which regulated the distribution of wealth. Corrective justice rested on the principle of equivalence; distributive justice was based on merit, the criteria of which might vary from one society to another. This whole concept of justice was later taken over by Thomas Aquinas and the Scholastics, almost without modification, and is still accepted by Roman Catholic social scientists.

Aristotle cited the story of Midas to emphasize the point that money is not identical with wealth. Agriculture and household management were honorable, but he frowned upon "krematistics," or such wealth-accumulating activities as trade. Above all, he deplored moneylending because it involved usury—"money bred of money" is unnatural because money was invented to serve as a medium of exchange. These views, too, were adopted by the Scholastics.

Roman thought.   In contrast with the Greeks, the Romans were not strong in speculative philosophy and made no significant contributions to economics, with the possible exception of treatises on agriculture which were practical rather than theoretical. The Romans, being administrators, excelled in legislation; and their great contribution is the body of law codified by Emperor Justinian, who reigned from 527 to 565. To be sure, Roman law is a compilation of legal texts containing nothing that even remotely approaches economic analysis; however, because of the use made of it by the Scholastics, it is very important to the evolution of economic thought.

Medieval or scholastic thought

Scope and method.   Scholastic economics is often regarded as a medieval doctrine; but this, strictly speaking, is incorrect. Although it had its roots in the Middle Ages, it outlived this period by more than two centuries. Far from dying around 1500, scholastic economics continued to flourish throughout the sixteenth century with the famous school of Salamanca, founded by the great jurist

Francisco de Vitoria, O.P. (c. 1480–1546). It reached its zenith of refinement and elaboration in the great works of synthesis and vulgarization of the seventeenth century and still had some vigor left in the eighteenth century, when Pietro Ballerini (1698–1769) and Daniel Concina, O.P. (1687–1756) took a last stand to defend the church's traditional doctrine on usury against the insidious attacks of Marchese Francesco Scipione Maffei (1675–1755) and Nicolas Broedersen (c. 1690–1772).

Even then scholastic economics did not die. It left its imprint, although unacknowledged and even disavowed, on the works of Abbé Ferdinando Galiani (1728–1787) and Abbé Antonio Genovesi (1712–1769), both Neapolitan forerunners of the classical school. Adam Smith (1723–1790), if Schumpeter is correct, owed more to Scholasticism than to mercantilism or physiocracy. In any case, scholastic doctrines were transmitted to him by Hugo Grotius (1583–1645) and Samuel von Pufendorf (1632–1694), whose works were used as textbooks when Smith attended the course in moral philosophy taught by Francis Hutcheson (1694–1746) at Glasgow College. This is a fact not to be denied. Regardless of controversies about who influenced whom and to what extent, there was continuity—not a sudden break—a point that should be stressed.

Like the Greek philosophers, the scholastic Doctors did not consider economics as an autonomous subject, but as a branch of moral philosophy (or moral theology). This is significantly the subject taught by both Smith and Genovesi, the former at Glasgow College and the latter at the University of Naples. However, Smith made economics into an independent science governed by expediency rather than by ethics.

In building their philosophical system, of which economics was a part, the scholastic Doctors combined elements from five different sources: the Bible, patristic literature, Greek philosophy, canon law, and Roman law. Greek philosophy, especially that of Aristotle, and Roman law were perhaps the most important for their economics. Canon law supplied only the canons outlawing usury and those denouncing trade as a sinful occupation. The scholastic writers took from Roman law the classification of contracts, which provided the framework for their whole doctrine. For example, the just price was discussed in connection with the *emptio–venditio*, or sales contract; and usury, in connection with the *mutuum*, or straight loan.

The medieval mind was legalistic. The question asked was not how the economic system functioned, but whether this or that was licit or illicit, just or unjust. In other words, the scholastic approach to economic problems was legal and ethical rather than mechanistic. The overemphasis on usury by many scholastic authors may have given the impression that this one question was the core of their doctrine, but this is not so. According to the Schoolmen, the scope of economics was to determine the rules of justice that applied to the exchange of goods or services (commutative justice) and to the distribution of income and wealth (distributive justice). This distinction between commutative and distributive justice was, of course, borrowed from Aristotle. Social justice is a new concept added by neoscholastic writers in recent times.

Like Marxian dialectics, the scholastic method follows a set pattern. One is certain to find economic questions discussed in any scholastic treatise dealing with moral theology or entitled *De contractibus* ("Concerning Contracts") or *De justitia et jure* ("Concerning Justice and Law"). Often it will be unnecessary to go beyond the title page or the table of contents in order to identify a treatise as belonging to the scholastic school.

The scholastic Doctors, following Aristotle, assumed that man was unable to minister to his own needs without assistance from his fellow men. According to Thomas Aquinas, o.p. (1225?–1274), the division of labor was ordained by a divine providence that endowed men with greater inclinations for one profession than for another (*Summa contra gentiles* III, 134).

In accordance with canon law, the community of goods was regarded as utopian, except when practiced on a small scale in monasteries or convents. While not an institution of natural law, private property, Thomas Aquinas declared, was an addition thereto devised by human reason (*Summa theologica* II–II, 66, 2, ad 1). He justified its existence on the same grounds that Aristotle did: first, because common property is apt to be neglected and, second, because public ownership only engenders confusion and discord. In the absence of planners, a planned economy was still inconceivable. Although property was privately owned, the use of it was common, and superfluities ought to be given to the poor. However, people were entitled to live as befitted their station in life. A knight, for example, was not required to give away his horses, because he might need them to fulfill his feudal obligations. Only in case of extreme necessity did all things revert to common ownership. Thus, a poor man on the point of starvation did not steal when he took a piece of bread without the permission of its owner.

The scholastic Doctors extolled agriculture as an occupation leading to virtue, but shared all the prejudices of Aristotle and of the Church Fathers against trade. Did not the canon law proclaim that merchants could scarcely, if ever, please God (*Decretum* Dist. 88, c. 11)? The attitude of the theologians mellowed only gradually. Thomas Aquinas approved of manufacturers and of importers who brought needed commodities from abroad. Later, the warehousing function was also recognized as legitimate, but retailing had to wait until the sixteenth century before receiving approval.

The scholastic doctrine centered on two main problems: the theory of the just price, and usury. Both have given rise to a great deal of misunderstanding.

Value theory. The scholastic Doctors were almost unanimous in recognizing utility as the source of value. In the words of Schumpeter, their analysis "lacked nothing but the marginal apparatus" (1954, p. 1054). Value was not regarded as an intrinsic quality, but as something dependent upon the mental process of valuation. To illustrate this point, the Schoolmen often cited St. Augustine (354–430), who stated in *The City of God* that, human superiority notwithstanding, a horse or a gem was often worth more than a slave. Some even turned this argument into a paradox by insisting that, if value were a matter of natural dignity, a living creature, such as a fly, would be more valuable than all the gold in the world. Value, in other words, was a function of utility. The other element of value—scarcity—was not overlooked. Perhaps one of the best scholastic expositions of value theory is found in the sermons of St. Bernardino of Siena, o.f.m. (1380–1444). However, he is not the original author of the passage, which he appropriated, without acknowledgment, from a manuscript—still unpublished—of Pierre Olivi, o.f.m. (1248–1298). He felt free to do this because Olivi had been accused of heresy. According to Olivi and Bernardino of Siena, there are three sources of value: scarcity (*raritas*), utility (*virtuositas*), and desirability (*complacibilitas*). Scarcity does not call for comment; utility is an objective quality: want-satisfying power; *complacibilitas* can only have one connotation: a subjective desire to gratify a want. This interpretation agrees with that of Schumpeter (1954, p. 98) who, however, wrongly regards St. Antoninus of Florence, o.p. (1389–1459) as the originator of this conception. It is regrettable that this line of thought was not pursued further. The Scholastics were certainly on the right track, although they did not quite succeed in solving the riddle of value.

The just price. Next to value comes price determination. Roman law had left this matter to the higgling and haggling between contracting parties. The medieval glossators added the phrase *sed communiter* ("but it must be commonly") to the principle that goods are worth as much as they sell for (*res tantum valet, quantum vendi potest*). Thus, price became a social phenomenon to be determined by the community. How can a community set a price? There are two possibilities: either spontaneously, by the chaffering of the market, or authoritatively, by public regulation. The first later became known as the "natural" or "vulgar" price; the second, as the "legal" price. In the absence of regulation, the market price was presumed to be just. This was the theory of both the civil law and canon law jurists. Among the theologians, only the Thomists acquiesced and arrived in their own way at the same conclusion; the Scotists and the nominalists dissented. Thus the Scholastics were divided and supported three rival, and partly conflicting, theories of the just price.

Albertus Magnus (1193–1280) stated unambiguously that the just price is set by the estimation of the market at the time of the sale. His pupil Thomas Aquinas was less specific and precise. Aquinas told a story (borrowed from Cicero) of a merchant who brought wheat to a country where there was a dearth. The question raised is whether this merchant may sell his grain at the prevailing price (*pretium quod invenit*) or whether he is bound to disclose that additional provisions are on the way. Thomas Aquinas answered his own question by stating that this merchant was not bound to do so by the rules of justice, but would act more virtuously if he did tell, or if he lowered his price. This answer, it seems, leaves no doubt as to the position of Thomas Aquinas.

The same point of view was taken by St. Bernardino of Siena, John Nider (1380–1438), and the majority of the theologians: the just price is set by "common estimation," which means the appraisal of the market place—with the reservation that they never questioned the right or even the duty of the public authorities to set and regulate prices in an emergency.

Nothing has been said thus far about the cost of production as a price determinant. Albertus Magnus and Thomas Aquinas, however, did not overlook this point entirely, and stated in their comments on Aristotle that arts and crafts would be doomed to destruction if the producer failed to recover his outlays in the selling price of his product. Albertus Magnus gave the example of a carpenter who will cease making beds if the price he receives does not compensate him for his expense and workmanship. In other words, according to Albertus Magnus and Aquinas, the market price cannot fall permanently below cost. Unfortunately this idea was lost; and the later Thomists focused all their attention on the market price, disregarding cost of production as if the two concepts were antithetic.

The champion of the importance of cost of production was John Duns Scotus (1265–1308). Starting with the observation that the merchant performs a useful function, he drew the conclusion that a just price should cover all the merchant's costs, including a normal profit and a compensation for risk. The weakness of this theory is, of course, that Scotus did not ask himself whether the merchant would be able to sell his wares above the market rate if his costs were too high. Scotus had very few followers; the best-known are another Scot, John Mayor (1469–1550), and a Portuguese, Johannes Consobrinus, also known as João Sobrinho (d. 1486), who taught for some time at Oxford.

Price regulation found strongest support among the nominalists. Jean de Gerson (1363–1429), for a while chancellor of the Sorbonne, even suggested entrusting to the public authorities the fixing of all prices—under the pretext that no one should presume to be wiser than the lawmaker. Since this scheme proved impractical, it found little support. Another nominalist, Henry of Langenstein the Elder (1325–1397), formulated the rule that if the authorities failed to set a fair price, the producer was allowed to set it himself; however, he ought not to charge more than would maintain him and his family suitably in his social condition. If he should overprice his wares in order to enrich himself or to better his status, he committed the sin of covetousness. The question whether such a producer would be able to obtain a price above that of his competitors was not raised by Langenstein. First published in 1874 by Wilhelm Roscher, Langenstein's rule received a great deal of publicity and was hailed by many, including Max Weber, Werner Sombart, R. H. Tawney, Heinrich Pesch, and Amintore Fanfani, as a typical formulation of the theory of the just price. There is, however, not the slightest justification for this enthusiasm. Far from being representative, Langenstein was a relatively minor figure; and his views were those of a minority group that exerted little influence in his time except perhaps in the German and Polish universities, which in the fifteenth century were bastions of nominalism.

Although the Schoolmen were unable to agree on a criterion of the just price, they were unanimous in their condemnation of monopoly, which was defined broadly as any collusion to manipulate prices. First of all, monopolies were branded as "conspiracies" against liberty; next, they were deemed injurious to the commonweal because they created artificial scarcity; and finally, they were blamed for raising prices above the competitive level—that is, above the level that would prevail if there were no monopoly. Profits derived from monopolistic exploitation were stigmatized as *turpe lucrum*, or illicit gain, which, like usury, was subject to restitution.

Since the Doctors favored market price, it should cause no surprise that they also were opposed to price discrimination. According to St. Bernardino of Siena, a seller ought not to take advantage of a buyer's ignorance, rusticity, or special need. In other words, prices ought to be the same to all, rich and poor alike. This was strictly in accordance with commutative justice, which, it is recalled, was based on equality and reciprocity.

The theory of the just price was applied to wages also, since wages were defined almost as if they were the price of labor (*pretium laboris*). Consequently, wages were determined by common estimation—that is, by the forces of supply and demand—excluding, of course, all attempts at exploitation. The author who gave the fullest treatment to this question was St. Antoninus, archbishop of Florence, to whom the purpose of wages was to enable the worker to support himself and his dependents on his social level. To achieve this purpose, St. Antoninus insisted upon punctual payment of the wage agreed upon and reproved employers who paid their workers in truck or in debased coin. He did not carry his criticism further, although he must have known that the wool and silk guilds of Florence attempted to keep wages down by using the antimonopoly legislation of the commune to prevent the formation of "brotherhoods" among the workers. In general, the Schoolmen were less favorable to the guilds than is generally assumed by Fabian socialists and Catholic historians who idealize the Middle Ages. Concerning wage differentials, Bernardino of Siena made the pertinent remark that skilled workers are better paid than unskilled because skill is scarce, for it is not acquired without toil and expensive training.

Monetary theory and usury. Monetary theory made little progress during the Middle Ages. The main author on this topic was Nicole Oresme (c. 1325–1382), who did not go much further than Aristotle. While neglecting monetary theory, most of the scholastic Doctors devoted an inordinate amount of space to usury, which they apparently regarded as a major social problem.

A great deal of misunderstanding exists about usury. According to modern concepts, usury is an exorbitant, oppressive interest rate; but the definition given by the Schoolmen was quite different. Usury was any increment, whether excessive or moderate, beyond the principal of a loan, or *mutuum*. Consequently, according to all the Doctors, usury occurred only in a loan. If it could be shown that a contract was neither explicitly nor implicitly a loan, there was no usury involved. Of course, a loan could be concealed under the color of another contract, which then became a contract *in fraudem usurarum*, or deceptively usurious.

With this approach to the problem, it is easy to see how the usury question became a hotbed of elusive discussion. The scholastic definition of usury allowed the merchants to make the most of legal technicalities and the Doctors to display their talents for casuistry and subtle distinctions.

Banking is as good an example as any. Since lending at interest was forbidden, the bankers found another way of making profits—by dealing in foreign exchange. The purchase of a foreign draft, because of the slowness of communications, always involved granting credit as well as dealing in exchange. Interest was, of course, concealed in the rate, or price, of exchange. Nevertheless, the bankers argued that a *cambium*, or foreign-exchange, contract was not a loan, but a legitimate business transaction. Although the argument rested on sheer sophistry, it was accepted by the theologians unless the *cambium* contract was too patently a disguised loan, as in the case of dry, or fictitious, exchange. The practical result of this tolerance was to outlaw discounting but to tie banking to exchange.

No charge could be made for lending, but the lender was sometimes entitled to compensation for reasons extraneous to the loan. Thus there emerged the theory of extrinsic titles: the three principal ones were *poena conventionalis, damnum emergens,* and *lucrum cessans. Poena conventionalis* was a penalty for tardy payment; *damnum emergens,* compensation for damages suffered by the lender. These two were readily admitted as valid; but not so *lucrum cessans,* or cessant gain, which meant that the lender might claim the same return as that yielded by rival or competing investments. Thus defined, *lucrum cessans* is in fact the same thing as the modern concept of opportunity cost. To admit this title, too, would have jeopardized the whole usury doctrine. *Lucrum cessans* was, therefore, rejected by Thomas Aquinas and most of the theologians. Later, in the sixteenth century, it was permitted by some latitudinarians, but only between merchants.

The usury doctrine was the Achilles heel of scholastic economics. It involved the Schoolmen and their sixteenth-century and seventeenth-century successors in insuperable difficulties that contributed greatly to bringing their whole doctrine into disrepute.

Later Scholasticism. As already mentioned, Scholasticism continued to prosper throughout the sixteenth century and afterward. The late Scholastics of the school of Salamanca made some new contributions, mainly in refining the old doctrines. The quantity theory of money was accepted as a matter of course. More than ever the adherents of the new school insisted upon the fairness of market price in the absence of public regulation. Some of them, such as Martin Azpilcueta (1493–1586), better known as Dr. Navarrus, were very skeptical about the merits of price fixing because it was unnecessary in normal times and ineffectual in times of dearth. Luis de Molina, s.j. (1535–1601), more famous for his views on grace than for his economic theories, formulated the law of supply and demand by stating that "a concourse [*concurrentium*] of buyers, more considerable at one time than at another, and their greater eagerness to buy will drive prices up, whereas paucity of purchasers will bring them down" (*De justitia et jure* II, disp. 348, no. 4). He also insisted that value depended upon consumers' preferences rather than upon qualities inherent in commodities. A Belgian Jesuit, Leonardus Lessius (1554–1623), made two minor contributions: allowing monopolies with regulated rates for the common good and giving an accurate description of the Antwerp money market, implicitly recognizing the presence of interest concealed in the exchange rates.

In the seventeenth century, the economic teachings of the scholastic school were systematically presented in the great synthetic works of cardinals Juan de Lugo, s.j. (1583–1660) and Giambattista de Luca (1613–1683), but they made no new contributions. Scholastic economics had reached maturity. By failing to renew its methods of analysis, scholastic thought fell into discredit and entered into a precipitous decline that involved other sciences and philosophy as well as political economy.

RAYMOND DE ROOVER

[*See also the biographies of* AQUINAS *and* ORESME.]

BIBLIOGRAPHY

BALDWIN, JOHN W. 1959 *The Medieval Theories of the Just Price: Romanists, Canonists, and Theologians in the 12th and 13th Centuries.* Philadelphia: American Philosophical Society.

BONAR, JAMES (1893) 1922 *Philosophy and Political Economy.* 3d ed. London: Allen & Unwin; New York: Macmillan.

DEMPSEY, BERNARD W. 1943 *Interest and Usury.* Washington: American Council on Public Affairs.

DE ROOVER, RAYMOND 1953 *L'évolution de la lettre de change, XIVᵉ–XVIIIᵉ siècles.* Paris: Colin. → Contains a detailed check list of scholastic authors.

DE ROOVER, RAYMOND 1955 Scholastic Economics: Survival and Lasting Influence From the Sixteenth Century to Adam Smith. *Quarterly Journal of Economics* 69:161–190.

DE ROOVER, RAYMOND 1958 The Concept of the Just Price: Theory and Economic Policy. *Journal of Economic History* 18:418–434.

ENDEMANN, WILHELM 1874–1883 *Studien in der romanisch-kanonistischen Wirtschafts und Rechtslehre bis gegen Ende des 17. Jahrhunderts.* 2 vols. Berlin: Guttentag. → Important for late Scholasticism.

FANFANI, AMINTORE 1933 *Le origini dello spirito capitalistico in Italia.* Milan (Italy): Società Editrice "Vita e Pensiero."

GRICE-HUTCHINSON, MARJORIE 1952 *The School of Salamanca: Readings in Spanish Monetary Theory, 1544–1605.* Oxford: Clarendon.

HÖFFNER, JOSEPH 1941 *Wirtschaftsethik und Monopole im 15. und 16. Jahrhundert.* Jena (Germany): Fischer.

HÖFFNER, JOSEPH 1955 *Statik und Dynamik in der scholastischen Wirtschaftsethik.* Veröffentlichungen der Arbeitsgemeinschaft für Forschung des Landes Nordrhein-Westfalen, Geisteswissenschaften, Vol. 38. Cologne (Germany): Westdeutscher Verlag.

NELSON, BENJAMIN N. 1949 *The Idea of Usury.* Princeton Univ. Press.

NOONAN, JOHN T. JR. 1957 *The Scholastic Analysis of Usury.* Cambridge, Mass.: Harvard Univ. Press.

O'BRIEN, GEORGE A. T. 1920 *An Essay on Mediaeval Economic Teaching.* New York: Longmans.

OERTMANN, PAUL 1891 *Die Volkswirtschaftslehre des Corpus juris civilis.* Berlin: Prager.

ROCHA, MANUEL 1933 *Travail et salaire à travers la scolastique.* École des Sciences Politiques et Sociales, Université Catholique de Louvain. Paris: Desclée de Brouwer.

SCHREIBER, EDMUND 1913 *Die volkswirtschaftlichen Anschauungen der Scholastik seit Thomas v. Aquin.* Beiträge zur Geschichte der Nationalökonomie, Vol. 1. Jena (Germany): Fischer.

SCHUMPETER, JOSEPH A. (1954) 1960 *History of Economic Analysis.* Edited by E. B. Schumpeter. New York: Oxford Univ. Press.

SOUDEK, JOSEF 1952 Aristotle's Theory of Exchange: An Inquiry Into the Origin of Economic Analysis. American Philosophical Society, *Proceedings* 96:45–75.

WEBER, WILHELM 1959 *Wirtschaftsethik am Vorabend des Liberalismus: Höhepunkt und Abschluss der scholastischen Wirtschaftsbetrachtung durch Ludwig Molina, S.J. (1535–1600).* Schriften des Instituts für Christliche Sozialwissenschaften der Westfälischen Wilhelms-Universität, Münster, Vol. 7. Münster (Germany): Aschendorffsche Verlagsbuchhandlung.

II
MERCANTILIST THOUGHT

"Mercantilism" is the label commonly given today to the doctrine and practices of nation-states in the period roughly from the fifteenth to the eighteenth centuries with respect to the nature and the appropriate regulation of international economic relations. In this doctrine great emphasis is put on the importance of maintaining an excess of exports of goods and services over imports as the sole means whereby a country without gold or silver mines can obtain a continuous net inflow of the precious metals, regarded as essential to national wealth and strength. In the eighteenth century the elder Mirabeau and Adam Smith applied to this doctrine the terms "mercantile system" and "commercial system" to emphasize its contrast with the doctrine of the physiocrats, which minimized the importance of foreign trade and put its emphasis instead on the importance of agricultural production. In the 1860s German writers introduced the term *Merkantilismus;* corresponding terms, such as "mercantilism" in English, thereafter gradually became standard in all the languages of the Western world. The term is sometimes objected to because it is often used in a pejorative sense, or because it is held, justly, that although often so used, it inadequately represents the varied content of the economic thought of some four centuries. Similar objections can, of course, be made against most general abstract terms ending in "ism," but it does not seem possible to do without them and it does seem possible to use them with disciplined restraint. In this article an attempt is made to limit the application of the term to the special and dominant aspects of thought and practice with respect to international economic relations during the fifteenth to eighteenth centuries.

The doctrine. The essentials of the doctrine can be summarized in terms of five propositions or attitudes: (1) policy should be framed and executed in strictly nationalistic terms, that is, national advantage alone is to be given weight; (2) in appraising any relevant element of national policy or of foreign trade, great weight is always to be put on its effect, direct or indirect, on the national stock of the precious metals; (3) in the absence of domestic gold or silver mines, a primary national goal should be the attainment of as large an excess of exports over imports as is practicable, as the sole means whereby the national stock of the precious metals can be augmented; (4) a balance of trade "in favor" of one's country is to be sought through direct promotion by the authorities of exports and restriction of imports or by other measures which will operate indirectly in these directions; (5) economic foreign policy and political foreign policy are to be pursued with constant attention to both plenty and "power" (including security under this latter term) as coordinate and generally mutually supporting national objectives, each capable of being used as a means to the attainment of the other.

This constituted the solid core of mercantilist doctrine, from which there was little dissent before the 1750s by writers on economic matters, but it left room for extensive debate within the ranks of adherents of the doctrine. There could be major differences in the reasoning presented for adherence to the respective propositions here listed, and there could be sharp differences of opinion as to the choice of means by which the accepted objectives could best be pursued.

Mercantilism was essentially a folk doctrine, evolved in the light of the prevailing historical circumstances and values by simple inference from the apparent facts. It was a doctrine of practical men not given to subtle economic analysis, which was in fact sparsely available in the age of mercantilism. The philosophers before the 1750s, the theologians, and the universities neither challenged it nor made any important contributions to it. It was not an area in which disciplined scholarship showed any deep interest.

Differences within the doctrine. The most striking difference of doctrine within the ranks of the mercantilists turned on why the indefinite accumulation of the precious metals should be regarded as an important national objective. The terms "wealth," "treasure," and "riches" were used with considerable ambiguity, sometimes in a broad sense to cover stocks of valuable goods of any kind which could command a price, but more often in a narrow sense to signify only the precious metals. The narrow usage was occasionally extended to commodities (other than the precious metals) which had great durability and high value per unit of bulk, such as precious stones and even tin and copper. The emphasis with respect to enrichment, to economic improvement, was never in terms of the level of consumption, and when it was in terms of the level of production or output, it was usually with reference to the contribution such production could make, directly or indirectly, to the acquisition and retention of "wealth" or "riches" or "treasure" in the narrow sense. It was on *accumulation* that the emphasis was put, and there was a widespread assumption, tacit or explicit, on the part of the mercantilist writers of the period that accumulation over long stretches of time could be achieved only or predominantly by the piling up of stocks of durable and high-value-per-unit commodities, especially of the precious metals. Often the only link with consumption as an economic objective was the recognition of their ready convertibility through exchange into essential consumers' goods as a reason why a limited number of specified durable goods were to be regarded as pre-eminently constituting items of national "wealth" or "riches."

The emphasis on the "store-of-wealth" function of the precious metals competed, however, with the emphasis of other mercantilist writers on the "circulation" function of the precious metals in their role as money, an emphasis which led to hostility to the use of the precious metals as hoards or in plate and jewelry. These writers believed that production and employment varied in physical volume in close proportion with the variations in the amount of money in circulation. They thus overlooked or denied that the main consequence of an increase in the amount of money might be a general rise of prices; they perhaps were taking for granted that there normally existed large amounts of unemployed labor and natural resources. At least for the later mercantilists emphasis tended to shift from the store-of-wealth to the circulation function of the precious metals. But when paper money was introduced, it became more difficult to reconcile emphasis on circulation with continuing stress on the importance of the precious metals and on a favorable balance of trade as the means of acquiring them.

One method used was to deny the advantages of paper money, or to support limitations on the issue of paper money which would prevent it from acting as a stimulus to the export and a deterrent to the import of the precious metals. But as long as the emphasis continued to be on the circulation function of the precious metals, the absence of any obvious answer to the question why paper money could not perform this function adequately and more cheaply tended to lead either to a return to the older emphasis on the store-of-wealth function of the precious metals or to the substitution—for stress on the monetary and balance-of-trade aspects of mercantilism—either of protectionist ideas resting in large part on nonmercantilist arguments or of a new receptivity toward free trade ideas.

An additional and widely expounded ground for emphasis on the desirability of indefinite national accumulation of the precious metals was based on the observation that the rate of interest and the availability of credit varied with the quantity of money, the former in the inverse direction and the latter in the same direction. It was argued that cheapness and abundance of credit would promote enterprise, employment, and production and would increase the ability to compete in foreign trade by lowering the interest element in the costs of production of domestic goods. Before the 1750s no one appears expressly to have pointed out that a given increase in the national stock of money, to the extent that it caused a rise in the price level, would either leave the rate of interest unchanged or cause it to rise rather than to fall and would leave unchanged the real availability of credit, as distinguished from its amount measured in monetary terms. With the advent of paper money, moreover, it was no longer necessary to have a net inflow of precious metals from abroad in order to have an increase in the national stock of money.

Writers who saw an inflow of the precious metals as increasing the rate of employment of human and other productive resources presumably perceived that this would result in increased consumption on the part of the owners of these resources. There was also widespread—but by no means universal—acceptance of the general desirability of an increase in the population and the number of potential workers and no doubt a recognition that such an increase would involve increased consumption. But the emphasis on increased production was made to rest much more on the contribution it could make to a favorable balance of trade, on the support it could give to an increase in population, and on its role in alleviating the moral and other evils of involuntary unemployment, of vagrancy, and of pauperism than on an acceptance in principle of the desirability of a higher level of per capita consumption for the general public. "Luxury" expenditures, for example, on the part of the working classes were almost universally deprecated, and even for the well-off were much more often disapproved than approved, except as they were believed to be necessary means to the employment of otherwise idle resources or to the maintenance of appropriate status and dignity for the upper classes. Increase in production was sought primarily for the contribution it could make to the accumulation of wealth in the form of durable, valuable commodities, at least if one judges by what the writers of the period expressly said.

Implementation. In the early stages of mercantilism it was often the practice to seek the general objectives by more or less direct and particular regulation of the details of individual commercial transactions involving trade with foreigners. Thus, in England there was for a time regulation by the Royal Exchanger of foreign exchange transactions and by other official agencies of transactions in commodity markets, so as to make sure that *each* individual transaction should as far as possible make a net contribution to the national stock of the precious metals. Later commentators on mercantilism labeled such practices as "bullionism" or "balance-of-(individual)-bargain system." It was believed that attention should be given not only to the aggregate balance of trade but also to the separate balances in the trade with particular countries or in particular sectors of commercial activity. There was considerable suspicion, for instance, that the trade with the East Indies was for all of Europe a "losing" trade involving a chronic drain of the precious metals to the East. Thomas Mun first formulated a persuasive defense of the English trade with the East Indies even if it did involve, in its first effect, a net drain from England of the precious metals. This drain, he claimed, was not an ultimate one, since by re-export at higher prices of its imports of Indian commodities, England more than regained the precious metals which had initially been sent to India. Mercantilist literature, however, long continued to support discrimination between countries in the regulation of imports according to the usual state of the trade balances with such countries, or as an incident to tariff bargaining, or as an instrument of power politics.

The mercantilists gave priority status with respect to eligibility for export to goods with a high labor content in relation to their value. Export of manufactures was favored over export of agricultural products ready for consumption; exports of raw materials such as raw wool, or minerals, was regarded as injurious or wasteful. The export of machines and tools and the emigration of skilled workers were regarded as specially injurious. Underlying these positions were the beliefs that labor was in such abundant supply that it was permissible to treat it as nearly equivalent nationally to a free good, and that restriction of export of raw materials or of machines would not substantially diminish their domestic rate of production and would result in their retention for domestic processing or use. Such restrictions would thus work to make the balance of trade favorable and to increase domestic employment.

The general mercantilist position was that imports of goods and services were in principle desirable only if (*a*) they were essentials which could not be produced, at whatever cost, at home, or (*b*) they were raw materials which could not be produced at home in the needed quantities except by the withdrawal of scarce resources from the production for domestic use or for export of goods with a higher labor content in proportion to their value, or (*c*) they needed to be imported as a *quid pro quo* for other countries' allowing their nationals to import from the country in question. The implicit mercantilist ideal was zero import, and export only in exchange for the precious metals. In France, Colbert and others gave this ideal express formulation in replying to objections raised by Frenchmen that the severity of French import restrictions

would result in other countries' prohibiting entry of French products. Colbert claimed that France alone had the potentiality to produce at home the whole range of commodities essential to national prosperity, whereas none of its neighbors could dispense with France's commodities.

A variant of mercantilist doctrine, expounded mostly but not exclusively by English writers, substituted for a favorable balance of trade in terms of monetary values a "balance of labor" in terms of the relative labor content of the exports and the imports—with an aggregate excess of the labor content in the exports over that in the imports treated as "favorable." This has been regarded by some modern commentators as a "refinement" or improvement of the balance of trade doctrine. It would, however, be easily possible for a given trade situation highly unfavorable by the trade balance criterion to be highly favorable by the balance of labor criterion, and vice versa. Under the balance of labor criterion, moreover, the fewer units of import commodities obtained on the average per unit of export commodity, other things being equal, the more "favorable" would be the balance of labor.

Political objectives. Mercantilism had political as well as strictly economic objectives in view. The *minimum* objectives were an even balance of trade and an even balance of power. But as large an excess of exports over imports as possible was an aspiration of all countries, and the great powers sought more than an even balance of power. They sought enough superiority of power to "give the law" to other countries, to enable conquest of adjoining territory or overseas colonies, or to defeat their enemies in war. It was general doctrine that strength was necessary as a means of protecting wealth and of augmenting it, while wealth was a strategic resource, necessary to produce strength and to support its exercise. With wealth one could finance and equip armies and navies, hire foreign mercenaries, bribe potential enemies, and subsidize allies. Power could be exercised to acquire colonies, to win access to new markets and to shut foreigners out of one's own markets, and to monopolize trade routes, high-seas fisheries, and the slave trade with Africa. "Power" was clearly and obviously a relative matter; what mattered was the ratio of power, not the terms of the ratio. It was also true of power that geography had great importance in determining what comparisons were relevant; landlocked countries had little occasion to concern themselves with their power relative to a distant maritime power, and being a neighbor to a strong country could mean being under constant threat. It was also a distinctive feature of political relations that comparisons of strength were relevant not only between pairs of countries but also between groups of actual or potential allies. The emphasis on international comparisons, on ratios, which was highly relevant in the political sphere in a world of power politics, whether the power was expected to serve national aggression or national security, was often carried over to the economic sphere, where it had little relevance. It could and did lead to gross confusion about the nature and significance of national wealth and national economic well-being.

When great emphasis was placed, in the economic sphere, as it logically was in the sphere of power rivalries, on an inherent conflict of interests, this had grave consequences both for economic policy and for international politics. If it was relative status that solely or mainly mattered, economic damage to a rival country could logically be treated as equivalent to economic benefit to one's own country, and famine abroad, to bountiful harvests at home. Such reasoning abounds in the mercantilist literature, and it was moral or sentimental revulsion against it more than superior economic analysis which brought much of the late eighteenth-century Enlightenment to the support of free trade ideas. Even among writers who were primarily interested in economic matters, the mercantilist "jealousy of trade" fostered, as overcompensation, an exaggerated belief in the harmony and mutuality of economic interests between countries.

The doctrine that low real wages (per hour or per day or per piece) were in the national interest was widely prevalent in England in the seventeenth and eighteenth centuries and has sometimes been labeled by modern writers as "the mercantilist labor doctrine." Many English writers did expound this doctrine, with favorable balance of trade considerations obviously in mind. But a substantial number of writers denied the proposition on which the doctrine was based, namely, that English laborers, once their minimum needs were taken care of, preferred idleness to more (or superior) commodities, or, as one eighteenth-century writer phrased it, that for workers in general "the luxury of indolence tends always to swamp the luxury of goods." Or, if they accepted the proposition as true to fact and regarded voluntary idleness as an evil, they proposed, on humanitarian and other grounds, the search for remedies less oppressive for the poor than low rates of real wages. It seems difficult to find on the Continent any trace of a special affinity between mercantilist thought in general and the low-wage doctrine, perhaps because it was generally impossible for the poor there to attain a basic minimum of subsistence without working to nearly the limits of their endurance, perhaps because in Catholic countries the frequency of religious holidays when work was prohibited satisfied their cravings for rest, leisure, and time-consuming dissipation.

Distinctive aspects of mercantilism. Mercantilism was a doctrine of extensive state regulation of economic activity in the interest of the national economy. It took for granted that man was inherently self-regarding and would pursue his own interests without concern about the consequences of such behavior for the interests of the community. It accepted as axiomatic that if individuals were in their economic behavior left free from tight regulation, the consequences for the community would be disastrous. But this had been practically universal doctrine from classical antiquity on, and therefore did not distinguish mercantilist from premercantilist thought.

Substantially new in mercantilist thought, however, was its systematic adjustment to the concentration of power and the monopolization of loyalty by nation-states, which in their relations with other states followed a "Machiavellian" or amoral code, and were more extensive in area of jurisdiction than the earlier city-states and feudal barons but less extensive than the empires of classical antiquity and than the universal Catholic church of the Middle Ages. Also substantially new in mercantilism were its greater concern with economic matters as one phase of the then prevalent secularization of thought and practice, the change in the specific character of the economic objectives of the political authorities, and the new administrative patterns of regulation of communal life. These new features were the product of the growth of commerce and of the changes in political organization associated with the breakdown of the Holy Roman Empire and of feudalism and the absorption of the hitherto substantially autonomous city-states by the new nation-states. Mercantilism was a doctrine of state intervention in economic life, but of state interventionism of a special pattern and with some special objectives. It was thus in sharp contrast with the later laissez-faire doctrine. It was also, however, in sharp contrast with some present-day systems of state interventionism, such as socialism, Russian communism, and the welfare state, for in principle at least these do not have the accumulation of the precious metals, favorable balances of trade, and national limits to moral obligations as central and ultimate objectives.

Differences in practice. Agreement on the general mercantilist objectives left abundant room for major differences both among periods and among countries in the choice of methods used in pursuing these objectives and in the degree of vigor of their pursuit. Practice was conditioned by limitations of administrative capacity; pressure of conflicting national objectives; domestic resistance arising out of regional, class, and occupational special interests; military weakness; and the idiosyncrasies, the apathy or enthusiasm, and the dynastic loyalties of monarchs.

The techniques adopted could be monetary ones, involving control of exchange markets and of the movement of the precious metals across national boundaries. They could take the form of regulation of individual commercial transactions; of regulation by general tariffs, prohibitions, or quantitative restrictions; or of subsidies to exports or to exporting or import-competing industries. The governments could themselves set up and operate factories producing for export or replacing imports; they could set up and operate companies engaged in foreign trade; they could grant monopoly privileges to privately owned chartered companies to produce and sell specified products in the domestic market, to engage in foreign trade on the basis of special privileges, and to administer overseas colonies. Governments could encourage immigration, restrict emigration, or promote early marriages in the belief that growth of population would serve the general mercantilist objectives. Wages and interest rates could be subjected to legal maxima in the belief that this would improve the national competitive position in foreign trade. Wars could be embarked upon for mercantilist reasons. On all of these matters, while ultimate objectives could be static within countries and uniform as between countries, the selection of means to serve these objectives could differ between countries and could undergo constant change through time within countries because of change of circumstances and of opinions.

Mercantilism in practice always in some measure fell short of what doctrine called for. Perhaps the most important deviations of practice from doctrine were those resulting from the fiscal necessities of government. All governments in the age of mercantilism found it difficult to finance their general activities. To adhere to mercantilist objectives without regard to fiscal considerations would often involve the exemption of important categories of exports from customs duties, the substitution of outright prohibition of specific exports and imports for customs duties—with a consequent loss of revenues—or the grant of subsidies to favored industries, shipping, fisheries, or colonies, all of these being measures which would involve an increase of government expenditures or decrease of government revenues.

Restraints on importation carried beyond some uncertain point could lead foreign countries injured thereby to adopt retaliatory or defensive measures, with the possible result that the gross contribution to a "favorable" balance of trade made by the import restrictions might even in the short run be more than offset by the adverse effect on exports.

Most mercantilist measures involved a burden on some occupational or regional sectors of the population. Such sectors, without challenging the general objectives of mercantilism, would commonly resort to all the forms of pressure and persuasion available to them to obtain a relaxation of the measures or a revision of them which would shift the burdens elsewhere. Thus, in England the graziers would press for a relaxation of the restrictions on the export of raw wool, and the independent merchants would protest vigorously against the special privileges granted to the trading companies. Even where absolute monarchy prevailed, governments found it necessary to make concessions to such dissenting groups.

Every measure restrictive of trade established a possibility of private profit from its evasion or violation, and no country was able to prevent extensive violation of the regulatory measures by smugglers, tax evaders, merchants operating illegally in restricted trades ("interlopers"), and bribed enforcement agents. Public resistance to particular restrictive measures and to the personnel endeavoring to enforce them, and lax administration at the top levels often led to apathy in enforcement. When Adam Smith, in 1778, entered into his duties as a commissioner of customs, he was astonished to find, expert though he already was, how much of his own personal effects consisted of articles of foreign manufacture which it was illegal not only to import but also to possess, and he warned a friend that the latter's wife, upon investigation, would probably find that she was even a worse offender.

In Britain in particular, although there was general approval in principle of mercantilism, there was almost equally general dislike of the administrative institutions and practices essential to its effective execution. The British public was jealous of the exercise of power by the executive branch of the national government, of administration conducted by the central authorities in London instead of locally, and of agents of the central government with powers of inspection and arrest. Legislation was more centralized than in most countries, but enforcement was highly decentralized and was largely left to unpaid local magistrates with considerable autonomy and to suits brought on their own initiative by interested parties or by voluntary informers who were remunerated from the monetary penalties imposed by the magistrates as a result of such suits. The higher the customs duties and the more burdensome the regulations and prohibitions, the greater was the incentive to evade or violate them, so that in many cases difficulty of enforcement led to restraint in the severity of legislation or to partial or complete abandonment of serious attempts at enforcement. It seems quite plausible, therefore, that at least in England mercantilist measures were in practice not nearly as severe a restraint on foreign trade in the eighteenth century as were, say, the transportation costs of the time or than are the ordinary tariffs of present-day protectionism.

While there was a substantial unity of doctrine throughout the Western world with respect to the proper objectives of commercial policy, the differences between countries in political organization, administrative structure, and geographical circumstances led to very substantial differences in the intensity with which, and the selection of devices whereby, they pursued these objectives. In the smaller Germanic states, for instance, mercantilism was little more than a vague general doctrine. The major interests of German intellectuals relating to economic and political matters, as represented by the contents of cameralist writings and university courses, were directed to the principles of management of the absolute rulers' finances, of organization and conduct of professionalized public administration, and of management of official property, including mints, mines, forests, and an occasional factory. In France, although public administration was on the whole centralized to an extent without parallel in England, taxation (including customs duties), property law, and guild regulations were largely under autonomous local administration following traditional and regionally diverse patterns and principles.

The decline of mercantilism. Criticism of the prevalent methods of pursuing mercantilist objectives was always fairly common in countries where some free discussion was tolerated. Much of this criticism, however, whatever its analytical merit, was special pleading by spokesmen for a political faction, an industry, a region, a particular port or town, or a particular privileged company.

In the 1750s there first began to appear comprehensive criticism of the basic principles of mercantilism by persons of stature with no visible private axes to grind. One major source of criticism was from exponents of an essentially new gospel of individualism which extolled the merits, on ethical and political as well as on economic grounds, of freedom of the individual from detailed regulation by the state. Here important voices were those of Adam Smith in Britain and of the marquis d'Argenson, the physiocrats, and Turgot in France. Important also was the widespread revulsion among intellectuals against the past record of almost continuous war and preparation for war, for which mercantilism was largely blamed. It was, in fact, much more the pacific and cosmopolitan views of the *philosophes* and the Illuminati on the Continent and of men like David Hume and Adam Smith in Britain than the more strictly economic argument of these and other writers which first put mercantilism seriously on the defensive among intellectuals.

In the early years of the nineteenth century the English classical school of economists rejected mercantilism on the basis of economic analysis, of which a part was substantially original with them. The school claimed that trade conducted under individual initiative and free from official regulation was inherently of mutual profit both to the individuals directly involved and to the community as a whole, and they applied this to domestic and international trade alike. Here they had had since the 1750s a number of important predecessors. They added, however, an analytical justification of this position which was essentially new, the principle that allocation of resources to production in accordance with comparative costs would maximize aggregate output and that the operations of individuals acting in their own interest in a free and competitive market would conform with this principle. They did not deny that this was subject to the qualification that producers knew both what their relevant costs were and what were the prices at which their products could be sold. But they claimed, as an obvious proposition, that businessmen were better informed on these matters than government could be. From this reasoning, they proceeded to the policy conclusion that the determination of what commodities and in what quantities a country could export and import to its greatest advantage should be left to the outcome of the decisions of individual businessmen operating to maximize their own incomes. This was a sharp break with mercantilism's insistence on the necessity of regulation of economic behavior and its ranking of the desirability of export and import of particular commodities according to whether they were manufactures or agricultural products or raw materials and according to their labor content. To the classical school these were more or less arbitrary classifications, whose correspondence, if any, in practice with classification according to the comparative cost principle would be fortuitous.

The classical school also rejected the mercantilist stress on the balance of trade and on the national supply of the precious metals. They claimed that in the absence of government regulation an international automatic equilibrating mechanism would bring each country the amount of specie appropriate to its needs and circumstances and would prevent trade balances from getting into serious disorder. Here they had predecessors in the eighteenth century, most notably, perhaps, Isaac Gervaise and David Hume.

It is to be noted that neither the mercantilists nor the classical school distinguished clearly and systematically between short-run and long-run effects, and that insofar as one can judge from the historical context and the implications of their writing, the mercantilists were as a rule thinking in terms of short-run effects and the classical school in terms of long-run effects. Appraisal by economists of the comparative analytical merits of the mercantilists and their classical school critics should therefore give careful consideration to the distinction between short-run and long-run analysis, if they regard this, as does the writer, as a crucial distinction.

The classical school doctrine with respect to international trade became dominant for a while in England and obtained a wide degree of qualified acceptance elsewhere. There followed in England over half a century of approximately complete free trade, and elsewhere it led to a substantial liberalization of foreign trade policy. The restrictions on foreign trade which continued to be imposed were supported on grounds which were largely nonmercantilist in character; they were often designed, in fact, to protect agriculture rather than manufactures. Survival into the present of mercantilist doctrine and practice is by no means rare. There are, however, important differences between mercantilist doctrine and the doctrines by which present-day state regulation of foreign trade are mainly supported, and major differences also in the respective patterns and techniques of regulation. As far as scholars are concerned, support of mercantilism as it operated in its prime, based on express acceptance of its objectives, its doctrine, and the appropriateness of its practices to its doctrine, seems today to be confined to a minority, mostly economic historians. The analytical grounds on which mercantilism has been supported or criticized are in

both cases sometimes of very disputable merit. Where policy is concerned, final appraisal, here, as generally in the social sciences, needs to deal expressly, as it often fails to do, with political, ethical, and socioeconomic values, as well as with the abstract logic of relations between actual and supposed matters of fact. It needs to call, therefore, on the resources of all the major social disciplines.

JACOB VINER

BIBLIOGRAPHY

PRIMARY SOURCES

COLBERT, JEAN BAPTISTE 1861–1873 Lettres, instructions et mémoires de Colbert. Edited by Pierre Clément. 7 vols. Paris: Imprimerie Impériale. → A general errata list and an analytical table by Pierre de Brotonne were published in 1882.

FORBONNAIS, FRANÇOIS VÉRNON D. DE 1754 Éléments du commerce. 2 vols. Paris: Briasson.

FRIEDRICH II, DER GROSSE, KING OF PRUSSIA Oeuvres de Frédéric le Grand. 31 vols. Berlin: Imprimerie Royale, 1846–1857. → See especially Volume 9, part 2, pages 212–240, "Exposé du gouvernement prussien" and "Essai sur les formes de gouvernement et sur les devoirs des souverains."

McCULLOCH, JOHN R. (editor) (1856) 1954 Early English Tracts on Commerce. Cambridge Univ. Press. → A photo-offset reprint of the 1856 edition was published by the Political Economy Club as A Select Collection of Early English Tracts on Commerce, From the Originals of Mun, Roberts, North and Others.

[MELON, JEAN F.] (1734) 1739 A Political Essay Upon Commerce. Dublin: Woodward & Cox. → First published in French.

STEUART DENHAM, JAMES (1767) 1805 The Works, Political, Metaphisical, and Chronological, of the Late Sir James Steuart of Coltness, Bart. Volumes 1–4: An Inquiry Into the Principles of Political Oeconomy: Being an Essay on the Science of Domestic Policy in Free Nations. London: Cadell & Davies.

UZTARIZ, GERÓNIMO DE (1742) 1751 The Theory and Practice of Commerce and Maritime Affairs. London: Rivington. → First published in Spanish.

SECONDARY SOURCES

BUCK, PHILIP W. (1942) 1964 The Politics of Mercantilism. New York: Octagon.

COLE, CHARLES W. 1931 French Mercantilist Doctrines Before Colbert. New York: Smith.

COLE, CHARLES W. (1939) 1964 Colbert and a Century of French Mercantilism. Hamden, Conn.: Shoe String Press.

COLE, CHARLES W. (1943) 1965 French Mercantilism: 1683–1700. New York: Octagon.

HECKSCHER, ELI F. (1931) 1955 Mercantilism. Rev. ed. 2 vols. London: Allen & Unwin; New York: Macmillan. → First published in Swedish.

JOHNSON, EDGAR A. J. 1937 Predecessors of Adam Smith: The Growth of British Economic Thought. Englewood Cliffs, N.J.: Prentice-Hall.

SCHMOLLER, GUSTAV VON (1884) 1931 The Mercantile System and Its Historical Significance: Illustrated Chiefly From Prussian History. New York: Smith. → A translation of a chapter from Schmoller's Studien über die wirtschaftliche Politik Friedrichs des Grossen.

SCHUMPETER, JOSEPH A. (1954) 1960 *History of Economic Analysis.* Edited by E. B. Schumpeter. New York: Oxford Univ. Press.

SUVIRANTA, BRUNO 1923 *The Theory of the Balance of Trade in England: A Study in Mercantilism.* Helsinki: Suomalaisen Kirjallisuuden Seura.

VINER, JACOB (1921–1951) 1958 *The Long View and the Short: Studies in Economic Theory and Policy.* Glencoe, Ill.: Free Press. → See especially pages 277–305, "Power Versus Plenty as Objectives of Foreign Policy in the Seventeenth and Eighteenth Centuries."

VINER, JACOB 1937 *Studies in the Theory of International Trade.* New York: Harper.

III
PHYSIOCRATIC THOUGHT

"Physiocrats" denotes the *économistes*, those who subscribed to the tenets of *physiocratie* (derived from *physeikratia*) and advocated governance of economic and political activity "in keeping with the laws implanted in Nature by Providence." Constituting the first "school" of political economy to emerge in the history of that science, they exercised considerable influence, mainly in France, where most lived, in the 1760s and early 1770s.

The climate of opinion in France in the 1750s was favorable to the ascendancy of a promise-laden set of principles such as the physiocrats put forward. The country's main industry, agriculture, was poorly carried on and generally in a bad way. Its system of taxation was vexatious, burdensome, and wasteful. Mercantilist policy and practice interfered with internal and external trade, retarded agriculture, and sustained privilege. It was believed in some quarters that adverse economic policies had brought about a diminution in population. Early in the century and again in the 1740s a number of works had appeared in which French agricultural and commercial policies were criticized and the country's economic experience was contrasted unfavorably with that of a progressive England. The merits of economic freedom and competition, though still poorly understood, had come to be appreciated by some administrators. Economic analysis was improving under the stimulus of such authors as Hume and Cantillon.

The beginning of the school may be dated as 1756, when François Quesnay published in the *Encyclopédie* his first economic article, "Fermiers," to be followed in 1757 by "Grains," in which the partially transitory influence of Cantillon's "rent" theory is present; these essays foreshadowed much of what was to become the school's body of principles. The formation of the school was facilitated by Quesnay's enjoyment of the patronage of Mme. de Pompadour and the sinecure of physician-in-ordinary to Louis XV. In 1757 the already famous Victor Riqueti, marquis de Mirabeau, author of the popular *L'ami des hommes, ou traité de la population* (1756–1760), after an interview with Quesnay at his *entresol* at the Palace of Versailles, became his first disciple and shortly his most enthusiastic and energetic co-worker.

The fundamental principles of the school were first set down in the *Tableau économique*, of which three "editions" seem to have been issued in 1758–1759, the last accompanied by explanations and maxims. Most of the later editions of the *Tableau* illustrated the advantages of compliance with physiocratic principles. By the middle 1760s Quesnay had acquired a number of faithful disciples, attracted by his and Mirabeau's writings, by discussions at their lodgings, and by the belief that in their principles might be found solutions for some of the nation's economic ills. Outstanding among these were Nicolas Baudeau, Pierre Paul Mercier de la Rivière, Guillaume François Le Trosne, Pierre Samuel Du Pont de Nemours, and Anne Robert Jacques Turgot, who subscribed to many, but not all, the tenets of the school. They, along with lesser members of the school, produced a stream of publications that popularized and clarified Quesnay's economic views, at first without modifying their fundamental content significantly. In time, however, some of Quesnay's disciples found themselves under pressure to make certain physiocratic economic tenets more compatible with current reality and to develop a doctrine of judicial control to balance that of legal despotism and thereby preserve the social order.

The intellectual influence of the physiocrats, great in the 1760s, underwent a rapid decline after 1770. A combination of circumstances generated political and intellectual opposition. Many special interest groups believed that they would be disadvantaged economically by physiocratic policies, among them tax farmers, financiers, manufacturers, landowners, possessors of exclusive privileges, and those who feared an increase in the price of bread. Turgot, who had risen to the office of comptroller-general, was relieved of his office in 1776, not long after he had introduced a number of physiocratic reforms; nearly all of these were suspended, and the remaining physiocratic journal was suppressed. The tenets and recommendations of the physiocrats were subjected to attack by both economic writers (e.g., Forbonnais, Galiani, Graslin, Mably) and noneconomists (e.g., Linguet, Necker, Voltaire). The residual authority of these tenets was gradually undermined by Smith's *Wealth of Nations*, which appeared in 1776, two years after Quesnay's death and eight years after he stopped writing on economic matters.

Interest in physiocracy did not completely disappear. Traces of it remain in early nineteenth-century economic literature. Physiocratic concerns continued to stimulate discussion, and some physiocratic reforms were finally introduced during the French Revolution. Physiocracy exercised some influence throughout Europe, particularly in Austria, Baden, Poland, Sweden, and Tuscany.

Presuppositions and theories. The physiocratic presuppositions and theories were largely imbedded in physiocratic models, the famous *Tableaux économiques*. Underlying the self-sustaining interclass flow of money, goods, and services incorporated in the idealized *tableaux* was a class structure more advanced than that then found in France. In the structure of the *tableaux*, the largest of the three classes, the *productive*, comprising one-half the population, engaged in agriculture, fishing, and mining. The *proprietary class*, made up of landed proprietors and those supported by proprietary income, comprised one-fourth the population, as did the *sterile*, or artisan, class, which included the balance of the population. In time, France's class structure presumably would correspond to this ideal; for the physiocrats, especially Turgot, were alert to evolutionary forces which, having generated the existing structure, could also generate its successor.

Aggregate national interclass flow of product and income was summarized in the *Tableau*. The *productive class* produced 5,000 million livres of output; it did this with the aid of land rented from the *proprietors*, an investment of 2,000 million livres *avances annuelles* in seeding, cultivation, etc., and a longer-period past investment of 10,000 million livres *avances primitives* in durable instruments, animals, etc., of which one-tenth was annually replaced. For expositive convenience, constant returns were assumed, with an increment of two units *avances annuelles* always resulting in an increment of five units in output. It was recognized that the response of output to increased *avances annuelles* was conditioned by the state both of *avances primitives* and of *avances foncières* (i.e., relatively permanent investments in buildings, clearing, drainage, etc.) made by proprietors in the past. Only Turgot discussed increasing and decreasing returns to inputs, but in a quite different connection. Of the 5,000 million livres of annual reproduction, or output, 3,000 million constituted *reprises*, or the return of expenses incurred by land-renting *fermiers*, 2,000 million in the form of *avances annuelles* and 1,000 million as outlay upon the maintenance of the *avances primitives*. The remaining 2,000 million represented the *net product*, the approximate monetary equivalent of which passed to the proprietors from the farmers

who cultivated the land under a competitively determined lease that normally stipulated an annual rent of approximately the anticipated *net product*; this money was in effect used by the proprietors to purchase 1,000 million livres of produce from the *productive class* and of output from the *sterile class*. The sterile class got from the productive class 2,000 million livres of produce, which it consumed or worked up into wrought goods and services for the other two classes and its own needs. It utilized little or no fixed capital and replaced its working capital in the current production period; for this reason Turgot compared its advances to the *avances annuelles* of the productive class.

Underlying the *Tableau* is the school's key postulate, that only the productive class cultivating the land produced a *net product*, whereas the sterile class merely recovered its outlay and the proprietary class, being *disposable* (i.e., not being actively involved in the continuation of the circular economic flow), could serve essentially public purposes. Expansion of the economy and the population therefore depended upon expansion of the expenditure of the productive class and the resultant expansion of the net product; hence the composition of expenditure was as important as its growth and stability. The physiocrats therefore condemned *luxe de décoration*, or excessive expenditure with the sterile class, but not *luxe de subsistance*, or heavy expenditure with the productive class; for usually diversion of expenditure from the productive class to the sterile class reduced the *net* expenditure of the former and thereby reduced the *net product*, and conversely. They also condemned man-made restrictions upon the sale of produce (among them duties and other barriers to internal and external trade in farm products); hoarding; the outflow of funds to foreign lands; and diversion of money into circuits that did not enter into agricultural markets. Some of these restrictions, they believed, had their origin in tax farming, flotation of government loans, monopolies and special privileges, and the absence of a regime of economic liberty. They noted that the demand for produce tended to rise as its quality improved and as the incomes of the masses rose above bare subsistence; and they sought to show that if produce commanded a *bon prix*, agricultural income, net product, and the economic condition of the population inclusive of the masses would improve.

The physiocrats' theory of taxation and such theory as they had of factor pricing and distribution were corollary to their postulate that only the product of land included a surplus. All taxes therefore were ultimately incident upon the *net product*.

From this it followed that this surplus should be taxed immediately; then the cost of collecting revenue for the support of the state, together with the adverse side effects of taxation, would be minimized. Not more than the completely *disposable* one-third of the net product should be devoted to state and church functions, among them *avances souveraines* for public capital; otherwise, investment in agriculture would be too little. The proprietors needed to invest about one-third of their rent (i.e., net product) in the repair and improvement of their property and to retain another third as compensation for *avances foncières* and the bearing of the risks and cares associated with ownership. Only the gross income of the productive class included a surplus. While the current price of labor might temporarily exceed its fundamental (or long-run supply) price, much as the current price of a product might temporarily exceed its fundamental price, the price of labor did not normally include a surplus; it corresponded to the conceivably upward-elastic subsistence and other costs of population replacement. Although Quesnay's scheme could not with consistency allow the farmer's income (or that of other entrepreneurs) to include a profit or surplus, his followers tried inadequately to explain away what appeared to be such a surplus, and Turgot went so far as to include a normal return on capital in "fundamental" price. Quesnay and some of his followers tried to treat interest as a surplus-free capital-replacement cost, but others finally had to conceive of interest as including more than such cost.

The physiocrats put great stress upon the role of investment. Quesnay and most of his disciples confined this role to agriculture. The stress on investment in discussions of net product appeared also in Quesnay's comparison of *grande* and *petite* agriculture. The former, involving large-scale and technologically advanced methods, required heavy capital investment; the latter, based upon traditional methods and backward owner–cultivator relations, utilized little capital. *Grande* agriculture was much more productive than *petite*; substitution of *grande* for *petite* might for a time permit increasing returns to capital. Turgot went beyond Quesnay to declare investment to be important in industry and commerce as well as in agriculture and to suggest how it gets allocated among alternative uses in keeping with prospective returns. In this and other respects, indeed, Turgot, together with Baudeau and Du Pont, among others, modernized the feudal framework within which Quesnay and Mirabeau had set their discussion.

The physiocrats sought to integrate their political and (not entirely homogeneous) philosophical views with their conceptions of actual and ideal economies. Although they appreciated, in somewhat varying measure, the power of self-interest and the workings of a system of interdependent prices, together with the roles of private property and a regime of economic liberty and competition, they also believed that the state might play an important part in making physiocracy function and realize individual-transcending purposes as well. For there existed a discoverable natural order, compliance with whose principles was essential to man's prosperity and happiness. Positive laws must reflect this order and a limited monarch, or "tutelary authority," must express and support it, subject to the ultimate approval of a judiciary competent to determine if natural law was being correctly interpreted.

The physiocratic contribution. Physiocracy contributed significantly to the development of economic science, and some of its concerns have continued to interest economists and others. In the first half of the nineteenth century physiocratic influence was reflected in discussions of such matters as underconsumption and the origin, form, and role of economic surplus, though these were examined within a quite different socioeconomic context than that envisaged by Quesnay. Detailed analysis of physiocracy was facilitated by the publication of a number of physiocratic works in 1846 under Daire's auspices. As early as the 1860s the circular flow model present in the *Tableau* commanded the attention of Marx, whose reproduction schemes probably were inspired by it; and not long after, Walras developed a *tableau* he considered "analogous" to Quesnay's. During the ensuing forty to fifty years much able scholarship was devoted to the physiocrats. With the emergence after 1930 of modern equilibrium and macroeconomic theory, together with national income accounting and input–output models, interest in relevant components of the physiocratic system increased, in Japan as well as in the West. This renewed attention was also stimulated by revival of interest in a major concern of the physiocrats, economic development. During the past half-century, moreover, the political and philosophical conceptions of the physiocrats have been subjected to renewed appraisal.

JOSEPH J. SPENGLER

[See also the biographies of QUESNAY; TURGOT.]

BIBLIOGRAPHY

EINAUDI, MARIO 1938 *The Physiocratic Doctrine of Judicial Control.* Cambridge, Mass.: Harvard Univ. Press.
François Quesnay et la physiocratie. 2 vols. Edited by Alfred Sauvy. 1958 Paris: Institut National d'Études

Démographiques. → Volume 1 consists of essays on Quesnay by various authors, and includes a chronological table of works by Quesnay on pages 301–316 and an annotated bibliography of works about Quesnay on pages 317–392. Volume 2 contains short essays and extracts by Quesnay.

HISHIYAMA, IZUMI 1960 The *Tableau économique* of Quesnay: Its Analysis, Reconstruction, and Application. *Kyoto University Economic Review* 30, no. 1:1–46.

MEEK, RONALD L. 1963 *The Economics of Physiocracy: Essays and Translations*. Cambridge, Mass.: Harvard Univ. Press. → The first part includes translations of extracts from various authors. The second part includes four essays by Meek, three of which were previously published in 1951–1960.

NEILL, THOMAS P. 1949 The Physiocrats' Concept of Economics. *Quarterly Journal of Economics* 63:532–553.

QUESNAY, FRANÇOIS 1756 Fermiers. Volume 6, pages 528–540 in *Encyclopédie, ou dictionnaire raisonné des sciences, des arts et des métiers*. Paris: Briasson.

QUESNAY, FRANÇOIS 1757 Grains. Volume 7, pages 812–831 in *Encyclopédie, ou dictionnaire raisonné des sciences, des arts et des métiers*. Paris: Briasson.

QUESNAY, FRANÇOIS (1758) 1766 *The Oeconomical Table: An Attempt Towards Ascertaining and Exhibiting the Source, Progress, and Employment of Riches, With Explanations by the Friend of Mankind, the Celebrated Marquis de Mirabeau*. London: Owen. → First published as *Tableau oeconomique*. Published also as part of Mirabeau's *L'ami des hommes*.

QUESNAY, FRANÇOIS *Oeuvres économiques et philosophiques de F. Quesnay, fondateur du système physiocratique*. Paris: Peelman, 1888.

SAMUELS, WARREN J. 1961 The Physiocratic Theory of Property and State. *Quarterly Journal of Economics* 75:96–111.

SAMUELS, WARREN J. 1962 The Physiocratic Theory of Economic Policy. *Quarterly Journal of Economics* 76:145–162.

SPENGLER, JOSEPH J. 1945 The Physiocrats and Say's Law of Markets. *Journal of Political Economy* 53:193–211, 317–347.

WEULERSSE, GEORGES 1910 *Le mouvement physiocratique en France de 1756 à 1770*. 2 vols. Paris: Alcan.

WEULERSSE, GEORGES 1950 *La physiocratie sous les ministères de Turgot et de Necker (1774–1781)*. Paris: Presses Universitaires de France.

WEULERSSE, GEORGES 1959 *La physiocratie à la fin du règne de Louis XV: 1770–1774*. Paris: Presses Universitaires de France.

WOOG, HENRI 1950 *The* Tableau économique *of François Quesnay: An Essay in the Explanation of Its Mechanism and a Critical Review of the Interpretations of Marx, Bilimovic and Oncken*. Staatswissenschaftliche Studien, New Series, Vol. 7. Bern: Francke.

IV

SOCIALIST THOUGHT

In the half-century prior to the Russian Revolution of 1917 the dominant doctrine inspiring the major socialist parties of continental Europe was Marxism (or was directly derived from Marxism). Since 1917 Marxism has become the official doctrine of the socialist sector of the world (i.e., of the Soviet Union and China and of the other countries of Europe and Asia associated with them). Treated historically, therefore, description and analysis of socialist thought must run predominantly in terms of Marxian doctrine. This is not to say that there have been no other different and rival socialist creeds that have been influential and continue to find an echo today. Marx spoke of the so-called "utopian socialists," who had preceded him and in contrast with whom he called his own doctrine "scientific socialism." Merging with these, there have been various brands of "ethical socialists," including the Christian socialists, basing themselves on this or that ethical principle as the preeminent one, such as "equality" or "community values," and on social motives, as against pursuit of "selfish" individual values and motives. Still others, such as the Fabians in England and the so-called *Kathedersozialisten* and their imitators on the Continent, advocated purely on grounds of expediency an extension of the economic functions and responsibilities of the state, thus identifying their "socialism" (and its consequential critique of individualism) with *étatisme*. Before coming to Marxism as a social philosophy something must accordingly be said about the historical origins and the varieties of these non-Marxian theories.

Utopian socialism. The author of one work on the socialist tradition (Gray 1946) starts with Moses, Lycurgus, and Plato, passing from them to the Essenes and the early Christian Fathers and thence to St. Thomas Aquinas and Sir Thomas More. Indeed, Plato and More have been cited as forerunners in many a work on the subject. But this article will not go so far back as this. It must be sufficient to distinguish those writers of the eighteenth or early nineteenth century who, in the shadows of the emerging modern world, sought to paint a picture of a perfect society of the future, deducible from first principles either of rationality or of morality and attainable only if mankind were sufficiently reasonable or good. Among these was Mably, a French contemporary of Adam Smith, who in a series of quasi-Platonic dialogues developed a critique of the institution of private property and who believed that nature had destined all men to be equal. He argued that the institution of private property both annihilates the primitive and natural equality of man and enables the indolent and unworthy to live at the expense of the active and industrious. Another eighteenth-century figure who both attacked the irrationality of existing society and went into considerable detail about the structure of an ideal society was Morelly (*Code de la nature* 1755).

The most quoted and influential of the architects of a utopian future were Saint-Simon and Fourier. The former, a count descended from an old and honored family who renounced his title during the French Revolution, became the founder of something of a school (which included the positivist philosopher Auguste Comte). After his death there was even established a Saint-Simonian church. Among other proposals for the reorganization of society on new principles he propounded a scheme for productive associations and a *projet de travaux* under the aegis of government and advocated the principle that the rights of property ought to be rooted solely in its contribution to the production of social wealth. Here his disciples, who developed his doctrines in notable respects, went further and preached the end of inheritance of property and its eventual transfer to the state. It was they who, incidentally, coined the formula "from each according to his ability, to each according to his needs." In his final work, *Nouveau christianisme*, 1825, Saint-Simon sought to expound a new religion dedicated to "the great aim of the most rapid improvement in the lot of the poorest class . . . the most numerous class." Persecuted and divided, the Saint-Simonian school disintegrated in the course of the 1830s.

Fourier is best known as the author of a scheme for the organization of *phalanstères*, communities in which both production and social life were to be organized on a cooperative or communal basis. This would allow the natural, inborn "harmony" of man to be realized—a harmony that existing commercial civilization had destroyed. In this new society work, instead of being a burden, would be enjoyed.

Another sketch of a communist utopia was Cabet's *Voyage en Icarie* of 1838. A more direct influence on French socialism in the middle and later nineteenth century was Proudhon, author of *Qu'est-ce que la propriété?*, 1840, and coiner of the aphorism "Property is theft." This aphorism was for him the answer to the Lockean right to property by labor. Yet, regarding property, he could be called a "distributivist" as much as, or even more than, a socialist. His influence has been more in the direction of anarchism than of socialism, since two of his central ideas were equality and individual freedom and he preached against communism and the authoritarian state. His remedy for the evil of taking (and living on) interest was a system of universal and interest-free credit to be organized through a mutual credit bank (his system of *mutualité*)—a proposal that not surprisingly drew the fire of Marx's criticism in the latter's *Misère de la philosophie*. [*See the biographies of* FOURIER; PROUDHON; SAINT-SIMON.]

The Ricardian socialists in England. The germ of socialist ideas in England before Marx lay in a critique of classical political economy by a group of writers and pamphleteers who have come to be loosely described as the Ricardian socialists. A centerpiece of this critique for the main figures of this group was a concept of exploitation couched in traditional eighteenth-century terms of "natural right." They were Ricardian in the sense that they sought to use Ricardo's theory of value in such a way as to turn it, with the aid of natural-right notions, against the main precepts of the Ricardian school.

By the end of the eighteenth century Spence and Ogilvie had derived from the principle of natural right the conclusion that ownership of land should be shared equally and that no man should have more than he could cultivate. Nature or God had given the land "in common to all men," and equal sharing of land by all was the basic guarantee and *sine qua non* of human freedom. By analogy, in the year after Ricardo's death William Thompson (in *An Inquiry Into the Principles of the Distribution of Wealth* 1824) deduced the right of labor to the whole produce of labor from the postulate that labor is the sole (active) creator of wealth. In existing society this was prevented by a system of "unequal exchanges" that resulted in part of labor's product being filched by the possessors of economic advantage. Apart from its injustice and its offense against the Benthamite maxim of "greatest happiness," this system deprived labor of much of its necessary incentive (substituting want as the spur to labor) and hence was inimical to national wealth. Such a notion could be held to have been implicit to some extent in Adam Smith's treatment of profit and rent as "deductions" and Ricardo's treatment of them as alternative and rival forms of surplus. But in Thompson's notion of appropriation, or exploitation, what was implicit in his forebears is given an explicit extension that those forebears would probably have disowned. Thompson, incidentally, also attempted a reply to Malthusian pessimism by stressing the historical relativity of population trends.

The year following Thompson's *Inquiry* there appeared Thomas Hodgskin's *Labour Defended Against the Claims of Capital*, which opens with the statement, "Throughout this country at present there exists a serious contest between capital and labour." (Two years later his lectures at the London Mechanics Institution were published as *Popular Political Economy*.) Hodgskin similarly distinguished property associated with one's own labor, which is a natural right, from property as the power to appropriate the product of the labor of others—that is, Lockean "natural right" from the "legal or artificial" right of ownership by conquest or appropriation. In a famous passage he declares, "I am certain that till the triumph of labour be complete; till productive industry alone be opulent, and till idleness alone be poor . . . till the right of property shall be founded on principles of justice and not those of slavery . . . there cannot and there ought not to be either peace on earth or goodwill amongst men." Halévy says of his ideas that, while they "have their starting point in the philosophy of Bentham, it is in the philosophy of Karl Marx that they find their resting place." Contemporaneously with Hodgskin, in 1825, John Gray published his *Lecture on Human Happiness*. Fourteen years later there appeared J. F. Bray's *Labour's Wrongs and Labour's Remedy*, which also contrasts "unequal exchanges" with equal and speaks of the exchange between capital and labor as "legalised robbery." Both writers ended by advocating somewhat vaguely a kind of Owenite cooperation.

These writers apparently had in common the a priori derivation of ideal precepts for rebuilding society from postulated first principles of "justice" or of "natural right." But what links them as forerunners of Marx is their common championship of productive labor against the appropriation of labor's product over and above a subsistence wage, in consequence of the concentration of property ownership in comparatively few hands.

Apart from the French utopians and English Ricardians, the German economic writer Rodbertus is sometimes included in the category of pre-Marxian socialists and with his generalized concept of rent has been called an anticipator of Marx's theory of surplus value. Certainly his theory at first sight has a good deal in common with that of the English Ricardian socialists. But the main concern of his theory was to provide an explanation of crises of overproduction (in terms of underconsumption) and of how these could be prevented. His critique of existing society must be classed as "conservative socialism," and the social reforms he advocated as a forerunner of "Bismarckian socialism" rather than of the popular socialist movement as we know it. Again, Lassalle (in some respects influenced by Rodbertus) was a popularizer and propagandist of socialist ideas rather than a theorist in his own right. [*See the biographies of* OWEN; RODBERTUS; THOMPSON.]

The Fabians and guild socialism. By the end of the century, when Fabian socialism arose in England as a rival both of nineteenth-century economic liberalism and of Marxism, the climate of thinking had changed. Gone was the influence of eighteenth-century rationalism and of the metaphysic of natural right, and gone with them was the habit of deriving ideal models for a future society from some mythical "natural" state of society in the past. The end of the Victorian era, the time of transition from the age of steam to that of electricity and from free trade to imperialism, had a more practical, more mundane, and more circumscribed cast of thought. The Fabians were not alone in their preoccupation with the inadequacies of laissez-faire and the propriety of extending the economic functions of the state. Certain academic economists, notably Sidgwick, had already opened this question, as earlier Jevons himself had done much more cautiously and as afterward Marshall and his disciple and successor Pigou were to do.

Among the authors of the *Fabian Essays* of 1889 were some famous names, such as Bernard Shaw, Sidney Webb, Graham Wallas, and Sidney Olivier, who, although sharing a common platform, spoke each with an individual accent. Bernard Shaw had been weaned from Marxism to the economic theories of Jevons (under the economist Wicksteed's influence) and from early revolutionary faith to a belief in evolutionary "gradualism," which was the hallmark of the group as a whole. Webb was the patient empiricist, versed in the literature of royal commissions and acts of Parliament, who could report voluminously and in detail on social ills and inefficiencies needing remedy and the practical steps by which governmental action could remove them. In his Fabian essay he remarks that "history shews us no example of the sudden substitution of Utopian and revolutionary romance," attacks the age of individualism as the age of anarchy, and advances a radical program of specific reforms as the necessary complement to political democracy. As a group, the Fabians were concerned with particular evils and remedial measures, rather than with any general philosophy of society or even (Shaw excepted) with the denunciation of private property and the receipt of rent, interest, and profit. Much emphasis was laid on efficiency, and their essential method would probably be called today "social engineering." Some have even denied them the name "socialists," owing to their lack of interest in any radical reconstitution of the property basis of society. Perhaps it is in Bernard Shaw, and in him only, that are found traces of continuity with earlier brands of socialism, whether of the English or the Continental variety, since he makes polemical use (in the *Fabian Essays* and in others of his works) of a generalized concept of rent as an "unearned surplus" reminiscent of Marxian surplus value—a socially created surplus, which ought to be appropriated by society and not by individuals.

Close on the heels of the Fabians—and to a large extent as a reaction against the strong element of *étatisme* in their outlook—came the comparatively short-lived but luminous movement known as "guild socialism." Originating in a group of writers connected with the journal *New Age* (edited by A. R. Orage) in the first decade of the present century, it was soon reinforced by recruits from the contemporary university generation (mainly Oxford Fabians and most notably G. D. H. Cole). It drew largely upon the ideas of the French syndicalists, with their emphasis on industrial direct action and the "industrial democracy" of direct workers' control, to correct the centralizing and bureaucratizing bias traditional to state socialism. (Cole's early work, *The World of Labour* of 1913, is eloquent of this French inspiration.) Their target of attack was less the particular inefficiencies of capitalist individualism than the evils and the hateful human degradation of "wage slavery," with labor treated as a commodity, the abolition of which required that the social ownership of industrial capital be combined with the organization of industry under the control of democratic guilds composed of the actual producers (i.e., workers by hand and brain in the industries in question). Industrial democracy in this form was necessary not only to emancipate the workers but also to complement, indeed to realize, political democracy. In their theory of the state, guild socialists tended to be pluralist and to reject the notion of state sovereignty. In its denunciation of wage slavery guild socialism had more affinity with earlier and with Continental socialist thought than had the more insular English Fabianism. [*See the biographies of* COLE; WALLAS; WEBB, SIDNEY AND BEATRICE.]

Marxian socialism.   Not surprisingly, in view of its Hegelian roots, Marxian socialism started with a philosophy of history and a methodology. In a much-quoted phrase, Marx spoke of finding Hegel standing on his head and of proceeding to set him on his feet. This he claimed to have done by enunciating his materialist interpretation of history. According to this, it was the mode of production of any given epoch that was the key to the interpretation of that epoch, including its "superstructure" of ideas and moral sentiments and its legal and political institutions. This mode of production was conceived of as embracing not only its productive technology but also the prevailing "social relations of production"—namely, relations between men that turned upon their relations to the process of production and in particular to ownership of the means of production. In effect, these were class relations, and the contradictions inherent in such relations were the basis of class struggle, the prime mover of historical change to date.

History since the end of tribal society had witnessed three main modes of production: slavery, feudal serfdom, and modern capitalism based on wage labor. All of these were forms of class society —each marked by class antagonism in its specific way—in which the producer was in a position of subjection to a ruling class whose power rested on ownership. In consequence of this subjection the surplus product, over and above what the producer himself retained for subsistence, was appropriated by the ruling and owning class, whether slaveowners, feudal *seigneurs*, or capitalists. In the first of these socioeconomic forms, the ruling class owned the person of the laboring producer as well as the impersonal, material means of production. In the second, it had the legal right to annex a certain portion of the labor time of the producer, whether in the form of direct labor services or of tribute in kind. In the third, the laborer was in legal status a free agent, the relation between him and the capitalist being that of a contractual market relationship, yet the economic compulsion of his propertyless status obliged the proletarian wage earner to sell his labor power for little more than a subsistence wage (or for even less in conditions of acute unemployment). Thus the wage-labor–capital relationship under capitalism bore a major analogy with earlier and more patently servile forms of class relationship; property right per se was able to draw to its possessor, independently of any productive activity, a share of the total product.

This, in brief, was Marx's concept of exploitation (and as fruit of exploitation, class struggle). His economic analysis, as expounded in *Das Kapital*, was designed to enlarge on this analogy with previous modes of appropriating surplus product and to show how the persistence of a difference between the value of labor power (sold for wages) and the value of its product was consistent with the "law of value"—that is, with conditions of a free market and of perfect competition. Unlike earlier socialist writers, he did not deduce the existence of surplus value or exploitation from some principle of natural right of labor to its product (all too often supposed by commentators and critics to be inherent in the labor theory of value). The analogy with earlier modes of appropriating a surplus product was for him a historical datum, which he sought to explain in terms of economic theory—doing so by penetrating below the market "appearance" of things to the "essence" of social relations under capitalism (the relationship between capitalist and proletarian as that of owner and propertyless). For this reason, the boundaries of economic analysis were drawn more widely than in the narrower market-equilibrium studies to which we have grown accustomed in post-Menger, post-Jevonian economics, from which property relations and their influence are excluded because they are thought to belong to social rather than to economic theory.

Marx's explanation turned on his distinction, to which he attached great importance, between labor and labor power. Labor power was what was sold as a commodity in return for wages and, like other commodities, sold for a price determined by the cost in labor necessary to produce and reproduce it. This was the cost of producing its own subsistence—its essential input (this being modified, as Marx, like Ricardo, allowed, by a historically relative factor of social habit and custom). Hence wages absorbed only *part* of the product of labor at work for any given length of time—the value of labor power as a productive input was never more than a fraction of the net output emerging from the productive process. The difference was surplus value, which accrued to title of ownership as profit, interest, or rent.

In this consisted the main part of his critical diagnosis of contemporary society. But it was also fundamental to his description of the dynamic of capitalist society and his prediction of its eventual replacement by socialism. With the development of the capitalist mode of production the class struggle would develop both in extent and in acuteness. With the widening and deepening of exploitation the proletariat would acquire class consciousness and would develop its own organization, both economic and political, as the eventual instrument of capital's overthrow. But there were two other agents of the dynamic process. First, there was a continuous tendency both toward concentration of production into larger units and toward centralization of capital itself, tendencies that at the same time encouraged more concentrated and more enduring organization of labor, while confronting labor with a more centralized, impersonal, and tyrannical foe. Second, because of its uncoordinated character (its characteristic "anarchy of production"), combined with a growing contradiction between the rate of growth of productive power and the slower rate of growth of markets, the process of capital accumulation was periodically interrupted by dislocating economic crises of overpro-

duction. Such crises served the function of re-creating the reserve army of the unemployed when it became depleted by the expanding demand for labor and wages showed signs of rising and encroaching upon surplus value. They also encouraged the tendency to concentration on the side of capital (the larger swallowing the smaller in lean years) and increased the instability of the worker's status and condition.

The inevitable outcome and only "solution" to these gathering contradictions was a revolt of organized labor against the growing tyranny of capital, as the latter showed itself increasingly to be a "fetter on production," no longer revolutionizing technique and expanding productive capacity as it had done in its halcyon days but restricting and wasting productive capacity and holding it in check. On its negative side such a revolt could only take the form of dispossessing the capitalists of their ownership rights—the famous "expropriation of the expropriators." On its positive side revolutionary transformation must take the form of the transfer of the means of production into social ownership and the social organization of production on a planned basis, since in conditions of modern technique and large-scale industrial production the kind of solution favored by Saint-Simon and Proudhon—the distribution of property in small units to all citizens—was clearly impracticable.

A social transformation of this kind, the most revolutionary known to history, would liquidate the class antagonism of previous class society by substituting the social equality of a community of active producers, where everyone was a worker drawing an income from society, for the unequal and divided society of those who owned and those who were dispossessed. The period of human history characterized by successive forms of class exploitation, each with its specific type of dominant and exploiting class appropriating surplus product in its own manner, would have closed. But this did not mean that historical change would have come to an end. The technical means of production would continue to develop, probably more rapidly than before; human organization, adapting to changing economic conditions and needs, would perennially undergo change. But the basic cause of social antagonism as known before in human history would have disappeared.

There was no pretense, however, that the relative social equality of all citizens as workers and producers would be the realization of an ideal of absolute justice among men. Socialists of the Marxian school have always spoken (since Marx wrote his *Critique of the Gotha Programme*) of two stages of socialism, a lower and a higher. In the former, although work incomes would constitute the sole category of income and inequalities due to the existence of property incomes would have disappeared, some differences of income would still remain, owing to the necessity of differentiating wages according to the amount and kind of work performed. Only at the latter stage, when the productive powers of society had been sufficiently developed and the moral standards of society sufficiently raised, would it be possible to achieve the fuller social equality of "from each according to his ability, to each according to his needs." It has become customary in recent decades to call the first "socialism" and to reserve the name "communism" for the second. One could say that the former would realize equality of opportunity for all, but the effect upon individual incomes of inequality of human capacities and talents would not be eliminated; only under "full communism" would differences of human capacities and needs cease to be of economic significance.

Marx and Engels and their followers always regarded it as inconsistent with their conception and method to prepare anything resembling a blueprint of the future socialist society. The attempt to do so was the hallmark of the utopian socialist, and in their ascetic refusal to emulate their predecessors in this respect, they stood at the opposite pole from Fourier and his obsessive love of detailed prescription. Socialism, it was stated, would be established by "the proletariat organized as the ruling class," which would forthwith "convert the means of production into State property"; it would "centralize all elements of production in the hands of the State" (i.e., of the proletariat organized as the ruling class) and would "increase the total of productive powers as rapidly as possible." There were some occasional hints in the writings of Marx and Engels that production would be organized consciously under some kind of prearranged social plan. But apart from the comments already quoted from the *Critique of the Gotha Programme*, that is virtually all. Lenin, who had the task of laying the foundations of the first socialist state, declared that "in Marx there is no trace of attempts to create utopias, to guess in the void at what cannot be known." [*See the biographies of* BERNSTEIN; KAUTSKY; LUXEMBURG; MARX.]

Post-1917 social democracy. In the years since the Russian Revolution the socialist world has been more or less sharply divided between those who recognized this event as a genuine socialist revolution and those who denied it such a name. The difference partly turned on the methods used to achieve and to consolidate the revolution, namely the use of insurrection and armed force and the regime of the "dictatorship of the proletariat." But there was also the deeper issue of whether socialism could be built at all in a backward country of weakly developed industry and predominantly peasant agriculture. The Russian Mensheviks denied that it could be and declared that the stage was set in Russia for no more than a "bourgeois revolution" against tsarist absolutism. What was distinctively new in Lenin's controversial interpretation when he arrived back in Russia in April 1917 was that, while accepting that a bourgeois revolution was in process, he nonetheless declared that the industrial proletariat could and should seize power in alliance with the peasantry. In doing so, the proletariat could transform a bourgeois revolution into a socialist one and eventually start to build socialism. The discussion about "socialism in one country" that was to develop within the Bolshevik ranks in the following decade was in large degree an extension of this same controversy, since it was concerned with the question of whether the transition to socialism, already started by the nationalization decrees of 1917–1918 and carried over into the "mixed economy" of the 1920s, could be *completed* unless the revolution spread to other, more technically advanced, countries of Europe.

Socialist parties in western Europe (with the exception of the Italian) generally followed the Menshevik line in their estimate of the Soviet revolution. They proceeded to affirm their devotion to democratic parliamentary methods and their intention of achieving socialism, not by a single revolutionary act, but by a series of modifying reforms in the existing structure and by a gradual extension of the economic functions of government. The rift in socialist thought and policy was deepened after the formation of the Third (or Communist) International in 1919, in opposition to the Second International, which after its collapse in 1914 was to be revived in 1920. The concept of socialism current in most social democratic circles increasingly approached that of Fabian gradualism and, in the course of two decades, in most cases ceased to be Marxian in anything but name. After World War II, partly under pressure of the "cold war," the leading parties of continental Europe and Scandinavia not only eschewed Marxism, but dropped from their programs any proposal for extensive socialization of production.

Some would say that the temper of the times is to eschew general social theories as speculative or metaphysical and that for this reason one can no longer speak of socialist theory apart from the

Marxist school. Certainly it is true that the tendency in England and elsewhere has been to favor an increasingly empirical approach. Sixty-three years after the appearance of the original *Fabian Essays* a number of younger thinkers of the English Labour party combined to produce in 1952 a collection of *New Fabian Essays* under the editorship of R. H. S. Crossman. What is remarkable about this new volume, in contrast with the emphasis of its forebear, is the playing down of socialization in the traditional sense of the transfer of means of production to state ownership (even to the point of dismissing it as an obsolete Marxian prejudice). If there is a single unifying theme in terms of which socialism as a credo is here definable, it is perhaps to be found in an emphasis on social equality. This is to be realized primarily through the extension of social services, a widening of educational opportunities, and progressive taxation. Indeed, one writer, C. A. R. Crosland, speaks as though the aims of the socialist movement were already achieved to a considerable extent, since the metamorphosis of capitalism "into a quite different system . . . is rendering academic most of the traditional socialist analysis," and state intervention in economic life has so increased as to "justify the statement that the capitalist era has now passed into history." Property rights, it is said, "no longer constitute the essential basis of economic and social power," which has passed to a new class of managers. Nationalization and "the early Fabian emphasis on collectivism" are expressly rejected as key to the definition of socialism, and equality of status is enthroned as the essence of the definition instead. Before the war, in 1937, Douglas Jay in *The Socialist Case* had already said, "If we are to have the substance and not the shadow, we must define socialism as the abolition of private unearned or inherited incomes rather than of the private ownership of the means of production"; while as for planning in any of its forms, these are "possible rather than necessary elements of socialism."

The economists' debate.   There remains to be said something in summary about the narrower discussion of socialism, by economists, which itself falls into two halves: discussion of the comparative merits of the two rival systems in the attainment of some postulated "optimum" and discussion of alternative mechanisms, or "models," for the operation of a socialist economy. The latter has become a lively subject of debate today in the socialist countries themselves.

As a result of the new economics of Jevons and Menger in the last quarter of the nineteenth century, two opposite tendencies arose among leading academic figures. First, as we have noted, there was a tendency in England especially (which Jevons himself cautiously initiated) to re-examine the case for laissez-faire and the exceptions to it. This re-examination, developed by Sidgwick and Marshall, drew attention to a number of "exceptions," in which public interest conflicted with private and in which production of wealth failed to be maximized when left to the free play of market forces. In the twentieth century, with the increasing prevalence of monopoly and restricted competition, this critique was extended to include the adverse effects of "imperfect competition" or "monopolistic competition"—the excess capacity latent in excessive product differentiation and also the swollen costs and distorting effects of salesmanship and advertising to which they give rise. Second and concurrently, the development of mathematical theories of general market equilibrium brought with it, as a signal corollary, a new justification of free enterprise: namely, that the general equilibrium toward which a competitive market always tends represents a maximum of utility (in given conditions of demand and of economic resources). This corollary of their analysis was underlined by Walras and popularized by his follower Pareto. What made this theorem on inspection less impressive than at first appeared was that the postulated optimum was relative to a given income distribution (or at least of a given structure of factor ownership taken as datum). Hence, it could not be used to pass judgment on income distribution itself. Its critics pointed out that the Walras–Pareto theorem defined, not a unique optimum position, but a whole series of positions. In a modified form, however, the theorem continued to be used as a justification of free competition as that which secures an optimum result *relative* to whatever income distribution existed (it being implicitly recognized that the state could, and should, modify that income distribution through taxation—so far as disincentive effects of taxation upon production allowed).

Soon, however, a counterattack was mounted upon the socialist case with the aid of this theorem, in the form of the contention that a socialist economy, since it would lack a market for factors of production, would have no way of attaining an optimum (of utility or welfare) or even of ascertaining in what direction this lay. Hence, in the words of Von Mises (the name chiefly associated with this argument), a socialist economy would be nonrational and uneconomic *ex natura* (1922). In the two decades that followed Von Mises's challenge socialist economists (in Germany in the course of the 1920s and in England and the United States in the 1930s) sought an answer to it by demonstrating various ways in which the problem could be solved. Most of the suggested mechanisms, however, involved the creation of actual markets or else of quasi-market processes for factors of production and "producers goods" (i.e., all productive inputs) and the simulation of competition under socialism. Henry Dickinson, for example, proposed actual markets; Lange proposed a system of accounting prices to be adjusted so as to equilibrate supply and demand by a trial-and-error process, with output decisions and investment decisions taken on the basis of these accounting prices according to certain rules (1936–1937). Such solutions mainly implied decentralized decision making (at the level of individual industries or enterprises) and accordingly set limits to the amount of centralized planning (other than "indicative planning") that could be used. This was not the case, however, with all the suggested solutions. In 1908, for example, the Italian economist Barone had already advanced one such solution in mathematical form. But doubt was expressed as to whether, as a centralized planning solution, it could be regarded as practicable in view of the complexity of the calculations involved. [*See the biographies of* BARONE; LANGE.]

It should be added that the further discussion of what has come to be called "welfare economics," especially in the course of the 1950s, has introduced considerable doubt as to whether the maximizing of welfare or of national output (or income) could be given any precise meaning. In both cases this doubt was primarily due to the aforementioned difficulty of income distribution; in the second case, for example, it was due to the dependence of prices, in terms of which output is summed into an aggregate, on income distribution. There was the difficulty introduced by a growing emphasis on the conventional element in wants and the influence of other people's consumption on an individual's satisfactions, as well as the effect of advertising propaganda ("the hidden persuaders") upon desires. Even if sense could still be conceded to the idea of maximizing something, it followed that the "tolerances" to be allowed to any mechanism for achieving it were considerably wider than had earlier been supposed [*See* WELFARE ECONOMICS.]

During the 1950s the question of more, or less, centralized or decentralized models and of the degree to which planning and a market mechanism could be combined also began to occupy economic discussion in the socialist countries of eastern Europe. On the one hand, this discussion was pro-voked by the need to give more initiative to the individual industrial enterprise in regard to the choice of inputs and outputs (within a general framework of planning) in a period when considerations of efficiency, quality, innovation, and attention to consumers' requirements were becoming more important than mere quantitative increase of output of a given range of products, which had been the main preoccupation of an earlier period. Combined with this was a reconsideration of the type of collective incentive to the enterprise that would be most conducive to the beneficial use of this initiative. On the other hand, the discussion was prompted by an increasing use of linear programming methods for selecting an optimum plan from among a range of alternative and self-consistent plans, according to the system of the Leningrad mathematician Kantorovitch. Such methods of optimal planning can be applied at various levels—that is, to decentralized or centralized decisions, to integral parts of a plan, or to a plan as a larger whole (at the time of writing they have been applied only to the former). In each optimal solution there is implicit a set of "shadow prices," in terms of which the cost of inputs necessary to yield a given output program is minimized (or alternatively the output yielded by a given quantity of available inputs is maximized). Accordingly, the question of what system of prices is consistent with the choice of optimum methods of production is immediately raised.

The Yugoslav economy was the first socialist economy to adopt a fairly drastic degree of decentralization, early in the 1950s. This took the form of giving economic enterprises greater discretion in their output programs (and even in large measure their investments) on the basis of contractual arrangements with other industries, enterprises, or wholesale and retail bodies. Yugoslavia is often cited, accordingly, as an example of a "decentralized market model." In recent years, however, other countries, including the Soviet Union, have in varying degrees moved in the direction of decentralization of planning and of freeing the enterprise as a decision-making unit from a surfeit of detailed directives. New "models" of decentralized (contractual) supply arrangements and enterprise autonomy linked with collective enterprise incentives have been experimented with, especially in consumer goods industries (e.g., the Liberman scheme in the U.S.S.R. and the Šik proposals in Czechoslovakia).

However, while in the socialist countries increased concern has been shown with optimal planning, among Western economists the focus of interest has been shifting away from questions of static equilibria to questions of growth. One could say that most economists are more concerned today to use growth potential as a criterion of judgment for an economic system than to use its capability either for attaining an economically perfect allocation of productive resources (defined in some way) or for ensuring an equitable distribution of income. On the relative weight to be attached to such criteria opinion naturally varies among economists, as it always has done and continues to do among socialists. But so far as a growth criterion is concerned, there can be little doubt that socialist economies have a distinctly good record: *vide* the high rates of growth in Soviet industry in the prewar decade and again in the planned economies as a whole in the postwar period. (In agriculture, on the other hand, although there have at times been successes, the record is less impressive.) Long-term planning in the Soviet Union in particular has set itself the goal of maintaining an industrial growth rate in the neighborhood of 10 per cent during this and the ensuing decade, and of overtaking the U.S. economy both in absolute production and in per capita production at an early date. Much in the comparative economic judgment of the two systems will no doubt turn on the result.

MAURICE DOBB

[*See also* COMMUNISM; COMMUNISM, ECONOMIC ORGANIZATION OF; MARXISM; PLANNING, ECONOMIC, *article on* EASTERN EUROPE; SOCIALISM; VALUE, LABOR THEORY OF.]

BIBLIOGRAPHY

BEER, MAX (1919–1920) 1953 *A History of British Socialism.* 2 vols. London: Allen & Unwin. → Based on Beer's *Geschichte des Sozialismus in England,* 1912.

BERGSON, ABRAM (1948) 1954 Socialist Economics. Volume 1, pages 412–448 in Howard S. Ellis (editor), *A Survey of Contemporary Economics.* Homewood, Ill.: Irwin.

BRUS, WLODZIMERZ 1961 *Ogólne problemy funkcjonowania gospodarki socjalistycznej* (General Problems in the Functioning of a Socialist Economy). Warsaw: Panstwowe Wydawnictwo Naukowe.

BURNS, EMILE 1935 *A Handbook of Marxism.* London: Gollancz.

CARR, EDWARD H. 1951–1964 *History of Soviet Russia.* 7 vols. New York: Macmillan. → Volumes 1–3: *The Bolshevik Revolution, 1917–1923,* 1951–1953. Volume 4: *The Interregnum, 1923–1924,* 1954. Volumes 5–7: *Socialism in One Country, 1924–1925,* 1958–1964. See especially Volume 1, Chapters 1–2, and Volume 2, Chapter 15.

COLE, G. D. H. 1953–1960 *A History of Socialist Thought.* 5 vols. New York: St. Martins; London: Macmillan. → Volume 1: *Socialist Thought: The Forerunners, 1789–1850,* 1953. Volume 2: *Marxism and Anarchism, 1850–1890,* 1954. Volume 3: *The Second International, 1889–1914,* 2 parts, 1956. Volume 4: *Communism and Social Democracy, 1914–1931,* 2 parts, 1958. Volume 5: *Socialism and Fascism, 1931–1939,* 1960.

DICKINSON, HENRY 1939 *Economics of Socialism.* Oxford Univ. Press.

GRAY, ALEXANDER 1946 *The Socialist Tradition: Moses to Lenin.* London: Longmans.

HAYEK, FRIEDERICH A. VON et al. 1935 *Collectivist Economic Planning: Critical Studies on the Possibilities of Socialism.* London: Routledge.

LANDAUER, CARL 1959 *European Socialism: A History of Ideas and Movements From the Industrial Revolution to Hitler's Seizure of Power.* 2 vols. Berkeley: Univ. of California Press. → Volume 1: *From the Industrial Revolution to the First World War and Its Aftermath.* Volume 2: *The Socialist Struggle Against Capitalism and Totalitarianism.*

LANGE, OSKAR (1936–1937) 1952 On the Economic Theory of Socialism. Pages 55–143 in Benjamin E. Lippincott (editor), *On the Economic Theory of Socialism.* Minneapolis: Univ. of Minnesota Press. → First published in Volume 4 of the *Review of Economic Studies.*

LICHTHEIM, GEORGE (1961) 1964 *Marxism: An Historical and Critical Study.* 2d ed., rev. London: Routledge.

MEHRING, FRANZ (1918) 1948 *Karl Marx: The Story of His Life.* London: Allen & Unwin. → First published in German. A paperback edition was published in 1962 by the Univ. of Michigan Press.

PIGOU, ARTHUR C. 1937 *Socialism Versus Capitalism.* London: Macmillan.

SCHLESINGER, RUDOLF 1950 *Marx: His Time and Ours.* New York: Kelley.

STEKLOV, IURII M. (1919?) 1928 *History of the First International.* London: Lawrence. → Translated from the 3d Russian edition.

VON MISES, LUDWIG (1922) 1959 *Socialism: An Economic and Sociological Analysis.* New ed., enl. New Haven: Yale Univ. Press. → First published as *Die Gemeinwirtschaft.*

V

THE HISTORICAL SCHOOL

The German historical school of economics reached its peak in the second half of the nineteenth century. It developed as a countermovement of romantic (that is, historical and universalist) thinking in opposition to classical economics, whose approach was timeless and atomistic.

The historical school embedded economic theory (often isolated by the classical economists) in a matrix of all the fields in which man is socially active and thereby laid the original foundations of a social theory of economics. Such thinkers as Adam Müller and Friedrich List were the precursors of the historical school.

The precursors. Adam Müller (1779–1829) did not regard the economy as a separate sphere of existence, dominated by the striving for profit. He considered the economy, rather, to be one element in the primordial social order, interrelated with custom, law, education, politics, and religion, and changing as these changed historically. In his theory of money, he went so far as to define money (intrinsically) as an expression of the desire for cooperation. He regarded governmental economic policy as a productive force and not merely as a necessity to be endured or, as did most of the classicists, as an organ of order and rule that should be kept in check. Yet Müller was not an avowed enemy of free enterprise and wanted to see it retained in a corporate state.

Müller's ideas had their philosophical foundation in the works of J. G. Fichte, especially in the latter's treatise *Der geschlossene Handelsstaat*, written in 1800. (Müller's fundamental ideas also resembled those of G. W. F. Hegel.) Starting from the same Enlightenment ideal of individual freedom as did the liberal classicists, Fichte reached an entirely different conclusion. He advocated enlarging the powers of the state, provided that the state was defined as having a social purpose. This romantic economic and social philosophy had as its practical objective the welfare state rather than the constitutional state. Fichte ultimately produced a defense of an autarkic state, isolated from the world market, whose planned economic constitution was "beneficent" domestically.

There is a bridge that leads to Marx both from Fichte and from Müller. In his *Lehre von Gegensatzen* of 1804, Müller laid down the philosophical foundations of his economic views. He asserted that all living phenomena arise from the interaction of opposites, and he considered the investigation of such interactions to be the task of economics. Like Marx, but a generation earlier, he viewed the economy and economics as evolving; indeed, he saw them as totally immanent in history. However, his interest was centered on the spiritual forces behind the material appearances of economic life; in this he was quite the opposite of Marx. (The relationship of base to superstructure was reversed.) He criticized classical economics as mechanistic, coldly rational, materialistic, and static.

The Romantic school, which included, in addition to Müller, such men as Edmund Burke, F. von Gentz, K. L. von Haller, J. Görres, and F. Baader, had almost no influence. Its imprecise, cloudy thought was unable to make headway against the dominant classical economics. Moreover, the economic developments of the era (the urge toward emancipation of the bourgeoisie, the Continental blockade, the tariff law, and later the Zollverein) were not such as to allow the politically conservative (corporate state) tendencies of the Romantics to prevail.

The more influential economic ideas of Friedrich List (1789–1804) were put forward in *Das nationale System der politischen Ökonomie*, written in 1841. The German idea of the nation, awakened in the struggle against Napoleon, was the starting point for List's economic thinking. He was primarily a practitioner of national economic integration, and his theoretical insights sprang from this soil. Starting from the historical fact that the economies of different countries are not equally strong, he advocated "educational" tariffs to protect infant industries and to enable weak, underdeveloped nations to rise to the standard of the richer, more industrialized ones. Only then would true international competition be possible.

List opposed his doctrine of a historical expansion of productive forces to the timelessness of liberal cosmopolitanism. He held that a nation's wealth is represented not by stocks of commodities but by the abilities and skills of its people. For Adam Smith, only material production was productive; List also considered education, administration, and communication to be historically important productive forces.

The older historical school.   The above were the roots of the older German historical school, whose principal representatives were W. Roscher (1817–1894), B. Hildebrand (1812–1878), and K. Knies (1821–1898). These men were Marx's contemporaries. At that time the bourgeois movement for the unification of Germany was flourishing, and Prussian-German power politics had begun its then victorious course. Following Müller, the older historical school (in particular Knies and Hildebrand) emphasized the inclusion of economics in the totality of the common moral and national life, whose historical, organic growth is based on free human deeds rather than on natural laws. In his methodological critique of classical economics, *Die Nationalökonomie der Gegenwart und Zukunft* (1848), Hildebrand denied the existence of natural laws applying to economic activity. He asserted that economics must seek for the laws of the historical evolution of the economy, rather than for immutable laws. Hildebrand did concede that an objective regularity of evolution operates in the economy. (The stages of this evolution he called the natural economy, the money economy, and the credit economy.)

As the most consistent advocate of the historical approach, Knies, in his *Die politische Ökonomie vom geschichtlichen Standpunkte* (1853), conceded no such absolute validity to evolutionary laws. He admitted that certain similarities can be observed in phenomena. But these do not involve necessity, for they are not linked by any causal nexus. They are merely analogies. Human action does not arise from an "innate" egotism but derives its motives from the spirit of the times.

Precisely because of this dubious substitution of subjective motivations for objective law, economic science is indebted to Knies for clearing the way for the methodologically significant insight that statistical rather than causal regularities apply in the historical–social realm. With this, Hildebrand and Knies broke definitively with the ideas of the classicists. Roscher, in his *Grundriss zu Vorlesungen über die Staatswirthschaft nach geschichtlicher Methode* (1843), remained somewhat dependent on classical ideas, though he stressed the historical method of research.

The similarities between the older historical school and Marx indicate a common intellectual background. For both, historical progress is a basic concept. Both take human actions in relation to productive forces as their point of departure, and both emphasize the concept of society. But Marx opposed his "rational" research into the laws of the historical process to the historical school's relativistic concept of societies, which it saw as based on an irrational flow of history. For Marx the base–superstructure relationship is the opposite; he regarded the social institutions as a superstructure dependent on the economy, rather than vice versa.

The later historical school. Thus the older historical school concentrated its attention on the fundamentals of universal historical economic development. The later historical school used this view as a point of departure and, at the beginning of the 1870s, turned to research into concrete details. The founder of this later school was Gustav Schmoller (1838–1917), and its adherents included L. Brentano, K. Bücher, G. F. Knapp, K. T. von Inama-Sternegg, and J. Conrad. Economic historicism also gained a more or less firm footing in England, France, Italy, and the United States. Men such as T. E. Cliffe Leslie, J. K. Ingram, W. J. Ashley, Charles Gide, L. Cossa, and Charles A. Beard were among its representatives in these countries.

The "great" dispute over method (*Methodenstreit*) with the marginalist neoclassicists forced the members of the later historical school to seek further clarification of their point of view, as in Schmoller's "Zur Methodologie der Staats- und Sozialwissenschaften" (1883). The antitheses were historical induction *vs.* deduction, individualizing *vs.* generalizing, and descriptive economics *vs.* economics that searches for laws or patterns. Another characteristic of the later school was its ethical and practical approach to questions of social policy, especially to

labor problems. Schmoller was instrumental in the founding of the Verein für Socialpolitik in 1872, whence the designation of the school as "professorial socialism" (*Kathedersozialismus*).

Brentano's resolution of the problems inherent in previous naively linear correlations of working time, labor output, and wages was a significant insight in political economy. So was Knapp's theory of money, presented in *The State Theory of Money* (1905), in which money is defined as a creation of the law rather than a "commodity."

At about the turn of the century there developed a German trend toward historical and sociological research which included such important thinkers as W. Sombart and Max Weber. This movement, which was a successor to and a critique of the historical school, was also influenced by W. Dilthey. Later on, O. Spann and his disciples went back directly to Adam Müller.

Influence on institutionalism. The influence of the historical school was not confined to Europe but was felt in America as well, particularly by the American institutionalists. After World War I they increasingly worked toward independence of economic thought. In the 1920s J. R. Commons, R. G. Tugwell, A. B. Wolfe, C. E. Ayres, W. H. Hamilton, M. A. Copeland, W. E. Atkins, and others tried to establish an American system of teaching and research. Characteristically they turned away from marginal utility and the entire abstractly theoretical approach of British neoclassical political economy. These were replaced by empirical studies of economic behavior along social-psychological and, to some extent, social-ethical lines.

Thorstein B. Veblen's economic relativism and his witty criticism of John Bates Clark's doctrine, based on marginal utility theory, demonstrated most clearly how weary a then influential group of American economists had become of the tutelage of their intellectual elders, the European theorists. The criticism of the institutionalists was aimed primarily at the fiction of the "economic man" and at the hypothesis of an exclusively hedonistic motivation for his actions. This institutionalist thinking had many links to European ideas. The initial general rejection of the classical theory by American economists, as well as their acceptance of the methodological principles of the older German historical school (especially in the form in which they were cast by Bruno Hildebrand), was inspired by personal and intellectual contacts at German universities while the historical school was at its peak.

Institutionalism and the closely related behaviorism proceed from the assumption that economic acts are not solely governed by the hedonistic principle. Man's economic behavior, his needs and desires, his ways and means, are merely functions of a constantly changing evolution that is infinitely complex, is molded by particular social institutions, and is in this sense "institutional." The true nature of economic relationships can be learned only by thorough study of economic institutions, of the changes they undergo in the course of their evolution, and of their interrelationships with the changes in the psychological peculiarities of men's economic behavior. Therefore the institutionalists demanded a dynamic concept of the economy.

This conceptual structure of institutionalism clearly echoes aspects of German experimental psychology and of Spencer's evolutionary doctrine, with the ideas of traditional British association psychology in its background. It cannot be denied, however, that the relativism central to this institutionalist way of thinking is close to the basic notions of the German historical school.

There is still another channel leading from the German historical school to American institutionalism. In the 1920s certain economists led by Commons became tired of neoclassicist research in general, and of the dispute about what is "free of value judgments" in particular. In their reaction they adopted the moderate standpoint that had earlier been advocated in Germany by Bruno Hildebrand, with his historical approach. They asserted that in establishing goals of economic policy, one must take into account the mass-psychological and social-ethical aspects of these goals.

A. T. Hadley, E. R. A. Seligman, and R. Mayo-Smith were among those who supported the "value-judgment-free" point of view and opposed Commons in this "value-judgment debate," which is often called the "little" dispute over method (*kleiner Methodenstreit*). Veblen was in the forefront of the challenge to John Bates Clark's economic theory, which was free of value judgments. As a young economist, Clark's son, John Maurice Clark, agreed with Veblen on particular issues.

These discussions had implications for economic policy. The institutionalists felt that the abstract-theoretical postulate of absolute economic freedom should be disregarded, and stress should be placed instead on the actual development of economic institutions and the behavior of individuals and of important socioeconomic groups. Governmental economic planning and control were justified, if necessary, to ensure the social-ethical ideal of welfare in the long run. This view was adopted by W. C. Mitchell, Commons, Hamilton, L. D. Edie, and Tugwell and, to a greater or lesser degree, by Wolfe, John Maurice Clark, F. C. Mills, O. F.

Boucke, D. Friday, and other economists. Still, American institutionalists did not simply accept the concepts of the German historical school. The methodological pragmatism of the majority of American institutionalists is manifested by their failure to evolve a unified cognitive procedure of a specific institutionalist nature. True, they accepted the deductive method. Yet their special interests lie in empirical–inductive, quantitative, mathematical–statistical, and causal–genetic analysis. For example, the work of W. C. Mitchell was primarily concerned with the analysis of business cycles and economic development. He is primarily responsible for the great growth of empirical research and of studies aimed at statistical and historical verification. It now appears that a more or less harmonious collaboration of abstract and empirical economic thought tends toward attaching increasing importance to the statistical, applied-mathematical, and historical approach.

THEO SURÁNYI-UNGER

[See the biographies of BÜCHER; COMMONS; HILDEBRAND; KNAPP; KNIES; LIST; MÜLLER, ADAM; ROSCHER; SCHMOLLER; VEBLEN.]

BIBLIOGRAPHY

WORKS BY MEMBERS OF THE HISTORICAL SCHOOL

HILDEBRAND, BRUNO (1848) 1922 *Die Nationalökonomie der Gegenwart und Zukunft, und andere gesammelte Schriften.* Jena (Germany): Fischer.

KNAPP, GEORG F. (1905) 1924 *The State Theory of Money.* 4th ed. enl. Munich: Duncker & Humblot. → First published as *Die staatliche Theorie des Geldes.*

KNIES, KARL (1853) 1930 *Die politische Ökonomie vom geschichtlichen Standpunkte.* New ed., enl. Leipzig: Buske. → First published as *Die politischen Ökonomie vom Standpunkte der geschichtlichen Methode.*

ROSCHER, WILHELM G. F. 1843 *Grundriss zu Vorlesungen über die Staatswirthschaft nach geschichtlicher Methode.* Göttingen (Germany): Dietrich.

SCHMOLLER, GUSTAV F. 1883 Zur Methodologie der Staats- und Sozialwissenschaften. *Jahrbuch für Gesetzgebung, Verwaltung und Volkswirtschaft* 7:975–994.

WORKS ABOUT THE HISTORICAL SCHOOL

ALBERY, M. 1955 Institucionalismo económico. *Revista de economía política* 6, no. 3:126–141.

BOULDING, KENNETH E. 1957 A New Look at Institutionalism. *American Economic Review* 47, no. 2:1–12. → Discussion on pages 13–27.

COATS, A. W. 1954 The Historist Reaction in English Political Economy: 1870–1890. *Economica* New Series 21:143–153.

COPELAND, MORRIS A. 1958 Institutionalism and Welfare Economics. *American Economic Review* 48:1–17.

DORFMAN, JOSEPH (1934) 1961 *Thorstein Veblen and His America.* New York: Viking; Kelley.

DOW, LOUIS A. 1961 Institutionalism and Contemporary Price Theory. *American Journal of Economics and Sociology* 20:181–193.

EISERMANN, GOTTFRIED 1956 *Die Grundlagen des Historismus in der deutschen Nationalökonomie.* Stuttgart (Germany): Enke.

ELLIS, JOHN M. 1961 Cannan and Veblen as Institutionalists. *American Journal of Economics and Sociology* 20:305–312.

GRUCHY, ALAN G. 1958 The Influence of Veblen on Mid-century Institutionalism. *American Economic Review* 48, no. 2:11–20.

HALL, FRANKLIN P. 1956 Toward Understanding Institutionalism. *Indian Journal of Economics* 37:177–186.

HAMILTON, DAVID B. 1962 Why Is Institutional Economics Not Institutional? *American Journal of Economics and Sociology* 21:309–317.

Institutional Economics; Veblen, Commons, and Mitchell Reconsidered: A Series of Lectures. 1963 Berkeley: Univ. of California Press. → By Joseph Dorfman, C. E. Ayres, and others.

JAHN, GEORG 1960 Die historische Schule der Nationalökonomie und ihr Ausklang: Von der Wirtschaftsgeschichte zur geschichtlichen Theorie. Pages 139–150 in Otto Stammer and Karl C. Thalheim (editors), *Festgabe für Friedrich Bülow zum 70. Geburtstag.* Berlin: Duncker & Humblot.

KNIGHT, FRANK H. 1952 Institutionalism and Empiricism in Economics. *American Economic Review* 42, no. 2:45–55.

MACARIO, SANTIAGO P. 1952 El institucionalismo como crítica de la teoría económica clásica. *Trimestre económico* 19:73–112, 250–300, 481–509.

MANN, FRITZ K. 1955 Wirtschaftstheorie und Institutionalismus in den Vereinigten Staaten. Pages 201–213 in Wilhelm Bernsdorf and Gottfried Eisermann (editors), *Die Einheit der Sozialwissenschaften: Franz Eulenburg zum Gedächtnis.* Stuttgart (Germany): Enke.

MANN, FRITZ K. 1960 Institutionalism and American Economic Theory: A Case of Interpenetration. *Kyklos* 13, no. 3:307–323.

PALOMBA, G. 1952 Storicismo e naturalismo nell'indagine economica. *Studi economici* 7:257–270.

POPPER, KARL R. 1957 *The Poverty of Historicism.* Boston: Beacon.

SPENGLER, JOSEPH J. 1959 Veblen and Mandeville Contrasted. *Weltwirtschaftliches Archiv* 82, part 1:35–65.

SPIETHOFF, ARTHUR 1952 The "Historical" Character of Economic Theories. *Journal of Economic History* 12:131–139.

STOCKING, GEORGE W. 1959 Institutional Factors in Economic Thinking. *American Economic Review* 49:1–21.

VIANELLO, MINO 1961 *Thorstein Veblen.* Milan (Italy): Edizioni di Comunità.

WAGNER, VALENTIN F. 1959 Die Armut des Historizismus: Theorie und Geschichte. *Schweizerische Zeitschrift für Volkswirtschaft und Statistik* 95:21–46.

WITTE, EDWIN E. 1954 Institutional Economics as Seen by an Institutional Economist. *Southern Economic Journal* 21:131–140.

VI

THE AUSTRIAN SCHOOL

Value theory before 1871. The "marginal revolution" of the 1870s is generally recognized as a major step in the advance of economic theory. Those who have been able to start with its established results often find it difficult to comprehend why an obvious and simple idea, which had occurred to many earlier thinkers, should have exercised such a great effect when W. S. Jevons, Carl Menger, and Léon Walras independently rediscovered it at about the same time and, particularly, why the tradition founded by Menger should so profoundly have affected economic theory for two generations. To account for this it is necessary to elaborate on the distinction that is commonly but inadequately expressed as a contrast between "objective" and "subjective" theories of value.

Since value is evidently an attribute possessed by certain things or services, it was natural to seek its determinants in some property or properties of the particular objects that possess it. This procedure had proved successful in the physical sciences, and the expectation that objects having the same value should have also other "intrinsic" properties in common therefore seemed reasonable. Of course, it had often been seen that the decisive factor might be something discoverable not in the object itself but rather in the relations of men to the object. Ever since the medieval scholastic philosophers (and even Aristotle), it had been pointed out again and again that to possess value an object must be useful and scarce. But this idea was rarely followed through systematically (though an exception must be made for the greatest of the early anticipators of modern theory, Fernando Galiani in his *Della moneta* of 1750) and never to the point of realizing that what was relevant was not merely man's relation to a particular thing or a class of things but the position of the thing in the whole means–end structure—the whole scheme by which men decide how to allocate the resources at their disposal among their different endeavors.

It was largely from approaching the problem of value through patient analysis of the character of economic choice in the various types of possible relations between different means and different ends that there ultimately emerged the explanation of value that made the work of Menger and his pupils so immediately effective. Although the answers supplied by Jevons and Walras to the old value paradox were no less correct, they were concealed from most contemporary economists by the mathematical notation employed. Moreover, these authors treated the solution of the utility paradox as merely a preliminary step to be gotten quickly out of the way in order to get on with the main business, the explanation of value in exchange. The Austrians, on the other hand, made the full analysis of the conditions of valuation, independent of the possibility of exchange, so much their central task that later they had to defend themselves against the misunderstanding that they believed marginal utility provided a direct explanation of price. Of course, the subjective value that it explains is merely a first step to the second stage, the theory of price.

On the Continent the utility-*cum*-scarcity approach had, since Galiani, remained an important tradition and considerable insight had been achieved in such works as E. B. de Condillac's *Le commerce et le gouvernement*, 1776, Louis Say's *Considérations sur l'industrie*, 1822, Auguste Walras's *De la nature de la richesse*, 1831, Jules Dupuit's *De la mesure de l'utilité des travaux publics*, 1844, and finally in the remarkable but at the time completely overlooked work of H. H. Gossen, *Entwicklung der Gesetz des menschlichen Verkehrs*, 1854. In England, on the other hand, the generally much more highly developed classical political economy had become wedded to an "objective" labor theory of value, and the utility tradition persisted only as a sort of undercurrent of protest, which reached a high point in 1834 with W. F. Lloyd's *The Notion of Value*. It was fully swamped when as late as 1848 J. S. Mill in his *Principles of Political Economy* not only re-expounded the classical position but calmly asserted, "Happily, there is nothing in the laws of value which remains for the present or any future writer to clear up; the theory of the subject is complete" (book 3, chapter 1, sec. 1). [*See the biographies of* DUPUIT; GALIANI; GOSSEN.]

Menger and the origins of the school.   While W. S. Jevons (who with his preliminary sketch of a theory of value based on "final utility" had anticipated Menger by nine years) was writing in direct opposition to dominant doctrine and had little more than Benthamite utilitarianism to draw upon, both Menger and Walras were able to build on a rich literary tradition favorable to the utility approach. But in Vienna, where Menger worked, there was little interest in economic theory. At that time economics was taught at the University of Vienna by Germans of chiefly sociological interests. The rapid rise of a distinct Austrian school of economic theory was thus entirely owing to Menger's work— though it did coincide with the university's rise to great eminence in a number of other fields, which for some fifty or sixty years made it an intellectual center of great influence.

Carl Menger was a civil servant in the prime minister's office at Vienna when at the age of 31 he published his first and decisive work, *Principles of Economics* (1871). It was the first part of an intended treatise, the rest of which never appeared. It dealt with the general conditions that create economic activity, value, exchange, price, and money. What made it so effective was that the explanation of value it offered arose from an analysis of the conditions determining the distribution of scarce goods among competing uses and of the way in which different goods competed or cooperated for the satisfaction of different needs—in short, what has been called above the "means–ends structure." It is this analysis that precedes the theory of value proper. Friedrich von Wieser was to develop this systematically into a *vorwerttheoretische* part of economic theory that made the Austrian form of marginal-utility analysis so suitable as a basis of further development. From this analysis springs most of what is known today as the logic of choice, or the "economic calculus."

Menger's exposition is generally characterized more by painstaking detail and relentless pursuit of the important points than by elegance or the use of graphic terms to express his conclusions. Though always clear, it is labored, and it is doubtful whether his doctrines would ever have had wide appeal in the form in which he stated them. However, he had the good fortune of finding at once avid and gifted readers in two young men who had left the University of Vienna some time before Menger became a professor there. They decided to make the fulfillment of his teaching their lifework. It was mainly through the work of Eugen von Böhm-Bawerk and Friedrich von Wieser, classmates and later brothers-in-law, that Menger's ideas were developed and spread. Gradually during the 1880s, when their most influential works appeared, they were joined by others working in the universities or elsewhere in Austria. Of these, Emil Sax, Robert Zuckerkandl, Johann von Komorzynski, and Robert Meyer particularly deserve mention. Somewhat later came Hermann von Schullern zu Schrattenhofen and Richard Schüller.

The year 1889, in which the greatest number of important publications of the group were concentrated, also saw the appearance of an important theoretical treatise by two Viennese businessmen, Rudolf Auspitz and Richard Lieben, *Untersuchungen über die Theorie des Preises* (1889). This can, however, only with qualifications be included in the works of the Austrian school. It moved on parallel but wholly independent lines and with its highly mathematical exposition was too difficult for most contemporary economists, so that its importance was recognized only much later.

Of great importance for spreading the teachings of the school, especially in Germany, was the fact that another Viennese professor, Eugen Philippovich von Philippsberg, though not himself an active theoretician, incorporated the marginal-utility doctrine into a very successful textbook, *Grundriss der politischen Ökonomie* (1893). For some twenty years after publication this remained the most widely used textbook in Germany and almost the only channel through which the marginal-utility doctrine became known there. In other foreign countries, especially England, the United States, Italy, the Netherlands, and the Scandinavian countries, the basic economic publications of the Austrians became known sooner, partly in English translations. Probably the most important foreign adherent was an exact contemporary of Böhm-Bawerk and Wieser, the Swede Knut Wicksell. Although he was also greatly indebted to Walras, Wicksell could write in 1921 that "since Ricardo's *Principles* there has been no other book —not even excepting Jevons' brilliant but somewhat aphoristic and Walras' unfortunately difficult work—which has had such a great influence on the development of economics as Menger's *Grundsätze*." [*See the biographies of* AUSPITZ *and* LIEBEN; MENGER; WICKSELL.]

Development by Böhm-Bawerk and Wieser. In the theoretical development of Menger's ideas the most important steps were Wieser's interpretation of costs as sacrificed utility (or "opportunity costs," as the concept later came to be called) and the theory of the determination of the value of the factors of production by "imputation" (*Zurechnung*). (This latter term and the term *Grenznutzen*— "marginal utility"—were introduced by Wieser.) In the field of value theory proper Böhm-Bawerk contributed mainly by the lucidity of his exposition and the great skill of his polemics. His most important original contribution was his theory of capital and interest, which was by no means accepted by all members of the school. In general it may be said that the school never developed a strict orthodoxy but that the development of Menger's ideas by its different members shows distinct differences. This applies particularly to Böhm-Bawerk and Wieser, who in many respects represented very different intellectual types and whose endeavors marked the starting points of two distinguishable traditions within the school. Böhm-Bawerk was a particularly consistent logical reasoner, a masterly debater, and at the same time, a man of great practical experience (he was three times Austrian minister of finance). He was able to ground his work on a thorough command of the whole of economic literature, and he was always ready to take issue with other views. He therefore kept closer in many ways to Menger's foundation than Wieser, who after the initial stimulus received from Menger, very much pursued his own ways. Wieser's work in consequence has a highly personal character, and though

in some respects (e.g., in the analysis of the role of different degrees of monopoly) he anticipated later development, in others, such as his insistence on the calculability and interpersonal comparability of utility, he developed in directions that had later to be abandoned. His *Social Economics* (1914), which constitutes the only complete systematization of the economic theory of the earlier Menger school, therefore cannot be regarded as representative but nonetheless constitutes a distinctly personal achievement. [*See the biographies of* BÖHM-BAWERK; WIESER.]

Controversy with the historical school. Carl Menger was a very effective teacher, and through his numerous pupils and his participation in the contemporary discussion of economic and financial policy he exercised considerable influence on Austrian public life. If after his first work, his literary contributions to pure theory, except in the field of money, are few, this is to be ascribed mainly to his involvement in the *Methodenstreit*, his dispute about method with the leader of the younger German historical school, Gustav Schmoller. That Menger's book had remained practically unnoticed in Germany was chiefly owing to the fact that the dominance of the historical school had almost eliminated the teaching of economic theory from German universities. In these circumstances it was natural that it should seem urgent to Menger to vindicate the importance of theoretical research. This he undertook in his *Problems of Economics and Sociology* (1883), which in several respects became as important for the development of the Austrian school as his earlier *Grundsätze*, although in detail his methodological views were not fully accepted even within his own school. But the systematic justification of what Schumpeter (1908, p. 94) was later to call "methodological individualism" and the analysis of the evolution of social institutions (in which he revived ideas originally conceived by Bernard Mandeville and David Hume) had a profound influence on all members of the school and, later, far beyond the limits of economics. Compared with this, the points immediately at issue with Schmoller are of lesser significance, although at the time they led to a passionate exchange of opinions to which several disciples on each side contributed. This exchange caused such a rift between the two groups that the German universities came to be filled more and more exclusively by members of the historical school and the Austrian universities by members of Menger's school. [*See the biography of* SCHMOLLER.]

The third and fourth generations. In 1903 Menger retired prematurely from teaching and in consequence exercised little direct influence on the formation of the third generation of the Austrian school, which grew up during the decade preceding World War I. These years, during which Böhm-Bawerk, Wieser, and Philippovich were teaching at Vienna, were the period of the school's greatest fame. It was particularly Böhm-Bawerk's seminar that provided the center of theoretical discussion and produced the leading members of the third generation. Among them, particular mention must be made of Ludwig von Mises, who continued the tradition of Böhm-Bawerk, and Hans Mayer, who continued that of Wieser. Joseph Schumpeter, although much indebted to Böhm-Bawerk, absorbed so many other influences (particularly that of the Lausanne school) that he cannot be wholly regarded as a member of this group. The same might be said of Alfred Amonn, who stood close to the English classical tradition. Somewhat younger but still wholly active at Vienna were Richard von Strigl, Ewald Schams, and Leo Illy (whose name was originally Leo Schönfeld).

In the 1920s a fourth generation appeared, to which Gottfried Haberler, Fritz Machlup, Alexander Mahr, Oskar Morgenstern, Paul N. Rosenstein-Rodan, and the author of this article belong. Most of these men, however, did the greater part of their work outside Austria. [*See the biography of* VON MISES, LUDWIG.]

FRIEDRICH A. VON HAYEK

BIBLIOGRAPHY

WORKS BY MEMBERS OF THE AUSTRIAN SCHOOL

AMONN, ALFRED (1911) 1927 *Objekt und Grundbegriffe der theoretischen Nationalökonomie.* Leipzig: Deuticke.

AUSPITZ, RUDOLF; and LIEBEN, RICHARD 1889 *Untersuchungen über die Theorie des Preises.* Leipzig: Duncker & Humblot. → A French translation was published in 1914.

BÖHM-BAWERK, EUGEN VON (1884–1912) 1959 *Capital and Interest.* 3 vols. South Holland, Ill.: Libertarian Press. → First published as *Kapital und Kapitalzins.* Volume 1: *History and Critique of Interest Theories,* 1884. Volume 2: *Positive Theory of Capital,* 1889. Volume 3: *Further Essays on Capital and Interest;* was first published as appendixes to Volume 2 of the 1909–1912 edition and was printed as a separate volume in 1921.

BÖHM-BAWERK, EUGEN VON (1896) 1949 *Karl Marx and the Close of His System.* Edited by Paul M. Sweezy. New York: Kelley. → First published in German.

BÖHM-BAWERK, EUGEN VON (1914) 1951 *Control or Economic Law?* South Holland, Ill.: Libertarian Press. → First published in German.

BÖHM-BAWERK, EUGEN VON 1924–1926 *Gesammelte Schriften.* 2 vols. Edited by Franz X. Weiss. Vienna: Hölder.

BÖHM-BAWERK, EUGEN VON 1926 *Eugen von Böhm-Bawerks kleinere Abhandlungen über Kapital und Zins.* Edited by Franz X. Weiss. Vienna: Hölder.

HAYEK, F. A. VON 1926 Bemerkungen zum Zurechnungs-problem. *Jahrbücher für Nationalökonomie und Statistik* 124:1–18.

ILLY, LEO 1948 *Das Gesetz des Grenznutzens.* Vienna: Springer. → Leo Illy was formerly called Leo Schönfeld.

KOMORZYNSKI, JOHANN VON 1889 *Der Werth in der isolirten Wirthschaft.* Vienna: Manz.

MAYER, HANS 1921–1922 Untersuchungen zu dem Grundgesetz der wirtschaftlichen Wertrechnung. *Zeitschrift für Volkswirtschaft und Sozialpolitik* New Series 1:431–458; 2:1–23.

MAYER, HANS 1932 Der Erkenntniswert der funktionellen Preistheorie. Volume 2, pages 147–239b in *Die Wirtschaftstheorie der Gegenwart.* Vienna: Springer.

MENGER, CARL (1871) 1950 *Principles of Economics: First General Part.* Edited by James Dingwall and Bert F. Hoselitz, with an introduction by Frank H. Knight. Glencoe, Ill.: Free Press. → First published as *Grundsätze der Volkswirtschaftslehre.*

MENGER, CARL (1871–1915) 1933–1936 *The Collected Works of Carl Menger.* 4 vols. With an introduction by F. A. von Hayek. The London School of Economics and Political Science. → Volume 1: *Grundsätze der Volkswirtschaftslehre,* (1871) 1934. Volume 2: *Untersuchungen über die Methode der Socialwissenschaften,* (1883) 1933. Volume 3: *Kleinere Schriften zur Methode und Geschichte der Volkswirtschaftslehre,* (1884–1915) 1935. Volume 4: *Schriften über Geldtheorie . . . ,* (1889–1893) 1936.

MENGER, CARL (1883) 1963 *Problems of Economics and Sociology.* Edited with an introduction by Louis Schneider. Urbana: Univ. of Illinois Press. → First published as *Untersuchungen über die Methode der Socialwissenschaften und der politischen Ökonomie insbesondere.*

MEYER, ROBERT 1887 *Das Wesen des Einkommens: Eine volkswirtschaftliche Untersuchung.* Berlin: Hertz.

PHILIPPOVICH VON PHILIPPSBERG, EUGEN 1893 *Grundriss der politischen Ökonomie.* Volume 1. Freiburg (Germany): Mohr.

SAX, EMIL 1887 *Grundlegung der theoretischen Staatswirtschaft.* Vienna: Hölder.

SCHAMS, EWALD 1934 Wirtschaftslogik. *Schmollers Jahrbuch für Gesetzgebung, Verwaltung und Volkswirtschaft im Deutschen Reiche.* 58:513–533.

SCHÖNFELD, LEO 1924 *Grenznutzen und Wirtschaftsrechnung.* Vienna: Manz. → Leo Schönfeld was subsequently called Leo Illy.

SCHÜLLER, RICHARD 1895 *Die klassische Nationalökonomie und ihre Gegner.* Berlin: Heymann.

SCHULLERN ZU SCHRATTENHOFEN, HERMANN VON 1889 *Untersuchungen über Begriff und Wesen der Grundrente.* Leipzig: Fock.

SCHUMPETER, JOSEPH A. 1908 *Das Wesen und der Hauptinhalt der theoretischen Nationalökonomie.* Leipzig: Duncker & Humblot.

SCHUMPETER, JOSEPH A. (1912) 1934 *The Theory of Economic Development: An Inquiry Into Profits, Capital, Credit, Interest, and the Business Cycle.* Harvard Economic Studies, Vol. 46. Cambridge, Mass.: Harvard Univ. Press. → First published as *Theorie der wirtschaftlichen Entwicklung.*

STRIGL, RICHARD VON 1923 *Die ökonomischen Kategorien und die Organisation der Wirtschaft.* Jena (Germany): Fischer.

VON MISES, LUDWIG (1912) 1953 *The Theory of Money and Credit.* New ed., enl. Translated by H. E. Batson. New Haven: Yale Univ. Press. → First published as *Theorie des Geldes und der Umlaufsmittel.*

VON MISES, LUDWIG (1922) 1959 *Socialism: An Economic and Sociological Analysis.* New ed. New Haven: Yale Univ. Press. → First published as *Die gemeinwirtschaft.*

VON MISES, LUDWIG (1949) 1963 *Human Action: A Treatise on Economics.* New rev. ed. New Haven: Yale Univ. Press.

WIESER, FRIEDRICH VON (1876–1923) 1929 *Gesammelte Abhandlungen.* Edited with an introduction by F. A. von Hayek. Tübingen (Germany): Mohr.

WIESER, FRIEDRICH VON (1889) 1956 *Natural Value.* Edited with a preface and analysis by William Smart. New York: Kelly & Millman. → First published in German.

WIESER, FRIEDRICH VON (1914) 1927 *Social Economics.* New York: Greenberg. → First published as *Theorie der gesellschaftlichen Wirtschaft.*

WIESER, FRIEDRICH VON 1926 *Das Gesetz der Macht.* Vienna: Springer.

ZUCKERKANDL, ROBERT (1889) 1936 *Zur Theorie des Preises mit besonderer Berücksichtigung der geschichtlichen Entwicklung der Lehre.* Leipzig: Stein.

WORKS ABOUT THE AUSTRIAN SCHOOL

ANTONELLI, ÉTIENNE 1953 Léon Walras et Carl Menger à travers leur correspondance. *Économie appliquée* 6:269–287.

BACHMANN, VERENA 1963 *Der Haushaltplan des Konsumenten und seine theoretische Erfassung durch die Grenznutzenlehre: Eine dogmengeschichtliche Untersuchung.* Züricher volkswirtschaftliche Forschungen, New Series, Vol. 7. Zürich: Polygraphischer Verlag.

BLAUG, MARK 1962 *Economic Theory in Retrospect.* Homewood, Ill.: Irwin. → Contains a good survey of recent literature.

BLOCH, HENRI S. 1937 *La théorie des besoins de Carl Menger.* Paris: Librairie Générale de Droit et de Jurisprudence.

HOWEY, RICHARD S. 1960 *The Rise of the Marginal Utility School: 1870–1889.* Lawrence: Univ. of Kansas Press.

HUTCHISON, TERENCE W. (1953) 1962 *A Review of Economic Doctrines, 1870–1929.* 2d ed. Oxford: Clarendon.

KAUDER, EMIL 1953 The Retarded Acceptance of the Marginal Utility Theory. *Quarterly Journal of Economics* 67:564–575.

KAUDER, EMIL 1957 Intellectual and Political Roots of the Older Austrian School. *Zeitschrift für Nationalökonomie* 17:411–425.

KIRZNER, ISRAEL M. 1960 *The Economic Point of View: An Essay in the History of Economic Thought.* Princeton, N.J.: Van Nostrand.

PIROU, GAËTAN (1932) 1945 *L'utilité marginale de Carl Menger à John Bates Clark.* 3d ed. Paris: Domat-Monchrestien.

ROSENSTEIN-RODAN, PAUL N. (1927) 1960 Marginal Utility. *International Economic Papers* 10:71–106. → First published as "Grenznutzen" in Volume 4 of *Handwörterbuch der Staatswissenschaften.* This edition contained a comprehensive bibliography which was omitted in the 1960 edition.

RUPPE-STREISSLER, MONIKA 1963 Zum Begriff der Wertung in der älteren österreichischen Grenznutzenlehre. *Zeitschrift für Nationalökonomie* 22:377–419.

SELIGMAN, BEN B. 1962 *Main Currents in Modern Economics: Economic Thought Since 1870.* New York: Free Press.

STIGLER, GEORGE J. 1941 *Production and Distribution Theories: The Formative Period.* New York: Macmillan.

STIGLER, GEORGE J. 1950 The Development of Utility Theory. *Journal of Political Economy* 58:307–327, 373–396.

WEBER, WILHELM 1949 Wirtschaftswissenschaft und Wirtschaftspolitik in Österreich, 1848–1948. Pages 624–678 in Hans Mayer (editor), *Hundert Jahre österreichischer Wirtschaftsentwicklung, 1848–1948.* Vienna: Springer.

WIEN-CLAUDI, FRANZ 1936 *Austrian Theories of Capital, Interest, and the Trade Cycle.* London: Nott.

VII

THE INSTITUTIONAL SCHOOL

Institutional economics is very largely an American intellectual product stemming from the work of Thorstein Veblen and other economists working in the Veblenian tradition. The term "institutional" was applied to this type of economics early in the current century because it examines the economic system as a part of human culture, which is a complex of many institutions. The concept of an "institutional school" can be used only very loosely—in the sense that the members of this school have the same philosophical orientation, the same broad cultural approach to economic studies, and the same way of viewing the American economic system.

The development of institutionalism can be divided into three major periods. The first period from 1890 to 1925 was the period when Veblen was laying the foundations of the institutionalist movement. The second period runs from 1925 to 1945; during these years a group of institutionalists, prominent among whom were John R. Commons, Wesley C. Mitchell, John M. Clark, and Rexford G. Tugwell, continued the work of institutional economics after Veblen had come to the end of his career. The third period includes the years since 1945 when work along similar lines has been continued by a new generation of institutionalists, conspicuous among whom are Clarence E. Ayres, John K. Galbraith, Leon H. Keyserling, Gardiner C. Means, and Gerhard Colm.

Veblen's cultural economics. An understanding of Thorstein Veblen's economics, which he described as "evolutionary" or "cultural" economics, must start with the fact that Veblen came to economics from the field of philosophy. Veblen started his economic analysis by asking the fundamental philosophical question: How does an economist or any other scientist comprehend the real world about him? Veblen's answer was that a scientist's comprehension of reality depends upon his intellectual or philosophical orientation, or mental set, which is a product of his life experience. This intellectual orientation of the scientist may induce him to regard the outside world as a static mechanism or as an evolving process. According to Veblen the intellectual orientation of Alfred Marshall and other orthodox economists led them to view the economic system as a static mechanism, whereas his own orientation led him to regard the economic system as a dynamic process.

In explaining the American economic system as a developing process, Veblen turned to the field of cultural anthropology as a model for economic science. In his hands economics became a study of the material aspect of human culture. Like human culture, the economic system is an evolving historical product that passes through an endless number of developmental stages. There is no one universal economic system, but rather there are many different ones, such as the capitalist, socialist, fascist, and communist systems. Although he carried economic inquiry back to the early Stone Age and projected it into a socialist state of the future, Veblen's main interest was always in explaining the nature and functioning of American capitalism in the period from 1875 to 1925. All institutionalists since Veblen have continued to make the study of the evolving American capitalist system their main concern.

The heuristic device Veblen used in constructing his theory of American capitalism is the dichotomy between "industry" (technology) and "business" (finance). This dichotomy is both psychological and cultural, since it finds expression in the conflict between the individual's drives (or instincts) for workmanship and acquisitiveness, and between society's industrial and business systems. The industrial system, Veblen held, is serviceable to mankind because it produces "economic" values, whereas the business system is disserviceable, since it can create only "pecuniary" values. Economic values are "real" values, goods of high social and private utility that contribute to race survival; pecuniary values are pseudo, or false, values that enlarge a person's financial assets but make no contribution to race survival. According to Veblen the evolution of American capitalism was leading to a widening of the conflict between industry and business; the time would eventually be reached when this conflict would be so intense that the common people, led by technocrats, would attempt to overthrow the capitalist system in order to establish a socialist regime based on workmanship. However, there was no guarantee that the working population would be successful in establishing socialism. Veblen thought it quite possible that the vested interests, in cooperation with the military class, would succeed in establishing a fascist type of society. If the technician-led working class were to succeed in replacing capitalism with socialism, the socialist society of the future would eliminate the dichotomy between industry and business and enable the industrial system to produce an abundant supply of economic values. Veblen did not think in terms of any early establishment of a regime of workmanship.

Although Veblen was very critical of the orthodox economics of his time, he never intended to dispense with all accumulated economic theory. Much of the economic theorizing since the time of Adam Smith concerning supply, demand, costs, and related matters is as useful to an institutionalist as to any other economist. What Veblen objected to was the normalistic philosophical underpinning, the rationalistic psychology, the particularistic methodology, and the mechanistic view of the economic system associated with orthodox or Marshallian economics. Veblen did not dispense with the pure theory of competitive economic behavior. He said that it was not very useful in explaining twentieth-century capitalistic behavior, and that economists should go far beyond the pure theory of competition to develop a theory of capitalism. For Veblen pure economic theory could only be a first approximation to economic reality. Above the level of pure economic theory it was necessary to construct a theory of the concrete evolving economic system (for the United States a theory of capitalism) before economic reality could be adequately comprehended.

Veblen's views about the nature of economic science are substantially those of all later members of the institutional school. Therefore, critics who assert that this school would do away with all inherited economic theory, that institutional economics is concerned only with the description of economic activity, or that it is not concerned with improving economic theory are misinformed about the nature of institutional economics as developed by Veblen and those who followed him.

Institutional economics after Veblen.   The post-Veblenian group of institutionalists that came into prominence in the 1920s and 1930s differed from Veblen in a number of important ways. Unlike Veblen they did not attempt to theorize about the whole sweep of economic development from the Stone Age to the contemporary phase of capitalist evolution. These later institutionalists denied that capitalism would come to a catastrophic end. Commons, Mitchell, Clark, and Tugwell in the 1930s were optimistic pluralists who did not accept Veblen's dualistic version of the class struggle. They did not agree with Veblen that capitalism must inevitably disappear and be replaced by either fascism or socialism. These men were antisocialistic solidarists who believed that class conflict could be replaced by class cooperation in a remodeled type of capitalism.

What the institutionalists of the 1930s took from Veblen was his basic view of the economic system as an evolving process, his division of the economic process into the technological (industrial) and the institutional (business) processes, and his view that conflict and not harmony is the fundamental characteristic of contemporary economic life. They also agreed with Veblen that the force that keeps the economic process in motion is technological change, which not only makes existing institutional arrangements obsolete but also opens the door to new institutional arrangements more in harmony with technological requirements. The post-Veblenian institutionalists accepted Veblen's view that it was possible, but not inevitable, that mankind would harmonize the industrial and business systems so as to produce an abundance of real, or economic, values.

John R. Common's primary interest was in the new industrial order which developed after 1875 and which replaced the equilibrium of the earlier competitive economy with a conflict-laden disequilibrium. In this new stage of capitalist development, collective action gave rise to major protectionist groups organized by businessmen, workers, and farmers to advance their sectional interests. In the period from 1875 to 1929 some of the conflicts between these interest groups were eliminated by the courts operating under the rule of judicial sovereignty. But after 1929, when "welfare capitalism" emerged and the government took a more positive role in economic affairs, numerous governmental administrative agencies took over the courts' work of domesticating the new industrial system and curbing economic conflict. Commons looked forward to seeing a form of "reasonable capitalism" in which conflict would be replaced by cooperation and reasonable values and practices would be established through administrative agencies working together with private economic groups.

In analyzing the era of finance capitalism that came after 1875, Wesley C. Mitchell made use of Veblen's dichotomy between industry and business. Mitchell's "money economy" is the financial superstructure that rests on the underlying real-product or industrial economy. The industrial economy deals with industrial technology and real output, whereas the money economy involves considerations of costs, prices, financial investment, and

profits. In Mitchell's "finance capitalism," or "high capitalism," of the period from 1875 to 1929, economic guidance was provided not by consumers but by large investors. This guidance led to much coordination within individual business enterprises but very little between them. A characteristic feature of Mitchell's high capitalism was the recurring, self-generating business cycle that periodically led to booms in the money economy which were followed by depression in both the money and real-product economies. By the early 1930s Mitchell had come to the conclusion that technological change had so fundamentally altered the structure and functioning of the American capitalist system that the only way to eliminate the business cycle and secure a satisfactory coordination of the money and real-product economies was to introduce limited democratic national economic planning. This planning would enlarge general welfare by stabilizing the economy, providing full employment, and turning out more of Veblen's economic values, or of what Mitchell described as goods that were "urgently needed."

John M. Clark looked at the American economy from a point of view that emphasizes the distinction between "social" and "commercial" efficiency. He contended that the market mechanism no longer functioned satisfactorily when the economy was dominated by large-scale business enterprises. Prices were no longer closely related to costs, surplus profits were not eliminated, and many rigidities were introduced into the economic system. The business concept of cost was restricted so as to exclude many important social costs such as unemployment, communal health hazards, unused productive capacities, and other costs associated with business fluctuations. Clark drew a distinction between social and market values and between social and market costs. Social values are those that the private market system ignores, such as clean air, scenic beauty, public health, and community welfare. Social costs such as unused productive capacity, unemployment, destruction of worker morale, and resource spoliation are also ignored by the private market mechanism. Clark's concerns were with bringing commercial efficiency closer to social efficiency and with making the economic system provide adequate supplies of both social and market values. He proposed to attack these problems in the 1930s through what he described as "social liberal" planning. This national planning would set forth the broad economic objectives of the nation in a social budget and would endeavor to achieve them by applying indirect economic controls only at certain strategic points.

In the 1930s Clark had hoped that this "social control of business" would be sufficient to enable the American economy to achieve a high level of social efficiency.

It was Rexford G. Tugwell's view that by the end of the 1920s the American industrial system had become mature but that the business system was still immature. Technological progress since 1875 had its own logic, which pointed toward large investments, mass production, low unit costs of production, low selling prices, and mass consumption. This logic of the industrial system, however, was unable to work itself out because of the obstacles placed in its path by the ideology of businessmen. Under the guidance of businessmen, large corporate enterprises have denied the logic inherent in technological progress by restricting output, keeping prices high enough to secure excessive profits, distorting income distribution, and by failing to assume responsibility for the social as well as the private costs of production.

The new equilibrium toward which Tugwell believed that the American economic system was moving in the 1930s could be hastened by establishing a fourth branch of government, namely, the directive branch. It would be the responsibility of this branch to improve the general welfare by democratically planning the nation's economic activities with the voluntary cooperation of private business enterprise. Tugwell suggested in the 1930s that large-scale business enterprises should be federally incorporated and that all the enterprises in each industry should be represented by a tripartite body representing business, labor, and consumers. The government with the aid of a central planning board would develop an investment policy that would keep private investment in line with the needs of planned economic growth. Price guidelines would be developed so that more of the advantages derived from technological progress would be passed on to consumers in the form of lower prices. Agricultural planning would be coordinated with industrial planning so that surplus farm population would find employment in the expanding industrial core of the economy. In this manner the logic of business enterprise would be harmonized with the logic of technological progress in a coming era of cultural equilibrium.

Institutionalism since World War II. Institutional economics since the end of World War II has been largely associated with the work of such economists as Clarence E. Ayres, Gardiner C. Means, Gerhard Colm, John K. Galbraith, and Leon H. Keyserling. These economists have worked along the lines laid down by Mitchell, Clark, and

Tugwell in the 1930s. A main difference, however, is that the institutionalists of the 1930s were dealing with welfare capitalism, whereas the institutionalists of the late 1940s and 1950s have been concerned with the problems of the next phase in the development of American capitalism, which may be called "guided capitalism."

The postwar institutionalists agree that the technological changes of the past few decades have so altered the structure and functioning of the American economic system that it does not, of its own accord, provide high levels of production and employment, an efficient use of resources, and an equitable distribution of income. Ayres, Colm, and Keyserling accept Means's view of "collective capitalism." According to this view large collective organizations, such as corporations and trade unions, have so much economic power that they can prevent the use of economic resources that would result in full employment and sustained economic growth at a high level. Administered prices and wages have introduced seriously disruptive rigidities into the economic system, which make it difficult for the economy to achieve its full employment growth potential. Gerhard Colm contends that the American capitalist system is not "coherent" enough to prevent a considerable disequilibrium from existing. The cultural forces that make for coherence are too weak to prevent the growth of conflicts between special interests and the general welfare. Like the institutionalists of the 1930s, present-day institutionalists have come to the conclusion that controlling the nation's major economic power groups, eliminating the economy's numerous rigidities, and curbing its tendencies toward a less than full use of capital and labor require a considerable remodeling of the American economic system, but within the traditional social and political framework.

In proposing to solve the nation's major economic problems with the aid of limited democratic national planning, present-day institutionalists have a large advantage over the earlier institutionalist proponents of national planning. In the 1930s national income analysis was in the earliest stages of its development; input–output analysis and econometrics were even less developed. Mitchell, Clark, and Tugwell could not quantify their planning proposals through projections of gross national product, since it was not then possible to make such projections. In other words, the planning proposals of the institutionalists of the 1930s were in no way operational and so could have little influence on economic decision making by the government. Since 1945 Colm, Keyserling, Means, and other advocates of limited democratic national planning have been able to turn to the national economic budgeting developed during World War II and now widely used in western Europe as a device for quantifying their national planning proposals and making them operational. Present-day institutionalists recommend the use of the national economic budget—what Keyserling describes as "the American economic performance budget"—to explore the pattern of future economic growth and to indicate the kind of balance among productive factors that would be necessary to reach sustained and adequate growth.

The institutionalists' "facilitative" or "indicative" national planning would be applied only at strategic points where the private market economy needs to be supplemented, if it is to achieve the desired growth goal. No such moderate planning could be successful without the active cooperation of business, agricultural, and labor groups. These major economic interest groups would become participants in the program of facilitative planning through a national economic council.

Institutionalism and the value problem. A matter of major interest to institutionalists is the objectives of their limited democratic national planning. From the institutionalist viewpoint, originating with Veblen, what ultimately provides direction for the economy is not the price system but the value system of the culture in which the economy is embedded. Economic guidance can only be as good as this cultural value system. John K. Galbraith calls attention to this value problem in stating his view that our affluent society suffers from an imbalance in which we produce too many private goods and too few public goods. Clarence E. Ayres tackles the same problem in his defense, based on his "technological theory of value," of the current "industrial way of life."

In Ayres's analysis all values originate in the life process; the basic criterion of value is whether or not a good contributes to an improvement of the life process, that is to say, to race survival. As science and technology progress and the industrial system becomes more complex, more real or "technological" values are created, and the life process is improved. Running through all values, economic and otherwise, is a unity of value in the sense that what is good or bad is in all circumstances determined by reference to the same criterion—science and technology. All such values as freedom, equality, security, abundance, and excellence are interrelated and are associated with the scientific and technological basis of the life process. For example, science and technology have made possible an economic abundance, which in turn has enlarged the

freedom of the consumer. The technological process gives rise to real, or "genuine," values that enhance the life process, but the institutional or "ceremonial" process is the source of pseudo values that weaken the life process. The latter values reflect inherited superstitions and attitudes toward status and privilege that have no foundation in science and technology and are detrimental to the welfare of the human race. Ayres regards the shift toward a more industrialized society as a favorable development, since in such a society science and technology undermine myth and superstition and substitute real for "ceremonial" values. He views industrialization as a movement toward a more "reasonable" or "rational" society; what is needed to expedite this movement, in Ayres's opinion, is more "pragmatic" national economic planning such as is proposed by Means, Colm, and Keyserling.

The influence of the institutional school. The number of economists in the United States who can be readily identified as institutionalists has never been very large. Much of the early influence of the institutional school was due to the fact that a few of its members, especially Veblen, Commons, Mitchell, and Clark, became very well known. Although the work of Veblen and other institutionalists in the years from 1890 to 1939 did not alter the general course of academic economics in the United States, it undoubtedly contributed to making economists in general somewhat more sophisticated about the limitations of their approach. Since Veblen's time economists have been more aware of the significance of the preconceptions underlying their work and of the limitations of their assumptions about human nature and the nature of the economic system. In recent years the institutionalist approach has been particularly useful in the study of developing countries, whose problems are most successfully handled when analyzed from the viewpoints of a number of social sciences. Institutional economics has also interested scholars concerned with an interdisciplinary approach to the social sciences.

The influence of the institutional school has been limited by the fact that its broad approach to economics has not been accepted by the majority of economists. Furthermore, the breadth of their approach leads the institutionalists to be interested in data that are of little concern to many other economists. These data relate to matters not readily amenable to mathematical or quantitative treatment, such as the impact of technological change, the relations between the economic system and its surrounding culture, and the development of a theory of capitalism.

Another factor restricting the influence of the

institutional school has been the nature of its economic policy recommendations, which are far less widely accepted than are Keynesian policy proposals. Since, in the United States, democratic national planning even of the moderate "indicative" type is neither politically acceptable nor of interest to the great majority of economists, the impact of institutionalist policy recommendations has been quite limited. Nevertheless, the institutionalist economic policy recommendations are sympathetically received in trade union quarters and by liberal elements in the Democratic party. Furthermore, economic trends in western Europe, where limited democratic national planning has been widely adopted in capitalist countries, suggest the possibility that the influence of the institutional school may be larger in coming decades than it has been recently. Should national economic planning cross the Atlantic, the institutional school could very well gain much more influence on the development of both economic theory and economic policy than it has at present.

ALLAN G. GRUCHY

[See also PLANNING, ECONOMIC; and the biographies of CLARK, JOHN MAURICE; COMMONS; MITCHELL; VEBLEN.]

BIBLIOGRAPHY

AYRES, CLARENCE E. 1961 Toward a Reasonable Society: The Values of Industrial Civilization. Austin: Univ. of Texas Press.

BERLE, ADOLF A.; and MEANS, GARDINER C. (1932) 1933 The Modern Corporation and Private Property. New York: Macmillan.

CLARK, JOHN MAURICE (1923) 1962 Studies in the Economics of Overhead Costs. Univ. of Chicago Press.

CLARK, JOHN MAURICE 1936 Preface to Social Economics: Essays on Economic Theory and Social Problems. New York: Farrar.

COMMONS, JOHN ROGERS (1924) 1959 Legal Foundations of Capitalism. Madison: Univ. of Wisconsin Press.

COMMONS, JOHN ROGERS (1934) 1959 Institutional Economics: Its Place in Political Economy. 2 vols. Madison: Univ. of Wisconsin Press.

COMMONS, JOHN ROGERS (1950) 1956 The Economics of Collective Action. Edited by K. H. Parsons. New York: Macmillan.

DORFMAN, JOSEPH (1934) 1961 Thorstein Veblen and His America. New York: Viking; Kelley.

GALBRAITH, JOHN K. 1958 The Affluent Society. Boston: Houghton Mifflin.

GAMBS, JOHN S. 1946 Beyond Supply and Demand: A Reappraisal of Institutional Economics. New York: Columbia Univ. Press.

GRUCHY, ALLAN G. 1947 Modern Economic Thought: The American Contribution. Englewood Cliffs, N. J.: Prentice-Hall.

MITCHELL, WESLEY C. (1912–1936) 1937 The Backward Art of Spending Money, and Other Essays. New York: McGraw-Hill.

VEBLEN, THORSTEIN (1891–1913) 1961 The Place of Science in Modern Civilisation, and Other Essays. New York: Russell.

VEBLEN, THORSTEIN (1899) 1953 The Theory of the Leisure Class: An Economic Study of Institutions. Rev. ed. New York: New American Library. → A paperback edition was published in 1959.

VEBLEN, THORSTEIN 1904 The Theory of Business Enterprise. New York: Scribner.

VEBLEN, THORSTEIN (1919) 1921 The Engineers and the Price System. New York: Huebsch.

ECONOMIC UNIONS
See under INTERNATIONAL INTEGRATION.

ECONOMIC WARFARE

Economic warfare is state interference in international economic relations for the purpose of improving the relative economic, military, or political position of a country. While the concept has a precise analytical content, it tends to have emotional overtones, especially under some of its many synonyms: economic aggression, penetration, infiltration, exploitation, assault, drive, offensive, imperialism, attack, aggression campaign, invasion, incursion, and many others.

The concept can best be understood against a background of what economists consider "normal" international economic relations. The world as visualized by the classical economists was one in which the individuals and enterprises of many nations strive to maximize utility and profits, using lowest-cost resources, wherever found. As a result each nation tends to specialize in the production of items in which its economic units have a comparative advantage, and private interests seeking profits buy in the cheapest markets and sell in the dearest. This search for the gains from trade is conducted within a framework of convertible currencies, with automatic mechanisms determining the principal economic variables—prices of goods and factors, and incomes—and carrying the burden of adjustment in the relatively free flow of goods and services across national borders. The role of the government is minimal and is primarily to assist the optimizing behavior of individual economic units.

This model is an abstract construction only. Historically, however, there have been approximations to it, particularly in the nineteenth century. Some permanent departures from the model have received widespread recognition and are not regarded as economic warfare. State interference with trade in order to foster high-cost but potentially competitive industries has long been accepted. Discrimination through various forms of exchange controls, multiple rates, tariffs, quotas, and bilateral balancing of trade has become ordinary policy with, in some cases, an economic justification. In most of these instances the government has acted primarily in support of domestic industry to achieve purely domestic economic and political goals.

State interference on behalf of the state itself is what distinguishes economic warfare from other types of international economic policies. It is the conscious attempt to enhance the relative economic, military, and political position of a country through its foreign economic relations. The action must be purposeful; otherwise a nation merely pursuing the benefits of trade for its citizens would be considered engaging in economic warfare if the action should in fact improve its relative position. It is the position of the country in the hierarchy of power, its position in relation to other countries, rather than any absolute accretion to its power, that is relevant. This can be accomplished by a country which gains more than other countries gain, gains while others lose, or loses while other countries lose more.

Economic warfare serves the purposes of the state, be they economic, political, or military, or some combination of the three. All of these purposes may be served simultaneously by the same action, or in some cases a course of action may serve one of them at the expense of another or the other two. The precise balance among purposes is determined by the total goals of the state. The state, in effect, has a utility function, and economic warfare is an effort to raise the value of one or more economic or noneconomic variables.

Military aspects

The military aspect of economic warfare has two basic dimensions. One involves the use of economic warfare as an adjunct to military operations. The other involves its use to strengthen the peacetime military establishment and prepare for war. In both, however, the aim is substantially the same. In peace, in preparation for war, or in war a nation wishes to acquire the maximum net resources available for military use and to deny the enemy or potential enemy any resources which may contribute to his war-making capability.

In peacetime or in preparing for military operations, the use of force may well be inappropriate, since it may jeopardize future plans. Economic warfare, however, may accomplish some of the same purposes as force. Resources may be acquired by improving the terms of trade of the country with respect to the rest of the world or with respect to a single nation or group of nations. A country may, through trade, acquire such influence over another country that the latter will be willing to form a military alliance rather than forgo the trade, or at least be willing to be neutral in a potential conflict. Furthermore, the victim may be induced to join in acts of economic warfare against still other countries. Economic relations may assume such importance and be subject to such manipulation that the trading partner will lose some or all of its sovereignty. Many techniques can and have been bent to these ends, such as the use of trade to disrupt markets, changing sources of supply or refusing to supply goods in an unpredictable manner, and manipulation of foreign exchange and gold holdings. So long as these actions are undertaken to acquire resources or to deprive a potential enemy of resources, economic warfare is being used in direct support of military operations.

In wartime, economic warfare is a natural and important adjunct to military actions. Again, the principal purpose is to prevent resources from falling into the hands of the enemy and to acquire as many resources as possible. These actions operate largely through nonbelligerents and will be used even though a military blockade may be neither feasible nor desirable. In some cases, action may be directed at weakening the enemy's economy, such as the counterfeiting of enemy currency during World War II.

Embargo. A special case of economic warfare is the full or partial embargo in anticipation of possible war, such as that maintained by the United States, with some western European support, against the Soviet Union, eastern Europe, and Communist China during the 1950s and 1960s. A country may fear the possibility of war with another country and decide that no trade should take place which might enhance the war-making potential of the prospective enemy. If and when war does come, the enemy will not be as well off as he would have been if there had been no embargo. This type of economic warfare has frequently been employed preceding military operations.

Embargoes generally confer short-run benefits on the perpetrator, but if war does not come, the long-run benefits may accrue to the embargoed nation. Because of modern technology most economies have such flexibility that there are few goods for which a substitute cannot be found, even if at a somewhat higher cost. When confronted with an embargo, a nation begins to develop substitutes, perhaps using resources formerly exported to bear most of the cost of the development. If the embargo period is long, the country will have made the necessary substitution, so that the complete embargo of wartime does not impose any further burden. This kind of economic warfare can backfire if the potential enemy is forced prematurely, at a time when it can perhaps better afford it, to prepare itself for war by developing self-sufficiency. In this case, the initiator has at most imposed some added costs on the enemy, but at the expense of facing an enemy not only more adequately prepared but also now insulated against this particular kind of economic warfare. Of course, a small country which has no alternate sources of supply or alternate markets can be reduced to impotence by an embargo by a large economic power.

Since World War II the United States has been the principal proponent of the embargo and the communist countries the principal victims. The United States first initiated a strategic embargo against the Soviet Union and eastern Europe when Czechoslovakia became a communist country in 1949. By "strategic" is meant that not all exports to those countries were eliminated, but only those considered important from the point of view of their war-making capability. During the Korean hostilities the embargo was strengthened and a complete embargo was applied against China. The United States tried to persuade most of its allies to initiate similar embargoes, but usually somewhat weaker ones were imposed.

There were many difficulties in applying the strategic concept, which has no precise economic meaning, since all economic goods are in reality substitutes for one another. After the Korean hostilities ended, most strategic controls were gradually relaxed almost to the vanishing point, except in the case of Communist China. When Cuba entered the Soviet sphere of influence, the United States applied an embargo, nominally strategic but in fact punitive. It was almost a complete embargo, excluding some foodstuffs and medicines. It is unlikely that the strategic embargoes have significantly benefited the United States. Although they may have created temporary bottlenecks and planning problems in the Soviet Union, they tend to make the communist world more self-sufficient and have increased intra-Soviet area trade. In the case of Cuba it has helped to drive that country into the Soviet economic sphere.

Economic aspects

Although it directly supports the military establishment, economic warfare, even when serving military purposes, is directed at the economy. If a country is at war or proposes to go to war, economic warfare serves a military goal. If a country is not at war and does not necessarily intend to engage in military hostilities, then economic warfare may be serving an economic function. All of the measures usable in wartime are also usable in peacetime. Some of them, however, are not generally employed because of their intimate association with active hostilities (e.g., preclusive buying).

For economic purposes, the actions constituting economic warfare generally fall into five categories: (1) guaranteeing sources of supply, (2) guaranteeing markets, (3) improving the terms of trade, (4) denial, and (5) economic take-over. The first three of these do not necessarily imply economic warfare; they may be normal commercial transactions undertaken in pursuit of private profits. They may, however, also be undertaken for the specific purpose of increasing the economic power of a country more rapidly than that of other countries. A wide variety of techniques are available for attaining these ends, ranging from those which are also usable in wartime to those apparently less predatory, such as gradually becoming a large trading partner and then threatening to withdraw trade, the building up of debts in other countries, and the extension of credit.

Political aspects

All of the above acts of economic warfare may also be used to further the third important purpose of economic warfare—the pursuit of political advantage. This purpose, always important, has gradually assumed greater and greater significance as nations have become increasingly cautious about the use of force to achieve aims which transcend the economic benefits that may be conferred by economic warfare. The search for political power may take three forms. It may be quite general. A country may simply desire respectability and status. Many countries on the way up, in process of political and economic development or in the consolidation of revolutionary gains, may want, initially at least, only to be recognized and noted as a member of the family of nations. Other countries, on the way back from a disastrous national experience, such as a lost war, may desire readmittance and a return to their former place.

The political purpose may also be manifested in a highly specific fashion. A country may wish to conclude an alliance or to obtain the vote of another in some international organization. Or it may want another country to eliminate a particular political or military leader, to undertake some change in domestic or foreign policy, or the like. The change may be either internal or external, or both. In most cases, however, it concerns foreign policy, since it is in this field that the power position of the initiating country is most directly affected.

The ability to employ economic warfare for these political goals is an indication of the relative economic power of the country. It implies either an economy significantly larger than that of the intended victim or an economy which is planned and can be directed by the government to the attainment of specific goals. Such is the case, for example, with the Soviet economy. Successful economic warfare implies growing economic strength of the protagonist relative to the intended victim, and even when such actions do not add directly to the economic capabilities of the initiator, they usually worsen the economic position of the victim.

The ultimate degree of political, as well as economic, influence is the take-over of another country. Just as economic warfare may be directed at reducing the flexibility of another country's economy to such an extent that the country can no longer make decisions with respect to its own resources, so economic warfare may also be used to pave the way for political amalgamation, to deprive a country of its national sovereignty. For some countries, e.g., Germany in the 1930s, the take-over has been the ultimate goal of economic warfare, and the other objects have been but stepping-stones to this end. This is true, however, only in the specific historic context in which a major power feels itself endowed with the truth and with the obligation to propagate it throughout the world. Throughout most of history, nations have been willing to set their sights much lower and have used economic warfare to attain much more limited objectives.

Strategies in economic warfare

Economic warfare is ordinarily a two-sided affair. When an intended victim of economic warfare discovers his position, he can be expected to retaliate. It is, of course, possible that he may go beyond economic warfare and may even initiate hostilities. Usually, however, the victim assumes one of three basic postures: (1) He may be passive and accept whatever solution the initiator of economic warfare proposes. This is a fairly rare phenomenon. (2) The victim fights back, attempts to defend himself, and only grudgingly gives in. The victim may choose to fight on the grounds already chosen—to break the embargo, to pay off accumulated debts by borrowing elsewhere or by selling accumulated balances at a discount, or to attempt to extricate himself from whatever other economic snares he is involved in. He may also fight back by using a different policy to inflict harm on his tormentor, so that the pressure will be relaxed. Thus, if country A holds large balances of the currency of country B and is using them to elevate its own position, country B may employ quotas or other discriminatory policies to raise the

siege. (3) Both countries may engage in economic warfare against one another but with different purposes, and both may be successful. The country with a narrow political purpose may achieve it through economic warfare against the country which is achieving its specific economic purposes in the same conflict. The political gains of the former may more than offset its economic losses. The economic gains of the latter may more than offset its political losses. Thus, in economic warfare each side can consider itself the winner and, by the same reasoning, each side can lose.

In the conduct of economic warfare, there are only two basic approaches. They are the carrot and the stick, cajolery and coercion, persuading the intended victim or forcing him through economic means into the desired course of action. Each has its applications. They may be used separately, but not infrequently they are used together.

Coercion. The stick, or coercion, has been used most frequently. After a country achieves a position of economic influence in another, it may threaten to stop making purchases, to cut off supplies, or to refuse to pay obligations unless some concession—economic, political, or military—is made. In two most common situations the victim is maneuvered into a position in which a substantial proportion of his trade is with the initiator, or the latter manages to become deeply indebted to the victim. Whether these devices will work depends heavily on the economic position of the victim and the market for his products. If that market is relatively brisk, the victim may chance switching his sales to other markets rather than make a concession. A victim in a favorable internal economic and trade position may be able to withstand non-payment of a debt for some time if it is not too large, expecting that it will eventually be repaid regardless of whether he gives in. On the other hand, a slow market for its product, depressed world economic conditions, a very large debt, or a large percentage of trade in the hands of the other country may leave a victim with no alternative but to pay premium prices for his supplies, to sell at a lower price to the other country, or to let his political and military policies be influenced by his trading partner. Usually this form of economic warfare damages the general prestige and standing of the country employing it, a cost which the initiator should calculate in advance.

Persuasion. The carrot, or persuasion, is a prestige builder. It consists of the use of foreign economic relations to favor another country and thereby win its good will and support. Favoritism is a delicate instrument and does not carry with it the sometimes unpleasant connotations of coercion; it may, however, be just as effective. The usual method is to give more favorable terms of trade—either lower export prices or higher import prices—than would be provided in the world market, or to loan or give resources to the other country. On the basis of these economic favors, a country may expect, in return, reciprocal favors in the form of political support, an alliance, or perhaps neutrality. The recipient, however, may not be swayed by the economic benefits, in which case the initiating country can only return to the *status quo ante*, leaving the recipient with some net economic gains.

It is possible and often likely that the two modes of economic warfare can be used in succession. For example, country A may pursue a policy of granting favors to country B, rewarding B for diverting an ever-increasing proportion of trade to A from its previous channels, making tied loans or grants which use capital equipment from country A only, and giving other forms of economic succor. Country B becomes used to these favors and comes to regard them as fundamental to its welfare. So important do these economic considerations become that the recipient is deluded into thinking that the concessions made to its benefactor are really in its own interest.

The method of persuasion, of course, works best when there is at least an ostensible similarity of outlook and interest between the two countries. In case the delusion breaks down, the initiator of economic warfare is in a position to employ the coercive method. While the recipient is being lulled by favors, the initiating country is gradually cornering a larger proportion of its trade, perhaps even approaching monopsony of some of the recipient's exports or monopoly of some of his imports. From this vulnerable position it is but a short step to being subject to massive coercion by the former benefactor. In its stupor, the recipient may not recognize what is happening until the initiator has maneuvered himself into a powerful and potentially damaging position. Then the latter, by withdrawing or threatening to withdraw, can often influence the policy of the victim.

It must be recognized that the use of persuasion may render the initiator vulnerable, particularly if the external economic relations of the two contending countries are of about the same size. If the trade is large for the recipient, it is also large for the initiator, and the recipient under some circumstances may subject the initiator to pressure through the same relations that the initiator is employing. If one country is substantially more powerful economically than the other, it can afford to pass up the debt repayment, can find other markets and new supplies. But the more comparable the countries are in economic power, or the more special economic considerations render them proximate, the greater is the likelihood that this form of economic warfare may backfire and hurt the country that initiated it.

Economic warfare and state trading

All the techniques of economic warfare, many of which have already been mentioned, may be classified as acts of buying or selling, borrowing or lending. The use of these techniques is consistent with either private or state trading. If private trading is the predominant form, however, then economic warfare can be waged only insofar as the government intervenes and acts, either positively or negatively, to influence the decisions of private traders.

A government-imposed quota or increased tariff in a country where private interests do the foreign buying may be an act of economic warfare if its intent is to improve the country's relative power position. A loan, sale, or purchase of some product, bilateral balancing of trade, and many other measures may also constitute economic warfare. The ingredient common to all these techniques is government action. Private actions may in some cases have the same result as economic warfare, although they are not necessarily so intended. Only government action is intended to be in the national interest and only government action, directly or through private traders, can constitute economic warfare.

Perhaps the most singular characteristic of state trading is that the nation which practices it is necessarily and automatically engaged in economic warfare. Comprehensive state trading stands alone in its power as an instrument that utilizes economic means to improve a country's relative economic, political, and military position. The concentration of all external transactions in the hands of the government implies that trade no longer is solely a means for increasing the income of the country. Economic decisions are automatically transmuted into economic–political–military decisions in which costs are balanced against benefits in all aspects of national life.

ROBERT LORING ALLEN

[*See also* FOREIGN AID; INTERNATIONAL TRADE CONTROLS; MILITARY POWER POTENTIAL; SANCTIONS, INTERNATIONAL. *Other relevant material may be found in* FOREIGN POLICY; WAR.]

BIBLIOGRAPHY

ALLEN, ROBERT L. 1960 *Soviet Economic Warfare.* Washington: Public Affairs Press.

ELLIS, HOWARD S. (1939–1940) 1941 *Exchange Control in Central Europe.* Harvard Economic Studies, Vol. 69. Cambridge, Mass.: Harvard Univ. Press.

HIRSCHMAN, ALBERT O. 1945 *National Power and the Structure of Foreign Trade.* Publications of the Bureau of Business and Economic Research, University of California. Berkeley and Los Angeles: Univ. of California Press.

VINER, JACOB 1923 *Dumping: A Problem in International Trade.* Univ. of Chicago Press.

WU, YUAN-LI 1952 *Economic Warfare.* Englewood Cliffs, N.J.: Prentice-Hall.

ECONOMICS

References to specific topics in economics will be found throughout this article. For articles giving an overview of some of the major fields of economics, see ECONOMETRICS; ECONOMIC GROWTH; ECONOMIC THOUGHT; HISTORY, *article on* ECONOMIC HISTORY; INCOME AND EMPLOYMENT THEORY; INTERNATIONAL TRADE; *and* WELFARE ECONOMICS. *For guides to major fields not summarized in single articles, see the entries under* AGRICULTURE; INDUSTRIAL ORGANIZATION; MONEY; PUBLIC FINANCE; *and* LABOR ECONOMICS.

Economics, according to a widely accepted definition, is the study of the allocation of scarce resources among unlimited and competing uses. It is the social science that deals with the ways in which men and societies seek to satisfy their material needs and desires, since the means at their disposal do not permit them to do so completely.

Much of the work of the discipline can be fitted into this framework, and no other comes so close to accommodating all of it. However, the framework has a serious shortcoming: it does not encompass the problem of depression, or the inadequacy of aggregate demand. Most modern market economies experience periods in which large quantities of resources are idle—particularly labor and plant capacity—so that the principal question is not in what way to use them, but how to put them to any use at all. The distinction between the problems of *allocating resources among uses* and of *achieving their full use* corresponds very roughly to the distinction between the two main branches of economics: *microeconomics* and *macroeconomics*. The latter, however, includes some aspects of money and the general level of prices that also have important implications for resource allocation.

Decisions about resource allocation are made in their simplest form within the household, in the familiar process of "making ends meet," or budgeting; the original meaning of economics was the practice of economy at the household level. What is now called economics was at first called political economy, to draw attention to its broader theater of action.

The concept of *scarcity* is crucial to an understanding of resource allocation. Almost all resources are scarce under most circumstances, in the sense that if they were available without cost, more would be used than could be supplied. Even air, the classic example of a limitless resource, can become scarce. Pure air is now the exception in crowded urban areas and air pollution can be prevented only at substantial costs. Water is free in many places but scarce and costly in arid or densely populated areas [*see* WATER RESOURCES]. Goods, such as sand or dirt, that may be free in their original location have costs when they are transported to the places at which they are needed.

The counterpart of pervasive scarcity is the unlimited extent of material wants. The overwhelming majority of the world's population would always like a little more (often a lot more) income and consumption than it has, almost regardless of the current level. The exceptions to this generalization are of two kinds—ascetics (a rare breed in modern societies) and the minute fraction of the world's population so wealthy that it need never, so to speak, consult the price column of the restaurant menu. Even among the very wealthy, with no desire to increase their consumption, there are some who seek to increase their incomes as a game or as a means of augmenting their power.

Economics as a social science does not examine what people *ought* to want, as distinguished from what they *do* want. The first question lies largely in the realm of ethics, aesthetics, or religion. Nevertheless, much writing by professional economists makes assumptions, explicit or implicit, about the proper goals of economic activity. Such writing can be considered economic philosophy rather than economic science narrowly defined. The former is often called *normative economics* and the latter *positive economics*. It is a positive statement to say that, other things being equal, a fall in the price of milk will increase its consumption—and the validity of such a statement can be tested against evidence. It is a normative statement to say that therefore the price of milk should be lowered. The second statement is not subject to disproof by evidence and implies that the speaker has personal or social values according to which the consumption of milk is "better" or more important than competing alternatives. If such values are widely shared, they may form an appropriate basis for social policy, but the validity of the values themselves nevertheless remains beyond the reach of scientific confirmation or testing.

The goals of economic activity are often subsumed under the heading "utility," a construct embracing all of the satisfactions to be obtained through consumption, production, and related behavior [see UTILITY]. It is generally assumed that the objective of economic activities is to maximize utility, subject to the limitations of resources, and that utility will be increased by the increased consumption of goods and services. In principle, utility can also be increased by such intangible factors as beautiful scenery, pleasant working conditions, amiable companions, or political power. However, such desiderata are seldom explicitly introduced into economic analysis, for a variety of reasons—some are not subject to measurement, some cannot be produced through economic activity—and when they are specified in detail almost all are very differently evaluated by different people. Moreover, some lie in the domains of other social science disciplines whose methods are better suited to analyze them. The assumption that the principal goal of economic activity is to produce goods and services, while clearly an oversimplification, is nevertheless useful in a wide variety of problems and can be modified in special cases, as seems appropriate.

In a dictatorship the utility to be maximized is that of the dictator; in a slave society it is that of the slave owners rather than the slaves. In free societies it is usually assumed that each person seeks to maximize his own utility and in general will be the best judge of how to do so.

An improved method of raising beef increases utility for beef-eating Americans or Argentines, although not for vegetarians; however, the explanation of such cultural, religious, or taste differences in assessing the value of additional output is not the economist's task. The national output includes bread and circuses, cathedrals and billboards, vitamins and poisons. The economist can study the forces affecting the market price or cost of each and under some circumstances can also say that a market price does not correctly reflect the underlying values of consumers and producers. Like any other citizen, he has personal opinions based on values that transcend market values, but if he cloaks these with the authority of his discipline, he arrogates wisdom.

The economic value of a particular good will not ordinarily depend on the use to which it is put—the price of a stick of dynamite is the same whether it is used to mine coal or to blow up a bridge.

Almost all societies would judge the value of the outcome to be positive in the first case and negative in the second, but the standards by which this judgment is made are not provided by economists in their scientific capacities.

The methodology of economics

The purpose of science is to achieve understanding either for its own sake—the satisfaction of "idle" curiosity—or as a basis for prediction and control. Although both elements are present in economics, the latter is particularly evident. [See PREDICTION AND FORECASTING, ECONOMIC.] The predictions sought generally refer to the aggregate behavior of sizable groups of people and not to the behavior of individuals. In most economic inquiries it is sufficient to reach such conclusions as that in a given market the consumption of milk increases 1 per cent in response to a 2 per cent reduction in its price; the economist ordinarily does not care whether this occurs because each family increases its consumption 1 per cent or because half the families increase their consumption 2 per cent and the other half not at all. (This indifference will disappear if the division of families into two groups is nonrandom; for example, it might be valuable to know that low-income families increase their consumption more than high-income families.) An economist almost never attempts to predict the consumption behavior of a particular individual in response to a price change. In some economic studies, data are used in which the observations refer to individuals; such studies as yet typically fail to explain a major part of the variance in individual behavior.

The focus on aggregates makes it possible to summarize the accumulation of economic knowledge in statements of observed regularities, or "laws," that do not apply to individuals considered singly. The preceding example about milk is a special case of the "law of demand"—the quantities of a commodity or service purchased move inversely with its price, other things being equal. This law is not contradicted by the discovery that some consumers stop buying a commodity whose price falls, because it no longer confers social distinction on the user (the so-called snob effect), so long as such behavior does not dominate the market for any commodity.

Partly because of the focus of economics on large-group behavior, economists can seldom use the method of laboratory experiment. (The few exceptions lie chiefly on the borderlines between economics and psychology; for example, subjects are given money to spend, gamble, or use in similar economic games.) The use of laboratory experiment is not, of course, a requisite of a science. Among natural sciences much of astronomy and meteorology are similarly disadvantaged. In economics the place of the laboratory experiment is largely taken by other methods of testing hypotheses, in which variables extraneous to the hypothesis being tested can, within limits, be held under statistical, rather than physical, control.

The use of statistical control of extraneous variables corresponds to the common theoretical device of "holding other things constant" in analyzing the functional relationship between two variables. For example, the statement that the consumption of milk increases in response to a fall in price can be represented as a demand curve, a downward sloping line on a graph whose vertical axis measures the price of milk and whose horizontal axis measures the rate of consumption. [See DEMAND AND SUPPLY.] This relationship assumes that other factors affecting milk consumption, such as consumer income and tastes, do not change. A change in one of these factors will cause the demand curve to shift. A more complicated relationship, which expresses the rate of consumption as a function of both price and income, is often more useful and can be estimated statistically. Such a three-dimensional demand surface is hard to show graphically and is therefore less common in elementary expositions.

A more complete analysis of the market for milk would include the conditions of supply as well as of demand. The relationship between the price of milk and the quantity supplied (generally positive, or upward sloping) is known as the supply schedule or the supply curve. Together the supply and demand curves determine the quantity sold and the price. For given supply and demand conditions, the position so determined is a stable equilibrium position, and quantity and price will tend to return to it if the market is subjected to a small accidental disturbance. [See ECONOMIC EQUILIBRIUM.] However, if the disturbance changes the underlying conditions of demand or supply, the market will move to a different equilibrium position. For example, if the taste for milk changed so that people wanted it more than before, the result would probably be a permanently higher consumption of milk, perhaps at a higher price.

The method that confines analysis to comparisons of the initial and final equilibrium positions of a market or system of markets is known as the method of comparative statics because it is not concerned with the path of the adjustment through time—that is, with such questions as whether milk consumption expands first quickly and then slowly in response to some initial impetus or expands at a steady rate. Dynamic analysis is concerned with the time path of movement. [See STATICS AND DYNAMICS IN ECONOMICS.] For example, in a study of hyperinflation the time pattern of response to a previous increase in the price level is a crucial attribute of a satisfactory theory. Although "static" is sometimes used as a term of reproach and "dynamic" as one of praise, the choice between dynamic and static analysis must rest on the nature of the problem, with no general presumption that one is superior. Dynamic analysis requires additional knowledge about human behavior—knowledge that is not always available, for it involves knowing not only how people respond to economic stimuli, but at what rate.

As the foregoing observations suggest, economics makes extensive use of quantitative data and has a large body of abstract theory that can be extended and explored for consistency through the use of formal logic. For this reason economists began to use mathematics and statistics earlier and more intensively than most other social scientists. [*The use of such methods in economics is discussed in* ECONOMETRICS.]

The functions of an economic system

We now turn to an overview of the substance of economics and in particular to the central problem of resource allocation. This will be approached through a classification of the functions of an economy devised by Knight (1933). Of his five functions, we shall consider four, designated here as: (a) determining the composition of output; (b) organizing production; (c) distributing the product (or income); and (d) providing for the future. (The fifth concerns the allocation of a fixed stock of goods over short periods of time.) Later we shall turn to the discussion of money, the price level, and the level of employment, which, as noted earlier, lie largely outside the resource-allocation framework.

Determining the composition of output. Modern societies determine what to produce in two basic ways—through political or governmental decisions and through the use of markets. These methods can be combined in varying proportions. Even in a country as noted for the use of markets as the United States, many important classes of goods and services—such as schools, roads, police protection, and national defense—are provided wholly or largely outside the market system in the sense that consumers pay for them through taxes rather than by the direct purchase of the services.

The nonmarket sector is much larger in such socialist countries as the Soviet Union, and their reliance on the market to guide production decisions is usually weaker where markets *are* used. However, even the Soviet Union has a few legal private markets, particularly for perishable farm produce. The activities in which government services are provided without explicit charge are not coextensive with the government sector of an economy—for example, government post offices sell mail services to users by means of postage stamps (though not always at prices that cover costs), much as private businesses sell their services.

In the market sector, consumer preferences are transmitted to producers through decisions to purchase the goods and services offered for sale. (Producers may also use survey techniques or experimental markets to test consumer acceptance of new products [*see* MARKET RESEARCH].) When consumers want more of a product that is sold on a free market, its price will tend to rise and its production will become more profitable. Existing producers will increase their output and new producers may enter the market. Conversely, if consumer desires for a product weaken, prices and output will tend to fall. [*See* DEMAND AND SUPPLY.] Although prices are in general the best signals to producers of changes in the pattern of demand, consumer preferences can also be transmitted through markets in which prices are fixed. In such markets, decreases in demand are indicated by unsold inventories of goods or by idle capacity to perform services; increases in demand are indicated by the disappearance of inventories and by queues. Most markets for consumer goods in socialist economies operate in this fashion, as do those monopolistic markets in capitalist economies in which prices are administered by sellers.

In socialist economies, decisions about the quantities of resources to devote to consumer goods are made centrally through government planning. Once these decisions are made, the planners have an incentive to heed market signals of surpluses and shortages and to allocate resources to particular products or to change product prices so as to achieve maximum consumer satisfaction with the allotted resources. However, the mechanisms for doing this in planned economies are not yet very successful. [*See* COMMUNISM, ECONOMIC ORGANIZATION OF; *and* PLANNING, ECONOMIC, *article on* EASTERN EUROPE.]

An economy in which all markets were fully responsive to changes in consumer tastes would exemplify consumer sovereignty [*see* CONSUMER SOVEREIGNTY]. Complete consumer sovereignty under free enterprise would require the absence of monopolies, so that consumers could be provided with that amount of each commodity whose costs of production they were just willing to pay. (A monopoly would be able to restrict output below this level to obtain a price in excess of costs.) In equilibrium such a system would have the property, given the distribution of income, that the composition of output could not be changed without reducing the satisfaction of one or more consumers. Informative advertising would be permissible, or even desirable, but advertising that persuades without informing represents a departure from consumer sovereignty [*see* ADVERTISING, *article on* ECONOMIC ASPECTS]. In principle, consumer sovereignty would be possible in a socialist economy if planners were willing to abide by decision rules that simulated the behavior of competitive markets.

The pattern of production resulting from consumer sovereignty depends not only on consumer tastes but also on the distribution of income and wealth. If income and wealth were redistributed more equally, there would be less production of goods and services consumed largely by the highest income groups (Cadillacs, domestic service) and by the lowest (potatoes, bus rides). Theoretically, there is less equality in decision making through the market than through democratic political processes, for in political elections each person has one vote, while in the market his "voting power" is proportional to his expenditures. The actual contrast is less sharp, for there are concentrations of political power as well, and not every citizen has equal influence on the outcome of political decisions.

An important advantage of a market system is that it characteristically provides for the tastes of minorities. It is often worthwhile for producers to make a product wanted by only a few people, provided that these few are willing to pay a little more than the price of a standard commodity. Consider, for example, the large number of different varieties, sizes, and shapes of bread offered for sale in a big city with a diverse population. By contrast, the provision of goods or services by governments has tended toward standardization and uniformity. Some critics of market economies view this variety as wasteful and argue that the efficiencies of standardization outweigh the importance of minor differences in tastes.

The market system also offers strong incentives to producers to develop new or improved products, in the hope that these will gain consumer acceptance and prove profitable. Innovation in consumer goods is a more conspicuous feature of market economies than of planned economies, although neither system can guarantee that innovations which would succeed will always be forthcoming.

Organizing production. Production is the combination of resources (factors of production) to produce desired output. Early in the history of economics the concept of production was associated with making physical products. Agriculture, mining, manufacture, and construction were considered productive activities, whereas transportation, trade, and such services as education were not. This distinction has long been abandoned. It is now recognized that transportation and trade add to the value of commodities by making them available where they are wanted and that furnishing services can contribute as much to the satisfaction of consumers as furnishing commodities [*see* INTERNAL TRADE].

Specialization and exchange and the division of labor are central concepts in the economics of production [*see* SPECIALIZATION AND EXCHANGE]. In undeveloped economies, much production is carried out by individuals and small groups (families, tribes, communities) which consume their own output. For example, in the early colonial period in North America, families usually grew or caught most of their own food, built their own houses, and made their own cloth, clothing, furniture, soap, and candles. In modern economies, most workers are specialized in the production of a particular commodity or service and usually perform a specialized task within the production process. Specialization increases output because workers acquire specialized skills and save time that would otherwise be spent in switching from one activity to another. Specialization usually enlarges the scale of production, and large-scale production justifies the use of expensive specialized tools and machinery. Moreover, the production of each good can be carried on in the most suitable locations. Although within some limits the division of labor undoubtedly increases output, it is sometimes argued that it deprives the worker of the satisfaction of creating a complete product and of variety in job content, thereby also diluting standards of craftsmanship and contributing to industrial unrest.

The possibility of specialization rests on the principle of *relative advantage*, which states that it is advantageous for a productive activity to be carried on by an inferior producer, provided that the superior producers are even more superior at doing something else. To take a familiar example, suppose that a doctor can mow his lawn in an hour, and the best gardener he can hire takes two hours. It will nevertheless pay him to hire the gardener

at $2 an hour if he can earn $5 in an additional hour of medical practice. (We assume that the doctor attaches less than $1 an hour of recreational value to lawn mowing.) The principle just illustrated also underlies the specialization of production among nations and is therefore the cornerstone of the theory of international trade. [*See* INTERNATIONAL TRADE, *article on* THEORY.]

Efficient production involves combining resources so as to minimize the cost of the output. We are all accustomed to partial measures of efficiency that relate useful output to the use of a single input—for example, miles per gallon of gasoline as a measure of the efficiency of an automobile. Partial measures of efficiency or productivity, such as output per man-hour, are also found in economics, but economists are usually more interested in the efficiency with which all resources together are used. A measure of this is "total factor productivity"—that is, useful output divided by the total input of economic resources, weighted by their respective prices or costs. [*See* PRODUCTIVITY.] This measure reflects the condition that it pays to conserve one factor by increasing the use of a second only if the added costs of the second factor are less than the value of the savings of the first. For example, an automobile that runs more miles per gallon is economically inefficient if the added cost of the better engine exceeds the cost of the gasoline saved over its lifetime, both valued at the same point in time.

Economists have long thought of resources, or inputs, in three traditional categories: land, labor, and capital. Land consists of the natural properties of soil, minerals, and climate; labor, of the current services (mental and physical) of humans; and capital, of such things as structures, machines, vehicles, livestock, inventories, and improvements to land such as clearing and terracing [*see* CAPITAL; LAND; NATIONAL WEALTH; AGRICULTURE, *article on* CAPITAL]. There is, however, nothing sacred about this particular trinity. The traditional factors are often very difficult to separate, as in the case of land and improvements to it. The factors can be more finely subdivided (for example, management can be distinguished from labor), or the scheme can be extended to recognize additional inputs, such as entrepreneurship [*see* ENTREPRENEURSHIP]. Humans can also be regarded as embodying investment made through education and training [*see* CAPITAL, HUMAN].

The relation between the combination of inputs in a production process and the resulting output is like a recipe in which labor, capital, and other classes of inputs replace such ingredients as butter, eggs, and milk. Such recipes are called production functions. [See PRODUCTION *and* ECONOMIES OF SCALE.] Cookbook recipes usually call for constant proportions of the various ingredients; in economic production, however, the proportions of inputs are generally varied in response to changes in factor prices so as to substitute less expensive for more expensive inputs. Although the possibility of substitution among factors may be limited by technology, it is often much greater than might at first be supposed. Steel mills in the United States, where labor is expensive, and in India, where labor is cheap, may use very similar basic production processes, yet Indian mills will find it economical to use much more labor and less capital in such auxiliary operations as materials handling.

For some purposes, the cost of an input is adequately represented by its market price. For others, one must turn to the more fundamental concept of *opportunity cost*, or alternative cost, which states that the cost of employing a unit of a factor of production in any activity is the output lost by the failure to employ that unit in its best alternative use. For example, the cost to the economy of changing the use of a tract of land on the outskirts of a city from farming to residences is represented by its value as farmland, which in turn depends on its contribution to farm output. However, if there were several residential or industrial development plans in each of which the value of the land was higher than in farming, the cost of using it in any one plan would be its highest value in any of the others. [See COST.]

Difficult problems arise when some of the outputs or inputs in a production process have no market value or when some of the costs of productive activity are not borne by the enterprise engaged in it. The evaluation of a proposal to convert farmland near a city into a free public recreation area is essentially a question of judging whether the benefits exceed the costs. Production costs imposed on parties not engaged in the production process are exemplified by air and water pollution from industrial wastes, especially where the losses are so widely diffused that individual lawsuits to recover damages are impractical. [See EXTERNAL ECONOMIES AND DISECONOMIES.] The presence of benefits or costs with no market valuation often leads to government regulation or intervention (such as the zoning of land or the prohibition of child labor) in the production processes of market economies.

In the classical period of economics, until about 1870, it was held that the cost of production determined the price or value of a commodity [see VALUE, LABOR THEORY OF]. The beginning of the neoclassical period is marked by the recognition that value is jointly determined by cost and by demand. The costs of producing a commodity often rise as total output is expanded and as resources less suited to its production are drawn into use. In such cases, an increase in demand requires the expansion of production into areas of higher costs and therefore causes an increase in price. However, changes in price can also arise on the supply side through changes in the underlying cost conditions, including changes in the supply of productive resources or in the technology of production, and through changes in the extent of monopoly power.

Once resources have been committed to a particular kind of production, they often cannot be easily withdrawn. For example, only a small fraction of the original construction cost of a railroad line could be retrieved as scrap value or from sale of the right of way. The remaining original construction costs, often called fixed costs or sunk costs, become irrelevant to day-to-day decisions about pricing and the nature of service. It will pay for the line to continue in operation if a pattern of prices and service is possible in which revenues cover current operating costs and interest on salvage value. Financial losses to the owners of specialized fixed capital are not social losses, and are not really costs, since such capital has no alternative use. As specialized capital equipment wears out, the costs of replacing it become relevant to decisions concerning the abandonment or continuation of the activity in which it is used. Analogous problems arise in the case of labor with specialized training.

The period within which some costs are fixed is called the short run; in the long run, all costs can be changed by changes in inputs. The length of the short run in chronological time varies with the nature of the production process and the durability of the capital goods used. It may be a hundred years for a hydroelectric project and a few weeks for an establishment making inexpensive cotton dresses.

Decisions about the organization of production also involve determining the lowest-cost location of productive facilities. Some kinds of facilities are located where raw materials are accessible (iron and steel mills, for example). Some activities take place close to sources of low-cost power (aluminum reduction and production of electrochemicals), others close to important markets for the product (automobile assembly), and still others where suitable labor is available or inexpensive (manufacture of garments). [See SPATIAL ECONOMICS.]

Distributing income. The third basic function of an economy is to distribute income. In a society based on subsistence agriculture most income is distributed in kind; each family consumes largely the products of its own labor and land. In complex economies most income is distributed in money, representing generalized purchasing power or command over all goods and services offered for sale. The dominant use of money-income payments results from both specialization in production and the increasing variety of things consumed. The producer uses money income to purchase small quantities of many products, not necessarily including the one that he himself makes.

Income is the net value of production during a period—the amount available for consumption or net saving after initial wealth or capital has been maintained. In other words, income is the maximum amount that an economy (or an individual) could consume during a period without becoming poorer. If actual consumption is less than this, there has been saving during the period, and wealth has increased.

The functional classification of income depends on the kind of productive services furnished by the income recipient [see INCOME DISTRIBUTION, *article on* FUNCTIONAL SHARE]. *Wages and salaries* are the return for furnishing labor services, *interest* is the return for furnishing capital, and *rent*, in one sense of the term, is the return for furnishing land [see WAGES; INTEREST; RENT]. (These categories are less neat in income statistics than in theory; a landlord who receives rent for a building, for example, is furnishing both land and capital.) The income share called *profit* is hard to identify with a particular factor of production. Much of what is called profit in both business and national accounts is a return to equity capital and corresponds to interest in economic theory. Some accounting profit represents a return to positions of monopoly power, sometimes called rent in another sense of the term. The residual, or "pure," profit is regarded by some economists as the return to entrepreneurship or to innovation and by others as a return (either positive or negative) for taking noninsurable risks. [See PROFIT.]

Certain streams of payments to individuals, called *transfer payments*, do not correspond to any current contribution to production, but are claims of one set of individuals against the income of another. Public assistance is one example. The sum of wages and salaries, rent, interest, and profits exhausts the national income, and transfer payments arise from a secondary redistribution of these shares.

The basic principle of income distribution in a private enterprise economy is that individuals should receive as income the value of their contribution to production, including both the value of their labor and of the services of any productive land or capital that they own. This system gives each person an incentive to use his resources fully and where their contribution to the value of output is greatest. In practice, differences between the contribution of a factor to production and the income it receives can be caused by some kinds of imperfections in the markets for productive services. The income distribution is also modified by transfer payments, which are received largely by low-income groups; by the provision of free government services; and by taxes, particularly progressive personal income taxes. For most capitalist countries, these modifications seem to work on balance in the direction of greater equality of incomes.

The distribution of incomes in capitalist societies has long been criticized by socialists and reformers as too unequal. The best known competing principle is that of Marx: "From each according to his abilities, to each according to his needs." No large, complex economy has ever operated on this principle for more than brief periods, although it may operate in certain religious orders and cooperative communities. Attempts to apply the Marxian principle have broken down because of two problems, assessing needs and maintaining incentives to work and to save.

The main difference between the principles of income distribution in contemporary capitalist and socialist countries lies in the treatment of nonlabor income. In both types of economies, workers are paid approximately in accordance with the value of their work. In the socialist countries, however, almost all productive capital is owned by the state, so that personal income from property is negligible. (In the Soviet Union some private income arises from interest on savings deposits and government bonds and from the private ownership of livestock by collective-farm families.) In capitalist economies, property income is much less equally distributed than labor income. It does not follow, however, that the distribution of income, as a whole, is more equal in socialist countries. In developed capitalist countries, labor income is the great bulk of total income; a somewhat less equal distribution of labor income in socialist than in capitalist countries could therefore offset the effect of the property share on the equality of total incomes and probably does offset much of it. However, there appears to be no counterpart in socialist economies to the very highest incomes under capitalism.

The distribution of income among persons is not only unequal but asymmetrical. Almost all income distributions are markedly skewed to the right; a concentration of individuals below the mean is balanced by a long "tail" much above the mean. Since natural abilities were long assumed to be symmetrically distributed and most income was seen as a return to various abilities, the skewness of real-world income distributions motivated much work by economists and statisticians. [*See* INCOME DISTRIBUTION, *article on* SIZE; *and* SIZE DISTRIBUTIONS IN ECONOMICS.]

The major social problem related to the personal distribution of income is poverty, an older and more pressing concern of economists and sociologists. In economies at a low level of development, most peasants and unskilled workers are considered poor. In the highly advanced economies, relatively few families with employed male heads are considered poor; poverty is largely a problem of the aged, the disabled, the long-term unemployed, and households with female heads. However, there are exceptions. For example, in the United States there are a substantial number of poor farm families and poor Negro families headed by employed men. [*See* POVERTY *and* CONSUMERS, *article on* CONSUMPTION LEVELS AND STANDARDS.]

The definition of poverty has varied with time and place. In the United States in the mid-1960s, a widely accepted definition was that families with incomes below $3,000 a year were poor; about one-fifth of all families fell below this mark. In earlier times or in underdeveloped countries, the standard of living embodied in this definition would be viewed as comfortable or even luxurious. If the accepted poverty line moves upward as fast as average income, the elimination of poverty becomes exceedingly difficult. But however elusive the definition of poverty, the social problem is real and serious. Low income is a major factor contributing to crime, disease, and ignorance, which in their turn can give rise to new generations of the poor.

Policies to combat poverty fall in three general categories: public assistance or relief, rehabilitation and retraining, and the regulation of product and factor prices. Economists have tended to criticize the simplest forms of direct relief, once on the ground that they raised the natural rate of increase of poor populations and more recently on the ground that they weaken the incentive to work. Education, rehabilitation, and retraining have been preferred because they attack and sometimes eliminate a fundamental cause of poverty—the small actual or potential contribution of low-income workers to production. For the aged or disabled, social insurance is increasingly viewed as the best approach to assuring a decent minimum standard of living [*see* AGING, *article on* ECONOMIC ASPECTS].

Greater equality of income is also an announced objective of numerous public policies that directly alter product or factor prices. For example, agricultural price and income policies in many countries raise the incomes of farm families, which are usually lower than those of urban families. Such policies may increase the income of the favored sector, but often not that of the poorest families within it. Such policies also tend to restrict output or distort the allocation of resources, so that the choice is between a given national income unequally shared and a smaller one somewhat more equally shared. Indeed, the result is sometimes to lower income without increasing equality at all. [*See* AGRICULTURE, *article on* PRICE AND INCOME POLICIES; SUBSIDIES.]

The demand for equalization policy is especially strong in times of war or disaster, when there is a general disposition to prevent the rich from bidding up the prices of goods in short supply. To achieve "fair shares" or "equality of sacrifice," the role of money in the distribution of income is often supplemented by the direct rationing of certain scarce items on a per capita basis or to users whose needs are judged to be greatest. Such policies also have substantial efficiency costs, which may reduce the income available for distribution. [*See* PRICES, *article on* PRICE CONTROL AND RATIONING.]

Providing for the future. The fourth major function of any economy is to provide for the future through the conservation of natural resources, the maintenance or replacement of existing stocks of physical capital, and the net accumulation of capital. Increases in the stock of human skills and in the fund of accessible knowledge also are important in providing for the future.

The views of economists on conservation often clash with those of others, including natural scientists [*see* CONSERVATION, *article on* ECONOMIC ASPECTS]. Two main kinds of conservation problems can be identified, the first of which arises when a resource, such as wild game or fish, cannot be owned. No hunter has an incentive to spare an animal today so that he may take it in the future, for if he fails to act now, the game may be taken by someone else. Conservation under these conditions requires such government controls as closed seasons and bag limits. Interesting economic problems arise in defining the optimum size of the population to be conserved.

Less severe policy problems arise where resources can be owned, as can land and solid minerals. (Oil and natural gas are an intermediate case.) If the owners of such a resource believe that it is becoming scarce and that few substitutes will be available, they have an incentive to conserve it in order to gain from the eventual rise in its price. The higher the cost of holding this asset, including the rate of return on alternative forms of wealth, the weaker will be this incentive. Nevertheless, overexploitation of resources can occur in such cases because of ignorance on the part of resource owners or because the interest rate confronting them does not correctly reflect the social cost of capital.

A larger part of the problem of providing for the future is that of maintaining and increasing physical capital. Capital is increased through saving, much of which is undertaken by individuals to provide for personal contingencies, such as illness and old age, and to accumulate wealth to bequeath to descendants or others. Saving is also undertaken because it yields income (interest), which corresponds to the productivity of capital in production. If the rate of interest is 6 per cent, refraining from consuming $100 of income this year will make possible consumption of $106 next year; alternatively it will make possible the consumption of an income stream of $6 in perpetuity. The return on capital provides both an incentive to accumulate and an incentive to refrain from using up present capital.

Investment provides capital for a growing population and also increases the amount of capital per person available to raise output per head. With unchanging technology the return on capital would tend to fall as the best investment opportunities were used up; however, this tendency is offset by technological changes that create new investment opportunities. The theoretical problems involved in measuring the stock of capital and discovering the principles that determine its yield are among the most difficult in economics. [See CAPITAL.]

Determining the optimum rate of investment in a growing economy also raises difficult problems, which have received increasing attention in mathematical economic theory [see INTEREST and ECONOMIC GROWTH, *article on* MATHEMATICAL THEORY]. The crucial elements in this analysis are the rate of growth of population, the rate of return on capital, the rate of technological change, and the weights to be attached to the satisfaction of present and future generations.

Society requires many kinds of capital. One important way of classifying these distinguishes capital used in production from that used directly in consumption, such as houses, private automobiles, and home appliances [*see* CONSUMERS, *article on*

CONSUMER ASSETS]. A second important classification distinguishes the capital used in the production of a particular product, such as livestock, machinery, or factories, from capital—such as roads, water supply systems, communications facilities—that enters indirectly into the production of many products. The latter, called social overhead capital, is often publicly owned. [*See* CAPITAL, SOCIAL OVERHEAD.] Adequate provision for overhead facilities may be prerequisite to investment in the production of specific products.

Investment in new physical capital or the acquisition of existing physical assets by individuals, corporations, or governments often requires the investor to raise funds externally by borrowing or issuing shares. In the public mind the resulting financial assets, such as mortgages, bonds, and stocks, are more often identified with capital than are the underlying physical assets. Savings are made available for investment when financial assets are purchased by individual savers or by financial institutions, such as savings banks and insurance companies, in which savers hold their funds. [*See* FINANCIAL INTERMEDIARIES.]

A third important way of providing for the future is through technological change, including the discovery of new products and processes. Technological change in its broadest sense involves a wide range of activities: the growth of fundamental scientific knowledge through basic research, the invention of machines and methods, the dissemination and diffusion of knowledge through education, and the introduction of new methods in particular applications. An increased stock of knowledge is a more important legacy to succeeding generations than an enlarged stock of physical capital. New technology is usually incorporated, or "embodied," in the stock of physical capital and in the skills of the labor force. [*See* INNOVATION; RESEARCH AND DEVELOPMENT; AGRICULTURE, *article on* PRODUCTIVITY AND TECHNOLOGY.]

Money, income, and the price level

So far our discussion of the functions of the economy has proceeded with little reference to money, yet all but the simplest economies would grind to a halt without this essential lubricant. Some specialization and exchange can take place with the aid of barter, the direct exchange of one commodity or service for another. However, barter requires that each party wants the exact kind and quantity of goods offered by the other, which would happen only by coincidence. Money, by freeing exchange from this coincidence of double demand, permits specialization to be greatly extended. The use of money as a medium of exchange therefore appears very early in economic development; money also furnishes the unit of account and, with other assets, serves as a store of value. [*See the general article on* MONEY.]

Early money consisted of scarce commodities of various kinds, especially precious metals, and the minting of metals into coins was one of the earliest economic functions of the state. In modern economies, banknotes and other paper currency have replaced coins, except in small transactions. These notes were originally redeemable in gold or silver; this has now become uncommon. Paper currencies were once thought to derive their value only from their convertibility into metallic money; however, experience has not supported this belief. It is now clear that money derives its value from its usefulness as a medium of exchange and that irredeemable paper currencies can have stable or even rising value if their issue is restricted.

The largest part of money in developed economies consists of bank deposits, usually transferable by check. Banks, through their lending operations, can create and destroy money in the form of bank notes and deposits. Recognition of this has led to their regulation by central banks (usually agencies of the government) as a means of controlling the quantity of money and thus affecting its value. [*See* BANKING *and* BANKING, CENTRAL.]

The value of money may be defined as the reciprocal of an index number of the general level of prices [*see* INDEX NUMBERS, *article on* PRACTICAL APPLICATIONS]. Changes in the price level are important because not all individual prices are equally affected and relative prices and resource allocation are therefore influenced. In particular, changes in the price level affect the distribution of real wealth and income; a sustained rise in prices, or inflation, enriches net debtors at the expense of net creditors because the debt is stated in nominal or monetary units rather than in terms of command over real goods. A sustained fall in prices, or deflation, has the opposite effect. [*See* INFLATION AND DEFLATION.]

One of the best developed theories of the value of money is the quantity theory [*see* MONEY, *article on* QUANTITY THEORY]. The demand for money, or cash balances, arises because money lowers the cost of making transactions. Recent formulations of the quantity theory express this demand as a function of real income or wealth, the expected rate of change of prices, the interest rate, and other variables. This function is thought to be reasonably stable in the long run, in which case the general level of prices is largely determined by changes in the quantity of money. Inflation results from sustained increases in the money supply relative to real income, and deflation from sustained decreases.

Changes in the demand for money under conditions of constant supply can often be inferred from the turnover rate of the money supply, usually called the *velocity of circulation* [*see* MONEY, *article on* VELOCITY OF CIRCULATION]. A decreased desire to hold money would lead to a rise in velocity as holders sought to dispose of excess balances; an increased desire to hold money would lower velocity.

A decrease in the stock of money or its failure to grow as fast as productive capacity can cause, or contribute to, a fall in aggregate demand, output, and employment. Similarly, increases in aggregate demand brought about by increases in the stock of money or by other means will cause increases in output and employment when there is unused productive capacity. Once capacity is fully used, further increases in aggregate demand only raise the price level. Since capacity output will not be reached at the same moment in all branches of the economy, an intermediate zone exists in which increases in demand will increase output and prices simultaneously. However, behavior in this zone need not be symmetrical for increases and decreases in demand. A decrease in demand is likely at first to reduce output with little effect on prices.

As this suggests, money is a crucial element in economic fluctuations—the business cycle or the alternation of periods of prosperity and depression and of rising or falling prices—which have been one of the most conspicuous features of modern capitalist economies [*see* BUSINESS CYCLES]. Economists have long studied the sequence of events in business cycles—the amplitudes of fluctuations, the length of expansions and contractions, and the leads and lags of turning points of series at cyclical peaks and troughs. Such observations have helped in the formation of theories of the causes of business cycles. Special attention has naturally been given to the causes of depression and widespread unemployment [*see* EMPLOYMENT AND UNEMPLOYMENT].

Interest in the construction of such macroeconomic theories was heightened by the great depression of the 1930s and in particular by the work of John Maynard Keynes. Central to Keynes's thinking was the concept of deficiency of aggregate demand. If income receivers spent their entire incomes on consumption, such a deficiency could not arise;

however, a portion of income is saved, and Keynes held that this portion rises as income rises. [*See* CONSUMPTION FUNCTION.] Still, no problem arises if desired investment equals saving. All savings will then be spent in the purchase of new investment goods, and the flow of income will continue undiminished. But Keynes argued that this equality need not hold—unfavorable investment opportunities and high interest rates can lead to a reduction in desired investment and an excess of saving. [*See* INVESTMENT.] Under these circumstances, aggregate demand will fall short of productive capacity, real income will drop until saving is equal to desired investment, and there will be persistent unemployment. In Keynes's view, governments should then create the required demand through an excess of government expenditures over tax receipts.

Until Keynes, orthodox economists had argued that unemployment was caused primarily by excessive wage rates and could be alleviated by wage cuts. Keynes assumed that in modern capitalist economies wages do not fall when output falls. In any case, his emphasis on the adequacy of demand led him to counsel against wage cuts. Wages, he pointed out, are incomes as well as costs, and their reduction could lower employment by diminishing the purchasing power of wage earners and their expenditures on consumption.

A crucial relationship in the Keynesian system is that between the quantity of money and the rate of interest, which takes a form that prevents the interest rate from falling below some minimum level. This "liquidity trap" implies that expansion of the money supply during a depression will fail to lower interest rates and therefore will not stimulate investment. [*See* LIQUIDITY PREFERENCE; *for a discussion of the full Keynesian model, see* INCOME AND EMPLOYMENT THEORY.]

During the 1930s, concern about aggregate demand stimulated work on systems of national income accounting that record the income and expenditures of the whole economy by sector [*see* NATIONAL INCOME AND PRODUCT ACCOUNTS]. The simultaneous development of macroeconomic theory and macroeconomic accounting, among other forces, has led to a fundamental change in the attitude of governments toward depression and unemployment. It is now generally accepted that governments can, and should, act to maintain aggregate demand at levels as close as possible to productive capacity, although there are still important disagreements about the best ways of doing this under particular circumstances. The principal possibilities are to increase the quantity of money and hold down or reduce interest rates through expansionary

policies of the central bank, to reduce taxes, and to increase government expenditure. [*See* MONETARY POLICY *and* FISCAL POLICY.] Opposite measures can be used to control inflation resulting from an excess of aggregate demand over capacity. The use of tax reductions or of increases in government expenditures as means of combatting deficient demand implies that the budgets of central governments should be in deficit in times of less than full employment.

Subfields of economics

The theory of resource allocation (microeconomic theory) and the theory of money, income, and the price level (macroeconomic theory) are the core of economics, whose outlines have been sketched above. Surrounding this core are several specialized fields. The mention of these here must be extremely brief, especially for fields described in single articles elsewhere in the encyclopedia.

Mathematical economic theory applies mathematical tools to theoretical problems in economics. *Econometrics* applies advanced statistical tools to empirical problems in economics. [*For a survey of both fields, see* ECONOMETRICS.] Scientists in these fields have an international association, the Econometric Society.

The history of economic thought is the study of the work of past economists and their influence on one another, on other disciplines, and on the world of affairs. In this encyclopedia several schools of economics are discussed as such [*see* ECONOMIC THOUGHT]. However, the article on economic thought does not discuss the English and American classical and neoclassical schools, whose ideas are reflected in many substantive articles and whose leading figures are discussed in biographies [*see* SMITH, ADAM; RICARDO; MILL *in the classical period*; MARSHALL; EDGEWORTH; JEVONS; CLARK, JOHN BATES, *in the neoclassical period*; KNIGHT; ROBERTSON; PIGOU *in more recent years*]. Similarly, the Keynesian school of economics is included not under economic thought, but under substantive entries and biographies [*see* KEYNES, JOHN MAYNARD; HANSEN].

Economic history applies economic analysis to problems that are outside the recent past, although such problems often have implications for the present and future [*see* HISTORY, *article on* ECONOMIC HISTORY]. There has been a strong recent movement toward the application of econometric methods to economic history. Interest in the field has been stimulated by concern about the economies of underdeveloped nations and by the lessons those nations can learn from the economic history of developed areas. Economic historians have an active international association and several specialized journals. Closely related to economic history is the rapidly expanding field of *economic development*, which covers both the theory of growth and the more practical application of economics to the problems of less developed areas [*see* ECONOMIC GROWTH].

Most other specialized fields in economics deal with problems of particular parts or aspects of the economy and the institutions peculiar to them.

Industrial organization considers problems arising from the structure of firms, industries, and markets. The firm is the entity that engages in production in the private sector of the economy. In simple economies, firms are owned by individuals or groups of partners, but large-scale economic activity is now carried out principally by corporations—firms that can be owned by many shareholders, who have no liability for corporate debts beyond the possible loss of value of their shares. Shareholders typically have little control over the affairs of the corporation; effective control is in the hands of professional managers. [*See* CORPORATION.]

An industry is the set of firms or establishments carrying out some branch of economic activity, although the boundaries of such a branch are not always easy to define usefully. A market in its simplest meaning is a place at which transactions are made; more broadly, it is the whole web of relationships between buyers and sellers. [*See* MARKETS AND INDUSTRIES.] The boundaries of markets, like those of industries, are often difficult to define.

A central concern of the field of industrial organization is the changes that take place in the character of markets as the number of buyers and sellers increases and as collusion among buyers or sellers becomes more difficult. At one extreme lies monopoly [*see* MONOPOLY]. In principle, a monopoly is a market with only one seller, although all sellers are affected to some degree by competition from other markets. A monopolist in aluminum production, for example, would face the competition of other metals in some uses of his product. Markets dominated by a few sellers (oligopolies) raise interesting theoretical problems concerning interaction and collusion among the sellers, which are often approached through game theory [*see* OLIGOPOLY]. At the other extreme are competitive markets with many sellers and buyers who do not collude [*see* COMPETITION].

With given technology, competition promotes economic efficiency; monopoly or oligopoly tend to produce restriction of output and higher prices.

However, it is sometimes argued that monopoly is indispensable to technological progress. The advocates of this controversial view contend that very large corporations are necessary for innovation because modern research is too expensive to be carried on by small competitive firms [*see* RESEARCH AND DEVELOPMENT].

Other topics considered in the field of industrial organization include processes that change the structure of industry and the government regulation of industry structure, output, and prices [*see* ANTITRUST LEGISLATION; MERGERS; REGULATION OF INDUSTRY].

Agricultural economics is concerned with the efficient use of resources in agriculture, the technology of food and fiber production, the distribution of farm products, and the income and welfare of farm populations [*see* AGRICULTURE]. Agricultural economists also study the migrations from rural areas that result from the high rate of natural increase of farm populations and the displacement of labor by improved farm technology. The organization of agricultural production differs sharply between different parts of the world—the family farm owned or rented by the operator, the large collective farm and state farm of the Soviet Union, the tropical plantation employing wage workers. The form of organization has important implications for efficiency and welfare. [*See* LAND TENURE; COMMUNISM, ECONOMIC ORGANIZATION OF; PLANTATIONS.]

Labor economics is both a branch of economics and of the interdisciplinary field of industrial relations. Although most of this broader field was once occupied by economists, it has increasingly attracted sociologists, psychologists, political scientists, and lawyers. Labor economists are therefore tending to specialize in the analysis of wages, hours of work, and employment [*see* WAGES; LABOR FORCE, *article on* HOURS OF WORK; EMPLOYMENT AND UNEMPLOYMENT]. They share with demographers an interest in labor force participation and also study government regulation of working conditions and the provision of social insurance and other wage supplements [*see* AGING, *article on* ECONOMIC ASPECTS; LABOR FORCE, *article on* PARTICIPATION; UNEMPLOYMENT INSURANCE; WORKMEN'S COMPENSATION].

A central institution in this field is the labor union—an association of workers formed to improve wages and working conditions through collective bargaining or political action [*see* LABOR RELATIONS *and* LABOR UNIONS]. Although labor economists concentrate on the impact of unions on wages and employment, they are still concerned with the growth and internal functioning of unions.

Public finance applies economic analysis to the activities of the state and their impact on the private economy, particularly on the level of income and employment [*see* BUDGETING; DEBT, PUBLIC; FISCAL POLICY]. A major part of the field is the study of tax systems, including the effect of taxes on income distribution: whether they fall proportionally on all levels of income, are regressive (take a larger share of the lower incomes), or are progressive (take a larger share of the higher incomes) [*see* TAXATION]. Other studies of taxes deal with the effect of alternative tax systems on incentives to work, to save, and to use resources efficiently. Another part of the field deals with government expenditures—with determining the kinds of economic activity most appropriate to the state and devising criteria for deciding which particular public projects are worth undertaking [*see* PUBLIC EXPENDITURES].

International economics extends economic analysis to the world economy. A country's transactions with other countries are summarized in its balance of payments [*see* INTERNATIONAL MONETARY ECONOMICS, *article on* BALANCE OF PAYMENTS]. Some of these transactions are trade in commodities and current services, which reflects specialization among countries in production [*see* INTERNATIONAL TRADE]. Economists study both the actual pattern of trade and the theoretical conditions underlying it; the theory of international trade is perhaps the best developed body of theory in any subfield of economics. The effect of tariffs or quotas on the world economy and on the nation imposing them is a central problem in international trade theory. [*See* INTERNATIONAL TRADE CONTROLS.]

Other international transactions are financial, such as the construction of branch plants in one country by companies owned in another and the flow of liquid capital through securities purchases [*for examples, see* INTERNATIONAL MONETARY ECONOMICS, *article on* PRIVATE INTERNATIONAL CAPITAL MOVEMENTS]. Conditions of international trade and capital flows are greatly affected by the relations between the values of various national currencies, now a frequent subject of study and of international discussion [*see* INTERNATIONAL MONETARY ECONOMICS, *articles on* EXCHANGE RATES *and* INTERNATIONAL MONETARY ORGANIZATION].

The preceding list of the fields of economics is not complete. Among the additional fields often set apart by professional associations, specialized journals, or special courses of instruction are *consumer*

economics, comparative economics, welfare economics, and *regional economics*. Space limitations preclude any discussion of these here, though they are covered elsewhere in the encyclopedia. [*See* CONSUMERS; CAPITALISM; COMMUNISM, ECONOMIC ORGANIZATION OF; ECONOMIC GROWTH; WELFARE ECONOMICS; SPATIAL ECONOMICS.]

Organization and growth of the profession

Economics has grown rapidly in recent years, as measured either by the membership of professional associations or by the volume of professional literature. The American Economic Association was founded in 1885 and the Royal Economic Society (then the British Economic Association) in 1890. The former had fewer than 200 members in 1886; it passed the 2,000 mark in 1912. The largest increases, however, occurred between 1940 and 1962, during which time the American Economic Association grew from just over 3,000 members to more than 11,000. In 1959 there were about 5,000 fellows of the Royal Economic Society. As of 1964 there were 37 national economic associations affiliated with the International Economic Association, including 20 in Europe, 7 in Asia, and 6 in the Americas.

The growth of professional literature has been just as impressive. In 1961–1962 an *Index of Economic Journals* was published, covering only articles in English. It requires 270 pages to index the articles published in the 38 years between 1886 and 1924, and 533 pages for the 5 years between 1954 and 1959. The oldest journal covered is the *Zeitschrift für die gesamte Staatswissenschaft* (Tübingen), founded in 1844. The next, the *Quarterly Journal of Economics* (Cambridge, Mass.), began in 1866. By 1900 there were seven—three in the United States, two in Germany, and one each in Britain and Sweden. The number of journals covered in 1961–1962 was 76, of which 29 were published in Europe, 24 in the United States and Canada, 19 in Asia, and 4 in Africa. The *Index* omits many more journals that publish no material in English.

Most economists are teachers in colleges and universities, although employment in business and government is increasing. Within universities most economists are in departments of economics, but in the United States there are also many on the faculties of schools of business, both graduate and undergraduate. Economists in business schools have worked closely with statisticians and applied mathematicians on problems of business decision theory and operations research.

Economists employed in business are sometimes

engaged largely in descriptive statistics and public relations and have had little professional training. A growing number of business firms, however, employ economists with graduate training to do economic analysis.

Perhaps the fastest growing use of economists, almost everywhere, is in government—at all levels from municipalities to international organizations, but particularly in national governments. Economists are involved in a large number of different government functions. Many are involved in collecting and analyzing statistics and preparing statistical estimates such as national income accounts and prices indexes. Economists in central banks and treasuries or ministries of finance are engaged in formulating and executing monetary and fiscal policies. Still others in such agencies as budget bureaus or ministries of defense may be making cost–benefit analyses of public works projects or weapons systems. One of the most important roles of government economists is in central planning organizations, ranging from the very large and powerful central planning agencies of the communist countries, through the highly influential planning agencies of France and the Netherlands, to the largely advisory bodies like the Council of Economic Advisers in the United States.

An example may suggest the impact of changes in economic thought on government policy in the past three decades. In 1932, at the depths of the great depression, when the unemployment rate was over 20 per cent, the United States sharply increased the rates of a number of excise taxes and introduced several new ones in an effort to reduce the budget deficit. Shortly afterward John Maynard Keynes was to argue that such a policy would prolong a depression. In 1964 the United States reduced income taxes sharply in the face of a budget deficit because the unemployment rate of 5.7 per cent was unacceptably high, and it is probably not accidental that unemployment soon began to fall.

The contrast between these opposite policies illustrates strikingly the influence, in this instance a salutary one, of economic thought on policy. This influence is an important force drawing students into the discipline, but it also imposes on economists obligations to develop skills and judgment commensurate with their responsibilities.

ALBERT REES

BIBLIOGRAPHY

WORKS ON THE METHODOLOGY OF ECONOMICS

FRIEDMAN, MILTON (1953) 1959 *Essays in Positive Economics.* Univ. of Chicago Press. → See especially Chapter 1.

KEYNES, JOHN N. (1891) 1955 *The Scope and Method of Political Economy.* 4th ed. New York: Kelley.
KNIGHT, FRANK H. (1933) 1951 *The Economic Organization.* New York: Kelley. → A paperback edition was published in 1966 by Harper.
KOOPMANS, TJALLING 1957 *Three Essays on the State of Economic Science.* New York: McGraw-Hill. → Makes considerable use of mathematics.
MACHLUP, FRITZ 1963 *Essays on Economic Semantics.* Edited by Merton H. Miller. Englewood Cliffs, N.J.: Prentice-Hall.
ROBBINS, LIONEL (1932) 1937 *An Essay on the Nature and Significance of Economic Science.* 2d ed., rev. & enl. London: Macmillan.

GENERAL TEXTBOOKS AND JOURNAL REFERENCES

AMERICAN ECONOMIC ASSOCIATION 1961–1965 *Index of Economic Journals.* 6 vols. Homewood, Ill.: Irwin.
BACH, GEORGE L. (1954) 1966 *Economics: An Introduction to Analysis and Policy.* 5th ed. Englewood Cliffs, N.J.: Prentice-Hall.
LIPSEY, RICHARD G.; and STEINER, PETER O. 1966 *Economics.* New York: Harper.
SAMUELSON, PAUL A. (1948) 1964 *Economics: An Introductory Analysis.* 6th ed. New York: McGraw-Hill.
STIGLER, GEORGE J. (1942) 1960 *The Theory of Price.* Rev. ed. New York: Macmillan. → First published as *The Theory of Competitive Price.*
STONIER, ALFRED W.; and HAGUE, DOUGLAS C. (1953) 1964 *A Textbook of Economic Theory.* 3d ed. New York: Wiley.

ECONOMICS OF DEFENSE

It is essential to see defense as an economic problem and to understand what economizing means. It is also important for nations to attempt to use an economic calculus (quantitative economic analysis) in making choices and to shape the institutional arrangements in defense planning with care. Although the setting for defense planning varies from nation to nation, these issues are similar everywhere.

The economic problem. Choosing among possible defense activities can be viewed as an economic problem: that of allocating available resources so as to get the greatest good from them. The alternatives include various possible sizes of the defense budget, i.e., various allocations of resources to defense, other governmental functions, and the private sector. The alternatives then include various allocations of the total defense budget among particular "outputs," or missions, such as nuclear retaliatory capability, limited-war capability, token forces, arms control, civil defense, various kinds of mobilization bases, sealift, and so on. As with outputs in the private sector, some of these are close to being final goods and some (like sealift) are intermediate outputs, which are used in turn to produce other outputs.

Choices among various ways of producing these outputs are sometimes called "lower-level" choices. Here are included such options as the use of alternative base locations, logistic arrangements, launch facilities, contract provisions, and personnel policies. In creating defense forces there are many substitution possibilities—larger regiments versus better-equipped regiments, electronic countermeasures versus numbers of missiles, truck transport versus airlift, rifles versus mortars. These lower-level choices are economic problems too. When one estimates the costs and gains of different submarine forces and deployments, one is concerned with the worth of resources in competing uses. When one considers alternative locations for air-defense missiles or sites for vehicle fuel storage and repairs, one is dealing with the worth of these resources in rival uses.

Needless to say, the choices at different levels are not independent of each other. The size of the budget should depend upon, among other things, the costs and gains of producing specific capabilities, i.e., the specific lower-level options that confront a nation. In turn, the choices at lower levels should often depend upon the size of the budget.

Another set of alternatives embraces various kinds of research and development intended to invent new defense policies or systems. Effective attempts to advance technology and efficient resource allocation within any given technology are both important; the absence of either would leave defense or any other activity at a comparatively primitive stage. Because relatively great uncertainties surround research and development alternatives, choosing among them calls for a different approach from decision making under conditions of comparative certainty (Klein & Meckling 1958; Nelson 1961).

Economizing. "Economizing" does not imply scrimping and penny-pinching in defense (or in any other activity), nor does it call for meeting all needs. Instead, in defense planning "economizing" implies cutting defense costs whenever resources can produce more-valuable outputs elsewhere and meeting defense needs whenever they are more important than other needs.

Many persons believe in or talk as if they believe in "needs" or "requirements" that should be met regardless of cost. Others seem to believe in cost or budget ceilings that must be adhered to no matter how large the gains that might be obtained by going above the ceiling. Still others believe that one should set up priority lists like the following: (1) laser; (2) new supersonic bomber; (3) improved long-range camera. What such a list means is hard to see: should all resources go to the first item? should resources go to the first item until an extra dollar there brings a zero return, even though the other items are worth something? should more money be spent on the first item than on the second and more on the second than on the third? The trouble is that a priority list does not face the real question: how *much* should be allocated to each item?

None of these beliefs give proper guidance. Hard though it may be to apply, the economic principle is the one to keep in mind: make any resource shift that yields more than it costs. When gain exceeds costs, a transfer of resources produces net gains and, thus, a greater total output. There are two major approaches to the application of this principle: improvement of the economic calculus (information about the costs and gains from alternative courses of action) and improvement of the institutional arrangements that shape defense choices. As in the private economy, both are important. Identification of the correct choice will not help much if institutions are such as to lead decision makers to make a different choice. On the other hand, better institutions are hard to devise if good choices cannot be identified. In making good decisions at every level—decisions about the size of budgets and about the allocation of given budgets—both the institutional arrangements and the economic calculus play an important role.

The possibility of an economic calculus. First of all, what does "economic efficiency" really mean? If one could calculate *all* gains and costs in commensurable terms, if these amounts were universally and unambiguously true, and if there were no uncertainties, the correct actions would be those that yielded net gains and they could be conclusively identified. In most activities, certainly in defense, these conditions do not hold. One major stumbling block is the fact that there is no generally accepted value that can be assigned to a change in the amount of defense as a whole or to an increment in any defense mission.

We can sometimes derive a production-possibility curve showing the various combinations of two defense outputs—say, ability to shoot down enemy missiles and ability to retaliate—attainable with the same total budget. But we have no indifference curves, and no price tags, to show how extra units of each capability should be valued. It is impossible, therefore, to identify the most valuable or optimal combination. (Even the most valuable combination would not necessarily be optimal, because there would be no assurance that the given budget was optimal.)

By exploring alternative ways of using the resources, however, one can sometimes show how to obtain more of one capability without sacrificing any of the other. Assuming there are no uncounted effects, such a change is an unambiguous improvement. In technical terminology, this constitutes moving to an *efficient point* on the production-possibility curve.

Moreover, when alternative actions affect only a single objective (seldom completely true), one can sometimes find a closely related type of improvement. By designing and comparing alternative ways to achieve that objective, one can often discover ways to achieve a specified amount of the objective at a lower cost or ways to achieve a larger amount of the objective at a specified cost. Such an improvement is akin to a shift toward an efficient point, because again the final result is the following: more of some desirable output can be produced without giving up anything else. This is the customary meaning of "economic efficiency."

Program budgeting.   One device that is intended to facilitate the use of an economic calculus in budgetary choices is program budgeting, which the U.S. Defense Department introduced in 1961. Its central feature is the presentation of costs for programs, or *output* categories (e.g., retaliatory capability, weapon systems, arms control), rather than for *input* categories (e.g., personnel, transportation). By thinking in terms of programs, officials can better take into account interdependencies—such as the effects of buying submarine-launched missiles or the worth of extra land-based ballistic missiles. Officials can presumably make better subjective judgments about the worth of output categories than they can make about the ultimate worth of inputs. These calculations also provide better clues to the worth of increments or decrements in output categories. Another feature of program budgeting is the presentation of the anticipated costs of a program decision for several years ahead rather than for one year at a time. This should help officials take into account the full-cost implications of decisions instead of merely the initial-payment implications.

Program budgeting is no panacea. Hard choices will still be relatively hard. There are difficulties, both conceptual and practical, in providing the most useful cost estimates. Also program budgeting, unless implemented with care, may be conducive to excessive centralization of authority, which itself entails disadvantages or costs. This will be considered below, in the discussion of the role of institutional arrangements. Our interest here is in program budgeting as an information system to facilitate economic calculations.

Cost–benefit analysis.   Increasingly, nowadays, there are direct attempts to prepare an economic calculus to help one choose among alternatives. These alternatives are often called *systems* because —whether they are physically small guidance mechanisms or vast combinations of missiles, aircraft, bases, command-and-control arrangements, personnel, and procedures—they are sets of interrelated parts. Such cost–gain comparisons are sometimes called *cost–effectiveness analyses* or *systems analyses*, especially when they pertain to defense; *operations research* or *operational analyses*, particularly when they compare alternative modes of operation; *cost–benefit analyses*, originally where they evaluated natural-resource projects [*see* WATER RESOURCES]; or simply *economic analyses*, where they examine conventional economic policies. The term "cost–benefit analyses" is now used rather widely, and it does seem to convey the underlying idea fairly well.

Cost–benefit analyses can be viewed as consisting of several elements: (1) the desired objectives, such as (in defense) being prepared to carry out specified missions; (2) the alternative systems, or means of trying to achieve the objectives; (3) the costs entailed by each of the systems; (4) models to help trace out the costs incurred and achievements provided; and (5) a criterion (involving both cost and achievement) to identify the best system. With regard to the last element, discussing the correct way to design criteria may seem like discussing the correct way to find the Holy Grail. In a world of uncertainty and *n*th best, judgments must help shape choices and no operational test of preferredness can be above suspicion. Moreover, analyses vary in their quality (which is hard to appraise) and in their applicability to different decisions. For these reasons the responsible decision makers must treat cost–benefit analyses as "consumer research" and introduce heroic judgments in reaching final decisions. In a sense, then, it may be both presumptuous and erroneous to discuss having a test of preferredness in these quantitative analyses.

Criteria should be discussed, nonetheless, in connection with such analysis. First, cost–benefit analysts must deal with a closely related set of issues: what *are* relevant impacts on achievement of objectives and what *are* relevant impacts on costs? (These issues confront one in the first four elements of cost–benefit analysis, of course, whether or not one includes a fifth element called criterion selection.) Second, cost–benefit analysts do apply criteria, especially in designing and redesigning the alternatives to be compared. They delete features that appear to be inefficient, add features that appear to be improvements, and probe for alternative combinations that are worth considering. This screening of possibilities and redesigning of alternative systems entails the use of criteria, and these should be explicitly considered and exhibited. Moreover, whether or not they ought to, analysts often present the final comparisons in terms of a criterion.

Thus, while it is wrong to talk as if a definitive criterion is an element of every analysis, we ought to emphasize certain points about criterion selection. First, many tests of preferredness can be quite misleading. For example, such tests as the ratio of gains to costs, the ratio of part of the gains to part of the costs, and the maximum gains for particular inputs should be avoided (Hitch & McKean 1960, pp. 158–181). Second, it should be stressed that good (although never perfect) criteria usually take one of the following forms: (1) maximum gains minus costs (to be used wherever possible); (2) maximum achievement of an objective for a given cost; or (3) minimum cost of achieving a specified amount of an objective.

Needless to say, analyses should attempt to take into account *all* gains and *all* costs. Some people feel that there are two types of gain or cost, economic and noneconomic, and that economic analysis has nothing to say about the latter. This distinction is neither very sound nor very useful. People pay for—that is, they value—paintings, as well as shoes; peace of mind, as well as aluminum pans; a lower probability of death, as well as garbage disposal. The significant categories are not economic and noneconomic items but (1) gains and costs that can be measured in monetary units, e.g., production or use of items, like steel, that have market prices to which users can adjust their transactions; (2) other commensurable effects, e.g., impacts on retaliatory capability of better warning systems as compared with the hardening of missile bases; (3) incommensurable effects that can be quantified separately but not in terms of a common unit, e.g., capability of destroying x targets and capability of showing resolve by putting y aircraft on forward bases; and (4) nonquantifiable effects. Examples of the latter are impacts on morale and thence on capability; impacts on the probability of limited war, of escalation, and of nuclear war; and impacts on the chances of working out mutually

acceptable arms controls. In taking a position on an issue, each of us implicitly quantifies such considerations. But there is no way to make generally valid quantifications that would necessarily agree with those of other persons. These distinctions between types of effects of alternative policies do serve a useful purpose, however, especially in warning us of the limitations of cost–benefit analysis.

Cost–benefit analysis necessarily involves groping and the making of subjective judgments, not just briskly proceeding with dispassionate scientific measurements. No one says, "This is the defense objective, and here are the three alternative systems to be compared; now trace out the impacts of each on cost and on achievement of the objective, and indicate the preferred system." What happens is that those making the analysis spend quite some time attempting an operational statement of an objective, for example, the capability, after receiving a specified strike, to destroy a designated set of targets with a stipulated probability. Then, a first attempt is made at designing the alternative ways of producing this capability. Preliminary costs are estimated. Members of the research team perceive that the alternative systems would affect other objectives, such as the deterring of minor aggressions or the providing of a flexible rather than a spasm response to major aggressions. Relations with other countries may be immediately involved. If the analysis is being made by a relatively small nation, for example, its defense posture would have subtle and crucial impacts on the reactions of neighboring countries and of large nations. The analysts redesign the alternatives in the light of these impacts, perhaps so that each alternative performs at least "acceptably" with respect to each objective. Next, it may appear that certain additional features, e.g., decoys or extra radar coverage, would add greatly to capability but not much to cost. Or the cost group may report that certain arctic installations are extremely expensive and that relocating them would reduce costs greatly with little impairment of effectiveness. In both cases the systems have to be modified again. This cut-and-try procedure is essential. Indeed, this process of redesigning the alternatives is probably a more important contribution than the final cost–effectiveness exhibits themselves. In any event, preparing such an analysis is a process of probing and not at all a methodical, scientific comparison following prescribed procedures (Quade 1964, chapter 3).

The incommensurables and uncertainties in cost–benefit analysis are pervasive. Consider the achievement of each of the multiple objectives mentioned above. The various achievements or effects of the alternative systems can perhaps be individually described, but they cannot be expressed in terms of a common denominator. Judgments about the extent of these effects and their worth have to be made. Similarly, some costs—the opportunity cost of devoting resources to defense, the sacrifice of crew lives, the impairment of morale and alertness in the performance of dull, monotonous tasks—if quantifiable at all, cannot validly be put in terms of a common denominator. Furthermore, because of uncertainties, whatever estimates can be prepared should in principle be probability distributions rather than unique figures for costs and gains. The system that performs the best in one contingency may perform the worst in another. This may call for redesigning the systems to insure against catastrophic outcomes, and it definitely calls for caution in interpreting the results of cost–benefit analyses. Finally, costs and gains occur over a period of time, not at a single point in time, and there is no fully acceptable means of handling these streams in analyzing defense options. To be compared, alternative cost–gain streams must each be reduced to a single number, such as present worth. Capabilities occurring in different years can hardly be so discounted satisfactorily. They must therefore be stipulated, and only the cost streams discounted. But when the time path or anything else is stipulated, this implies that there are no trade offs. Also, discounting the cost streams alone poses some problems. For example, most persons would be inclined to discount risky proposals at high rates—but with the gains stipulated, unless risks under alternative systems are carefully equalized, the risky proposals would be relatively cheap and attractive! (For more detail on the difficulties regarding incommensurables, uncertainties, and time, see Hitch & McKean 1960, chapters 10, 11.)

These difficulties are present because life is complex and choice is hard. They are not created by cost–benefit analysis. Moreover, they do not render such quantitative economic analysis useless. They simply mean that the analysts have to be discriminating about when and how to use various tools. Cost–benefit analyses are less helpful in applications where uncertainties are great, as in the case of choosing between disarmament options or between exploratory research and development proposals, and in cases where incommensurables are highly significant, as in selecting the size of defense programs, than they are in choosing between certain force-structure alternatives, such as alternative mixes of Polaris and Minuteman missiles or alternative base locations.

Perhaps the main conclusion, however, is that we must *always* regard analyses as only aids or inputs to decisions, not as oracular touchstones. (And, needless to say, fragments of cost–benefit analyses, interaction models, games that force people to consider the reactions of allies and enemies, improvements in computational and analytical techniques—any activities that help shed light on costs or gains— are also inputs to decisions and can help increase economic efficiency in defense.) Even the most comprehensive of cost–benefit analyses must be interpreted, not applied mechanically. If employed cautiously and with institutional checks and balances to insure against misuse, cost–benefit analyses can be quite useful. They can sometimes help eliminate really bad choices, allowing the decision makers to choose from a short list of reasonably good options. They can sometimes point with considerable clarity to improvements, even though neither they nor any other technique can identify truly optimal choices. Most important of all, cost–benefit analyses can provide the right framework for decision makers, bargainers, or anyone else "to think in." It is the right kind of framework to use in organizing the evidence and one's thoughts and intuitions regarding alternatives.

The role of institutional arrangements.   In defense, as in other problems of choice, we must recognize that factors other than information and exhortation play a role in shaping actual choices. The hypothesis that each individual, including the official, attempts to maximize his own utility should be kept in mind, and the way in which rules and institutions shape the costs and rewards confronting the individual should be recognized.

The utility-maximization hypothesis does not imply that people are extremely selfish and brutish or anything of the sort. It merely holds that individuals get satisfaction from many things—play, power, material goods, spiritual well-being, helping others, getting their own way—and that these things are to some extent substitutes for each other. That being the case, if the cost to consumers or officials of one item or action increases, they will demand less of it and more of other things. An increase in the rewards to officials or other individuals from one item or action will cause them to demand more of it and less of other items. (For a discussion of the utility-maximization hypothesis, see Alchian & Allen 1964, chapter 2.) This general theorem can lead to many testable hypotheses regarding both private and public activities, including defense.

Models of the private economy make use of this hypothesis, and they yield many good predictions.

In the private sector of the economy, the *price mechanism* causes individuals to feel most of the costs of and gains from their actions. In the public sector the *bargaining mechanism*, although a very imprecise instrument, performs some of the same function (Lindblom 1955). If a decision maker contemplates an action, he will consider some of the costs he would impose on others, at least on those who have the power to retaliate. He will consider some of the gains he would bestow on others, at least on those with whom he can bargain for favors. Spill-over costs and gains prompt one to consider central intervention as a mechanism to capture these, yet central control can actually so blunt the bargaining mechanism as to lead to the neglect of such externalities. If there are more checks and balances, top management may be impelled to take more of the costs and gains into account. In any organization there is a whole spectrum of possible bargaining arrangements, each with its own advantages and disadvantages.

These points are pertinent to defense planning. A high degree of centralization brings some advantages, but it also means that bargaining power is less dispersed, and so ultimately important considerations may be disregarded (Schlesinger 1966). In a defense department, as in any bureaucracy, there are natural tendencies to centralize authority. With five-year program budgeting, this tendency may be unduly reinforced. Although the defense minister or chief may wish to coordinate interrelated choices, as long as the military branches have the authority to allocate their own budgets they will do much as they please anyway. So the program budget may become, not an information system, but an approved five-year plan that serves as an institutional instrument of control.

This arrangement can correct some of the undesirable effects of the rivalry between military branches in shaping programs that are interrelated. But, as I have argued above, the fact that centralization brings gains does not automatically mean that it is an improvement. For it also brings some ill effects or costs, which should be weighed against the gains. With centralization one set of views plays a greater role in decision making, and dissenting views play lesser roles. In other words, there are fewer checks and balances on the views of the central group. Also, if central managers try to control in much detail, they find it imperative to simplify decision making and to discourage program changes. Finally, lower-level incentives to dissent and criticize and urge changes may diminish if such activities begin to be unrewarding. All these forces can in the long run produce disadvantages:

(1) the suppression of alternatives; (2) a neglect of part of the costs and gains from alternative policies; and (3) a neglect of uncertainties.

One group's view of the future will be less diversified than the separate judgments of a multiplicity of groups. Dominance of one group may lead to the disregarding of trade offs and options that others may take seriously, to the treating of certain costs and gains more lightly than others would, and to the regarding of a particular subset of contingencies and uncertainties as the major ones. The need to simplify—to use half-page summaries and rules of thumb—strengthens these same tendencies. They may be further reinforced by a loss of incentives at lower levels, perhaps by tacit agreements to refrain from introducing disturbing considerations. For some choices, such as force-structure decisions that have crucial interrelationships, central control is appropriate. For other choices, such as exploratory research and development decisions that are dominated by uncertainty, a greater degree of decentralization may be desirable.

We need to learn more about institutional arrangements for harnessing the efforts of individuals to promote various objectives. We have much to learn about the effects on incentive of alternative bargaining structures, procedures, "rules of the game," relationships between defense agencies and contractors, and so on. In the U.S. Department of Defense and in similar organizations in other nations, numerous institutional modifications are being tried, such as organizational changes, program budgeting, incentive contracts, contracts in which savings resulting from the use of cheaper components are shared, and stock funds under which certain activities are managed almost like private businesses (Hitch & McKean 1960, chapter 12). In the long run, institutional arrangements will turn out to be fully as important as the use of an economic calculus in improving defense choices.

ROLAND N. MCKEAN

[*See also* BUDGETING; CIVIL–MILITARY RELATIONS; MILITARY POLICY; *and the detailed guide under* MILITARISM.]

BIBLIOGRAPHY

ALCHIAN, ARMEN A.; and ALLEN, WILLIAM R. (1964) 1965 *University Economics.* Belmont, Calif.: Wadsworth.

DAVIS, OTTO A.; and WHINSTON, ANDREW B. 1963 Welfare Economics and the Theory of Second Best. Unpublished manuscript. → A paper jointly sponsored by the Cowles Commission for Research in Economics and the Graduate School of Industrial Administration of the Carnegie Institute of Technology.

DEVONS, ELY 1950 *Planning in Practice: Essays in Aircraft Planning in War-time*. Cambridge Univ. Press.

ENKE, STEPHEN 1954 Some Economic Aspects of Fissionable Material. *Quarterly Journal of Economics* 68:217–232.

ENTHOVEN, ALAIN; and ROWEN, HENRY 1961 Defense Planning and Organization. Pages 365–417 in Universities–National Bureau Committee for Economic Research, *Public Finances: Needs, Sources, and Utilization; A Conference. . . .* Princeton Univ. Press.

HARRIS, SEYMOUR E. 1951 *The Economics of Mobilization and Inflation*. New York: Norton.

HIRSHLEIFER, JACK 1963 *Disaster and Recovery: A Historical Survey*. Selected RAND Abstracts, Vol. 1. Research Memorandum RM-3079-PR. Santa Monica, Calif.: RAND Corp.

HITCH, CHARLES J. 1958 Economics and Military Operations Research. *Review of Economics and Statistics* 40:199–209.

HITCH, CHARLES J. 1965 *Decision-making for Defense*. Berkeley: Univ. of California Press.

HITCH, CHARLES J.; and McKEAN, ROLAND N. 1960 *The Economics of Defense in the Nuclear Age*. Cambridge, Mass.: Harvard Univ. Press.

HOAG, MALCOLM W. 1959 Some Complexities in Military Planning. *World Politics* 11:553–576.

KLEIN, BURTON H.; and MECKLING, WILLIAM H. 1958 Application of Operations Research to Development Decisions. *Operations Research* 6:352–363.

KNORR, KLAUS 1956 *The War Potential of Nations*. Princeton Univ. Press.

LEVINE, ROBERT A. 1963 *The Arms Debate*. Cambridge, Mass.: Harvard Univ. Press.

LINCOLN, GEORGE A. (1950) 1954 *Economics of National Security: Managing America's Resources for Defense*. 2d ed. Englewood, Cliffs, N.J.: Prentice-Hall.

LINDBLOM, CHARLES E. 1955 *Bargaining: The Hidden Hand in Government*. Research Memorandum RM-1434-RC. Santa Monica, Calif.: RAND Corp.

McKEAN, ROLAND N. 1963 Cost–Benefit Analysis and British Defense Expenditure. Pages 17–35 in Alan T. Peacock and D. J. Robertson (editors), *Public Expenditure: Appraisal and Control*. Edinburgh: Oliver & Boyd.

MARSHALL, ANDREW W.; and MECKLING, WILLIAM H. 1962 Predictability of the Costs, Time and Success of Development. Pages 461–475 in Universities–National Bureau Committee for Economic Research, *The Rate and Direction of Inventive Activity: Economic and Social Factors*. Princeton Univ. Press.

MASSÉ, PIERRE 1959 *Le choix des investissements: Critères et méthodes*. Paris: Dunod.

NELSON, RICHARD R. 1961 Uncertainty, Learning, and the Economics of Parallel Research and Development Efforts. *Review of Economics and Statistics* 43:351–364.

NOVICK, DAVID (editor) 1965 *Program Budgeting: Program Analysis and the Federal Budget*. Cambridge, Mass.: Harvard Univ. Press.

PECK, MERTON J.; and SCHERER, FREDERIC M. 1962 *The Weapons Acquisition Process: An Economic Analysis*. Boston: Harvard Univ., Graduate School of Business Administration, Division of Research.

QUADE, EDWARD S. (editor) 1964 *Analysis for Military Decisions*. Chicago: Rand McNally.

RAND CORPORATION 1958 *Report on a Study of Nonmilitary Defense*. Santa Monica, Calif.: The Corporation.

ROBBINS, LIONEL 1947 *The Economic Problem in Peace and War: Some Reflections on Objectives and Mechanisms*. London: Macmillan.

SCHELLING, THOMAS C. 1960 *The Strategy of Conflict*. Cambridge, Mass.: Harvard Univ. Press.

SCHERER, FREDERIC M. 1964 *The Weapons Acquisition Process: Economic Incentives*. Boston: Harvard Univ., Graduate School of Business Administration, Division of Research.

SCHLESINGER, JAMES R. 1960 *The Political Economy of National Security: A Study of the Economic Aspects of the Contemporary Power Struggle*. New York: Praeger.

SCHLESINGER, JAMES R. 1963 Quantitative Analysis and National Security. *World Politics* 15:295–315.

SCHLESINGER, JAMES R. 1966 Organizational Structure and Planning. Unpublished manuscript, National Bureau of Economic Research (New York).

ECONOMIES OF SCALE

It is commonly observed that in producing and distributing almost every economic good there is some systematic relationship between the size or scale of the plant and the production cost per unit of output, and a similar relationship between the scale of the firm and the unit cost of producing and distributing the good. Let scale be measured as the rate of output per unit of time which a plant or firm is best designed to produce (can produce more economically than any other size of plant or firm). Let us also suppose that any plant or firm is operated at its best rate of output. Producing at that output rate, a plant or firm will have a certain cost per unit of output for production, and a firm a certain unit cost for production plus distribution. But these unit costs will not necessarily be invariant to the scale of the plant or firm. (For formal analysis of the relationship of the scale to the rate of utilization of the plant or firm and for definition of the scale curve, or long-run average cost curve, see Viner 1931 and Stigler 1946, pp. 128–142.)

As the scale of a plant is enlarged from the smallest feasible size through progressively larger sizes, increases in the scale of plant will generally result in lower production costs per unit of output until some critical scale is reached beyond which further increases in scale will leave unit production costs unchanged. This critical plant scale may be designated as the *minimum optimal scale* of plant in any given industry. Similarly, as the scale of a firm operating a plant or plants in an industry is progressively increased to and beyond the size required for the operation of one plant of minimum optimal scale, the firm may realize reductions in the cost of producing and distributing a good, possibly until it is large enough to operate two or more such plants, although again it apparently tends to reach a critical scale beyond which further scale increases will not result in lower unit costs of production and distribution.

"Plant" in this context means a factory, mill, or other assemblage of connected productive facilities located on a single site (frequently also called an "establishment"), and "firm" means an independent administrative and control unit which manages a plant or plants and distributes their outputs. The reductions of costs with increases in the scales of plants or firms reflect, in general, economies of scale; in particular, economies of large-scale plant and economies of large-scale firm (in essence economies of the multiplant firm). The economies in question are in general "internal economies" (economies internal to the plant or firm in the sense that they are attributable to increased size of the individual unit), as distinguished from "external economies," which are reductions in unit costs that may occur as the result of increases in the size of an industry, accomplished by an increase in the number of firms.

Realization of scale economies results in the decline of unit costs of production in a plant until a minimum optimal (lowest-unit-cost) scale is reached; thereafter, further increases in scale will not tend either to reduce or to increase unit production costs, and there will be an indefinitely wide range of optimal plant scales that are larger than the minimum optimal scale. The same may also be true of firms in that, once they have attained minimum optimal scales, further growth will neither increase nor decrease their unit costs. But there is the possibility that the growth of firms to very large size will result in an increase in their unit costs—that there are diseconomies of very large scale firms which place an upper limit on firm scales that are optimal. The actual existence of such diseconomies is both debatable and debated.

Economies of scale may be either "real" economies, reflecting a reduction in the physical quantities of productive factors needed to produce a unit of output (and a corresponding reduction in money costs), or "strictly pecuniary" economies, reflecting only a reduction in the prices at which the firm acquires productive factors, no real cost savings being involved. Economies of large-scale plant typically have a technological basis and are real economies. They are generally attributed to real savings in production costs resulting from specialization of labor, specialization of capital equipment, and specialization of management functions that large plant scales permit. Economies of the large or multiplant firm, so far as they are

realized, may be real economies of specialization of management, or real savings in shipping costs through the operation of geographically dispersed plants where nationwide distribution is for some reason advantageous to the firm. They may also be strictly pecuniary economies resulting from lower prices paid for productive factors as a result of the monopsonistic power of large-volume buyers, or from access to financing on preferential terms. The realization of strictly pecuniary economies is of no advantage to society except insofar as "passing them on" to customers of large firms through lower output prices may have desired effects on the distribution of income. (An extensive analysis of the bases of scale economies is found in Robinson 1931.)

Real economies of large-scale plant are due fundamentally to indivisibilities or "lumpiness" in the particular forms of specialized factors or agencies of production, which can be acquired or used only in certain finite sizes and in some cases are more efficient in larger than in smaller sizes. With infinite divisibility of every productive factor and agent, there would be no plant scale-economies. This fact explains why progressive expansion of a plant will lead to a minimum optimal scale beyond which the plant will be neither more nor less efficient. At some critical finite scale, the indivisibilities of specialized factors or agencies which favor large plant-size will be fully overcome (the advantages of specialization will be exhausted), and further increases in scale can do no better than duplicate plants of minimum optimal scale on a single site. (For more extensive analysis of this and related matters, see Bain 1952, pp. 110–117. For analysis of the reflection of scale economies in production functions, see Boulding [1941] 1955, chapter 34.) The same phenomenon of exhaustion of scale economies at some finite scale is encountered with any real economies of the multiplant firm, and probably with its strict pecuniary economies as well.

If diseconomies of very large firms are encountered (and the evidence bearing on this issue is inconclusive), it is because of the inherent inefficiency of very large administrative organizations, afflicted with inflexible regulations, red tape, and extensive internal communication problems. Some theorists have argued that management is essentially a "fixed factor" which cannot be expanded in size beyond certain limits without assuming an altered and less efficient form.

Quantitative importance. What has been said so far refers entirely to the qualitative character of the relationship of the scale of the plant or firm to the unit cost of production and distribution of a good, and to the theoretical explanation of such a relationship. The important economic issues turn upon the question of how quantitatively important these scale economies (and diseconomies) are in various industries. This is because the extent of their importance in any industry determines the minimal degree of plant concentration and minimal degree of concentration of industry control by firms which are consistent with plants and firms of reasonably efficient scale; it also determines (if diseconomies of very large firms are involved) the maximal degree of concentration by firms which is consonant with efficiency.

Specifically, therefore, we wish to know for each of a large group of industries and for types of industries similar in the relevant respects: (1) the approximate percentage of industry output which would be supplied by one plant of minimum optimal scale; (2) the approximate percentage of industry output which would be supplied by one firm of minimum optimal scale; (3) the extent to which production costs per unit of output of plants of progressively less than minimum optimal scale exceed lowest attainable costs (i.e., the slope of the plant "scale curve" relating unit costs to scale, over a range of suboptimal plant scales); (4) the extent to which unit production costs plus distribution costs of firms of progressively less than minimum optimal scale exceed lowest attainable costs (i.e., the slope of the firm "scale curve"); and (5) whether or not (and if so, to what extent) diseconomies of very large firms are encountered in practice.

This information should permit us to determine for any industry, or for groups of similar industries, how large a number of reasonably efficient plants and how large a number of reasonably efficient firms the industry can support (as well as how small a number of firms, should diseconomies of very large firms be significant). And this determination should in turn indicate the extent to which the pursuit of efficiency in scale of plants and firms is consistent with degrees of concentration of industry control by firms which are respectively compatible with competition, oligopoly, and monopoly. It should also allow us to appraise existing degrees of concentration of control in individual industries, and particularly the development of large multiplant firms, with an eye to finding to what degree they are justified by the pursuit of scale economies and conversely to what degree concentration is greater, and market structures less competitive, than considerations of economy actually require.

There is not as yet available an adequate body of evidence on the quantitative importance of scale economies in large numbers of industries in all of the several sectors (e.g., agriculture, manufacturing, wholesale and retail trade, the service trades, construction, and so on) of any national economy. Bain has, nevertheless, developed data (1956*b*) on the importance of scale economies in a sample of 20 manufacturing industries in the United States as of the early 1950s, the majority of them having moderate to high concentration of control by relatively few firms. The findings for this sample may be viewed as tentatively and roughly indicative of the importance of economies of large plants and firms in American manufacturing industries generally.

As for economies of large-scale plant, it appears that the proportion either of national industry capacity (where the industry has a unified national market) or of capacity supplying the largest regional submarket (where the industry is fragmented into regional submarkets) that would be provided by one plant of minimum optimal scale is from 15 to 25 per cent in two out of 20 cases, from 10 to 15 per cent in four cases, from 5 to 7½ per cent in six cases, from 2½ to 5 per cent in three cases, and below 2½ per cent in five cases. In a number of industries in which the proportion of the market supplied by one plant of minimal optimal scale is appreciable, however, the elevation of unit costs at appreciably smaller plant scales is relatively slight, so that plants with substantially less than minimal optimal scale would be reasonably efficient; in only about 40 per cent of the industries do plants with scales from one-half to one-fourth the minimum optimal scale experience significantly higher production costs. Taking into account both the ratio of the output of a plant of minimum optimal scale to the size of the market and the relative flatness of many plant scale curves at suboptimal scales, we draw the following tentative conclusions about the 20 manufacturing industries.

(1) In two, plant-scale economies are very important, in the sense that the output of a plant of minimum optimal scale exceeds 10 per cent of the designated market output and that unit costs would be at least moderately higher at half-optimal scale.

(2) In five, plant-scale economies are moderately important in that the output of a plant of minimum optimal scale is 4 or 5 per cent of the designated market output and that unit costs would be moderately higher at half-optimal scale.

(3) In nine, plant-scale economies are relatively unimportant, either because a plant of minimum

optimal scale would supply a small percentage of the output in the designated market or because plants of suboptimal scale experience only slightly higher costs, or for both reasons.

(4) In four, information does not permit definite classification, but important plant-scale economies may be present in two of the four cases.

So far as we may generalize from these findings (1956*b*, pp. 71–82), the importance of plant-scale economies is widely variable among industries generally and among industries with high concentration of control by a few firms. In a distinct minority of cases, plant-scale economies are sufficiently important to justify a moderately high degree of plant and firm concentration. In the substantial majority of cases, plant-scale economies are such that reasonably efficient production is consistent with the existence of a substantial number of individual plants serving an unsegmented national or principal regional submarket; high concentration of control by firms is not required to take advantage of economies of large-scale plants.

For the same sample of industries, economies of the large-scale or multiplant firm appeared to be relatively unimportant. In half of 12 industries for which pertinent data can be found, there appear to be no economies of multiplant firm whatever. In the other half, from slight to modest economies (involving a cost advantage of from 2 to 4 per cent) are found for firms controlling several optimal-sized plants. These economies are attributed in some cases to large-scale management and in others to reduced costs of distribution, typically through the use of regional plants to supply regional markets (1956*b*, pp. 83–93). In the latter case, the economies are generally conditional on nationwide sales promotion of goods with appreciable transportation costs, and although they represent savings to the firms involved, they are not savings to the economy, which could be as efficiently supplied by regional firms not engaging in this type of sales promotion. (Economies of large-scale distribution are discussed at greater length in Bain 1956*a*, pp. 343–345.) With a few exceptions, realization of reasonably efficient production and distribution by manufacturing industries does not really require multiplant firms; efficiency requires firms with outputs no larger than one plant of minimum optimal scale. In the few exceptional cases, the efficient multiplant firm would ordinarily not need to have more than plant of minimum optimal scale in any regional submarket. Realization of economies of the multiplant firm, therefore, would not require higher concentration of control by firms in such submarkets than would realization

of economies of large-scale plants alone—as seems generally to be the rule. Economies of the multiplant firm appear to have been greatly overrated by various observers making casual judgments.

Our investigation in general reveals no firm or systematic evidence that diseconomies of large scale tend necessarily to be encountered by very large firms in manufacturing industries. Some instances are found in which the largest firms in an industry have higher unit costs than somewhat smaller firms, but their cost disadvantages appear to be attributable to a variety of special circumstances not intrinsically linked with scale of firm per se. Diseconomies of large-scale firm thus do not tend to provide an effective check on degrees of concentration of industry control by firms that are much higher than required for efficiency in production and distribution. Indeed, the incidence of dominant firms which are from four or five to twenty or more times as large as is required for exploiting all visible economies of large-scale production and distribution is quite high in the 20 American manufacturing industries sampled.

One reason that economies of large scale are not such as to justify high degrees of concentration of industry control by firms in the United States is that the national and major regional submarkets in this country are very large—most usually large enough to absorb the outputs of numerous plants and firms of reasonably efficient scale. In other industrialized countries outside the communist bloc, national and regional markets range from moderately smaller to much smaller, but in most such industries production techniques and methods do not differ enough from those of the United States that the scales of reasonably efficient plants are appreciably different. In these other countries, therefore, realization of efficiency in scale of plants and firms typically would require from moderately to substantially greater degrees of plant and firm concentration than is required in the United States. But actual plant concentration in their industries most frequently is not high enough for reasonable efficiency, although concentration of industry control by firms may be. (Findings on this matter are presented in Bain 1966, chapters 3–5.)

As to attained efficiency in the United States, the findings based on the sample of 20 manufacturing industries are that between 70 and 90 per cent of the output of a manufacturing industry is typically supplied by plants and firms of reasonably efficient scale, whereas the remaining 10 to 30 per cent is supplied by plants (and typically one-plant firms) that suffer from appreciable diseconomies of unduly small scale. Such an inefficient fringe of small plants appears generally to supply a larger proportion of industrial output in most other industrialized countries outside the communist bloc (Bain 1966, pp. 55–66).

Large-scale sales promotion. This discussion has not dwelled on possible "economies of large-scale promotion," in part because the proper term would be "advantages" rather than "economies"— cost additions rather than savings generally being associated with sales promotion. The question nevertheless remains as to whether there are systematic advantages to firms in large-scale sales promotion programs and expenditures. The evidence is largely negative. Although it is true that, in industries selling differentiated products, large established firms are frequently able to maintain large market shares with smaller sales-promotion costs per unit of sales than those incurred by smaller firms to maintain smaller shares of the market, it is not generally true that the smaller firms can match the advantaged position of the larger ones by simply increasing their sales-promotion outlays. In effect, there is no unique functional relationship between size of promotional outlays and volume of sales, exploitable by all firms, comparable to the unique relationship between scale of plant and production costs. The term "economies of large-scale sales promotion" is thus inherently misleading (Bain 1956a, pp. 339–343).

The foregoing discussion has emphasized the fact that although appreciable economies of large-scale plant are encountered at least in manufacturing, as well as some slight economies of multiplant firms, they are not important enough quantitatively to justify high degrees of plant and firm concentration in the great majority of manufacturing industries in the United States. It is still true, however, that plants of absolutely very large size are required for efficiency in many lines of manufacturing and that substantially smaller plants suffer diseconomies of insufficient scale. Various findings which have been made to the effect that the smallest plants and one-plant firms in most manufacturing industries are, or can be, as efficient as or more efficient than plants and firms of larger sizes generally rest on statistical misinterpretation of defective cost data and of irrelevant profit data (see, for example, U.S. Federal Trade Commission 1941, pp. 12–92; Kaplan 1948, chapter 5) and can at present be regarded as thoroughly invalidated. Inefficiencies of unduly small-scale plants indeed exist, and, as noted above, are encountered in an inefficient fringe of firms in most manufacturing industries.

Much has of necessity been left unsaid about scale economies, particularly concerning their importance in industries outside the manufacturing sector. Scattered evidence suggests that economies of large-scale plant are exceedingly important in most public-utility industries and have some importance in construction industries. Significant economies of the large-scale firm are definitely encountered in some of the distributive trades, including especially the food-distribution industry. We lack systematic data, however, to support a general appraisal of the importance of scale economies in these sectors.

JOE S. BAIN

[*See also* INDUSTRIAL CONCENTRATION.]

BIBLIOGRAPHY

BAIN, JOE S. 1952 *Price Theory.* Rev. & enl. ed. New York: Holt. → The first edition was published in 1948.
BAIN, JOE S. 1956a Advantages of the Large Firm: Production, Distribution and Sales Promotion. *Journal of Marketing* 20:336–346.
BAIN, JOE S. 1956b *Barriers to New Competition: Their Character and Consequence in Manufacturing Industries.* Harvard University Series on Competition in American Industry, No. 3. Cambridge, Mass.: Harvard Univ. Press.
BAIN, JOE S. 1966 *International Differences in Industrial Structure.* New Haven: Yale Univ. Press.
BOULDING, KENNETH E. (1941) 1955 *Economic Analysis.* 3d ed. New York: Macmillan. → A fourth revised edition was published in 1966 by Harper.
KAPLAN, ABRAHAM D. H. 1948 *Small Business: Its Place and Problems.* New York: McGraw-Hill.
ROBINSON, EDWARD A. G. (1931) 1959 *The Structure of Competitive Industry.* Rev. ed. Univ. of Chicago Press.
STIGLER, GEORGE J. (1946) 1966 *The Theory of Price.* Rev. ed. New York: Macmillan.
U.S. FEDERAL TRADE COMMISSION 1941 *Relative Efficiency of Large, Medium-sized, and Small Business.* U.S. Temporary National Economic Committee, Investigations of Concentration of Power, Monograph No. 13. Washington: Government Printing Office.
VINER, JACOB (1931) 1952 Cost Curves and Supply Curves. Pages 198–232 in American Economic Association, *Readings in Price Theory.* Homewood, Ill.: Irwin. → First published in Volume 3 of the *Zeitschrift für Nationalökonomie.*

ECONOMY, DUAL

About the turn of the century, Dutch politicians and scholars interested in the economic condition of the East Indian colony—now called Indonesia—were confronted with a baffling situation. According to the economic views generally held by Dutch economists in the last decades of the nineteenth century, the unhampered development of free enterprise should have favored not only the European plantation owners but eventually the Javanese peasantry as well. The establishment of Western-style, rationally operated plantations should have had a stimulating effect on the peasants, encouraging them to cultivate crops for the world market after the example of the European planters.

About 1900, however, it was clear that the liberal policy had failed, and it was officially recognized that a state of "diminishing welfare" prevailed in the East Indies. Dutch economists started to investigate the causes of the failure, and they asked themselves to what extent the main theses of classical economics were valid for the economic situation in tropical colonies.

In 1910, the young Dutch economist J. H. Boeke, in his doctoral dissertation, denied that the tenets of the classical school were at all applicable to tropical colonial conditions and posited the need for a separate theoretical approach to the specific problems of what today would be called the underdeveloped territories (Koninklijk Instituut 1961, pp. 8 ff.).

In so doing, Boeke inaugurated a prolonged discussion on the fundamentals of economic dualism in underdeveloped territories, a discussion that has continued until the present day.

Boeke's theory. On closer investigation of Boeke's argument, the basis for his dualistic theory (not only in his dissertation, but in his later work as well) proves to be a distinction between "economic" and "social" needs. While economic activity in the West, according to prevailing economic theory, was based on the all-powerful stimulus of economic needs, the Indonesian peasant, according to Boeke, was guided fundamentally by social needs. On this basis, Boeke has evolved a dualistic theory, the core of which is that the economic laws that were found valid for capitalistic society are not applicable to societies in which capitalism lives side by side with a peasant economy still largely ruled by precapitalistic relationships. It was Boeke's view that the introduction of mature capitalism into a precapitalist peasant economy not only disturbed the equilibrium of the latter economic system, but obstructed the gradual development of capitalistic forms comparable to those in the evolution of the Western economy.

In Boeke's view, this type of dualism prevailed in politically independent countries outside the Western world as well as in colonial territories. He included southeastern Europe and the whole of Asia, Africa, and Latin America in this dualistic world, not even excepting Japan. Therefore, even if, in a specific region, an end were put to colonial rule and political independence were achieved, this would not put an end to economic dualism: indigenous capitalists are as far removed from the precapitalist peasant society as foreign ones.

Today, hardly any scholar acquainted with the evolution of theoretical economics during the past decades will find the theoretical formulation of Boeke's views acceptable. The Dutch economist P. Hennipman, for example, sharply attacked the distinction between economic and noneconomic needs, which indeed he pronounced untenable (Koninklijk Instituut 1961, pp. 21–24). Boeke's comparison between Western and non-Western society was not based on a profound intrinsic knowledge of the former; he compared Indonesian society, which he really knew, with a picture of Western society based on the assumption of an all-pervading dominance of a fictitious *homo economicus.* Scholars better acquainted with Western society, among them agronomists who knew the Dutch countryside well, argued that many phenomena considered by Boeke to be typical of "dualistic" societies could be found in rural areas of western Europe as well.

Still, the lack of validity of Boeke's theoretical assumptions hardly detracts from the significance of many of his factual observations, if these are stripped of their too absolute formulation. As a general typology of most nonindustrial societies, Boeke's analysis remains fully relevant. One of his main arguments against the application of Western economic theory to phenomena in the rural sphere of tropical dependencies is the inefficacy there of all kinds of economic incentives. Although the "inverse elasticity of supply" (the decrease of economic effort in the face of higher profits or higher wages), considered by Boeke to be typically dualistic, may be well known in Western societies as the "backward-sloping supply curve," still the general lack of response in non-Western rural societies to all kinds of economic stimuli, official pressures, and expert advice remains one of the crucial problems in the modern world.

There exists a sharp cleavage between those countries that have been able to achieve economic maturity in the past and those that are still in a preindustrial stage. Notwithstanding its theoretical weaknesses, Boeke's analysis of actual conditions in those nonindustrial countries still contains a valid challenge for the present time.

Boeke's views on policy. As far as practical policy is concerned, Boeke's dualism, in the more extreme formulation presented in his later works, comes down to the thesis that in nonindustrial countries, because of the unbridgeable gulf between those elements actively engaged in capitalistic enterprise and the rural masses still living in a pre-capitalistic economy, the road toward gradual development is blocked (Boeke 1946). The latecomers in the race for economic advancement play against odds that exceed by far the obstacles overcome by the Western world in the past. According to Boeke, the historical processes of the past century, which amounted to a subservience and subordination of the precapitalistic countryside to the interests of an energetic and expansive capitalism, have obstructed a spontaneous growth of capitalistic forms in those areas. In essence, Boeke's argument is directed against any cheap belief in a smooth evolution. His works were an antidote to the rosy optimism prevailing in United Nations circles and elsewhere in the late 1940s.

The core of Boeke's factual analysis is formed by his view that in densely populated areas like the island of Java no actual economic development occurs. At best, one could speak of "static expansion"—a spread of existing patterns of land use and economic relationships over an ever-widening territory (Boeke 1953, p. 174). The increase in aggregate production is fully drained off by a congruent increase in population, thus preventing any attempt to raise per capita production.

At present, the vicious circle characteristic of the actual state of the rural economy in underdeveloped countries is being more generally recognized. It becomes increasingly clear that any assumption that a rise in production will automatically result in saving and investment is unrealistic and that still less realistic would be an assumption that investment will automatically involve a rise in production. Any planning that starts from a preconception about valid input–output ratios in underdeveloped areas misreads the actual conditions in the countryside. What is needed is not a purely economic approach based on some arbitrary mathematical model; one should first acquire an insight into the sociological preconditions for economic development. Boeke's dualistic approach essentially forms a first attempt in this direction, although he wrongly expressed his theory in economic instead of sociological terms. Only very recently have sociologists started to provide economists with the background information needed to build a relevant model.

Geertz's agricultural involution.   The idea that Boeke launched as the concept of "static expansion" has been elaborated by the American cultural anthropologist Clifford Geertz in much greater detail, and in a somewhat different sense, as the phenomenon of "agricultural involution." Geertz holds that actual developments in the countryside of Java

were contrary to what should be considered an evolutionary pattern. There was increasing tenacity and internal elaboration of basic social patterns; tenure systems grew more intricate; tenancy relationships more complicated; cooperative labor arrangements more complex—all in an effort to provide everyone a basis, however small, for living in the over-all system (Geertz 1963, p. 82). The size of the individual farm remained Lilliputian.

A social system that Geertz calls "shared poverty" developed, stressing social justice and obstructing efficiency and economic progress. The way the Javanese peasantry manage to keep alive and abreast of the population increase in a process of steady intensification of traditional farming and a progressive elaboration of repetitive basic patterns amounts, according to Geertz, to "treading water."

There are some differences between Boeke's and Geertz's analyses. Although both of them view the outcome—the existing impasse—as a consequence of a historical process, Geertz stresses the colonial factor more than Boeke did. Accordingly, his interpretation of the Japanese case is different from Boeke's: in his view, the Japanese economy is no longer dualistic, since a dynamic interaction between the agrarian and the industrial sectors "kept Japan moving and ultimately pushed her over the hump to sustained growth" (1963, p. 135).

The greatest difference between Java and Japan, according to Geertz, is that in Java the increase in output was soon swamped by the attendant spurt in population; in Japan the population relegated to farming remained virtually constant (1963, p. 137).

The difference in approach between Geertz and Boeke also leads to a somewhat different outlook on the future. Boeke's view of an inherent dualism gradually developed into an extreme pessimism. On the basis of the economic theories considered by him to be valid for dualistic societies, Boeke declared the poverty of the masses of Asia unchangeable—at least as far as the densely populated areas are concerned. Instead of aiming at economic development for the rural masses, which is anyhow unattainable, the authorities should put stress on spiritual values. Boeke thus adopted, for the rural masses in these areas, the Gandhian philosophy of "plain living and high thinking" ([1946] 1948, pp. 88–89).

Although Geertz is not less gloomy about the present state and actual trends, he does not endorse this pessimistic conclusion. He once caustically dismissed Boeke's formula as a "combination of plain living and high thinking on the part of the mass and high living and plain thinking on the part of the elite" (1956, p. 160). Although he is not able to show a clear way out of the impasse either, he does not pronounce that all the roads to material progress are blocked forever.

"Betting on the strong." What both Boeke's and Geertz's analyses should make fully clear is that the situation, as it has developed in areas such as Java, precludes any solution that takes for granted that "development" can only be slow and gradual. Yet actual policies are still largely dominated by the philosophy of gradualism. Those who are aware that poverty and ignorance are severe impediments to introducing technical innovations tend to look for specific agents for introducing the innovations needed to increase agricultural per capita production. It is always the more advanced farmers who are almost automatically selected as such agents. It is they who show a greater responsiveness to all kinds of innovations and technical improvements and who are much easier to approach by government agencies or special services. Such a method starts implicitly from the assumption that the advanced farmers will set an example for the backward ones, who are expected to follow the model that they are able to observe from close by. The innovation is intended to spread, like an oil stain, to other layers of rural society. It is this approach that could be called "betting on the strong."

Boeke's view regarding this "betting on the strong" approach has not been too consistent. In 1910, writing on the basis of literature and without personal experience in the colony, he had expressed a distrust of the "well-to-do Natives," among whom were many *hadjis* (the affluent and prestigeful pilgrims to Mecca), as agents for economic development. Their progress would only amount to a situation in which "the rich grow richer and the poor grow poorer" (Koninklijk Instituut 1961, p. 33).

Paradoxically enough, in 1927, Boeke himself, after a prolonged stay in Indonesia, reversed his stand. At that time, he did not see any possibility of promoting native welfare except through the intermediary of a small elite, consisting of "the vigorous, energetic, advanced elements" in Indonesian rural society. Boeke said that these wealthier landowners, working their way upward, should not be blackened and branded as usurers and bloodsuckers (see Koninklijk Instituut 1961, p. 293).

These elements of rural society should be approached, by the specialized welfare agencies, in a way that Boeke called "person-centered." Not compulsion, but patient persuasion should be the method used by the welfare agencies. The effort should not be directed toward the poor masses, in order to achieve specific objectives, but toward individuals differentiating themselves from the mass by certain personal qualities. The basic assumption is,

evidently, that the improvement of native welfare can only be a slow, gradual process. The person-centered welfare policy should be guided, above all, by "faith and patience" (Koninklijk Instituut 1961, p. 298).

In his later publications, when Boeke had lost faith even in a slow process of spreading development, the wealthy "progressive" farmers more or less disappear from the center of his attention. His approach to problems of economic policy becomes truly dualistic, insofar as he has no faith any more in the possibility that the advance of the progressive farmers will slowly extend to the rural masses. A new policy has to be conceived for the latter group; as we have observed, it is the spiritual values that, according to Boeke's teachings in his later years, should be stressed in an approach that he called one of "village reconstruction."

The Indonesian experience. It is interesting to know how the oil-stain approach, actually applied by the agricultural extension service in postwar Indonesia, worked out in practice. As recorded by the capable Dutch rural sociologist H. ten Dam in an article based on a study of the western Java village of Tjibodas in the early 1950s, the fruits of such a policy are far from promising (Koninklijk Instituut 1961, pp. 347–382). In this village, the representatives of the government agencies came into personal contact only with the large landowners, who constitute roughly $1\frac{1}{2}$ per cent of the total village population. It was they who profited most from all the facilities provided by the agricultural extension services. It was they who, through a cooperative society in which they had the largest stake, got, at prices set by the extension service, artificial fertilizers and chemical preparations needed for the cultivation of profitable commercial crops. There was a group of smaller independent farmers with economic holdings, a number of whom attempted to follow the example of large landowners. But even if taken together, the large landowners and the independent farmers do not exceed 10 per cent of the total village population. The great majority, the farm hands and the part-time farmers with uneconomic holdings who have to work for the larger landowners as wage laborers or sharecroppers, do not profit at all from all the innovations introduced in local agriculture.

Boeke's early prophecy appears to have come true: as a consequence of a policy of "betting on the strong," the rich grew richer and the poor grew, if not poorer, then at least more numerous—and more restive.

The Indian experience. In India, whenever the "betting on the strong" approach was attempted, the results were exactly the same as in Java. Dube, in the villages investigated by him, assesses the results of the community development project, as far as the agricultural extension work is concerned, as follows:

A closer analysis of the agricultural extension work itself reveals that nearly 70 per cent of its benefits went to the *élite* group and to the more affluent and influential agriculturists. The gains to poorer agriculturists were considerably smaller. Being suspicious of government officials they did not seek help from the Project as often. . . . For the economic development of this group, as well as for that of the artisans and agricultural labourers, no programmes were initiated by the Project.   (Dube 1958, pp. 82–83)

The main obstacle to the oil-stain effect can be reduced to the obvious cause that following the example of the "progressive farmers" presupposes the possession of sufficient land and capital, besides the required "progressive" outlook and a mental preparedness to follow the example of the "strong" (India [Republic] 1957, vol. 1, p. 81; vol. 3, part 1, pp. 254–255). The small peasants in India are no more able to follow the example of the progressive farmers than their counterparts in Java had been able to follow, in the past, the example of the European planters. Those possessing uneconomic holdings are more likely to be forced, in the long run, to sell their holdings in order to pay off debts. The larger landowners, profiting from technical innovations, may be tempted to extend their holdings; a progressive outlook as far as farming technique is concerned is by no means a guarantee for a progressive outlook concerning principles of social justice.

The prospect is complicated still more by the existence of a large category of landless farm hands. Can they be expected to profit from the improvements in farming techniques, even if they *are* introduced by a wealthier master–landowner? There is a wealth of evidence indicating that, on the average, real wages in rural India have not appreciably increased since the country gained its independence. Against certain local increases of rural employment opportunities, largely as a consequence of the introduction of irrigation works, we have to take into account not only the strong social, political, and economic position of the landowning castes in the countryside, but also the rapid natural increase of the population in the rural areas.

Only if most of the natural increase of the rural population is absorbed into nonagricultural occupations could a slowly mounting productivity per unit of land be turned, in the long run, into higher real wages for agricultural labor, through a raising of per capita production. In order to make mech-

anization of agriculture profitable, the absolute number of people dependent on agriculture would even have to be reduced, except insofar as a reclamation of wastelands could increase the total cultivated area. But even the former condition—an approximately stationary population engaged in farming—is far from being realized in most parts of India, since urbanization and industrialization are developing much too slowly to be able to reduce considerably the percentage of the total population employed in agriculture, let alone to absorb the natural increase.

The conclusion to be drawn from this constellation is obvious. Modern farm techniques are not likely to spread in a situation in which cheap agricultural labor is abundant. The gains to be derived from "community development" largely aimed at the "progressive farmers" will predominantly accrue to a restricted landowning group. A "betting on the strong" policy is likely to amount to a policy of "the devil take the hindmost."

In countries where the hindmost are restricted in numbers, a large proportion of them may be driven away from the countryside to seek employment in an urban area; the remaining ones may, if they are not too numerous in comparison with the land surface available for cultivation, profit in the long run from the increased productivity per surface area and eventually learn improved farming techniques from the more prosperous farmers.

But in countries where the hindmost form a large majority, either as peasants with uneconomic holdings or as landless laborers, the "betting on the strong" policy cannot work. The large masses of the rural population are, for the time being, tied to their traditional rural occupations as farm hands or sharecroppers, which means that a gradual oil-stainlike spread of modern farming techniques to them is out of the question. These poor masses form a drag upon any attempt to solve the rural problem in a gradual way.

Involution, evolution, and revolution.   From the foregoing, it appears that sociology has not yet been able to establish a way to break through the rural impasse. It is important, however, that some scholars have been able to analyze its main causes. Their analyses may provide a more consistent and more refined way of defining the pre-take-off situation with which both economists and politicians are concerned. Rather than Boeke's concept of dualism, Geertz's concept of "involution" appears to be the crucial one. But, at the same time, this concept may point the way toward a solution of what seemed to Boeke to be an inherent and permanent dualism. If the prevailing process is one of involution, it is clear why a gradual evolution is out of the question. Sociologists and political scientists should investigate if the only response to the challenge of involution should not be "revolution"—in the sense of a thorough reversal of the prevailing trends. Some thought should be given as to what extent such a revolution would use the substitution for the "betting on the strong" approach of one of "betting on the many," who, mainly through organization and intensive education toward efficiency and self-reliance, will be made strong.

Boeke held that any innovations brought about by pressure were of no avail and that the only viable approach could be a personal one, based on persuasion and directed to the "happy few." But if persuasion and education could be combined with activating the masses, which was never seriously attempted in a colonial setting, the outcome of such an approach might prove much more promising, even though a certain amount of pressure would be needed.

Therefore the problems, if not the theoretical cadre and the solutions forwarded by Boeke in connection with the dualism prevailing in many parts of the world, are still as topical as they were fifty years ago.

W. F. WERTHEIM

[See also ASIAN SOCIETY, article on SOUTHEAST ASIA; DIFFUSION, articles on THE DIFFUSION OF INNOVATIONS and INTERPERSONAL INFLUENCE; ECONOMIC ANTHROPOLOGY; ECONOMIC GROWTH, article on NONECONOMIC ASPECTS.]

BIBLIOGRAPHY

BOEKE, JULIUS H. (1946) 1948 The Interests of the Voiceless Far East: Introduction to Oriental Economics. Rev. & enl. ed. Leiden (Netherlands): Universitaire Pers Leiden. → First published as Oosterse economie.

BOEKE, JULIUS H. 1953 Economics and Economic Policy of Dual Societies as Exemplified by Indonesia. New York: Institute of Pacific Relations. → Revised and enlarged version of the author's two earlier studies: The Structure of the Netherlands Indian Economy (1942) and The Evolution of the Netherlands Indies Economy (1946).

DUBE, S. C. 1958 India's Changing Villages: Human Factors in Community Development. London: Routledge.

GEERTZ, CLIFFORD 1956 The Social Context of Economic Change: An Indonesian Case Study. Unpublished manuscript, M.I.T., Center for International Studies.

GEERTZ, CLIFFORD 1963 Agricultural Involution: The Process of Ecological Change in Indonesia. Association of Asian Studies, Monographs and Papers, No. 11. Berkeley: Univ. of California Press.

HIGGINS, BENJAMIN H. (1955) 1956 The "Dualistic Theory" of Underdeveloped Areas. Economic Development and Cultural Change 4:99–115. → A revised and condensed version of an article first published in Volume 8 of Ekonomie dan kerrangan Indonesia.

INDIA (REPUBLIC), COMMITTEE ON PLAN PROJECTS 1957 Report of the Team for the Study of Community Projects and National Extension Service. 3 vols. New Delhi: Manager of Publications.

KONINKLIJK INSTITUUT VOOR DE TROPEN 1961 Indonesian Economics: The Concept of Dualism in Theory and Policy. The Hague: van Hoeve. → A collection of essays and addresses by Dutch authors, including J. H. Boeke, on economic dualism, with an extensive editorial introduction.

SADLI, MOHAMAD 1957 Some Reflections on Prof. Boeke's Theory of Dualistic Economics. Economics and Finance in Indonesia 10:363–384.

WERTHEIM, W. F. (1964) 1965 East–West Parallels: Sociological Approaches to Modern Asia. Chicago: Quadrangle Books. → A collection of essays, the final one dealing in detail with the "betting on the strong" approach.

ECONOMY AND SOCIETY

The discipline of economics commonly focuses on only one aspect of social life—how people employ scarce resources to produce, distribute, and exchange goods and services for consumption. Economists acknowledge that there are other aspects—political, legal, educational, for instance—and that these aspects influence economic life significantly. However, they usually assume that, for purposes of economic analysis, these influences are constant and thus do not modify economic processes; or, as it is often put, tastes and institutions are "given." By thus limiting the number of variables they study, economists have been able to advance their science, but they have also greatly oversimplified the relations between economic and other types of social variables.

The field of economic sociology relaxes, as it were, these stringent assumptions about the relations between economic and other types of social variables and explicitly focuses on explaining variations in the ways these different types of variables impinge on one another. For example, in studying wages the economist concentrates mainly on the features of the market that influence and are influenced by wage levels, whereas the sociologist inquires into a wider range of causes and consequences. If management, for instance, persistently tinkers with wage levels, the sociologist may find out that this strengthens informal cliques of workmen and inclines them to subvert the authority of management; or it may foster the formation of a labor union or excite activity on the part of an existing one. Both these social consequences may then themselves "feed back" and influence the level of wages.

Economic sociology. The relations between economic and other social variables may be studied at three levels. At the most concrete level, the economic sociologist applies the standard tools of sociology to the study of roles and organizations that specialize in economic activities. He may, for example, study the sources of recruitment, career patterns, life styles, and role strains of skilled workers in an industrial firm; or he may study the organization of the firm itself, analyzing the status systems, power and authority relations, patterns of deviance, cliques and coalitions, and the relations among these phenomena.

At the second level, the economic sociologist analyzes the relations between economic structures and other structures. The work of Max Weber, especially, exemplifies this level of analysis. In particular, Weber was preoccupied with the conditions under which industrial capitalism of the modern Western type could arise and flourish. Initially, he was careful to distinguish between industrial capitalism and other forms, such as finance capitalism and colonial capitalism; industrial capitalism refers to the systematic and rational organization of *production* itself. Having identified industrial capitalism, Weber sought to identify the historical conditions most conducive to its rise and continuing existence. One of his most famous arguments is that the rise of ascetic Protestantism, especially Calvinism, established social and psychological conditions conducive to this particular form of capitalism (1904–1905). Another well-known argument developed by Weber is that bureaucracy provides the most rational form of social organization for perpetuating industrial capitalism (1922). He also found in the political–legal complex, especially in property laws and monetary systems, many other institutional structures conducive to industrial capitalism.

Weber never developed his economic sociology into a full theoretical system. Rather, he remained at the level of generating historical insights about the pattern of institutional structures surrounding important economic phenomena. Even so, it is possible to see his distinctive contribution to economic sociology. Unlike traditional economists, Weber was not interested in the regularities produced *within* the capitalist system of production (regularities such as the business cycle); instead, he was interested in establishing the important institutional conditions under which capitalist systems —and their regularities—came into being.

At the third, most abstract, level the economic sociologist considers the economic and other types of social variables as organized into analytic systems, which cut across concrete social structures, and he studies the relations among these systems. This approach is exemplified in the works of Tal-

cott Parsons and Neil J. Smelser (see Parsons 1937; Parsons & Smelser 1956; Smelser 1963). The economic system, for example, consists of suppliers of factors of production, producers, and consumers, none of which should be identified with any particular social structure but all of which can be viewed, at this abstract level, as interacting with one another in a network of markets. Furthermore, the economic system interacts with other social systems. For example, the economy provides wage payments and consumer goods and services in exchange for the motivation and skills, so necessary for a viable labor force, that are generated by the "pattern-maintenance" social system, which includes familial, educational, and specialized-training structures.

The economy and cultural factors

By culture is meant that complex of existential and evaluational symbols which provide meaning and legitimacy to the conduct of social life. Concrete cultural items are cosmologies, values, ideologies, aesthetic productions, and scientific knowledge. The economic sociologist is concerned with the ways in which these symbols facilitate or inhibit various types of economic activity and the ways in which economic behavior leads to modifications of cultural symbols.

Little research has been conducted on the role of cultural factors *within* economic organizations. What has been done focuses mainly on problems of effective communication. One of the persistent problems of bureaucracies, for example, is the disruption that occurs when necessary information is altogether lacking, withheld, distorted in passage, or too slow in arriving. Numerous studies of industrial bureaucracy have uncovered typical points of distortion and omission: subordinates "cover up" information they do not wish their superiors to know, and foremen "soften" orders from above out of sympathy with workmen. [*See* ORGANIZATIONS, *article on* ORGANIZATIONAL INTELLIGENCE.]

Stimulated mainly by the Marxian and Weberian traditions, sociologists have conducted a more substantial amount of research on the relations *between* economic organization and cultural symbols. Some research, such as that of Robert N. Bellah on Tokugawa Japan (1957), focuses directly on Weber's problem concerning the ways in which religious beliefs stimulate or inhibit economic development. Other scholars have inquired into the relations between ideologies and economic activity. The most thorough study of ideologies as instruments of social control in industry is the comparative research of Reinhard Bendix (1956) on managerial ideologies as they have developed in four industrializing countries—Great Britain, the United States, Russia, and East Germany. Bendix's main concern is with the justifications that managerial classes have generated in the process of inducing workers to submit to their authority. The effects of ideology in relieving role-strains are emphasized in a study of the American business creed by Francis Sutton and his associates (1956). These investigators attribute the tenacity of the free-enterprise ideology among businessmen to strains in their roles: for example, their own ambivalence toward the phenomenon of bigness in the American economy is smoothed over by a defiant reassertion of the values of traditional free enterprise. Ely Chinoy's study of automobile workers (1955) also stresses the frustration-reducing elements of ideology, which often serves to rationalize the discrepancies between the expectations generated by the "American dream" of equality of opportunity and the actual life situations of the workers.

The economy and solidary groupings

Solidary groupings include families, friendship groups, and diffuse collectivities, such as neighborhood, racial, and ethnic groupings. Solidary groupings, which occupy an important place in the integrative system of society, are typically characterized by face-to-face interaction and close personal understandings and loyalties among members. The economic sociologist asks how these groupings influence, and are influenced by, economic behavior.

Industrial sociology. Recognition of the importance of solidary groupings *within* industrial organizations is closely associated with the rise of the "human-relations" approach in industrial sociology during the interwar period. Before the rise of this school, industrial sociology in the United States was mainly under the influence of the "scientific-management" approach associated with the name of Frederick W. Taylor. According to this approach, workers in industrial organizations can be treated primarily as isolated neurophysiological organisms with definite capacities and skills; their efficiency, moreover, is largely a product of such factors as speed of work, amount of effort expended, and amount of rest allowed for recovery of strength. The scientific-management school more or less ignored the social-psychological determinants of morale and efficiency.

In the mid-1920s, when the famous Hawthorne experiments on productivity began in the Western Electric Company in Chicago, the initial emphasis was on the effects of various nonsocial factors (lighting and rest periods, for example) on worker performance. During the course of the experiments, however, it became apparent to the investigators that these "physical" factors were not nearly so important in fostering high morale and productivity as various "human" factors, such as receiving status, being accepted in a meaningful primary group, and being allowed to express grievances to a patient and responsive authority. The investigators, in short, isolated the solidary grouping as a determinant of economic behavior (see Roethlisberger & Dickson 1939). Further experiments conducted in the Bank Wiring Room revealed that cliques of workmen could also affect productivity adversely by setting and enforcing their own informal standards of production rates, which were different from those established by management. These kinds of findings have given rise to a whole tradition of research on the diverse relations between the formal and informal organizations within a bureaucracy and on how these relations affect organizational functioning. [See ORGANIZATIONS, article on THEORIES OF ORGANIZATIONS.]

Family structure. Most research on the relations *between* economic organization and solidary groupings concerns the ways in which certain kinds of family structure may facilitate or inhibit economic activity. For example, primogeniture may facilitate the formation of an urban-industrial labor force, since this type of inheritance system ejects younger sons from the land and makes them possible candidates for other lines of employment; thus, research by Conrad M. Arensberg and Solon T. Kimball (1940) found that younger sons constituted many of the migrants in rural Ireland. On the other hand, certain types of family life may inhibit economic activity. David Landes (1951) has argued that the peculiar structure of the French business family has kept the typical firm small and has thus inhibited economic growth. In his study of the Chinese family (1949), Marion J. Levy isolated the factors of particularism, favoritism, and functional diffuseness as features of classical Chinese kinship that tended to inhibit industrialization.

With respect to the influence of urban-industrial life on the family, most research in the interwar period—for example, the work of Ernest W. Burgess and Harvey J. Locke (see Burgess et al. 1945) —was based on the assumption that urbanization and industrialization lead to the isolation and disintegration of the family. More recent research has challenged or modified this thesis. Talcott Parsons has argued that the urban-industrial complex does not cause the family to deteriorate but rather gives rise to a more highly specialized, and in some ways more effective, family system (Parsons et al.

1955). In a massively documented study, William J. Goode (1963) has attempted to demonstrate and explain the fact that the conjugal nuclear family is the more-or-less universal concomitant of modernization.

Studies of consumption. In one respect the economists' traditional concern with personal consumption reflects a preoccupation with the relations between solidary groupings and the economy, since this type of consumption commonly refers to the demands made by the household sector on the production sector. Throughout most of the history of economic thought, scholars have postulated some rather simple psychological principles that are assumed to govern consumers' behavior—principles such as the hedonistic calculus, diminishing marginal utility, or indifference-curve maps. Manifestly, however, as the work of Thorstein Veblen has so well demonstrated, social position and attitudes directly affect tastes and, by implication, make for variation in individual and aggregate consumption functions (Veblen 1899). In recent decades economists and sociologists have attempted to mobilize a number of social and psychological variables to explain differential consumption and saving patterns. James Duesenberry, for example, formally incorporates a principle of imitative spending into his theory of consumer behavior (1949). Milton Friedman posits age and composition of family as determinants of tastes, which in turn affect the consumption function (1957). George Katona, using the survey method, has undertaken to study consumer attitudes extensively and to predict consumer behavior from these attitudes (1951; 1960). Finally, sociologists and economists have produced a plethora of empirical studies showing how social-structural variables such as age, stage in family cycle, race, home-ownership status, and degree of urbanization determine spending and saving patterns. On the whole, these efforts have not produced a formally adequate theory of consumption that systematically incorporates social-structural variables. The closest approximation to such a theory is found in the work of Guy H. Orcutt and his associates (1961), who have introduced variables such as marital status and duration of marriage, as well as age, education, and race of head of household, into probability models of spending and saving behavior.

Role differentiation and stratification

From at least the time of Adam Smith, who paid particular attention to the division of labor as a determinant of the wealth of a nation, economists have recognized the importance of role differentiation in economic life. By and large, however, their concern has been restricted to the relations between the specialization of labor and economic variables, such as productivity, wage differentials, the distribution of the shares of income, and selected aspects of labor–management relations. Sociologists have introduced more and different kinds of variables into the analysis of occupations and, in particular, have focused explicitly on the organization of differentiated roles into stratified systems.

Economists' versions of the attitudes and behavior of individuals in occupational roles generally follow the logic of supply and demand. They assume that the amount of work a person offers in the market is some function of the economic rewards available to him. While a number of different labor-supply functions have been advanced, most of these ignore the effects on the worker of social factors other than economic incentives. By contrast, sociologists conceive of roles (including occupational roles) as organized clusters of activities involving interaction with the physical, social, and cultural environments. These activities are structured and regulated by values, norms, and sanctions. Economic rewards and deprivations are important, but they constitute only one of several types of sanctions. Roles, furthermore, are subject to a number of types of strains, reactions to which influence the incumbent's attitudes and behavior. In analyzing the foreman's role in industry, for example, sociologists have discovered that his role is subject to considerable strains because it has been emasculated in past decades in two important ways: first, centralized management of control has made him less an independent authority over production and more an implementor of ready-made decisions; second, the centralization of the handling of grievances in the unions has relieved him of certain "human-relations" functions. The foreman, caught in a role that is simultaneously limited in function and beset by cross-pressures, often wavers between identification with management, with workers, and with other foremen (Leiter 1948). Contemporary sociological research has yielded similar types of descriptions and analyses of behavior in executive, professional, worker, and miscellaneous service roles.

Above and beyond wage conditions and level of prosperity, which are perhaps the most important determinants, economists and sociologists have uncovered a number of variables that influence labor turnover and absenteeism (for example, see Parnes 1954). Social factors influencing turnover are occupation (the average turnover of teachers, for instance, is much lower than that of factory workers); age (older workers tend to change jobs less often than younger workers); sex (women move in and out of the labor force more than men but probably do not move geographically and occupationally so much); and race (Negro men tend to change jobs more often than white men). Some of the conditions that affect absenteeism, besides wages, are distance of residence from plant; size of firm (which is undoubtedly related to morale); occurrence of holidays (absenteeism drops just before holidays); age (young men display absenteeism more than old); marital status (single men are absent more than married men); and arduousness of work (which encourages absenteeism). [See LABOR FORCE, *article on* MARKETS AND MOBILITY.]

Stratification systems.   Much of the sociological research on role differentiation *within* economic organizations has concerned the relations between formal and informal organization (reviewed above). In addition, sociologists have studied status systems of industrial organizations and their relations to behavior. As a general rule, status in an organization is determined by the degree of skill, the level of authority and responsibility, and the level of remuneration of an occupational position. However, additional criteria that are imported from "outside" the workplace, such as age, sex, and racial or ethnic background, affect the status of the individual in the organization.

Because of the multiplicity of determinants of general status, individuals in organizations frequently experience a sense of ambiguity as to their actual status (Homans 1953). This leads to a focus on the symbolic aspects of status, such as the number of telephones or amount of floor space per office. Many conflicts in organizations revolve around the distribution of symbols rather than the distribution of the determinants of status underlying these symbols. Another characteristic of industrial organizations that arises from the multiplicity of determinants of status is the tendency toward "status crystallization"—that is, bringing all aspects of status roughly into line with one another. If an individual is paid much for performing a low-skill job, for example, dissatisfactions both for him and his fellow workers, as well as pressures to balance wage and skill levels, arise. This tendency for all aspects of status to be brought into line underlies many conflicts in industrial settings: for example, opposition to promoting a young executive too rapidly for his age and experience, to placing women in positions of authority, and to elevating Negroes to high-level jobs.

With respect to the relations *between* economic systems and stratification systems, two strands of research dominate the contemporary scene. The first, stemming from the Marxian tradition, con-cerns the degree to which specific types of economic systems appear to give rise to distinctive types of stratification systems. Alex Inkeles and Peter Rossi (1956), for instance, found that in a number of industrialized nations, occupations associated with industrial production (engineer, foreman, machine worker, etc.) were assigned very similar positions in the general prestige hierarchy of occupations. The second strand of research, stemming perhaps from an ideological preoccupation with equality of opportunity, concerns the degree to which rates of upward social mobility increase or decrease in industrial society. Basing their case on extensive comparative data, Seymour M. Lipset and Reinhard Bendix (1959) argued that rates of social mobility are very similar in all the industrial societies of the West and that these similarities are traceable to common features of the occupational structures of these societies. Additional research, the most conspicuous of which is the work of Natalie Rogoff (for example, 1953), concerns the degree to which opportunities for upward mobility are "closing" under conditions of advanced industrial development in the United States.

The economy and political factors

The term "political" here refers to the creation, institutionalization, and utilization of power in a social setting. Defined this broadly, the term encompasses the study of authority systems in organizations, the study of governments, and the study of competition and conflict among groups. The economic sociologist is concerned with studying the mutual relations between economic activities and these diverse political phenomena.

Most studies of authority systems *within* industrial firms involve the relations between the types of supervision (typically described in terms of an authoritarian–democratic dimension) and worker morale, productivity, and receptivity to innovations. The most common finding is that worker morale and productivity are higher under "employee-centered" leadership than under leadership oriented to technical standards of efficiency (Viteles 1953). Most of the experiments and field studies on supervision have been carried out in countries with democratic traditions, especially the United States and Great Britain; obviously, studies of societies with different political traditions might show different results.

Research on the political relations *between* economic organizations and other social units has advanced on a variety of fronts. Under the heading of "the economics of imperfect competition," economists have studied a variety of political involvements of business firms: ways in which large firms are able to control, and perhaps dominate, prices and output under monopolistic conditions; ways in which wealth and power become concentrated in the economy; and ways in which government policies (e.g., antitrust policies) influence the structure and behavior of firms (for example, Mason 1959). Economists and sociologists have devoted a modest amount of research to the power relations between stockholders and managers and between consumers and business firms, but far more research has been done on the power relations and conflicts between business firms and labor unions. In particular, scholars have devoted much study to the causes of labor disputes (see Kornhauser et al. 1954; Knowles 1952). Some causes have been fairly well established: strikes occur more frequently under conditions of prosperity, more frequently in isolated industries with homogeneous worker populations, and less frequently under totalitarian governments and in periods of national crisis.

Finally, much contemporary research and discussion focuses on the relations between business and government. This research is shrouded in ideological controversy and confused findings. One school of thought, advanced by the late C. Wright Mills (1956), argues that national political power in the United States has become increasingly concentrated in recent decades and that the holders of power and makers of important decisions are a small group of corporate executives and military officials; this view, however, has been challenged on both methodological and substantive grounds. The empirical research on economic controls over local politics also shows a mixed picture. For example, in a study of a Southern community, Floyd Hunter (1953) concluded that the major decisions were guided by a small group of economically dominant individuals. Other research—for example, that of Delbert Miller (1958) and Robert Schulze (1958)—indicates that the degree to which business groups dominate local politics varies considerably from community to community and over time.

NEIL J. SMELSER

[*Directly related are the entries* ECONOMIC THOUGHT; INDUSTRIAL RELATIONS; INDUSTRIALIZATION; SYSTEMS ANALYSIS, *article on* SOCIAL SYSTEMS. *Other relevant material may be found in* CONSUMERS; ECONOMY, DUAL; PEASANTRY; *and in the biographies of* BARNARD; DURKHEIM; KEYNES, JOHN MAYNARD; LE PLAY; MARSHALL; MARX; PARETO; SMITH, ADAM; SOMBART; WEBER, MAX.]

BIBLIOGRAPHY

ARENSBERG, CONRAD M.; and KIMBALL, SOLON T. (1940) 1961 *Family and Community in Ireland*. Gloucester, Mass.: Smith.

BALDWIN, GEORGE B. 1955 *Beyond Nationalization: The Labor Problems of British Coal*. Cambridge, Mass.: Harvard Univ. Press.

BELLAH, ROBERT N. 1957 *Tokugawa Religion: The Values of Pre-industrial Japan*. Glencoe, Ill.: Free Press.

BENDIX, REINHARD 1956 *Work and Authority in Industry: Ideologies of Management in the Course of Industrialization*. New York: Wiley.

BURGESS, ERNEST W.; LOCKE, HARVEY J.; and THOMAS, MARY M. (1945) 1963 *The Family: From Institution to Companionship*. 3d ed. New York: American Book Co.

CHINOY, ELY 1955 *Automobile Workers and the American Dream*. Garden City, N.Y.: Doubleday.

DUESENBERRY, JAMES S. 1949 *Income, Saving, and the Theory of Consumer Behavior*. Harvard Economic Studies, Vol. 87. Cambridge, Mass.: Harvard Univ. Press.

FRIEDMAN, MILTON 1957 *A Theory of the Consumption Function*. National Bureau of Economic Research General Series, No. 63. Princeton Univ. Press.

GALBRAITH, JOHN K. (1952) 1956 *American Capitalism: The Concept of Countervailing Power*. 2d ed., rev. Boston: Houghton Mifflin.

GOODE, WILLIAM J. 1963 *World Revolution and Family Patterns*. New York: Free Press.

HOMANS, GEORGE C. 1953 Status Among Clerical Workers. *Human Organization* 12:5–10.

HUNTER, FLOYD 1953 *Community Power Structure: A Study of Decision Makers*. Chapel Hill: Univ. of North Carolina Press. → A paperback edition was published in 1963 by Doubleday.

INKELES, ALEX; and ROSSI, PETER H. 1956 National Comparisons of Occupational Prestige. *American Journal of Sociology* 61:329–339.

KATONA, GEORGE 1951 *Psychological Analysis of Economic Behavior*. New York: McGraw-Hill. → A paperback edition was published in 1963.

KATONA, GEORGE 1960 *The Powerful Consumer: Psychological Studies of the American Economy*. New York: McGraw-Hill.

KNOWLES, KENNETH G. J. C. 1952 *Strikes: A Study in Industrial Conflict; With Special Reference to British Experience Between 1911 and 1947*. Oxford University, Institute of Statistics, Monograph No. 3. Oxford: Blackwell; New York: Philosophical Library.

KORNHAUSER, ARTHUR; DUBIN, ROBERT; and ROSS, ARTHUR M. (editors) 1954 *Industrial Conflict*. New York: McGraw-Hill.

LANDES, DAVID M. 1951 French Business and the Businessman: A Social and Cultural Analysis. Pages 334–353 in E. M. Earle (editor), *Modern France: Problems of the Third and Fourth Republics*. Princeton Univ. Press.

LEITER, ROBERT DAVID 1948 *The Foreman in Industrial Relations*. New York: Columbia Univ. Press.

LEVY, MARION J. 1949 *The Family Revolution in Modern China*. Cambridge, Mass.: Harvard Univ. Press.

LIPSET, SEYMOUR M.; and BENDIX, REINHARD 1959 *Social Mobility in Industrial Society*. Berkeley: Univ. of California Press.

MASON, EDWARD S. (editor) 1959 *The Corporation in Modern Society*. Cambridge, Mass.: Harvard Univ. Press.

MILLER, DELBERT C. 1958 *Industry and Community Power Structure: A Comparative Study of an American and an English City. American Sociological Review* 23:9–15.

MILLS, C. WRIGHT 1956 *The Power Elite.* New York: Oxford Univ. Press.

NIMKOFF, M. F.; and MIDDLETON, RUSSELL 1960 Types of Family and Types of Economy. *American Journal of Sociology* 66:215–225.

ORCUTT, GUY H. et al. 1961 *Microanalysis of Socioeconomic Systems: A Simulation Study.* New York: Harper.

PARNES, HERBERT S. 1954 *Research on Labor Mobility: An Appraisal of Research Findings in the United States.* Bulletin No. 65. New York: Social Science Research Council.

PARSONS, TALCOTT 1937 *The Structure of Social Action: A Study in Social Theory With Special Reference to a Group of Recent European Writers.* New York: McGraw-Hill.

PARSONS, TALCOTT; and SMELSER, NEIL J. 1956 *Economy and Society: A Study in the Integration of Economic and Social Theory.* Glencoe, Ill.: Free Press.

PARSONS, TALCOTT et al. 1955 *Family, Socialization and Interaction Process.* Glencoe, Ill.: Free Press.

ROETHLISBERGER, FRITZ J.; and DICKSON, WILLIAM J. (1939) 1961 *Management and the Worker: An Account of a Research Program Conducted by the Western Electric Company, Hawthorne Works, Chicago.* Cambridge, Mass.: Harvard Univ. Press. → A paperback edition was published in 1964 by Wiley.

ROGOFF, NATALIE 1953 *Recent Trends in Occupational Mobility.* Glencoe, Ill.: Free Press.

SCHULZE, ROBERT O. 1958 The Role of Economic Dominants in Community Power Structure. *American Sociological Review* 23:3–9.

SMELSER, NEIL J. 1963 *The Sociology of Economic Life.* Englewood Cliffs, N.J.: Prentice-Hall.

SUTTON, FRANCIS X. et al. 1956 *The American Business Creed.* Cambridge, Mass.: Harvard Univ. Press.

VEBLEN, THORSTEIN (1899) 1953 *The Theory of the Leisure Class: An Economic Study of Institutions.* Rev. ed. New York: New American Library. → A paperback edition was published in 1959.

VITELES, MORRIS S. 1953 *Motivation and Morale in Industry.* New York: Norton. → A psychological approach.

WEBER, MAX (1904–1905) 1930 *The Protestant Ethic and the Spirit of Capitalism.* Translated by Talcott Parsons, with a foreword by R. H. Tawney. London: Allen & Unwin; New York: Scribner. → First published in German. The 1930 edition has been reprinted frequently.

WEBER, MAX (1922) 1957 *The Theory of Social and Economic Organization.* Edited by Talcott Parsons. Glencoe, Ill.: Free Press. → First published as Part 1 of *Wirtschaft und Gesellschaft.*

EDGEWORTH, FRANCIS YSIDRO

Francis Ysidro Edgeworth (1845–1926) was raised on the family estate of Edgeworthstown, County Longford, Ireland. His father died when Edgeworth was two years old. Edgeworth studied under tutors and spent considerable time reading and memorizing the classics and English poetry. From an early age he also read widely in Spanish, French, German, and Italian. This interest in Continental literature may well have been strengthened by the fact that his mother was the daughter of a Spanish political refugee. One of Edgeworth's aunts was the famous novelist Maria Edgeworth, and the poet Thomas Lovell Beddoes was his cousin.

At the age of 17, Edgeworth entered Trinity College, Dublin, and then proceeded to Balliol College, Oxford, where he received first class honors in *litterae humaniores.* After several years of practicing law in London, he accepted a lectureship in logic at King's College and was later appointed Tooke professor of political economy.

In 1891 he became Drummond professor of political economy at Oxford and a fellow of All Souls College. Never marrying, he resided principally at All Souls for the remainder of his life, although he maintained rooms in London for over fifty years and inherited the family estate in 1911.

Although he was highly respected as a teacher and original thinker by both economists and statisticians of his time, Edgeworth does not seem to have profoundly influenced the then current thinking in either field. Present readers, however, find much that is stimulating and informative in Edgeworth and not uncommonly note with some surprise that ideas they believe to have originated recently are, sometimes clearly, sometimes vaguely, anticipated in Edgeworth's work.

When he became professor emeritus at Oxford in 1922, Edgeworth was serving his second term as president of the economic section of the British Association and was a vice-president of the Royal Economic Society. He had earlier served as president (1912) and council member of the Royal Statistical Society; he had been awarded its Guy medal in 1907. He was also a fellow of the British Academy.

Undoubtedly, Edgeworth's greatest professional contribution, in addition to teaching and writing, was his editorship of the *Economic Journal.* He became its first editor in 1891 and was later chairman of the editorial board. At the time of his death in 1926, Edgeworth was joint editor with Keynes.

He is reported (L. L. P. 1926) to have been an effective and stimulating teacher, attracting good students and encouraging many vigorous discussions. Frequently he would become one of the less active participants, intervening occasionally to expose an error or to bring a neglected but fruitful problem to the attention of his class.

Edgeworth's main written contributions to economics are contained in seven small books and numerous journal articles and reviews. In 1925 his principal articles and reviews were published in three volumes entitled *Papers Relating to Political Economy* (see 1891–1921) under his own editorship and under the sponsorship of the Royal Economic Society.

Mathematical Psychics, published in 1881, is probably Edgeworth's most important writing. His "contract curve" and its generalization, the set of "Edgeworth-allocations" (Debreu & Scarf 1963; Vind 1964) or "core," are still basic concepts for the theoretical study of exchange equilibrium and welfare economics; and his theory of barter has provided a valuable point of departure for recent research on dynamic economic adjustments (Uzawa 1962). Edgeworth discussed a number of interesting bargaining situations in light of the theory presented.

Edgeworth's arguments in the first section of *Psychics* against the common view that mathematics could be applied only to numerical phenomena were quite advanced and provocative then but will appear awkward and unnecessary to a current reader who has studied set theory and topology. Much of the remainder of the book is concerned with attempts to establish practical implications of utilitarian ethics. These views were, and remain, highly controversial.

Edgeworth's collected works include a group of related papers (1897a; 1897b; 1899; 1911; 1912) on taxation, price discrimination, and monopoly that involve original theoretical developments, which are still of considerable interest. In these papers are a number of famous paradoxes, such as: A tax on one of two monopolized commodities which are appropriately related in production, consumption, or both may cause prices of both commodities to fall; and the introduction of price discrimination into a competitive market might benefit both producers and consumers (where consumer benefit is taken to be aggregate consumer surplus). The 1912 paper contains a very good discussion of the difficulties of establishing a theoretical equilibrium for duopolists or monopolists who sell related commodities. A number of other papers deal with tax problems of Edgeworth's time and with utilitarian principles for determining equitable taxation. Quantitative problems encountered in contemplated applications of utilitarianism are also treated in his first book, *New and Old Methods of Ethics* (1877).

Edgeworth served several years as secretary of the Committee on Value of the Monetary Standard of the British Association for the Advancement of Science. This interest is reflected in ten articles on index numbers and the value of money. Two memoranda prepared for the British Association for the Advancement of Science (1887–1889) contain what can still be regarded as a fairly comprehensive discussion of theoretical problems of index number constructions.

Metretike draws a number of interesting parallels beween utility and its measurement and application, on the one hand, and probability and its measurement and application, on the other (1887a). Although there are some interesting observations, there is no fundamental interrelationship such as that later achieved through the axiom systems of Ramsey, Savage, and others.

The other four of Edgeworth's books are lectures on war finance delivered during the war and immediately afterward (1915a; 1915b; 1917; 1919). These works, like most of his writings on current policy issues, drew more criticism than praise from his colleagues: "[He] might descend eventually on one side or the other of the fence, but, . . . he kept himself so long poised evenly midway that the final movement when, and if, it happened, was apt to be unnoticed" (L. L. P. 1926). Keynes remarked:

He feared a little the philistine comment on the strange but charming amalgam of poetry and pedantry, science and art, wit and learning, of which he had the secret; and he would endeavor, however unsuccessfully, to draw a veil of partial concealment over his native style, which only served, however, to enhance the obscurity and allusiveness and half-apologetic air with which he served up his intellectual dishes. (Keynes [1926] 1963, p. 227)

Some basis for these complaints must be admitted. Even in his theoretical and highly mathematical writings, Edgeworth's expository skill is notably less than his insight and logical ability. The overapologetic tone Keynes mentions is frequently apparent; it is illustrated by Edgeworth's description of his correction of a colleague's misinterpretation as: "points of detail on which the critical shoemaker corrected the masterpiece of the Grecian painter ([1891–1921] 1963, vol. 1, p. 143).

Another factor which frequently led to lengthy and sometimes complicated passages in Edgeworth and drew critical comments from his contemporaries was his desire to account explicitly for every logically possible combination of circumstances. Many current readers are more patient on this score. A more mathematically inclined generation is better aware of the advantages of carefully keeping track of the exact relations that exist between alternative conditions and consequences.

Among Edgeworth's other publications that should be noted are his article on the law of error in the 1902 *Encyclopædia Britannica*, his article on probability in the 1911 edition, and his biography of Mill and article on index numbers in *Palgrave's Dictionary of Political Economy*.

Edgeworth's best-known work on distribution theory is a series which gives an asymptotic approximation to a fairly general class of distribution functions and is still sometimes used (Cramer 1945, pp. 228–231). Under the heading "The law of error," Edgeworth used this series to derive several versions of the central limit theorem and to approximate a number of empirical frequency distributions (1883; 1898–1900; 1905; 1926; and with Bowley, 1902). He also extended Galton's work on correlation, and he developed a formula for the general multivariate normal density, and considered some of its properties (1893; 1905).

Following Bernoulli, Laplace, and Mill, Edgeworth was basically Bayesian in his approach to statistical inference. His "genuine inverse method" (1908–1909) consisted of finding a normal approximation to the posterior distribution of unknown parameters (*quaesita*, or frequency constants, in his terminology), assuming a diffuse prior distribution, and equating the means of the posterior distribution to their maximum likelihood estimates (called "most probable values"). He properly objected to forming a uniform prior on the basis of ignorance, since this would imply a specific non-uniform prior on any transformation of the original parameters. However, as Edgeworth also recognized, any reasonably smooth and unconcentrated prior will lead to results that differ little from those obtained from either a uniform distribution or a diffuse distribution when the number of observations is large. Thus Edgeworth's genuine inverse method was based on some of the same underlying ideas as the theory of stable estimation examined earlier by Fisher and Jeffreys and recently emphasized by Bayesian statisticians (Edwards et al. 1963).

Not all of Edgeworth's work on inference was developed from this approach. He believed the prior distribution would often be unknown and looked for other principles and devices. He discussed the difference of two means (1905; 1908–1909) and the possible significance of an estimate of trend (1886) in language much like that of the Neyman–Pearson theory of hypothesis testing.

Several of Edgeworth's papers are concerned with the problem of the "best" mean (e.g., 1887*a*). This usually means an estimate of a population parameter, optimal according to some stated criterion; but the case of finding a suitable descriptive representative for a collection of empirical data is also considered. A criterion frequently employed is that of minimizing expected loss (called "least detriment" or "minimum disadvantage"), and a number of inquiries proceed under the assumption that all that is known of the loss function is that it is symmetric and an increasing function of the deviation of an estimate from the true value. This assumption led Edgeworth to criticize Laplace for advocating widespread use of least-squares. Edgeworth advocated use of the median in many circumstances. Noting that the median of a univariate sample minimizes the sum of absolute deviations, he developed a method for fitting a straight line to bivariate data to minimize this sum (1923).

Edgeworth never developed his many original contributions to either economics or statistics to make a comprehensive coordinated work. He dealt with questions only dimly understood in his time (many are still controversial and not fully developed), and although he made significant contributions, I suspect that he himself was not satisfied with the state in which he left most of his topics. He was still working with enthusiasm shortly before his death at the age of 81. His work, however, has retained much more interest than that of some who had greater impact on their contemporaries. Modern mathematical economists and statisticians find him a stimulating and reassuring intellectual forebear, surprisingly up-to-date in many respects and still instructive.

CLIFFORD HILDRETH

[*For discussion of the subsequent development of Edgeworth's ideas, see* BAYESIAN INFERENCE; UTILITY.]

WORKS BY EDGEWORTH

1877 *New and Old Methods of Ethics.* London: Parker.

(1881) 1953 *Mathematical Psychics: An Essay on the Application of Mathematics to the Moral Sciences.* New York: Kelley.

1883 The Law of Error. *London, Edinburgh and Dublin Philosophical Magazine and Journal of Science* Fifth Series 16:300–309.

1886 Progressive Means. *Journal of the Royal Statistical Society* [1886]:469–475.

1887*a* *Metretike: Or the Method of Measuring Probability and Utility.* London: Temple.

1887*b* Observations and Statistics: An Essay on the Theory of Errors of Observation and the First Principles of Statistics. Cambridge Philosophical Society, *Transactions* 14, part 2:138–169.

(1887–1889) 1963 Measurement of Change in the Value of Money. Volume 1, pages 195–297 in Francis Ysidro Edgeworth, *Papers Relating to Political Economy.* New York: Franklin. → Consists of two memoranda prepared for the British Association for the Advancement of Science.

(1891–1921) 1963 *Papers Relating to Political Economy.* 3 vols. New York: Franklin. → Contains and reviews articles which appeared in the *Economic Journal . . .* 1891–1921 inclusive.

1893 Exercises in the Calculation of Errors. *London, Edinburgh and Dublin Philosophical Magazine and Journal of Science* Fifth Series 36:98–111.

(1897*a*) 1963 The Pure Theory of Monopoly. Volume 1, pages 111–142 in Francis Ysidro Edgeworth, *Papers Relating to Political Economy.* New York: Franklin. → First published in Italian.

(1897*b*) 1963 The Pure Theory of Taxation. Volume 2, pages 63–125 in Francis Ysidro Edgeworth, *Papers Relating to Political Economy.* New York: Franklin.

1898–1900 On the Representation of Statistics by Mathematical Formulae. *Journal of the Royal Statistical Society* 61:671–700; 62:125–140, 373–385, 534–555; 63 (Supplement):72–81.

(1899) 1963 Professor Seligman on the Theory of Monopoly. Volume 1, pages 143–171 in Francis Ysidro Edgeworth, *Papers Relating to Political Economy.* New York: Franklin. → First published as "Professor Seligman on the Mathematical Method in Political Economy."

1902 EDGEWORTH, FRANCIS YSIDRO; and BOWLEY, A. L. Methods of Representing Statistics of Wages and Other Groups Not Fulfilling the Normal Law of Error. *Journal of the Royal Statistical Society* 65:325–354.

1905 The Law of Error. Cambridge Philosophical Society, *Transactions* 20:36–65; 113–141.

1908–1909 On the Probable Errors of Frequency Constants. *Journal of the Royal Statistical Society* 71: 381–397; 72:81–90.

(1911) 1963 Use of Differential Prices in a Regime of Competition. Volume 1, pages 100–107 in Francis Ysidro Edgeworth, *Papers Relating to Political Economy.* New York: Franklin. → First published as "Monopoly and Differential Prices."

(1912) 1963 Contributions to the Theory of Railway Rates. Part III. Volume 1, pages 172–191 in Francis Ysidro Edgeworth, *Papers Relating to Political Economy.* New York: Franklin.

1915*a* *The Cost of War and Ways of Reducing It Suggested by Economic Theory: A Lecture.* Oxford: Clarendon.

1915*b* *On the Relations of Political Economy to War.* Oxford Univ. Press; New York and London: Milford.

(1917) 1918 *Currency and Finance in Time of War: A Lecture.* Oxford: Clarendon; New York and London: Milford.

1919 *A Levy on Capital for the Discharge of Debt.* Oxford: Clarendon.

1923 On the Use of Medians for Reducing Observations Relating to Several Quantities. *London, Edinburgh and Dublin Philosophical Magazine and Journal of Science* Sixth Series 46:1074–1088.

1926 Mr. Rhodes' Curve and the Method of Adjustment. *Journal of the Royal Statistical Society* New Series 89:129–143.

WORKS ABOUT EDGEWORTH

BOWLEY, ARTHUR L. 1928 *F. Y. Edgeworth's Contributions to Mathematical Statistics.* London: Royal Statistical Society.

KEYNES, JOHN MAYNARD (1926) 1963 Francis Ysidro Edgeworth: 1845–1926. Pages 218–238 in John Maynard Keynes, *Essays in Biography.* New York: Norton.

L. L. P. [Obituary of] F. Y. Edgeworth. 1926 *Journal of the Royal Statistical Society* 89:371–377.

[Obituary of] F. Y. Edgeworth. 1926 *London Times* February 16, p. 21, cols. 2–3.

UZAWA, HIROFUMI 1962 On the Stability of Edgeworth's Barter Process. *International Economic Review* 3:218–232.

VIND, KARL 1964 Edgeworth: Allocations in an Exchange Economy With Many Traders. *International Economic Review* 5:165–177.

SUPPLEMENTARY BIBLIOGRAPHY

CRAMER, HAROLD (1945) 1951 *Mathematical Methods of Statistics.* Princeton Mathematical Series, No. 9. Princeton Univ. Press.

DEBREU, GERARD; and SCARF, HERBERT 1963 A Limit Theorem on the Core of an Economy. *International Economic Review* 4:235–246.

EDWARDS, WARD; LINDMAN, HAROLD; and SAVAGE, LEONARD J. 1963 Bayesian Statistical Inference for Psychological Research. *Psychological Review* 70:193–242.

MARSHALL, ALFRED 1881 Review of *Mathematical Psychics. Academy* 19:457 only.

ROBERTSON, D. H. 1916 Review of *On the Relations of Political Economy to War. Economic Journal* 26: 66–68.

EDUCATION

The articles under this heading are for the most part devoted to discussions of education as an institutionalized form of socialization to adult roles. The articles under SOCIALIZATION *describe other and broader aspects of this concept. Education as an occupation is described in* TEACHING. *Particular institutions that have an educational function are described in* ADULT EDUCATION; COMMUNICATION, MASS; RELIGIOUS ORGANIZATION; UNIVERSITIES; VOLUNTARY ASSOCIATIONS. *The economic aspects of education are discussed in* CAPITAL, HUMAN; *the psychological aspects in* ACHIEVEMENT TESTING; EDUCATIONAL PSYCHOLOGY; INTELLECTUAL DEVELOPMENT; INTELLIGENCE AND INTELLIGENCE TESTING; LEARNING. *Other relevant material may be found in* EQUALITY; LEISURE; OCCUPATIONS AND CAREERS; PROFESSIONS; *and the biographies of* DEWEY; DURKHEIM; MANNHEIM; MONTESSORI; VEBLEN; WALLER; WEBER, MAX.

I. THE STUDY OF EDUCATIONAL
        SYSTEMS   *Burton R. Clark*
II. EDUCATION AND SOCIETY   *C. Arnold Anderson*
III. EDUCATIONAL ORGANIZATION   *A. H. Halsey*

I

THE STUDY OF EDUCATIONAL SYSTEMS

Instruction is a basic activity of mankind. Men inform one another, conveying belief, knowledge, and skill, as they raise a family, earn a living, govern a polity, minister a church, nurse the ill, encounter friends, or communicate through a mass medium. All social systems, large or small, contain occasions for learning and participate to some degree in transmitting culture and in socializing the individual. But the degree of educational involvement is often minor, since many systems of regular transaction leave instruction undifferentiated and incidental and are not characterized by their educational effort. Some webs of human relations, however, are designed to instruct: they raise instruction to purpose; they possess roles of teacher and learner; they receive social definitions—school, college, education—that signify their emphasis. They are set apart in society precisely to differentiate instruction from other activities and make it a form of adult work. When educational activities are thus concentrated, we call them educational systems.

The study of education, while prepared to pursue instruction in its weaker expressions, focuses on these units that constitute a distinctive sector. What transpires within the school and college to determine human behavior and the relations of men? What activities besides instruction emerge to characterize the educational enterprise? How are educational systems shaped by, and how do they in turn affect, the structures of society that allocate resources, exercise power, and provide social order?

Education fascinates the citizen and the scholar alike in the modern era, as it grows in importance but retreats from the view of the amateur. New and expanding economic, political, and social functions pull education into the mainstream of society. At the same time, growing size, deepening complexity, and ever greater specialization mask the processes of education—in the recesses of the city school district, the privacy of the boarding school, the esoteric divisions of the giant university, the educational subsystems of religious, industrial, and military establishments. Rapid change undermines the understanding of education that everyone possesses from the remembrance of things past. Caring more but knowing less, practical men support systematic study of education in the hope it will inform the conventional wisdom and advise educational policy. Aware that political, economic, social, and psychological theory must comprehend the educational domain, social scientists have turned a forgotten realm into a field of special interest. As they point out, a major social institution that touches the lives of all and incorporates a fifth or fourth or third of the population at one time is

overlooked only at considerable peril to social practice and social theory.

Among the attending social sciences, sociology casts a wide net in its pursuit of educational behavior. The sociology of education is partly a holding company for men who study particular social forms and processes and happen to have followed their interests into the educational domain. Students of small-group behavior, childhood and adolescence, deviancy, stratification, occupations, science, law, formal organizations, and leadership are found wandering in schools and colleges in search of findings that would develop a perspective, suggest a concept, or warrant a generalization. The ties of the sociology of education to general sociology are thus many and intimate, defined and redefined by the shifting interests and locales of sociological research. This research field is also, however, a search for unique features of social structure that characterize educational systems. Every major social institution has dynamics of its own, special social functions, and particular problems of performance. When society locates so much cultural transmission and socialization in a separate major institution, the distinctive social qualities of that institution will have significant consequence for the rest of society. The need for social research here is that of clarifying the major implications of concentrating instruction in administered settings, where it becomes the business and vested interest of a segment of the population.

Dividing along lines of social structure, there are four broad sectors of sociological approach: the connection of education to the rest of society; the character of education as a broad institution composed of many organizations and practitioners; the internal life of the school or college; and the systems of organized instruction that arise in major institutions other than education itself.

Education and society

Education, economy, and politics. As a society undergoes industrialization and modernization, its instruction of the young becomes extensively differentiated, internally complex, and elaborately connected with other features of society. Education becomes more necessary for the economy and linked closely to it as a major mediator between manpower demand and labor supply. Occupational competence, general and specific, is increasingly certified by schooling, and achievement is thereby prefigured, as labor shifts from manual to mental and from low to high degree of skill. In the aggregate, those who leave school early are designated for unskilled work, and those who remain on the educational escalator are carried to the jobs for which their general education and specialized vocational training have earmarked them. Higher education is also deeply involved in technological advance, as a location for scientific work and as the enterprise that trains the modern researcher and technologist. Thus, education becomes a way of investing in human capital across many levels of skill.

If brain workers are *the* economic need of societies in advanced industrialism, governmental as well as industrial leaders must become interested in the agencies that attempt systematically to develop mental capacities. The relation of education to government becomes extensive as public officials scrutinize schools and colleges for labor-force effectiveness and worry about the costs and benefits of different programs for training educated labor. The relation of education to the main stream of politics grows as mass education creates new publics—some active, some passive—that attract the politician and the political party to issues of what the government is and should be doing in education.

Mass education also deepens the role of the school in political socialization. In the past, the central political contribution of the schools has been the training of a small governmental elite, as in the case of the Victorian public school in England (Wilkinson 1964). In modern society, education becomes a prime source of differences in political perspectives across large populations. The more highly educated are more aware of the impact of government and are more likely to consider themselves free to engage in political discussions and competent to influence governmental affairs; they "possess the keys to political participation and involvement" (Almond & Verba 1963, p. 318). Among the settings that shape belief, the school is also pre-eminently within the reach of political control, tempting new governments or revolutionary regimes to use it as an instrument for legitimating particular forms of government and reform. Strong pressures exist to move education from elite to mass indoctrination.

Thus, education increasingly becomes a branch of political economy. The sociology of education here converges with the growing body of inquiry into the economics and politics of education and with the interests of political scientists and political sociologists in governance and political socialization.

Social stratification and mobility. As education connects more closely to the economy and the po-

litical order, the role of education in assigning status to individuals and groups also sharpens and intensifies. The paths of social mobility run through the school; the system divides the young and assigns them to adult statuses by means of years of schooling and specific occupational preparation. Thus, the equality of educational provision and access, across divisions of class, ethnicity, and race, becomes a critical social and educational problem. Does the educational system function primarily as an institution of social inheritance, stabilizing social position across generations, or as an institution of social mobility, appointing sons to statuses different from their fathers'? Whatever else education in advanced industrial societies is about, it is about equality.

Massive inequality is generated in modern society when there is considerable difference in the quantity and quality of schooling between rural and urban areas, among regions of a country, and among the neighborhoods and suburbs of the metropolis. Where schooling is of slight consequence to the fate of the masses, such patterned differences matter little. But as schooling becomes the precursor of adult status, the demand to equalize educational provision is heightened. In the United States, where social and educational doctrines have emphasized equal opportunity, the comprehensive school was for some time considered an assurance of equal treatment. But the pulling apart of the classes and the races in the major metropolitan areas, often into separate educational districts, has turned the public schools into agencies that are unequally equipped. Extensive regional differences have also been revealed, especially in the education of the Negro minority. With this, equality becomes a political and administrative issue of planning across larger sectors of population to equalize school resources, personnel, and climates of learning.

Personal aspiration and the capacity to use education—or be processed by it—also varies greatly by the class- and ethnic-linked characteristics of the home, the age group, the neighborhood, and the state or region of country. These shaping environments of youth, external to the school, are ascribed rather than achieved. When these early and systematic inequalities of background are put alongside the growing importance of education in adult status, they appear unfair, and their reduction becomes a matter of social justice. Certain social settings of child rearing—the slums—are deemed educationally incompetent, giving the child so little educational capacity and drive that he appears culturally stunted and destined to be shunted to the depths of the lower class (Work Conference . . . 1963). Democratic doctrine and the politics of democracy then urge that the educational domain be extended into earlier years of life, so that formal agents of care and instruction may blunt and overcome the educationally negative effects of family and neighborhood. The extending and deepening connections of education to the economy and social status thus move educational institutions into a deeper encroachment upon the domains of socialization that in early society were monopolized by family, church, and community.

Modern research (e.g., Halsey et al. 1961) suggests the existence of deep and systematic differences in educability that are a product of the early preschool and extraschool environments. A society's pool of ability is socially as well as biologically defined; "talent" is a function of social strata, educational provision, and the interaction between the two.

Education and culture. Education's broadest function has been to act as caretaker and dispenser of certain cultural resources of society. The raising of the culturally unformed—the child and the immigrant—to the state of capable adult is the activity on which the formal institution of education was founded. Formal education is therefore an effort to do explicitly and systematically what family and community had long accomplished in an undifferentiated fashion before society became so complex that the task had to be performed by specialists.

Of all the relations of education to society, the primordial function of cultural transmission is the one most seriously disturbed by modern social forces. There is some slippage of this function to other institutions: thus, educational subsystems emerge and develop extensively in the institutions of adult work. Moreover, there is a growing amount of unsystematic cultural indoctrination through the mass media—television, radio, movies, records—where instruction is combined with entertainment and commerce. The media blend, competing with the school and affecting its performance, is new in its near-universal coverage. The child tunes in daily to central molders of taste and transmitters of lore; a significant part of traditional and emergent culture is surely now communicated through these new channels. The problem for research is to ascertain what part of the imagery and knowledge of youth is transmitted in these extraeducational ways, what alterations in the emphases of the core culture are made, and how the work of the school and college is affected. The possibility exists that the very form of new means of communication, particularly the visual sensing of television, affects the relation of the person to the environment (McLuhan 1964).

The transmission of culture also becomes segmental in the upper levels of the educational system, as formal instruction is both extended and differentiated to prepare men for an elaborating structure of skilled occupations. Men must be differentially socialized to the spreading variety of adult statuses. The professional school is a purveyor of specialized culture, and even the disciplines of the liberal arts grow less liberal in modern times as academic men respond to proliferating knowledge by developing expertise in a narrow segment. These tendencies weaken rather than strengthen understanding among educated men, as experts discourse in esoteric languages and gaze down the tunnels of special perspectives.

But the relation of education to culture is perhaps most changed, not by alterations in the transmitting of a heritage, but by expansion in the creating of knowledge. This historically minor role evolves toward dominance in higher education as nations increase their commitment to research. The involvement of the university, as locus of research and trainer of the researcher, makes education an active, intrusive force in culture as well as social and political affairs. The university has helped to instigate and propel the explosion in knowledge and the ascendance of science that characterize technological societies. This dynamic relation constitutes part of the awesomeness of the educational enterprise in modern times.

Social change and social integration. The greater the scope of the educational institution, the more complex is its relation to social order. Schools and colleges, as noted above, increasingly undertake broad functions for the mass of the population that were formerly fulfilled by family, community, and church. The educational system, when socially effective, becomes a device for orderly change across generations in the class and elite location of individuals and groups. But the system may weaken the integration of society through lack of articulation or incapacity to adapt. Articulation is partly a problem of how well educational output matches occupational demand. An oversupply of men educated in public administration and law, or otherwise prepared to seize coveted posts in the civil service, is a source of a discontented and restless intelligentsia in industrializing societies that are at the same time short of scientists and engineers. A vast supply of men trained below a general threshold of functional literacy offers the possibility in advanced industrial societies of a mass of unskilled workers ill-fitted for the job-upgrading and retraining that spreads throughout the modern economy.

Adaptation is partly a problem of how the major training institution confronts rapid social change. Mannheim (1950, p. 248) maintained that the school of the past was "a training ground for imitative adjustment to an established society," while the modern school is (or ought to be) "an introduction into an already dynamic society." To face only tradition is potentially malintegrative; new knowledge must be brought into the curriculum, and the new and the old made coherent. Estimates must be made of behavior appropriate to an unknown future, increasing the pressure to educate for "adaptability." But this is to risk loss of age-old values, cultural discontinuity, and crisis in personal identity. Flexibility, a training ideal suggested by rapid change, may cause confusion and lend a hand to chaos. Social integration, in its instructional bases, depends in part on the capacity of the school to blend adaptive flexibility with stable imitation of the past, working to avoid both atomized individualism and cultural orthodoxy.

Since education faces many forces in complex societies, its adaptation in one direction may generate serious strain in another. The close link to the economy in advanced industrial societies turns education into a talent farm, a massive "people-processing" enterprise preparing manpower to the specifications of occupational demand and governmental blueprint. Such an enterprise is also characteristically large in scale and highly specialized in internal operation. One outcome of massive processing is a callous relation between those who administer and teach and those who occupy the chairs of the student. The processing hardly bothers the student with only vocational objectives in mind, but it seriously disturbs intellectual interests of faculty and students. Idealistic youth, concerned about personal identity and social justice in the mass society, sees itself poorly served by instructional systems that are hooked to the requirements of technological advance. Thus, as education becomes "Establishment," it contributes to modern intellectual discontent and alienation.

When the educational system is hypnotized with occupational demand, it will also overlook the requirements of a man when he is off the job. Clearly, education must learn to contribute substantially to the use of free time. Yet the orientation to duty and the tight schedules of schools that prepare the young for bureaucratized work are antithetical to the sensibilities appropriate for leisure. Fixation on utilitarian study also renders art a frill in the curriculum, reducing the aesthetic experience of the young and leaving it to other institutions to sustain the arts in society.

In the short span of a generation or two an educational system may even prove critical to the identity and integration of a nation. In the rapid change characteristic of the last half of the twentieth century, new nations and traditional societies struggle to bring their populations to modernity. One example is Israel, where mass immigration focuses national energies on assimilation of traditional folk. By 1960 Israel was a secular, Western-type democracy, with an economy rooted in science and technology. But over a half of the country's large wave of immigrants in the 1950s were Afro–Asian Jews, illiterate and poor and Eastern in terms of values. In such circumstances, the socialization that takes place in the immigrant family threatens rather than supports national integration. The youth of the traditional families must be captured by such arms of the state as the school and the army, rapidly weaned from tradition, and transformed into modern citizens and workers; or else when the children of today come to adulthood and the ballot, there may be two nations or a nation with a different identity. [*See* REFUGEES, *article on* ADJUSTMENT AND ASSIMILATION.]

Many other nations in Asia, Africa, and Latin America, some newly formed as well as undergoing rapid modernization, find the educational system playing a critical role in nationhood and national change. The educational system strains to provide the trained men for the expanding upper sectors of a rapidly changing structure of occupations, particularly the men who can plan and lead modern government and industry. The teachers and graduates of the system, far ahead of the masses in capacity to understand the modern polity, challenge traditional ruling elites, by means ranging from the barricades of the street demonstration to the desks of the civil servant. Critical problems of national identity sometimes center on the capacity of the schools to promote a national language in a multilingual new society; for example, there has been an attempt in Malaya, peopled by Malays, Chinese, Indians, and Europeans, to make Malay the unifying language of the nation. Whatever else education in the modernizing society is about, it is about national integration and modern competence. Here the sociology of education becomes preeminently a part of the sociology of national development [*see, for example,* Foster 1965; Coleman 1965; *see also* LINGUISTICS, *article on* THE SPEECH COMMUNITY; MODERNIZATION].

Finally, education has become a peculiarly creative force in society. Its laboratories may serve industry and government, but its scholars and scientists also create the knowledge that opens new vistas and undermines existing economic and political structures. Its teachings may prepare the compliant worker, but its teachers also create attitudes critical of established ways and acquaint the young with ideals and institutions of freedom. Complex systems of prolonged education lead toward change as well as stability, critical thought as well as unthinking imitation, discontinuity and eruption as well as continuity and slow evolution. The tendencies are plural, leaving the outcome open to the play of values, the effectiveness of group action, and the exercise of political power.

The major educational institution

The major educational institution of a society has a division of labor, a structure of control, and a work force. Important social phenomena in their own right, these components of the system at large affect the educational process and its impact on the individual and society. The institutional features in part reflect the larger society, but they also have dynamics of their own and consequences not planned by political leaders and administrative staffs. Several issues involved in the division of labor and the structure of control will be reviewed here.

As education is extended to a larger share of the population, lengthened to occupy more years in the life cycle, and linked more closely to the allocation of occupation and status, the tasks of education are diversified. More educational sectors form around permutations of program, personnel, and clientele, intensifying problems of division of labor and control. In societies characterized by central control of educational policy, national governmental authorities attempt systematically to allocate tasks to sectors and to standardize programs and requirements of entry and exit within those major segments. In decentralized educational structures, tasks may be defined and seized by private initiative and dispersed public authorities, resulting in greater variation in the wares that schools offer parents and students.

Centralization of educational control in a national ministry, or, at a lower level, in a regional or state department, serves certain ends and presents certain institutional problems, while decentralization serves other ends and leads to problems of a different order. Centralization serves integration, orderly procedure, the uniform application of

standards, and innovation from the top. It allows for redistribution of resources across a large system to reduce the disparity among local educational settings, between the poor and the rich and the backward and the advanced. The problems posed by central control are ones of bureaucratic rigidity, massive error, and the lessening of initiative in the provinces; such an establishment may not have the foresight, sensibility, and planning capacity to make the myriad adjustments required of a diversified institution in a rapidly changing society.

Decentralization serves local adaptation to the diverse values of plural societies and the tailoring of school interests to specific group interests, for example, the preparation of Philadelphia gentlemen, the maintenance of Lutheranism, the acculturation of a minority. It allows for grass-roots initiative. The problems posed by decentralized control are ones of local initiative becoming subservient to local *status quo* and of piecemeal response to needs and interests that extend across society. A locally adaptive system becomes a case of institutional drift as authority moves upward in other institutions: for example, as national corporations, unions, and regulatory agencies come to dominate the economy and as the work of education comes to relate closely to the national economy and such concerns as the technology of national advance and protection. The perceived costs of drift and the natural insensitivity of local authority to national problems promote efforts to centralize control or to construct national mechanisms for influencing the scattered authorities who retain formal control.

The modern state needs to order the educational division of labor. Where a national bureaucratic machinery is weak or lacking, the effort to coordinate the division of labor will encourage the strengthening of that machinery and also the growth of an ancillary structure, composed of voluntary associations, interorganization compacts, study committees, accrediting bodies, and testing organizations, that helps to knit together separate public and private authorities. The ancillary groups, lacking command, operate primarily through the persuasion of money, prestige, and competitive advantage of large organization over solitary effort. At the same time, the modern state also needs to support research, to diversify its advanced education, and to develop sectors of creative adjustment to rapid change that cannot be anticipated in all its complexity in the central office. Where decentralization or federalism is lacking, the effort to diversify and provide for widespread initiative will encourage the proliferation of centers of influence within the system and result in a loosening of the tight integration of the traditional structure.

Thus, decentralized educational structures are under pressure to change the internal division of labor and control toward national order, through ancillary organization as well as stronger national bureaucracy. On the other hand, centralized educational systems are under pressure to loosen the traditional bureaucracy in order to admit new forms of secondary and higher education and to exploit the role of education in research and innovation. The strain toward coordinated order and the strain toward individual and organizational autonomy are fundamental conflicting tendencies inherent in education in advanced industrial societies. With different cultural traditions and different structures of political power, societies will pursue somewhat different resolutions of this basic conflict. But we may also expect some convergence among nations to occur on a model of the educational system that weds central direction to extensive consultation and persuasion and that places preparation for unguided change on a par with direct implementation of national policy.

The educational organization

The school or college is a formal social system with external relations and internal patterns that condition the educational process (Bidwell 1965). The individual agency has a particular part to play in the educational division of labor, and its place in the institutional web affects the status of the organization and its members. A school is judged externally by public perception of how its main tasks connect with the general status system of society. "Vocational" secondary schools that lead to low-status occupations, compared to "academic" secondary schools leading to high-status occupations, everywhere labor under a stigma that affects the recruitment and morale of teachers and the self-conception and ambition of students. It is virtually an iron law of school status that a parity of esteem cannot be achieved by schools performing different educational and social tasks (Banks 1955). In systems of specialized secondary schools, for example, the tripartite English structure, the difficulties of school esteem turn some educators and laymen toward the more comprehensive forms of school organization, grouping curricular streams within a common school in order to avoid the status degradation of a good share of the teachers and the students. As schools and colleges grow in number and variety, the status of one among the others is increasingly affected by a contest composed of the effort of favored organizations to protect and proclaim their acknowledged superiority, the attempts of consuming publics to discriminate and label, and the maneuvers of some reformers, administrators, and the less-favored teachers to screen the division of work from the public assessments that define status inequalities (Clark 1960).

In the internal structure of the educational organization, the growing scale and proliferation of work activities induce a differentiation of roles. Administration becomes separated from teaching; because of the need for coordination, a hierarchy of administrative levels comes into being. Teaching itself becomes more specialized as knowledge proliferates. The magnitude of the task of advising and channeling students produces the nonteaching counselor. As the role structure of the school becomes more complicated, there is a bureaucratization of relations, with responsibilities and jurisdictions formally circumscribed and rules formally elaborated to preform decisions for maximum fairness and dependability. As written records shadow the student and experts assess him and assign him to treatments, the formal apparatus takes on such weight that it is able to compete with the home and neighborhood in determining the future of the young. Parental and student orientations must interact with the increasingly more systematized means of achievement. The orientations are sometimes defined, sometimes redefined, and always processed by the everyday activities of a bureaucracy (Cicourel & Kitsuse 1963).

The weight of bureaucracy varies among schools and colleges, however, depending on the exercise of other forms of influence, particularly the collegial authority of faculties, and on the informal counterpressures of faculty and student subcultures. The importance of bureaucracy also depends on whether the large school or college is a unitary organization or a federation of quasi-independent clusters of faculty and students. Indeed, organizational structure may possibly have strong and lasting effects on individual character. Personal identity is hard to establish in the modern fast-changing world, and the campus is one of the critical locales of identity formation. If identity is dependent on personal relations, then the decline in community typical of the large mass campus will disturb and weaken identity processes. Growing impersonality in schools and colleges apparently has greater social consequence than impersonality in nearly all other types of organizations. The effort of some educational reformers to structure large campuses as federations of small states is a response to this growing belief. On this apparently critical issue, the sociological imagination is still largely imprisoned by clichés and uninformed by research.

Education in other institutions

The immense appetite of modern society for systematic instruction extends educational work throughout society. Substantial educational subsystems develop within the military, industry, and the church to instill specific skill, knowledge, or perspective not provided in the regular line of schools and colleges. This development is particularly powered by rapid change in work skills and the complex demands of modern organization. A modern business firm takes care of its competence by systematic training of personnel, from top management to the rank and file. Men alternate between production and instruction, with blocs of hours or weeks or months given over to the classroom within or outside the firm. The modern military establishment is a vast educational enterprise: its competence depends on the capacity to transform raw recruits into technicians and to create an officers' corps in which the manager and the technologist assume places alongside the fighting commander of old. Military careers increasingly depend on effective performance in the schools that train officers to successively higher levels of complex skill and thought.

New nations also find the military a primary educational workshop. In Israel, the army plays an important role alongside the schools in the acculturation of immigrants: young men learn Hebrew, their own history and geography, the modern-style discipline of working with others, and new work skills. In most modernizing societies, military officers are among the best educated groups, gaining particular competence in engineering and administration. Combining modern expertise with access to means of power, they play a critical role in the politics of national development.

Religious organizations, long educational in their formal and quasi-formal indoctrination of the flock, plunge further into organized instruction as they turn the church basement into community center and the church official into social worker and adult educator, broadening activities to maintain a central place in secularizing societies. In the United States of the 1960s, more persons participate in the adult classes of churches and synagogues than in those offered by colleges and universities, particularly in the South. The established churches capture educational audiences more effectively than the educational courses of television (Johnstone & Rivera 1965, pp. 10 ff., 53–55, 111). When to the formal classes we add the deliberate socialization performed from the pulpit, it is clear that a broad definition of education would have to include much investigation of the church as an instructional medium.

Similar trends obtain in the public bureau, the union, and the professional association. Institutions of adult work and pleasure find it to their self-interest to encourage the emergence of an educational subsystem and thus to spread formal education throughout society. Thus, for an ever larger share of the population, formal education is the main means to cultural as well as occupational qualification. Knowledge is a prime ingredient of the society based on science, technology, and expertise, and the primacy of knowledge is the primacy of education. In the face of large dangers and uncertainty, a learning society offers the opportunity that very large numbers of men may participate effectively in a complex culture and in the social and political affairs of a complex society. In this possibility lies the educational promise of modern man.

BURTON R. CLARK

BIBLIOGRAPHY

ALMOND, GABRIEL A.; and VERBA, SIDNEY 1963 *The Civic Culture: Political Attitudes and Democracy in Five Nations.* Princeton Univ. Press.

BANKS, OLIVE 1955 *Parity and Prestige in English Secondary Education: A Study in Educational Sociology.* London: Routledge; New York: Humanities.

BECKER, HOWARD S. et al. 1961 *Boys in White: Student Culture in Medical School.* Univ. of Chicago Press.

BIDWELL, CHARLES E. 1965 The School as a Formal Organization. Pages 972–1022 in James G. March (editor), *Handbook of Organizations.* Chicago: Rand McNally.

CHARTERS, W. W. JR. 1963 The Social Background of Teaching. Pages 715–813 in Nathaniel L. Gage (editor), *Handbook of Research on Teaching.* Chicago: Rand McNally.

CICOUREL, AARON V.; and KITSUSE, JOHN I. 1963 *The Educational Decision-makers.* Indianapolis: Bobbs-Merrill. → An analysis of the confounding of educational guidance by psychological assumptions and social bias.

CLARK, BURTON R. 1960 *The Open Door College: A Case Study.* New York: McGraw-Hill.

CLARK, BURTON R. 1964 Sociology of Education. Pages 734–769 in Robert E. L. Faris (editor), *Handbook of Modern Sociology.* Chicago: Rand McNally.

COLEMAN, JAMES S. 1961 *The Adolescent Society: The Social Life of the Teenager and Its Impact on Education.* New York: Free Press.

COLEMAN, JAMES S. (editor) 1965 *Education and Political Development.* Princeton Univ. Press.

DURKHEIM, ÉMILE (1902–1911) 1956 *Education and Sociology.* Glencoe, Ill.: Free Press. → Contains four articles first published in French.

FOSTER, PHILIP J. 1965 *Education and Social Change in Ghana.* London: Routledge; Univ. of Chicago Press.

FRASER, W. R. 1963 *Education and Society in Modern France.* New York: Humanities; London: Routledge.

GROSS, NEAL; MASON, WARD S.; and McEACHERN, ALEXANDER W. 1958 *Explorations in Role Analysis: Studies of the School Superintendency Role.* New York: Wiley.

HALSEY, A. H.; FLOUD, JEAN; and ANDERSON, C. ARNOLD (editors) 1961 *Education, Economy, and Society: A Reader in the Sociology of Education.* New York: Free Press.

JOHNSTONE, JOHN W. C.; and RIVERA, RAMON J. 1965 *Volunteers for Learning: A Study of the Educational Pursuits of American Adults.* Chicago: Aldine.

McLUHAN, MARSHALL 1964 *Understanding Media: The Extensions of Man.* New York: McGraw-Hill. → A paperback edition was published in 1965.

MANNHEIM, KARL 1950 *Freedom, Power, and Democratic Planning.* New York: Oxford Univ. Press. → Published posthumously.

VEBLEN, THORSTEIN (1918) 1957 *The Higher Learning in America: A Memorandum on the Conduct of Universities by Business Men.* New York: Sagamore.

WALLER, WILLARD W. (1932) 1961 *The Sociology of Teaching.* New York: Russell.

WEBER, MAX (1906–1924) 1946 *From Max Weber: Essays in Sociology.* Translated and edited by Hans H. Gerth and C. Wright Mills. New York: Oxford Univ. Press. → See especially pages 129–156, 240–244, and 426–434.

WILKINSON, RUPERT 1964 *Gentlemanly Power: British Leadership and the Public School Tradition; A Comparative Study in the Making of Rulers.* Oxford Univ. Press. → Also published as *The Prefects: British Leadership.* . . .

WILSON, LOGAN (1942) 1964 *The Academic Man: A Study in the Sociology of a Profession.* New York: Octagon Books.

WORK CONFERENCE ON CURRICULUM AND TEACHING IN DEPRESSED URBAN AREAS, 1962 1963 *Education in Depressed Areas.* Edited by A. H. Passow. New York: Columbia Univ., Teachers College, Bureau of Publications.

II
EDUCATION AND SOCIETY

Education can be viewed as including all communicating of knowledge and shaping of values; in this sense it is synonymous with socialization. During most of human history deliberate instruction has been incidental and sporadic, and even in the most complex societies much instruction, in the broader sense of the term, devolves upon agencies other than schools. In this article, however, the focus is mainly upon formalized education as carried out by distinctive institutions, especially schools. The aim of formal education is to prepare the child for the transition from the confined but diffuse relationships of the family to the more impersonal and diversified relationships of the larger society. In its core sense, education rests on tutelage of child by adult; only in the complex societies is instruction often given by one adult to another. There are multiple explanations for the appearance of schools, and these same causes continue to generate new sorts and levels of schools as societies become more complex.

Rise of formal education

In many preliterate tribes an age group undergoes tuition in adult skills, and particularly in cult rituals and in religious beliefs and symbolisms, under the care of a specially designated adult. Ideological and ritual components appear in every example of formal education, although they become less definite and presumably less effective as schools are given more diversified and preponderantly secular responsibilities. Occasionally we observe a ruling group attempting to convert youth to beliefs not shared by most parents; typically, however, schools are expected to create consensus among a numerous citizenry around certain unifying themes.

A second source of formal schooling lies in the necessity that some youths acquire proficiency in a set of skills that may not only differ from those of the parents but may also be too complicated for the parents to teach. Until a late stage in the technological development of a society most individuals learn their livelihood skills as a by-product of growing up. The first deviation from that pattern is exemplified by apprenticeship under a master in a different household; the youth's parents may teach the same craft, but the required impersonality of instruction encourages shifting the responsibility to another family. In many societies schools are set up to teach bookkeeping and correspondence arts to children of traders and artisans; this type of instruction is sometimes given in elementary schools, but wherever vocational training is organized in special schools, it normally occurs in a second or third level of school that builds upon the basic education of a "common" school. In most societies schools contribute little of the specialized training for manual occupations but function rather to prepare the child for later training in both manual and nonmanual skills on the job.

Although various sorts of extra-school and informal education are common to all societies, the full development of instruction occurs only after the appearance of writing. The adoption of writing adds a new dimension to the life of a society: a sense of the past, sometimes also anticipation of the future, and new agencies for coordinating the activities of scattered and heterogeneous groups. Writing may become the monopoly of a priesthood and its secular use be confined mainly to officials, or it may become widely used. Within a priesthood diversified and graded schools may develop; likewise, instruction and the certifying of competence may become highly elaborated among officials.

It has been pointed out that clocks came into use in order to give precision to the temporal coordination of activities extending beyond direct observation and the range of the voice. Likewise, literacy became diffused as it proved useful to coordinate activities over space as well as time. A society is defined by the area within which interchange is frequent and over which men are responsive to influences from shared focal centers; crystallization and preservation of this unity come to depend progressively upon formal training in basic literacy skills and in the unifying themes of the culture. However, deliberate efforts by ruling groups to spread literacy widely were rare until modern times —although schools were widespread some centuries ago in China and also in less elaborate form in India and parts of the Islamic world. Common schools were established usually in an effort to ensure unity of sacred or secular ideology throughout a population; more direct economic and political considerations have become important only in modern times.

Even in societies with a relatively simple technology, schooling beyond simple literacy is fostered by the need to keep records and chronicles and conduct correspondence, and by the desire to read holy books. As shown by the initiative displayed among craftsmen and traders, ability to keep simple accounts and to handle transactions in distant markets provides another incentive. As trading and other contacts proliferate, the services of the occasional scribe prove inadequate. The advantages of literacy become important to more and more of the populace as ordinary men acquire the capacity and the right to choose among alternative ways of life. Useful books are published as well as uplifting ones, along with tales about the enlarging world and melodramas of social life. The exhilaration of widening experience through symbols of what is not immediately present in time or space should not be underestimated.

Schooling, unlike less formal training and apprenticeship, does not include participation in adult activities; instead, school subjects and adult life are mediated through the teacher, who becomes one of the key specialists in society, alongside the warrior, priest, trader, official, and master craftsman. In societies in which literacy is not widely diffused, such as Europe in the early medieval period, book learning takes on the character of a special apprenticeship for entry into an intellectual elite. Unless they happen to be born into this elite, students in such societies will not ordinarily meet with adults outside the schools who make use of school learning in their daily life, for this is a feature only of societies in which the printed word is both widely available and commonly understood. But even in highly literate societies the student's opportunities for observing the uses of learning are severely limited. One reason for this is the increasing length of the period of compulsory education. The school pupil vicariously anticipates adult activities, but his perception of them is filtered through the teacher and the school environment. As the school years pass he will increasingly anticipate his own social future and come to perceive the relevance of his lessons. However, only if the education is vivid and learning meaningful will he incorporate his school experiences into his conception of himself so that learning becomes a development of self rather than authoritarian drill. In varying degrees, schooling enables the pupil to acquire skills that facilitate joint activities and that enable him to participate imaginatively in the lives of other people (including men who are dead or not yet living), to relate himself to activities not embraced in the life of his kin group, and to conceptualize social entities, such as the nation.

At all levels the lessons of the schoolroom are surrounded by moral and value judgments, regardless of curriculum. One of the most significant tendencies is for the formalized pattern of school lessons themselves to become instruments of moral teaching through the discipline or mastery of a subject that is "outside" the pupil. There are right ways to solve a problem; there is a correct spelling; an essay is ordered or disjointed. This morality characterizes the growing number of specialties and professions whose members have been subjected to the discipline of impersonal assessment of achievement. Direct moral instruction that is not linked to cognitive achievement is less likely to succeed.

As societies become larger and more complex, literacy must become more widely dispersed and more firmly inculcated, for the organization of virtually all aspects of national life depends upon it. A growing proportion of youths need an extended basic schooling in the common language of political, economic, and social intercourse; only with this will they be able to undertake the further specialized training made necessary by the increasing diversification of adult roles. Schooling is at once a homogenizing and differentiating process. Also, as social change accelerates and acquiescence in or commitment to change spreads, the adaptive or tradition-conserving function of schools is replaced in part by the support and creation of change. The growing complexity of society and the associated expansion and elaboration of the school system are reflected in an alteration and multiplication of procedures relating to selection of pupils for retention in higher schools and for their allocation among types of schools and curricula. The roles of teachers are first differentiated from other vocations and then internally divided in myriad ways.

Schools and society

Individuation and socialization: this duality runs through the history of education. Educational participation gives people things in common, but it also sets them apart into special worlds of discourse and of activity. Schools are expected to give youth the common skills that are simple and universal, as well as to identify those few individuals who can excel, rise to eminence in learning, and rule their fellows. Shared arts of communication and consensus on cherished values are prime aims of schools everywhere, but teachers are relied upon also to nourish the talented and indulge the privileged. How large a part schools play in homogenization and differentiation (and in what patterns) is at once a reflection of and a factor in the scale of the society and its realized or perceived need for integration. It depends also upon whether the society is elitist or democratic in orientation.

In premodern societies, where each community or district has its own dialect, costume, and even units of measure, schools may be nonexistent and unnecessary as agencies of social integration. However, the unifying of societies and nations has required the virtual obliteration of provincial cultures and the imposition of common expectations and practices to override local customs. Historically, the most frequent function of schools in this process has been the cultural homogenization of an elite. However, the molding of a linguistically and ideologically unified elite has reinforced status distinctions and thus has also been divisive, setting the elite apart. Parallel events are observable today in the newer nations, where secondary school (especially if residential) and university graduates make up the new leadership that strives to weld local cultures into a nation. Even where underlying ideologies are democratic, these few leaders risk becoming alienated from other citizens who do not participate at all in the "high culture."

The unification of nations and larger societies cannot progress far without the common school for widening circles of ordinary folk. This was exemplified in the flourishing of the English "dame schools," with their modicum of training in literacy and ciphering and their preoccupation with teaching of the proper behavior to the "lower orders." With its gradual extension and improvement, the common school both challenges elitism and takes on responsibility for fostering consensus among all citizens around selected themes. The national language slowly spreads through successive generations of pupils, accommodating them to acknowledgment of the ruler's writs, participation in the rituals of patriotism, and familiarity with the heroes and events of literature and history. The diffusion of literacy both incites and broadens participation in political life, and the spreading of facility in numbers underlies the knitting together of the larger economy.

The common schools perform an interclass assimilating function, however limited and crude. Through the common schools children of peasants and laborers acquire a less abrasive speech, less violent habits of conduct, some insight into the attractions of cultural amenities, and a few folkways of complex social living. Slowly increasing numbers learn the advantages of deferred gratification and of systematic work. In the more democratic school systems, this social assimilation may go on even within the university. Meanwhile, the high evaluation of education that motivates some to enter the preferred occupations stimulates the further spread of schooling throughout the population.

In the early stages of the diffusion of schools, the divisiveness produced by them extends spatially, as well as along the lines of status. Acceptance of schools beyond (and even below) the compulsory level is uneven among the districts and regions of a society. Common education proves to be more useful in some areas than in others, and in some districts it may quickly lead to the adoption of secondary and higher education. Residents of some areas draw ahead of residents of others in learning and in prosperity, in active sharing of the national culture, and in accessibility to the amenities of an advancing society. This disparity is most extreme in plural societies lacking a single mother tongue and especially in the new nations where, to a degree hitherto unparalleled in history, schools are being relied upon to create a unified people out of a throng of tribes. If vernacular languages are used in the early grades, the common schools may have little unifying effect.

Where schools are operated by religious groups —even where there is central inspection—the value content of curricula may become equivocal. Each nation's history affects the balance of those influences that bridge the religions or strengthen their inward-looking tendencies. However, the contest for autonomy and for central financial aid can increase central control over curricula. Where many forces work to create a broad underlying national unity, separate schools may have little divisive effect. Indeed, for religious as for other minorities, "parochial" schools commonly serve as way stations on the road to assimilation, especially where a single language is used by all. What is common to these lessons and the atmosphere of all schools leads each group into assimilation of pervasive national ways of life.

As the duration of common schooling is extended, so also are both the duration of the period in which schools may carry out their socially integrating functions and the further years of school life for those who continue into the increasingly elaborated programs of middle and higher education. Again, we see both merging and separating forces at work as schools play a growing role in the society. The special cultures of the various better-educated groups that are fostered by their schooling are less exclusive than those in simpler elitist societies; these restricted cultures are in greater degree an extension in depth of the themes and practices that pervade the lower schools as well.

Thus, education continuously raises barriers to communication among the members of a society, even as it is also continuously eroding isolation. Associated with schooling are the occupational specialties of a complex society, and some of these groups exploit the schools to reinforce their favored positions by restricting numbers of qualified entrants. However, rising demands from the economy and populist pressures also force the breaking of such obstructions. Meanwhile, the rising standard of average schooling means that fewer occupational boundaries are chasms between sodden ignorance and genteel learning.

Diffusion of both schooling and consumer goods creates increasing diversity of ways of life even while fostering status continuities within the society. This process finds its most complete expression in the university, for no matter how much a society may press toward "comprehensive" rather than differentiated education for its various subpopulations, there is no escaping extreme specialization at the university level. And it is in the universities, in recent years, that there has arisen the greatest concern that learned men shall share a common culture.

Conservation and innovation

The principal task of formal education in the past was to inculcate accepted bodies of information and sets of beliefs—to conserve and pass down

a heritage. However, in the more dynamic societies schools are called upon to play a more creative role by supporting or fostering change; everywhere they have indirectly provided support for change by giving men the basic tools with which to enlarge their knowledge indefinitely and to manipulate it creatively. The counterpoint of socialization and individuation is thus again at work.

Educational conservatism that finds its source in established religion or ethics was exemplified in Confucian learning and the bureaucratic examinations in China and in the development of clerkly schooling in medieval Europe. Yet even in those or similar situations, schooling did not function solely to rigidify ideas, for among the elites philosophical speculation could not be confined. And alongside the erudite education there arose also more popular and pragmatic kinds. Soon after the introduction of printing, books expounding practical novelties for daily life and craft practice poured from the press—and in China over the centuries from the hands of the copyist—opening new possibilities to men with even a minimum of literacy. The same funds of ideas stimulated religious and political innovation, enhanced in some societies by popular reading of the holy books.

The modern age takes it for granted that change is natural. Literacy has meant exposure to novelty and has prepared men of the most diverse stations to react to new ideas from many quarters. Preserving the continuity of expanding knowledge has become a principal source of innovation. It is significant that much of the Western technological revolution was the work of artisans who fused their ingenuity with published manuals to accelerate the rate of invention. Indeed, learned men and literate artisans were in more intensive interaction in past generations than they are today. Progressively, the potentialities of written communication were exploited by advocates of political and social reform, by religious leaders, and by the sellers of goods. In our much-schooled age we have forgotten how little schooling men need in order to put literacy to use, as we have forgotten also the capacity of oral traditions.

Modernization of new nations. The many educational developments that unfolded slowly throughout the history of Western countries are telescoped in the nations that are today borrowing educational systems, but similar borrowing had gone on among the Western countries as they were shaping their educational systems to changing conceptions of social need. The new nations find the task of adaptation more difficult because they are anxious to communicate an ill-defined and often nonexistent traditional unitary culture and equally eager to use schools to produce a technology for which traditional culture has little pertinence. Often, then, the implanted Western education has created mainly a small deviant group devoted to modernization. Although it is possible to absorb folklore into history and literature courses, other features of the traditional culture cannot be adapted so easily to meet the demands of modernization. In the societies where the fusion of traditional with technological folkways occurred more gradually, more of the traditional culture was preserved.

As school attendance diffuses, one principal result is deeper appreciation of the utility of education and thus the emergence of impulses for additional and different kinds of education. These attitudes spread through a population much as do other new cultural traits, with patterned foci and gradients of educational development; the climax areas correspond generally to those where other impulses to social change are also vigorous.

Wherever Western-type schools have taken root, their activity is associated with receptivity to new ideas and practices in many spheres of life, and the individual with more schooling possesses more traits of modernity. He is more informed about the world, more likely to accept the new, more appreciative of the complexities of his society, and better able to comprehend the more complex forces at work around him. Assimilation of schooling by females adds a special multiplier to these changes and serves also to transform family life in ways that foster more adaptive children. However, in all these respects there is much overlapping among subpopulations. The less educated are often better informed in pragmatic matters than the highly educated, and they can be more open-minded to novelty. Illiterate men in societies with strong oral traditions may have broad perspectives.

As common schooling is extended, its conserving function with respect to high culture spreads to more people. At the same time, the change-supporting influence of the schools permeates larger parts of the society and challenges elitist practices. Moreover, the more dynamic and creative ways of teaching begin to be effective even in the common schools, which come to embrace elements of science and social studies along with the three Rs—the whole in a context of change. Secondary and especially university education becomes predominantly oriented to subjects relating to the less conservative parts of the culture.

Of particular importance is the transformation of the language skills of children by the school. Not only does the working language of the typical child expand but it also becomes increasingly oriented to use in ways instrumental to change. However, in this process the handicaps of those groups least affected by informal as well as formal education become more visible. Laggard groups may become more than nominally absorbed into the schools only slowly, and in many advanced societies the task of making formal education effective for such groups has emerged as crucial in a time of rapid occupational change.

Schools as agencies of change. It is Western education, that of the civilization whose science and technology is now spreading everywhere, that has seen the most explicit use of schools as agencies of change. Response to technological requirements appeared first at intermediate levels of the schools. Apart from the proliferation of apprenticeship and ciphering and similar schools, demands for formal technical instruction were met in many countries by a diversification of secondary vocational programs, by technical institutes, and by university-level technological training that was often segregated from the university proper. The "agricultural and mechanical" colleges of the United States borrowed many components from Europe and with them created a more permissive and diversified system, which in turn was copied in Europe and elsewhere. Outside the prestige branches of education, varied practical training supplanted the traditional "cultural" subjects and initiated a reorientation of education toward programs more supportive of change.

However, in almost all societies universities have been the sanctuaries for critical analysis of the society; even where they have made little use of that privilege, it has usually been available. And insofar as high-level intellectual training has been required by practical activities, universities have been persuaded to provide that instruction. However belatedly they may have responded, the universities now constitute centers for induced change; they train more and more segments of the national elite. In a few countries it has come to be accepted that many kinds of occupations deserve university sponsorship, that new vocations call for new kinds of professors, and that varied motives and standards of competence may legitimately be part of university life.

Schools resist change both by passivity and by active opposition. It is easier to continue on well-trod, familiar paths, and typically the new is not welcomed by teachers, most of whom have spent their lives within schools. At the higher levels, resistance in part reflects devotion to particular intellectual traditions, often confounded with conventions as to the "standards" that a university must uphold. These conventions lose their power only after science and technology have manifested self-sustaining powers and critical importance for national survival.

Regardless of intent, schools assist change when they provide the simple literacy that enables men to read and the core training in the traditional branches of learning. They favor change also by identifying and promoting the talented who, even when co-opted into presumably constraining prestige positions, often prove recalcitrant to custom. They foster change more directly when they accept new materials into classrooms or accept responsibility to train for new vocations. They are completely involved when or if they encourage independent and critical thinking (at whatever level) and when they undertake scientific research and carry on the special kind of apprenticeship called graduate study. Finally, expansion of adult education and refresher courses at all levels of schooling is becoming an integral part of social organization to counter obsolescence and foster more rapid change.

Combining the homogenizing–differentiating dichotomy with the conserving–changing dichotomy gives us four categories in terms of which the different stages of education may be described. It is in common schooling (which may last as long as 12 or even 14 years) that the homogenizing and conserving functions are most distinctly merged. Furthermore, any separation of schools for different subpopulations, relegating most children to inferior schools, also upholds tradition. On the other hand, as more individuals share schooling through many years, change is favored simply because individuals begin to learn the scientific and technical ideas that link them to other influences making for change. It is at the university level that specialization accompanied by advanced instruction combines differentiation with facilitation of change.

Education and social class

Structuring of a school system so that pupils pass from one class or grade to the next by promotion is in part a response to problems of scale and in part associated with a more elaborated content of teaching. It may also reflect a shift away from an elitist system, manifested, for example, by the decline of gentlemanly prerogatives at the university and the adoption of merit competition for entry. The oldest formal promotion system, that of China, emphasized advancement from one examination level to eligibility to sit for the next. Over

much of its history that system used achievement criteria for advancement with only minor complication by status considerations, and China was the source of the now world-wide examinations for testing competence.

Once schooling extended beyond ecclesiastical bounds or tutorial practice for formation of an elite, a three-level system emerged in the countries of western Europe: universities for an elite, grammar schools for clerks and as preparation for the university, and primary schools (if any) for the populace. This system became entrenched even as schooling became widely diffused. Meanwhile, it has been economic limitation as much as snobbery that has preserved the idea that the proportion of children enrolled should diminish rapidly at each successive level of school. Tacitly or explicitly, it has been assumed also that lessons grow in difficulty with level and that progressively fewer children can cope with them. In premodern economies relatively few men are needed for the nonmanual occupations. These conditions and assumptions have been slowly modified in the more advanced countries, as people come to believe both that more education is needed among the citizenry of a democracy and that education is a satisfying good in its own right to which all are entitled. However, the pyramidal form persists, and among the functions of the educational system are selection of those pupils who may move to successively higher courses and also, as schools are diversified, allocation of those who do continue among various types and qualities of school.

In societies that have developed school systems there are sets of adult vocations for which corresponding levels or varieties of schooling are normally the minimal conditions of entry. Selection for continuation in school thus becomes at the same time one factor in the allocation of ultimate roles in society, and allocation among specialized courses of study establishes links to particular subsets of adult positions within the broader categories anticipated by educational selection. Thus, the schools become related in ever more complex ways to economic and social stratification and to the mobility structures of the society. At the same time, the procedures adopted for intraschool selection and allocation have repercussions on pedagogical processes, teacher orientations, and the general atmosphere of the school.

Education-determined status. A formal school system, then, never exists solely as an ornament to the leisure of a privileged stratum but serves also as a means for determining which individuals will occupy various positions in the society. Traditionally, few children from humble families gained admittance to the "classical" schools. Since passage through the upper levels of such schools facilitated entry into elitist occupations and positions, education contributed as much to intergenerational stability as to mobility in status. However, as lower-status children come to form an appreciable proportion of postprimary enrollments, schooling plays a more important part in distributing individuals among occupations and status levels; educated and able sons of workers fill the expanding white-collar and professional positions and even displace some of the less able sons of the older elites. In open and nonrestrictive economies, however, once prolonged schooling becomes widespread the separate and distinctive effect of the sheer amount of schooling upon economic and social status is blurred. Parental status will play a small part, but native ability, drive, health, and luck make for wide status variability among men of equivalent schooling.

Thus neither the association of schooling with parental status nor its association with the individual's own adult status is simple or stable. The clearest instances of education-determined status exist where the individual's status is defined by his position in a bureaucracy and where such a position is conditional upon possession of particular certificates. Developing societies during the period when school opportunities are still distributed narrowly (in proportionate enrollments but not necessarily in terms of parental status) provide the most striking contemporary examples of education-determined status; however, they also display the precarious political influence of educated elites as populist political practices take root. Moreover, in such societies the status associated with years of schooling is status in a new structure growing up beside the old system. The connections between old and new status systems may be tenuous and the roles of schooled men in them quite disparate, although as yet we know little about these relationships.

Selection and allocation

In the intraschool sorting operations many factors are at play. In all societies self-selection (or, conversely, dropping out) is important. In earlier periods when the schools retained a literary or religious flavor throughout, self-selection (which always incorporates some ability factors) occurred sometimes mainly within the elite and sometimes more broadly, especially in recruitment to the clergy. As enrollments have broadened and schooling has become prolonged and diversified, self-selection—as well as self-allocation to lines of study or types of schools—has been extended to increasing proportions of the population.

However, even in the most egalitarian societies, readiness to use schools is unevenly distributed through both geographic and social space. These imparities exceed what might be explained by differences in financial capacity or native ability. In part, they are associated with area and ethnic differentials in what schooling can contribute to subsequent incomes and positions, but the degree of awareness of both the pragmatic and the more esoteric values of schooling reflects also the communication structure of the society. Interacting with self-selection are the practices and policies of teachers and the rules for promotion and allocation that have become educational customs. These range from informal guidance to the most formal and rigid examination systems.

Examination systems.   Especially pervasive are the difficulties associated with the use of examinations, although a clear appreciation of this problem is comparatively recent. So long as schooling beyond simple literacy was confined to small minorities, Western countries relied primarily upon self-selection and status selection, with informal identification of talent by performance in the lower school. However, as school systems grew this procedure became inadequate, and teachers' assessments and classroom exercises were supplemented and even replaced by systematic testing, often by examinations prepared by outside experts. Whereas standardized external examinations were adopted in China at a time when they could be limited to classical literary material, in the more recent Western systems such examinations were introduced at a time when schools and curricula were rapidly diversifying. No single traditional set of criteria comparable to that of the Chinese could suffice, and in the West standardized examinations have seldom become so central a feature of an entire school system as in some Oriental lands. By the same token, rote learning has been less pervasive, and it is no accident that "progressive" education emerged in the United States—the least rigid and least examination-prone of the Western nations.

In the West testing shifted to a mass basis in response to several circumstances: growing enrollments, pressures from new subpopulations for entry to postprimary schools, concern for protecting or imposing "standards" (which extended in some nations to intellectual life outside the schools), rising aspirations for equality of educational opportunity, and most recently anxiety about identifying the unutilized "reserves of talent." Increasing reliance upon examinations has injected into previously looser systems the well-known pressures upon teachers to orient their lessons to expected tests rather than to exploration of the subject or to the child's mental and creative development. On the other hand, mass testing has led to increasing awareness of irregularities in standards among schools and the educational poverty of the poorest schools, particularly in decentralized systems. The counterpoints of quality versus quantity and of conformity to set standards versus diversity of educational outcomes have been laid out with a new clarity in recent years.

Selection procedures. Meanwhile, there has been a growing concern about the validity of tests as bases for selection and allocation, however reliable they may be for measuring a restricted set of accomplishments. Tests in the traditional academic core subjects may satisfactorily predict future academic success along the same lines; however, they are of limited help in predicting occupational success in nonacademic positions that nevertheless presuppose a strong educational preparation. Indeed, as we become more familiar with the intricacies of selection in practice (of which examinations are only a part), doubts about its validity multiply. Errors can be diminished by postponing the age at which selection (or allocation to preferred streams) must occur; by giving children a good number of years in which to manifest their potentialities, underestimation of talent is less likely. Indeed, the present reaction in favor of more "general" education shows that some hoary educational traditions contain much merit.

Systematic investigation, reinforced by changing social philosophies, is revealing more about how the capacity of children to benefit from school is modified by their home environments, including participation in diverse kinds of outside supportive activities; educability is now considered to be a function of prior educational experiences. These relationships are dramatized also in the schools of newly developing countries and among the "culturally deprived" in the backward rural areas and city slums of Western countries.

Again we face conflicting considerations: many of the educationally handicapped will be reluctant pupils if held in school—or marginal workers if they leave. Some respond by apathy or rebellion because they dislike school and think that what they study is useless. Among many who wish to continue but who do poorly in lessons, repeated failure induces withdrawal and lethargy, which sometimes turns into open aggression. Others resent being treated perpetually as nonadults and still others, while surviving in school, see no connection between what they do as pupils and what they expect to do as adults. The growing tendency in contemporary society to impose formal educational requirements for entry to even the least skilled jobs therefore presents schools with an unprecedented task.

Many of these problems reflect unimaginative teaching, while others arise from pressures on schools to orient their programs to selection and allocation standards for admission to a next level of school. As professionals, teachers face a dilemma. Selecting a minority of superior pupils is an obligation, and their own prestige is affected by the outcome, not to mention that encouragement of superior performance is what many teachers most enjoy. However, there is also a primary obligation to maximize the learning of all pupils. Teachers have both the instrumental task of impelling pupils to learn set lessons and the expressive task of making learning pleasant. The process of selection throws the balance to the instrumental side.

Effects of the type of schooling and the type of curriculum upon the choice of a particular vocation shift with technological advances and changing societal structures. Traditionally, only a small proportion of families have relied upon formal instruction for vocational training; manual workers and large parts of the middle stratum have relied largely upon apprenticeship. As the typical individual's schooling was lengthened, three things have happened. First, additional general education has become a prerequisite for a rising proportion of jobs, and hence specialized vocational training has been deferred; most of higher education remains, as it has always been, vocational. Second, much of what previously would have been learned on the job has been formalized and incorporated in vocational and technical schools. Third, on-the-job training has also multiplied, and the age-cycle pattern of vocational and refresher or upgrading study has become more complex and extended.

As the first and third of these tendencies go further, schools can decrease their responsibility for allocation, but insofar as the second tendency predominates, schools are expected to assign children early to courses that prepare for particular kinds of occupation. This is not a task for which schools are well qualified. In practice they identify the pupils that are ready for further academic education—although with less validity than is commonly believed—while giving little useful pedagogical guidance to others. The problem is most critical, although often least recognized, where postschool occupational selection and allocation processes are the most rigidly geared to diplomas (whether by convention, rulings of vocational associations, or government regulation), and it is exacerbated to the degree that status of pupils' families strongly affects educational aspirations or performance. Allocation by the school may range from a formal priority system based on examinations through less formal constraints on pupil choices. Even though guidance may be offered, this rests on a shaky scientific basis and much of it reflects social bias as well as pedagogic rigidity. Moreover, specialized capacities are rare; most pupils will have aptitudes in almost equal degree for a wide range of courses and of occupations, at least within a broad band of general ability.

Recently a tendency toward "manpower planning" has emerged and is rapidly being diffused throughout the world. Its aim is to forecast the numbers of individuals with different occupational qualifications needed by the society, to ration school places accordingly, and then to direct individuals toward the "right" preparation. The validity of these forecasts remains unproved in the present state of research, quite apart from the value question of how much direction should be given to individual choices of education or vocation.

C. Arnold Anderson

[*Directly related are the entries* Literacy; Teaching; Universities. *Other relevant material may be found in* Socialization; Social mobility.]

BIBLIOGRAPHY

Ben-David, Joseph 1963/1964 Professions in the Class System of Present Day Societies: A Trend Report and Bibliography. *Current Sociology* 12:247–330. → In addition to providing a social history of the transformation of the professions, this article emphasizes their relationships with higher education; it includes an extensive bibliography.

Campbell, Roald F.; and Brunnell, Robert A. (editors) 1963 *Nationalizing Influences on Secondary Education.* Univ. of Chicago, Midwest Administration Center. → A demonstration of the forces making for educational uniformity in a highly decentralized administrative system.

Cicourel, Aaron V.; and Kitsuse, John I. 1963 *The Educational Decision-makers.* Indianapolis: Bobbs-Merrill. → An analysis of the confounding of educational guidance by psychological assumptions and social bias.

Davis, James A. 1965 *Undergraduate Career Decisions.* Chicago: Aldine.

Floud, Jean E.; and Halsey, A. H. 1958 The Sociology of Education: A Trend Report and Bibliography. *Current Sociology* 7, no. 3. → Traces the emergence of the

discipline and assesses its main contributions. Contains an extensive bibliography.

Gage, Nathaniel L. (editor) 1963 *Handbook of Research on Teaching.* Chicago: Rand McNally. → A symposium of research and interpretation on all aspects of teaching: assessment of methods, recruitment to the profession, etc.

Goody, Jack; and Watt, Ian 1963 The Consequences of Literacy. *Comparative Studies in Society and History* 5:304–345. → An analysis of the social consequences of the introduction of writing into a society.

Halsey, A. H. (editor) 1961 *Ability and Educational Opportunity.* Paris: Organization for Economic Cooperation and Development. → Comparison of educational selection and allocation in various countries.

Halsey, A. H.; Floud, Jean; and Anderson, C. Arnold (editors) 1961 *Education, Economy, and Society: A Reader in the Sociology of Education.* New York: Free Press.

Henry, Jules 1960 A Cross-cultural Outline of Education. *Current Anthropology* 1:267–305.

National Society for the Study of Education, Committee on Education for the Professions 1962 *Education for the Professions.* Edited by Nelson B. Henry. Univ. of Chicago Press.

Sanford, Nevitt (editor) 1962 *The American College.* New York: Wiley. → A symposium of research on virtually every aspect of higher education, with special attention to variations in selection.

Stinchcombe, Arthur L. 1964 *Rebellion in a High School.* Chicago: Quadrangle Books. → An analysis of the sources of educational apathy induced by compulsory education under existing pedagogical conditions.

Waller, Willard W. (1932) 1961 *The Sociology of Teaching.* New York: Russell.

Znaniecki, Florian 1936 *Social Actions.* New York: Farrar & Rinehart. → See pages 189–230 on "Educational Guidance" for a discussion of the social relationships that constitute education.

III

EDUCATIONAL ORGANIZATION

The study of educational organization has its place in the social sciences mainly as an application of theories of organization. In such theories any organization, whether a national system of education, an industry, or a single institution, such as a school, hospital, or prison, is treated as if it were a self-contained system of social relationships. The link to the wider network of social relationships, of which any organization must be a part, is then treated in terms of boundary maintenance, functional exchange, or the distinction between internal structure and external environment. At the most macroscopic level, studies of education concentrate on the functional relations between education and the other great institutional orders of society—the economy, the polity, religion, and kinship—and form part of general comparative sociology.

Educational organizations—that is, the social

structure and functioning of an educational system or its constituent units—are studied at descending levels of generality. An educational system or subsystem, an individual school or a university, will have a formal constitution defining the distribution of roles within it, the allocation of resources and disciplinary powers, and the content and method of teaching. It will also have an informal pattern of power, influence, and communication and a characteristic value system. Initially, organizations are formal arrangements made to pursue defined ends; however, within them arise spontaneous friendships, loyalties, habits of work, and routines of communication that may support or subvert, but that will in any case modify and complicate, the functioning of the system as defined in its formal charter.

These aspects of organization may be studied both individually and in relation to one another; but in the case of the sociology of the school, the effectiveness of any study depends upon knowledge at a more macroscopic level. There is what W. W. Waller termed "a separate culture of the school," but this is responsive to the structure of the wider society. Wider social trends can and do affect and alter the functions of schools, colleges, and universities, with or without any explicit redirection of aim or overt reorganization. In any case, they give rise to the stresses and strains that underlie and permeate the daily life of educational institutions. Thus, the analysis of the role of the teacher or the pupil must sooner or later go beyond the boundary of the school or college as a social system and take account of those influences in the external environment that support or frustrate tacit or explicit educational goals as they are interpreted within the organization. The structure and culture of a school derive partly from the logic of a teaching and learning situation, but they are also, and usually more importantly, shaped by outside influences. Persons entering the organization bring with them expectations and assumptions about their own rights and obligations. The family, neighborhood, class, and ethnic environment of pupils send them into school with varying attitudes toward their educational experience. To understand the internal life of the school, it is necessary to see it in a wider social context; in this way the sociology, anthropology, and social psychology of the school is necessarily linked to the study of the family, the neighborhood, the religious community, and, ultimately, to the whole of society.

Sociological studies. Education is a topic as old as civilization, but only in recent years has educational organization, as described above, been defined as a special area for sociological study. There is no article on educational organization in the *Encyclopaedia of the Social Sciences*, which was published in the early 1930s. However, the general field of the sociology of education has a recognizable, if checkered, history, which dates perhaps from the publication of Lester Ward's *Dynamic Sociology* in 1883 and certainly from the delivery of Durkheim's lectures (1902–1911) at the Sorbonne in the early years of the twentieth century. Thorstein Veblen's satirical and bitter classic on *The Higher Learning in America*, which constituted a landmark in the analysis of the university as a social system, appeared in 1918, and Willard W. Waller's treatment of the school in sociologically similar, if politically more urbane, terms was published in 1932.

However, it is only since World War II that the study of educational organization has begun to flourish as an integral part of the social sciences. This development owes much to the rise of a group of American and European sociologists who have been determined to treat education in the same terms as any other social institution, that is, as an object intrinsically worthy of scientific study, apart from any concern for social policy or human betterment.

Education and society

Appreciation of the character and significance of educational systems is becoming increasingly important for the understanding of contemporary society. Education has expanded rapidly with the advance of industrialization; it is being extended to new nations and new classes of students, and new pedagogical methods are continually being developed. Now that as much as 5 per cent of national income may be spent on education, economists, sociologists, and psychologists are all drawn to analyze the comparative costs, efficiency, and functioning of the various systems of teaching, research, and administration.

Educational planning plays a prominent part in the modern government of both advanced and so-called underdeveloped countries, and in the recent past it has produced a large literature of official reports and academic studies that illustrate the problems of educational organization at widely varying levels of educational development. In California the problem is to devise a system of mass higher education, whereas in underdeveloped countries like Nigeria the problem is to develop higher education while at the same time creating adequate primary and secondary education. One of these official planning reports deserves special mention:

the Robbins Report, which has provided a detailed description (and prescription) for higher education in Britain, has also yielded an excellent comparative sociography of the secondary and higher educational systems of Australia, Canada, France, Germany, the Netherlands, New Zealand, Switzerland, the United States, and the Soviet Union (Great Britain . . . 1963).

Types of educational organization

Educational systems have one universal characteristic: they transmit knowledge and belief. They consist, therefore, of a disciplined relation between teacher and taught, but they can and do vary according to what is to be taught, how, by whom, and to whom. Accordingly, the classification of types and the analysis of variations may proceed from all or any of the following four points of reference. First, the *aims* of the organization define its role in relation to knowledge and belief, whether as guardian, critic, or innovator. Second, the *control* of the organization refers to its relations—of control and subservience, service and support—with other social institutions, notably the state, the church, the family, and the employer. Third, the *formal organization* refers to the allocation of roles within the organization, the rights and duties attaching to them, and the methods of selection for the various positions of administration, teaching, research, and learning. Finally, the *informal organization* consists of the "subcultures," or spontaneous groupings and patterns of interaction that form within the formal framework of the organization.

Weber's typology of educational systems. No typology of educational organization based on all these sources of variation exists as yet in the literature, although the accumulation of case studies and comparative work promises to make the task feasible. A beginning is to be found in Max Weber's discussion of charisma and bureaucracy and their application to the social roles of the Chinese literati (Weber 1906–1924). Weber's principal reference is to the aims and functions of whole systems of education rather than to the differentiation of functions among particular organizations within them. His attention is, moreover, largely confined to those forms of education aimed at producing members of the elite or ruling strata of societies, and thus he has little or nothing to say about modern mass education.

Most educational systems have been restricted to elites, and from this point of view Weber distinguished three broad types of social personality: the *charismatic,* that of the *cultivated man,* and

the *expert.* These three social types correspond to three types of power and authority in society. The first is that of the charismatic leader whose personal gift or mission is magically or divinely inspired. The second includes a wide range of forms of authority sanctioned by custom and tradition— for example, that of the Chinese mandarins, the minority leisure class of citizens in ancient Greece or Rome, or the gentlemanly strata of eighteenth-century Europe. The third type corresponds to the rational and bureaucratic forms of authority typical of advanced industrial societies, for example, that of the special expertise of scientists and professional men. In the total range of educational systems, the first and third of Weber's types are polar opposites, and the most numerous actual examples are found within the intermediate range. In reality there are no pure cases of these types, as Weber took care to emphasize.

Strictly speaking, the qualities necessary for charismatic leadership cannot be transmitted by a system of education in the sense that this would be understood in the modern world. By definition, charisma cannot be created by training; it is a personal gift of grace that either exists in a person or infiltrates him through magical rebirth. In contrast, the cultivation of the pupil for the style of life of a secular or religious status group is in principle possible for anyone, and this is likewise true for the type of organization that sets out to train experts for practical usefulness in a public authority, a business enterprise, or a scientific laboratory. Although entry to either the second system (that of "education") or the third (that of "training") is open in principle to individuals of any social origin, the goals will nevertheless vary —in the former case, according to the idea of cultivation held by the dominant stratum; in the latter, according to the internal requirements of the expertise. Thus, the second type of organization includes a wide range of actual educational goals. The goal may be the production of a socially distinctive type of knight or courtier, as in the case of the Japanese samurai; it may be the education of a scribe or intellectual, where a priestly class is dominant; or it may be the amateur gentlemanly administrator, as in imperial Britain.

Systems of education for membership in a cultivated status group have usually been under religious control. This is true of the Christian, Islamic, and Judaic traditions, but the Chinese literati and the Hellenic philosophers' schools are important exceptions. The education of the Chinese mandarin, although based on sacred texts, consisted in laymen teaching laymen, and the Hellenic schools were completely secular and designed for the education of a leisured ruling class.

Bureaucratization. The characteristic mark of the type of education that aims at imparting specialized expert training is the standardized examination system. This is not to say that examination systems are either indispensable to bureaucratic forms of authority or unknown to prebureaucratic systems. For example, the special examination system came late to the French, English, and American bureaucracies, whereas classical China for many centuries enjoyed a politically organized examination system for official careers. However, the Chinese system was not designed to examine special skills but rather to ensure that successful candidates were broadly equipped with the high culture of the literati. In the case of the modern bureaucracies, qualifications for entry are increasingly defined in terms of specialized scientific and technological training, at the expense of wide humanistic cultivation. As Weber put it: "Behind all the present discussions of the foundations of the educational system, the struggle of the 'specialist type of man' against the older type of 'cultivated man' is hidden at some decisive point. This fight is determined by the irresistibly expanding bureaucratization of all public and private relations of authority and by the ever-increasing importance of expert and specialized knowledge" ([1906–1924] 1946, p. 243).

Educational systems in industrial society

Bureaucratic organization of authority and the specialization of knowledge are the starting points for the analysis of educational systems in modern industrial society. Education is a planned process of cultural transmission, consisting of three elements: preservation, innovation, and dissemination. Whereas in simple cultures only preservation is important, in modern industrial society all three elements are essential to the maintenance of a culture that is cumulative in its complexity. Such cultures require long and specialized education for increasing proportions of the population, as well as the organization of innovation in institutions of research and development. The translation of these processes of cultural transmission into forms of educational organization varies according to the political and social structure of nations, but the basic trend toward large-scale specialization and bureaucratization is unmistakable.

The major force for change has been the pressure in industrial society to incorporate a scientific culture into the organization of studies. Thus, since the second half of the nineteenth century,

educational systems have expanded in numbers of students, range of teaching, and provision for research. They have also become increasingly dependent on governments for financial support and increasingly controlled by the state. Primary education is compulsory for all, and secondary education is available for an increasing majority.

The structure of systems of higher education is the outcome of a long process of historical adaptation, with the dominant line of descent stemming from the European medieval universities. There are other more ancient traditions of higher learning in the Islamic world and in China and India. But the spread of Western technological civilization has carried the European conception of a university throughout the world and especially to those parts of Africa, Latin America, and Asia that at some time have been dominated or ruled by European countries.

There are considerable variations in the place retained by universities in expanded systems of higher education. The general trend has been toward functional specialization among different kinds of colleges and institutes, although, of course, the new professions based on technology and the social sciences meet with greater or lesser acceptance in the teaching schedule of different institutions. It is in the United States that the newer branches of higher education are most likely to be included within the university systems; American graduate schools have been particularly willing to incorporate almost every kind of vocational course. The Soviet Union represents the opposite tendency; the Russian institutes are highly differentiated, providing education in a single specialized field and entirely separated from the universities. The western European universities occupy an intermediate position, with technology and teacher training commonly provided in separate institutions that are often of lower prestige.

Aims. Education in industrial societies is characteristically aimed at the production of experts; consequently, it is organized in a complex of schools and colleges with more or less specialized aims in relation to education, training, and research. Quite apart from the need in all societies (industrial or preindustrial) to ensure the communication of some kind of common value system, the economic functions of education require that secondary and higher forms of schooling be based on universal or near-universal primary schooling.

Primary schooling. All advanced industrial countries have universal compulsory schooling at the primary stage and curricula designed to equip the whole population with basic literacy and numeracy in preparation for possible entry to more specialized education at the secondary stage. Primary schools are at the same time the major agencies of socialization into groups beyond the family. According to Parsons (1959), the American primary school weans children from complete reliance on the moral assumptions of particularism and diffuseness, which are characteristic of kin relations, and inculcates acceptance of universalism and specificity as the essential basis for role playing in a differentiated industrial economy.

Secondary schooling. Economic demand for trained scientific and professional manpower and a growing political demand for equality of educational opportunity result everywhere in educational expansion. Throughout the world the systems vary enormously. In Soviet Russia the school system has been centrally organized to meet estimated demands for labor through selective technical education; and it has incorporated both political indoctrination and a fusing of school and work at the secondary level in order to foster loyalty to Soviet society and its political and social ideology. It is significant, in terms of both of these aims of Russian education, that plans have been anounced for secondary boarding schools to be established for 80 per cent of pupils by 1980 (Great Britain . . . 1963). In western Europe the organization of education still preserves its traditional form, reflecting the demands of the class system for schooling according to social origin and as preparation for a particular social position. Secondary schools are differentiated, with a minority offering curricula that prepare pupils for entry to higher education. In most European countries entry to skilled trades is accomplished by some form of apprenticeship or learnership system within industry; however, the trend is toward transferring industrial training to technical schools and colleges, along either American or Russian lines.

In the United States secondary schooling developed from a movement to Americanize large numbers of immigrants and to raise the educational and social level of new and growing communities. However, in many countries there has generally been opposition to the integrated extension of compulsory common schooling. The problem in Europe, and in many of its Asian and African colonial or former colonial territories, is to develop comprehensive types of secondary education out of systems of separate schools with unequal social prestige, which were designed historically for different social classes (see, for instance, Pedley 1963). Attempts in this direction have met with varying success. In Czechoslovakia, Yugoslavia, and else-where in eastern Europe the break with tradition has been sharp. There is also a strong movement in Scandinavia in favor of "comprehensive schools" (in which all children of compulsory school age are given various types of training within the same institution); weaker movements in favor of such schools exist in France and Britain.

Universities. The European universities remain elitist in conception. Although in many countries (with the notable exceptions of England and the Soviet Union) they are formally open to all secondary school graduates, compared with American universities they are highly restricted both in numbers and in terms of the social origins of their students.

Universities are usually defined as self-governing communities of scholars. In practice, they may be neither self-governing nor communities nor entirely composed of scholars. Nevertheless, the idea of a corporate body that acts as the "guardian" of a world-wide intellectual culture is what enables the term "university" to be applied to institutions of widely ranging size, quality, and purpose. Intellectual culture is preserved in universities through teaching directed particularly at those students capable of forming the academic succession. In modern times, especially since the rise of the natural sciences, the universities have come to be concerned as much with extending as with preserving knowledge, that is, with research as much as with teaching.

Control. The state exercises a large measure of control over the educational system in all industrial countries. The degree to which religious and private control is permitted varies, and private education may be of crucial social significance, as in the case of the British "public" schools. The degree of centralization also varies; this determines the level at which religious bodies, political parties, teachers' unions, and parents' associations exert pressure in favor of their particular interests. Centralized government may be combined with centralized administration as in France or with decentralized administration as in Sweden, or both may be decentralized as in the United States. But decentralization does not guarantee the autonomy of individual schools. There is, for example, a marked contrast between Britain and the United States in terms of the greater degree of insulation of the British school from outside influences and the greater freedom of the classroom teacher to determine his own methods of teaching and choice of textbooks.

In most countries the financing of universities is mainly borne by the state, although in some countries, for example the United States, there are many purely private institutions. The British universities, although increasingly dependent for their finance on state funds, are nevertheless independent of direct state control and are linked to the government through the University Grants Committee. In the former British colonial territories similar arrangements for state financial support have been made, coupled with self-government in individual universities. Frequently, however (as in Nigeria and Ghana), there is greater stress than in England on the right of the state to control the university according to what is conceived as the national interest.

Principles of authority

Burton Clark (1962, p. 152) distinguished three principles of authority in the control of schools and colleges: *public trusteeship, bureaucracy,* and *colleagueship.* The dominant form is that of the public trust, through which control is exercised by a lay body representing state, community, religious, or other interests. This type of control is common among both state and private schools and colleges. In the public trust the formal position of the internal administration of the school is subordinate to the policy of the lay governors. But in practice the line between policy and administration is often difficult to determine. In any case, the increasing size and specialization of educational organizations favor the growth of bureaucracy and/or the collegiate type of authority. Bureaucratic and trustee types of authority share the characteristic of a hierarchical allocation of jurisdictions and duties, whereas the collegiate type presupposes the equal sharing of power and responsibility among peers.

Bureaucratic organization is typical of large and internally differentiated groups that aim at producing a specified and standardized "product." In schools or colleges that concentrate on instruction rather than education and that standardize their product by regular examinations, bureaucratic organization is correspondingly viable. But educational organizations, and especially universities, usually have other functions, and where the relationship between teacher and students involves character training, there must be an element of particularism that cannot be bureaucratized. For example, the collegiate ideal associated with traditional Oxford and Cambridge is one of a community of established older and aspiring younger scholars living closely together and cooperating in the task of preserving and transmitting a cultivated way of life. This collegiate system is not conceived as narrowly intellectual in its scope, and far less

as a tradition of occupational training. It is intended to pass on to each new generation of scholars a total culture or style of life, including carefully nurtured elements of mind and aesthetic taste and character in due measure. Relations of teachers and taught within this system are particularistic, affective, and attended by diffuse obligations.

By contrast, in the kind of college that trains the student for a lucrative, specialized technical position in business or the professions, the typical organization is bureaucratic. The institution assumes no responsibility for the values or social character of the novitiate; teacher and taught meet only in the context of formal instruction. The relationship is segmental rather than comprehensive, and the obligations specific rather than diffuse.

Specialization and professionalization. The modern social context of higher education increasingly favors the bureaucratic type of institution. A technological economy seeks to fashion the institution of higher learning as an antechamber for its manpower demands and as a source of marketable technical innovation. As systems of higher education expand, they recruit students from wider and wider ranges of social origin, a practice that no longer guarantees the homogeneity of family and school backgrounds, on which the traditional collegiate life of the ancient universities depended. Students seek a degree course to earn a living, rather than college residence to complete their induction into a style of life. Similarly, in the same context, the career interests of professors and lecturers encourage research, which brings academic and professional recognition, or administration, which brings local reward, rather than teaching, which commonly brings neither.

The trend toward increasingly large schools and colleges is coupled with the proliferation of more specialized administrative, teaching, and research roles, especially, although by no means exclusively, at the higher stages of education. Teaching has become an elaborate hierarchy of specialized professions, with specific qualifications for entry and increasing social and professional distance between the positions at the apex of the university system and the classroom teacher in a primary school. For example, the traditional integration of secondary and university teaching careers in France is breaking down under this pressure. At the same time, the geographical and social range of recruitment to teaching at all levels is widening into a national and even international market. Administration of large schools and colleges has also created specialized careers in educational administration, ancillary health and welfare services, and especially student counseling or vocational guidance.

Conflicts within the organization.   The professionalization and specialization of the teaching professions constitute another force favoring colleagueship rather than bureaucratic authority. "Rationality in academic settings often seems best served by flat structures with relatively little hierarchy, a minimum of rules, and much freedom for the typical practitioner" (Clark 1962, pp. 161–162). Conflicts within schools and universities often express themselves as struggles between the administration and the faculty over the degree of "flatness" of organization and its application to the multiple functions of education. Thus, if the formal organization of schools and colleges is made more bureaucratic through increasing scale, conflicts are typically brought about through specialization and take the form of opposition between bureaucratic and professional definitions of roles. In another guise similar conflicts emerge between "locals" and "cosmopolitans" (Lazarsfeld & Thielens 1958; cf. Caplow & McGee 1958), with the former oriented toward the organization, especially its teaching functions, and the latter oriented toward a profession extending beyond the boundaries of the institution, especially toward the world-wide pursuit of new knowledge in a specialist field of science or scholarship. The informal organization of educational institutions is also conditioned by these conflicts as well as by accommodations to the formal disciplinary relations between teachers and students.

Student subcultures

The conception of an organization as defined in its formal charter or organization chart, or its normative conception as expressed, for example, in "the idea of a university" (Newman 1852), may or may not faithfully reproduce an objective description of the statistical norms of behavior within it. Typically, both the formal organization and the normative conception are extensively modified by the existence of an informal organization, and in the case of schools and universities this informal structure appears as a set of subcultures among teachers and students. The distinction between "locals" and "cosmopolitans" referred to above is now commonplace in studies of university teachers. Student subcultures have also been identified in recent studies of colleges and high schools. Martin Trow and Burton Clark have distinguished four types of subcultures that flourish in varying degrees on different types of campuses (Clark 1962,

chapter 6). The traditional culture is *collegiate;* it is pleasure seeking and manifests intense loyalty to the organization, although not to the intellectual purposes of the organization. Where the latter is also present, that is, where the loyalties of students to their college are articulated through the intellectual concerns of the senior members, there emerges an *academic* culture, symbolized by the library and the seminar. Where neither is present there is a *consumer–vocational* culture—a time-serving college attendance for the sake of acquiring a degree or diploma and, hence, a claim to a job. The fourth possibility occurs where a high value is attached to ideas and the institution is disesteemed; those circumstances encourage the *nonconformist* or bohemian culture which is sometimes found on the edge of academic life.

It should be emphasized that the authors have tried to distinguish cultures in terms of shared or group norms rather than to suggest classifications of either students or universities. All four subcultures may be found in any university and may influence any student. The four student cultures are derived from two variables, namely, degree of attachment to the institution and degree of attachment to intellectual ideas. The reference to "intellectual ideas" is intended to distinguish knowledge and techniques that are "useless" from those that are "useful" in the sense of being marketable or defined in terms of an occupational requirement. The distinction between academic and vocational subcultures is close to the distinction made earlier between "education" for a nonprofessional elite position and "training" for a clearly defined professional occupation.

Institutional and intellectual loyalties are strengthened or weakened by the modes of recruitment, social origins and destiny of the student, the social organization of the university, and the interests of the teaching, research, and administrative staff. In all industrial societies the increasing importance of the examination system, the intrusion of science, and the growth of the professions and of governmental administration mark the beginning of a double shift from the collegiate toward both the academic and the vocational types of culture among students.

Vocational culture is fostered under circumstances in which students are recruited widely from all social classes, especially from those that need and want to use educational qualifications to gain occupational advantage and security. It grows most readily in large, impersonal, nonresidential institutions, where the administration is highly bureaucratic and the interests of the staff are inclined toward research and administration rather than teaching. Scientific industrialism generates precisely these conditions. It encourages, over a widening range of occupations, the allocation of roles according to achievement rather than by ascription, with a consequent endemic search for talented people and the proliferation of educational institutions as training centers for a society that exhibits an increasingly complex division of labor. Modern universities in industrial towns, as well as (even more clearly) technical and commercial colleges and evening institutes, have recruited students and organized their studies in ways that unavoidably tend to promote a vocational rather than an academic alternative to traditional collegiate culture.

Rejection of educational aims. Rather similar subcultures are also found in schools where the nonconformist variant shades over into, or is replaced by, a delinquent subculture that expresses rejection of the educational aims of the school. In a study of American high schools Coleman (1961) argued that these variations in patterns of values and behavior inside the school reflect the existence of a general adolescent culture in the wider society. He points out that diverse organizations—including factories, jails, armies, and hospitals—consist of an administrative corps controlling a larger subordinate group. The relationship takes the form of an exchange bargain or wages being exchanged for work; in the case of a school, "grades" and promotion are exchanged for learning and good behavior. Under all such circumstances, pressure is put on individuals by the subordinate group to conform to the group's norms in order to prevent excessive competition and ensure a maximum return for minimum effort on the part of the average member. Where the adolescent culture is collegiate, vocational, or delinquent rather than academic, the result is to thwart high scholastic standards and to reduce the correlation between high intelligence and high academic performance. The challenge then becomes one of devising an organization that will harness the energy of the adolescent culture to educational aims.

A. H. HALSEY

[See also ACADEMIC FREEDOM; ADULT EDUCATION; BUREAUCRACY; TEACHING; UNIVERSITIES; and the biography of WALLER.]

BIBLIOGRAPHY

CAPLOW, THEODORE; and McGEE, REECE J. 1958 *The Academic Marketplace.* New York: Basic Books. → A paperback edition was published in 1961 by Wiley.

CLARK, BURTON R. 1962 *Educating the Expert Society.* San Francisco: Chandler.

COLEMAN, JAMES S. 1961 *The Adolescent Society: The Social Life of the Teenager and Its Impact on Education.* New York: Free Press.

CURLE, ADAM 1963 *Strategy for Developing Societies: A Study of Educational and Social Factors in Relation to Economic Growth.* London: Tavistock.

DE WITT, NICHOLAS 1961 *Education and Professional Employment in the U.S.S.R.* Washington: National Science Foundation.

DURKHEIM, ÉMILE (1902–1911) 1956 *Education and Sociology.* Glencoe, Ill.: Free Press.

FLOUD, JEAN E. 1962 Teaching in the Affluent Society. *British Journal of Sociology* 13:299–308.

FLOUD, JEAN E.; and HALSEY, A. H. 1958 The Sociology of Education: A Trend Report and Bibliography. *Current Sociology* 7, no. 3.

GORDON, C. WAYNE 1957 *The Social System of the High School: A Study in the Sociology of Adolescence.* Glencoe, Ill.: Free Press.

GRANT, NIGEL 1965 *Soviet Education.* Gloucester, Mass.: Smith.

GREAT BRITAIN, COMMITTEE ON HIGHER EDUCATION 1963 *Higher Education.* Report of the Committee appointed by the Prime Minister, under the Chairmanship of Lord Robbins, 1961–1963. Papers by Command, Cmnd. 2154. London: H.M. Stationery Office. → See especially Appendix No. 5.

GROSS, NEAL 1958 *Who Runs Our Schools?* New York: Wiley.

GROSS, NEAL; MASON, WARD S.; and McEACHERN, ALEXANDER W. 1958 *Explorations in Role Analysis: Studies of the School Superintendency Role.* New York: Wiley.

HALSEY, A. H.; FLOUD, JEAN; and ANDERSON, C. ARNOLD (editors) 1961 *Education, Economy, and Society: A Reader in the Sociology of Education.* New York: Free Press. → See especially parts 5 and 6.

LAZARSFELD, PAUL F.; and THIELENS, WAGNER JR. 1958 *The Academic Mind: Social Scientists in a Time of Crisis.* A report of the Bureau of Applied Social Research, Columbia University. Glencoe, Ill.: Free Press.

MEAD, MARGARET 1951 *The School in American Culture.* Cambridge, Mass.: Harvard Univ. Press.

NEWMAN, JOHN H. (1852) 1957 *The Idea of a University: Defined and Illustrated.* New York: Longmans. → The classic formulation of the ideals of a Christian liberal education. First published as *On the Scope and Nature of University Education.*

PARSONS, TALCOTT (1959) 1961 The School Class as a Social System: Some of Its Functions in American Society. Pages 434–455 in A. H. Halsey, Jean Floud, and C. Arnold Anderson (editors), *Education, Economy, and Society.* New York: Free Press. → First published in Volume 29 of the *Harvard Educational Review.*

PEDLEY, ROBERT 1963 *The Comprehensive School.* Baltimore: Penguin.

RIESMAN, DAVID (1956) 1958 *Constraint and Variety in American Education.* Garden City, N.Y.: Doubleday.

TAYLOR, WILLIAM 1963 *The Secondary Modern School.* London: Faber & Faber.

VEBLEN, THORSTEIN (1918) 1957 *The Higher Learning in America: A Memorandum on the Conduct of Universities by Business Men.* New York: Sagamore.

WALLER, WILLARD W. (1932) 1961 *The Sociology of Teaching.* New York: Russell.

WARD, LESTER F. (1883) 1926 *Dynamic Sociology: Or, Applied Social Science, as Based Upon Statical Sociology and the Less Complex Sciences.* 2d ed., 2 vols. New York: Appleton.

WEBER, MAX (1906–1924) 1946 *From Max Weber: Essays in Sociology.* Translated and edited by Hans H. Gerth and C. Wright Mills. New York: Oxford Univ. Press.

WILSON, BRYAN R. 1962 The Teacher's Role: A Sociological Analysis. *British Journal of Sociology* 13:15–32.

WILSON, LOGAN 1942 *The Academic Man: A Study in the Sociology of a Profession.* New York: Oxford Univ. Press.

The World Year Book of Education, 1965: The Education Explosion. Edited by George Z. F. Bereday and Joseph A. Lauwerys. 1965 New York: Columbia Univ., Teachers College.

EDUCATIONAL PSYCHOLOGY

A definitive history of educational psychology is still wanting. Existing histories of areas of psychology are generally addressed to other purposes, with the development of educational psychology treated incidentally (for example, Boring 1929; Murphy 1929). Burt (1957) prepared a history of educational psychology but it was limited to Britain.

Early origins. The beginnings of recorded speculation about the relationships between human nature and the educational process may be found in the classical Greek period (Brubacher 1947). The writings of such pre-Socratic philosophers as Democritus (5th century, B.C.) stressed the effects of the home on the learner and anticipated, among modern notions, the belief in the value of training children to manage property by sharing property with them.

The most detailed treatment of psychological matters relevant to education in this early Greek period is found in the works of Aristotle. Of particular significance for the course of subsequent developments in education were his emphasis on the intellectual aspects of behavior and education and his support for a "faculty" psychology, which asserted some independence among components of mental activity and the possibility of training these components, or "faculties," through their "exercise." Aristotelian influence remained strong through ensuing centuries and may still be found in some current views on the conduct of education.

Possibly the next major influence on educational–psychological thought occurred in the efforts of Scholastics to rationalize Aristotelian thinking in terms of the doctrines of Christianity. The most complete and influential product of this effort lies in the magnum opus of Aquinas, *Summa theologica,* which for the most part continues to constitute the educational frame of reference for a significant group of Catholic educators and psychologists.

Faculty psychology versus associationism. In the seventeenth century came the first strong attack by empiricists on the entrenched faculty psychology of Aristotle and on Descartes's thesis that "true knowledge" is based on ideas that are innate in man rather than learned. According to the protest, epitomized by Locke (Brett 1921), the mind at birth is blank (*tabula rasa*), rather than a repository of preformed ideas. Ideas, Locke maintained, result from the sensory experiences of the child and his reflection upon these sensations. This empiricist position found many adherents—although many of them rejected the postulated "faculty" of reflection—and led to a psychology of learning called "associationism," in which Aristotelian "faculties" were firmly rejected in favor of explanations of learning through the association of sensory experiences and ideas. It is ironical that this "non-Aristotelian" explanation was quite congruent with some of Aristotle's own thinking. It was Aristotle who first enunciated the principles of learning through "similarity," "contrast," and "contiguity."

By the eighteenth century, there had emerged two sharply competing educational psychologies: faculty psychology and associationism. The conflicting viewpoints controlled the pedagogical scene through the next century, with faculty psychology in the more influential position. Toward the close of the nineteenth century, the two schools of thought, then even more sharply differentiated, were represented in two textbooks, one written by Alexander Bain and the other by James Sully. In *Outlines of Psychology With Special Reference to the Theory of Education* (1884), Sully emphasized the faculty-psychology position. Bain utilized the associationist position in *Education as a Science* (1879).

Formal discipline. In the principles and practices of education in the United States and England during the nineteenth century, formal discipline was the pedagogical rule, and curriculum content was largely selected not for the instrumental value of the knowledge area, but rather for its promise of providing rigorous and systematic exercise of the postulated mental faculties. Nor were those educators with associationist views free of this formal-discipline approach to education. Apparently their practices partook of the same type of discipline, providing formal training of the senses in the same fashion in which their counterparts were training mental faculties (Brubacher 1947, p. 143).

Child-centeredness.   A resistance to both faculty psychology and formal discipline began to develop early in the nineteenth century. Johann Pestalozzi, the Swiss social reformer, and Friedrich Froebel, the German mystic, made strong petitions for the recognition of the importance of the learner's unique interests and abilities in selecting educational ends and curriculum content. At the same time, another German, Johann Friedrich Herbart, introduced the concept of "apperceptive mass," the totality of conscious ideas, constituting the synthesizing agent of experience—and implied the importance of the learner's interests in structuring the procedures of education. Those who later were to adopt the "child-centered" orientation in education and child rearing found frequent cause to refer to the ideas of Pestalozzi, Froebel, and Herbart, as well as to those of the earlier Rousseau.

Emergence of a scientific posture.   In contrast to the earlier, almost exclusively speculative, approach to the nature and nurture of learning, the closing decades of the nineteenth century saw the rise of systematically empirical and experimental treatments of relevant questions. It has been suggested that the formal beginning of educational psychology should be placed in the 1880s, when the experimental and empirical studies of Sir Francis Galton (association, reaction time, sensory acuity), G. Stanley Hall ("contents" of children's minds), and Hermann Ebbinghaus (memory) were published.

In the next decade, Hall began the publication of the *Pedagogical Seminary*, and William James effectively began to popularize psychology in education through his *Talks to Teachers* and public lectures.

Intelligence testing.   It was also in the 1890s that Alfred Binet, of France, began the work that was to dominate the thinking about intelligence and educability in the twentieth century. Faced with the task of developing procedures for identifying mental retardation among Parisian pupils, and in collaboration initially with V. Henri and finally with Theodore Simon, Binet developed an intelligence test around the concept of "mental age," in which complex mental processes were examined rather than merely reaction time and sensory discrimination skill.

The 1905 Binet–Simon Scale was translated into English by Henry Goddard in 1908 and used in American schools. Frederick Kuhlmann produced a revision for the United States in 1912. Louis Terman, in 1916, extended and modified the Binet–Simon Scale (the Stanford–Binet); with subsequent revisions, the Stanford–Binet became the most widely known and used individual intelligence test in the world, and this led to translations and adaptations for widely different cultures (for example, the Tanaka–Binet in Japan). Terman's monumental inquiries into giftedness (*Genetic Studies of Genius*, 1925–1929) partially relied upon and sprang from his work in the development of the Stanford–Binet Scale.

Thorndike and connectionism.   At the beginning of the twentieth century, the first identifiable "giant" in educational psychology emerged—Edward Lee Thorndike, who is generally acknowledged as the first man who might appropriately deserve the label "educational psychologist." Although Thorndike had previously made a significant contribution to the field of animal learning in 1901, he made a dramatic impact on pedagogy when he and Woodworth produced the classic studies that "slew the dragon of formal discipline" (McDonald 1964). The import of the findings was —and continues to be—that what is learned in one sphere of activity "transfers" to another sphere only when the two spheres share common "elements." That is, the transfer of training is not inherently a property of a mental faculty or of a disciplinary content.

Later findings, including those of another pioneer in educational psychology, Charles H. Judd, suggested that the "common elements" might be as broad as the level of generalization. In any event, the implications for a teaching method and the selection of curriculum content were clear and influential on school practices—the necessity for deliberate teaching for transfer through seeking or demonstrating commonalities among different spheres, content, problems, and so on. The most recent development of this transfer-of-training "theory" is found in Bruner's (1960) argument for identifying and teaching the basic "structure" of any knowledge area—the hypothesis being that there is a basic defining structure to any domain of concern which provides an area of knowledge with the greatest part of its generalizing and heuristic power.

The contributions of Thorndike went far beyond his transfer-of-training theory. In addition to effecting more interest in rigorous and objective research on educational problems, he proposed a utilitarian theory of learning through the formation of "connections" between stimuli and responses (now referred to as "connectionism"), advising that desirable connections be rewarded and undesirable connections punished (Thorndike 1913, p. 20). Of the many assessments of Thorndike's work and influence, McDonald's (1964) is particularly penetrating.

Dewey and progressive education. No discussion of educational psychology in the Western Hemisphere, eastern Europe, or the Far East can ignore the thinking of John Dewey, whose major intellectual image is not that of an educational psychologist. Dewey, easily acknowledged as the sponsor, if not the father, of the "progressive education" movement, produced ideas that effectively became embedded in psychological thinking and teaching in professional education and that continued to influence the conduct of education in the second half of the twentieth century. Of the massive elements of the philosophy proposed (known as "instrumentalism"), those most clearly bearing on the psychology of learning and teaching are his concepts of "growth" and "intelligent action." For Dewey, learning was "intelligent action," in which the learner continuously evaluates his experience in view of what his purposes are and what consequences he actually experiences. The product of this continued evaluation is a redefinition of purposes, continued criticized experiences, and so on without end. "Growth" (more effective purposing and more intelligent action) is the end sought by teachers and learners. In this conception, respect for the interest of the learner is a matter of high priority; similarly, the utilization of the learner's purposes is both important and, indeed, inescapable. Individuality of the pupil and the utilization of problem solving as a pedagogical technique became shibboleths of education in the 1930s and 1940s, although there is a good reason to believe that many teachers who professed Dewey's views failed to understand them adequately.

Between the world wars. In the period between World War I and World War II, three additional influences were at work on the character of educational psychology: psychoanalysis, gestalt psychology, and developments in mental measurement.

Psychoanalysis. The image of Freud's theorizing, which loomed large over psychological thinking throughout the world at the turn of the twentieth century, began to have visible impact on the emphases and practices in education, particularly in non-Catholic areas of Europe and in the United States. The conclusion that there were crucial formative influences in human behavior led to a strong interest in early childhood education and the relationship between home background and schooling. A mental health movement was born, and educators began to express interest in the nonintellectual domain of the learner, not only as a

legitimate educational concern in its own right, but for its possible relationship to the problems of teaching and learning the intellectual content of curricula.

Gestalt psychology. From Germany came a strong dissent to the learning principles propounded by Thorndike. The gestaltists thought that Thorndike's connectionism was too analytical and mechanical to account for the *organization* of behavior. They proposed that behavior is "wholistic"; the search should be for patterns, or "gestalten," rather than for linkage of discrete experiences. There emerged from this view an emphasis on the "education of the whole child," a view that was reinforced by, and in turn reinforced, the mental-hygiene developments in education and the views of Dewey. Insight and reorganization became the new watchwords, although confirming experimental evidence was difficult to find. Textbooks on educational psychology appeared with gestalt, "field," and "organismic" biases (for example, Ogden 1926; Commins 1937).

Development in mental measurement. Although the development of mental tests had begun in the previous century, the need for effective and rapid selection and description devices in mobilizing and assigning military personnel during World War I led to intensification of activity in the measurement field. It was here that the prototype of pencil-and-paper personality scales was born and group intelligence tests were first used (Yerkes 1921). The strong popularization of these scales led quickly to their appearance in the testing programs of schools and in the programs of teacher education. The ready availability of usable measures also fostered more study of individual differences in the schools and made possible the provision of more information about pupils for use in planning curricula and in dealing with learning problems.

Present status and concerns

In general, the procedures of education since World War II have been formulated somewhat independently of the formal theories of learning elaborated by psychologists, who have had little interest in the specifics of the school context (Buswell 1956). Relating the two domains is difficult, in part because theories of learning are not sufficiently mature to offer reliable and confirmable predictions about particular events. Equally relevant, however is the realization that behavioral situations in the schools are complex and heterogeneous (Spence 1959, p. 88). At present, while the school represents an enormously complex psychological arena, the science of psychology is still struggling with its basic concepts and laws. The beginnings of a resolution of this dilemma are presently found in two forms: reconceptualizations of (*a*) the focus of research in educational psychology and (*b*) the nature of "teaching."

Reconception of research. The change in the conception of research in educational psychology is best demonstrated by the difference between two yearbooks of the National Society for the Study of Education (NSSE), published more than twenty years apart and addressed to the implications of the psychology of learning for educational practice. In the first yearbook (NSSE 1942), an attempt was made to identify the necessary implications for education from each of several competing theories of learning. Twenty-two years later (NSSE 1964), however, the earlier intention was overlooked in favor of finding general cues for education in learning theories by looking primarily to the daily problems of the classroom as a source of research activity in educational psychology. That is, an earlier *deductive* approach has given way to a less rigid *inductive* orientation focused on the school. An examination of the literature on educational psychology suggests that the foregoing interest is represented in research activity. Journals representing research and thinking in educational psychology have increased in number and distribution in all major areas of the world and increasingly include studies and conclusions more closely relevant to the affairs of the classroom teacher and the school administrator. At the same time, however, attempts to clarify the relevance of learning theory for pedagogy have also been accelerated.

Reconception of "teaching." Historically, attempts to make psychology meaningful to teachers have been handicapped by a tendency to think of teaching as the application of reliable rules and principles—that is, teachers have tended to look to psychology for immediately applicable and valid procedures—despite the fact that such dogmatic assistance is precluded by the relative instability of psychological data and the highly situational nature of teaching. In the second half of the present century, several attempts have been made to elaborate models and paradigms for teaching that would place the utilization of psychology in more reasonable perspective (Gage 1963). One implication of these reconceptions is that the act of teaching is inherently a *hypothesizing act* (Coladarci 1963). The educator, focused on desired changes in the learner, views his operations and arrangements as "hypotheses" about the conditions produc-

ing a change in the learner; the educator explicitly generates these hypotheses from the best available human knowledge, which is in itself hypothetical in character. There have been recent applications of this position in many areas of the world, and its impact is evidenced in changes in the curriculum of teacher education (for example, Carpenter & Haddan 1964; Calonghi 1956; Derbolav 1961; Moreira 1955).

Status of the educational psychologist. It is generally conceded that the prestige of educational psychology and educational research has tended to be low among social scientists in general and psychologists in particular (Haggard 1954). The marked exception appears to be in the Soviet Union, where the psychology of education is given high priority at national and local levels; for example, it is clear that education is viewed as the major field of application for psychology, since the Institute of Psychology in Moscow, the official center for Russian psychological research, is responsible to the Academy of Educational Sciences (Simon & Simon 1963, p. 3). Elsewhere, however, it has been thought that educational psychologists, after the Thorndike era, have been less than adequately prepared in psychology and insufficiently productive of ideas and research.

In the middle of the present century, systematic attention has been devoted to this matter by professional organizations in psychology and by universities offering doctoral programs in this field of specialization. The American Psychological Association in 1954 formed the Committee on Relations between Psychology and Education to assess the situation and make recommendations. As a result of this, among other pressures, the gulf between the standards of psychology in general and those of educational psychology is gradually narrowing. In 1964 the Division of Educational Psychology of the American Psychological Association provided for the Edward Lee Thorndike Award for distinguished psychological contributions to education. With increased visibility and professional acknowledgment, the specialization is gradually achieving more effective status and more rigorous training requirements. Carroll (1963), after measuring educational psychology against the criteria for a discipline, has concluded that the field may be so classified at this time.

Specializations. Although specific specializations in educational psychology vary with emerging needs and changes in education, some subareas have remained stable over time and in most areas of the world. The field of *tests and measurements* is well defined and popular, particularly in North America, England, the Continent, and Japan. Developments in this special field have been increased markedly by recent advances in mathematical statistics and electronic computers.

School psychology, representing the special diagnostic–clinical function in school systems, is represented in most countries and provides the bridge between clinical psychology and educational psychology. *Mental hygiene*, although frequently classified with school psychology, continues to carry the influence brought to bear on education initially by Freud's work and more recently by psychiatry in general (Krugman 1958). *Guidance and counseling*, where it is distinguished from school psychology, represents the interests of those who provide individual counsel for students with nonpathological personal and academic problems, including vocational guidance at the secondary school and college levels.

School psychometry, rapidly becoming acknowledged as an identifiable and appropriate role, is composed of the administration of individual intelligence and personality tests in schools, together with assistance in the planning of testing programs and construction of achievement tests in various subjects. Because of the crucial importance of reading skill in education and society, the *psychology of reading* is attracting a growing number of psychologists. The importance of the early childhood years in education and the increase in preschool programs has led to the *child development* specialization, comprising both those who engage in preschool education and those with primarily research interests.

Most recently, a new specialization has emerged, *social psychology of education*, prompted by research and theory that emphasize the social nature of school instructional groups and the social-psychological factors in learning, motivation, aspiration, and identification. Evidence of this particular aspect has been seen in the United States, Sweden, Denmark, and France [*see* READING DISABILITIES].

Topics in educational psychology. Specific topics of study in educational psychology vary considerably over time and across cultural–national lines. Four general categories represent most of those subjects presently pursued in this field: (*a*) learning, which is by far the most frequent topic in the field; (*b*) readiness for learning, which includes the phenomena of interests, aptitudes, and motivation; (*c*) mental health and social adjustment, which focus on the noncognitive purposes of the school and correlates of intellectual learning;

and (*d*) measurement and evaluation, which comprise the techniques for assessing the educational growth of learners, diagnosing learning problems, and clarifying the criteria to be used in an evaluation of the school.

Three specific aspects of educational psychology merit particular mention in view of their continuing importance, widespread concern, and critical relevance in pedagogy: the educability of the learner, individual differences, and educational technology.

Educability. The degree to which a pupil is ready to profit from instruction and the rate at which he is able to learn are patently vital considerations in education. The earlier point of view on educability supported a unitary and genetic explanation of pupil ability. The general assumption was that success in the various demands of school curricula is attributable to a general underlying ability of genetic origin. Although this view still continues in many quarters, two developments that would support a contrary view have occurred. On the basis of the work of many investigators, primarily in England and the United States, the general concept of intelligence can be seen to comprise subabilities that are not very highly correlated with one another (for example, memory, verbal fluency, arithmetic computation, and spatial perception). As a result, differential intelligence tests have been developed and are widely used in today's schools. These tests, instead of providing a single index, such as intelligence quotient, produce a set of scores (a profile) that shows the relative ability of the learner in each of several areas. The second development is the ideological rejection of genetic explanations of educability on the part of educators and psychologists in the Soviet Union and similarly persuaded political states. The Soviet assumption is that internal conditions of the child (for example, "intelligence") are themselves products of external forces (for example, educative treatments) (Bogoiavlenski & Menchinskaia 1959).

One development consistent with almost any conception of educability is the attempt to construct intelligence tests that are "culture fair," that is, satisfy the assumption that each examinee has had equal opportunity to learn the demands posted in the tests. Piaget and his colleague Inhelder have attracted considerable interest in their attempt to discover a genetic order in the development of various concepts in children (Inhelder & Piaget 1955); their conclusions, however, have been met largely with reservations thus far in non-French cultures.

Individual differences. Although research in individual differences has a long history in psychology and education, work in this field continues to increase in quantity and scope. Among recent data, those affecting school procedures most significantly are the findings that differences "within" a child are almost as extensive as differences between children. That is, the various skills and achievement levels of a particular learner are not homogeneous; indeed, achievement in some areas, such as music, may be uncorrelated with achievement in others, such as mathematics. The import of this for the school was quickly realized and is exemplified in such practices as ungraded schools, differential assignment of pupils to instructional groups in curricular areas, and increased use of differential aptitude tests in pupil assignment and educational diagnosis.

Educational technology. When the radio and motion picture became available to the schools, studies in educational psychology demonstrated the effectiveness of these media in attitude change and information learning. Television, a later arrival in the technological resources of education, has been undergoing similar assessment and appears to serve the schools' purposes at least as well as the more traditional devices. However, the foregoing media largely provided stimulus situations only; there was no incorporation of the learner's responses. This limitation, noted by Porter (1957), has apparently been overcome in the later technological development in instruction—programmed instruction, including the use of "teaching machines."

The development of programmed instruction, stemming from earlier work by the American psychologists S. L. Pressey and B. F. Skinner, occupied a large portion of research activity among educational psychologists in the 1960s. The basic characteristics of the procedure are: (*a*) breaking down the task (or content) to be learned into small sequential steps; (*b*) presenting the organized material to the individual learner (sometimes by machine processes) in such a way that he must respond correctly to each step before continuing to the next; (*c*) informing the learner of the correctness of his response; and, in some variations, (*d*) selecting the next step for the learner in terms of the correctness or incorrectness of his previous response. A considerable amount of research on the validity of this procedure has been completed, but much is still under way. Excellent summaries have been published by Lumsdaine (1963; 1964) and Stolurow (1961). The findings seem to indicate that such programming procedures not only reduce the amount of the teacher's time needed for each pupil but also produce at least as much, if not more, learning in the curriculum areas involving a great deal of structure, such as algebra, and information, such as biology [*see* LEARNING, *article on* PROGRAMMED LEARNING].

ARTHUR P. COLADARCI

[*See also* EDUCATION; TEACHING. *Other relevant material may be found in* ACHIEVEMENT TESTING; COUNSELING PSYCHOLOGY; DEVELOPMENTAL PSYCHOLOGY; INTELLIGENCE AND INTELLIGENCE TESTING; LEARNING; LEARNING THEORY; *and in the biographies of* DEWEY; MONTESSORI; THORNDIKE.]

BIBLIOGRAPHY

BAIN, ALEXANDER 1879 *Education as a Science.* New York: Appleton.

BOGOIAVLENSKI, D. N.; and MENCHINSKAIA, N. A. (1959) 1963 The Relation Between Learning and Mental Development in School Children. Pages 50–67 in Brian Simon and Joan Simon (editors), *Educational Psychology in the U.S.S.R.: Papers by D. N. Bogoiavlenski and Others.* Stanford (Calif.) Univ. Press. → First published in Russian.

BORING, EDWIN G. (1929) 1950 *A History of Experimental Psychology.* 2d ed. New York: Appleton.

BRETT, GEORGE S. 1921 *A History of Psychology.* Volume 2: Medieval and Early Modern Period. New York: Macmillan.

BRUBACHER, JOHN S. 1947 *A History of the Problems of Education.* New York: McGraw-Hill.

BRUNER, JEROME S. (1960) 1965 *The Process of Education.* Cambridge, Mass.: Harvard Univ. Press.

BURT, CYRIL L. 1957 Impact of Psychology Upon Education. *Yearbook of Education* [1957]:163–180.

BUSWELL, GUY T. 1956 Educational Theory and the Psychology of Learning. *Journal of Educational Psychology* 47:175–184.

CALONGHI, LUIGI 1956 *Testi e esperimenti: Metodologia della ricerca pedagogico-didattica.* Turin (Italy): Pontificio Ateneo Salesiano.

CARPENTER, FINLEY; and HADDAN, EUGENE E. 1964 *Systematic Application of Psychology to Education.* New York: Macmillan.

CARROLL, JOHN B. 1963 The Place of Educational Psychology in the Study of Education. Pages 101–119 in John Walton and James L. Kuethe (editors), *The Discipline of Education.* Madison: Univ. of Wisconsin Press.

COLADARCI, ARTHUR P. 1963 The Relevance of Psychology to Education. Pages 380–404 in George F. Kneller (editor), *Foundations of Education.* New York: Wiley.

COMMINS, WILLIAM D. 1937 *Principles of Educational Psychology.* New York: Ronald Press.

DERBOLAV, JOSEF 1961 *Die gegenwärtige Situation des Wissens von der Erziehung.* Bonn: Bouvier.

DEWEY, JOHN (1910) 1933 *How We Think: A Restatement of the Relation of Reflective Thinking to the Educative Process.* Boston: Heath.

DEWEY, JOHN 1964 *On Education: Selected Writings.* Edited by Reginald D. Archambault. New York: Random House. → A posthumously published collection.

GAGE, NATHANIEL L. 1963 Paradigms for Research on Teaching. Pages 94–141 in Nathaniel L. Gage (editor), *Handbook of Research on Teaching*. Chicago: Rand McNally.

HAGGARD, ERNEST A. 1954 The Proper Concern of Educational Psychologists. *American Psychologist* 9:539–543.

INHELDER, BÄRBEL; and PIAGET, JEAN (1955) 1958 *The Growth of Logical Thinking From Childhood to Adolescence*. New York: Basic Books. → First published as *De la logique de l'enfant à la logique de l'adolescent*.

KRUGMAN, MORRIS (editor) 1958 *Orthopsychiatry and the School*. New York: American Orthopsychiatric Association.

LUMSDAINE, ARTHUR A. 1963 Instruments and Media of Instruction. Pages 583–682 in Nathaniel L. Gage (editor), *Handbook of Research on Teaching*. Chicago: Rand McNally.

LUMSDAINE, ARTHUR A. 1964 Educational Technology, Programed Learning, and Instructional Science. Pages 371–401 in National Society for the Study of Education, *Theories of Learning and Instruction*. Univ. of Chicago Press.

McDONALD, FREDERICK J. 1964 The Influence of Learning Theories on Education (1900–1950). Pages 1–26 in National Society for the Study of Education, *Theories of Learning and Instruction*. Univ. of Chicago Press.

MOREIRA, JOÃO ROBERTO 1955 *Introdução ao estudo do currículo da escola primária*. Rio de Janeiro (Brazil): Instituto Nacional de Estudos Pedagógicos.

MURPHY, GARDNER (1929) 1949 *Historical Introduction to Modern Psychology*. Rev. ed. New York: Harcourt.

NATIONAL SOCIETY FOR THE STUDY OF EDUCATION 1942 *The Psychology of Learning*. 41st Yearbook, part 2. Edited by Nelson B. Henry. Bloomington, Ill.: Public School Publishing Co.

NATIONAL SOCIETY FOR THE STUDY OF EDUCATION 1964 *Theories of Learning and Instruction*. 63d Yearbook, part 1. Edited by Ernest R. Hilgard. Univ. of Chicago Press.

OGDEN, ROBERT M. 1926 *Psychology and Education*. New York: Harcourt.

PORTER, DOUGLAS 1957 A Critical Review of a Portion of the Literature on Teaching Devices. *Harvard Educational Review* 27:126–147.

SIMON, BRIAN; and SIMON, JOAN (editors) 1963 *Educational Psychology in the U.S.S.R.* Stanford (Calif.) Univ. Press.

SPENCE, KENNETH W. 1959 The Relation of Learning Theory to the Technology of Education. *Harvard Educational Review* 29:84–95.

STOLUROW, LAWRENCE M. 1961 *Teaching by Machine*. U.S. Office of Education, Cooperative Research Monograph No. 6. Washington: Department of Health, Education and Welfare.

SULLY, JAMES (1884) 1896 *Outlines of Psychology With Special Reference to the Theory of Education*. Rev. ed. New York: Appleton.

THORNDIKE, EDWARD L. (1913) 1921 *Educational Psychology*. Volume 2: The Psychology of Learning. New York: Columbia University, Teachers College.

THORNDIKE, EDWARD L.; and WOODWORTH, ROBERT S. 1901 The Influence of Improvement in One Mental Function Upon the Efficiency of Other Functions. *Psychological Review* 8:247–261, 384–395, 553–564.

YERKES, ROBERT M. (editor) 1921 Psychological Examining in the United States Army. Volume 15 of National Academy of Sciences, *Memoirs*. Washington: Government Printing Office.

EFFICACY, POLITICAL
See POLITICAL EFFICACY.

EGO IDENTITY
See IDENTITY, PSYCHOSOCIAL.

EGO PSYCHOLOGY
See under PSYCHOANALYSIS.

EHRENBERG, RICHARD

Richard Ehrenberg, economist and economic historian, was born in 1857 in Wolfenbüttel in the Grand Duchy of Brunswick, Germany. He was the son of a Jewish educator and the brother of a famous Göttingen law professor and authority on insurance law. Coming from an impecunious family, Ehrenberg was not able to finish his secondary school education but instead had to work as a bank clerk to earn his living. However, after saving a little money, he applied for admission at the University of Tübingen and was accepted as a student despite the fact that he did not have his *Abitur*. Eventually, after further studies at Munich and Göttingen, he acquired a doctoral degree in economics.

Ehrenberg then became the secretary of the Altona chamber of commerce, a position that gave him unusual insight into the way business was conducted in one of Europe's largest commercial ports. At the same time, he devoted himself to historical studies and, in 1896, published one of his most important works, *Das Zeitalter der Fugger*, a book that has remained so fresh that a French edition was published as recently as 1955. Its appearance brought Ehrenberg the appointment of associate professor at Göttingen. He moved to the University of Rostock as a full professor in 1898 and taught there until his sudden death in 1921.

Throughout his life, Ehrenberg was interested in new problems and in new solutions for old problems. He was a prolific writer and did research in many areas. Because the University of Rostock owned the papers of Heinrich von Thünen, Ehrenberg was drawn into studying the work and ideas of this important nineteenth-century German economic theorist, whose influence can clearly be discerned in Ehrenberg's writings. Thünen had made important contributions not only to economic theory but also to agricultural economics, and since Rostock was located in one of the fertile regions of the German Empire, it was natural that Ehrenberg's attention would be attracted to that area of research also. German economic thinking at that time was dominated by problems of *Sozialpolitik,* and it is not surprising that Ehrenberg shared an interest in labor problems. In this sphere, he strove to achieve a reconciliation of businessmen and workers, based on the recognition of their community of interest.

However, none of these are the fields in which Ehrenberg did his most creative work. By inclination he was a historian, and his early work on the Fuggers, in fact a book on sixteenth-century financial institutions, is evidence that talent coincided with inclination. This historical bent was complemented by experience with modern business acquired in his former chamber-of-commerce position. As a result, his interest turned from economic history proper to what today we would call "business history." In 1902 and 1905, respectively, Ehrenberg published the first and second volumes of *Grosse Vermögen*: the first treats Jakob Fugger, the Rothschilds, and Krupp; the second, based on the autobiography of John Parish, a Hamburg merchant, deals with the house of Parish in Hamburg. In 1906, Ehrenberg published *Die Unternehmungen der Brüder Siemens*, a book in which he proved a pioneer in the particular brand of business history developed some thirty years later by N. S. B. Gras at the Graduate School of Business, Harvard University. In fact, Ehrenberg exerted some influence on Gras.

It was neither Ehrenberg's historical bent nor his own experience with business that alone moved him to study business and businessmen in historical perspective. As a matter of fact, he also belonged to that group of German economists who first promoted the study of business administration, a research area then designated in Germany as *Privatwirtschaftslehre*. Consequently, he became one of the first to propose an academic education for businessmen and was active in efforts to promote that goal by establishing the so-called *Handelshochschulen*.

According to Ehrenberg, economic theory, too, could profit from the study of business records, especially of the accounts of enterprises, as well as of household budgets, in that it might thereby become more "exact." To this end he founded the Vereinigung für Exakt-vergleichende Wirtschaftsforschung, whose name conveys Ehrenberg's idea that the use of business records for improving economic theory could be combined with the comparative study of economic life in various places and periods. To promote this program, he founded, in 1905, the *Thünen-Archiv: Organ für exakte Wirtschaftsforschung* (with Volume 3 the title was changed to *Archiv für exakte Wirtschaftsforschung*).

Nine volumes appeared, the last in 1922; many of Ehrenberg's important papers appeared in this periodical and a bibliography of his writings is in the last volume. However, he was unsuccessful in his attempt at promoting the use of business records in economic research. Economists had not yet learned to distinguish between macroeconomics and microeconomics, a fact that made his suggestions premature and led to some confusion.

Ehrenberg's outstanding achievements have never received the recognition they deserve. His work was not compatible with that of the younger historical school, then dominating German economics, and he himself was on bad terms with Gustav Schmoller, its master. In Germany, this assessment has persisted: the *Neue deutsche Biographie*, a biographical dictionary in the process of publication, does not contain an article on Ehrenberg.

FRITZ REDLICH

[*For discussion of the subsequent development of Ehrenberg's ideas, see the biography of* GRAS.]

WORKS BY EHRENBERG

(1896) 1928 *Capital and Finance in the Age of the Renaissance: A Study of the Fuggers and Their Connections*. New York: Harcourt. → A translation, with some sections omitted, of the author's two-volume work *Das Zeitalter der Fugger*.

(1902–1905) 1925 *Grosse Vermögen: Ihre Entstehung und ihre Bedeutung*. 2 vols. 2d ed. Jena (Germany): Fischer.

1906 *Die Unternehmungen der Brüder Siemens*. Jena (Germany): Fischer.

EHRLICH, EUGEN

Eugen Ehrlich (1862–?1918) is commonly considered the founder of the sociology of law, a discipline standing somewhere between jurisprudence and pure sociology.

Ehrlich was born in Czernowitz, the capital of the province of Bukovina, then a part of the Austrian Empire (now Russia). He studied law at the University of Vienna and, after receiving his law degree, became a *Privatdocent* at that university. In 1897 he accepted an appointment as professor of Roman law at the university in his native town and remained there until his death in 1918 or 1919. (The exact death date is not known because the transfer of this province to Rumania at that time was accompanied by much disorder.)

From the beginning of his academic career, Ehrlich supported the theory of free law (*freie Rechtswissenschaft*) put forward at that time in Germany by Hermann Kantorowicz and his followers. This school was opposed to the jurisprudence of concepts (*Begriffsjurisprudenz*), then the dominant theory in almost all countries except perhaps the United States and England. According to the jurisprudence of concepts, a judicial decision is always based on pre-established statements of the so-called written law; all cases, foreseen or unforeseen, can be solved on the basis of the existing system of statutes and of authoritative judicial decisions. Against this view Kantorowicz argued that the judge must form his decision on the basis of his sense of justice, using the facts accumulated during the trial.

Ehrlich did not entirely support the teachings of the school of free law. Instead he suggested that the law as expressed in judicial decisions should be distinguished from the law as expressed in social conduct (*lebendes Recht*). The latter can be ascertained by observing human behavior in society; it is particularly apparent in organized activity. To study it Ehrlich advocated using the methods of the most progressive sociologists of his time: the observation, generalization, and arrangement of findings into a consistent system, followed by the application of the results to concrete cases.

Ehrlich's views were first published in his *Fundamental Principles of the Sociology of Law* (1913). In addition to its discussion of sociological jurisprudence, the book contains several interesting and important chapters on the development of law in different countries. Although the book greatly influenced the further development of the science of law, the two chapters explicitly devoted to the sociology of law are not systematic enough to provide the basis of a genuine science.

As one of the originators of a new science, Ehrlich discussed at length the methods that should be applied to develop it but did not venture to predict future findings. The two concluding chapters of his *Sociology of Law* are devoted to the methods to be applied to build up the science: in the first, he emphasizes the importance of legal history and juristic science (roughly, jurisprudence); in the second, he speaks of a study of "living law," very similar to the study of the current customary law, but hinting also at some sociological methods of studying social reality. Among other things, he published a questionnaire concerning the "living law" of the peoples of Bukovina, predominantly Rumanians and Ukrainians.

Ehrlich was by no means the first to suggest that statute law does not explain the whole nature of the law. The Russo-Polish jurist Lev Petrazhitskii had expressed such views in his *Vvedenie v izuchenie prava i nravstvennosti* and *Teoriia prava*

i gosudarstva v sviazi s teoriei nravstvennosti ("Introduction to the Study of Law and Morals" and "Theory of Law and State," respectively; both are in Petrazhitskii 1905–1907). The nature of the law, according to Petrazhitskii, is primarily psychological and is determined by individual psychology. His three closest followers, Pitirim A. Sorokin, Georges D. Gurvitch, and Nicholas Timasheff, considered his emphasis on individual psychology a grave error and shifted their focus to collective psychology, ultimately going still further and transferring the entire subject to sociology.

Another contemporary of Ehrlich, Roscoe Pound, also published articles on sociological jurisprudence. Although he expressed ideas that were more moderate than those of Ehrlich, he did distinguish between law in books and law in life. Many other American jurists of that period were also arguing against the jurisprudence of concepts.

Also in the Ehrlich tradition, there arose in Sweden the Uppsala school, headed by Axel Hägerström (see *Inquiries Into the Nature of Law and Morals* 1953, a compilation of Hägerström's theoretical contributions). The Uppsala school taught that the basic concepts of law had been misconceived: there are no such things as rights and obligations; there are only human ideas about these subjects. This point of view is similar to that of Petrazhitskii, although Hägerström was not familiar with Petrazhitskii's work.

Although the sociology of law is still in its infancy, Ehrlich's work has given a new impetus to the idea of the study of the law as a social fact and not just as a system of ideas expressed in books.

N. S. TIMASHEFF

[*For the historical context of Ehrlich's work, see the biographies of* KANTOROWICZ *and* POUND. *For discussion of the subsequent development of his ideas, see* JURISPRUDENCE; LAW, *article on* THE SOCIOLOGY OF LAW; *and the biography of* SOROKIN.]

BIBLIOGRAPHY

EHRLICH, EUGEN (1913) 1936 *Fundamental Principles of the Sociology of Law.* Translated by Walter L. Moll, with an introduction by Roscoe Pound. Cambridge, Mass.: Harvard Univ. Press. → First published as *Grundlegung der Soziologie des Rechts.* See especially Walter L. Moll's "Translator's Preface." Also contains a list of Ehrlich's major works.

GURVITCH, GEORGES D. (1940) 1947 *Sociology of Law.* Preface by Roscoe Pound. London: Routledge. → First published in French.

HÄGERSTRÖM, AXEL 1953 *Inquiries Into the Nature of Law and Morals.* Uppsala (Sweden): Almqvist & Wiksells.

PETRAZHITSKII, LEV I. (1905–1907) 1955 *Law and Morality.* Translated by Hugh W. Babb, with an introduction by Nicholas S. Timasheff. Cambridge, Mass.: Harvard Univ. Press. → An abridgment and translation of *Vvedenie v izuchenie prava i nravstvennosti*, 1905, and *Teoriia prava i gosudarstva v sviazi s teoriei nravstvennosti*, 1907.

SOROKIN, PITIRIM A. (1947) 1962 *Society, Culture, and Personality; Their Structure and Dynamics: A System of General Sociology.* New York: Cooper Square Publishers.

TIMASHEFF, NICHOLAS S. 1939 *An Introduction to the Sociology of Law.* Harvard Sociological Studies, Vol. 3. Cambridge, Mass.: Harvard University, Committee on Research in the Social Sciences.

TIMASHEFF, NICHOLAS S. 1957 Growth and Scope of Sociology of Law. Pages 424–449 in Howard Becker and Alvin Boskoff (editors), *Modern Sociological Theory in Continuity and Change.* New York: Dryden.

EINAUDI, LUIGI

Luigi Einaudi (1874–1961), Italian economist and statesman, was born at Carrù, in the province of Cuneo. He studied with Salvatore Cognetti de Martis at the University of Turin and was appointed a fellow in political economy there in 1899 and professor of financial science in 1907. He taught for a short time at a secondary school and held an appointment as teacher of economics at the Luigi Bocconi Commercial University in Milan, and for more than forty years he was on the faculty at Turin.

Forced to flee Italy after the 1943 armistice, Einaudi taught for a while at the University of Geneva. After his return to Italy, he became successively governor of the Bank of Italy in 1945, deputy to the Constituent Assembly in 1946, vice-president of the Council and minister of the budget in De Gasperi's fourth cabinet in 1947, senator in 1948, and on May 11, 1948, president of the republic.

He returned to private life in 1955 at the end of his presidential term. For the rest of his life he lived on an estate near his birthplace, taking particular pleasure in his magnificent library of economic works. As late as 1961 he was working on the problem of Italian monetary reform, suggesting that a new unit of currency be adopted, to be worth 1,000 lire and to be called the scudo.

Although he found some merit in Pareto and his followers, Einaudi is reputed to have considered Adam Smith, David Ricardo, and John Stuart Mill the greatest of all economists. Always a strong supporter of freedom and an opponent of monopoly, Einaudi's economic writings included a defense of trade union freedom, yet he never observed the degree to which the state and the trade unions themselves were becoming monopolies.

Many of Einaudi's most important writings are in the field of finance and taxation. The best known is probably his *Principî di scienza della finanza* (1932), which was published in many editions. He also made studies of the Italian fiscal system, the relationship between taxes and savings, the myths and paradoxes of fiscal justice, and the relationships between taxes and land.

During his period of exile in Switzerland, he published, under the pseudonym of Junius, *I problemi economici della federazione europea* (1945). His commitment to federation dated back to the turn of the century, and he had long been concerned with the problems it involved.

Einaudi's primary interest was, however, history—both economic history and the history of economic thought. His study of the Piedmont financial system during the War of the Spanish Succession, 1701–1714, is a model of patient inquiry, and it produced material of significance to twentieth-century problems. An earlier work, *Un principe mercante: Studio sulla espansione coloniale italiana* (1900b), is a study of the expansion of a "developing" country. He also analyzed the works of individual economists, including those of Ferrari, Adam Smith, and Sismondi.

In addition to teaching and writing on economics, Einaudi was active as an editor and journalist. He brought out in 1933, for example, a new edition of Jules Dupuit's *De l'utilité et de sa mesure*, in Italian. For many years he was editor of the journal *La riforma sociale.* The title was an accurate reflection of his liberal social views, and the journal was suppressed in the 1930s. He later started another journal, the *Rivista di storia economica*, intending to imply by the title change that the contents were politically safe. Since this was not the case, the new journal survived only three years. Einaudi remained throughout his life a classicist in economics and an old-fashioned liberal in politics.

UGO PAPI

WORKS BY EINAUDI

1900a *La rendita mineraria* (Mining Income). Turin: Unione Tipografico-Editrice.

1900b *Un principe mercante: Studio sulla espansione coloniale italiana* (A Merchant Prince: Essay on Italian Colonial Expansion). Turin: Bocca.

1902 *Studi sugli effetti delle imposte: Contributo allo studio dei problemi tributari municipali* (Studies in the Effects of Taxes). Turin: Bocca.

1924 *La terra e l'imposta* (The Land and the Tax). Milan: Università Commerciale Bocconi.

1927 *La guerra e il sistema tributario italiano* (The War and the Italian Taxation System). Bari: Laterza & Figli.

1929 *Contributo alla ricerca dell' "ottima imposta"* (Contributions to Research on the Optimum Tax). Milan: Università Commerciale Bocconi.

(1932) 1948 *Principî di scienza della finanza.* (Principles of Financial Science). 4th ed., rev. Turin: Einaudi.

1933 *La condotta economica e gli effetti sociali della guerra italiana* (The Economic Conduct and Social Effects of the First World War). New Haven: Yale Univ. Press.

1945 *I problemi economici della Federazione Europea* (The Economic Problems of European Federation). Milan: La Fiaccola.

1949 *Lezioni di politica sociale* (Social Politics). Turin: Einaudi.

(1954) 1955 *Il buongoverno: Saggi di economia e politica, 1897–1954* (Good Government). Bari: Laterza.

1955 *Prediche inutili* (Useless Sermons). Turin: Einaudi.

1956 *Lo scrittoio del presidente (1948–1955)* (The President's Desk). Turin: Einaudi.

SUPPLEMENTARY BIBLIOGRAPHY

BERNARDINO, ANSELMO 1954 *Vita di Luigi Einaudi.* Padua: CEDAM.

BOUSQUET, G. H. 1962 Luigi Einaudi (1874–1961). *Revue d'économie politique* 72:5–12.

DIVISIA, FRANÇOIS 1963 Luigi Einaudi: 1874–1961. *Econometrica* 31:240–241.

ELASTICITY

The quantity of a commodity that people want to purchase (demand) per unit of time or want to sell (supply) per unit of time depends in part upon the price of the commodity. Economists have sought ways to describe and measure the relationship between changes in the rate of quantity demanded or supplied and changes in price.

Alfred Marshall (1885, p. 260) first used the term *elasticity* to refer to the percentage change in quantity demanded ($\Delta q/q$) divided by the percentage change in price ($\Delta p/p$), and indicated that elasticity at C, on the demand curve $ABCDE$ (see Figure 1), is CG divided by CF. He elaborated these ideas in his *Principles* (1890, book 3, chapter 3) and the concept has since been adopted by the profession.

Prior to Marshall, there had been no generally accepted terminology or measure of the relationship between price and quantity, although concepts similar to elasticity had been suggested. For example, Mill (1848, book 3, chapter 2, sec. 4) compared percentage changes in price and in quantity, but he did not divide the two to get what we now call elasticity. Cournot (1838, chapter 4, sec. 24) showed the relationship between elasticity and total revenue (see below) by comparing the ratio of the change in quantity demanded to the change in price ($\Delta q/\Delta p$) and the ratio of quantity de-

manded to price (q/p), but he did not suggest dividing the two ratios to measure elasticity.

Elasticity of demand. Elasticity of demand is defined as the percentage change in the quantity demanded, divided by the percentage change in price. It is derived from the demand curve, which shows the absolute quantity demanded as a function of price. Since the rate of demand rises if the price falls, and vice versa, the elasticity of demand is actually negative, except that it is common to ignore the algebraic sign and use the absolute value. By definition, demand is inelastic if the elasticity is less than one and is elastic if the elasticity is greater than one. An elasticity of one is called *unit*, or *unitary*, *elasticity*.

Elastic demand. If demand is elastic, a given percentage increase in price causes a larger percentage decline in the quantity demanded, or a given percentage reduction in price causes a larger percentage increase in quantity demanded. In the limiting case of perfectly (infinitely) elastic demand, which is illustrated by the horizontal line segment DE in Figure 1 (if it is visualized as extended horizontally so as to constitute the entire demand curve), any increase in price, no matter how small, will cause the quantity demanded to decline to zero; and any reduction in price, again no matter how small, will cause the quantity demanded to increase without limit.

Demand is usually elastic for commodities for which there are good substitutes, so that the de-

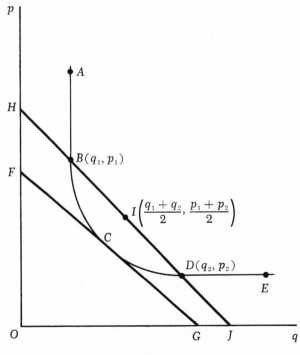

Figure 1

mand facing a firm is more elastic than the demand facing an industry, since a buyer may substitute the products of other firms in the industry. It is part of the definition of perfect competition that there must be so many firms in the industry producing such excellent substitutes that the demand facing the firm is perfectly (infinitely) elastic, even though the demand facing the industry may be inelastic. [See COMPETITION.]

Inelastic demand.   Conversely, if demand is inelastic the percentage change in quantity is smaller than the percentage change in price. An increase in price therefore causes a proportionately smaller decline in the quantity demanded, and a reduction in price causes a proportionately smaller increase in the quantity demanded. In the limiting case of zero elasticity (perfectly inelastic demand), which is illustrated by the vertical line segment *AB* in Figure 1 (if it is visualized as extended vertically so as to constitute the entire demand curve), neither an increase nor a reduction in price has any effect upon the quantity demanded.

Products that have no good substitutes, like tobacco, or that require a very small proportion of the consumer's income, like salt, frequently have inelastic demands.

Relation to total revenue.   Elasticity of demand also shows how the total dollar value of sales of the commodity responds to a change in its price. For example, if the price of a commodity with inelastic demand is increased, the total revenue of the seller will increase even though the quantity demanded declines somewhat, since the increase in price more than offsets the reduction in volume. This creates a presumption that a seller faced with an inelastic demand will raise his price and will continue to do so until demand becomes elastic. Similar reasoning shows that a reduction in price reduces total revenue if demand is inelastic but increases total revenue if demand is elastic, since the increase in volume more than offsets the reduction in price. Finally, an increase in price reduces total revenue if demand is elastic and does not change total revenue if demand has unit elasticity.

Relation to marginal revenue.   There is also a logical relationship between the elasticity of demand and marginal revenue. Marginal revenue is defined as the change in the total revenue per unit change in quantity sold, if the relationship between the price and the quantity sold is given by the demand curve. Positive marginal revenue therefore implies that total revenue increases if the quantity sold increases, or declines if the quantity sold declines. Since the relation between price and quantity is given by the demand curve, an increase in sales volume must be accompanied by a decline in price. Thus, a positive marginal revenue means that total revenue increases as volume increases and price declines. Since a decline in price increases total revenue only if demand is elastic, positive marginal revenue must be associated with elastic demand. Furthermore, since profit maximization requires that marginal cost equal marginal revenue, and marginal cost is always positive, it follows that the marginal revenue of the profit-maximizing firm must be positive and the demand elastic.

Similar reasoning shows that negative marginal revenue is associated with inelastic demand: if demand is inelastic, an increase in price reduces volume and increases total revenue, so that marginal revenue is negative. The intermediate case of unit elasticity of demand implies zero marginal revenue, since any change in price is just balanced by a change in volume, and total revenue is the same at any price or at any volume.

Relation to price.   Elasticity of demand usually changes with the price of the product. Thus, it is incorrect to say that the demand for cigarettes is inelastic or that the demand for butter is elastic. The correct statement is that these demands are elastic or inelastic at the prices that are currently charged. At higher prices the demand for cigarettes might well become elastic, while the demand for butter might well become inelastic if its price fell far enough below the price of oleomargarine.

In the particular case of the straight-line demand curve, which is so frequently used for illustrative purposes in economics, the demand is elastic and marginal revenue is positive throughout the upper half of the possible price range, while demand is inelastic and marginal revenue negative throughout the lower half of the price range.

Elasticity of supply.   Defined as the percentage change in the quantity offered for sale divided by the percentage change in price, elasticity of supply is derived from the supply curve, which shows the absolute amount producers wish to sell as a function of price. Since sellers wish to sell more at a higher price, the elasticity of supply is positive. If the supply curve is inelastic, a relatively larger increase in price is required to produce a given (percentage) increase in quantity supplied. If the supply curve is elastic, the sellers are more responsive to a change in price, and the increase in the quantity supplied is larger, on a percentage basis, than the increase in price.

Other elasticities.   Marshall originally introduced the concept of elasticity in connection with demand and supply curves, but economists soon started to use the ratio of the percentage changes to describe the relationship between any two variables, provided only that the variables are functionally related. By 1913, Johnson (p. 503) was able to write, "This form of expression [the ratio of percentage changes] corresponds to the general notion of elasticity."

The most important elasticities, other than demand and supply, are income elasticity of demand and cross-elasticity of demand.

Income elasticity of demand. The demand for a commodity depends upon its price, consumers' incomes, the prices of other commodities on which consumers might spend their incomes, and perhaps on other variables. Quantity demanded is therefore functionally related to price, if incomes and other prices do not change; and the (price) elasticity of demand is a property of this function. Quantity demanded is also functionally related to income, if the price of the commodity and other prices do not change. The *income elasticity of demand* is a property of this function and is defined as the percentage change in the quantity demanded divided by the percentage change in income.

If income elasticity of demand is negative, consumers purchase less of the commodity as their incomes rise, and the commodity is, by definition, an inferior good. If income elasticity is positive, but less than one, consumers buy more of the product as their incomes rise (if prices do not change), but spend a smaller proportion of their incomes on the commodity. For commodities with income elasticities greater than one, consumers spend a higher proportion of a higher income on the commodity, and the quantity demanded grows at a faster (percentage) rate than income grows.

Cross-elasticity of demand. Quantity demanded is also functionally related to the prices of other commodities, if the commodity's own price and consumers' incomes do not change. Cross-elasticity of demand is a property of this function and is defined as the percentage change in the quantity demand of commodity A divided by the percentage change in the price of commodity B.

The commodities A and B are, by definition, substitutes if the cross-elasticity is positive, since an increase in the price of B then causes a reduction in the demand for B and an increase in the demand for A. Conversely, if cross-elasticity is negative, the commodities are complements, since an increase in the price of B causes consumers to demand less of both commodities.

Mathematical definitions. *Point elasticity.* If the variables q, p, and y are related by the function $q = f(p, y)$, the p elasticity of q, or the elasticity of q with respect to p, is customarily defined as $\eta_{qp} = (\partial q/\partial p)(p/q)$, no matter what variables the letters represent.

If, as is customary, q represents the quantity demanded, p the price, and y the consumers' incomes, then η_{qp} is the (price) elasticity of demand and is negative. Marginal revenue, M, is defined as $M = \partial(pq)/\partial q$, and it can be shown that $M = p(1 + 1/\eta_{qp})$.

Arc elasticity. Sometimes the functional relationship between p and q is unknown, but two points, B and D, with coordinates (q_1, p_1) and (q_2, p_2) as in Figure 1, are known; and the arc elasticity between the two points is desired. The usual practice is to assume that the demand curve passing through these points is a straight line, $HBIDJ$, and to calculate the point elasticity at I, the point midway between B and D. The formula for the arc elasticity, so defined, is

$$\eta = \frac{q_2 - q_1}{q_2 + q_1} \cdot \frac{p_2 + p_1}{p_2 - p_1}.$$

While this procedure is arbitrary, it has two advantages over calculating the elasticity at either B or D. First, the elasticity has the same value whether the change is from B to D or from D to B. More important, however, is the fact that the relationships between elasticity, total revenue, and marginal revenue, which were discussed above, are valid if elasticity is calculated at I, but not if it is calculated at either B or D.

DIRAN BODENHORN

[*See also* DEMAND AND SUPPLY; *and the biographies of* COURNOT; MARSHALL; MILL.]

BIBLIOGRAPHY

COURNOT, ANTOINE AUGUSTIN (1838) 1960 *Researches Into the Mathematical Principles of the Theory of Wealth.* New York: Kelley. → First published in French.

JOHNSON, W. E. 1913 The Pure Theory of Utility Curves. *Economic Journal* 23:483–513.

MARSHALL, ALFRED 1885 On the Graphic Method of Statistics. Pages 251–260 in Royal Statistical Society, London, *Jubilee Volume of the Statistical Society.* London: Stanford.

MARSHALL, ALFRED (1890) 1961 *Principles of Economics.* 9th ed., 2 vols. New York and London: Macmillan. → A variorum edition. The eighth edition is more convenient for normal use.

MILL, JOHN STUART (1848) 1961 *Principles of Political Economy, With Some of Their Applications to Social Philosophy.* 7th ed. Edited by W. J. Ashley. New York: Kelley.